PRACTICAL
POLISH-ENGLISH
ENGLISH-POLISH
DICTIONARY

PRACTICAL POLISH-ENGLISH ENGLISH-POLISH DICTIONARY

by

Iwo Cyprian Pogonowski

REVISED EDITION
1985

HIPPOCRENE BOOKS

New York

This edition printed in HIPPOCRENE PRACTICAL DICTIONARY format

1985

Second revised edition

Hippocrene Books, Inc.
171 Madison Avenue
New York, New York 10016

Printed in the United States or America

Library of Congress Cataloging in Publication Data

Pogonowski, Iwo Cyprian, 1921–
    Dictionary, Polish-English, English-Polish

    1. Polish language—Dictionaries—English.
    2. English language—Dictionaries—Polish.
    I. Title.
    PG6640.P54   491.8′5321   82-9211
                                AACR2

ISBN 0-87052-064-4

TO MY WIFE MAGDALENA

ACKNOWLEDGMENTS AND WORDS OF APPRECIATION

To Ms.Melanie Tomaszkiewicz for help in preparation of the phonetic guide.
To Ms.Teresa Widomska for typing and proof-reading.
To Mr.Robert Czarnek, Mr.Emil J.Skibiński, Mr.Jerzy A. Starczewski,Drs. Kazimierz Sowiński, Wiesław Zdaniewski and Zdzisław Mach for proof-reading and checking of the spelling against
current standard dictionaries.
To Ms.Janina Czarnek and Mr. Zdzisław Mach for help in preparation of information on the Polish cuisine.
To Dr.Magdalena J. Pogonowska for help in editing "SAY IT IN
POLISH!"conversations for travelers to Poland.

<u>CONTENTS - SPIS TREŚCI</u>

INTRODUCTION

The Polish-English part of this dictionary contains about 16,000 entries. The large Polish-English dictionaries usually contain some 180,000 entries, which give basic forms only and do not include ending changes, etc. discussed below. The term dictionary entry is used here as defined by the U.S. Bureau of Federal Supply, which indicates that each word variant explained constitutes an entry.

The word choice and translation are updated for current usage in America and Poland. Characteristic idiomatic usages are included. Each entry includes a pronunciation guide for sound and stress. A stress mark is placed over the stressed vowel.

The pronunciation guide, following the listing of all entries in this dictionary, gives also an illustrated discussion of Polish and English sounds and an explanation of the phonetic symbols. For practical reasons, the number of phonetic symbols are expressed in Latin letters only. Special care is given to explain and illustrate the pronunciation of Polish consonants and vowels which do not occur in the English language and vice versa. The information presented stresses whenever possible the familiar pronunciation and meaning in common usage in both languages.

Linguists define the language as a raw material for the creative activity of speaking. It is a rule-governed creativity in which we are creating and understanding sentences within rules of grammar. A grammatical rule is a description of a pattern habitually followed in a given language; changes in pattern render changes in meaning. This is true, of course, in both Polish and English languages.

An active language changes at varying rates but always at a rate faster than its changes in rules of grammar. Grammar has greater stability than syntax and vocabulary. Every language offers a special way of seeing and interpreting. Languages within the same Indo-European group are not simply equivalent.

The abundance of Polish grammatical forms that do not occur in English should be noticed. A multitude of inflectional forms of Polish nouns and adjectives is reflected in their structure and spelling. Changes in endings of nouns and adjectives correspond to their function in a sentence, their gender and number. Thus, Polish declension requires seven ending changes in nouns and adjectives for both singular and plural, in each gender. Polish personal verb forms correspond by gender and number to the subject of the sentence; thus, nine verb endings occur in the present tense alone. Impersonal forms and various moods expand this number. Both the perfect and imperfect of Polish verbs are indicated by structural variation (In informal Polish, the distinction between perfect and imperfect forms is not always carefully observed.). Verbs "dać" and "dawać" and "zabrać" and "zabierać" illustrate the structural difference between perfect and imperfect forms characteristic of the Polish language.

If every possible structural form of every Polish noun, adjective, verb, adverb, etc. inclusive of all ending changes was a dictionary entry, the number of Polish words listed would be in millions. The number of Polish words is further increased by multitudes of augmentative and diminutive forms which give expression to emotional values by word structure. These augmentative and diminutive forms serve to make the meaning of nouns and adjectives precise by often achieving broadening and clarifying. Augmentative and diminutive forms in Polish are often used to express feelings and attitudes both positive and negative. A comparison of a Polish, German and English word may be useful in order to illustrate the relative usage of augmentatives and diminutives. The use of the German word offers a chance to see the transition between Slavic and Germanic languages. In German diminutives and augmentatives we see the influence of the languages of the Elbe River Slavs, the Polabians, the Lusatians and the Czechs as well as the influence of the Polish language./Also see page VII/.

Language:	Basic word:	Augmentative Form:	Diminutive Form:
ENGLISH	BOY	BIG BOY	LITTLE BOY
GERMAN	KNABE	KNAB	KNABCHEN, KNABLEIN
POLISH	CHŁOPIEC	CHŁOPAK CHŁOPACZYSKO CHŁOPCZYSKO ETC.	CHŁOPCZYK CHŁOPACZEK CHLOPTAS CHLOPACZYNA ETC.

It should be noticed that in this example the Polish word "chlopiec" is a diminutive form derived from the Polish word "chłop" which among other meanings stands for a grown man. In the Polish language there is a middle voice of verb inflection not used in English. The middle voice represents the subject as acting on and for itself in a way different than the usual active and passive form common to both the Polish and English languages. The middle voice in Polish describes self-reflectiveness not directly describable in English. The Polish middle voice occurs within the reflexive form of verb followed by "się." The gender of nouns in Polish is structurally indicated in conjugation of verbs (See p.VIII). The designation of gender of the Polish nouns is influenced by the sound of the ending. Thus, inanimate things in the Polish, as in most Indo-European languages, often are of masculine or feminine grammatically designated gender. The Polish word "robota," for example, meaning "work," is of feminine gender because of

the ending "a"; a derivative noun "robot" which means a mechanical man or brain is of masculine gender indicated by ending
sound of the letter "t." The profound differences between the
Polish and English language make literal translation of common
expressions usually impossible which is the main cause of the
difficulty of learning Polish by English speakers and vice
versa. The relative difficulty of learning a foreign language
depends on the characteristics of one's own language as illustrated on Table 1, (page VI) showing the relative difficulty
of languages for English speakers based on the experience of
the Foreign Service Institute (1973).

The Slavic languages, including Polish, are a family of languages evolved directly from the original Indo-European language by relatively undisturbed evolution. Any two of the
fourteen Slavic languages are sufficiently similar to allow
their speakers to communicate quite effectively if each speaks
his own language slowly and explains to the other the words
that are not common to both languages. All the Slavic languages have almost the same flexional characteristics with the
exception of Bulgarian, which like English lost the decle-
sions. It happened in Bulgaria after the imposition of Greek
in place of the Old Slavic liturgical language and during the
lengthy Turkish occupation. Polish speakers have to learn to
express meaning by word structure within the grammatical rules
of flexional changes. The English and Bulgarian speakers a-
chieve logical clarity of meaning by order or position of
words. Thus, English and Bulgarian are defined as isolating
or position languages. Polish speaker learning English en-
counters much simpler grammatical forms and basic concepts in
the English language than does his English counterpart in Polish. Assuming the same intensity of foreign language teaching program Polish speakers learn English about 20 to 30% faster than vice versa. The English language is mixed so much
that it does not have a close sister language. However, what
remained in English of the Old Anglo-Saxon grammar, is of Germanic character, even though, to the English speakers today,
the Old Anglo-Saxon is a foreign language. Also Germanic is
the majority of the high-frequency vocabulary in the modern
English. Thus, English is usually classified by the linguists
as a Germanic language, even though, the Romance languages,
including Latin, contribute to English about half of its vocabulary. Both, Romance and Germanic languages have much simpler grammar than do the Slavic languages with exception of
Bulgarian. The Polish language belongs to the inflective
group of languages and it utilizes the active voice to a
greater extent than does the English language. Numerous diacritical markings in Polish give good correlation of sound to
spelling. The difficulties of correlating sound to spelling
in English result mainly from the fact that two different
sound correlations to the Latin alphabet occurred in Britain,
first to the Anglo-Saxon and then to the French (brought with
the Norman invasion). Polish pronunciation is rather stable
and clear. English vowels are relatively less stable and un-

dergo variations under stress. On the other hand, the voiced consonants that occur at the end of an English word are often pronounced clearly. The word "love," for example, has a clear "v" at the end and not an "f" as it would be pronounced in Polish. In Polish, all consonants that occur at the end of a Polish word are voiceless. The word "woz," for example, is pronounced with an "s" at the end: "voos." Typically, rules of grammar and phonetics in English start with words "often," "sometimes," etc. while in Polish similar rules are stated: "always, with very few exceptions." The foreign words enrich English vocabulary and remain relatively unchanged. In Polish the foreign borrowings are assimilated into declension of nouns (single and plural) and adjectives (both subject to expansion in to augmentative and diminutive forms) and conjugation of verbs (each in perfect and imperfect form) and grammatical forms derived from verbs. The English language is much simpler in this respect because each noun without any change in spelling potentially may be used as a verb and sometimes as an adjective. In Polish the vigorous growth of abstract and scientific terms was based mainly on the indigenous words with parallel foreign borrowings. The Polish language achieves the size of its vocabulary by use of prefixes and suffixes to a much greater extent than does the English language. For example the mystical ancient Indo-European root-word "god," common to both Polish and English is expanded in Polish to over 3,000 structurally different words. Meanings of these words include weather, agreements, disagreements, harmony, adventure, comfort, discomfort, toilet (wy-god-ka), injury, dignity, decency, indecency, mystical union, time measurement, reconciliation, hiring etc.(VII).Total vocabulary in English and Polish is about one half a million words. However the make up of each vocabulary is different. English has some 120,000 root-words or about double the 60,000 root-words that are characteristic of an inflective language such as Polish. A practical dictionary is based on the frequency of use of words. Table II (p. VI) includes the plot of high frequency words as a percent of the words printed on an average English page. Thus knowing 1,000 most frequently used words one would know about 70% of words on an average page; and knowing 5,000 would give 86% and knowing 10,000 would give one about 92% of words on an average English page. The size of a person's vocabulary and the degree of comprehension of a native language learned with age and education is shown approximately on Table III (p. VI).

It is interesting to note that throughout Europe, including Poland, many professional and business people with rudimentary knowledge of English prefer to read factual reports in English, rather than in their native language. English is recognized by them as a methodical, energetic, businesslike and sober language, that is somewhat short on finery and elegance, but flexible and unrestrained by strict rules of grammar and lexicion. Centuries of colonial expansion brought English to all corners of the world where hundreds of millions use it.

English today is a dominant world language, while less than sixty million people know the Polish language. However, the Polish language with its logic, finery and elegance will continue to give a good start to abstract thinkers such as mathematicians, logicians, philosophers, anthropologists, novelists and poets and thus contribute to the pluralistic culture of the world.

TABLE I __RELATIVE DIFFICULTY OF LANGUAGES FOR ENGLISH SPEAKERS__
Class time for average student to reach between minimal and working professional proficiency according to Foreign Service Institute (1973).
__24 weeks=720 hours:__ Afrikaans;Danish;Dutch;French;German;Haitian;
Creole;Italian;Norwegian;Spanish;Swedish;Swahili.
__38 weeks=1140hours:__ Bulgarian;Dari:Farsi:Greek:Hindi:Indonesian;
Malay;Urdu.
__44 weeks=1320hours:__ Amharic;Bengali;Burmese;Czech;Finnish;Hebrew;
Hungarian;Cambodian-Khmer;Lao;Nepali:Philipino;Polish;Russian;Ser-
bo-Croatian;Sinhala;Thai;Tamil;Turkish;Vietnamese.
__65 weeks=1950hours:__ Arabic;Chinese;Japanese;Korean.

TABLE II __HIGH FREQUENCY ENGLISH WORDS VS. PERCENTAGE OF WORDS ON
AN AVERAGE PRINTED PAGE__ according to H.Kučera and W.N.
Francis"Computational Analysis of Present-day American English"1967.

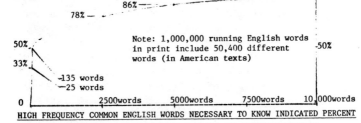

PERCENTAGE OF WORDS UNDERSTOOD ON AN AVERAGE PRINTED PAGE : 100%
92%
86%
78%

50%
33%

Note: 1,000,000 running English words
in print include 50,400 different
words (in American texts) -50%

-135 words
-25 words

0 | 2500words | 5000words | 7500words | 10,000words

HIGH FREQUENCY COMMON ENGLISH WORDS NECESSARY TO KNOW INDICATED PERCENT

TABLE III __APPROXIMATE GROWTH OF VOCABULARY AND UNDERSTANDING OF
WORDS WITH AGE AND EDUCATION IN A NATIVE LANGUAGE__
Compare with estimated median vocabulary size for each age group by
K.C.Diller "The Language Teaching Controversy" 1978.

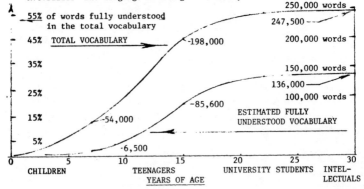

55% of words fully understood
in the total vocabulary
250,000 words
247,500
45% TOTAL VOCABULARY -198,000 200,000 words
35% 150,000 words
25% 136,000
100,000 words
15% ESTIMATED FULLY
UNDERSTOOD VOCABULARY
-54,000 -85,600
5%
-6,500

0 | 5 | 10 | 15 | 20 | 25 | 30
CHILDREN | TEENAGERS | UNIVERSITY STUDENTS | INTEL-
| YEARS OF AGE | | LECTUALS

EXAMPLE OF NOUN AND ADJECTIVE DECLENSION IN POLISH LANGUAGE

DOBRY DOM = GOOD HOME, GOOD HOUSE

SINGULAR:

NOMINATIVUS	= MIANOWNIK	DOBRY DOM	GOOD HOME
GENETIVUS	= DOPEŁNIACZ	DOBREGO DOMU	OF A GOOD HOME
DATIVUS	= CELOWNIK	DOBREMU DOMOWI	FOR A GOOD HOME
ACCUSATIVUS	= BIERNIK	DOBRY DOM	A GOOD HOME
INSTRUMENTALIS	=NARZĘDNIK	DOBRYM DOMEM	BY A GOOD HOME
LOCATIVUS	= MIEJSCOWNIK	W DOBRYM DOMU	IN A GOOD HOME
VOCATIVUS	= WOŁACZ	O DOBRY DOMU!	OH! GOOD HOME

PLURAL:

NOMINATIVUS	= MIANOWNIK	DOBRE DOMY (2,3,4)	GOOD HOMES
		DOBRYCH DOMOW (5...)	GOOD HOMES
GENETIVUS	= DOPEŁNIACZ	DOBRYCH DOMOW	OF GOOD HOMES
DATIVUS	= CELOWNIK	DOBRYM DOMOM	FOR GOOD HOMES
ACCUSATIVUS	= BIERNIK	DOBRE DOMY (2,3,4)	GOOD HOMES
		DOBRYCH DOMOW (5...)	GOOD HOMES
INSTRUMENTALIS	=NARZĘDNIK	DOBRYMI DOMAMI	BY GOOD HOMES
LOCATIVUS	= MIEJSCOWNIK	W DOBRYCH DOMACH	IN GOOD HOMES
VOCATIVUS	= WOŁACZ	O DOBRE DOMY!(2,3,4)	OH!GOOD HOMES
		O (PIĘC) DOBRYCH	OH! (FIVE)
		DOMOW! (5...)	GOOD HOMES

NOTE: (2,3,4) = Small Polish plural of two, three and four.
(5...) = Large Polish plural of five and more.

DIMINUTIVES: SING.: DOBRY DOMEK - PLUR.: DOBRE DOMKI (2,3,4)
                                     DOBRYCH DOMKOW (5...)
              DOBRY DOMECZEK   DOBRE DOMECZKI (2,3,4)
                                   DOBRYCH DOMECZKOW (5...)
AUGMENTATIVES: SING.:DOBRE DOMISKO   PLUR.:DOBRE DOMISKA(2,3,4)
                                     DOBRYCH DOMISK (5...)

EXAMPLE OF CONJUGATION OF A VERB IN THE POLISH LANGUAGE

CZYTAC (chi-tach) = TO READ

- PAST TENSE -

PERFECT FORM = SINGLE TIME COMPLETED OCCURENCE

MASCULINE	"I"	(JA)	CZYTAŁEM	I READ
FEMININE	"I"	(JA)	CZYTAŁAM	
MASCULINE	"YOU"	(TY)	CZYTAŁES	YOU READ
FEMININE	"YOU"	(TY)	CZYTAŁAS	
		(ON)	CZYTAŁ	HE READ
		(ONA)	CZYTAŁA	SHE READ
		(CNO)	CZYTAŁO	IT READ
MASCULINE	"WE"	(MY)	CZYTALISMY	WE READ
FEMININE	"WE"	(MY)	CZYTAŁYSMY	
MASC.PLUR.	"YOU"	(WY)	CZYTALISCIE	YOU READ
FEM. PLUR.	"YOU"	(WY)	CZYTAŁYSCIE	
		(ONI)	CZYTALI	THEY READ
FEM.& NEUTER		(CNE)	CZYTAŁY	

CZYTYWAC (chi-ti-vach)=TO READ (OFTEN)

IMPERFECT FORM = MULTIPLE INCOMPLETE OCCURENCE IN THE PAST

MASCULINE	"I"	(JA)	CZYTYWAŁEM	I USED TO READ
FEMININE	"I"	(JA)	CZYTYWAŁAM	
MASCULINE	"YOU"	(TY)	CZYTYWAŁES	YOU USED TO READ
FEMININE	"YOU"	(TY)	CZYTYWAŁAS	
		(ON)	CZYTYWAŁ	HE USED TO READ
		(ONA)	CZYTYWAŁA	SHE USED TO READ
		(CNO)	CZYTYWAŁO	IT USED TO READ
MASCULINE	"WE"	(MY)	CZYTYWALISMY	WE USED TO READ
FEMININE	"WE"	(MY)	CZYTYWAŁYSKY	
MASC.PLUR.	"YOU"	(WY)	CZYTYWALISCIE	YOU USED TO READ
FEM. PLUR.	"YOU"	(WY)	CZYTYWAŁYSCIE	
		(ONI)	CZYTYWALI	THEY USED TO READ
FEM.& NEUTER		(ONE)	CZYTYWAŁY	

EXAMPLES OF WORDS DERIVED FROM THE VERB "CZYTAC"= TO READ

DOCZYTAC, DOCZYTAC SIE, DOCZYTYWAC, DOCZYTYWAC SIE, NACZYTAC SIE, NACZYTYWAC SIE, OCZYTAC SIE, ODCZYTAC, ODCZYTYWAC, POCZYTAC, POCZYTAC SOBIE, POCZYTYWAC, POCZY-TYWAC SOBIE, PRZECZYTAC, ROZCZYTAC SIE, ROZCZYTYWAC SIE, WCZYTAC SIE, WCZYTYWAC SIE, WYCZYTAC, WYCZYTYWAC, ZACZY-TYWAC, SIE, ZACZYTAC SIE describe all the possible ways and conditions of reading with the exception of "reread-ing" which can not be translated into Polish in one word. Besides the twenty three verbs are nouns: CZYTANKA, CZY-TELNICTWO, CZYTELNIK, CZYTELNIA, CZYTELNOSC, ODCZYT, POCZY-TALNOSC, NIEPOCZYTALNOSC, POCZYTNOSC, and adjectives as: CZYTELNY, NIECZYTELNY, OCZYTANY, NIEOCZYTANY, POCZYTALNY, NIEPOCZYTALNY, POCZYTNY etc.

PRZEDMOWA

Angielsko-polska część słownika zawiera około 15,000 haseł.
Jak wiadomo pojęcia i myśli formuje się w poszczególnych ję-
zykach w różny sposób. Nawet języki należące do tej samej grupy / jak np polski i angielski do grupy indoeuropejskiej/ nie
są równoznaczne.

Bogactwo polskich form gramatycznych nie ma odpowiednika w
angielskim. Odmiana rzeczowników i przymiotników przez siedem
przypadków oraz czasowników przez wszystkie możliwe osoby z od-
powiednimi zmianami końcówek, typowymi dla języka polskiego,
nie istnieje w angielskim. Język angielski bogatszy jest w wyrażenia zwyczajowo-idiomatyczne; więcej też jest w nim przyim-
ków i zaimków.

Język polski zawiera liczne formy gramatyczne poszczególnych
słów i gdyby wprowadzić każdą z nich jako odrębne hasło słownika to takich haseł byłoby kilka milionów.

Polska forma zwrotna zawiera określenia pośrednie między for-
mami czynną i bierną charakterystycznymi dla obu języków. Tej
formy nie można dosłownie przetłumaczyć na angielski. Na przykład powiedzenie "wzruszyłem się" nie znaczy dokładnie "I am
touched", co równa się polskiemu "jestem wzruszony". "I touched
myself" natomiast wcale nie znaczy "wzruszyłem się".

Inną cecha charakterystyczną języka polskiego jest odróżnienie
małej liczby mnogiej /2,3 i 4/ od dużej /5 i więcej/: tego roz-
różnienia nie ma w języku angielskim.

Ogólnie biorąc język polski ma więcej form rzeczownikowych,
przymiotnikowych oraz czasownikowych. W angielskim natomiast
prawie każdy rzeczownik bez zmiany pisowni może być użyty jako
czasownik a nieraz także jako przymiotnik. Polskie zasady gramatyczne można wyrazić słowami "zawsze z kilkoma wyjątkami", an-
gieskie zasady gramatyczne i fonetyczne są bardziej płynne - mówi się w nich: "często", "czasem" i "nieraz". W angielskim prze-
ważają wyrażenia i fonetyka zwyczajowe.

W części angielsko-polskiej słownika oznaczono formy gramatyczne poszczególnych haseł: rzeczowniki, przymiotniki, czasowniki,
przysłówki, zaimki, przyimki i częste zwroty.

Angielskie czasowniki nieregularne podano w trzech podstawo-

wych formach /infinitive, past and past participle = bezokolicznik, czas przeszły i imiesłów czasu przeszłego/.

Hasła wybrano z uwzględnieniem słownictwa używanego obecnie
w Polsce i w Ameryce; są wśród nich ważniejsze wyrażenia poto-
czne.

Podano wymowę i akcent.

BIBLIOGRAPHICAL NOTE

The spelling used in this dictionary was checked against standard current dictionaries.

The semantic aspects of phrases was analysed in accordance with Korzybski's General Semantics. Alfred Korzybski, Polish philosopher, mathematician and engineer founded in 1938 the Institute of General Semantics in Lakeland, Connecticut. The works of Jens Otto Jespersen were used as references for linguistic comments.

POLISH-ENGLISH

a (a)(as"a" in car) conj. and; or; but; then: at that time

a to (a to) conj. and so

abażur (a-bá-zhoor) m. lamp shade; a device to screen light

abdykować (ab-di-kó-vach) v. abdicate, abdicate the throne

abecadło (a-be-tsá-dwo) n. A.B.C., alphabet

abonament (a-bo-ná-ment) m. subscription, season ticket

abonent (a-bó-nent) m.subscriber, holder of a season ticket

abonować (a-bo-nó-vach) v. subscribe to a periodical etc.

absencja (ab-sén-tsya) f. absence, non-attendance

abstrakcja(ab-strák-tsya) f. abstraction; abstract

absurd (áb-soord) m. absurdity

aby (á-bi) conj. to; in order to, in order that, only to

ach ! (akh) excl.:oh ! ah!

aczkolwiek (ach-kól-vyek) conj. though; although, albeit, tho

adapter (a-dáp-ter) m. record player, adapter: pick-up

administracja (ad-mee-ńees-tráts-ya) f.administration; (management) authorities

admirał (ad-mée-raw) m.admiral

adres (ád-res) m.address

adwokat (ad-vó-kat) m. lawyer

afera (a-fé-ra) f. swindle

aferzysta (a-fe-zhís-ta) m. swindler: confidence man

afisz (á-feesh) m. poster

afiszować (a-fee-shó-vach) v. advertise: flaunt: parade

agrafka (a-gráf-ka) f. safety pin: hist.: buckle: brooch

agrest (ág-rest) m.gooseberry

aha ! (ákh-a!) excl.:oh yes...

a jakże ! (a-yák-zhe) excl. oh yes...: yes indeed!

akacja (a-káts-ya) f. acacia; locust tree: black locust

akcja (ák-tsya) f. action; share; plot; campain

akord (ák-ort) m. chord; piece work; contract work

AK (a-ká) f. Polish Home Army (W.W.II) (Armia Krajowa)

akowiec (a-kóv-yets) m. soldier of the Polish Home Army (W.W.II)

aksamit (ak-sá-meet) m. velvet

akt (akt) m. deed; act; cer- tificate; painting of a nude

akta (ák-ta) pl. documents; deeds; dossier: files; records

aktualny (ak-too-ál-ni) m. timely; current; up to date

akumulator (a-koo-moo-lá-tor)m. battery: storage battery

akuszerka (a-koo-sher-ka) f. midwife: accoucheuse

akwarela (ak-va-ré-la) f. water- color; painting in water color

albo (á-lbo) conj. or; else

albowiem (al-bó-vyem) conj. for; as; since;because; on account of

ale (á-le) conj. however; but; still; yet; not at all; n.defect

aleja (a-le-ya) f. avenue: alley

aleź (á-lesh) conj. why (yes)

alfa (ál-fa) f. alpha

alfabet (al-fá-bet) m. alphabet

alfons (ál-fons) m. pimp: cadet

alimenty (a-lee-mén-ti) pl. alimony for separated wife

alkohol (al-kó-khol) m. alcohol

alpejski (al-peý-skee) adj. m. Alpine: of the Alps

aluzja (a-lóoz-ya) f. hint: allusion: insinuation: dig

ałun (á-woon) m. alum

amant (á-mant) m. lover: beau

ambasada (am-ba-sá-da) f. embassy: ambassador and his staff

ambicja (am-beéts-ya) f. ambi- tion: aspiration: self esteem

ambona (am-bó-na) f. pulpit

Amerykanin (A-me-ri-ká-ńeen) m. American: man native of America

Amerykanka (A-me-ri-kán-ka) f. American: American women

amerykański (a-me-ri-kań-skee) adj. m. American: of America

amnestia (am-nést-ya) f.amnesty

amory (a-mó-ri) pl. flirtation; courting; love affairs

amortyzacja (a-mor-ti-záts-ya) f. depreciation; amortization

amperomierz (am-pe-ró-myesh) m. ammeter: meter of amperes

amputować (am-poo-tó-vach) v.
amputate; to cut off
amunicja (a-moo-neets-ya) f.
ammunition: munitions
analfabeta (a-nal-fa-bé-ta) m.
illiterate: an ignorant
analiza (a-na-lée-za) f. analysis ; parsing
analogia (a-na-lóg-ya) f. analogy; parallelism; parity
ananas (a-ná-nas) m. pineapple;
rascal; rogue; blighter
andrus (án-droos) m. rough kid
andrut (ánd-root) m. wafer
anegdota (a-neg-dó-ta) f.
anecdote; story; theme
aneksja (a-neks-ya) f. annexation; rape of a country
anemia (a-ném-ya) f. anemia
angażować (an-ga-zhó-vach) v.
engage; undertake; hire;bind
angielski (an-gél-skee) adj.
m. English; English language
ani (á-ñee) conj. neither; nor;
no; not; or; not even
anielski (a-ñel-skee) adj. m.
angelic: cherubic; angelical
animusz (a-ñee-moosh) m.
courage; verve; vigor; zest
anioł (á-ñow) m. angel
aniżeli (a-ñee-zhé-lee) part.
rather; than; rather than
ankieta (an-ké-ta) f. poll;
inquiry; questionnaire
anons (a-nons) m. advertisement in a newspaper; ad
antybiotyki (an-ti-bee-yó-ti-
kee) pl. antibiotics
antyk (án-tik) antique
antypatyczny (an-ti-pa-tich-
ni) adj. m. repugnant
apartament (a-par-tá-ment) m.
residence: suite of rooms
aparat (a-pá-rat) m. apparatus;
appliance; camera; gadget;gear
apel (áp-el) m. appeal; roll-
call; appeal; muster; parade
apetyt (a-pé-tit) m. appetite
apostolski (a-pos-tól-skee)
adj. m. apostolic: missionary
aprobować (a-pro-bó-vach) v.
approve; endorse; sanction

aprowizacja (a-pro-vee-záts-ya)
f. food supply; provisions
apteczka (ap-téch-ka) f. first
aid kit; medicine chest
apteka (ap-té-ka) f. pharmacy
arbiter (ar-bée-ter) m. umpire;
arbitrator; moderator; mediator
arbuz (ár-boos) m. watermelon
architekt (ar-khée-tekt) m.
architect
arcydzieło (ar-tsi-dźhé-wo) n.
masterpiece
arena (a-ré-na) f. arena; stage
areszt (á-resht) m. arrest; jail
argument (ar-góo-ment) m.
argument; reason; contention
arkusz (ár-koosh) m. sheet
armata (ar-má-ta) f. cannon
armator (ar-má-tor) m. shipowner; skipper; charterer
armia (árm-ya) f. army; array
arogancja (a-ro-gán-tsya) f.
arrogance; insolence; conceit
arteria(ar-tér-ya) f. artery
artykuł (ar-ti-koow) m. article
artretyzm (ar-tré-tizm) m.
arthritis; gout
artyleria (ar-ti-lér-ya) f.
artillery; gunnery; ordnance
artysta (ar-ti-sta) m. artist
arytmetyka (a-rit-mé-ti-ka) f.
arithmetic
as (as) m. ace ; A flat
asceta (as-tsé-ta) m. ascetic
asekuracja (a-se-koo-ráts-ya)
f. insurance; assurance
aspiryna (as-pee-rí-na) f.
aspirin
astma (ást-ma) f. asthma
asygnata (a-sig-ná-ta) f.
order (of payment)
asymilować (a-si-mee-ló-vach)
v. assimilate: absorb; liken
asystować (a-sis-tó-vach) v.
accompany; attend; court; assist
atak (á-tak) m. attack; charge
(fit); spasm; offensive
atlas (at-las) m. atlas
atleta (at-lé-ta) m. athlete
atłas (át-was) m. satin
atmosfera (at-mos-fé-ra) f.
atmosphere: air; climate; tone

atom (á-tom) m. atom

atol (á-tol) m. atoll

atomowy (a-to-mó-vi) adj. m. atomic

atrakcja (a-trák-tsya) f. attraction; high light

atrament (a-trá-ment) m. ink

atut (á-toot) m. trump

audycja (aw-díts-ya)f. broadcast; program; pop

aukcja (áwk-tsya) f. auction

autentyczny (aw-ten-tích-ni) adj. m. authentic; genuine

auto (áw-to) n. motor car

autor (áw-tor) m. author

autostrada (aw-to-strá-da) f. superhighway; freeway

awans (á-vans) m. promotion; advancement; preferment

awantura (a-van-too-ra) f. brawl; fuss; row: scandal

azot (á-zot) m, nitrogen

aż (ásh) part. as much; up to; til ; until; as far as

ażeby (a-zhé-bi) conj. that; in order that; so that

ażurowy (a-zhoo-ró-vi) adj. m. lace-like; transparent

ba (bá) excl.: hey ?; nay; indeed..; and even; what more

baba (bá-ba) f. woman (old, simple); grandmother; rammer

babiarz (báb-yash) m. lady chaser: ladies' man

babie lato (bá-bye lá-to) n. Indian Summer ;lass;chick;cake

babka (báb-ka) f. grandmother;

babrać (báb-rach) v. smear; stain; dabble; soil: fumble

bachor (bá-khor) m. kid; brat

baczność (bách-noshćh) f. attention; care

bać się (bach shah) v. fear

badacz (bá-dach) m. researcher

badać (bá-dach) v. investigate; examine; research ; explore

badyl (bá-dil) m. stem: weed

badylarz (ba-dí-lash) m. marketing gardener (slang)

bagatela (ba-ga-té-la) f. trifle ; easy matter

bagaż (bá-gash) m. luggage

bagażowy (ba-ga-zhó-vi) m. porter; adj.m. baggage-; luggage-

bagnet (bág-net) m. bayonet

bagno (bág-no) m. swamp; morass

bajka (báy-ka) f. fairy-tale; gossip; scandal; story; fable

bajoro (ba-yó-ro) n. muddy pool

bak (bak) m. gasoline tank; side whisker ;bacteria;

bakterie (bak-tér-ye) pl.germs

bal (bal) m. ball; bale; log

balet (bá-let) m. ballet

balia (bál-ya) f. wash tub

balkon (bál-kon) m. balcony

balustrada (ba-loos-trá-da) f. railing; hand rail; guard rail

bałagan (ba-wá-gan) m. mess; disorder; disarray; confusion

bałamucić (ba-wa-moo-tseéch) v. lead astray; loiter; flirt; coax

bałwan (báw-van) m. snowman; ass; breaking wave crest; blockhead; fool; nitwit; fetish; idol; lump

banał (bá-naw) m. stock phrase; tag; banality; truism; triviality

banan (bá-nan) m. banana

banda (bán-da) f. band; gang

bandaż (bán-dash) m. bandage

bandera (ban-dé-ra) f. flag

bandyta (ban-dí-ta) m. bandit

bank (bank) m. bank; pool

bankiet (bán-ket) m. banquet

banknot (bánk-not) m. banknote

bankrut (bánk-root) m. bankrupt

babtysta (bap-tís-ta) m. baptist

bar (bar) m. bar; barium

barman (bár-man) m. barman

barak (bá-rak) m. barrack

baran (bá-ran) m. ram;tup; idiot

baraszkować (ba-rash-kó-vach) v. frolic: gambol; romp; caper

barbarzynca (bar-ba-zhiń-tsa) m. barbarian: savage; vandal

barczysty (bar-chís-ti) m. broad-shouldered; square built

bardziej (bár-dzhey) adv.more; (emphatic "bardzo"); worse

bardzo (bár-dzo) adv. very

bariera (bar-yé-ra) f. rail; barrier; hand rail; obstacle

barki (bár-kee) pl. shoulders

barłóg (bár-woog) m. litter bed

barszcz (barshch) m. beet soup
barwa (bár-va) f. color; hue
bary (bá-ri) pl. large
  shoulders: parallel bars
barykada (ba-ri-ká-da) f.
  barricade; barrier
baryłka (ba-riw-ka) f. barrel
basen (bá-sen) m. pool; tank
bastard (bás-tard) m. bastard
baśń (baśhń) f. fable; myth
bat (bat) m. whip; lash
bateria (ba-tér-ya) f. battery
bawełna (ba-véw-na) f. cotton
bawialnia (ba-vyál-ña) f.
  sitting room; parlor
bawić (bá-veech) v. amuse;
  entertain; recreate; stay
bawidamek (ba-vee-dá-mek) m.
  ladies man; gallant
bawół (bá-voow) m. buffalo
baza (bá-za) f. base; basis
bazgrać (báz-grach) v. scribble;
  scrawl; scratch; daub; splotch
bażant (bá-zhant) m. pheasant
bąbel (bówn-bel) m. blister
bądź (bownch) v. be this
bądź (bownch) conj. either-or
bąk (bownk) m. horse fly;
  blunder; vulg. ; fart
bąkać (bówn-kach) v. mumble;
  hint ; mutter; hum
bebechy (be-bé-khi) pl. guts
beczka (béch-ka) f. barrel
bednarz (béd-nash) m. cooper
befsztyk (béf-shtik) m. beefsteak
beksa (bék-sa) f. cry baby
beletrystyka (be-le-trís-ti-
  ka) f. fiction ; letters
belka (bél-ka) f. beam; bar
bełkot (béw-kot) m. mumbling
benzyna (ben-zína) f. gasoline
berbeć (bér-bech) m. small kid;
  toddler ; brat; dot
berek (bé-rek) m. tag play
beret (bé-ret) m. beret ; cap
besztać (bésh-tach) v. scold;
  rebuke ; chide; rebuke:trounce
bestia (bés-tya) f. beast
beton (bé-ton) m. concrete
bety (bé-ti) pl. bedding
bez (bes) prep. without

bez (bes) m. lilac;prep.without
bez-(bes) prefix = suffix less
beza (bé-za) f. meringue
bezbarwny (bez-bárw-ni) adj.
  m. colorless; plain; drab; dull
bezbłędny (bez-bwáňd-ni) adj.
  m. faultless; correct; perfect
bezbolesny (bez-bo-lés-ni) adj.
  m. painless
bezbronny (bez-brón-ni) adj.
  m. defenseless; helpless;unarmed
bezcelowy (bez-tse-ló-vi) adj.
  m. aimless; pointless; useless
bezcenny (bez-tsén-ni) adj.m.
  priceless; invluable; inestimable
bezchmurny (bez-khmoó-rni)
  adj. m. cloudless; serene; clear
bezdomny (bez-dóm-ni) adj. m.
  homeless; houseless; shelterless
bezdzietny (bez-dzhét-ni) adj
  m. childless; without offspring
bezdźwięczny (bez-dzhvánch-ni)
  adj. m. soundless; voiceless
bezecny (be-zéts-ni) adj. m.
  wicked; infamous; ignominious
bezgotówkowy (bez-go-toov-kó-
  vi) adj. m. without cash
bezgrzeszny (bez-gzhésh-ni)
  adj. m. sinless;inocent; chaste
bezkonkurencyjny (bez-kon-koo-
  ren-tsíy-ni) adj. m. unrivaled
bezkrwawy (bez-krvá-vi) adj.
  m. bloodless; free of bloodshed
bezkształtny (bez-kshtáwt-ni)
  adj. m. shapeless; formless
bezład (béz-wat) m. disorder
bezmiar (béz-myar) m. immen-
  sity; boundlessness; vastness
bezmyslność (bez-míshl-noshch)
  f. thoughtlessness; wantonness
beznadziejny (bez-na-dzhéy-ni)
  adj. m. hopeless; desperate
bez ogródek (bez o-groó-dek)
  adv. bluntly; unequivocally
bezokolicznik (bez-o-ko-leech-
  ñeek) m. infinitive (mood)
bezowocny (bez-o-vóts-ni) m.
  fruitless; vain; unsuccessful
bezpieczeństwo (bez-pye-cheñ-
  stvo) m. security; safety
bezpłatnie (bez-pwát-ñe) adv.
  free of charge; gratuitously

bezpłciowy (bez-pwchó-vi) adj.
m. sexless; neutral; insipid
bezpodstawny (bez-pod-stáv-ny)
adj. m. groundless; baseless
bezpośrednio (bez-po-shred-ño)
adv. directly; directly
bezprawny (bez-práv-ni) adj.
m. lawless; illegal; illicit
bezprzedmiotowy (bez-przed-myo-
tó-vi) adj. m.   aimless
bezprzykładny (bez-pzhi-kwád-
ni) adj. m. unprecedented
bezradny (bez-rád-ni) adj. m.
helpless; baffled; at a loss
bezręki (bez-rán-kee) adj.m.
armless; handless (cripple)
bezrobotny (bez-ro-bó-tni)
adj. m. unemployed
bezrolny (bez-ról-ni) adj.m.
landless; with no land
bezsenny (bez-sén-ni) adj. m.
sleepless; restless; wakeful
bezsens (béz-sens) m. nonsense
bezsilny (bez-sheel-ni) adj.
m. powerless; weak; helpless
bezskuteczny (bez-skoo-téch-
ni) adj. m. to no avail;
futile; ineffective; nugatory
bezsporny (bez-spór-ni) adj.
m. incontestable; undebatable
bezsprzeczny (bez-spzhech-ni)
adj. m. indisputable; evident
bezstronność (bez-stron-noshch)
f. impartiality; fairness
beztroski (bez-trós-kee) adj.
m. carefree; careless;jaunty
bezustanny (bez-oos-tán-ni)
adj. m. ceaseless; endless
bezużyteczny (bez-oo-zhi-téch-
ni) adj. m. useless; idle
bezwartościowy (bez-var-tosh-
 chó-vi) adj. m. worthless
bezwarunkowy (bez-va-roon-kó-vi)
adj. m. unconditional; utter
bezwładność (bez-vwád-noshch)
f. inertia; torpor; decline
bezwstydny (bez-vstíd-ni) adj.
m. shameless; lewd; flagrant
bezwyznaniowy (bez-viz-na-ño-
vi) adj. m. nonsectarian
bezwzględny (bez-vzgláhd-ni)
adj. m. ruthless; despotic
bezzębny (bez-zánb-ni) adj. m.
toothless; edentate

bezzwłoczny (bez-zvwóch-ni)
adj. m. immediate; prompt
bezzwrotny (bez-zvrót-ni) adj.
m. not to be refunded
beż (besh) m. beige
bęben (bán-ben) m. drum; kid;
brat; barrel; cylinder;tumbler
bęcwał (bánts-vaw) m. nincompoop; dullard; chickle head
bękart (bán-kart) m. bastard
biadać (byá-dach) v. moan
białaczka (bya-wách-ka) f.
leukemia
białko (byá-wko) n. egg white;
protein; white of the eye
biały (bya-wi) adj. m. white
biba (bee-ba) f. drinking spree
biblia (beeb-lya) f. Bible
biblioteka (beeb-lyo-té-ka) f.
library: bookcase; book series
bibuła (bee-boo-wa) f. blotting
paper; illegal political
publication; literary trash
bicz (beech) m. whip; whiplash
bić (beéch) v. beat; defeat(etc)
biec (byets) v. run; trot; flow
bieda (bye-da) f. poverty; want;
trouble; distress; evil days
biedny (byéd-ni) adj. m. poor
bieg (byeg) m. run; race; course
biegle (bye-gle) adv. fluently
biegun (bye-goon) m. pole;
rocker; spindle; trunnion
biegunka (bye-goon-ka) f.
diarrhea; dysentery
biel (byel) f.whiteness; white
bielizna (bye-leéz-na) f. linen
bielmo (byel-mo) n. cataract
bierny (byer-ni) adj. m. passive
bieżący (bye-zhówn-tsi) adj. m.
current; flowing; running
bieżnia (byézh-ña) f. runway;
track; racecourse; tyre tread
bigos (bee-gos) m. hashed meat
and cabbage (Polish style)
bijatyka (bee-ya-tí-ka) f.
fight; brawl; tussle; scrimmage
bila (bee-la) f. billiard ball
bilans (bee-lans) m. balance
sheet; balance; rest; outcome
bilet (bee-let) m. note; ticket
biodro (byód-ro) n. hip; huckle
biszkopt (beesh-kopt) m.
biscuit; sponge cake; cracer

bitny (beet-ni) adj. m. valiant

bitwa (beet-va) f. battle; fight

biuro (byoo-ro) n. office

biust (byoost) m. bust; breast

biustonosz (byoos-tó-nosh) m. brassiere; bra; bust bcdice

biżuteria (bee-zhoo-tér-ya) f. jewelry: jewels

blacha (blá-kha) f. sheet metal; cook top; tinware

blady (blá-di) adj. m. pale

blaga (blá-ga) f. lie; bluff

blankiet (blán-ket) m. blank form; printed form: blank

blask (blask) m. flush; luster

bliski (blées-kee) adj. m. near; imminent; near by:close

blizna (bleéz-na) f. scar

bliźni (bleéźh-nee)m. fellow man; twin: identical; neighbor

blokować (blo-kó-vach) v.block; blockade; obstruct; stall

blondynka (blon-dín-ka) f. blonde (girl); fair haired girl

bluzka (blóoz-ka) f. blouse

bluźnić (blóoźh-ńeech) v. curse; blaspheme; talk nonsense

błahość (bwa-khoshch) f. trifle

błagać (bwá-gach) v. beseech

błazen (bwa-zen) m. clown; buffoon

błąd (bwownt) m. error; slip-up; ⎰mistake; lapse

błąkać się (bwówn-kach shán)v. wander; stray; roam; rove

błękit (bwan-keet) m. blue; azure; blue pigment; sky

błocić (bwo-cheech) v. get muddy: soil with mud; spatter

błogi (bwo-gee) adj. m.blissful: delightful; sweet

błogosławić (bwo-go-swa-veech) v. bless; praise; exalt; thank

błona (bwona) f. membrane; coat; film; tunic; velum; web

błonie (bwo-ńe) n. meadow; plain; public grassy land

błotnik (bwot-ńeek) m.(car) fender; mudguard; splash board

błoto (bwo-to) n. mud; muck

błysk (bwisk) m. flash; flare

bo (bo) conj. because; for; or; as; since; or else; but then

bochenek (bo-khé-nek) m. loaf

bocian (bó-chan) m. stork

boczny (bóch-ny) adj. m. lateral; side ; collateral (line)

boczyć się (bó-chych shán) v. sulk; be angry; look askance

bodaj (bó-day) part. may be; should be…; would be...;

bodziec (bó-dźhets) m. stimulus

bogactwo (bo-gáts-tvo) n.riches; wealth; means; fortune; plenty

bogaty (bo-gá-ti) adj. m. rich

bogobojny (bo-go-bóy-ni) adj. m. pious; devout; church going

bohater (bo-kha-ter) m. hero

boisko (bo-ées-ko) n. stadium; field; threshing floor;gridiron

bojaźń (bó-yaźhń) f. fear; fright

boja (bó-ya) f. buoy ; beacon

bojkot (bóy-kot) m. boycott

bojownik (bo-yóv-ńeek) m. fighter; militant; champion

bok (bok) m. side; flank

boks (boks) m. boxing; stall

boleć (bó-lech) v. pain; ache

bolesny (bo-lés-ni) adj. m. sore; painful; sad; woeful; dismal

bomba (bóm-ba) f. bomb; sphere

bombowiec (bom-bó-vyets) m. bomber ; bombing plane

borykać się (bo-rí-kach shán) v. cope; struggle; wrestle

bosak (bo-sak) m. boat hook

boso (bó-so) adv. barefoot

bosy (bó-si) adj. m. barefoot

bowiem (bó-vyem) conj. for; because; since; as; hence

boży (bo-zhi) adj. m. God's

Bóg (book)m. God

bój (booy) m. fight; battle

ból (bool) m. pain; ache; sore

bór (boor) m. forest; wood

bóść (booshch) v. gore; sting

bóźnica (boozh-ńee-tsa) f. synagogue: house of prayer

bractwo (bráts-tvo) n. fraternity; brotherhood; guild

brać (brach) v. take; hold etc.

brak (brak) m. lack; need;want; scarcity; shortage;absence;fault

brama (brá-ma) f. gate; gateway; front door; wicket

bransoletka (bran-so-lét-ka) f.
  bracelet; wristlet; bangle
brat (brat) m. brother; mate
bratać (brá-tać) v. unite;
  fraternize; chum up
bratanek (bra-tá-nek) m. nephew
bratanica (bra-ta-ńée-tsa) f.
  niece
brednie (bréd-ńe) n. nonsense
brew (brev) f. eyebrow
brewerie (bre-vér-ye) n. brawl
brezent (bré-zent) m. tarpau-
  lin; canvas
brnąć (brnównch) v. wade
broczyć (bró-chich) v. bleed
broda (broda) f. beard; chin
brodzić (bró-dźheech)v. wade
broić (bró-eech) v. make
  mischief; frolic; romp;gambol
brom (brom) m. bromine
brona (bró-na) f. harrow
bronić (bró-ńeech) v. defend
bronz (bronsı m. bronze
broń (broń) f. weapon; arms
broszka (brósh-ka) f. brooch
broszura (bro-shóo-ra) f.
  pamphlet; folder; booklet
browar (bró-var) m. brewery
bród (broot) m. ford
brud (broot) m. dirt; filth
bruk (brook) m. pavement
brukiew (broo-kęv) f. turnip
brulion (brool-yon) m. rough
  draft; notebook; exercise book
brunatny (broo-ná-tni) adj. m.
  brown; tawny; tan colored
brunetka (broo-nét-ka) f.
  brunette
brutal (broo-tal) m. brute
bruzda (brooz-da) f. furrow;
  groove; deep wrinkle; streak
brwi (brvee) pl. eye brows
brykać (brí-kach) v. prance
bryła (brí-wa) f. lump; mass
bryzg (brizk) m. splash
bryzgać (briz-gach) v. splash
brzeg (bzhek) m. shore; margin
brzemię (bzhe-myáń) n. burden
brzęk (bzháńk) m. clink;chink;
  rattle; ping; buzz; hum:drone
brzuch (bzhookh) m. belly; abdomen; stomach; tummy; guts

brzydki (bzhíd-kee) adj. m.
  ugly; unsightly; hideous; foul
brzydzić się (bzhí-dźheech śháń)
  v. feel disgust; loathe; abhor
brzytwa (bzhít-va) f. razor
buchać (boo-khach) v. squirt;
  spout;burst forth; flare; blaze
bucik (boo-cheek) m. shoe; boot
buda (boo-da) f. shed (stall)
budowa (boo-dó-va) f. construction; erection; framework
budowla (boo-dov-la) f. building (large); edifice;structure
budynek (boo-dí-nek) m. building; edifice; house
budzić (boo-dźheech)v. wake up
budzik (boo-dźheek)m. alarm
  clock; alarum clock
budżet (boo-jet) m. budget
bujać (boo-yach) v. rock; lie
bufor (boo-for) m. buffer
bułka (boow-ka) f. roll (breakfast); bread roll; loaf
bunt (boont) m. mutiny
bura (boo-ra)f. reprimand
burak (boo-rak) m. beet
burda (boo-r-da) f. scuffle;row;
  brawl; disturbance; rough neck
burmistrz (boor-meestsh) m.
  mayor
bursztyn (boor-shtin) m. amber
burta (boor-ta) f. ship's side
bury (boo-ri)adj. m. dark gray
burza (boo-zha) f. tempest;
  storm; wind storm; rain storm
burżuazja (boor-zhoo-áz-ya) f.
  bourgeoisie; middle class
busola (boo-só-la) f. compass
but (boot) m. boot; shoe; sabot
buta (boo-ta) f. arrogance
butelka (boo-tél-ka) f. bottle
butny (boot-ni) adj. m. arrogant; insolent; overbearing
buzia (boo-zha) f. face; mouth
by (bi) conj. in order that;
  (conditional)as if; at least
byczy (bí-chi) adj. m. 1. bull's
  2. very good; glorious
być (bich) v. be; exist; live
bydlę (bid-láń) n. beast; brute
byle (bi-le) conj. in order to;
  so as to; pron. any; slap-dash

byży (bí-wi) adj. m. former

bynajmniej (bi-náy-mñey) adv.
by no means,; not at all

bystrość (bíst-roshćh) f.
swiftness; shrewdness

byt (bit) m. existence

bytność (bít-noshćh) f. stay

bywać (bí-vach) v. frequent

bywalec (bi-vá-lets) m.patron
frequenter; man of the world

bzdura (bzdoo-ra) f. nonsense

bzik (bżheek)adj. m. crank;
loony; crazy; m. fad; craze

bzykać (bzí-kach) v. buzz

cackać się (tsáts-kach shań)v.
fondle; pamper; humor;coddle

cacko (tsáts-ko) n. jewel;
trinket; plaything;toy;beauty

cal (tsal) m. inch

całka (tsáw-ka) f. integral

całkiem (tsáw-ḱem) adv.quite;
entirely; completely; totally

całkowity (tsaw-ko-vée-ti)
adj. m. total; complete

cało (tsá-wo) adv. (in one
piece) safely; safe and sound

całować (tsa-wó-vach) v. kiss;
embrace; give a kiss

całus (tsá-woos) m. kiss

cap (tsap) m. billy goat

caber (tsówn-ber) m. rump;
fillet

cążki (tsównzh-kee) pl. small
tongs; pliers; pincers

ceber (tsé-ber) m. bucket

cebula (tse-bóo-la) f. onion

cech (tsekh) m. trade; guild

cecha (tsé-kha) f. feature;
mark; trait; stamp; character

cechować (tse-khó-vach) v.
mark; characterize; calibrate

cedr (tsedr) m. cedar

cedzić (tsé-dżheećh)v. strain;
filter; percolate;sip;trickle

cegielnia (tse-ǵel-ña) f.
brickyard; brick factory

cegła (tséǵ-wa) f. brick

cel (tsel) m. purpose; aim

cela (tsé-la) f. cell

celnik (tsél-ñeek) m. customs
inspector: customs officer

celować (tse-ló-vach) v. aim;
excel; exceed

celuloza (tse-loo-ló-za) f.
cellulose

cembrować (tsem-bró-vach) v.
case(well); timber (a shaft)

cement (tsé-ment) m. cement

cena (tsé-na) f. price; value

cenić (tsé-ñeećh) v. value;rate;
esteem; prize; evaluate

cennik (tsén-ñeek) m. price
list; price catalogue

centnar (tsént-nar) m. hundredweight

centrala (tsen-trá-la) f. head
office ; main office ; exchange

centrum (tsént-room) n. center

centryfuga (tsen-tri-foo-ga) f.
centrifuge; separator

centymetr (tsen-tí-metr) m.
centimeter ⌐blockhead

cep (tsep) m. flail; darn; mend

cera (tsé-ra) f. complexion

ceramiczny (tse-ra-meéch-ni)
adj. m. ceramic; earthenware

cerata (tse-rá-ta) f. oilcloth

ceregiele (tse-re-ǵe-le) n.
fuss: petty formalities

certować sie(tser-to-vach shan)v.
pretend;stand on ceremony;fuss

cewka (tsév-ka) f. spool

cęgi (tsáñ-gee) pl. tongs

cętka (tsáñt-ka) f. dot

chałat (khá-wat) m. lab.coat

chałastra (kha-wás-tra) f. mob

chałupa (kha-woo-pa) f. hut

cham (kham) m. roughneck; boor

charakter (kha-rák-ter) m.
disposition; chara.cter

charczeć (khár-chech) v.
wheese; snort; be hoarse

chata (khá-ta) f. hut; cabin

chcieć (khćhećh) v. want

chciwiec (khćhee-vyets) m.
greedy man; grasping man

chełpić się (khew-peećh sháń)
v. boast; brag; bluster:vaunt

chemia (khém-ya) f. chemistry

chemiczny (khe-meéch-ni) adj.m.
chemical

cherlak (khér-lak) m. weakling

chęć (kháńch) f. wish; desire

chędogi (kháń-do-gi) adj. m.
neat; clean; tidy; orderly

chichot (khee-khot) m. giggle;
laughter; chuckle; titter
chimera (khee-mé-ra) f. whim
chinina (khee-ńee-na) f. quinine
chiński (kheeń-skee) adj.m.
Chinese
chirurg (khee-roorg) m. surgeon; sawbones (slang)
chlapać (khlá-pach) v. splash
chleb (khleb) m. bread
chlew (khlev) m. pigsty;pigpen
chlor (khlor) m. chlorine
chluba (khloo-ba)f.glory,pride
chlubić się (khloo-beech sháń)
v. boast; flatter oneself
chlusnąć (khloos-nówńch) v.
splash; fling; spout; spurt
chłeptać (khwep-tach) v. lap up
chłodzić (khwo-dźheech)v. cool
chłonąć (khwo-nówńch) v. absorb;
devour; drink in; inhale
chłop (khwop) m. peasant; man
chłosta (khwos-ta) f. lashing
chłód (khwoot) m. cold; freshness; coolness; iciness:shiver
chłystek (khwis-tek) m. squirt
chmara (khma-ra) f. swarm
chmiel (khmyel) m. hop; hops
chmura (khmoo-ra) f. cloud
chociaż (kho-chash) conj.albeit;
even if; though, tho'; while
chociaż = chocby = chociazby
choć (khoch) conj. at least
chodnik (khod-ńeek) m. sidewalk; pathway; stair carpet
chodzić (kho-dźheech) v. go;
walk; move; creep; pace;attend
choina (kho-ee-na) f. fir
cholera (kho-lé-ra) f. cholera
excl.:damn ! hell! the devil!
cholewa (kho-le-va) f. boot
chorągiew (kho-równ-gev) f.
flag; standard; ensign
choroba (kho-ro-ba) f. sickness
chory (khó-ri) adj. m. sick;
ill; ailing; infirm; unwell
chować (kho-vach) v. hide
chód (khoot) m. gait; walk
chór (khoor) m. choir
chów (khoof) m. breeding
chrabąszcz (khrá-bówńshch) m.
beetle;May -bug

chrapać (khrá-pach) v. snore
chroniczny (khro-ńeech-ni) adj.
m. chronic
chronić (khró-ńeech) v. shelter;
protect; quard; shield; fence
chropowaty (khro-po-vá-ti) adj.
m. rough; callous; coarse;harsh
chrust (khroost) m. kindling
chrupać (khroo-pach) v. crunch
chrypka (khrip-ka) f. hoarse -
ness; sore throat
Chrystus (khris-toos) m. Christ
chrzan (khzhan) m. horseradish
chrząstka (khzhównst-ka) f.
cartilage; gristle; copula
chrząszcz (khshównshch) m.
May bug; beetle; cockchafer
chrzcić (khzhćheech) v. baptize
chrzest (khzhest) m. baptism
chrześcijanin (khzhe-śhćhee-
yá-ńeen) m. Christian
chrzęst (khzháńst) m. clatter
chrzęścić (khzháń-śhćheech) v.
clank; jangle; grate; crunch
chuchać (khoo-khach) v. puff
chuchro (khóokh-ro) m. weakling
chuć (khooćh) f. lust
chudnąć (khood-nówńch) v.lose
weight; grow thin; lose flesh
chuligan (khoo-lee-gan) m.
hoodlum; ruffian; roughneck
chustka (khoóst-ka) f. handkerchief; kerchief; scarf
chwacki (khvats-kee) adj. m.
brave; plucky; gallant; rakish
chwalić (khvá-leech) v. praise
chwała (khvá-wa) f. praise;
glory; splendor; pride
chwast (khvast) m. weed
chwiać (khvyach) v. waver
chwila (khvee-la) f. moment
chwycić (khvi-ćheech) v. grasp
chwyt (khvit) m. grasp; grip
chyba (khí-ba) part. maybe
chybotać (khi-bo-tach) v. rock
chybić (khi-beech) v. miss
chylić (khi-leech) v. bow
chyłkiem (khíw-kem) adj.
stealthily; on the sly
chytry (khit-ri) adj. m. sly
chyży (khi-zhi) adj. m. swift
ci (ćhee) pron. these; they;
part.: for you

ciało (chá-wo) n. body; substance; frame; anatomy;corpse
ciarki (char-kee) pl. shudder
ciasnota (chas-nó-ta) f.
tightness; narrow-mindedness
ciastko (chast-ko) n . cake;pie
ciasto (chás-to) n, dough
ciąć (chowńch) v. cut; clip
ciagnac(chówng-nównch)v.pull
ciągnik (chówng-ńeek) m. tractor; agrimotor; crawler
ciąża (chówn-zha) f. pregnancy
ciążenie (chówn-zhe-ńe) v.
gravitation;tendency
cichaczem (chee-khá-chem) adv.
stealthily; on the quiet
cichnąć (cheekh-nównch) v.
quiet down; subside; abate
cicho (chee-kho) adv. silently;
noiselessly; softly:privately
cichy (chee-khi) adj. m. quiet;
still; low;gentle; calm; serene
ciec (chets) v. leak; flow
ciecz (chech) f. liquid
ciekawy (ché-kav) adj. m.cute;
curious;interesting;prying
cielak (che-lak) m. calf
cielesny (che-lés-ni) adj. m.
carnal; bodily; sexual
ciemię (che-myáń) n. crown of
the head; septum of the skull
ciemiężenie (che-myáń-zhe-ńe)
n. oppression; subjugation
ciemnia (chem-ńa) f. dark room
ciemno (chem-no) adv. darkly
ciemny (chém-ni) adj. m. dark
cieniować (che-ńo- vach) v.
shade; modulate; grade
cienisty (che-ńees-ti) adj.
m. shady; shade giving
cienki (chen-kee) adj. m. thin
cień (cheń) m. shade; shadow
cieplarnia (che-plár-ńa) f.
greenhouse; hothouse; stove
ciepło (che-pwo) adv. warm
cieplawy (che-pwa-vi) adj.
m. lukewarm; tepid
ciepły (chép-wi) adj. m. warm
cierń (cherń) m. thorn;pricle
cierpiący (cher-pyówn-tsi)
adj. m., suffering; ailing;ill
cierpieć (cher-pyech)v.suffer;
anguish; be troubled; endure

cierpki (cherp-kee) adj. m.
tart; acid;surly;acrid;sour
cierpliwosc (cher-plee-voshch)
f. patience; endurance
cierpliwy (cher-plee-vi) adj.
m. enduring; patient: forbearing
cierpnąć (cherp-nównch) v.
grow numb; creep; go to sleep
ciesielstwo (che-shel-stvo) n.
carpentry (in construction)
cieszyc (che-shich) v. cheer
ciesla (cheśh-la) m. carpenter
(constr.);wood worker;shipwright
cietrzew (che-tzhev) m. black-
cock; black grouse; grey hen
cieśnina (cheśh-ńee-na) f. strait
cięcie (cháń-che) n. cut; gash
cięciwa (chań-chee-va) f. chord;
bow string; string; subtense
cięgi (cháń-gee) pl. lashing
cięty (cháń-ti) adj. m. sharp-
tongued; biting;dogged;incisive
ciężar (cháń-zhar) m. weight;
burden; gravity; onus; duty;task
ciężec (cháń-zhech) v. grow
heavy; become a burden;encumber
ciężki (cháńzh-kee) adj. m.
heavy; weighty: bulky; oppressive
ciężko (cháńzh-ko) adv. heavily
ciocia (chó-cha) f. auntie;aunt
cios (chos) m. blow; stroke;
hit; shock; ashlar; block; joint
cioteczny brat (cho-tech-ni
brat) m. cousin
ciotka (chót-ka) f. aunt
ciosac (chó-sach) v. hew; chop out
cis (chees) m. yew
cisawy (chees-ávi) adj. m.
chesnut (horse)
ciskac (chees-kach) v. fling;cast;
throw; hurl: sling; plunk;let fly
cisnąć (chees-nównch) v. press;
squeeze; bear; urge; pinch;crowd
cisza (chee-sha) f. calm; silence
ciśnienie (cheesh-ńé-ńe) n.
pressure; blood pressure; thrust
ciuch (chookh) m. used clothing
ciułać (choo-wach) v. hoard
ciurkiem (choor-kem) adv. in
a trickle; with big drops
ciupa (choo-pa) f. jail; clink
ciupasem (choo-pá-sem) adv.
under convoy under armed convoy

ciżba (chéezh-ba) f. crowd
ckliwy (tsklée-vi) adj. m.
   qualmy; sickly; faint;sloppy
clic (tsleech) v. collect
   custom duty;lay a custom duty
cło (tswo) n. customs
cmentarz (tsmén-tash) m. cemetery; burial ground
cmokac (tsmó-kach) v. smack
cnota (tsnó-ta) f. virtue
co (tso) pron. part. what;which
codzień (tsó-dżeń)adv. daily
cofac się (tsó-fach shan) v.
   back up; remove; withdraw
cokolwiek (tso-kól-vyek) pron.
   anything; whatever; somewhat
comber (tsom-ber) m. saddle
   (of mutton);rump;loin; haunch
coraz (tsó-raz) adv. ever
coś (tsosh) pron. something
corka (tsoor-ka) f. daughter
cóż (tsoosh) pron. what then
cuchnąc (tsookh-nównch) v.
   stink foul; smell foul
cucic (tsoo-cheech) v. revive
cud (tsoot) m. wonder; miracle
cudzołożyc (tsoo-dzo-wó-zhich)
   v. commit adultery
cudzoziemiec (tsoo-dzo-zhé-
   myets) m. alien; foreigner
cudzy (tsoo-dzi) adj. m.
   someone else's; alien;foreign
cudzysłów (tsoo-dzi-swoof)m.
   quotation marks
cukier (tsoo-ker) m. sugar
cuma (tsoo-ma) f. mooring
cwał (tsvaw) m. full gallop
cwaniak (tsvá-ñak) m. city
   slicker; sly dog;crafty guy
cwany (tsvá-ni) adj. m. sly;
      cunning; crafty; artful
cyc (tsits) m. nipple (vulg.)
cyfra (tsíf-ra) f. number
cygan (tsí-gan) m. gipsy;
   cheat; Gypsy;swindler; liar
cykl (tsikl) m. cycle
cylinder (tsi-léen-der) m.
   cylinder; barrel; top hat
cyna (tsi-na) f. tin
cynamon (tsi-na-mon)m.cinnamon
cynober (tsi-nó-ber) m.vermil-
   ion

cyngiel (tsín-gel) m. trigger
cynik (tsi-ñeek) m. cynic
cynk (tsink) m. zinc; tutenag
cypel (tsi-pel) m. cape; tip
cyprys (tsi-pris) m. cypress
cyrk (tsirk) m. circus
cyrkiel (tsír-kel) m. compass
cysterna (tsis-tér-na) f.
   cistern; tank car; vat
cytadela (tsi-ta-de-la) f.
   citadel; fortress
cytata (tsi-tá-ta) f. quotation
cytryna (tsi-trí-na) f. lemon
cywil (tsi-veel) m. civilian
cyzelowac (tsi-ze-ló-vach) v.
   engrave; carve; elaborate
czad (chat) m. carbon monoxide
czaic się (chá-eech shan) v.
   lie in wait; lurk; stalk;crouch
czajnik (cháy-ñeek) m. tea-pot
czajka (cháy-ka) f. gull
czako (chá-ko) f. shako
czapka (cháp-ka) f. cap; pileus
czapla (cháp-la) f. heron
czaprak (cháp-rak) m. horse
   blanket; caparison; trappings
czar (char) m. spell; charm
czarno (chár-no) adv. blackly
czart (chart) m. devil; deuce
czas (chas) m. time; duration
czaszka (chásh-ka) f. skull
czaty (chá-ti) pl. watch;
   lookout; wait; ambush
cząstka (chownst-ka) f. particle
czcic (chcheech) v. adore;
   worship; idolize; venerate
czcigodny (chchee-god-ni) adj.
   m. honorable; revered; venerable
czcionka (chchyon-ka) f. type;
   character; letter in print
czczo (chcho) adv. empty (stomach); emptily; vainly; idly
czego (che-go) conj. why? what?
czek (chek) m. check (in banking)
czekac (ché-kach) v. wait;
   expect; waste time; be in store
czekanie (che-ka-ñe) n. wait
czekan (ché-kan) f. pickhammer
czekolada (che-ko-lá-da) f.
   chocolate; slab of chocolate
czeladnik (che-lád-ñeek) m.
   apprentice; journeyman

czelność (chél-noshch) f. impudence ; effrontery; nerve
czelusć (che-looshch) f. abyss;
gulf; precipice; depths[to what?
czemu (ché-moo) part. why?what
czepek (ché-pek) m. bonnet;
hood ; night cap; caul;calyptra
czepiać się (chep-yach shán)
v. cling; hang on; peck at
czereda (che-ré-da) f. gang;
throng ; crowd; swarm: pack
czerep (ché-rep) m. shell;
skull; fragment: splinter;shard
czeresnia (che-résh-ña) f.
cherry; cherry tree; gean
czernić (chér-ñeech) v, black-
en ; black; paint black
czern (chern) f. black color
czerpać (chér-pach) v. scoop;
draw; ladle; derive (benefit)
czerstwy (chérs-tvi) adj. m.
stale; robust(man); firm
czerw (cheŕv) m. worm ; grub
czerwienić sie (cher-vye-
ñeech shán) v. blush (redden)
czerwony (cher-vó-ni) adj. m.
red ; scrlet; crimson; ruddy
czesać (ché-sach) v. comb ;brush
czeski (chés-kee) adj. m. Czech
czesne (chés-ne) n. tuition
czesć (cheshch) f. honor; cult;
respect ; adoration;good name
często (cháns-to) adv. often
częstokroć (chan-stó-kroch)
adv. often ; repeatedly
częstość (cháns-toshch) f.
frequency ; recurrence
częstotliwosc (chan-sto-tlee-
woshch) f. frequency ;recurrence
częstować (cháh-stó-vach) v.
treat to something ; regale
częsty (cháns-ty) adj. m.
frequent ; repeated often
częsciowy (chán-shchó-vi) adj.
m. partial ; fragmentary
częsc (cháhshch) f. part:share
czkawka (chkáv-ka) f. hiccups
człon (chwon) m. element; segment ; link ; member; clause
członek (chwo-nek) m. limb;
member; man's sex organ
człowiek (chwó-vyek) m. man ;
individual; chap; somebody

czmychnąć (chmíkh-nównch) v.
bolt; steal out; whisk away
czochrać (chókh-rach) v. tousle; ripple; hackle ;scratch
czołg (chowg) m. tank (military): reptile
czołgać (chow-gach) v. crawl
czoło (chó-wo) n. forehead
czop (chop) m. peg; plug; pin
czosnek (chós-nek) m. garlic
czterdziesci (chter-dzhésh-
chee) num. forty
czternaście (chter-nash-che)
num. fourteen
czteropiętrowy (chte-ro-pyán-
tró-vi) adj. m. four stories
high ; four storeyed
cztery (chté-ri) num. four
czub (choop) m. tuft; crest
czucie (choo-che) n. feeling;
smelling ; sense perception
czuć (chooch) v. feel; smell
czujka (chóoy-ka) f. sentry
czułość (choo-woshch) f.
tenderness ; affection: caress
czuły (choo-wi) adj. m. tender;
affectionate; sensitive;keen
czupurny (choo-poor-ni) adj. m.
pugnacious; boastful;defiant
czuwać (choo-vach) v. watch;
nurse ; look-out ; stay up;tend
czwartek (chvar-tek) m. Thursday
czwarty (chvar-ti) num. fourth
czworobok (chvo-ró-bok) m.
quadrilateral; square;tetragon
czworokąt (chvo-ró-kownt) m.
quadrangle; quad; tetragon
czwórka (chvoor-ka) f. four-
some; crew of four; good mark
czy (chi) conj. if; whether
czychać (chi-khach) v. lurk
czyj (chiy) pron. whose
czyjs (chiysh) pron. somebody's
anybody's; someone else's
czyli (chi-lee) conj. or;
otherwise; that is to say
czym...tym (chim...tim) adv.
the sooner... the; the more
the...: the less... the...
czyn (chin) m. act. deed
czynsz (chinsh) m. rent
czynić (chi-ñeech) v. do;
render ; act: amount;cause

czyrak (chi-rak) m. boil; furuncle ; boil; anbury; rising
czynnik (chin-ñeek) m. factor
czysto (chi-sto) adv. clean
czysty (chis-ti) adj. m. clean
czyszczenie (chish-che-ñe) n.
  cleaning ; brushing;diarrhoea
czyścić (chish-cheech) v.
  clean ; scour; brush; rub;purge
czyściec (chish-chets) m.
  purgatory ; woundwort
czytać (chi-tach) v. read
czytelnia (chi-tel-ña) f.
  reading room ;lending library
czytelnik (chi-tel-ñeek) m.
  reader ; reading individual
czytelny (chi-tel-ni) adj. m.
  legible ; readable
czyż (chish) part.if; whether
ćma (chma) f. obscurity; swarm;
  night butterfly ;night moth
ćmić (chmeech) v. obscure;dim;
  darken ; eclipse; smoke; sicken
ćwiartka (chvyart-ka) f. one
  quarter ; one fourth of a liter
ćwierć (chwyerch) f. one
  fourth (of a liter etc.)
ćwiczenie (chvee-che-ñe) n.
  exercise ; instruction; drill
ćwiek (chvyek) m. nail ; stud
ćwikła (chveek-wa) f. beetroot
  with horseradish (salad)
dach (dakh) m. roof ; shelter
dać (dach) v. give ; pay;result
daktyl (dak-til) m. date
dal (dal) f. distance; remoteness ; far away; aloof
dalece (da-le-tse) adv. further;
  by far; so far;(so)much so
dalej (da-ley) adv. further;
  moreover : further on; so on
dalmierz (dal-myesh) m. range
  finder ; telemeter
dalszy (dal-shi) adj. m. further;
  farther ; later; another
dama (da-ma)f. lady ; partner
dana (da-na)adj.f.given (data)
danie (da-ñe) m. serving;
  dish ; course
danser (dan-ser) m. dancer
dane (da-ñe) pl. data
dar (dar) m. gift ; present
daremnie (da-rem-ñe) adv.
  in vain ; without success

daremny (da-rem-ni) adj. m.
  futile; vain; idle; ineffective
darmo (dar-mo) adv. free;
  gratuitously; to no avail
darować (da-ro-vach) v. give;
  forgive; overlook; spare
data (da-ta) f. date
datek (da-tek) n. small gift
dawać (da-vach) v. give (often)
dawno (dav-no) adv. long ago
dąb (domp) m. oak tree (wood)
dąć (downch) v. blow; resound
dąsać się (down-sach shañ) v.
  sulk; be in the pouts; mump
dążyć (down-zhich) v. aspire;
  tend; aim; be bound; trend
dbać (dbach) v. care;set store
dech (dekh) m. breath; gust
decydować (de-tsi-do-vach) v.
  decide; resolve; determine
decyzja (de-tsis-ya) f. decision; ruling; resolve
delikatność (de-lee-kat-noshch)
  f. delicacy; gentleness; tact
defekt (de-fekt) m. defect
demaskować (de-mas-ko-vach) v.
  unmask: uncover; denounce
demokracja (de-mo-krats-ya) f.
  democracy
denerwować (de-ner-vo-vach) v.
  bother; make nervous; irritate
dentysta (den-tis-ta) m.
  dentist
depesza (de-pe-sha) f. wire;
  telegram; cable; dispatch
deponować (de-po-no-vach) v.
  deposit; put in safe keeping
depozyt (de-po-zit) m. deposit
deptać (dep-tach) v. trample;
  tread; pace up and down;stain
derka (der-ka) f. rug; blanket
deseń (de-señ) m. pattern;
  design; decorative design
deska (des-ka) f. plank; board
desperacja (des-pe-rats-ya) f.
  desperation; despair
deszcz (deshch) m. rain
detal (de-tal) m. retail; detail; trifling matter
determinacja (de-ter-mee-nats-
  ya) f. determination
dewiza (de-vee-za) f. foreign
  money ; motto; slogan; device

dębina (dăn-bee-na) f. oak
wood; oak bark

dętka (dănt-ka) f. pneumatic
tire; tube; air chamber

diabeł (dyá-bew) m. devil

dieta (dye-ta) f. diet;regimen

dla (dla) prep. for; to;towards

dlaczego (dla—che-go)prep. why;
what for

dlatego (dla—te-go)prep.
because; this is why; and so

dławić (dwa-veech) v. choke;
squash; throttle; strangle

dłoń (dwoń) f. palm of the
hand; hand; metacarpus; quart

dłubać (dwoo-bach)v. groove;
poke; tinker; pick one's teeth

dług (dwoog) m. debt; obligation

długi (dwoo-gee) adj. m. long

długo (dwoo-go) adv. a long
time; a long way; long before

dłuto (dwoo-to) n. chisel

dłutować (dwoo-to-vach) v.
chisel; cut with chisel

dłużnik (dwoozh-ñeek) m. debtor

dmuchać (dmoo-khach)v. blow

dniówka (dñoov-ka) f. day's
work; work by day; time work

dno (dno) n. bottom; utterness

do (do) prep. to; into; up;till

doba (do-ba) f. 24 hours

dobić (do-beech) v. deal
a death blow; drive home

dobierać (do-bye-rach) v.
match; take more; select

dobitny (do-beet-ni) adj. m.
expressive; emphatic; distinct

doborowy (do-bo-ro-vi) adj. m.
choice; select; picked

dobosz (do-bosh) m. drummer

dobór (do-boor) m. selection;
assortment; choice;assortment

dobra (do-bra) n. riches

dobranoc (do-bra-nots)(indecl)
good-night

dobrany (do-bra-ni) adj. m.
matching; becoming;accordant

dobre (do-bre) adj. n. good

dobro (do-bro) n. good; right

dobrobyt (do-bro-bit) m. well-
being; prosperity; welfare

dobroczynnosc (do-bro-chin-
noshch) f. charity; works of
mercy; philanthropy

dobroc (do-roch) f. kindness

dobroduszny (do-bro-doosh-ni)
adj. m. kindhearted; kindly

dobrodziej (do-bro-dzhey) m.
benefactor ; his reverence

dobrotliwy (do-bro-tlee-vi)
adj. m. kind; good natured

dobrowolny (do-bro-wol-ni)
adj. m. voluntary; gratuitus

dobry (do-bri) adj. m. good;
kind; right; hearty; retentive

dobrze (do-brze) adv. well;
O K; rightly; properly;okay

dobudowka (do-boo-doov-ka) f.
building extension

dobyc (do-bich) v. pullout

dobytek (do-bi-tek) m. belongings; effects; livestock

doceniac (do-tse-ñach) v.
duly appreciate; value

docent (do-tsent) m. associate
professor; lecturer

dochodzenie (do-kho-dze-ñe) n
investigation; inquiry

dochodzic (do-kho-dzheech)v.
draw near; investigate; reach

dochod (do-khoot) m. income;
revenue; profit; returns

dociac (do-chownch) c. sting;
taunt; fit by cutting off

dociec (do-chets) v. find out

dociekac (do-che-kach) v.
search; investigate; find out

docierac (do-chye-rach) v.
draw near; reach; reduce
friction ; rub up; get at

docinek (do-chee-nek) m. taunt

doczekac (do-che-kach) v. wait;
live to see; wait 'til

doczepiac (do-chep-yach) v. fix
append; attach; hitch; link

doczesny (do-ches-ni) adj. m.
temporal; worldly; mundane

dodac (do-dach) v. add; sum up

dodatek (do-da-tek) m. supplement; addition; fixture; extra

dodatni (do-dat-ñee) adj. m.
positive; advantageous; active

dodawanie (do-da-va-ñe) n.
addition

dogadac sie (do-ga-dach shañ)v.
come to terms;communicate well

dogadzac (do-ga-dzach) v.
please; accommodate; satisfy

doglądać (do-glówn-dach) v.
supervise; tend; oversee

dogmat (dóg-mat) m. dogma

dogodny (do-gód-ni) adj. m.
convenient; suitable; handy

dogonić (do-go-ñeech) v. catch
up; overtake; be in hot pursuit

dogryzać (do-gri-zach) v. vex;
tease; finish munching;disturb

doić (do-eech) v. milk; fleece

dojarka (do-yár-ka) f. milk
maid; milking machine

dojazd (do-yazt) m. access;drive;
approach; means of transport

dojechać (do-ye-khach) v. reach;
arrive; approach; bang; hit

dojeżdżać (do-yezh-jach) v.
commute; be coming; pull in

dojmujący (doy-moo-yówn-tsi) adj.
m. acute; piercing; sharp:keen

dojrzały (doy-zha-wi) adj. m.
ripe; mellow; mature: adult

dojrzeć (doy-zhech) v. glimpse;
notice;;ripen; be ripe;mellow

dojście (doy-shche) n. approach

dok (dok) m. dock

dokarmić (do-kár-meech) v.
nourish additionally

dokazać (do-ká-zach) v. prove;
achieve; accomplish;do the trick

dokazywać (do-ka-zí-vach) v.
frolic: gambol; romp and play

dokąd (do-kównt) adv. where;when?
whither; where to ? how far?till

dokładać (do-kwa-dach) v. add;
throw in; pay more; give moore

dokładny (do-kwad-ni) adj. m.
accurate; exact; precise

dokoła (do-ko-wa) adv. round;
round about; all round

dokonać (do-kó-nach) v. achieve;
accomplish; carry out;fulfil;do

dokończenie (do-koń-che-ñe) n.
conclusion: completion; end

doktor (dók-tor) m. doctor

dokręcać (do-kráń-tsach) v.
tighten; screw tight; turn off

dokuczać (do-koo-chach) v. vex;
annoy; nag; bully: sting;trouble

dola (do-la) f. fortune; lot

dolar (dó-lar) m. dollar

doliczyć (do-lee-chich) v.
count up ; add; charge more

dolina (do-lee-na) f. valley;
dale; glen; coomb; pocket

dolny (dól-ny) adj. m. lower

dołączyć (do-wówn-chich) v.add;
join; enclose; affix; tack on

dołek (do-wek) m. dimple; pit

dom (dom) m. house   v. demand

domagać się (do-ma-gach sháñ)

domiar (do-myar) m. additional
assessment; surtax;on top of it

domniemany (do-mñe-ma-ni) adj.
m. supposed; assumed; alleged

domostwo (do-mós-tvo) n. household; homestead; farmstead

domownik (do-mow-ñeek) m.
inmate   ; housemate

domowy (do-mó-vi) adj. m.
domestic; homemade; private

domysł (do-misw) m. guess

doniesienie (do-ñe-she-ñe) n.
denunciation; report; news

doniosły (do-ño-swi) adj. m.
significant; far reaching

donosiciel (do-no-shee-chel)
m. denunciator: informer

donośny (do-nósh-ni) adj. m.
resounding; renging; loud

dookoła(do-o-ko-wa) adv. round;
round about; all around; around

dopaść (do-pashch) v. catch up;
overtake: reach at a run;seize

dopalać (do-pa-lach) v. after-
burn; finish burning; burn up

dopasować (do-pa-so-vach) v.
fit; adapt; adjust; match;tone

dopatrywać (do-pa-tri-vach) v.
see to it; find out; keep an eye

dopełnić (do-pew-ñeech) v.fulfil;
fill up; complete ; make up

dopędzić (do-páñ-dźheech) v.
catch up with; overtake;gain on

dopiąć (do-pyównch) v. attain;
buckle up; button up; obtain

dopiero (do-pye-ro) adv. only;
just; hardly;barely ;not till

dopilnować (do-peel-no-vach) v.
see something done ;supervise

dopisek (do-pée-sek) m. postscript; foot note

dopłata (do-pwa-ta) f. extra
payment; surcharge;extra fare

dopływ (do-pwif) m. tributary

dopomagać (do-po-má-gach) v. help; be of assistance

dopominać się (do-po-mee-nach shán) v. put in claim; demand

dopóki (do-pooki) conj. as long; as far; while; until; till

dopóty (do-poó-ti) conj. 'til ; until ; so far; up to here

dopraszać się (do-pra-shach shán) v. solicit; beg; insist

doprawdy (do-práv-di) adv. truly; indeed; really

doprawiać (do-práv-yach) v. add (to taste); replace

doprowadzić (do-pro-vá-dźheech) v. lead to; cause; provoke

dopust Boży (dó-poost Bo-zhi) m. calamity; scourge; act of God

dopuszczać (do-poosh-chach) v. admit; allow; permit; be open

dopytać się (do-pi-tach shán) v. find out; inquire; question

dorabiać (do-ráb-yach) v. make additionally; replace; finish

doradca (do-rád-tsa) m. adviser; counselor ; guide

dorastać (do-rás-tach) v. mature; grow up; reach

doraźnie (do-ráźh-ńe) adv. (immediately) on the spot

doręczyć (do-rán-chich) v. hand in; deliver; transmit

dorobek (do-ró-bek) m. acquisition; rise to affluence

dorobkiewicz (do-rob-ké-veech) m. upstart; parvenu

doroczny (do-róch-ni) adj. m. yearly; annual; recurring yearly

dorodny (do-ród-ni) adj. m. handsome; fine-looking; shapely

dorosły (do-rós-wy) adj. m. adult; grown up; mature ; grown

dorożka (do-rozh-ka) f. cab

dorównywać (do-roov-ni-vach) v. match; equal; catch up with

dorsz (dorsh) m. cod (fish)

dorywczy (do-riv-chi) v. occasional; improvised; fitful; off-and-on; hit-and-run

dorzecze (do-zhe-che) n. river basin; drainage area

dorzeczny (do-zhéch-ni) adj. m. reasonable; sensible; efficient; adequate; acceptable; logical

dorzucać (do-zhoo-tsach) v. throw in; add; throw as far as

dosadny (do-sád-ni) adj. m. forceful ; expressive; crisp

dosiadać (do-sha-dach) v. mount (horse); bestride

dosięgać (do-shán-gach) v. reach; attain; catch up with

doskonalić (dos-ko-na-leech) v. perfect; improve; cultivate

doskwierać (do-skvye-rach) v. pinch; gripe ; trouble; worry

dosłowny (do-swóv-ni) adj. m. literal ; verbal; textual

dosłyszeć (do-swi-shech) v. hear well; catch a sound

dostać (dos-tach) v. get; obtain; reach; take out

dostarczyć (dos-tar-chich) v. provide; supply ; deliver

dostateczny (do-sta-téch-ni) adj. m. sufficient ; adequate

dostatek (do-stá-tek) m. abundance; wealth; affluence

dostawca (do-stáw-tsa) m. supplier ; provider

dostawa (do-stá-va) f. delivery

dostawać (do-stá-vach) v. reach; receive ; be attended to

dostęp (do-stáňp) m. access

dostojnik (do-stoy-ńeek) m. dignitary; notable of high rank

dostosować (do-sto-so-vach) v. accommodate; subordinate; fit

dostroić (do-stro-yeech) v. tune up ; conform; adapt

dostrzec (do-stzhets) v. notice; behold ; perceive; spot; spy; see

dostudzić (do-stoo-dźheech) v. cool off plenty; sufficient

dosyć (do-sich) adv. enough;

dosztukować (do-shtoo-kó-vach) v. piece on; eke out; sew on

dość (dóshch) adv. enough

dośrodkowy (do-śhrod-kó-vi) adj. m. centripetal; concentric

doświadczyć (do-śhvyad-chich) v. experience ; sustain; feel

dotarcie (do-tár-che) n. reaching; overcoming friction

dotąd (dó-townt) adv. up till now; here to fore ; hitherto; thus far; so far; yet; by then; till then; still; not...as yet

dotkliwy (dot-klee-vi) adj. m.
painful ; keen; intense; severe
dotknąć (dot-known'ch) v. touch
dotknięcie (dot-kñan—che) n.
touch; contact; feeling;stroke
dotrzec (do-tzhech) v. reach;
overcome friction; rub up
dotrzymać (do-tzhi-mach) v.
keep; stick to one's
commitment ; adhere;redeem
dotychczas (do-tikh-chas) adv.
up to now; hitherto; to date
dotyczyć (do-ti-chich) v.
concern; relate; regard; affect
dotyk (do-tik) m. touch;feel
dowcip (dov-cheep) m. wit;
joke; jest; gag; quip; sally
dowiedziec się (do-vye-dzhech
shan) v. get to know; learn
dowidzenia (do-vee-dze-na)
good bye; see you later
dowierzać (do-vye-zhach) v.
trust; have confidence in
dowieść (do-vyesh'ch) v. prove
dowieżć (do-vyezhch) v.
1. supply 2. drive to
dowodzić (do-vo-dźheech)v.
conduct;keep proving
dowolnie (do-vol-ñe) adv. at
will; optionally; freely
dowolny (do-vol-ni) adj. m.
optional; any; whichever
dowód (do-voot) m. proof;
evidence; record; token
dowódca (do-vood-tsa) m.
commander ∫delivery
dowóz (do-voos) m. supply;
doza (do-za) f. dose
dozbroić (do-zbro-eech) v.
rearm; supplement weapons
dozgonny (do-zgón-ni) adj. m.
lifelong; lasting til' death
doznać (do-znach) v. go through;
undergo ; endure; feel;suffer
dozorca (do-zor-tsa) m. caretaker; watchman; overseer
dozorować (do-zo-ro-vach) v.
oversee; supervise; attend
dozór (do-zoor) m. surveillance
dozwolic (do-zvo-leech) v.
allow to happen; let happen
dożynki (do-zhin-kee) pl.
harvest festivities

dożywocie (do-zhi-vo-che)n.
life estate; life pension
dół (doow) m. pit; bottom part
drab (drap) m. ruffian; scamp
drabina (dra-bee-na) f. ladder
dramat (dra-mat) m. drama
draň (draň) m. scoundrel; crumb
drapacz (dra-pach) m. scraper
drapać (dra-pach) v. scratch)
drapieżnik (dra-pyezh-ñeek) m.
beast of prey; plunderer
drastyczny (dra-stich-ni) adj.
m. drastic; rough; violent
dratwa (drat-va) f. pitched-
thread; shoemaker's twine
drażliwy (drazh-lee-vi) adj.
m. touchy; irritable; ticklish
drażnic (drazh-ñeech) v. tease;
irritate; whet; vex; annoy; jar
drąg (drowñk) m. pole; bar
drążyć (drown-zhich) v. hollow
out; bore; torment; fret;gnaw
drelich (dre-leekh) m. denim
dren (dren) n. drain (pipe)
dreptać (drep-tach) v. trip-
trot; toddle; totter; patter
dreszcz (dreshch) m. chill;
shudder; thrill; flutter; shiver
dreszczowiec (dresh-cho-vyets)
m. thriller (novel or movie)
drewno (drev-no) n. piece of
wood; timber ; log; xylem
dręczyć (drañ-chich) v. torment
drętwiec (drań-tvyech) v. grow
numb; grow stiff; stiffen
drgać (drgach) v. tremble;
vibrate; quiver; throb; wobble
drobiazg (drób-yazk) m. trifle;
detail; trinket; small fry
drobina (dro-bee-na) f. particle
drobne (drób-ne) n. small
change; petty cash ; small coin
drobnica (drob-ñee-tsa) f.
small goods; packages
drobnostka (drob-nóst-ka) f.
trifle; small matter; trinket
drobny (dro-bni) adj. m. small;
tiny ; trivial; petty; slight
droga (dro-ga) f. 1. road;
2.journey; 3.adj.f. dear
drogeria (dro-gér-ya) f. drugstore ; drysaltery

drogi (dró-gee) adj. m. dear;
expensive; costly; beloved
drogowskaz (dro-góv-skas) m.
road sign; signpost
drozd (drozt) m. thrush
drożdże (dróżh-je) pl. yeast
drożec (dró-zhech) v. grow
dear; rise in price;appreciate
drożyzna (dro-zhíz-na) f. high
cost of living; high prices
drób (droop) pl. paltry
dróżka (dróozh-ka) f. path
druciany (droo-cha-ni) adj. m.
of wire; made out of wire
drugi (droo-gee) num. second;
other; the other one; latter
druh (drookh) m. buddy;
companion; friend; boy scout
druk (drook) m. print; printing
drut (droot) m. wire
druzgotać (drooz-go-tach) v.
smash; shatter; crush to pieces
drużba (dróozh-ba) m. best man
drużyna (droo-zhí-na) f. team
drwal (drval) m. lumber jack
drwić (drveech) v. mock;deride
drwiny (drvee-ny) pl. mockery
dryg (drik) m.knack; flair for
drzazga (dzház-ga) f. splinter
drzeć (dzhech) v. tear; pull
drzemka (dshem-ka) f. nap
drzewo (dshe-vo) n. tree
drzeworyt (dshe-vó-rit) m.
woodcut; wood engraving
drzwi (dzhvee) n. door
drżeć (drzhech) v. shiver;shake
dubeltówka (doo-bel-toóv-ka) f.
double barrel gun; shotgun
duch (dookh) m. spirit; ghost;
state of mind; intent; life
duchowieństwo (doo-khov-yeń-stvo)
pl. clergy; priesthood
dudek (doo-dek) m. 1. hoopoe;
2. dupe; fool; dolt: booby
dudnić (dood-neech) v. resound
dudy (doo-di) pl. bagpipe
dukat (doo-kat) m. ducat
dulka (dool-ka) f. oarlock
duma (doo-ma) f. pride; epic
dumać (doo-mach) v. meditate
dumny (doom-ni) adj. m. proud
dupa (doo-pa) f. ass (vulg.)
dur (door) m. typhoid fever

duren (doo-reń) m. fool; ass
durzyć (doo-zhich) v. fool;
infatuate; bewilder; dupe
dusić (doo-sheech) v. strangle
dusigrosz (doo-shee-grosh) m.
penny pincher; niggard
dusza (doo-sha) f. soul;psyche
dużo (doo-zho) adv. much; many
duży (doo-zhi) adj. m. big;
large; great; fair-sized
dwa (dva) num. two
dwakroć (dva-kroch) num. twice
dwanaście (dva-násh-che) num.
twelve
dwieście (dvyésh-che) num. 200
dwoić (dvo-eech) v. double
dwojaczki (dvo-yách-kee) pl.
twins; double pot;the two;
dwoje (dvo-ye) num. two;in two;
couple; two(fold);two(ways)
dwór (dvoor) m. country manor
dworski (dvór-skee) adj. m.
courtly; manorial; of court
dworzec (dvó-zhets) m. (railway) station; depot
dwukrotnie (dvoo-krot-ńe) adv.
twice; twice over
dwunastka (dvoo-nást-ka) f.
twelve ;(team)of twelve
dwustronny (dvoo-stron-ni)adj.
m. two-sided; bilateral
dyg (dik) m. curtsy; bob
dygnitarz (dig-ńee-tash) m.
dignitary; high ranking man
dygotać (di-go-tach) v. tremble
dykta (dik-ta) f. plywood
dyktator (dik-tá-tor) m.
dictator ;absolute ruler
dylemat (di-le-mat) m. dilem-
ma; perplexity; fix
dym (dim) m. smoke; fumes
dymić (di-meech) v. smoke
dynamit (di-na-meet) m. dynamite; W.W II German ersatz bread
dyndać (din-dach) v. dangle
dynia (di-ńa) f. pumpkin
dyplom (di-plom) m. diploma
dyplomacja (di-plo-máts-ya) f.
diplomacy; policy; tact
dyrekcja (di-rek-tsya) f.
management; headquarters
dyrygent (di-ri-gent) m.
orchestra conductor

dyscyplina (dis-tsɨ-plee-na) f. discipline; branch; line

dysk (disk) m. disc; discus

dyskrecja (dis-krets-ya) f. discretion; management

dyskusja (dis-koos-ya) f. discussion; debate

dysponować (dis-po-no-vaćh) v. dispose; control; order

dysputa (dis-poo-ta) f. dispute; debate; controversy

dystans (dis-tans) m. distance

dystyngowany (dis-tin-go-va-ni) adj. m. distinguished

dysza (di-sha) f. nozzle; blast pipe; snout; twyer

dyszeć (di-shech) v. gasp;pant

dywan (di-van) m. carpet; rug

dywidenda (di-vee-den-da) f. dividend

dywizja (di-veez-ya) f. division

dyżurny (di-zhoor-ny) adj. m. on call; on duty; orderly

dzban (dzban) m. jug; pitcher

dziać się (dżhaćh shań) v. occur; happen; take place

dziadek (dżha-dek) m. grandfather; nut cracer

dział (dżhaw) m. section

działacz (dżha-wach) m. activist(in politics, religion etc)

działać (dżha-waćh) v. act; work; be active; be effective

działka (dżhaw-ka) f. parcel

działo (dżha-wo) n. cannon

dziarski (dżhar-skee) adj. m. brisk; lively; swinging; rakish

dziąsło (dżhown-swo)n. gum

dzicz (dżheech)pl. savages

dzida (dżhee-da) f. spear;pike

dzieci (dżhe-chee) pl. children

dzieciństwo (dżhe-cheeń-stvo) n. childhood; boyhood;infancy

dziecko (dżhets-ko) n. child; baby; trot; brat; kiddie; kid

dziedziczyć (dżhe-dżee-chićh) v. inherit(property,features)

dziedzina (dżha-dżhee-na) f. realm; area;sphere; domain

dziedziniec (dżhe-dżhee-ńets)m. yard; court; backyard

dziegieć (dżhe-gećh) m. tar

dzieje (dżhe-ye) pl. history

dziejowy (dżhe-yo-vi) adj. m. historical; historic

dziekan (dżhe-kan) m. dean

dzielić (dżhe-leećh) v. divide; share; split; distribute

dzielnica (dżhel-ńee-tsa) f. province; quarter; section

dzielny (dżhel-ni) adj. m. brave; resourceful; efficient

dzieło (dżhe-wo) n. achievement; work; composition

dziennik (dżhen-ńeek)m. daily-news; daily; journal; diary

dzienny (dżheń-ni) adj. m. daily; diurnal; day's

dzień (dżheń)m. day; daylight

dzień dobry(dżheń dob-ri)good morning

dzierżawa (dżher-zha-va) f. lease; rental; holding

dzierżyć (dżher-zhićh) v. wield (power); hold; grip

dziesiątka (dżhe-shownt-ka) f. ten;(team of)ten

dziesięć (dżhe-shańćh) num. ten

dziewczyna (dżhev-chi-na) f. girl; lass; wench; maid

dziewica (dżhe-vee-tsa) f. virgin; maiden

dziewięć (dżhe-vyańćh) num. nine

dziewiętnaście (dżhe-vyańt-nashćhe) num. nineteen

dzięcioł (dżhań-chow) m. woodpecker

dziękczynienie (dżhańk-chi-ńe-ńe)n. thanks-giving

dziękować (dżhań-ko-vaćh) v. thank; give thanks

dzik (dżheek) m. boar; tusker

dziobać (dżho-baćh)v. peck

dziób (dżh-oob) m. beak; bill

dzisiejszy (dżhee-shey-shi) adj. m. today's; modern

dziś (dżheesh) adv. today

dziupla (dżhoop-la) f. (tree) hollow(in a trnk)

dziura (dżhoo-ra) f. hole

dziurawy (dżhoo-ra-vi) adj. m. leaky; full of holes

dziw (dżheef) m. wonder

dziwactwo (dżhee-vats-tvo) n.
crank; fad; craze; peculiarity
dziwić (dżhee-veech) v. astonish
dziwny (dżheev-ni)adj.m.strange;
dzwon (dzyon) m. bell; chime
dźwięczeć (dżhvyań-chech) v.
ring; sound; jingle; clang
dźwięk (dżhvyánk) m. sound
dźwig (dżhveek) n. crane
dźwigać (dżhvee-gach)v. lift;
hoist; raise; heave; erect;carry
dżdżysty (j-jis-ti) adj. m. wet;
rainy ; drizzly (weather)
dżem (jem) m. jam; fruit jam
dżet (jet) m. jet
dżinsy (jeen-si) pl. blue
jeans (pants)
dżokey (jó-key) m. jockey
dżudo (joo-do) m. judo (sport)
dżuma (joo-ma) f. plague
dżungla (joon-gla) f. jungle
echo (ekho) n. echo; response
edukacja (e-doo-kats-ya) f.
education; schooling;instruction
efekt (e-fekt) m. effect
efektowny (e-fek-tóv-ni) adj.
m. showy ; striking; attractive
efektywny (e-fek-tiv-ni) adj.
m. efficient ; effective; real
egida (e-gee-da) f. protection;
auspices ; protectorate
egoista (e-go-ees-ta) m.egotist
egoistyczny (e-go-ees-tich-ni)
adj. m. selfish; self seeking
egzamin (eg-za-meen) m. examination; exam ; standing a test
egzekucja (eg-ze-koots-ya) f.
execution ; seizure; flogging
egzemplarz (eg-zem-plash) m.
copy (sample); specimen
egzystencja (eg-zis-ten-tsya)
f. existence; livelihood
ekierka (e-ker—ka) f. set
square ;draftsman's triangle
ekipa (e-kee-pa) f. team;crew
ekonomia (e-ko-nóm-ya) f.
economics; thrift; economy
ekran (ék-ran) m. screen;shield
ekspedient (ex-pe-dyent) m.
salesperson ; clerk;salesman
ekspedycja (ex-pe-dits-ya) f.
1. dispatch 2. expedition

ekspert (éx-pert) m. expert
eksploatować (ex-plo-a-to-vach)
v. exploit; sweat; utilize
eksponat (ex-po-nat) m. exhibit
ekspozytura (ex-po-zy-too-ra)
f. agency; branch office
ekwipować (ek-vee-po-vach) v.
equip; fit out; provide with
elaborat (e-la-bo-rat) m. study (elaboration)
elastyczność (e-las-tich-nośhch)
elasticity; resilience;flexibility
elegancja (e-le-gánts-ya) f.
elegance; fashion; style
elektrociepłownia (e-lek-tro-
chep-wóv-ńa) f. steamplant
elektryczność (e-lek-trich-
nośhch) f. electricity
element (e-le-ment) m. element
elementarny (e-le-men-tar-ni)
adj. m. fundamental; primary
elewator (e-le-va-tor) m.
elevator ; hoist
emalia (e-mál-ya) f. enamel
emeryt (e-me-rit) m. retired
person; pensioner; pensionary
emigracja (e-mee-gráts-ya) f.
emigration; exile; emigrants
emisja (e-mees-ya) f. emission
emocja (e-mo-tsya) f. thrill
entuzjazm (en-tóoz-yazm) m.
enthusiasm; rapture
energia (e-nérg-ya) f. energy
energiczny (e-ner-geech-ni)
adj. m. energetic; vigorous
epoka (e-pó-ka) f. epoch
epitet (e-pee-tet) m. epithet
era (era) f. era; epoch
erotyczny (e-ro-tich-ni) adj.
m. erotic; sexual
eskadra (es-kad-ra) f. squadron; aerial fleet: flight
eskorta (es-kór-ta) f. escort
estetyczny (es-te-tich-ni)
adj. m.esthetic; in good taste
etap (é-tap) m. stage (of development) ; halting place
etatowy (e-ta-tó-vi) adj. m.
permanent (job): full time
eter (é-ter) m. ether
etyczny (e-tich-ni) adj. m.
ethical; moral

etykieta (e-ti-ke—ta) f. label; etiquette; formality;ceremonial
ewakuacja (e-va-koo-a-tsya) f. evacuation
ewangielia (e-van-gél--ya) f. gospel; gospel truth
ewangielik (e-van-gé—leek) m. protestant ; Lutheran
ewentualnosc (e-ven-too-al-noshćh) f. possibility
ewentualnie (e-ven-too-ál-ńe) adv. possibly; if need be
ewidencja (e-vee-dén-tsya) f. records; list; files ; roll
ewolucja (e-vo-loo-tsya) f. evolution; development
fabryczny (fa-brich-ni) adj. m. manufactured
fabryka (fa-bri-ka) f. factory
fabuła (fa-boo-wa) f. fable; plot of a novel etc.; story
facet (fa-tset) m. guy
fachowiec (fa-kho-vyets) m. expert; specialist;connoisseur
fajdac (fay-dać) v. shit (vulg.)
fajans (fáy-ans) m. earthenware
fajerka (fa-yér-ka) f.cook-top unit; stove lid
fajka (fáy-ka)f. pipe (for smoking); wild boar's tusk
fajtłapa (fayt-wá-pa) m. all thumbs guy(awkward,clumsy man)
fakt (fakt) m. fact
faktor (fák-tor) m. broker; agent; factor; intermediary
faktycznie (fak-tich-ńe) adv. in fact;actually; indeed; truly
fala (fa-la) f. wave; tide;surge
falisty (fa-lees-ti) adj. m. wavy; rolling; corrugated
falochron (fa-ló-khron) m. breakwater : pier; jetty; mole
falsyfikat (fal-si-fée-kat) m. forgery; counterfeit; fake
fałd (fawt) f. fold (wrinkle)
fałsz (fawsh) m. falsehood
fałszowac (faw-shó-vać) v. falsify; fake; forge; sing flat
fama (fa-ma) f. fame; rumor
fanaberie (fa-na-bér-ye) pl. whims ; fads; frills; ostentation
fanatyk (fa-ná-tik) m. fanatic; enthusiast; bigot; maniac

fanfaron (fan-fa-ron) m. braggart; coxcomb; swaggerer
fantastyczny (fan-tas-tich-ni) adj. m. fantastic; wild; odd
fantazja (fan-taz-ya) f. dash; imagination; fiction; whim
fara (fá-ra) f. parish church
farba (fár-ba) f. paint; dye color; dyeing; blood
farbowac (far-bó-vać) v. dye
farsa (fár-sa) f. farce;mockery
farsz (farsh) m. stuffing
fartuch (fár-tookh)m. apron
fasola (fa-só-la) f. bean
fasonowac (fa-so-no-vać) v. fashion; shape; mold model
fatalny (fa-tal-ni) adj. m. fatal; ill-fated; awful;fateful
fastryga (fas-tri-ga) f. tack; basting; baste; tacks
faszyzm (fa-shizm) m. fascism
fatyga (fa-ti-ga) f. trouble; fatigue ; trouble; bother;pains
fatałaszki (fa-ta-wash-kee) pl. knik-knacks; frippery; trinkets
febra (féb-ra) fever;the shakes
faworyzowac (fa-vo-ri-zo-vać) v. favor; play favorites
felczer (fél-cher) m. male nurse : medical assistant
federacja (fe-de-rats-ya) f. federation : union
feralny (fe-rál-ni) adj. m. unlucky; ill fated; hapless
ferie (fér-ye) pl. holidays
ferma (fér-ma) f. farm ; ranch
ferment (fér-ment) m. ferment
festyn (fés-tin) m. festival
fetor (fé-tor) m. stench
figa (fee-ga) f. fig ; nix
figiel (fee-gel) m. practical joke ; prank; trick; ill turn
figura (fee-góo-ra) f. figure; shape ; form; image; big wig
fikcja (feek-tsya) f. fiction
filar (fee-lar) m. pillar
filatelista (fee-la-te-lees-ta) m. stamp-collector
filc (feelts) m. felt
filia (feel-ya) f. branch (store); branch-office
filiżanka (fee-lee-zhan-ka) f. cup ; cupful; coffee-cup

film (feelm) m. film

filolog (fee-ló-lok) m. philologist; linguist

filozof (fee-ló-zof) m. philosopher

filtr (feeltr) m. filter

filut (fee-loot) m. jester; rogue; sly boots; joker

finanse (fee-nán-se) pl. finances; finance; funds

finisz (fee-ńeesh) m. end (of a run); the finish

fiołek (fyo-wek) m. violet

fiołkowy (fyow-ko-vi) adj. m. purple; violet; of the violet

firanka (fee-rán-ka) f. curtain; drapery

firma (feer-ma) f. business; firm; name of a firm

fisharmonia (fees-har-món-ya) f. harmonium

fizjognomia (feez-yo-gnóm-ya) f. face; external aspect

fizjonomia (feez-yo-nóm-ya) f. face; physiognomy

fizjolog (feez-yo-lok) m. physiologist

fizyczny (feez-ích-ni) adj. m. physical; bodily; manual

fizyk (fee-zik) m. physicist

flaczki (flách-kee) pl. tripe

flaga (flá-ga) f. banner; flag; ensign; standard

flaki (fla-kee) pl. bowels

flakon (fla-kon) m. vase

flanela (fla-ne-la) f. flannel

flaszka (flásh-ka) bottle

flama (flá-ma) f. lady-love

flądra (flówn-dra) f. flounder

flegma (fleg-ma) f. phlegm

flejtuch (fléy-tookh) m. slut

flet (flet) m. flute

flirt (fleert) m. flirt

flisak (flee-sak) m. raftsman

flora (fló-ra) f. flora

floret (fló-ret) m. foil

flota (fló-ta) f. navy; fleet

fluksja (flooks-ya) f. tooth-infection swelling

fluid (floo-eet) m. fluid

fochy (fó-khi) pl. blues; whims; sulks; pouts

foka (fó-ka) f. seal

folgować (fol-gó-vaćh) v. slacken; relax; indulge; abate

folklor (fólk-lor) m. folklore

folusz (fo-loosh)m.fulling mill

folwark (fól-vark) m. farm

fonetyczny (fo-ne-tích-ni) adj. phonetic

fontanna (fon-tán-na) f. fountain; spurt; waterworks

foremny (fo-rém-ni) adj. m. shapely; handsome; symmetrical

forma (fór-ma) f. shape; mold

format (fór-mat) m. size

formularz (for-móo-lash) m. (application) form; blank

formuła (for-móo-wa) f. formula

fornir (fór-ńeer) m. veneer

forsa (fór-sa) f. (money); dough; bread; tin; chink

forsować (forsó-vaćh) v. force; strain; urge; exhort;overcome

fort (fort) m. fort; stronghold

forteca (for-té-tsa) f. fortress; citadel; stronghold

fortel (for-tel) m. stratagem; trick; ruse; subterfuge

fortepian (for-té-pyan) m. grand piano; piano

fortuna (for-tóo-na) f. fortune

fosa (fó-sa) f. moat

fosfat (fós-fat) m. phosphate

fosfor (fós-foor) m. phosphorus

fotel (fó-tel) m. armchair

fotograf (fo-tó-graf) m. photographer

fotografia (fo-to-gráf-ya) f. photograph; snap shot; picture

fracht (frákht) m. freight

fragment (frág-ment) m. fragment; episode; excerpt;scrap

frak (frak) m. evening formal

framuga (fra-móo-ga) f. recess (structure); bay; embrasure

frant (frant) m. sly dog; knave

frasunek (fra-soo-nek) m. worry; grief; sorrow; care; trouble

fraszka (frász-ka) f. trifle

frazes (frá-zes) m. platitude

frekwencja (fre-kvén-tsya) f. attendance; turnout; frequency

frędzla (frańdz-la) f. fringe

fresk (fresk) m. fresco

front (front) m. front ;face,etc

froterować (fro-te-ro-vach) v.
 rub ; polish; wax (floors)

frunąć (froo-nownch) v. fly
 away ; fly about; flee

frymarczyć (fri-mar-chich) v.
 barter ; trade; traffic

fryzjer (friz-yer) m. barber;
 hairdresser ; beautician

fujara (foo-ya-ra) m. & f. all-
 thumbs; nincompoop; pan-pipe

fukać (foo-kach) v. scold

fundacja (foon-dats-ya) f.
 foundation ; endowment

fundament (foon-da-ment) m.
 foundation; substructure

fundusz (foon-doosh) m. fund

funkcja (foonk-tsya) f.
 function; office; duties

funt (foont) m. pound

fura (foo-ra) f. cart; wagon

furgon (foor-gon) m. truck

furia (foo-ya) f. fury; rage

furiat (foor-yat) m. madman

furman (foor-man) m. carter

furora (foo-ro-ra) f. sensation

furtka (foort-ka) f. gate

fusy (foo-si) pl. grounds

fuszer (foo-sher) m. bungler

futerał (foo-te-raw) m.
 (gun)case; holster

futro (foo-tro) n. fur

futryna (foo-tri-na) f. door-
 frame ; window-frame

futrzarz (foot-zhash) m. furrier

fuzja (fooz-ya) f. fusion;
 rifle ; shotgun

gabardyna (ga-bar-di-na) f.
 gabardine

gabinet (ga-bee-net) m. study;
 (ruling)cabinet; office

gablotka (ga-blot-ka) f.showcase

gad (gat) m. reptile;mean guy

gadać (ga-dach) v. talk; yak;
 prattle; talk nonsense

gaduła (ga-doo-wa) m. clapper

gaj (gay) m. grove

gala (ga-la) f. gala

galanteria (ga-lan-ter-ya) f.
 haberdashery

galareta (ga-la-re-ta) f. jelly

galeria (ga-ler-ya) f. gallery

galimatias (ga-lee-mat-yas) m.
 gibberish; hotchpotch; mess

galon (ga-lon) m. gallon

galop (ga-lop) m. gallop; run

galwaniczny (gal-va-neech-ni)
 adj. m. galvanic ; voltaic

gałąź (ga-wownzh) f. branch

gałgan (gaw-gan) m. rag; rascal; good-for-nothing;scamp

gałganiarz (gaw-ga-nash) m.
 ragtagman; ragpicker

gałka (gaw-ka) f. knob

gama (ga-ma) f. scale

gamoń (ga-mon) m. lout; oaf

ganek (ga-nek) m. balcony

gangrena (gan-gre-na) f.
 gangrene; depravity; corruption

ganić (ga-neech) v. blame

gapa (ga-pa) f. sucker

gapić się (ga-peech shan) v.
 gape; star-gaze ; moon; stare

gapie (ga-pye) pl. gapers

garaż (ga-rash) m. garage

garb (garb) m. hunch; hump

garbarnia (gar-bar-na) f.
 tannery ; tan-yard

garbować (gar-bo-vach) v. tan

garbaty (gar-ba-ti) adj. m.
 hunch-backed; humpy; uneven

garbus (gar-boos) m.=garbaty

garbić (gar-beech) v. stoop

garderoba (gar-de-ro-ba) f.
 wardrobe; dressing-room

gardło (gard-wo) n. throat

gardłować (gard-wo-vach) v.
 v. talk big; clamor; cry for

gardłowy (gard-wo-vi) adj. m.
 guttural; punishable by death

gardzić (gar-dźheech)v. scorn;
 despise; have in contempt

gardziel (gar-dźhel) f. throat;
 fauces; choke; gorge; jaws

garnąć (gar-nownch) v. gather

garncarz (garn-tsash) m. potter

garnek (gar-nek) m. pot; potful

garnirować (gar-nee-ro-vach) v.
 garnish; trim (a dress etc.)

garnitur (gar-nee-toor) m. set;
 suit; suite; assortment

garnizon (gar-nee-zon) m.
 garrison

garnuszek (gar-noo-shek) m. cup
garstka (garst-ka) f. handful
garsc (garshch) f. handful
gasic (ga-sheech) v. extinguish; quench ; put out;eclipse
gasnac (gas-nownch) v. die out
gasnica (gash-nee-tsa) f.
 fire-extinguisher
gastronomiczny (gas-tro-no-
 meech-ni) adj. m. gastronomic
gastryczny (gas-trich-ni)
 adj. m. gastric
gatunek (ga-too-nek) m. kind;
 quality; sort; class; species
gaweda (ga-van-da) f. chat
gawiedz (ga-vyedzh) f. mob;
 rabble ; populace; gaping crowd
gawron (ga-vron) m. rook
gaz (gas) m. gas; open throttle
gaza (ga-za) f. gauze
gazeciarz (ga-ze-chash) m.
 newspaperboy; newsstand
gazeta (ga-ze-ta) f. newspaper
gazolina (ga-zo-lee-na) f.
 gasoline; gasolene: petrol
gazomierz (ga-zo-myesh) m.
 gas-meter
gazownia (ga-zov-na) f. gas-
 plant; gas works
gaznik (gazh-neek) m. carburet-
 or
gaza (ga-zha) f. wage; salary
gabczasty (gownb-cha-sti) adj.
 m. spongy; squashy; mushy
gabka (gownb-ka) f. sponge
gasienica (gown-she-nee-tsa)
 f. caterpillar; band; track
gasior (gown-shor) m. gander;
 jar; demijohn; ridge tile
gaszcz (gownshch) m. thicket
gbur (gboor) m. rude; boor
gburowaty (gboo-ro-va-ti) adj.
 m. boprish; rude ; churlish
gdakac (gda-kach) v. cackle;
 yak
gderac (dge-rach) v. grumble
gdy (gdi) conj. when; as; that
gdyby (gdi-bi) conj. if
gdyz (gdish) conj. for; because
gdzie (gdzhe) adv. conj. where
gdzie indziej(gdzhe-een-dzhey)
 adv. elsewhere

gdziekolwiek (gdzhe-kol-vyek)
 adv. anywhere; wherever
gdzie niegdzie (gdzhe-neg-dzhe)
 adv. here and there; in places
gdzies (gdzhesh) adv. somewhere ; somewhere round
gejzer (gey-zer) m. geyser
gen (gen) m. (biol.) gene
genealogia (ge-ne-a-log-ya) f.
 genealogy; origin
generacja (ge-ne-rats-ya) f.
 generation
generalny (ge-ne-ral-ni) adj.
 m. general ; widespread
general (ge-ne-raw) m. general
genetyczny (ge-ne-tich-ni)
 adj. m. genetic
geneza (ge-ne-za) f. origin;
 genesis ; birth
genialny (ge-nal-ni) adj. m.
 ingenious; genial ; great
geniusz (ge-nyoosh) m. genius
geodezja (ge-o-dez-ya) f.
 geodesy
geografia (ge-o-graf-ya) f.
 geography
geologia (ge-o-log-ya) f.
 geology
geometra (ge-o-met-ra) m.
 surveyor ; land surveyor
geometria (ge-o-metr-ya) f.
 geometry ; geometry book
georginia (ge-or-gee-na) f.
 dahlia
germanski (ger-man-skee) adj.
 m. Germanic
gest (gest) m. gesture ;motion
gestykulowac (ges-ti-koo-lo-
 vach) v. gesticulate
getto (get-to) n. ghetto
geba (gan-ba) f. mug; mouth;
 puss ; snout; muzzle; face
gegac (gan-gach) v. cackle
ges (gansh) f. goose
gesl (ganshl) f. lute
gestosc (gan-stoshch) f. density; thickness; closeness
gestwina (gan-stvee-na) f.
 thicket; array; accumulation
giac (gyownch)v. bow; bend
gibki (geeb-kee) adj. m.
 pliant; flexible; limber

giełda (gew-da) f. stock-exchange; money-market
giez (ges) m. gadfly; breeze
giętki (gańt-kee) adj. m. flexible; nimble; elastic
gigant (gee-gant) m. giant
gilza (geel-za) f. (cartridge) case; shell; cigarette tube
gimnastyczny (geem-nas-tich-ni) adj. m. gymnastic
gimnazjum (geem-náz-yoom) n. high-school; middle-school
ginąc (gee-nównch) v. perish
ginekolog (gee-ne-ko-log) m. gynecologist
gips (geeps) m. gypsum
gitara (gee-tá-ra) f. guitar
glazura (gla-zoo-ra) f. glaze
gleba (glé-ba) f. soil
glejt (gleyt) m. safe-conduct
gledzic (glań-dźheech)v. talk-through one's hat; talk-nonsense;twaddle; blather
gliceryna (glee-ce-ri-na) f. glycerin
glin (gleen) m. aluminum
glina (glee-na) f. clay; loam
glista (glees-ta) f. earth-worm; ascaris; nema
glob (glop) m. globe; sphere
gładki (gwad-kee) adj. m. plain; smooth; sleek;even; level;glib
gładzic (gwa-dźheech)v. smooth; (put to death);mangle; stroke
głaskac (gwas-kach) v. caress; fondle; stroke;pet; tickle
głaz (gwas) m. boulder; rock
głąb (gwównp) f, depth
głąb (gwównp) m. stalk
głębia (gwanb-ya) f. depth; deep; interior; intensity
głęboki (gwan-bó-kee) adj. m. deep; distant; remote; intense
głębokosc (gwan-bó-koshch) f. depth; profundity; keenness
głodny (gwod-ni) adj. m. hungry
głodowac (gwo-do-vach) v. starve; hunger; lay off food
głodzic (gwo-dźheech)v. starve (somone); underfeed; deprive
głos (gwos) m. voice; sound;tone
głosowac (gwo-so-vach) v. vote

głosnik (gwosh-ńeek) m. loud-speaker;public-address system
głosno (gwosh-no) adv. loud
głosny (gwosh-ni) adj. m. loud
głowa (gwo-va) f. head; chief
głowic się (gwo-veech shań) v. beat one's brains out;puzzle
głod (gwoot) m. hunger; famine
głog (gwook) m. hawthorn
głowka (gwoo-vka) f. pinhead; knob; tip; top; boss; heading
głownodowodzący (gwoov-no-do-vo-dzówn-tsi) m. commander-in-chief
głowny (gwoov-ni) adj. m. main; predominant; foremost
głuchy (gwoo-khi) adj. m. deaf
głupi (gwoo-pee) adj. m. silly; stupid; foolish; asinine
głupiec (gwoop-yets) m. dumb-head; fool; idiot;loony; goof
głupota (gwoo-po-ta) f. stu-pidity;imbecility; foolishness
głupstwo (gwoop-stwo) n. nonsense; trifle; blunder
głuszec (gwoo-shets) m. grouse
gmach (gmakh) m. large building
gmatwac (gma-tvach) v. tangle; embroil; mix up; complicate
gmerac (gme-rach) v. rummage
gmin (gmeen) m. populace
gmina (gmee-na) f. county subdivision ; parish
gnat (gnat) m. bone (slang)
gnębic (gnań-beech) v. oppress
gniady (gńa-di) adj. m. bay (horse); dark brown horse
gniazdo (gńaz-do) n. nest
gnic (gńeech) v. rot; decay
gnida (gńeeda) f. nit
gniesc (gńeshch) v. squeeze
gniew (gńev) m. anger; wrath
gnieździc się (gńeźh-dźheech shań) v. nestle ; cluster
gnilny (gńeel-ni) adj. m. putrid; of rot; septic
gnoic (gno-eech) v. putrefy
gnojowka (gno-yoov-ka) f. liquid manure; manure pit
gnoj (gnooy) m. manure; dung; stinker (vulg.); lousy bum
gnusny (gnoosh-ni) adj. m. sluggish; lazy; idle; listless

godło (gód-wo) n. emblem
godność (gód-noshch) f. dignity; name; pride; self-esteem
godny (gód-ni) adj. m. worthy
gody (go-di) n. nuptials; mating
godzić (go-dźheech) v. reconcile; hire; square; engage
godzien (go-dźhen) adj. m.
deserving ; worth; worthy
godzina (go-dźhee-na) f. hour
godziwy (go-dźhee-vi) adj. m.
proper; suitable; just; fair
goić (go-eech) v. heal; cure
goleń (go-leń) m. shin-bone
golić (go-leech) v. shave
golonka (go-lón-ka) f. pig's
feet dish ; knuckle
gołąb (go-wównp) m. pigeon
gołoledz (go-wo-ledźh) f.
glazed frost ;frozen dew
gołosłowny (go-wo-swov-ni) adj.
m. unfounded; proofless; vain
goły (go-wi) adj. m. naked
gonić (go-ńeech) v. chase; hunt
goniec (go-ńets) m. messenger
gonitwa (go-ńeet-va) f. chase
gont (gont) m. shingle
gorąco (go-równ-tso) n. heat
gorący (go-równ-tsi) adj. m.
hot; sultry; warm; hearty;lively
gorączka (go-równch-ka) f. fever; shakes; excitement; heat
gorczyca (gor-chi-tsa) f.
mustard; charlock
gorętszy (go-rant-shi) adj.
m.hotter; fervent; intense
gorliwiec (gor-lee-vyets) m.
zealot; ardent supporter
gorliwy (gor-lee-vi) adj. m.
zealous; keen; eager; devout
gorset (gor-set) m. girdle
gorszy (gor-shi) adj. m. worse
gorszyć (gor-shich) v. demoralize; scandalize; shock;deprave
gorycz (go-rich) f. bitterness
goryl (go-ril) m. gorilla
gorzałka (go-zhaw-ka) f. brandy spirits ; booze; spirit
gorzeć (go-zhech) v. be ablaze
gorzej (go-zhey) adv. worse
gorzelnia (go-zhel-ńa) f.
distillery ; still
gorzki (gozh-kee) adj. n.bitter

gospoda (gos-pó-da) f. inn
gospodarczy (gos-po-dar-chi)
adj. n. economic;farm; charring
gospodarka (gos-po-dar-ka) f.
economy;housekeeping; farming
gospodarny (gos-po-dar-ni) adj.
m. economical; thrifty
gospodarstwo (gos-po-dar-stvo)
n. household; farm; possessions
gospodarz (gos-po-dash) m.
landlord; host; farmer;manager
gospodyni (gos-po-di-ńee) f.
landlady; hostess; manageress
gosposia (gos-po-sha) f.
housekeeper; maid; servant
gościć (gosh-cheech) v. receive; entertain; treat; stay at
gościna (gosh-chee-na) f.
visit; stay at sb house
gościnność (gosh-cheen-noshch)
f. hospitality
gość (goshch) m. guest;caller
gościec (gosh-chets) m. gout;
arthritis
gotować (go-to-vach) v. cook;
boil ; get ready; prepare
gotowość (go-to-voshch) f.
readiness ; willingness
gotowy (go-to-vi) adj. m.
ready; done; complete;willing
gotówka (go-toov-ka) f. cash
gotyk (go-tik) m. Gothic
goździk (gozh-dźheek)m. carnation; clove; gilly-flower
góra (goo-ra) f. mountain
góral (goo-ral) m. mountaineer
górnictwo (goor-ńeets-tvo) n.
mining; mining industry
górnik (goor-ńeek) m. miner
górnolotny (goor-no-lot-ni)
adj. m. lofty; soaring;gaudy
górny (goor-ni) adj. m. upper
górować (goo-ro-vach) v. prevail ; excel; dominate ; rise
górski (goor-skee) adj. m.
mountainous ; mountain
górzysty (goo-zhis-ti) adj.
m. hilly ; mountainous
gówniarz (goov-ńash) m.
(vulg): shitass; whipster
gówno (goov-no) m. shit (vulg.)
gra (gra) f. game ;sham; acting
grab (grap) m. hornbeam; hardbeam

grabarz (gra-bash) m. grave-
digger;sexton; burying beetle
grabić (gra-beech) v. rake;
plunder ; rob; sack; rake up
grabie (gra-bye) n. rake
grabież (gra-byesh) f. plunder
graca (gra-tsa) f. scraper
gracja (grats-ya) f. grace
gracować (gra-tso-vach) v.
scrape; rake; mix mortar
gracz (grach) m. player; gambler; double-dealer; sly fox
grać (grach) v. play; act;
gamble ; pretend; pulsate
grad (grad) m. hail; volley
grafika (fra-fee-ka) f. graphic
art ; graphics; art of writing
gram (gram) m. gram
gramatyka (gra-ma-ti-ka) f.
grammar; grammar book
gramofon (gra-mo-fon) m. record player; phonograph
gramolić się (gra-mo-leech
shań) v. clamber;climb
granat (gra-nat) m. grenade
granatnik (gra-nat-ńeek) m.
mortar ; howitzer
granatowy (gra-na-to-vi) adj.
m. navy blue ; of grenades
granda (gran-da) f. swindle
graniastosłup (gra-ńa-sto-
swoop) m. prism
granica (gra-ńee-tsa) f. boundary; limit; border; range
granit (gra-ńeet) m. granite
granulować (gra-noo-lo-vach)
v. granulate
grań (grań) f. (mountain) ridge;
crest; edge; razor's edge
grasować (gra-so-vach) v. roam
about; prowl; maraud; stalk
grat (grat) m. run down furniture (or man); crock; trash
gratis (gra-tees) adv. free of
charge; something given free
gratka (grat-ka) f. windfall
gratulacja (gra-too-lats-ya)
f. congratulations;felicitation
grawer (gra-ver) m. engraver
grawitacja (gra-vee-tats-ya)
f. gravitation
grdyka (grdi-ka) f. Adam's
apple

grecki (grets-kee) adj. m.
Greek
gremialnie (grem-yal-ńe) adv.
in-a-mass; completely;altogether
grobla (grob-la) f. dike; dam
grobowiec (gro-bov-yets) m.
tomb ; sepulchre ;family vault
grobowy (gro-bo-vi) adj. m.
grave ; deathly; gloomy;dismal
groch (grokh) m. pea; pea plant
grom (grom) m. thunderclap
gromada (gro-ma-da) f. crowd;
throng; community; team
gromadzić (gro-ma-dźheech) v.
amass; hoard; gather;attract
gromić (gro-meech) v. storm;
rout ; reprimand; defeat
grono (gro-no) n. bunch of
grapes ; cluster; group;body
gronostaj (gro-no-stay) m.
ermine
grosz (grosh) m. penny (copper)
groszek (gro-shek) m. green
pea(s) ; spotted pattern
grot (grot) m. dart; spike
grota (gro-ta) f. grotto; care
groza (gro-za) f. dread; horror
grozić (gro-źheech)v. threaten
groźba (gróźh-ba) f. threat
grób (groop) m. grave ; tomb
gród (groot) m. (fortified) town
gródź (groodźh)f. bulkhead
grubiański (groob-yań-skee)
adj. m. rude ; coarse; obscene
grubość (groo-boshch) f. thickness ; girth; size; grist
gruby (groo-by) adj. m. thick;
fat; stout; big;low-pitched
gruchotać (groo-kcho-tach) v.
shatter ; batter; rattle;crash
gruczoł (groo-chow) m. gland
gruda (groo-da) f. lump; clod
grudzień (groo-dźheń) m.
December
grunt (groont) m. ground; soil
grupa (groo-pa) f. group ; class
grusza (groo-sha) f. pear-tree
gruz (groos) m. rubble ; ruins
gruzeł (groo-zew) m. clot
gruzy (groo-zi) pl. debris
gruźlica (groozh-lee-tsa) f.
tuberculosis; consumption

gryka (grí-ka) f. buckwheat
grymas (grí-mas) m. grimace
grypa (grí-pa) f. flu;influenza
grysik (grí-sheek) m. grits
gryzoń (grí-zoń) m. rodent
gryzć (grizhćh) v. bite;torment
grzać (gzhach) v. warm;thrash;fire;
grządka (gzhownd-ka) f. flower
   bed ; patch ; (hen-)roost
grząsć (gzhowńshćh) v. wade
grząski (gzhown-skee) adj. m.
   quaggy; slimy; slushy; miry
grzbiet (gzhbyet) m. back;
   spine ; ridge; butt; edge;rib
grzebać (gzhe-baćh) v. bury;
   rummage; dig;rake up; fumble
grzebień (gzhe-byeń) m. comb;
   crest of a wave; ridge;teaser
grzech (gzhekh) m. sin; fault
grzechotka (gzhe-khót-ka) f.
   rattle; flapper; clapper
grzechotnik (gzhe-khot-ńeek)
   m. rattlesnake
grzeczność (gzhech-nośhćh) f.
   politeness; favor; attentions
grzęznąć (gzhańz-nowńćh) v.
   get stuck;wade; flounder;sink
grzmiący (gzhmyowń-tsi) adj. m.
   thundering; booming;fulminatory
grzmot (gzhmot) m. thunder; hag
grzyb (gzhip) m. mushroom;
   fungus; snuff
grzywa (gzhí-ya) f. mane
grzywna (gzhív-na) f. fine
gubernator (goo-ber-ná-tor) m.
   governor(general)
gubić (goo-beećh) v. loose;ruin
gula (goo-la) f. knob; bump
gulasz (goo-lash) m. meat soup
gulgotać (gool-go-taćh) v.
   gurgle; bubble; gobble
guma (goo-ma) f. rubber
gumno (goom-no) n. barn (yard)
gust (goost) m. taste; palate
guz (goos) m. bump; tumor
guzdrać się (gooz-draćh śhań) v.
   dawdle; dally; waste time;lag
gwałcić (gvaw-ćheećh) v. rape;
   violate; compel; coerce;force
gwałt (gvawt) m. rape; outrage
gwałtowny (gvaw-tóv-ni) adj.
   m. 1. outrageous 2. urgent

gwar (gvar) m. hum; noise
gwara (gva-ra) f. dialect;
   slang; jargon; lingo; cant;
   patter ; colloquial language
gwarancja (gva-ran-tsya) f.
   warranty; guarantee; pledge
gwardia (gvar-dya) f. guard
gwarny (gvar-ni) adj. m. noisy
gwarzyć (gva-zhich) v. chat
gwiazda (gvyáz-da) f. star
gwint (gveent)m.thread (mech.)
gwintować (gveen-to-vaćh) v.
   cut thread ; tap; rifle
gwizd (gveezt) m. whistle
gwoli (gvo-lee) conj. for the
   sake of ; because of;in order
gwoźdź (gwoożhdźh) m. nail to
gzyms (gzims) m. molding
   cornice; mantelpiece
habit (khá-bit) m. monk's
   frock ; habit ; nun's frock
haczyk (kha-chik) m. small
   hook ; barb; snag; catch
hafciarka (haf-char-ka) f.
   embroideress
haft (khaft) m. embroidery
haftka (kháft-ka) f. clasp
hak (khak) m. hook ; clamp
hala (khá-la) f. (sports) hall
halka (khál-ka) f. petticoat
halny wiatr (hal-ni vyátr)
   Tatra wind (foehn)
halucynacja (kha-loo-tsi-nats-
   ya) f. hallucination
hałas (kha-was) m. noise; din
hałasować (kha-wa-só-vaćh) v.
   make noise ; be noisy
hałastra (kha-wás-tra) f. mob;
   rabble; riff-raff; ragtag mob
hałaśliwy (kha-waśh-lee-vi)
   adj. m. noisy ; loud; rowdy
hamak (khá-mak) m. hammock
hamować (kha-mó-vaćh) v.apply
   brakes; restrain; hamper;curb
hamulec (kha-moo-lets) m. brake
hamulec ręczny (kha-moo-lets
   rańch-ni) handbrake
handel (khandel) m. commerce
handlarz (khánd-lash) m. merchant;shopkeeper; peddler
handlować (khan-dlo-vaćh) v.
   trade; deal; be in business

hangar (khan-gar) m. hangar
haniebny (kha-ńeb-ni) adj. m.
 disgraceful; dirty; foul; vile
hanba (khań-ba) f. disgrace
hanbić (khań-beech) v. disgrace
haracz (kha-rach) m. tribute
harcerstwo (khar-tser-stvo) n.
 scouting
harcerz (khar-tsesh) m. boy
 scout
hardy (kha-rdy) adj. m. haughty
harfa (khar-fa) f. harp
harmider (khar-mee-der) m.
 hullabaloo; clatter; din; row
harmonia (khar-moń-ya) f. harmony; accordion; harmonics
harować (kha-ro-vach) v. toil
harpun (khar-poon) m. harpoon
hart (khart) m. fortitude;
 hardness; sternness;temper;grit
hartować (khar-to-vach) v.
 temper; harden; anneal;quench
hasać (kha-sach) v. frisk;
 frolic; romp;gambol; dance
hasło (kha-swo) n. password
haubica (khau-bee-tsa) f.
 howitzer
haust (khaust) m. gulp; swig
hazard (kha-zard) m. risk;
 hazard; the gaming table
heban (khe-ban) m. ebony
hebel (khe-bel) m. plane
hebrajski (kheb-ray-skee) adj.
 m. Hebrew
heca (khe-tsa) f. fun; fuss
hegemonia (khe-ge-moń-ya) f.
 hegemony
hej (khey) excl.: hey! ho!
hejnał (khey-naw) m. trumpet-
 call; bugle-call; reveille
hektar (khek-tar) m. hectare
hełm (khewm) m. helmet; dome
hemoroidy (khe-mo-roy-di) pl.
 piles;hemorrhoids
hen (khen) adv. far; away
herb (kherp) m. coat-of-arms
herbaciarnia (kher-ba-char-ńa)
 f. teahouse
herbata (kher-ba-ta) f. tea
herbatnik (kher-bat-ńeek) m.
 biscuit
heretyk (khe-re-tik) m. heretic

herezja (khe-rez-ya) f. heresy
hermetyczny (kher-me-tich-ni)
 adj. m. air-tight; hermetic
heroiczny (khe-ro-eech-ni) adj.
 m. heroic
heroizm (khe-ro-eezm) m. heroism
herszt (khersht) m. ringleader
het (khet) adv. far; away
hetman (khet-man) m. commander
hiacynt (khya-tsint) m.hyacinth
hiena (khee-e-na) f. hyena
hierarchia (khye-rar-khya) f.
 hierarchy
hieroglif (khye-ro-gleef) m.
 hieroglyph; illegible writing
higiena (khee-ge-na) f. hygiene;
 sanitation; hygienics
hinduski (kheen-doos-kee) adj.
 m. Hindu
hiperbola (khee-per-bo-la) f.
 hyperbola; hyperbole
hipnotyczny (kheep-no-tich-ni)
 adj. m. hypnotic; mesmeric
hipochondryk (khee-po-khon-drik)
 m. hypochondriac
hipokryta (khee-po-kri-ta) m.
 hypocrite; pretender;dissembler
hipopotam (khee-po-po-tam) m.
 hippopotamus
hipoteka (khee-po-teka) f.title;
 mortgage ; records office
hipoteza (khee-po-te-za) f.
 hypothesis ; assumption
histeria (khees-ter-ya) f.
 hysteria; hysterical fit
historia (khees-tor-ya) f. story; history ; affair; show;fuss
hiszpański (kheesh-pań-skee)
 adj. m. Spanish
hitlerowiec (kheet-le-ro-vyets)
 m. hitlerite
hodować (kho-do-vach) v. breed
hodowca (kho-dov-tsa) m. breeder; grower ; farmer;cultivator
hojny (khoy-ni) adj. m. generous; lavish; liberal; profuse
hokej (kho-key) m. hockey
holenderski (kho-len-der-skee)
 adj. m. Dutch
holować (kho-lo-vach) v. tow;
 haul; drag; tug; haul; truck

hołd (khowd) m. tribute

hołota (kho-wó-ta) f. riffraff

honor (kho-nor) m. honor

honorarium (kho-no-ıar-yoom)
n. fee; honorarium

horda (khor-da) f. horde; throng

horrendalny (kho-ren-dal-ni)
adj. m. awful; horrible

hormon (khor-mon) m. hormone

horoskop (kho-ros-kop) m.
horoscope ; prophesy ;prospect

horyzont (kho-ri-zont) m.hor-
izon; vistas; prospects

hotel (kho-tel) m. hotel

hoży (kho-zhi) adj. m. brisk;
handsome; comely; fresh

hrabia (khrab-ya) m. count

hrabina (khra-bee-na) f.
countess

hrabianka (khra-byan-ka) f.
countess (miss)

hrabstwo (khrab-stwo) n. county

hreczka (khrech-ka) f. buckwheat

hreczkosiej (khrech-ko-shey)
m.country bumpkin

hubka (khoob-ka) f. tinder

huczeć (khoo-chech) v. roar

hufnal (khoof-nal) m. horse-
shoe nail

huk (khook) m. bang; roar

hulać (khoo-lach) v. carouse;
riot; make merry; run wild

hulajnoga (khoo-lay-no-ga) f.
scooter (without motor)

hulaka (khoo-la-ka) m. carous-
er; debaucher; rioter: rake

hulanka (khoo-lan-ka) f. riot;
debauch ; junket: carouse;revel

hultaj (khool-tay) m. libertine;
rascal; rogue

humanista (khoo-ma-ñees-ta) m.
humanist ; classical scholar

humanitarny (khoo-ma-ñee-tár-
ni) m. humane ; humanitarian

humor (khoo-mor) m. humor

hura (khoo-ra) f. hurrah !
cheers ! long live !

huragan (khoo-ra-gan) m. hurricane ; cyclone

hurmem (khoor-mem) adv. in
swarms ; in a mass; altogether

hurt (khoort) m. wholesale

humus (khoo-moos) m. humus

husarz (khoo-sash) m. Polish
winged-armor cavalryman (hist.)

huśtać (khoosh-tach) v. swing;
rock; dandle; toss up and down

huśtawka (khoosh-tav-ka) f.
swing ; seesaw; swing boat

huta (khoo-ta) f. metal or
glass mill; smelting works

hutnik (khoot-ñeek) m. metal
or glass(man)worker ;metalurgist

hycel (khi-tsel) m. dogcatcher;
rascal; good for nothing

hydrant (khid-rant) m. hydrant

hydraulika (khi-drau-leé-ka)
f. hydraulics ; plumbing

hymn (himn) m.anthem; hymn

i (ee) conj. and; also; too

ichtiologia (eekh-tyo-lóg-ya)
f. ichthyology

idea (ee-de-a) f. idea; aim

idealista (ee-de-a-lees-ta) m.
idealist; dreamer; visionary

idealny (ee-de-al-ni) adj. m.
ideal ; perfect; visionary

identyczny (ee-den-tich-ni)
adj. m. identical ; similar

ideologia (ee-de-o-log-ya) f.
ideology ; world view

idiosynkrazja (ee-dyo-sin-kráz-
ya) f. idiosyncrasy

idiota (ee-d-yo-ta) m. idiot

idiotka (eed-yot-ka) f. idiot

iglaste drzewo (ee-glas-te
dzhe-vo) m. coniferous tree

iglica (eeg-leé-tsa) f. spire

igła (eeg-wa) f. needle

ignorancja (eeg-no-ran-tsya) f.
ignorance; lack of knowledge

igrać (eeg-rach) v. play; trifle

igrzysko (ee-gzhis-ko) n.
spectacle (games); contest

ikra (eek-ra) f. spawn; roe

ile (ee-le) adv. how much

ilekroć (ee-le-kroch) adv.
every time; whenever ; when

iloczas (ee-ló-chas) m. quantity (of a vowel or syllable)

iloczyn (ee-lo-chin) m. (multiplication) product

iloraz (ee-lo-raz) m. (division)
quotient

iloŝciowy (ee-loŝh-ĉhó-vi)adj.
m. quantitative; numerical
iloŝć (ee-loŝhćh) f. quantity
iluminacja (ee-loo-mee-náts-ya)
f. illumination; floodlight
ilustracja (ee-loos-trats-ya)
f. illustration; figure;picture
iluzja (ee-looz-ya) f. illusion
ił (eew) m. loam
im (eem) conj. the more...
imać (ee-maćh) v. size upon
imadło (ee-mád-wo) n . (shop)
vice ; chuck; holder ; vise
imaginacja (ee-ma-gee-náts-ya)
f. imagination; empty fancy
imbir (eém-beer) m. ginger
imbryk (eém-brik) m. teapot
imieniny (ee-mye-ńee-ni) n.
name-day; name-day party
imiennie (ee-myen-ńe) adv. by
name; personally; individually
imiennik (ee-myen-ńeek) m.
namesake
imiesłów (ee-mye-swoov) m.
participle
imię (ee-myáń) n. name (given)
imigracja (ee-mee-gráts-ya) f.
immigration; the immigrants
imigrant (ee-mee-grant) m.
immigrant;foreign settler
imigrować (ee-mee-gro-vaćh) v.
immigrate;settle in a new land
imitacja (ee-mee-táts-ya) f.
imitation; counterfeit; fake
imitować (ee-mee-to-vaćh) v.
imitate; mimic; simulate
impas (eém-pas) m. deadlock
imperialista (eem-per-ya-lees-
ta) m. imperialist
imperium (eem-per-yoom) n.
empire
impertynent (eem-per-tí-nent) m.
arrogant; pert,impertinent man
impet (eém-pet) m. impetus
imponować (eem-po-nó-vaćh) v.
impress; impose on sb; dazzle
import (eém-port) m. import
impregnować (eem-preg-nó-vaćh)
v. impregnate; make waterproof
impreza (eem-pré-za) f. enterprise; spectacle; show; stunt
improwizować (eem-pro-vee-zo-
vaćh) v. improvise; extemporize

impuls (eém-pools) m. impulse
inaczej (ee-ná-chey) adv. otherwise; differently; unlike
inauguracja (ee-na-goo-ráts-ya)
f. inauguration; opening
inaugurować (ee-na-goo-ro-vaćh)
v. inaugurate; initiate
in blanko (een-blán-ko) adv.
in blank ; blank,check
incydent (een-tsi-dent) m.
incident; happening; event
indagacja (een-da-gats-ya) f.
investigation; questioning
indeks (eén-deks) m. index
indemnizacja (een-dem-ńee-
záts-ya) f. indemnity
indukcja (een-dóok-tsya) f.
induction; generalized reasoning
indyk (een-dik) m. turkey
indyczka (een-dích-ka) f.
turkey-hen
indywidualny (een-di-vee-doo-
ál-ni) adj. m. individual
inercja (een-érts-ya) f. inertia ; inaction; inertness
infekcja (een-fékts-ya) f.
infection; contamination
infiltracja (een-feel-trats-ya)
f. infiltration
inflacja (een-fláts-ya) f.
inflation
influenza (een-floo-én-za) f.
influenza ; flu ; grippe
informacja (een-for-mats-ya) f.
information ; intelligence;news
informacyjny (een-for-ma-tsiy-
ni) adj. m. information (office)
informować (een-for-mó-vaćh) v.
inform ; instruct; post up
ingerencja (een-ge-rén-tsya) f.
interference; meddling
inhalacja (een-kha-lats-ya) f.
inhalation: breathing in
inicjał (ee-ńeets-yaw) m. initial (letter); ornate letter
inicjator (ee-ńeets-ya-tor) m.
originator ; mover; founder
inicjatywa (ee-ńeets-ya-ti-va)
f. initiative; enterprise
inkasować (een-ka-so-vaćh) v.
collect (money); get a blow
inklinacja (een-klee-nats-ya)
f. inclination ; liking

inkwizycja (een-kvee-zits-ya)
f. inquisition; investigation
innowacja (een-no-vats-ya) f.
innovation ; novelty ,
innowierca (een-no-vyer-tsa)
m.dissenter; heretic
inny (een-ni) adj. m. other;
different; another (one)
inscenizacja (een-stse-ñee-záts-
ya) f. putting on stage
inspekcja (een-spek-tsya) f.
inspection; review; inspectorate
inspekty (een-spek-ti) n. hotbed ; glass covered frame
inspiracja (een-spee-ráts-ya)
f. inspiration ; breathing in
instalacja (een-sta-láts-ya) f.
installation ; plumbing, etc
instalator (een-sta-la-tor) m.
plumber; fitter; electrician
instrukcja (een-strook-tsya)
f. instruction ; order;training
instrument (een-stroo-ment) m.
instrument; tool; deed;appliance
instynkt (een-stinkt) m. instinct ; aptitude; knack
instytucja (een-sti-toots-ya) f.
institution ; establishment
insynuacja (een-si-noo-áts-ya)
f. insinuation; innuendo
integralny (een-te-gral-ni)
adj. m. integral; whole; entire
intelekt (een-te-lekt) m. intellect; intelligence; mind
intelektualista (een-te-lek-
too-a-lees-ta) m. intellectual
inteligencja (een-te-lee-gén-
tsya) f.intelligensia ; intelligence; (quick)understanding
inteligentny (een-te-lee-gen-
tni) adj. m. intelligent
intencja (een-tén-tsya) f. intention ; purpose; view;finality
intensywny (een-ten-siv-ni)
adj. m. intensive; strenuous
interes (een-té-res) m. interest; business:store; matter
interesowny (een-te-re-sów-ni)
adj. m. selfish; greedy
interesujący (een-te-re-soo-
yown-tsi) adj. m. interesting
internat (een-tér-nat) m. boarding school

interpretacja (een-ter-pre-
táts-ya) f. interpretation
interwencja (een-ter-vén-tsya)
f. intervention;interference
intratny (een-trát-ni) adj. m.
lucrative; profitable;paying
introligator (een-tro-lee-ga-
tor) m. bookbinder
intruz (een-troos) m. intruder
intryga (een-tri-ga)f. plot;
intrigue ; machination
intuicja (een-too-eéts-ya) f.
intuition ; insight; feeling
intuicyjny (een-too-ee-tsiy-ni)
adj. m. intuitive
inwalida (een-va-lee-da) m.
invalid; disabled (soldier)
inwazja (een-váz-ya) f. invasion
inwencja (een-vén-tsya) f. in-
ventiveness; invention
inwentarz (een-vén-tash) m.
inventory; stock; list
inwestycja (een-ves-títs-ya)
f. investment ; capital outlay
inżynier (een-zhi-ñer) m.
engineer (with college degree)
inżynieria (een-zhi-ñer-ya) f.
engineering
ircha (eér-kha) f. suede-
leather; chamois ; shammy
irlandzki(eer-landz-kee) adj.
Irish ,
irys (ee-ris) m. iris
ironia (ee-ro-ñya) f. irony
irygacja (ee-ri-gáts-ya) f.
irrigation : watering
irytacja (ee-ri-tats-ya) f.
irritation ; vexation; chafe
iskać (eesk-ach) v. v. seek
lice; cleanse of vermin
iskra (ees-kra) f. spark
istnieć (eest-ñech) v. exist
istnienie (eest-ñé-ñe) n.
existence;being; entity
istny (eest-ni) adj. m. real;
veritable ;downright; sheer
istota (ees-tó-ta) f. being;
essence ; gist; sum; entity
istotny (ees-tót-ni) adj. m.
real; substantial ; vital
istotnie (ees-tót-ñe) adv.
indeed; truly ; really;in fact
iscie (eésh-che) adv. indeed;
truly ; really; in truth

iść (eeshch) v. go; walk

izba (eez-ba) f. room; chamber

izba handlowa (eez-ba khan-dlo-va) f. Chamber of Commerce

izolacja (ee-zo-láts-ya) f. isolation; insulation; seal

izolator (ee-zo-lá-tor) m. insulator; non-conductor

izolacyjna taśma (ee-zo-la-tsiy-na táśh-ma) f. insulating tape

izoterma (ee-zo-ter-ma) f. isotherm:line of equal temperature

izotop (ee-zo-top) m. isotope

izraelicki (eez-ra-e-leets-kee) adj. m. Israeli; of Israel

izraelita (eez-ra-e-lee-ta) m. Israelite; citizen of Izrael

iż (eezh) conj. that(literary)

iżby (eezh-bi) conj.m. in order that; in order to; lest

ja (ya) pron. I;(indecl.):self

jabłecznik (yab-wech-ñeek) m. apple cider; apple pie

jabłko (yáp-ko) n. apple

jabłoń (ya-bwoñ) f. apple tree

jacht (yakht) m. yacht

jachtklub (yákht-kloob) m. yacht club

jad (yat) m. venom; poison

jadalnia (ya-dál-ña) f. dining-room; mess; mess-hall

jadalny (ya-dál-ni) adj. m. eatable; edible; dining-

jadło (yád-wo) n. food;edibles

jadłodajnia (ya-dwo-dáy-na) f. restaurant; eating house

jadłospis (yad-wo-spees) m. menu; bill of fare

jaglana kasza (yag-lá-na ká-sha) f. millet-groats

jaglica (yag-lee-tsa) f. trachoma; viral eye infection

jagnię (yag-ñáñ) n. lamb

jagoda (ya-gó-da) f. berry

jajko (yáy-ko) n. egg(small)

jajo (yá-yo) n. egg; ovum

jajko na twardo(yáy-ko na twár-do) hard-boiled egg

jajko na miekko(yáy-ko na myáñ-ko) soft-boiled egg

jajecznica (ya-yech-ñee-tsa) f. scrambled eggs

jajnik (yáy-ñeek) m. ovary

jak (yak) adv. how;as;if; than

jakby (yák-bi) adv. as if; if

jakgdyby (yak-gdi-bi) adv. as if; seemingly; sort of

jaka (yá-ka) pron. f. what; which; f. jacket

jaki (yá-kee) pron. m. what; which one? that;some; like

jakie (yá-ke) pron. n. what; which=jąki(fem.& neuter)

jakiś (yak-eeśh) pron. some

jakkolwiek (yak-kol-vyek) conj. though: pron. somehow;anyhow

jakkolwiek (yak-kol-vyek) adv. somehow; anyhow; however

jako (yá-ko) adv. as;by way of

jako tako(ya-ko ta-ko) adv. so-so; tolerably well

jakoś (yá-kosh) adv. somehow

jakość (ya-kośhch) f. quality

jakościowo (ya-kosh-chó-vo) adv. m. qualitatively

jakże (yák-zhe) pron. how;sure

jałmużna (yaw-moozh-na) f. alms; charity;(hist.endowment)

jałowcówka (ya-wov-tsoov-ka) f. gin; juniper-flavored vodka

jałowiec (ya-wo-vyets) m. juniper(Juniperus)

jałowieć (ya-wo-vyech) v. grow-sterile; grow unproductive

jałowy (ya-wo-vi) adj. m. barren;sterile;arid;aseptic

jałówka (ya-woov-ka) f. heifer

jama (yá-ma) f. pit; hole; den; cavity; cave; burrow; hollow

jamnik (yam-ñeek) f. dachshund

jankes (yán-kes) m. Yankee

Japończyk (ya-poñ-chik) m. Japanese

japoński (ya-poñ-skee) adj. m. Japanese; of Japan

jar (yar) m. canyon; ravine

jarmark (yár-mark) m. fair

jarosz (ya-rosh) m. vegetarian

jarski (yár-skee) adj. m. vegetarian; meatless

jary (yá-ri) adj. robust; vigorous; hale; spring-

jarzębiak (ya-zháñ-byak) m. sorb brandy; rowan-berry vodka

jarzębina (ya-zhán-bée-na) f.
sorb tree; rowan;rowan berry
jarzmo (yázh-mo) n. yoke
jarzyć (yá-zhich) v. sparkle;
glitter; glow; shimmer
jarzyna (ya-shí-na) f. vegetable ; dish of vegetables
jasełka (ya-séw-ka) pl. crib;
Nativity play; créche
jasiek (yá-shek) m. little
pillow ; bean; beans
jaskinia (yas-kee-ńa) f. cave
jaskiniowiec (yas-kee-ńó-vyets)
m. cave dweller; cave man
jaskółka (yas-koów-ka) f.
swallow; martin; harbinger
jaskrawy (yas-kra-vi) adj. m.
glowing ; showy ; vivid;extreme
jasno (yás-no) adv. clearly;
brightly ; cheerfully;plainly
jasny (yás-ny) adj. m. clear;
, bright ; light; shining;noble
jasnowidz (yas-no-veets) m.
clairvoyant ; cristal gazer:seer
jastrząb (yas-tzhównp) m. fal-
kon; hawk; goshawk
jaszczyk (yash-chik) m. muni-
tion box; ammunition trailer
jaśmin (yaśh-meen) m. jasmine
jaśnieć (yaśh-ńech) v. shine;
sparkle, radiate; gleam; pale
jatka (yát-ka) f. shambles;
butcher's shop ; massacre
jatki (yát-kee) pl. shambles
jaw (yav) m. reality;v.expose
jawić (ya-veéch) v. appear;show
jawny (yáv-ni) adj. m. evident;
public ; open; notorious;sheer
jawor (ya-vor) m. plane tree;
maple; sycamore:sycamore wood
jaz (yas) m. weir ; milldam
jazda (yáz-da) f. ride ;driving
jaźń (yáżhń) f. ego; self;
the I ; the inner man ; psyche
jąć (yównch) v. seize; begin
jądro (yówn-dro) n. nucleus;
testicle; kernel; core
jąkać (yówn-kach) v. stutter
jątrzyć (yówn-tzhich) v. irritate; fester ;vex; embitter
jechać (yé-khach) v. ride;drive
jeden (yé-den) num. one; some

jedenaście (ye-de-náśh-che)
num. eleven
jedlina (yed-leé-na) f. fir
grove; fir and spruce branches
jednać (yéd-nach) v. conciliate
jednak (yéd-nak) conj. however;
yet; still;but; after all;though
jednaki (yed-ná-kee) adj. m.
identical; similar; equal;alike
jedno (yéd-no) n. num. one; one-
jednocześnie (yed-no-cheśh-ńe)
adv. simultaneously; also
jednoczyć (yed-nó-chich) v.
unify; merge; join; unite
jednogłośnie (yed-no-gwóśh-ńe)
adv. unanimously; in chorus
jednokrotnie (yed-no-krot-ńe)
adv. one time; once
jednostka (yed-nost-ka)f. unit;
individual;entity;measure;digit
jedność (yéd-nośhch) f. unity
jedwab (yéd-vab) m. silk
jedynaczka (ye-di-nách-ka) f.
only daughter
jedynak (ye-di-nak) m. only son
jedynie (ye-di-ńe) adv. only;
merely ; solely; nothing but
jedyny (ye-di-ni) adj. m. the
only one; the sole; unique
jedzenie (ye-dze-ńe) n. meat;
food; victuals; feed; eats
jemioła (ye-myó-wa) mistletoe
jeleń (yé-leń) m. stag; deer
jelito (ye-leé-to) n. intestine;
bowel ; gut
jełczeć (yew-chech) v. grow-
rancid ;become rancid
jeniec (ye-ńets) m. captive
jerzyna (ye-zhi-na) f. blackberry
jesień (ye-śheń) f. autumn;
fall; the fall of the leaf
jesienny (ye-śhen-ni) adj. m.
autumnal; of autmn
jesion (ye-śhon) m. ash tree
jesionka (ye-śhón-ka) f. fall
overcoat; light overcoat
jesiotr (ye-śhotr) m. sturgeon
jestestwo (yes-tes-tvo) m.
being; nature; creature
jeszcze (yesh-che) adv. still;
besides; more; yet; way back

jeść (yeshch) v. eat; feed sb
jeśli (yesh-lee) conj. if
jezdnia (yézd-ña), f. roadwav
jezuita (ye-zoo-ée-ta) m. Jesuit: member of Jesuit Order
jeździec (yeźh-dzhets) m.
horseman; rider; equestrian
jeż (yesh) m. porcupine
jeżdżenie (yezh-dzhe-ñe) n.
riding; driving; tyrannizing
jeżeli (ye-zhé-lee) conj. if
jeżyć się (yé-zhich śhań) v.
bristle up; stand on end
jeżyna (ye-zhí-na) f. blackberry; blackberry bush;bramble
jęczeć (yáñ-chech) v. moan;
groan; wail; whine;complain
jęczmień (yáñch-myeń) m. barley
jędrny (yáñdr-ni) adj. m. firm;
robust; strong; terse; pithy
jędza (yáñ-dza) f. witch; shrew
jęk (yáñk) m. groan; moan; wail
jęknąć (yáñk-nowńch) v. moan;
groan; whine; bellyache(once)
język (yáñ-zik) m. tongue
jod (yod) m. iodine
jodła (yód-wa)f.fir tree; spruce
jodyna (yo-dí-na) f. tincture
of iodine; iodine
jon (yon) m. ion
jowialny (yo-vyál-ni) adj. m.
jovial; debonair; genial
jubiler (yoo-bee-ler) m. jeweler (store or profession)
jubileusz (yoo-bee-lé-oosh) m.
jubilee; anniversary
jucht (yoo-kht) m. Russian
leather: water-proof leather
juczny koń (yooch-ni koń) adj.
m. pack-horse: beast of burden
judzić (yoo-dzheech)v.instigate
juki (yoo-kee) pl. packsaddle
junak (yoo-nak) m. brave; swaggerer; dashing fellow
jurysdykcja (yoo-ris-dík-tsya)
f. jurisdiction;legal authority
juta (yoo-ta) f. jute;jute plant
jutro (yoo-tro) adv. tomorrow
jutrzejszy (yoo-tshéy-shi) adj.
m. tomorrow's : future
jutrzenka (yoo-tzhén-ka) f.
day-break; morning star; dawn

już (yoozh) conj. already;
at any moment; by now;no more
juźci (yoóżh-ćhee) conj. of
course; certainly;sure thing!
kabalarka (ka-ba-lár-ka) f.
fortune teller (by cards)
kabała (ka-bá-wa) f. cabbala
kabaret (ka-bá-ret) m. cabaret
kabel (ká-bel) m. cable
kabestan (ka-bé-stan) m. cap-
stan; winch; windlass
kabina (ka-bée-na) f. cabin
kabłąk (káb-wowńk) m. bow;hoop
kabotyn (ka-bó-tin) m. poser;
buffoon; second-rate actor
kabriolet (ka-bryó-let) m.
convertible car; gig
kabza (káb-za) m. purse
kac (kats) m. hangover
kacerz (ká-tsesh) m. heretic
kacet (ká-tset) m. Nazi concentration camp
kaczka (kách-ka) f. duck
kaczor (ká-chor) m. drake
kadłub (kád-woop) m. trunk;
hull; fuselage; framework
kadra (kád-ra) f. staff; cadre
kadzić (ká-dzheech)v. incense;
flatter; fart (vulg.)
kadzidło (ka-dźheéd-wo)n.
incense; fragrance;frankincense
kadź (kadźh) f. tub; tubful
kafar (ká-far) m. piledriver
kafel (ká-fel) m. tile (ceramic)
kaftan (káf-tan) m. jacket
kaftan bezpieczeństwa (káf-tan
bez-pye-cheñ-stva) m. straight
jacket ;"waistcoat"
kaftanik (kaf-tá-ñeek) m. bodice; vest;jacket; caftan
kaganiec (ka-gá-ñets) m. muzzle;
torch ; oil lamp; lamp; cresset
kajać się (káy-ach śhań) v.
repent; confess with contrition
kajak (ká-yak) m. kayak:canoe
kajdany (kay-dá-ni) pl. hand-
cuffs;shackles; chains; bonds
kajuta (ka-yoo-ta) f. ship-
cabin; living qyarter at sea
kajzerka (kay-zér-ka) f. fancy
roll of bread ; kaiser roll
kakao (ka-ká-o) n. cacao

kaktus (kák-toos) m. cactus
kalać (ká-lach) v. pollute;
foul up; stain;befoul: sully
kalafior (ka-lá-fyor) m. cauliflower ; form of snow
kalarepa (ka-la-ré-pa) f.
turnip-cabbage; kohlrabi
kalectwo (ka-lets-tvo) n. disability; lameness; cripplehood
kaleczyć (ka-le-chich) v. wound;
mutilate; hurt; injure;cripple
kalejdoskop (ka-ley-dos-kop) m.
kaleidoscope; medley:miscellany
kaleka (ka-le-ka) m; f. cripple
kalendarz (ka-len-dash) m.
calendar; almanach
kalesony (ka-le-só-ni) pl.
underware;drawers;under pants
kalina (ka-lee-na) f. guelder-
rose; cranberry shrub (tree)
kalka (kál-ka) f. carbon paper
kalkulacja (kal-koo-láts-ya) f.
calculation; computation
kalkulować (kal-koo-ló-vach) v.
calculate; compute; work out
kaloria (ka-lór-ya), f. calorie
kaloryfer (ka-lo-rí-fer) m.
radiator; steam heater; heater
kalosz (ká-losh) m. rubber
overshoe; galosh; rubber boot
kalumnia (ka-lóom-ña) f.
calumny; slander; aspersion
kalwin (kál-veen) m. Calvinist
kał (kaw) m. excrement; stool
kałamarz (ka-wá-mash) m. ink-
stand; ink bottle; ink pot
kałuża (ka-woo-zha) f. puddle
kamelia (ka-mél-ya) f. camellia
kameralna muzyka (ka-me-rál-na
moo-zi-ka) chamber music
kamerdyner (ka-mer-dí-ner) m.
butler ; valet (de chambre)
kamerton (ka-mér-ton) m.
tuning-fork"U", shaped
kamfora (kam-fó-ra) f. camphor
kamgarn (kám-garn) m. worsted
kamienica (ka-mye-ñée-tsa) f.
apartment house; tenants
kamienieć (ka-mye-ñech) v.
petrify; turn into stone
kamieniołom (ka-mye-ño-wom) f.
quarry; stone pit

kamień (ká-myeń) m. stone
kamizelka (ka-mee-zél-ka) f.
waistcoat; vest; camisole
kampania (kam-pá-ña) f. campaign ; drive(promotional)
kamrat (kám-rat) m. chum
kamyk (kám-ik) m, pebble
kanadyjski (ka-na-diy-skee) adj.
m. Canadian ; of Canada
kanalia (ka-nál-ya) f. scoundrel
kanalizacja (ka-na-lee-záts-ya)
f. sewers ;sanitation; drainage
kanał (ká-naw) m. channel; dyke:
sewer; duct; ditch; conduit:tube
kanapa (ka-ná-pa) f. sofa
kanapka (ka-náp-ka) f. sandwich; small size sofa
kanarek (ka-ná-rek) m, canary
kancelaria (kan-tse-lár-ya) f,
office: chancellery; archives
kancerować (kan-tse-ró-vach) v.
damage: mangle; lacerate; hack
kanciarz (kán-chash) m. swindler; trickster ; con man
kanciasty (kan-cha-sti) adj.
m. angular; awkward: stiff
kanclerz (kán-tslesh) m.
chancellor(chief of government)
kandelabr (kan-dé-labr) m.
chandelier; street lamp
kandydat (kan-di-dat) m. candidate; applicant; aspirant
kangur (kán-goor) m. kangaroo
kanon (ká-non) m. canon (priest)
kanonierka (ka-no-ñér-ka) f.
gunboat; patrol boat
kanonik (ka-nó-ñeek) m. canon
(priest); monsignor; prelate
kanonizować (ka-no-ñee-zó-vach)
v. canonize ; glorify
kant (kant) m. edge; crease;
swindle; trick; racket; chant
kantar (kan-tar) m. halter
kantor (kán-tor) m. office;
counter; counting office
kantyna (kan-tí-na) f. canteen
kanwa (kán-va) f. canvas
kapa (ká-pa) f. bedspread;cover
kapać (ká-pach) v. dribble;
trickle; drip;fall drop by drop
kapela (ka-pé-la) f. (music)
band; choir

kapelan (ka-pé-lan) m. chap-
lain(in armed forces, hospital)
kapelusz (ka-pé-loosh) m. hat
kapilarny (ka-pee-lár-ni) adj.
m. capillary
kapiszon (ka-pée-shon) m. hood
kapitalista (ka-pee-ta-leés-
ta) m. capitalist
kapitalizm (ka-pee-tá-leezm) m.
capitalism
kapitał (ka-pée-taw) m. capital
kapitan (ka-pée-tan) m. captain
kapitulacja (ka-pee-too-lá-
tsya) f. surrender; capitula-
tion ; giving up
kapitulować (ka-pee-too-ló-
vać) v. surrender; give up
kaplica (kap-leé-tsa) f. chapel
kapliczka (kap-leéch-ka) f.
shrine; wayside shrine
kapłan (ká-pwan) m. priest
kapłon (ká-pwon) m. capon
kapota (ką-pó-ta) f. long coat
kapral (káp-ral) m. corporal
kaprys (káp-ris) m. caprice;
fad; whim; fency; freak;vagary
kaptować (kap-tó-vać) v.
win over; bring over; canvas
kaptur (káp-toor) m. hood
kapturowy sąd (kap-too-ró-vi
sownd) kangaroo court
kapusta (ka-poós-ta) f. cabbage ; a dish of cabbage
kapuś (ká-poosh) m. stool-
pigeon ; informer; police spy
kapuśniak (ka-poósh-ñak) m.
cabbage soup; drizzle;mizzle
kara (ká-ra) f. penalty; fine;
punishment; correction;nuisance
karabin (ka-rá-been) m. rifle
karać (ká-rać) v. punish
karafka (ka-ráf-ka) f. serving-
bottle; water bottle; flagon
karakuły (ka-ra-koó-wi) pl.
astrakhan sheep fur
karalny (ka-rál-ni) adj. m.
punishable ;deserving a fine
karaluch (ka-rá-lookh) m.
cockroach ; black beetle
karambol (ka-rám-bol) m. collision ; cannon; carom
karaś (ká-rash) m. crucian

karat (ká-rat) m. carat
karawaniarz (ka-ra-vá-ñash) m.
undertaker; coffin bearer
karb (karb) m. notch; score;
crease; fold: nick; tally;curl
karbid (kár-beed) m. carbide
karbol (kár-bol) m. carbolic
acid ; phenol
karbować (kar-bó-vać) v.
notch; curl; tally; crimp;fold
karbunkuł (kar-boón-koow) m.
ulcer ; carbuncle
karburator (kar-boo-rá-tor) m.
carburetor
karcer (kár-tser) m. prison;
dark cell; detention
karciarz (kár-ćhash) m. (cards)
gambler; card player; gamester
karcić (kár-ćheećh) v. reproof;
admonish; scold; castigate
karczemny (kar-chém-ni) adj.
m. rude ; vulgar; coarse
karczma (kárch-ma) f. tavern
karczoch (kár-chokh) m. arti-
choke (thistlelike plant)
karczować (kar-chóv-ać) v.
dig up (stumps); clear land
kardiografia (kar-dyo-gráf-ya)
f. cardiography
kardynalny (kar-di-nál-ni) adj.
m. fundamental; essential
kardynał (kar-di-naw) m. cardinal; prince(Catholic Church)
karetka (ka-rét-ka) f. ambulance;
(prison or mail) van; chaise
kariera (kar-yé-ra) f. career
kark (kark) m. neck; nape
karkołomny (kar-ko-wóm-ni) adj.
m. neckbreaking; breakneck
karłowaty (kar-wo-vá-ti) adj.
m. dwarfish ; undersized
karamel (ka-rá-mel) m. caramel
karmić (kár-meećh) v. feed;
nourish ; nurse; suckle;nurture
karmin (kar-meen) m. carmine
karnawał (kar-ná-vaw) m. carnival   penally
karnie (kár-ñe) adv. in order;
karność (kár-noshćh) f. discipline ; orderly conduct
karny (kar-ni) adj. m. disciplined; penal ; punitive

karo (ká-ro) n. diamonds (in
cards); square cut; décolleré
karoseria (ka-ro-sér-ya) f.
car body ; truck body
karp (karp) m. carp (fish)
karta (kár-ta) f. card; page;
note; sheet; ticket; charter
kartel (kár-tel) m.(industrial)
trust ; cartel; combine; pool
kartofel (kar-tó-fel) m. potato
kartoflanka (kar-to-flán-ka) f.
potato soup; type of onion
kartograf (kar-tó-graf) m.
cartographer ; map maker
karton (kár-ton) m. cardboard
kartoteka (kar-to-té-ka) f.
card index ; file
karuzela (ka-roo-zé-la) f.
merry-go-round ; carousel
kary koń (ká-ri koń)m.black
horse; horse of black color
karygodny (ka-ri-gód-ni) adj.
m. unpardonable ; guilty;gross
karykatura (ka-ri-ka-too-ra)
f. cartoon ; caricature;parody
karykaturzysta (ka-ri-ka-too-
zhís-ta) m. cartoonist
karzeł (ká-zhew) m. dwarf
kasa (ká-sa) f. cashier'sdesk;
cash register; ticket office
kasjer (kás-yer) m. cashier
kask (kask) m. helmet ; tin hat
kaskada (kas-ká-da) f. cascade
kasować (ka-só-vaćh) v. cancel
kasta (kás-ta) f. caste
kastrować (kas-tro-vaćh) v.
castrate; geld
kasyno (ka-sí-no) n. casino;
club ; mess-hall; mess room
kasza (ká-sha) f. grits; groats;
cereals ; gruel; porridge;mess
kaszel (ká-shel) m. cough
kaszkiet (kásh-ket) m. cap
kasztan (kásh-tan) m. chestnut
kat (kat) m. executioner
katafalk (ka-tá-falk) m. bier
kataklizm (ka-ták-leezm) m.
cataclysm ; disaster; calamity
katalizator (ka-ta-lee-zá-tor)
m. catalyst
katalog (ka-tá-lok) m. catalog
katar (ká-tar) m. headcold ;
running nose ; catarrh

katarakta (ka-ta-rák-ta) f.
cataract; opaque eye-lens
kataryniarz (ka-ta-ri-nash) m.
organ grinder
katarynka (ka-ta-rin-ka) f.
barrel organ; street organ
katastrofa (ka-tas-tró-fa) f.
catastrophe; disaster; crash
katecheta (ka-te-khé-ta) m.
teacher of catechism
katedra (ka-té-dra) f. pulpit;
univ. dept. chair; cathedral
kategoria (ka-te-gór-ya) f.
category; division; class
kategoryczny (ka-te-go-rich-ni)
adj. m. absolute; categorical
katoda (ka-tó-da) f. cathode
katolicki (ka-to-leets-kee)
adj. m. Catholic
katować (ka-tó-vaćh) v. torture; beat cruelly; hack
kaucja (káw-tsya) f. bail; deposit; security: recognizance
kauczuk (káw-chook) f. India
natural rubber; caoutchouc
kaukaski (kaw-kás-kee) adj. m.
Caucasian; of Caucasus
kawa (ká-va) f. coffee
kawaler (ka-vá-ler) m. bachelor; suitor; beau; cavalier
kawaleria (ka-va-ler-ya) f.
cavalry ; young folks
kawalkada (ka-val-ká-da) f.
cavalcade
kawał (ká-vaw) m. piece; joke;
cheat; lump; funny business
kawałek (ka-vá-wek) m. bit;
morsel; scrap; chunk;1000zł.
kawiarnia (kav-yár-ńa) f. café
kawior (káv-yor) m. caviar
kawka (káv-ka) f. jackdaw
kawon (ká-von) m. watermelon
kawowy (ka-vó-vi) adj. m. (of)
coffee; coffee-
kazać (ká-zaćh) v. order;tell;
preach; make sb. do something
kazanie (ka-zá-ńe) n. sermon
kazić (ká-żheećh)v. pollute;
corrupt; blemish;contaminate
kazirodztwo (ka-żhee-ródz-tvo)
n. incest
kaznodzieja (kaz-no-dźhe-ya) m.
preacher; evangelist

kaźń (kaźhń) f. execution,
każdorazowy (kazh-do-ra-zó-vi)
  adj.m.every;each;every single
każdy (kázh-di) pron. every;
  each; respective; any; all
kącik (kówń-cheek) m. nook
kąkol (kowń-kol) m. cockle-
  weed; corn cockle
kąpać (kówń-pach) v. bathe;soak
kąpiel (kówń-pyel) f. bath
kąpielisko (kowń-pye-lees-ko)
  n. resort;spa; public bath
kąsać (kówń-sach) v. bite
kąsek (kówń-sek) m. bit; nip
kąt (kownt) m. corner; angle
kątomierz (kówń-tó-myesh) m.
  protractor ; dial-sight
kciuk (kchook) m. thumb
kelner (kél-ner) m. waiter
kelnerka (kel-nér-ka) f.
  waitress; bar maid
keson (ke-son) m. caisson
kędzierzawy (káń-dźhe-zha-vi)
  adj. m. curly, curled; fuzzy
kędzior (káń-dźhor) m. curl;
  lock; ringlet
kępa (káń-pa) f. cluster;
  holm ; hurst; clump; tuft
kęs (káńs) m. bit; mouthful
kibic (kee-beets) m. kibitzer
kibić (kee-beech) f. figure;
  waist ; middle
kichać (kee-khach) v. sneeze
kiecka (kéts-ka) f. frock;
  skirt; petticoat (inelegant)
kiedy (ke-di) conj. when; as;
  ever; how soon?;while; since
kiedy indziej (ke-di een-dźhey)
  adj. some other time
kiedykolwiek (ke-di-kól-vyek)
  adv. whenever; at any time
kiedyś (ke-diśh) adv. someday; in the past; once;one day
kiedyż ? (ke-dish) adv. when-
  then ? when on earth?
kielich (ke-leekh) m. goblet;
  chalice; cup; cupful; glassful
kielnia (kel-ńa) f. trowel
kieł (kew) m. tusk; canine-
  tooth; fang;cutting bit
kiełbasa (kew-ba-sa) f. sausage

kiełek (ke-wek) m. sprout
kiełkować (kew-kó-vach) v.
  sprout. germinate; spring up
kiełzać (k ew-zach) v. bridle
kiep (kep) m. oaf; fool; gull
kiepski (kép-skee) adj. m.
  mean; bad; poor; second-rate
kier (ker) m. (cards) hearts
kierat (ke-rat) m. thrasher
kiermasz (ker-mash) m. fair
kierować (ke-ró-vach) v.steer;
  manage; run; show the way
kierownik (ke-rov-ńeek) m.
  manager; director ;supervisor
kierunek (ke-roo-nek) m.
  direction ; course; trend;line
kiesa (ke-sa) m. purse
kieszeń (ke-sheń) f. pocket
kij (keey) m. stick cane; staff
kijanka (kee-yan-ka) f. tadpole
kikut (kee-koot) m. stump ;stub
kilim (kee-leem) m. rug ;carpet
kilka (keel-ka) num. a few;some
kilkakroć (keel-ká-kroch) adv.
  repeatedly ;again and again
kilkakrotny (keel-ka-krót-ni)
  adj. m. repeated ;recurring
kilkudniowy (keel-koo-dńo-vi)
  adj. m. of several days
kilkoro (keel-kó-ro) num. some;
  several ; one or two; a number
kilof (kee-lof) m. pick; hack
kilogram (kee-ló-gram) m. kilogram ; 2.2 pounds
kilometr (kee-ló-metr) m. kilometer; 3,280.8 feet
kiła (kee-wa) f. syphilis
kinetyka (kee-ne-tí-ka) f.
  kinetics; science of motion
kino (kee-no) n. cinema;movies
kiosk (kyosk) m. kiosk; booth
kipieć (kee-pyech) v. boil
kisić (kee-śheech) v. ferment
kisnąć (kees-nówńch) v. turn
  sour ; ferment; pickle; fug
kiszka (keesh-ka) f. intestine
kiść (keeśhch) f. bunch; wrist
kit (keet) m. putty ; mastic
kiwać (kee-vach) v. rock; nod;
  wag; dangle;fool dodge; jink
klacz (klach) f. mare
klajster (kláy-ster) m. glue;
  paste ; water base glue

klakson (klák-son) m. car horn
klamka (klám-ka) f. door knob
klamra (klám-ra) f. buckle;
clasp ; bracket; fastener;staple
klapa (klá-pa) f. lapel: valve
klapsy (kláp-si) pl. spanking
klarować (kla-ró-vach) v. clarify ; filter;clear; purify
klarnet (klár-net) m. clarinet
klasa (klá-sa) f. class; classroom ; rank; order; division
klaskać (klás-kach) v. clap
klasowy (kla-só-vi) adj. m.
class ; of classes; class-
klasyczny (kla-sich-ni) adj. m.
classic ; standard;conventional
klasyfikować (kla-si-fee-kó-
vach) v. classify ;sort; grade
klasztor (klásh-tor) m. monastery ; convent; cloister
klatka (klát-ka) f. cage ; crate
klatka schodowa (klát-ka skho-
dó-va) staircase ; stairway
klatka piersiowa (klát-ka
pyer-shó-va) ribcage; chest
klauzula (klaw-zóo-la) f.
clause ; proviso; reservation
klawisz (klá-veesh) m. (piano)
key;stool pigeon; jailer
kląć (klownch) v. curse; swear
klatwa (klównt-va) f. curse;
ban; excommunication; anathema
klecić (kle-cheech) v. botch
kleić (kle--eech) v. glue;
stick together; fudge; shape
kleik (kle—eek) m. gruel
klej (kley) m. glue ; cement
klejnot (kley-not) m. jewel
klekotać (kle-kó-tach) v. clatter; rattle ; chatter; prate
kleks (kleks) m. blot;ink-spot
klepać (klé-pach) v. hammer;
flatten ; prattle; pat;blab;clap
klepka (klep-ka) f. stave
klepsydra (klep-síd-ra) f. hour-
glass; obituary notice
kleptomania (klep-to-má-ña) f.
kleptomania: impulse to steal
kler (kler) m. clergy;priesthood
kleszcz (kleshch) m. tick
kleszcze (klésh-che) n. pliers;
tongs ; claws; pincers; nippers

klękać (klan-kach) v. kneel
down; bend the knee; kneel
klęska (kláns-ka) f. defeat;
disaster; calamity
klęsnąć (kláns-nownch) v.
shrink; subside; go down
klient (klee—ent) m. customer
klika (klee-ka) f. clique
klimat (klee-mat) m. climate
klin (kleen) m. wedge;cotter
klinga (kleen-ga) f. (sword)
blade; sabre-blade
kliniczny (klee-ñeech-ni) adj.
clinic ; clinic-
klinika (klee-ñee-ka) f. clinic
klisza (klee-sha) f. (photo)
plate; printing plate
klitka (kléet-ka) f. cell
kloc (klots) m. log; block
klomb (klomp) m. flower bed
klon (klon) m. maple
klops (klops) m. meat loaf
klosz (klosh) m. glass cover;
lamp shade; dish cover
klozet (kló-zet) m. toilet
klub (kloob) m. club; union
klucz (klooch) m. key; wrench
kluska (klóos-ka) f. boiled
dough strip; dumpling
kładka (kwád-ka) f. foot-
bridge; gangway; brow
kłaki (kwá-kee) pl. oakum;
shaggy hair; matted hair
kłam (kwam) m. lie; falsehood
kłamać (kwá-mach) v. lie
kłamca (kwám-tsa) m. liar
kłaniać się (kwá-ñach shan) v.
salute; bow; greet; worship
kłaść (kwashch) v. lay; put
dawn; place; set; deposit
kłąb (kwównp) m. clew; ball
kłąbek (kwówn-bek) m. ball
(of thread); hunk of yarn
kłębic się (kwán-beech shán) v.
whirl; swirl; surge; billow
kłoda (kwo-da) f. log; clog
kłopot (kwo-pot) m. trouble
kłopotać (kwo-pó-tach) v.
trouble; disturb; worry
kłopotliwy (kwo-pot-lée-vi) adj.
troublesome: baffling
kłos (kwos) m. (corn) ear

kłócić (kwoó-cheech) v. quarrel
kłódka (kwoód-ka) f. padlock
kłotliwy (kwoot-lee-vi) adj.
 m. quarrelsome; cantankerous
kłótnia (kwoó-tña) f. quarrel
kłuć (kwooch) v. stab; prick
kłus (kwoos) m. trot;jog trot
kłusownik (kwoo-sóv-ñeek) m.
 poacher; trespassing hunter
kmieć (kmyech) m. peasant
kminek (kmeé-nek) m. cumin
knajpa (knáy-pa) f. tavern
knebel (kné-bel) m. gag
knocić (knó-cheech) v. bungle
knot (knot) m. wick;fuse;bungle
knuć (knooch) v. plot; scheme
koalicja (ko-a-leéts-ya) f.
 coalition: temporary union
kobiałka (ko-byáw-ka) f.
 wicker-basket; chip basket
kobieciarz (ko-bye-chash) m.
 ladychaser; lady's man
kobiecość (ko-bye-tsoośhch) f.
 womanhood; femininity
kobiecy (ko-bye-tsi) adj. m.
 female; womanish; feminine
kobierzec (ko-bye-zhets) m.
 carpet; anything like a carpet
kobieta (ko-bye-ta) f. woman
kobyła (ko-bi-wa) f. mare
kobza (kób-za) f. bagpipe
koc (kóts) m. blanket; coverlet
kochać (kó-khach) v. love
kochanie (ko-khá-ñe) n. love;
 darling; sweetheart; affection
kochany (ko-khá-ni) adj. m.
 beloved; loving; affectionate
kochliwy (kokh-leé-vi) adj. m.
 easily in love; amorous
koci (ko-chee)adj. m. catlike
kociak (kó-chak) m. kitty;
 lassie; lass; pinup girl
kocioł (ko-chow) m. kettle;
 boiler; pot; encirclement
kocur (ko-tsoor) m. tomcat
koczować (ko-chó-vach) v. nomad-
 ize; wander about;be encamped
koczownik (ko-chóv-ñeek) m.
 nomad; wanderer; vagrant
kodeks (kó-deks) m. (legal)code
koedukacja (ko-e-doo-káts-ya)
 f. coeducation

koegzystencja (ko-eg-zis-tén-
 tzya) f. coexistence
kofeina (ko-fe-eé-na) f.
 caffeine; alkaloid in coffee
kogut (ko-goot) m. cock;rooster
koić (kó-eech) v. soothe
kojarzenie (ko-ya-zhé-ñe) n.
 matching ; association; union
kojarzyć (ko-yá-zhich) v. unite;
 bind; join; link; connect
kojący (ko-yówn-tsi) adj. m.
 soothing;comforting; balmy
kojec (kó-yets) m. coop ; pen
kokaina (ko-ka-eé-na) f.' co-
 caine; an alkaloid drug
kokarda (ko-kár-da) f. rosette;
 bow ; slip-knot; knot
kokietka (ko-két-ka) f. flirt
kokietować (ko-ke-tó-vach) v.
 flirt ; court; woo; coquet
koklusz (kók-loosh) m.
 whooping-cough
kokos (ko-kos) m. 1. coconut
 2. good business ; a grand thing
kokoszka (ko-kósh-ka) f. brood-
 hen; laying hen
koks (koks) m. coke; gas coke
koksownia (kok-sóv-ña) f. cok-
 ing plant ; cokery
kolaboracja (ko-la-bo-ráts-ya)
 f.collaboration ; collaborators
kolacja (ko-láts-ya) f. supper
kolano (ko-lá-no) m. knee
kolarstwo (ko-lár-stvo) n.
 cycling ; bicycle sport
kolarz (kó-lash) m. cyclist
kolący (ko-lówn-tsi) adj. m.
 prickly; thorny; spiked
kolba (kól-ba) f. (rifle) butt
kolczasty (kol-chás-ti) adj. m.
 barbed ; thorny; spiny
kolczyk (kól-chik) m. earring;
 earmark; ear tag; eardrop
kolebka (ko-léb-ka) f. cradle
kolec (kó-lets) m. thorn
kolega (ko-lé-ga) m. buddy;
 colleague; fellow worker
koleina (ko-le-eé-na) f. truck
 rut; groove; wheel trace
kolej (kó-ley) f. railroad
kolejka (ko-léy-ka) f. (waiting)
 line;narrow-gage railroad; turn

kolejno (ko-léy-no) adv. by turns; one after the other

kolejny (ko-léy-ni) adj. m. next; successive; following

kolekcja (ko-lék-tsya) f. collection ; things collected

kolektywizacja (ko-lek-ti-vee-záts-ya) f. collectivization

koleżeństwo (ko-le-zhéń-stvo) n. fellowship; comradeship

kolęda (ko-lán-da) f. Christmas carol; song of joy or praise

kolędować (ko-lan-dó-vach) v. sing carols; wait a long time

koliber (ko-lee-ber) m. hummingbird

kolia (kól-ya) f. necklace

kolidować (ko-lee-dó-vach) v. collide ; interfere

koligacja (ko-lee-gáts-ya) f. (family) relationship

kolisty (ko-leés-ti) adj. m. circular ; round

kolizja (ko-leéz-ya) f. collision; clash; interference

kolka (kól-ka) f. colic

kolokwium (ko-lók-vyoom) m. oral examination; test

kolonia (ko-lóń-ya) f. colony

kolonista (ko-lo-nées-ta) m. settler; colonist; colonial

kolońska woda (ko-lóń-ska vo-da) cologne water

kolor (kó-lor) m.color;tint;hue

koloryt (ko-ló-rit) m. coloring

kolosalny (ko-lo-sál-ni) adj. m. colossal; vast;tremendous

kolportaż (kol-pór-tash) m. (paper) distribution

kolumna (ko-loóm-na) f. column

kołatać (ko-wá-tach) v. knock; rattle; beg; throb; bang;

kołczan (ków-chan) m. quiver

kołdra (ków-dra) f. quilter-cover; quilt; coverlet

kolek (ko-wek) m. peg ;stake

kolnierz (ków-ñesh) m. collar

koło (kó-wo) n. wheel; circle

kolo (kó-wo) prep. around; near; about; by; in vicinity

kołodziej (ko-wo-dżhey) m. wheelwright

kołowacizna (ko-wo-va-chéez-na) f. dizziness

kołować (ko-wó-vach) v. revolve; confuse ; circle; stray; whirl

kołowrotek (ko-wo-vró-tek) m. spinning-wheel; reel; winch

kołowrót (ko-wó-vroot) m. windlass ; hoist; gin; whip;turnpike

kołowy ruch (ko-wó-vi rookh) vehicular traffic

kołpak (ków-pak) m. pointed fur cap ; calpack

kołtun (ków-toon) m. hair.snarl; bigot; moron; obscurant

kołysać (ko-wi-sach) v. rock; sway ; toss to and fro; roll

kołysanka (ko-wi-sán-ka) f. lullaby ; cradle song;berceuse

kołyska (ko-wís-ka) f. cradle

komar (kó-mar) m. mosquito

kombajn (kóm-bayn) m. combine

kombinacja (kom-bee-náts-ya) f. combination ;union; scheme;slip

kombinować (kom-bee-nó-vach) v. combine; speculate ; scheme

komedia (ko-méd-ya) f. comedy

komenda (ko-mén-da) f. command ; headquarters; an order

komentarz (ko-mén-tash) m. commentary ; glossary; remark

kometa (ko-mé-ta) f. comet

komfort (kóm-fort) m. comfort

komiczny (ko-meéch-ni) adj. m. comic ; amusing; funny;droll

komin (kó-meen) m. chimney

kominek (ko-mee-nek) m. fireplace ; hearth; open fire

kominiarz (ko-mee-ñash) m. chimney-sweep

komis (kó-mees) m. (on) commission sale; commission shop

komisariat (ko-mee-sár-yat) m. police station : commissariat

komisja (ko-meés-ya) f. commission; board (of inquiry etc.)

komitet (ko-mee-tet) m. committee ; board

komitywa (ko-mee-ti-va) f. intimacy ; good friendly terms

komiwojażer (ko-mee-vo-ya-zher) m. traveling salesman

komnata (kom-ná-ta) f. chamber

komoda (ko-mó-da) f. chest of drawers ; loy-boy;commode

komora (ko-mó-ra) f. chamber

komora celna (ko-mó-ra tsél-na) customsoffice; custom house

komorne (ko-mór-ne) n. (appartment) rent ; rental

komórka (kom-moo-rka) f. cell

kompan (kóm-pan) m. chum ;pal

kompania (kom-páń-ya) f. company ; stock company; society

kompas (kom-pas) m. compass

kompensata (kom-pen-sá-ta) f. compensation; indemnity

kompetentny (kom-pe-teń-tni) adj. m. competent; qualified

kompleks (kóm-pleks) m. complex; group;(inferiority)complex

komplement (kom-plé-ment) m. compliment ;complement

komplet (kóm-plet) m. set

kompozytor (kom-po-zí-tor) m. composer (of music)

kompot (kóm-pot) m. compote

kompres (kóm-pres) m. compress

kompromis (kom-pró-mees) m. compromise ;accomodation

kompromitacja (kom-pro-mee-tá-tsya) f. disgrace; loss of face

komuna (ko-moo-na) f. commune

komunał (ko-moo-naw) m. platitude; banality; commonplace

komunia (ko-mooń-ya) f. communion;part of Catholic mass

komunikacja (ko-moo-ńee-kats-ya) f. communication ;contact

komunikat (ko-moo-ńee-kat) m. bulletin ; communiqué; report

komunikować (ko-moo-ńee-ko-vach) v. inform; give news; report

komunista (ko-moo-ńees-ta) m. communist(advocate or supporter)

konać (ko-nach) v. agonize; expire; be dying;die(with greed)

konar (ko-nar) m. limb; branch

koncentryczny (kon-tsen-trich-ni) adj. m. concentric

koncept (kon-tsept) m. concept; idea; joke; plan ;brain wave

koncert (kon-tsert) m. concert

koncesja (kon-tsés-ya) f. concession; license; license to do...

koncha (kón-kha) f. shell; lobe

kondensator (kon-den-sá-or) m. condenser ; capacitor

kondolencja (kon-do-lén-tsya) f. condolence ;words of sympathy

kondukt (kón-dookt) m. funeral procession ;funeral service

konduktor (kon-dook-tor) m. conductor (train-ticket inspector in charge of passengers

kondycja (kon-dits-ya) f. condition; form; status

konewka (ko-név-ka) f. (watering) can; pot;jug;pewter

konfederacja (kon-fe-de-ráts-ya) f. confederation; confederacy

konfekcja (kon-fék-tsya) f. ready-made clothes (pl.)

konferencja (kon-fe-rén-tsya) f. conference ; meeting(official)

konferować (kon-fe-ró-vach) v. confer ;hold a conference

konfesjonał (kon-fes-yó-naw) m. confessional

konfiskata (kon-fees-ká-ta) f. seizure ; confiscation

konfitura (kon-fee-too-ra) f. jam ; preserve ; candied fruits

konfrontować (kon-fron-tó-vach) v. confront ;bring face to face

kongres (kón-gres) m. congress

koniak (kó-ńak) m. brandy;cognac

koniczyna (ko-ńee-chi-na) f. clover ; trefoil; shamrock

koniec (kó-ńets) m. end; conclusion; tip; point ;close

koniecznie (ko-ńech-ńe) adv. absolutely; necessarily

konieczny (ko-ńech-ni) adj. m. indispensable ;vital;necessary

konik (ko-ńeek) m. pony

konik polny (kó-ńeek pól-ni) grasshopper; cricket (Locusta)

konina (ko-ńee-na) f. horse-meat; horseflesh

koniunktura (kon-yoonk-too-ra) f. market condition ;situation

konkluzja (kon-klooz-ya) f. conclusion ; inference

konkretny (kon-krét-ni) adj. m. concrete; definite ;real

konkurencja (kon-koo-rén-tsya)
f. competition; rivalry;contest
konkurs (kón-koors) m. contest
konnica (kon-ñee-tsa) f. cavalry ; cavalry unit; horse
konno (kón-no) adv. on horseback ; sit astraddle ;mounted
konny (kón-ni) adj. m. mounted
konopie (ko-nóp-ye) n. hemp
konował (ko-nó-vaw) m. farrier;
quack doctor ; sawbones
konserwa (kon-sér-va) f. preserve; conservatists
konserwatorium (kon-ser-va-tór-
yoom) n. conservatory
konsola (kon-só-la) f. console
konspirować (kon-spee-ró-vach)
v. plot ; conspire; keep secret
konstatować (kon-sta-tó-vach)
v. state; ascertain ; find
konsternacja (kon-ster-náts-ya)
f. consternation ; dismay
konstrukcja (kon-strook-tsya)
f. construction ;design; plan
konstruować (kon-stroo-ó-vach)
v. construct ;build; make
konstytucja (kon-sti-toóts-ya)
f. constitution; physique
konsulat (kon-soo-lat) m. consulate (office or term of office)
konsumować (kon-soo-mó-vach) v.
consume ; eat; drink; use up
konsylium (kon-sil-yoom) n.
consultation (usually medical)
konszachty (kon-shakh-ti) pl.
collusion ; scheming
kontakt (kón-takt) m. contact
kontaktować się (kon-tak-tó-
vach shañ) v. contact :touch
konto (kón-to) n. account
kontrabanda (kon-tra-bán-da)
f. smuggling ;contraband
kontrakt (kón-trakt) m. contract enforcable by law
kontraktować (kon-trak-tó-vach)
v. contract; hire; engage
kontrast (kón-trast) m. contrast (pointing the differences)
kontrastować (kon-tras-tó-vach)
v. contrast ;stand in contrast
kontratak (kontr-á-tak) m.
counter-attack

kontrola (kon-tró-la) f. control; checking; check up
kontrolny (kon-tról-ni) adj.
m. of control;of supervision
kontrolować (kon-tro-ló-vach)
v. control; check; verify
kontrpropozycja (kontr-pro-po-
zíts-ya) f. counterproposal
kontrrewolucja (kontr-re-vo-
loóts-ya)f.counterrevolution
kontrowersja(kon-tro-vérs-ya)
f. controversy; a quarrel
kontuar (kon-too-ar) m. counter
kontur (kon-toor) m. outline
kontusz (kón-toosh) m. split-
sleeve Polish overcoat (of old)
kontuzja (kon-toóz-ya) f. shock
kontynent (kon-tí-nent) m.
continent; mainland ;land mass
konwalia (kon-vál-ya) f. lily
of the valley ; convallaria
konwikt (kón-veekt) m. boarding school (for boys or girls)
konwój (kón-vooy) m. convoy
konwulsja (kon-voóls-ya) f.
convulsion; a fit; a spasm
koń (koñ) m. horse ; steed
koń mechaniczny (koñ me-kha-
ñeech-ni) mechanical horsepower; horsepower
końcowy (koñ-tso-vi) adj. m.
final; terminal; last; late
końcówka (koñ-tsoov-ka) f.
ending; remainder;tail-piece
kończyć (kóñ-chich) v. end;
finish; quit; be dying; stop
kończyna (koñ-chi-na) f. extremity; limb; member; leg
kooperacja (ko-o-pe-ráts-ya)
f. cooperation ; acting together
koordynacja (ko-or-di-náts-ya)
f. coordination (mental&phys.)
kopa (kó-pa) threescore (60);
pile; dozens; stack
kopa siana (kó-pa shá-na) haystack ; hayrick
kopać (kó-pach) v. dig; kick
kopalnia (ko-pál-ña) f. mine
koparka (ko-pár-ka) f. excava-
tor; mechanical shovel
kopcić (kop-cheech) v. soot;
smoke; blacken with smoke

kopciuszek (kop-choo-shek) m.
Cinderella; drudge

kopeć (ko-pech) m. soot

koper (ko-per) m. dill; fennel

koperta (ko-per-ta) f. envelope; quilt-case;(watch-)case

kopiasty (kop-yas-ti) adj. m.
heaped; piled up;heaped(plate)

kopiec (kop-yets) m. mound;
barrow; mound;heap; knoll

kopiować (kop-yo-vach) v. copy

kopuła (ko-poo-wa) f. dome

kopyto (ko-pi-to) n. hoof

kora (ko-ra) f. bark; cortex

koral (ko-ral) m. coral (red)

korale (ko-ra-le) pl. bead
necklace; coral beads; gills

korba (kor-ba) f. crank; winch

kordon (kor-don) m. cordon

korek (ko-rek) m. cork; fuse;
stopper; traffic jam; tie-up

korekta (ko-rek-ta) f. proof

korepetycja (ko-re-pe-tits-ya)
f. tutoring; private lessons

korespondencja (ko-res-pon-den-
tsya) f. correspondence;letters

korespondent wojenny (ko-res-
pon-dent vo-yen-ni) war correspondent; war reporter

korkociąg (kor-ko-chownk) m.
cork-screw; tail-spin; twist

korniszon (kor-nee-shon) m.
pickled cucumber; gherkin

korny (kor-ni) adj. m. humble

korona (ko-ro-na) f. crown

koronacja (ko-ro-nats-ya) f.
coronation; crowning

koronka (ko-ron-ka) f. lace

koronować (ko-ro-no-vach) v.
crown ; be crowned

korowód (ko-ro-vood) m. procession; pageant; train;difficulty

korporacja (kor-po-rats-ya) f.
corporation ; association;guild

korpulentny (kor-poo-len-tni)
adj. m. fat; corpulent; obese

korpus (kor-poos) m. body;
staff; (army) corps, etc

korsarz (kor-sash) m. pirate

kort tenisow (kort te-nee-so-
vi) tennis court

korupcja (ko-roop-tsya) f. corruption; venality; bribery

korygować (ko-ri-go-vach) v.
correct; rectify; put right

korytarz (ko-ri-tash) m. corridor; passage-way; lobby

koryto (ko-ri-to) n. through;
river-bed; channel; chute

korzec (ko-zhets) m. bushel

korzeń (ko-zheń) m. root; spice

korzyć (ko-zhich)v. humble;
humiliate ; prostrate

korzystać (ko-zhis-tach) v.
profit; gain;enjoy a right

korzystny (ko-zhist-ni) adj.
m. profitable; favorable

korzyść (ko-shishch) f. profit

kos (kos) m. blackbird

kosa (ko-sa) f. scythe; tress

kosiarka (ko-shar-ka) f. mower

kosić (ko-sheech) v. mow;scythe

kosmaty (kos-ma-ti) adj. m.
shaggy ; hairy; fleecy

kosmetyczka (kos-me-tich-ka) f.
vanity bag ; beautician

kosmetyk (kos-me-tik) m. cosmetic : makeup(skin and hair)

kosmiczny (kos-meech-ni) adj.
m. cosmic ; outer space

kosmopolita (kos-mo-po-lee-ta)
m. cosmopolite ;cosmopolitan

kosmyk (kos-mik) m. wisp ; strand

kosodrzewina (ko-so-dzhe-vee-
na) f. dwarf mountain pine

kosooki (ko-so-o-ki) adj. m.
with slanting eyes; with scowl-
ing eyes; cross-eyed

kostium(kos-tyoom) m. suit;dress

kostka (kost-ka) f. small bone;
ankle; knuckle; die; lump

kostnica (kost-nee-tsa) f.
morgue ; mortuary ;dead house

kostnieć (kost-nech) v. grow
stiff ; ossify; freeze

kosy (ko-si) adj. m. slanting

kosz (kosh) m. basket ;Tartar camp

koszary (ko-sha-ry) pl. barracks (military); caserns

koszenie (ko-she-ne) n. mowing

koszerny (ko-sher-ni) adj. m.
kosher (clean or fit to eat)

koszmar (kosh-mar) m. nightmare ; frightening experience

koszt (kosht) m. cost ; price;
expense; charge; economic costs

kosztorys (kosh-tó-ris) m.
  estimate (of cost),
kosztowny (kosh-tov-ni) adj.
  m. expensive ; costly;precious
koszula (ko-shoo-la) f. shirt
koszyk (kó-shik) f. small
  basket; grab bag; hilt guard
koszykówka (ko-shi-koov-ka) f.
  basketball
kościany (kośh-cha-ni) adj. m.
  bone ; osseous;made out of bone
kościec (kośh-chets) m. skeleton ; framework ; frame
kościelny (kośh-chel-ni) adj.
  m. of church ; ecclesiastical
kościotrup (kośh-cho-troop) m.
  skeleton (vulg.)
kościół (kośh-choow), m. church
kościsty (kośh-chee-sti) adj.
  m. bony; angular ; rawboned
kość (kośhch) f. bone ; spine
koślawić (ko-śhla-veech) v.
  deform ; distort; crook
koślawy (ko-śhla-vi) adj. m.
  crooked; lame ; lopsided
kot (kot) m. cat; pussy cat;puss
kotara (ko-ta-ra) f. curtain
kotek (kó-tek) m. kitten ;puss
kotlet (kót-let) m. cutlet
kotlina (kot-lee-na) f. dale
kotłować (ko-wó-vach) v.whirl;
  seethe; surge; drive crazy
kotłownia (kot-wov-ńa) f.
  boiler room ;boiler house
kotwica (kot-vee-tsa) f. anchor
kotwiczyć (kot-vee-chich) v.
  anchor ; lie at anchor
kowadło (ko-vad-wo) m. anvil
kowal (kó-val), m. blacksmith
kowalny (ko-val-ni) adj. m.
  malleable ; ductile; forgeable
koza (kó-za)f. goat; jail
kozioł (kó-zhow) m. buck;gambol
koźlę (kóźh-ań) n. kid;goatling
kożuch (ko-zhookh) m. sheepskin
  furcoat ;coating on hot milk
kół (koow) m. stake; post
kółko (ków-ko) m. small wheel;
  small circle: (soc.) circle
kpiarz (kpyash) m. scoffer
kpić (kpeech) v. jeer; sneer
kpiny (kpee-ni) n. mockery ;
  this is preposterous ! (exp.)

kra (kra) f. ice floe
krach (krakh) m. crash
kraciasty (kra-chás-ti) adj.
  m. checquered ; grated;checkered
kradzież (krá-dżhesh) f. theft
kradziony (kra-dżho-ni) adj.
  m. stolen ; robbed
kraina (kra-eé-na) f. land;
  region ; province ;country
kraj (kray) m. country; verge;
  edge; hem of a garment; land
krajać (krá-yach) v. cut;slice;
  carve; operate; hack; saw
krajobraz (kray-ob-ras) m.
  landscape; scenery painting
krajowy (kra-yo-vi) adj. m.
  native; nationally made,
krajoznawczy (kra-yo-znav-chi)
  adj. m. hiking, touring
krakać (krá-kach) v. croak
kram (krám) m. booth; mess;
  trouble; stall;odds and ends
kramarz (krá-mash) m. huckster
kran (kran) m. tap; faucet
kraniec (krá-ńets) m. border;
  edge; end; extremity; margin
krańcowy (krań-tsó-vi) adj. m.
  extreme; marginal; excessive
krasa (krá-sa) f. grace;
  beauty; loveliness ; splendor
krasić (kra-śheech) v. decorate
krasomówca (kra-so-moóv-tsa) m.
  orator(very eloquent)
kraść (kráśhch) v. steal; rob
kraśnieć (kráśh-ńech) v. blush;
  grow beautiful; redden
krata (krá-ta) f. grate
krater (krá-ter) m. crater
krawat (krá-vat) m. (neck) tie
krawcowa (krav-tsó-va) f.
  seamstress ;tailor's wife
krawędź (kra-vándżh) f. edge
krawężnik (kra-vánzh-ńeek) m.
  curb(stone); roof-hip
krawiec (krá-vyets) m. tailor
krąg (krownk) m. ring ; ver-
  tebre ; disk; range; sphere
krążek (krówn-zhek) m. small
  disk; potter's wheel;pulley
krążyć (krówn-zhich) v. circulate; rotate; wander; stray
kreacja (kre-áts-ya) f. (dress)
  creation; theatre part

kreda (kre-da) f. chalk
kredens (kre-dens) m. china
cabinet ; cupboard; buffet
kredka (kred-ka) f.crayon;
lipstick; chalk for writing
kredowy (kre-do-vi) adj. m.
cretaceous;chalky;made of chalk
kredyt (kre-dit) m. credit
krem (krem) m. cream;custard
krematorium (kre-ma-tor-yoom)
n. crematorium ; crematory
kremowy (kre-mo-vi) adj. m.
creamcolored; cream yellow
kreować (kre-o-vach) v. create;
act; set up; institute; appoint
krepa (kre-pa) f. crape
kres (kres) m. end; limit;term
kreska (kres-ka) f. dash(line);
stroke; hatch; scar; accent
kreślić (kresh-leech) v. draw;
trace; sketch; cross out
kret (kret) m. mole ; schemer
kretowisko (kre-to-vees-ko) n.
krew (krev) f. blood molehill
krewetka (kre-vet-ka) f. shrimp
krewki (krev-kee) adj. m. rash;
quick-tempered; impetuous
krewny (krev-ni) m. relative
kręcić (kran-cheech) v. twist;
turn; shoot film;fuss; boss
krecony (kran-tso-ni) adj. m.
twisted; curled;winding;spiral
kręgle (krang-le) n. bowling
(ninepin)game of bowles;tenpins
kręgosłup (kran-gos-woop) m.
spine; vertebral column
kręgowiec (kran-go-vyets) m.
vertebrate ;animal with spine
krepować (kran-po-vach) v. bind;
embarass; hamper; hinder
krepy (kran-pi) adj. m. stocky;
thickset; sturdy; short
kretactwo (kran-tats-tvo) n.
cheat; foul dealing; shuffle
kretacz (kran-tach) m. double-
dealer; dodger; quibbler;cheat
kręty (kran-ti) adj. m. curved;
curly; winding; tortuous
krnąbrny (krnownbr-ni) adj. m.
stubborn; unruly; restive;balky
krochmal (krokh-mal) m. starch
krochmalić (krokh-ma-leech) v.
starch ; beat up; stiffen

krocie (kro-che) pl. thousands
kroczyć (kro-chich) v. stride
kroić (kro-eech) v. cut; slice
krok (krok) m. step ;pace;march
krokiew (kro-kev) f. rafter
krokodyl (kro-ko-dil) m. crocodile ; split flap (aviation)
kromka (krom-ka) f. slice
kronika (kro-nee-ka) f.chronicle
kropić (kro-peech) v. sprinkle
kropka (krop-ka) f. dot ; point
kropkować (krop-ko-vach) v. dot
kropla (krop-la) f. drop
krosno (kros-no) n. loom
krosta (kros-ta) f. pimple
krotochwila (kro-to-khvee-la)
f. joke; burlesque; farce
krowa (kro-va) f. cow; mine
krój (krooy) m. cut; fashion
król (krool) m. king; rabbit
królestwo (kroo-les-tvo) n.
kingdom; the realms; sphere
królewicz (kroo-le-veech) m.
crown prince ; king's son
królewski (kroo-lev-skee) adj.
m. royal; king's; queen's
królik (krool-eek) m. rabbit
królikarnia (kroo-lee-kar-ña)
f. warren ; rabbit warren
królowa (kroo-lo-va) f. queen
krótki (kroot-kee) adj. m.
short; brief ;terse; concise
krótko (kroo-tko) adv. briefly;
shortly; tersely;(hold) tightly
krtań (krtañ) f. larynx
kruchy (kroo-khi) adj. m. brittle;
frail; tender; crisp; crusty
krucjata (kroots-ya-ta) f. crusade ; action for some cause
krucyfiks (kroo-tsi-feeks) m.
crucifix ; cross of Jesus
kruczek (kroo-chek) m. trick
kruczy (kroo-chi) adj. m. jet-
black; raven's (color)
kruk (krook) m. raven
krupy (kroo-pi) pl. groats
kruszec (kroo-shets) m. (metal)
ore ; metal; gold; silver
kruszeć (kroo-shech) v. crumble;
grow brittle; repent
kruszyć (kroo-shich) v. crush;
crumb; destroy; shatter;disrupt

kruszyna (kroo-shí-na) f. crumb
kruźganek (kroozh-gán-ek) m.
portico ; gallery; ambulatory
krwawica (krva-vee-tsa) f. hard-
won money; toil ; labor
krwawić (krvá-veech) v. bleed
krwawy (krvá-vi) adj. m. bloody;
bloodthirsty; bloodstained
krwiobieg (krvee-ó-byeg) m.
blood circulation
krwisty (krvées-ti) adj. m.
sanguineous; blood-red
krwotok (krvó-tok) m. hemorrhage : bleeding
kryć (krićh) v. hide; conceal;
cover ;roof over;shield; mask
kryjówka (kri-yoov-ka) f.
hiding-place ; hide-out
kryminalista (kri-mee-na-leés-
ta) m. criminal. crime;thriller
kryminał (kri-mée-naw) m. prison;
krynica (kri-née-tsa) f. spring
krystalizować (kris-ta-lee-zó-
vach) v. crystallize ; shape
kryształ (krish-taw) m. crystal
kryterium (kri-tér-yoom) n.
criterion; touchstone; test
kryty (krí-ti) adj. m. covered
krytyczny (kri-tích-ni) adj. m.
critical; decisive; crucial
krytyk (krí-tik) m. critic
krytyka (kri-tí-ka) f. criticism; review; censure
kryzys (krí-zis) m. crisis
krzaczasty (kzha-chás-ti) adj.
m. bushy; shaggy; beetle
krzak (kzhak) m. bush
krzątać (kzhówn-tach)v. bustle
krzątanina (kzhown-ta-née-na)
f. bustle ; comings and goings
krzem (kzhem) m. silicone
krzemień (kzhe-myen) f. flint
krzepić (kzhe-peech) v. brace
up; refresh; invigorate;fortify
krzepki (kzhep-kee) adj. vigorous; lusty; robust; husky
krzepnąć (kzhep-nownch) v. coagulate; gather strength
krzesać (kzhe-sach) v. strike
fire ; strike sparks
krzesiwo (kzhe-shee-vo) n.
tinder-box ; flint

krzesło (kzhés-wo) n. chair
krzew (kzhev) m. shrub
krzewić (kzhe-veech) v. spread;
propagate; teach; graft
krzta (kzhta) f. whit; bit
krztusiec (kzhtoo-shets) m.
whooping-cough
krztusić się (kzhtoo-sheech
shán) v. choke; stifle
krzyczeć (kzhí-chech) v. shout;
cry ; scream; yell; clamor
krzyk (kzhik) m. cry; scream;
shriek ; yell; outcry; call
krzykacz (kzhí-kach) m. bawler;
crier ; shouter; agitator
krzykliwy (kzhik-lee-vi) adj.
m. noisy ; clamorous; loud
krzywa (kzhí-ya) f. curve
krzywda (kzhív-da) f. harm;
wrong ; a sense of wrong
krzywdzący (kzhiv-dzówn-tsi)
adj. m. harmful; injurious
krzywdzić (kzhiw-dźheech)v.
harm; wrong ;damage;be unfair
krzywica (kzhi-vee-tsa) f.
rickets ;rachitis;sweep saw
krzywić (kzhi-veech) v. bend
krzywić się (kzhi-veech shán)
v. make faces; bend ; warp
krzywo (kzhí-vo) adv. crooked
krzywy (kzhi-vi) adj. m. crooked; skew; distorted;slanting
krzyż (kzhish) m. cross
krzyżować (kzhi-zhó-vach) v.
cross; thwart; crucify
krzyżówka (kzhi-zhoóv-ka) f.
crossword puzzle
ksiądz (kshóynts) m. priest
książę (kshown-zhan) m. prince;
duke; ruler of a duchy
książka (kshównzh-ka) f. book
księga (kshan-ga) f. register;
large book; volume; tome
księgarnia (kshan-gar-ña) f.
bookstore ; bookshop
księgarz (kshan-gash) m. bookseller; owner of a bookstore
księgować (kshan-go-vach) v.
keep-books ;enter in the books
księgowy (kshan-go-vi) m. bookkeeper ; accountant
księgozbiór (kshán-go-zbyoor)
m. book collection; library

księstwo (kshahn-stvo) n. duchy
księżna (kshahzh-na) f. princess ; wife of a prince
księży (kshahn-zhi) adj. m.
priestly ;belonging to a priest
księżyc (kshahn-zhits) m. moon
kształcić (kshtaw-cheech) v.
educate ; train; form;school
kształt (kshtawt) m. form;
shape ; configuration; figure
kształtny (kshtawt-ni) adj. m.
shapely ; neat; nicely made
kształtować (kshtaw-to-vach) v.
shape ; form; mold ; fashion
kto (kto) pron. who ; all;those
kto inny (kto een-ni) pron.
somebody else ; someone else
kto bądź (kto bowndch) pron.
anybody ; nayone;just anyone
ktoś (ktosh) pron. somebody
którędy (ktoo-rahn-di) adv.
which way, how to get there?
który (ktoo-ri) pron. who;
which; that ; any; whichever
któż (ktoosh) pron. whichever
ku (koo) prep. towards; to
kubatura (koo-ba-too-ra) f.
(building) volume;cubature
kubek (koo-bek) m. cup: mug
kubeł (koo-bew) m. pail;bucket
kucharka (koo-khar-ka) f. cook
kucharz (koo-khash)m. cook
kuchenka gazowa (koo-khen-ka
ga-zo-va)f.(gas) hotplate
kuchnia (kookh-na) f. kitchen
stove; cooking range; kitchen
kucnąć (koots-nownch)v. squat
kucyk (koo-tsik) m. small pony
kuć (kooch) v. hammer; shoe a
horse; cram lessons: peck;coin
kudłaty (kood-wa-ti) adj. m.
shaggy; hairy ; hirsute
kudły (kood-wi) pl. shaggy hair
kufel (koo-fel) m. beer mug
kufer (koo-fer) m. trunk
kuglarz (koog-lash) m. juggler
kukiełkowy teatr (koo- kew -ko-
vi teatr) puppet-show
kukła (kook-wa) f. puppet
kukułka (koo-koow-ka) f. cuckoo
bird; cuckoo clock
kukurydza (koo-koo-ri-dza) f.
maize; corn; Indian corn

kula (koo-la) f. sphere; bullet
crutch; ball; globe; shot
kulawy (koo-la-vi) adj. m. lame
kulbaczyć (kool-ba-chich) v.
saddle (a horse)
kuleć (koo-lech) v. limp
kulić się (koo-leech shan) v.
snuggle; crouch; cringe;nestle
kulinarny (koo-lee-nar-ni) adj.
m. culinary; of cooking
kulisy (koo-lee-si) pl. theatre
scenes; the inner facts; links
kulisty (koo-lee-sti) adj. m.
spherical; ball-shaped
kulminacyjny (kool-mee-na-tsiy-
ni) adj. m. culminant; climactic
kult (koolt) m. cult;worship
kultura (kool-too-ra) f. culture; good manners;cultivation
kuluar (koo-loo-ar) m. lobby
kułak (koo-wak) m. fist;punch
kum (koom) m. godfather; crony
kumoterstwo (koo-mo-ter-stvo)
n. favoritism; log rolling
kumulacja (koo-moo-lats-ya) f.
cumulation; merger; fusion
kuna (koo-na) f. marten
kundel (koon-del) m. mongrel
kunszt (koonsht) m. art;skill
kunsztowny (koon-shtov-ni) adj.
m. artistic; artful;ingenious
kupa (koo-pa) f. heep; pile;
lot; excrement; assemblage
kupczyć (koop-chich) v. bargain;
trade; influence peddling
kupić (koo-peech) v. buy
kupiec (koop-yets) m. shopkeeper; merchant; dealer
kupno (koop-no) n. purchase
kupon (koo-pon) m. coupon
kur (koor) m. cock; cock crow
kura (koo-ra) f. hen; hen bird
kuracja (koo-rats-ya) f. cure
kuratorium (koo-ra-tor-yum) n.
board of trustees (of schools)
kurcz (koorch) m. cramp;shrinking
kurczę (koor-chan) n. chicken
kurczyć (koor-chich) v. shrink
kurek (koo-rek) m. tap; cock
kurier (koor-yer) m. courier
kurnik (koor-neek) m. chicken
house; hen house; hen roost
poultry house; hen cote

kuropatwa (koo-ro-pát-va) f.
partridge (game bird)
kurować (koo-ró-vaćh) v. heal;
cure ; treat for an illness
kurs (koors) m. course;rate;fare
kursować (koor-só-vaćh)v.
circulate; ferry; run; ply
kurtka (koór-tka) f. jacket
kurtyna (koor-tí-na)f. curtain
kurwa (koór-va) f. whore (vulg.)
kurz (koosh) m. dust
kurza ślepota (koózha shle-pó-
ta) night blindness
kusić (koó-sheech) v. tempt
kustosz (koós-tosh) m. custo-
dian; curator; conservator
kusy (koosi) adj. m. short
kusza (koó-sha) f. crossbow
kuśnierz (koósh-nesh) m. furrier
kuter (koó-ter) m. cutter
kutwa (koót-va) f. miser
kuty (koó-ti) adj. m. forged;
shod; cunning; sly; shrewd
kuzyn (koó-zin) m. cousin
kuzynka (koo-zín-ka) f. cousin
kuźnia (koóźh-na) f. forge
kwadra (kvád-ra) f. quarter moon
kwadrans (kvád-rans) m. quarter
of an hour; fiftee minutes
kwadrat (kvád-rat) m. square
kwakać (kvá-kaćh) v. quack
kwalifikacja (kva-lee-fee-káts-
ya) f. qualification;evaluation
kwalifikować (kva-lee-fee-kó-
vaćh) qualify ; class;appraise
kwapić się (kva-peećh shań) v.
be eager; be in a hurry
kwarantanna (kva-ran-tán-na) f,
quarantine; period of isolation
kwarc (kvarts) m. quartz
kwarta (kvár-ta) f. quart
kwartalny (kvar-tál-ni) adj. m.
quarterly;occuring quarterly
kwas (kvas) m.acid; pl.discord
kwasić (kvá-sheech) v. sour;
ferment; pickle;embitter;be idle
kwaskowaty (kvas-ko-vá-ti) adj.
m. sourish ; acidulous
kwasy (kvá-si) pl. fusses; bad-
blood; ill humor; dissent
kwaśny (kvash-ni) adj. m. sour
kwatera (kva-té-ra) f. quarters;
lodging; living accommodation

kwaterka (kva-tér-ka) f. quarter
of a liter; quarter liter bottle
kwesta (kves-ta) f. collection
(for); passing the hat around
kwestia (kvést-ya) f. question
kwestionariusz (kves-tio-nár-
yoosh) m. questionnaire
kwękać (kvań-kaćh) v. complain
kwiaciarka (kvya-chár-ka) f.
florist; flower girl
kwiaciarnia (kvya-chár-na) f.
flower shop; florist's
kwiat (kvyat) m. flower
kwiczeć (kvee-chech) v. squeak
kwiczoł (kvee-chow) m. field-
fare (Turdus pilavis)
kwiecień (kvye-ćheń) m. April
kwiecisty (kvye-ćhees-ti) adj.
m. flowery; colorful; ornate
kwietnik (kvyet-neek) m. flower-
bed; carpet bed
kwik (kveek) m. squeal; squeak
kwit (kveet) m. receipt
kwitnąć (kveet-nównćh)v. blossom ;grow moldy;look healthy
kwitować (kvee-to-vaćh) v. give
receipt; relinquish; forgo
kwoka (kvó-ka) f. sitting hen
kwota (kvó-ta) f. amount (of
money); amount; allocation
kynologiczny związek (ki-no-lo-
geéch-ni zvyown-zek) kennel
club ; kennel association
labirynt (la-bee-rint) m. la-
byrinth; maze
laborant (la-bó-rant) m. lab.
technician; assistant chemist
laboratorium (la-bo-ra-tor-
yoom) m. laboratory ; lab
lać (laćh) v. pour; shed; (spill)
lada (lá-da) f. counter; chest
lada (lá-da) part. any; whatever; the least; paltry
lada kto (lá-da kto) anybody
ladacznica (la-dach-née-tsa) f.
harlot; prostitute; strumpet
laik (lá-eek) m. layman
lak (lak) m. sealing wax
lakier (la-ker) m. varnish
lakmus (lak-moos) m. litmus
lakoniczny (la-ko-neéch-ni) adj.
m. terse; brief; curt; laconic
stating much in few words

lakować (la-ko-vach) v. seal
lalka (lál-ka) f. doll ;puppet
laktoza (lak-to-za) f. lactose
lament (la-ment) m. lament
lamować (la-mo-vach) v. laminate
lamówka (la-moov-ka) f. trim;
border ; edge; trimming: piping
lampa (lám-pa) f. lamp
lampart (lam-part) m. leopard
lampas (lám-pas) m.stripe;lampas
lampion (lam-pyon) m. lampion
lamus (la-moos) m. storeroom
lanca (lan-tsa) f. lance; spear
lancet (lan-tset) m. lancet ;fleam
landara (lan-da-ra) f. jalopy;
old crate ; rumble-tumble
lanie (la-ńe) n. pouring; cast-
ing; beating ;thrashing; licking
lanolina (la-no-lee-na) f. lanolin ; wool-fat (in ointments)
lansady (lan-sa-di) pl. pranc-
ing gait ; skips; leaps; bounds
lansować (lan-so-vach) v. launch
lapidarny (la-pee-dar-ni) adj.
m. terse; concise ;curt; crisp
lapis (la-pees) m. silver nitrate ; lunar caustic
lapsus (lap-soos) m. lapse(slip)
laryngologia (la-rin-go-lóg-ya)
f. laryngology
las (las) m. wood; forest ;thicket
lasek (la-sek) m. grove
laska (lás-ka) f. cane ; stick
laskowy orzech (las-ko-vi
ó-zhekh)m. hazelnut
lasować (la-so-vach) v. slake
lata (la-ta) pl. years
latać (la-tach) v. fly;be running
latarka (la-tar-ka) f. flashlight ; torch : small lamp
latarnia (la-tar-ńa) f. street-
light ; lantern; beacon
latarnia morska (la-tar-ńa morska) lighthouse
latarnik (la-tar-ńeek) m. lighthouse keeper
latawiec (la-tav-yets) m. kite
lato (la-to) n. Summer
latorośl (la-to-roshl) f. shoot;
offspring: scion; sprig; sprout
laubzega (lawb-ze-ga) f. fret-
saw; jigsaw: scroll saw

laufer (law-fer) m. runner;
(chess) bishop
laury (law-ri) pl. laurels
laureat (law-re-at) m. laure-
ate ; prize-winner
lawa (la-va) f. volcanic lava
lawenda (la-ven-da) f. lavender ; lavender water
laweta (la-ve-ta) f. gun-
carriage; heavy gun base
lawina (la-vee-na) f. avalanche ; shower(of words)
lawirować (la-vee-ro-vach) v.
veer; tack; intrigue
lazaret (la-za-ret) m. field
hospital(for infections)
lazur (la-zoor) m. azure; sky
blue; blue pigment
ląd (lownd) m. 1. land;
2. mainland; 3. continent
lądować (lown-do-vach) v. land;
disembark; go ashore; alight
lecieć (le-chech) v. fly; run;
hurry;wing; drift; drop; fall
leciutko (le-choot-ko) adv.
bearly touching;very lightly
leciwy (le-chee-vi) adj. m.
up in years;advanced in years
lecz (lech) conj. but;however
leczenie (le-che-ńe) n. healing ; cure; treatment
lecznica (lech-nee-tsa) f. hospital; clinic;nursing home
leczyć (le-chich) v. heal;
treat; nurse;practice medicine
ledwie (led-vye) adv. hardly;
scarcely ; barely;almost;nearly
ledwo że nie (le-dvo zhe ńe)
adv. almost; nearly; hardly
legacja (le-gats-ya) f. legation; legacy; bequest
legalizować (le-ga-lee-zo-vach)
legalize; certify; attest
legalny (le-gál-ni) adj. m.
legal; lawful;allowed by law
legat (le-gat) m. bequest;
papal muncio
legawiec (le-ga-vyets) m.
pointer : setter
legenda (le-gen-da) f. legend
legendarny (le-gen-dar-ni) adj.
m. legendary ; fabulous;storied

legia (leg-ya) f. legion
legion (leg-yon) m. legion
legitymacja (le-gee-ti-máts-ya)
f. i-d card; identification
papers; membership card etc
legitymować się (le-gee-ti-mo-
vach shań) v. prove one's
identity; identify oneself
lęgnąć (leg-nównch) v. fall
in battle; perish; lie down
legowisko (le-go-vee-sko) n.
berth; bedding;encampment;den
legumina (le-goo-mee-na) f.
dessert; sweet dish;legumin
lej (ley) m. crater; funnel
lejce (ley-tse) pl. reins
lejek (le-yek) m. small funnel
lek (lek) m. medicine; drug
lekarski (le-kár-skee) adj. m.
medical; medicinal
lekarz (le-kash) m. physician
lekceważący (lek-tse-va-zhówn-
tsi) adj. m. disrespectful
lekceważenie (lek-tse-va-zhe-
ńe) n. disdain;disrespect
lekceważyć (lek-tse-vá-zhich)
v. slight; scorn; neglect
lekcja (lék-tsya) f. lesson
lekki (lék-kee) adj. m. light;
light-hearted;graceful; slight
lekko (lék-ko) adv. easily
lekkoatleta (lek-ko-at-le-ta) m.
field&track man
lekkomyślny (lek-ko-miśhl-ni)
adj. m. careless; thoughtless;
reckless; rash; fickle
lektura (lek-too-ra) f. reading
matter ; reading list; reading
lemiesz (le-myesh) m. plough-
share : blade; vomer
lemoniada (le-mo-ńá-da) f. lemonade; lemon squash
len (len) m. flax ;linen;
lenić się (le-ńeech shań) v.
be idle; be lazy; shed hair
lenieć (le-ńech) v. shed hair
leninizm (le-ńee-ńeezm) m. Le-
ninism;Lenin's interpretation
lenistwo (le-ńees-tvo) n. laziness ; idleness; sluggishness
leniwy (le-ńee-vi) adj. m. lazy
lennik (len-ńeek) m. vassal
pledging fealty to overlord

lenno (lén-no) n. fief
len (leń) m. lazy-bones; idler;
lazy bum ; sluggard
lep (lep) m. glue ; flypaper
lepianka (lep-yán-ka) f. adobe;
mud hut; mud cabin
lepić (le-peech) v. stick; glue
lepiej (lép-yey) adv. better;
rather ;(feel) better
lepki (lep-kee) adj. m. sticky
lepszy (lép-shi) adj. m. better
lesbijka (les-beéy-ka) f. les-
bian :homosexual women
lesisty (le-śhees-ti) adj. m.
wooded; woody; forest-
leszcz (léshch) m. bream
leszczyna (lesh-chi-na) f.
hazelnut tree ; hazel grove
leśnictwo (leśh-ńeets-tvo) n.
forestry ; forest-range
leśniczówka (leśh-ńee-choóv-ka)
f. ranger's house (forester's)
leśniczy (leśh-ńee-chi) m. ranger ; forest-ranger;forester
leśnik (leśh-ńeek) m. forester
leśny (leśh-ni) adj. m. of
forest; of forestry;forest-
letarg (le-targ) m. lethargy
letni (let-ńee) adj. m. lukewarm; half-hearted; summer
letnik (let-ńeek) m. vacationer
letnisko (let-ńees-ko) n. summer
resort ;summer vacation spot
lew (lev) m. lion; lady's man
lewa (le-ya) f. left (side)
lewar (le-var) m. lever; jack
lewatywa (le-ya-ti-va) f. enema
lewica (le-vee-tsa) f. the left
(polit.) ; left-hand side
lewo (lé-vo) adv. to the left
lewy (le-vi) adj. m. left; false
leźć (leźhch) v. crowl; creep-
along; plod along; climb;jostle
leżak (le-zhak) m. folding
(canvas) chair;deck-chair
leżeć (le-zhech) v. lie; (fit)
lędźwie (lańdźh-vye) pl. loins
legnąć (lang-nównch) v. hatch
lęk (lank) m. fear;anxiety;dread
lękać się (lán-kach shań) v.
be afraid; dread;stand in awe
lękliwy (lánk-lee-vi) adj. m.
timid ;faint-hearted;apprehensive

lgnąć (lgnównch) v. adhere;sink; stick; be partial; feel attracted

libacja (lee-báts-ya) f. drinking party; drinking bout

liberalny (lee-be-rál-ni) adj. m.liberal; broad-minded

liberał (lee-bé-raw) m. liberal

libertyn (lee-ber-tin) m. libertine; free thinker

lice (lee-tse) n. face; cheek; the right side; evidence

licencja (lee-tsén-tsya) f. license (ermission to practice)

licho (lee-kho) adv. poorly

licho (lee-kho) n. evil; devil

lichota (lee-kho-ta) f. rubbish

lichtarz (leékh-tash) m. candlestick ; candelabrum;candelabra

lichwa (leékh-va) f. usury

lichwiarz (leékh-vyash) m. usurer; loan shark; money lender

lichy (lee-khi) adj. m. shoddy; shabby; poor; mean;rotten;petty

lico (lee-tsom.face; cheek; surface; front; outer part

licować (lee-tsó-vach) v. fit for... ; comport ;veneer; face

licytacja (lee-tsi-táts-ya) f. auction ; bidding; the bid

licytować (lee-tsi-tó-vach) v. auction; bid; offer; call

liczba (leéch-ba) f. number; figure; integer; group; class

liczbowy (leech-bó-vi) adj. m. numerical ;numeral

licznik (leech-neek) m. counter; numerator; gasmeter; electrometer, etc,;taximeter; register

liczny (leéch-ni) adj. m.numerous ; large; abundant;plentiful

liczyć (lee-chích) v. count ; reckon;compute; calculate

liczydło (lee-chíd-wo) n. abacus; counter; register

liga (lee-ga) f. league ;alliance

lik (leék) m. lot ;countless

lignina (leeg-nee-na) f. lignin

likier (lee-ker) m. liquor

likwidacja (leek-vee-dáts-ya) f. liquidation ;closing down

likwidować (leek-vee-do-vach) v. liquidate ;do away with

lila (lee-la) adj. m. (color) pale-violet; lily-

lilia (leel-ya) f. lily

liliowy (leel-yó-vi) adj. m. lilac (color) ; lily-

liliput (lee-lee-poot) m. little dwarf ; midget; pygmy

limfa (leém-fa) f. lymph

limit (lee-meet) m. limit

limuzyna (lee-moo-zí-na) f. limousine; pilot's enclosure

lin (leen) m. tench

lina (lee-na) f. line; rope

lincz (leénch) m. lynch

linczować (leen-chó-vach) v. lynch; kill by mob action

lingwista (leen-gveés-ta) m. linguist (specialist)

linia (leén-ya) f. line; lane

linijka (lee-neéy-ka) f. ruler

liniować (lee-ñyo-vach) v. rule; line (paper)

liniowy okręt (leen-yó-vi okrant) liner (ship);battleship

linoleum (lee-no-lé-oom) n. linoleum (floor covering)

linoskoczek (lee-no-skó-chek) m. tightrope artist

linotyp (lee-nó-tip) m. linotype (typesetting machine)

linowa kolejka (lee-nó-va ko-léy-ka) cable car

lipa (lee-pa)f.l·linden tree 2. fake; cheat; fraud

lipiec (leep-yets) m. July

lira (lee-ra) f. lyre

liryczny (lee-rích-ni) adj. m. lyric; lyrical

liryk (lee-rik) m. lyrist;lyric

liryka (lee-rí-ka) f. lyric poetry ; lyricism

lis (lees) m. fox; sly man

list (leest) m. letter;note

lista (leés-ta) f. list;roll

listonosz (lees-to-nosh) m. postman

listopad (lees-tó-pad) m. November

listownie (lees-tóv-ñe) adv. by letter ; by mail

listwa (leés-tva) f. trim

liszaj (lee-shay) m. herpes

liszka (leesh-ka) f. caterpillar; vixen; sly fox
liściasty (leesh-chas-ti) odj.
m. leafy; leafed; foliaceous
liść (leeshch) m. leaf; frond
litania (lee-tah-ya) f. litany
litera (lee-te-ra) f. letter
literacki (lee-te-rats-kee)
adj. m. literary; of letters
literat (lee-te-rat) m. writer
literatura (lee-te-ra-too-ra)
f. literature; writings
litewski (lee-tev-skee) adj. m.
Lithuanian; Lithuanian language
litograf (lee-to-graf) m.
lithographer
litościwy (lee-tosh-chee-vi)
adj. m. merciful; compassionate
litość (lee-toshch) f. pity;
mercy; compassion
litować się (lee-to-vach shan)
v. have pity; feel pity
litr (leetr) m. liter
liturgia (lee-toor-gya) f.
liturgy; religious ritual
lity (lee-ti) adj. m. massive
solid; cast; pure-
lizać (lee-zach) v. lick
lizol (lee-zol) m. lysol
lizus (lee-zoos) m. bootlicker
lniany (lña-ni) adj. m. linen;
flaxen; linseed
loch (lokh) m. dungeon; cellar
lodołamacz (lo-do-wa-mach) m.
icebreaker: ice shield
lodowaty (lo-do-va-ti) adj. m.
icy; ice-cold; chilling; frigid
lodowiec (lo-do-vyets) m. glacier; mass of ice and snow
lodowisko (lo-do-vees-ko) n.
skating-rink; ice rink
lodownia (lo-dov-ña) f. ice-
chamber; ice-cellar; icy cold
lodowy (lo-do-yy) adj. m. of ice
lodówka (lo-dov-ka) f. refrigerator; ice box; ice chest
lody (lo-di) pl. ice cream
logarytm (lo-ga-ritm) m. loga-
rithm
logiczny (lo-geech-ni) adj. m.
logical; consistent; sound
logik (lo-geek) m. logician;
expert in logic

logika (lo-gee-ka) f. logic
lojalność (lp-yal-noshch) f.
loyalty; straightforwardness
lojalny (lo-yal-ni) adj. m.
loyal; staunch; low-abiding
lok (lok) m. curl; coil
lokaj (lo-kay) m. lackey
lokal (lo-kal) m. premises
lokalizować (lo-ka-lee-zo-vach)
localize; locate; range
lokalny (lo-kal-ni) adj. m.
local; regional; of a place
lokata (lo-ka-ta) f. investment
lokator (lo-ka-tor) m. tenant
lokomocja (lo-ko-mots-ya) f.
locomotion; communication
lokomotywa (lo-ko-mo-ti-va) f.
train engine; locomotive
lokować (lo-ko-vach) v. place
lombard (lom-bard) m. pawnshop
lont (lont) m. fuse; slow-match
lornetka (lor-net-ka) f. field
glasses; opera glasses
los (los) m. lot; fate; chance;
lottery-ticket; destiny; hazard
losować (lo-so-vach) v. draw
lots; raffle; draw cuts
lot (lot) m. flight; speed
loteria (lo-ter-ya) f. lottery
lotnia (lot-ña) f. hang glider
lotnictwo (lot-ñeets-tvo) n.
aviation; aeronautics; air force
lotnik (lot-ñeek) m. aviator
lotnisko (lot-ñees-ko) n. airport; airfield; aerodrome
lotniskowiec (lot-ñees-kov-
yets) m. aircraft carrier
lotny (lot-ni) adj. m. bright;
quick; swift; sharp; subtle
lotos (lo-tos) m. lotus
loża masońska (lo-zha ma-soñs-
ka) shriner's lodge
lód (loot) m. ice; pl. ice cream
lśniący (lshñown-tsi) adj. m.
shining; bright; glossy; sleek
lśnić (lshñeech) v. glitter;
shine; gleam; glimmer; shimmer
lub (loop) conj. or; or else
luba (loo-ba) f. sweetheart
lubić (loo-beech) v. like;
be fond; enjoy; be partial
lubieżny (loo-byezh-ni) adj.
m. lustful; voluptuous; lewd

lubość (loo-boshćh) f. delight
lubować się (loo-bó-vaćh śháń)
v. take delight ; find pleasure
lud (loot) m. people; nation
ludność (loód-noshćh) f. population (of a given territory)
ludny (loód-ni) adj. m. populous ; teeming; crowded
ludobójstwo (loo-do-bóoy-stvo)
n. genocide;killing of a nation
ludowy (loo-do-vi) adj. m.pop-
ulist; popular; country
ludożerca (loo-do-zhér-tsa) m.
cannibal ; man man-eater
ludzie (loo-dźhe) pl. people
ludzkość (loódz-koshćh) f.
mankind; humaneness; humanity
lufa (loo-fa) f. gunbarrel
luk (look) m. hatch ;skylight
luka (loo-ka) f. gap;blank;break
lukier (loo—ker) m. sugar-
icing ; frosting
lukratywny (look-ra-tiv-ni) adj.
m. lucrative ; profitable
luksus (look-soos) m. luxury
lunatyk (loo-ná-tik) l. sleepwalker; 2. loony
lunąć (loo-nównćh) v. rain in
torrents;slap ;lash down;whack
luneta (loo-né-ta) f. field-
glass ;spy-glass; telescope
lupa (loo-pa) f. magnifying
glass ; jeweler's glass (loop)
lusterko (loos-tér-ko) n. hand-
glass ; rear-view mirror(in a car)
lustro (loós-tro) n. mirror
lustrować (loos-tró-vaćh) v.
inspect; review ; check; audit
lut (loot) m. solder,
luteranin (loo-te-ra-ńeen) m.
Lutheran
lutnia (loot-ńa) f. flute
lutować (loo-tó-vaćh) v. solder
luty (loo-ti) m. February
luty (loo-ty) adj. m. bleak;
grim ; severe; bleak
luz (loos) m. clearance; play
luzak (loo-zak) m. loose (replacement) horse
luzować (loo-zó-vaćh) v. replace;
relieve ; loosen;slacken;ease off
luźny (loozh-ni) adj. m. loose

lwi (lvee) adj. m. lion's
lżej (lzhey) adv. lighter;
easier; with less weight
lżenie (lzhé-ńe) n. abuse; insults;vituperation
lżyć (lzhićh) v. abuse; insult
łabędź (wa-báńdźh)m. swan
łach (wakh) m. rag ; clout
łacha (wa-kha) f. sandbank
łachman (wákh-man) m. rag
łachudra (wa-khoód-ra) m.
ragtagman; ragamuffin
łaciarz (wa-ćhash) m. patcher
łaciaty (wa-ćhá-ti) adj. m.
in patches ; pinto(horse)
łacina (wa-ćhee-ņa) f. Latin
łaciński (wa-cheéń-skee) adj.
m. Latin; of Latin
ład (wad) m. order;orderliness
ładnie (wad-ńe) adv. nicely
ładnieć (wad-ńećh) v. grow
pretty; grow prettier
ładny (wad-ny) adj. m. nice
ładować (wa-do-vaćh) v. load;
charge; cram; fill
ładownica (wa-dow-ńee-tsa) f.
cartridge pouch (or box)
ładunek (wa-doó-nek) m. load;
cargo; charge ; shipload;burden
łagodność (wa-gód-noshćh) f.
gentleness ; kindliness;suavity
łagodny (wa-gód-ni) adj. m.
gentle ;mild;soft;meek;easy
łagodzący (wa-go-dzówń-tsi) adj.
m. alleviating; extenuating
łagodzić (wa-gó-dźheećh)v.
soothe; relieve; alleviate
attenuate; mitigate; smooth
łajać (wá-yaćh) v. scold; chide
łajdactwo (way-dáts-tvo) n.
mean trick;scoundrels;rabble
łajdak (wáy-dak) m. scoundrel
łajno (wáy-no) n. dung; shit
łaknąć (wak-nównćh) v. hunger
for; thirst for ;crave for
łakocie (wa-kó-ćhe) pl. deli-
cacies; sweets;tidbits;candy
łakomić się (wa-ko-meećh śháń)
v. covet; lust;be tempted
łakomy (wa-kó-mi) adj. m.
greedy; covetous; avid
łakomstwo (wa-kóm-stvo) n.
greed; gluttony;greediness

Łamać (wa-mach) v. break;crush; quarry;shatter; crack; snap

Łamigłowka (wa-mee-gwoow-ka) f. riddle; puzzle;jig-saw puzzle

Łamistrajk (wa-mee-strayk) m. scab; strikebreaker

Łamliwy (wam-lee-vi) adj. m. fragile;frail;brittle;breakable

Łan (wan) m. stand of wheat

Łania (wa-ña) f. hind; doe

Łańcuch (wań-tsookh) m. chain; range; series; train;succession

Łańcuchowa reakcja (wań-tsoo-khó-va re-ák-tsya) chain reaction

Łapa (wa-pa) f. paw ;claw;arm

Łapać (wá-pach) v. catch;snatch

Łapanka (wa-pan-ka) f. roundup

Łapcie (wáp-che) n. bast sandals : moccasins

Łapczywosc (wap-chi-voshch) f. greed; greediness; avidity

Łapczywy (wap-chi-vi) adj. m. greedy; money-grubbing

Łapka (wáp-ka) f. (mouse) trap

Łapowka (wa-poóv-ka) f. bribe

Łapserdak (wap-sér-dak) m. rogue; ragamuffin;scoundrel

Łasica (wa-shée-tsa) f. weasel

Łasić się (wa-sheech shäñ) v. fawn on sb.; toady

Łaska (wás-ka) f. grace ; clemency; favor; generosity;mercy

Łaskawy (was-ká-vi) adj. m. gracious; kind; generous

Łaskotac (was-ko-tach) v. tickle; titillate

Łaskotliwy (was-kot-lee-vi) adj. m. ticklish; titillating

Łasy (wa-si) adj. m. greedy

Łaszczyć się (wash-chich shäñ) v. covet; lust

Łata (wa-ta) f. patch

Łatać (wá-tach) v. patch up

Łatanina (wa-ta-nee-na) f. patch work; bungling

Łatwo (wát-vo) adv. easily

Łatwopalny (wat-vo-pál-ni) adj. m. inflammable ; combustible

Łatwosc (wát-voshch) f. ease; facility;aptitude; fluency

Łatwowierny (wat-vo-vyér-ni) adj. m. credulous ;gullible

Łatwy (wát-vi) adj. m. easy

Ława (wá-va) f. bench ;footing

Ławica (wa-vée-tsa) f. (fish) shoal ; sandbank; shelf; layer

Ławka (wáf-ka) f. pew; bench

Ławnik (wav-ñeek) m. juror; alderman; assessor

Łazić (wa-żheech)v. crawl; loiter ; slouch about;creep

Łazienka (wa-żhén-ka) f. bathroom; toilet: bath

Łazik (wa-żheek) m. tramp; jeep

Łaznia (wáżh-ña) f. bath

Łażący (wa-zhówn-tsi) adj. m. dragging; crawling;scansorial

Łączący (wówn-chówn-tsy) adj. m. uniting; joining; unitive

Łącznica (wównch-ñeé-tsa) f. junction ;switchboard

Łącznie (wówn-chñe) adv. together; including; inclusive of

Łącznik (wownch-ñeek) m. hyphen; liaisonman ;link; tie; bond

Łączność (wownch-noshch) f. contact; communication; unity; signal service; connection

Łączny (wownch-ni) adj. m. joint; combined;total; global

Łączyć (wown-chich) v. join; unite ;merge;link;bind;weld

Łąka (wown-ka) f. meadow

Łeb (wep) m. head; pate

Łechtac (wékh-tach) v. tickle; flatter ; titillate; lure

Łęk (wäñk) m. saddlebow; syncline; arch; bow; pommel

Łgać (wgach) v. lie;brag;boast

Łgarstwo (wgár-stvo) n. lie

Łgarz (wgásh) m. liar; braggart

Łkać (wkach) v. sob

Łobuz (wó-boos) m. rogue; rascal; scamp; scoundrel

Łodyga (wo-dí-ga) f. stem

Łoic (wo-eech) v. tallow; beat up; wallop; curry

Łokiec (wó-kech) m. elbow

Łom (wom) m. crowbar;scrap;junk

Łomot (wó-mot) m. crash; crack

Łono (wo-no) n. lap; bosom;womb

Łopata (wo-pá-ta) f. spade

Łopot (wó-pot) m. (sail)flutter

Łoskot (wos-kot) n. clatter; bang; din; rumble;racket;boom

łosoś (wo-sosh) m. salmon

łoś (wosh) m. elk; moose

łotewski (wo-tev-skee) adj. m.
Latvian : Latvian language

łotr (wotr) m, vicious scoundrel; knave; rascal; rogue

łowczy (wov-chi) adj. m. hunting; huntsman's; hunter's

łowić (wov-eech) v. trap;
fish; catch; hunt; chase

łowiectwo (wov-yets-tvo) n.
hunting; game shooting

łowy (wo-vi) pl. hunt; chase

łozina (wo-zhee-na) f. wicker;
sallow; osier; osier-bed

łoże (wo-zhe) n. bed; cradle

łożyć (wo-zhich) v. spend

łożysko (wo-zhis-ko) n.(river)
bed; (ball) bearing

łódka (wood-ka) f. small boat

łódź (woodzh) f. boat;craft

łój (wooy) m. tallow;suet;sebum

łów (woov) m. hunt; chase

łóżeczko (woo-zhech-ko) n.
(child's) bed ; small bed

łóżko (woozh-ko) n. bed;bunk

łubin (woo-been) m. lupin

łucznik (wooch-ñeek) n. archer

łuczywo (woo-chi-vo) n. resinous kindling;resinous chips

łudzący (woo-dzown-tsi) adj.
m. delusive; deceptive

łudzić (woo-dzheech)v. delude;
deceive; give false hope

ług (woog) m. lye

ługować (woo-go-vach) v. leach;
lixiviate

łuk (wook) m. bow; arch; bent;
vault

łuna (woo-na) f. glow (of sun
or fire)

łup (woop) m. booty; spoils

łupać (woo-pach) v. cleave;
split; ache; give shooting pain

łupek (woo-pek) m, slate

łupić (woo-peech) v. plunder

łupież (woo-pyezh) f. dandruff

łupieżca (woo-pyezh-tsa) m.
plunderer; looter; pillager

łupina (woo-pee-na) f. husk;
shell; peel; skin; hull;rind

łuska (woos-ka) f. scale; husk;
shell; pod; flake; rind

łuskać (woos-kach) v. scale;
husk; peel; pod; hull (rice)

łuszczyć (woosh-chich) v. peel;
pare; flake off; shell off

łuza (woo-za) f. billiard
pocket

łydka (wit-ka) f. calf(leg-shank)

łyk (wik) m. gulp; sip; draft

łykać (wi-kach) v. swallow;
gulp; sip; bolt; gorge; drink

łyko (wi-ko) n. bast; phoem

łykowaty (wi-ko-va-ti) adj. m.
wiry; tough; fibrous

łypać (wi-pach) v. blink

łysek (wi-sek) m. (boldhead)
boldy; bold-faced animal

łysieć (wi-shech) v. become
bold; grow bold; lose hair

łysina (wi-shee-na) f. pate

łyskać (wis-kach) v. flash

łysy (wi-si) adj. m. bold

łyżeczka (wi-zhech-ka) f. teaspoon; dessert spoon; curette

łyżka (wizh-ka) f. spoon;spoonful

łyżwa (wizh-va) f. skate

łyżwiarz (wizh-vyash) m.skater

łyżwowy (wizh-vo-vi)adj.of skates

łza (wza) f. tear

łzawy (wza-vi) adj. m. tearful

łzowy kanał (wzo-vi ka-naw)
tear canal; tear duct

maca (ma-tsa) f. matzos

macać (ma-tsach) v. feel; grope

machać (ma-khach) v. wave;whisk;
swing; wag; lash; flap;brandish

macher (ma-kher) m. trickster

machina (ma-khee-na) f. (large)
machine; bureaucratic machine

machinacja (ma-khee-nats-ya) f.
machination; dodge; intrigue

machlojka (ma-khloy-ka) f.
swindle; defraudation

macica (ma-chee-tsa) f. uterus;
womb; screw nut; tap root

macierz (ma-chesh) f. mother
country; matrix; mother

macierzanka (ma-che-zhan-ka) f.
thyme : wild thyme

macierzyński (ma-che-zhiñ-ski)
adj. m. maternal; mother's

macierzyństwo (ma-che-zhiñ-stvo)
n. maternity; motherhood

macierzysty (ma-che-zhis-ti)
adj. m. maternal; (parental)
maciora (ma-cho-ra) f. sow
macka (mats-ka) f. tentacle;
feeler; antenna; horn
macocha (ma-tso-kha) f. stepmother; not as good as mother
maczac (ma-chach) v. dip; soak
maczuga (ma-choo-ga) f. bat;
club; bludgeon; cudgel
magazyn (ma-ga-zin) m. store;
warehouse; repository; store
magazynier (ma-ga-zi-ner) m.
warehouseman; storekeeper
magia (mag-ya) f. sorcery
magiczny (ma-geech-ni) adj. m.
magic; conjuring tricks
magiel (ma-gel) m. mangle
magik (ma-geek) m. magician
magister (ma-gees-ter) m.mas-
ter (diplomat); chemist
magisterium (ma-gees-ter-yoom)
n. master's degree
magistrat (ma-gees-trat) m.
city hall; municipality
maglowac (mag-lo-vach) v, mangle; calender; bother; crush
magnat (mag-nat) m. magnate
magnes (mag-nes) f. magnet
magnetofon (mag-ne-to-fon) m.
tape-recorder
magnetyczny (ma-gne-tich-ni)
adj. m. magnetic;magnetical
magnetyzm (mag-ne-tizm) m.
magnetism;personal charm
magnez (mag-nes) m. magnesium
magnezja (mag-nez-ya) f. mag-
nesia; magnesium
magnolia (mag-nol-ya) f. magnolia (Magnolia)
mahometanin (ma-kho-me-ta-neen)
m. Mohammedan; Moslem
mahon (ma-khon) m. mahogany
maic (ma-eech) v. decorate
with green leaves
maj (may) m. May
majaczyc (ma-ya-chich) v. rave;
loom ; be delirious
majatek (ma-yown-tek) m. fortune; estate; property;wealth
majdan (may-dan) m. parade-
ground; personal junk; traps

majeranek (ma-ye-ra-nek) m.
marjoram; fragrant mint(cooking)
majestat (ma-yes-tat) m. majesty; kingship; stateliness
majetnosc (ma-yant-noshch) f.
wealth; fortune; property
majetny (ma-yant-ni) adj. m.
well to do ;wealthy; affluent
majonez (ma-yo-nes) m. mayonnaise; egg yoke dressing
major (ma-yor) m. major
majowka (ma-yoov-ka) f. May-
outing ; picnic; junket
majster (may-ster) m. qualified
craftman; boss; master;foreman
majstersztyk (may-ster-shtik) m.
masterpiece;greatest work
majstrowac (may-stro-vach) v.
tinker ; make (an object)
majtek (may-tek) m. deckhand
majtki (mayt-kee) pl. panties
mak (mak) m. poppy seed
makaron (ma-ka-ron) m. macaroni
makata (ma-ka-ta) f. tapestry
makler (mak-ler) m. broker
makolagwa (ma-ko-lowng-va) f.
linnet; lass; lassie
makrela (ma-kre-la) f. mackerel
maksyma (ma-ksi-ma) f. axiom;
maxim ; adage :rule of conduct
maksymalny (ma-ksi-mal-ni) adj.
m. maximum ;top-;peak-;most-
makulatura (ma-koo-la-too-ra) f.
waste-paper;spoilage; rubbish
makuch (ma-kookh) m. oilcake
malaria (ma-lar-ya) f. malaria
malarstwo (ma-lar-stvo) m.
painting (art); house painting
malarz (ma-lash) m. painter
malec (ma-lets) m. youngster
malec (ma-lech) v. shrink;dwindle
malenki (ma-len-kee) adj. m.
very small; tiny; insignificant
malenstwo (ma-len-stvo) n. tiny
thing; little one; little mite
malina (ma-lee-na) f. raspberry
malowac (ma-lo-vach) v. paint;
stain; color; make up;depict
malowidlo (ma-lo-veed-wo) n.
painting; picture (painted)
malowniczy (ma-lov-nee-chi)
adj. m. picturesque; vivid

maltretować (mal-tre-tó-vach)
v. abuse; mistreat; il, treat
malwersacja (mal-ver-sáts-ya)
f. embezzlement; peculation
mało (má-wo) adv. little; few;
seldom; lack; not enough
małoduszny (ma-wo-doosh-ni)
adj. m.small- minded; narrow-
minded; cheap ;fainthearted
małoletni (ma-wo-lét-ñee)adj.
m. minor; under age ;juvenile
małomówny (ma-wo-moóv-ni) adj.
m. reticent; laconic;taciturn
małostkowy (ma-wost-kó-vi) adj.
m. fussy; petty; mean
małpa (máw-pa) f. ape; monkey
małpować (maw-po-vach) v. ape
mały (má-wi) adj. m. little;
small size; low; modest;slight
małżeński (maw-zheń-skee) adj.
m. matrimonial ;conjugal
małżeństwo (maw-sheń-stwo) n.
married couple; wedlock
małżonek (maw-zhó-nek) m. husband ; spouse; consort; mate
małżonka (maw-zhón-ka) f. wife
mama (má-ma) f. mamma ; mother
mamałyga (ma-ma-wí-ga) f.
maize gruel ; hominy
mamić (ma-meéch) v. deceive;
delude ;beguile; lure;tempt
mamidło (ma-meéd-wo) n. illusion ; delusion;lure;seduction
mamona (ma-mó-na) f. mammon
mamlać (mám-lach) v. mumble
mamrotać (mam-ró-tach) v. mutter ; mumble; gibber
mamut (ma-moot) m. mammoth
manatki (ma-nát-kee) pl.person-
al belongings; traps
mandaryn (man-dá-rin) n. man-
darin; Chinese digninitary.
mandat (man-dat) m. mandate;
traffic ticket ; fine
mandolina (man-do-lee-na) f.
mandolin with 8 to 10 strings
manekin (ma-ne-keen)m.mannequin
manewr (má-nevr) m. maneuver
manewrować (ma-nev-ró-vach) v.
maneuver; steer;handle; switch
maneż (ma-nesh) m. riding-
school; horse-driven thrasher

mangan (man-gan) m. manganese
mania (ma-ñya) f. mania ;fad
maniak (ma-ñyak) m. maniac;crank
manicure (ma-ñee-keer) m.
manicure;doing one's fingernails
manic (ma-ñeech) v. deceive;tempt
maniera (ma-ñe-ra) f. manner
manierka (ma-ñer-ka) f. canteen
manifest (ma-ñee-fest) m. man-
ifesto: a public declaration
manifestacja (ma-ñee-fes-táts-ya)
f. manifestation; demonstration
manifestować (ma-ñee-fes-tó-
vach) v. demonstrate; display
manipulacja (ma-ñee-poo-láts-ya)
f. manipulation ; handling
manipulować (ma-ñee-poo-lo-vach)
v. manipulate;handle; tinker
mankiet (man-Ket) m. cuff;turn-up
mankament (man-ka-ment) m. defect; shortcoming; fault
manko (mán-ko) n. (acc.) shortage; allowance for cash errors
manna (mán-na) f. cream of
wheat; a godsend manna
manometr (ma-no-metr) m. pressure gauge; steam gauge
manowce (ma-nóv-tse) pl. road-
less area; misguided direction
manufaktura (ma-noo-fak-too-ra)
f. fabrics; manufacture; shop
manuskrypt (ma-noós-kript) m.
manuscript(hand or typewritten)
mankuctwo (mań-koóts-tvo) n.
left-handedness
mapa (má-pa) f. map; chart
mara (ma-ra) f. ghost; apparition; nightmare; dream; vision
marazm (ma-razm) m. sluggishness
marchew (mar-khev) f. carrot
marcepan (mar-tse-pan) m. mar-
zipan; marchpane
margaryna (mar-ga-ri-na) f.
margarine ; marge (slang)
margines (mar-gée-nes) m. margin; edge; border;minor thing
mariaż (mar-yazh) m. marriage
marionetka (mar-yo-nét-ka) f.
puppet;dummy ; figurehead
marka (már-ka) f. mark; brand;
stamp; trade mark; reputation
markotno (mar-kót-no) adv. sad

markotny (mar-kót-ni) adj. m.
peevish; moody; sullen; sad
marksistowski (mark-shees-tóvs-
kee) adj. m. Marxist: of Marx
marksizm (márk-sheezm) m.
Marxism; Marxist believes
marmolada (mar-mo-lá-da) f.
marmalade; jam; shambles
marmur (már-moor) m. marble
marniec (már-ñech) v. deteriorate; waste; decline; perish
marnosc (már-noshch) f. futil-
ity; flimsiness; vanity
marnotrawny (mar-no-tráv-ni)
adj. m. wasteful; prodigal
marnowac (mar-nó-vach) v. waste
marny (már-ni) adj. m. poor;
meagre; sorry; of no value
marsz(marsh) m. march; walk
marsz ! (marsh) excl.: (command)
forward march; split ! get
out ! off you go !
marszałek (mar-shá-wek) m.
marshal; Polish Seym speaker
marszczyc (mársh-chich) v.
wrinkle; frown; crease; ripple
marszruta (marsh-róo-ta) f.
route ; itinerary
martwica (mart-vée-tsa) f.
necrosis ; sinter; travertine
martwic (márt-veech) v. distress;grieve; vex; worry;afflict
martwy (márt-vi) adj. m. dead
martyr (már-tir) m. martyr
maruder (ma-róo-der) m. maraud-
er; straggler; loiterer
marudzic (ma-róo-dżheech)v.
loiter; grumble; lag behind
mary (má-ri) pl. mar; bier
marynarka (ma-ri-nár-ka) f.
jacket; sportscoat; navy
marynarz (ma-ri-nash) m. mariner; sailor; seaman;jack(tar)
marynata (ma-ri-ná-ta) f. pickle
marynowac (ma-ri-nó-vach) v.
pickle; marinade; side-track
marzec (ma-zhets) m. March
marzenie (ma-zhé-ñe) n. dream;
reverie; day dream; pensiveness
marznąc (márzh-nównch) v. freeze
marzyciel (ma-zhi-chel) m.
dreamer; fantast; visionary

marzyc (má-zhich) v. dream
masa (má-sa) f. bulk; mass
masa perłowa (má-sa per-wó-va)
f. mother of pearl
masakra (ma-sák-ra) f. massacre; carnage; butchery
masakrowac (ma-sak-ró-vach) v.
massacre; slaughter;butcher;
masarnia (ma-sár-ña) f. pork·
meat shop; pork butcher's shop
masarz (má-sash) m. pork-
butcher; pork meat worler
masaż (má-sash) m. massage
masażysta (ma-sa-zhis-ta) m.
masseur ; rubber
maselniczka (ma-sel-ñeech-ka)
f. butter-dish; small churn
maska (más-ka) f. mask; hood
maskowac (mas-kó-vach) v.
disguise; mask;hide; screen
masło (más-wo) n. butter
masonski (ma-són-skee) adj. m.
masonic; freemason's
masowac (ma-só-vach) v. massage
masowo (ma-só-vo) adv. wholesale; in a mass; in masses
masywnosc (ma-siv-noshch) f.
massiveness ; solidity
masywny (ma-siv-ni) adj. m.
massive ; solid; bulky; massy
maszerowac (ma-she-ró-vach) v.
march ; march on; keep marching
maszkara (mash-ká-ra) f. monster; scarecrow; eyesore
maszt (masht) m. mast;flagstaff
maszyna (ma-shí-na) f. machine
maszynka do golenia (ma-shín-
ka do go-lé-ña) safety razor
maszyneria (ma-shi-nér-ya) f.
machinery ; mechanism
maszynista (ma-shi-ñées-ta) m.
railroad engineer
maszynistka (ma-shi-ñeest-ka)
f. typist
maszynopis (ma-shi-nó-pees) m.
typescript; typewritten copy
masc (mashch) f. ointment;
horse color; unguent
maslanka (ma-shlán-ka) f.
buttermilk; product of churning
mat (mat) m. flat color; check-
mate (one's opponent)

mata (ma-ta) f. mat; matting
matactwo (ma-táts-tvo) n. legal
  trickery; fraudulence; deceit
matczyny (mat-chi-ni) adj. m.
  maternal ; mother's
matematyczny (ma-te-ma-tich-ni)
  adj. m. mathematical
matematyk (ma-te-ma-tik) m.
  mathematician (also student)
matematyka (ma-te-má-ti-ka) f.
  mathematics ;science of numbers
materac (ma-te-rats) m.mattress
materia (ma-ter-ya) f. matter;
  stuff; subject;point;puss;cloth
materialista (ma-ter-ya-lees-ta)
  m. materialist
materialistyczny (ma-ter-ya-
  lees-tich-ni) adj. m. materia-
  listic (opposite to spiritual)
materiał (ma-ter-yaw) m. material; substance; stuff; cloth
matka (mát-ka) f. mother
matnia (mát-ńa) f. snare; trap
matowy (ma-tó-vi) adj. m. flat
  color; dull; without luster
matrona (ma-tró-na) f. matron
matryca (ma-trí-tsa) f. matrix;
  die ; type;mold ; stencil;swage
matrykuła (ma-tri-koo-wa) f.
  register of university students
matrymonialny (ma-tri-mo-ñal-ni)
  adj. m. matrimonial ;marital
matura (ma-too-ra) f. final
  highschool examination
mauretański (maw-re-tań-skee)
  adj. m. Moorish ; of Moors
mazać (ma-zach) v. smear; daub
mazgaj (máz-gay) m. crybaby
mazur (ma-zoor) m. mazurka
  rythm; Mazurian ; Mazovian
maź (maźh) f. grease;tallow
mącić (moẃn-cheech) v. blur;
  ruffle ; muddy; cloud;confuse
mączka (mownch-ka) f. fine
  flour;powder; dust; starch
mądrość (mown-droshch) f. wisdom; intelligence; sagacity
mądry (mowń-dri) adj. m. sage
mąka (mown-ka) f. flour; meal
mąż (mownsh) m. husband; man
mąż stanu (mowńsh stá-noo)
  statesman ; outstanding politician: outstanding diplomat

mdleć (mdlech) v. faint;weaken
mdlić (mdleech) v. nauseate
mdłosc (mdwoshch) f. nausea
mdło (mdwo) adv. dull; nauseating; sickening; faintly;dimly
meble (méb-le) pl. furniture
mecenas (me-tse-nas) m. lawyer
mech (mekh) m. moss ; down
mechaniczny (me-kha-ñeech-ni)
  adj. m. mechanical;automatic
mechanik (me-khá-ñeek) m. mechanic; Jack of all trades
mechanika (me-kha-ñee-ka) f.
  mechanics ;practical mechanics
mechanizm (me-khá-ñeesm) m.
  mechanism;gear ; device
mecz (mech) m. sport match
meczet (me-chet) m. mosque
medal (me-dal) m. medal
mediacja (med-yáts-ya) f. me-
  diation; settling of differences
meduza (me-doo-za) f. jellyfish
medycyna (me-di-tsi-na) f. medicine: art of healing
medyczny (me-dich-ni) adj. m.
  medical ; medicinal
medyk (me-dik) m. medical student; medic(hist. :physician)
medykament (me-di-ká-ment) m.
  drug; medicine (hist. expr.)
medytacja (me-di-táts-ya) f.
  meditation: thinking deeply
megafon (me-gá-fon) m. loud-
  speaker; megaphone,
megaloman (me-ga-lo-man) m. meg-
  alomaniac;self appointed boss
melancholia (me-lan-khól-ya) f.
  melancholy; the blues;dejection
melasa (me-la-sa) f. molasses
meldować (mel-do-vach) v. report; register; announce
meldunek (mel-doo-nek) m. report; announcement; notification
melioracja (mel-yo-ráts-ya) f.
  reclamation of land; drainage
melodia (me-lód-ya) f. melody
meloman (me-lo-man) m. music
  lover: music enthusiast
melon (me-lon) m. melon
melonik (me-lo-ñeek) m. bowler
  hat; derby; bowler;billycock
memoriał (me-mor-yaw) m. memorial;minutes' journal(commercial)

menażeria (me-na-zhér-ya) f.
menagerie ;animal collection
menażka (me-nazh-ka) f. mess kit
mennica (men-ńée-tsa) f. mint
menstruacja (men-stroo-áts-ya)
f. menstruation ; menses
mentalność (men-tál-noshch) f.
mentality ; a way of thinking
menu (mé-noo) m. menu ;bill of
mer (mer) m. mayor   [fare
merdać (mér-dach) v. wag tail
merytoryczny (me-ri-to-rích-ni)
adj. m. of substance ;essential
meszek (mé-shek) m. down; nap
meta (me-ta) f. goal; hang-out
metafizyka (me-ta-fée-zi-ka) f.
metaphysics (speculative phil.)
metal (mé-tal) m. metal
metalowy (me-ta-ló-vi) adj. m.
metallic[luster, sound etc)
metalurgia (me-ta-lúr-gya) f.
metallurgy : science of metals
metamorfoza (me-ta-mor-fo-za)
f. metamorphosis ;metamorphism
meteor (me-té-or) m. meteor
meteorologia (me-te-o-ro-lóg-
ya) f. meteorology[system
metoda (me-tó-da) f. method;
metodyczny (me-to-dích-ni) adj.
m. methodical ;systematic
metr (metr) m. meter : 39.37in.
metro (mét-ro) n. subway
metropolia (me-tro-pól-ya) f.
metropolis ; main large city
metryczny (me-trích-ni) adj. m.
metric ; metrical
metryka (me-tri-ka) f. birth-
certificate;the public register
metys (mé-tis) m. metis
mewa (mé-va) f. sea-gull
mezalians (me-zál-yans) m. mis-
alliance; improper alliance
mezanin (me-za-ńeen) m.mezzanine
męczarnia (mań-chár-na) f. torture; torment; anguish; agony
męczennik (man-chen-ńeek) m.
martyr : sufferer for faith etc.
męczyć (man-chich) v. bother;
torment; oppress;tire; exhaust
mędrek (man-drek) m. smart
aleck;knowyall; wiseacre
mędrzec (man-dzhets) m. sage

męka (mán-ka) f. fatigue; torment ;pain;distress; nuisance
męski (máńs-kee) adj. m. masculine; manly ; man's; virile;male
męskość (máńs-kóshch) f. manhood; virility; manliness
męstwo (máńs-tvo) n. bravery
mętny (mańt-ni) adj. m. turbid;
dull;dim; blurred;vague; fishy
męty (mań-ti) n. dregs; scum of
society; underworld; raffle
mężatka (máń-zhát-ka) f. married woman; femme covert (legal.)
mężczyzna (mánzh-chiz-na) m. man
mężniec (mánzh-ńech) v. grow
manly ; muster courage;take heart
mężny (mánzh-ni) adj. m. brave
mglisty (mglées-ti) adj. m.
foggy; misty; dim;nebulous;vague
mgła (mgwa) f. fog; mist; cloud
mgławica (mgwa-vée-tsa) f, neb-
ula ; cloud;hazy idea; haze
mgnienie (mgńe-ńe) n. blink;
twinkle ; wink; flash;jiffy;trice
miał (myaw) m. dust; powder
miałki (myaw-kee) adj. m. fine
(sugar ; sand etc.)(powdered
miano (myá-no) n. name ;designation
mianować (mya-nó-vach) v. appoint ; promote; give a title
mianowicie (mya-no-vee-che)
adv. namely ; to wit : that is ...
mianownik (mya-nov-ńeek) m.
denominator; nominative
miara (myá-ra) f. measure; gauge
yard-stick;foot-rule;amount;limit
miarkować (myar-ko-vach) v.
guess; note; mitigate one's self
miarodajny (mya-ro-dáy-ni) adj.
m. authoritative; competent
miarowy (mya-ró-vi) adj. m.
rythmic ; steady; regular

miasteczko (myas-tech-ko) n.
borough ;country town
miasto (myas-to) n. town
miałczeć (myaw-chech) v. mew
miazga (myáz-ga) f. pulp ; squash
miażdżyć (myazh-dzhich) v. crush;
squash ; smash; grind;lacerate
miąć (myownch) v. crumple ;wrinkle
miąższ (myównzhsh) m. pulp;
flesh of fruit; pomace; squash

miech (myekh) m. bellows

miecz (myech) m. sword

mieć (myeć) v. have;hold; run

miednica (myed-ńee-tsa) f. hand washtub ; pelvis;wash basin

miedza (mye-dza) f. farm boundary strip ; bounds; balk

miedź (myedżh) f. copper

miedziak (mye-dżhak) m. copper penny; copper coin

miedziany (mye-dźha-ni) adj. m. of copper; of brass

miedzioryt (mye-dżho-rit) m. copper engraving

miejsce (myejs-tse) n. place; location; spot; room; space; seat; employment;berth; scene

miejscowość (myey-stso-vośhćh) f. locality ; place;town;village

miejscowy (myeys-tso-vi) adj. m. local; native; indigenous

miejski (myeys-kee) adj. m. of town; of city ;urban

mielizna (mye-leez-na) f. shoal; shallow water ; sandbank; shelf

mielenie (mye-lé-ńe) n. grinding; milling; mincing; jabber;prattling

mielony (mye-lo-ni) adj. m. ground ; milled; minced;chewed up

mieniać (mye-ńać) v. change; swap; exchange; convert

mienić (mye-ńeećh) v. call; glitter; shimmer; change color

mienić się (mye-ńeech śhań) v. change one's color; glitter

mienie (mye-ńe) n. property; belongings ;estate; effects

miernictwo (myer-ńeets-tvo) m. surveying; land measuring

mierniczy (myer-ńee-chi) m. surveyor; adj. m. geodetic

mierność (myer-nośhćh)f.mediocrity ; average range

miernota (myer-no-ta) f. average intelligence; mediocrity

mierny (myer-ny) adj. m. mediocre; mean; moderate;indifferent

mierzeja (mye-zhe-ya) f. sand-bar

mierzić (myer-żheećh) v. be disgusting; sicken;make unbearable

mierznąć (myezh-nównćh) v. become disgusting; pall on sb

mierzwa (myesh-va) f. litter

mierzwić (myezh-veećh) v. tousle

mierzyć (mye-zhićh) v. measure; judge; try on; aim;tend towards

miesiąc (mye-śhownts) m. month; moon ; lunar month [massage

miesić(mye-śheećh)v. knead;

miesięcznie (mye-śhańch-ńe) adv. monthly ; every month

miesięcznik (mye-śhańch-ńeek) m. monthly paper ; monthly

mieszać (mye-shać) v. mix; mingle; shuffle; confuse

mieszać się (mye-shaćh śhań) v. meddle; become confused

mieszanina (mye-sha-ńee-na) f. mixture; compound,; medley

mieszanka (mye-shan-ka) f. blend ;mix; mixture;miscellany

mieszczanin (myesh-cha-ńeen) m. burgher ; townsman; citizen

mieszczaństwo (myesh-chań-stvo) n. middle class ;narrow-minded-

mieszek (mye-shek) m.small ness bellows; bag; money-bag

mieszkać (myesh-kać) v. dwell; live; stay ;have a flat; lodge

mieszkalny (myesh-kál-ny) adj. m. inhabitable; habitable

mieszkanie (myesh-ká-ńe) n. apartment; rooms; lodgings

mieszkaniec (myesh-ká-ńets) m. inhabitant; lodger; resident

mieść (myeśhćh) v. sweep; fling

mieścić (myeśh-ćheećh) v. contain; fit ;hold; store; place

mieścina (myeśh-ćhee-na) f. small town, out-of-the-way

miewać (mye-vaćh) v. have occasionally; feel sometimes

mięczak (myań-chak) m. mollusk

międlić (myańd-leećh) v. bruise; hackle; crush; hold forth

między (myań-dzi) prep. between; among; in the midst

międzymorze (myań-dzi-mo-zhe) n. isthmus : narrow strip between sea

międzynarodowy (myań-dzi-na-ro-do-vi) adj. m. international

międzyplanetarny (myań-dzi-plane-tár-ni) adj. m. interplanetary ; of cosmic space

miękczyc (myáńk-chićh) v. soften; move; touch; palatalize
miękisz (myán-keesh) m. pulp
miękki (myáńk-kee) adj. m.
soft ; flabby; limp; supple
miękko (myáńk-ko) adv. softly
miękkosc (myáńk-kośhćh) f.
softness ; irresolution;pliancy
mięknąc (myáńk-nównćh) v.
soften up ;relax; relent
mięsien (myáń-śheń) m. muscle
mięsisty (myáń-śhees-ti) adj.
m. fleshy ;meaty; pulpous
mięsiwo (myáń-śhee-vo) n. meat
mięso (myáń-so) n. flesh; meat
mięsozerny (myáń-so-zhér-ni)
adj. m. carnivorous;meat eating
mięta (myáń-ta) f. mint ;trifle
miętosic (myáń-to-śheećh) v.
crumble; knead ; crush up
mig (meeg) m. split second;
twinkle; sign language
migac (meé-gaćh) v. twinkle
migawka (mee-gáv-ka) f. camera
shutter; news in brief
migdał (meeg-daw) m. almond;
tonsil ; good and tasty thing
migi (mee-gee) pl. sign language; speaking by signs
migotac (mee-go-taćh) v. twinkle; flicker; waver;whisk;flit
migracja (mee-gráts-ya) f. migration : migrating (of groups)
migrena (mee-gre-na) f. migraine; sick headache
mijac (meé-yaćh) v. go past;
pass by; pass away; go by
mijac się z prawdą (mee-yaćh
śháń z práv-dówn) swerve from
the truth; to be untrue
mika (meé-ka) f. mica
mikrob (meé-krob) m. microbe
mikrofon (mee-kró-fon) m. microphone ;transmitter
mikroskop (mee-krós-kop) m. microscope
mikroskopijny (m ee-kros-kopeéy-ni) adj. m. microscopic
mikstura (meeks-tóo-ra) f. mixture; concoction; medicine
mila (mee-la) f. mile (1609,35m)
mila morska (meé-la mór-ska) f.
nautical mile (1853,2 meters)

milczący (meel-chówn-tsi) adj.
m. silent; reticent ; mum;tacit
milczec (meel-chećh) v. be silent; quit talking; be quiet
milczenie (meel-che-ńe) n. silence: keeping still; stillness
milczkiem (meelch-ḱem) adv.
secretly; stealthily;on the sly
mile (mee-le) adv. pleasantly;
kindly ; warmly; courteously
miliard (meel-yard) m. thousand
million; billion
milicja (mee-leéts-ya) f. militia; police; constabulary
milicjant (mee-leéts-yant) m.
policeman; constable
miligram (mee-leé-gram) m. milligram ; 1/1,000 of a gram
milimetr (mee-leé-metr) m. millimeter: 1/1,000 of a meter
milion (meel-yon) m. million
milioner (meel-yo-ner) m. millionaire; a very wealthy man
milionowe miasto (meel-yo-no-ve
mya-sto) city of million people
militarny (mee-lee-tár-ni) adj.
m. military; of soldiers
militaryzowac (mee-lee-ta-rizo-vaćh) v. militarize
milknąc (meélk-nównćh) v. abate;
quit talking; die away;subside
miło (mee-wo) adv. nicely;
pleasantly; agreeably
miło poznac (mee-wo póz-naćh)
glad to meet ; nice to meet
miłosierdzie (mee-wo-śher-dźhe)
m. charity; mercy;compassion
miłosierny (mee-wo-śhér-ni) adj.
m. merciful; charitable
miłosny list (mee-wós-ni leest)
love letter
miłostka (mee-wost-ka) f. little
love affair
miłosc (meé-wośhćh) f. love
miłosnik (mee-wosh-ńeek) m.
fancier; amateur ; fan
miłowac (mee-wo-vaćh) v. love
miły (mee-wy) adj. m. pleasant;
beloved; likable;nice;enjoyable
mimiczny (mee-meéch-ni) adj. m.
mimic; imitative:make-believe
mimo (meé-mo) prep. in spite of;
notwithstanding ; (al)though

mimo (mee-mo) adv. past; by
mimochodem (mee-mo-kho-dem) adv.
by the way; incidentally
mimo woli (mee-mo vo-lee) adv.
involuntarily; unintentional
mimowolny (mee-mo-vol-ni) adj.
m. involuntary; unintentional
mimo wszystko (mee-mo vshist-ko)
after all; in spite of all
mina (mee-na) f. 1. facial
expression; 2. mine ; air
minaret (mee-na-ret) m. minaret
minąć (mee-nownch) v. pass by
mineralny (mee-ne-ral-ni) adj.
m. mineral;containing minerals
mineralogia (mee-ne-ra-log-ya)
f. mineralogy
minerał (mee-ne-raw) m. mineral
minia (meen-ya) f. minium; red
lead base; red lead
miniatura (meen-ya-too-ra) f.
miniature; miniature copy
minimalny (mee-nee-mal-ny) adj.
m. minimal;the least possible
minimum (mee-nee-moom) m. minimum;adv. at the very least
miniony (mee-no-ni) adj. m. bygone; of long ago; olden
minister (mee-nees-ter) m. minister; cabinet member
ministerialny (mee-nees-ter-
yal-ni) adj. m. ministerial
ministerstwo (mee-nees-ter-stvo)
n. ministry;department of state
minorowy (mee-no-ro-vi) adj. m.
in minor key; low-spirited
minuta (mee-noo-ta) f. minute
minutowy (mee-noo-to-vi) adj.
m. of one minute
miodownik (myo-dov-neek) m.
gingerbread
miodowy miesiąc (myo-do-vi mye-
shownts) honeymoon
miodosytnia (myo-do-sit-na) f.
meadbar
miot (myot) m. throw; cast; lit-
ler; brood ;animal birth; fling
miotacz (myo-tach) m. thrower
miotacz ognia (myo-tach og-na)
m. firethrower
miotać (myo-tach) v. throw; fling;
toss ;hurl; stir; rave; storm
miotła (myot-wa) f. broom

miód (myoot) m. honey ; mead
mir (meer) m. esteem ;respect
miriady (meer-ya-di) pl. myr-
iads : large numbers
mirra (meer-ra) f. myrrh
mirt (meert) m. myrtle
misa (mee-sa) f. platter; bowl
misja (mees-ya) f. mission
misjonarz (mees-yo-nash) m.
missionary
miska (mees-ka) f. dish; pan
misterny (mees-ter-ni) adj. m.
fine; delicate; subtle;clever
mistrz (meestsh) m. master;
maestro; champion; expert
mistrzostwo (mees-tzhos-tvo)
m. championship; mastery
mistrzowski ruch (mees-tzhovs-
kee rookh) masterstroke
mistycyzm (mees-ti-cizm) m.
mysticism ;intuitive knowledge
mistyczny (mees-tich-ni) adj.
m. mystic ; mystical: occult
mistyfikacja (mees-ti-fee-
kats-ya)f.mystification
mistyfikować (mees-ti-fee-ko-
vach) v. mystify; hoax;deceive
mistyk (mees-tik) m. mystic
misyjny (mee-siy-ni) adj. m.
missionary; mission-
miś (meesh) m. teddy bear;
nylon fur coat or jacket
mit (meet) m. myth; mythology
mitologia (mee-to-log-ya) f.
mythology : study of myths
mitologiczny (mee-to-lo-geech-
ni) adj. m. mythologic
mitra (mee-tra) f. mitre
mitręga (mee-tran-ga) f. delay;
waste of time; delay; dawdler
mitrężyć (mee-tran-zhych) v.
loiter; waste time;dally; lag
mityczny (mee-tich-ni) adj. m.
mythical; mythic ; fictitious
mitygować (mee-ti-go-vach) v.
quiet; appease ;check;restrain
mityng (mee-ting) m. (mass)
meeting ; a gathering of people
mizantrop (mee-zan-trop) m.
misanthrope ; hater of people
mizdrzyć się (meez-dzhich shan)
v. ogle; wheedle ;make eyes

mizerak (mee-zé-rak) m. poor
soul; weakling; poor devil
mizeria (mee-zér-ya) f. cucumber salad; shabby possessions
mizerny (mee-zér-ni) adj. m.
meager; ill-looking; mean;paltry
mknąć (mknównch) v. fleet;rush
mlaskać (mlás-kach)v.lap; smack
mlecz (mlech) m. marrow ;milt
mleczarnia (mle-chár-ña) f.
dairy ; creamery ; milk bar
mleczny (mlech-ni) adj. m. milk;
milky; dairy; lactic;milk-white
mleć (mlech) v. grind; mill
mleko (mlé-ko) n. milk
młocarnia (mwo-tsár-ña) f.
thresher ;threshing-machine
młocka (mwots-ka) f. threshing
młoda (mwo-da) adj. f. young
młode (mwo-de) adj. pl. young
n.pl. the young; litter
młodociany (mwo-do-chá-ni) adj.
m. juvenile; youthful
młodość (mwo-doshch) f. youth
młody (mwo-di) adj. m. young
młodzian (mwo-dżhan) m. young
man ; lad ; youth
młodzieniaszek (mwo-dżhe-ña-
shek) m. sprig; stripling;lad
młodzieniec (mwo-dżhé-ñets) m.
young man ; lad: youth
młodzieńczy (mwo-dżheñ-chi)
adj. m. youthful
młodzież (mwo-dżhesh) f. youth;
young generation
młodzik (mwo-dżheek)m. youngster; teenager; youngling
młokos (mwo-kos) m. kid
młot (mwot) m. sledge; hammer
młotek (mwo-tek) m. hammer;
tack-hammer ;clapper
młócić (mwoo-cheech) v. thrash
młyn (mwin) m. mill; grinder
młynarz (mwi-nash) m. miller
młynek (mwi-nek) m. handgrinder
młyński (mwiñ-skee) adj. m.
mill-; of a mill
mnich (mñeekh) m. monk; friar
mniej (mñey) adv. less; fewer
mniej wiecej (mñey vyań-tsey)
more or less ; about; round
mniejsza o to (mñey-sha o to)
never mind that (exp.)

mniejszość (mñey-shoshch) f.
minority; the lesser part
mniejszy (mñey-shi) adj. m.
smaller; lesser ;less; minor
mniemać (mñe-mach) v. suppose;
deem ; imagine;think; consider
mniemanie (mñe-ma-ñe) n. opinion ;notion;conviction
mniszka (mñeesh-ka) f. nun
mnoga (mno-ga) num. plural
mnogi (mno-gee) adj. m. nume-r-
ous ;-of the plural
mnogość (mno-goshch) f. abundance; plurality; multitude
mnożenie (mno-zhe-ñe) n. multiplication ;increase; breeding
mnożyć (mno-zhich) v. multiply
mnóstwo (mnoos-tvo) n. very
many; multitude; swarm; loads
mobilizacja (mo-bee-lee-zats-
ya) f. mobilization ;call-up
mobilizować (mo-bee-lee-zó-
vach) v. mobilize; call up
moc (mots)f. might; great-
deal; power;vigor;strength
mocarstwo (mo-tsár-stvo) n.
strong country;(world)power
mocarz (mo-tsash) m. strong
man; potentate; powerful man
mocny (mots-ni) adj. m. strong
mocować się (mo-tsó-vach shañ)
v. wrestle; exert oneself
mocz (moch) m. urine
moczar (mo-char) m. bog; marsh
moczopędny (mo-cho-pañd-ni)
adj. m. diuretic
moczowy (mo-chó-vi) adj. m.
uric; urinary; of urine
moczyć (mo-chich) v. wet;
drench; steep; soak;urinate
moda (mo-da) f. fashion
model (mo-del) m. model
modelować (mo-de-ló-vach) v.
model; shape; mold; fashion
modernizować (mo-der-ni-zó-vach)
v. modernize;bring up to date
modlić się (mod-leech shañ) v.
pray; say one's prayers
modlitewnik (mod-lee-tev-ñeek)
m. prayer-book
modlitwa (mod-leet-va) f.
prayer ; grace(at meal time)

modła (mód-wa) f. mold; standard; fashion; model; pattern
modniarka (mod-ńár-ka) f. milliner ; modiste ; hat maker
modny (mód-ni) adj. m. fashionable ; in fashion;in vogue
modry (mód-ri) adj. m. azure-
blue ; deep blue:cerulean blue
modrzew (mód-zhev) m. larch
modulacja (mo-doo-láts-ya) f.
modulation ;inflection
modulować (mo-doo-ló-vach) v.
modulate ; inflect; regulate
modyfikacja (mo-di-fee-káts-ya)
f. modification ; alteration
modyfikować (mo-di-fee-kó-vach)
v. modify ; alter; qualify
modystka (mo-dist-ka) f. modiste ; milliner; hat maker
mogący (mo-gówn-tsi) adj. m.
able; capable ; competent
mogiła (mo-gee-wa) f. tomb
mojżeszowy (moy-zhe-shó-vi)
adj. m. Mosaic : of Moses
mokka (mók-ka) f. natural coffee :,mocha: Mocha coffee
moknąć (mók-nownch) v. get wet;
get soaked, drenched:be soaked
mokradło (mo-krád-wo) n. bog
mokry (mók-ri) adj. m. wet;
moist ; watery;rainy; sweaty
molekularny (mo-le-koo-lár-ni)
adj. m. molecular; of molecule
molekuła (mo-le-koó-wa) f. molecule ; smallest particle
molestować (mo-les-tó-vach) v.
molest; annoy; vex; trouble
molo (mó-lo) n. pier; mole;
jetty; breakwater ; quay
moment (mo-ment) m. moment
momentalny (mo-men-tál-ni) adj.
m. instantaneous ;immediate
monarcha (mo-nár-kha) m. monarch ; sovereign: king
monarchista (mo-nar-khees-ta)
m. monarchist; royalist
moneta (mo-né-ta) f. coin ;chink
moneta brzecząca (mo-né-ta
bzhań-chówn-tsa) cash;coins
mongolski (mon-gól-skee) adj. m.
Mongol : of Mongolia
monitor (mo-ńee-tor) m. monitor

monitować (mo-ńee-tó-wach) v.
admonish; monitor : check on
monogram (mo-nó-gram) m. monogram; initials in a design
monokl (mo-nokl) m. eye-glass
monolog (mo-nó-log) m. mono-
logue; soliloquy of one actor
monopol (mo-nó-pol), m. monopoly
monoteizm (mo-no-té-eezm) m.
monotheism; belief in one god
monotonia (mo-no-tóń-ya) f. monotony ; sameness : no variety
monotonny (mo-no-tón-ni) adj.
m. monotonous ;drab; dull
monstrualny (mon-stroo-ál-ni)
adj. m. monstrous ; horrible
monstrum (mon-stroom) n. monster ; monstrosity
montaż (món-tazh) m. mounting;
assembling;installation; set-up
monter (món-ter), m. installator
montować (mon-tó-vach) v. in-
stall; put together; put up
monumentalny (mo-noo-men-tál-
ni) adj. m. monumental
mops (mops) m. pug-dog
moralizator (mo-ra-lee-zá-tor)
m. moralizer
moralizować (mo-ra-lee-zó-vach)
v. moralize ; discuss morality
moralność (mo-rál-noshch) f.
morals; morality; ethics
moralny (mo-rál-ni) adj. m.
moral; ethical:of good conduct
morał (mó-raw) m. moral lesson
moratorium (mo-ra-tór-yoom) n.
moratorium; legalized delay
mord (mord) m. murder; slaughter
morda (mór-da) f. snout; muzzle;
vulg: mug; kisser; puss; phiz
morderca (mor-dér-tsa) m. murderer; assassin;cutthroat
morderczy (mor-dér-chi) adj. m.
murderous ; cutthroat; deadly
morderstwo (mor-dér-stvo) n.
murder; assassination
mordęga (mor-dań-ga) f. toil;
drudge; moil;fag; strain
mordować (mor-do-vach) v. kill;
torment;harass;toil;sweat;worry
mordować się (mor-do-vach shań)
v. toil; kill oneself with work

morela (mo-ré-la) f. apricot

morena (mo-ré-na) f. moraine

morfina (mor-fée-na) f. morphine (derivative of opium)

morfologia (mor-fo-lóg-ya) f. morphology: science of forms

morga (mór-ga) f. acre

morowy (mo-ró-vi) adj. m. pestilential; clever; good buddy; fine fellow; first-rate

mors (mors) m. walrus

morska choroba (mors-ka kho-ró-ba) seasickness; dizziness

morski (mórs-kee) adj. m. maritime; sea; nautical; naval

morwa (mór-va) f. mulberry

morze (mozhe) n. sea ; ocean

morzyć (mo-zhich) v. starve

mosiądz (mo-shownts) m. brass

moskit (mos-keet) m. mosquito

most (most) m. bridge

mościć (mosh-cheech) v. pad (nest); make a bed of straw

motać (mo-tach)v. reel; embroil; entangle; intrigue; spool

motek (mo-tek) m. reel ; ball

motłoch (mot-wokh) m. mob

motocykl (mo-to-tsikl) m. motorcycle (a two-wheeled vehicle)

motor (mo-tor) m. motor

motorówka (mo-to-róov-ka) f. motorboat

motoryzacja (mo-to-ri-záts-ya) f. motorization;mechanization

motoryzować (mo-to-ri-zo-vach) v. motorize; mechanize

motyka (mo-ti-ka) f. hoe

motyl (mo-til) m. butterfly

motyw (mó-tiv) m. motif; motive

motywować (mo-ti-vó-vach) v. give reasons; explain;justify

mowa (mo-va) f. speech; language

mozaika (mo-záy-ka) f. mosaic

mozolić (mo-zo-leech) v. toil; take pains; exert oneself

mozolny (mo-zol-ni) adj. m. toilsome;;strenuous arduous

mozół (mo-zoow) m. exertion

moździerz (mozh-dzhesh) m. mortar ; mine thrower

może (mo-zhe) adv. perhaps; maybe; very likely; how about?

możliwość (mozh-lee-voshch) f. possibility; chance; contigency

możliwości (mozh-lee-vosh-chee) pl. scope ;vistas; capabilities

możliwy (mozh-lee-vi) adj. possible ; fairly good; passable

można (mozh-na) v. imp. it is possible; one may; one can

możność (mozh-noshch) f. power; freedom to; free choice to

możny (mózh-ni) adj. m. potent; powerful; mighty

móc (moots) v. (potentially) to be able ; be capable

mój (mooy) pron. my; mine

mól (mool) m. moth

mól książkowy (mool kshoownzh-kó-vi) bookworm

mór (moor) m. pestilence; epidemic ;plague ; pest

mórg (moorg) m. acre

mówca (moóv-tsa) m. speaker

mówić (moo-veech) v. speak; talk; say; tell ;say things

mównica (moov-nee-tsa) f. (pulpit); speaker's platform

mózg (moozk) m. brain

mózgowy (mooz-gó-vi) adj. m. cerebral ; of the brain

mroczny (mroch-ni) adj. m. dusky; gloomy ;obscure;dark

mrok (mrok) m. dusk; twilight

mrowić się (mró-veech shán) v. swarm ; teem; be alive

mrowie (mróv-ye) n. swarm; tingle ;gooseflesh;creeps

mrowisko (mro-vées-ko) n. anthill ; ants'nest

mrozić (mro-zheech) v. freeze; congeal; refrig erate ; chill

mroźny (mróźh-ni) adj. m.frosty; icy ; freezing

mrówka (mroov-ka) f. ant :emmet

mróz (mroos) m. frost ;the cold

mruczeć (mroo-chech) v. mumble; mutter ; purr; murmur; grumble

mrugać (mroo-gach) v. twinkle; blink; wink ; flicker; flinch

mruk (mrook) m. mumbler; grumbler; man of few words;growler

mrukliwy (mrook-lee-vi) adj. m. mumbling; sulky; gruff;taciturn

mrużyć (mroo-zhich) v. blink;
wink ; squint; half-shut(eyes)
mrzonka (mzhon-ka) f. illusion
msza (msha) f. mass (in church)
mszalny (mshál-ni) adj. m. for
mass; of mass (in the church)
mszał (mshaw) m. missal
mściciel (mshchee-chel) m.
avenger ; retaliator
mścić (mshcheech) v. avenge
mściwy (mshchee-vi) adj. m.
vindictive; vengeful
mszczenie (mshche-ñe) n. vengeance ; retaliation
mszyca (mshi-tsa) f. mite
mszysty (mshis-ti) adj. m. mossy
mucha (moo-kha) f. fly
mufka (moof-ka) f. muff
mularz (moo-lash) m. mason
mulat (moo-lat) m. mulatto
mulisty (moo-lees-ty) adj. m.
muddy; oozy; slimy ; sludgy
muł (moow) m. ooze; slime
muł (moow) m. mule
mumia (moom-ya) f. mummy
mundur (moon-door) m. uniform
municypalny (moo-ñee-tsi-pál-ni)
adj. m. municipal
munsztuk (moon-shtook) m. (bridle) bit; mouthpiece
mur (moor) m. brick wall
murarz (moo-rash) m. bricklayer
murawa (moo-rá-va) f. lawn
murować (moo-ró-vach) v. lay-
bricks ; build in brick(in stone)
murowany (moo-ro-vá-ni) adj. m.
of bricks; of stone : certain
murzyn (moo-zhin) m. negro
mus 1, (moos) m. necessity; compulsion ; constraint
mus 2., (moos) m. froth ;mousse
musieć (moo-shech) v. be obliged
to; have to ;be forced; must
muskać (moos-kach) v. touch
lightly ; skim; stroke
muskularny (moos-koo-lár-ni) adj.
m. muscular ; strong;hefty;beefy
muskuł (moos-koow) m. muscle
musować (moo-só-vach) v. foam;
froth ; bubble; fizz; sparkle
muszka (moosh-ka) f. fly; gun-
bead; face skin-spot ;bow-tie;
midge; dry-fly; patch (on skin)

muszkat (moosh-kat) m. nutmeg
muszkiet (moosh-ket) m. musket ; smooth bore firearm
muszla (moosh-la) f. shell;conch
musztarda (moosh-tár-da) f.
mustard seasoning
musztra (moosh-tra) f. (drill)
training; exercise
muślin (moosh-leen) m. muslin
mutacja (moo-táts-ya) f. muta-
tion; change; variation
muterka (moo-ter-ka) f. (bolt)
nut; female screw
muza (moo-za) f. Muse
muzealny (moo-ze-ál-ni) adj. m.
of museum
muzeum (moo-ze-oom) n. museum
muzułmanin (moo-zoow-ma-ñeen)
m. Moslem (Mussulman)
muzyczny (moo-zich-ni) adj. m.
musical: set to music
muzyk (moo-zik) m. musician
muzyka (moo-zi-ka) f. music
muzykalność (moo-zi-kál-noshch)
f. ear for music
muzykalny (moo-zi-kál-ni) adj.
m. having ear for music
muzykant (moo-zí-kant) m. low
class musician : bandsman
my (mi) pron. we ; us
myć (mich) v. wash
mycka (mits-ka) f. skull-cap
mydlarnia (mid-lár-ña) f. soap-
store; soap-works; perfumery
mydlarstwo (mid-lár-stvo) n.
soap-making; soap-boiling
mydlarz (mid-lash) m. soap-maker
mydlić (mid-leech) v. soap;
froth; dress someone down
mydlić oczy (mid-leech o-chi) v.
pull wool over eyes
mydliny (mid-lee-ni) pl. soap-
suds; lather
mydło (mid-wo) n. soap; soft soap
mylić (mi-leech) v. mislead;
misguide;confuse; deceive
mylny (mil-ni) adj. m. wrong
mysz (mish) f. mouse
myszkować (mish-kó-vach) v.
covertly explore; trace scent
myśl (mishl) f. thought; idea
myślący (mish-lówn-tsi) adj. m.
thoughtful; reflective

myśleć (mish-lech) v. think
myśliciel (mish-lee-chel) m.
  thinker;one who thinks a lot
myśliwiec (mish-leev-yets) m.
  fighter plane: fighter pilot
myśliwy (mish-lee-vi) m. hunter
myślnik (mishl-ñeek) m. dash
  (mark); hyphen
myślowy (mish-lo-vi) adj. m.
  mental; reflective; intellectual
myto (mi-to) n. toll; tollgate
mżyć (mzhich) v. drizzle
na (na) prep. on; upon; at;
  for; by; in;
  NOTE: verbs with prefix na
  NOT INCLUDED HERE: CHECK WITH-
  OUT THE PREFIX na
nabawić się (na-ba-veech shañ)
  v. bring upon oneself; incur
nabawić strachu (na-ba-veech
  stra-khoo)v.frighten
nabiał (na-byaw) m. dairy
  products including eggs
nabiegać się (na-bye-gach shañ)v.
  have run a lot; exert oneself
nabić (na-beech) v. load weapon;
  beat up(somebody); whack
nabiegły krwią (na-byeg-wi
  krvyown) adj.m. bloodshot
nabierać (na-bye-rach) v. take;
  take in; tease; cheat; amass
nabijać (na-bee-yach) v. stud;
  (repeatedly) load gun
nabijać się (na-bee-yach shañ)
  v. make fun of (somebody)
nabożeństwo (na-bo-zheñ-stvo)
  n. church service
nabożny (na-bozh-ni) adj. m.
  pious; religious; godly;devoutly
nabrać (na-brach) v. take; take
  in; tease; cheat; gather;swell
nabój (na-booy) m. charge; car-
  trige; round of ammunition
nabrzeże (na-bzhe-zhe) n. wharf;
  embankment; landing-pier
nabrzmiały (na-bzhmya-wi) adj.
  m. swollen : distended
nabytek (na-bi-tek) m. acquisition; purchase;new recruit
nabrzmiewać (na-bzhmye-vach) v.
  swell ;plump up; plump out
nabywać (na-bi-vach) v. acquire;
  obtain; gain ; buy; purchase

nabywca (na-biv-tsa) m. buyer
nacechowany (na-tse-kho-va-ni)
  adj. m. marked; characterized
nachodzić (na-kho-dzheech)v.
  intrude; (abstr.) haunt
nachylać (na-khi-lach) v. stoop;
  bend; incline; lean;tilt;slant
nachylenie (na-khi-le-ñe) n.tilt
  slope; inclination;batter;slant
nacięcie (na-chan-che) n. incision; notch; cut :nick:score
naciągać (na-chown-gach) v.
  streach; draw; strain; pull
  one's leg;take sb in; infuse
naciek (na-chek) m. infiltration; leak ; swelling
nacierać (na-che-rach) v. rub;
  attack; harass ; demand
nacinać (na-chee-nach) v. notch;
  cut; score; nick;hoax;dupe
nacisk (na-cheesk) m. pressure;
  stress; accent;thrust; push
naciskać (na-chees-kach) v.
  press; urge ;bear on; push
nacjonalista (na-tsyo-na-lees-
  ta) m. nationalist
nacjonalizacja (na-tsyo-na-lee-
  záts-ya) f. nationalization
nacjonalizm (na-tsyo-na-leezm)
  m. nationalism
nacjonalizować (na-tsyo-na-lee-
  zó-vach) v. nationalize
naczekać się (na-che-kach shañ)
  v. wait too long:tire of waiting
na czczo (na chcho) adv. on an
  empty stomach; unfed; fasting
naczelnik (na-chel-ñeek) m.
  manager; chief; head; master
naczelny (na-chel-ni) adj. m.
  chief; head; paramount; primate; principal;main;paramount
naczerpać (na-cher-pach) v.
  dip up; draw (fluid);scoop up
naczynie (na-chi-ñe) n. vessel
nad (nad) prep. over; above; on
  upon; beyond; at; of;for
nadajnik (na-day-ñeek) m.
  transmitter: feeder
nadal (na-dal) adv. still; in
  future; continue (to do)
nadaremnie (na-da-rém-ñe) adv.
  in vain; unsuccessfully; to no
  purpose; without result

nadaremny (na-da-rém-ni) adj.
m. fruitless; vain;unsuccessful
nadarzać się (na-da-zhać śhǎn)
v. happen; occur; turn up
nadawać (na-da-vać) v. confer
bestow ;grant; endow; christen
nadawca (na-dáv-tsa) m. sender
nadąć (na-dównch) v., puff up
nadąsany (na-dówn-sá-ni) adj.
m. sulky; sullen; stuffy
nadążać (na-dówn-zhać) v. keep
up with; cope with :keęp pace
nadbałtycki (nad-baw-tits-kee)
adj. m. on the Baltic ;Baltic
nadbiec (nád-byets) v. come
running up; hasten up :run up
nadbrzeże (nad-bzhé-zhe) n.
shore; coast; littoral
nadbrzeżny (nad-bzhézh-ni) adj.
m. coastal; sea-shore
nadbudowa (nad-boo-dó-va) f.
superstrycture :added floor
nadbudować (nad-boo-do-vać)
v. build on ;add an upper floor
nadchodzić (nad-khó-dźheećh)v.
approach; arrive; come
nadciągać (nad-ćhówn-gać) v.
draw near; be nearing; come
nadciśnienie (nad-ćheeśh-ńé-ńe)
n. excess pressure;hypertension
nadczłowiek (nad-chwó-vyek) m.
superman; superhuman man
nadejście (na-déy-śhche) v.
coming; arrival; oncoming
nadepnąć (na-dep-nównch) v.
step on ;, tread on (crushing)
nader (na-der) adv. greatly;
excessively; highly; most
nadesłać (na-de-swach) v. send
in; forward; remit
nade wszystko (na-de vshist-ko)
adv. above all (else)
nadęty (nad-ắn-ti) adj. m.
puffed up; inflated; superior
nadgraniczny (nad-gra-ńeéch-ni)
adj. m. near-border;frontier-
nadjechać (nad-yé-khać) v.
drive up; come up; arrive
nadlecieć (nad-lé-ćhech) v. fly
in; arrive in a hurry
nadleśniczy (nad-leśh-ńee-chi)
m. chief ranger; forest inspector: head of rangers

nadliczbowy (nad-leech-bó-vi)
adj. m. overtime; additional
nadludzki (nad-loodz-ki) adj.
m. superhuman ; divine
nadmiar (nád-myar) m. excess
nadłamać (nad-wá-mać) v. break
slightly; cause a slight break
nadmienić (nad-myé-ńeech) v.
mention ; allude;hint; add
nadmierny (nad-myér-ni) adj.
m. excessive; extravagant;undue
nadmorski (nad-mor-skee) adj.
m. seaside-;maritime
nadmuchać (na-dmoo-khać) v.
inflate; blow up with air
nadobny (na-dób-ny) adj. m.
handsome; comely; pretty
nadobowiązkowy (nad-o-bo-vyównz-
kó-vi) adj. m. optional
na dół (na doow) down; down
stairs; downwards
nadpić (nád-peech) v. take a
sip; start overfilled drink
nadpłynąć (nad-pwi-nównch) v.
sail in; swim in; arrive
nadprodukcja (nad-pro-dook-
tsya) f. excess production
nadprogramowy (nad-pro-gra-mo-
vi) adj. m. extra; additional
nadprzyrodzony (nad-pzhy-ro-dzó-
ni) adj. m. supernatural
nadpsuty (nad-psó-ti) adj. m.
partly spoiled; impaired
nadrabiać (nad-ráb-yach) v.
catch up with; make up; work
ahead of schedule:compensate for
nadruk (na-drook) m. overprint
nadrzędny (nad-zhánd-ni) adj.
m. superior; primary;precedent
nadskakiwać (nad-ska-kee-vać)
v. try to ingratiate oneself
nadsłuchiwać (nad-swoo-khee-
vać) v. strain to listen
nadspodziewany (nad-spo-dżhe-vá-
ni) adj. m. unexpected
nadstawiać (nad-stáv-yach) v.
expose; risk; hold out; cock
nadto (nád-to) adv. moreover;
besides; too much; too many
nadużycie (nad-oo-zhi-che) n.
abuse; excess; misuse
nadużywać (nad-oo-zhi-vać) v.
abuse; take advantage ;strain

nadwaga (nad-vá-ga) f. overweight;allowed extra weight
nadwartość (nad-vár-tośhćh) f.
overvalue in economics
nadwątlić (nad-vównt-leećh) v.
weaken; impair; damage
nadwiślański (nad-veeśh-láń-
skee) adj. m. on the Vistula
nadwodny (nad-vód-ni) adj. m.
near water; riverside; aquatic
nadwozie (nad-vó-zhe) m. car-
body; body of a car or truck
nadwyrężać (nad-vi-rán-zhać)
v. impair; strain; weaken
nadwyżka (nad-vízh-ka) f. surplus; excess amount
nadymać (na-di-mać) v. puff up
nadymić (na-dí-meeć) v. fill
with smoke;make a lot of smoke
nadzieja (na-dźhe-ya) f. hope
nadziemski (nad-żhém-skee) adj.
m. celestial; heavenly;divine
nadzienie (na-dźhe-ńe) n.
stuffing ; filling; forcemeat
nadziewać (na-dźhe-vać) v.
stuff;pierce with;put on; fill
nadzorca (nad-zór-tsa) m. overseer; superintendent;supervisor
nadzór (nád-zoor) m. supervision
nadzwyczaj (nad-zvi-chay) adv.
unusually; extremely; most
nadzwyczajny (nad-zvi-cháy-ni)
adj. m. extraordinary; extreme
nafta (náf-ta) f. petroleum
naftalina (naf-ta-lée-na) f,
naphthalene; naphthaline
nagabywać (na-ga-bi-vać) v.
annoy; accost; trouble;molest
nagana (na-gá-na) f. blame
nagi (na-gi) adj. m. naked;
bare ; nude; bald; empty
naginać (na-gee-nać) v. bend
down; submit to; adapt; bow
nagle (nág-le) adv. suddenly
naglić (nág-leećh) v. urge
nagłość (nág-wośhćh) f. urgency
nagłówek (na-gwoo-vek) m. heading; caption; title; headline
nagły (nág-wi) adj. m. sudden;
urgent;instant;abrupt; pressing
nagminny (na-gmeen-ni) adj. m.
universal;usual;current;general

nagniotek (na-gńó-tek) m.
(skin) corn; callus on the skin
nagonka (na-gón-ka) f. campaign
against; hue and cry against
nagosc (ná-gośhćh) f. nudity
nagradzać (na-grá-dzaćh) v.
reward; give prize;recompense
nagrobek (na-gró-bek) m. tomb
nagroda (na-gró-da) f. reward
nagrodzić (na-gró-dźheećh)v.
reward; requite; recompense
nagromadzić (na-gro-má-dźheećh)
v. accumulate; amass; heap up
nagrzewać (na-gzhé-vać) v.
warm up ; heat up; preheat
naigrawać (na-ee-gra-vać) v.
mock; scoff; deride;ridicule
naiwny (na-eev-ni) adj. m. naive
najazd (ná-yazt) m. invasion
najbardziej (nay-bár-dźhey)
adv. most(of all)
najechać (na-yé-khać)v.overrun;
invade; run into;ram; crowd
najedzony (na-ye-dzó-ni) adj.
m. full (of food); satiated
najem (ná-yem) m. hire
najemnik (na-yém-ńeek) m.
hireling; mercenary;free lance;
soldier of fortune;wage earner
najemny (na-yém-ni) adj. m.venal;
mercenary; hired labor
najeść się (ná-yeśhćh śháń) v.
eat plenty of; eat a lot
najeźdźca (na-yeźhdźh-tsa) m.
invader; assailant; violator
najeżdżać (na-yezh-dzhać) v.
invade; run into; attack; ram
najeżony (na-ye-zhó-ni) adj. m.
bristling; bristly ; beset
najgorszy (nay-gor-shi) adj. m.
worst; the worst of all
najgorzej (nay-go-zhey) adv.
worst of all : worst possible
najlepiej (nay-lép-yey) adv.
best ; best of all
najlepszy (nay-lép-shi) adj. m.
best; best of all; best possible
najmniej (náy-mńey) adv. least
najmniejszy (nay-mńéy-shi) adj.
m. least; smallest; least of all
najmować (nay-mó-vać) v. rent;
hire; engage; lease

najpierw (náy-pyerv) adv. first
of all ;in the first place
najscie (náysh-che) n. intrusion; inroad; invasion;incursion
najsc (nayshch) v. intrude
najwięcej (nay-vyan-tsey) adv.
most of all (worst of all)
najwiekszy (nay-vyank-shi) adj.
m. biggest; largest; extreme
najwyzej (nay-vi-zhey) adv.
highest; at the very most
najwyzszy (nay-vizh-shi) adj.
m. highest; top; utmost
nakarmic (na-kár-meech) v. feed
nakaz (ná-kas) m. order ;writ
nakazywac (na-ka-zi-vach) v.
order; demand; command
nakleic (na-klé-eech) v. stick
on ; paste up; mount; post
nakład (ná-kwad) m. outlay
nakładac (na-kwa-dach) v. lay
on; put on; place; set;spread
nakładca (na-kwad-tsa) m. publisher (of printed work)
nakłaniac (na-kwa-nach) v. persuade ;induce; bring;get;urge
na koniec (na kó-nets) adv.
finally ; at the end
nakreslac (na-krésh-lach) v.
delineate ; sketch;draft;write
nakręcac (na-kran-tsach) v. wind
up; shoot (movie);turn ;direct
nakrętka (na-kránt-ka) f.(screw)
nut; female screw; jam nut
nakrycie (na-kri-che) n. cover
nakrywac (na-kri-vach) v. cover
nakrywka (na-kriv-ka) f. lid
na kształt (na kshtawt) in form
of...;in shape of; a kind of...
nalac (ná-lach) v. pour in; pour
on (liquid only,no sand etc.)
nalegac (na-lé-gach) v. insist
naleganie (na-le-gá-ne) n. in-
sistence ; urgent demand
nalepiac (na-lép-yach) v. stick
on; paste on; mount; glue on
nalepka (na-lép-ka) f. label
naleśnik (na-lésh-neek) m. pancake wrap around stuffing
nalewac (na-le-vach) v. pour in
należec (na-lé-zhech) v. belong
należnosc (na-lézh-noshch) f.
due; ration ; charge; fee

należny (na-lézh-ni) adj. m.
due. owing; rightful; proper
należycie (na-le-zhi-che) adv.
properly; duly; suitably
należyty (na-le-zhi-ti) adj.
m. proper; right; appropriate
nalot (na-lot) m. air raid;
(skin) rush ; coating
naładowac (na-wa-do-vach) v.
load; charge; cram
nałogowiec (na-wo-go-vyets) m.
addict; chain-smoker
nałogowy (na-wo-gó-vi) adj. m.
addicted ; inveterate;habitual
nałogowy pijak (na-wo-gó-vi
pee-yak) alcoholic
nałog (ná-woog) m. addiction
namacalny (na-ma-tsál-ni) adj.
m. tangible; substantial
namaszczac (na-mash-chach)v.
anoint ; grease; smear
namaszczenie (na-mash-che-ne)
n. unction ;anointing
namawiac (na-máv-yach) v.
persuade ; prompt; urge;egg on
namazac (na-ma-zach) v. daub-
over; anoint ; scrawl(scribble)
namiastka (na-myást-ka) f.
substitute; ersatz; stopgap
namiernik (na-myér-neek) m.
direction finder; pelorus
namiestnik (na-myest-neek) m.
regent; governor; viceroy
namiętnosc (na-myánt-noshch) f.
passion ; infatuation; fervor
namiętny (na-myánt-ni) adj. m.
passionate ; keen; ardent;lusty
namiot (ná-myot) m. tent
namoczyc (na-mo-chich) v. wet;
soak ; soak; steep; drench
namoknąc (na-mok-nownch) v. get
soaked ; become saturated
namowa (na-mó-va) f. persuasion
namulic (na-moo-leech) v. slime
up ; silt up; mud up; ooze up
namydlic (na-míd-leech) v.
soap up ; put soap lather on
namysł (ná-misw) m. reflection
namyslac się(na-mish-lach chan)v.
ponder; reflect ; think over
nanosic (na-nó-sheech) v.bring;
deposit; plot; track (mud)
na nowo (na nó-vo) adv. anew

naocznie (na-och-ńe) adv. by
eye; visually ; clearly
naoczny świadek (na-och-ni
shvya-dek) eyewitness; bystander
na odwrót (na od-vroot) adv.
inversely; the other way round
na ogół (na o-goow) adv. (in
general) generally; on the whole
na około (na o-ko-wo) adv. all
around; about; right round
naokoło (na-o-ko-wo) prep. round
naonczas (na-on-chas) adv. at
that time; then; in those days
naoliwić (na-o-lee-veech) v. oil;
lubricate ; grease; make slippery
na opak (na o-pak) adv. backward; perversely; the wrong way
na ostatek (na o-sta-tek) adv.
finally; in the end; at last
naostrzyć (na-os-tzhich) v.
sharpen up ; become sharp
na oścież (na osh-chesh) adv.
wide open; opened all the way
na oślep (na osh-lep) adv. blind-
ly; full tilt; headlong
na ówczas (na oov-chas) adv. at
that time ; then; in those days
napad (na-pad) m. assault; attempt
napadać (na-pa-dach) v. assail
napar (na-par) m. infusion;
brew ; a beverage brewed
naparstek (na-par-stek) m. thimble; dram; thimble full
naparzyć (na-pa-zhich) v. infuse
napaskudzić (na-pas-koo-dżeech)
v. soil up; make a mess; dirty
napastliwy (na-past-lee-vi) adj.
m. aggressive ; malicious; bitter
napastnik (na-past-ńeek) m. aggressor; forward center (sport)
napastować (na-pas-to-vach) v.
pester; attack; wax; molest; worry
napaść (na-pashch) f. assault
napawać (na-pa-vach) v. fill up
(with feelings ; panic, wander)
napatrzyć się (na-pat-shich shán)
v, see enough ; have a good look
napełniać (na-pew-nach) v. fill
up ; inspire; imbue; pervade
napewno (na-pev-no) adv. surely;
certainly; for sure ; without fail
napęd (na-pand) m. propulsion;
drive; force; driving gear

napędowy (na-pan-do-vi) adj.
m. motive; driving; impulsive
napędzać (na-pan-dzach) v. chase
in; propel ; round up; drift in
napić się (na-peech shán) v.
have a drink ; quench one's thirst
napierać (na-pye-rach) v. press
forward; insist, ; advance
napięcie (na-pyan-che) n. tension; strain; voltage; intensity
napiętek (na-pyan-tek) m. heel
napiętnować (na-pyant-no-vach)
v. brand; stigmatize; censure
condemn as being very bad; stamp
napięty (na-pyan-ty) adj. m.
tense; taut; strained; tight
napinać (na-pee-nach) v. strain
napis (na-pees) m. inscription
napitek (na-pee-tek) m. drink
napiwek (na-pee-vek) m. tip
napluć (na-plooch) v. spit on
napływ (na-pwiv) m. influx
napływać (na-pwi-vach) v. inflow; flow in; flock; pour in
napływowy (na-pwi-vo-vi) adj.
m. alluvial; immigrant; allien
napoczynać (na-po-chi-nach) v.
start up; open; broach
napominać (na-po-mee-nach) v.
admonish; reprimand: rebuke
napomknąć (na-pom-knownch) v.
mention; hint at; allude to
napomnienie (na-pom-ńe-ńe) n.
admonition; reprimand; rebuke
na pomoc ! (na po-mots) excl;
help ! give help! please, help!
napotny (na-pot-ni) adj. m.
sudatory ; perspiratory
napotykać (na-po-ti-kach) v.
run in; come across; be faced with
napowietrzny (na-po-vyetzh-ni)
adj. m. aerial; overhead
na powrót (na pov-root) adv.
return; again; on the way back
na pozór (na po-zoor) adv. apparently; on the face of it
napój (na-pooy) m. drink
na pół (na poow) adv. in half
napór (na-poor) m. pressure
naprawa (na-pra-va) f. repair;
redress: renovation; reform
naprawdę (na-prav-dán) adv. indeed; really; truly; positively

naprawiać (na-praw-yach) v. repair: fix; mend; rectify:reform
naprędce (na-pránd-tse) adv.
hastily: in a hurry;slapdash
naprężenie (na-prăn-zhe-ńe) n.
tension; strain; tautness
naprężyć (na-prăn-zhich) v.
tauten; stretch;strain
naprowadzać (na-pro-vá-dzach)
v. lead in; direct to:advise
na próżno (na proozh-no) adv.
in vain: uselessly;to no avail
naprzeciw (na-pzhe-cheev) adv.
opposite: vis-a-vis
naprzec (na-pzhech) v. press;
urge : press hard;;insist on
na przekór (na pzhe-koor) adv.
in despite: just to spite
na przełaj (na pzhe-way) adv.
shortcut (across obstacles)
na przemian (na pzhe-myan) adv.
alternately : by turns
naprzód (na-pzhoot) adv. forwards;first;in the first place
na przykład (na pzhik-wat) adv.
for instance; for example
naprzykrzac się(na-pshik-shach
śhăń)v bother;molest:pester
napuchnąć (na-pookh-nowńch)v.
swell ; become swollen
napuchły (na-pookh-wi) adj. m.
swollen ;bulging; distended
napuścić (na-poosh-cheech) v.
set up ; impregnate; let in
napuszony (na-poo-sho-ni) adj.
m. puffed up; bristling;ruffled
napychać (na-pi-khach) v. stuff;
cram ;cram:fill;pack:crowd,stow
narada (na-rá-da) f. consultation ; council; conference
naradzać się (na-rá-dzach śhăń)v.
consult; confer with:deliberate
naramiennik (na-ra-myeń-ńeek)
m. epaulet; shoulder-strap
narastać (na-rás-tach) v. grow
on :increase; accumulate:accrue
naraz (ná-ras) adv. suddenly
na razie (na rá-źhe) adv. for
the time being ;for the present
narażać (na-rá-zhach) v. expose
to endanger
narciarstwo (nar-chár-stvo) n.
skiing

narciarz (nár-chash) m. skier
narcyz (nár-tsis) m. narcissus
nareszcie (na-résh-che) adv.
at last : finally;at long last
naręcze (na-rań-che) n. armful
narkotyczny (nar-ko-tich-ni)
adj. m. narcotic :causing numbness
narkotyk (nar-kó-tik) m.narcot-
ic :drug for sleep and relief
narkoza (nar-kó-za) f. anesthe-
sia ; anaesthetization
narobić (na-ró-beech) v.mess up;
cause nuisance; make a mess
narodowość (na-ro-dó-vośhch) f.
nationality :national status
narodowy (na-ro-dó-vi) adj. m.
national;of national character
narodzenie (na-ro-dzé-ńe) n.
birth; a being born;the beginning
narodzić się (na-ró-dźheech śhăń)
v. be born; originate; arise
narodziny (na-ro-dźhee-ni)n.
birth; origin; the beginning
narosł (ná-roshl) f. tumor;
growth;excrescence; wart;knar
narowisty (na-ro-vees-ti) adj.
m. restive;vicious:skittish
narożnik (na-rózh-ńeek) m. corner;angle; cross-roads:gusset
narożny (na-rózh-ni) adj. m.
corner-; at the street corner
naród (ná-root) m. nation;people
narów (ná-roof) m. vice (res-
tivness); bad habit; fault
narta (nár-ta) f. ski; sleigh
naruszać (na-roo-shach) v. disturb; violate; injure; harm
naruszenie (na-roo-shé-ńe) n.
offense; disturbance; breach
narwany (na-rvá-ni) adj. m.
hot-head; reckless; rash
narybek (na-ri-bek) m. small
fry; coming generation
narząd (na-zhownt) m. organ
narzecze (na-zhe-che) n. (primitive)dialect
narzeczona (na-zhe-chó-na) f.
fiancée: an engaged woman
narzeczony (na-zhe-chó-ni) m.
fiance
narzekać (na-zhe-kach) v. complain: grumble: lament

narzekanie (na-zhe-ká-ñe) n.
 complaints;kick: bitching
narzędzie (na-zhán-dźhe) n.
 tool; utensil; implement
narzucać (na-zhoo-tsaćh) v.
 throw over; impose;shovel on
nasada (na-sá-da) f. base
nasenna pigułka (na-sén-na pi-
 goów-ka) sleeping-pill
nasiadówka (na-śha-doóv-ka) f.
 sitzbath; hip-bath
nasiąkać (na-shoun-kaćh) v.
 soak up;become saturated;imbibe
nasienie (na-śhe-ñe) m. seed;
 sperm; semen: posterity
nasilenie (na-śhee-le-ñe) n.
 intensification; intensity
naskórek (na-skoó-rek) m. outer
 skin; epidermis; cuticle
naskarżyć (na-skár-zhićh) v.
 denounce; lodge a complain
nasłuchać się (na-swoo-khaćh
 śhán) v. hear plenty
nasłuchiwać (na-swoo-khee-vaćh)
 v. monitor (radio);listen
nasmarować (na-sma-ro-vaćh) v.
 smear over: grease; lubricate
nastać (ná-staćh) v. set in;
 enter; occur; come about
nastanie (na-stá-ñe) n. arrival;
 setting-in; advent; coming
nastarczyć (na-stár-chićh) v.
 supply enough; keep pace; cope
nastawać (na-stá-vaćh) v. insist
nastawiać (na-stáv-yaćh) v. set
 up; set right; tune in; point
nastawienie (na-sta-vyé-ñe) n.
 attitude; bias; disposition
następca (na-stánp-tsa) m. successor ; heir
następnie (na-stanp-ñe) adv.
 next; then; subsequently
następny (na-stánp-ni) adj. m.
 next; the next: the following
następować (na-stáñ-po-vaćh) v.
 follow; tread; come after:ensue
następstwo (na-stánp-stvo) n.
 result; succession; upshot
następujący (na-stáñ-poo-yoẃn-
 tsi) adj. m. successive; following; the following
nastraszyć (na-stra-shićh) v.
 frighten; intimidate

nastręczać (na-strán-chaćh) v.
 afford; present; offer; procure
nastroić (na-stró-eećh) v. at-
 tune; tune up ; dispose to
nastroszyć (na-stró-shićh) v.
 bristle up; perk up; heap up
nastrój (ná-strooy) m. mood
nasturcja (na-stoor-tsya) f.
 nasturtia ; lark-heel
nasuwać (na-soó-vaćh) v. shove
 up ; draw over: afford;overthrust
nasycać (na-si-tsaćh) v. satiate; satisfy ; sate; saturate
nasycenie (na-si-tsé-ñe) n. sa-
 tiation; saturation :satisfaction
nasycony (na-si-tsó-ni) adj. m.
 satiate; saturated ; replete
nasyłać (na-sí-waćh) v. send on
nasyp (ná-sip) m. embankment
nasypać (na-sí-paćh) v. pour in;
 spread up (dry powder etc)
nasz (nash) pron. our; ours
naszyć (na-shićh) v. sew on;
 trim with; trim
naszkicować (na-shkee-tsó-vaćh)
 v. sketch ; make a sketch
naszyjnik (na-shiy-ñeek) m.
 necklace ; neck jewelry
naśladować (na-śhla-dó-vaćh) v.
 imitate ; mimic; reproduce
naśladowanie (na-śhla-do-vá-ñe)
 n. imitation; copy
naśladowca (na-śhla-dóv-tsa)
 m. imitator
naśmiewać się (na-śhmyé-vaćh
 śhán) v. laugh at; deride
naświetlać (na-śhvyet-laćh) v.
 explain; irradiate; expose
natarcie (na-tár-ćhe) n.
 1. rubbing; 2. onslaught; attack; offensive; advance
natarczywość (na-tar-chi-vośhćh)
 n. insistency; obtrusiveness
natarczywy (na-tar-chí-vi) adj;
 n. insistent; pressing;urgent
natchnąć (nát-khnoẃnćh) v. inspire ; infuse; penetrate
natchnienie (nat-khñe-ñe) n.
 inspiration; brain wave;impulse
natenczas (na-ten-chas) adv.
 then: at that time; as
natężać (na-tán-zhaćh) v. strain;
 intensify: strenghten; exert

natężenie (na-tán-zhé-ńe) n.
tension;strain: effort;pitch
natężony (na-tán-zho-ni) adj.
m. intense : strained
natknąć (nát-knównch) v. come
across ;butt; stick; stud
natłoczony (na-two-cho-ni) adj.
m. crowded: packed; huddled
natłoczyć (na-two-chích) v.
cram: pack: crowd; huddle
natłok (ná-twok) m. crowd;
throng; pressure accumulation
natomiast (na-tó-myast) adv.
however; yet; on the contrary
natłuscić (na-twoósh-ćheech) v.
oil; grease; lubricate
natrafić (na-trá-feećh) v. encounter; come across
natręctwo (na-tráńts-tvo) n.
intrusiveness; importunity
natręt (ná-tráńt) m. intruder
natrętny (na-tráńt-ni) adj. m.
intrusive; bothersome
natrysk (ná-trisk) m. shower-
bath: shower; sprying
natrząsać się (na-tzhówn-sach
śháń)v.scoff at: sneer;poke fun
natrzeć (ná-tzhech) v. rub;
attack; harass: scold; rate
natura (na-tóo-ra) f. nature
naturalizacja (na-too-ra-lee-
záts-ya) f. naturalization
naturalizować (na-too-ra-lee-zó-
vach) v. naturalize
naturalny (na-too-rál-ni) adj.
m. natural; true to life
natychmiast (na-tikh-myast) adv.
at once;instantly; right away
natychmiastowy (na-tikh-myas-
tó-vi) adj. m. instantaneous
nauczać (na-oo-chách) v. teach;
instruct; tutor; train
nauczanie (na-oo-cha-ńe) n.
teaching; instruction
nauczka (na-oóch-ka) f. (pointed) lesson (unpleasant)
nauczyciel (na-oo-chi-ćhel) m.
teacher; instructor
nauczyć się (na-oo-chich śháń)
v. learn: come to know
nauka (na-oo-ka) f. science;
learning; study; teaching

naukowiec (na-oo-kóv-yets) m.
scientist; scholar; researcher
naukowość (na-oo-kó-vośhćh) f.
erudition; scholarship;learning
naukowy (na-oo-kó-vi) adj. m.
scientific; scholarly;academic
naumyślnie (na-oo-míshl-ńe)
adv. on purpose; of set purpose
nawa (ná-va) f. nave; aisle
nawadniać (na-vád-ńach) v.
irrigate; saturate with water
nawalić (na-vá-leećh) v. pile
up; fail; bungle;break down
nawał (ná-vaw) m. no end of
nawała (na-vá-wa)f. overwhelm-
ing mass; swarms; onslaught
nawałnica (na-vaw-ńée-tsa) f.
tempest; storm; hurricane
nawarstwienie (na-var-stvyé-ńe)
n. stratification
nawarzyć (na-vá-zhich) v. brew;
cook; concoct; get in trouble
nawet (ná-vet) adv. even
nawet gdyby (na-vét gdí-bi)
adv. even if; even though
nawias (ná-vyas) m. parenthesis
nawiasem (na-vyá-sem) adv. incidentally; by way of digression
nawiasowy (na-vya-só-vi) adj.
m. parenthetical; incidental
nawiązać (na-vyówn-zać) v.
tie to; refer to; enter in
nawiązanie (na-vyówn-za-ńe) n.
connection; reference to
nawiedzać (na-vyé-dzach) v.
visit; haunt; afflict; obsess
nawierzchnia (na-vyezh-khńa) f.
surface (finish); pavement
nawijać (na-vee-yach) v. wind
up;reel; roll up; spool: coil
nawlekać (na-vlé-kach) v. thread;
string; slip on
nawodnienie (na-vod-ńe-ńe) n.
irrigation; saturation with water
nawoływać (na-vo-wi-vach) v.
call; hail; exhort to; halloo
nawozić (na-vó-zheech) v. fertilize; manure :truck:cart: fill
nawóz (ná-voos) m. manure :dung
na wpół (na vpoow) adv. half;
semi-: half-(finished, boiled)
nawracać (na-vra-tsách) v. turn
around; convert ; turn back

nawrócenie (na-vroo-tsé-ńe) n.
conversion; being converted
nawrót (ná-vroot) m. return;
relapse; recurrence; set-back
na wskros (na vskrosh) adv.
throughout; from end to end
nawyk (ná-vik) m. habit; wont
nawykać (na-vi-kach) v. accustom; fall into a habit
nawykły (na-vik-wi) adj. m.
accustomed; get used to...
na wylot (na vi-lot) adv. through
and through; right through
nawymyslać (na-vi-miśh-lach) v.
revile; abuse;insult; invent
na wyrywki (na vi-riv-kee) adv.
at random;at haphazard
nawzajem (na-vzá-yem) adv. mu-
tually; same to you
na wznak (ná vznak) adv. on
one's back; on one's supine
nazad (ná-zat) adv. back (wards)
nazajutrz (na-zá-jootsh) adv.
next morning; next day
nazbierać (na-zbyé-rach) v.
gather up; collect;assemble
nazbyt (ná-zbit) adv. too much
na zewnątrz (na zév-nówntsh)
adv. out; outwards; outside
naznaczyć (na-zna-chich) v.
mark;fix; appoint;outline;scar
nazwa (náz-va) f. designation;
name; appellation; title
nazwisko (naz-vee-sko) m. family name; surname;reputation
nazywać (na-zi-vach) v. call;
name;term; denominate; christen
nażarty (na-zhar-ti) adj. m.
gorged; stuffed(greedily)
nażreć się (ná-zhreth śháń) v.
gorge; stuff oneself (vulg.)
negacja (ne-gáts-ya) f. negation; opposite of positive
negatyw (ne-gá-tiv) m. negative
negatywny (ne-ga-tív-ni) adj.
m. negative; saying "no"
negliż (nég-leesh) m. undress;
morning dress; dishabille
negocjacje (ne-go-tsyáts-ye) pl.
negotiations;settling a treaty
negować (ne-gó-vach) v. deny
nekrolog (ne-kró-log) m. obituary notice ; obituary

nektar (nék-tar) m. nectar
neofita (ne-o-fée-ta) m. convert; neophyte; proselyte
neologizm (ne-o-ló-geezm) m.
neologism; new word;new meanning
neon (né-on) m. neon light
nepotyzm (ne-pó-tizm) m. nepo-
tizm; favoritism to relatives
nerka (ner-ka) f. kidney
nerw (nerv) m. nerve;vigor;ardor
nerwica (ner-vée-tsa) f. neurosis; nervous disturbance
nerwoból (ner-vo-bool) m. neuralgia; severe pain along a nerve
nerwowość (ner-vó-voshch) f.
nervosity; irritability; fidgets
nerwowy (ner-vo-vi) adj. m. nervous;made up of nerves; fearful
neseser (ne-sé-ser) m. dressing
case; make-up case; toilet case
netto (net-to) adv. net (cost)
neutralizować (ne-oo-tra-lee-
zó-vach) v. neutralize
neutralność (ne-oo-trál-noshch)
f. neutrality; neutral status
neutralny (ne-oo-trál-ni) adj.
m. neutral; indifferent
neutron (ne-oo-tron) m. neutron
newralgia (ne-vrál-gya) f.
neuralgia; pain along a nerve
newroza (ne-vro-za) f. neurosis
nęcić (nań-cheech) v. entice;
court; allure; tempt;be seductive
nędza (nań-dza) f. misery
nędzarz (nań-dzash) m. destitute
wretch; beggar; pauper
nędznik (nańdz-ńeek) m. villain
nędzny (nańdz-ni) adj. m. wretched;miserable ; shabby; sorry
nękać (nań-kach) v. molest; hurry;
torment; harass; annoy; worry
ni to ni owo (ńee to ńee o-vo)
adv. neither this nor that
ni stąd ni zowąd (ńee stównt
ńee zo-vównt) without reason;
suddenly ; for no reason whatever
niania (ná-ńa) f. (baby's)
nurse ; nanny; dry nurse
niańczyć (náń-cheech) v. nurse
niańka (náń-ka) f. nurse
niby (ńee-bi) adv. as if; pre-
tending ;as it were; like
nic (ńeets) pron. nothing; nought

nic nie szkodzi (ńeets ńe shko-dźhee) expr.: does not matter

nic z tego (ńeets z te-go) expr.: no use: to no avail: to no purpose;

nicość (ńee-tsoshćh) f. nothing-ness; oblivion; nonentity

nicpoń (ńets-poń) m. good-for-nothing; "nogoodnik"; scamp

niczyj (ńee-chiy) adj. m. no-man's: nobody's; no one's

nici (ńee-ćhee) pl. 1. threads 2. nothing; nothing of it

nić (ńeećh) f. thread

nie (ńe) part. no ; not(any)

nie jeszcze (ńe yesh-che) not-yet; not for a long time

nieagresja (ńe-a-gres-ya) f. nonaggression (treaty)

niebaczny (ńe-bach-ni) adj. m. imprudent; rush; inconsiderate

niebawem (ńe-ba-vem) adv. soon

niebezpieczeństwo (ńe-bez-pye-cheń-stvo) m. danger: peril

niebezpieczny (ńe-bez-pyech-ni) adj. m. dangerous; risky; tricky

niebiański (ńe-byań-skee) adj. m. heavenly ; divine

niebieskawy (ńe-byes-ka-vi) adj. m. bluish

niebieski (ńe-byes-kee) adj. m. blue; heavenly; of the sky

niebieskooki (ńe-byes-ko-o-kee) adj. m. blue-eyed

niebiosa (ńe-byo-sa) pl. Hea-vens: the visible sky

niebo (ńe-bo) ŋ. sky

nieborak (ńe-bo-rak) m. poor soul; poor soul; poor devil

nieboszczyk (ńe-bosh-chik) m. deceased; dead person

niebosiężny (ńe-bo-shańzh-ni) adj. m. sky-high: towering

niebotyczny (ńe-bo-tich-ni) adj. m. sky-high ; sky reaching

niebożę (ńe-bo-żań) n. poor soul; poor thing; poor devil

nie byle jak (ńe bi-le yak) expr. not just any way: not carelessly

niebyły (ńe-bi-vi) adj. m. null and void ; unexisting

niebywale (ńe-bi-va-le) adv. unusually; exceptionally

niebywały (ńe-bi-va-wi) adj. m. unheard-of ; unusual; uncommon

niecały (ńe-tsa-wi) adj. m. incomplete :defective; less than

niecenzuralny (ńe-tsen-zoo-rál-ni) adj. m. indecent; un-printable : obscene; suggestive

niech (ńekh) part. let :suppose

niechcący (ńe-khtsówn-tsi) adv. unintentionally ; unawares

niechęć (ńe-khańćh) f. disincli-nation; aversion; ill-will

niechętny (ńe-khańt-ni) adj. m. unwilling; reluctant: averse

niechluj (ńe-khlooy) m. grub; sloppy ; slut: dirty: sloven

niechybny (ńe-khib-ni) adj. m. without fail :certain:unerring

niechże (ńekh-zhe) part. let

niecić (ńe-ćheećh) v. kindle; stir up ; light (a fire)

nieciekawy (ńe-ćhe-ka-vi) adj. m. blank; void of interest

niecierpliwić się (ńe-ćher-plee-veećh shań) v. be impatient

niecierpliwy (ńe-ćher-plee-vi) adj. m. impatient; restless

niecnota (ńe-tsno-ta) m. scamp; rogue ; rascal: scoundrel

niecny (ńets-ni) adj. m. vile

nieco (ńe-tso) adv. somewhat; a little: a trifle; slightly

niecodzienny (ńe-tso-dżhen-ni) adj. m. uncommon: unusual

nieczesany (ńe-che-sa-ni) adj. m. unkempt : disorderly

nieczęsty (ńe-chań-sti) adj. m. infrequent: not frequent

nieczuły (ńe-choo-vi) adj. m. callous : heartless: insensible

nieczynny (ńe-chin-ni) adj. m. inert; inactive:out of order

nieczysty (ńe-chis-ti) adj. m. unclean:polluted: dirty; shady

nieczytelny (ńe-chi-tel-ni) adj. m. illegible ; cramped:crabbed

niedaleki (ńe-da-le-kee) adj. m. near; not distant:at hand

niedaleko (ńe-da-le-ko) adv. near; not far; a short way off

niedawno (ńe-dav-no) adv. re-cently; not long ago;newly

niedbale (ńe-dba-le) adv. care-lessly; casually: nonchalantly

niedbalstwo (ńe-dbál-stvo) n. negligence; laxity:carelessness

niedbały (ńe-dba-wi) adj. m.
negligent;untidy;lax;careless
niedługi (ńe-dwoo-gee) adj. m.
short; not long
niedługo (ńe-dwoo-go) adv. soon;
not long; before long;by and by
niedobitki (ńe-do-beet-kee) pl.
survivors; routed soldiers
niedobór (ńe-do-boor) m. deficit; shortage; scarcity; loss
niedobrany (ńe-do-bra-ni) adj.
m. ill-suited; ill-matched
niedobry (ńe-dob-ri) adj. m.
no-good; bad; wicked; nasty
niedobrze (ńe-dob-zhe) adv. not
well; badly;wrong;improperly
nie doceniać(ńe-do-tse-ńach) v.
underestimate; estimate too low
niedociągnięcie (ńe-do-chown-
gnan-ćhe) n. shortcoming
niedogodność (ńe-do-god-noshćh)
f. inconvenience; drawback
niedogodny (ńe-do-god-ni) adj.
m. inconvenient; undesirable
nie dogotowany(ńe-do-go-to-va-
ni) adj. m. underdone; half-
cooked; half-raw; under done
nie dojadać(ńe-do-ya-dach) v.
not eat enough;starve
niedojda (ńe-doy-da) m. nitwit;
bungler; fumbler; lout
niedojrzały (ńe-doy-zha-wi) adj.
m. unripe; immature; under age
niedokładny (ńe-do-kwad-ni) adj.
m. inaccurate; inexact
niedokończony (ńe-do-koń-cho-ni)
adj. m. unfinished;incomplete
niedokrwisty (ńe-do-krvees-ti)
adj. m. anemic; anaemic
niedola (ńe-do-la) f. adversity
niedołęga (ńe-do-wan-ga) m.
blunderer; cripple;duffer
niedołęstwo (ńe-do-wan-stvo) m.
inefficiency; clumsiness
niedomagać (ńe-do-ma-gach) v.
be unwell; be ailing
nie domknięty(ńe-do-mknan-ti)
adj. m. ajar; slightly open,
niedomówienie (ńe-do-moo-vye-ńe)
n. vague hint; insinuation
niedomyślny (ńe-do-miśhl-ni)
adj. m. slow thinking

niedopałek (ńe-do-pa-wek) m.
(cigarette) butt: stub;ember
niedopatrzenie (ńe-do-pa-tzhe-
ńe) n. oversight; neglect
niedopuszczalny (ńe-do-poosh-
chal-ni) adj. m. inadmissible
niedorozwinięty (ńe-do-roz-
vee-ńan-ti) adj. m. underdeveloped; mentally retarded
niedorzeczny (ńe-do-zhech-ni)
adj. m. absurd; ridiculous
niedoskonały (ńe-dos-ko-na-wi)
adj. m. imperfect;deficient
niedosłyszalny (ńe-do-swi-shal-
ni) adj. m. inaudible
niedosmażony (ńe-do-sma-zho-ni)
adj. m. underdone : half-raw
nie dospać(ńe-dos-pach) v.
sleep too short time; not sleep
enough; not to have enough sleep
niedostateczny (ńe-dos-ta-tech-
ni) adj. m. insufficient
niedostatek (ńe-dos-ta-tek) m.
shortage; indigence; poverty
niedostępny (ńe-do-stanp-ni)
adj. m. inaccessible;out of reach
niedostosowanie (ńe-dos-to-so-
va-ńe)n. maladjustment
niedostrzegalny (ńe-do-stzhe-
gal-ni) adj. m. imperceptible
niedościgły (ńe-do-śhćheeg-wi)
adj. m. matchless; inimitable
niedoświadczenie (ńe-do-śhvyad-
ché-ńe) n. inexperience
niedouczony (ńe-do-oo-cho-ni)
adj. n. half-educated
nie dowarzony (ńe do-va-zho-ni)
adj. m. half-boiled; rough
niedowarzony (ńe-do-va-zho-ni)
adj. m. immature;undereducated
niedowiarek (ńe-do-vya-rek) m.
unbeliever;atheist; skeptic
niedowidzieć (ńe-do-vee-dźech)
v. be short-sighted
nie dowierzać(ńe-do-vye-zhach)
v. distrust; disbelieve
niedowład (ńe-do-vwat) m. pare-
sis: partial paralysis
niedozwolony (ńe-doz-vo-lo-ni)
adj. m. not allowed;illicit
niedrogi (ńe-dro-gee) adj. m.
cheap; inexpensive

nieduży (ňe-doo-zhi) adj. m. small; little;not big;not tall

niedwuznaczny (ňe-dvoo-znach-ni) adj. m. unequivocal; clear

niedyskrecja (ňe-dis-krets-ya) f. indiscretion;indelicacy,

niedyspozycja (ňe-dis-po-zits-ya) f. indisposition

niedziela (ňe-dźhé-la)f. Sunday

niedźwiadek (ňe-dźhvyá-dek) m. bear cub; Teddy bear.

niedźwiedzica (ňe-dzhvye-dźhée-tsa) f. female bear:she-bear

niedźwiedź (ňe-dźhvyedźh) m. bear: bearskin; clumsy man

nieelastyczny (ňe-e-las-tích-ni) adj. m. inelastic

nieestetyczny (ňe-es-te-tích-ni) adj. m. unesthetic

nieetyczny (ňe-e-tích-ni) adj. m. unethical; immoral

niefachowy (ňe-fa-khó-vi) adj. m. incompetent; inexpert

nieforemny (ňe-fo-rém-ni) adj. m. shapeless; deformed

nieformalnie (ňe-for-mál-ňe) adv. informally; illegally

niefortunny (ňe-for-tóon-ni) adj. m. unlucky; regrettable

niefrasobliwy (ňe-fra-sob-lee-vi) adj. m. care-free;jaunty

niegdyś (ňeg-dish) adv. former-ly; once; at one time

niegodny (ňe-gód-ni) adj. m. unworthy;undignified;vile;base

niegodziwy (ňe-go-dźhée-vi)adj. m. wicked;vile;base;mean;foul

niegościnny (ňe-gosh-chéen-ni) adj. m. inhospitable;desolate

niegrzeczny (ňe-gzhéch-ni) adj. m. rude; impolite;unkind: bad

niegustowny (ňe-goos-tóv-ni) adj. m. tasteless:in bad taste

niehigieniczny (ňe-khee-ge-ňéech-ni) adj. m. unsanitary

niehonorowy (ňe-kho-no-ró-vi) adj. m. dishonorable; unfair

nieistotny (ňe-ees-tó-tni) adj. m. inessential; immaterial

niejaki (ňe-yá-kee) adj. m. a; one; certain:some;slight

niejasno (ňe-yás-no) adv. dimlv: vaguely;ambiguouslv;obscurely

niejasny (ňe-yás-ni) adj. m.dim; unclear;indistinct;vague;obscure

niejeden (ňe-yé-den) adj. m. many a: quite a number

niejednokrotnie (ňe-yed-no-krót-ňe) adv. repeatedly;recurrently

nie karany (ňe ka-rá-ni) adj. m. with a clean record; not con-victed before

niekiedy (ňe-kyé-di) adv. now and then; sometimes; at times

niekonsekwentny (ňe-kon-se-kvent-ni) adj. m. inconsistent

niekorzystny (ňe-ko-zhist-ni) adj. m. disadvantageous

niekorzyść (ňe-kó-zhishch) f. disadvantage; detriment

niekształtny (ňe-kshtáwt-ni) adj. m. unshapely; formless

niektóry (ňe-ktoó-ry) adj. m. some;one here and there

nieledwie (ňe-léd-vye) adv. all but: almost;practically

nielegalny (ňe-le-gál-ni) adj. m. illegal;unlawful:illicit

nieletni (ňe-lét-ňe) adj. m. under age;juvenile; minor

nieliczny (ňe-léech-ni) adj. m. not numerous; scarce;rare;small

nielitościwy (ňe-lee-tośh-chée-vi) adj. m. unmerciful

nielogiczny (ňe-lo-géech-ni) adj. m. illogical: nonsensical

nieludzki (ňe-loódz-kee) adj. inhuman: atrocious;ruthless

nieład (ňe-wat) m. disorder; disarray; confusion:mess

nieładnie (ňe-wád-ňe) adv. not nicely: unattractively;wrongly

niełaska (ňe-wás-ka) f. disgrace; disfavor;loss of respect

niemal (ňe-mal) adv. almost; nearly ;pretty nearly;well-nigh

niemało (ňe-má-wo) adv. not a few; pretty much :not a little

niemały (ňe-má-wi) adj. m. pret-ty big ;fair-sized;goodly;no mean

niemądry (ňe-mownd-ri) adj. un-wise; ill-judged ;silly;stupid

niemczyć (ňem-chich) v.Germanize

niemęski (ňe-máň-kee)adj.m.unmanly

niemiecki (ňem-yéts-kee) adj. m. German ; German language

niemiły (ñe-mée-wi) adj. m. unpleasant;unsightly;harsh;surly
niemniej jednak (ñe-mney yed-
nak) nevertheless; all the
same;none the less: however
niemoc (ñe-mots) f. impotence
niemodny (ñe-mod-ni) adj. m.
outmoded; out of fashion
niemoralny (ñe-mo-rál-ni) adj.
m. immoral: dishonest
niemowa (ñe-mo-ya) m.∝ f. mute
niemowlę (ñe-mov-lán) n. baby
niemożliwy (ñe-mozh-leé-vi)
adj. m. impossible
niemrawy (ñe-mra-vi) adj. m.
sluggish; tardy; indolent
niemy (ñie-mi) adj. m. dumb
nienaganny (ñe-na-gán-ni) adj.
m. blameless; faultless
nienaruszalny (ñe-na-roo-shál-
ni) adj. m. inviolable
nienaruszony (ñe-na-roo-sho-ni)
adj. m. intact·undisturbed
nienasycony (ñe-na-si-tso-ni)
adj. m. insatiable; (chem.
unsaturated); voracious
nienaturalny (ñe-na-too-rál-ni)
adj. m. unnatural; insincere
nienawistny (ñe-na-veest-ni)
adj. m. hateful;full of hatred
nienawisc (ñe-na-veeshch) f.
hate: abomination:detestation
nie nazwany (ñe naz-vá-ni) adj.
m. unnamed: not maned
nienormalny (ñe nor-mál-ni)
adj. m. abnormal; insane
nieobecnosc (ñe-o-béts-noshch)
f. absence; non-attendance
nieobecny (ñe-o-bets-ni) adj.
m. absent: not present:not in
nieobeznany (ñe-o-bez-ná-ni)
adj. m. uninformed; ignorant
nieobliczalny (ñe-o-blee-chál-
ni) adj. m. unreliable; incalculable;irresponsible
nieobyczajny (ñe-o-bi-cháy-ni)
adj. m. immoral:ill-mannered
nieoceniony (ñe-o-tse-ño-ni)
adj. m. inestimable
nieoczekiwany (ñe-oche-kee-vá-
ni) adj. m. unexpected
nieodłączny (ñe-od-wown-ni)
adj. m. inseparable

nieodmienny (ñe-od-myén-ni)
adj. m. invariable;undeclinable
nieodparty (ñe-od-pár-ti) adj.
m. irrefutable; compelling
nieodpowiedni (ñe-od-po-vyéd-ñee)
adj. m. inadequate; wrong
nieodpowiedzialny (ñe-od-po-vye-
dźhál-ni) adj. m. irresponsible
nieodstępny (ñe-od-stáp-ni)
adj. m. inseparable;ever present
nieodwołalny (ñe-od-vo-wál-ni)
adj. m. irrevocable; final
nieodzownie (ñe-od-zóv-ñe) adv.
inevitably; absolutely
nieodzowny (ñe-od-zóv-ni) adj.
m. indispensable;irrevocable
nieodżałowany (ñe-od-zha-wo-vá-
ni) adj. m. never enough regretted; much regretted
nieoględny (ñe-o-glánd-ni) adj.
m. inconsiderate;reckless;rash
nieograniczony (ñe-o-gra-ñee-chó
ni) adj. m. infinite; boundless
nieokiełzany (ñe-o-kew-za-ni)
adj. m. unbridled; uncontrollable
nieokreslony (ñe-o-kresh-ló-ni)
adj. m. indefinite;undetermined
nieokrzesany (ñe-o-kzhe-sa-ni)
adj. m. rude:crude;ill-mannered
nieomal (ñe-o-mal) adv. almost;
nearly; pretty nearly;practically
nieomylny (ñe-o-mil-ni) adj. m.
infallible:unerring;sure
nieopatrzny (ñe-o-patzh-ni) adj.
m. unguarded: inconsiderate
nieopisany (ñe-o-pee-sa-ni) adj.
m. indescribable;excessive;extreme
nieopłacalny (ñe-o-pwa-tsál-ni)
adj. m. unprofitable
nieopłacony (ñe-o-pwa-tso-ni)
adj. m. unpaid;not paid for
nieopodal (ñe-o-pó-dal) adv.
near by: close at hand;next door
nieorganiczny (ñe-or-ga-ñeech-
ni) adj. m. inorganic;inanimate
nieosobowy (ñe-o-so-bó-vi) adj.
m. inpersonal; not personal
nieostrożny (ñe-os-trozh-ni)
adj. m. careless; imprudent
nieoswojony (ñe-os-vo-yo-ni)
adj. m. untamed; unfamiliar
nieoświecony (ñe-osh-vye-tso-
ni) adj. m. dark; ignorant

nieoznaczony (ńe-oz-na-chó-ni)
adj. m. indefinite;unmarked
niepalący (ńe-pa-lówn-tsi) adj.
m. not smoking; non smoking
niepalność(ńe-pál-noshćh)f.in-
combustibility;non-inflammability
niepalny (ńe-pál-ni) adj. m.
incombustible;uninflammable
niepamięć (ńe-pá-myáńćh) f.
oblivion; forgetfulness
niepamiętny (ńe-pa-myánt-ni)
adj. m. forgetful; immemorial
nieparlamentarny (ńe-par-la-
men-tár-ni) adj. unparliamen-
tary rough (language)
nieparzysty (ńe-pa-zhis-ti)
adj. m. odd;uneven; unpaired
niepełnoletni (ńe-pew-no-let-
ńee) adj. m. minor; underage
niepewność (ńe-pév-noshćh) f.
uncertainty; incertitude
niepewny (ńe-pév-ni) adj. m.
uncertain ;insecure; unsafe
niepisany (ńe-pee-sá-ni) adj.
m. unwritten; not in writing
niepiśmienny (ńe-peesh-myén-ni)
adj. m. illiterate;unlettered
niepłacący (ńe-pwa-tsówn-tsi)
adj. m. non-paying
niepłodny (ńe-pwód-ni) adj. m.
sterile; barren; infertile
niepłonny (ńe-pwon-ni) adj. m.
well-founded ; motivated
niepochlebny (ńe-po-khléb-ni)
adj. m. unfavorable
niepocieszony (ńe-po-ćhe-shó-
ni) adj. m. desolate
niepoczciwy (ńe-poch-ćhee-vi)
adj. m. wicked; unkind
niepoczytalny (ńe-po-chi-tál-ni)
adj. m. irresponsible ;insane
niepodejrzany (ńe-po-dey-zhá-ni)
adj. m. unsuspected
niepodległość (ńe-pod-lég-woshćh)
f. independence :sovereignty
niepodległy (ńe-pod-lég-wi) adj.
m. independent; sovereign
niepodobieństwo (ńe-po-do-byeń-
stvo) n. impossibility
niepodobna (ńe-po-dób-na) adv.
it's impossible ;there is no way
niepodobny (ńe-po-dób-ni) adj.
m. unlike; unlikely ;dissimilar

niepodzielny (ńe-podźhél-ni)
adj. m. indivisible;undivided
niepogoda (ńe-po-gó-da) f. bad
weather; foul weather
niepogwałcony (ńe-po-gvaw-tsó-
ni) adj. m. inviolate
niepohamovany (ńe-po-ha-mo-
vá-ni) adj. m. unrestrained
niepojętny (ńe-po-yánt-ni)
adj. m. dull(man);stupid
niepojęty (ńe-po-yań-ti) adj.
m. inconceivable ; incomprehensible; unimaginable
niepokalany (ńe-po-ka-lá-ni)
adj. m. immaculate;faultless
niepokaźny (ńe-po-káźh-ni) adj.
m. inconspicuous;modest:shabby
niepokoić (ńe-po-kó-eećh) v.
disturb; trouble; annoy;pester
niepokonany (ńe-po-ko-ná-ni)
adj. m. invincible;irresistible
niepokój (ńe-pó-kooy) m. anxiety; unrest:trouble;agitation
niepolityczny (ńe-po-lee-tich-
ni) adj. m. impolitical; in-
expedient; improper:impolitic
niepomierny (ńe-po-myér-ni)
adj. m. excessive ; extreme
niepomny (ńe-póm-ni) adj. m.
forgetful; oblivious
niepomyślny (ńe-po-mishl-ni)
adj. m. adverse ; unlucky
niepopłatny (ńe-po-pwát-ni)
adj. m. unprofitable
niepoprawny (ńe-po-práv-ni)
adj. m. incorrigible
niepopularny (ńe-po-poo-lár-ni)
adj. m. unpopular
nieporadny (ńe-po-rád-ni) adj.
m. awkward ;helpless
nieporęczny (ńe-po-rańch-ni)
adj. m. cumbersome ;unhandy
nieporozumienie (ńe-po-ro-zoo-
myé-ńe) n. misunderstanding
nieporównany (ńe-po-roov-ná-
ni) adj. m. incomparable
nieporuszony (ńe-po-roo-shó-ni)
adj. m. immovable; firm
nieporządek (ńe-po-zhówn-dek)
adj. m. disorder; mess
nieporządny (ńe-po-zhównd-ni)
adj. m. disorderly; untidy;
messy;slipshod;chaotic

nieposłuszeństwo (ńe-po-swoo-sheń-stvo) n. disobedience
nieposłuszny (ńe-po-swoosh-ni) adj. m. disobedient:unruly
niepospolity (ńe-pos-po-lee-ti) adj. m. uncommon: rare
niepostrzeżenie(ńe-po-stshe-zhé-ńe)adv.imperceptibly;unnoticeably
niepotrzebny (ńe-po-tzhéb-ni) adj. m. unnecessary; useless
niepowetowany (ńe-po-ve-to-vá-ni) adj. m. irreparable
niepowodzenie (ńe-po-vo-dzhé-ńe) n. failure; adversity
niepowołany (ńe-po-vo-wá-ni) adj. m. uncalled for; incompetent; unfit; undesirable
niepowrotny (ńe-pov-rót-ni) adj. m. irrevocable; irrecoverable; beyond recall
niepowstrzymany (ńe-pov-stzhi-má-ni) adj. m. irresistible
niepowszedni (ńe-pov-shed-ńee) adj. m. uncommon: exceptional
niepowściągliwy (ńe-pov-shćhówng-lée-vi) adj. m. intemperate
niepozorny (ńe-po-zór-ni) adj. m. inconspicuous; modest
niepożądany (ńe-po-zhówn-da-ni) adj. m. undesirable: undesired
niepożyteczny (ńe-po-zhi-téch-ni) adj. m. useless;unprofitable
niepraktyczny (ńe-prak-tích-ni) adj. m. impractical;unwieldy
niepraktykujący (ńe-prak-ti-koo-yówn-tsi)adj. m. noncommunicant ; retired (professional)
nieprawda (ńe-práv-da) f. untruth; falsehood; lie
nieprawdopodobny (ńe-prav-do-po-dób-ni) adj. m. improbable
nieprawdziwy (ńe-prav-dżhee-vi) adj. m. untrue; false :faked
nieprawidłowość (ńe-pra-vee-dwó-voshćh) f. anomaly; irregularity; falsity;incorrectness
nieprawidłowy (ńe-pra-vee-dwó-vi) adj. m. anomalous; irregular; contrary to the rules
nieprawny (ńe-práv-ni) adj. m. illegal; unlawful: invalid
nieprawomyslny (ńe-pra-vo-míshl-ni) adj. m. unorthodox:disloyal

nieprawy (ńe-pra-vi) adj. m. unrighteous; adulterous; bastard: unlawful; illegitimate
nieproporcjonalny (ńe-pro-por-tsyo-nál-ni) adj. m. disproportional:out of proportion
nieproszony (ńe-pro-shó-ni) adj. m. uncalled for; self-invited: unwelcome (guest)
nieprzebaczalny (ńe-pzhe-ba-chál-ni) adj. m. unpardonable
nieprzebłagany (ńe-pzhe-bwa-ga-ni) adj. m. implacable
nieprzebrany (ńe-pzhe-brá-ni) adj. m. inexhaustible;countless
nieprzebyty (ńe-pzhe-bí-ti) adj. m. impassable: unfordable
nieprzejednany (ńe-pzhe-yed-ná-ni) adj. m. irreconcilable
nieprzejrzysty (ńe-pzhey-zhís-ti) adj. m. not clear
nieprzekupny (ńe-pzhe-koóp-ni) adj. m. unbribable;incorruptible
nieprzemakalny (ńe-pzhe-ma-kál-ni) adj. m. waterproof
nieprzenikniony (ńe-pzhe-ńeek-ńo-ni) adj. m. impenetrable
nieprzepuszczalny (ńe-pzhe-poosh-chál-ni) adj. m. impervious :impenetrable
nieprzerwany (ńe-pzher-vá-ni) adj. m. continuous ;ceaseless
nieprzescigniony (ńe-pzhesh-ćheeg-ńo-ni) adj. m. unsurpassable ; unexcelled
nieprzewidziany (ńe-pzhe-vee-dżhá-ni) adj. m. unforeseen
nieprzezorny (ńe-pzhe-zór-ni) adj. m. improvident; unforseeing ;wanting of foresight
nieprzezroczysty (ńe-pzheżh-ro-chí-s-ti) adj. m. opaque
nieprzezwyciężony (ńe-pzhez-vi-ćhan-zhó-ni) adj. m. invincible ;insurmountable
nieprzychylny (ńe-pzhi-khíl-ni) adj. m. unfriendly :prejudiced
nieprzydatny (ńe-pzhi-dát-ni) adj. m. useless ; unserviceable
nie przygotowany(ńe-pzhi-go-to-va-ni) adj. m. unprepared
nieprzyjaciel (ńe-pzhi-ya-ćhel) m. enemy; foe :ill-wisher

nieprzyjacielski (ńe-pzhi-ya-
chél-skee) adj. m. enemy; hostile: enemy's: enemy-
nieprzyjazny (ńe-pzhi-yaz-ni)
adj. m.unfriendly; inimical
nieprzyjaźń (ńe-pzhi-yazń) f.
hostility: unfriendliness
nieprzyjemnosc (ńe-pzhi-yém-
nośhćh) f. unpleasantness
nieprzyjemny (ńe-pzhi-yém-ni)
adj. unpleasant; disagreeable
nie :.vmuszory (ńe-pzhi-moo-
shó-ni) adj. m. free; uncon-
strained ; voluntary
nieprzystępny (ńe-pzhis-tanp-
ni) adj. m. inaccessible
nieprzytomnosc (ńe-pzhi-tóm-
nośhćh) f. unconsciousness;
absentmindedness
nieprzytomny (ńe-pzhi-tóm-ni)
adj. m. unconscious; absent-
minded ;frantic:mad; wild
nieprzyzwoitosc (ńe-pzhi-zvo-
eé-tośhćh) f. indecency
nieprzyzwoity (ńe-pzhiz-vo-eé-
ti) adj. m. indecent; obscene
nieprzyzwyczajony (ńe-pzhi-zvi-
cha-yó-ni) adj. m. unaccustomed: lacking of habit
niepunktualny (ńe-poon-ktoo-ál-
ni) adj. m. unpunctual; late
nierad (ńe-rad) adj. m. unwilling; discontent : annoyed
nieraz (ńe-ras) adv. often;
again and again ;many a time
nierdzewny (ńe-rdzév-ni) adj.
m. rustproof ;stainless
nierealny (ńe-re-ál-ni) adj. m.
imaginary; unreal; unrealizable
nieregularnosc (ńe-re-goo-lár-
nośhćh) f. irregularity
nieregularny (ńe-re-goo-lár-ni)
adj. m. irregular ; erratic
nиereligijny (ńe-re-lee-geéy-
ni) adj. m. irreligious
nierogacizna (ńe-ro-ga-cheéz-
na) f. pl. swines pl.
nierozdzielny (ńe-roz-dźhél-ni)
adj. m. inseparable
nierozerwalny (ńe-ro-zer-vál-ni)
adj. m. indissoluble
nierozgarnięty (ńe-roz-gar-ńań-
ti) adj. m. dull; (dim-witted)

nierozłączny (ńe-roz-wównch-ni)
adj. m. inseparable
nierozmyslny (ńe-roz-míshl-ni)
adj. m. unintentional
nierozpuszczalny (ńe-roz-poosh-
chál-ni) adj. m. indissoluble
nierozsądny (ńe-roz-sównd-ni)
adj. m. unwise; unreasonable
nierozwaga (ńe-roz-vá-ga) f.
inconsideration; rashness
nierozważny (ńe-roz-vázh-ni)
adj. m. imprudent; inconside-
ate; thoughtless; rush: hasty
nierównosc (ńe-roov-nośhćh) f.
inequality ;unevenness
nierówny (ńe-roov-ni) adj. m.
unequal; crooked; uneven
nieruchliwy (ńe-rookh-leé-vi)
adj. m. slow ; unwieldy
nieruchomość (ńe-roo-khó-mośhćh)
f. real estate : immobility
nieruchomy (ńe-roo-khó-mi) adj.
m. immobile; fixed ;still:at rest
nierychło (ńe-rikh-wo) adv. not
soon : slowly: not forthcoming
nierzadko ńe-zhád-ko) adv. often : now and then; not seldom
nierzad (ńe-zhównt) m. prostitution; anarchy : debauchery
nierzeczowy (ńe-zhe-chó-vi) adj.
m. pointless; futile
nierzeczywisty (ńe-zhe-chi-veés-
ti) adj. m. unreal ;fictitious
nierzetelny (ńe-zhe-tél-ni) adj.
m. dishonest: unreliable
niesamowity (ńe-sa-mo-veé-ti)
adj. m. weird; uncanny : unearthy
niesforny (ńe-sfór-ni) adj. m.
unruly; disorderly ;turbulent
nieskalany (ńe-ska-lá-ni) adj.
m. immaculate ; spotless: pure
nieskazitelny (ńe-ska-zhee-tél-
ni) adj. m. unblemished; upright : spotless: moral
nieskładny (ńe-skwad-ni) adj.
m. awkward ;discordant;clumsy
nieskończonosc (ńe-skon-cho-
nośhćh) f. infinity
nieskończony (ńe-skoń-chó-ni)
adj. m. unfinished; infinite
nieskromny (ńe-skróm-ni) adj.
m. indecent : immodest ;morally
offensive: improper

nieskuteczny (ńe-skoo-téch-ni)
adj. m. ineffective: futile
niesłabnący (ńe-swab-nówn-tsi)
adj. m. unabated;unflagging
niesława (ńe-swá-va) f. infamy
niesławny (ńeswáv-ni) adj. m.
infamous ;inglorious:disgraceful
niesłowny (ńe-swóv-ni) adj. m.
unreliable; undependable
niesłuszność (ńe-swoósh-noshch)
f. injustice :groundlessness
niesłuszny (ńes-swoósh-ni) adj.
m. unjust; wrong :groundless
niesłychany (ńe-swi-khá-ni) adj.
m. unheard of; unprecedented
niesmaczny (ńe-smách-ni)adj. m.
tasteless: unsavory: unseemly
niesmak (ńes-mak) m. bad taste;
disgust: repugnance:nasty taste
niesnaski (ńes-nás-kee) pl. dissension :discord; quarrels
niespełna (ńes-pêw-na) adv. nearly; not all;not quite: about
niespodzianka (ńe-spo-dźhán-ka)
f. surprise : surprise gift
niespodziewany (ńe-spo-dźhe-vá-ni)
adj. m. unexpected ;unlooked for
niespokojny (ńe-spo-kóy-ni) adj.
m. restless; fussy :upset;fretful
niesporo (ńe-spo-ro) adv. slowly
nie sposób (ńe spó-soop) adv.
it's impossible :by no means
niespożyty (ńe-spo-zhi-ti) adj.
m. durable; indefatigable
niesprawiedliwość (ńe-spra-vyed-
leé-voshch) f. injustice
niesprawiedliwy (ńe-spra-vyed-
leé-vi) adj. m. unjust;unfair
niesprawny (ńe-správ-ni) adj. m.
ineffective; inefficient
nie sprzyjający (ńe spzhi-ya-
yówn-tsi) adj. m. adverse
niestały (ńe-stá-wi) adj. m. unsteady; inconsistent;variable
niestaranny (ńe-sta-rán-ni) adj.
m. careless;sloppy: dowdy
niestateczny (ńe-sta-téch-ni) adj.
m. unstable: fickle; flighty
niestety (ńe-sté-ti) adv. alas;
unfortunately: I am sorry
niestosowny (ńe-sto-sóv-ni) adj.
m. improper; unsuitable:unfit:
inappropriate: out of place

niestrawność (ńe-strav-noshch)
f. indigestion: dyspepsia
niestrawny (ńe-strav-ni) adj.
m. indigestible: stodgy; dull
niestrudzony (ńe-stroo-dzo-ni)
adj. m. indefatigable; untiring
niestworzony (ńe-stvo-zho-ni)
adj. m. unreal; nonsense
niesumienny (ńe-soo-myén-ni)
adj. m. unscrupulous ;unreliable
nieswojo (ńe-svo-yo) adv. un-
easily;strangely; qualmishly
nieswój (ńe-svooy) adj. m. ill
at ease; uncomfortable;seedy;
strange : off color
niesymetryczny (ńe-si-me-trich-
ni) adj. m. asymmetrical
niesympatyczny (ńe-sim-pa-tich-
ni) adj. m. unpleasant
nieszczególny (ńe-shche-goól-ni)
adj. m. mediocre: so-so
nieszczelny (ńe-shchel-ni) adj.
m. leaky; not shut tight
nieszczery (ńe-shché-ri) adj.
m. insincere; double;dealing
nieszczęsny (ńe-shcháns-ni) adj.
m. miserable; ill-fated
nieszczęście (ńe-shchań-shche)
n. misfortune; disaster
nieszczęśliwy (ńe-shćhań-shlee-
vi) adj. m. unhappy;ill-starred
nieszkodliwy (ńe-shkod-lee-vi)
adj. m. harmless: not grave
nieszlachcic (ńe-shlakh-tseets)
m. commoner: man not of gentry
nieszpetny (ńe-shpet-ni) adj.
m. fairly good-looking
nieszpory (ńe-shpo-ri) pl. ves-
pers; evening prayers
nieścisły (ńe-shćhees-wi) adj.
m. inexact; inaccurate; faulty
nieścisliwy (ńe-shćheesh-lee-vi)
adj. m. incompressible
nieść (ńeshch) v. carry; bring;
bear; lay; afford, drive;waft
nieślubny (ńe-shloob-ni) adj. m.
illegitimate; out of wedlock
niesmiały (ńe-shmyá-wi) adj. m.
coy; shy; timid; bashful
niesmiertelny (ńe-shmyer-tel-ni)
adj. m. immortal: everlasting
nieświadomy (ńe-shvya-dó-mi) adj.
m. ignorant; unaware :involuntary

nietakt (ńe-takt) m. lack of tact; slip: taktlessness

nietaktowny (ńe-tak-tóv-ni) adj. m. tactless: indelicate

nietknięty (ńe-tknań-ti) adj. m. intact;virgin;untouched

nietolerancja (ńe-to-le-rants-ya) f. intolerance

nietoperz (ńe-to-pesh) m. bat

nietowarzystki (ńe-to-va-zhís-kee) adj. n. unsociable

nietrafny (ńe-tráf-ni) adj. m. wrong; missing the mark

nietrzeźwy (ńe-tzheźh-vi) m. drank; tipsy;unsound

nietutejszy (ńe-too-téy-shi) adj. m. stranger; non-resident

nietykalny (ńe-ti-kál-ni) adj. m. immune; inviolable

nie tyle (ńe ti-le) adv.not so much: not exactly; but;rather

nie tylko (ńe til-ko) adv. not only; anything but

nieubłagalny (ńe-oo-bwa-gál-ni) adj. m. implacable;irrevocable

nieuchronny (ńe-oo-khrón-ni) adj. inevitable; inescapable

nieuchwytny (ńe-oo-khvít-ni) adj. m. elusive;evasive;inaudible

nieuctwo (ńe-oóts-tvo) n. lack of education: ignorance

nieuczciwy (ńe-ooch-chée-vi) adj. m. dishonest; foul;unfair

nieuczynny (ńe-oo-chín-ni) adj. m. unobliging; disobliging

nieudolny (ńe-oo-dól-ni) adj. m. awkward; clumsy: decrepit

nieufny (ńe-oóf-ni) adj. m. distrustful; suspicious

nieugaszony (ńe-oo-ga-shó-ni) adj. m. unextinguished; unquenchable; unsuppressible

nieugięty (ńe-oo-gyáń-ti) adj. m. inflexible;unyielding

nieuk (ńe-ook) m. know-nothing

nieukojony (ńe-oo-ko-yó-ni) adj. m. inconsolable

nieuleczalny (ńe-oo-le-chál-ni) adj. m. incurable

nieumiarkowany (ńe-oo-myar-ko-vá-ni) adj. m. intemperate

nieumiejętny (ńe-oo-mee-yáńt-ni) adj. m. inexpert; unskilled

nieumyślny (ńe-oo-míśhl-ni) adj. m. unintentional

nieunikniony (ńe-oo-ńeek-ńo-ni) adj. m. unavoidable;inevitable

nieuprzedzony (ńe-oo-pzhe-dzó-ni) adj. m. unbiased; not forwarned; not prejudiced

nieuprzejmy (ńe-oo-pzhey-mi) adj. m. impolite; discourteous

nieurodzaj (ńe-oo-ró-dzay) m. bad harvest; bad crops;scarcity

nie usprawiedliwiony (ńe-oos-pra-vyed-lee-vyó-ni) adj. m. unexcused;unjustified; wantom

nieustanny (ńe-oos-tán-ni) adj. m. constant: perpetual;unceasing

nieustraszony (ńe-oos-tra-shó-ni) adj. m. fearless: intrepid

nieusuwalny (ńe-oo-soo-vál-ni) adj. m. immovable: irremovable

nie uszkodzony (ńe oosh-ko-dzó-ni) adj. m. unhurt; undamaged

nieuwaga (ńe-oo-vá-ga) f. inattention; absentmindedness

nieuważny (ńe-oo-vázh-ni) adj. m. inattentive;careless

nieuzasadniony (ńe-oo-za-sad-ńó-ni) adj. m. unfounded;unjustified

nieuzbrojony (ńe-ooz-bro-yó-ni) adj. m. unarmed: disarmed

nieużyteczny (ńe-oo-zhi-téch-ni) adj. m. useless: superfluous

nieużyty (ńe-oozhí-ti) adj. m. unused; uncooperative;disobliging

niewart (ńe-vart) adj. m. not worth; unworthy; not deserving

nie warto (ńe vár-to) adv. not worth (talking):not worth while

nieważny (ńe-vázh-ni) adj. m. invalid; trivial;null and void

niewątpliwy (ńe-vównt-plée-vi) adj. m. sure; doubtless

niewczesny (ńe-vchés-ni) adj. m. untimely; late; inopportune

niewdzięczny (ńe-vdzháńch-ni) adj. m. ungrateful; thankless

niewesoły (ńe-ve-só-wi) adj. m. sad; joyless; pretty bad

niewiadomy (ńe-vya-dó-mi) adj. m. unknown(direction, origin etc.)

niewiara (ńe-vyá-ra) f. disbelief; mistrust; unbelief

niewiasta (ńe-vyás-ta) f. woman

niewidomy (ńe-vee-do-mi) adj.
m. blind:lacking insight
niewidzialny (ńe-vee-dżhal-ni)
adj. m. invisible
niewiedza(ńe-vyé-dza) adj. m.
ignorance: unawarness
niewiele (ńe-vye-le) adv. not
much; not many: little: few
niewielki (ńe-vyel-kee) adj. m.
small; little: unimportant
niewierny (ńe-vyer-ni) adj. m.
disloyal; infidel; unfaithful
niewieści (ńe-vyésh-ćhee) adj.
m. womanly: feminine
niewinność (ńe-veen-noshćh) f.
innocence: purity: chastity
niewinny (ńe-veen-ni) adj. m.
not guilty: innocent:harmless
niewłaściwy (ńe-vwash-ćhee-vi)
adj. m. improper: unsuitable
niewola (ńe-vó-la) f. captivity:
slavery; bondage:servitude
niewolić (ńe-vó-leećh) v. enslave; compel oppress
niewolnica (ńe-vol-ńee-tsa) f.
slave: serf: prisoner of war
niewolnik (ńe-vól-ńeek) m. slave
nie wolno (ńe vól-no) v. not
allowed not permitted
niewód (ńe-voot) m. dragnet
niewprawny (ńe-vpráv-ni) adj.
m. unversed; unskilled; inexpert: incompetent: inefficient
niewspółmierny (ńe-wspoow-myer-
ni) adj. m. incommensurable
nie wtajemniczony(ńe-vta-yem-
nee-chó-ni) adj. m. uninitiat-
ed; outsider: not privy
niewyczerpany (ńe-vi-cher-pá-ni)
adj. m. inexhaustible
niewygoda (ńe-vi-gó-da) f. discomfort: trouble: hardship
niewygodny (ńe-vi-gód-ni) adj.
m. uncomfortable: awkward
niewykonalny (ńe-vi-ko-nál-ni)
adj. m. unfeasible: unworkable
niewykształcony (ńe-vi-kshtaw-
tsó-ni) adj. m. uneducated
niewymierny (ńe-vi-myér-ni) adj.
m. irrational; surd
niewymowny (ńe-vi-móv-ni) adj.
m. unspeakable:inexpressible

niewymuszony (ńe-vi-moo-shó-ni)
adj. m. free (and easy)
niewymyślny (ńe-vi-miśhl-ni)
adj. m. unsophisticated
niewypał (ńe-vi-paw) m. dud
niewypłacalny (ńe-vi-pwa-tsál-
ni) adj. m. insolvent
niewypowiedziany (ńe-vi-po-vye-
dżhá—ni) adj. m. untold
niewyraźnie (ńe-vi-ráźh-ńe) adv.
indistinctly: seedily
niewyraźny (ńe-vi-ráżh-ni) adj.
m. queer; indistinct
niewyrobiony (ńe-vi-ro-byó-ni)
adj. m. raw; inexperienced
niewyrozumiały (ńe-vi-ro-zoo-
myá-wi) adj. m. intolerant
niewysłowiony (ńe-vi-swo-vyó-
ni) adj. m. ineffable
niewyspany (ńe-vis-pá-ni) adj.
m. sleepy; not slept enough
niewystarczający (ńe-vis-tar-
cha-yówn-tsi) adj. m. insufficient : inadequate
niewystawny (ńe-vis-táv-ni) adj.
m. frugal; modest; simple
niewytłumaczony (ńe-vi-twoo-ma-
chó-ni) adj. m. inexplicable
niewytrwały (ńe-vi-trvá-wi)
adj. m. not persistent
niewytrzymały (ńe-vi-tzhi-má-wi)
adj. m. not enduring
niewzruszony (ńe-vzroo-shó-ni)
adj. m. unmoved:rigid
niezachwiany (ńe-za-khvyá-ni)
adj. m. unshaken undeterred
niezadowolenie (ńe-za-do-vo-le-
ńe) n . discontent:displeasure
niezadowolony (ńe-za-do-vo-ló-ni)
adj. m. dissatisfied:displeased
niezakłócony (ńe-za-kwoo-tsó-ni)
adj. m. undisturbed:unmarred
niezależność (ńe-za-leżh-nośhćh)
f. independence :self-sufficiency
niezależny (ńe-za-leżh-ni) adj.
m. independent: self contained
niezamężna (ńe-za-mańzh-na) adj.
f. unmarried :single woman
niezamożny (ńe-za-mozh-ni) adj.
m. rather poor: indigent
niezapominajka (ńe-za-po-mee-
náy-ka) f. forget-me-not

niezapomniany (ně-za-pom-ňa-ni)
adj. m. not-to-be-forgotten
niezaprzeczalny (ňe-za-pzhe-
chál-ni) adj. m. undeniable
niezaradny (ně-za-rád-ni) adj.
m. helpless: resourceless
niezasłużony (ňe-za-swoo-zhó-
ni) adj. m. undeserved
niezawisły (ňe-za-vees-wi) adj.
m. independent:self-dependent
niezawodnie (ňe-za-vód-ňe) adv.
surely; without fail:infallibly
niezawodny (ňe-za-vód-ni) adj.
m. sure: never failing: safe
niezbadany (ňe-zba-da-ni) adj.
m. unexplorable:,inscrutable
niezbędny (ňe-zbánd-ni) adj.
m, indispensable: essential
niezbity (ňe-zbée-ti) adj. m.
irrefutable: uncontrovertible
niezbyt (ňe-zbit) adv. not very
(much): none too; not too
niezdarny (ňe-zdar-ni) adj. m.
clumsy: awkward;,bungled
niezdatny (ňe-zdat-ni) adj. m.
unfit: unqualified:unserviceable
niezdecydowany (ňe-zde-tsi-do-
vá-ni) adj. m. undecided
niezdolność (ňe-zdol-noshćh)
f. inability: unfitness
niezdolny (ňe-zdol-ni) adj. m.
incapable; unable:unfit: dull
niezdrowy (ňe-zdro-vi) adj. m.
unhealthy: unwell:ill:sickly
niezdyscyplinowany (ňe-zdis-tsi-
plee-no-vá-ni) adj. m. un-
disciplined : unruly
niezgłębiony (ňe-zgwańb-yo-ni)
adj. m. inscrutable; abyssal
niezgoda (ňe-zgó-da) f. discord;
disagreement: dissension
niezgodność (ňe-zgod-noshćh)
f. inconsistency.; clash
niezgodny (ňe-zgód-ni) adj. m.
discordant; incompatible
niezgrabny (ňe-zgráb-ni) adj.
m. unhandy; clumsy:shapeless
niezliszczalny (ňe-zeesh-chál-
ni) adj. m. unattainable
niezliczony (ňe-zlee-chó-ni)
adj. m. uncountable:countless
niezłomny (ňe-zwóm-ni) adj. m.
inflexible; firm: steadfast

niezmącony (ňe-zmówn-tsó-ni)
adj. m. unruffled:undisturbed
niezmienny (ňe-zmyen-ni) adj.
m. invariable: constant;fixed
niezmierny (ňe-zmyer-ni) adj.
m. immense: vast: boundless
niezmordowany (ňe-zmor-do-va-ni)
adj. m. indefatigable:tireless
nieznaczny (ňe-znach-ni) adj.
m. trivial; insignificant
nieznajomość (ňe-zna-yo-moshćh)
f. ignorance; unawareness
nieznajomy (ňe-zna-yo-mi) adj.
m. unknown: strange (faces etc.)
nieznany (ňe-zná-ni) adj. m.
unknown: unfamiliar: obscure
nieznośny (ňe-znósh-ni) adj. m.
unbearable: annoying:nasty;pesky
niezręczny (ňe-zrańch-ni) adj.
m. awkward: clumsy:tactless
niezrozumiały (ňe-zro-zoo-mya-
wi) adj. m. unintelligible
niezrównany (ňe-zroov-ná-ni)
adj. m. matchless; incomparable;peerless: unique: grand
niezwłoczny (ňe-zvwóch-ni) adj.
m. instant:prompt: immediate
niezwyciężony (ňe-zvi-chán-zho-
ni) adj. m. invincible
niezwykły (ňe-zvík-wi) adj. m.
unusual:extreme: rare: odd
nieżonaty (ňe-zho-ná-ti) adj.
m. unmarried: single: bachelor
nieżyczliwy (ňe-zhich-lee-vi)
adj. m. unfriendly;ill-disposed
nieżyt (ňe-zhit) m. inflamma-
tion:catarrh: hay fever;colitis
nieżywy (ňe-zhi-vi) adj. m.
dead; lifeless: inanimate
nigdy (ňeeg-di) adv. never
nigdzie (ňeeg-dźhe) adv. nowhere: anywhere(after negation)
nijaki (ňee-ya-kee) adj. m.
none; neuter (gender)
nikczemnik (ňeek-chém-ňeek) m.
villain: scoundrel: wretch
nikczemny (ňeek-chém-ni) adj.
vile:abject; despicable: base
nikiel (ňee-kel) m. nickel
nikły (ňeek-wi) adj. m. scanty
niknąć (ňeek-nównćh) v. vanish
nikotyna (ňee-ko-tí-na) f. ni-
otine: poisonous tabacco extract

nikt (ńeekt) pron. nobody

nim (ńeem) conj. before:till

nimb (ńeemp) m. halo:aureole

niniejszy (ńee-ńey-shi) adj. m. this; present: the present

niski (ńees-kee) adj. m. low

nisko (ńees-ko) adv. low

nisza (ńee-sha) f. niche:recess

niszczący (ńeesh-chown-tsi) adj. m. destructive: disruptive

niszczeć (ńeesh-chech) v. waste away: deteriorate: decay:waste

niszczyciel (ńeesh-chi-chel) m. devastator: destroyer:waster

niszczyć (ńeesh-chich) v. destroy;spoil:ruin: wreck;damage

nit (ńeet) m. rivet

nitka (ńeet-ka) f. thread

nitować (ńee-to-vach) v. rivet

niwa (ńee-va) f. field:soil

niweczyć (ńee-ve-chich) v. destroy: annihilate· lay waste

niwelacja (ńee-ve-láts-ya) f. leveling; survey: surveying

niwelować (ńee-ve-lo-vach) v. level: survey

nizina (ńee-zhee-na) f. lowland

niż (ńeezh) m. lowland;atmospheric low

niż (ńeesh) conj. than

niżej (ńee-zhey) adv. lower; below; down: further down

niższość (ńeesh-shoshch) f. inferiority

niższy (ńeezh-shi) adj. m. lower; inferior: shorter

no (no) part. why; well; now; then: just: there· there now!

noc (nots) f. night

nocleg (nots-leg) m. place to sleep : night's lodging

nocny (nots-ni) adj. m. nocturnal; night-

nocować (no-tso-vach) v. spend night· stay overnight: sleep

noga (no-ga) f. leg : foot

nogawica (no-ga-vee-tsa) f. legging : trouser leg

nomenklatura (no-men-kla-too-ra) f. nomenclature

nominacja (no-mee-náts-ya) f. appointment : nomination

nominalny (no-mee-nál-ni) adj. m. nominal : face(value)

nonsens (nón-sens) m. nonsense

nora (no-ra) f. burrow

norma (nór-ma) f. standard;

norm: rule: general principle

normalizacja (nor-ma-lee-záts-ya) f. normalization:standard

normalizować (nor-ma-lee-zo-vach) v. normalize· standardize

normalny (nor-mál-ni) adj. m. normal: standard: ordinary

normować (nor-mo-vach) v. regulate: standardize:normalize

nos (nos) m. nose : snout

nosić (no-sheech) v. carry; wear: bear :have about one

nosorożec (no-so-ro-shets) m. rhinoceros (with horn)

nostalgia (nos-tál-gya) f. nostalgia: homesickness

nosze (no-she) pl. stretchers

nota (no-ta) f. note; grade

notariusz (no-tár-yoosh) m. notary public·

notatka (no-tát-ka) f. note

notatnik (no-tát-ńeek) m. notebook· diary: notes

notes (no-tes) m. pocket notebook· notebook

notoryczny (no-to-rich-ni) adj. m. notorious : flagrant:arrant

notować (no-to-vach) v. make notes; take notes: write down

notowanie (no-to-va-ńe) n. quotation : record

nowela (no-ve-la) f. short story : amendment

nowelista (no-ve-lees-ta) m. short story writer

nowicjat (no-veéts-yat) m. novitiate : novitiate

nowicjusz (no-veéts-yoosh) m. novice : beginner: tiro

nowina (no-vee-na) f. news

nowinka (no-veén-ka) f. fad

nowiutki (no-vyóot-kee) adj. m. brand-new; spick-and-span

nowoczesny (no-vo-chés-ni) adj. m. modern :up to date:newest

noworoczny (no-vo-róch-ni) adj. m. New Year's · of New Year

nowość (nó-voshch) f. novelty

nowotwór (no-vo-tvoor) m. tumor : new coined word

nowożytny (nu-vo-zhít-ní) adj.
m. (of) modern (peric
nowy (no-vi) adj. m. new
nozdrze (nóz-dzhe) n. nostrii
nożownik (no-zhov-neek) m.
knifer; knife-fighter
nożyce (no-zhi-tse) pl. shears;
clippers ' large shears
nożyczki (no-zhich-kee) pl.
scissors; small scissors
nożyk (no-zhik) m. pocketknife
nów (noov) m. new moon
nóż (noosh) m. knife ;cutter
nucić (noo-cheech) v. hum
nuda (noo-da) f. boredom
nudności (nood-nosh-chee) pl.
nausea ' impulse to vomit
nudny (nood-ni) adj. m. boring;
nauseating :dull: sickening
nudysta (noo-dis-ta) m. nudist
nudziarz (noo-dzhash) m. bore
nudzić (noo-dzheech) v. bore
numer (noo-mer) m. number
numerować (noo-me-ro-vach) v.
number ' give a number to
numerowy (noo-me-ro-vi) adj. m.
porter; bell-boy: hotel waiter
numizmatyka (noo-meez-ma-ti-ka)
f. numismatics :study of coins
nuncjusz (noon-tsyoosh) m. nun-
cio ; papal ambassador
nurek (noo-rek) m. diver
nurkować (noor-ko-vach) v. dive
nurt (noort) m. current (flowing): stream: trend: wake
nurtować (noor-to-vach) v. fret;
penetrate ; pervade: ferment
nurzać (noo-zhach) v. dip; welter in; plunge :immerse:steep
nuta (noo-ta) f. (sound) note
nuty (noo-ti) pl. written music: printed music: score
nuż (noozh) adv. if; and if
nużący (noo-zhown-tsi) adj. m.
tiring :tiresome: wearisome
nużyć (noo-zhich) v. tire :weary
nygus (ni-goos) m. lazybones
nygusować (ni-goo-só-vach) v.
lounge about; loiter ; loaf
nylon (ne-lon) m. nylon
nyża (ni-zha) f. niche; alcove

o (o) prep. of; for; at; by;
about; against; with ' to: over
oaza (o-a-za) f. oasis
oba (o-ba) pron. both
obabrać (o-ba-brach) v. besmear
obaj (o-bay) pron. both
obalenie (o-ba-le-ne) n. overthrow: subversion: abolition
obalić (o-ba-leech) v. overthrow :knock down: fell;refute
obarczyć (o-bar-chich) v. encumber; saddle :load: burden
obarzanek (o-ba-zha-nek) m.
round cracknel torus shaped
obawa (o-ba-va) f. fear; apprehension : phobia;anxiety
obawiać się (o-bav-yach shan) v.
be anxious ; fear' dread
obcas (ob-tsas) m. heel
obcążki (ob-tsownzh-kee) pl.
(small) tongs : pincers:pliers
obcesowo (ob-tse-so-vo) adv.
headlong; outright :abruptly
obcęgi (ob-tsan-gee) pl. tongs
obchodzić (ob-kho-dzheech) v.
go around; evade; elude;
celebrate :inspect :by-pass
obchód (ob-khoot) m. (daily)
beat; celebration 'circuit
obciągać (ob-chown-gach) v.
pull down; cover; pull tight
obciążać (ob-chown-zhach) v.
burden; charge (account)
obcierać (ob-che-rach) v. wipe
obcinać (ob-chee-nach) v. cut
off; clip :crop:chop off
obcisły (ob-chees-wi) adj. m.
tight ' close fitting:clinging
obcokrajowiec (ob-tso-kra-yo-
vyets) m. foreigner: alien
obcokrajowy (ob-tso-kra-yo-vi)
adj. m. foreign : alien
obcować (ob-tso-vach) v. associate :have an intercourse
obcowanie (ob-tso-va-ne) n. intercourse; association
obcy (ob-tsi) adj. m. strange;
foreign :unfamiliar: unrelated
obczyzna (ob-chiz-na) f.foreign
country ; exile: foreign land
obdarować (ob-da-ro-vach) v.
bestow :lavish gifts on ...

obdarty (ob-dar-ti) adj. m. ragged;in rags: tattered
obdarzyc (ob-da-zhich) v. bestow: lavish gifts on ...
obdzielic (ob-dzhe-leech)v. divide; distribute;deal;endow
obdzierac (ob-dzhe-rach)v. rip
off; skin off;strip; fleece
obecnie (o-bets-ne) adv. at
present;just now;to-day
obecnosc (o-bets-noshch) f.
presence: attendance
obejmowac (o-bey-mo-vach) v.
embrace; enfold; span; include;
take over; take in; grasp
obejrzec (o-bey-zhech) v. inspect; glance at; see
obejscie (o-bey-shche) n. bypass; farmyard : manner
obejsc (o-beyshch) v. go around
obelga (o-bel-ga) f. insult;
outrage; abuse affront
obelzywy (o-bel-zhi-vi) adj. m.
insulting; abusive;opprobrious
oberwac (o-ber-vach) v. tear
off; cop it; pluck;get a knock
oberza (o-ber-zha) f. inn
oberzysta (o-ber-zhis-ta) m.
innkeeper;owner of an inn
oberznac (o-ber-zhnownch) v.
cut off; trim; clip
obeschnac (o-bes-khnownch) v.
dry up; get dry; dry
obetrzec (o-be-tzhech) v. wipe
out: dust: rub sore: skin
obezwladnic (o-bez-vwad-neech)
v. overpower;subdue: disable
obeznany (o-bez-na-ni) adj. m.
familiar: acquainted;conversant
obfitosc (ob-fee-toshch) f.
plenty: abundance:profusion
obfity (ob-fee-ti) adj. m.abun-
dant: ample: profuse:liberal
obgadywac (ob-ga-di-vach) v.
talk ill; talk over: crab
obgryzac (ob-gri-zach) v. nibble
bare: gnaw: pick a bone: bite
obiad (ob-yat) m. dinner
obicie (o-bee-che) n. upholstery;
padding; chip; beating :drubbing
obiecywac (o-bye-tsi-vach) v.
promise: look forward to

obieg (o-byek) m. circulation
obiegac (o-bye-gach) v. run-
around; circulate;revolve
obiekcja (o-byek-tsya) f. objection: demur
obiekt (ob-yekt) m. object;
target: subject: building
obiektyw (o-byek-tiv) m.object-
lens: object-glass; objective
obiektywny (o-byek-tiv-ni) adj.
m. objective;impartial
obierac (o-bye-rach) v. choose;
elect; peel : pick: strip
obierzyny (o-bye-zhi-ni) pl.
peelings; parings
obieralny (o-bye-ral-ni) adj.
m. elective: eligible
obietnica (o-byet-nee-tsa) f.
promise: engagement
obijac (o-bee-yach) v. chip;
hoop; loaf :hurt: injure
objadac sie (ob-ya-dach shan)
v. gorge; overeat : cram
objasniac (ob-yash-nach) v.
explain: make clear: gloss
objaw (ob-yav) m. symptom
objawic (ob-ya-veech) v. reveal
objazd (ob-yazt) m. tour; circuit;detour:diversion:by-pass
objac (ob-yownch) v. embrace;
assume: grasp: encompass:span
objezdzac (ob-yezh-dzhach) v.
ride; around:break in a horse
objetosc (ob-yan-toshch) f.
volume; bulk:capacity: content
obkladac (ob-kwa-dach) v. wrap;
cover: line: impose:hit:buffet
oblegac (ob-le-gach) v. besiege
oblac (ob-lach) v. pour on(water)
oblekac (ob-le-kach) v. clothe;
put on; cover; encase: don
oblepiac (ob-le-pyach) v. paste
over: stick: post:plaster over
oblewac (ob-le-vach) v. pour
on: drench: bathe: sprinkle:wash
oblezenie (ob-lan-zhe-ne) m.
siege: state of siege
obliczac (ob-lee-chach) v.
count: reckon; figure out: mean
oblicze (ob-lee-che) n. face
obliczenie (ob-lee-che-ne) n.
calculation: evaluation: count

obligacja (ob-lee-gáts-ya) f.
 obligation; bond ; share
oblizać (ob-leé-zach) v. lick
obŕadowac (ob-wa-do-vach) v.
 load down;heap; burden
obława (ob-wá-va) f. roundup;
 posse ; man hunt: chase: raid
obłąkany (ob-wówn-ká-ni) adj.
 m. insane; loony; madman
obŕęd (ób-waĥt) m. insanity
obŕędny (ob-waĥd-ni) adj. m.
 mad; wild ; insane: crazy
obŕok (ób-wok) m. cloud
obŕowić się (ob-wó-veech shaĥ)
 v. pick up a lot·make a pile
obŕożnie (ob-wózh-ne) adv. bedridden; severely (ill)
obŕożyc (ob-wo-zhich) v. cover;
 wrap: line:impose: hit:buffet
obŕuda (ob-woo-da) f. hypocrisy
obŕudnik (ob-wood-neek) m.hyp-
 ocrite:snuffler:dissembler
obŕudny (ob-wood-ni) adj. m.
 hypocritical:false: canting
obŕupac (ob-woo-pach) v. shell;
 peel:bark: flay:skin
obŕuszczac (ob-woosh-chach) v.
 scale; shell: husk; flay: skin
obŕy (ob-wi) adj.oval;tapering;
 terete; cylindrical: oval
obmacac (ob-ma-tsach) v. feel
 about; explore with fingers
obmawiac (ob-mav-yach) v. slander; backbite; gossip:speak ill
obmierznąć (ob-myerzh-nownch) v.
 get sick of (something)
obmowa (ob-mo-va) f. slander;
 detraction: backbiting
obmurować (ob-moo-ró-vach) v.
 brick in; brick veneer
obmyslac (ob-mish-lach) v. design; contrive; reflect
obmywac (ob-mi-vach) v. wash-
 up:sponge·down·give a wash
obnażac (ob-na-zhach) v. denude;
 bare; unclothe:strip:uncover
obnižac (ob-nee-zhach) v. lower;
 sink; drop; abate; level down
obniženie (ob-nee-zhé-ne) n.
 decrease; reduction; lowering
obnižka (ob-neezh-ka) f. reduction; depreciation:drop:fall

obojczyk (o-bóy-chik) m. collar
 bone;clavicle; amice:gorget
obnosic (ob-nó-sheech) v. take
 around; flaunt ; parade
obojętnie (o-bo-yaĥt-ñe) adv.
 indifferently:slang:no matter
obojętność (o-bo-yaĥt-noshch)
 f. indifference: neutrality
obojętny (o-bo-yaĥt-ni) adj. m.
 indifferent; neutral
obok (ó-bok) adv. prep. beside;
 next; about:close by:by:close
obopólny (o-bo-pool-ni) adj. m.
 common; mutual:reciprocal
obora (o-bó-ra) f. cowbarn
obosieczny (o-bo-shéch-ni) adj.
 m.two-edged: double edged
obowiązek (o-bo-vyówn-zek) m.
 duty; obligation: responsibility
obowiązkowy (o-bo-vyównz-ko-vi)
 adj. m. dutiful; compulsory
obowiązany (o-bo-wyówn-za-ni)
 adj. m. obligated:compelled
obowiązujący (o-bo-vyówn-zoo-
 yówn-tsi) adj. m. obligatory
obowiązywac (o-bo-vyówn-zi-vach)
 v. be in force (law etc)
obozowac (o-bo-zó-vach) v. camp;
 camp out: tent encamp:bivouac
obój (o-booy) m. oboe, (horn)
obóz (o-boos) m, camp
obrabiac (ob-ra-byach) v. machine (metal, wood etc.); work-
 over; fashion; shape;till:hem
obrabiarka (ob-rab-yar-ka) f.
 machine tool: lathe
obrabowac (ob-ra-bo-vach) v. rob
obracac (ob-ra-tsach) v. turnover; rotate: crank
obrachowac (ob-ra-kho-vach) v.
 compute· figure out: calculate
obrachunek (ob-ra-khoo-nek) m.
 settlement; bill;"day of reckoning":count· reckoning
obrada (ob-ra-da) f, conference
obradowac (ob-ra-do-vach) v.
 confer; deliberate: debate: sit
obradzac (ob-ra-dzach) v. bear
 crops: vield a crop:be plentiful
obramowac (ob-ra-mó-vach) v.
 frame:encircle; encase:hem:edge
obrastac (ob-ras-tach) v. overgrow: grow .:grow all over

obraz (ob-raz) m. picture;
image : painting:drawing
obraza (ob-ra-za) f. affront;
offense :insult:outrage:offence
obrazek (ob-ra-zek) m. illustration; small picture
obrazić (ob-ra-żheech) v. offend: affront: insult:sting
obrazowy (ob-ra-zo-vi) adj. m.
pictorial ; picturesque:vivd
obrażenie (ob-ra-zhe-ńe) n.
offense; injury: insults
obraźliwy (ob-rażh-lee-vi) adj.
m. offensive; touchy:resentful
obrażać (ob-ra-zhach) v. offend;
(repeatedly)insult: affront
obrąb (ob-rownb) m. cutoff
obrąbek (ob-rown-bek) m. hem
obrączka (ob-rownch-ka) f. ring
obręb (ob-rainb) m. compass;
area:reach:extent:precincts
obrębiać (ob-rainb-yach) v. hem
obręcz (ob-rainch) f. hoop; tire;
rim: band: gridle: ring:circle
obrobić (ob-ro-beech) v. machine
obrok (ob-rok) m. feed;fodder
obrona (ob-ro-na) f. defense
obronność (ob-ron-nośhch) f.
defense capability:defences
obronny (ob-ron-ni) adj. m. de-
fensive:fortified:protective
obrońca (ob-roń-tsa) m. defender
guard; barrister:advocate
obrośnięty (ob-rośh-ńań-ti) adj.
m. overgrown; unshaven
obrotny (ob-rot-ni) adj. m.
active; skillful; nimble:agile
obrotowy (ob-ro-to-vi) adj. m.
turnover (tax):rotary;revolving
obroża (ob-ro-zha) f. (dog) collar: neck band
obrócić (ob-roo-cheech) v. rotate ;revolve :turn: go
obrót (ob-root) m. turn; turnover: revolution: slew: sales
obrus (ob-roos) m. tablecloth
obruszać (ob-roo-shach) v. loos-
en up: irritate: bring down
obrywać (ob-ri-vach) v. tear
off: tear away:pluck:wrench off
obryzgiwać (ob-riz-gee-vach) v.
splash; spatter

obrzęd (ob-zhańd) m. rite; ceremony : custom
obrzęk (ob-zhańk) m. swelling
obrzękły (ob-zhańk-wi) adj. m.
swollen: oedemous: tumid
obrzmiały (obzh-mya-wi) adj.
m. swollen: oedemous: tumid
obrzucać (ob-zhoo-tsach) v.
throw upon: hurl:pelt; fell
obrzydliwy (ob-zhid-lee-vi)
adj. m. revolting; disgusting
obrzydzenie (ob-zhi-dze-ńe) n.
aversion: nausea: disgust
obrzynać (ob-zhi-nach) v. clip;
cut: cut off; edge: trim;cheat
obsada (ob-sa-da) f. cast; crew;
garrison; staff: mounting
obsadka (on-sad-ka) f. penholder: small mounting
obsadzać (ob-sa-dzach) v. plant;
staff: set: fix: occupy:stock
obserwacja (ob-ser-váts-ya) f.
observation: remark
obserwator (ob-ser-va-tor) m.
observer: look out man:witness
obserwatorium (ob-ser-va-tor-
yoom) m. observatory
obserwować (ob-ser-vo-vach) v.
watch; observe; take stock
obsługa (ob-swoo-ga) f. attendance; service: staff
obsługiwać (ob-swoo-gee-vach)
v. wait-upon; service
obstalować (ob-sta-lo-vach) v.
order (a suit of clothes etc.)
obstalunek (ob-sta-loo-nek) m.
order: a request to supply
obstawać (ob-sta-vach) v. insist on; hold to; stand by;
persist in; abide by
obstąpić (ob-stown-peech) v.
surround: form a circle;cluster
obstrzał (ob-stzhaw) m. gunfire; scope of fire: firing
obstrukcja (ob-strook-tsya) f.
obstruction; constipation
obsuwać (ob-soo-vach) v. slide
down; creep: lower:bring down
obsuwisko (ob-soo-vees-ko) n.
landslide ; landslip
obsychać (ob-si-khach) v. dry
up : get parched: run dry:go dry

obsyłać (ob-si-wach) v. send around (messengers,etc.)

obspypywac (ob-si-pi-vach) v. strew: sprinkle: shower:heap

obszar (ob-shar) m. area; range

obszarnik (ob-shar-ñeek) m. landowner:large scale farmer

obszerny (ob-sher-ni) adj. m. spacious: extensive:vast:broad

obsztorcowac (ob-shtor-tso-vach) v. snub; give hard time

obszukac (ob-shoo-kach) v. search : ransack:make a search

obszyc (ob-shich) v. sew around

obuch (o-bookh) m. back of axe; sledge: head of an axe

obudzic (o-boo-dżeech)v. wake up:awaken: excite; stir up

obumarły (o-boo-mar-wi) adj. m. deadened; half dead:decaying

obumierac (o-boo-myé-rach)v. wither; atrophy:decay: shrink

oburącz (o-boo-rownch) adv. with both hands:with both arms

oburzac (o-boo-zhach) v. revolt; shock: provoke indignation

oburzony (o-boo-zho-ni) adj. m. indignant; resentful

obustronny (o-boo-stron-ni) adj. m. bilateral;mutual:reciprocal

obuwie (o-boo-vye) n. footwear

obwarowywac (ob-va-ro-vi-vach) v. fortify; entrench: secure

obwąchiwac (ob-vown-khee-vach) v. sniff around:smell around

obowiązywac (ob-vyown-zi-vach) v. bind up; bandage; tie

obwieszczac (ob-vyesh-chach) v. announce; proclaim: notify

obwieszczenie (ob-vyesh-che-ñe) n. proclamation: notice

obwiniac (ob-vee-ñach) v. accuse

obwisac (ob-vee-sach) v. sag; droop: hang loosely: flag

obwodowy (ob-vo-do-vi) adj. m. circumferential; district

obwoluta (ob-vo-loo-ta) f. wrapper; book-jacket: file cover

obwoływac (ob-vo-wach) v. acclaim; proclaim: call names

obwód (ob-voot) f. perimeter

oby (obi) part. may...:may you

obycie (o-bi-che) n. good manners: experience:familiarity

obyczaj (o-bi-chay) m. custom

obyczajnosc (o-bi-chay-noshch) f. decency; morality: morals

obyczajny (o-bi-chay-ni) adj. m. decent: moral

obydwaj (o-bi-dvay) num. both

obyty (o-bi-ti) adj. m. familiar; easy mannered:polished

obywac sie (o-bi-vach shañ) v. do without: dispense with

obywatel (o-bi-va-tel) m. citizen; squire: inhabitant

obywatelka (o-bi-va-tél-ka) f. citizen: inhabitant: citizeness

obywatelstwo (o-bi-va-tél-stvo) m. citizenship;nationality

obznajomic (ob-zna-yo-meech)v. familiarize: acquaint:inform

obżarstwo (ob-zhar-stvo) n. gluttony: stuffing oneself

ocalec (o-tsá-lech) v.survive (danger)·rescue: save

ocalenie (o-tsa-lé-ñe) n. rescue: salvation: escape

ocalic (o-tsa-leech) v. rescue

ocean (o-tsé-an) m. ocean

ocena (o-tse-na) f. grade; estimate; appraisal

ocet (o-tset) m. vinegar

och!(okh !) excl.: oh !

ochędożyc (o-khań-do-zhich) v. clean: put in order

ochlapac (o-khla-pach) v. splash: splatter(with mud)

ochładzac (o-khwa-dzach) v. cool; chill: refresh

ochłap (ó-khwap) m. offal; trash; scrap of meat

ochłonąc (o-khwo-nownch) v. calm down: get cooler: cool

ochoczo (o-khó-cho) adv.eagerly; cheerfully: gladly:gaily

ochota (o-khó-ta) f. eagerness; forwardness; willingness

ochotnik (o-khot-ñeek) n. volunteer: serving of free will

ochraniac (o-khra-ñach) v. protect; preserve: shield

ochrona (o-khró-na) f. (shelter) protection; conservation

ochronny (o-khron-ni) adj. m.
protective; preventive

ochrypły (o-khrip-wi) adj. m.
hoarse; husky; raucous

ochrypnąć (o-khrip-nownch) v.
hoarsen; grow hoarse

ochrzcić (okh-zhcheech) v. baptize; christen; name: dub

ociągać się(o-chown-gach shan)
v. linger: delay:put off

ociec (o-chets) v. drain; drip

ociekać (o-che-kach) v. drain;
drip: stream: overflow: drv

ociemniały (o-chem-na-wi) adj.
m. blind: blind man

ocieniać (o-che-nach) v. shade
over: protect from the sun

ocieplać (o-chep-lach) v. warm
up: make warmer: get warm

ocierać (o-che-rach) v. wipe
off: rub sore: gall; abrade

ociężały (o-chan-zha-wi) adj.
m. inert; (lazy) heavy; tardy;
dull: ponderous: languid:bovine

ociosać (o-cho-sach) v. hew

ocknąć się (ots-knownch shan)
v. wake up (from a nap) awake

oclić (ots-leech) v. assess custom duty; levy duty;pay duty

oczarować (o-cha-ro-vach) v.
charm; enchant;fascinate:ravish

oczekiwać (o-che-kee-vach) v.
wait for; await; expect;hope

oczekiwanie (o-che-kee-va-ne)
n. expectation: prospect

oczerniać (o-cher-nach) v.
slander; malign; defame; vilify

oczko (och-ko) n. (needle) eye-
let; little eye:mesh:stitch

oczny (och-ni) adj. m. optic

oczyszczać (o-chish-chach) v.
clean; purify; dust: clear

oczytany (o-chi-ta-ni) adj. m.
well-read : of wide reading

oczywisty (o-chi-vees-ti) adj.
m. obvious; self-evident;plain

oczywiście (o-chi-veesh-che)
adv. obviously; of course

od (od) prep. from; off; of;
for; since; out of; with; per;
by; then (idiomatic)

odbarwić (od-bar-veech) v.
bleach; decolorize

odbicie (od-bee-che) n. reflection; bounce; ricochet; beating
back; deflection: repercussion

odbić (od-beech) v. bounce back;
rescue; recover: reflect:print

odbiegać (od-bye-gach) v. desert; deviate; stray; digress

odbijać (od-bee-yach) v. reflect; print; put off; fend
off; recapture: leave a trace

odbiorca (od-byor-tsa) m. receiver; customer; addressee

odbiornik (od-byor-neek) m.
(radio) receiver: collector

odbiór (od-byoor) m. receipt;
reception; collection

odbitka (od-beet-ka) f. copy;
reprint: impression: proof:slip

odblask (od-blask) m. reflection
of light: gleam: irradiation

odbudowa (od-boo-do-va) f. reconstruction: restoration

odbudować (od-boo-do-vach) v.
rebuild: restore: reconstruct

odbyt (od-bit) m. 1. sale
2. anus: end of alimentary tract

odbywać (od-bi-vach) v. do;
perform; be in progress

odcedzić (od-tse-dzeech) v.
strain: strain out: drain away

odchodzić (od-kho-dzhaech)v.
go away; leave; walk off;
split;sail; retire; withdraw

odchudzać (od-khoo-dzach) v.
reduce (weight); slim:slenderize

odchylać (od-khi-lach) v. deflect; slant; slope:bend back

odchylenie (od-khi-le-ne) n.
deviation: declination:variation

odciągać (od-chown-gach) v.
draw aside : retract:divert:delay

odciążać (od-chown-zhach) v.
relieve;unburden; lighten:ease

odcień (od-chen) m. shade; tint;
undertone; tinge:hue:cast: tone

odcierpieć (od-cher-pyech) v.
suffer for; expiate; atone

odcinać (od-chee-nach) v. cut
off; sever; amputate; detach

odcinek (od-chee-nek) m. sector;
segment; space; period; receipt

odcisk (od-cheesk) m. imprint;
skin-corn: stamp:trace: squeeze

odcyfrować (od-tsi-fró-vach) v.
decipher; make out

odczekać (od-che-kach) v. wait
out· wait for the right moment

odczepić (od-che-peech) v. detach; unhook; get rid:clear out

odczuć (od-chooch) v. feel;
notice; resent; smart from

odczyn (od-chin) m. (chem) reaction: chemical change

odczynnik (od-chin-neek) m.
reagent; reacting substance

odczyt (od-chit) m. lecture

odczytać (od-chi-tach) v. read
over; take the reading; call

oddać (od-dach) v. give back;
pay back; render; deliver

oddalać (od-da-lach) v. remove;
send away; drive away

oddalony (od-da-lo-ni) adj. m.
distant; remote ;far away

oddany (od-da-ni) adj. m. given
up; devoted ;loving; intent

oddawać (od-da-vach) v. give
back; pay back; return:repay

od dawna (od dav-na) since a
long time ·long since

oddech (ód-dekh) m. breath

oddychać (od-di-khach) v.
breathe; take breath; respire

oddział (od-dżhaw) m. division;
section; ward; branch; detail

oddziaływać (od-dżha-wi-vach)
v. influence; affect

oddzielać (od-dżhé-lach) v. separate; divorce; split

oddzielny (od-dżhél-ni) adj. m.
separate ;individual;discrete

oddzierać (od-dżhe-rach) v.
tear off; pull off;pull away

oddźwięk (od-dżhvyank) m. echo;
resonance; repercussion

odebrać (o-dé-brach) v. take
away; receive; withdraw;regain

odechcieć się (o-dekh-chech shan)
v. lose interest:cease liking

odegnać (o-deg-nach) v. chase
away; drive away; drive off

odegrać się (o-dé-grach shan) v.
win back; recover;take place

odejmować (o-dey-mo-vach) v.
subtract; deduct; take away
diminish;withdraw; deprive

odejście (o-dey-shche) n. departure ;,withdrawal;deviation

odejść (o-deyshch) v. depart;
go away; leave; abandon

odemknąć (o-dem-known/ch) v.
open; half open;set ajar:unbolt

odepchnąć (o-dep-khnownch) v.
shove away; beat back;reject

odeprzeć (o-dep-zhech) v. repel;
repulse; fight off; retort

oderwać (o-der-vach) v. tear
off; break off; detach;sever

odesłać (o-des-wach) v. send
back: return;refer; direct

odetchnąć (o-det-known/ch) v.
breathe (freely); respire

odetkać (o-det-kach) v. unstop;
open; uncork· unchoke: fall out

odezwa (o-déz-va) f. proclamation; appeal;urgent request

odgadywać (od-ga-di-vach) v.
guess: surmise; solve a riddle

odgałęziać (od-ga-wàn-żhach) v.
branch away; fork off; ramify

odganiać (od-ga-nach) v. chase
away: drive off; dismiss

odgarniać (od-gar-nach) v. shove
away: rake aside; push aside

odginać (od-gée-nach) v. unbend;
fold back; straighten· curve

odgłos (od-gwos) m. echo; resonance: sound; noise; thud

odgniatać (od-gna-tach) v. bruise; wrinkle; crease (the skin)

odgrażać się (od-gra-zhach shán)
v.talk big; threaten

odgradzać (od-gra-dzach) v.
fence off; separate; shut out

odgrodzić (od-gro-dżheech) v. divide off; fence off; shut off

odgruzować (od-groo-zo-vach) v.
clear off rubbish from a space

odgrywać (od-gri-vach) v. play
off; perform; act; make believe

odgryzać (od-gri-zach) v. bite
off; snap off; gnaw off

odgrzebywać (od-gzhe-bi-vach) v.
dig up; rake up;unearth; turn up

odgrzewać (od-gzhe-vach) v. re-
warm; rehash; warm up (food)

odjazd (od-yazt) m. departure

odjeżdżać (od-yézh-dżhach) v.
depart; be off; abandon ;start

odjęcie (od-yán-che) n. deduction; amputation; weaning
odkazić (od-ka-źheećh) v. disinfect; sterilize
odkażać (od-ka-zhaćh) v. disinfect (repeatedly); sterilize
odkażenie (od-ka-zhe-ńe) n.dis-
infection: sterilization
odkąd (od-kównt) adv. since;
since when ? ever since;from
odkleić (od-kle—eećh) v. unglue; unstick; detach; ungum
odkładać (od-kwa-daćh) v. put
aside; save; put back;put off
odkłonić się (od-kwo-ńeećh
śhań) v. greet back
odkopać (od-ka-paćh) v. dig up
odkorkować (od-kor-kó-waćh) v.
uncork; unjam (the traffic)
odkręcić (od-krán-cheećh) v.
unscrew; turn around
odkroić (od-kró-yeećh) v. cut —
off; carve off; slice off
odkryć (od-krićh) v. discover;
uncover: lay bare;expose;notice
odkrycie (od-kri-ćhe) n. discov-
ery;exploration; exposure
odkupić(od-koo-peećh) v. repurchase; redeem; buy ;replace
odkupienie (od-koo-pye-ńe) n.
redemption ; repurchase
odkurzacz (od-kóo-zhach) m. vac-
cuum cleaner; carpet sweeper
odkuwać się (od-kóo-vaćh śhań)
v. recoup losses;forge;knock off
odlać (od-laćh) v.pour off;cast
odlatywać (od-la-tí-vaćh) v.
fly away; fly off· take off
odległość (od-leg-woshćh) f.
distance: remotness; interval
odległy (od-leg-wi) adj. m. distant; remote; far away;long ago
odlepiać (od-lep-yaćh) v. unglue; unstick; detach; ungum
odlew (od-lev) m. cast; pour
odlewać (od-lé-vaćh) v. pour
off; cast; mould; pour out
odlewacz (od-le-vach) m. founder
odlewnia (od-lev-ńa) f. foundry
odliczać (od-lee-chaćh) v. deduct; count;reckon·off;allow
odliczenie (od-lee-che-ńe) n.
deduction; allowance

odlot (ód-lot) m. departure
(by plane): take-off; start
odludek (od-loó-dek) m. recluse
odludny (od-loód-ni) adj. m.
solitary; lonely; secluded
odłam (ód-wam) m. fraction
odłamać (od-wa-maćh) v. break
off; sever; snap off
odłamek (od-wa-mek) m. chip;
splinter; fragment;chip;stub
odłazić (od-wá-źheećh) v. crawl
away; get unstuck; come off
odłączyć (od-wówn-chićh) v.
sever; disconnect; separate
odłożyć (od-wó-zhićh) v. set
aside; put off; put back
odłóg (ód-wook) m. fallow
odłupać (od-woo-paćh) v. split
off; chip off; break off
odma płucna (ód-ma pwoots-na)
f. pneumothorax; pneumatosis
odmarznąć (od-mar-znównćh) v.
thaw; melt; get warm:unfreeze
odmawiać (od-mav-yaćh) v.refuse;
say prayers; decline;recite
odmeldować (od-mel-do-vaćh) v.
take a formal leave
odmęt (ód-mánt) m. chaotic
whirlpool; confusion; depths
odmiana (od-mya-na) f. change;
alteration;modification
odmieniać (od-mye-ńaćh) v. change;
alter; decline ;   conjugate
odmienny (od-myén-ni) adj. m.
mutable; different; unlike
odmierzać (od-myé-zhaćh) v.
measure off ;mark off
odmłodzić (od-mwo-dźheećh) v.
rejuvenate;make (look) younger
odmowa (od-mó-va) f. refusal;
denial; saving "no"
odmówić (od-moo-veećh) v.refuse;
say prayers ; say "no"
odmrozić (od-mro-źheećh) v. get
frostbite ; get frozen; thaw
odmrożenie (od-mro-zhe-ńe) n.
frostbite; kibe
odmruknąć (od-mrook-nównćh) v.
mutter back; grunt out
odnając (od-na-yównćh) v. sublet
odnawiać (od-náv-yaćh) v. renew;
renovate ; restore;reform

odnajdywać (od-nay-di-vach) v. recover; find; discover

od niechcenia (od ne-khtse-ńa) adv. carelessly; willy-nilly

odniemczać (od-ńem-chach) v. de-Germanize (language etc.)

odniesienie (od-ńe-she-ńe) n. carrying back; reference (line)

odnieść (od-ńeshch) v. bring back; take back; sustain

odnoga (od-no-ga) f. spur; branch; offshoot; river pass

odnosić (od-no-sheech) v. take back; carry back (repeatedly)

odnośnie (od-nosh-ńe) prep. concerning; in comparison

odnośnik (od-nosh-ńeek) m. reference; footnote (in a text)

odnośny (od-nosh-ni) adj. m. relative; respective; proper

odnotować (od-no-to-vach) v. check off; note down; state

odnowa (od-no-va) f. renewal; restoration; regeneration

odnowić (od-no-veech) v. renew; renovate: reform; revive

odosobnić (od-o-sob-ńeech) v. isolate; confine; stand alone

odosobnienie (od-o-sob-ńe-ńe) n. isolation; privacy; seclusion

odor (o-door) m. reek; smell

odpad (od-pat) m. refuse; dropout; waste; muck; scraps

odpadać (od-pa-dach) v. drop off; fall off; peel off; come off

odpadki (od-pad-kee) pl. waste

odparcie (od-par-che) n. repulsion; rejection; refutation

odparować (od-pa-ro-vach) v. parry; repel; evaporate

odparzenie (od-pa-zhe-ńe) n. gall; scald; chafe (skin)

odparzyć (od-pa-zhich) v. blister; chafe one's skin

odpędzać (od-pan-dzach) v. chase away; repel: expel; banish

odpiąć (od-pyońch) v. unfasten; unbutton; unbuckle; unclasp

odpieczętować (od-pye-chań-to-vach) v. unseal; open (a letter)

odpinać (od-pee-nach) v. unbutton; disconnect; undo; unclasp

odpierać (od-pye-rach) v. repel; refute; force back; disprove

odpiłować (od-pee-wo-vach) v. saw off; file off; cut off

odpis (od-pees) m. copy

odpisać (od-pee-sach) v. copy; write back; answer; deduct

odpłacić (od-pwa-cheech) v. repay; reciprocate; get back at

odpłata (od-pwa-ta) f. retribution; repayment; retaliation

odpłynąć (od-pwi-nownch) v. float away; sail away; swim away; put to sea; low tide

odpływ (od-pwif) m. ebb; outflow; odpoczynek (od-po-chi-nek) m. rest; repose; relax from work

odpoczywać (od-po-chi-vach) v. rest; have a rest; take a rest

odpokutować (od-po-koo-to-vach) v. expiate; atone; pay dearly

odporność (od-por-noshch) f. immunity; resistance; hardiness

odpowiadać (od-po-vya-dach) v. answer to; correspond to

odpowiedni (od-po-vyed-ńee) adj. m. respective; adequate; suitable; fit; right; due; opportune

odpowiedzialność (od-po-vye-dźhal-noshch) f. responsibility; liability; civil liability

odpowiedzialny (od-po-vye-dźhal-ni) adj. m. responsible; liable; accountable; trustworthy

odpór (od-poor) m. opposition; resistance; opposition

odprasować (od-pra-so-vach) v. press; iron; press out; express

odprawa (od-pra-va) f. dispatch; rebuff; briefing; debriefing

odprawiać (od-prav-yach) v. dispatch; dismiss; celebrate (mass); order away; send away

odprężać (od-pran-zhach) v. relax; slacken; let down; recoil

odprężenie (od-pran-zhe-ńe) m. relax; easing of tension; détente

odprowadzać (od-pro-va-dzach) v. divert; drain off; escort

odpruwać (od-proo-vach) v. rip off (buttons); rip away

odprzedać (od-pzhe-dach) v. resell

odprzedaż (od-pzhe-dash) f. re-
sale;sale at second hand
odpust (od-poost) m. indulgence
odpuszczenie (od-poosh-che-ñe)
n.foregiveness; remission
odpychać (od-pi-khach) v. repel
odpychanie (od-pi-kha-ñe) n.
repulsion; repelling
odra (ód-ra) f. measles pl. ru-
beola(high fever&skin eruption)
odrabiać (od-rab-yach) v. work
off; work out, get done;undo
odraczać (od-ra-chach) v. put
off; postpone;defer: delay
odradzać (od-ra-dzach) v. advise
against; regenerate; revive
odrapać (o-dra-pach) v. scratch
up; dilapidate; scrape off
odrastać (od-ras-tach) v. grow
back; sprout again; shoot again
odraza (od-ra-za) f. aversion
odrazu (od-ra-zoo) adv. at once
odrażający (od-ra-zha-yówn-tsi)
adj. m. repulsive; hideus
odrąbać (od-równ-bach) v. chop
off; hew away; cut off
odrębność (od-ránb-noshch) n.
distinction; individuality
odrębny (od-ránb-ni) adj. m.
distinct; individual:separate
odręczny (od-ránch-ni) adj. m.
freehand; personal; longhand
odrętwiały (od-ránt-vya-wi) adj.
m. numbed; torpid : stiff
odrobić (od-ro-beech) v. work
off; work out; get done· do
odrobina (od-ro-bee-na) f. small
bit; particle; shred; a dash
odroczenie (od-ro-che-ñe) n.
adjournment; postponment
odroczyć (od-ro-chich) v. put
off; delay; defer; postpone
odrodzenie (od-ro-dze-ñe) m.
rebirth; renaissance
odrodzić (od-ro-dźheech) v.
regenerate :renew; revive
odróżniać (od-roozh-ñach) v. dis-
tinquish; differentiate
odróżniać się (od-roozh-ñach
shán) v. differ :be different
odruch (od-rookh) m. reflex
odrywać (od-ri-vach) v. tear
off; sever;separate;break off

odrzec (od-zhech) v. reply
odrzucać (od-zhoo-tsach) v.
reject; repulse; cast away
odrzutowiec (od-zhoo-tov-yets)
m. jet (plane)
odrzwia (od-zhvya) pl. door-
frame: mine prop set
odrzynać (od-zhi-nach) v. cut
off; cut away; detach· sever
odsądzać (od-sówn-dzach) v.
deny; infamize;deprive of merit
odsetka (od-set-ka) f. interest
point; percentage; proportion
odsiadywać (od-sha-di-vach) v.
sit out; serve (sentence)
odsiecz (od-shech) f. rescue
odskoczyć (od-sko-chich) v.
jump off; spring back·dart away
odsłonić (od-swo-ñeech) v. un-
veil;expose; display: show
odsprzedać (od-spzhe-dach) v.
resell; sale at second hand
odstawać (od-sta-vach) v. hang-
loose; not fit; come off
odstawić (od-sta-veech) v. put
aside ; deliver; play(dumb)
odstąpić (od-stówn-peech) v.
step back; secede; cede
odstęp (od-stánp) m. margin;
space: interval; lapse (of time)
odstępca (od-stánp-tsa) m. renegade; deserter; turncoat
odstępne (od-stánp-ne) n. payment for giving up a lease
odstraszyć (od-stra-shich) v.
deter; frighten away;scare
odstręczyć (od-strán-chich) v.
dissuade; turn away;repel;deter
odstrzał (od-stzhaw) m. shooting
off; firing (game, mine)
odsunąć (od-soo-nownch) v. push
away; shove away; brush aside
odsyłacz (od-si-wach) m. reference mark; footnote mark
odsyłać (od-si-wach) v. send
back; refer;return; direct
odsypać (od-si-pach) v. pour
off (not liquid);alluviate
odsypiać (od-sip-yach) v. catch
up on sleep ; sleep off
odszkodowanie (od-shko-do-va-ñe)
n. indemnity : compensation

odszukać (od-shoo-kach) v. retrieve; run down;seek out;find
odśrodkowy (od-śhrod-ko-vi)
adj. m. centrifugal
odświeżyć (od-śhvye-zhich) v.
refresh; recondition·restore
odświętny (od-śhvyant-ni) adj.
m. festive;ceremonial·showy
odtąd (ód-townt) adv. henceforth; from now on; from here
odtłuścić (od-twoosh-cheech)
v. degrease; reduce weight
odtrącać (od-trown-tsach) v.
repel; jostle; knock off; deduct (charges);thrust aside
odtrutka (od-troot-ka) f.anti-
dote! counterpoison
odtwarzać (od-tva-zhach) v.
reproduce; reconstitute
odtwórca (od-tvoor-tsa) m. re-
producer; performer
oduczać (od-oo-chach) v. un-
teach; unlearn; break a habit
odurzać (o-doo-zhach) v. stun;
make dopey; stupefy;daze;dizzy
odurzenie (o-doo-zhe-ňe) n.
stupor; giddiness;intoxication
odwadniać (od-vad-ňach) v.
drain; dehydrate· dewater
odwaga (od-va-ga) f. courage
odwalić (od-va-leech) v. push
away; beat it; copy; get over
with; roll aside;remove:sham
odwar (od-var) m. decoction
odważnik (od-vazh-ňeek) n.
scale—weight
odważny (od-vazh-ni) adj. m.
brave; courageous;bold;daring
odważyć (od-va-zhich) v. weigh
odważyć się (od-va-zhich śhäň)
v. dare;have the courage·risk
odwdzięczyć się(od-vdzhäň-chich
śhäň) v. repay (with gratitude; return; requite:repay
odwet (od-vet) m. retaliation;
retort; revenge; requital
odwiązać (od-vyown-zach) v.
untie; unfasten;unbuckle;undo
odwieczny (od-vyech-ni) adj. m.
eternal; immemorial·age long
odwiedzać (odvye-dzach) v.vis-
it; call on; pay a visit;
pay a call; come to see

odwiedziny (od-vye-dźhee-ni)n.
visit; call; coming to see
odwijać (od-vee-yach) v. unwrap
odwilż (ód-veelzh) f. thaw
odwlekać (od-vlé-kach) v. put
off; postpone;delay;drag away
odwodnić (od-vod-ňeech) v. drain
odwodzic (od-vo-dźheech)v. draw
off;draw aside;dissuade
odwoływać (od-vo-wach) v. take
back; appeal; refer; recall
odwołanie (od-vo-wa-ňe) n. recall; appeal;repeal;cancellation
odwozić (od-vo-żheech) v. take
back (by car); drive back
odwód (ód-voot) m. reserve
odwracać (od-vra-tsach) v. reverse: turn around;invert
odwrotny (od-vrót-ni) adj. m.
reverse;opposite;converse
odwrót (ód-vroot) m. retreat;
reverse; withdrawal
odwykać (od-vi-kach) v. break
a habit; loose the habit
odwzajemniać (od-vza-yem-ňach)
v. reciprocate;repay;return
odyniec (o-di-ňets) m. boar
odzew (od-zev) m. echo; reply
odziedziczyć(o-dźhe-dźhee-chich)
v. inherit; succeed(to a title)
odzienie (o-dźhe-ňe) n. clothing
odzież (o-dźhezh) f. clothes
oznaczać (od-zna-chach) v.
distinguish; decorate;mark off
odznaczenie (od-zna-che-ňe) n.
distinction;award;decoration
odznaka (od-zna-ka) f. badge
odzwierciadlać (od-zvyer-chad-
lach) v. reflect (something)
odzwyczajać (od-zvi-chá-yach)
v. break a habit;make loose a
habit
odzyskać (od-zis-kach) v. retrieve; regain; recover:win back
odzywać się (od-zi-vach śhäň) v.
speak up;drop a line;respond
odźwierny (od-dźhvyer-ni) m.
doorman; janitor;caretaker
odżyć (ód-zhich) v. come back to
life; revive;be reborn:reappear
odżywczy (od-zhiv-chi) adj. m.
nutritious;nourishing;alimentary
odżywiać (od-zhiv-yach) v.nour-
ish; feed ;supply with food

odżywienie (od-zhiv-yé-ńe) n. food; nourishment; diet

ofensywa (o-fen-si-va) f. offensive; push; attack

oferma (o-fér-ma) f. sad sack

oferta (o-fér-ta) f. offer

ofiara (o-fyá-ra) f. victim; offering; sacrifice; dune

oficer (o-fée-tser) m. (military) officer

oficjalny (o-feets-yál-ni) adj. m. official; formal; reserved

oficyna (o-fee-tsí-na) f. backhouse; printing shop; annex

ofuknąć (o-fook-nównćh) v. rebuke; reprimand; trounce; rate

ogar (ó-gar) m. bloodhound

ogarek (o-ga-rek) m. candleend; stump; stub: cigarette end

ogarniac (o-gár-ńach) v. seize; comprehend; take in; grasp

ogien (ó-geń) m. fire; flame

ogier (ó-ger) m. stallion

ogladać (o-glówn-dach) v. inspect; consider; see

ogledny (o-glánd-ni) adj. circumspect; moderate; cautious

oglada (o-gwa-da) f. good manners; refinement; urbanity: polish

ogłaszac (o-gwa-shach) v. advertize; declare; publish

ogłuchnąc (o-gwookh-nównćh) v. become deaf; be hushed

oglupiec (o-gwoop-yech) v. become stupid; grow silly

ognie sztuczne (óg-ńe shtóoch-ne) pl. fireworks

ogniotrwały (o-gńo-trva-wi) adj. fireproof; incombustible·

ognisko (od-ńees-ko) n. hearth; focus; camp fire·fire place

ognisty (og-nées-ti) adj. m. fiery; flaming; passionate

ogniwo (og-ńee-vo) n. link

ogolic (o-gó-leech) v. shave

ogon (ó-gon) m. tail; trail; scut

ogonek (o-gó-nek) m. waiting line; queue; diacritical mark

ogorzały (o-go-zhá-wi) adj. m. sunburnt; tanned; weather beaten

ogólnie (o-gool-ńe) adv. generally; as a rule; universally

ogólny (o-goól-ni) adj. m. general; prevailing; global; total

ogół (ó-goow) m. people; public

ogółem (o-goo-wem) adv. on the whole; as a whole; altogether

ogórek (o-goo-rek) m. cucumber

ogórkowy sezon (o-goor-ko-vi se-zon) slack time (season)

ograbic (o-gra-beech) v. rob

ograniczony (o-gra-ńee-cho-ni) adj. m. narrow-minded; limited

ogrodnik (o-gród-ńeek) m. gardener; horticulturist

ogrodzic (o-gro-dźheech)v. fence in; enclose; wall in; rail in

ogromny (o-grom-ni) adj. m. huge

ogród (ó-good) m. garden

ogryzac (o-gri-zach) v. gnaw away; nimble at; pick (a bone)

ogrzewac (o-gzhe-vach) v. heat

ohydny (o-khid-ni) adj. m. hideous; ghastly; abonimable: vile

o ile (o ée-le) conj. as far as

ojciec (oy-chets) m. father

ojciec chrzestny (oy-chyets khzhést-ni) godfather

ojczym (oy-chim) m. stepfather

ojczysty język (oy-chís-ti yáńzik) native tongue

ojczyzna (oy-chíz-na) f. native country; motherland; homeland

okaleczyc (o-ka-le-chich) v. maim; cripple; lame; mutilate

oka mgnienie (o-ka mgńe-ńe) n. eye blink; split second

okap (ó-kap) m. eaves; overlap

okaz (ó-kas) m. specimen; type

okazac (o-ka-zach) v. show; demonstrate; evidence; exhibit

okazały (o-ka-zá-wi) adj. m. magnificent; stately; grand

okaziciel (o-ka-żhee-chel) m. bearer (of a check etc.)

okazja (o-kaz-ya) f. opportunity

okazyjny (o-ka-zíy-ni) adj. m. occasional; chance (acquaintance)

okazywac (o-ka-zí-vach) v. demonstrate; show; manifest; display

oklaski (o-klas-kee) pl. applause; clapping; acclamations

oklaskiwać (o-klas-kee-vach) v. applaud; clap (one's hands)

okleić (o-klé-eech) v. paste-
over;stick over; smear over
oklepany (o-kle-pá-ni) adj. m.
commonplace; (well) worn
okład (ó-kwat) m. compress;
hotpad ; lining;wrapping
okładka (o-kwád-ka) f. (book)
cover; book binding
okłamać (o-kwa-mach) v. deceive; tell a lie; delude
okno (ók-no) n. window
oko (ó-ko) n. eye; eye sight
okolica (o-ko-lee-tsa) f. region; surroundings;vicinity
okoliczność (o-ko-leech-noshch)
f. circumstance; fact;occasion
około (o-kó-wo) prep. near;
about; more or less;at;on;or so
okoń (ó-koń) m. perch; bass
okop (ó-kop) m. trench
okopcić (o-kóp-cheech) v. soot
okostna (o-kóst-na) f. perios-
teum; lining of the bones
okólnik (o-kool-neek) m. circular; corral;poultry yard
okpić (ó-kpeech) v. pool wool
over eyes; deceive;cheat;gull
okradać (o-kra-dach) v. pickpocket; burglarize; rob
okrakiem (o-kra-kem) adv.
astraddle;with legs wide apart
okrasa (o-kra-sa) f. fat; ornament ; seasoning ;gravy;lard
okrasić (o-kra-sheech) v. adorn;
season ;add a condiment
okratować (o-kra-to-vach) v.
grate; bar (a window)
okratowanie (o-kra-to-va-ne)
m. grating; railings; bars
okrąg (o-krownk) m. district
okrągły (o-krówng-wi) adj. m.
round; spherical·full(month etc)
okrążać (o-krówn-zhach) v. encircle; circle;revolve:detour
okres (ó-kres) m. period;phase
określać (o-kresh-lach) v.
define; qualify;fix;appoint
okręcać (o-kran-tsach) v. coil
around;wrap; turn around
okręt (o-krant) m. ship:boat
okrężny (o-kranzh-ni) adj. m.
roundabout;indirect;devious
circuitous; circular:travelling-
pedlar's(trade etc.)

okropność (o-krop-noshch) f.
horror; atrocity;outrage
okropny (o-krop-ni) adj. m.
horrible;fearful;awful;extreme
okruch (o-krookh) m. crumb
okrucieństwo (o-kroo-chyeń-
stvo) n. cruelty;atrocities
okrutny (o-kroot-ni) adj. m.
cruel;savage;excessive; sore
okrycie (o-kri-che) n. covering; wrap;garment;overcoat
okrywać (o-kri-vach) v. cover
okrzyczany (o-kzhi-chá-ni) adj.
m. notorious;famous;renowned
okrzyk (ó-kzhik) m. outcry
okrzyknąć (o-kzhik-nównch) v.
proclaim;declare; brand
oktawa (ok-ta-va) f. octave
okucie (o-koó-che) n. hardware; ferrule; fitting
okuć (o-kooch) v. shoe a horse;
shackle; fit a lock and hinges
okular (o-koo-lar) m. eyeglass
okularnik (o-koo-lár-neek) m.
cobra;poisonous snake of Asia
okulista (o-koo-lees-ta) m.
eye doctor;eye surgeon;oculist
okultyzm (o-kool-tizm) m. oc-
cultism; hidden knowledge
okup (o-koop) m. ransom
okupacja (o-koo-páts-ya) f.
occupation; occupancy
okupować (o-koo-po-vach) v.
occupy;invade a territory
okupywać (o-koo-pi-vach) v. pay
ransom; compensate;redeem;atone
olbrzym (ól-bzhim) m. giant
olbrzymi (ol-bzhi-mee) adj. m.
gigantic;huge;cllossal;excessive
olcha (ól-kha) f. alder tree
oleander (o-le-án-der) m. oleander (an evergreen shrub)
olej (ó-ley) m. oil; oil paint
olej lniany (ó-ley lña-ni) adj.
m. linseed-oil
oligarchia (o-lee-gár-khya) m.
oligarchy;the ruling persons
oliwa (o-lee-va) f. olive; oil
oliwić (o-lee-veech) v. oil
oliwka (o-leev-ka) f. olive-tree
olszyna (ol-shi-na) f. alder-
tree stand; alder wood
olśniewać (ol-shńe-vach) v.
dazzle; ravish;enchant·

ołów (owoof) m. lead;lead shot
ołówek (o-woo-vek) m. lead
pencil;drawing in pencil
ołtarz (ow-tash) m. altar
omackiem (o-máts-'kem) adv.
gropingly ; blindfold
omal (ó-mal) adv. nearly
omamić (o-má-meech) v. deceive
omaścić (o-másh-cheech) v. add
fat; add butter(on bread etc.)
omawiac (o-máv-yach) v. discuss
omdlały (om-dlá-wi) adj. m.
fainted; faint; languid
omdlec (om-dlech) v. faint
omen (ó-men) m. omen
omieszkac (o-myesh-kach) v.
fail;omit;neglect
omijac (o-mee-yach) v. pass
omlet (om-let) m. omelet
omłócić (o-mwoo-cheech) v.
thresh out; give a thrashing
omotac (o-mo-tach) v. entangle
omowic (o-moo-veech) v. discuss
omylic (o-mi-leech) v. mislead
omylny (o-mil-ni) adj. m. fal-
lible;misleading;deceitful
omyłka (o-miw-ka) f. error
on; ona; ono (on; o-na; ó-no)
pron. he; she; it
oni (o-ńee) m. pl. they;
one (o-ne) f. pl. they
ondulacja (on-doo-láts-ya) f.
(hair) wave;permanent wave
ondulacja trwała (on-doo-lats-
ya trvá-wa) permanent (wave)
onegdaj (o-nég-day) adv. the
other day;two days ago
ongis (on-geesh) adv. (arch)
at one time;once upon a time
oniemiały (o-ńe-mya-wi) adj.
m. mute; dumb; speechless
oniesmielac (o-ńe-shmye-lach)
v. intimidate;browbeat;cow
opactwo (o-páts-tvo) n. abbey
opaczny (o-pách-ni) adj. m.
wrong;mistaken;improper
opad (o-pat) m. (rain) fall
opadac(o-pa-dach) v. subside
(na)opak (na o-pak) adv. up-
side down; reverse;wrong way
opakowanie (o-pa-ko-va-ńe) n.
wrapping ; packing

opal (o-pal) m. opal
opalac się (o-pa-lach shań) v.
suntan; tan;bronze;lie on the sun
opalanie (o-pa-la-ńe) n. heating (house etc.);fire marking
opalenizna (o-pa-le-ńeez-na) f.
suntan; tan; scorched remains
opał (o-paw) m. fuel for heating
opamiętac (o-pa-myań-tach) v.
sober down; bring to reason
opanowac (o-pa-no-vach) v.
master;conquer;seize; learn
opanowany (o-pa-no-vá-ni) adj.
m. cool-headed;composed;calm
opary (o-pá-ri) pl. fumes
oparcie (o-par-che) n. support
oparzyć (o-pá-zhich) v. scald
opasac (o-pa-sach) v. belt;
girdle;grid;encircle;surround
opaska (o-pás-ka) f. band
opasły (o-pás-wi) adj. m. obese
opasc (o-pashch) v. drop; sink;
hang loose;settle;collapse;slope
opatentowac (o-pa-ten-to-vach)
v. patent ;take out a patent
opatrunek (o-pa-troo-nek) m.
dressing; bandage; field dressing
opatrywac (o-pa-tri-vach) v.
fix; dress; provide;prepare
opera (o-pé-ra) f. opera; opera
house; no end of a joke
operacja (o-pe-ráts-ya) f. surgery; operation; action;process
operowac (o-pe-ro-vach) v.oper-
ate; manipulate; act; handle
opętanie (o-pań-tá-ńe) n. obsession;demonical possession
opieczętowac (o-pye-chań-to-
vach) v. seal up; seal
opieka (o-pyé-ka) f. care
opiekowac (o-pye-ko-vach) v.
take care; care for;have charge
opiekun (o-pye-koon) m. guardian; curator; foster-parent
opierac się (o-pye-rach shań)
v. lean; base; relay;rest;defy
opieszały (o-pye-shá-wi) adj.
m. slow; tardy; lazy; inert
opinia (o-peeń-ya) f. opinion;
view; reputation; sentiment
opis (o-pees) m. description
oplątać (o-plown-tach) v. ensnare; entangle; entwine

opluwać (o-ploo-vach) v. spit
on ;spit at; slander; defame

opłacać (o-pwa-tsach) v. pay;
bribe ;cover the cost;reward

opłakany (o-pwa-ka-ni) adj. m.
deplorable ;sad; pitiful

opłakiwać (o-pwa-kee-vach) v.
lament; deplore ;mourn

opłata (o-pwa-ta) f. fee

opłatek (o-pwa-tek) m. wafer

opłucna (o-pwoots-na) f. pleu-
ra ;membrane around the lungs

opłukiwać (o-pwoo-kee-vach) v.
rinse; wash with water

opływać (o-pwi-vach) v. sail
around; abound ;encircle;roll

opływowy (o-pwi-vo-vi) adj. m.
streamlined; streamline

opodal (o-po-dal) adv. near by

opodatkować (o-po-dat-ko-vach)
v. tax; impose a tax

opona (o-po-na) f. tire

oponować (o-po-no-vach) v.
oppose ; take exception

opornie (o-por-ne) adv. with
difficulty ; arduosly

oporny (o-por-ni) adj. m. balky;
recalcitrant; refractory

opowiadać (o-pov-ya-dach) v.
tell - tale ;relate;record

opozycja (o-po-zits-ya) f. opposition ; resistance

opór (o-poor) m. resistance

opóźniać (o-poożh-nach) v. delay; retard;slow dawn;defer

opóźnienie (o-poożh-ne-ne) n.
delay ;deferment;tardiness

opracować (o-pra-tso-vach) v.
work up; elaborate:compile

oprawa (o-pra-va) f. frame;
binding;framework:handle

oprawca (o-prav-tsa) m. skinner;
executioner:torturer:assassin

opresja (o-pres-ya)f.oppression

oprocentowanie (o-pro-tsen-to-
wa-ne) n. interest(on money)

oprowadzać (o-pro-va-dzach) v.
show around; act as a guide

oprócz (o-prooch) prep.: except;
besides:,apart from:but:save

opróżniać (o-proożh-nach) v.
empty ;clear:evacuate·unload

opryskliwy (o-prisk-lee-vi)
adj. m. peevish;gruff;harsh

opryszek (o-pri-shek) m. hood-
lum:hooligan:rowdy:rough-neck

oprzec (op- zhech) v. lean; base;
resist:become inffamed;inflame

oprzytomnieć (o-pzhi-tom-ńech)
v. recover; collect oneself

optyk (op-tik) m. optician

optymista (op-ti-mees-ta) m.
optimist: one of cheerful views

opublikować (o-poo-blee-ko-
vach) v. publish;make public

opuchły (o-pookh-wi) adj. m.
swollen; dilated

opuchlina (o-pookh-lee-na) f.
swelling :dilatation

opuszczać (o-poosh-chach) v.
leave; omit; abandon· lower

opustoszały (o-poos-to-sha-vi)
adj. m. deserted:desolate:empty

opuszczenie (o-poosh-che-ńe) n.
omission·lowering:reduction

orać (o-rach) v. till; plough

oranżeria (o-ran-zher-ya) f.
greenhouse: hothouse:orangery

oraz (o-raz) conj. as well as

orbita (or-bee-ta) f. orbit

order (or-der) m. decoration;
order(for service rendered etc.)

ordynarny (or-di-nar-ni) adj.
m. gross; coarse:vulgar:trashy

orędzie (o-rań-dzhe) n. (official) message;proclamation

oręż (o- rańsh) m. weapon

organiczny (or-ga-ńeech-ni)
adj. m. organic:constitutional

organista (or-ga-ńees-ta) m.
organist :organ player

organizacja (or-ga-ńee-záts-
ya)f.organization:organized group

organizm (or-ga-ńeezm) m. organism; any living thing

orgia (org-ya) f. orgy

orka (or-ka) f. tillage

orkiestra (or-kes-tra) f. orchestra: orchestra pit

orny (or-ni) adj. m. arable

orszak (or-shak) m. retinue

ortodoksja (or-to-doks-ya) f.
orthodoxy: conventionality

ortografia (or-to-gra-fya) f.
orthography;correct spelling

oryginalny (o-ri-gee-nál-ni)
adj. m. original;inventive;new

orzech (o-zhekh) m. nut;walnut

orzeczenie (o-zhe-che-ńe) m.
decision; sentence; ruling

orzeł (o-zhew) m. eagle;genius

orzeźwiać (o-zheźh-vyach) v.
refresh; brace up; invigorate

osa (o-sa) f. wasp; vixen;shrew

osad (o-sat) m. sediment; dregs

osada (o-sa-da) f. settlement

osadnik (o-sad-ńeek) m. settler

osadzać (o-sa-dzach) v. plant;
seat; settle; place;fix;steady

osamotnienie (o-sa-mot-ńe-ńe)
n. isolation;loneliness

osądzać (o-sown-dzach) v.
sentence ; judge ;prejudge

oschły (oskh-wi) adj. m. arid;
dry; cold; stiff; stand-offish

oselka (o-sew-ka) f. whetstone

oset (o-set) m. thistle;teasel

osiadać (o-sha-dach) v. settle;
subside; make a settlement

osiągnąć (o-showng-nownch) v.
attain;achieve;gain;reach

osiedlać (o-shed-lach) v.
settle;make a settlement

osiem (o-shem) num. eight

osiemdziesiąt (o-shem-dźhe-
shównt) num. eighty

osiemnaście (o-shem-nash-che)
num. eighteen

osiemset (o-shem-set) num.
eight hundred

osierocić (o-she-ro-cheech)
v. be orphaned

osika (o-shee-ka) f. aspen

osikać (o-shee-kach) v. sprinkle; piss on (vulg.)

osiodłać (o-shod-wach) v. saddle; reduce to subjugation

osioł (o-shyow) m. donkey; ass

oskarżać (o-skár-zhach) v.
accuse ;charge with;indict

oskrzela (o-skzhe-la) pl. n.
bronchia;main part of windpipe

oskrzydlać (o-skzhid-lach) v.
outflank ;go beyond; cut off

oskubać (o-skoo-bach) v. fleece;
feather;pluck;skin; soak

osłabiać (o-swab-yach) v. weak-
en ;reduce; lessen;diminish

osłabienie (o-swa-bye-ńe) n.
weakness ; diminuation;debilitation

osłona (o-swo-na) f. shield;
cover ; protection; defense

osładzać (o-swa-dzach) v. sweet-
en; put sugar; cheer up

osłupiały (o-swoo-pya-wi) adj.
m. amazed; aghast ; astounded

osmarować (o-sma-ro-vach) v.
besmear; libel ; run down; soil

osoba (o-só-ba) f. person

osobisty (o-so-beés-ti) adj.
m. personal; private ;particular

osobiście (o-so-beésh-che) adv.
personally ; in person

osobnik (o-sób-ńeek) m. individual; specimen; person

osobny (o-sób-ni) adj. m. separate; private; individual

osobowość (o-so-bo-vośhch) f.
personality; individuality

osowiały (o-so-vya-wi) adj. m.
depressed; dejected ;glum;monish

ospa (ós-pa) f. smallpox

ospały (os-pa-wy) adj. m.
drowsy; sleepy; sluggish; dull

ostatecznie (o-sta-tech-ńe) adv.
finally; after all; at last

ostateczny (o-sta-tech-ni) adj.
m. final ;ultimate; eventual

ostatek (o-sta-tek) m. reminder; rest; remains; scrap

ostatni (o-stát-ńee) adj. m.
last; late; end;closing; parting

ostatnio (o-stát-ńo) adv. of late;
lately; not long ago; recently

ostoja (o-sto-ya) f. mainstay

ostroga (o-stró-ga) f. spur

ostrokątny (o-stro-kównt-ni)
adj. m. sharp-angled

ostrożność (o-strozh-nośhch)
f. caution; prudence; care

ostrożny (o-strozh-ni) adj. m.
careful; prudent;cautious; wary

ostry (ó-stri) adj. m. sharp

ostryga (o-stri-ga) f. oyster

ostrze (o-stzhe) n. cutting
edge; spike ;blade; point;prong

ostrzegać (o-stzhe-gach) v.
warn of; warn against;admonish

ostrzeliwać (o-stzhe-lee-vach)
v. shoot at; strafe; fire at;
accustom to gun fire

ostrzeżenie (o-stzhe-zhé-ńe)
n. warning ;danger sign·notice
ostrzyć (o-stzhich) v. sharp-
en : whet;grind;put an edge
ostrzygać (o-stzhi-gach) v.
cut (hair) ; shear sheep;trim
ostudzać (o-stoó-dzach) v. cool
ostygać (o-sti-gach) v. cool
down ; chill, cool off: abate
osuszać (o-soó-shach) v. dry;
drain: dehumidify;wine; mop
oswobodzić (o-svo-bo-dźheech)
v. free; liberate:rescue:rid
oswoić (o-svó-eech) v. tame;
familiarize; tame;domesticate
oszacować (o-sha-tso-vach) v.
evaluate; estimate;appraise
oszczep (osh-chep) m. javelin
oszczerstwo (osh-chér-stvo) n.
calumny; libel; defamation
oszczędności (osh-chańd-nosh-
ćhee) pl. savings;money)
oszklenie (o-shkle-ńe) n. glaz-
ing (of windows)
oszołomić (o-sho-wó-meech) v.
stun: daze:stupefy:bewilder
oszpecić (o-shpe-ćheech) v. deface; disfigure:deform; mar
oszukać (o-shoo-kach) v. cheat
oszust (o-shoost) m. cheater
oś (osh) f. axle (axis)
ościenny (o-shchen-ni) adj. m.
bordering: adjoining: adjacent
ość (oshch) f. (fish) bone
oślepiać (o-shle-pyach) v.
blind; dazzle; strike blind
ośmieszać (o-shmye-shach) v.
ridicule;deride;make fun of
ośrodek (o-shró-dek) m. center
oświadczenie (o-shviad-ché-ńe)
n. declaration; pronouncement
oświadczyny (c-shvyad-chi-ni)
pl. marriage proposal
oświata (o-shvya-ta) f. education; learning
oświecać (o-shvye-tsach) v.
light up; enlighten; educate
oświetlenie (o-shvyet-le-ńe) n.
lighting ;light: illumination
otaczać (o-ta-chach) v. surround;enclose:turn on a lathe
otchłań (ot-khwań) f. abyss

otępienie (o-tań-pye-ńe) n.
dullness ;stupor:stupefaction
oto (o-to) part. here; there
otoczenie (o-to-ché-ńe) n. environment;setting; associates
otoczyć (o-tó-chich) v. surround: enclose;turn on a lathe
otomana (o-to-ma-na) f. couch
otóż (o-toósh) conj. now
otruć (o-trooch) v. poison
otrucie (o-troo-ćhe) n. poisoning
otrzaskać (o-tshas-kach)v.acquaint
otrząsać (o-tzhóuwn-sach) v.
shake loose; shudder; strew
otrzewna (o-tzhév-na) f. peri-
toneum; lining of abdomen
otrzeźwieć (o-tzhézh-vyech) v.
sober up;be disillusioned:brisk up
otrzymać(o-tzhi-mach) v. receive ; get; be given;acquire
otulić (o-too-leech) v. tuck in;
wrap;wrap up: shroud:enfold: lag
otwarcie (o-tvar-ćhe) adv.openly;
frankly; in plain words;outright
otwarty (o-tvar-ti) adj. m.
open; frank:overt;professed
otwierać (ot-vye-rach) v. open
otwór (ót-voor) m. opening
otyły (o-ti-wi) adj. m. obese
owacja (o-váts-ya) f. ovation
owad (ó-vad) m. insect
owal (ó-val) m. oval
owca (óv-tsa) f. sheep
owczarek (ov-cha-rek) m. sheep-dog
owczarnia(ov-chár-ña)f. sheen-fold
owdowiały (ov-do-vya-wi) adj.
m. widowed : one who lost wife
owies (ó-vyes) m. oats
owiewać (o-vyé-vach) v. blow
upon;sweep over: encompass:inspire
owijać (o-vee-yach) v. wrap up
owłosiony (o-vwo-sho-ni) adj.
m. hairy; hirsute; shaggy; pilose
owo (ó-vo) pron. that : that thing
owoc (ó-vots) m. fruit ;fruitage
owrzodzenie (o-vzho-dze-ńe) n.
ulceration : sore: sores
owsianka (ov-shan-ka) f. oatmeal; kasha; porridge
owszem (óv-shem) part. yes;
certainly; on the contrary
ozdabiać (o-zdáb-yach) v. dec-
:orate; adorn :trim: garnish

ozdoba (oz-dó-ba) f. decoration
oziębiac (o-zháń-byach) v. cool
off; chill; cool down; damp
oziębły (o-zhánb-wi) adj. m.
frigid ; cold; reserved; dry
oznaczac (o-zná-chach) v. mark;
signify ; indicate; fix; spell
oznajmiac (o-znay-myach) v.
announce ;inform; notify;state
oznaka (o-zná-ka) f. sign;
symptom; badge; mark
ozor (o-zoor) m. (bull's)
tongue; gossiping tongue
oženic (o-zhe-ńeech) v. marry
oźywiac (o-zhiv-yach) v. bring
to life; animate;brisk up
oźywienie (o-zhi-vye-ńe) n.
animation ;liveliness; stir
oźywiony (o-zhiv-yo-ni) adj. m.
animated; lively; brisk,
ósemka (oo-sém-ka) f. eight
ósma godzina (oós-ma go-dzhee-
na) eight o'clock
ósmak (oós-mak) m. eighth grad-
er; eighth grade pupil
ów (oof) m. pron. that
owa (ó-va)f. pron. that
owo (ó-vo)n. pron. that
owi (ó-vee)pl. m. pron. that
owe (ó-ve)pl. f. pron. that
owczesny (oov-chés-ni) adj. m.
the then;of those days
ówdzie (oóv-dzhe) adv. elsewhere; there
pa ! (pa) excl.: bye-bye !
pacha (pá-kha) f. armpit
pachnąc (pákh-nównch) v. smell
(good) ;have a fragrance
pachołek (pa-kho-wek) m. boy;
page;servant;menial; flunkey
pachwina (pakh-vee-na) f. groin
pacierz (pá-chesh) m. prayer
pacierzowy stos (pa-che-zhó-vi
stos) spinal column; spine
paciorki (pa-chór-kee) pl.
string of beads ;short prayer
pacjent (páts-yent) m. patient
pacyfista (pa-tsi-fees-ta) m.
pacifist ;believer in peace
pacyfizm (pa-tsi-feezm) m.
pacifism; ideology of peace
paczka (pách-ka) f. parcel

paczyc (pá-chich) v. warp
padac (pá-dach) v. fall down
padalec (pa-dá-lets) m. blind-
worm: slow warm
padlina (pad-lée-na) f. carrion
pagorek (pa-góo-rek) m. hill
pająk (pá-yównk) m. spider
pajęczyna (pa-yáń-chi-na) f.
cobweb ; spider web;gossamer
paka (pá-ka) f. crate;lock-up
pakowac (pa-kó-vach) v. pack;
cram; wrap ; pack off; pack up
pakunek (pa-koo-nek) m. baggage
pal (pál) m. pile ; stake·picket
palący (pa-lówn-tsi) m. smoker
palec (pá-lets) m. finger : toe
palenie (pa-le-ńe) n. smoking
palenisko (pa-le-ńees-ko) n.
hearth ; fireplace; grate
paleta (pa-lé-ta) f. palette
palic (pa-leech) v. burn; smoke
cigarette; heat;scorch;shoot
paliwo (pa-lee-vo) n. fuel
palma (pál-ma) f. palm-tree
palnik (pál-ńeek) m. burner
palto (pál-to) n. overcoat
pałac (pá-wats) m. palace
pałka (páw-ka) f. stick; club
pamflet (pám-flet) m. pamphlet
pamiątka (pa-myównt-ka) f.
souvenir; token of remembrance
pamięc (pá-myańch) f. memory
pamiętac (pa-myáń-tach) v. remember; recall;be careful
pamiętnik (pa-myáńt-ńeek) m.
diary; memoirs; album
pan (pan) m. lord ; master;
mister; you ;gentleman: squire
pan młody (pan mwo-di) m. bridegroom; man about to be married
pani (pa-ńee) f. lady; you;
madam ; mistress(in school etc.)
panika (pa-ńee-ka) f. panic· scare
panna (pán-na) f. miss; girl:lass
panna młoda (pán-na mwó-da) f,
bride; woman about to be married
panoszyc się (pa-nó-shich sháń)
v. domineer ; boss : run the show
panowac (pa-nó-vach) v. rule;
reign; be master of; command;rife
panteizm (pan-té-eezm) m. pan-
theism

pantera (pan-té-ra) f. panther

pantoflarz (pan-to-flash) m. henpecked husband

pantofel (pan-to-fel) m. slipper; shoe; light low shoe

pantomima (pan-to-mee-ma) f. pantomime; gestures no words

panujący (pa-noo-yówn-tsi) adj. m. prevailing; ruling

pański (pań-skee) adj. m. lord's; your's

państwo (pań-stvo) n. state; married, couple

papa (pá-pa) f. feltpaper

papier (pá-pyer) m. paper

papieros (pa-pyé-ros) m. cigarette;tabacco rolled in paper

papieski (pa-pyés-kee) adj. m. papal; of the Pope

papież (pá-pyesh) m. pope

papka (páp-ka) f. pulp; mash; pap; gruel; paste; slurry

paplać (páp-lać) v. prattle

paproć (pá-proć) f. fern

papryka (pa-prí-ka) f. redpepper; paprica; paprika

papuga (pa-poo-ga) f. parrot

para 1. (pá-ra) f. couple

para 2. (pá-ra) f. steam

parabola (pa-ra-bó-la) f. parabola

parada (pa-rá-da) f. parade

paradoks (pa-rá-doks) m. paradox; apparent, contradiction

parafia (pa-ráf-ya) f. parish

parafina (pa-ra-fée-na) f. paraffin(waxy petroleum)

paragraf (pa-ra-graf) m. paragraph(a distinct section)

paraliż (pa-ra-leesh) m. paralysis;crippling of activities

parametr (pa-rá-metr) m. parameter;element of an orbit

parapet (pa-ra-pet) m. windowsill; stool rail; breastwork

parasol (pa-rá-sol) m. umbrella

parawan (pa-ra-van) n. screen

parcelować (par-tse-ló-vać) v. parcel out(land);cut up

parcie (pár-će) n. thrust

park (park) m. park

parkan (pár-kan) m. fence; net; hoarding

parlament (par-lá-ment) m. parliament; national legislature

parny (pár-ni) adj. m. sultry

parobek (pa-ró-bek) m. farmhand; plough man; rustic

parodia (pa-ród-ya) f. parody

parokrotnie (pa-ro-krot-ńe) adv. repeatedly; a couple of times

parostatek (pa-ro-stá-tek) m. steamboat; steamer; steamship

parować (pa-ró-vać) v. evaporate; vaporize; cook by steam

parowiec (pa-ró-vyets) m. steamboat; steamer; steamship

parowóz (pa-ró-voos) m. steam locomotive : railroad engine

parów (pá-roov) m. ravine

parówki (pa-roóv-kee) pl. hot dogs; sausages; frankfurters

parszywy (par-shi-vi) adj. m. mangy; scabby; lousy; horrid

partacki (par-táts-kee) adj. m. bungled up; botched; fudged

partacz (pár-tach) m. bungler

parter (par-ter) m. ground floor; first floor; parterre

partia (párt-ya) f. party; card game; political party; game

partner (pár-ner) m. partner

partyjny (par-tíy-ni) adj. m. party(member); party member

partykuła (par-ti-koo-wa) f. particle;

partyzantka (par-ti-zánt-ka) f. guerrilla; partisan war

parytet (pa-ri-tet) m. parity

parzyć (pá-zhich) v. scald; steam; burn; percolate; couple

parzysty numer (pa-zhis-ti noo-mer) even number

pas (pas) m. belt; traffic lane

pasat (pá-sat) m. trade wind

pasażer (pa-sá-zher) m. passenger : chap; fellow; liner

pasek (pá-sek) m. belt; band

pasieka (pa-shé-ka) f. apiary

pasierb (pa-sherb) m. stepson

pasierbica (pa-sher-bee-tsa) f. stepdaughter

pasja (pás-ya) f. passion

paskarz (pás-kash) m. profiteer

pasmo (pás-mo) n. streak; tract; range; traffic lane

pasożyt (pa-só-zhit) m. parasite ; sponger

pasta (pás-ta) f. paste

pasterka (pas-tér-ka) f. midnight mass; shepherdess

pasterz (pás-tesh) m. shepherd

pastwa (pás-tva) f. prey

pastwisko (pas-tvees-ko) n. pasture ; grassland

pastylka (pas-til-ka) f. tablet

pasywny (pa-sív-ni) adj. m. passive; acted upon

pasza (pá-sha) f. fodder

paszcza (pásh-cha) f. jaw

paszport (pásh-port) m. passport ; certificate

paść (paśhćh) v. fall down; graze ; tend cattle; feed

patelnia (pa-tél-ña) f. frying-pan with a handle

patent (pá-tent) m. patent

patetyczny (pa-te-tích-ni) adj. m. pathetic ; pompous; turgid

patolog (pa-tó-lok) m. pathologist ; specialist in pathology

patriarcha (pa-tree-ár-kha) m. patriarch

patriota (pa-tree-ó-ta) m. patriot

patron (pá-tron) m. sponsor; stencil; pattern ; protector

patronat (pa-tró-nat) m. patronage ; power to grant favors

patroszyc (pa-tro-shich) v. disembowel; gut ; draw (a fowl)

patrzec (pá-tzhech) v. look

patyk (pá-tik) m. stick

patyna (pa-tí-na) f. patina

pauza (páw-za) f. pause

paw (pav) m. peacock

paznokieć (paz-nó-kyech) m. (finger) nail ; toe nail

pazur (pá-zoor) m. claw

paź (paśh) m. page

październik (paźh-dzhér-ñeek) m. October

pączek (pówn-chek) m. bud

pąsowy (pówn-só-vi) adj. m. red; crimson : bright red; poppy red

pchać (pkhach) v. push; thrust

pchła (pkhwa) f. flea

pchnięcie (pkhñáń-che) n. push; thrust; jostle : shove; lunge

pech (pekh) m. bad luck

pechowiec (pe-khó-vyets) m. unlucky fellow; lackless chap

pedagog (pe-dá-gok) m. pedagogue; educator; educationist

pedał (pe-daw) m. 1. pedal; 2. gay; homosexual; pansy boy

pedant (pé-dant) m. pedant

pejcz (peych) m. horsewhip

pejzaż (pey-zash) m. landscape

peleryna (pe-le-ri-na) f. cape

pelikan (pe-lee-kan) m. pelican

pełnia (pew-ña) f. fullness

pełnić (pew-ñeech) v. fulfill

pełno (pew-no) adv. plenty

pełnoletni (pew-no-lét-ñee) adj. m. adult; of age

pełnomocnictwo (pew-no-mots-ñeets-tvo) n. power of attorney; full powers (legal)

pełny (pew-ni) adj. m. full

pełzać (pew-zach) v. creep; crawl ; fawn; drag; cringe

penicylina (pe-ñee-tsi-lee-na) f. penicillin

pensja (pén-sya) f. salary; pension; allowance; wages

pensjonat (pen-syó-nat) m. boarding house

perfidny (per-féed-ni) adj. m. perfidious; double dealing

perfumy (per-foo-mi) pl. scent; perfume ; perfumes

pergamin (per-gá-meen) m. parchment; sheep skin

period (pér-yod) m. period

perkal (pér-kal) m. calico

perła (pér-wa) f. pearl

peron (pé-ron) m. train-platform at railroad station

perski (pér-skee) adj. m. Persian; Iranian; of Iran

personalny (per-so-nál-ni) adj. m. personal; personnel officer

personel (per-só-nel) m. staff; personnel; employees

perspektywa (per-spek-tí-va) f. perspective; sense of pornortion

perswazja (per-svaz-ya) f. persuasion; power of persuading

pertraktacja (per-trak-táts-ya) f. negotiation; parley

peruka (pe-róo-ka) f. wig

peruwiański (pe-roo-vyań-skee) adj. m. Peruvian: of Peru

peryskop (pe-rís-kop) m. periscope

pestka (pést-ka) f. kernel;pip; drupe; stone; trifle

pesymista (pe-si-meés-ta) m. pessimist

petent (pé-tent) m. petitioner

pewien (pé-vyen) adj. m. certain; one; a; an; some; sure

pewnik (pév-ñeek) m. axiom

pewniak (pév-ñak) m. cinch; surefooted man; certainty

pewny (pév-ni) adj. m. sure; secure; dependable· safe

pęcak (pán-tsak) m. peeled barley; hulled barley

pęcherz (pán-khesh) m. bladder

pęczniec (pánch-ñech) v. swell

pęd (pánd) m. rush; dash; run; speed;impetus;urge;shoot;sprout

pędzel (pán-dzel) m. (paint) brush; tuft of hair

pędzic (pán-dzeech) v. drive; run; lead; distill;hurry

pęk (pánk) m. bunch

pękać (pán-kach) v. burst;split; crack;go off; burst; snap

pępek (pán-pek) m. navel

pętac (pán-tach) v. shackle; hobble;knock about

pętak (pán-tak) m. squirt

pętelka (pán-tél-ka) f. loop; noose; knot

piac (pyach) v. crow ; sing

piana (pyá-na) f. foam

pianino (pya-ñee-no) n. piano

piasek (pyá-sek) m. sand

piasta (pyás-ta) f. hub; nave

piastowac (pyas-tó-vach) v. nurse; tend; hold

piąc się (pyównch śhań)v.climb

piątek (pyówn-tek) m. Friday

piątka (pyównt-ka) f. five

piąty (pyówn-ti) num. fifth

picie (pee-che) n. drinking

pic (peech) v. drink; booze

picus (pee-tsoosh) m. dandy

piec (pyets) m. stove; oven; furnace; kitchen stove; kiln

piec (pyets) v. bake; roast ; burn; scorch; sting; smart

piechota (pye-khó-ta) m. infantry ;a variety of beans

piechotą (pye-khó-town) adv. on foot; (go) on foot

piecza (pyé-cha) f. care; charge

pieczarka (pye-chár-ka) f. meadow mushroom

pieczątka (pye-chównt-ka) f. seal; stamp; signet

pieczeń wołowa (pye-cheń vo-wó-va) f. roast beef

pieczyste (pye-chis-te) n. roast meat; meat course; joint; roast

pieczywo (pye-chi-vo) n. bakerygoods; bread; baking

pieg (pyeg) m. freckle ;ephelis

piegowaty (pye-go-vá-ti) adj. m. freckled

piekarnia (pye-kár-ña) f. bakery; baker's shop

piekarz (pye-kash) m. baker

piekielny (pye-ḱel-ni) adj. m. infernal; of hell; hellish

piekło (pyék-wo) n. hell

pielęgniarka (pye-lang-nár-ka) f. nurse; hospital nurse

pielęgnowac (pye-lang-no-vach) v. nurse; tend; care;cultivate

pielgrzym (pyél-gzhim) m. pilgrim ;wanderer to holy place

pielucha (pye-loo-kha) f. diaper; baby's napkin

pieniądz (pye-ñównts) m. money; coin; currency; funds

pienic (pye-ñeech) v. foam; sparkle; cover with foam

pieniężny (pye-ñánzh-ni) adj. m. monetary; pecuniary;moneyed

pień (pyeń) m. trunk; stem; stump ; snag; stock; root

pieprz (pyepsh) m. pepper

pierdziec (pyér-dzhech) v. fart (vulg.): stink up

pierdzioch (pyér-dzhokh)m. old fart (vulg.); old stinker

piernat (pyer-nat) m. featherbed ; bedding

piernik (pyer-ñeek) m. gingerbread; duffer

piers (pyersh) f. breast;chest

pierscien (pyersh-cheń) m. ring

pierscionek (pyersh-chó-nek) m. ring (small)

pierwej (pyer-vey) adv. of
first; sooner; before; first

pierwiastek (pyer-vyas-tek) m.
root; element; radical

pierworodny (pyer-vo-rod-ni)
adj. m. firstborn

pierwotny (pyer-vot-ni) adj.
m. primitive; primary;original

pierwszenstwo (pyerv-shen-stvo)
n. priority; precedence

pierwszy (pyer-vshi) num. first

pierzchac (pyezh-khach) v. run
away; flv; flee; disperse;scutter

pierze (pye-zhe) n. feathers

pierzyna (pye-zhi-na) f.feather-
bed; eider down; quilt

pies (pyes) m. dog

pieszczota (pyesh-cho-ta) f.
caress; endearment

pieszo (pye-sho) adv. on foot

piescic (pyesh-cheech) v. fondle;caress;pet;hug; babble

piesn (pyeshn) f. song

pietruszka (pyet-roosh-ka) f.
parsley

pieciobój (pyan-cho-booy) m.
pentathlon

piecioletni (pyan-cho-let-nee)
adj. m. five year old

pięc (pyanch) num. five

piedz (pyandzh) m. palm; span

pięcdziesiąt (pyan-dzhe-shownt)
num. fifty

pięcset (pyanch-set) num. five-
hundred

pięknosc (pyank-noshch) f.
beauty; good looks; loveliness

piękny (pyan-kni) adj. m.beau-
tiful; lovely; fine:handsome

piesciarz (pyansh-chash) m.
boxer ; pugilist

pięsc (pyanshch) f. fist

piesciarstwo (pyansh-char-stvo)
m. box; boxing; pugilism

pięta (pyan-ta) f. heel

piętnastoletni (pyant-nas-to-
let-ni) adj. m. fifteen years
old

piętnasty (pyant-nasti) num.
fifteenth

piętnascie (pyant-nash-che) num.
fifteen

piętno (pyant-no) n. mark;stig-
ma; brand; stamp; impress

piętro (pyant-ro) n. story;
floor ;storey

piętrzyc (pyant-zhich) v. pile
up ; bank un;heap; accumulate

pigułka (pee-goow-ka) f. pill

pijak (pee-yak) m. drunk

pijany (pee-ya-ni) adj. m.
drunk ; tipsy; intoxicated;elated

pijawka (pee-yav-ka) f. leech

pikantny (pee-kant-ni) adj. m.
spicy; piquant; pungent; sharp

piknik (peek-neek) m. picnic

pilnik (peel-neek) m. file

pilnosc (peel-noshch) f. diligence; urgency;industry; care

pilny (peel-ni) adj. m. diligent; urgent; industrious:careful

pilot (pee-lot) m. pilot

pilsn (peelshn) f. felt

piła (pee-wa) f. saw; bore

piłka (peew-ka) f. ball; hand-
saw : football; socker; shot

piłowac (pee-wo-vach) v. file;
saw : bore; rasp

pingwin (peen-gveen) m. penguin

piołunowka (pyo-woo-noov-ka) f.
absinth flavored liqueur

pion (pyon) m. plumb (line)

pionek (pyo-nek) m. pawn

pionier (pyo-ner) m. pioneer

pionowy (pyo-no-vi) adj. m.
vertical; upright; plumb

piorun (pyo-roon) m. thunder-
bolt; lightning shaft

piorunochron (pyo-roo-no-khron)
m. lightning-rod

piosenka (pyo-sen-ka) f. song

piórko (pyoor-ko) n. (small)
feather; pen ; plumelet

pióro (pyoo-ro) n. feather; pen

piramida (pee-ra-mee-da) f.
pyramid

pirat (pee-rat) m. pirate

pirotechnika (pee-ro-tekh-nee-
ka) f. pyrotechnics

pisac (pee-sach) v. write

pisarz (pee-sash) m. writer

pisemnie (pee-sem-ne) adv. in
writing; in black and white

pisk (peesk) m. squeal

piskliwy (peesk-lee-vi) adj. m.
shrill; squeaky; thin; strident;
piping; reedy

pisklę (peesk-lañ) n. chicken;
nestling; squealer
piskorz (pees-kosh) m.loach;eel
pismo (pees-mo) n. writing;
letter; newspaper; scripture;
alphabet; type; print
pisownia (pee-sóv-ña) f. spelling; orthography
pistolet (pees-tó-let) m. pistol; handgun : gun ; spray gun
pisuar (pee-soo-ar) m. urinal
piszczec (peesh-chech) v.creak:
squeak; screech; squeal;peep
piszczel (peesh-chel) m. shin-
bone; tibia; blow pipe
piśmiennictwo (peesh-myen-ñeets-
tvo) n. literature
piśmiennie (peesh-myén-ñe) adv.
in writing;in black and white
piwiarnia (peev-vyár-ña) f.
beer hall;beer house;saloon
piwnica (peev-ñee-tsa) f. cellar; basement; coal cellar
piwny (peev-ni) adj. m. brown
(color); hazel; beer-
piwo (pee-vo) n. beer
piwonia (pee-vó-ña) f. peony
piwowar (pee-vó-var) m. brewer
piżama (pee-zhá-ma) f. pyjamas
plac (plats) m. square; area;
ground;building site; field
plac boju (plats bó-yoo) battle
field; field of battle
placek (plá-tsek) m. cake; pie
placówka (pla-tsoov-ka) f.
sentry; post; outpost:agency
plaga (plá-ga) f. plague
plagiator (plag-yá-tor) m.
plagiarist
plakat (plá-kat) m. poster
plama (plá-ma) f. blot; stain
plamić (plá-meech) v. blot;
stain; soil; tarnish; defile
plan (plan) m. plan; design:map
planeta (pla-né-ta) f. planet
planować (pla-nó-vach) v. plan
planowo (pla-nó-vo) adv. according to plan; systematically
plantacja (plan-táts-ya) f.
plantation
plaster (plás-ter) m. plaster;
patch; tape; adhesive; slice

plastyczne sztuki (plas-tích-ne
shtoo-kee) fine arts
plastyczny (plas-tích-ni) adj.
m. plastic; artistic; vivid
plastyk (plás-tik) m. artist;
plastic (substance)
platerować (pla-te-ró-vach) v.
plate (with an other metal)
platforma (plat-fór-ma) f. platform :train; lorry; shelf
platoniczny (pla-to-ñeech-ni)
adj. m. Platonic;unsubstantial
platyna (pla-tí-na) f. platinum
plazma (pláz-ma) f. plasma
plaża (plá-zha) f. beach
plażować (pla-zho-vach)v.sun-bathe
plądrować (plown-dró-vach) v.
plunder; ransack
pląsy (plown-si) pl. dance
plątać (plown-tach) v. entangle
plebania (ple-bá-ña) f. rectory
plebiscyt (ple-bees-cit) m. pleb-
iscite; people's direct vote
plecak (ple-tsak) m. rucksack
plecionka (ple-chon-ka) f. plaid
braid; wattle; basket work
plecy (ple-tsi) pl. back;backing
pleć (plech) v. weed (a garden)
plemienny (ple-myen-ni) adj. m.
tribal; of a trbe
plemię (ple-myañ) n. tribe
plemnik (plém-ñeek) m. sperm
plenum (ple-noom) n. plenary
session; plenary assembly
pleść (pleshch) v. twist; blab;
weave;interlace; talk nonsense
pleśnieć (plesh-ñech) v. mold
pletwa (plet-va) f. fin;dovetail
plewić (ple-veech) v. weed
plik (pleek) m. bundle; sheaf
plisa (plee-sa) f. pleat
plomba (plom-ba) f. lead seal;
tooth filling; stopping
plon (plon) m. crop;yield
plotka (plót-ka) f. gossip; rumor; piece of gossip
pluć (plooch) v. spit; abuse
plugawy (ploo-gá-vi) adj. m.
filthy; squalid:foul;obscene
plus (ploos) m. plus; asset
plusk (ploosk) m. splash
pluskać (ploos-kach) v. splash

pluskiewka (ploos-kév-ka) f.
thumbtack;drawing pin
pluskwa (ploos-kva) f. bedbug
plusz (ploosh) m. plush
plutokracja (ploo-to-kráts-ya)
f. plutocracy
pluton (ploó-ton) m. platoon
plwocina (plvo-chée-na) f.
spittle;expectoration; spit
płaca (pwa-tsa) f. wage;salary
płachta (pwákh-ta) f. sheet
płacić (pwá-cheech) v. pay
płacz (pwach) m. cry; weep
płakać (pwá-kach) v. cry; weep
płaski (pwás-kee) adj. m. flat
płaskorzeźba (pwas-ko-zhéźh-ba)
f. (bas) relief; bas-relief
płaskowyż (pwas-kóvish) m. pla-
teau; table land
płaszcz (pwashch) m. overcoat
płaszczyć (pwásh-chich) v. flatten; become flat;fall,flat
płaszczyzna (pwash-chíz-na) f.
plane;surface;area;sheet:plain
płat (pwat) m. slice; lobe
płatać (pwá-tach) v. cut; play
(tricks);slice;split;fell
płatek (pwa-tek) m. flake
płatność (pwát-noshch) f. payment ; remittance
pławić (pwá-veech) v. float;
wallow : duck; drown;soak
płaz (pwas) m. reptile
płaz (pwas) m. flat of sabre
płciowy (pwchó-vi) adj. m.
sexual: genital; sex-(urge etc.)
płeć (pwech) f. sex; complexion
płetwa (pwét-va) f. fin
płochliwy (pwo-khlee-vi) adj.
m. timid ; shy; skittish
płochy (pwo-khi) adj. m. fri-
volous ;shy;timid;fickle
płodny (pwod-ni) adj. m. fertile :productive; prolific
płodzić (pwo-dźheech)v. beget
płomień (pwo-myeń) m. flame
płonąć (pwo-nównch) v.be on
fire :blaze;be inflamed;glow
płonny (pwon-ni) adj. m. sterile ;useless;vain;of no avail
płoszyć (pwo-shich) v. frighten
płot (pwot) m. fence;hoarding

płowieć (pwo-vyech) v. fade
płowy (pwó-vi) adj. m. flaxen;
fair; buff; fallow; fawn
płód (pwoot) m. fetus; fruit
płócienny (pwoo-chén-ni) adj.
m. linen; canvas-(sail,shoes etc.)
płótno (pwoot-no) n. linen;canvas
płuco (pwoo-tso) n. lung
płucny (pwoots-ni) adj. m. pul-
monary
pług (pwook) m. plough; plow
płukać (pwoo-kach) v. rinse;
wash; gargle
płyn (pwin) m. liquid: fluid
płynąć (pwi-nównch) v. flow;
swim; sail; drift; go by;come
płynny (pwin-ni) adj. m. liquid;
fluent; fluid;smooth;graceful
płyta (pwi-ta) f, plate; slab;
disk; sheet: board;record
płyta gramofonowa (pwi-ta gra-
mofo-nó-va) f. (musical) record : disk
płytki (pwit-kee) adj. m. shallow; flat; trivial; poinless
pływać (pwi-vach) v. swim; float;
navigate; be afloat; be evasive
pływak (pwi-vak) m. swimmer;
float; quibler; buoy
pniak (pnak) m. stump; trunk
po (po) prep. after; to; up to;
till; upon; for; at; in; up;
of; next; along; about; over;
past; behind ; as far as
pobicie (po-bee-che) n. battery
pobić (po-beech) v. beat up;
defeat ; beat in; thrash; spank
pobielac (po-bye-lach) v. whiten;
tin : make white; paint white
pobierać (po-byé-rach) v. take;
collect ; receive;get;draw:charge
pobliski (pob-lees-kee) adj. m.
nearby ; neighboring
pobłażać (po-bwa-zhach) v. indulge; forbear ; be tolerant
pobłażliwy (po-bwazh-lee-vi)
adj. m. lenient; forgiving
poboczny (po-bóch-ni) adj. m.
lateral; secondary : accessory
poborca (po-bor-tsa) m. (tax)
collector : tax gatherer
poborowy (po-bo-ró-vi) m. recruit; recruiting

pobory (po-bó-ri) pl. salary

pobrać (po-brać) v. receive; collect; get; draw; gather

pobudka (po-bood-ka) f. incentive; motive; reveille

pobudliwy (po-bood-leé-vi) adj. m. excitable: ebullient

pobyt (pó-bit) m. stay; visit

pocałować (po-tsa-wó-vach) v. kiss: give a kiss

pocałunek (po-tsa-woo-nek) m. kiss: caress with the lips

pochlebiać (po-khle-byach) v. flatter: adulate; expect:fawn

pochlebny (po-khleb-ni) adj. m. flattering: complimentary

pochłaniać (po-khwa-ñach) v. absorb: swallow up;engulf

pochmurny (po-khmoor-ni) adj. m. gloomy; cloudy: overcast

pochodnia (po-khód-ña) f. torch

pochodny (po-khód-ni) adj. m. derivative: derived

pochodzenie (po-kho-dze-ñe) n. origin; descent; source

pochopny (po-khop-ni) adj. m. hasty; eager; rush: ready

pochować (po-kho-vach) v. bury

pochód (pó-khoot) m. march; procession; parade

pochwa (pókh-va) f. sheath; _vagina_

pochwała (po-khva-wa) f. praise; eulogy; approval: applouse

pochylić (po-khí-leech) v. incline; slope: slant: droop

pochyły (po-khi-wi) adj. m. inclined; stooped: sloping:oblique

pociać (pó-chownch) v. cut up; slash; sting; saw up: intersect

pociąg (póch-ownk) m. train; affinity: inclination

pociągać (po-chown-gach) v.pull; draw; attract;tug: attract:coat

pociągnięcie (po-chówng-ñan-che) n. pull; move; stroke: pluck

po cichu (po chee-khoo) adv. secretly; silently; softly

pocić (pó-cheech) v. sweat

pociecha (po-ché-kha) f. comfort; joy:solace:;satisfaction

po ciemku (po chem-koo) adv. in the dark:while in the dark

pocierać (po-ché-rach) v. rub

pocieszać (po-ché-shach) v. console; comfort;cheer up; solace

pocieszenie (po-che-she-ñe) n. consolation: comfort; solace

pocieszny (po-chesh-ni) adj. m. funny; amusing;droll; comic

pocisk (pó-cheesk) m. missile; bullet; projectile

po co ? (po tso) what for ?

poczać (po-chównch) v. begin; conceive; become pregnant

początek (po-chown-tek) m. beginning; start:outset;fore-part

początkujący (po-chownt-koo-yówn-tsi) m. beginner

poczciwy (poch-chee-vi) adj. m. good-hearted ; friendly ;kindly

poczekać (po-ché-kach) v. wait

poczekalnia (po-che-kál-ña) f. waiting room

poczęstować (po-chown-stó-vach) v. treat: entertain; serve

poczęstunek (po-chown-stoo-nek) m. treat; drinks; entertainment

poczta (póch-ta) f. post; mail

pocztówka (poch-toóv-ka) f. postcard: picture postcard

poczucie (po-choo-che) n. feeling; sense; consciousness

poczwórny (po-chvoór-ni) adj. m. fourfold;four times as large, as tall;as long, as strong,as big

poczynać (po-chi-nach) v. begin (aggressively); conceive

poczytalny (po-chi-tál-ni) adj. m. accountable;, sane

poczytny (po-chit-ni) adj. m. popular (book):widely read

pod (pod) prep. under; below; towards;, on; in ; underneath

podać (po-dach) v. give; hand; pass ;serve; shake (hand)

podanie (po-dá-ñe) n. application : request; legend

podarek (po-da-rek) m. gift

podarty (po-dár-ti) adj. m. torn

podatek (po-dá-tek) m. tax ;duty

podatnik (po-dat-neek) m. taxpayer; rate payer

podaż (pó-dazh) f. supply

podążać (po-down-zhach) v. make for; draw to: make ons's way

podbicie (pod-bee-che) n. conquest; instep; lining ;ceiling

podbiec (pŏd-byets) v. run up
podbiegunowy (pod-bye-goo-nó-vi) adj. m. polar;near pole
podbój (pŏd-booy) m. conquest
podbudowa (pod-boo-dó-va) f. substructure; base course
podbródek (pod-broo-dek) m. chin; bib; feeder
podburzać (pod-boo-zhach) v. stir up; incite to revolt
podchmielony (pod-khmye-ló-ni) adj. m. tipsy; in drink
podchodzić (pod-khó-dźheech)v. approach; assume an attitude
podchwycić (pod-khvi-cheech) v. catch up; snatch up; spot
podchwytliwy (pod-khvit-lee-vi) adj. m. captious (question etc.)
podciągać (pod-chown-gach) v. draw up ;pull up;improve;class
podczas (pod-chas) prep. during; while ;when; whereas
podczerwony (pod-cher-vo-ni) adj. m. infrared
poddać (pŏd-dach) v. surrender; suggest ;submit; expose
pod dostatkiem (pod dos-tat-kyem) adv. plenty; enough
podejmować (po-dey-mo-vach) v. take up; entertain ;pick up
podejrzany (po-dey-zha-ni) adj. m. suspect ;suspicious; shady
podejrzliwy (po-dey-zhlee-vi) adj. m. suspicious ;distrustful
podeptać (po-dep-tach) v. tramp (under foot);bustle about
poderwać (po-der-vach) v. jerk up; pick up; weaken ;rouse
podeszwa (po-desh-va) f. sole
podginać (pod-gee-nach) v. tuck up; cock ;turn up; bend(a knee)
podglądać (pod-glown-dach) v. spy; peep ; pry; snoop
podgórski (pod-goor-skee) adj. m. foot-hill ;piedmont
podjechać (pod-ye-khach) v. drive up ;ride uphill; come up
podgrzewać (pod-gzhe-vach) v. warm up; heat up
podjudzać (pod-yoo-dzach) v. stir up; incite (to evil)
podkasać (pod-ká-sach) v. tuck up ; turn up; rise

podkład (pŏd-kwat) m. base; railroad tie ;undercurrent;bedding
podkładać (pod-kwa-dach) v. lay under; put under;plant as evidence
podkop (pŏd-kop) m. mine; sap
podkowa (pod-kó-va) f. horse-shoe; semicircle
podkradać (pod-krá-dach) v.thieve; pilfer; creep up
podkreślać (pod-kresh-lach) v.stress underline; emphasize; accentuate
podkuwać (pod-koo-vach) v. shoe(horse) ;hobnail a shoe; cram
podlegać (pod-le-gach) v. be subject; be liable ;succomb;undergo
podległość (pod-leg-woshch) f. dependence; subjection;subordination
podlewać (pod-le-vach) v. water
podlizywać się (pod-lee-zi-vach shan) v. suck up to ;make up to
podlotek (pod-ló-tek) f. fledgling; flapper;girl in her teens
podłoga (pod-wó-ga) f. floor
podłość (pod-woshch) f. meanness
podług (pŏd-wook) prep. : according to ;in conformity with
podłużny (pod-woozh-ni) adj. m. oblong; longitudinal; elongated
podły (pŏd-wi) adj. m. mean
podmiejski (pod-myey-skee) adj. m. suburban
podminować (pod-mee-nó-vach) v. undermine; sap
podmiot (pod-myot) m. subject
podmuch (pod-mookh) m. gust; blow; puff; waft; breath;blast
podmywać (pod-mi-vach) v. wash under; sap; undermine;wash away
podniebienie (pod-ńe-bye-ńe) n. palate ;roof of the mouth
podniecać (pod-ńe-tsach) v.flurry excite ;agitate ;rouse;egg on
podnieść (pod-ńeshch) v. lift; hoist ;rise;elevate;rear;incerease
podnieta (pod-ńe-ta) f. stimulus ;impulse;spur;stimulant
podniosły (pod-ńos-wi) adj. m. sublime ;elevated; lofty
podnosić (pod-no-sheech) v.hoist; raise; lift; take up; elevate
podnóżek (pod-noo-zhek) m. foot-stool; ottoman ;leg rest

podobać się (po-do-bach shãn)
v. please; be attractive;like

podobny (po-dob-ni) adj. m.
similar; like; congenial

podoficer (pod-o-fee-tser) m.
noncommissioned officer

podołać (po-do-wach) v. be up
to;be equal to;cope;manage

podomka (po-dom-ka) f. house-
robe; dressing gown

podówczas (pod-oov-chas) adv.
at that time;at the time;then

podpadać (pod-pa-dach) v. be
spotted; fall under a category

podpalenie (pod-pa-le-ñe) n.
arson; setting of fire

podpatrzyć (pod-pa-tzhich) v.
spy; peep; find out; pry

podpierać (pod-pye-rach) v.
prop up; support; bolster

podpinać (pod-pee-nach) v.pin;
buckle up; strap;fasten;gird

podpis (pod-pees) m. signature

podpływać (pod-pwi-vach) v.
swim up; sail up; row up

podpora (pod-po-ra) f. prop

podporucznik (pod-po-rooch-
ñeek) m. second lieutenant

podporządkować (pod-po-zhõwnt-
ko-vach) v. subordinate

podprowadzić (pod-pro-va-
dźheech) v. bring near

podpułkownik (pod-poow-kov-
ñeek) m. lieutenant colonel

podrażnić (pod-razh-ñeech) v.
displease; irritate;vex;gall

podręcznik (pod-rañch-ñeek) m.
handbook; textbook; manual

podrożeć (pod-ro-zhech) v. go
up; grow dear; rise in price

podróż (pod-roozh) f. travel;
voyage; journey; passage

podróżnik (pod-roozh-ñeek) m.
traveler; voyager; wayfarer

po drugie (po droo-ge) adv.
in the second place; second

podrzeć (pod-zhech) v. tear up

podrzędny (pod-zhãnd-ni) adj.
m. subordinate; secondary

podsądny (pod-sownd-ni) m. defendant; the person sued

podskakiwać (pod-ska-kee-vach)
v. leap; jump up;hop;skip

podsłuch (pod-swookh) m. eavesdropping; wire tapping;listen in

podstawa (pod-sta-va) f. base;
basis;footing;mount;principle

podstawić (pod-sta-veech) v.
substitute;put under;bring round

podstęp (pod-stãp) m.trick;ruse;
guile; deceit;piece of deceit

podstępny (pod-stãp-ni) adj. m.
deceitful; tricky; crafty;insidious

podstrzygać (pod-stzhi-gach) v.
trim the hair; shorten the hair

podsuwać (pod-soo-vach) v. push
near; plant; suggest; slip under

podsycać (pod-si-tsach) v. foment; feed; fan (a quarrel etc.)

podsypywać (pod-si-pi-vach) v.
pour (sand etc.);strew; sprinkle

podszept (pod-shept) m. suggestion; prompting; insinuation

podszeptywać (pod-shep-ti-vach)
v. prompt; suggest;hint;insinuate

podszewka (pod-shev-ka) f. lining ; inside information

podświadomy (pod-shvya-do-mi)
adj. m. subconscious(mental process)

podupadać (pod-oo-pa-dach) v.
decline; deteriorate;fall into decay

poduszka (po-doosh-ka) f. pillow;
pad; cushion; ball (of the thumb)

podwajać (pod-va-yach) v. double;
duplicate; increase twofold

podważyć (pod-va-zhich) v. lever
up; pry up; shake (an opinion)

podwiązka (pod-vyowns-ka) f.
garter; suspender; ligature

podwieczorek (pod-vye-cho-rek)
m. afternoon tea; afternoon snack

podwieźć (pod-vyeżhch) v. give
a ride; give a lift(in one's car)

podwładny (pod-vwad-ni) adj. m.
subordinate (to somebody);inferior

podwodna łódź (pod-vod-na woodźh)
f. submarine (under water warship)

podwoić (pod-vo-eech)v. double

podwozie (pod-vo-zhe) n. chassis

podwórko (pod-voor-ko) n. backyard ;farmyard;court;courtyard

podwyżka (pod-vizh-ka) f. raise

podzelować (pod-ze-lo-vach) v.
resole (shoes, boots, foot ware)

podziać (po-dźhach) v. loose

podział (po-dźhaw) m. division

podziałka (po-dźhaw-ka) f.
scale; graduation; division
podzielać (po-dźhe-lach) v.
share; participate; concur
podzielić (po-dźhe-leech) v.
divide (into parts)
podzielny (po-dźhel-ni) adj. m.
adj. m. divisible(easily)
podziemie (pod-źhem-ye) n.basement; underworld
podziemny (pod-źhem-ni) adj. m.
underground; secret
podziękować (po-dźhan-ko-vach)
v. thank; decline with thanks
podziewać (po-dźhe-vach) v.
loose; mislay;leave somewhere
podziw (po-dźheef) m. admiration; wander
podzwrotnikowy (pod-zvrot-nee-ko-vi) adj. m. tropical
podżegacz (pod-zhe-gach) m. instigator; warmonger; abettor
poemat (po-e-mat) m. poem
poeta (po-e-ta) m. poet
poetka (po-et-ka) f. poet
poezja (po-ez-ya) f. poetry
pogadanka (po-ga-dan-ka) f,
talk; chat; chatty lecture
poganiać (po-ga-nach) v. drive;
egg on; urge on; prod on;hustle
poganin (po-ga-neen) m. pagan
pogarda (po-gar-da) f. contempt
pogarszać (po-gar-shach) v.
make worse; aggravate;worsen
pogawędka (po-ga-vand-ka) f.
chat; chit-chat
pogląd (po-glownd) m. opinion
pogłębiać (po-gwanb-yach) v.
deepen; dig deeper; dredge
pogłoska (po-gwos-ka) f. rumor
pogniewać się (po-gńe-vach śhan)
v. get angry; be angry
pogoda (po-go-da) f. weather;
cheerfulness; fine weather
pogodny (po-god-ni) adj. m.
serene; cheerful; sunny
pogodzić (po-go-dźheech) v.
reconcile; square (things)
pogoń (po-goń) f. pursuit;
chase; hunt; quest; pursuers
pogorszenie (po-gor-she-ńe) n.
worsening; deterioration

pogorszyć (po-gor-shich) v.
make worse: aggravate
pogorzelisko (po-go-zhe-lees-ko) n. after fire ruins
pogotowie (po-go-to-vye) n.
ambulance service; readiness
pogranicze (po-gra-ńee-che) n.
borderland; border line
pogrom (po-grom) m. rout
pogromca (po-grom-tsa) m.tamer; conqueror
pogróżka (po-groozh-ka) f.
threat;threatening expression
pogrzeb (po-gzhep) m. funeral
pogrzebacz (po-gzhe-bach) m.
poker (for stirring a fire)
pogwałcić (po-gvaw-cheech) v.
violate; outrage;transgress
poić (po-eech) v. water; ply
pojawić się (po-ya-veech śhan)
v. appear; emerge; occur;arise
pojazd (po-yazt) m. car;vehicle
pojąć (po-yownch) v. grasp;
marry; comprehend;understand
pojechać (po-ye-khach) v. go;
leave; take (train, boat etc.)
pojednać (po-yed-nach) v. reconcile (two or more parties)
pojednawczy (po-yed-nav-chi)
adj. m. conciliatory
pojedynczy (po-ye-din-chi) adj.
m. single; individual; onefold
pojedynek (po-ye-di-nek) m.
duel; encounter; single combat
pojemnik (po-yem-neek) m. container; vessel; receptacle
pojemnosc (po-yem-noshch) f.
capacity; cubic content
pojezierze (po-ye-zhe-zhe) n.
lake land; lake district
pojęcie (po-yan-che) n. notion;
idea; concept; comprehension
pojętny (po-yant-ni) adj. m.
intelligent; sharp; teachable
pojmować (poy-mo-vach) v.grasp;
comprehend; conceive;imagine
pojutrze (po-joot-zhe) adv. day
after tomorrow
pokarm (po-karm) m. food; feed
pokaz (po-kas) m. display; shaw
pokazywać (po-ka-zi-vach) v.
show; point; exhibit; let see

pokaźny (po-kazh-ni) adj. m.
respectable; appreciable
pokład (pók-wad) m. deck; layer
pokątny (po-kównt-ni) adj. m.
underhanded; secret; illegal
pokłon (pók-won) m. bow; homage
pokłócicsię (po-kwoo-cheech
shań)v. fall out with;quarrel
pokochać (po-kó-khach) v. fall
in love; become fond of
pokoik (po-kó-eek) m. little
room; little cozy room
pokojówka (po-ko-yoov-ka) f.
maid; housemaid; chamber maid
pokolenie (po-kole-ne) n. generation; about 30 years
pokonać (po-ko-nach) v. defeat
pokorny (po-kor-ni) adj. m.
humble; meek; submissive
pokost (pó-kost) m. varnish
pokrajać (po-kra-yach) v. cut
up; carve up; slice; slash
pokój (pó-kooy) m. room; peace
pokrapiać (po-kra-pyach) v.
sprinkle; wash down (a meal)
pokrewieństwo (po-krev-yeń-stvo)
n. kinship; kindred;relation
pokrewny (po-krev-ni) m. related; kindred; akin; cognate
pokrotce (po-kroot-tse) adv.
in short; in brief;concisely
pokrycie (po-kri-che) n. cover
pokryć (po-krich) v. cover
po kryjomu (po-kri-yó-moo) adv.
secretly; on the sly; in secret
pokrywa (po-kri-va) f. lid
pokrywać (pokri-vach) v. cover;
upholster; serve (mare)
pokrzepić (po-kzhé-peech) v.
invigorate; refresh; fortify
pokrzywa (po-kzhee-va) f. nettle
pokrzyżować (po-kzhi-zho-vach)
v. cross up; confound ;tangle
pokup (pó-koop) m. demand
pokupny (po-koop-ni) adj. m.
in demand ; selable
pokusa (po-koo-sa) f. temptation
pokuta (po-koo-ta) f. penance
pokwitować (po-kvee-tó-vach) v.
receipt ; acknowledge receipt
pokwitowanie (po-kvee-to-va-ne)
n. receipt   (liquid)
polać (pó-lach)v. pour over

Polak (pó-lak) m. Polonian;
Pole; Polonius; vulg.:polack
polana (po-lá-na) f. glade
polano (po-lá-no) n. billet; log
polarny (po-lár-ni) adj. m. polar ; of the polar axis
pole (po-le) n. field
polec (pó-lets) v. fall; be
killed (in battle)
polecać (po-le-tsach) v. recommend; commend; instruct; order
polegać (po-le-gach) v. rely
polemika (po-le-mee-ka) f. po-
lemics; controversy
polepszać (po-lep-shach) v. improve; ameliorate; mend; better
polerować (po-le-ro-vach) v.
polish; furbish; burnish;refine
polewać (po-le-vach) v. water;
glaze; glaze; enamel; ice
polewka (po-lev-ka) f. broth
polędwica (po-lánd-vee-tsa) f.
sirloin; loin; fillet(of beef)
policja (po-leets-ya) f. police
policzek (po-lee-chek) m. cheek
politechnika (po-lee-tekh-nee-
ka) f. polytechnic college
politowanie (po-lee-to-va-ne)
n. pity; compassion
polityk (po-lee-tik) m. politician; statesman
polka (pól-ka) f. polka; Polish
girl; Polish woman; Pole
polny (pól-ni) adj. m. field
polon (pó-lon) m. polonium
(chem.)
polonez (po-ló-nez) m.polonaise
(dance)
Polonia (po-loń-ya) f. Polish
colony ; Polish emigrants
Polonus (po-ló-noos) m. Pole of
old ;typical Pole of the past
polot (pó-lot) m. elan ;imagination
polować (po-ló-vach) v. hunt
polski (pól-skee) adj. m. Polish ; Polish language
polszczyć (polsh-chich) v.Polo-
nize ;invest with Polish traits
polszczyzna (pol-shchiz-na) f.
Polish language ; Polish traits
polubić (po-loo-beech) v. get to
like ; become fond;take a fancy

polubownie (po-loo-bóv-ñe) adv.
amicably; by compromise
połamać (po-wa-maćh) v. break
połączenie (po-wówn-che-ñe) n.
connection; linkage;contact
połknąć (pów-knówñćh) v. swallow;gulp down; drink down
połowa (po-wó-va) f. half
położenie (po-wo-zhé-ñe) n.
position; situation; site
położna (po-wózh-na) f. midwife
położnica (po-wozh-ñee-tsa) f,
woman in childbed
położyć (po-wo-zhićh) v. lay
down; place;deposit;fell;ruin
połóg (po-wook) m. childbirth
połów ryb (pó-woov rib) fish
catch; fishing; fish haul
południe (po-wood-ñe) n. noon;
south; midday; the South
południk (po-wood-ñeek) m. meridian; the line of longitude
południowo-wschodni (po-wood-
ño-vo wskhód-ñee) south-east
południowo-zachodni (po-wood-
ño-vo za-khod-ñee) south-west
południowy (po-wood-ño-vi) adj.
m. south; midday; southerly
połykać (po-wi-kaćh) v. swallow
połysk (pó-wisk) m. glitter;
gloss; luster; sheen; sparkle
pomadka (po-mád-ka) f. lipstick
pomagać (po-má-gaćh) v. help
pomalenku (po-ma-leñ-koo) adv.
little by little; very slowly
pomału (po-má-woo) adv. little
by little; slowly; leisurely
pomarańcza (po-ma-rań-cha) f.
orange; orange tree
pomarszczony (po-marsh-chó-ni)
adj. m. wrinkled; creased
pomazać (po-má-zaćh) v. smearover; anoint; soil; scrawl
pomawiać (po-máv-yaćh) v. accuse; impute; charge with
pomiar (po-myar) m. measurement;
survey; surveying;mensuration
pomiatać (po-myá-taćh) v. push
around; spurn; hold in contempt
pomidor (po-mee-dor) m. tomato
pomieszać (po-myé-shaćh) v. mix
up; mingle; blend;stir;tangle;
muddle up;embroil;mistake

pomieszanie zmysłów (po-mye-sha-
ñe zmis-woov) insanity; madness
pomieszczać (po-myesh-chaćh) v.
admit; contain; accomodate
pomiędzy (po-myán-dzi) prep.
between; among; in the midst
pomijać (po-mee-yaćh) v. pass
over; omit; overlook; leave out
pomimo (po-mee-mo) prep. in
spite of; notwithstanding
pomnażać (po-mna-zhaćh) v. multiply; increase; intensify
pomniejszać (po-mñey-shaćh) v.
diminish; lessen;reduce;belittle
pomnik (póm-ñeek) m. monument
pomoc (pó-mots) f. help; aid
pomocnik (po-móts-ñeek) m. helper; assistant: helpmate; aid
pomocny (po-móts-ni) adj. m.
helpful; instrumental
pomorski (po-mór-skee) adj. m.
Pomeranian; of Pomerania
pomost (pó-most) m. platform
pomóc (pó-moots) v. help; assist
pompa (póm-pa) f. pump; pomp
pompować (pom-pó-vaćh) v. pump
pomsta (póm-sta) f. vengeance
pomruk (póm-rook) m. murmur;
grumble; growl;purr; rumble
pomstować (pom-stó-vaćh) v.
curse; swear; revile;vituperate
pomyje (po-mí-ye) pl. dishwater; hog-wash; swill; lap
pomylić (po-mí-leećh) v. confound; be mistaken; mislead
pomyłka (po-miw-ka) f. error
pomysł (pó-misw) m. idea
pomyslność (po-mishl-noshćh) f.
prosperity; success; happiness
pomyślny (po-mishl-ni) adj. m.
successful; favorable; good
pomywaczka (po-mi-vach-ka) f.
dishwasher; scullery maid
ponad (po-nád) prep. above;
over; beyond;upwards of;super-;
more than;over and above;besides
ponadto (po-nád-to) prep. moreover; besides; furthermore;also
ponaglać (po-nág-laćh) v. rush;
urge; remind:press; urge on
ponaglenie (po-nag-le-ñe) n.
reminder; pressure
ponawiać (po-náv-yaćh) v. renew

ponętny (po-nant-ni) adj. m.
seductive; attractive; alluring
poniechać (po-ńe-khach) v.give
up;relinquish; renounce;desist
poniedziałek (po-ńe-dzha-wek)
m. Monday
poniekąd (po-ńe-kownt) adv.
partly;in a way; in a sense
ponieść (po-ńeshch) v. sustain;
carry;bear; suffer;incur;push
ponieważ (po-ne-vash) conj. because; as; since; for
poniewczasie (po-ńev-cha-she)
adv. too late;after the event
poniewierać (po-ńe-vye-rach) v.
kick around;slight;mishandle
poniżej (po-ńee-zhey) adv. below; beneath;hereunder;under
poniżyć (po-ńee-zhich) v. degrade; humble;tread down
ponosić (po-no-sheech) v. bear;
carry (away);suffer;incur
ponowić (po-no-veech) v. renew
ponownie (po-nov-ńe) adv. anew;
again; afresh; a second time
ponowny (po-nov-ni) adj. m. repeated; renewed;reiterated
ponton (pon-ton) m. pontoon
ponury (po-noo-ri) adj m.gloomy
dismal; sullen; dreary; sullen
pończocha (poń-cho-kha) f.
stocking
popadać (po-pa-dach) v. fall in
poparcie (po-pár-che) n. support; backing; promotion;push
popaść (po-pa-shch) v. fall in
popatrzeć (po-pa-tzhech) v. look
popelina (po-pe-lee-na) f.
poplin;a ribbed cloth
popchnąć (pop-khnownch) v. push;
shove;hastle; jostle;steer
popełniać (po-pew-nach) v. commit;perpetrate
popęd (po-pant) m. impulse
popędliwy (po-pand-lee-vi) adj.
impetuous; rush;hot headed
popędzać (po-pan-dzach) v. drive
on; urge; push on; prod;spur
popielaty (po-pye-la-ti) adj. m.
charcoal-grey; ashen; gray
popielec (po-pye-lets) m. Ash
Wednesday

popielniczka (po-pyel-ńeech-
ka) f. ash-tray; ash pan
popierać (po-pye-rach) v. support; back;promote;favor;uphold
popiersie (po-pyer-she) n. bust
popić (po-peech) v. rinse down
popiół (po-pyoow) m. ashes;ash;
cinders; slag
popis (po-pees) m. show; parade
popisywać się (po-pee-si-vach
shań)v.show off;flaunt;parade
poplecznik (po-plech-ńeek) m.
backer; upholder; partisan
popłatny (po-pwat-ni) adj. m.
profitable; lucrative
popłoch (po-pwokh) m. panic
popołudnie (po-po-wood-ńe) n.
afternoon
po południu (po po-wood-ńoo) in
the afternoon
poprawa (po-pra-va) f.improve-
ment;change for the better
poprawka (po-prav-ka) f. correction;amendment; alteration
poprawny (po-prav-ni) adj. m.
correct;faultless;proper
po prostu (po pros-too) adv.
simply;openly;unceremoniously
poprzeczka (po-pzhech-ka) f.
crossbar; crossbeam;the bar
poprzedni (po-pzhed-ńee) adj.
m. previous; preceding;former
poprzedzać (po-pzhe-dzach) v.
precede;orelude;go before
poprzestać (po-pzhes-tach) v.
settle for; be satisfied
popularny (po-poo-lar-ni) adj.
m. popular; prevalent
popychać (po-pi-khach) v. push;
shove; ill treat; hustle; jostle
popychadło (po-pi-khad-wo) n.
drudge; scapegrace
popyt (po-pit) m. demand
pora (po-ra) f. time; season
porachunek (po-ra-khoo-nek) m.
reckoning; a bone to pick
porada (po-ra-da) f. advice
poradnia (po-rad-ńa) f. information bureau;dispensary;clinic
poradnik (po-rad-ńeek) m. guide;
handbook; reference book
poradzić (po-ra-dzhech) v. advise

poranek (po-rá-nek) m. morning
porastać (po-rás-tać) v. overgrow; grow; become overgrown
poratować (po-ra-tó-vać) v.
help in distress; recuperate
porażenie (po-ra-zhé-ne) n.
stroke; shock; paralysis
porażka (po-rázh-ka) f. defeat; set back; reverse
porcelana (por-tse-lá-na) f.
china; porcelain
porcja (pór-tsya) f. portion
poręcz (pór-anch) f. banister
poręczenie (po-ran-che-ne) n.
guarantee; bail;warranty;pledge
poręka (po-ran-ka) f. guaranty;
pledge;sponsorship; surety
poronić (po-ro-ńeech) v. abort;
miscarry; have a miscarriage
porost (po-rost) m. growth
porowaty (po-ro-vá-ti) adj. m.
porous; full of pores
porozdawać (po-roz-dá-vać) v.
give away; pass around
porozumienie (po-ro-zoo-myé-ne)
m. understanding;agreement
poród (po-root) m. child delivery; childbirth; partitution
porównać (po-roóv-nać) v. compare; draw a comparison; liken
porównanie (po-roov-ná-ńe) n.
comparison;equalization
poróżnić (po-roozh-ńeech) v.
disunite; divide; embroil
port (port) m. port; harbor
portfel (pórt-fel) m. wallet
portier (pórt-yer) m. doorman
portki (pórt-kee) pl. pants
(vulg.);breeches; trousers
portmonetka (port-mo-nét-ka) f.
purse; billfold; wallet
porto (por-to) n. postage
portret (pór-tret) m. portrait
portugalski (por-too-gál-skee)
adj. m. Portuguese
poruczać (po-roó-chach) v. entrust; charge with
porucznik (po-roóch-ńeek) m.
lieutenant
poruszać (po-roó-shach) v. move;
touch; sway; set in motion
poruszenie (po-roo-she-ńe) n.
agitation;movement; stir;touch

poryw (pó-riv) m. impulse; rapture; gust; onrush; elation
porywać (po-rí-vach) v. snatch;
carry off; whisk away;grab;thrill
porywacz (po-ri-vach) m. kid-
naper; abductor; ravisher
porywczy (po-riv-chi) adj. m.
rash;irritable;impetuous;hasty
porządek (po-zhówn-dek) n.
order;tidiness;regularity;system
porządny (po-zhównd-ni) adj. m.
neat; decent; accurate;reliable
porzucać (po-zhoo-tsach) v.
abandon; desert;forsake; leave
porzucić (po-zhoo-cheech) v.
abandon; give up; cast away
posada (po-sá-da) f. employment
posadzka (po-sádz-ka) f. parquet floor; tile floor
posąg (po-sównk) m. statue
poselstwo (po-sél-stvo) n. legation; deputation; envoys
poseł (po-sew) m. envoy; con-
gressman; deputy; legate
posępny (po-sánp-ni) adj. m.
gloomy; dismal; dreary; dark
posiadacz (po-sha-dach) m. bearer; holder; possessor;owner
posiadać (po-sha-dać) v. hold;
own; possess; acquire;dominate
posiadłość (po-shad-woshch) f.
estate; property; dominion
posiedzenie (po-she-dze-ne) n.
session; conference; meeting
posilać (po-shee-lać) v. refresh; nourish; feed
posiłek (po-shee-wek) m. meal;
refreshment; reinforcement
posłać (po-swać) f. send; make a
bed; dispatch somewhere
posłanie (po-swá-ne) n. bed;
bedding; message;dispatch
posłaniec (po-swa-ńets) m. messenger; commissionaire
posłuchać (po-swoo-khać) v.
listen; obey; take advice
posługa (po-swoo-ga) f. service
posługacz (po-swoo-gach) m. servant; attendant; commissionaire
posłuszny (po-swoosh-ni) adj. m.
obedient; submissive;docile
pospolity (pos-po-lee-ti) adj. m.
vulgar; common;commonplace

posrebrzać (po-sréb-zhach) v. silver (plate);silver foil

post (post) m. fast; fast day

postać (pó-stach) f. form;shape; figure;human shape;personage

postanowić (po-sta-nó-veech) v. decide; enact;resolve;determine

postanowienie (po-sta-no-vye-ñe) n. decision; resolve; provision

postarać się (po-stá-rach śhañ) v. procure; obtain;get;try;find

postawa (po-stá-va) f. attitude, posture; pose;bearing; position

postawny (po-stáw-ni) adj. m. portly;handsome;well made

postawić (po-stá-veech) v. set up; put up;set on;put on;raise

postąpić (po-stóm-peech) v. proceed; act; deal;follow;treat

posterunek (po-ste-roo-nek) m. outpost; sentry; police station

postęp (pó-stämp) m. progress; advance;march;headway

postępowanie (postán-po-va-ñe) n. behavior; advance;procedure

postojowe (po-sto-yo-ve) n. demurrage;adj.n.parking

postój (pó-stooy) m. halt;stop; stand; parking;stopping place

postrach (pó-strakh) m. terror; dread;scare;fright;bugaboo

postrzał (pó-stzhaw) m. gunshot; wound;shot;rifle shot;lumbago

postrzelony (po-stzhe-ló-ni) adj. m. wounded; crazy;cracked

postulat (po-stoo-lat) m. demand; claim; requirement

postument (po-stoo-ment) m. pedestal; socle

posucha (po-sóo-kha) f. drought

posuw (pó-soov) m. feed (of a drill); feed of a lathe

posuwać (po-sóo-vach) v. move; shove; push on;carry;dash;speed

posyłać (po-sí-wach) v.send over

posyłka (po-síw-ka) f. errand

posypywać (po-si-pi-vach) v. dust; pour; sprinkle (dry)

poszanowanie (po-sha-no-va-ñe) n. respect; observance(of a law)

poszarpać (po-shár-pach) v.maul; tear up; jag up;mangle;rend

poszczególny (po-shche-goól-ni) adj. m. individual

poszerzać (po-she-zhach) v. widen;broaden;extend;ream;spread

poszewka (po-shév-ka) f. pillow-case ; pillow slip

poszkodowany (po-shko-do-vá-ni) adj. m. victim ;sufferer

poszlaka (po-shlá-ka) f.trace: circumstantial evidence; sign

poszukiwać (po-shoo-kee-vach) v. search;look for;inquire;claim

poszukiwanie (po-shoo-kee-va-ñe) n. search;quest;research

pościć (póśh-cheech) v. fast

pościel (póśh-chel) f. bed-clothes sheets and blankets

pościg (póśh-cheeg) m. chase

pośladek (po-śhlá-dek) m. buttock; rump; bum

pośliznąć się (po-śhleéz-nównch śhañ) v. slip ;make a slip

poślubić (po-śhloó-beech) v. marry; take in marriage

pośmiertny (po-śhmyert-ni) adj. m. posthumous (child, works etc.)

pośmiewisko (po-śhmye-veés-ko) n.,laughingstock;butt of ridicule

pośpiech (póśh-pyekh) m. haste; hurry; dispatch

pośredni (po-śhréd-ñee) adj. m.,intermediate; indirect

pośrednik (po-shred-ñeek) m. go-between; intermediary

pośredniczyć (po-shred-ñee-chích) v.,mediate;be a go-between

pośród (po-śh-rood) prep. among

poświadczać (po-shvyád-chach) v., attest; certify;testify;witness

poświadczenie (po-shvyad-che-ñe) n. certificate;attestation

poświęcać (po-shvyań-tsach) v. sacrifice; sanctify

poświęcenie (po-shvyáñ-tse-ñe) n. devotion; sacrifice

pot (pot) m. sweat; perspiration

potajemny (po-ta-yem-ni) adj. m. secret; clandestine;underhand

potakiwać (po-ta-kée-vach) v. assent; agree; acquiesce

potas (pó-tas) m. potassium

potaż (pó-tash) m. potash

potąd (po-townt) adv. up to
here ;up to this place
potem (po-tem) adv. after ;
afterwards; then; later on
potencjalny (po-ten-tsyál-ni)
adj. m. potential ;virtual
potęga (po-tán-ga) f. power;
might ;force;impressiveness
potęgowac (po-tán-go-vach) v.
intensify ;raise to a power
potępiac (po-tán-pyach) v.
damn; run down ;condemn
potępienie (po-tán-pye-ńe) n.
damnation ;disapproval;blame
potężny (po-tánzh-ni) adj. m.
mighty,;tremendous;powerful
potknąc sie (pot-knównch shán)v.
slip ;trip; stumble;make a slip
potknięcie (pot-kñan-che) n.
slip; stumble; trip ; a lapse
potoczny (po-toch-ni) adj. m.
current; common ;everyday;daily
potok (po-tok) m. stream;brook
potomek (po-tó-mek) m. descendant ; offspring; scion
potomnosc (po-tom-noshch) f.
posterity ;future generations
potomstwo (po-tom-stvo) pl. issue; progeny; offspring;breed
potop (po-top) m. deluge; flood
potrafic (po-tra-feech) v. know
how to do ;manage;be able to do
potrawa (po-tra-ya) f. dish
potrawka (po-tráv-ka) f. fricassee ;ragout
potrącic (po-trówn-cheech) v.
knock; deduct ;poke;push;jostle
po trochu (po-tro-khoo) adv.
little by little ;gradually
potrojny (po-trooy-ni) adj. m.
triple ;triplicate;treble
potrzask (pot-shask) m. trap
potrząsac (po-tzhówn-sach) v.
shake ; brandish; agitate;strew
potrzeba (po-tzhé-ba) f. need;
want;call;emergency;extremity
potrzebny (po-tzhéb-ni) adj. m.
necessary ;needed;wanted
potulny (po-tool-ni) adj. m.
docile ;submissive;humble;meek
poturbowac (po-toor-bo-vach) v.
manhandle; rough up ;beat;maul
batter;knock about;ill-treat;
give a rough handling; hurt

potwarz (po-tvash) f. slander
potwierdzac (po-tvyer-dzach) v.
confirm; attest;corroborate
potwór (po-tvoor) m. monster
potykac się (po-ti-kach shán)
v. stumble; skirmish;joust
potylica (po-ti-lee-tsa) f.
occiput; back part of skull
pouczac (po-oo-chach) v. instruct; teach ;give instructions
pouczenie (po-oo-che-ńe) n.
instruction;giving instructions
poufalic się(po-oo-fá-lich shán)v
take liberties; familiarize
poufały (po-oo-fá-wi) adj. m.
intimate;unceremonious;free with
too familiar; maty;hob-nobbing
poufny (po-oof-ni) adj. m. confidential ;private;secret
powab (po-vap) m. charm;attrac-
tion;lure;seduction;loveliness
powabny (po-váb-ni) adj. m. attractive; charming;alluring
powaga (po-va-ga) f. gravity;
seriousness;dignity;prestige
powalac (po-va-lach) v. soil;
dirty; overthrow;kill;slay
powalic (po-va-leech) v. knock
down;overthrow;kill;slay;fell
powała (po-va-wa) f. ceiling
poważac (po-va-zhach) v. respect;esteem;have regard
poważny (po-vazh-ni) adj. m.
earnest; grave;dignified;serious
powątpiewac (po-vównt-pye-vach)
v. doubt;have doubts; be dubious
powetowac (po-ve-to-vach) v.
make up;idemnify oneself;retrieve
powiadac (po-vyá-dach) v. say;
tell; speak ;(the legend)has it
that
powiadomic (po-vya-do-meech) v.
inform; notify; let know
powiastka (po-vyast-ka) f. tale
powiat (po-vyat) m. county;
district; district authorities
powicie (po-vee-che) n. swad-
dling clothes; child delivery
powidła (po-veed-wa) pl. jam;
marmalade; jam
powiedziec (po-vye-dźhech) v.
say; tell; declare
powieka (po-vye-ka) f. eyelid
powielacz (po-vye-lach) m.
mimeograph

powiernica (po-vyer-nee-tsa) f.
confidante;trusted friend
powierzac (po-vye-zhach) v.
confide;charge with a task
powierzchnia (po-vyezhkh-ña) f.
surface;plane; area; acreage
powiesic (po-vye-sheech) v.
hang;supend; hung up;ring off
powiesc (po-vyeshch) f. novel
powiesc się (po-vyeshch shan)
v. succeed; be successful
powietrze (po-vyet-zhe) n. air
powiew (po-vyev) m, breeze
powiększac (po-vyank-shach) v.
enlarge;augment;extend; add
powiększenie (po-vyank-she-ñe)
n. enlargement; magnification
powijaki (po-vee-ja-kee) pl.
swathings;initial stage
powiklac (po-veek-wach) v.
complicate; embroil
powinnosc (po-veen-noshch) f.
duty; obligation
powinowaty (po-vee-no-va-ti)
adj. m. related; akin
powitac (po-vee-tach) v. welcome; salute; bid welcome
powlekac (po-vle-kach) v. cover; drag; coat;smear; spread
powloczka (po-vwoch-ka) f. pillowcase; envelope;covering
powloka (po-vwo-ka) f. (paint)
coat; covering;envelope; shell
powloczysty (po-vwoo-chis-ti)
adj. m. trailing; enticing
powodowac (po-vo-do-vach) v.
cause; bring about; touch off;
effect; induce; give occasion
powodzenie (po-vo-dze-ñe) n.
success; well-being;prosperity
powodzic się (po-vo-dzhech shan)
v. fare (well; ill);be well off
powojenny (po-vo-yen-ni) adj.
m. post-war; after-war
powoli (po-vo-lee) adv. slow
powolny (po-vol-ni) adj. m.
slow; tardy;leisurely;gradual
powolanie (po-vo-wa-ñe) n. vocation; call;appointment;quot.
powonienie (po-vo-ñe-ñe) n.
sense of smell; smell
powod (po-voot) m. cause: reason;ground; motive;plaintiff

powodz (po-voodzh) f. flood
powoj (po-vooy) m. bindweed
powoz (po-woos) m. carriage
powracac (po-vra-tsach) v. return; come back;resume;recover
powrotny (po-vrot-ni) adj. m.
return; return(ticket)
powrot (po-vroot) m. return
powroz (po-vroos) m. rope
powstanie (po-vsta-ñe) n. rising; uprising; insurrection
powstaniec (po-vsta-ñets) m.
insurgent(against a government)
powstawac (po-vsta-vach) v.
rise up; stand up;revolt
powstrzymac (po-vstzhi-mach) v.
restrain; refrain; hold back
powszechny (po-vshekh-ni) adj.
m. universal; general; public
powszedni (po-vshed-ñee) adj.
m. everyday; commonplace;daily
powsciągliwosc (povshchowng-
lee-voshch) f. abstinence;
temperance; moderation;restraint
powsciągliwy (povshchowng-lee-
vi) adj. m. reserved; absti-
nent; moderate;temperate
powtarzac (pov-ta-zhach) v. say
again; go over; repeat;reproduce
po wtore (po vtoo-re) adv. secondly; in the second place; then
powtornie (pov-toor-ñe) adv.
anew; again; a second time
powtorny (po-vtoor-ni) adj. m.
repeated; renewed; second-
powyżej (po-vi-zhey) adv. above;
here in before; higher up; over
powziąc (pov-zhownch) v. take
up; form ;decide;conceive(a plan)
poza (po-za) f. pose; attitude;
sham
poza (po-za) prep. : beyond; besides; except; apart;outside;extra-
pozagrobowy (po-za-gro-bo-vi)
adj. m. beyond the grave;
hereafter; from beyond the grave
pozbawiac (po-zbav-yach) v.
deprive;dispossess;take away
pozbyc się (poz-bich shan) v.
rid oneself; get rid;shake off
pozdrawiac (po-zdra-vyach) v.
greet; send one's greetings
pozew (po-zef) m. summons; writ;
citation

poziom (po-żhom) m. level

poziomka (po-żhom-ka) f. wild strawberry(fruit or plant)

poziomy (po-żho-mi) adj. m. horizontal;level;uninspired

pozłota (po-zwo-ta) f. gilding

poznać (po-znać) v. get to know; recognize;taste;acquaint

poznajomić (po-zna-yo-meeć) v. acquaint; introduce

poznanie (po-zna-ńe) n. cognition; acquaintance; learning

pozornie (po-zor-ńe) adv. apparently; on the surface

pozostać (po-zos-tać) v. remain; stay behind;continue

pozostały (po-zos-ta-wi) adj. m. remaining; residual;left

pozostawiać (po-zos-tav-yać) v. leave (behind);bequeath

pozór (po-zoor) m. appearance; pretext; sham;look;mask;cloak

pozwać (poz-vać) v. summon

pozwalać (po-zva-lać) v. let; allow; permit;tolerate;suffer

pozwany (po-zva-ni) m. defendant; person sued or accused

pozwolenie (po-zvo-le-ńe) n. permission;consent; permit

pozycja (po-zyts-ya) f. position; item; status;posture

pozyskać (po-zis-kać) v. gain; win over; conciliate

pozytywny (po-zi-tiv-ni) adj. m. positive; affirmative

pozywać (po-zi-vać) v. sue; cite; summon; cite(to court)

pożałować (po-zha-wo-vać) v. repent; regret; take pity

pożar (po-zhar) m. fire (woods, buildings);conflagration

pożądać (po-zhówn-dać) v. desire; covet; lust after

pożądany (po-zhówn-da-ni) adj. m. desirable; welcome;desired

pożądliwy (po-zhownd-lee-vi) adj. m. greedy; covetus;lewd

pożegnać (po-zheg-nać) v. bid goodbye; see off; dismiss

pożerać (po-zhe-rać) v. devour

pożoga (po-zhó-ga) f. fire; conflagration; ravages (of war)

pożółknąć (po-zhoówk-nownć) v. grow yellow;turn yellow

pożycie (po-zhi-će) v. intercourse; conjugal life

pożyczka (po-zhich-ka) f. loan

pożyteczny (po-zhi-tech-ni) adj. m. useful;profitable

pożytek (po-zhi-tek) m. use; advantage;usefulness; benefit

pożywić (po-zhi-veeć) v. feed; nourish; refresh;give food

pożywny (po-zhiv-ni) adj. m. nutritious; nourishing

pójść (pooyshćh) v. go; go away; go up.;leave;fly;drift;pan out

póki (poo-kee) conj. till; untill; as long as;while; when

pół (poow) num. half;semi- ; demi-;one half; mid(way);hemi-

półbucik (poow-boo-cheek) m. half boot; low shoe

półgłosem (poow-gwo-sem) adv. in a low voice;in an undertone

półgłówek (poow-gwoo-vek) m. half-wit; fool; simpleton; dolt

półka (poow-ka) f. shelf;ledge

półkole (po-kó-le) n. semicircle; half-circle;hemicycle

półksiężyc (poow-kshan-zhits)m. half-moon; crescent;the Crescent

półkula (poow-koo-la)f. hemisphere ;half of a sphere

półmisek (poow-mee-sek) m. charger dish; dish

półnagi (poow-na-gee) adj. m. half naked ; half dressed

północ (poow-nots) f. midnight; north; North; the North

północno-wschodni (poow-nóts-no wskhód-ńe)north-east

północno-zachodni (poow-nóts-no zakhód-ńe)north-west

północny (poow-nóts-ni) adj. north ; Northern; Northerly

półroczny (poow-roch-ni) half-yearly; semi-annual

półświatek (poow-shvya-tek) m. love industry;demimonde

półtora (poow-tó-ra) num. one and half; a (day etc.) and half półwysep (poow-vi-sep) m. peninsula; almost an island

póty (poo-ti) conj. as long

później (poozh-ney) adv. later on; afterwards ;at a later date

późno (poozh-no) adv. late ;late-późny (poozh-ni) adj. m. late

prababka (pra-báb-ka) f. great grandmother

praca (prá-tsa) f. work; job

pracodawca (pra-tso-dáv-tsa) m. employer (employing for wages)

pracowity (pra-tso-vée-ti) adj. m. industrious; hard-working

pracownik (pra-tsóv-ñeek) m. worker ;employee ; clerk;official

praczka (prách-ka) f. washwoman; laundress;washerwoman

prać (prach) v. wash; beat up

pradziad (pra-dźhad) m. great grandfather; ancestor

pragnąć (prag-nównćh) v. be thirsty; desire; wish;long for

pragnienie (prag-ñe-ñe) n.wish; thirst; desire; lust for

praktyczny (prak-tích-ni) adj. m. practical;sensible;expedient

praktyka (prak-ti-ka) f. practice; usage;apprenticship

praktykować (prak-ti-kó-vach) v. practice; be in training

pralka (prál-ka) f. washing machine; washer;wash board

pralnia (prál-na) f. laundry

pranie (prá-ñe) n. washing

praojciec (pra-óy-ćhets) m. forefather; ancestor

prasa (prá-sa) f. press; print

prasować (pra-só-vach) v. iron (linen etc.);press; print

prawda (práv-da) f. truth

prawdomówność (prav-do-moóv-nośhćh) f. truthfulness

prawdopodobny (prav-do-po-dób-ni) adj. m. probable; likely

prawdziwie (prav-dźhéev-ye) adv. truly; genuinely; indeed

prawdziwy (prav-dźhée-vi) adj. m. true; real; authentic

prawica (pra-vée-tsa) f. the Right; right hand; right wing

prawić (prá-veech) v. talk; say

prawidło(pra-veéd-wo) n. rule; boot tree ; law; centering

prawidłowy (pra-veed-wó-vi) adj. m. regular; correct;proper

prawie (práv-ye) adv. almost; nearly ;practically; all but

prawnik (prav-ñeek) m. lawyer

prawnuczka (prav-noóch-ka) f. great granddaughter

prawnuk (práv-nook) m. great grandson

prawny (práw-ni) adj. m. legal; lawful;legitimate;rightful

prawo (prá-vo) adv. right;law

prawo (prá-vo) n. law; (driving) license;statute; claim

prawodawca (pra-vo-dáv-tsa) m. legislator;lawmaker;lawgiver

prawodawstwo (pra-vo-dáv-stvo) n. legislation; legislature

prawomocny (pra-vo-móts-ni) adj. m. legal; valid

prawosławny (pra-vo-swáv-ni) adj. m. orthodox

prawość (pra-vośhćh) f. honesty; integrity; righteousness

prawować się (pra-vó-vach śhãn) v. litigate; sue; be engaged in a lawsuit; be at law with...

prawowity (pra-vo-vée-ti) adj. m. legal (heir etc.)

prawy (prá-vi) adj. m. honest; right; rigth hand-;upright;lawful

prażyć (pra-zhich) v. grill;roast burn;keep heavy gunfire on

prąd (prównd) m. current; flow stream ;air flow;tendency; trend

prądnica (prownd-nee-tsa) f. generator ;dynamo

prąd stały (prównd stá-wi) m. direct current

prąd zmienny (prównd zmyén-ni) alternating current

prążek (prówñ-zhek) m. stripe

precyzja (pre-tsíz-ya) f. precision ;accuracy;exactness

precyzować (pre-tsi-zó-vach) v. define; state precisely ;define

precz ! (prech) adv. go away; do away with; down with

prefabrykować (pre-fa-brí-ko-vach)v.prefabricate

prefiks (pre-feeks) m. prefix
prelegent (pre-le-gent) m. lecturer (presenting a lecture)
prelekcja (pre-lek-tsya) f.
lecture (informative talk)
preliminarz (pre-lee-mee-nash)
m. estimate of a budget
premedytacja (pre-me-di-tats-
ya) f. premeditation
premia (prem-ya) f. premium;
bonus;bounty; prize; gift
premier (pre-myer) m. prime
minister ; premier
premiera (pre-mye-ra) f. first
night show;first night
prenumerata (pre-noo-me-ra-ta)
f. subscription(to a paper etc.)
preparat (pre-pa-rat) m. pre —
paration;concoction;specimen
prerogatywa (pre-ro-ga-ti-va)
f. privilege; prerogative
presja (pres-ya) f. pressure
prestiż (pres-teesh) m. prestige; high esteem
pretekst (pre-tekst) m. pretext;
excuse; false reason or motive
pretensja (pre-tens-ya) f. claim;
grudge;debt;pretentiousness
prezerwatywa (pre-zer-va-ti-va)
f. contraceptive sheath
prezent (pre-zent) m. gift
prezes (pre-zes) m. chairman
prezydent (pre-zi-dent) m. president; mayor; Lord Mayor
pręcik (pran-cheek) m. (small)
stick; stamen ;rod; graphite
prędki (prand-kee) adj. m. swift;
quick; rapid; fast; prompt;hasty
prędko (prand-ko) adv. quickly;
fast; 2. soon;at once
prędkość (prand-koshch) f. speed;
swiftness; velocity;impetuosity
prędzej (pran-dzey) adv. quicker
sooner; rather; with all haste
pręga (pran-ga) f. stripe; wale
pręgierz (pran-gesh) m. pillory
pręgowaty (pran-go-va-ti) adj.
m. striped ;with stripes
pręt (prant) m. rod; bar; pole;
switch;stick;wand;twig;perch
prężność (pranzh-noshch) f. resilience; elasticity;energy

prężny (pranzh-ni) adj. m.
elastic; resilient;supple
prężyc (pran-zhich) v. strain
probierczy kamień (pro-byer-
chi kam-yen) m. touch-stone
problem (prob-lem) m. problem
probostwo (pro-bos-tvo) n.
parsonage; parish; rectory
proboszcz (pro-boshch) m. pastor; parish priest;parson
probówka (pro-boov-ka) f.
test-tube; test glass
proca (pro-tsa) f. sling
proceder (pro-tse-der) m.trade;
(shady)dealings; a plot
procedura (pro-tse-doo-ra) f.
procedure; legal practice
procent (pro-tsent) m. percentage; interest on money
procentować się (pro-tsen-to-
vach shan) v. bring interest
proces (pro-tses) m. lawsuit
procesja (pro-tses-ya) f. procession; moving as in parade
procesować (pro-tse-so-vach)
v. sue; be engaged in a liti-
gation ;litigate a cause
proch (prokh) m. powder; dust
proch strzelniczy (prokh
stzhel-nee-chi) m. gunpowder
producent (pro-doo-tsent) m.
producer; manufacturer; maker
produkcja (pro-dook-tsya) f.
production ;output;performance
produkować (pro-doo-ko-vach)
v. produce; grow;generate;stage
produkt (pro-dookt) m. produtt
profanować (pro-fa-no-vach) v.
profane; desecrate :despoil
professor(pro-fe-sor) m. professor ; teacher
profil (pro-feel) m. profile
profilaktyczny (pro-fee-lak-
tich-ni) adj. m. prophylactic
prognoza (prog-no-za) f. prognosis ; forcast(of weather etc.)
program (prog-ram) m. program
progresja (pro-gres-ya) f.
progression ; sequence
prohibicja (pro-hee-beets-ya)
f. prohibition ;forbiddind
projekcja (pro-yek-tsya) f.
projection (on a screen etc.)

projekt (pró-yekt) m. project
projektować (pro-yek-tó-vach)
  v. design ;plan;lay out;draft
proklamować (pro-kla-mo-vach)
  v. proclaim ;announce officially
prokurator (pro-koo-ra-tor) m.
  public prosecutor
proletariat (pro-le-tár-yat) m.
  proletariat ;working class
prolog (pro-lok) m. prologue
prolongować (pro-lon-gó-vach)
  v. prolong; extend
prom (prom) m. ferry (boat)
promieniec (pro-mye-ńech) v.
  radiate; beam(with joy etc.)
promieniotwórczy (pro-mye-ńo-
  tvoor-chi) adj. m. radio-
  active(matter, isotopes, etc.)
promieniować (pro-mye-ńo-vach)
  v. radiate;beam;glow;brim over
promienisty (pro-mye-ńees-ti)
  adj. m. radial ;radiant;rediate
promienny (pro-myen-ni) adj.
  m. radiant; beaming ;bright
promień (pro-myeń) m. beam;
  ray; gleam;radius; fin ray
promocja (pro-mots-ya) f. promotion;conferment of a degree
propaganda (pro-pa-gan-da) f.
  propaganda;publicity;boosting
propagować (pro-pa-go-vach) v.
  propagate; publicize;boost
proponować (pro-po-no-vach) v.
  propose;put forwards;suggest
proporcja (pro-ports-ya) f.
  proportion;ratio; relation
proporcjonalny (pro-por-tsyo-
  nál-ni) adj. m. proportional
proporzec (pro-pó-zhets) m.
  pennon; banner;streamer;jack
propozycja (pro-po-zits-ya) f.
  proposal; offer; suggestion
proroctwo (pro-rots-tvo) n.
  prophecy; prediction
prorok (pro-rok) m. prophet
prosić (pró-sheech) v. beg;
  pray; ask; invite; request
prosię (pro-shań) n. young pig
proso (pro-so) n. millet
prospekt (prós-pekt) m. prospect;folder;view;panorama
prosperować (pros-pe-ró-vach)
  v. prosper;be prosperous;thrive

prostacki (pros-táts-kee) adj.
  m. boorish; rude ;vulgar;coarse
prostak (prós-tak) m. boor; gull
prostata (pros-tá-ta) f. prostate (gland at the of male bladder)
prosto (prós-to) adv. straight;
  right; upright;simply;candidly
prostoduszny (pros-to-doosh-ni)
  adj. m. simple- hearted ;naive
prostokąt (pros-tó-kownt) m.
  rectangle(with four right angles)
prostolinijny (pros-to-lee-ńeey-
  ni) adj. m. straightforward
prostopadła (pros-to-pád-wa) f.
  perpendicular ;normal; sheer
prostota (pros-tó-ta) f. simplic-
  ity ; neatness; boorishness
prostować (pros-to-vach) v.
  straighten; correct;revise
prosty (prós-ti) adj. m. straight;
  right; direct simple;vulgar;plain
prostytucja (pros-ti-too-tsya) f.
  prostitution; streetwalking
prostytutka (pros-ti-toot-ka) f.
  prostitute; streetwalker
proszek (pro-shek) m. powder
  (for baking etc.); wafer
proszę (pró-shań) please
prośba (prósh-ba) f. request;
  demand; petition; application
proszkować (prosh-kó-vach) v.
  pulverize; grind to powder
protegowany (pro-te-go-vá-ni)
  adj. m. protégé
protekcja (pro-ték-tsya) f. pull;
  patronage; backing;influence;push
protest (pro-test) m. protest
protestant (pro-tés- tant) m.
  Protestant ; evangelical
protestantyzm (pro-tes-tan-tizm)
  m. Protestantism
proteza (pro-té-za) f. artificial limb or denture
protokół (pro-tó-koow) m. record;
  protocol;minutes; official record
prototyp (pro-tó-tip) m. proto-
  type; archetype; protoplast
prowadzenie (pro-va-dzé-ńe) n.
  management; conduct;leadership
prowadzić (pro-va-dzheech) v. steer; •
  lead;conduct; guide; keep; live;
  carry on ;show the way;escort;run;
  manage (an institution)

prowadzić auto (pro-vá-dźheećh) áu-to) drive a car

prowiant (pro-vyant) m. provisions;eatables; rations

prowincjonalny (pro-veen-tsyonál-ni) adj. m. provincial

prowizja (pro-veéz-ya) f. commission; percentage; brokerage

prowizoryczny (pro-vee-zo-richni) adj. m. provisional

prowodyr (pro-vo-dir) m. ringleader; gang leader

prowokacja (pro-vo-kats-ya) f. provocation; stirring trouble

proza (pró-za) f. prose;dullness

próba (proo-ba) f. trial; test; proof; ordeal;acid test;try;go

próbka (proob-ka) f. sample

próbny (proob-ni) adj. m. experimental; tentative ;test-

próbować (proo-bó-vach) v. try; test; taste;put to test;offer

próchnica (prookh-nee-tsa) f. moulder; (tooth) decay;humus

próchno (proókh-no) n. rotten wood; mould;rot; wood dust

procz (prooch) prep. save; except;besides;apart from

próg (prook) m. threshold

prószyć (proo-shích) v. sift; flake; make dust;sprinkle;spray

próżnia (proozh-ña) f. vacuum

próżniaczy (proozh-ña-chi) adj. m. lazy; idle;inactive;leisured

próżniak (proozh-ñak) m. idler

próżno (proozh-no) adv. vainly; empty-;in vain; to no avail

próżność (proozh-noshćh) f. vanity; false pride;futility

próżny (proozh-ni) adj. m. 1. empty; void; 2. vain

pruć (prooćh) v. rip; unsew

pruski (proós-kee) adj. m. Prussian (of Prussia

prychać (pri-khach) v. snort

prycza (pri-cha) f. plank-bed

pryk stary (prik sta-ri) adj. m. old goat; old duffer

prym (prim) m. lead; first place; superiority;the lead

prymas (pri-mas) m. primate

prymka (prim-ka) f. chewing tobacco;plug of chewing tobacco

pryskać (pris-kach) v. splash; spray; fly;clear out;bolt;burst

pryszcz (prishch) m. pimple

prysznic (prish-ñeets) m. shower bath; shower

prywatny (pri-vat-ni) adj. m. private; personal;confidential

pryzmat (priz-mat) m. prism

prządka (pzhównd-ka) f. spinner

prząść (pzhównshćh) v. spin

przebaczać (pzhe-ba-chach) v. forgive; pardon; condone

przebaczenie (pzhe-ba-che-ñe) n. pardon; forgiveness;remittal

przebąkiwać (pzhe-bówn-kee-vach) v. mutter ;hint;allude;mention

przebić (pzhe-beech) v. pierce; perforate; puncture;stab;recoin

przebieg (pzhe-byeg) m. curse; run ;progress;process; milage

przebiegać (pzhe-bye-gach) v. run cross ;take place;proceed

przebiegły (pzhe-byeg-wi) adj. m. cunning; sly ;wily;crafty

przebierać (pzhe-bye-rach) v. choose; sort;change clothes;sift

przebijać (pzhe-bee-yach) v. pierce; puncture;show through

przebłysk (pzhe-bwisk)m.glimpse; ray; flash; sparkle;glimmer

przebłyskiwać (pzhe-bwis-keevach) v. gleam ;shine;flash

przebolec (pzhe-bo-lech) v. get over; put up with ;get over it

przeboj (pzhe-booy) m. hit; success; breakthrough ; clou

przebranie (pzhe-brá-ñe) m. disguise ;being disguised

przebrnąć (pzhe-brnównch) v. muddle through; wade through

przebrzmiały (pzhe-bzhmya-wi) adj. m. overblown; has-been

przebudowa (pzhe-boo-dó-va) f. remodeling; rebuilding

przebudzić (pzhe-boo-dźheech)v. wake up; awake ;rouse;revive

przebyć (pzhe-bićh) v. be over through; surmount; ride out storm ;travel;cross;pass;dwell

przebywać (pzhe-bi-vach) v. stay; reside ;dwell;inhabit

przecedzać (pzhe-tse-dzach) v. filter;strain through a sieve

przeceniać (pzhe-tse-ńach) v.
overrate ;lower the price
przechadzka (pzhe-chádz-ka) f.
walk ;stroll;tour; airing
przechadzać się (pzhe-kha-
dzach śhań) v. take a walk;
stroll ;go for a walk;saunter
przechodzić (pzhe-kho-dżheech)
v. pass (through)
przechodzień (pzhe-kho-dżheń)
m. passerby ; pedestrian
przechowanie (pzhe-kho-va-ńe)
n. safekeeping;storage
przechowywać (pzhe-kho-vi-vach)
v. store ;preserve;harbor;keep
przechrzcić (pzhekh-zhćheech)
v. convert; change name
przechwalać (pzhe-khva-lach) v.
talk big ;overpraise;extol;puff
przechwycić (pzhe-khvi-ćheech)
v. intercept; seize
przechylić (pzhe-khi-leech) v.
tilt; lean; tip; incline
przechytrzyć (pzhe-khit-zhich)
v. outwit; overreach;outsmart
przeciąg (pzhe-chownk) m.
draught; span;spell;time lapse
przeciąć (pzhe-chownch) v. cut;
cross; intersect;slice;cleave
przeciągać (pzhe-chown-gach) v.
draw; drag; delay; stretch
przeciążać (pzhe-chown-zhach)
v. overload;overburden
przecie (pzhe-che) conj. yet;
still; of course but;after all
przeciekać (pzhe-che-kach) v.
leak; ooze; drain; percolate
przecierać (pzhe-che-rach) v.
rub; wipe clear; threadbare;
fret ;polish (shoes) ;clear up
przecierpieć (pzhe-cher-pyech)
v. endure; bear; suffer
przecież (pzhe-chezh) conj. yet;
still; after all; now ;though
przeciętny (pzhe-chant-ni) adj.
m. average ;ordinary;mediocre
przecinać (pzhe-chee-nach) v.
cut; intersect ;slice;cleave
przecinek (pzhe-chee-nek) m.
comma ; point (in mathematics)
przeciskać się (pzhe-chees-kach
śhań) v. squeeze through ;push
through;elbow one's way

przeciw (pzhe-cheev) prep.
against; versus ;contrary to
przeciwko (pzhe-cheev-ko) prep.
against; contrary ; versus
przeciwdziałać (pzhe-cheev-
dżha-wach) v. counteract
przeciwległy (pzhe-cheev-leg-wi)
adj, m. opposite; contrary
przeciwlotniczy (pzhe-cheev-
lot-ńee-chi) adj. m. antiair-
craft(artllery, defence etc.)
przeciwnie (pzhe-cheev-ńe) adv.
on the contrary; reverse
przeciwnik (pzhe-cheev-ńeek) m.
opponent ; adversary;enemy;foe
przeciwność (pzhe-cheev-noshch)
f. adversity;set-back;reverse
przeciwstawiać (pzhe-cheev-stav-
yach) v. oppose; set against
przeciwwaga (pzhe-cheev-va-ga)
f. counterweight;balance weight
przecudny (pzhe-tsood-ni) adj.
m. most wonderful;just marvellous
przeczący (pzhe-chown-tsi) adj.
m. negative; contradictory
przeczenie (pzhe-che-ńe) n.
negation;negative;denial
przecznica (pzhech-ńee-tsa) f.
side-street ;cross street
przeczucie (pzhe-choo-che) n.
foreboding ;presentiment
przeczulony (pzhe-choo-lo-ni)
adj. m. high-strung; over-
-sensitive;touchy; irritable
przeczyć (pzhe-chich) v. deny;
belie; negate; contradict
przeczyszczać (pzhe-chish-chach)
v. purge; cleanse; scour ;wipe
przeczytać (pzhe-chi-tach) v.
read through ;peruse;read over
przed (pzhech) v. insist on;urge;
press on ;push;exert pressure;
impel;drive;insist;bear down;strl-
przed (pzhet) prep. before; in
front of; ahead of; previous
to; from ;since;ago ;against
przedajny (pzhe-day-ni) adj. m.
venal;open to bribery
przedawnienie (pzhe-dav-ńe-ńe)
n. expiration of validity
przedawniony (pzhe-dav-ńo-ni)
adj. m. of expired validity
przeddzień (pzhéd-dżheń) m. eve

przede wszystkim (pzhe-de vshist-keem) adv. above all; first; first of all; in the first place; to begin with

przedhistoryczny (pzhed-hees-to-rich-ni) adj. m. prehistoric;before recorded hist.

przedimek (pzhed-ée-mek) m. article (in grammar)

przedkładać (pzhed-kwa-dach) v. submit; refer; propose; present; prefer;give priority

przedłużać (pzhed-woo-zhach) v. lengthen; prolong;extend

przedmieście (pzhed-myesh-che) n, suburb;outskirts of a city

przedmiot (pzhed-myot) m. object; subject; subject matter

przedmiotowy (pzhed-myo-tó-vi) adj. m. objective; at issue

przedmowa (pzhed-mó-va) f. preface; foreword;introduction

przedmówca (pzhed-moóv-tsa) m. previous speaker

przedni (pzhéd-ńee) adj. m. leading; front; forward; choice; fine ;foremost;superior

przedostać się (pzhe-dos-tach shań) v. penetrate;pass through

przedostatni (pzhed-os-tát-ńee) adj. m. last but one

przedpłata (pzhed-pwa-ta) f. advance payment;subscription

przedpokój (pzhed-pó-kooy) m. (waiting-room) lobby; antechamber; anteroom; hall

przedpole (pzhed-pó-le) n. foreground; foreland

przedpołudnie (pzhed-po-wood-ńe) n. morning; forenoon

przedpotopowy (pzhed-po-to-pó-vi) adj. m. fossil; antediluvian; fossilized; obsolete

przedramię (pzhed-ram-yań) n. forearm; antebrachium

przedrostek (pzhed-ros-tek) m. prefix (in grammar)

przedruk (pzhed-rook) m. reprint; reimpression;impression

przedrzeć (pzhéd-zhech) v. tear up; tear through; rend; break through;penetrate;burst

przedrzeźniać (pzhed-zhéźh-ńach) v. ape; mimic; mock; take off; immitate like an ape

przedsiębiorca (pzhed-shań-byor-tsa) m. contractor;businessman

przedsiębiorstwo (pzhed-shań-byor-stvo) n. business; concern; enterprise; firm

przedsiębrać (pzhed-shań-brach) v. undertake;embark upon

przedsionek (pzhed-shó-nek) m. lobby; vestibule; porch;auricle

przedsmak (pzhed-smak) m. foretaste;earnest(of future events)

przedstawić (pzhed-sta-veech) v. present; represent;recommend

przedstawiciel (pzhed-sta-vee-chel) m. representative

przedstawicielstwo (pzhed-sta-vee-chél-stvo) n. agency

przedstawienie (pzhed-sta-vyé-ńe) n. performance;show;version

przedszkole (pzhed-shko-le) n. kindergarten; nursery school

przedświt(pzhéd-shveet)m. predawn; daybreak;dawn; harbinger

przedtem (pzhéd-tem) adv. before; formerly;in advance;earlier

przedterminowy (pzhed-ter-mee-nó-vi) adj. m. advance; premature; done ahead of time

przedwczesny (pzhed-vches-ni) adj. m. premature; untimely

przedwczoraj (pzhed-vcho-ray) adv. the day before yesterday

przedwieczny (pzhed-vyéch-ni) adj. m. eternal;primeval;ancient

przedwiośnie (pzhed-vyosh-ńe) n. early spring

przedwojenny (pzhed-vo-yén-ni) adj. m. prewar; before the war

przedział (pzhe-dźhaw) m. partition; compartment; section

przedzielić (pzhe-dźhe-leech) v. divide; part;separate

przedzierać (pzhe-dźhe-rach) v. tear down; tear up; rend

przedziurawić (pzhe-dźhoo-ra-veech) v. perforate; puncture; riddle; pierce ;make a hole

przedziwny (pzhe-dźhéev-ni) adj. m. prodigious; admirable; odd

przeforsować (pzhe-for-so-vach) v. ram through; force through

przegapić (pzhe-ga-peech) v. let slip; over look; miss

przeginać (pzhe-gee-nach) v. bend (over); turn up; turn down

przegląd (pzhe-glownt) m. review; inspection; survey

przegłosować (pzhe-gwo-so-vach) v. outvote; take a vote

przegonić (pzhe-go-neech) v. overtake; drive out; drive through; drive away; rush past

przegotować (pzhe-go-to-vach) v. boil; overcook; overboil

przegrać (pzhe-grach) v. lose (war; game etc.); gamble away

przegradzać (pzhe-gra-dzach) v. partition; divide; separate

przegrana (pzhe-gra-na) f. defeat; loss; beating; licking

przegryzać (pzhe-gri-zach) v. bite through; bite in two

przegroda (pzhe-gro-da) f. partition; division; stall; cell

przegub (pzhe-goop) m. wrist; ball-and-socket joint

przeholować (pzhe-kho-lo-vach) v. overshoot; rush into excess

przeistoczyć (pzhe-ees-to-chich) v. transform; remould; convert

przejaśnienie (pzhe-yash-ne-ne) n. clearing up; bright interval

przejaw (pzhe-yav) m. symptom; sign; indication; manifestation

przejawiać (pzhe-ya-veeach) v. reveal; display; manifest; show

przejazd (pzhe-yazt) m. crossing; passage; thoroughfare

przejąć (pzhe-yownch) v. take over; seize; adopt; master; thrill

przejechać (pzhe-ye-khach) v. pass; ride; cross; run over

przejęty (pzhe-yan-ti) adj. m. impressed; upset; deeply stirred; perturbed; wrapped up

przejmować (pzhey-mo-vach) v. take over; seize; penetrate

przejrzeć (pzhey-zhech) v. see through; recover sight; revise

przejrzysty (pzhey-zhis-ti) adj. m. transparent; clear; sheer

przejście (pzhey-shche) n. pass; transition; conversion; roadway

przejściowo (pzhey-shcho-vo) adv. temporarily; provisionally

przejść (pzheyshch) v. pass; cross; experience; go across

przekaz (pzhe-kas) m. transfer; money order; remittance

przekazywać (przhe-ka-zi-vach) v. transfer; pass on; send on; transmit; deliver; direct

przekaźnik (pzhe-kazh-neek) m. relay; repeater; transmitter

przekąsem (pzhe-kown-sem) adv. ironically; mockingly; spitefully

przekąska (pzhe-kowns-ka) f. snack; refreshment

przekątna (pzhe-kownt-na) f. diagonal (line)

przekleństwo (pzhe-klen-stvo) n. curse; profanity; damnation

przekład (pzhe-kwat) m. translation; rendering; rearrangement

przekładać (pzhe-kwa-dach) v. shift; transfer; prefer; move; translate; reach; put between

przekładnia (przek-wad-na) f. gearbox; clutch; transposition

przekłuć (pzhe-kwooch) v. prick; pierce; puncture; perforate

przekonać (pzhe-ko-nach) v. convince; persuade; bring round

przekonanie (pzhe-ko-na-ne) n. conviction; persuasion; opinion

przekop (pzhe-kop) m. trench; ditch; tunnel; cutting; piercing

przekopać (pzhe-ko-pach) v. dig-through; turn over; excavate; cut

przekora (pzhe-ko-ra) f. spite

przekraczać (pzhe-kra-chach) v. overstep; cross; surpass

przekradać się (pzhe-kra-dach shan) v. steal through

przekreślić (pzhe-kresh-leech) v. cross out; delete; annul

przekręcić (pzhe-kran-cheech) v. twist; distort (a statement)

przekroczenie (pzhe-kro-che-ne) n. trespass; offence; transgression

przekroczyć (pzhe-kro-chich) v. cross; trespass; exceed; offend; violate; transgress (the law)

przekroić (pzhe-kró-eećh) v. cut
przekrój (pzhé-krooy) v. cross
section; profile;review,
przekrwienie (pzhe-krvye-ńe) n.
hyperemia;congestion
przekształcić (pzhe-kshtaw-
ćheećh) y. transform
przekupić (pzhe-koó-peećh) v.
bribe; buy over; corrupt
przekupka (pzhe-koóp-ka) f.
huckstress; vendor;wrangler
przekupny (pzhe-koóp-ni) adj.
m. venal; bribable
przekupstwo (pzhe-koóp-stvo) n.
bribery ;graft; corruption
przekwitać (pzhe-kvee-tach) v.
wither; fade; decay;shed blossom
przelatywać (pzhe-la-ti-vach)
v. fly through;cross;run;pass
przelew (pzhé-lef) m. transfusion; transfer;over flow
przelewać (pzhe-le-vach) v.
overfill; transfer; shed
przelękły (pzhe-lán-kwi) adj.
m. frightened ;intimidated
przelęknąć (pzhe-lańk-nównch)v.
frighten ;scare; terrify
przelicytować (pzhe-lee-tsi-
tó-vach) y. outbid
przeliczyć (pzhe-lee-chich) v.
miscalculate; count over
przelot (pzhe-lot) m. over-
flight; flight; passage
przelotny (pzhe-lót-ni) adj. m.
fleeting; passing; transient
przeludnienie (pzhe-lood-ńe-ńe)
n. overpopulation; congestion
przeładować (pzhe-wa-dó-vach)
v. overload; transship;reload
przeładunek (pzhe-wa-doo-nek)
m. load transfer,; reloading
przełamać (pzhe-wa-mach) v.
break through;break in two
przełazić (pzhe-wa-żheech) v.
climb over ;creep across
przełącznik (pzhe-wównch-ńeek)
m. switch; shift;commutator
przełęcz (pzhe-wańch) v. (mountain) pass;saddle; col
przełknąć (pzhew-knównch) v.
swallow; swollow down
przełom (pzhe-wom) m. breakthrough; turning point;gorge

przełożony (pzhe-wo-zhó-ni)
adj. m. principal, superior
przełożyć (pzhe-wo-zhich) v.
transfer; prefer; shift;reach
przełyk (pzhé-wik) m. gullet;
esophagus
przemakać (pzhe-má-kach) v.
ooze; get wet;,be permeable
przemarsz (pzhe-marsh) m.
marching past; march of troops
przemarznąć (pzhe-mar-znównch)
v. be chilled ;freeze stiff
przemawiać (pzhe-ma-vyach) v.
speak; harangue; address
przemądrzały (pzhe-mównd-zha-
wi) adj. m. smart aleck
przemęczać (pzhe-mań-chach) v.
overstrain; overwork ;spend
przemęczenie (pzhe-mań-che-ńe)
n. strain ;overwork; tiredness
przemiał (pzhe-myaw) m. grinding; milling ;meal;grist;shoal
przemiana (pzhe-mya-na) f.change;
transformation; alteration
przemianować (pzhe-mya-no-vach)
v. rename ; change name
przemienić (pzhe-mye-ńeech) v.
change; transform ;alter;turn
przemieścić (pzhe-myesh-ćheech)
v. displace ;dislocate; shift
przemijać (pzhe-mee-yach) v.
go by;be over; pass; cease
przemilczeć (pzhe-meel-chech)
v. keep secret;leave unsaid
przemoc (pzhe-mots) f. force;
violence ;constraint;compulsion
przemoczyć (pzhe-mo-chich) v.
soak; drench ;wet;seep; sop
przemoknąć (pzhe-mok-nównch) v.
be soaked ;be permeable;get wet
przemowa (pzhe-mo-va) f. speech;
oration; address :harangue
przemóc (pzhe-moots) v. overcome ;conquer;defeat;master;prevail
przemówić (pzhe-moo-veech) v.
speak up ;make a mistake(speaking)
przemówienie (pzhe-moov-ye-ńe)
n. speech ;address; oration
przemycać (pzhe-mi-tsach) v.
smuggle (into a country,a room etc.)
przemyć (pzhe-mich) v. rinse; scrub;
wash ;give a wash; lavage; flush
przemysł (pzhe-misw) m.industry

przemysłowy (pzhe-mis-wo-vi) adj.
m. industrial;manufacturing

przemyśliwać (pzhe-miśh-lee-
vach) y. ponder; think over

przemyślny (pzhe-miśhl-ni) adj.
m. ingenious;clever;cunning

przemyt (pzhe-mit) m. smuggling

przemytnik (pzhe-mit-ñeek) m.
smuggler; contrabandist

przemywać (pzhe-mi-vach) v.
rinse; wash; scrub;lavage;flush

przenieść (pzhe-ñeshch) v.
transfer; surpass; carry over;
remove;convey; move; retrace

przenigdy (pzhe-ñeeg-di) adv.
nevermore; never; never

przenikać (pzhe-ñee-kach) v.
penetrate; pierce; permeate

przenikliwy (pzhe-ñeek-lee-vi)
adj. m. penetrating; acute;
sharp; piercing;keen;shrewd

przenocować (pzhe-no-tso-vach)
v. pass the night;put up

przenośnia (pzhe-nosh-ña) f.
metaphor; figure of speach

przenośny (pzhe-nosh-ni) adj. m.
portable; mobile;metaphorical

przeobrażać (pzhe-o-bra-zhach)
v. transform; modify;change

przeoczenie (pzhe-o-che-ñe) m.
oversight; omission

przeoczyć (pzhe-o-chich) v.
overlook; leave out;omit

przepadać (pzhe-pa-dach) v. be
lost; be extremely fond;vanish

przepalić (pzhe-pa-leech) v.
burn through;overheat;scorch

przepasać (pzhe-pa-sach) v.
gird ;belt;tie;overfeed

przepaska (pzhe-pas-ka) f. band

przepaść (pzhe-pashch) f. abyss

przepchać (pzhep-khach) v. push
through; pass through;clean out

przepełniać (pzhe-pew-ñach) v.
overfill; cram ; over cram

przepełnienie (pzhe-pew-ñe-ñe) n.
overfill; crowd;excess

przepędzać (pzhe-pan-dzach) v.
drive away; spend ;distil;stay

przepić (pzhe-peech) v. spend
on drinking ; drink away;waste

przepierać (pzhe-pye-rach) v.
launder; wash clothes

przepierzenie (pzhe-pye-zhe-ñe)
n. partition (wall etc.)

przepiękny (pzhe-pyań -kni)
adj. , very beautiful; gorgeous

przepiłować (pzhe-pee-wo-wach)
v. saw through; file through

przepiórka (pzhe-pyoor-kni) f.
quail(migratory game bird)

przepis (pzhe-pees) m. 1. regulation; 2. recipe

przepisać (pzhe-pee-sach) v.
1. prescribe; 2. copy

przepłacać (pzhe-pwa-tsach) v.
overpay; pay too much; bribe

przepłukać (pzhe-pwoo-kach) v.
rinse; gargle ;scour; wash

przepłynąć (pzhe-pwi-nownch) v.
swim across ;row across

przepływać (pzhe-pwi-vach) v.
flow; float across; swim
across; row across;sail across

przepocić (pzhe-po-cheech) v.
sweat through ;sweat (a shirt)

przepoić (pzhe-po-eech) v. impregnate ;saturate; fill

przepona (pzhe-po-na) f. diaphragm ;midriff; stiffener

przepowiadać (pzhe-po-vya-dach)
v. predict ;foretell;repeat

przepracować się (pzhe-pra-tso-
vach śhañ) v. overwork (oneself) ;overstrain oneself

przepraszać (pzhe-pra-shach) v.
apologize ;excuse oneself

przeprawa (pzhe-pra-va) f.
1. passage; crossing ;journey
2. fight ;incident;scene; row

przeprawiać (pzhe-prav-yach) v.
cross over ;carry across

przeproszenie (pzhe-pro-she-ñe)
n. apology ; apologies

przeprowadzać (pzhe-pro-va-dzach)
v. convey; lead; move ;pass

przeprowadzka (pzhe-pro-vadz-ka)
f. moving(form a house etc.)

przepuklina (pzhe-poo-klee-na)
f. hernia; rupture

przepustka (pzhe-poost-ka) f.
pass; permit ;liberty; sluice

przepuszczać (pzhe-poosh-chach)
v. let pass ;promote;leak;miss;
let slip;waste;squander away

przepuszczalność (pzhe-poosh-chál-noshćh) f. permeability

przepych (pzhe-pikh) m. luxury; pageantry;splendor;ostentation

przepychać (pzhe-pi-khaćh) v. push through; force through

przepytywać (pzhe-pi-ti-vaćh) v. examine;inquire ;question

przerabiać (pzhe-ra-byaćh) v. do over; revise ;remodel;alter

przerachować (pzhe-ra-kho-vaćh) v. miscalculate; count over

przeradzać się (pzhe-ra-dzaćh shán) v. change (into)

przerastać (pzhe-ras-taćh) v. outgrow; rise above ;surpass

przerazić (pzhe-ra-zheećh) v. terrify; appal; consternation

przeraźliwy (pzhe-razh-lee-vi) adj. m. appalling; terrifying shrill ; awesome; acute;sharp

przerażenie (pzhe-ra-zhe-ñe) n. terror ;horror;dread;dismay

przerażony (pzhe-ra-zho-ni) adj. m. horror stricken

przeróbka (pzhe-roob-ka) f. revision ;reshaping; alteration

przerwa (pzher-va) f. pause; break; recess ; interval

przerys (pzhe-ris) m. tracing

przerysować (pzhe-ri-so-vaćh) v. trace; copy ;retrace

przerwać (pzher-vaćh) v. interrupt; pause; cut off

przerzedzic(pzhe-zhe-dzheećh)v. thin out ; decimate(a population)

przerzucać (pzhe-zhoo-tsaćh) v. throw over; shift; move; flip; browse;transfer; ransack

przerzynać (pzhe-zhi-naćh) v. cut through;cut in two

przesada (pzhe-sá-da) f. exaggeration ;overstatement

przesadzać (pzhe-sa-dzaćh) v. 1. exaggerate; 2. transplant

przesalać (pzhe-sa-laćh) v. oversalt ;put too much salt

przesąd (pzhe-sównt) m. prejudice; superstition;fallacy

przesądny (pzhe-sównd-ni) adj. m. superstitious ;prejudiced

przesiadać się (pzhe-sha-daćh shán) v. change(places; seats)

przesiedlać (pzhe-shed-laćh) v. displace; migrate;transplant

przesiewać (pzhe-she-vaćh) v. sift; sieve ;screen out;riddle

przesilać się (pzhe-shee-laćh shán) v. subside ;get over; culminate;overcome;overstrain

przesilenie (pzhe-shee-le-ñe) n. crisis ;turning point

przeskoczyć (pzhe-sko-chićh) v. jump over;vault ;outstrip;skip

przesłać (pzhe-swaćh) v. 1.send; 2. make bed over ;rearrange a bed

przesłaniać (pzhe-swa-ñaćh) v. screen off ;veil;cover;hide;shade

przesłanka (pzhe-swan-ka) f. premise ;prerequisite;condition

przesłuchiwać (pzhe-swoo-khee-vaćh) v. interrogate;question

przesmyk (pzhes-mik) m. strait

przesolony (pzhe-so-ló-ni) adj. m. oversalted;with excess salt

przespać (pzhes-paćh) v. sleep over ;fail to wake up for...

przestać (pzhes-taćh) v. cease

przestanek (pzhes-tá-nek) m. pause; rest ; stop

przestankować (pzhe-stan-kó-vaćh) v. punctuate (written matter)

przestarzały (pzhe-sta-zha-vi) adj. m. obsolete;time worn

przestawać (pzhe-stá-vaćh) v. 1.cut out; break off; 2. associate; hobnob ;keep company

przestawiać (pzhe-stáv-yaćh) v. displace; transpose;shift

przestąpić (pzhe-stówn-peećh) v. step over;transgress ;cross

przestępca (pzhe-stánp-tsa) m. criminal;felon;law beaker

przestępny (pzhe-stánp-ni) adj. m. leap (year) ;felonious

przestępstwo (pzhe-stánp-stvo) n. offense; crime;transgression

przestrach (pzhe-strakh) m. fright; alarm; fear; terror

przestraszyć (pzhe-stra-shićh) v. scare; startle;alarm

przestroga (pzhe-stro-ga) f. warning; admonition;caution

przestronny (pzhe-stron-ni) adj. m. spacious; roomy

przestrzegać (pzhe-stzhe-gach)
v. observe (rules); caution

przestrzelić (pzhe-stzhe-leech)
v. shoot through;shoot down

przestrzenny (pzhe-stzhen-ni)
adj. m. spatial; roomy

przestrzeń (pzhe-stzheń) f.
space ; outer space; room

przestworze (pzhe-stvo-zhe) n.
expanse; infinity ; space

przesunięcie (pzhe-soo-ńań-che)
n. shift; transfer;displacement

przesuwać (pzhe-soo-vach) v.
move; shift ; shove; transfer

przesycać (pzhe-si-tsach) v.
saturate; glut; impregnate

przesyłać (pzhe-si-wach) v.
send ; dispatch; forward

przesyłka (pzhe-siw-ka) f.
shipment ; mail; parcel

przesypiać (pzhe-sip-yach) v.
oversleep; sleep away

przesyt (pzhe-sit) m. glut

przeszczep (pzhe-shchep) m.
transplant; graft; grafting

przeszkadzać (pzhe-shka-dzach)
v. hinder; trouble ;prevent

przeszkoda (pzhesh-ko-da) f.
obstacle ; hitch; obstruction

przeszkolenie (pzhe-shko-le-
ńe) n. training ; course

przeszło (pzhesh-wo) adv.
more than ; over(an amount)

przeszłość (pzhesh-woshch) f.
past ; record;antecedents

przeszukać (pzhe-shoo-kach) v.
search over ; ransack

przeszyć (pzhe-shich) v. sew-
through; pierce; gore;quilt

prześcieradło (pzhesh-che-rad-
wo) n. bedsheet; sheet

prześcignąć (pzhe-shcheeg-
nownch) v. outdistance; outdo; outstrip;overtake;excel

prześladować (pzhe-shla-do-
vach) v. persecute;harass;haunt

prześladowanie (pzhe-shla-do-
va-ńe) n. persecution;obsession

prześliczny (pzhe-shleech-ni)
adj. m. most beautiful;lovely

prześlizgnąć (pzhe-shleez-nownch)
v. slip through;glide past

przeświadczenie (pzhe-shvyad-
che-ńe) n. conviction;certitude

prześwietlać (pzhe-shvyet-lach)
v. shine through; fluoroscope

przetak (pzhe-tak) m. riddle

przetaczać (pzhe-ta-chach) v.
1. rollover; 2. transfuse

przetapiać (pzhe-tap-yach) v.
recast; smelt(metals); melt

przetarg (pzhe-tark) m. auction

przetarty (pzhe-tár-ti) adj. m.
threadbare; rubbed through

przetłumaczyć (pzhe-twoo-ma-
chich) v. translate ; explain

przeto (pzhe-to) conj. therefore;accordingly;consequently

przetrawić (pzhe-tra-veech) v.
digest;ruminate;etch;corrode

przetrwać (pzhe-trvach) v.
survive; outlast;remain;keep

przetrwonić (pzhe-trvo-ńeech)
v. squander;waste;fritter away

przetrząsnąć (pzhe-tzhowns-
nownch) v. search (shake
through);ransack;comb out

przetrzymać (pzhe-tzhi-mach) v.
endure; outdo; keep waiting

przetwarzać (pzhe-tva-zhach)
v. remake; manufacture

przetwórnia (pzhe-tvoor-ńa) f.
factory; processing plant

przewaga (pzhe-va-ga) f. pre-
dominance ; overbalance ;lead

przeważać (pzhe-va-zhach) v.
outweigh; prevail; overbalance

przeważający (pzhe-va-zha-yown-
tsi) adj. m. prevailing; superior; predominant

przeważnie (pzhe-vazh-ńe) adv.
mainly; mostly; chiefly;largely

przewiązać (pzhe-vyown-zach) v.
bind up; change dressing

przewidywać (pzhe-vee-di-vach)
v. anticipate; foresee

przewiercić (pzhe-vyer-cheech)
v. drill through (pierce)

przewiesić (pzhe-vye-sheech)v.
sling over;hang over;rehang

przewietrzyć (pzhe-vyet-zhich)
v. ventilate

przewiew (pzhe-vyev) m. draught;
breeze; breath of air;whiff

przewiezienie (pzhe-vye-zhe-ńe)
n. transport ;transportation;
carriage; conveyance

przewijac (pzhe-vee-yach) v.
wrap up; change dressing
przewinienie (pzhe-vee-ńe-ńe)
n. offense; delinquency
przewlekły (pzhe-vlek-wi) adj.
m. protracted; lingering;lasting
przewodni (pzhe-vod-ńee) adj.
m. leading ;guiding(principle)
przewodniczący (pzhe-vod-ńee-
chown-tsi) m. chairman
przewodnik (pzhe-vod-ńeek) m.
guide; conductor; leader
przewodzic (pzhe-vo-dzheech) v.
head; command ;lead;conduct
przewozic (pzhe-vo-zheech) v.
convey; transport;cart across
przewoznik (pzhe-vozh-ńeek) m.
ferryman;carter; carrier
przewod (pzhe-voot) m. conduit;
channel; wire;procedure
przewoz (pzhe-voos) m. transport; freight ; cartage
przewracac (pzhe-vra-tsach) v.
overturn; turn over; upset;
toss ; topple; invert;reverse
przewrotnosc (pzhe-vrot-noshch)
f. perversity; perfidy;deceit
przewrot (pzhe-vroot) m. revolution;upheaval;coup d'état
przewyższac (pzhe-vizh-shach)
v. out do; exceed; surpass
przez (pzhes) prep. ; across;
over; through; during; within; in; on;on the other side
przeziębic się (pzhe-zhań-beech
shań) v. catch cold;grow cold
przezimowac (pzhe-zhee-mo-vach)
v. winter; hibernate
przeznaczac (pzhe-zna-chach) v.
intend; earmark ; mean; destine; assign; allocate;design
przeznaczenie (pzhe-zna-che-ńe)
n. destiny; destination
przezornosc (pzhe-zor-noshch) f.
caution; prudence;foresight
przezrocze (pzhe-zhro-che) n.
transparency; slide;open work
przezroczysty (pzhe-zhro-chis-
ti) adj. m. transparent
przezwisko (pzhes-vees-ko) n.
1. nickname; 2. abusive name
przezwyciężac (pzhez-vee-chan-
zhach) v.overcome; conquer

przezywac (pzhe-zi-vach) v. revile; abuse; call names
przeżegnać się (pzhe-zheg-nach
shań) v. cross oneself
przeżuwac (pzhe-zhoo-vach) v.
chew;masticate; ponder over
przeżycie (pzhe-zhi-che) n.
experience; survival
przeżyc (pzhe-zhich)v.survive;
live through;outlive
przeżytek (pzhe-zhi-tek) m.
relic of the passd;old timer
przędza (pzhań-dza) f. yarn
przędzalnia (pzhań-dzal-ńa) f.
spinning mill;spinning room
przęsło (pzhańs-wo) n. (bridge)
bay; (stair) flight; span
przodek (pzho-dek) m. 1. ancestor; 2. front;heading;end;top
przodowac (pzho-do-vach) v.
lead; excel; be the best
przodownictwo (pzho-dov-ńeets-
tvo) n. leadership; hegemony
przodownik (pzho-dov-ńeek) m.
leader;foreman;police inspector
przod (pzhoot) m. front; ahead
przy (pzhi) prep. by; at; near
by; with; on; about; close to
przybic (pzhi-beech)v. nail down
przybiec (pzhi-byets) v. run
up ; hasten;come up running
przybierac (pzhi-byé-rach) v.
dress up; put on; adopt;adorn
przybliżac (pzhi-blee-zhach) v.
bring near;draw near;magnify
przybliżony (pzhi-blee-zho-ni)
adj. m. approximate;very near
przyboczny (pzhi-boch-ni) adj.
m. side(kick); personal (aide);
body (guard);adjutant (officer)
przybory (pzhi-bo-ri) pl. accessories;outfit; tools;tackle
przybor (pzhi-boor) m. rise
(of flood);rise (of a river)
przybrac (pzhi-brach) v. adorn;
put on; assume; adopt;rise;grow
przybrzeżny (pzhi-bzhezh-ni)
adj. m. coastal; riverside
przybudowka (pzhi-boo-doov-ka)
f. annex;addition(to a building)
przybycie (pzhi-bi-che) n. arrival;gain;growth; accession
przybysz (pzhi-bish) m. newcomer

przybytek (pzhi-bi-tek) m. increase; sanctuary;repository
przybywać (pzhi-bi-vać) v.
1. arrive 2. increase;rise
przychodnia (pzhi-khod-ńa) f. outpatient,clinic;ambulatory
przychodzić (pzhi-kho-dźheeć) v. come over, around, along, to, again; turn up; arrive
przychód (pzhi-khoot) m. income;profit; takings;proceeds
przychylać (pzhi-khi-lać) v. incline: comply; bend
przychylny (pzhi-khil-ni) adj. m. favorable; kind;friendly
przyciągać (pzhi-ćhown-gać) v. attract; draw near;appeal;lure
przyciąganie ziemskie (pzhi-ćhown-ga-ńe zhem-ske) gravitation; gravitational,pull
przyciemniać (pzhi-ćhem-ńać) v. dim; darken;shade;black out
przycinać (pzhi-ćhi-nać) v.
1. cut; slip; 2. make fun of
przycisk (pzhi-ćheesk) m.
1. pressure; 2. accent; 3. paper-weight; weight;emphasis
przyciskać (pzhi-ćhis-kać) v. press; keep down;squeeze
przycupnąć (pzhi-tsoop-nownć) v. squat,down;crouch;lie in wait
przyczaić się (pzhi-cha-eeć shań) v. lurk; sulk; ambush;hide
przyczepić (pzhi-che-peećh) v. attach; fasten;link;fix;pin;hook
przyczepić się (pzhi-che-peech shań) v. cling; pick a quarrel; find fault; hold tight; attach
przyczepka (pzhi-chep-ka) f. trailer
przyczółek (pzhi-choo-wek) m. abutment; bridgehead; beachhead;fronton;frontal;pediment
przyczyna (pzhi-chi-na) f.cause; reason; ground; intercession
przyczynek (pzhi-chi-nek) m. contribution(to science etc.)
przyczyniać (pzhi-chi-ńać) v. add; add to; contribute
przyczynowość (pzhi-chi-no-voshćh) f. causation;causality
przyćmiewać (pzhi-ćhmye-vać) v. dim; tarnish; obscure; outshine; overshadow;darken; eclipse

przydać (pzhi-dać) v. add; apend; lend; add weight
przydatny (pzhi-dat-ni) adj. m. useful;helpful;serviceable
przydawka (pzhi-dav-ka) f. attribute,(gram.);qulifier
przydeptać (pzhi-dep-tać) v. thread upon; step on
przydługi (pzhi-dwoo-gee) adj. m. lengthy;somewhat too long
przydomek (pzhi-do-mek) m. by-name; surname;nickname
przydreptać (pzhi-drep-tać) v. trip along; come tripping
przydrożny (pzhi-drozh-ni) adj. m. roadside(shrine etc.)
przydusić (pzhi-doo-sheećh) v. throttle; smother;press down
przydybać (pzhi-di-bać) v. overtake; take unawares;nab
przydymać (pzhi-dimać) v. foot it along; run up(slang)
przydymiony (pzhi-dim-yo-ni) adj. m. smoky; tinted
przydział (pzhi-dżhaw) m. allotment; ration;allowance
przydzielać (pzhi-dżhe-lać) v. assign; allocate;allot
przyganiać (pzhi-ga-ńać) v. blame; find fault with; criticize;rebuke;reprimand
przygarnąć (pzhi-gar-nownć) v. take up; adopt;hug;grasp;shelter
przygasać (pzhi-ga-sać) v. dim; subside; abate;go out;die down
przyglądać się (pzhi-glown-dać shań) v. observe;look on;scan;see
przygnać (pzhi-gnać) v. drive near; bring; run up; hasten
przygnębiać (pzhi-gnań-byać) v. depress; deject;dishearten
przygnębienie (pzhi-gnań-bye-ńe) n. depression; low spirits
przygniatać (pzhi-gńa-tać) v. crush;overwhelm; oppress; burden; press down;squeeze; pinch
przygoda (pzhi-go-da) f. adventure; accident; experience
przygodny (pzhi-god-ni) adj. m. occasional; casual; accidental
przygotować (pzhi-go-to-vać) v. prepare; get ready; worn ; fit; coach; train; make ready; pack up; turn on (the bath)

przygotowanie (pzhi-go-to-va-ñe) n. preparation;getting ready
przygotowawczy (pzhi-go-to-vav-chi) adj. m. preparatory;initial
przygrywac (pzhi-gri-vach) v. 1. accompany; 2. play(music)
przygrzewać (pzhi-gzhe-vach) v. warm up; heat up;swelter
przygwozdzic (pzhi-gvozh-dzheech) v. nail down;pin down
przyimek (pzhi-eé-mek) m. preposition(relation word)
przyjaciel (pzhi-ya-chel) m. friend;good friend;close friend
przyjaciołka (pzhi-ya-choow-ka) f. girl friend;close friend
przyjazd (pzhi-yazt) m. arrival; time of arrival
przyjazny (pzhi-yaz-ni) adj. m. friendly; amicable; kindly
przyjazń (pzhi-yazhñ) f. friendship; friendly relations;amity
przyjaznic się (pzhi-yazh-ñeech shañ) v. be friends;pal;chum
przyjechac (pzhi-ye-khach) v. come (over); arrive; come
przyjemnosc (pzhi-yém-noshch) f. pleasure; enjoyment; gusto;zest
przyjemny (pzhi-yém-ni) adj. m. pleasant;attractive;nice;cosy
przyjezdny (pzhi-yézd-ni) m. stranger; sightseer;visitor
przyjeżdżac (pzhi-yezh-dżhach) v. arrive (by transportation)
przyjęcie (pzhi-yán-che) n. admission; adoption; reception
przyjęty (pzhi-yan-ti) adj. m. customary; acceptable
przyjmowac (pzhiy-mó-vach) v. receive; accept; entertain
przyjscie (pzhiysh-che) n. arrival; coming; advent
przyjsc (pzhiyshch) v. come-over; come along; come around
przykazac (pzhi-ka-zach) v. order; tell; enjoin to do
przykazanie (pzhi-ka-za-ñe) n. commandment; injunction
przyklasnąc (pzhi-klas-nównch) v. applaud;commend;praise
przykleic (pzhi-kle-eech) v. stick; glue; paste; stick on (stamp etc.)

przyklękac (pzhi-klan-kach) v. genuflect; bend the knee
przykład (pzhi-kwat) m. example; instance; pattern; sample
przykładac (pzhi-kwa-dach) v. 1. apply;affix; lend a hand; 2. beat up with;apply a force
przykładny (pzhi-kwad-ni) adj. m. exemplary; model/husband)
przykrajac (pzhi-kra-yach) v. cut off; cut out(garments etc.)
przykrawac (pzhi-kra-vach) v. cut out(garments etc.);cut off
przykręcac (pzhi-kran-tsach) v. screw on; 2. turn tight
przykrosc (pzhi-kroshch) f. annoyance;irritation;vexation
przykry (pzhi-kri) adj. m. disagreeable;painful;nasty;bad
przykrywac (pzhi-kri-vach) v. cover; roof over
przykrywka (pzhi-kriv-ka) f. lid; cover (of friendship etc.)
przykrzyc się (pzhi-kzhich shañ) v. be bored; have nothing to do;pall on;weary;long
przykucnąc (pzhi-koots-nównch) v. squat down;crouch; squat
przykuc (pzhi-kooch) v. 1. hammer; 2. arrest(attention);chain;grip;rivet;fascinate
przylatywac (pzhi-la-ti-vach) v. fly in; fly into (a room)
przylądek (pzhi-lówn-dek) m. cape; tip of land; headland
przyleciec (pzhi-le-chech) v. fly in; arrive;come running
przylegac (pzhi-le-gach) v. 1. fit; cling; 2. adjoin
przyległy (pzhi-lég-wi) adj. m. adjacent;adjoining;contiguous
przylepic (pzhi-le-peech) v. stick; glue on;stick to;post
przylepiec (pzhi-le-pyets) m. adhesive; tape; court plaster
przylgnąc (pzhi-lgnównch) v. stick; cling; adhere;nestle up
przylot (pzhi-lot) m. plane arrival(of an airplane)
przylutowac (pzhi-loo-to-vach) v. solder on; sweat on
przyłączac (pzhi-wówn-chach) v. annex; join; add;connect;attach

przyłączenie (pzhi-wown-che-ne) n. annexation;incorporation

przyłbica (pzhiw-bee-tsa) f. visor; beaver;welder's helmet

przymawiać (pzhi-mav-yach) v. criticize;rebuke;pinprick;nettle

przymawiać się (pzhi-mav-yach shan) v. hint around for

przymiarka (pzhi-myar-ka) f. fitting on; trying on clothes

przymierać (pzhi-mye-rach) v. starve;be half dead;be dying

przymierzać (pzhi-mye-zhach) v. try on;set to; apply to

przymierze (pzhi-mye-zhe) n. alliance; covenant; Testament

przymierzyć (pzhi-mye-zhich) v. try on; set on; apply to

przymieszka (pzhi-myesh-ka) f. admixture;addition;modicum;dash

przymiot (pzhi-myot) m. (man's) quality; trait; attribute

przymiotnik (pzhi-myot-neek) m. adjective (grammar)

przymknięty (pzhim-knan-ti) adj. m. half-closed; shut up

przymocować (pzhi-mo-tso-vach) v. fasten; fix; secure;attach

przymówka (pzhi-moov-ka) f.gibe; hint; allusion;scoff;jeer

przymrozek (pzhi-mro-zek) m. slight frost;ground frost

przymrużyć oczy (pzhi-mroo-zhich o-chi) blink; narrow one's eyes; wink

przymus (pzhi-moos) m. compulsion; constraint; coersion

przymusić (pzhi-moo-sheech) v. compel;force;oblige;coerce

przymusowy (pzhi-moo-so-vi) adj. m. obligatory;coercive;forced

przynaglać (pzhi-nag-lach) v. urge; haste; push on;hustle;spur

przynajmniej (pzhi-nay-mney) adv. at least;at any rate;anyway

przynależeć (pzhi-na-le-zhech) v. belong; be member(of a party)

przynależność (pzhi-na-lezh-noshch) f. (nationality) member-ship;affiliation;(national)status

przynależny (pzhi-na-lezh-ni) adj. m. belonging; appurtenant

przynęta (pzhi-nan-ta) f. bait; lure; enticement; lure; decoy

przynosić (pzhi-no-sheech) v. 1. bring; fetch; 2. bear; yield; bring(profit);afford

przyobiecać (pzhi-obye-tsach) v. promise; give a promise

przyobiecywać (pzhi-ob-ye-tsi-vach) v. promise;give a promise

przypadać (pzhi-pa-dach) v. be due; fall; come; happen

przypadek (pzhi-pa-dek) m. event; chance; case; incident

przypadkiem (pzhi-pad-kem) adv. by chance; accidentally

przypadkowo (pzhi-pad-ko-vo) adv. accidentally;unintentionally

przypadłość (pzhi-pad-woshch) f. affliction; ailment; disease

przypalić (pzhi-pa-leech) v. singe; burn; smoke;scorch;sear

przypasać (pzhi-pa-sach) v. attach (to belt); grid on

przypatrywać się (pzhi-pa-tri-vach shan) v. observe; look at; contemplate;have a look at

przypatrzyć się (pzhi-pa-tzhich shan) v. observe;contemplate

przypędzać (pzhi-pan-dzach) v. 1. come in haste; 2. drive (to)

przypiąć (pzhi-pyownch) v. pin; fasten;attach;buckle; pin on

przypieczętować (pzhi-pye-chan-to-vach) v. seal up; confirm

przypisek (pzhi-pee-sek) m. note; postscript; added note

przypisywać (pzhi-pee-si-vach) v. ascribe; attribute; credit

przypłacać (pzhi-pwa-tsach) v. pay (with life; health; property etc.); pay (dearly)

przypłynąć (pzhi-pwi-nownch) v. arrive sailing or swimming; come to shore; swim up;sail up

przypływ (pzhi-pwif) m. high tide; inflow;influx; high water

przypodobać się(pshi-po-do-bach shan)v.get into good graces

przypominać (pzhi-po-mee-nach) v. remind; recollect;resemble

przypomnienie (pzhi-pom-ne-ne) n. reminder; memento;souvenir

przypowieść (pzhi-póv-yeshch)
f. tale; parable; allegory
przyprawa (pzhi-prá-va) f. seasoning; spice;relish;sause
przyprawiać (pzhi-práv-yach)
v. 1. season; 2. cause a loss
przyprowadzać (pzhi-pro-vá-
dzach) v. bring along; fetch
przypuszczać (pzhi-poosh-chach)
v. suppose;let approach;admit
przypuszczalnie (pzhi-poosh-
chál-ñe) adv. supposedly
przypuszczalny (pzhi-poosh-
chál-ni) adj. m. supposed
przypuszczenie (pzhi-poosh-che-
ñe) n. guess; supposition
przyroda (pzhi-ro-da) f. nature
przyrodni brat (pzhi-ród-ñee
brát) half brother
przyrodnia siostra (pzhi-ród-ña
shós-tra) half sister
przyrodnik (pzhi-ród-ñeek) m.
naturalist;natural historian
przyrodzony (pzhi-ro-dzo-ni)
adj. m. innate;natural;inborn
przyrost naturalny (pzhi-rost
na-too-rál-ni) birthrate
przyrostek (pzhi-ros-tek) m.
suffix (grammar)
przyrząd (pzhi-zhownd) m. instrument;tool; appliance;device
przyrządzać (pzhi-zhown-dzach)
v. make ready; prepare;cook
przyrzeczenie (pzhi-zhe-che-ñe)
n. promise; plighted word
przyrzekać (pzhi-zhe-kach) v.
promise to do(something)
przysadka (pzhi-sád-ka) f. pi-
tuitary gland; stipule
przysądzać (pzhi-sówn-dzach) v.
award; adjudge; allocate
przysiad (pzhi-shad) m. squat
przysiadać (pzhi-shá-dach) v.
sit down; crouch; sit up
przysięga (pzhi-shan-ga) f.
oath; sworn attestation
przysięgać (pzhy-shan-gach) v.
swear to do; take an oath
przysięgły (pzhy-shang-wi)adj.
m. sworn (jury man)
przysłać (pzhi-swach) v. send in
przysłaniać (pzhi-swa-ñach) v.
shade; vail;cover up;screen

przysłona (pzhi-swó-na) f. veil;
shade; screen; diaphragm; stop
przysłowie (pzhi-swóv-ye) n.
proverb; by word
przysłówek (pzhi-swoo-vek) m.
adverb (grammar)
przysłuchiwać się (pzhi-swoo-
khee-vach shañ) v. listen to
przysługa (pzhi-swoo-ga) f.
service;good turn;favor;kindness
przysługiwać (pzhi-swoo-gee-
vach) v. to have right;be vested
przysłużyć się (pzhi-swoo-shich
shañ) v. render service
przysmak (pzhis-mak) m. delicacy
przysmażyć (pzhi-sma-zhich) v.
roast; fry a little; brown;devil
przysparzać (pzhi-spá-zhach) v.
1. increase; add to 2. cause
(trouble);bring unpleasantness
przyśpieszać (pzhish-pye-shach)
v. accelerate; urge;speed up
przyśpieszenie (pzhish-pye-she-
ñe) n. acceleration;speeding up
przysposabiać (pzhis-po-sáb-yach)
prepare; adapt; adopt;fit;qualify
przystać (pzhis-tach) v. join;
comply;cohere;fit together;befit
przystanąć (pzhi-sta-nównch) v.
stop; pause; halt
przystanek (pzhi-stá-nek) m.
stop; station; bus stop etc.
przystań (pzhi-stañ) f. small
(boat) harbor(inland); port
przystawać (pzhi-sta-vach) v.
fit; enlist; coincide; halt
przystawiać (pzhi-stáv-yach) v.
place near; set against; put
przystawka (pzhi-stáv-ka) f.
side dish; hors-doeuvre
przystęp (pzhi-stanp) m. access
przystępny (pzhi-stánp-ni) adj.
m. 1. accessible; 2. moderate
przystojny (pzhi-stóy-ni) adj.
m. handsome; decent; suitable
przystosować (pzhi-sto-so-vach)
v. adjust; fit;accomodate;adapt
przystrajać (pzhi-stra-yach) v.
decorate; adorn; dress; trim
przysunąć (pzhi-soo-nównch) v.
move near; push nearer
przyswajać (pzhi-sva-yach) v.
acquire; assimilate; adopt(ways)

przysyłać (pzhi-si-wach) v.
send; send along; send up

przysypac (pzhi-si-pach) v. cover (with earth; snow etc.)

przyszłość (pzhish-woshch) f. future; days to come; the future

przyszyc (pzhi-shich) v. sew on

przyszykować (pzhi-shi-ko-vach) v. prepare; make ready

przysnić się (pzhish-neech shan) v. appear in a dream

przyśrubować (pzhi-shroo-bo-vach) v. screw on; screw down

przyswiadczyc (pzhi-shviad-chich) v. agree with; attest

przytaczac (pzhi-ta-chach) v. quote; cite; wheel up; bring up

przytakiwac (pzhi-ta-kee-vach) v. say yes; assent; acquiesce

przytepic (pzhi-tan-peech) v. dull; blunt somewhat; dim; befog

przytepienie (pzhi-tan-pye-ne) n. dullness; bluntness

przytknąc (pzhit-knownch) v. place touching; set to; apply to

przytłaczac (pzhi-twa-chach) v. overwhelm; press to earth; crush

przytłumic (pzhi-twoo-meech) v. damp; deaden; stifle; subdue; dim

przytoczyc (pzhi-to-chich) v. quote; cite; roll up; bring up

przytomnie (pzhi-tom-ne) adv. with presence of mind; lucidly

przytomnosc (pzhi-tom-noshch) f. consciousness; (one's) senses

przytomny (pzhi-tom-ni) adj.m. conscious; quickwitted

przytrafiac się (pzhi-traf-yach shan) v. happen; occur; befall

przytrzymac (pzhi-tzhi-mach) v. hold; detain; keep in place; arrest

przytulic (pzhi-too-leech) v. snuggle; cuddle; hug; cuddle; fold

przytułek (pzhi-too-wek) m. shelter; alms house; poor house

przytwierdzic (pzhi-tvyerdźheech) v. fasten; fix; attach; assent

przytyk (pzhi-tik) m. dig; allusion; tilt; reference; junction

przytykac (pzhi-ti-kach) v. 1. adjoin; 2. set; apply; border

przy tym (pzhi-tim) adv. besides

przyuczac (pzhi-oo-chach) v. train; accustom an animal

przywabiac (pzhi-vab-yach) v. decoy; allure; lure

przywara (pzhi-va-ra) f. vice; fault; defect; shortcoming

przywiązac (pzhi-vyown-zach) v. bind; tie; attach; hitch; lash; fasten

przywdziewac (pzhi-vdźhe-vach) v. put on (clothes)

przywidzenie (pzhi-vee-dźe-ne) n. illusion; delusion; phantasm

przywiezc (pzhi-vyeżhch) v. import; bring; drive up; recall

przywilej (pzhi-vee-ley) m. privilege; prerogative; charter

przywitac (pzhi-vee-tach) v. welcome; greet; bid good morning

przywłaszczac (pzhi-vwash-chach) v. usurp; appropriate

przywodzic (pzhi-vo-dźeech) v. lead; bring about; remind; drive

przywłaszczenie (pzhi-vwash-che-ne) n. appropriation; usurpation (of rights etc.)

przywołac (pzhi-vo-wach) v. summon; call in; signal; sign

przywozic (pzhi-vo-żheech) v. bring (by car); import; deliver

przywodca (pzhi-vood-tsa) m. leader; ringleader; chietain

przywoz (pzhi-voos) m. import; delivery; transport; carriage

przywracac (pzhi-vra-tsach) v. restore; bring back; reappoint

przywrocenie (pzhi-vroo-tse-ne) n. restoration; reinstatement

przywyknąc (pzhi-vik-nownch) v. get accustomed; get used

przyznac (pzhi-znach) v. award; admit; allow; acknowledge; grant

przyzwalac (pzhi-zva-lach) v. consent; approve; agree; concede

przyzwoitosc (pzhi-zvo-ee-toshch) f. decency; propriety

przyzwoity (pzhi-zvo-ee-ti) adj. m. decent; proper; seemly; suitable

przyzwolenie (pzhi-zvo-le-ne) n. consent; acquiescence

przyzwyczajac (pzhi-zvi-cha-yach) v. accustom; habituate

przyzwyczajenie (pzhi-zvi-cha-ye-ne) n, habit; custom
przyzywać (pzhi-zi-vach) v. call in ; call sb;beckon;sign
psalm (psalm) m. psalm
pseudonim (psew-do-neem) m. pseudonym; pen name
psiarnia (pshar-ña) f. kennel
psie pieniądze (pshe pye-nown-dze) dirt cheap; dog cheap
psikus (pshee-koos) m. prank
psota (pso-ta) f. prank; mischief; practical joke; trick
psotnik (psot-ñeek) m. prankster; practical joker;scamp
pstrąg (pstrowng) m. trout; kelt
pstry (pstri) adj. m. 1. mottled; speckled; 2. uncertain;freaked
psuć (psooch) v. spoil; decay; waste; corrupt; deprave; damage;put out of order;mess up
psychiatra (psi-khyat-ra) m. psychiatrist; shrink; alienist
psychiczny (psi-kheech-ni) adj. m. mental(state,disease etc.)
psycholog (psi-kho-lok) m. psychologist; behaviorist
pszczelarstwo (pzhche-lar-stvo) n. beekeeping ; apiculture
pszczelarz (pshche-lash) m. beekeeper; apiarist
pszczoła (pshcho-wa) f. bee
pszenica (pshe-ñee-tsa) f. wheat
ptactwo (ptats-tvo) pl. fowl; birds; the species of birds
ptak (ptak) m. bird;fowl
ptaszek (pta-shek) m. little bird; small bird; rogue
publicysta (poo-blee-tsis-ta) m. columnist; journalist
publiczność (poo-bleech-noshch) pl. public;community; audience
publikacja (poo-blee-kats-ya) f. publication;something published
puch (pookh) m. down;fluff
puchacz (poo-khach) m. eagle owl(night bird of prey)
puchar (poo-khar) m. cup; bowl
puchlina wodna (poo-khlee-na wod-na)f.dropsy ;hydropsy
puchnąć (pookh-nownch) v. swell
puchowy (poo-kho-vi) adj. m. downy;fluffy;eiderdown

pucołowaty (poo-tso-wo-va-ti) adj. m. chubby cheeked
pucz (pooch) m, Putsch
pudełko (poo-dew-ko) n. box (small); tin ; can;hand box
puder (poo-der) m. powder
puderniczka (poo-der-ñeech-ka) f. powder box; compact;puff box
pukać (poo-kach)v. knock ;rap
pugilares (poo-gee-la-res) m. billfold; pocket book;wallet
pukiel (poo-kel) m. curl;lock
pula (poo-la) f, pool;kitty
pularda (poo-lar-da) f. poularde; fowl
pulchny (pool-khni) adj. m. plump;mellow;loose;spongy
pulower (poo-lo-ver) m. pullover (sweater)
pulpit (pool-peet) m. desk; lectern; shelf;book rest
puls (pools) m. pulse;vibration
pulsować (pool-so-vach) v. pulsate;palpitate;throb;vibrate
pułap (poo-wap) m. ceiling
pułapka (poo-wap-ka) f. trap
pułk (poowk) m. regiment;group
pułkownik (poow-kov-ñeek) m. colonel; group captain
pumeks (poo-meks) m. pumice
punkt (poonkt) m. point; mark
punktualny (poonk-too-al-ni) adj. m. punctual;exact;prompt
pupa (poo-pa) f. behind; buttocks; bottom
pupil (poo-peel) m. ward; pupil; favorite
purchawka (poor-khav-ka) f. 1. puff-ball; 2. grumpy fellow
purpura (poor-poo-ra) f. purple
purytanin (poo-ri-ta-ñeen) m. Puritan;man of strict religion
pustelnia (poos-tel-ña) f. hermitage;solitary secluded place
pustelnik (poos-tel-ñeek) m. hermit; recluse
pustka (poost-ka) f. solitude; empty (place);emptiness;void
pustkowie (poost-kov-ye) n. deserted place;desert;solitude
pustoszyć (poos-to-shich) v. devastate;ravage;lay waste;ruin
pusty (poos-ti) adj.m. empty

pustynia (poos-ti-ña) f. desert
puszcza (poosh-cha) f. primeval
forest; wilderness
puszczac (poosh-chach) v. let
go; let fall; set afloat; free;
fade; drop; let out; emit; start
puszczać się (poosh-chach shañ)
v. draw apart; let go; be a
permissive girl;go to bed with
puszek (poo-shek) m. down
puszka blaszana (poosh-ka bla-
sha-na) tin can; tin box
puszysty (poo-shis-ti) adj. m.
downy;fluffy;flossy;flaky;nappy
puścić (poosh-cheech) v. let go;
let free; release; let fall
puzon (poo-zon) m. trombone
(one octave lower than trumpet)
pycha (pi-kha) f. 1. pride;
2. excellent tidbit;fine stuff
pykac (pi-kach) v. puff; pop
pylić (pi-leech) v. dust;be dusty
pył (piw) m. dust; powder
pyskować (pis-ko-vach) v. be
saucy; bark; bawl
pysk (pisk) m. muffle; snout;
mug;muzzle;phiz; rowdyism
pyskaty (pis-ka-ti) adj. m.
foulmouthed;saucy;pert;bawling
pyszałek (pi-sha-wek) m. boaster; braggart;,coxcomb
pysznic się (pish-ñeech shañ)
v. swagger;prance;swank;strut
pysznie (pish-ñe) adv. proudly;
admirably;in grand fashion
pytać (pi-tach) v. ask; inquire;
question; interrogate
pytanie (pi-ta-ñe) n. question;
inquiry; query; interrogation
pytel (pi-tel) m. bolter
pytlować (pi-tlo-vach) v. sift;
bolt(flour);be a chatterbox
pyton (pi-ton) m. python
pyza (pi-za) f. dumpling
pyzaty (pi-za-ti) adj. m. chubby
rab (rab) m. slave; servant
rabarbar (ra-bar-bar) m. rhubarb
rabat (ra-bat) m. discount; rebate;reduction (in price)
rabin (ra-been) m. rabbi
rabować (ra-bo-vach) v. rob;
maraud;plunder; pirate; take
by force; steal

rabunek (ra-boo-nek) m. robbery; plunder; holdup;spoliation
rabuś (ra-boosh) m. robber;
plunderer; pillager
rachityczny (ra-khee-tich-ni)
adj. m. rickety; rachitic
rachmistrz (rakh-meestsh) m.
accountant;calculator;reckoner
rachować (ra-kho-vach) v. calculate;count;reckon;compute;rely
rachunek (ra-khoo-nek) m. bill;
account;count;calculation;sum
rachunkowość (ra-khoon-ko-
voshch) f. bookkeeping
racica (ra-chee-tsa) f. cloven
hoof; cow hoof
racja (rats-ya) f. reason;right;
ration;propriety;correctness
racjonalizować (ra-tsyo-na-lee-
zo-vach) v. rationalize;improve
racjonalny (ra-tsyo-nal-ni)
adj. m. rational; reasonable
raczej (ra-chey) adv. rather;
sooner; rather than
raczkować (rach-ko-vach) v. go
on all fours; crawl on all four
raczyć (ra-chich) v. deign; be
pleased; treat;condescend;stoop
rad (rad) adj. m. 1. pleased;
glad 2., m. radium
rada (ra-da) f. advice; counsel
radar (ra-dar) m. radar
radca (rad-tsa) m. advisor;
counselor;legal advisor
radcostwo (rad-tsos-tvo) n.
councillorship;post of advisor
radio (rad-yo) n. radio; wireless; broadcasting (system)
radiofonia (ra-dyo-fo-ña) f.
broadcasting;radiotelephony
radioaktywny (rad-yo-ak-tiv-ni)
adj. m. radioactive
radiostacja (rad-yi-stats-ya)
f. radio station
radiodepesza (rad-yo-de-pe-sha)
f. radiotelegram
radioterapia (rad-yo-te-rap-ya)
f. radiotherapy;X-ray therapy
radny (rad-ni) m. alderman
radosny (ra-dos-ni) adj. m. gay;
glad; festive(day etc.)
radość (ra-doshch) f. joy; gladness;delight;merriment;glee

radykalny (ra-di-kál-ni) adj. m.
radical;man of radical views
radykał (ra-di-kaw) m. radical
radzić (ra-dźheeĆh) v. deliberate; suggest; advice;counsel
radziecki (ra-dźhets-kee) adj.
m. Soviet;of Soviet Union
rafa (rá-fa) f. reef;rim;ripple
rafineria (ra-fee-nér-ya) f.
refinery; refining works
rafinować (ra-fee-no-vach) f.
refine; purify; distil
raid (rayd) m.sport rally (race)
raj (ray) m. paradise; heaven
rak (rak) m. crayfish; cancer
rakieta (ra—ke-ta) f. 1. rocket; flare; 2. (tennis) racket
rama (rá-ma) f. frame;scheme;case
ramię (ra-myáń) n. shoulder
ramowy (ra-mó-vi) adj. m. frame
rampa (rám-pa) f. ramp; loading
platform;bar;barier; float
rana (rá-na) f. wound;injury;sore
randka (ránd-ka) f. date
ranek (rá-nek) m. morning; day-
break; break of day
ranga (rán-ga) f. rank; standing
ranic (rá-neech) v. wound; hurt
ranny (rán-ni) adj. m. 1. wounded; injured; 2. morning; early
rano (rá-no) adv. 1. early;
2. morning; forenoon;too early
rapier (rá-pyer) m. rapier
raport (rá-port) m. report; account; statement; log
raptem (ráp-tem) adv. suddenly;
abruptly;no more than;all in all
raptowny (rap-tóv-ni) adj. m.
abrupt; sudden;impulsive;heady
rasa (ra-sa) f. race; stock;
breed ;(plant)variety; blood
rasizm (ra-śheezm) m. racism
rasowy (ra-só-vi) adj. m. racial;
thoroughbred;purebred;racy
raszpla (rásh-pla) f. rasp
rata (rá-ta) f. instalment (payment);part payment(system)
ratować (ra-tó-vach) v. rescue;
save; deliver(from danger)
ratownictwo (ra-tov-ńeets-tvo) n.
life saving (system)
ratownik (ra-tov-ńeek) m. lifeguard; rescuer; life saver

ratunek (ra-tóo-nek) m. rescue;
salvation;help;assistance;resort
ratunkowy pas (ra-toon-ko-vi
pas) m. life belt; life jacket
ratusz (rá-toosh) m. city hall
ratyfikacja (ra-ti-fee-káts-
ya) f. ratification
raut (ráwt) m. evening party
raz (ras) m. 1. one time;
2. blow; stroke; buffet
raz (ras) adv. once; at one
time; at last; time being
razem (ra-zem) adv. together
razic (ra-źheećh) v. 1. strike;
2. offend; 3. dazzle; shock;hit
razowy (ra-zó-vi) adj. m. brown
(bread); whole meal (bread)
razowiec (ra-zó-vyets) m. whole
meal bread; brown bread
rażący (ra-zhówn-tsy) adj. m.
1. glaring; 2. flagrant; rank
raźnie (ráźh-ńe) adv. cheerfully; briskly; at a lively pace
rąb (równb) m. rim;pane;clearing
rąbać (równ-bach) v. 1. chop;hew;
2. say truth to face ; slash
rączka (równch-ka) f. handle;
small hand; handgrip;holder
rączy (równ-chi) adj. m. swift
rdza (rdza) f. rust;mildew;blight
rdzenny (rdzeń-ni) adj. m.
essential; original;specific
rdzeń (rdzeń) m. core; pith;
marrow; gist; essence; log
rdzoodporny (rdzo-od-pór-ni)
adj. rust-proof;stainless
reagować (re-a-gó-vach) v.
react; respond;be suscrptible
rdzewieć (rdze-vyećh) v. corrode;
rust; get rusty; gather rust
reakcja (re-ak-tsya) f. reaction
reakcjonista (re-ak-tsyo-ńees-
ta) m. reactionary
reakcyjny (re-ak-tsíy-ni) adj.
m. reactionary;retrograde
reaktywować (re-ak-ti-vo-vach)
v. 1. start again; 2. reacti-
vate;bring back to life;recall
realia (re-al-ya) pl. realia;
realities
realista (re-a-lées-ta) m. re-
alist advocate of realism
realizm (re-a-leezm) m. realism

realizować (re-a-lee-zó-vach) v. actualize; realize;cash(assets)
realność (re-al-noshch) f. 1. real estate;2. reality;the real
realny (re-ál-ni) adj. m. real; concrete; actual;genuine;true
rebelia (re-bél-ya) f. rebellion;uprising against government
recenzent (re-tsen-zent) m.critic; reviewer (of books, plays, etc.)
recenzja (re-tsen-zya) f. review (of books, plays, etc.)
recepcja (re-tsep-tzya) f. reception;formal social function
recepis (re-tsé-pees) m. receipt; recipe;written receipt
recepta (re-tsép-ta) f. prescription; doctor's order
rechot (re-khot) m. shrieking laughter; croak(of forgs)
recydywista (re-tsi-di-vées-ta) m. recidivist;old offender
recytować (re-tsi-to-vach) v. recite;give a recitation
redagować (re-da-go-vach) v. edit;draw up;formulate;draft
redakcja (re-dak-tsya) f. 1. editing; 2. editors office
redaktor (re-dák-tor) m. editor
redukcja (re-dóok-tsya) f. reduction (in size,price etc.)
redukować (re-doo-ko-vach) v. reduce; lay off;cut down
referat (re-fé-rat) m. report
referencja (re-fe-rén-tsya) f. reference; testimonial
referent (re-fe-rent) m. clerk
refleks (re-fleks) m. reflex
refleksja (re-fléks-ya) f. reflection; thought; cogitation
reflektor (re-flek-tor) m. reflector; searchlight;headlight
reflektować (re-flek-to-vach) v. 1. apply for; want; 2. reflect;bring to reason;moderate
reforma (re-for-ma) f. reform
reformacja (re-for-máts-ya) f. reformation; Reformation
reformować (re-for-mo-vach) v. reform; reorganize
regaty (re-gá-ti) pl. boat race
regencja (re-gén-tsya) f. regency; regency style

regionalny (re-gyo-nál-ni) adj. regional; local
regulacja (re-goo-láts-ya) f. regulation;control;regulator
regularny (re-goo-lar-ni) adj. m. regular; even;systematic
regulować (re-goo-ló-vach) v. 1. regulate control 2. settle
reguła (re-góo-wa) f. rule
rehabilitować (re-kha-bee-lee-tó-vach) v. rehabilitate
reja (re-ya) f. yardarm
rejent (re-yent) m. notary public; notary; regent
rejestr (re-yestr) m. register; file; index;roll;register mark
rejestracja (re-yes-tráts-ya) f. registration; licensing
rejestrować (re-yes-tró-vach) v. register; enroll;record
rejon (re-yon) m. region
rejwach (rey-vakh) m. uproar; hullabaloo;row;hurly-burly
rekin (ré-keen) m. shark
reklama (rek-lá-ma) f. advertising; commercial publicity
reklamacja (re-kla-máts-ya) f. complaint;demand for compensation
reklamować (re-kla-mo-vach) v. 1. complain; 2. advertise
rekolekcje (re-ko-lék-tsye) pl. retreat;period of contemplation
rekomendacja (re-ko-men-dáts-ya) f. recommendation;reference
rekompensata (re-kom-pen-sá-ta) f. compensation;recompense
rekonvalescent (re-kon-va-lés-cent) m. convalescent
rekord (ré-kord) m. (sports) record; (world) record
rekordzista (re-kor-dzhees-ta) m. record holder;champion
rekreacja (re-kre-áts-ya) f. recreation;opposing action
rekrut (rék-root) m. recruit; conscript;recently enlisted man
rekrutować (re-kroo-to-vach) v. recruit; enlist(new people)
rektor (rék-tor) m. university president;university head
rektyfikować (rek-ti-fee-kó-vach)v. rectify;correct; put right; purify

rekwizycja (rek-vee-zits-ya) f.
requisition;seizure
relacja (re-lats-ya) f. 1. report; 2. rate; relation
relatywizm (re-la-ti-veezm) m.
relativity; relativism
relegacja (re-le-gats-ya) f.
expulsion; relegation
religia (re-leeg-ya) f. religion
religijny (re-lee-geey-ni) adj.
m. religious; godly
relikwia (re-leek-vya) f. relic
remanent (re-ma-nent) m. remainder; inventiry;stock
remis (re-mees) m. (sport)draw
remiza (re-mee-za) f. engine-
shed ; engine-house; depot;barn
remont (re-mont) m. 1. repair;
2. (horse) remount
remontować (re-mon-to-vach) v.
repair; recondition;overhaul
renumeracja (re-noo-me-rats-ya)
f. renumeration;recount
ren (ren) m. reindeer; caribou
renegat (re-ne-gat) m. renegade
renifer (re-nee-fer) m. reindeer;(domesticated)arctic deer
renoma (re-no-ma) f. renown
renta (ren-ta) f. rent ; fixed
income; annuity; pension
rentowność (ren-tov-noshch) f.
profitability;earning capacity
rentgenolog (rent-ge-no-lok) m.
radiologist; roentgenologist
rentowny (ren-tov-ni) adj. m.
profitable;renumerative
reorganizacja (re-or-ga-nee-
zats-ya) f. reorganization
reparacja (re-pa-rats-ya) f.
1. repair; 2. reparation
repatriacja (re-pa-tree-ats-ya)
f. repatriation
reperować (re-pe-ro-vach) v.
mend; repair;fix; set right
repertuar (re-per-too-ar) m.
repertory; repertoire
repetycja (re-pe-tits-ya) f.
repetition(of a lesson etc.)
replika (rep-lee-ka) f. 1, re-
plica; 2. rebuttal; 3. (theatre)cue; retort;rejoinder
replikować (re-plee-ko-vach) v.
answer back; rejoin; retort

reportaż (re-por-tash) m. 1.
account; 2. reporting; commentary;coverage (of event etc.)
represja (re-pres-ya) f.
reprisal;repressive measures
reprezentacja (re-pre-zen-tats-
ya) f. representation
reprezentant (re-pre-zen-tant)
m. representative
reprezentować (re-pre-zen-to-
vach) v. represent; display
reprodukcja (re-pro-dook-tsya)
f. reproduction;copy;replica
republika (re-poob-lee-ka) f.
republic
republikański (re-poob-lee-kań-
skee) adj. m. republican
reputacja (re-poo-tats-ya) f.
reputation; (character)
resor (re-sor) m. (car) spring
resort (re-sort) m. 1. agency;
2. competence;scope;province
respekt (res-pekt) m. respect
restauracja (res-taw-rats-ya)
f. 1. restaurant; 2. restoration (of objects of art etc.)
restrykcja (res-trik-tsya) f.
restriction; reservation
restytucja (res-ti-toots-ya)
f. restitution; restoration
reszta (resh-ta) f. rest; reminder; change; residue
retoryka (re-to-ri-ka) f. rhetoric;manual of rhetoric
retusz (re-toosh) m. retouch
retuszować (re-too-sho-vach)
v. touch up; retouch
reumatyczny (re-oo-ma-tich-ni)
adj. m. rheumatic
reumatyzm (re-oo-ma-tizm) m.
rheumatism(pain in joint etc.)
rewanż (re-vansh) m. 1. rematch;
2. revenge; get back at
rewelacja (re-ve-lats-ya) f.
revelation;striking disclosure
rewers (re-vers) m. 1. receipt;
2. reverse (side etc.)
rewia (rev-ya) f. 1. parade;
2. (theatre) revue
rewidować (re-vee-do-vach) v.
1. revise; 2. search; 3. audit
rewizja (re-veez-ya) f. revision
search;audit;inspection;retrial

rewizjonizm (re-veez-yo-neezm)
m. revisionism
rewizyta (re-vee-zi-ta) f. return visit
rewolucja (re-vo-loots-ya) f.
revolution;complete change
rewolucyjny (re-vo-loo-tsiy-ni)
adj. m. revolutionary
rewolwer (re-vol-ver) m. revolver; gun (with revolv.cylinder)
rezerwa (re-zer-va) f. reserve
rezerwat (re-zer-vat) m. reservation;game preserve
rezerwować (re-zer-vo-vach) v.
reserve; set aside; book
rezerwuar (re-zer-voo-ar) m.
reservoir;(storage)tank
rezolutny (re-zo-loot-ni) adj.
m. resolute;determined; game
rezonans (re-zo-nans) m. resonance(intesifying vibrations)
rezultat (re-zool-tat) m. result; effect; numerical answer
rezydencja (re-zi-den-tsya) f.
residence;dwelling place
rezydent (re-zi-dent) m. resident(not a transient)
rezygnacja (re-zig-nats-ya) f.
resignation;patient submission
reżim (re-zheem) m. regime
reżyser (re-zhi-ser) m. stage
manager; (film) director
ręcznie (ranch-ne) adv. by hand
ręcznik (ranch-neek) m. towel
ręczny (ranch-ni) adj. m. manual;
hand made; wrist(watch)
ręczyć (ran-chich) v. guarantee
ręka (ran-ka) f. hand; arm;touch
rękaw (ran-kav) m. sleeve
rękawica (ran-ka-vee-tsa) f.
mitten; gauntlet;mitt;glove
rękawiczka (ran-ka-veech-ka) f.
glove(fur lined,velvet, etc.)
rękodzielnik (ran-ko-dzhel-neek)
m. craftsman;handicraftsman
rękojeść (ran-ko-yeshch) f. hilt;
handle; handgrip; helve
rękojmia (ran-koy-mya) f. guaranty; pledge; gage;warranty
rękopis (ran-ko-pees) m. manuscript; script; MS
robactwo (ro-bats-tvo) n.vermin

robak (ro-bak) m. worm;beetle;grub
rober (ro-ber) m. (bridge) rubber (in card game)
robić (ro-beech) v. make; do;act;
work; become; get;feel;turn;knit
robociarz (ro-bo-chash) m. common laborer (slang); mechanic
robocizna (ro-bo-cheez-na) f.
wages;cost of labor; labor
roboczogodzina (ro-bo-cho-go-dzhee-na)f. man-hour
robot (ro-bot) m. robot
robota (ro-bo-ta) f. work; job
robotnica (ro-bot-nee-tsa) f.
worker (bee) ; operative;mechanic
robotnik (ro-bot-neek) m. worker; worker;operative;mechanic
robótki (ro-boot-kee) pl.
needlework; fancy work
rocznica (roch-nee-tsa) f.
anniversary
rocznie (roch-ne) adv. yearly
rocznik (roch-neek) m. annual;
yearbook; annual set; age group
roczny (roch-ni) adj. m. annual; one year's (duration etc.)
rodak (ro-dak) m. compatriot
rodowity (ro-do-vee-ti) adj.
m. native; by birth; trueborn
rodowód (ro-do-voot) m. genealogy; origin;pedigree;descent
rodzaj (ro-dzay) m. kind; sort;
gender;type; race; manner;aspect
rodzajnik (ro-dzay-neek) m. article (definite or indefinite)
rodzeństwo (ro-dzen-stvo) n.
brothers and sisters
rodzice (ro-dzhee-tse)pl. parents;father and mother
rodzić (ro-dzheech)v. bear;
procreate breed; yield (crops)
rodzina (ro-dzhee-na)f. family
rodzinny (ro-dzheen-ni)adj. m.
family; native; home(life etc.)
rodzynek (ro-dzi-nek) m. raisin;
currant
rogacz (ro-gach) m. 1. stag;
2. cuckold;deceived husband
rogatka (ro-gat-ka) f. tollgate; toll bar; turnpike
rogaty (ro-ga-ti) adj. m.
horned; haughty; deceived
(husband)

rogatywka (ro-ga-tív-ka) f.
four-cornered cap(Polish style)
rogowacieć (ro-go-va-chech) v.
grow horny;become corneous
rogowaty (ro-go-va-ti) adj.
corneous ; horny
rogówka (ro-góov-ka) f. cornea
rogóżka (ro-góozh-ka) f. (door)
mat(flat,woven of straw etc.)
roić (ro-yeech) v. 1. dream;
imagine; 2. swarm; teem; run
rojalista (ro-ya-lees-ta) m.
royalist; supporter of the king
rojny (róy-ni) adj. m. teeming;
swarming(crowds etc.)
rojowisko (ro-yo-vees-ko) n.
hive; swarm;gathering place
rok (rok) m. year;a twelvemonth
rok przestępny (rok pzhe-stáňp-
ni) leap year
rokować (ro-kó-vach) v. 1. negotiate 2. expect; promise
rokowania (ro-ko-va-ña) pl. 1.
negotiations; 2. prognosis
rola (ró-la) f. 1. arable land
2. (theatre) part;scroll;weight
rolka (ról-ka) f. roll; spool;
reel;runner;pulley;castor
rolnictwo (rol-ñeets-tvo) v.
agriculture;farming;husbandry
rolnik (rol-ñeek) m. farmer
romans (ró-mans) m. 1. novel;
2. love affair; laison
romantyczny (ro-man-tich-ni) adj.
m. romantic;full of romance
romantyk (ro-man-tik) m. romantic
romantyzm (ro-man-tizm) m. ro-
manticism(literary style etc.)
romański (ro-mań-skee) adj. m.
Romance; Romanesque
romb (romb) m. rhomb;diamond
rondel (ron-del) m. stewpan
rondo (ron-do) n. brim; circular
plaza; traffic circle;circus
ronić (ro-ñeech) v. 1. shed;
2. miscarry;drop;cast;emit;moult
ropa (ró-pa) f. 1. puss; 2. crude
oil;rock oil; naphta;petroleum
ropieć (róp-yech) v. fester;have
oozing sore; suppurate
ropień (róp-yeň) m. abscess
ropny (róp-ni) adj. m. purulent;
oil fired; oil-(derrick etc.)

ropucha (ro-poó-kha) f. toad
rosa (ró-sa) f. dew
rosły (rós-wi) adj. m. tall;
big frame; stalwart
rosnąć (rós-nównch) v. grow
rosół (ró-soow) m. broth;
bouillion; clear soup;pickle
rostbef (rost-bef) m. roast-
beef; baked beef
rosyjski (ro-siy-skee) adj. m.
Russian; of Russia
roszczenie (rosh-che-ñe) n.
claim; pretension; pretence
rościć (rosh-cheech) v. claim
roślina (rosh-lee-na) f. plant;
vegetable; living plant
roślinność (rosh-leen-noshch)
f. flora, ; vegetation
rowek (ró-vek) m. (small) channel; groove; gutter; rut;furrow
rower (ró-ver) n. bike; cycle
rowerzysta (ro-ve-zhis-ta) m.
cyclist
rozbawiony (roz-ba-vyó-ni) adj.
m. merry; amused;in high spirits
rozbestwić (roz-bést-veech) v.
enrage;turn into a wild beast
rozbicie (roz-bee-che) n. break;
wreck;jumble;defeat;rout; hurt
rozbić (roz-beech) v. smash;
defeat; wreck;shatter;disrupt
rozbiegać się (roz-byé-gach śhań)
v. scatter; run; swarm (through)
rozbierać (roz-byé-rach) v. undress; strip; dismount; analyze
rozbieżny (roz-byézh-ni) adj. m.
divergent;different;discordant
rozbijać (roz-bee-yach) v. break
up; rout; crush;bluster;storm
rozbiór (róz-byoor) m. 1. analysis; 2. dismemberment;partition
rozbiórka (roz-byoor-ka) f. de-
molition;taking to pieces
rozbitek (roz-bee-tek) m. shipwreck person; castaway; wreck
rozbój (roz-booy) m. robbery;
piracy; banditry;highjacking
rozbójnik (roz-booy-neek) m.
bandit;robber;cutthroat;brigand
rozbrajać (roz-bra-yach) v.
disarm(a person etc.);dismantle
(a ship);appease; pacify

rozbrat (róz-brat) m. split;
disunion;break with somebody
rozbrojenie (roz-bro-ye-ńe) n.
disarmament;reduction of arms
rozbrojeniowy (roz-bro-ye-ńo-vi)
adj. m. disarmament
rozbrzmiewać (roz-bzhmyé-vach)
v. resound;ring out; (re)echo
rozbudowa (roz-boo-dó-va) f.
build up; extension;expansion
rozbudować (roz-boo-dó-vach) v.
extend;enlarge;expand;develop
rozbudzić (roz-boo-dźheéch) v.
rouse up; wake up ;excite;stir
rozchmurzyć (roz-khmoo-zhich)
v. clear up; brighten up
rozchodzić (roz-khó-dźheéch) v.
1. stretch (shoes); 2. spread;
3. come apart
rozchód (róz-khoot) m. expendi-
ture; expenses; outgoings
rozchwytać (roz-khvi-tach) v.
snatch up;scramble for;sweep off
rozchylać (roz-khi-lach) v.
open; force apart, spread
rozciągać (roz-chówn-gach) v.
stretch; extend;widen;expand
rozcieńczyć (roz-chen-chich) v.
thin; dilute; rarefy;attenuate
rozcierać (roz-che-rach) v. rub;
grind;crush;spread (ointment)
rozcinać (roz-chee-nach) v.
cut up; dissect; rip open
rozczarować (roz-cha-ro-vach) v.
disappoint;disenchant
rozczesać (roz-che-sach) v. comb
down;brush out(one's hair),
rozczłonkować (roz-chwon-kó-vach)
v. dismember;divide;break up
rozczulić (roz-choo-leech) v.
move; touch;affect;stir(feelings)
rozczyn (róz-chin) m. solution
(chem.); leaven (yeast)
rozdać (róz-dach) v. distribute
rozdarcie (roz-dár-che) n.
1. tear; 2. disruption
rozdeptać (roz-dép-tach) v.
trample out under foot;tread on
rozdęcie (roz-dáń-che) n. swelling; inflation;expansion
rozdmuchać (roz-dmoo-khach) v.
fan; inflate;blow about;amplify

rozdrapać (roz-drá-pach) v.
1. scratch; 2. snatch up
rozdrażnić (roz-drázh-ńeech)
v. irritate; exaspreate; vex
rozdrobnić (roz-dró-bńeéch) v.
split up; divide;crumble;morsel
rozdroże (roz-dró-zhe) n.
crossroads; parting of the ways
rozdwoić (roz-dvó-eech) v.
split; cleave; divide in two
rozdymać (roz-dí-mach) v. inflate; swell;expand;puff out
rozdział (róz-dźhaw) m. distribution; disunion; parting
(hair);dispensation;chapter
rozdzielać (roz-dźhe-lach) v.
divide; distribute;set at odds
rozdzierać (roz-dźhé-rach) v.
tear up;tear asunder;rend;pierce
rozdźwięk (róz-dźhvyánk) m.
discord ;dissonance; clash
rozebrać (ro-zéb-rach) v. undress; analyze; take apart
rozedma (ro-zéd-ma) f. emphy-
sema(swelling produced by gas)
rozejm (ro-zeym) m. truce
rozejrzeć się (ro-zéy-zhech
śhań) v. look around
rozejść się (ro-zeyśhch śhań)
v. split; part; separate
rozerwać się (ro-zér-vach śhań)
v. divert oneself;get torn
rozgałęzic (roz-ga-wáń-źheech)
v. branch out; fork off
rozgałęzienie (roz-ga-wáń-zhe-
ńe) n. branching;ramification
rozgardiasz (roz-gárd-yash) m.
bustle; chaos; confusion
rozgarnąc (roz-gár-nównch) v.
rake aside; part;brush apart
rozgarnięty (roz-gar-ńáń-ti)
adj. m. bright; clever; sharp
rozglądać się (roz-glówn-dach
śhań) v. look around;look for
rozgłaszać (roz-gwá-shach) v.
make known; broadcast
rozgłos (róz-gwos) m. publicity;
fame; renown;repute;notoriety
rozgłosnia (roz-gwóśh-ńa) f.
broadcasting station
rozgmatwać (roz-gmát-vach) v.
disentangle; extricate

rozgnieść (roz-gneśhch) v.
flatten; squash (once)
rozgniatać (roz-gña-tach) v.
squash; flatten (often)
rozgniewać (roz-gñe-vach) v.
anger; vex; irritate
rozgoryczenie (roz-go-ri-che-ñe)
n. bitterness; exasperation
rozgoryczyć (roz-go-ri-chich) v.
embitter; exacerbate; disgust
rozgotować (roz-go-to-vach) v.
cook to a pulp; cook to rags
rozgraniczyć (roz-gra-ñee-chich)
v. delimit; mark boundaries
rozgromić (roz-gró-meech) v.
rout(the enemy); crush(an army)
rozgrywać (roz-gri-vach) v. play
one's game; put through; carry out
rozgryźć (roz-griżhch) v. bite
through; bite in two; crack(nuts)
rozgrzać (roz-gzhach) v. warm up
rozgrzebać (roz-gzhe-bach) v.
dig up; rake up; scatter
rozgrzeszyć (roz-gzhe-shich) v.
absolve(of sins); forgive
rozgrzewać (roz-gzhe-vach) v.
warm up; rouse; stimulate
rozhukany (roz-khoo-ka-ni) adj.
m. wild; unruly; riotus
rozhuśtać (roz-khoosh-tach) v.
set swinging; set rocking
roziskrzyć (roz-eesk-zhich) v.
start sparkle; make sparkle
rozjaśnić (roz-yash-ñeech) v.
brighten; clear up; clarify
rozjątrzyć (roz-yownt-zhich) v.
exasperate; irritate; chafe
rozjemca (roz-yém-tsa) m. referee; arbiter; umpire
rozjeżdżać się (roz-yézh-dzhach
śhañ) v. disperse; part
rozjuszyć (roz-yoo-shich) v.
enrage; infuriate; exasperate
rozkapryszony (roz-ka-pri-sho-
ni) adj. m. whimsical; fitful
rozkaz (roz-kas) m. order
rozkiełznać (roz-ḱewz-nach) v.
unbridle; unchain; let loose
rozkleić (roz-kle-eech) v. 1.
unglue; weaken; 2. post up
rozkład (roz-kwat) m. dissolution;
decay; disposition; timetable ;
train schedule; breakdown

rozkładać (roz-kwa-dach) v. decompose; spread; display; stagger (hours); lay out; distribute
rozkołysać (roz-ko-wi-sach) v.
set rocking; set swinging; agitate
rozkopywać (roz-ko-pi-vach) v.
dig up; rip up; make excavations
rozkosz (roz-kosh) f. delight
rozkrajać (roz-kra-yach) v.
cut up; carve; slice; divide
rozkręcić (roz-kran-cheech) v.
unscrew; unreel; take to pieces
rozkruszyć (roz-kroo-shich)
v. crush up; grind; disintegrate
rozkrzewić (roz-kzhe-veech) v.
propagate; increase; diffuse
rozkuć (roz-kooch) v. unshackle;
unshoe (horse); unchain; hammer out
rozkulbaczyć (roz-kool-ba-chich)
v. unsaddle; take the saddle off
rozkupić (roz-koo-peech) v. buy
up; buy everything; buy all
rozkwit (roz-kveet) m. bloom
rozkwitać (roz-kvee-tach) v.
flower; burst into flower; beam
rozlatywać się (roz-la-ti-vach
śhañ) v. fly away; break up;
scatter; disperse; run away; burst
rozlazły (roz-laz-wi) adj. m.
slack; loose; spread out; sloppy
rozległy (roz-lég-wi) adj. m.
spacious; vast; wide; extensive
rozleniwiać (roz-le-ñeev-yach)
v. make lazy; induce to laziness
rozlepić (roz-le-peech) v. post;
put up; paste up; stick; unstick
rozlew (roz-lev) m. flood
rozlew krwi (roz-lev krvee) m.
bloodshed; killing; slaughter
rozlewać (roz-le-vach) v. spill;
shed; pour(out); ladle out(soup)
rozliczenie (roz-lee-che-ñe) n.
settling; reckoning; settlement
rozliczny (roz-leech-ni) adj.
m. manifold; diverse; numerous
rozliczyć (roz-lee-chich) v.
settle up (accounts); calculate
rozlokować (roz-lo-ko-vach) v.
put up; make at home; quarter
rozlosować (roz-lo-so-vach) v.
allot; distribute by lot
rozluźnić (roz-loożh-ñeech) v.
slacken; relax; unfasten

rozluźnienie (roz-loozh-ńe-ńe)
n. loosening;laxity;slackness
rozładować (roz-wa-do-vać) v.
unload; discharge(a battery)
rozłam (róz-wam) m. breach;
split;break;division;dissent
rozłamać (roz-wa-mać) v.
break (in two); split
rozłazić się (roz-wa-zheećh
śhań) v. fall apart; disperse
rozłączenie (roz-wown-ché-ńe)
n. separation; disjunction
rozłączyć (roz-wówn-chićh) v.
disconnect;sever;uncouple
rozłąka (roz-wówn-ka) f. separation (of people)
rozłożyć (roz-wó-zhićh) v.
spread;lay out;disassemble
rozłupać (roz-woo-pać) v.
split; cleave; rift; slit;
crack(nuts,etc.); rive
rozmach (róz-makh) m. impetus;
dash; grand style;force;swing
rozmaitości (roz-ma-ee-tośh-
chee) pl. miscellanea; vaude-
ville theater;variety theater
rozmaity (roz-ma-ee-ti) adj.
m. various; miscellaneous
rozmaryn (roz-má-rin) m. rose-
mary (Rosmarinus)
rozmarzenie (roz-ma-zhe-ńe) n.
daydream;dreaminess;reverie
rozmawiać (roz-máv-yać) v.
converse; talk; speak with
rozmazać (roz-ma-zać) v. blur;
smear;daub; let out (a secret)
rozmiar (roz-myar) m. dimension;
extent;size;proportion;scale
rozmienić (roz-mye-ńeećh) v.
change (money);get the change
rozmieszczać (roz-myesh-chać)
v. arrange; dispose;place;put
rozmieszczenie (roz-myesh-ché-
ńe) n. distribution; layout
rozmiękczyć (roz-myánk-chićh) v.
soften; soak;steep;make soft
rozmięknąć (roz-myánk-nownćh)
v. become soft ;get soaked;sop
rozmijać się (roz-mee-yać śhań)
v. miss; swerve from;fail to meet
rozmiłować się (roz-mee-wo-vać
śhań) v. take a liking to

rozminąć się(roz-mee-nównćh śhań)v.
miss (on road):pass each other
rozmnażać (roz-mna-zhać) v.breed;
multiply; propagate; imcrease
rozmoczyć (roz-mó-chićh) v.soak;
steep; wet thoroughly: sodden
rozmoknąć (roz-mok-nównćh) v.
become soaked;, get soggy
rozmowa (roz-mo-va) f. conversation; talk ;discourse
rozmowny (roz-mov-ni) adj. m.
communicative; talkative
rozmówca (roz-moov-tsa) m.
interlocutor (in conversation)
rozmówić się (roz-moo-veećh
śhan) v. talk over;get understood
rozmysł (róz-misw) m. premeditation; consideration; intention
rozmyślać (roz-miśh-lać) v.
meditate; ponder how to do
rozmyślanie (roz-miśh-la-ńe) n.
meditation; contemplation
rozmyślić się (roz-miśh-leećh
śhań), v. change one's mind
rozmyślny (roz-miśhl-ni) adj.
m. deliberate;intentional;wilful
roznamiętnić (roz-na-myánt-
ńeećh) v. impassion; excite
rozniecić (roz-ńe-ćheećh) v.
inflame; enkindle a fire;inspire
roznosić (roz-no-śheećh) v.
carry around; serve;rout;cut up
rozochocić (roz-o-kho-ćheećh)
v. make merry;enliven; animate
rozogniać się (roz-og-nać
śhań) n. inflame; excite;flare up
rozpacz (róz-pach) f. despair
rozpad (róz-pat) m. decay;break up
rozpakować (roz-pa-kó-vać) v.
unpack(one's luggage);unwrap
rozpalić (roz-pa-leećh) v.fire up;
ignite; start a fire; set ablaze
rozpamiętywać (roz-pa-myán-ti-
vać) v. contemplate ;reflect upon
rozpaplać (roz-pá-plać) v.
blab out;divulge ; babble out
rozpasany (roz-pa-sá-ni) adj. m.
unbridled; dissolute; licentious
rozpatrywać (roz-pa-tri-vać)
v. consider; act upon ;examine
rozpęd (róz-pánt) m. impetus;
dash ;momentum; taking a run

rozpędzać (roz-pán-dzać) v. pick
up speed; scatter;disperse
rozpętać (roz-pán-tać) v. unshackle; unleash;let loose
rozpiąć (róz-pyównch) v. unbuckle; undo; stretch; set (sail)
rozpieczętować (roz-pye-chán-
to-vach) v. unseal;open
rozpierać (roz-pye-rach) v. expand; extend; push aside
rozpierzchnąć się (roz-pyezh-
khównch shán) v. scatter
rozpieszczać (roz-pyésh-chach)
v. pamper; spoil;coddle up
rozpiętość (roz-pyán-toshch) f.
span; spread; range;strech
rozpinać (roz-pee-nach) v. unbutton; stretch; spread (sails etc.)
rozplątać (roz-plown-tach) v.
untangle;untie(a knot);unravel
rozpleść (roz-leshch) v. unbraid;
untwine; unplait(hair);unravel
rozpłakać się (roz-pwa-kach shán)
v. burst into tears;start weeping
rozpłaszczyć (roz-pwash-chich) v.
flatten out; flat(metal)
rozpłatać (roz-pwa-tach) v.slit;
split; cleave; split in two
rozpłodowy (roz-pwo-do-vi) adj.
m. (for) breeding; breeding-
rozpłodzić (roz-pwó-dźheech) v.
propagate;cause reproduction
rozpłód (roz-pwoot) m. propagation; reproduction
rozpływać się(roz-pwi-vach shán)v.
melt away;dissolve; flow;spread
rozpoczęcie (roz-po-chán-che) n.
start; outbreak;beginning;start
rozpoczynać (roz-po-chi-nach) v.
begin; start going; open;initiate
rozpogodzić się (roz-po-go-
dźheech shán) v. clear up
brighten up;cheer up;rise spirit
rozporek (roz-po-rek) m. fly; slit
rozporządzać (roz-po-zhówn-dzach)
v. dispose; decree; order;control
rozpościerać (roz-posh-che-rach)
v. unfurl; spread out;expand
rozpowiadać (roz-po-vya-dach) v.
tell tales;divulge; talk about
rozpowszechniać (roz-pov-shekh-
ñach) v. widespread; diffuse
disseminte;propagate; spread

rozpowszechnienie (roz-pov-
shekh-ñe-ñe) n. propagation;
spread;diffusion;prevalence
rozpoznać (roz-póz-nach) v.
recognize; spot; diagnose
rozpoznanie (roz-po-zná-ñe) n.
diagnosis; identification;
reconnaissance;recognition
rozpoznawczy (roz-poz-náv-chi)
adj. m. diagnostic;distinctive
rozpraszać (roz-prá-shach) v.
scatter; dispel; distract;disperse
rozprawa (roz-prá-va) f. trial;
showdown; dissertation; debate
rozprawiać (roz-práv-yach) v.
debate: argue; dispute; reason; talk at length;discuss
rozprawić się (roz-pra-veech
shán) v. settle matters;
fight out;dispose of; floor
rozprężyć (roz-prán-zhich) v.
distend; expand; dilate; re-
sile;deprive of elasticity
rozprostować (roz-pros-to-vach)
v. straighten;unbend;stretch(legs)
rozproszyć (roz-pró-shich) v.
disperse;scatter;dispel;distract
rozprowadzić (roz-pro-va-
dźheech) v. spread; retail;
distribute; dilute; convey;smear
rozpruć (róz-prooch) v. rip up;
open; unsew;unravel;rip open
rozprzedać (roz-pzhe-dach) v.
sell out;sell(successively)
rozprzedaż (roz-pzhe-dash) f.
sale;complete sale;retailing
rozprzestrzenić (roz-pzhe-
stzhe-ñeech) v. spread;propagate
rozprzęgać (roz-pzhán-gach) v.
1. unhitch; 2. disorganize
rozprzężenie (roz-pzhan-zhé-ñe)
n. anarchy; demoralization
rozpusta (roz-poos-ta) f. debauch; riot; libertinism
rozpustnica (roz-poost-ñee-tsa)
f. rake; rip; libertine; debauchee; profligate; libertine
rozpustnik (roz-poost-ñeek) m.
libertine; debauchee; rake;
profligate;rip; reprobate
rozpuszczać (roz-poosh-chach)
v. dissolve; dismiss; let go;
disband;thaw;melt;defrost;unfreeze

rozpuszczalnik (roz-poo-chál-neek) m. solvent; paint thinner

rozpuszczalny (roz-poos..ch l-ni) adj., m. soluble;dissolvable

rozpychać się (roz-pi-khách shán) v.shove aside; jostle; elbow one's way;push one's way

rozpylacz (roz-pi-lach) m. sprayer; nozzle; atomizer

rozpylać (roz-pi-lach) v. spray; pulverize; atomize

rozpytywać (roz-pi-ti-vach) v. ask for;inquire for;ask questions

rozrachować (roz-ra-kho-vach) v. settle accounts; calculate

rozrachunek (roz-ra-khoo-nek) m. squaring up accounts

rozradzać się (roz-ra-dzach shán) v. breed;propagate

rozrastać się (roz-ras-tach shán) v. grow larger; in-crease; develop; expand

rozrąbać (roz-rown-bach) v. cut asunder; hew apart;chop up

rozrobić (roz-ro-beech) v. stir up; dilute;scheme;intrigue;brawl

rozrodczość (roz-rod-choshch) f. reproduction;reproductiveness

rozróżniać (roz-roozh-ñach) v. distinguish; tell apart;discern

rozruchy (roz-roo-khy) pl. riots; disturbances

rozruszać (roz-roo-shach) v. start up; stir up; put in mo-tion;set in motion;animate

rozrywać (roz-ri-vach) v. burst; disrupt;tear open;entertain

rozrywka (roz-riv-ka) f. amuse-ment; recreation; pastime

rozrzadnica (roz-zhownd-ñee-tsa) f. control panel

rozrzedzić (roz-zhe-dzheech) v. dilute; rarefy;thin down;weaken

rozrzewnić (roz-zhev-ñeech) v. move; touch;affect;stir(the soul)

rozrzucać (roz-zhoo-tsach) v. scatter;, squander;distribute

rozrzutność (roz-zhoot-noshch) f. extravagance;lavishness

rozrzutny (roz-zhoot-ni) adj. m. wasteful; extravagant; thriftless;squandering;prodigal; spendthrift; lavish

rozsada (roz-sá-da) f. seed-ling; seedlings

rozsadzać (roz-sa-dzach) v. space-out;place; seat sepa-rately; blow up;explode;split

rozsądek (roz-sown-dek) m. good sense; discretion;reason

rozsądny (roz-sownd-ni) adj. m. sensible; reasonable; advisable;sound;judicious

rozsiadać się(roz-shá-dach shan)v. sit stretched; sprawl round

rozsiekać (roz-she-kach) v. cut up; slash asunder; hack up

rozsiewać (roz-she-vach) v. saw; disseminate;spread;shed

rozsiodłać (roz-shod-wach) v. unsaddle;take the saddle off

rozsławiać (roz-swav-yach) v. glorify; make famous; extol

rozstać się (roz-stach shán) v. part; give up; part with

rozstanie (roz-sta-ñe) n. parting; separation

rozstawać się (roz-sta-vach shan) v. part with; give up

rozstawiać (roz-stav-yach) v. disperse; place apart; space; spread;put at intervals

rozstąpić się(roz-stown-peech shán) v. step aside;come apart;split

rozstęp (roz-stanp) m. gap; space; slit;interval;heave

rozstroić (roz-stro-eech) v. put out of tune; upset; disar-ray;derange;disorder; untune

rozstrój (roz-strooy) m. upset; disorder;confusion;derangement

rozstrzelać (roz-stzhe-lach) v. 1. scatter; 2. execute by shooting;put before a firing squad

rozstrzygać (roz-stzhi-gach) v. try out; decide; fight out; judge

rozstrzygnięcie (roz-stzhig-nan-che) v. decision; settlement

rozsuwać (roz-soo-vach) v. part; draw aside;separate;expand(a compas)

rozsyłać (roz-si-wach) v. dis-tribute; circulate; send out

rozsypać (roz-si-pach) v. dis-perse(a granular substance);spill

rozszarpać (roz-shar-pach) v. tear up; claw; disjoin;mangle

rozszczepiać (roz-shchep-yach)
v. split; cleave; fissure
rozszczepienie (roz-shche-pye-
ne) n. split; diffraction
rozszerzać (roz-she-zhach) v.
widen; broaden; enlarge; expand; spread out; extend; open
rozszerzenie (roz-she-zhe-ne)
n. enlargement; dilation
rozsznurować (roz-shnoo-ro-
vach) v. unlace; loosen the lace
rozszyfrować (roz-shif-ro-vach)
v. decode; break the code
rozścielać (roz-shche-lach) v.
spread; make the bed
rozśmieszać (roz-shmye-shach) v.
amuse; make laugh; be amusing
rozświecić (roz-shvye-cheech) v.
light up; throw light on; shine on
roztaczać (roz-ta-chach) v. roll
out; spread; unfold; display; bore
roztajać (roz-ta-yach) v. thaw
roztapiać (roz-tap-yach) v.
melt; smelt(metal); thaw (ice)
roztargać (roz-tar-gach) v.
tear to pieces; ruffle; dishevel
roztargniony (roz-targ-no-ni)
adj. m. absentminded; distracted; scatterbrained ; far-away
rozterka (roz-ter-ka) f. tearing
between; dissension; suspense
roztkliwiać (roz-tklee-vyach) v.
feel for; touch; move; stir
roztłuc (roz-twoots) v. smash up
roztopy (roz-to-pi) pl. thaw
roztratować (roz-tra-to-vach)
v. run over; trample; tread
under foot; trample to death
roztrąbić (roz-trown-beech) v.
broadcast; blaze abroad
roztrącić (roz-trown-cheech) v.
push aside; elbow; part; jostle
roztropność (roz-trop-noshch) f.
prudence; thoughtfulness
roztropny (roz-trop-ni) adj. m.
wise; cautious; circumspect; politic
roztrwonic (roz-trvo-neech) v.
squander(a fortune, money etc.)
roztrzaskać (roz-tzhas-kach) v.
smash; shatter; crash to pieces
roztrzepanie (roz-tzhe-pa-ne) n.
scatterbrain; fickleness

roztrzepany (roz-tzhe-pa-ni)
adj. m. scatterbrain; giddy
roztwór (roz-tvoor) m.(chem.)
solution(colloidal,molal etc.)
roztyć się (roz-tich shan) v.
grow fat; become fat
rozum (ro-zoom) m. mind; reason; intellect; understanding;
wit; senses; judgment; brains
rozumieć (ro-zoom-yech) v.
understand; get; perceive
rozumny (ro-zoom-ni) adj. m.
rational; reasonable; wise
rozumować (ro-zoo-mo-vach) v.
reason; argue
rozwaga (roz-va-ga) f. thoughtfulness; prudence; reflection;
deliberation; consideration
rozwalać (roz-va-lach) v. shatter; demolish; smash; sprawl
rozwarty kąt (roz-var-ti kownt)
m. obtuse angle
rozważać (roz-va-zhach) v.
1. weigh out; 2. consider
rozweselić (roz-ve-se-leech) v.
cheer up; put in good humor
rozwiać (roz-vyach) v. blow
away; blow to and fro; scatter
rozwiązać (roz-vyown-zach) v.
untie; solve; undo; dissolve;
loosen; unbind; unravel; undo
rozwiązanie (roz-vyown-za-ne)
n. solution; way out; (child)
delivery; realization; execution
rozwiązły (roz-vyownz-wi) adj.
m. fast; dissolute; debauched
rozwidniać (roz-veed-nach) v.
dawn; be lit up; become lit up
rozwiedziony (roz-vye-dzho-ni)
adj. m. divorced(f.divorcee)
rozwierać (roz-vye-rach) v.
open wide; fling open
rozwieszać (roz-vye-shach) v.
hang about; stretch; spread out
rozwieść się (roz-vyeshch shan)
v. divorce; dwell upon
rozwijać (roz-vee-yach) v. unwrap; unfold; develop; spread
rozwikłać (roz-veek-wach) v.
disentangle; unravel; clear up
rozwikłanie (roz-veek-wa-ne) n.
unraveling; disentanglement

rozwlekać (roz-vle-kać) v.
drag out; protract; spread

rozwlekły (roz-vlek-wi) adj. m.
verbose; lengthy; long-spun

rozwodnić (roz-vod-neech) v.
dilute; water down; weaken

rozwodnik (roz-vod-neek) m. divorced man; divorcee

rozwodowy (roz-vo-do-vi) adj. m.
divorce-(proceedings etc.)

rozwodzic (roz-vo-dźheećh) v.
divorce (a married couple)

rozwojowy (roz-vo-yo-vi) adj.
evolutional; developmental

rozwolnienie (roz-vol-ne-ne) n.
diarrhea; lax bowels; open bowels

rozwozic (roz-vo-żheećh) v.
transport; deliver (mail etc.)

rozwód (roz-vood) m. divorce

rozwódka (roz-vood-ka) f. divorcee; divorced woman

rozwój (roz-vooy) m. development; evolution; growth

rozwścieczony (roz-všhćhe-cho-
ni) adj. m. enraged; furious

rozwydrzony (roz-vid-zho-ni)
adj. m. rampant; wild; lawless

rozzłościć (roz-zwośh-ćheećh)
v. irritate; make angry; provoke

rozżalenie (roz-zha-le-ne) n.
grudge; resentment; bitterness

rozżarzyć (roz-zha-zhićh) v.
inflame; set on fire; fire

rożek (ro-zhek) m. small horn;
croissant; small corner

rożen (ro-zhen) m. roasting spit

ród (rood) m. clan; breed; family; stock; race; origin; line

róg (roog) m. horn; corner; bugle; antler; corner kick (sport)

rój (rooy) m. swarm; hive; cluster

rosć (rooshćh) v. grow; age; go up

rów (roov) m. ditch; trench; trough

rówieśnik (roov-vyesh-neek) m.
peer of same age; contemporary

równać (roov-nać) v. equalize;
level; make even; smooth out

równanie (roov-na-ne) n. equation; equalization; comparison

równia (roov-na) f. plane; level

równie (roov-ne) adv. equally

również (roov-nesh) conj. also;
too; likewise; as well

równik (roov-neek) m. equator

równina (roov-nee-na) f. plain;
flat country; level landscape

równo (roov-no) adv. even; (equi-)

równoboczny (roov-no-boch-ni)
adj. m. equilateral

równoczesny (roov-no-ches-ni)
adj. m. simultaneous

równoległobok (roov-no-leg-wo-
bok) m. parallelogram

równoległy (roov-no-leg-wi) adj.
m. parallel to; collateral

równoleżnik (roov-no-lezh-neek)
m. parallel (of latitude)

równomierny (roov-no-myer-ni)
adj. m. even; uniform; steady

równoramienny (roov-no-ra-myen-
ni) adj. m. isosceles (triangle)

równorzędny (roov-no-zhand-ni)
adj. m. equal rank; equivalent

równość (roov-nośhćh) f. equality; parity; identity

równouprawnienie (roov-no-oo-
prav-ne-ne) n. equality of
rights (of women, men etc.)

równowaga (roov-no-va-ga) f.
equilibrium; balance; poise

równowartościowy (roov-no-var-
tosh-cho-vi) adj. m. equivalent; equipollent

równoważny (roov-no-vazh-ni)
adj. m. equivalent; equiponderant

równoważyć (roov-no-vazhićh)
v. balance; equalize; even up

równoznaczny (roov-no-znach-ni)
adj. m. synonymous; tantamount

rozga (rooz-ga) f. switch; cane

róż (roozh) m. rouge; pink

róża (roo-zha) f. rose (flower etc.)

różaniec (roo-zha-nets) m. ro-
sary; beads; telling one's beads

różdżka (roozhdzh-ka) f. dowsing
rod; twig; divining rod (or wand)

różnica (roozh-nee-tsa) f. difference; disparity; dissent

różniczka (roozh-neech-ka) f.
differential; small difference

różnic się (roozh-neech shan) v.
differ; be at variance

różnobarwny (roozh-no-barv-ni)
adj. m. many colored; motley

różnojęzyczny (roozh-no-yan-
zich-ni) adj. m. many-tongued

różnolity (roozh-no-lee-ti)
adj. m. diverse ; varied
różnorodny (roozh-no-ród-ni)
adj. m. heterogeneous ;varied
różnoznaczny (roozh-no-znach-
ni) adj. m. ambiguous
różny (roozh-ni) adj. m. different miscellaneous;sundry
różowy (roo-zho-vi) adj. m.
pink; rosy ; ruddy ;rose color
rtęciowy (rtăn-chó-vi) adj.m.
mercuric(compounds etc.)
rtec (rtănch) f. mercury
rubaszny (roo-básh-ni) adj. m.
coarse ; ill-mannered
rubin (roo-been) m. ruby (red)
rubryka (roo-bri-ka) f. space;
column;blank space; rubric
ruch (rookh) m. move; movement;
traffic; motion; gesture stir
ruchawka (roo-kháv-ka) f. riot
ruchliwy (rookh-lee-vi) adj.m.
busy; mobile; agile;active
ruchomości (roo-kho-mósh-chee)
pl. movables (personal property);belongings;(one's things)
ruchomy (roo-khó-mi) adj. m.
mobile ;moving; shifting flexile
ruczaj (roo-chay) m. brook
.ruda (roo-da) f. ore(metallic)
rudera (roo-dé-ra) f. run-down
house ; shanty; ruin ;hovel
rudy (roo-di) adj. m. red(haired);russet;ginger;foxy;ruddy
rufa (roo-fa) f, stern ;poop
rugować (roo-go-vach) v. eject;
oust; evict; eliminate;displace
ruina (roo-ee-na) f. ruin;wreck
ruja (roo-ya) f. heat; rut
rujnować (rooy-no-vach) v.
ruin; undo; destroy;wreck
ruleta (roo-lé-ta) f. roulette
rulon (roo-lon) m. roll;rouleau
rum (room) m. rum (drink)
rumak (roo-mak) m. charger;
steed; palfrey; courser
rumianek (roo-mya-nek) m. camomile ; chamonile(tea)
rumiany (roo-mya-ni) adj. m.
rosy ; ruddy; browned;florid
rumienić (roo-mye-neech) v.
blush; brown;redden;color
rumieniec (roo-mye-ñets) m.
blush; ruddiness; floridity

rumor (roo-mor) m. racket; uproar; rumble; clatter; din
rumowisko (roo-mo-vees-ko) n.
debris; rubble; brash
rumuński (roo-moon-skee) adj.
m. Rumanian ;of Rumania
runąc (roo-nównch) v. fall down;
collapse; crash; swoop;resound
runda (roon-da) f. bout; round;
lap; fall (in wrestling)
runo (roo-no) n. fleece; nap
rupiecie (roo-pye-che) n. rubbish; trash; junk; stuff;oddments
ruptura (roop-too-ra) f. hernia
rura (roo-ra) f. tube; pipe
rurka (roor-ka) f. small pipe
rurociąg (roo-ro-chówng) m.
pipeline ;run of pipes;piping
rusałka (roo-sáw-ka) f. undine;
naiad;water nymph; vanessa
ruszac (roo-shach) v. move; stir;
touch; start;take away;withdraw
rusznikarz (roosh-nee-kash) m.
gunsmith (man or shop)
rusztowanie (roosh-to-va-ñe) n.
scaffold; cradle (hanging)
rutyna (roo-ti-na) f. routine
rutynowany (roo-ti-no-va-ni)
adj. m. experienced;conpetent
rwać (rvach) v. pluck; tear;
pull out; pull up; rush ;burst
rwący (rvówn-tsy) adj. m. rapid;
racking (pain);swift flowing
rwetes (rvé-tes) m. bustle; ado;
racket ; turmoil ;agitation; stir
ryba (ri-ba) f. fish; the Fish
rybak (ri-bak) m. fisherman
rybny staw (rib-ni stav) fish
pond (artficially made)
rybołostwo (ri-bo-woos-tvo) n.
fishery; fishing
rycerski (ri-tser-skee) adj. m.
chivalrous ; courteous
rycerz (ri-tsesh) m. knight
rychło (rikh-wo) adv. soon;
quickly; early; soon after
rychły (rikh-wi) adj. m. speedy;
quick; early; prompt;approaching
rycina (ri-chee-na) f. engraving;
illustration;cartoon;drawing;plate
rycynus (ri-tsi-noos) m. castor
oil; castor oil plant
ryczałt (ri-chawt) m. lump sum;
global sum

ryczeć (ri-chech) v. roar; moo;
bellow;low;growl;bray;hoot;yell
ryć (rich) v. dig; root: engrave;
carve;excavate;burrow;plough
rydel (ri-del) m. spade; spud
rydwan (rid-van) m. chariot
rygiel (ri-gel) m. bolt;bar;lock
rygor (ri-gor) m. rigor;severity
ryj (riy) m. snout;phiz;mug(vulg.)
ryk (rik) m. roar;moo;low;yell
rylec (ri-lets) m. burin; graver;
chisel; etching needle;dry point
rym (rim) m. rhyme;rhyme word
rymarz (ri-mash) m. saddler
rymować (ri-mo-vach) v. rhyme
rynek (ri-nek) m. market(square)
rynna (rin-na) f. gutter; chute
rynsztok (rin-shtok) m. sewer
rynsztunek (rin-shtoo-nek) m.
armor; armature; outfit ; kit
rys (ris) m. feature; trait
rysa (ri-sa) f.crack; flow; fissure;scratch;rift;crevice;chink
rysopis (ri-so-pees) m. descrip-
tion(of a person for a passport)
rysować (ri-so-vach) v. draw;
design; sketch;draft;trace;show
rysownica (ri-sov-nee-tsa) f.
drawing board;drafting table
rysownik (ri-sov-neek) m. draftsman; illustrator; designer
rysunek (ri-soo-nek) m. sketch;
drawing ; draft; outline;cartoon
rysunkowy (ri-soon-ko-vi) adj.m.
tracing; drawing; cartoon;drawn
ryś (rish) m . lynx
rytm (ritm) m. rhythm ;cadence
rytmiczny (rit-meech-ni) adj. m.
rhythmic;regular; measured
rytownictwo (ri-tov-neets-tvo)
n. engraving; die sinking
rytownik (ri-tov-neek) m. engraver; die sinker
rytuał (ri-too-aw) m. ritual
rywal (ri-val) m. rival;contestant
rywalizacja (ri-va-lee-zats-ya)
f. rivalry;competition;emulation
ryza (ri-za) f. ream; restraint
ryzyko (ri-zi-ko) n. risk;venture
ryzykować (ri-zi-ko-vach) v.
risk; venture; gamble; hazard
ryzykowny (ri-zi-kov-ni) adj.m.
risky; hazardous;venturesome

ryż (rizh) m. rice
ryży (ri-zhi) adj. m. red (haired);russet;ginger;foxy;red-brown
rzadki (zhad-kee) adj. m. rare;thin
rzadko (zhad-ko) adv. seldom;thinly
rarely;far apart;exceptionally
rzadkość (zhad-koshch) f. rar-
ity:sparseness;curiosity; curio
rząd (zhownt) m. row; rank;
file; line, up; government
rządca (zhownd-tsa) f. administrator; ruler;land steward
rządowy (zhown-do-vi) adj. m.
governmental;government-;state-
rządzić (zhown-dzheech) v. rule;
govern; control; direct;be in power
rzec (zhets) v. say; utter
rzecz (zhech) f. thing; matter; act;
stuff; deal,; work; subject;theme
rzeczka (zhech-ka) f. small river;
river; brook; stream
rzecznik (zhech-neek) m. spokesman; attorney ; patent agent
rzeczownik (zhech-ov-neek) m.
noun; substantive (grammar)
rzeczowo (zhe-cho-vo) adv.
factually; terse; business
like ; to the point ;objectively
rzeczoznawca (zhe-cho-znav-tsa)
m. expert;specialist(authority)
rzeczpospolita (zhech-pos-po-
lee-ta) f. republik; commonwealth
rzeczywistość (zhe-chi-vees-
toshch) f. reality;actuality
rzeczywisty (zhe-chi-vees-ti)
adj. m. real; actual; virtual
rzednieć (zhed-nech) v. grow
thin; become rare;scatter;thin
rzeka (zhe-ka) f. river; stream
rzekomo (zhe-ko-mo) adv. would
be; allegedly ; supposedly;ostensibly
rzekomy (zhe-ko-mi) adj.m.make
believe; reputed; supposed
sham; alleged; immaginary;so called
rzemień (zhe-myen) m. leather
strap; leather band; leather belt
rzemieślniczy (zhe-myeshl-nee-
chi) adj. m. trade; craft-
rzemieślnik (zhe-myeshl-neek)
m. artisan; craftsman;tradesman
rzemiosło (zhe-myos-vo) n. (handi)
craft;trade;job;business

rzemyk (zhé-mik) m. small leather strap;chin strap; thong

rzepa (zhé-pa) f. turnip

rzepak (zhé-pak) m. rapeseed;cole

rzesza (zhé-sha) f. crowd; Reich

rzeszoto (zhe-shó-to) n. sieve

rześki (zhésh-kee) adj. m. lively; brisk; spry; fresh;brisk

rześkość (zhesh-kóshch) f. vigor

rzetelny (zhe-tel-ni) adj. m. honest; upright; fair; real

rzewny (zhév-ni) adj. m. wistful

rzezać (zhé-zach) v. slaughter; castrate; circumcise

rzezimieszek (zhe-żhee-mye-shek) m. cutpurse; thief; pickpocket

rzeź (zheżh) f. carnage; massacre;slaughter; shambles;carnage

rzeźba (zheżh-ba) f. sculpture

rzeźbiarstwo (zheżh-byár-stvo) n. sculpture; sculpturing

rzeźbiarz (zheżh-byash) m. sculptor;artist creating sculptures

rzeźbić (zheżh-beech) v. carve; cut;sculpture;weather(the earth)

rzeźnia (zheżh-ña) f. slaughterhouse

rzeźnik (zheżh-ñeek) m. butcher

rzeźwić (zheżh-veech) v. refresh

rzeźwość (zheżh-vóshch) f. agility; briskness;sprightliness

rzeźwy (zheżh-vi) adj. m. agile; brisk; smart;spry;lively;bracing

rzeżączka (zhe-zhównch-ka) f. gonorrhea

rzędem (zhán-dem) adv. in a row

rzędna (zhand-na) f. ordinate

rzepolić (zhan-pó-leech) v. scrape (on fiddle);rasp(the fiddle)

rzęsa (zhan-sa) f. eyelash

rzęsisty (zhan-shées-ti) adj. m. profuse; heavy; abundant;copious

rzężić (zhan-żheech) v. death rattle; ruckle (in sickness)

rżnąć (zhnównch) v. cut,carve; butcher; vulg.:screw;have sex

rzodkiew (zhod-kev) f. radish

rzodkiewka (zhod-kév-ka) f. radish(the pungent root eaten raw)

rzucać (zhoo-tsach) v. throw; fling; pitch; dash;hurl; toss

rzucić (zhoo-cheech) v. throw; cast; plunge; dash; pitch; fling

rzut (zhoot) m. throw; cast; projection; view; sketch

rzutki (zhoot-kee) adj. m. brisk;lively; enterprising

rzutkość (zhoot-kóshch) f. briskness; initiative

rzyć (zhich) f. (vulg.) ass

rzygać (zhi-gach) v. vomit; belch; spew; eject;emit

rzymski (zhim-skee) adj. m. Roman; of Rome(church;rite)

rżeć (rzhech) v. whinny; neigh

rżnąć (rzhnównch) v. cut; saw; engrave; carve; butcher; bang; play cards; (vulg.):screw

rżniecie (rzhñán-che) n. colic; bellyache; (slang): beating

rżysko (rzhis-ko) n. stubblefield; rye field

sabat (sá-bat) m, Sabbath

sabotaż (sa-bó-tash) m. sabotage; act of sabotage

sacharyna (sa-kha-ri-na) f. saccharine

sad (sad) m. orchard

sadło (sád-wo) n. leaflard

sadowić (sa-do-veech) v. place; show to a seat; seat

sadownik (sa-dóv-ñeek) m. fruitgrower;fruit farmer; orchardist

sadyba (sa-di-ba) f. dwelling; house; human habitation; home

sadysta (sa-dis-ta) m. sadist

sadza (sá-dza) f. soot; black

sadzać (sá-dzach) v. show to a seat; seat;make sit down

sadzawka (sa-dzáv-ka) f. pool

sadzić (sa-dżheech) v. plant; set; run; speed;stud(decorate)

sadzonka (sa-dzón-ka) f. seedling; quickset; cutling

sadzonejajka (sa-dzo-ne yáy-ka) s. fried eggs sunny side up

safanduła (sa-fan-doó-wa) f. bungler; yes-man; oaf;muff;duffer

safian (sá-fyan) m. morocco (lather); saffian

sagan (sá-gan) m. kettle ;pot

sak (sak) m. dipnet; sack

sakrament (sa-krá-ment) m. sacrament (of matrimony etc.)

sakwa (sák-va) f. wallet;purse money-bag; feed-bag ;nose bag

sala (sá-la) f. 1. hall; 2. audience (in a hall)

salaterka (sa-la-tér-ka) f. salad bowl; vegetable dish

salceson (sal-tsé-son) m. headcheese; (mock)brawn

saletra (sa-let-ra) f. niter; saltpeter;potassium nitrate

salina (sa-lee-na) f. saltworks; saline; salt mine

salmiak (sal-myak) m. ammoniumchloride; sal-ammoniac

salon (sa-lon) m. drawing-room

salonka (sa-lón-ka) f. club car (railroad);parlor car

salutować (sa-loo-to-vach) v. salute; dip the flag

salwa (sál-va) f. volley;salvo

sałata (sa-wá-ta) f. 1. lettuce; salad; 2. cabman (slang)

sam (sam) adj. m. alone; oneself; myself; yourself; nothing but

samica (sa-mee-tsa) f. female

samiec (sam-yets) m. male

samobójca (sa-mo-bóoy-tsa) m. suicide; suicidal man

samobójczy (sa-mo-booy-chi) adj. m. suicidal;leading to suicide

samobójstwo (sa-mo-booy-stvo) n. suicide;act of killing oneself

samochód (sa-mo-khood) m. automobile; car;motor car

samochwał (sa-mo-khvaw) m. braggart; boaster; blow hard

samodział (sa-mo-dżhaw) m. homespun (cloth)

samodzielność (sa-mo-dżhel-noshch) f. independence

samodzielny (sa-mo-dżhel-ni) adj. m.self-reliant; independent; self-contained

samogłoska (sa-mo-gwos-ka) f. vowel; vocal

samogon (sa-mo-gon) m. moonshine

samoistny (sa-mo-eest-ni) adj. m. independent;autonomous

samokrytyka (sa-mo-kri-ti-ka) f. self-criticism;self-accusation

samokształcenie (sa-mo-kshtaw-tse-ńe) n. self-education

samolot (sa-mo-lot) m. airplane

samolub (sa-mo-loob) m. egoist

samolubstwo (sa-mo-loob-stvo) n . selfishness ; egoism

samolubny (sa-mo-loob-ni) adj. m. selfish; self-seeking;egoistic

samoobrona (sa-mo-o-bró-na) f. f. self-defense

samopas (sa-mó-pas) adv. alone; by oneself; loosely; unheeded

samopoczucie (sa-mo-po-choo-che) n. frame of mind; feeling

samopomoc (sa-mo-pó-mots) f. self-help; mutual aid (society)

samorodek (sa-mo-ró-dek) m. (gold) nugget

samorodny (sa-mo-ród-ni) adj. m. autogenous; natural; virgin

samorząd (sa-mo-zhownt) m. autonomy; self-government

samotnik (sa-mot-ńeek) m. recluse; hermit;solitary;rogue

samostanowienie (sa-mo-sta-no-vyé-ńe) n. self-determination

samotność (sa-mot-noshch) f. solitude; loneliness

samouctwo (sa-mo-oots-tvo) n. self-education;self instruction

samouczek (sa-moo-oo-tchek) m. handbook (for self-instruction)

samouk (sa-mo-ook) m. self-taught (man);self taught person

samowładczy (sa-mo-vwad-chi) adj. m. autocratic; arbitrary

samowola (sa-mo-vó-la) f. license (arbitrariness);lawlessness

samowystarczalny (sa-mo-vis-tar-chál-ni) adj. m. self-sufficient;self contained;unsubsidized

samozachowawczy instynkt (sa-mo-za-kho-vav-chi een-stinkt) m. self-preservation instinct

samozapalenie się (sa-mo-za-pa-lé-ńe shań) n. spontaneous combustion; self ignition

samozwaniec (sa-mo-zva-ńets) m. usurper; pretender

sanatorium (sa-na-tor-yoom) m. sanitorium; sanatorium

sandacz (sán-dach) m. perch-pike

sandał (sán-daw) m. sandal

sanie (sá-ńe) pl. sleigh; sledge

sanitariuszka(sa-ńee-tar-yoosh-ka) f. nurse(emergency, military)

sanitarny (sa-nee-tar-ni) adj.
m. sanitary; health-
sankcja (sank-tsya) f. sanction
sankcjonować (sank-tsyo-no-
vach) v. sanction;authorize
sanki (san-kee) pl. sled
sanskryt (san-skrit) m. San-
skrit; Sanscrit
sapać (sa-pach) v. gasp; pant;
heave; snort;puff and blow;chug
saper (sa-per) m. combat engineer;army engineer; sapper
sardynka (sar-din-ka) f. sardine
sarkać (sar-kach) v. grumble
sarkastyczny (sar-kas-tich-ni)
adj. m. sarcastic(smile etc.)
sarna (sar-na) f. roe deer
sarnia skóra (sar-na skoo-ra)
f. buckskin;roe-deer's hide
satelita (sa-te-lee-ta) m. satellite; attendant
satyna (sa-ti-na) f. satin
satyra (sa-ti-ra) f. satire
satysfakcja (sa-tis-fak-tsya)
f. satisfaction; compensation
sączyć się (sown-chich shan)
v. drip; trickle; distill;
sift ; ooze out; seep;percolate
sąd (sownd) m. judgment ; court
sądownictwo (sown-dov-neets-tvo)
n. judicature ;jurisdiction
sądowy (sown-do-vi) adj. m. judicial; of court;judiciary
sądzić (sown-dzheech) v. judge;
think; believe; expect; guess
sąg (sowng) m. cord (of wood)
sasiad (sown-shad) m. neighbor
sąsiadka (sown-shad-ka) f.
neighbor; lady next door
sąsiedni (sown-shed-nee) adj.
m. adjacent;neighboring
sąsiedztwo (sown-shedz-tvo) n.
neighborhood; nearness;proximity
sążeń (sown-zhen) m. fathom;
cord;approximately six feet
scalić (stsa-leech) v. integrate
scedzić (stse-dzheech) v. strain
off;decant; pour off(a liquid)
scena (stse-na) f. scene; stage
scenariusz (stse-nar-yoosh) m.
scenario; script; screenplay
sceneria (stse-ner-ya) f. scen—
ery;srage decorations;backdrops

sceptyczny (stsep-tich-ni) adj.
m. sceptic; skeptical(smile etc.)
sceptyk (stsep-tik) m. skeptic
schab (skhab) m. pork chop
schadzka (skhadz-ka) f. date
scheda (skhe-da) f. inheritance; inheritance; heirloom
schemat (skhe-mat) m. scheme;
plan;draft;outline; diagram
schematyczny (skhe-ma-tich-ni)
adj. m. schematic (drafting...)
schizma (skheez-ma) f. schism
schlebiać (skhleb-yach) v.
flatter;wheedle;adulate;gratify
schludny (skhlood-ni) adj. m.
neat; clean;trim;slick;tidy
schnąć (skhnownch) v. dry; dry
up; wane; waste;parch;wither
schodki (skhod-kee) pl. steps
(small);small stairs
schodowa klatka (skho-do-va
klat-ka) staircase
schody (skho-di) pl. stairs
schodzić (skho-dzheech) v. get
down; go down stairs;step down
scholastyka (zkho-las-ti-ka) f.
scholasticism; Scholasticism
schorowany (skho-ro-va-ni) adj.
m. invalid;ailing;ill;sick
schować (skho-vach) v. hide;
pocket;conceal;put away; save
schowek (skho-vek) m. closet;
safe; hiding place; cubby;recess
schód (skhood) m. stair; step
schron (skhron) m. shelter;
pillbox; air raid shelter etc.
schronić sie (skhro-neech shan)
v. take refuge;take cover
schronisko (skhro-nees-ko) n.
shelter;hiding place;refuge
schudnięcie (skhood-nan-che) n.
loss of fat (weight);slimming
schwycić (skhvi-cheech) v.
seize; catch; get hold of
schylać (skhi-lach) v. bend;
bow; incline; stoop down
schyłek (skhi-wek) m. decline
scyzoryk (stsi-zo-rik) m. pocketknife; clasp knife;pen knife
seans (se-ans) m. seance; sitting;showing;performance
secesja (se-tses-ya) f. seces-
sion:Secession style(architecture)

sedes (se-des) m. toilet seat

sedno (sed-no) n. crux; core; gist; essence(of the matter)

sejm (seym) m. Polish parliament (600 years old)

sekcja (sek-tsya) f. dissection; section; cross-section ;division

sekret (sek-ret) m. secret

sekretarz (se-kre-tash) m. secretary;reporter; minuter

seksualny (se-ksoo-al-ni) adj. m. sexual; sex-(appeal,urge etc)

sekta (sek-ta) f. sect

sektor (sek-tor) m. sector

sekunda (se-koon-da) f. second

sekundnik (se-koond-neek) m. second -hand(of a watch)

sekutnica (se-koot-nee-tsa) f. shrew; scold; vixen

seledynowy (se-le-di-no-vi) adj. m. aquamarine;willow green

selekcja (se-lek-tsya) f. selection(by elimination,natural etc)

seler (se-ler) m. celery

semafor (se-ma-for) m. semaphore

semicki (se-meets-kee) adj. m. Semitic (character etc.)

seminarium (se-mee-nar-yoom) n. seminar;seminary;trainning school

sen (sen) m. sleep; dream

senat (se-nat) m. senate (in Poland evolved from royal council in XV c.);Upper House

senator (se-na-tor) m. senator

senior (sen-yor) m. senior

senny (sen-ni) adj. m. sleepy

sens (sens) m. sense; significance;gist;drift;meaning;point

sensacja (sen-sats-ya) f. sensation; a hit;making a hit

sensacyjny (sen-sa-tsiy-ni) adj. m. sensational; exciting

sentencja (sen-tents-ya) f. maxim; dictum; pronouncement

sentyment (sen-ti-ment) m. sentiment;partiality;fondness;feeling

separacja (se-pa-rats-ya) f. separation(from bed and board)

separatka (se-pa-rat-ka) f. private-room; solitary cell

separować (se-pa-ro-vach) v. separate;isolate

seplenić (se-ple-neech) v. lisp; have a lisp;speak with lisp

ser (ser) m. cheese

serce (ser-tse) n. heart;kindness

sercowy (ser-tso-vi) adj. m. cardiac ; love-(affair,secret etc.)

serdak (ser-dak) m. sleeveless (furred) waistcoat

serdeczność (ser-dech-noshch) f. cordiality;heartiness;caresses

serdeczny (ser-dech-ni) adj. m. hearty; cordial;sincere

serdelek (ser-de-lek) m. small sausage (specially smoked)

serenada (se-re-na-da) f. serenade (music and song at night)

seria (ser-ya) f. series; chain; set;train (of events etc.)

serio (ser-yo) adv. seriously

sernik (ser-neek) m. cheesecake ; casein

serwatka (ser-vat-ka) f. whey

serweta (ser-ve-ta) f. (small) table cloth;doily;serviette

serwetka (ser-vet-ka) f. napkin

serwilizm (ser-vee-leezm) m. servility; humbly submission

serwis (ser-vees) m. dinner set; service (tennis),turn of serving

serwować (ser-vo-vach) v.(tennis) serve; do services;aid;help

seryjny (se-riy-ni) adj. m. serial; consecutive

sesja (ses-ya) f. session

setka (set-ka) f. hundred

setny (set-ni) num. hundredth

sezon (se-zon) m. season

sędzia (san-dzha) m. judge; umpire; referee; magistrate

sędziwy (san-dzhee-vi)adj. m. aged; old;grey headed;ancient

sęk (sank) m. knot;knag;knar

sękaty (san-ka-ti) adj. m. knotty;knaggy;gnarly;nodose;rugged

sęp (sanp) m. vulture

sfera (sfe-ra) f. sphere;zone

sferyczny (sfe-rich-ni) adj. m. spherical(geometry,triangle etc.)

sfinks (sfeenks) m. sphinx

sfora (sfo-ra) f. pack of dogs

siać (shach) v. sow(corn,terror...)

siadać (sha-dach) v. sit down; take a seat;get stranded;go flat

siano (śha-no) n. hay
sianokosy (śha-no-ko-si) pl.
  haymaking; hay cutting
siarczan (śhar-chan) m. sulfate
siarka (śhar-ka) f. sulfur
siarkowy (śhar-ko-vi) adj. m.
  sulfuric(acid etc.)
siatka (śhat-ka) f. net; screen
siatkówka (śhat-koov-ka) f. ret-
  ina; volley-ball
siąść (śhanśhch) v. sit down
sidło (śhid-wo) n. snare; trap
siebie (śhe-bye) pron. (for)
  self; oneself;one;each other
siec (śhets) v. cut; mow; whip
sieczka (śhech-ka)f.chop straw;
  chaff; empty head(slang)
sieczna (śhech-na) f. secant
sieczna broń (śhech-na broń) f.
  cutting weapons
sieć (śhech) f. net; network;
  grid;fishing net;trap;snare;web
siedem (śhe-dem) num. seven
siedemdziesiąt (śhe-dem-dźhe-
  shownt) num. seventy
siedemdziesiąty (śhe-dem-dźhe-
  shown-ti) num. seventieth
siedemnasty (śhe-dem-nas-ti)
  num. seventeenth
siedemnaście (śhe-dem-nash-che)
  num. seventeen
siedemset (śhe-dem-set) num.
  seven hundred
siedlisko (śhed-lees-ko) n, seat;
  abode;habitation;hotbed;nest
siedmiokrotny (śhed-myo-krot-ni)
  adj. m. sevenfold
siedmioletni (śhed-myo-let-nee)
  adj. m. seven year (old; lasting)
siedzący (śhe-dzown-tsi) adj. m.
  sitting(posture);sedentary
siedzenie (śhe-dze-ne) n. seat;
  bottom; behind
siedziba (śhe-dzhee-ba) f. seat;
  abode;habitat(of an animal)
siedzieć (śhe-dzhech) v. sit
  (stay);be perched;be settled
siejba (śhey-ba) f. sowing; sowing time
siekacz (śhe-kach) m. incisor;
  chopping knife; chopper

siekanina (śhe-ka-nee-na) f.
  hash;chopping up;cutting up
siekiera (śhe-ke-ra) f. axe
siekierka (śhe-ker-ka) f.
  hatchet; small axe
sielanka (śhe-lan-ka) f. idyll
sielankowy (śhe-lan-ko-vi) adj.
  m. idyllic; pastoral;bucolic
sielski (śhel-skee) adj. m.
  rural;idyllic; pastoral
siemię (śhe-myań) n. bird seed
siennik (śhen-neek) m. straw-
  mattress;pallet;paillasse
sień (śheń) f. hallway; corridor;vestibule;entrance hall
siepacz (śhe-pach) m. (rough)
  henchman;hired assassin
sierota (śhe-ro-ta) m. f. orphan;lonsome person;poor fellow
sierp (śherp) m. sickle
sierpień (śher-pyeń) m. August
sierść (śherśhch) f. hair (coat)
sierżant (śher-zhant) m. sergeant (military rank)
siew (śhev) m. sowing; seeds
siewca (śhev-tsa) m. sower
siewnik (śhev-neek) m. seeder;
  sowing-machine
się (śhań) pron. self (oneself;
  myself etc.;of itself)each other
sięgać (śhań-gach) v. reach
sikać (śhee-kach) v. squirt;
  spout; gush; piss (vulg.)
sikawka (śhee-kav-ka) f. fire
  hose; squirt; fire engine
sikora (śhee-ko-ra) f. titmouse
siksa (śheek-sa) f. hussy; small
  girl piddler
silnik (śhil-neek) m. motor
silnik spalinowy (śhil-neek spa-
  lee-no-vi) combustion engine
silny (śhil-ni) adj. m. strong;
  powerful;mighty;hefty;lusty;stiff
silos (see-los) m. silo;(store)pit
siła (śhee-wa) f. 1. force; might;
  strength; power; 2. many; much
siłacz (śhee-wach) m. strongman
siłownia (shee-wov-na) f. power
  plant;power station;power house
sinawy (shee-na-vi) adj. m.
  bluish; somewhat blue
siniak (shee-nak) m. bruise

sinus (see-noos) m. sine (of
  an angle)
siny (shee-ni) adj. m. livid;
  blue; purple;blue in the face
siodełko (sho-dew-ko) n. bicycle seat;small saddle
siodlarz (shod-lash) m. saddler
siodłać (shod-wach) v. saddle
siodło (shod-wo) n. saddle
sioło (sho-wo) m. hamlet;village
siostra (shos-tra) f. sister
siostrzenica (shos-tshe-nee-
  tsa) f. niece
siostrzeniec (shos-tshe-nets)
  m. nephew
siostrzyczka (shos-tzhich-ka)
  f. little sister
siodemka (shoo-dem-ka) f. seven
siodmy (shood-mi) num. seventh
sito (shee-to) n. sieve;strainer
sitowie (shee-tov-ye) n. bulrush
siusiać (shoo-shach) v. tinkle;
  urinate ; piss;pee;piddle
siwek (shee-vek) m. grey horse
siwieć (sheev-yech) v. grow gray
siwucha (shee-voo-kha) f. low
  grade vodka; rot gut
siwy (shee-vi) adj. m. gray;
  blue; grizzly;grey haired;hoary
skafander (ska-fan-der) m. diving
  suit ; pressure suit;wind jacket
skakać (ska-kach) v. jump; spring;
  bounce; leap; pop; skip ; dive
skakanka (ska-kan-ka) f. jumping
  rope; skipping rope
skala (ska-la) f. scale;extent
skaleczenie (ska-le-che-ne) n.
  cut; injury; hurt;wound
skaleczyć (ska-le-chich) v. hurt;
  injure; cut;prick;wound
skalisty (ska-lees-ti) adj. rocky
skalp (skalp) m. scalp
skała (ska-wa) f. rock
skamieniały (ska-mye-na-wi) adj.
  m. petrified ;fossil-;stone-
skamienieć (ska-mye-nech) v. become petrified ;turn into stone
skandal (skan-dal) m. scandal
skarb (skarb) m. treasure; treasury; riches;beloved person;hoard
skarbiec (skar-byets) m. treasury;
  strong room;safe deposit

skarbnik (skarb-neek) m.treas-
  urer;cashier;paymaster
skarbonka (skar-bon-ka) f.
  piggy bank;money box;poor box
skarcić (skar-cheech) v. admonish;rebuke;reprimand;scold
skarga (skar-ga) f. complaint;
  suit; claim; charge;grievance
skarłowaciały (skar-wo-va-
  cha-wi) adj. m. stunted;
  dwarfish
skarpa (skar-pa) f. scarp; buttress;slope;escarpment
skarpetka (skar-pet-ka) f.
  sock;a short stocking
skarżyć (skar-zhich) v. sue;
  denounce;complain;tell tales
skarżypyta (skar-zhi-pi-ta) m.
  squealer; informer; telltale
skaza (ska-za) f. tarnish;brab;
  blot; flaw;defect;spot;speck
skazać (ska-zach) v. condemn;
  sentence;pass judgement;doom
skazaniec (ska-za-nets) m.
  condemned man (to death)
skazić (ska-zheech) v. spoil;
  corrupt; adulterate;pollute
skąd (skownt) adv. from where;
  since when; where from?
skądinąd (skownd-ee-nownt) adv.
  otherwise; on the other hand
skąpić (skown-peech) v. skimp;
  stint; begrudge (food,money...)
skąpiec (skownp-yets) m. miser
skąpstwo (skownp-stvo) n. par-
  simony;avarice;stinginess
skąpy (skown-pi) adj. m. stingy; scanty; meager; scant
skiba (skee-ba) f. clod
skinąć (skee-nownch) v. signal;
  motion;nod; bow (one's head)
skinienie (skee-ne-ne) m. nod;
  bow; sign ;call;gesture;motion
sklejać (skle-yach) v. glue
  together;stick;paste; patch
sklejka (skley-ka) f. plywood
sklep (sklep) m. store; shop
sklepienie (skle-pye-ne) n.
  vault ;vaulting; dome
sklepikarz (skle-pee-kash) m.
  shopkeeper; tradesman
sklepowa (skle-po-va) f. saleslady; saleswoman

skleroza (skle-ró-za) f. scle-
rosis;hardening of body

skład (skwat) m. composition;
warehouse; store;framework

składać (skwa-dać) v. make up;
compose; piece;fold;set together

składacz (skwa-dach) m. type-
setter; compositor

składany (skwa-da-ni) adj. m.
compound; folding;miscellaneous

składka(skwad-ka) f. contribution;collection;membership fee

składnia (skwad-ña) f. syntax

składnica (skwad-ñee-tsa) f.
depository; warehouse;depot

składnik (skwad-ñeek) m. ingredient; component;element

składowe (skwa-dó-ve) n. warehouse fee; storage charges

skłamać (skwa-mach) v. tell
a lie;tell an untruth; lie

skłaniać (skwa-ñach) v. bend;
lean; incline;induce;impel;rest

skłon (skwon) m. slope; bow

skłonność (skwon-noshćh) f.
inclination;tendency;disposition

skłonny (skwon-ni) adj. m. disposed; inclined;prone;apt

skłócić (skwoo-ćheech) v. stir
up; agitate; cause to disagree

sknera (skne-ra) m.& f. miser

skobel (sko-bel) m. staple

skoczek (sko-chek) m. jumper

skocznia (skóch-ña) f. ski-
jump (ramp);take off ramp

skoczny (skóch-ni) adj. m. brisk;
lively; vivacious;saltary

skoczyć (sko-chich) v. leap;
jump; spring;make a dash;hurry

skojarzenie (sko-ya-zhé-ñe) n.
association; union;conjunction

skok (skok) m. jump; leap; hop

skok tłoka (skok two-ka) m. piston stroke

skołatany (sko-wa-tá-ni) adj. m.
worn; battered; shattered

skołować (sko-wo-vach) v. confound; muddle; exhaust

skomleć (skom-lech) v. whine

skomplikowany (skom-plee-ko-va-
ni) adj. m. complex; intricate

skonać (sko-nach) v. expire; die

skończyć (skon-chich) v. finish; end;stop;have done

skoro (sko-ro) conj. after;at;
since; as;quickly;soon;if;once
adv. very soon; by and by

skoroszyt (sko-ro-shit) m.
folder ;letter file

skorowidz (sko-ro-veets) m.
index; indexed note book

skorpion (skor-pyon) m. scor-
pion; Scorpio

skorupa (sko-roo-pa) f. crust;
shell;hull;incrustation;carapace

skory (sko-ri) adj. m. quick;
eager;prompt(to act); swift

skostniały (skost-ña-wi) adj.
m. ossified;numb;stiff;fossilized

skosny (skósh-ni) adj. m. slanting; oblique; inclined

skotłować (skot-wo-vach) v. whirl;
bewilder;agitate;swirl; seethe

skowronek (sko-vró-nek) m.
lark; skylark

skowyczeć (sko-vi-chech) v.
yelp; whipe;squeal;whimper;whine

skowyt (sko-vit) m. yelp;squeal

skóra (skoo-ra) f. skin; hide;
leather; hide;skin;coat;pelt;derm

skórka (skoor-ka) f. skin; peel;
crust; cuticle;agnail;pelt;fur

skórny (skoor-ni) adj. m. cuta-
neous; dermal;skin-(disease etc.)

skórzany (skoo-zha-ni) adj. m.
leather made; leathery;leather-

skra (skra) f. spark (poetic)

skracać (skra-tsach) v. short-
en; cut down;lessen;abridge

skradać się (skra-dach śhan) v.
steal; creep up;advance stealthily

skraj (skray) m. border; edge;
brink; margin;fringe;rand;outskirts

skrajać (skra-yach) v. cut off;cut
(cloth); cut up (to pieces)

skrajność (skray-noshćh) f.
extremism; extreme

skrajny (skray-ni) adj. m.
extreme;intense;utmost;ultra;utter

skrapiać (skrap-yach) v.damp;
sprinkle ;moisten; water

skraplać (skrap-lach) v. liquefy; condense;precipitate

skrawek (skra-vek) m. shred;snip;
strip; patch; chip;fragment;patch

skreslić (skresh-leech) v.
sketch; cancel; jot down;delete

skręcać (skrań-tsach) v. twist;
turn off; break (neck);strand

skrępować (skrań-po-vach) v. tie
up; restrict;embarrass;impede

skręt (skrańt) m. twist; twist-
ing; coil; turn; torsion

skrobaczka (skro-bach-ka) f.rasp;
scraper; foot scraper(for mud)

skrobać (skro-bach) v. scrape;
rasp; scratch; scale (fish)

skromny (skrom-ni) adj. m.coy;
modest;unassuming;simple;lowly

skroń (skron) f. temple

skropić (skro-peech) v. liquefy;
sprinkle;water;moisten;damp

skrócić (skroo-cheech) v. abbreviate; shorten ;cut down;curtail

skrót (skroot) m. abbreviation

skrucha (skroo-kha) f. contrition; repentance;compunction

skrupulatny (skroo-poo-lát-ni)
adj. m. scrupulous;precise,exact

skrupuł (skroo-poow) m. scruple

skruszyć (skroo-shich) v. crumble;crush;bring to repentance

skrycie (skri-che) adv. secretly

skryć (skrich) v. hide;obscure

skrypt (skript) m. script; mi-
meographed lecture; I.O.U.

skrytka pocztowa (skrit-ka poch-
tó-va) post office box

skrytość (skri-toshch) f. secrecy; secretiveness

skryty (skri-ti) adj. m. underhanded; secret; reticent

skrzek (skzhek) m. scream; croak

skrzep (skzhep) m. clot; coagu-
lation(of blood);grume;thrombus

skrzepnąć (skzhep-nownch) v. clot;
coagulate;set;freeze;solidify

skrzętnie (skzhant-ne) adv. sed-
ulously ; diligently;busily

skrzętny (skzhant-ni) adj. m.
industrious; busy; diligent

skrzydlaty (skzhid-la-ti) adj.
m. winged;wing-shaped;winglike

skrzydło (skzhid-wo) n. wing;
leaf; brim; (fan) arm extension

skrzynia (skzhi-ña) f. chest;bin;
box;hutch;case;crate;coffer

skrzynka (skzhin-ka) f. box;chest

skrzynka biegów (skzhin-ka
bye-goov) f. gearbox;gear case

skrzypce (skzhip-tse) n. violin; fiddle;person playing fiddle

skrzypek (skzhi-pek) m. violinist; fiddler

skrzypieć (skzhi-pyech) v. crunch;
creak; screech;grind;squeak;gride

skrzywiać (skzhi-vyach) v. bend;
distort; twist;contort;put awry

skrzyżowanie dróg (skzhi-zho-
vá-ñe droog) pl. f. crossroads;crossing;intersection

skrzyżowany (skzhi-zho-vá-ni)
adj. m. crossbred; cross-
legged

skubać (skoo-bach) v. nibble;
pluck; pick; fleece;graze;tease

skuć (skooch) v. shackle; chain

skulić (skoo-leech) v. curl up;
cuddle up; squat; lie low;crouch

skup (skoop) m. purchasing center

skupiać (skoop-yach) v. concentrate; bring together; gather

skupienie (skoop-yé-ñe) n. concentration;focussing;compression

skupiony (skoop-yo-ni) adj. m.
collected; concentrated ;dense

skupować (skoo-po-vach) v. buy;
buy up ;keep buying; buy out

skurcz (skoorch) m. cramp; shrinking;
spasm; twitch; systole;contraction

skurczyć (skoor-chich) v. draw in;
shrink; contract; lessen;diminish

skuteczność (skoo-tech-noshch)
f. efficiency; efficacy;good trsult

skutecznie (skoo-tech-ñe) adv.
with good result;effectively

skuteczny(skoo-tech-ni) adj. m.
effective;efficient; operative

skutek (skoo-tek) m. effect;
result; outcome; consequence

skuter (skoo-ter) m. motor-
scooter

skutkować (skoot-ko-vach) v.
have effect; work; operate

skwapliwy (skwap-lee-vi) adj.
m. eager; willing;ready

skwar (skvar) m. scorching heat

skwarek (skva-rek) m. crackling
skwaśniały (skvash-na-wi) adj.
m. sour;turned sour; glum
skwer (skver) m. square
słabiutki (swa-byoot-kee) adj.
m. very weak(in diminutive)
słabnąć (swab-nownch) v. weaken;
grow feeble;decline;diminish
słabość (swa-boshch) f. weakness;
illness;debility;fragility
słabowity (swa-bo-vee-ti) adj.
m. weakly; feeble;fragile;puny
słaby (swa-bi) adj. m. weak;frail;
feeble;infirm;faint;flimsy;poor
słać (swach) v. send; make bed;
spread(a table cloth etc.);strew
słaniać się (swa-nach shan) v.
totter; stagger;lurch; reel
sława (swa-va) f. glory; renown;
fame; celebrity;reputation;repute
sławetny (swa-vet-ni) adj. m.
notorious;famous;ill famous
sławić (swa-veech) v. praise;
celebrate; glorify;laud;blazon
sławny (swav-ni) adj. m. famous;
glorious;celebrated;illustrious
słodkawy (swod-ka-vi) adj. m.
sweetish; slightly sweet
słodki (swod-kee) adj. m. sweet
słodycze (swo-di-che) pl. sweets
słodzić (swo-dżheech) v. sweeten
słoik (swo-eek) m. jar; gallipot;
glass;pot ;small jar;little jar
słojowaty (swo-yo-va-ti) adj. m.
grained;veined;shownig grain
słoma (swo-ma) f. straw
słomianka (swo-myan-ka) f. straw
mat;doormat;straw plaited basket
słomiany wdowiec (swo-mya-ni
vdo-vyets) m. grass widower
słomka (swom-ka) f. small straw
słonecznik (swo-nech-neek) m.
sunflower
słoneczny (swo-nech-ni) adj. m.
sunny;solar(system,year etc.)
słonina (swo-nee-na) f. lard
słoniowa kość (swo-no-va koshch)
f. ivory
słonka (swon-ka) f. wood-cock
słony (swo-ni) adj. m. salty
słoń (swon) m. elephant
słońce (swon-tse) n. sun;sunlight

słota (swo-ta) f. foul weather
słotny dzień (swot-ni dżheń) m.
rainy day; bad weather day
słowacki (swo-vats-kee) adj.
m. Slovak; Slovakian
słowianin (swo-vya-neen) m.
Slav
słowiański (swo-vyan-skee) adj.
m. Slav; Slavonic
słowik (swo-veek) m. nightingale; good singer
słownictwo (swov-neets-tvo) n.
vocabulary; list of words
słownik (swov-neek) m. dictionary; vocabulary; language
słowny (swov-ni) adj. m. verbal; reliable; dependable
słowo (swo-vo) n. word; verb
słoworod (swo-vo-rood) m. etymology; origin of words
słowotworstwo (swo-vo-tvoor-
stvo) n. word formation
słód (swood) m. malt
słój (swooy) m. jar; (tree)
ring;pot;vain;grain
słówko (swoov-ko) n. (little
or sweet) word;nice word
słuch (swookh) m. hearing
słuchacz (swoo-khach) m. listener; student ;hearer;auditor
słuchać (swoo-khach) v. hear;
obey;listen;obey orders
słuchawka (swoo-khav-ka) f.
(tel.) receiver; earphone
słuchowisko (swoo-kho-vees-ko)
m. radio drama;broadcast drama
słuchy (swoo-khy) pl. rumors;
(animal) ears;uncertain news
sługa (swoo-ga) f. servant
słup (swoop) m. pillar; column;
post; pole pylon; landmark
słupek (swoo-pek) m. pillaret;
small post;stake;stud; rail
słuszność (swoosh-noshch) f.
rightness; equity; rightful-
ness; legitimacy;aptness;justice
słuszny (swoosh-ni) adj. m.
just; fair; right;pertinent;apt
służalczy (swoo-zhal-chi) adj.
m. servile ;cringing;subservient
służąca (swoo-zhown-tsa) f.
maid ;servant; cleaning woman

służący (swoo-zhówn-tsi) m. servant;manservant;domestic

służba (swoozh-ba) f. service

służbowy (swoozh-bó-vi) adj. m. official;business(trip etc.)

służyć (swoo-zhich) v. serve

słychać (swi-khach) v. people say; one hears;be heard

słynąć (swi-nównch) v. be famed

słynny (swin-ni) adj. m. famous

słyszalny (swi-shál-ni) adj. m. audible;within hearing range

słyszeć (swi-shech) v. hear

smacznego ! (smach-né-go) exp. good appetite

smaczny (smach-ni) adj. m. tasty

smagać (smá-gach) v. lash; whip

smagły (smag-wi) adj. m. swarthy

smak (smak) m. taste; relish; savor;palate;liking;appetite

smakołyk (sma-ko-wik) m. tidbit; delicacy;dainty;choice morsel

smakować (sma-ko-vach) v. taste

smakowity (sma-ko-vee-ti) adj. m. savory;appetizing;tasty

smalec (sma-lets) m. lard; fat

smar (smar) m. grease; lubricant

smarkać (smár-kach) v. blow nose

smarkacz (smar-kach) m. squirt; snot; whippersnapper;raw lad

smarkaty (smar-ká-ti) adj. m. snotty; callow; raw

smarować (sma-ro-vach) v. smear

smarowidło (sma-ro-vid-wo) n. grease ; lubricant; ointment

smażyć (sma-zhich) v. fry

smętny (smán-tni) adj. m. melancholy; blue;doleful; dolorous

smoczek (smó-chek) m. nipple; pacifier;dummy;comforter

smok (smok) m. dragon

smoking (smó-king) m. dinner jacket; tuxedo;formal jacket

smolny (smól-ni) adj. m. resinous; pitchy;tarry

smoła (smó-wa) f. pitch; tar

smrodliwy (smrod-lee-vi) adj. m. rank; stinky; smelly; foul

smród (smroot) m. stench; fetor

smucić (smoo-cheech) v. sadden

smukły (smook-wi) adj. m. slender; slim; willowy; gracile

smutek (smoo-tek) m. sorrow; sadness ; grief; mournfulness

smutny (smoot-ni) adj. m. sad

smycz (smich) f. leash;dog lead

smyczek (smi-chek) m. (violin) bow; fiddle stick

smyk (smik) m.whippersnapper; brat; kid; small boy

snop (snop) m. sheaf; bunch

snop światła (snop shvyat-wa) light beam;light shaft

snuć (snooch) v. spin;reel off

snycerz (sni-tsesh) m. sculptor

sobek (so-bek) m. egoist

sobota (so-bó-ta) f. Saturday

sobowtór (so-bóv-toor) m. double

soból (só-bool) m. sable (fur)

sobór (só-boor) m. synod

socjalista (so-tsya-leés-ta) m. socialist

socjalizacja (so-tsya-lee-zá-tsya) f. socialization

socjalizm (so-tsyá-leezm) m. socialism

socjologia (so-tsyo-lóg-ya) f. sociology ; social science

soczewica (so-che-vee-tsa) f. lentil; lentils

soczewka (so-chev-ka) f. lens

soczysty (so-chís-ti) adj. m. juicy ; sappy; mellow; coarse

soda (so-da) f. soda

sodowa woda (so-dó-va vo-da) f. soda water

sofa (só-fa) f. lounge; sofa

sofistyczny (so-fees-tích-ni) adj. m. sophistical; captious

sojusz (só-yoosh) m. alliance

sojusznik (so-yoosh-neek) m. ally;associate joined for a common purpose

sok (sok) m. sap; juice

sokół (so-koow) m. falcon

solanka (so-lan-ka) f. salt spring; solted bread roll;brine

solić (so-leéch)v.salt;add salt

Solidarność (so-lee-dár-noshch)s. Solidarity Labor Union;solidarity

solidarny (so-lee-dár-ni) adj. m. solidary; sympathetic

solidny (so-leéd-ni) adj. m. solid; firm;sound:reliable;safe

solista (so-leés-ta) m. soloist

soliter (so-lee-ter) m. tapeworm: solitary tree; solitaire (gem stone)

solniczka (sol-neech-ka) f.
saltshaker; saltcellar
solo (so-lo) adv. solo
solny (sol-ni) adj. m. saline
solony (so-lo-ni) adj. m. salt-
ed ; corned(beef);salt cured
sołtys (sow-tis) m. village
head(officer below wójt)
sonata (so-na-ta) f. sonata
sonda (son-da) f. probe; feeler;
lead;plummet;sounding ballon
sonet (so-net) m. sonnet
sopel (so-pel) m. icicle
sopran (sop-ran) m. soprano
sortować (sor-to-vach) v. sort
sos (sos) m. gravy; sauce
sosna (sos-na) f. pine
sośnina (sosh-nee-na) f. pine-
wood;pine tree;pine branches
sowa (so-va) f. owl
sowity (so-vee-ti) adj. m. lav
ish;ample;abundant;rich
sód (sood) m. sodium
sól (sool) f. salt
spacerować (spa-tse-ro-vach) v.
walk; stroll; walk about
spacja (spa-tsya) f. (print)
space
spaczać (spa-chach) v. warp;
pervert; twist;distort
spaczenie (spa-che-ne) n. dis-
tortion; perversion; warp
spać (spach) v. sleep;slumber
spad (spat) m. slope; drop
spadać (spa-dach) v. fall; drop
spadek (spa-dek) m. fall; inheritance; downfall;slope;dip
spadkobierca (spad-ko-byer-tsa)
m. heir;inheritor;successor
spadochron (spa-do-khron) m.
parachute
spadzisty (spa-dzhees-ti) adj.
m. steep;sloping;precipitous
spajać (spa-yach) v. weld; solder; link;join;unite;bond
spalenizna (spa-le-neez-na) f.
(smell of) burning (smoke)
spalić (spa-leech) v. burn out
spalony (spa-lo-ni) adj. m.
adust; (sport) offside
sparzyć (spa-zhich) v. burn;
sting ; scald;blister;scorch

spasły (spas-wi) adj. m. fat
spaść (spashch) v. fall; fatten
spawacz (spa-vach) m. welder
spawać (spa-vach) v. weld; solder; weld metal
spawanie (spa-va-ne) n. weld-
ing(of metals etc.)
spazm (spazm) m. spasm;convulsion
spec (spets) m. specialist;expert;
craftsman; dab hand; dab
specjalizacja (spe-tsya-lee-
zats-ya) f. specialization
specjalność (spe-tsyal-noshch)
f. specialty;peculiarity
specjalny (spe-tsyal-ni) adj.
m. special;express;particular
specificzny (spe-tsi-feech-ni)
adj. m. specific;peculiar
spedytor (spe-di-tor) m. shipping agent; forwarding agent
spekulacja (spe-koo-lats-ya) f.
speculation; venture
spekulant (spe-koo-lant) m.
profiteer; speculator;gambler
spekulować (spe-koo-lo-vach) v.
speculate; profiteer; gamble
spelunka (spe-loon-ka) f. joint
spełniać (spew-nach) v. perform;
fulfill;comply with;accomplish
spędzać (span-dzach) v. round
up (cattle); spend (time);
abort;drive away;gather;pass time
spichlerz (spee-khlesh) m. gran-
ary
spiczasty (spee-chas-ti) adj. m.
pointed;peaked;tapering;sharp
spiec (spyets) v. burn;scorch;
sunblister;blush; parch;sinter
spieniężyć (spye-nan-zhich) v.
cash(checks);sell property)
spieniony (spye-no-ni) adj. m.
foamy;foaming;covered with foam
spierać się (spye-rach shañ) v.
argue;contend;quarrel;dispute
spieszny (spyesh-ni) adj. m.
hasty; quick; hurried
spieszyć się (spye-shich shañ)
v. hurry; dismount;be eager
spięcie (spyan-che) n. buckle;
short circuit;collision; clash
spiętrzyć (spyan-tzhich) v.
pile up; heap up;bank up;dam up

spiker (spee-ker) m. (radio) announcer; disc jokey;Speaker

spinacz (spee-nach) m. fastener

spinać (spee-nach) v. fasten; pin up; clasp; spur (horse)

spinka (speen-ka) f. clasp

spirala (spee-ra-la) f. spiral; coil;volute;helix;spiral glide

spiralny (spee-ral-ni) adj. m. spiral;helical;involuted

spirytus (spee-ri-toos) m. spirit; alcohol; spirits

spis (spees) m. list; register; inventory;record;roll;census

spis rzeczy (spees zhe-chi) table of contents

spisać (spee-sach) v. record; write down;acquit oneself(well...)

spisek (spee-sek) f. plot; conspiracy; hatching a plot

spiskowiec (spees-ko-vyets) m. conspirator; plotter

spiż (speezh) m. brass; bronze

spiżarnia (spee-zhar-ńa) f. pantry; buttery; cupboard

spiżowy (spee-zho-vi) adj. m. brass ; bronze; booming(voice)

splatać (spla-tach) v. braid; interlace;interlock;plait

splątać (splown-tach) v. snarl up; mat;ravel;confuse;muddle up

spleśniały (splesh-ńa-wi) adj. m. moldy: musty ;mildewy

splot (splot) m. twine; twist; coil;tangle;plaitcoincidence

splunąć (sploo-nownch) v. spit

spluwaczka (sploo-vach-ka) f. spittoon ;cuspidor

spłacić (spwa-ćheech) v. pay off

spłaszczyć (spwash-chich) v. flatten out; humble (another)

spłata (spwa-ta) f. refund; instalment payment; repayment

spłatać figla (spwa-tach feeg-la) v. play a trick;play a joke

spław (spwav) m. rafting;floating

spławiać (spwav-yach) v. float; get rid;shunt; raft (timber etc.)

spławik (spwa-veek) m. (fishing) float(dipping when fish bites)

spławny (spwav-ni) adj. m. navigable (river, waterway etc.)

spłodzić (spwo-dźheech)v. beget; generate;put out;produce

spłonąć (spwo-nownch) v. burn down;go up in flames; redden

spłonka (spwon-ka) f. percussion cap; primer;detonator

spłoszyć (spwo-shich) v. scare away; frighten;startle; flush

spłowiały (spwo-vya-wi) adj. m. faded (appearance)

spłukać (spwoo-kach) v. rinse; flush;swill out;wash away

spływać (spwi-vach) v. flow (down);drift;float(down stream)

spochmurnieć (spo-khmoor-ńech) v. grow cloudy; gloomy

spocić się (spo-ćheech śhań) v. sweat; become sweaty;prespire

spoczynek (spo-chi-nek) m. rest

spoczywać (spo-chi-vach) v. sit; rest; lie down;be at rest;rest on

spod (spot) prep. form under

spodek (spo-dek) m. saucer

spodenki (spo-den-ki) pl. (knee) pants; shorts

spodlić (spod-leech) v. debase; degrade; disgrace; demean

spodnie (spod-ńe) n. trousers; pants; slacks; breeches

spodobać się (spo-do-bach śhań) v. take a liking; take a fancy

spodziewać się (spo-dźhe-vach śhań)v.expect; hope for

spoglądać (spo-glown-dach) v. look out; look at; contemplate

spoić (spo-eech) v. make drunk; weld; ply with liquor

spoistość (spo-ees-toshch) f. cohesion; compactness; density

spoisty (spo-ees-ti) adj. m. compact;cohesive;dense;tenacious

spojenie (spo-ye-ńe) n. weld; joint; pubic symphysis

spojówka (spo-yoov-ka) f. conjunctiva

spojrzeć (spoy-zhech) v. look; glance at; gaze at;view

spojrzenie (spoy-zhe-ńe) n. glance; look; gaze;peep

spokojny (spo-koy-ni) adj. m. quiet; calm; peaceful;still

spokój (spó-kooy) m. peace;
calm ;quiet;serenity;placidity

spokrewniony (spo-krev-ño-ni)
adj. m. related to; related

spoliczkować (spo-leech-ko-vaćh)
v. slap face

społeczeństwo (spo-we-cheń-stvo)
n. society; public;community

społeczny (spo-wéch-ni) adj. m.
social (evil etc.);public;welfare

społem (spo-wem) adv, together
in common ;jointly; unitedly

spomiędzy (spo-myán-dzi) prep.
from among.;from the midst

sponad (spo-nat) prep. from
above ; from over (the top of...)

sponiewierać (spo-ñe-vye-raćh)
v. abuse; ill-treat; maltreat

spontaniczny (spon-ta-ñeech-ni)
adj. m. spontaneous ; voluntary

sporadyczny (spo-ra-dich-ni)
adj. m. sporadic; occasional

sporny (spor-ni) adj. m. controversial;debatable;questionable

sporo (spo-ro) adv. good deal;
a lot of; briskly;quite a few

sport (sport) m. sport;athletics

sportowiec (spor-tó-vyets) m.
sportsman;athlete;sporting man

spory (spó-ri) adj. m. pretty
big; fast; useful; lasting

sporządzać (spo-zhówn-dzaćh) v.
make up;draw up; make out

sposobić (spo-só-beećh) v. prepare; make ready(colloquial exp.)

sposobność (spo-sób-noshćh) v.
opportunity;occasion;chance

sposobny (spo-sób-ni) adj. m.
convenient; capable; able

sposób (spó-soop) m. means; way

spostrzegać (spo-stzhé-gaćh) v.
notice; perceive;observe;spot

spostrzegawczy (spo-stzhe-gáv-
chi) adj. m. quick to notice;
keen;observant;perceptive

spostrzeżenie (spo-stzhe-zhe-ńe)
n. observation ;awareness;notice

sposród (spó-shrood) prep. from
amongst;from the midst

spotęgować (spo-tán-gó-vaćh) v.
intensify; increase ;strengthen

spotkać (spot-kaćh) v. come
across; meet ;run across;befall

spotkanie (spot-ka-ńe) n. meeting; date; encounter

spotwarzać (spo-tva-zhaćh) v.
calumniate ;defame; slander

spoufalać się (spo-oo-fa-laćh
shań) v. become intimate

spowiadać (spo-vya-daćh) v.
confess; listen to confession

spowiednik (spo-vyed-ñeek) m.
confessor (priest)

spowiedź (spo-vyedzh) f. confession; confided secrets

spowijać (spo-vee-yaćh) v.
swathe; wrap;shroud; cover

spowodować (spo-vo-dó-vaćh) v.
cause ; induce; set off

spoza (spó-za) prep. from
behind;from beyond;from outside

spozierać (spo-zhe-raćh) v.
glance at;look;gaze at

spożycie (spo-zhi-ćhe) n. consumption;intake (food,calories)

spożywać (spo-zhi-vaćh) v. consume; eat; drink; have a meal

spożywca (spo-zhiv-tsa) m. consumer

spożywcze artykuły (spo-zhiv-
che ar-ti-koo-wi) pl, n.
groceries;food products

spód (spoot) m. bottom; foot

spódnica (spood-ñee-tsa) f.
skirt ; petticoat;apron strings

spójnia (spóoy-ña) f. bond;
union; tie; bond; link

spójnik (spóoy-ñeek) m. conjunction

spółdzielczość (spoow-dzhel-
choshćh) f. cooperation

spółdzielnia (spoow-dzhel-ña)
f. coop; cooperative

spółgłoska (spoow-gwos-ka) f.
consonant (grammar)

spółka (spoow-ka) f. partnership; company ;society

spór (spoor) m. strife; dispute

spóźniać się (spoozh-ñaćh shań)
v. be late; be slow;come late

spóźnienie (spoozh-ñe-ńe) n.
delay; late coming;late arrival

spóźniony (spoozh-ño-ni) adj.
m. late ;delayed;belated;tardy

spracować się (spra-tso-vaćh
shań) v. be tired; be exhaust-
ed ; have worked hard

spracowany (spra-tso-va-ni) adj.
m. overworked;exhausted; tired
spragniony (sprag-ño-ni) adj.
m. thirsty;thirsting for
sprawa (spra-va) f. affair; matter; cause; case;question;job
sprawca (sprav-tsa) m. doer;
author; culprit;originator
sprawdzic (sprav-dźheech) v.
verify;examine; test; check
sprawdzian (sprav-dżhan) m.
test; gauge; criterion;template
sprawiac (sprav-yach) v. cause;
bring to pass;occasion;afford
sprawiedliwosc (spra-vyed-lee-
vošhch) f. justice; equity
sprawiedliwy (spra-vyed-lee-vi)
adj. m. just;righteous;fair
sprawka (sprav-ka) f. doing;
trick; small offense; prank
sprawnosc (sprav-ñoshch) f. efficiency; dispatch; skill
sprawny (sprav-ni) adj. m. able;
efficient; deft; dexterous
sprawowac (spra-vo-vach) v. perform;discharge; hold; exercise
sprawowanie (spra-vo-va-ñe) n.
conduct; behavior;performance
sprawozdanie (spra-voz-da-ñe) n.
report; account;statement
sprawozdawca (spra-voz-dav-tsa)
m. reviewer; reporter
sprawunek (spra-voo-nek) m.
purchase(made while shopping)
sprezac (spran-zhach) v. compress; tense;prestress
sprezarka (spran-zhar-ka) f.
compressor; air compressor
sprezenie (spran-zhe-ñe) n.
compression;prestress;pretension
sprezyna (spran-zhi-na) f.
spring; mainspring; impulse
sprezystosc (spran-zhis-toshch)
f. elasticity; energy;resilience
sprezysty (spran-zhis-ti) adj.
m. elastic; springy; energetic
sprostowac (spros-to-vach) v.
rectify; correct; right
sprostowanie (spros-to-va-ñe)
v. rectification;correction
sproszkowac (sprosh-ko-vach) v.
pulverize; levigate;triturate

sprosny (sprošh-ni) adj. m.
obscene; lewd ;foul(language)
sprowadzac (spro-va-dzach) v.
bring; import; fetch; call in
sprochnialy (sprookh-ña-wi)
adj. m. rotten;decayed
sprochniec (sprookh-ñech) v.
rot; decay; moulder;grow carious
spryciarz (spri-chash) m. dodger; trickster; slyboots
spryskac (spris-kach) v. splash
spryt (sprit) m. shrewdness;
cunning; gumption; knack
sprytny (sprit-ni) adj. m.
tricky; clever; cunning; cute
sprzaczka (spzhownch-ka) f.
buckle ;clasp
sprzataczka (spzhown-tach-ka)
f. cleaning woman;charwoman
sprzatac (spzhown-tach) v.
tidy up; clean up; clear up;
pich up; take away;snatch away
sprzatanie (spzhown-ta-ñe) n.
clearing; tidying up;housework
sprzeciw (spzhe-cheev) m. objection; opposition; resistance
sprzeciwiac sie (spzhe-cheev-
yach šhan) v. object; oppose
sprzeczac sie (spzhe-chach
šhan) v. fight; argue; dispute;
squabble; quarrel;contend about
sprzeczka (spzhech-ka) f. quarrel; squable;altercation; tiff
sprzecznosc (spzhech-noshch) f.
contradiction; discrepancy
sprzeczny (spzhech-ni) adj. m.
contradictory; incompatible
sprzedac (spzhe-dach) v. dispose of; sell; trade away
sprzedajny(spzhe-day-ni) adj.
m. venal;corrupt; corruptible
sprzedawca (spzhe-dav-tsa) m.
salesman; shop keeper;dealer
sprzedawczyni (spzhe-dav-chi-
nee) f. saleslady;saleswoman
sprzedaz (spzhe-dash) f. sale
sprzedaz detaliczna (spzhe-
dash de-ta-leech-na) f. retail;sale at retail prices
sprzedaz hurtowa (spzhe-dash
khoor-to-va) f. wholesale
sprzeniewierzenie (spzhe-ñe-
vye-zhe-ñe) n. embezzlement

sprzęgać (spzhan-gach) v. couple; tie; link; team up; connect

sprzęgło (spzhan-gwo) n. clutch; coupling ; coupler;attachment

sprzęt (spzhant) m. implement; furniture; accessories; utensils; tackle; outfit; chattels

sprzyjać (spzhi-yach) v. favor

sprzykrzyć (spzhik-zhich) v. get sick of; get fed up with

sprzymierzeniec(spzhi-mye-zhe-nets) m. ally; confederate

sprzymierzony (spzhi-mye-zho-ni) adj. m. allied;confederated

sprzysięgać się (spzhi-shan-gach shan) v. conspire; plot

sprzysiężenie (spzhi-shan-zhe-ne) n. plot; conspiracy

spuchnąć (spookh-nownch) v. swell

spulchniać (spoolkh-nach) v. fluff up;loosen;cultivate(soil)

spust (spoost) m. release; catch; slip; trigger; appetite; drain

spustoszenie (spoos-to-she-ne) n. devastation; ravage;ruin

spustoszyć (spoos-to-shich) v. devastate; ravage; make havoc

spuszczać (spoosh-chach) v. let down; drop; droop; lower; drain

spuścizna (spoosh-cheez-na) f. inheritance; legacy;heritage

spychacz (spi-khach) m. bulldozer; stripper

spychać (spi-khach) v. push down; relegate; drive away

spytać się (spi-tach shan) v. ask; ask a question

srać (srach) v. shit (vulg.)

srebrnik (srebr-neek) m. silvercoin; silversmith

srebrny (srebr-ni) adj. m. silver; of silver

srebro (sreb-ro) n. silver

srebrzyć (sreb-zhich) v. silverplate ;silver;wash with silver

srebrzysty (sreb-zhis-ti) adj. m. silvery (glow,color etc.)

srogi (sro-gee) adj. m. fierce; cruel; severe; srict; grim

sroka (sro-ka) f. magpie

srokaty (sro-ka-ti) adj. m. piebald (horse) ;with patches

srom (srom) m. disgrace; vulva

sromota(sro-mo-ta)f.shame;ignomity; disgrace

sromotny (sro-mot-ni) adj. m. shameful; disgraceful;infamous

srożyć (sro-zhich) v. rage; torment; storm;oppress;be severe

ssać (ssach) v. suck; exploit

ssak (ssak) m. mammal;mammalian

ssawka (ssav-ka) f. sucker

ssąca pompa (ssown-tsa pom-pa) f. suction pump

stabilizować (sta-bee-lee-zo-vach) v. stabilize; fix

stacja (stats-ya) f. station

stacja benzynowa (stats-ya ben-zi-no-va) f. filling or service station

stacjonować (sta-tsyo-no-vach) v. be stationed;be in garrison

staczać (sta-chach) v. roll down; fight (battle)

staczać się (sta-chach shan) v. roll down; go from bad to worse;be on the down grade

stać (stach) v. stand; be stopped; farewell; ill-afford;rise

stać się (stach shan) v.become; grow; occur; happen

stadion (sta-dyon) m. stadium

stadło (sta-dwo) n. couple

stadnina (stad-nee-na) f. stud

stado (sta-do) n. flock; herd

stagnacja (stag-nats-ya) f. stagnation; recession;stagnancy

stajnia (stay-na) f. stable

stal (stal) f. steel

stale (sta-le) adv. constantly; always; for ever;incessantly

stalownia (sta-lov-na) f. steelmill; steel plant; steel works

stalowy (sta-lo-vi) adj. m. steel; steely; steel gray

stała (sta-wa) f. constant

stałość (sta-woshch) f. stability; firmness; steadiness

stały (sta-wi) adj. m. stable; permanent; solid; fixed;firm

stamtąd (stam-townd) adv. from there; from over there;out of it

stan (stan) m. state; status; condition;order; estate; class

stanąć (sta-nownch) v. stand up; stop at; put up; rise; set foot

standaryzować (stan-da-ri-zo-
vаć) v. standardize

stanik (sta-neek) m. bodice;
bra; brassière;waste; corsage

staniol (stań-yol) m. tin foil

stanowczość (sta-nóv-chośhch)
f. determination; finality

stanowczy (sta-nóv-chi) adj. m.
final; positive; decided ;firm

stanowić (sta-no-veech) v. establish; determine; constitute;; decide; proclaim

stanowisko (sta-no-vees-ko) n.
position; post; status; stand

starać się (sta-rаćh śhań) v.
take care; try one's best

staranie (sta-ra-ńe) n.care;
endeavor; exertion; pains

staranny (sta-rán-ni) adj. m.
careful; accurate; nice;exact

starcie (star-ćhe) n. clash;
collision; friction ; squabble

starczy (star-chi) adj. m. se-
nile; v.:it is enough (exp.)

starczyć (star-chich) v. suffice

starodawny (sta-ro-dáv-ni) adj.
m. old time; ancient;antique

staromodny (sta-ro-mod-ni) adj.
m. old fashioned;outmoded

starosta (sta-ros-ta) m. county-
head; wedding host; foreman

starość (sta-rośhćh) f. old age

staroświecki (sta-rosh-vyéts-
kee) adj. m. old fashioned

starożytność (sta-ro-shít-nośhćh)
f. antiquity; ancient times

starożytny (sta-ro-zhít-ni) adj.
m. ancient; antique ;old world

starszeństwo (star-sheń-stvo) n.
seniority ; superiority

starszy (star-shi) adj. m. old-
er; elder; superior(officer)

starszyzna (star-shiz-na) f. the
elders; the seniors;the chiefs

start (start) m. take-off; start

startować (star-to-vаćh) v.
start; take off; make a start

staruszek (sta-roó-shek) m. old
fellow;old man;old gentleman

stary (sta-ri) adj. m. old

starzec (sta-zhets) m. old man

starzeć się (sta-zhećh śhań) v.
grow old ;age;grow stale;go bad

stateczny (sta-téch-ni) adj.
m. stable; bouyant; staid

statek (sta-tek) m. ship;
craft; vessel;boat;steamship

statki (stat-kee) pl. kitchen
pots & pans

statua (sta-too-a) f. statue

statut (sta-toot) m. statute

statyka (sta-ti-ka) f. statics

statysta (sta-tis-ta) m. supernumerary (actor);dummy;mute

statystyczny (sta-tis-tích-ni)
adj. m. statistical; statistic

statystyka (sta-tis-ti-ka) f.
statistics ;returns

statyw (sta-tiv) m. stand;
support; tripod

staw (stav) m. pond; joint

stawać się (sta-vаćh śhań) v.
become; grow (scarce,big etc.)

stawiać (sta-vyаćh) v. place;
erect; put; stand; offer; lay
down ;post; station;put upright

stawka (stav-ka) f. stake

stąd (stównd) adv. from here;
away;therefore;that is why

stągiew (stówn-gyev) f. vat

stąpać (stówn-páćh) v. pace;
tramp;tread;plod along;lumber

stchórzyć (stkhoo-zhíćh) v.
show fear; shrink with fright

stearyna (ste-a-rí-na) f. stea-
rin (glyceryl tristearate)

stek (stek) m. steak; pile of...
(lies; insults etc.); pack of...

stelmach (stél-makh) m. cart-
wright;wheelwright

stempel (stém-pel) m. stamp;
prop; ramrod; punch; die

stemplowany (stem-plo-vá-ni)
adj. m. cancelled; used

stenograf (ste-nó-graph) m.
stenographer;shorthand writer

stenografia (ste-no-graph-ya)
f. shorthand ;stenography

stenotypistka (ste-no-ti-peest-
ka) f. stenotypist ; steno

step (step) m. steppe

ster (ster) m. helm; rudder

sterczeć (stér-chećh) v. stand
out; stick out; tower; bulge

stereoskop (ste-re-ós-kop) m.
stereoscope

stereotypowy (ste-re-o-ti-po-vi) adj. m. stereotyped
sternik (ster-ńeek) m. pilot
sterować (ste-ro-vach) v. steer
sterta (ster-ta) f. stack
stebnować (stan-bno-vach) v. stitch; quilt
stęchlizna (stan-khleez-na) f. fusty smell; musty smell
stęchły (stankh-wi) adj. m. musty; stale; foul; fusty; frowsty
stękać (stan-kach) v. moan; groan; utter a groan; complain
stępić (stan-peech) v. blunt; dull; take the edge off
stępienie (stan-pye-ńe) n. dullness (of knife; mind etc.)
stęskniony (stan-skńo-ni) adj. m. sick for; yearning for; hankering for; nostalgic
stężały (stan-zha-vi) adj. m. hardened; stiff; concentrated; solidified; coagulated
stężeć (stan-zhech) v. harden; stiffen ; coagulate; concentrate
stężenie (stan-zhe-ńe) n. concentration; strength (solutions)
stłoczyć (stwo-chich) v. cram; compress; jam; squize; pack; pile up
stłuc (stwoots) v. smash; break; bruise; shatter; injure; beat up
stłuczenie (stwoo-che-ńe) n. bruise; break; contusion; injury
stłumiać (stwoom-yach) v. dampen; muffle; deaden; suppress; stifle
sto (sto) num. hundred
stocznia (stoch-ńa) f. shipyard
stodoła (sto-do-wa) f. barn
stoik (sto-eek) m. Stoic
stoisko (sto-ees-ko) n. stand
stojak (sto-yak) m. stand
stojący (sto-yown-tsi) adj. m. standing; stagnant; erect; upright
stok (stok) m. slope; hillside
stokroć (sto-kroch) adv. hundred times; a hundred times; hundredfold
stokrotka (sto-krot-ka) f. daisy
stokrotny (sto-krot-ni) adj. m. hundredfold repeated
stolarnia (sto-lar-ńa) f. joiner's shop; carpinter's shop
stolarz (sto-lash) m. cabinetmaker; joiner; carpenter

stolec (sto-lets) m. stool (large); bowel movement
stolica (sto-lee-tsa) f. capital(of a country)
stolik (sto-leek) m. small table; nice little table
stolnica (stol-ńee-tsa) f. molding board ; paste board
stołeczny (sto-wech-ni) adj. m. metropolitan (taxes); capital (city)
stołek (sto-wek) m. stool
stołować (sto-wo-vach) v. board
stołownik (sto-wov-ńeek) m. boarder
stołówka (sto-woov-ka) f. mess hall; mess; cantine
stonka (ston-ka) f. potato beetle; potato bug; Colorado beetle
stonoga (sto-no-ga) f. centipede; wood louse
stop (stop) m. (metal) alloy; melt; traffic sign :stop; halt
stopa (sto-pa) f. foot; standard
stopa procentowa (sto-pa protsen-to-va) f. interest rate
stopa życiowa (sto-pa zhi-chova) f. living standard
stoper (sto-per) m. stopwatch
stopić (sto-peech) v. melt
stopień (sto-pyeń) m. (stair) step; degree; grade; extent
stopniały (stop-ńa-wi) adj. m. molten away; dwindled; shrunk
stopnieć (stop-ńech) v. melt down; melt away; srink; dwindle
stopniowo (sto-ńo-vo) adv. gradually; little by little
stopniowy (stop-ńo-vi) adj. m. gradual; progressive
stora (sto-ra) f. shade; blind
storczyk (stor-chik) m. orchid
stos (stos) m. (wood) pile
stos atomowy (stos a-to-mo-vi) m. atomic pile
stosować (sto-so-vach) v. use
stosownie (sto-sov-ńe) adv. accordingly; properly
stosowny (sto-sov-ni) adj. m. proper; convenient; opportune
stosunek (sto-soo-nek) m. rate; relation; proportion; attitude
stosunek płciowy (sto-soo-nek pwcho-vi) m. sexual intercourse

stosunki handlowe (sto-soon-kee khand-ló-ve) pl. trade relations ;commercial relations

stosunkowy (sto-soon-kó-vi) adj. m. relative; proportional

stowarzyszenie (sto-va-zhi-she-ńe) n. association; club

stożek (stó-zhek) m . cone

stożkowaty (stozh-ko-vá-ti) adj. m., conical; cone shaped

stóg (stoog) m. stack (rick)

stół (stoow) m. table

stracenie (stra-tse-ńe) n. execution; loss ; doom

straceniec (stra-tse-ńets) m. desperado; madcap

strach (strakh) m. fear; fright

stracić (stra-ćheech) v. lose; execute(a man);shed(teeth etc.)

stragan (stra-gan) m. booth; stand; (market) stall

straganiarz (stra-gá-ńash) m. stand owner; stall holder

strajkować (stray-kó-vach) v. go on strike; strike

strapienie (stra-pyé-ńe) n. worry; distress; heartbreak

strapiony (stra-pyó-ni) adj. m. worried; dejected; distressed

straszak (strá-shak) m. noisy toy pistol; scarecrow; bugaboo

straszliwy (strash-lee-vi) adj. m. horrible; fearsome;awful

straszny (strash-ni) adj. m. awful; terrible;awesome;frightful

straszyc (stra-shich) v. frighten; haunt; threaten; bluff

straszydło (stra-shid-wo) n. scarecrow; fright

strata (stra-ta) f. loss

strategia (stra-tég-ya) f. strategy ;generalship

strategiczny (stra-te-geech-ni) adj. m. strategic

stratny (strát-ni) adj. m. one that lost;being the looser

strawa (stra-ya) f. food ; meal

strawić (stra-veech) v. digest; consume; bear;stomach; stand

strawne (stráv-ne) n. food ration (in the army etc.)

straż (strash) f. guard; watch ; safe custody;strict guard;escort

straż pożarna (strash po-zhar-na) f. fire brigade

straż przednia (strash pzhéd-ńa) f. vanguard ;advance guard

straż tylna (strash til-na) f. rearguard ; rear guard

strażak (stra-zhak) m. fireman

strażnica (strazh-ńee-tsa) f. guardhouse; watchtower

strażnik (strazh-ńeek) m. guard; watchman ;sentry

strącić (strown-ćheech) v. knock off (apples) ; throw down

strączek (strown-chek) m . (small) pod ;hull;husk;legume

strąk (strownk) m. pod;hull;husk

strefa (stre-fa) f. zone ;area

streszczać (stresh-chach) v. sum up; summarize;abbreviate

streszczenie (stresh-ché-ńe) n. resume; summary ;digest

stręczyciel (strań-chi-chel) m. pimp; procurer ; broker

stręczyć (stran-chich) v. procure (women) ; recommend

strofa (stró-fa) f. strophe

strofować (stro-fo-vach) v. reprimand ;admonish;scold;chide

stroić (stro-eech) v. dress up; tune up; make fun ;add beauty

strojny (stróy-ni) adj. m. dressed up; elegant; smart

stromy (stro-mi) adj. m. steep

strona (stró-na) f. side; page; region ; aspect; part; party

stronnictwo (stron-ńeets-tvo) n. party (political)

stronniczy (stron-ńee-chi) adj. m. partial; biased;unfair

stronnik (stron-ńeek) m. partisan; supporter;follower;henchman

strop (strop) m. ceiling ;roof

stropić (stro-peech) v. discourage ; confound; abash;disconcert

stroskany (stros-ka-ni) adj.m. worried; sorrowful; dejected

strój (strooy) m. attire ;dress

stróż (stroosh) m. watchman

strudzony (stroo-dzó-ni) adj. m. weary ; tired;exhausted

strug (stroog) m. plane (tool)

struga (stroo-ga) f. stream; creek ; trickle;flow in streams strugać (stroo-gach) v. whittle

struktura (strook-too-ra) f. structure ;flow; flux;jet;torrents

strumień (stroo-myeń) m. stream;

struna (stroo-na) f. string; chord; wire; (metal)wire

struna głosowa (stroo-na gwo-so-va) vocal cord

strup (stroop) m. scab; crust

struś (stroosh) m. ostrich

strych (strikh) m. attic

strychnina (strikh-nee-na) f. strychnine

stryczek (stri-chek) m. (hanging) rope ;noose;the halter

stryj (striy) m. uncle

stryjeczny brat (stri-yech-ni brat) m. cousin

strzał (stzhaw) m. shot

strzała (stzha-wa) f. arrow

strzaskać (stzhas-kach) v. smash to pieces; shatter

strząsać (stzhown-sach) v. shake off: shake down; flick off

strzec (stzhets) v. guard; protect; watch; keep an eye on

strzelać (stzhe-lach) v. shoot; fire; slap; score; blunder

strzelanie (stzhe-la-ńe) n. shooting (practice); gunfire

strzelanina (stzhe-la-ńee-na) f. gunfire ; shots; gunplay

strzelba (stzhel-ba) f. shotgun

strzelec (stzhe-lets) m. shooter; rifleman; sniper; gunner; scorer

strzelnica (stzhel-ńee-tsa) f. shooting range;rifle range

strzelniczy proch (stzhel-ńee-chi prokh) m. gunpowder

strzemienne (stzhe-myen-ne) n. parting drink;stirrup cup

strzemię (stzhe-myań) n. stirrup

strzepać (stzhe-pach) v. brush off; flick off;shake off(away)

strzęp (stzhańp) m. shred; tatter

strzępić (stzhań-peech) v. shred

strzępić język (stzhań-peech yań-zik) v. wag one's tongue; waste breath;talk nonsense

strzyc (stzhits) v. cut; clip; shear; cut (hair);mow;trim;graze

strzyc uszami (stzhits oo-sha-mee) v. prick up ears

strzykać (stzhi-kach) v.squirt; spray;inject; ache

strzykawka (stzhi-kav-ka) f. syringe; hypodermic syringe

strzyżenie (stzhi-zhe-ńe) n. (hair) cut ; sheep shearing

strzyżony (stzhi-zho-ni) adj. m. cropped; cut; clipped

student (stoo-dent) m. student

studenteria (stoo-den-tér-ya) pl. students ;student folks

studiować (stoo-dyo-vach) v. study ;investigate;peer

studnia (stood-na) f. well

studzić (stoo-dzheech) v. cool down (one's tea,etc.)

studzienny (stoo-dzhen-ni) adj. m. well (shaft;water etc.)

stuk (stook) m. knock ;clutter

stukać (stoo-kach) v. knock; tap; hit;rap;patter;rattle;drum

stulecie (stoo-le-che) n. century ;an age;hundred years

stuletni (stoo-lét-ńee) adj. m. hundred years old ;age old

stulić (stoo-leech) v. press tight; close up; coil up

stwardnieć (stvard-ńech) v. harden; stiffen ;grow callous

stwardniały (stvard-ńa-wi) adj. m. hardened; hard ;sclerotic

stwardnienie(stvard-ńe-ńe) n. hardening; callosity

stwierdzać (stvyer-dzach) v. state; find out; confirm

stwierdzenie (stvyer-dze-ńe) n. statement; ascertainment

stworzenie (stvo-zhe-ńe) n. creature; formation;creation

stworzyciel (stvo-zhi-chel) m. creator; maker(of the world)

stworzyć (stvo-zhich) v. create :produce;set up;compose

Stwórca (Stvoor-tsa) m. Creator; Maker

styczeń (sti-cheń) m. January

styczna (stich-na) f. tangent

styczność (stich-noshćh) f. contact; tangency ;adjacency

stygmat (stíg-mat) m. stigma

stygnąć (stig-nównch) v. cool down; cool off; cool

styk (stik) m. contact; butt

stykać się (sti-kach shan) v.
contact; touch;adjoin;meet

styl (stil) m. style; fashion

stylista (sti-lees-ta) m. styl-
ist

stylistyka (sti-lees-ti-ka) f.
art of composition ;syntax

stylowy (sti-lo-vi) adj. m. stylish; of style;in a given style

stypa (sti-pa) f. wake; funny
confusion; funeral banquet

stypendium (sti-pend-yoom) n.
scholarship; stipend; grant

subiektywny (soo-byek-tiv-ni)
adj. m. subjective

sublokator (soob-lo-ka-tor) m.
lodger ;subtenant

subordynacja (soob-or-di-nats-
ya) f. subordination

subskrypcja (soob-skrip-tsya) f.
subscription

substancja (soob-stan-tsya) f.
substance; matter

subsydiowac (soob-sid-yo-vach)
v. subsidize

subtelnosc (sub-tel-noshch) f.
subtlety; niceness; delicacy

subtelny (soob-tel-ni) adj. m.
subtle;nice;fine;refined

subwencja (soob-ven-tsya) f.
subsidy; grant in aid

suchar (soo-khar) m. dry-bread
ration; cracker; biscuit

sucharek (soo-kha-rek) m. cracker ; biscuit

suchosc (soo-khoshch) f. dryness

suchotnik (soo-khot-neek) m. con-
sumptive

suchoty (soo-kho-ti) pl. consumption; phthisis

suchy (soo-khi) adj. m. dry

sufit (soo-feet) m. ceiling

sugerowac (soo-ge-ro-vach) v.
suggest;allude;hint

sugestia (soo-ges-tya) f. suggestion; motion; proposal

sugestywny (soo-ges-tiv-ni) adj.
m. suggestive(speech etc.)

suka (soo-ka) f. bitch

sukces (sook-tses) m. success

sukcesja (sook-tses-ya) f. succession; inheritance; devolution

sukienka (soo-ken-ka) f. dress

sukiennice (soo-ken-nee-tse)
n. weaver's or draper's market
hall ; cloth hall

sukiennik (soo-ken-neek) m.
draper; clothier

suknia (sook-na) f. gown

sukno (sook-no) n. cloth

sultan (soow-tan) m. sultan

sum (soom) m. sheatfish

suma (soo-ma) f. sum; total;
high mass ;entirety;whole

sumaryczny (soo-ma-rich-ni)
adj. m. summary; total;global

sumienie (soo-mye-ne) n. conscience

sumienny (soo-myen-ni) adj. m.
conscientious;scrupulous

sumowac (soo-mo-vach) v. sum up

sunac (soo-nownch) v. glide;
slide; push; move; skim along

supel (soo-pew) m. knot

surdut (soor-doot) m. frock
coat; overcoat

surogat (soo-ro-gat) m. surro-
gate ; substitute for

surowica (soo-ro-vee-tsa) f.
serum

surowiec (soo-ro-vyets) m.
raw material;staple; rawhide

surowosc (soo-ro-voshch) f.
severity; crudeness ;rigor

surowy (soo-ro-vi) adj. m.
severe; raw ; coarse; harsh

surowka (soo-roov-ka) f. pig
iron;fruit salad;raw hide

susza (soo-sha) f. drought;
dryness ;dry weather

suszarka (soo-shar-ka) f. (hair)
dryer ; desciccator

suszarnia (soo-shar-na) f. dry-
ing shed ;drying plant;kiln

suszka (soosh-ka) f. blotter

suszyc (soo-shich) v. dry

sutanna (soo-tan-na) f. cassock

sutener (soo-te-ner) m. cadet;
souteneur ; bully ;ponce

suterena (soo-te-re-na) f.base-
ment

sutka (soot-ka) f. nipple

suty (soo-ti) adj. m. copious;
abundant ; lavish ;plentiful;rich

suwać (soo-vach) v. shove
suwak (soo-vak) m. slide rule
swada (sva-da) f. eloquence
swar (svar) m. squabble; quarrel;rife;dissension
swarliwy (svar-lee-vi) adj. m.
quarrelsome;cantankerous
swastyka (svas-ti-ka) f. swas-
tica; swastika
swat(svat) m. matchmaker
swatać (sva-tach) v. matchmake
swaty (sva-ti) n. matchmaking
swawola (sva-vo-la) f. anarchy
swawolny (sva-vol-ni) adj. m.
unruly;playful;frolicsome;wilful
swąd (svownd) m. reek; stench
sweter (sve-ter) m. sweater
swędzenie (svan-dzhe-ne) n.
itch; an itch; tingle
swędzić (svan-dzheech) v. itch
swoboda (svo-bo-da) f. freedom;
ease; latitude;liberty
swoboda działania (svo-bo-da
dzha-wa-na) v. freedom to act
swobodny (svo-bod-ni) adj. m.
free; easy;at liberty;loose;lax
swoisty (svo-ees-ti) adj. m.
specific;characteristic
swojski (svoy-skee) adj. m.
homely;familiar;friendly;tame
sworzeń (svo-zheń) m. carriage
bolt; lug bolt;cotter;pin
swój (svooy) pron. his; hers;my;
its;our;your;their;one's own
swój człowiek (svooy chwo-vyek)
m. trustworthy man
sybaryta (si-ba-ri-ta) m. Sy-
barite;sybarite; voluptuary
syberyjski (si-be-riy-skee) adj.
m. Siberian; of Siberia
sycić (si-cheech)v. satiate
syczeć (si-chech) v. hiss
syfon (si-fon) m. siphon
sygnalizować (sig-na-lee-zo-
vach) v. signalize; signal
sygnał (sig-naw) m. signal
sygnatura (sig-na-too-ra) f.
(official) signature
sygnet (sig-net) m. signet;
seal ring; imprint;colophon
syk (sik) m. hiss;sizzle;fizzle
sylaba (si-la-ba) f. syllable

sylogizm (si-lo-geezm)m. syllo-
gism;rozumowanie dedukcyjne
sylweta (sil-ve-ta) f. silhou-.
ette; outline;profile;figure
symbioza (sim-byo-za) f. symbio-
sis:living together
symbol (sim-bol) m. symbol
symboliczny (sim-bo-leech-ni)
adj. m. symbolic ;symbolical
symbolizować (sim-bo-lee-zo-
vach) v. symbolize
symetria (si-metr-ya) f. symmetry
symetryczny (si-me-trich-ni)
adj, m. symmetrical
symfonia (sim-fon-ya) f. symphony
symfoniczny (sim-fo-neech-ni)
adj. m. symphonic
sympatia (sim-pat-ya) f. liking
sympatyczny (sim-pa-tich-ni)
adj. m. congenial;attractive
sympatyk (sim-pa-tik) m. well-
wisher; sympathizer
sympatyzować (sim-pa-ti-zo-vach)
v. like; go along; feel with
symptom (simp-tom) m. symptom
symulacja (si-moo-lats-ya) f.
simulation;make believe;sham
symulować (si-moo-lo-vach) v.
simulate;feign;pretend;affect
syn (sin) m. son
synagoga (si-na-go-ga) f. synagogue
syndykat (sin-di-kat) m. syndi-
cate;syndicat;labor union
synek (si-nek) m. sonny
synekura (si-ne-koo-ra) f.
sinecure; cosy job;fat job
synod (si-nod) m. synod
synonim (si-no-neem) m. synonym
synowa (si-no-va) f. daughter
in law
synowiec (si-no-vyets) m. nephew
syntetyczny (sin-te-tich-ni)
adj. m. synthetic
synteza (sin-te-za) f. synthesis
sypać (si-pach) v. strew; pour;
scatter (dry matter);betray secrets
sypialnia (si-pyal-ña) f. bedroom ;bedroom furniture suite
sypki (sip-kee) adj. m. loose
(dry);granular(substance);friable

sypki towar (syp-kee tó-var) m.
 granular goods; dry goods
syrena (si-re-na) f. siren;
 mermaid;hooter;Warsaw's emblem
syrop (si-rop) m. syrup
syryjski (si-riy-skee) adj. m.
 Syrian; of Syria
system (sís-tem) m. system
systematyczny (sys-te-ma-tich-
 ni) adj. m. systematic; neat
syt (sit) adj. m. satiate; full
sytny (sit-ni) adj. m. filling
 up; nourishing; satiating
sytuacja (si-too-ats-ya) f.
 situation;circumstances;things
sytuować (si-too-o-vać) v. sit-
 uate ; locate; position
sytuowany (si-too-o-va-ni) adj.
 m. situated ; placed;located
syty (si-ti) adj. m. satiate;
 dilled up; well-fed;nourishing
szabla (shab-la) f. sabre
szablon (shab-lon) m. stencil;
 pattern; model; stereotype
szablonowy (sha-blo-nó-vi) adj.
 m. routine; stereotype
szach-mat (shakh-mat) m. check-
 mate (in a chess game etc.)
szachista (sha-khees-ta) m.
 chess player
szachować (sha-kho-vać) v.
 check (in chess); check
szachownica (sha-khov-nee-tsa)
 f. chessboard ;checker board
szachraj (shakh-ray) m. cheat
szachrować (zhakh-ro-vać) v.
 cheat; swindle; jockey
szachy (sha-khi) pl. chess
szacować (sha-tso-vać) v.
 evaluate; estimate ;size up
szacunek (sha-tsoo-nek) m.
 1. valuation; 2. respect
szafa (sha-fa) f. chest; wardrobe; bookcase ; cupboard
szafir (sha-feer) m. sapphire
szafka nocna (shaf-ka nóts-na)
 f. night table;bedside table
szafot (sha-fot) m. (execution)
 scaffold
szafować (sha-fó-vać) v. lavish ; squander;be liberal
szafran (shaf-ran) m. saffron

szajka (shay-ka) f. gang
szakal (sha-kal) m. jackal
szal (shal) m. shawl ;scarf
szala (sha-la) f. scale
szalbierstwo (shal-byer-stvo)
 n. swindle ; fraud;imposition
szalbierz (shal-byesh) m.fraud;
 swindler ; quack ;impostor
szaleć (sha-lech) v. rage ;rave
szalenie (sha-le-ńe) adv. mad-
 ly; terribly;awfully;like mad
szaleniec (sha-le-ńets) m. madman; daredevil ; desperado
szaleńczy (sha-leń-chi) adj. m.
 frantic;mad;insane;reckless
szaleństwo (sha-leń-stvo) n.
 fury; madness ; craze;frenzy
szalik (sha-leek) m. scarf
szalony (sha-ló-ni) adj. m. mad
szał (shaw) m. rage;fury;frenzy
szałas (sha-was) m. tent; shanty ; shed; shelter; chalet;hut
szamotać się (sha-mó-tach shań)
 v. scuffle;.struggle; tussle
szampan (sham-pan) m. champagne
szaniec (sha-ńets) m. bastion
szanować (sha-nó-vach) v. respect; honor; have regard;esteem
szanowny (sha-nóv-ni) adj. m.
 honorable;worthy; dear(sir)
szansa (shán-sa) f. chance
szantaż (shan-tazh) m. blackmail ; extortion
szantażować (shan-ta-zho-vach)
 v. blackmail ;make squeal
szantażysta (shan-ta-zhis-ta)
 m. blackmailer ;extortioner
szarak (sha-rak) m. hare; average man of the street ;yeoman
szarańcza (sha-rań-cha) v. locust ;swarm of locust;swarm
szarfa (shar-fa) f. scarf; sash
szargać (shar-gach) v. besmear;
 foul up; slander; tarnish;slur
szarlatan (shar-la-tan) m. confidence man; charlatan
szarotka (shar-ót-ka) f. edelweiss
szarość (sha-rośhćh) f. greyness;
 drabness ;dullness; duskiness
szarpać (shar-pach) v. jerk; pull;
 tear; tousle ; knock about;assail

szaruga (sha-roo-ga) f. gray,
foul weather; gray skies

szary (sha-ri) adj. m. gray;drab

szarzec (sha-zhech) v. loom;
gray ; grow dusky; show grey

szarzyzna (sha-zhiz-na) f.
grayness; drabness; duskiness

szarża (shar-zha) f. (cavalry)
charge;(military)rank; officer

szarżować (shar-zho-vach) v.
charge (recklessly);overact

szastać (shas-tach) v. squander

szata (sha-ta) f. garment;gown

szatan (sha-tan) m. satan; devil ; very strong coffee

szatański (sha-tań-skee) adj.
m. devilish; infernal;satanic

szatkować (shat-ko-vach) v.
cut; chop ; shred;slice

szatnia (shat-na) f. locker
room; coat room

szatynka (sha-tin-ka) f. dark-
blond girl;auburn haired woman

szczać (shchach) v. piss (vulg.)

szczapa (shcha-pa) f. split log;
splint; chip ; sliver;thin man

szczaw (shchav) m. sorrel

szczątek (shchown-tek) m. remnant; vestige ;fragment

szczebel (shche-bel) m.(ladder)
rung; spoke; grade ;round

szczebiot (shche-byot) m. chatter; chirp;babble;prattle;warble

szczebiotać (shche-byo-tach) v.
chirrup ; chirp; chatter;bable

szczebiotanie (shche-byo-ta-ne)
n. chatter; prattle;chirp;warble

szczecina (shche-chee-na) f.
bristle (of hogs);stubble beard

szczególność (shche-gool-noshch)
f. peculiarity;singularity

szczególny (shche-gool-ni) adj.
m. peculiar; special; specific

szczegół (shche-goow) m. detail

szczegółowy (shche-goo-wo-vi)
adj. m. detailed ; minute

szczekać (shche-kach) v. bark

szczekanie (shche-ka-ne) n. bark

szczelina (shche-lee-na) f. slot;
crevice; cleft ;slit; rift;crack

szczelny (shchel-ni) adj. m.
(water) tight; (air) tight etc.

szczeniak (shche-ńak) m. puppy ; kid ; pup

szczep (shchep) m. graft; tribe;
seedling

szczepić (shche-peech) v. graft;
vaccinate; inoculate

szczepienie (shche-pye-ne) n.
grafting; vaccination

szczepionka (shche-pyon-ka) f.
vaccine

szczerba (shcher-ba) f. jag;
notch; gap ;nick; chip; dent

szczerbaty (shcher-ba-ti) adj.
m.gap-toothed; jagged

szczerbić (shcher-beech) v. jag

szczerość (shche-roshch) f.
sincerity ; open-heartedness

szczerozłoty (shche-ro-zwo-ti)
adj. m. pure golden

szczery (shche-ri) adj. m.
sincere ;frank; candid

szczędzić (shchan-dzheech) v.
spare; economize ;grudge;stint

szczęk (shchank) m. clink; clash;
clang ;jangle; rattle

szczęka (shchan-ka) f. jaw

szczękac (shchan-kach) v.
clink; clang ;jangle;rattle

szczęścic się (shchansh-cheech
shan) v. have good luck

szczęście (shchansh-che) n.
happiness; good luck; success

szczęśliwy (shchan-shlee-vi)
adj. m. happy; lucky ;successful

szczodrość (shchod-roshch) f.
generosity ;open-handedness

szczodry (shchod-ri) adj. m.
generous ;abundant; ample

szczoteczka (shcho-tech-ka) f.
small brush; toothbrush

szczotka (shchot-ka) f. brush

szczotkarski (shchot-kar-skee)
adj. m. brush ;brush maker's

szczotkować (shchot-ko-vach) v.
brush down; bursh;polish(a floor)

szczuć (shchooch) v. hiss; bait;
embitter against ;set dogs on

szczudło (shchood-wo) n. stilt ;
crutch

szczupak (shchoo-pak) m. pike

szczuplec (shchoop-lech) v.
slim down; reduce; diminish

szczupłość (shchoop-wośhch) f.
slimness; scarcity;scantiness

szczupły (shchoop-wi) adj. m.
slim; slender; thin; lean

szczur (shchoor) m. rat

szczycić się (shchi-cheech śhăn)
v. boast; take pride; be proud

szczypać (shchi-pach) v. pinch

szczypce (shchip-tse) pl. tongs;
pliers; pincers; clippers

szczypczyki (shchip-chi-kee) pl.
tweezers; forceps

szczypiorek (shchi-pyo-rek) m.
chive

szczypta (shchip-ta) f. pinch

szczyt (shchit) m. top; summit

szczytny (shchit-ni) adj. m.
lofty; sublime ;commendable

szczytowy (shchi-to-vi) adj.m.
pick; culminant ; uppermost;top

szef (shef) m. boss; chief

szelest (she-lest) m. rustle

szeleścić (she-lesh-cheech) v.
rustle; whisper(in the wind)

szelki (shel-kee) pl. suspenders; straps; belts; braces

szelma (shel-ma) f. rogue;
scoundrel; wretch; knave

szelmostwo (shel-most-vo) n.
roguery;rascally trick

szemrać (shem-rach) v. murmur;
grumble;prattle;repine against

szept (shept) m. whisper

szeptać (shep-tach) v. whisper

szepnąć (shep-nownch) v. whisper; murmur; conspire; scheme

szereg (she-reg) m. row; file;
series;range;chain(of events)

szeregować (she-re-go-vach) v.
rank; classify; arrange

szeregowy (she-re-go-vi) adj.m.
series; soldier in the ranks

szermierka (sher-myer-ka) f.
fencing

szermierz (sher-myesh) m. fencer

szeroki (she-ro-kee) adj. m.
wide;broad; ample; extensive

szerokość (she-ro-koshch) f.
width; latitude; breath

szerokotorowa kolej (she-ro-ko-
to-ro-va ko-ley) f. wide gauge
railroad (Russian)

szerszeń (sher-sheń) m. hornet;
wasp

szerzenie (she-zhe-ne) n. spread

szerzyć (she-zhich) v. spread

szesnasty (shes-nas-ti) num.
sixteenth

szesnaście (shes-nash-che) num.
sixteen

sześcian (shesh-chan) m. cube

sześcienny (shesh-chen-ni) adj.
m. cubic

sześciokrotny (shesh-cho-krot-
ni) adj. m. sixfold

sześcioro (shesh-cho-ro) num.
six

sześć (sheshch) num. six

sześćdziesiąt (sheshch-dzhe-
shownt) num. sixty

sześćdziesiąty (sheshch-dzhe-
shown-ti) adj. m. sixtieth

sześćset (sheshch-set) num.
six hundred

szew (shev) m. seam ;stitch

szewc (shevts) m. shoemaker

szewstwo (shev-stvo) n. shoe-
making;shoemaking;trade

szkalować (shka-lo-vach) v.
slander;defame; calumniate

szkapa (shka-pa) f. jade

szkaradny (shka-rad-ni) adj.m.
hideous; ugly; abominable;nasty

szkarlatyna (shkar-la-ti-na) f.
scarlet fever ;scarlatina

szkarłat (shkar-wat) m. scarlet

szkarłatny (shkar-wat-ni) adj.
m. scarlet;crimson; purple

szkatuła (shka-too-wa) f. casket

szkic (shkeets) m. outline;
sketch; essay; study;draught

szkicować (shkee-tso-vach) v.
sketch; outline; draw up;design

szkicownik (shkee-tsov-neek) m.
sketch pad; sketchbook

szkielet (shke-let) m. skeleton;
framework; shell; carcass

szkiełko (shke w-ko) n. small
glass; pane;slide

szklanka (shklan-ka) f. (drinking)
glass; glassful (of water etc.)

szklany (shkla-ni) adj. m. glass;
glassy(eyes); vitreous

szklarz (shklash) m. glazier

szklić (shkleech) v. glaze;brag
szklisty (shklees-ti) adj. m.
glassy;glazy;vitreous;hyaline
szkliwo (shklee-vo) n. enamel;
glaze;(desert)varnish
szkłó (shkwo) n. glass;pane
szkocki (shkots-kee) adj.m.
Scottish; of Scottland
szkoda (shko-da) f. damage;
harm;detriment;mischief
szkodliwy (shkod-lee-vi) adj.m.
harmful;detrimental;damaging
szkodnik (shkod-ñeek) m. wrongdoer pest;nuisance
szkodzić (shko-dżheech) v. harm;
injure;be harmful;cause damage
szkolenie (shko-le-ñe) n. training;instruction; schooling
szkolić (shko-leech) v. school;
train;give instruction;instruct
szkolnictwo (shkol-ñeets-tvo) n.
school system; education
szkolny (shkól-ni) adj. m.
school; scholastic; school-
szkoła (shko-wa) f. school
szkop (shkop) m. Kraut; Hun(vulg.)
szkopuł (shko-poow) m. obstacle
szkorbut (shkór-boot) m. scurvy
szkuner (shkoo-ner) m. schooner
szkwał (shkvaw) m. squall;flaw
szlaban (shla-ban) m. tollgate ;
barrier;train crossing barrier
szlachcic (shlakh-cheets) m.
squire ; nobleman; gentleman
szlachecki (shla-khets-kee) adj.
m. noble ; gentle; gentleman's
szlachetny (shla-khet-ni) adj.
m. noble ; noble-minded ;elegant
szlachta (shlakh-ta) f. gentry
szlafrok (shlaf-rok) m. house-
robe ; wrapper; dressing gown
szlak (shlak) m. trail; track;
border;route;band;selvage;scent
szlam (shlam) m. slime;ooze;slit
szlem (shlem) m. big slam
(bridge)(card game)
szlemik (shle-meek) m. little
slam (card game,bridge)
szlifa (shlee-fa) f. epaulette
szlifierka (shlee-fyer-ka) f.
grinding machine;grinder
szlifierz (shlee-fyesh) m. pol-
isher; cutter;grinder

szlifować (shlee-fo-vach) v.
polish; burnish;cut(diamonds)
szlochać (shlo-khach) v. sob
szmaciany (shma-cha-ni) adj.
m. rag; made out of rags
szmaragd (shma-ragd) m. emerald; emerald green
szmat (shmat) m. large piece;
long way;a good bit;expanse
szmata (shma-ta) f. clout; rag
szmatławiec (shma-twa-vyets)
m. shabby newspaper; smear
sheet;rag
szmelc (shmelts) m. scrap
szmer (shmer) m. murmur;rustle
szmergiel(shmer-gel)m. emery
szminka (shmen-ka) f. lipstick; paint;rouge;make up
szmugiel (shmoo-gel) m. smuggle;smuggling;contraband
szmuglować (shmoo-glo-vach) v.
smuggle(goods)
szmonces (shmon-tses) m. Jewish
quip or joke; nonsense(slang)
szmuklerstwo (shmook-ler-stvo)
n. haberdashery
szmuklerz (shmook-lesh) m.
haberdasher
sznur (shnoor) m. rope; cord
sznurek (shnoo-rek) m. string
sznurować (shnoo-ro-vach) v.
lace up; lace; tie
sznurowadło (shnoo-ro-vad-wo)
n. shoe lace;lace;shoe string
sznurowany (shnoo-ro-va-ni) adj.
m. laced
sznycel po wiedeńsku (shni-tsel
po vye-deñ-skoo) m. Wiener
cutlet
szofer (sho-fer) m. chauffeur;
driver;(bus)driver;truck driver
szopa (sho-pa) f. shed;lark;fun
szopka (shop-ka) f. puppet show
szorować (sho-ro-vach) v. rub;
scour; scrub; wash;grate;run
szorstki (shorst-kee) adj. m.
coarse; rough; crude; harsh
szorstkość (shorst-koshch) f.
roughness; harshness;bluntness
szosa (sho-sa) f. highway;road
szowinizm (sho-vee-ñeezm) m.
chauvinism
szósty (shoos-ti) adj.m. num.
sixth

szpada (shpá-da) f. sword

szpagat (shpá-gat) m. string; (ballet) split;cord;twine;twist

szpaler (shpá-ler) m. double (tree) row; lane; hedge

szpalta (shpál-ta) f. (newspaper) column;(printer's)slip

szpara (shpá-ra) f. gap; slot; rift;chink;crack;slit;crevice

szparag (shpa-rak) m. asparagus

szpargał (shpár-gaw) m. scrappaper;scrap of paper

szpecić (shpe-cheech) v. disfigure; make ugly;mar beauty

szperacz (shpe-rach) v. ferreter; scout;sniper;searcher

szperać (shpe-rach) v. forage; burrow;poke about;search books

szpetny (shpét-ni) adj. m. ugly

szpic (shpeets) m. spike;peak; (sharp) point;Pomeranian dog

szpicel (shpee-tsel) m. stool pigeon; informer;plainclotheman

szpiczasty (shpee-chás-ti) adj. m. pointed; tapering

szpieg (shpyeg) m. spy; sleuth

szpiegostwo (shpye-gós-tvo) n. espionage ; spying

szpiegować (shpye-gó-vach) v. spy upon;shadow;watch;eavesdrop

szpik (shpeek) m. marrow

szpikować (shpee-kó-vach) v. stuff (meat);lard(meat etc.)

szpilka (speel-ka) f. pin(small)

szpilkowy (shpeel-kó-vi) adj.m. conifer; pegged (soles)

szpinak (shpee-nak) m. spinach

szpital (shpee-tal) m. hospital

szpon (shpon) m. claw; talon

szponder (shpon-der) m. flank (meat); sirloin

szprotka (shprot-ka) f. sprat

szpryca (shpri-tsa) f. syringe

szprycha (shpri-kha) f. spoke

szprycować (shpri-tso-vach) v. sprinkle ; syringe

szpulka (shpool-ka) f. bobbin

szpunt (shpoont) m. plug; stopper; bung ;peg; tongue;feather

szpuntować (shpoon-to-vach) v. bung (barrel) ; plug;peg

szrama (shrá-ma) f. scar

szranki (shrán-kee) pl. lists; bounds; reins;tilt yard;barriers

szreń (shreń) f. neve ; frost

szron (shron) m. hoar-frost; rime; coat of rime

sztab (shtab) m. staff;headquarters

sztaba (shtá-ba) f. bar;(gold) ingot ;ingot(of silver)

sztabowy (shta-bó-vi) adj. m. staff (officer)

sztachety (shta-khé-ti) pl.(picket) fence; railing

sztafeta (shta-fe-ta) f. relay (race); relay race

sztaluga (shta-loo-ga) f. easel

sztanca (shtan-tsa) f. die; stamp ; punch

sztandar (shtan-dar) m. banner

sztokfisz (shtok-fish) m. stockfish; cod; codfish

sztolnia (shtol-ña) f. gallery

sztucer (shtoo-tser) m. rifle (gun); sporting rifle

sztuciec (shtoo-chets) m. fork

sztuczka (shtooch-ka) f. trick; small piece; dodge;manoeuvre

sztuczne tworzywo (shtooch-ne tvo-zhi-vo) n. plastic

sztuczny (shtooch-ni) adj. m. artificial;sham;false;immitation-

sztućce (shtooch-tse) pl. (table) silver;knife,fork and spoons

sztuka (shtoo-ka) f. art; piece; cattlehead; (stage) play;stunt

sztukateria (shtoo-ka-tér-ya) f. stucco work; stucco

sztukować (shtoo-ko-vach) v.piece; patch up; eke out; lengthen

szturchać (shtoor-khach) v. poke; dig; prod; jab; push; jostle

szturm (shtoorm) m. attack; storm; assault ;onslaught

szturmować (shtoor-mo-vach) v. storm; attack; assault; harass

sztych (shtikh) m. stab; engraving ;etching;woodcut; spade

sztyft (shtift) m. tag; pin; peg

sztylet (shti-let) m. stiletto; dagger; poniard; bodkin; spike

sztywnieć (shtiv-ñech) v. stiffen ;grow stiff;become stiff

sztywny (shtiv-ni) adj. m. stiff

szubienica (shoo-bye-nee-tsa)
f. gallows; hanging matter
szubrawiec (shoo-bra-vyets) m.
scoundrel; rascal; rogue
szubrawstwo (shoob-rav-stvo) n.
villainy; rascally trick; rabble
szufla (shoof-la) f. shovel
szuflada (shoof-la-da) f. drawer; shunting; shelving
szuja (shoo-ya) f. scoundrel
szukać (shoo-kach) v. look for;
seek; search; cast about for
szukanie (shoo-ka-ńe) n. search
szuler (shoo-ler) m. gambler
szum (shoom) m. (wind) noise; hum;
roar; uproar; scum; frost
szumieć (shoom-yech) v. buzz;
roar; froth; hum; rustle; fizz
szumny (shoom-ni) adj. m. roar-
ing; boistrous; noisy; frothy
szumowiny (shoo-mo-vee-ni) pl.
scum; scum of the society
szurgać (shoor-gach) v. shuffle
noisily; scrape foot on the floor
szuter (shoo-ter) m. gravel
szwaczka (shvach-ka) f. seamstress; needlewoman
szwadron (shvad-ron) m. squadron; (cavalry) squadron; troop
szwagier (shva-ger) m. brother-
-in-law
szwagierka (shva-ger-ka) f.
sister-in-law
szwajcar (shvay-tsar) m. doorman; (Szwajcar = Swiss)
szwajcarski (shvay-tsar-skee)
adj. m. Swiss; of Switserland
szwalnia (shval-ńa) f. underwear
factory; tailoring shop
szwargot (shvar-got) m. gibberish; jabber; lingo
szwedzki (shvedz-kee) adj. m.
Swedish; of Sweden
szyb (shib) m. shaft; (oil) well
szyba (shi-ba) f. (glass) pane
szybki (shib-kee) adj. m. quick;
fast; prompt; rapid; sharp; smart
szybko (shib-ko) adv. quickly;
fast; promptly; swiftly; apace
szybkość (shib-koshch) f. speed;
velocity; rate; fastness
szybować (shi-bo-vach) v..glide;
soar; tower; sail; plane

szybowiec (shi-bo-vyets) m.
glider (motorless)
szychta nocna (shikh-ta nots-
na) v. night shift
szycie (shi-che) n. sewing
szyć (shich) v. sew; sew up
szydełko (shi-dew-ko) n. crochet needle; crochet hook
szydełkować (shi-dew-ko-vach)
v. crochet
szyderca (shi-der-tsa) m.
scoffer; giber; railer
szyderczy (shi-der-chi) adj.
m. scoffing; sarcastic
szyderstwo (shi-der-stvo) n.
scoff; jeer; sneer; gibe; derision
szydło (shid-wo) n. awl; pricker
szydzić (shi-dzheech) v. scoff
szyfr (shifr) m. code; cipher
szyja (shi-ya) f. neck; bottleneck
szyk (shik) m. order; elegance;
(battle) array; order; formation
szykana (shi-ka-na) f. chica-
nery; vexation; difficulties; style
szykanować (shi-ka-no-vach) v.
vex; chicane; annoy; nag; pick at
szykować (shi-ko-vach) v. make
ready; prepare; get ready
szykować się (shi-ko-vach shań)
v. get ready; be in prospect
szykowność (shi-kov-noshch) f.
elegance; smartness; style; chic
szykowny (shi-kov-ni) adj. m.
smart; elegant; fashionable; chic
szyld (shild) m. sign-board
szyldwach (shild-vakh) m. sentry; military guard
szyling (shi-ling) m. shilling
szympans (shim-pans) m. chim-
panzee
szyna (shi-na) f. rail
szynk (shink) m. bar; saloon; pub
szynka (shin-ka) f. ham
szynkarz (shin-kash) m. barman
szyszak (shi-shak) m. helmet
szyszka (shish-ka) f. (tree)
cone; trobile; bigwig; topdog
ściana (shcha-na) f. wall
ścianka (shchan-ka) f. partition; bulkhead; small wall
ściągać (shchown-gach) v. draw
down or together; cheat in class;
assemble; collect (taxes)

ściągaczka (śhchówn-gach-ka) f. cheat note; crib

ścieg (śhcheg) m. stitch

ściec (śhchets) v. drain off; run off;trickle down; drip

ściek (śhchek) m. sewer; gutter; sink; sewage;drain;sewer;gully

ściekać (śhche-kach) v. drain off; flow down;trickle down

ściemniać (śhchem-ñach) v. dark-en; dim; obscure;dim the lights

ścienny (śhchen-ni) adj. m. mu-ral(painting);wall (map etc.)

ścierać (śhche-rach) v. rub off; dust off;grind down;wear off

ścierka (śhcher-ka) f. duster; rug; kitchen towel;clout

ściernisko (śhcher-nees-ko) n. stubble field; stubble

ściern (śhcherñ) m. stubble

ścierpły (śhcherp-wi) adj. m. numb; gone to sleep

ścierwo (śhcher-vo) n. carrion

ścieśniać (śhcheśh-ñach) v.cramp; tighten;narrow;restrict;close

ścieżka (śhchezh-ka) f. trail; pass ;(foot) pass; alley

ścięcie (śhchan-che) n. behead-ing; cutting off;truncation

ścięgno (śhchang-no) n. tendon

ścięty (śhchan-ti) adj. m. truncated;cut off; beheaded

ścigacz (śhchee-gach) m. tor-pedo boat;motor gun boat

ścigać (śhche-gach) v. chase; pursue;run after;hunt;procecute

ścinać (śhchee-nach) v. cut off; cut down; fell (tree);clip;clot

ścinać się (śhchee-nach śhañ) v. coagulate; congeal;fix;clot;fail

ściółka (shchoow-ka) f. litter bed; litter,bedding;barn litter

ścisk (śhcheesk) m. throng;press; crowd; squeeze ;crush;clamp

ściskać (śhchees-kach) v. com-press; shake (hand); squeeze; embrace;clasp;harass;hamper;hug

ścisłość (śhchees-woshch) f. exactness; accuracy; compact-ness; density; reliability

ścisły (śhchees-wi) adj. m. exact; precise; compact;dense

ściśle (śhcheesh-le) adv. ex-actly;tightly; compactly

ślad (śhlat) m. trace; track; (foot) print; footstep

ślamazara (śhla-ma-za-ra) f. sluggard; slowheaded person

ślamazarny (śhla-ma-zár-ni) adj. m. sluggish

śląski (śhlówns-kee) adj. m. Silesian ;of Silesia

śledczy (śhled-chi) adj. m. inquisitional ; of inquiry

śledzić (śhle-dżheech) v. spy; watch; investigate; observe

śledziona (śhle-dżho-na) f. spleen ; milt

śledziowy (śhle-dzhó-vi) adj. m. herring (oil,salad etc.)

śledztwo (śhledz-tvo) n. investigation ;inquest;inquiry

śledź (śhledzh) m. herring

ślepie (śhlep-ye) n. (animal's) eye ; eye; lights

ślepnąć (śhlep-nównch) v. go blind ;loose one's eyesight

ślepa ulica (śhle-pa oo-lee-tsa) s. dead end street

ślepota (śhle-pó-ta) f. blind-ness ;cecity;lack of foresight

ślepy (śhle-pi) adj. m. blind

ślęczeć (śhlan-chech) v. drag study or reading; drudge; pore; plod; slog away; boggle

śliczny (śhleech-ni) adj. m. pretty; lovely; dandy

ślimacznica (śhlee-mach-ñee-tsa) s. road access ramp;helix

ślimak (śhlee-mak) m. snail

ślina (śhlee-na) f. saliva

śliniak (śhlee-ñak) m. bib

śliski (śhlees-kee) adj. m. slippery ; slimy;scabrous

śliwa (śhlee-va) f. plum tree

śliwka (śhleev-ka) f. plum

śliwowica (śhlee-vo-vee-tsa) f. plum brandy;plum vodka

ślizgacz (śhleez-gach) m.speed-boat; gliding boat

ślizgać się (śhleez-gach śhañ) v. slide; glide; slip; skate

ślizgawka (śhleez-gáv-ka) f. skating rink ;kid's slide

ślizgowiec (śhleez-gó-vyets) m. hydrofoil; gliding boat; speed boat

ślub (śhloob) m. wedding; vow

ślubna obrączka (śhloob-na ob-rówńch-ka) f. wedding ring

ślubny (śhloob-ni) adj. m. nuptial; wedding-(ring);legitimate

ślubować (śhloo-bo-vach) v. vow

ślusarz (śhloó-sash) m. locksmith; ironworker;metal worker

śluz (śhloos) m. slime; phlegm

śluza (śhloo-za) f. sluice

śmiać się (śhmyách śháń) v. laugh;chuckle;scoff;make sport

śmiałek (śhmya-wek) m. daredevil; mad cap

śmiałość (śhmya-woshch) f. boldness;courage;bravery;daring;guts

śmiały (śhmya-wi) adj. m. bold

śmiech (śhmyekh) m. laughter

śmieci (śhmye-chee) pl. rubbish; garbage;rag;shred;scrap;refuse

śmiecić (śhmye-cheech) v. litter; throw litter about

śmiecie (śhmye-che) pl. rubbish; garbage;refuse;litter;scrap

śmieć (śhmyech) m. litter; rag

śmiercionosny (śhmyer-cho-nóśhni) adj. m. lethal; deadly

śmierć (śhmyerch) f. death

śmierdzieć (śhmyér-dźhech) v. stink; smell; reek(of nicotine)

śmiertelnik (śhmyer-tél-ńeek) m. mortal man

śmiertelność (śhmyer-tel-nośhch) f. mortality; deadliness

śmiertelny (śhmyer-tel-ni) adj. m. mortal;deadly;death(throes)

śmieszność (śhmyesh-nośhch) f. comic trait; the ridiculous

śmieszny (śhmyésh-ni) adj. m. funny; ridiculous;comic;absurd

śmieszyć (śhmyé-shich) v. make laugh; cause laughter;amuse

śmietana (śhmye-tá-na) f. sourcream; clotted cream

śmietanka (śhmye-tán-ka) f. cream; flower(of society etc.)

śmietnik (śhmyét-ńeek) m. garbage can; garbage dump

śmiga (śhmee-ga) f. (wind mill) sail

śmigło (śhmeég-wo) n. propeller

śmigłowiec (śhmeeg-wóv-yets) m. helicopter

śniadanie (śhńa-dá-ńe) n. breakfast ; luncheon

śniady (śhńa-di) adj. swarthy; sun-tanned;dusky;tawny

śnić (śhńeech) v. dream (about something);have a dream

śniedź (śhńedźh) f. verdigris

śnieg (śhńeg) m. snow;snowscape

śniegowce (śhńe-góv-tse) pl. snowboots;overshoes; galishes

śnieg pada (śhńeg pa-da) exp.: it snows

śnieżka (śhńezh-ka) f. snowball

śnieżnobiały (śhńezh-no-bya-wi) adj. m. snow-white

śnieżny (śhńezh-ni) adh. m. snowy;snow white; snow-storm; blizzard

śnieżyca (śhńe-zhi-tsa) f. snow-storm; blizzard

śpiący (śhpyówn-tsi) adj. m. sleepy;drowsy;slumberous

śpiączka (śhpyówn-ka) f. sleeping sickness

śpieszyć się (śhpye-shich śháń) v. hurry;hasten;be in a hurry

śpiew (śhpyev) m. song;singing

śpiewaczka (śhpye-vach-ka) f. singer (girl or woman)

śpiewać (śhpyé-vach) v. sing

śpiewak (śhpyé-vak) m. singer

śpiewnik (śhpyev-ńeek) m. songbook; hymn-book

śpiewny (śhpyév-ni) adj. m. melodious; singsong-(accent)

śpioch (śhpyokh) m. sleepy head; lie-abed; slug-abed

śpiwór (śhpee-voor) m. sleeping bag

średni(śhred-ńee) adj. m. average; medium; mean(temperature)

średnica (śhred-nee-tsa) f. diameter; bore; middle register

średnik (śhréd-ńeek) m. semicolon

średnio (śhréd-ńo) adv. average ; medium- ;fairly well

średniowiecze (śhred-ńo-vye-che) n. Middle Ages

średniowieczny (śhred-ńo-vyéch-ni) adj. m. medieval

środa (śhro-da) f. Wednesday

środek (śhro-dek) m. center; middle; measures; means; remedy;midst;inside;agent;medium

środkowy (śhrod-ko-vi) adj. m. central; center-(line);middle

środowisko (śhro-do-vees-ko) n. surroundings; environment;circle

śródmieście (śhrood-myesh-che) n.city center; center of town

Sródziemne morze (śhrood-źhem-ne mo-zhe) n. Mediterranean sea; Mediterranean

śruba(śhroo-ba) f. screw

śrubokręt (śhroo-bo-krant) m. screwdriver; turn-screw

śrut (śhroot) m. (lead) shot

świadczenie (śhvyad-che-ńe) n. benefit; charge; testimony

świadczyć (śhvyad-chich) v. witness;attest;bear witness

świadectwo (śhvya-dets-tvo) n. certificate; bill of health

świadek naoczny (śhvya-dek na-och-ni) exp.:eyewitness

świadomość (śhvya-do-moshch) f. consciousness; awareness

świadomy (śhvya-do-mi) adj.m. conscious; aware; wilful

świat (śhvyat) m. world

światło (śhvyat-wo) n. light

światłomierz (śhvyat-wo-myezh) m. lightmeter ; photometer

światopogląd (śhvya-to-pog-lownd) m. ideology ;outlook on life

światowy (śhvya-to-vi) adj. m. world; worldly;global;society-

świąteczny (śhvyown-tech-ni) adj. m. festive;holiday(mood...)

świątynia (śhvyown-ti-ńa) f. temple;place of worship

świder (śhvee-der) m. drill; auger; bore; borer;perforator

świdrować (śhvid-ro-vach) v. drill;bore;perforate;pierce

świeca (śhvye-tsa) f. candle

świecić (śhvye-cheech) v. light up; shine; glitter; sparkle

świecki (śhvyets-kee) adj. m. secular;mundane;laic;lay

świecki ksiądz (śhvyets-kee kshownts) m. secular priest

świeczka (śhvyech-ka) f. (small) candle

świecznik (śhvyech-ńeek) m. chandelier; candlestick

świergot (śhvyer-got) m. twitter; chirp; warble; chirrup; tweet

świergotać (śhvyer-go-tach) v. chirp;chirrup;warble; tweet

świerk (śhvyerk) m. fir tree

świerkowy (śhvyer-ko-vi) adj. m. fir;spruce; of spruce

świerszcz (śhvyershch) m. cricket; grasshopper

świerzb (śhvyezhb) m. scabies

świerzbieć (śhvyezh-byech) v. itch; be itching

świetlica(śhvyet-lee-tsa) f. reading hall;community center

świetlik (śhvyet-leek) m. fire-bug ;glow worm; skylight;fire fly

świetlny(śhvyetl-ni)adj.m. lighting (gas etc.)

świetność (śhvyet-noshch) f. splendor; magnificence;glamor

świetny (śhvyet-ni) adj. m. splendid ;excellent;first rate

świeżo (śhvye-zho) adv. fresh

świeży (śhvye-zhi) adj. m. fresh; new; recent; fresh;raw;ruddy

święcenie (śhvyan-tse-ńe) n. celebration; blessing ;observance

święcić (śhvyan-cheech) v. celebrate ;keep a holiday; bless

święcone (śhvyan-tso-ne) n. Easter blessed food (Polish style)

święta (śhvyan-ta) pl. holidays

święto (śhvyan-to) n. holiday

świętokradztwo (śhvyan-to-krads-tvo) n. sacrilege

świętoszek (śhvyan-to-shek) m. bigot;sanctimonious hypocrite

świętość (śhvyan-toshch) f. sanctity; holiness; sainthood

święty (śhvyan-ti) adj. m. saint; holy; saintly; pious;sacred

świnia (śhvee-ńa) f. swine;hog;pig

świnić (śhvee-ńeech) v. make a mess; litter up; play dirty

świnka morska (śhveen-ka mor-ska) f. guinea-pig ;cavy

świństwo (śhveen-stvo) n. dirty deed ;meanness;nasty stuff;dross

świsnąć (śhvees-nównch) v.
whistle; pilfer; bolt

świst (śhveest) m. whistle
sound; bullet sound

świstak (śhvees-tak) m. marmot

świstawka (śhvees-táv-ka) f.
whistle

świstek (śhvees-tek) m. scrap
of paper; slip of paper

świt (śhveet) m. daybreak; dawn

świtać (śhvee-tach) v. dawn
(upon) ; rise (of sun or moon)

świtezianka (śhvee-te-źhán-ka)
f. water-nymph

tabaka (ta-bá-ka) f. snuff

tabakierka (ta-ba-kér-ka) f.
snuffbox

tabela (ta-bé-la) f. table;
index; list

tabletka (tab-lét-ka) f. tablet;
pill;blackboard;switchboard;slab;

tablica (tab-lee-tsa) f. board;

tablica rozdzielcza (tab-lee-
tsa roz-dźhél-cha) switchboard

tabliczka mnożenia (tab-leéch-ka
mno-zhe-ña) f. multiplication
table

tabor kolejowy (ta-bor ko-le-
yó-vi) m. rolling stock (r.r.)

taboret (ta-bo-ret) m. taboret

tabu (ta-boo) n. taboo

tabun (ta-boon) m. horse herd

taca (tá-tsa) f. tray; salver

taczki (tách-kee) m. wheelbarrow

tafla (taf-la) f. plate; slab

taić (tá-eech) v. hide; conceal

tajać (tá-yach) v. thaw; melt

tajemnica (ta-yem-nee-tsa) f.
secret; mystery;secrecy

tajemniczy (ta-yem-ñee-chi) adj.
m. mysterious;inscrutable'weird

tajny (táy-ni) adj. m. secret

tak (tak) part. yes; adv. thus;
as;indecl.:like this;so

tak czy tak (tak chi tak) exp.
anyhow ; either way;in any case

taki (tá-kee) adj. m. such

taki sam (tá-kee sam) adj. m.
identical ; similar

takielunek (ta-ke-lóo-nek) m.
rig; rigging; tackle

taksa (ták-sa) f. tariff; rate

taksacja (tak-sáts-ya) f. tax-
appraisal

taksować (tak-só-vach) v. estimate; rate; appraise;value

taksówka (tak-sóov-ka) f. taxi

takt (takt) m. tact

taktowny (tak-tóv-ni) adj. m.
tactful;cosiderate

taktyczny (tak-tích-ni) adj.m.
tactical; political

taktyka (tak-ti-ka) f. tactics

także (ták-zhe) adv. also; too;
as well; likewise; alike

talent (ta-lent) m. talent

talerz (tá-lesh) m. (food)plate;
plateful; disk ;planting scalp

talerzyk (ta-le-zhik) m. small
plate; ski-stick disk; scale

talia (tál-ya) f. waist; card
deck; tackle; middle

talk (tá-lk) m. talcum ;talc

talon (tá-lon) m. coupon

tam (tam) adv. there; yonder

tama (tá-ma) f. dam; dike

tamować (ta-mó-vach) v. dam up;
block ; check; stem; clog

tamtejszy (tam-tey-shi) adj. m.
from there; living there

tamten (tám-ten) pron. that

tamtędy (tam-dé-di) adv. that
way; the other way

tamże (tam-zhe) adv. there in;
in the same place;ay which place

tancerka (tan-tsér-ka) f. dancer ; ballet-dancer; partner

tancerz (tán-tsesh) m. dancer

tandeta (tan-dé-ta) f. trashy
products; shoddy goods

taneczny (ta-néch-ni) adj. m.
dancing ;dance-(step;music etc.)

tangens (tán-gens) m. tangent

tani (tá-ñee) adj. m. cheap

taniec (tá-ñets) m. dance

tanieć (tá-ñech) v. get cheaper; cheapen grow cheaper

taniość (tá-ñośhch) f. cheap-
ness; low prices

tańczyć (tań-chich) v. dance

tankowiec (tan-kó-vyets) m.
tanker

tapczan (táp-chan) m. couch;
convertible bed

tapeta (ta-pé-ta) f. wallpaper
tapicer (ta-pée-tser) m. upholsterer ;upholsterer's shop
taran (ta-ran) m. battering ram
tarapaty (ta-ra-pá-ti) pl.
  trouble; predicament;sad fix
taras (tá-ras) m. terrace
tarasować (ta-ra-só-vach) v.
  block;stand in the way plank
tarcica (tar-chee-tsa) f. deal;
tarcie (tár-che) n. friction;
  frictional resistance
tarcza (tár-cha) f. shield;disk
tarczowa piła (tar-chó-va pee-
  wa) circular saw
tarczyca (tar-chí-tsa) f. thy-
  roid gland
targ (targ) m. country market
targać (tár-gach) v. tear;jerk
targować (tar-gó-vach) v. sell;
  bargain; trade; haggle;deal
tarka (tár-ka) f. rasp; grater
tartak (tár-tak) m. sawmill
taryfa (ta-rí-fa) f. tariff
tarzać się (tá-zhach shan) v.
  wallow;welter; roll(in mud)
tasak (tá-sak) m. chopper;
  cleaver
tasiemiec (ta-she-myets) m.
  tapeworm; cestoid; taenia
tasiemka (ta-shem-ka) f. ribbon;
  tape
tasować (ta-só-vach) v. shuffle
taśma (tásh-ma) f. band; tape
taśma ruchoma (tásh-ma roo-kho-
  ma) f. belt conveyor
tatarka (ta-tár-ka) f. buckwheat
taternik (ta-tér-neek) m. mountain climber;alpinist
tatuować (ta-too-o-vach) v. tattoo; make a tattoo mark
tatuś (tá-toosh) m. daddy;dad
tchawica (tkha-vée-tsa) f. tra-
  chea; windpipe
tchnąć (tkhnownch) v. inspire
tchnienie (tkhñe-ñe) n. breath
tchórz (tkhoosh) m. skunk; coward;craven;poltroon; funk
tchórzliwy (tkhoo-zhlee-vi)
  adj. m. cowardly;chicken-hearted
tchórzostwo (tkhoo-zhoost-vo)
  n. cowardice

teatr (té-atr) m. theatre;the stage
teatralny (te-a-tral-ni) adj.
  m. theatrical; scenic; stage-
techniczny (tekh-ñeech-ni) adj.
  m. technical(terms,school,staff…)
technik (tekh-ñeek) m. technician; engineer; mechanic
technika (tekh-ñee-ka) f. technique; engineering;technology
technologia (tekh-no-lóg-ya) f.
  technology;production engineering
teczka (tech-ka) f. briefcase;
  folder;portfolio;jacket;binder
tegoroczny (te-go-roch-ni)adj.m.
  this year's
teka (té-ka) f. (large) briefcase; portfolio;file;folder
tekst (té-kst) m. text;wording
tekstylny (teks-tíl-ni) adj.m.
  textile;textile-;draper-;clothier-
tektura (tek-tóo-ra) f. cardboard; pasteboard(corrugated)
telefon (te-le-fon) m. telephone;phone;phone receiver
telefonistka (te-le-fo-ñeest-
  ka) f. telephone operator
telefonować (te-le-fo-nó-vach)
  v. ring up; telephone;call up
telegraf (te-le-graph) m. telegraph;telegraph office
telegraficzny (te-le-gra-feech-
  ni) adj. m. telegraphic
telegrafować (te-le-gra-fo-
  vach) v. cable; wire; telegraph
telegram (te-le-gram) m. telegram; cable; wire;cablegram
telepatia (te-le-pát-ya) f. te-
  lepathy;thought transference
teleskop (te-les-kop) m. telescope; telescopic spring
teleskopowy (te-les-ko-pó-vi)
  adj. m. telescopic
telewizja (te-le-veéz-ya) f.
  television; TV
telewizor (te-le-vée-zor) m.
  television set;TV set
temat (té-mat) m. subject
temblak (tém-blak) m. sling
temperament (tem-pe-rá-ment)
  m. temper;nature;mettle
temperatura (tem-pe-ra-tóo-ra)
  f. temperature; fever

temperować (tem-pe-ro-vach) v.
temper; sharpen; mitigate
temperówka (tem-pe-roov-ka) f.
pencil sharpener
tempo (tém-po) n. rate; tempo
temu (té-mu) adv. ago
ten;ta, to (ten, ta, to) m.f.n.
pron. this
ten sam (ten sam) pron. the
same (man, pencil, etc.)
tendencja (ten-den-tsya) f. tendency;inclination;proclivity
tendencyjny (ten-den-tsiy-ni)
adj. m. biased;tedentious
tenis (té-ñees) m. tennis
tenor (té-nor) m. tenor(voice)
tenuta (te-noo-ta) f. land holding; rent;tenure; lease
tenże (tén-zhe) m. pron. the
same (individual etc.)
teolog (te-o-lok) m. theologian
teologia (the-o-lóg-ya) f. theology; Faculty of Theology
teoretyczny (te-o-re-tich-ni)
adj. m. theoretical;speculative
teoretyk (te-o-ré-tik) m. theo-
retician; theorist
teoria (te-ór-ya) f. theory
terapia (te-ráp-ya) f. therapeut-
ics; therapy
teraz (té-ras) adv. now;nowadays
teraźniejszość (te-razh-ney-
shoshch) f. present (time)
teraźniejszy kurs (te-razh-ney-
shi koors) m. present rate
teren (té-ren) m. terrain
terenowy samochód (te-re-no-vi
sa-mó-khood) m. cross-country
car (four wheel drive)
terkotać (ter-ko-tach) v. rattle; clatter;chatter(away)
termin (ter-meen) m. term; apprenticeship;time limit(fixed)
termin ostateczny (ter-meen os-
ta-tech-ni) m. deadline
terminator (ter-mee-ná-tor) m.
apprentice;terminator
terminarz (ter-mee-nash) m. appointment calendar; agenda
terminologia (ter-mee-no-log-
ya) f. terminology;nomenclature
terminowo (ter-mee-nó-vo) adv.
on time;in due time;punctually

termit (ter-meet) m. termite
termometr (ter-mo-metr) m.
thermometer
termos (ter-mos) m. thermos-
bottle;vacuum bottle(flask)
terpentyna (ter-penti-na) f.
turpentine(oil)
terror (ter-ror) m. terror
terroryzować (ter-ro-ri-zo-
vach) v. terrorize; bully
terytorialny (te-ri-tor-yal-
ni) adj. m. territorial
terytorium (te-ri-tor-yoom) n.
territory
testament (tes-ta-ment) m.
testament;(last)will
teściowa (tesh-chó-va) f.
mother-in-law
teść (téshch) m. father-in-law
teza (té-za) f. thesis;argument
też (tesh) adv. also; too;likewise
tęchnąć (tankh-nownch) v. get
musty; grow mouldy;reduce swelling
tęcza (tán-cha) f. rainbow
tęczówka (tán-choov-ka) f. iris
tędy (tán-di) adv. this way
tęgi (tán-gee) adj. m. stout;
strong; solid; fat;big;portly
tęgo (tán-go) adv. stoutly;ably;
amply; mightly;powerfully
tępak (tán-pak) m. dullard
tępić (tán-peech) v. dull;
blunt; destroy; combat; exterminate; oppose;persecute
tępota (tan-pó-ta) f. dullness;
stupidity;obtuseness; stolidity
tępy (tan-pi) adj. m. dull;
point less; slow-witted
tęsknić (tánsk-neech) v. long
(for); yearn ; be nostalgic
tęsknota (tánsk-nó-ta) f. longing ; hankering; nostalgia
tęskny (tánsk-ni) adj. m. melancholy;wietful;longing;yearning
tętent (tán-tent) m. hoof beat
tętnica (tán-tñee-tsa) f. artery
tętnic (tánt-ñeech) v. pulsate
tętno (tánt-no) n. pulse;vibrations
tężec (tán-zhets) m. tetanus
teżec (tán-zhech) v. stiffen;
solidify;set;clot;curdle;coagulate;
grow stronger;acquire vigor

tężyzna (tan-zhiz-na) f. vigor
tkacki (tkats-kee) adj. m. textile; weaver's;of textiles
tkactwo (tkats-tvo) n. weaving
tkacz (tkach) m. weaver (man)
tkać (tkach) v. weave; poke
tkanina (tka-nee-na) f. fabric
tkanka (tkan-ka) f. tissue
tkliwość (tklee-voshch) f. tenderness;love;affection
tkliwy (tklee-vi) adj. m. tender;loving;affectionate;sensitive
tknąc (tknownch) v. touch;size
tkwić (tkveech) v. stick;stay
tlec (tlech) v. smoulder
tlen (tlen) m. oxygen
tlenek (tle-nek) m. oxide
tlic się (tleech shan) v.
smoulder; glow; burn lightly
tło (two) n. background
tłocznia (twoch-na) f. press
tłoczyć (two-chich) v. press;
crowd; print; stamp; crush
tłok (twok) m. piston; crowd
tłuc (twoots) v. pound; hammer;
batter; smash; shatter
tłuczek (twoo-chek) m. pestle
tłuczeń (twoo-chen) m. macadam;
broken stone; road gravel
tłum (twoom) m. crowd;mob;host
tłumacz (twoo-mach)m. interpreter ; translator
tłumaczenie (twoo-ma-che-ne) n.
translation;explanation;excuse
tłumaczyć (twoo-ma-chich) v.
translate; interpret;justify
tłumić (twoo-meech) v. muffle;
put down; dampen;suppress;stifle
tłumik (twoo-meek) m. muffler
tłumny (twoom-ni) adj. m. crowded ; numerous ;populous
tłumok (twoo-mok) m. bundle
tłusty (twoos-ti) adj. m. obese;
fat(meat,pig etc.);podgy; oily
tłuszcz (twooshch) m. fat ;
grease
tłuszcza (twoosh-cha) f. mob
tłuścic (twoosh-cheech) v.
grease; smear with grease
to (to) pron. it; this; that;so
toaleta (to-a-le-ta) f. toilet
toaletowe przybory (to-a-le-to-
ve pzhi-bo-ri) pl. toilet-
articles; cosmetics

toast (to-ast) m. toast
tobół (to-boow), m. pack; bundle
toczony (to-cho-ni) adj. m.
turned; shaped;rounded
toczyć (to-chich) v. roll; machine; wage (war);wheel;carry on
toga (to-ga) f. gown;Roman toga
tok (tok) m. course; progress
tokarka (to-kar-ka) f. lathe
tokarnia (to-kar-na) f. lathe
tokarz (to-kash) m. machinist;
turner; lathe operator
tokować (to-ko-vach), v. toot
tolerancja (to-le-ran-tsya) f.
tolerance;broad-mindedness
tolerować (to-le-ro-vach) v.
tolerate;suffer;stand for
tom (tom) m. volume
ton (ton) m. sound; tone;note
tona (to-na) f. ton(metric etc.)
tonacja (to-nats-ya) f. pitch ;
key ; mode; tone
tonaż (to-nash) m. tonnage
tonąć (to-nownch) v. drown
toń (ton) f. deep (water);
flood;deep sea;depth of water
topaz (to-pas) m. topaz
topic (to-peech) v. drown;thaw;
melt down; smelt (metals);sink
topiel (to-pyel) f. abyss;gulf
topliwy (top-lee-vi) adj. m.
meltable;fusible;liquescent
topniec (top-nech) v. melt
topografia (to-po-gráf-ya) f.
topography;lay of the land
topola (to-po-la) f. poplar
toporek (to-po-rek) m. hatchet
topor (to-poor) m. (big) hatchet; axe; battle axe
tor (tor) m. track;lane;path
tor kolejowy (tor ko-le-yo-vi)
m. rail-track;railroad track
torba (tor-ba) f. bag; bagful
torcik (tor-cheek) m. small
layer cake
torebka (to-reb-ka) f. (hand)
bag; purse; small bag(or pouch)
torf (torf) m. peat
torfowisko (tor-fo-vees-ko) n.
peat bog; turbary
torować (to-ro-vach) v. clear;
pave; clear a path;show the way
torpeda (tor-pe-da) f. torpedo;motor driven rail car

torpedować (tor-pe-do-vach) v.
torpedo; scuttle;obstruct
torpedowiec (tor-pe-do-vyets)
m. torpedo boat
tors (tors) m. torso
tort (tort) m. tort (multi-lay-
er) fancy cake
tortura (tor-too-ra) f. torture
torturować (tor-too-ro-vach) v.
torture;torment;put to torture
totalny (to-tal-ni) adj. m. totalitarian; total;entire
towar (to-var) m. merchandise
towarowy dom (to-va-ro-vi dom)
m. department store
towarzystki (to-va-zhis-kee)
adj- m. sociable; social
towarzystwo (to-va-zhist-vo) n.
company;society;companionship
towarzysz (to-va-zhish) m. companion;pal;associate;camerade
towarzyszka (to-va-zhish-ka) f.
companion(female);associate
towarzyszyć (to-va-zhi-shich) v.
accompany;escort;keep company
tożsamość (tozh-sa-moshch) f.
identity; sameness
tracić (tra-cheech) v. lose;
waste;shed(leaves); execute
tradycja (tra-dits-ya) f. tradition;handing down customs etc
tradycyjny (tra-di-tsiy-ni) adj.
m. traditional
traf (traf) m. happenstance;
chance;luck; coincidence
trafem (tra-fem) adv. by chance
trafiać (traf-yach) v. hit
(target);guess right; home
trafność (traf-noshch) f. accuracy; rightness; soundness
trafny (traf-ni) adj. m. exact;
correct; right; fit; apt
tragarz (tra-gash) m. porter
tragedia (tra-ged-ya) f. tragedy;very sad or tragic event
tragiczny (tra-geech-ni) adj. m.
tragic; disastrous;very sad
tragikomedia (tra-gee-ko-med-
ya) f. tragicomedy
trajkotać (tray-ko-tach) v.
chatter; jabber;rattle;gabble
trak (trak) m. square saw;frame
saw

trakcja (trak-tsya) f. traction
trakt (trakt) m. highway; course
traktat (trak-tat) m. treaty
traktor (trak-tor) m. tractor
traktować (trak-to-vach) v.deal;
treat; negotiate; discuss
trampolina (tram-po-lee-na) f.
spring board; diving board
tramwaj (tram-vay) m. tramway
tramwajarz (tram-va-yash) m.
tramway worker
tran (tran) m. (cod or whale)
oil; cod liver oil
trans (trans) m. trance;ectasy
transakcja (trans-akts-ya) f.
transaction; deal
transatlantycki (trans-at-lan-
tits-kee) adj. m. transatlantic
transformator (trans-for-ma-tor)
m. transformer;converter
transfuzja (trans-fooz-ya) f.
transfusion(of blood etc.)
transmisja (trans-mees-ya) f.
transmission; broadcast
transmitować (trans-mee-to-vach)
v. transmit; broadcast
transparent (trans-pa-rent) m.
(marching) slogans; banner
transport (trans-port) m. transport; haulage; consignment
tranzyt (tran-zit) m. transit
tranzytowy (tran-zi-to-vi) adj.
m. transit-;through(traffic etc.)
trapez (tra-pes) m. trapeze
trapić (tra-peech) v. molest;
pester; worry; annoy; bother
trasa (tra-sa) f. route;(bus)line
trasa podróży (tra-sa pod-roo-
zhi) f. itinerary
tratować (tra-to-vach) v. trample; tred down
tratwa (trat-va) f. raft;float
trawa (tra-va) f. grass
trawić (tra-veech) v. digest
trawienie (tra-vye-ne) n. digestion;consumption
trawnik (trav-neek) m. lawn
trąba (trown-ba) f. trumpet;
trunk (elephant); tornado;
twister;horn;whirlwind; ninny
trąba wodna (trown-ba vod-na) f.
waterspout; wind spout

trąbić (trown-beech) v. bugle;
toot ;hoot; roar; proclaim

trąbka (trownb-ka) f. horn;bugle

trącać (trown-tsach) v. jostle;
elbow; tip; knock; nudge;strike

tracić (trown-cheech) v. jostle;
smell;be fusty;be out of date

trąd (trownd) m. leprosy

trel (trel) m. trill

trelować (tre-lo-vach) v. trill

trema (tre-ma) f. stage fright

trener (tre-ner) m. coach;trainer

trening (tre-neeng) m. training

trenować (tre-no-vach) v. train;
coach; practise(shooting)

trepanacja (tre-pa-nats-ya) f.
trepanation

trepki (trep-kee) pl. sandals

tresować (tre-so-vach) v. train;
tame; drill; break in(horses)

tresura (tre-soo-ra) f. taming;
training(of animals)

treściwy (tresh-chee-vi) adj.m.
concise ; substantial;meaty;pithy

treść (treshch) f. content;jist;
substance; essence;pith;marrow

trębacz (tran-bach) m. trumpeter

trędowaty (tran-do-va-ti) adj.m.
leprous; leper

triumfować (tree-oom-fo-vach) v.
triumph;achieve triumphs;prevail

trochę (tro-khan) adv. a little
bit; a few ;some;awhile;a spell

trociny (tro-chee-ni) pl. sawdust; scraps (of writings etc.)

trofea (tro-fe-a) pl. trophies

trojaki (tro-ya-kee) adj. m.
threefold; triple;treble;triplex

troje (tro-ye) num. three

troki (tro-kee) pl. straps

trolejbus (tro-ley-boos) m.
trolleybus

tron (tron) m. throne;the throne

trop (trop) m. track; trace

tropic (tro-peech) v. track

tropikalny (tro-pee-kal-ni) adj.
m. tropical;of the tropics

troska (tros-ka) f. care; anxiety; worry; concern;solicitude

troskać się (tros-kach shan) v.
care and worry about;be cocerned

troskliwość (tros-klee-voshch)
f. thoughtfulness; care; heed

troskliwy (tros-klee-vi) adj.m.
careful; attentive;thoughtful

troszczyć się (trosh-chich
shan) v. care; be anxious
about ; take care;look after

trotuar (tro-too-ar) m. sidewalk; pavement(for pedestrians)

trójbarwny (trooy-barv-ni) adj.
m. tricolor ;three-colored

trójca (trooy-tsa) f. trinity

trójka (trooy-ka) f. three

trójkąt (trooy-kownt) m.
triangle; set square

trójnasób (trooy-na-soob)
three times as much

trójnik (trooy-neek) m. three-
way (pipe) connection;"T"(-tee)
joint; "Y" joint; wye ; tee

truchtem (trookh-tem) adv. by
jogging ; by trot;at a trot

trucizna (troo-cheez-na) f.
poison; venom

truć (trooch) v. poison; bother
(slang); molest; worry

trud (troot) m. pains; toil

trudnić się (trood-neech shan)
v. occupy oneself;be engaged

trudno (trood-no) adv.with
difficulty; too bad ;hard

trudność (trood-noshch) f.
difficulty; hardshiphandicap

trudny (trood-ni) adj. m.
difficult;hard;tough;laborious

trudzić (trood-dzheech)v. trouble; disturb; cause trouble

trujący (troo-yown-tsi) adj. m.
poisonous; toxic; poison-

trumna (troom-na) f. coffin

trunek (troo-nek) m. drink

trup (troop) m. corpse;cadaver

trupiarnia (troop-yar-na) f.
mortuary; morgue

truskawka (troos-kav-ka) f.
strawberry

truteń (troo-ten) m. drone

trwać (trvach) v. last; persist; stay; remain;linger on

trwały (trva-wi) adj. m. durable

trwanie (trva-ne) n. duration

trwoga (trvo-ga) f. awe; fright

trwonić (trvo-neech) v. waste;
squander; trifle away; fritter
away (money,time, energy etc.)

trwoźliwy (trvozh-leé-vi) adj.
m. timid; fearful; shy

trwożny (trvozh-ni) adj. m.
anxious; fearful; timid;shy

trwożyć (trvo-zhich) v. startle;
frighten; scare;be frightening

tryb (trib) m. manner; mode;
mood; gear; procedure;course

trybuna (tri-boo-na) f. tribune;
stand; speaker's platform

trybunał (tri-boo-naw) m.tribunal

trychina (tri-khee-na) f. trichina; trichinosis

trygonometria (tri-go-no-metr-ya)
f. trigonometry(spherical etc.)

tryk (trik) m. 1.ram(ing);2.trik

trykot (tri-kot) m. tricot

trykotowy (tri-ko-to-vi) adj.m.
tricot; made of tricot

trykotaże (tri-ko-ta-zhe) pl.
hosiery; knittings

trykotowy (tri-ko-to-vi) adj.m.
knitted(goods,fabric,wear etc.)

trylion (tril-yon) num. trillion

tryskać (tris-kach) v. spurt;
spout; gush ;jet;squirt;flow

trywialny (tri-vyal-ni) adj.m.
trivial; vulgar; coarse; trite

trzask (tzhask) m. crack ; bang

trzaska (tzhas-ka) f. chip(wood)

trzaskać (tzhas-kach) v. crack;
bang ; smash; shatter;knock;hit

trząść (tzhownshch) v. shake

trzcina (tzhchee-na) f. cane;
reed(of bamboo etc.)

trzcina cukrowa (tzhchee-na
coo-kro-va) f. sugar cane

trzcinowy (tzhchee-no-vi) adj.
m. cane(chair);made out of cane

trzeba (tzhe-ba) v. imp. ought
to;one should ___[gut;geld

trzebić (tzhe-beech) v. clear;

trzeci (tzhe-chee) num. third

trzeć (tzhech) v. rub; grate

trzepaczka (tzhe-pach-ka) f.
whisk; beater;carpet beater

trzepać (tzhe-pach) v. hit
dust out ; beat(carpet); slap

trzepnąć (tzhep-nownch) v. hit;
crump; strike;spank;slap;wag

trzepotać (tzhe-po-tach) v.
flap; flutter;flicker; toss

trzeszczeć (tzhesh-chech) v.crack;
crackle;creak;crunch:rustle

trzewia (tzhev-ya) pl. bowels;guts

trzewik (tzhe-veek) m. shoe;slipper

trzeźwic (tzheźh-veech) v. sober up;bring back to consciousness

trzeźwość (tzheźh-voshch) f.
sobriety;level-headedness

trzeźwy (tzheźh-vi) adj. m.
sober;clear headed;wide awake

trzęsawisko (tzhań-sa-vees-ko)
n. bog;swamp;quagmire;slough

trzęsienie ziemi (tzhań-she-ne
źhe-mee) n. earthquake

trzmiel (tzhmyel) m. bumblebee

trznadel (tzhna-del) m. yellow
bunting;yellow hammer;bunting

trzoda (tzho-da) f. herd;
flock; heard(of swine,pigs etc.)

trzon (tzhon) m. handle; hilt;core

trzonek (tzho-nek) m. shaft;shank;
handle(of a hammer, axe etc.)

trzonowy ząb (tzho-no-vi zownb)
m. molar; grinder

trzpień (tzhpyeń) m. pin

trzpiot (tzhpyot) m. giddy; gay

trzustka (tzhoost-ka) f. pan-
creas; sweetbread

trzy (tzhi) num. three

trzydziestokrotny (tzhi-dzhes-
to-krot-ni) adj. m. thirtyfold

trzydziestoletni (tzhi-dzhes-to-
let-nee) adj. m. thirty year
old(man,oak,house,horse etc.)

trzydziesty (tzhi-dzhes-ti) num.
thirtieth

trzydzieści (tzhi-dzhesh-chee)
num. thirty

trzykrotny (tzhi-krot-ni) adj.
m. threefold

trzylampowy (tzhi-lam-po-vi)
adj. m. three-lamp

trzyletni (tzhi-let-nee) adj.
m. three year old(boy,car etc.)

trzymać (tzhi-mach) v. hold;
keep;cling;clutch;hold on to

trzynasty (tzhi-nas-ti) num.
thirtcenth

trzynaście (tzhi-nashche) num.
thirteen

trzypiętrowy (tzhi-pyań-tro-vi)
adj. m. three-story high(house)

trzysta (tzhís-ta) num.
three hundred
tu (too) adv. here;in here
tuba (too-ba) f. tube;horn
tubka (toób-ka) f. small tube
tuberkuliczny (too-ber-koo-
leéch-ni) adj. m. tuberculous
tubylczy (too-bíl-chi) adj. m.
native;indigenous; local
tubylec (too-bí-lets) m. native;
aboriginal; local inhabitant
tucznik (tóoch-ñeek) m. porker
tuczyc (too-chích) v. fatten
tulejka (too-léy-ka) f. socket
tulic (too-leéch) v. hug; fondle
tulipan (too-lée-pan) m. tulip
tułacz (too-wach) m. wanderer;
vagrant ;exile ;homeless wander-er
tułaczka (too-wách-ka) f. homeless wandering;wandering life
tułac się (too-wach shañ) v.
wander;be homeless;be in exile
tułów (tóo-woov) m. torso
tum (toom) m. cathedral;minster
tuman (too-man) m. 1. dust-cloud;
2. dummie;nitwit;duffer
tunel (too-nel) m. tunnel
tupac (too-pach) v. stamp;tramp
tupet (too-pet) m. nerve;chutz-
pah; self-assurance;impudence
tur (toor) m. bison; aurochs
turbina (toor-beé-na) f. turbine
turecki (too-réts-kee) adj. m.
Turkish(saddle,fashion etc.)
turkawka (toor-káv-ka) f. turtledove;wild dove
turkot (toor-kot) m. rumble;rattle
turkotac (toor-ko-tach) v.
rumble ;bump along; rattle
turkus (toor-koos) m. turquoise
turniej (toor-ñey) m. tournament
turysta (too-ris-ta) m. tourist
turystyczny (too-ris-tích-ni)
adj. m. tourist; touring-
tusz (toosh) m. 1. shower; hit;
2. India ink;mascara
tusza (too-sha) f. corpulence
tuszowac (too-shó-vach) v.
1. draw with ink; 2. cover up;
hush up; stifle (a scandal etc.)
tutaj (too-tay) adv. here
tutejszy (too-téy-shi) adj. m.
local;of this place;of our place

tuzin (too-zheen) m. dozen
tuż (toosh) adv. near by;
close by; just before;just after
tuż obok (toosh o-bok) adv.
next too; near by: close by
twardniec (tvárd-ñech) v. hard-
en; stiffen; fix; bind
twardosc (tvar-doshch) f. hardness ; stiffness; severity
twardy (tvar-di) adj. m. hard
twarożek (tva-ró-zhek) m. cottage cheese;small cottage cneese
twarog (tvá-roog) m. cottage
cheese curds; cottage cheese
twarz (tvash) f. face;physionomy
twarzowy (tva-zhó-vi) adj. m.
becoming; facial(bone etc.)
twierdza (tvyér-dza) f. fortress ; stronghold ;citadel
twierdzący (tvyer-dzown-tsi)
adj. m. affirmative(answer etc.)
twierdzenie (tvyer-dzé-ñe) n.
affirmation; theorem;assertion
twierdzic (tvyér-dźheech) v.
assert; maintain ;affirm; say
twornik (tvor-ñeek) m. armature
tworzyc (tvo-zhích) v. create;
form; compose; produce; make
tworzywo sztuczne (tvo-zhi-vo
shtooch-ne) n. plastic
twoj (tvooy) pron. yours; your
twor (tvoor) m. creation; piece
of work ; origination;outgrowth
tworca (tvoor-tsa) m. creator;
author; maker ;originator
tworczosc (tvoor-choshch) f.
creation;output ;production
tworczy (tvoor-chi) adj. m.
creative ; originative;formative
ty (ti) pron. you(familiar form)
tyczka (tích-ka) f. pole; perch
tyczyc się (ti-chích shañ) v.
concern; regard;refer to
tyc (tich) v. grow fat
tydzień (ti-dźheń) m. week
tyfus (ti-foos) typhus
tygiel (ti-gel) m. crucible
tygodnik (ti-god-ñeek) m.
weekly (magazine etc.)
tygodniowy (ti-god-ño-vi) adj.
m. weekly (pay etc.)
tygrys (tíg-ris) m. tiger ;type
of German tank in World War II

tygrysica (tig-ri-sheé-tsa) f.
tigeress

tyka (ti-ka) f. perch: pole

tyka miernicza (ti-ka myer-née-
cha) f. surveyor's rod [affect;

tykać (ti-kach) v. touch; tick;
tykwa (tik-va) f. pumpkin [strike

tyle (ti-le) adv. so much; as
many; as much; so many: that much

tylekroć (ti-le-kroch) adv. so
many times: that many times

tylko (til-ko) adv. only: but: just
tylko co (til-ko tso) adv. just
now: a moment ago: this instant

tylna straż (til-na strash) f.
rear guard

tylny (til-ni) adj. m. back;
hind(leg etc.): rear (light etc.)

tył (tiw) m. back; rear; stern

tym lepiej (tim le-pyey) adv.
so much better

tymczasem (tim-cha-sem) adv.
meantime: during ; at the time

tymczasowo (tim-cha-só-vo) adv.
provisionally: temporarily

tymczasowy (tim-cha-só-vi) adj.
m. temporary; provisional

tynk (tink) m. plaster(work)

tynkować (tin-ko-vach) v.
plaster· rough cast (a wall)

tynktura (tink-too-ra) f. tincture; tinge; light color

typ (tip) m. type ; model; guy

typowy (ti-pó-vi) adj. m. typical; standard(article etc.)

tyrada (ti-rá-da) f. tirade

tyran (ti-ran) m. tyrant; bully

tyrania (ti-rán-ya) f. tyranny

tyrański (ti-rań-skee) adj. m.
tyrannical; tyrannous; bullying

tysiąc (ti-shownts) num. thousand

tysiąclecie (ti-shownts-le-che)
n. millennium

tysiącletni (ti-shownts-let-ńi)
adj. m. millenary

tysięczny (ti-shanch-ni) num.
thousandth

tytan (ti-tan) m. titan; tita-
nium ; demon(of work etc.)

tytaniczny (ti-ta-neech-ni) adj.
m. titanic ; huge

tytoniowy (ti-to-nó-vi) adj. m.
tobacco ; of tobacco leaves

tytoń (ti-toń) m. tobacco

tytularny (ti-too-lár-ni) adj.
m. titular; nominal

tytuł (ti-toow) m. title

tytułowa strona (ti-too-wo-va
stro-na) f. title page

tytułować (ti-too-wo-vach) v.
entitle; address; style as a...

u (oo) prep. beside; at; with;
by; on; from; in; (idiomatic)

u boku (oo bo-koo) exp.: at one's
side (to have a helper, a sabre...)

ubarwić (oo-bar-veech) v. color

ubawić się (oo-bá-veech shań)
v. have fun; have a good laugh

ubezpieczać (oo-bez-pye-chach)
v. insure; secure; protect

ubezpieczalnia (oo-bez-pye-chál-
ńa) f. health insurance center; insurence company

ubezpieczenie (oo-bez-pye-che-
ńe) n. insurance; protection

ubezpieczenie życia (oo-bez-pye-
che-ńe zhi-cha) n. life insurance; life assurance

ubezpieczenie społeczne (oo-bez-
pye-che-ńe spo-wéch-ne) n.
social security insurance

ubiec (oo-byets) v. run; pass

ubiegać się (oo-byé-gach shań)
v. solicit; compete for

ubiegły (oo-byeg-wi) adj. m.
past; last (year, week etc.)

ubierać (oo-bye-rach) v. dress

ubijaczka (oo-bee-yach-ka) f.
stamper; compactor; kitchen whisk

ubijać (oo-bee-yach) v. stamp;
churn; chip; kill; pack; ram

ubijać interes (oo-bee-yach
een-te-res) v. strike a bargain; strike a deal

ubikacja (oo-bee-kats-ya) f.
toilet; rest room; powder room; W.C.

ubiór (oob-yoor) m. attire; grab

ubliżać (oo-blee-zhach) v. insult ; offend; affront

ubliżający (oo-blee-zha-yown-
tsi) adj. m. offensive; insulting;
disparaging

uboczny produkt (oo-boch-ni
pró-dookt) m. byproduct

ubogi (oo-bo-gee) adj. m. poor

ubolewać (oo-bo-le-vach) v, deplore; feel sympathy for...

ubolewanie (oo-bo-le-va-ńe) n, regret; lamentation;sympathy

ubożeć (oo-bo-zhech) v. become poor; become impoverished

ubój (oo-booy) m. slaughter

ubóstwiać (oo-boost-vyach) v. idolize; love;be crazy about

ubóstwo (oo-boost-vo) n. poverty;destitution;meagerness

ubość (oo-booshch) v. gore

ubrać (oob-rach) v. dress

ubranie (oob-ra-ńe) n. clothes; decoration:putting in a fix

ubytek (oo-bi-tek) m. decrease

ubytek krwi (oo-bi-tek krvee) blood loss

ubywać (oo-bi-vach) v. retire; go; lessen; reduce; decrease

ucałować (oo-tsa-wo-vach) v. kiss (good night,good bye etc.)

ucho (oo-kho) n. ear; handle; (needle) eye;ring(of anchors)

uchodzić (oo-kho-dźheech)v. go away; flee; pass (for)

uchodźca (oo-khodzh-tsa) m. refugee;displaced person

uchować (oo-kho-vach) v. save; preserve;save;retain;keep;rear

uchronić (oo-khro-ńeech) v. guard; preserve;protect;keep

uchwalać (oo-khva-lach) v. pass a law ; resolve; decide

uchwała (oo-khva-wa) f. resolution; vote; law

uchwycić (oo-khvi-chich) v. grasp; catch; seize; see ;get

uchwyt (ookh-vit) m. handle

uchwytny (oo-khvit-ni) adj.m. graspable; palpable;audible

uchybiać (oo-khib-yach) v. fail; offend ; transgress

uchybienie (oo-khi-byé-ńe) n. offense; transgression;insult

uchylać (oo-khi-lach) v. put aside ; half-open; set ajar

uciążliwy (oo-chown-zhlee-vi) adj. m. burdensome ; heavy

ucichać (oo-chee-khach) v. calm down ; be hushed;abate

uciecha (oo-ché-kha) f. joy

ucieczka (oo-chéch-ka) f. escape ; flight; desertion;recourse

ucieleśnić (oo-che-lésh-ńeech) v. embody ; personify

uciekać (oo-che-kach) v. flee

uciemiężać (oo-che-myań-zhach) v. oppress ; burden;tread down

ucierać (oo-che-rach) v. wipe off; grind ; grate; level;pound

ucierpieć (oo-cher-pyech) v. suffer ; be hard hit;sustain a loss

ucieszny (oo-chesh-ni) adj. m. funny ; comical; droll;amusing

ucieszyć (oo-che-shich) v. gladden ; please; gratify ; delight

uciąć (oo-chee-nach) v. cut off

ucisk (oo-cheesk) m. oppression

uciskać (oo-chees-kach) v. press; pinch; opress ; hurt ;compress

uciszyć (oo-chee-shich) v. silence ; quiet; still; soothe;lull

uciułać (oo-choo-wach) v. scrape together ; save ;put aside

uczcić (ooch-cheech) v. honor; dignify ; celebrate ;commemorate

uczciwy (ooch-chee-vi) adj. m. honest ; upright; straight

uczelnia (oo-chel-ńa) f. school; college ; academy ;university

uczenie (oo-che-ńe) adv. learnedly ; n. learning ; teaching

uczennica (oo-chen-ńee-tsa) f. schoolgirl;(girl) pupil

uczeń (oo-cheń) m. schoolboy

uczepić (oo-che-peech) v. hang on ; hitch; hook; attach;fasten

uczesać (oo-che-sach) v. comb (hair);brush hair;dress hair

uczesanie (oo-che-sa-ńe) n. hairdo; hairstyle; coiffure

uczestniczyć (oo-chest-ńee-chich) - v. take part; share in;participate

uczestnik (oo-chest-ńeek) m. participant;(sport)competitor

uczęszczać (oo-chansh-chach) v. frequent; attend(concerts,school...)

uczony (oo-cho-ni) m. scientist; learned; erudite; scholarly man

uczta (ooch-ta) f. feast;banquet

uczucie (oo-choo-che) n. feeling

uczuciowy (oo-choo-cho-vi)adj. m. sensitive ; emotional;sentimental

uczuć (oo-chooch) v. feel ;realize

uczyć (oo-chich) v. teach; train
uczyć się (oo-chich shan) v.
learn; study; take lessons
uczynek (oo-chi-nek) m. deed
uczynić (oo-chi-neech) v. make
uczynność (oo-chin-noshch) f.
kindness ; helpfulness
uczynny (oo-chin-ni) adj. m.
obliging ; helpful ;cooperative
udany (oo-da-ni) adj. m. successful; put on; sham
udar słoneczny (oo-dar swo-
nech-ni) m. sunstroke
udaremnić (oo-da-rem-neech) v.
frustrate; foil; upset; defeat
udawać (oo-da-vach) v. pretend
udawać się(oo-da-vach shan)v.go;
succeed;manage;pan out;make for
udeptać (oo-dep-tach) v. tread
down; beat a path ;tread on
uderzać (oo-de-zhach) v. hit
uderzenie (oo-de-zhe-ne) n.
blow; stroke; hit; bump;impact
udo (oo-do) n. thigh
udobruchać (oo-do-broo-khach)
v. appease; win over; coax
udogodnić (oo-do-god-neech) v.
facilitate; improve
udoskonalenie (oo-dos-ko-na-le-
ne) n. perfection;improvement
udoskonalić (oo-dos-ko-na-leech)
v. perfect; improve
udostępnić (oo-dos-tanp-neech)
v. give access;put within reach
udowodnić (oo-do-vod-neech) v.
prove; demonstrate;substantiate
udowodnienie (oo-do-vod-ne-ne)
n. evidence; proof;demonstration
udręka (ood-ran-ka) f. anguish;
torment; distress; worry
udusić (oo-doo-sheech) v. strangle; smother; stifle; throttle
udział (oo-dzhaw) m. share;
part; quota;participation
udziałowiec (oo-dzha-wo-vyets)
m. shareholder; partner
udzielać (oo-dzhe-lach) v.
give; grant; furnish; apply
udzielenie (oo-dzhe-le-ne) n.
giving; granting;dispensing
ufać (oo-fach) v. trust;confide
ufność (oof-noshch) f. confidence; trust; reliance

ufny (oof-ni) adj. confident;
trustful;hopeful;reliant;sanguine
ufundować (oo-foon-do-vach) v.
found; set up ;endow;establish
uganiac się (oo-ga-nach shan)
v. chase after;seek(graces,job...)
ugaszczać (oo-gash-chach) v.
entertain ; treat; feast;treat to
uginać (oo-gee-nach) v. bend-
down; deflect; inflect;bow before
ugłaskać(oog-was-kach) v. tame
ugniatać (oog-ña-tach) v. press-
down ; exert pressure; pinch
ugoda (oo-go-da) f. agreement
ugodowiec (oo-go-do-vyets) m.
compromiser;advocate of conciliation
ugodowy (oo-go-do-vi) adj.m.
conciliatory ; amicable
ugodzić (oo-go-dzheech)v.hit;hire
ugór (oo-goor) m. fallow
ugryźć (oog-rishch) v. bite off
ugrzeznać (oo-gzhañz-nownch)
v. stick; be stuck; get bogged
uiszczenie (oo-eesh-che-ne) n.
payment(of a bill,rent etc.)
uiścić (oo-eesh-cheech) v. pay
up ; remit(a sum); acquit(a debt)
ujadać (po-ya-dach) v. yelp;quarrel
ujarzmić (oo-yazh-meech) v.
subdue ; enslave ; enthrall;
subjugate
ujawniać (oo-yav-nach) v. reveal ; disclose;expose;unmask;show
ująć (oo-yownch) v. conceive;
deduct ; seize; grasp; lessen;win
ujednolicić (oo-yed-no-lee-
cheech) v. standardize ;unify
ujemny (oo-yem-ni) adj. m.
negative(value,etc.);unfavorable
ujeżdżać (oo-yezh-dzhach) v.
break in (a horse);smooth(a road)
ujeżdżalnia (oo-yezh-dzhal-ña)
f. riding school ;manege
ujęcie (oo-yañ-che) n. grasp
ujma (ooy-ma) f. detraction
ujmować (ooy-mo-vach) v. seize
restrain;embrace;apprehend;express
ujmujący (ooy-moo-yown-tsi) adj.
m. winsome;egaging;prepossessing
ujrzeć (ooy-zhech) v. see;glimpse
ujście (ooysh-che) n. escape;
(river) mouth;withdrawal;retreat;
outlet;issue;vent (to indignation)

ukamienⁿwaⁿ (oo-ka-mye-no-vach) v. stone to death; lapidate

ukazac (oo-ka-zach) v. show (appear) ; exhibit; reveal

ukąsic (oo-kown-sheech) v. bite

ukąszenie (oo-kown-she-ne) n. bite ; sting

uklęknąc (oo-klank-nownch) v. genuflect; kneel down

układ (ook-wat) m. scheme; agreement; disposition ;system

układac się (ook-wa-dach shan) v. lay down; negotiate;pan out

układanka (oo-kwa-dan-ka) f. jigsaw puzzle;building blocks

układny (ook-wad-ni) adj. m. polite; urbane; affable;mannerly

ukłon (ook-won) m. bow (greeting)

ukłonic się (oo-kwo-neech shan) v. bow; tip one's hat ; greet

ukłucie (oo-kwoo-che) n. prick; sting ; sharp pain; prod;twinge

ukochac (oo-ko-khach) v. take a fancy ; grow fond; hug

ukochana (oo-ko-kha-na) adj. f. beloved ; darling; pet (female)

ukochany (oo-ko-kha-ni) adj. m. beloved ; darling; pet (male)

ukoic (oo-ko-eech) v. soothe

ukojenie (oo-ko-ye-ne) n. relief ; consolation;allevivtion

ukonczyc (oo-kon-chich) v. complete; finish ; end (school etc.)

ukos (oo-kos) m. slant ; incline

ukosny (oo-kosh-ni) adj. m. oblique ; sloping; skew; diagonal

ukracac (oo-kra-tsach) v. curb; subdue ; reform; check;put an end

ukradkiem (oo-krad-kem) adv. stealthily ; by stealth;furtively

ukraiński (ook-ra-een-skee) adj. m. Ukrainian; of Ukraine

ukrajac (oo-kra-yach) v. cut off

ukręcic (ook-ran-cheech) v. twist off ; roll up; wrench off

ukrop (ook-rop) m. boiling water ; feverish bustle

ukrocic (oo-kroo-cheech) v. repress; curb; reform;put an end to

ukrycie (ook-ri-che) n. hiding place ; hideaway; hideout;cover

ukrywac (oo-kri-vach) v. hide; cover up ; conceal; hold back

ukryty (ook-ri-ti) adj. m. hidden; concealed;put out of sight

ukrywac (ook-ri-vach) v. hide

ukształtowac (ook-shtaw-to-vach) v. shape; fashion; cast

ukształtowanie (oo-kshtaw-to-va-ne) n. configuration; formulation ; form; shape

ukuc (oo-kooch) v. hammer out

ul (ool) m. beehive ; hive

ulac (oo-lach) v. pour off; cast(metal);pour off water

ulatac (oo-la-tach) v. fly off

ulatniac się (oo-lat-nach shan) v. evaporate; volatize; vanish ; melt away; leak; escape

ulatywac (oo-la-ti-vach) v. fly away; leak (vapors; odors, smells) ; rise in the air

uleczalny (oo-le-chal-ni) adj. m. curable; remediable; medicable

uleczenie (oo-le-che-ne) n. cure; successful recovery

uleczyc (oo-le-chich) v. heal

ulegac (oo-le-gach) v. yield

ulegly (oo-leg wi) adj. m. submissive; docile; compliant

ulepszac (oo-lep-shach) v. improve; better; ameliorate

ulepszenie (oo-lep-she-ne) n. improvement; amelioration

ulewa (oo-le-va) f. rainstorm

ulewac (oo-le-vach) v. pour off; cast (metals);pour(water)

ulga (ool-ga) f. relief;solace

uleżec się (oo-le-zhech shan) v. mellow; settle;lie quiet

ulica (oo-lee-tsa) f. street

uliczka (oo-lech-ka) f. lane

ulicznica (oo-leech-nee-tsa) f. prostitute; streetwalker

ulicznik (oo-leech-neek) m. gamin; guttersnipe ;nipper

ulitowac się (oo-lee-to-vach shan) v. have pity;take pity

ulotka (oo-lot-ka) f. hand - bill ; leaflet;throwaway

ultimatum (ool-tee-ma-toom) n. ultimatum;final order(demand)

ultrafioletowy (ool-tra-fyo-le-to-vi) adj. m. ultraviolet

ulubieniec (oo-loo-bye-nets) n. favorite ; darling; pet

ulubiony (oo-loo-byo-ni) adj.
m. beloved;favorite; pet
ulżyc (ool-zhićh) v. relieve
ułamać (oo-wa-mać) v. break
off ; be broken off;come off
ułamek (oo-wa-mek) m. fraction;
fragment;mathematical fraction
ułamkowy (oo-wam-ko-vi) adj.m.
fractional(number,report etc.)
ułan (oo-wan) m. uhlan (Polish
light cavalryman (lancer)
ułaskawić (oo-was-ka-veećh) v.
pardon(a condemned person)
ułaskawienie (oo-was-ka-vyé-ñe)
n. pardon; reprieve
ułatwić (oo-wat-veećh) v. facilitate; simplify;make easier
ułatwienie (oo-wat-vyé-ñe) n.
facilitation; simplification
ułomność (oo-wóm-noshćh) f. de-
formity; defect ; frailty
ułomny (oo-wóm-ni) adj. m. disabled; defective; lame;faulty
ułożony (oo-wo-zhó-ni) adj.m.
arranged; well-mannered; set
umacniać (oo-mats-ñać) v.
strengthen; fortify; secure
umaczać (oo-ma-chach) v. dip;
wet; soak; sop;have hand in;
umarły (oo-már-wi) adj. m. deceased; dead
umartwiać (oo-márt-vyach) v.
mortify(a person)
umarzać (oo-ma-zhać) v. amortize; discontinue ; remit
umawiać się (oo-mav-yach śhäñ)
v. make a date (or plan)
umeblować (oo-meb-lo-vać) v.
furnish; fit out; fit up
umeblowanie (oo-meb-lo-va-ñe)
n. furniture ;furnishings
umiar (oóm-yar) m. moderation
umiarkowany (oo-myar-ko-va-ni)
adj. m. moderate; temperate
umieć (oó-myech) v. know how
umiejętność (oo-mye-yáñt-noshćh)
f. science; skill; know how
umiejscowić (oo-myey-stsó-veećh)
v. locate; assign a place;place
umierać (oo-myé-rach) v. die
umieszczać (oo-myésh-chach) v.
place; put; set;insert;seat

umilać (oo-mee-lać) v. make
pleasant; add charm;give charm
umilknąć (oo-meelk-nównch) v.
fall silent ; cease talking
umiłowany (oo-mee-wo-va-ni) adj.
m. beloved ; favorite; dear
umizgać się (oo-meez-gach śhäñ)
v. flirt; woo; court; ogle
umizgi (oo-meez-gee) pl. flirt-
ing ; courtship; love making
umniejszać (oo-mney-shach) v.
diminish; lessen; belittle;abate
umocnić (oo-mots-ñeećh) v.
strengthen; fortify; beef up
umocnienie (oo-mots-ñe-ñe) n .
consolidation; fortification
umocować (oo-mo-tsó-vach) v.
fasten; hitch; fix; secure
umorzyć (oo-mó-zhićh) v. absolve;
amortize; extinguish
umowa (oo-mó-ya) f. contract
umowny (oo-móv-ni) adj. m.
contractual; conventional
umożliwić (oo-mozh-leé-veećh)
v. make possible; enable
umówić ≈ umawiać
umundurowanie (oo-moon-doo-ro-
va-ñe) n. uniforms; uniform
umyć (oó-mićh) v. wash up
umykać (oo-mi-kać) v. run away
umysł (oó-misw) m. mind; intellect
umysłowy (oo-mis-wó-vi) adj.m.
mental; intellectual; brain-
umyślnie (oo-mishl-ñe) adv. on
purpose ; specially; purposely
umyślny (oo-mishl-ni) adj. m.
intentional; deliberate;special
umywać się (oo-mi-vać śhäñ) v.
wash up; be fit for comparison
umywalnia (oo-mi-wal-ña) f.
washbasin ; washroom;washstand
unaocznić (oo-na-óch-ñeećh) v.
make evident; visualize
unarodowić (oo-na-ro-dó-veećh)
v. nationalize;put to state control;
unarodowienie (oo-na-ro-do-vye-
ñe) nationalization
uncja (oón-tsya) f. ounce
unia (oóñ-ya) f. union
unicestwić (oo-ñee-tses-tveećh)
v. annihilate ; frustrate

unicestwienie (oo-ñee-tses-tvye-ñe) n. annihilation;frustration

uniemożliwić (oo-ñe-mozh-lee-veech) v. make impossible

unieruchomić (oo-ñe-roo-kho-meech) v. immobilize ; tie up

unieszkodliwić (oo-ñe-shkod-lee-veech) v. render harmless

unieść (oo-ñeshch) v. lift up

uniewaźnić (oo-ñe-vazh-ñeech) v. annul ; void; cancel; repeal

uniewaźnienie (oo-ñe-vazh-ñe-ñe) n. annulment; invalidation

uniewinnić (oo-ñe-veen-ñeech) v. acquit;exculpate; excuse

uniewinnienie (oo-ñe-veen-ñe-ñe) n. acquittal

uniezależnić (oo-ñe-za-lezh-ñeech) v. make independent

uniform (oo-ñee-form) m. uniform

unikać (oo-ñee-kach) v. avoid; shun; steer clear;abstain from

unikat (oo-ñee-kat) m. unique item; rare specimen;curiosity

uniwersalny (oo-ñee-ver-sal-ni) adj. m. universal;versatile

uniwersytet (oo-ñee-ver-si-tet) m. university

uniżać się (oo-ñee-zhach shañ) v. humble oneself;be servile

uniżony (oo-ñee-zho-ni) adj.m. humble ; servile; cringing

unormować (oo-nor-mo-vach) v. normalize; regulate:regularize

unosić (oo-no-sheech) v. carry up; lift off;bear (a weight)

unowocześnić (oo-no-vo-chesh-ñeech) v. modernize

uodpornić (oo-od-por-ñeech) v. immunize; harden; inure

uogólnić (oo-o-gool-ñeech) v. generalize (rules,observations)

uogólnienie (oo-o-gool-ñe-ñe) n. generalization

uosabiać (oo-o-sa-byach) v. personify;embody;typify

uosobienie (oo-o-so-bye-ñe) n. personification;embodiment

upadać (oo-pa-dach) v. fall down; collapse; topple over

upadek (oo-pa-dek) m. fall;drop

upadłość (oo-pad-woshch) f. bankruptcy ; insolvency

upadły (oo-pad-wi) adj. m. fallen; bankrupt; insolvent

upajać (oo-pa-yach) v. intoxicate; elate; fuddle ; make drunk

upalny dzień (oo-pal-ni dzheñ) m. hot day :very hot day

upał (oo-paw) m. (intense) heat

upaństwowić (oo-pan-stvo-veech) v. nationalize: socialize

upaństwowienie (oo-pan-stvo-vye-ñe) n. nationalization

uparty (oo-par-ti) adj. m. stubborn; obstinate;pigheaded

upatrywać (oo-pa-tri-vach) v. look for; suspect; perceive

upełnomocnić (oo-pew-no-mots-ñeech) v. give powers (of attorney); empower; commission

upewnić (oo-pev-ñeech) v. assure ; reassure ; make sure

upić się (oo-peech shañ) v. get drunk; be intoxicated

upierać się (oo-pye-rach shañ) v. persist; insist; stick to

upinać (oo-pee-nach) v. fasten on; pin up; tie(one's hair)

upiór (oo-pyoor) m. ghost

upiorny (oo-pyor-ni) adj. m. ghostly;weird;nightmarish;ghastly

upłynnienie (oo-pwin-ñe-ñe) n. make fluid;flux; liquefaction

upływ (oop-wiv) m. run off; (blood) loss; lapse; expiration

upływać (oo-pwi-vach) v. flow away; pass; lapse; go by;flow

upłynąć (oo-pwi-nownch) v. elapse; pass; expire ;sail away

upodobać (oo-po-do-bach) v. take a liking ; take to; fancy

upodobanie (oo-po-do-ba-ñe) n. liking; fancy; predilection for

upodobnić się (oo-po-dob-ñeech shañ) v. assimilate; conform to

upoić (oo-po-eech) v. intoxicate; make drunk; elate

upojenie (oo-po-ye-ñe) n. inebriation; rapture ;intoxication

upokorzenie (oo-po-kozhe-ñe) n. humiliation; abasement

upokorzyć (oo-po-ko-zhich) v. humiliate ;make eat crow;abase

upominać (oo-po-mee-nach) v. admonish; warn; scold;rebuke

upominek (oo-po-mee-nek) m.
gift; souvenir;present;token
uporać się (oo-po-rach shan)
v. get over;cope with;negotiate
uporczywy (oo-por-chi-vi) adj.
m. stubborn;obstinate;severe
uporządkować (oo-po-zhownd-ko-
vach) v. put in order;tidy up
uposażenie (oo-po-sa-zhe-ne)
n. pay; allowance;salary;wages
uposażyć (oo-po-sa-zhich) v.
endow; give allowance
uposledzenie (oo-poshle-dze-ne)
n. handicap(mental,physical etc.)
uposledzony (oo-po-shle-dzo-ni)
adj. m. feebleminded;deprived
upoważnic (oo-po-vazh-neech) v.
authorize;commission;entitle
upoważnienie (oo-po-vazh-ne-ne)
n. authorization;full powers
upowszechniac (oo-pov-shekh-
nach) v. put into general use
upór (oo-poor) m.
upragniony (oo-prag-no-ni) adj.
m. desired; longed for
upraszać (oo-pra-shach) v. request; beg; beseech
uprawa (oo-pra-va) f. culture;
cultivation;agriculture;tillage
uprawiac (oo-prav-yach) v.
cultivate;till(the soil)
uprawnic (oo-prav-neech) v. entitle; qualify; legalize
uprawniony (oo-prav-no-ni)
adj. m. entitled
uprosic (oo-pro-sheech) v. get
by begging; persuade;ask to do
uproscic (oo-prosh-cheech) v.
simplify; reduce; cancel
uprowadzic (oo-pro-va-dzheech)
v. abduct; kidnap;lead away
uprzątać (oo-pzhown-tach) v.
clean up; tidy up;put away;kill
uprząż (oop-zhownsh) f. harness;
(horse) ;gear of draught animals
uprzedni (oo-pzhed-nee) adj.
m. previous;prior;foregoing
uprzedzac (oo-pzhe-dzach) v.
anticipate; warn; have bias
uprzedzenie (oo-pzhe-dze-ne) n.
anticipation; prejudice;notice
uprzedzony (oo-pzhe-dzo-ni) adj.
m. prejudiced; forewarned

uprzejmosc (oo-pzhey-moshch) f.
polite kindness;courtesy
uprzejmy (oo-pzhey-mi) adj.m.
kind ; polite; nice; suave;affable
uprzemysłowic (oo-pzhe-mi-swo-
veech) v. industrialize
uprzemysłowienie (oo-pzhe-mi-
swo-vye-ne) n. industrializa-
tion ;development of industry
uprzykrzyc się (oo-pzhik-zhich
shan) v. get fed up with
uprzystepnic (oo-pzhis—tanp-
neech) v. facilitate; make
available; make accessible
uprzytomnic (oo-pzhi-tom-neech)
v. realize; impress upon (sb)
uprzywilejowany (oo-pzhi-vee-le-
yo-va-ni) adj. m. privileged
upuscic (oo-poosh-cheech) v.
let fall;let drop; bleed
upychac (oo-pi-khach) v. staff;
pack tight;cram;ram; fill
urabiac (oo-rab-yach) v. fashion
uraczyc (oo-ra-chich) v. treat
uradowac (oo-ra-do-vach) v.
gladden ; delight; rejoice
uradzic (oo-ra-dzheech) v. agree
decide; resolve; contrive
uran (oo-ran) m. uranium
urastac (oo-ras-tach) v. grow
uratowac (oo-ra-to-vach) v.
save ; salvage; rescue
uraz (oo-ras) m. injury; complex; resentment; grudge
uraza (oo-ra-za) f. grudge;
rancor; soreness; ill feeling
urazic (oo-ra-zheech) v. hurt;
offend ; wound sb's feelings
uragac (oo-rown-gach) v. insult
uregulowac (oo-re-goo-lo-vach)
v. stettle; put in order; pay
urlop (oor-lop) m. leave; fur-
lough ; vacation; holiday
urna (oor-na) f. urn;ballot box
uroczy (oo-ro-chi) adj. m.
charming;enchanting ;delightful
uroczystosc (oo-ro-chis-toshch)
f. celebration; festivity
uroczysty (oo-ro-chis-ti) adj.
m. solemn; ceremonial;festive
uroda (oo-ro-da) f. beauty;
loveliness; attraction; charm

urodzaj (oo-ró-dzay) m. good
harvest ;abundance; harvest;crop
urodzajny (oo-ro-dzáy-ni) adj.
m. fertile; fecund
urodzenie (oo-ro-dze-ńe) n.
birth
urodzić (oo-ro-dźheećh)v. give
birth ; breed; bear; yield
urodziny (oo-ro-dźhee-ni)n.
birthday ; birth
urodzony (oo-ro-dzó-ni) adj.
m. born ; born and bred
uroić (oo-ro-eećh) v. imagine
urojenie (oo-ro-ye-ńe) n.
fiction; fancy; illusion
urojony (oo-ro-yo-ni) adj.m.
imaginary; abstract; fictitious
urok (oo-rok) m. charm; spell
uronić (oo-ró-neećh) v. shed;
drop; let fall; lose;shed;miss
urozmaicenie (oo-roz-ma-ee-tse-
ńe) n. variety; diversity;change
urozmaicić (oo-roz-ma-ee-ćheećh)
v. diversify; vary ;while away
uruchomić (oo-roo-khó-meećh) v.
start; put in motion;set going
urwać (oor-vach) v. tear off;
pull off; wrench away; deduct
urwis (oor-vees) m. urchin
urwisko (oor-vees-ko) n. precipice; crag; cliff ; steep rock
urwisty (oor-vees-ti) adj. m.
steep; precipitous; abrupt
urywek (oo-ri-vek) m. fragment
urząd (oozh-ownt) m. office
urzadzać (oozh-own-dzáćh) v.
arrange; settle; set up
urządzenie (oo-zhówn-dze-ńe) n.
furniture; installation;gear
urzec (oo-zhets) v. enchant;
bewitch; fascinate;cast a spell
urzeczywistnić (oo-zhe-chi-
veést-ńeećh) v. make real;fulfil
urzeczywistnienie (oo-zhe-chi-
veest-ńe-ńe) n. realization
urzędnik (oo-zhánd-ńeek) m.
official; white-collar worker
urzędowanie (oo-zhań-do-va-ńe)
n. office hours;clerical duties
urzędowy (oo-zháń-do-vi) adj.
m. official(document,capacity...)
urzynać (oo-zhi-nach) v. cut off

usadowić się (oo-sa-dó-veećh
śhań) v. sit or settle down
uschły (oós-khwi) adj. m.
dried up; withered;wasted away
usiąść (oo-śhównśhćh) v. sit
down; take a seat;perch;alight
usidłać (oo-śheed-wach) v.
entrap; ensnare ;enmesh;inveigle
usilny (oo-śheel-ni) adj.m.
strenuous; intense; pressing
usiłować (oo-śhee-wó-vach) v.
strive; try hard; attempt
usiłowanie (oo-śhee-wo-va-ńe)
n. attempt; efford; endeavor
uskarżać się(oos-kár-zhaćh śhań)
v.complain; grumble (about...)
uskutecznić (oo-skoo-tech-
ńeećh) v. bring about;effect
usłuchać (oo-swoo-khach) v.
follow order (advice);obey
usługa (oo-swoo-ga) f. service;
favor; good turn; help
usługiwać (oo-swoo-gée-vaćh)
v. wait on; serve;attend
usłużyć (oo-swoo-zhićh) v.
do a service; do a good turn
usnąć (oo-snównćh) v. fall
asleep; go to sleep
uspokoić(oo-spo-kó-eećh) v.
calm down; soothe; set at ease
uspołecznić (oos-po-wéch-ńeećh)
v. socialize; civilize;collectivize
usposobić (oos-po-so-beećh) v.
dispose; predispose; incline
usposobienie (oos-po-so-bye-
ńe) n. disposition;temper;mood
usprawiedliwić (oos-pra-vyed-
leé-veećh) v. justify;explain
usprawiedliwienie (oos-pra-
vyed-lee-vyé-ńe) n. excuse;
apology; plea; reason;justification
usprawnić (oos-práv-ńeećh) v.
rationalize; make efficient
usta (oós-ta) n. mouth; lips
ustalenie (oo-sta-lé-ńe) n.
determination; settlement
ustalić (oo-stá-leećh) v. determine; settle; fix; set
ustały (oo-stá-wi) adj. m.
settled (fluid)
ustanawiać (oo-sta-ná-vyaćh)
v. constitute; enact; set up

ustanowienie (oo-sta-no-vye-ńe) n. instituting; establishing

ustatkować się (oo-stat-ko-vach shań) v. settle down

ustawa (oo-sta-ya) f. law; rule

ustawać (oo-sta-vach) v. cease; be weary; hardly stand

ustawiać (oo-stav-yach) v. arrange; place; put; set up

ustawiczny (oo-sta-veech-ni) adj. m. constant; continual

ustawienie (oo-sta-vye-ńe) n. dispositon; installation

ustawodawca (oo-sta-vo-dav-tsa) m. legislator

ustawodawstwo (oo-sta-vo-dav-stvo) n. legislation

usterka (oo-ster-ka) f. defect

ustęp (oos-tańp) m. restroom; paragraph ; passage

ustępliwy (oos-tań-plee-vi) adj. m. yielding ; compliant

ustępować (oos-tań-po-vach) v. yield ;withdraw; recede;cease

ustępstwo (oos-tańp-stvo) n. concession;meeting half way

ustnik (oost-neek) m. mouthpiece

ustny (oost-ni) adj. m. oral; verbal; spoken

ustosunkowany (oo-sto-soon-ko-va-ni) adj. m. influential

ustrój (oos-trooy) m. structure; government system; organism

ustrzec (oos-tzhets) v. guard; avoid; safeguard ;protect from

usunięcie (oo-soo-nań-che) n. removal; withdrawal

usuwać (oo-soo-vach) v. remove

usychać (oo-si-khach) v. wither

usypać (oo-si-pach) v. pile up; pour out; pour off (sand etc.)

usypiać (oo-sip-yach) v. put to sleep;lull to sleep;send to sleep

uszanować (oo-sha-no-vach) v. respect; spare(life etc)

uszanowanie (oo-sha-no-va-ńe) n. respect; respects

uszczelka (oosh-chel-ka) f. gasket;seal; packing

uszczelniać (oosh-chel-ńach) v. pack; caulk; stop(a leak etc.)

uszczęśliwić (oosh-chan-shlee-veech) v. make happy ;delight

uszczerbek (oosh-cher-bek) m. harm ; damage; loss

uszczuplić(oosh-choop-leech) v. curtail; reduce ;lessen

uszczypliwy (oosh-chip-lee-vi) adj. m. sarcastic; biting

uszko (oosh-ko) m. (small) ear; (needle) eye ; ravioli

uszkodzenie (oosh-ko-dze-ńe) n. damage; injury ;imperment

uszkodzić (oosh-ko-dzheech) v. damage ;injure; impair; spoil

uszny (oosh-ni) adj. m. ear

uścisk dłoni (oósh-cheesk dwo-ńe'e)m.handshake

uścisnąć (oosh-chees-nownch) v. embrace; grasp;hug;squeeze(hand)

uśmiać się (oosh-myach shań) v. laugh heartily;have a good lough

uśmiech (oosh-myekh) m. smile

uśmiechać się (oosh-mye-khach shań) v. smile; give a smile

uśmiercić (oosh-myer-cheech) v. kill ; put to death

uśmierzyć (oosh-mye-zhich) v. calm down;mitigate;alleviate

uśpić (oosh-peech) v. put to sleep; anesthetize ;etherize

uświadomić (oosh-vya-do-meech) v. instruct; initiate;realize

uświadomienie (oosh-vya-do-mye-ńe) n. consciousness;information

uświetnić (oosh-vyet-ńeech) v. give prestige; add splendor

utaić (oo-tá-eech) v. conceal

utajony (oo-ta-yo-ni) adj.m. secret ; latent; potential

utalentowany (oo-ta-len-to-va-ni) adj. m. talented ; gifted

utarczka (oo-tarch-ka) f. skirmish; encounter; squabble

utarg (oo-tark) m. receipts ; take ; takings

utargować (oo-tar-go-vach) v. make a bargain; realize

utarty (oo-tar-ti) adj. m. usual; well-worn;wide spread

utęsknienie (oo-tańs-khe-ńe-ńe) n. longing; earnest desire

utknąć (oot-knownch) v. get stuck stall; stick fast; get to a stop

utlenić (oo-tle-ńeech) v. oxidize(metals);peroxidize(hair)

utłuc (oót-woots) v. pound;
bruise;crush; pestle;mash;grind
utonąć (oo-to-nównch) v. be
drowned ; sink;be lost
utopia (oo-top-ya) f. Utopia
utopic (oo-tó-peech) v. sink;
drown (an animal etc.)
utorować (oo-to-ró-vach) v.
clear a path; show the way
utożsamić (oo-tozh-sa-meech) v.
identify with
utracić (oo-tra-ćheech) v.loose;
waste ; forfeit a right(etc)
utracjusz (oo-tráts-yoosh) m.
spendthrift; squanderer
utrapienie (oo-trap-ye-ńe) n.
worry; torment; nuisance
utrata (oo-trá-ta) f. loss
utrącać (oo-trówn-tsach) v.
chip; knock of; blackball
utrudniać (oo-trood-ńach) v.
make difficult; hinder
utrudnienie (oo-trood-ńe-ńe) n.
difficulty; hindrance
utrwalić (oo-trva-leech) v.
make permanent; fix; record
utrzymanie (oo-tzhi-ma-ńe) n.
living; upkeep; board;support
utuczyć (oo-too-chích) v.
fatten; grow fat;fatten up
utulić (oo-too-leech) v. comfort; console;nestle (face...)
utwierdzić (oo-tvyer-dżheeć) v.
confirm; fix; set; consolidate
utworzenie (oo-tvo-zhe-ńe) n.
formation ; initiation;creation
utworzyć (oo-tvo-zhích) v.
create; form; compose;initiate
utwór (oot-voor)m. work; composition; production;creation
utyć (oo-tích) v. become fat
utykać (oo-ti-kach) v. limp
utylitarny (oo-ti-lee-tar-ni)
adj. m. utilitarian; useful
utyskiwać (oo-tis-kee-vach) v.
complain; grumble (at,about)
uwaga (oo-vá-ga) f. attention;
remark ; notice;exp.: Caution!
uwalniać (oo-val-ńach) v. set
free ; rid; let off; dismiss
uważać (oo-va-zhach) v. pay
attention ; be careful; mind;
take care; look after;
watch out;consider;reckon

uważny (oo-vázh-ni) adj. m.
careful; attentive; watchful
uwiąd (oov-yównt) m. atrophy
uwiązać (oo-vyówn-zach) v.
attach; bind; tie; fasten
uwidocznic (oo-vee-doch-ńeech)
v. make evident; show; expose
uwiecznić (oo-vyech-ńeech) v.
perpetuate; immortalize
uwielbiać (oo-vyel-byach) v.
adore; worship; admire
uwielbienie (oo-vyel-bye-ńe) n.
adoration;admiration;worship
uwierać (oo-vye-rach) v. (shoe)
pinch; rub; hurt
uwierzytelnic (oo-vye-zhi-tel-
ńeech) v. legalize;certify;attest
uwierzytelnienie (oo-vye-zhi-
tel-ńe-ńe) n. certification;
accreditation; authentication
uwięzić (oo-vyán-żheech) v.
imprison;throw into prison
uwijac się (oo-vee-yach śhań)
v. be busy; bustle about
uwikłać (oo-veek-wach) v. entangle;involve;get entangled
uwłaczać (oov-wa-chach) v. belittle ; insult; outrage;affront
uwłosiony (oo-vwo-śho-ni) adj.
m. hairy; hirsute; pilose
uwodziciel (oo-vo-dżhee-ćhel)
m. seducer (of women);inveigler
uwodzic (oo-vó-dżheech) v. seduce (men or women)
uwolnic (oo-vol-ńeech) v. free
uwolnienie (oo-vol-ńe-ńe) n.
liberation;rescue; acquittal
uwydatnic (oo-vi-dat-ńeech) v.
accentuate; set off; bring out
uwypuklic (oo-vi-pook-leech) v.
accentuate; set off;protrude
uwzględnic (oovz-gländ-ńeech)
v. consider; comply; acquiesce
uwzględnienie (oovz-gländ-ńe-ńe)
n. allowance for;compliance
uzależnic (oo-za-lezh-ńeech) v.
make dependent; subordinate
uzasadnic (oo-za-sád-ńeech) v.
substantiate; justify;motivate
uzasadnienie (oo-za-sad-ńe-ńe)
n. justification; motive
uzbrajać się (ooz-bra-yach śhań)
v. arm oneself; equip oneself

uzbrojenie (ooz-bro-ye-ńe) n.
arming; armament; weapons
uzda (ooz-da) f. bridle
uzdolnić (ooz-dol-ńeech) v.
enable; qualify;capacitate
uzdolnienie (ooz-dol-ńe-ńe) n.
talent; gift; aptitude
uzdolniony (ooz-dol-no-ni) adj.
m. gifted; talented;capable;apt
uzdrawiać (ooz-dra-vyach) v.
heal; cure;bring back to health
uzdrowisko (ooz-dro-vees-ko)
n. health resort
uzębienie (oo-zań-bye-ńe) n.
dentition;toothing(of gears..)
uzgadniać (ooz-gad-ńach) v.
reconcile;coordinate;adjust
uziemienie (oo-żhe-myé-ńe) n.
grounding; earth
uzmysłowić (ooz-mi-swo-veech)
v. visualize; convey (meaning)
uznawać (ooz-na-vach) v. acknowledge; do justice;confess
uznanie (ooz-na-ńe) n. recognition; admission; approval
uzupełniać (oo-zoo-pew-ńach) v.
complete; fill up;make up
uzurpator (oo-zoor-pa-tor) m.
usurper(who takes without right)
uzyskać (oo-zis-kach) v. obtain;
gain; win;get; acquire;secure
uźerać się (oo-zhe-rach śhań)
v. fight over;,quarrel;wrangle
użyczać (oo-zhi-chach) v.
grant; give; lend; spare;impart
użyć (oo-zhich) v. use; exert;
take (medicine); profit;employ
użyteczny (oo-zhi-tech-ni) adj.
m. useful; serviceable;helpful
użytek (oo-zhi-tek) m. use
użytkownik (oo-zhit-kov-ńeek)
m. user (of appartment etc.)
używać (oo-zhi-vach) v. use;
enjoy; exercise right;make use
używalność (oo-zhi-val-nośhch)
f. use;enjoyment;utilization
używalny (oo-zhi-val-ni) adj.m.
usable; in working order
używany (oo-zhi-vá-ni) adj.m.
used; second-hand;worn
użyźniać (oo-zhiżh-ńach) v.
fertilize; enrich(the soil)

w (v) prep. in ; into; at
we (ve) prep. in; into; at
wabić (va-beech) v. lure
wabik (va-beek) m. decoy; lure
wachlarz (vákh-lash) m. fan;
range(of questions, subjects..)
wada (va-da) f. fault; defect;flaw
wadliwy (wad-leé-vi) adj. m.
faulty;defective;;imperfect
wafel (va-fel) m. wafer; cornet
waga (vá-ga) f. weight; balance;
pair of scales; importance
wagary (va-ga-ri) pl. skipping
school; playing truant; the wag
wagon (va-gon) m. car; wagon
wagon restauracyjny (va-gon res-
taw-ra-tsiy-ni) dining car
wahać się (va-khach śhań) v.
hesitate ;sway; rock; swing
wahadło (va-khá-dwo) n. pendu-
lum(swinging backwards and forwards)
wahadłowy (va-khad-wo-vi) adj.
m. rocking; swinging; oscilatory
wakacje (va-káts-ye) pl. vacation; holidays;taking a holiday
walać (va-lach) v. soil; stain;dirty
walc (valts) m. waltz
walcować (val-tso-vach) v. roll;
flatten; mill; laminate
walczyć (val-chich) v. fight; vie;
straggle;be in conflict;contend
walec (vá-lets) m. cylinder; roller
waleczność (va-lech-nośhch) f.
bravery ; valor;gallantry;courage
waleczny (va-lech-ni) adj. m.
valiant; brave; gallant;courageous
walić (vá-leech) v. demolish;hit;pile
walijski (va-leey-skee) adj.m.
Welsh; of Wales
walizka (va-leez-ka) f. suitcase; valise; portmanteau
walka (val-ka) f. struggle;
fight; war; battle; wrestling
walny (val-ni) adj. m. general;
complete; decisive;outstanding
walor (va-lor) m. value;quality
waluta (va-loo-ta) f. currency
wał (vaw) m. 1. rampart; dike;bank:
2. shaft;arbor; billow
wałach (va-wakh) m. gelding
wałek (vá-wek) m. roller; shaft;
cylinder; rolling pin ;wad; roll

wałęsać się (va-wáń-sach shán)
v. rove; loaf; idle about
wałkoń (vaw-koń) m. loafer;
do-nothing; idler
wałkować (vaw-kó-vach) v. roll;
mangle; debate; thresh out
wampir (vam-peer) m. vampire
wandal (ván-dal) m. vandal
wanienka (va-ńen-ka) f. little
tub ; bathtub; laboratory dish
wanna (van-na) f. bath tub
wapienny (va-pyen-ni) adj.m.
limy; limestone;calcareus
wapień (va-pyeń) m. limestone
wapno (váp-no) n. lime
wapń (vapń) m. calcium
warcaby (var-tsá-bi) pl. check-
ers; draughts (game)
warchlak (várkh-lak) m. boar-
cub;young wilde boar; piglet
warchoł (var-khow) m.brawler ;
discord sower; squabbler
warczeć (var-chech) v. growl
warga (vár-ga) f. lip; labium
wariant (vár-yant) m. variant
wariactwo (var-yáts-tvo) n.
madness;piece of folly; folly
wariat (var-yat) m. lunatic;
insane ; madman; fool;crazy man
wariować (var-yo-vach) v. go
insane ; rave ;go mad; be mad
warkocz (var-koch) m. braid
warkot (vár-kot) m. growl;
whirr; throb; rattle; drone
warowny (va-róv-ni) adj. m.
fortified;made into fortress
warować (va-ró-vach) v. fortify
warstwa (várs-tva) f. layer;
stratum; coat;coating; class
warstwowy (var-stvo-vi) adj.
m. laminar; stratal;foliated
warsztat (varsh-tat) m. workshop; workbench;(weaver's)loom
warsztatowy (var-shta-tó-vi)
adj. m. workshop-(equipment etc)
warta (vár-ta) f. watch; guard
wartki (várt-kee) adj. m. rapid; fast(current);animated
wartko(várt-ko) adv. fast; rap-
idly ; impetuously
warto (vár-to) adv.   it's
worth (while); it's proper; it's
worth one's while; it pays

wartościowy (var-tosh-chó-vi)
adj. m. valuable; precious
wartość (var-toshch) f. value;
worth ;quality;power;magnitude
wartownik (var-tov-ńeek) m.
guard; sentry; sentinel
warunek (va-roo-nek) m. condition; requirement; term;stipulation
warunkowy (va-roon-kó-vi) adj.
m. conditional;contingent;provisory
warząchew (va-zhówn-khev) v.
ladle
warzyć (va-zhich) v. cook; brew
warzywa (va-zhí-va) pl. vegetables: pot herbs;truk garden produce
warzywny (va-zhiv-ni) adj. m.
vegetable ; vegetable-
wasz (yash) pron. your; yours
waśnić (vash-ńeech) v. saw
discord (among men or women)
waśń (vaśhń) f. quarrel
wata (vá-ta) f. cotton wool
watować (va-tó-vach) v. pad;
quilt ;wad (a jacket etc.)
wawrzyn (vav-zhin) m. laurel
waza (vá-za) f. vase;soup tureen
wazelina (va-ze-lee-na) f.
vaseline.
wazon (va-zon) m. flower pot
ważki (vázh-kee) adj. m. grave;
weighty ; ponderable
ważny (vazh-ni) adj. m. important;valid; significant
ważyć (vá-zhich) v. weigh
ważyć się (va-zhich shán) v.
dare; weigh oneself;poise;venture
wąchać (vówn-khach) v. smell
wągr (vowngr) m. blackhead;
scolex; comedo;tapeworm larva
wąs (vówns) m. moustache;whisker
wąski (vówn-skee) adj. m. narrow; tight(fitting);narrow-(gage)
wąskotorowa kolej (vówns-ko-to-
ro-va ko-ley) f. narrow gauge
railroad
wątek (vówn-tek) m. weft; plot
wątły (vównt-wi) adj. m. frail
wątpić (vównt-peech) v. doubt
wątpliwy (vownt-plee-vi) adj.
m. doubtful;open to doubt;toss-up
wątroba (vown-tro-ba) f. liver
wątróbka (vown-troob-ka) f.
liver (dish);(calf's) liver

wąwóz (vówn-voos) m. ravine;
gorge; gully ; canyon ; defile
wąż (vównsh) m. snake; hose
wbiec (vbyets) v. run in;run up
wbijać (vbee-yaćh)v.hammer in
wbrew (vbrev) prep. in spite
of ; in defiance; against
wbudować (vboo-do-vaćh) v.
build in; incorporate
w bród (v broot) adv. l. in
abundance; 2. fording (river)
wcale (vtsa-le) adv. quite
wcale nie (vtsa-le ńe) not at
all (exp,);not in the least
wchłaniać (vkhwa-ńach) v. absorb; soak up; take in;soak in
wchodzić (wkhó-dźheećh) v. enter; get in; set in; climb
w ciągu (v chown-goo) adv.
during ;while; in time of
wciągać (vchown-gaćh) v. pull
in; drag in; inhale;implicate
wciąż (vchównsh) adv. continual-
ly; constantly;persistently
wcielać (vćhe-laćh) v. incorporate; embody; merge; realize
wcielenie (vćhe-le-ńe) n. in-
carnation; embodiment;merger
wcierać (vćhe-raćh) v. rub in
wcięcie (vchán-ćhe) n. incision
notch ;narrow,waist;low cut neck
wciskać (vćhees-kaćh) v. press
in; squeeze in ;wedge; cram
w czas (v chas) on time
wczasy (vcha-si) pl. vacations
wczesny (vches-ni) adj. m.
early;in the small hours
wcześnie (vcheśh-ńe) adv. early
wczoraj (vcho-ray) adv. yesterday; during yesterday
wczoraj wieczorem (vchó-ray vye-
chó-rem) adv. last night
wczuwać się (vchoo-vaćh śhań)
v. sympathize; get in spirit
wdarcie (vdár-ćhe) n. invasion
wdawać się (vdá-vaćh śhań) v.
l. intervene; 2. associate
wdech (vdekh) m. aspiration
wdowa (vdó-va) f. widow
wdowiec (vdó-vyets) m. widower
w dół (v doow) adv. down; downwards ; downstairs; (go)lower

wdrapać się (vdra-paćh śhań) v.
climb up ; shin up(a tree)
wdrażać (vdra-zhaćh) v. train;
implant ; accustom to;enter upon
wdychać (vdi-khaćh) v. breathe;
inhale ; breathe in; imbibe
wdzierać się (vdźhe-raćh śhań)
v. break in; struggle up hill
wdziewać (vdźhe-vaćh) v. put
on (clothes); slip on;take(the veil
wdzięcznosć (vdźhańch-nośhćh)
f. gratitude ; thankfulness
wdzięczny (vdźhańch-ni) adj.
m. grateful; thankful;graceful;cute
wdzięk (vdźhańk) m. grace;charm
według (veď-wook) prep. according to; after; along;near;next
wegetacja (ve-ge-táts-ya) f.
vegetation; bare existence
wegetarianin (ve-ge-tar-ya-ńeen)
m. vegetarian(on meatless diet)
wegetować (ve-ge-to-vaćh) v.
exist barely; vegetate
wejrzeć (véy-zhećh) v. glance
in;look in;get an insight;inspect
wejrzenie (vey-zhe-ńe) n.glance
in; (eye)expression; insight
wejście (veysh-ćhe) n . entrance; way in; admission;entry
wejściowy (veysh-ćho-vi) adj.
m. entrance-(door;gate,etc.)
wejść (veyshćh) v. enter;get in
weksel (vék-sel) m. loan note
welon (vé-lon) m. veil
wełna (vew-na) f. wool
wełniany (vew-ńa-ni) adj. m.
woolen; worsted, wool-(fabric...)
wełnisty (vew-ńees-ti) adj.m.
wooly; fleecy;wool bearing
weneryczna,choroba (ve-ne-rich-
na kho-ro-ba) f. venereal
disease
wenezuelski (ve-ne-zoo-él-skee)
adj. m. Venezuelan;of Venezuela
wentyl (ven-til) m. vent;valve
wentylacja (ven-ti-láts-ya) f.
ventilation;ventilation system
wentylator (ven-ti-la-tor) m.
ventilator; ventilating-fan
weranda (ve-ran-da) f. porch
werbel (vér-bel) m. ruffle;
drum-call; drumbeat ;drum

werbować (ver-bo-vach) v. enlist; recruit; canvas
werbunek (ver-boo-nek) m. draft; recruitment;enlisting;recruting
wersja (vee-sya) f. version
werwa (ver-ya) f. verve;zip;pep
weryfikować (ve-ri-fee-ko-vach) v. verify;confirm
wesele (ve-se-le) n. wedding
wesołość (ve-so-wośhćh) f.joy gaiety; glee; hilarity
wesoły (ve-so-wi) adj. merry; gay; jolly; gleeful; funny
wespoł (ves-poow) adv. together; jointly; all together
westchnienie (vest-khne-ne) n. sigh(of relief etc.)
wesz (vesh) f. louse
wet za wet (vet za vet) exp.: tit for tat; retaliate
weteran (ve-te-ran) m. veteran
weterynarz (ve-te-ri-nash) m. vet; veterinary; farrier
wetknąć (vet-knownch) v. stick in;slip in;tuck away; stuff
wewnątrz (vev-nowntsh) prep., adv. inside; within; intra-
wewnętrzny (vev-nantzh-ni) adj. m. inner;internal; inward
wezbrać (vez-brach) v. swell
wezbrany (vez-bra-ni) adj. m. flush; overflowing; swollen
wezwać (vez-vach) v. call in
wezwanie (vez-va-ne) n. call
węch (vankh) m. smell; nose
wędka (vand-ka) f. fishing rod
wędkarz (vand-kash) m. angler
wędlina (vand-lee-na) f. meat products; pork products
wędliniarnia (vand-lee-nar-na) f. pork-butcher's shop
wędrować (van-dro-vach) v. wander; roam; rove; hike
wędrowiec (van-dro-vyets) m. wanderer; tramp; rover
wędrówka (van-droov-ka) f. migration; roam; tramp;wandering
wędzic (van-dźeech) v. smoke; cure; meat; bloat fish
wędzidło (van-dźheed-wo) n. (horse) bit;bridle;curb
wędzonka (van-dzon-ka) f. bacon

węgiel (van-gel)m. coal;crayon
węgielny kamień (van-gel-ni kamyeń) m. corner stone;corner stone
węgiel (van-gew)m. corner; quoin
węgierski (van-ger-skee) adj. m. Hungarian; of Hungary
węglan (van-glan) m. carbonate
węglowodan (van-glo-vo-dan) m. carbohydrate (chemical compound)
węglowodor (van-glo-vo-door) m. hydrocarbon ;rock oil etc.
węglowy (van-glo-vi) adj. m. carbonic; coal; carboniferous; carbon-
węgorz (van-gosh) m. eel
węzeł (van-zew) m. knot; junction; noose; loop; snarl;hitch
węższy (vanzh-shi) adj. m. narrower(than)
wgląd (vglownt) m. insight; view
wglądać (vglown-dach) v. look into; get an insight;inquire
wgłębic się (vgwan-beech śhan) v. sink; study; go into (matter)
wgryźć się (vgrizhćh śhan) v. penetrate; get teeth into...
wiać (vyach) v. blow; beat it
wiadomo (vya-do-mo) v. (imp.) it is known;everybody knows
wiadomość (vya-do-mośhćh) f. news; information; message
wiadomy (vya-do-mi) adj. m. known; a certain;well known
wiadro (vya-dro) n. bucket;pail
wiadukt (vya-dookt) m. viaduct
wianek (vya-nek) m. flower crown; wreath; maidenhead
wiara (vya-ra) f. faith;belief
wiarogodny (vya-ro-god-ni) adj. m. reliable; credible;veracious
wiarołomny (vya-ro-wom-ni) adj. m. unfaithful; treacherous
wiarus (vya-roos) m. veteran (old guard) [breeze
wiatr (vyatr) m. wind;gale;
wiatrak (vyat-rak) m. windmill
wiatrówka (vya-troov-ka) f. air gun; wind breaker (jacket)
wiąz (vyowns) m. elm (Ulmus)
wiązać (vyown-zach) v. tie; bind
wiązanie (vyown-za-ne) n. tie; truss; bond; link;fixation;weave

wiązanka (vyőwn-zan-ka) f. garland; bunch; banquet;cluster

wiązka (vyőwnz-ka) f. bundle; bunch; cluster; beam(of rays)

wibracja (vee-bra-tsya) f. vibration; jarring ; jar

wichrowac się (vee-khro-vach shań) v. warp; curl

wicher (vee-kher) m. windstorm ; gale;strong wind

wichrzyciel (veekh-zhi-chel) m. warmonger; firebrand;instigator

wichrzyc (veekh-zhich) v. make trouble; create discord;tousle

wichura (vee-khoo-ra) f. windstorm; gale; strong wind

wichura snieżna (vi-khoo-ra-śhneźh-na) snowstorm;blizzard

wic (veech) v. wind; meander; build nest; curl;m.twig;osier

widelec (vee-de-lets) m. fork

widełki (vee-dew-kee) pl. fork (small) ;forked branch

widełkowaty (vee-dew-ko-va-ti) adj. m. forked;fork shaped

widły (veed-wi) pl. pitch fork

widmo (veed-mo) n . ghost; phantom ;spectrum;specter

widno (ved-no) adv. 1. evidently; 2. in daylight ;in light

widnokrąg (veed-no-krőwnk) m. horizon ; sea-line ;true horizon

widocznie (vee-doch-ńe) adv. evidently ;apparently; clearly

widocznosc (vee-doch-noshch) f. visibility ;field of vision

widoczny (vee-doch-ni) adj. m. visible; evident noticeable

widok (vee-dok) m. view; sight

widokówka (vee-do-koov-ka) f. picture postcard

widowisko (vee-do-vees-ko) n. show; spectacle ; pageant

widownia (vee-dov-ńa) f. audience; theatre house ;scene

widz (veets) m. spectator

widzenie (vee-dze-ńe) n. sight; vision ; visit; hallucination

widzialny (vee-dzhal-ni) adj. m. visible (to the naked eye...)

widziec (vee-dzhech) v. see

wiec (vyets) m. meeting;rally

wieczerza (vye-zhe-zha) f. supper ;Lord's Supper

wiecznosc (vyech-noshch) f. eternity; ages ;eternal life

wieczny (vyech-ni) adj. m. eternal; perpetual; endless

wieczorek (vye-cho-rek) m. evening (party); nice evening

wieczorem (vye-cho-rem) exp.; in the evening ;during the evening

wieczorny (vye-chor-ni) adj. m. evening -(dress,newspaper,etc.)

wieczorowy (vye-cho-ro-vi) adj. m. nightly; evening (performance)

wieczór(vye-choor) m. evening

wieczysty (vye-chis-ti) adj. m. eternal; perpetual;imperishable

wiedza (vye-dza) f. knowledge; learning;erudition; science

wiedziec (vye-dźhech) v. know

wiedzma (vyedźh-ma) f. witch

wiejska droga (vyey-ska dro-ga) f. village road, country road

wiejski (vyey-skee) adj. m. village; rural; rustic;country

wiek (vyek) m. age; century

wiekowy (vye-ko-vi) adj. m. secular; ancient; aged;very old

wiekuistosc (vye-koo-ees-toshch) f. eternity ; all time

wiekuisty (vye-koo-ees-ti) adj. m. eternal; everlasting

wielbiciel (vyel-bee-chel) m. devotee; admirer; idolator (man)

wielbicielka (vyel-bee-chel-ka) f. devotee; idolatress (woman)

wielbłąd (vyel-bwőwnd) m. camel

wielce (vyel-tse) adv. very; greatly; extremely ;very much

wiele (vye-le) adj. m. many; a lot;much; far out;a great deal

wielebny (vye-leb-ni) adj. m. reverend (Father etc.)

Wielkanoc (vyel-ka-nots) f. Easter

wielkanocny (vyel-ka-nots-ni) adj. m. Easter; of Easter

wielki (vyel-kee) adj. m. big; large; great; vast; keen;mighty

wielkoduszny (vyel-ko-doosh-ni) adj. m. magnanimous ;generous

wielkolud (vyel-kő-lood) m.giant

wielkomiejski (vyel-ko-myey-skee) adj. m. metropolitan; urban ; of a large city

wielkość (vyel-koshćh) f. greatness; size; dimension

wielobarwny (vye-lo-barv-ni) adj. m. multicolor (ed)

wieloboczny (vye-lo-boch-ni) adj. m. multilateral ;polygonal

wielokrążek (vye-lo-krown-zhek) m. set of pulleys ; pulley-block

wielokrotny (vye-lo-krót-ni) adj. m. repeated; multiple

wieloletni (vye-lo-let-ńi) adj. m. long; years long;many years'

wielopiętrowy (vye-lo-pyan-tro-vi) adj. m. multistory

wieloraki (vye-lo-rá-kee) adj. m. manifold ; varied ;multiple

wieloryb (vye-lo-rib) m. whale

wielorybnik (vye-lo-rib-ńeek) m. whaler;whaleman;whaling ship

wielostronny (vye-lo-stron-ni) adj. m. multilateral; many-sided ; versatile; various

wielozgłoskowy (vye-lo-zgwos-ko-vi) adj. m. polysyllabic

wieloznaczny (vye-lo-znach-ni) adj. m. multivocal; ambiguous

wielożeństwo (vye-lo-zheń-stvo) n. polygamy,

wieniec (vye-ńets) m. wreath; garland; crown ; chaplet

wieńczyć (vyeń-chich) v. crown

wieprz (vyepsh) m. hog; pig

wieprzownina (vyep-zho-vée-na) f. pork (meat)

wieprzowy (vyep-zho-vi) adj.m. pork ;pork's;pig's;hog's;porcine

wiercenie (vyer-tse-ńe) n. drilling ; perforation;boring

wiercić (vyer-chich) v. bore; drill ; pester; bother

wierność (vyer-noshćh) f. fidelity; loyalty ; faith; truth

wierny (vyer-ni) adj. m. faithful ; true;loyal;exact

wiersz (vyersh) m. verse; poem

wiertarka (vyer-tár-ka) f. drill

wiertnictwo (vyert-ńeets-tvo) n. drilling(activity)

wierutny (vye-root-ni) adj.m. stark(liar); notorious; through-and-through ; rank; arrant;born

wierzący (vye-zhown-tsi) adj. m. believer; believing Christian

wierzba (vyezh-ba) f. willow

wierzch (vyezhkh) m. top; brim head; surface; cover; lid

wierzchni (vyezh-khńee) adj. m. upper ; top; outer;outside

wierzchołek (vyezh-khó-wek) m. top; peak; summit; apex;vertex

wierzyciel (vye-zhi-ćhel) m. creditor; mortgagee; obligee

wierzycielka (vye-zhi-ćhel-ka) f. creditor (woman)

wierzyć (vye-zhich) v. believe; trust;rely; believe in God

wierzytelność (vye-shi-tel-noshćh) f. debt; claim

wieszać (vye-shach) v. hang

wieszadło (vye-shad-wo) v. hanger; peg; ;coat-stand

wieszak (vye-shak) v. rack

wieszcz (vyeshch) m. bard; seer; poet (leading,national)

wieszczy (vyesh-chi) adj. m. prophetic ;visionary

wieś (vyesh) f. village; countryside; hamlet;the villagers

wieść (vyeshćh) 1. f. news 2. v. lead; conduct; draw; succeed ;stand at the head

wieśniaczka (vyesh-ńach-ka) f. countrywoman ;peasant woman

wieśniak (vyesh-ńak) m. countryman; villager; yokel ;rustic

wietrzeć (vyet-zhech) v. decay

wietrzyć (vyet-zhich) v. ventilate; smell; nose;aerate

wietrzenie (vyet-zhe-ńe) n. ventilation; decay (of rocks)

wiewiórka (vye-vyoor-ka) f. squirrel; squirrel fur

wieźć (vyezhćh) v. carry (on wheels) ;transport ;convey;drive

wieża (vye-zha) f. tower; rook

wieżowiec (vye-zho-vyets) m. skyscraper;high-rise(building)

wieżyczka (vye-zhićh-ka) f. turret; pinnacle;small tower

więc (vyańts) conj. now; well; therefore; so;consequently

więcej (vyań-tsey) adv. more

więdnąć (vyańd-nownćh) v. wither; fade; wilt

więcierz (vyáń-chezh) m. fishing net (set taut or hoops)

większość (vyáńk-shoshch) f. majority; the bulk; most

większy (vyáńk-shi) adj. m. bigger; larger; greater

więzić (vyáń-zheech) v. imprison ;confine; detain;restrain

więzienie (vyáń-zhe-ñe) n. prison; confinement; jail;restraint

więzień (vyáń-zheñ) m. prisoner

więzy (vyáń-zi) pl. fetters; restrains; chains; bonds

wigilia (vee-geel-ya) f. Xmas Eve; eve

wiklina (vee-klee-na) f. osier

wikłać (veek-wach) v. entangle

wikt (veekt) m. board; keep

wilczur (veel-choor) m.wolf dog

wilgoć (veel-goch) f. humidity

wilgotny (veel-got-ni) adj. m. moist; humid ; damp; wet

wilia (veel-ya) f. eve

wilk (veelk) m. wolf;wolfskin

wilżyć (veel-zhich) v. moisten

wina (vee-na) f. guilt; fault

winda (veen-da) f. elevator

winiarnia (vee-ñar-ña) f. wineshop ;vine vault; winery

winić (vee-ñeech) v. accuse; blame for ;fix the blame on

winien (vee-ñen) adj. m. indebted; owing; guilty; at fault

winnica (veen-ñee-tsa) f. vineyard; vine growing plantation

winny (veen-ni) adj. m. guilty

winny (veen-ni) adj. m. of wine; vineous-; vine-; winy

wino (vee-no) n. wine ;grapevine

winogrono (vee-no-gró-no) n. grape

winorośl (vee-no-roshl) f. vine

winowajca (vee-no-vay-tsa) m. culprit; evildoer; the guilty one

winszować (veen-sho-vach) v. congratulate (on having success)

wiosenny (vyo-sén-ni) adj. m. spring -(flowers,month etc.)

wioska (vyós-ka) f. hamlet

wiosło (vyós-wo) n. oar;paddle

wiosłować (vyos-wó-vach) v. row

wiosna (vyós-na) f. Spring(time)

wioślarz (vyósh-lash) m. oarsman ; rower

wiotki (vyót-kee) adj. m. limp

wiór (vyoor) m. shaving ; chip

wir (veer) m. whirl; eddy ;vortex

wiraż (vee-rash) m. curve; bend

wirować (vee-ro-vach) v. whirl

wirówka (vee-roóv-ka) f. centrifuge ;hydro-extractor

wirtuoz (veer-too-os) m. virtuoso ;maestro; great musician etc.

wirus (vee-roos) m. virus

wisieć (vee-shech) v.hang; sag

wisiorek (vee-shó-rek) m. pendant

wiśnia (veesh-ña) f. cherry (tree)

wiśniak (veesh-ñak) m. cherry-brandy; cherry liqueur

witać (vee-tach) v. greet; welcome; meet to welcome;bid welcome

witamina (vee-ta-mée-na) f. vitamin (A,B,C,D,E etc.)

witryna (vee-tri-na) f. shop-window ; glass case

wiza (vee-za) f. visa

wizerunek (vee-ze-roo-nek) m. likeness; image;picture; effigy

wizja (veez-ya) f. vision ;view

wizyta (vee-zí-ta) f. call; visit; be on a visit

wizytówka (vee-zi-toov-ka) f. calling card; visiting card

wjazd (vyazt) m. (car) entrance

wjeżdżać (vyézh-dzhach) v. drive in ;ride to the top

wkleić (vkle-eech) v. stick in

wklęsłodruk (vklañ-swo-drook) m. copper plate print

wklęsły (vklañs-wi) adj. m. concave; hollow; sunken

wkład (vkwat) m. input; deposit; investment; outlay; inset

wkładać (vkwa-dach) v. put in

w koło(vkó-wo) adv. round;in circles; over and over again

wkoło (vkó-wo)prep. round; about; in circles [appear;

wkraczać (vkra-chach) v. step in; invade; intervene; enter; stalk

wkradać się (vkra-dach shañ) v. steal in; slip in; creep in

wkrapiać (vkráp-yach) v. put drops in; beat up

wkręcać (vkráń-tsach) v. screw
in ; drive in; push into a job
wkroczyć (vkro-chich)v. enter
(formally) ; appear ; invade
wkrótce (vkroot-tse) adv. soon
wkupić się (vkoó-peech śhań) v.
buy way in;pay one's footing
wlac (vlach) v. pour in
wlatywać (vla-ti-vach) v. fly
in ; rush in; dart in;run in
wlec (vlets) v, drag ; tow
wlepić (vle-peech) v. l. paste
in; 2, glare at; stare at
wlewać (vlé-vach) v. pour in
wlezć (vleżhch) v. crawl in ;
climb up; barge in; step in
wliczenie (vlee-che-ńe) n. inclusion; counting in
wliczyć (vlee-chich) v. count
in ; reckon in ;include
w lot (v lot) adv. in a flash;
quickly; in a hurry
wlot (vlot) m. inlet ; intake
wlot kuli (vlot koo-lee) m.
bullet entry
władać (wa-dach) v. rule ;wield
władca (vwad-tsa) m. ruler
władny (wád-ni) adj. m. sovereign ; having the authority
władza (wa-dza) f. authority
włamać się (vwa-mach śhań) v.
break in; burglarize
włamanie (vwa-má-ńe) n. burglary ; house breaking
włamywacz (vwa-mi-vach) m. burglar; housebreaker; picklock
własnoręcznie (vwa-sno-ráńch-ńe)
adv. personally; with one's
hand ; with one's own hand
własność (vwas-noshch) f. property ; characteristic feature
własnowolny (vwas-no-vól-ni)
adj. m. spontaneous;voluntary
własny (vwas-ni) adj. m. own;very
właściciel (vwaśh-chee-chel) m.
proprietor ; holder;owner
właściwy (vwaśh-chee-vi) adj.m.
proper ; right; suitable; due
właściwość (vwaśh-chee-voshch) f.
propriety ; characteristic
właśnie (vwaśh-ńe) adv. exactly;
just so; precisely; very;just
as;just now;just then;only just

właz (vwas) m. manhole ;hatch
włazić (vwa-żheech) v. crawl
in ; barge in; step in;go deep
włączac (vwowń-chach) v. include; switch on; plug in
włącznie (vwówńch-ńe) adv. in-
clusively; inclusive;including
włączenie (vwówń-che-ńe) n.
inclusion ; merger ;incorporation
włochaty (vwo-khá-ti) adj. m.
hairy ; shaggy; hirsute;nappy
włos (vwos) m. hair ; fur
włosień (vwo-śheń) m. trichina
włoski (vwos-kee) adj.m. Italian; of Italy
włoskowaty (vwos-ko-vá-ti) adj.
m. capillary ; hairlike (tubes)
włoszczyzna (vwozh-chíz-na) pl.
vegetables ; Italian studies
włościanin (vwośh-cha-ńeen) m.
farmer ; peasant ; country man
włożyć (vwo-zhich) v. put in
włóczęga (vwoo-cháń-ga) m.
tramp ;rover; vagrant;roam
włóczka (vwooch-ka) f. yarn
włócznia (vwooch-ńa) f. spear
włóczyć (vwoo-chich) v. drag
włókienniczy (vwo-kyen-ńee-chi)
adj. m. textile(trade,fiber etc.)
włókniarz (vwook-ńash) m.
weaver; textile worker
włóknisty (vwook-ńees-ti) adj.
m., fibrous; stringy;thready
włókno (vwook-no) n. fibre
wmawiać (vmáv-yach) v. talk
into; persuade; make believe
wmieszać się (vmye-shach śhań)
v. interfere; join; mix;mingle
wmuszać (vmoo-shach) v. force
(upon) ; press upon ∫directly
wnet (vnet) adv. soon; shortly;
wneka (vnáń-ka) f. niche;recess
wnetrze (vnáń-tzhe) n. interior
wnętrzności (vnantzh-nóśh-chee)
pl. bowels ; intestines ;entrails
Wniebowzięcie (vńe-bo-vżhán-che)
n. Assumption ∫put in; infer;
wnieść (vńeśhch) v. carry in ;
⌐—⌐gather;conclude
wnikać (vńee-kach) v. penetrate
wnikliwy (vńee-klee-vi) adj. m.
penetrating; discerning;piercing
wniosek (vnó-sek) m. conclusion;
proposition; suggestion;motion

wnioskodawca (vnos-ko-dav-tsa)
m. mover; giver of a motion
wnioskować (vnos-ko-vach) v.
conclude; deduct;infer; gather
wnioskowanie (vnos-ko-va-ne)
n. conclusion; inference
wnosić (vno-sheech) v. carry in;
conclude; infer; gather
wnuczka (vnooch-ka) f. granddaughter
wnuk (vnook) m. grandson
wnyk (vnik) m. snare
woalka (vo-al-ka) f. veil(hat)
wobec (vo-bets) prep. in the
face of; before; towards
woda (vo-da) f. water;froth; bull
wodnisty (vod-nees-ti) adj. m.
watery; wishy-washy;aqueous
wodno-płatowiec (vod-no-pwa-to-
vyets) m. hydroplane;water plane
wodny (vod-ni) adj. m. water-
wodociąg (vo-do-chownk) m. waterworks ; water tap
wodolecznictwo (vo-do-lech-neets-
tvo); n. hydrotherapy;water cure
wodopój (vo-do-pooy) m. watering spot ; cow-pond;water hole
wodorost (vo-do-rost) m. seaweed; alga
wodorowa bomba (vo-do-ro-va
bom-ba) f. H-bomb
wodospad (vo-do-spat) m. waterfall; cascade
wodotrysk (vo-do-trisk) m. fountain; waterspout
wodować (vo-do-vach) v. launch
on water ; splash down(on water)
wodowstręt (vo-do-vstrent) m.
hydrophobia; rabies
wodór (vo-door)m. hydrogen
wodza (vo-dza) f. rein;hold;sway
wodzić (vo-dżheech) v. lead;run
wodzirej (vo-dżhee-rey) m. dance
leader; ringleader;bell wether
w ogóle (vo-goo-le) adv. generally; on the whole; in the main
wojak (vo-yak) m. warrior;soldier
wojenny (vo-yen-ni) adj. m. military; war;wartime; of war
wojewodztwo (vo-ye-voodz-tvo) n.
province; voivodeship
wojłok (voy-wok) m. felt (thick)

wojna (voy-na) f. war ;warfare
wojna domowa (voy-na do-mo-va)
f. civil war
wojować (vo-yo-vach) v. wage
war ; combat; contend
wojowniczy (vo-yov-nee-chi)
adj. m. warlike; aggresive
wojownik (vo-yov-neek) m.
(tribal) warrior
wojsko (voy-sko) n. army;troops
wojskowość (voy-sko-voshch) f.
military science;the army
wojskowy (voy-sko-vi) adj.m.
military ; army(post etc.)
wokalny (vo-kal-ni) adj. m.
vocal _ all around
wokoło (vo-ko-wo) adv. round;
wola (vo-la) f. will;volition
wolec (vo-lech) v. prefer
wolno (vol-no) adv. slowly
wolnomyśliciel (vol-no-mi-
shlee-chel) m.freethinker
wolność (vol-noshch) f. liberty; freedom ; independence
wolnościowy (vol-nosh-cho-vi)
adj. m. for liberation
wolny (vol-ni) adj. m. free
wolt (volt) m. volt
woltomierz (vol-to-myesh) m.
voltmeter
wołać (vo-wach) v. call;cry
wołanie (vo-wa-ne) n. call;cry
wołowina (vo-wo-vee-na) f.
beef
wonny (von-ni) adj. m. fragrant; aromatic; sweet-smelling
woniec (vo-nech) v. scent;
smell ; be fragrant
woń (voń) f. fragrance
woreczek (vo-re-chek) m. small
bag ; pouch; cyst
worek(vo-rek) m. bag ; sack
wosk (vosk) m. wax
woskować (vos-ko-vach) v. wax
wozić (vo-żheech) v. carry (on
wheels); transport;drive;cart
wozownia (vo-zov-na) f. coach
house
woźnica (vożh-nee-tsa) m. coach-
man ;driver; waggoner
woženie (vo-zhe-ne) n. transport; transportation;carriage

wódka (vood-ka) f. vodka
wódz (voots) m. commander;chief
wójt (vooyt) m. village mayor
wół (voow) m. ox ;steer;bullock
wór (voor) m. (big) sack(ful)
wówczas (voov-chas) adv. then;
   that time; at the time
wóz (voos) m. car; cart;wagon
wózek (vóo-zek) m. (small) car
wpadać (vpa-dach) v. fall in;
   rush in; drop in;run into
wpajać (vpa-yach) v. put in
   (head); implant; instill
wpatrywać się (vpa-tri-vach
   shañ) v. stare;look intently
wpełzać (vpew-zach) v.crawl in;
   creep in(into a cave etc.)
wpędzać (vpañ-dzach) v. drive
   sb in;bring on sb...(death etc)
wpić się (vpeech shañ) v. sink
   into; penetrate; bury(teeth)
wpierw (vpyerv) adv. first
wpis (vpees) m. enrollment
wpisać (vpee-sach) v. write in
wpisowe (vpee-só-ve) n. registration fee;inscription fee
wplatać (vpla-tach) v. twine
   in; weave; braid ;intersperse
wplątać (vplown-tach) v. entangle;implicate;involve
wpłacać (vpwa-tsach) v. pay in
wpłata (vpwa-ta) f. payment
wpław (vpwaf) adv. (swim)across
wpływ (vpwif) m. influence; income ; effect; impact of
wpływać (vpwi-vach) v. flow in;
   influence; have effect
wpływowy (vpwi-vó-vi) adj. m.
   influential
w pobliżu (v po-blee-zhoo) adv.
   near ;in the vicinity;close by
w poprzek (v pó-pzhek) prep.
   adv. across; crosswise
wpół (vpoow) adv. in half; halfway ; half past;half-;semi-
w pośród (v pósh-rood) adv.
   among ;in the midst of
wprawa (vpra-va) f. skill;
   practice ; proficiency
wprawdzie (vpráv-dzhe) adv. in
   truth ; to be sure; indeed
wprawić (vpra-veech) v. set in;
   train in ; insert; put in

wprawny (vpráv-ni) adj. m.
   skillful;trained; experienced
wprost (vprost) adv. directly;
   straight ahead; outright;simply
wprowadzenie (vpro-va-dze-ñe) n.
   introduction; initiation
wprowadzać (vpro-va-dzach) v.
   usher; introduce; lead in;put in
wprzęgać (vpzhañ-gach) v. harness, (horse, river etc)
wprzód (vpshoot) adv. ahead; before; first; in the first place
wpuszczać (vpoosh-chach) v. let
   in; admit; insert;allow to enter
wpychać (vpi-khach) v. push in
wracać (vra-tsach) v. return
wrastać (vras-tach) v grow in
wraz (vras) prep., together
wrażenie (vra-zhé-ñe) n. impression;sensation;feeling;thrill
wrażliwość (vrazh-lee-voshch) f.
   sensitivity; susceptibility
wrażliwy (vrazh-lee-vi) adj. m.
   sensitive; thin-skinned;tender
wreszcie (vrésh-che) adv. at
   last;finally; after all;eventually
wręcz (yránch) adv. down right
wręczać (vran-chach) v. hand in
wrodzony (vro-dzó-ni) adj. m.
   innate; inborn; inbred;congenital
wrogi (vro-gee) adj. m. hostile
wrogość (vró-goshch) f. hosti-
   ity; ill-will; enmity;malevolence
wrona (vró-na) f. crow
wrota (vró-ta) n. gate
wrotki (vrót-kee) pl. roller
   skates
wróbel (vroo-bel) m. sparrow
wrócić (vroo-cheech) v. return
wróg (vrook) m. foe; enemy
wróżba (vroozh-ba) f. omen
wróżbiarz (vroozh-byash) m.
   fortune-teller; soothsayer
wróżka (vroozh-ka) f. fortune-
   teller;palmist; fairy
wróżyć (vroo-zhich) v. tell
   fortunes; foretell ;predict
wryć się (vrich shañ) v. dig in;
   sink in; imbed
wrzask (vzhask) m. scream ;yell
wrzaskliwy (vzhas-klee-vi) adj.
   m. shrill;piercing; clamorous

wrzawa (vzha-va) f. noise
wrzący (vzhówn-tsi) adj. m.
boiling ; scalding (hot)
wrzątek (vzhówn-tek) m. boiling
water
wrzeciono (vzhe-ćho-no) n.
spindle ; verge
wrzeć (vzhech) v. boil ; rage
wrzesien (vzhe-śheň) m. September
wrzeszczec (vzhesh-chech) v.
shriek ; yell; scream; cry
wrzos (vzhos) m. heather
wrzosowisko (vzho-so-vees-ko)
n. heath; moor
wrzód (vzhoot) m. abscess
wrzucac (vzhoo-tsach) v. throw
in; drop in; put in; cast
wsadzac (vsa-dzach) v. put in;
plant ; stick; lock sb up
wschodni (vskhod-nee) adj. m.
east; easterly; eastern
wschodzic (vskho-dźheech) v.
shoot up; rise; sprout
wschod słonca (vskhood swoń-
tsa) m. sunrise
wsiadac (vsha-dach) v. get in;
mount; get on board; take seat
wsiąkac (vshówn-kach) v. sink
in; infiltrate ;percolate
wskazany (vska-za-ni) adj. m.
advisable;indicated;desirable
wskazówka (vska-zoov-ka) f.
hint; direction; (clock) hand
wskazujący palec (vska-zoo-yown-
tsi pa-lets) m. forefinger
wskazywac (vska-zi-vach) v.
point out;show; indicate
wskaźnik (vskaźh-neek) m. index; pointer; indicator;signal
wskos (v skos) adv. slant
wskros (vskrosh) prep. through
wskutek (vskoo-tek) prep. as
a result; due to; thanks to
wskrzesic (vskzhe-sheech) v.
resuscitate; revive;wake;recall
wspaniałomyslny (vspa-na-wo-
mishl-ni) adj. m. magnanimous
wspaniałosc (vspa-na-woshch) f.
splendor; grandeur;lordliness
wspaniały (vspa-na-wi) adj. m.
superb; glorious; grand;great;
smashing; magnificient;splendid

wsparcie (vspar-che) n. support
wspierac (vspye-rach) v. support ; prop up; assist; help
wspinac się (vspee-nach śhań)
v. climb up;toil up hill;rear
wspomagac (vspo-ma-gach) v. help
wspominac (vspo-mee-nach) v.
remember; recall; mention
wspornik (vspor-neek) m. canti-
lever (beam);bracket; support
wspólnik (vspool-neek) m. partner; accomplice; associate
wspólny (vspool-ni) adj. m. common; joint; combined ;collective
współczesnosc (vspoow-ches-noshch)
f. the present time (day,age)
współczesny (vspoow-ches-ni) adj.
m. contemporary ; modern ;present
współczucie (vspoow-choo-che) n.
sympathy ; compassion ;pity
współczynnik (vspoow-chin-neek)
m. coefficient ; factor
współdziałac (vspoow-dźha-wach)
v. cooperate ; act jointly
współistniec (vspoow-eest-ńech)
v. coexist
współistnienie (vspoow-eest-ńe-
ńe) n. coexistence
współpraca (vspoow-pra-tsa) f.
cooperation ; team-work
współrzędna (vspoow-zhánd-na) f.
coordinate axis
współudział (vspoow-oo-dźhaw) m.
participation; share
współwłasciciel (vspoow-vwash-
chee-chel) m. joint owner
współzawodnictwo (vspoow-za-vod-
ńeets-tvo) m. competition
współzawodnik (vspoow-za-vod-
ńeek) m. competitor; rival
współzyc (vspoow-zhich) v. get
along; live together; coexist
wstawac (vsta-vach) v. get up
wstawiac (vsta-vyach) v. set in
wstawiac się (vsta-vyach śhań) v.
get tipsy; plead for sb
wstąpic (vstówn-peech) v. step
in; drop in; step up; enter
wstążka (vstownzh-ka) f. ribbon
wstecz (vstech) adv. backwards
wsteczny (vstech-ni) adj. m.
reactionary; reverse;backward

wstęga (vstáú-ga) f. (large)
ribbon ; band;sash;wreath;wisp

wstęp (vstáṅp) m. entrance;
admission ; preface; opening

wstępny (vstáṅp-ni) adj. m.in-
troductory ; initial;preliminary

wstręt (vstráṅt) m. aversion

wstrętny (vstráṅt-ni) adj. m.
hideous ; foul;vile; nasty

wstrząs (vstzhówns) m. shock

wstrząsający (vstzhówn-sa-yówn-
tsi) adj. m. shocking; thrilling

wstrzemięźliwość (vstzhe-myáṅ-
żhleé-vośhćh) f. moderation

wstrzemięźliwy (vstzhe-myáṅ-
żhleé-vi) adj. m. moderate

wstrzykiwać (vstzhi-keé-vach)
v. inject; give a shot

wstrzymać (vstzhi-mach) v. stop;
abstain; put off; hold back

wstyd (vstid) m. shame; dis -
grace;dishonor;indecency

wstydliwy (vstid-leé-vi) adj.m.
shy; bashful; timid;embarassing

wstydzić się (vsti-dźheećh shaṅ)
v. be ashamed; blush for sb

wsunąć (vsoo-nównćh) v. slip in;
put in; insert into;tuck in

wsypa (vsí-pa) f.a bad break;
gaffe; give-away of a plot

wsypać (vsí-pach) v. pour in;
tell on somebody; pour (grain)

wszakże (vshák-zhe) conj. adv.
yet; however; nevertheless

wszcząć (vshównćh) v. start; begin; institute; enter(talks)

wszechmocny (vshekh-móts-ni) adj.
m. omnipotent; almighty

wszechnica (vshekh-neé-tsa) f.
university

wszechstronny (vshekh-strón-ni)
adj. m. universal; versatile

wszechświat (vshékh-śhvyat) m.
universe; cosmos : macrocosm

wszelki (vshel-kee) adj. m.
every; all; any; whatever

wszerz (vshesh) adv. broadside

wszędzie (vsháṅ-dźhe) adv. everywhere; on all sides ;all over

wszystek (vshís-tek) adj. m.
whole; all; ever; the whole

wszywać (vshí-vach) v. sew in

wścibski (vśhćheeb-skee) m.
busybody; meddler; snooper

wściekać się (vśhćhé-kaćh shaṅ)
v. rage; rave; be furious

wścieklizna (vśhćhe-kleéz-na) f.
rabies ; madness;hydrophobia

wściekłość (vśhćhék-wośhćh) f.
fury; rage; tantrums;madness

wślad (vshlad) adv. following
in tracks; following closely

wśliznąć się (vśhleéz-nównćh
shaṅ) v. sneak in; slip in

wśród (yshroot) prep. among

wtaczać (vta-cháćh) v. roll in

wtajemniczyć (vta-yem-neé-chićh)
v. initiate; acquaint;instruct

wtargnąć (vtarg-nównćh) v. invade; break into; interrupt

wtedy (vte-di) adv. then

wtem (vtem) adv. suddenly

wtenczas (vtén-chas) adv. then;
at that time; at this junction

wtoczyć (vtó-chićh) v. roll in

wtorek (vto-rek) m. Tuesday

wtórny (vtoór-ni) adj. m. secondary ; incidental;repeated

wtrącać się (vtrówn-tsaćh shaṅ)
v. meddle; cut into; butt in

wtyczka (vtích-ka) f. plug

wtykać (vti-kaćh) v. insert

w tył (vtiw) adv. back

wuj (vooy) m. uncle

wujenka (voo-yén-ka) f. aunt

wulgarny (vool-gár-ni) adj. m.
vulgar; coarse; low

wulkan (vool-kan) m. volcano

wulkanizować (vool-ka-neé-zó-
vaćh) v. vulcanize ;cure(rubber)

wwozić (v-vó-żheećh) v. import

wwóz (v-voos) m. import;importation

wy (vi) pron. you; you people

wybaczać (vi-ba-cháćh) v. forgive; pardon; buckle out of line

wybawca (vi-báv-tsa) m. savior;
rescuer; liberator ;redeemer

wybawić (vi-bá-veećh) v. save;
deliver ; free;rescue; rid

wybebeszyć (vi-be-bé-shićh) v.
gut (chicken etc.)

wybić (vi-beećh) v. knock out
(something); strike; cover;kill

wybiec (vi-byets) v. run out

wybieg (vi-byek) m. evasion; runway; playground; fowl run

wybielić (vi-bye-leech) v. whitewash; bleach; coat with tin

wybierać (vi-bye-rach) v. choose elect; select; pick out ;mine

wybierak (vi-bye-rak) m. selector (technical term)

wybieralny (vi-bye-rál-ni) adj. m. elective; eligible ;electable

wybitny (vi-beet-ni) adj. m. prominent; eminent ; marked

wybladły (vi-blád-wi) adj. m. pale; dim; faded; colorless

wybłagać (vi-bwa-gach) v. get by entreaty; impetrate

wyblakły (vi-blák-wi) adj. m. faded; dim; dilute;weathered

wyboisty (vi-bo-ees-ti) adj.m. rough; full of holes; bumpy

wyborca (vi-bór-tsa) m. voter

wyborczy (vi-bór-chi) adj. m. electoral;election-(precinct...)

wyborny (vi-bór-ni) adj. m. excellent; prime; choice;splendid

wyborowy (vi-bo-ro-vi) adj. m. choice; select; first rate

wybory (vi-bo-ri) pl. election

wybór (vi-boor) m. choice;option

wybrany (vi-bra-ni) adj. m. elected; chosen; selected

wybredny (vi-bréd-ni) adj. m. fastidious; particular;exacting

wybrnąć (vibr-nownch) v. get out; pull through; wade;clear out of

wybrukować (vi-broo-kó-vach) v. pave (the road, the street etc.)

wybryk (vi-brik) m. prank; freak; antic; whim; frolic;caprice

wybrzeże (vi-bzhe-zhe) n. coast; beach; sea-shore; sea-coast

wybrzuszenie (vi-bzhoo-she-ñe) n. bulge; swelling; knob; belly

wybuch (vi-bookh) m. explosion; eruption; outbreak; outburst

wybudować (vi-boo-do-vach) v. build ; erect; raise;construct

wycelować (vi-tse-lo-vach) v. take aim; level a gun at

wychodek (vi-khó-dek) m. privy

wychodzić (vi-kho-dzheech) v. get out; walk out; climb out

wychodźca (vi-khódzh-tsa) m. emigrant ; émigré

wychować (vi-khó-vach) v. bring up ; rear; rise; train; educate

wychowanek (vi-kho-vá-nek) m. pupil;alumnus; ward ;foster child

wychowanie (vi-kho-vá-ñe) n. upbringing; manners ; education

wychowawca (vi-kho-váv-tsa) m. tutor; educator;foster father

wychudły (vi-khóod-wi) adj. m. gaunt; skinny; haggard ;emaciated

wychwalać (vi-khvá-lach) v. praise; exalt; extol;speak highly

wychylać (vi-khi-lach) v. stick out;empty (glass);bend;incline

wychylać się (vi-khi-lach shán) v. lean out; stick one's neck out; hang out; appear ;be visible

wyciąg (vi-chownk) m. extract; elevator; hoist; winch ;excerpt

wyciągać (vi-chown-gach) v. pull out; stretch out; derive; wycie (vi-che) n. howl ;scream

wycieczka (vi-chéch-ka) f. trip; excursion; outing ;ramble;hike

wyciekać (vi-ché-kach) v. leak out; flow out; ooze out ;scamper

wycieńczać (vi-cheñ-chach) exhaust

wycieńczenie (vi-cheñ-che-ñe) n. exhaustion; weakness; debility

wycieraczka (vi-che-rach-ka) f. wiper; doormat

wycierać (vi-che-rach) v. wipe; erase; efface;dust;wear out

wycięcie (vi-cháñ-che) n. opening; cut; décolleté ;notch;jag

wycinać (vi-chee-nach) v. cut out ; carve out; fell;cut down

wycisk (vi-cheesk) m. press; squeeze; beating (slang)

wyciskać (vi-chées-kach) v. squeeze out; impress; wring

wycofać (vi-tsó-fach) v. withdraw; remove;retract;call off

wycofanie (vi-tso-fá-ñe) n . withdrawal; recall;retirement

wyczerpać (vi-cher-pach) v. exhaust; drain; deplete;scoop

wyczerpanie (vi-cher-pa-ñe) n. exhaustion; depletion;prostration

wyczesywać (vi-che-si-vach) v. comb out; dress hair (beard etc.)

wyczuwać (vi-choo-vach) v. sense;
feel; scent; ascertain;perceive
wyczyn (vi-chin) m. feat; stunt
wyczyszczać (vi-chish-chach) v.
clean; brush; clean out; polish
wyć (vich) v. howl; roar;shriek
wyćwiczony (vich-vee-cho-ni)
adj. m. trained; skilled
wydajność (vi-day-noshch) f.
yield; productivity; output
wydajny (vi-day-ni) adj. m.
productive ; effective
wydalać (vi-da-lach) v. dismiss;
sack ; expel; eliminate;excrete
wydalenie (vi-da-le-ne) n. expulsion ; dismissal; excretion
wydanie (vi-da-ne) n. edition
wydarty (vi-dar-ti) adj. m.
torn out;plucked out;snached out
wydarzać się (vi-da-zhach shan)
v. happen; turn out well;occur
wydarzenie (vi-da-zhe-ne) n.
event ; happening;circumstance
wydatek (vi-da-tek) m. expense
wydatkować (vi-dat-ko-vach) v.
spend ; lay out funds;expend
wydatny (vi-dat-ni) adj. m.
prominent; salient; distinct
wydawać (vi-da-vach) v. spend;
give the change; publish
wydawca (vi-dav-tsa) m. publisher; editor;publishing house
wydawnictwo (vi-dav-neets-tvo)
n. publication; publishing
house;publishing firm
wydąć (vi-downch) v. expand;
puff up; inflate ; blow up
wydech (vi-dekh) m. exhalation
wydeptać ścieżkę (vi-dep-tach
shchezh-kan) beat a path (exp.)
wydłubywać (vi-dwoo-bi-vach) v.
scrape out; poke;hollow out
wydłużać (vi-dwoo-zhach) v. prolong; lengthen; elongate
wydma (vid-ma) f. dune;snowdrift
wydobrzeć (vi-dob-zhech) v. recover; get better ; improve
wydobycie (vi-do-bi-che) n, output; yield; production
wydobywać (vi-do-bi-vach) v. extract; mine; wring; get;obtain
wydostać (vi-dos-tach) v. bring
out; extricate; obtain;pull out

wydra (vi-dra) f. otter; vulg.:
bitch; hussy; minx;vixen
wydrapać (vi-dra-pach) v.
scratch out; erase a stain
wydrapać się (vi-dra-pach shan)
v. climb up; scramble up (out)
wydrążać (vi-drown-zhach) v.
hollow out ; drill; excavate
wydrwić (vi-drveech) v. jeer;
mock; cheat; gibe; deride
wydrwigrosz (vi-drvee-grosh)
m. swindler; fraud; take-in
wydusić (vi-doo-sheech) v.
squeeze out; extort; strangle
wydychać (vi-di-khach) v.
breathe out; exhale; emit
wydymać (vi-di-mach) v. puff out;
inflate; belly out;blow up;bulge
wydział (vi-dzhaw) m. department
wydziedziczać (vi-dzhe-dzhee-
chach) v. disinherit
wydzielać (vi-dzhe-lach) v.emit;
detach; distribute; secrete
wydzielenie (vi-dzhe-le-ne) n.
secretion; assignment; elimination; emanation ;issue
wydzieliny (vi-dzhe-lee-ni) pl.
sercreta; excretions; discharge
wydzielony (vi-dzhe-lo-ni) adj.
m. emited; segregated; alloted
wydzierać (vi-dzhe-rach) v. tear
out; roar out; blare out;scramble
wydzierżawić (vi-dzher-zha-veech)
v. lease; farm out; rent; let out
wydzierżawienie (vi-dzher-zha-
vye-ne) n. leasing;renting
wyegzekwować (vi-eg-zek-vo-vach)
v. exact; enforce; carry out
wyekwipowanie (vi-ek-vee-po-va-
ne) n. outfit; equipment
wyeleganciec (vi-e-le-gan-chech)
v. acquire elegance;become elegant
wyeliminowanie (vi-e-lee-mee-no-
va-ne) n. elimination;exclusion
wyga (vi-ga) m. old experienced
hand; sly fox; old stager
wygadać (vi-ga-dach) v. blab out
wygadany (vi-ga-da-ni) adj. m.
glib; eloquent; wordy ;talkative
wyganiać (vi-ga-nach) v. expel;
chase out; turn out(cattle)
wygarniać (vi-gar-nach) v. rake
out; tell off ; say openly ;shoot

wygasać (vi-ga-sach) v. extinguish; expire; go out; die out
wyginać (vi-gee-nach) v. bend
wygląd (vig-lównd) m. appearance;aspect; air;looks;semblance
wyglądać (vig-lówn-dach) v. look out; appear;appear;look
wygładzać (vi-gwa-dzach) v. smooth;level;even; sleek
wygłodzić (vi-gwo-dżheech) v. starve out; underfeed; famish
wygłosić (vi-gwo-sheech) v. pronounce; utter;deliver(speech)
wygnać (vig-nach) v.expel;banish
wygnanie (vig-na-ne) n. exile
wygniatać (vi-gna-tach) v. press out; squeeze out; extort; kill
wygoda (vi-go-da) f. comfort
wygodny (vi-god-ni) adj. m. comfortable; cozy; handy
wygolony (vi-go-lo-ni) adj. m. clean-shaven; well shaven
wygotować (vi-go-to-vach) v. boil away; distill; prepare
wygórowany (vi-goo-ro-va-ni) adj. m. excessive; stiff(price)
wygrać (vi-grach) v. win; score
wygramolić się (vi-gra-mo-leech shań) v. scramble up (out)
wygrana (vi-gra-na) f. winning; victory; prize; a win
wygryzać (vi-gri-zach) v. 1.bite out; corrode; 2. drive out by harassment;oust;bore a hole
wygrzebywać (vi-gzhe-bi-vach) v. dig out; unearth; rake out
wygrzewać się (vi-gzhe-vach shań) v. bask; warm oneself
wygwizdać (vi-gveez-dach) v. hiss off (stage); whistle away
wyjałowić (vi-ya-wo-veech) v. sterilize; exhaust(brain,soil...)
wyjaśnić (vi-yash-neech) v. explain; clear up; elucidate
wyjaśnienie (vi-yash-ne-ne) n. explanation; interpretation
wyjawić (vi-ya-veech) v. disclose; reveal; bring to light
wyjazd (vi-yazt) m. departure
wyjąkać (vi-yówn-kach) v. stammer out;stutter out; falter out
wyjątek (vi-yówn-tek) m. exception; excerpt; extract

wyjątkowy (vi-yówn-ko-vi) adj. m. exceptional;unusual;unique
wyjechać (vi-ye-khach) v. drive away; come out with
wyjeżdżać (vi-yezh-dzhach) v. leave; drive away; set out
wyjmować (viy-mo-vach) v. take out; remove; extract; excerpt
wyjście (viysh-che) n. exit; way out; departure;egress
wyka (vi-ka) f. vetch ; tare
wykadzić (vi-ka-dżheech) v. smoke out; fumigate; perfume
wykałaczka (vi-ka-wach-ka) f. toothpick
wykarczować (vi-kar-cho-vach) v. grub out; clear;dig up(trees)
wykaz (vi-kas) m. list; register; roll; schedule;docket
wykąpać (vi-kówn-pach) v. bathe
wykipieć (vi-keep-yech) v. boil over (milk,water,soup etc.)
wyklęty (vi-klań-ti) adj. m. cursed; excommunicated
wykluczyć (vi-kloo-chich) v. exclude;expel; shut out;except
wykład (vik-wat) m. lecture
wykładać (vi-kwa-dach) v. lecture; lay out; display; cover
wykładnik (vi-kwad-neek) m. exponent; expression; ratio
wykładowca (vi-kwa-dov-tsa) m. lecturer; instructor
wykłuwać (vi-kwoo-vach) v. stab out; put out; tattoo;prick out
wykoleić (vi-ko-le-eech) v. derail; lead astray;ditch(a train)
wykombinować (vi-kom-bee-no-vach) v. contrive; think out
wykonać (vi-ko-nach) v. execute; do; fulfil ; carry out; perform
wykonalny (vi-ko-nal-ni) adj.m. feasible; workable;realizable
wykonanie (vi-ko-na-ne) n. execution;realization;fulfilment
wykonawczy (vi-ko-nav-chi) adj. m. executive ;executory(details...)
wykończenie (vi-koń-che-ne) n. finish ; trimming;last touch
wykończyć (vi-koń-chich) v. finish off ; dress; do sb in
wykop (vi-kop) m. excavation ; potato lifting; flying kick

wykopać (vi-ko-pach) v. dig out
wykopalisko (vi-ko-pa-lees-ko)
n. find (archaeological)
wykorzenić (vi-ko-zhe-ńeech) v.
root out ; uproot; eradicate
wykorzystać (vi-ko-zhis-tach) v.
take advantage ; exploit:use up
wykpić (vik-peech) v. deride
wykraczać (vi-kra-chach) v. step
over; break law ; transgress
wykradać (vi-kra-dach) v. steal;
kidnap ;purloin;pilfer;abduct
wykrajać (vi-kra-yach) v. cut
out ; carve out;make a low cut
wykres (vi-kres) m. graph; chart
wykreślić (vi-kresh-leech) v.
trace; cross out ; draw ;erase
wykręcać (vi-krań-tsach) v. screw
out; distort; elude; twist
wykręt (vi-krant) m. shift;
excuse ; dodge ;guibble
wykrętny (vi-krant-ni) adj. m.
shifty ;evasive; sophistical
wykroczenie (vi-kro-che-ńe) n.of-
fense ; misdemeanor;delinquency
wykroić (yi-kro-eech) v. cut out
wykruszyć (vi-kroo-shich) v.
crumble out ; shell(corn etc.)
wykryć (vi-krich) v. discover;
detect ; reveal(the truth etc.)
wykrztusić (vi-kzhtoo-sheech) v.
cough up; choke out ;hawk up
wykrzyknąć (vi-kzhik-nownch) v.
call out ; shout; cry out
wykształcić (vi-kzhtaw-cheech) v.
educate ; train; shape; form
wykup (yi-koop) m. ransom
wykupić (vi-koo-peech) v. buy up
wykurzać (vi-koo-zhach) v. smoke
out (foxes,bees, etc.)
wykwintny (vi-kveent-ni) adj.m.
elegant; exquisite ; urbane
wyleczalny (vi-le-chal-ni) adj.
m. curable;possible to cure
wyleczyć (vi-le-chich) v. cure
wylew krwi (vi-lev krvee)
hemorrhage; blood effusion
wylewać (vi-le-vach) v. pour out;
overflow;spill;bail out water
wylęgać (vi-lan-gach) v. hatch
wylękły (vi-lańk-wi) adj. m.
frightened ; scared ;terrified

wyliczać (vi-lee-chach) v.
count up; count out; recite
wylosować (vi-lo-so-vach) adj.
m. draw out by lots ;toss for
wylot (vi-lot) m.flight departure; nozzle; exhaust; exit
wyludniać (vi-lood-ńach) v.
depopulate;desolate;devastate
wyładować (vi-wa-do-vach) v.
unload; discharge; cram;pack
wyładowanie (vi-wa-do-va-ńe)
n. unloading; discharge
wyłamać (vi-wa-mach) v. break
out;break loose;break away
wyławiać (vi-wav-yach) v. fish
out; spot out; catch (a sound)
wyłaniać (vi-wa-ńach) v. evolve;
emerge; show; appoint;form
wyłączać (vi-wown-chach) v.
exclude; switch off;disconnect
wyłącznik (vi-wownch-ńeek) m.
switch; circuit-breaker;cut off
wyłączny (vi-wownch-ni) adj.
m. exclusive; sole; only;entire
wyłudzić (vi-woo-dźheech) v.
coax; beguile; trick; fool
wyłom (vi-wom) m. breach; gap
wyłuskać (vi-woos-kach) v. husk;
scale; fleece; shell; hull; pod
wymaczać (vi-ma-chach) v. soak
wymagać (vi-ma-gach) v. require;
expect; demand; need; exact
wymaganie (vi-ma-ga-ńe) n. requirement; demand;requisite;need;
want
wymawiać (vi-mav-yach) v. pronounce; reproach; cancel;express
wymazać (vi-ma-zach) v. erase;
efface; blot out; smear;use up
wymiana (vi-mya-na) f. exchange
wymiar (vi-myar) m. dimension
wymiatać (vi-mya-tach) v.
sweep out; clean out; sweep
wymieniać (vi-mye-ńach) v.
exchange; convert; replace
wymierać (vi-mye-rach) v. die
out; become extinct(gradually)
wymierzać (vi-mye-zhach) v. aim;
measure; assess; survey;mete out
wymię (yi-myań) n. udder ∫evade
wymijać (vi-mee-yach) v. pass by;
wymiotować (vi-myo-to-vach) v.
vomit; be sick;spew up(one's food)

wymogi (vi-mo-gee) pl. require-
ments; exigencies:needs
wymowa (vi-mo-va) f. pronunciation; significance(of facts...)
wymowny (vi-mov-ni) adj. m.
eloquent; telltale; telling
wymóc (vi-moots) v. extort;
compel; wring; force;prevail
wymówienie (vi-moov-ye-ne) n.
notice (to quit or dismiss)
wymówka (vi-moov-ka) f. reproach;
pretext; excuse; put-off;evasion
wymusić (vi-moo-shich) v. extort
wymuszenie (vi-moo-she-ne) n.
extortion;blackmail;shakedown
wymykać się (vi-mi-kach shan)
v. escape;slip away;sneak out
wymysł (vi-misw) m. fiction;
invention ;fiction; abuse
wymyślać (vi-mish-lach) v. think
up; call names; invent; abuse
wymyślny (vi-mishl-ni) adj. m.
clever ; ingenious;sophisticated
wymywać (vi-mi-vach) v. wash out
wynagradzać (vi-na-gra-dzach) v.
reward; pay; indemnify;make up
wynagrodzenie (vi-na-gro-dze-ne)
n. reward; pay; fee; reparation
wynajdywać (vi-nay-di-vach) v.
find (out); invent; devise
wynajmować (vi-nay-mo-vach) v.
hire ; rent ; rent; hire
wynajem (vi-na-yem) m. lease ;
wynalazca (vi-na-laz-tsa) m.
inventor; contriver
wynalazek (vi-na-la-zek) m. invention ; device;contrivance
wynaleźć (vi-na-lezhch) v. invent
wynaradawiać (vi-na-ra-dav-yach)
v. denationalize ; divest
wynik (vi-neek) m. result; score
wyniosłość (vi-nos-woshch) f.
eminence; haughtiness ; prance
wyniosły (vi-nos-wi) adj. m.
lofty; high-handed ;insolent
wyniszczać (vi-neesh-chach) v.
ruin ; exhaust; weaken;devastate
wynosić (vi-no-sheech) v. carry
out; elevate; amount ;wear out
wynudzać (vi-noo-dzach) v. get
by bothering; bore stiff
wynurzenie (vi-noo-zhe-ne) n.
emergence; (personal) outpouring

wyobraźnia (vi-o-brazh-na) f.
imagination ; fancy;empty fancy
wyobrażać (vi-o-bra-zhach) v.
imagine; picture; fancy;suppose
wyobrażenie(vi-o-bra-zhe-ne) n.
notion; idea ; image;representation
wyodrębniać (vi-od-ranb-nach)
v. single out; separate; isolate
wyodrębnienie (vi-od-ranb-ne-
ne) n. separation; isolation
wyolbrzymiać (vi-ol-bzhi-myach)
v. magnify; exaggerate(very much)
wypaczyć (vi-pa-chich) v. warp
wypad (vi-pat) m. sally; attack
wypadać (vi-pa-dach) v. fall
out; rash out; become; turn
out; happen; occur; work out
wypadek (vi-pa-dek) m. accident;
case ;event; chance;instance
wypadkowa (vi-pad-ko-va) f. resultant (force, effect etc.)
wypakować (vi-pa-ko-vach) v.
unpack; cram ; pack tight
wypalać (vi-pa-lach) v. burn out
wypaplać (vi-pap-lach) v. babble
out ; blurt out(the truth,secret)
wyparcie się (vi-par-che shan)
n. disclaimer ; repudiation
wyparować (vi-pa-ro-vach) v.
evaporate; vanish into thin air
wypatrywać (vi-pa-tri-vach) v.
watch (for) ; look out;espy;descry
wypełniać (vi-pew-nach) v. fulfil; fill up ; while away;fill in
wypełnienie (vi-pew-ne-ne) n.
fulfilment ; order execution;filler
wypędzać (vi-pan-dzach) v. drive
out; expel ; discharge;dislodge
wypiekać (vi-pye-kach) v. bake;
wypierać (vipye-rach) v. oust;
push out;force out;supplant
wypierać się (vi-pye-rach shan)
v. deny ; repudiate;disown;abjure
wypijać (vi-pee-yach) v. drink
(empty); drink to; drink off
wypinać (vi-pee-nach) v. extend;
strech out ; show one's back side
wypis (vi-pees) m. extract;passage
wypisywać (vi-pee-si-vach) v.
(write) extract;make out(a check)
wyplątać (vi-plown-tach) v.
extricate; disentangle;disengage;
free from tangles

wyplątany (vi-plown-tá-ni) adj.
m. disembroiled;extricated
wyplenić (vi-ple-ńeech) v. weed
out; root out; eradicate
wypluć (vi-plooch) v. spit out
wypłacać (vi-pwa-tsach) v. pay
out; pay up; pay off; repay
wypłacalny (vi-pwa-tsal-ni) adj.
m. solvent; sound(financially)
wypłata (vi-pwa-ta) f. pay (day)
wypłoszyć (vi-pwó-shich) v.
scare away; drive away (cats...)
wypłowieć (vi-pwo-vyech) v. fade
wypłukać (vi-pwoo-kach) v. rinse;
wash out; swill out;give a rinse
wypływ (vi-pwiv) m. outflow;
discharge; efflux; leakage
wypływać (vi-pwi-vach) v. flow
out; sail out; swim out; rise
wypocić (vi-po-cheech) v. sweat
out; perspire ;be soaked in sweat
wypoczynek (vi-po-chi-nek) m.
rest; repose
wypoczywać (vi-po-chi-vach) v.
rest;have a rest;take a rest
wypogadzać się (vi-po-ga-dzach
shań) v. clear up; cheer up
wypomnieć (vi-pom-ńech) v. reproach; remind ;keep reminding
wypornośc (vi-por-noshch) f.
displacement; draught ;buoyancy
wyposażać (vi-po-sa-zhach) v.
equip; endow; fit out; stock
wyposażenie (vi-po-sa-zhe-ńe) n.
equipment; outfit; wages ;dowry
wyposażyć (vi-po-sa-zhich) v.
endow; equip; fit out;stock
wypowiadać (vi-po-vya-dach) v.
pronounce; declare ; express
wypowiedzenie (vi-po-vye-dze-ńe)
n.(discharge) notice; (war) declaration; renunciation;utterance
wypożyczać (vi-po-zhi-chach) v.
lend out;borrow from;hire to
wypożyczalnia (vi-po-zhi-chal-ńa)
f. rental business ;rental agency
wypracowanie (vi-pra-tso-vá-ńe)
n. (school) composition; elaboration ;essay; exercice
wyprać (vi-prach) v. wash out
wypraszać (vi-pra-shach) v.
1. plead; 2. show (the door) ;
give somebody the gate;turn out

wyprawa (vi-prá-va) f. expedition; outfit; tanning;dowry
wyprawiac (vi-pra-vyach) v.
send; tan;plaster;give(a party)
wyprężać (vi-pran-zhach) v.
stretch out; tense(a muscle etc.)
wyprostować (vi-pros-tó-vach)
v. straighten;set streight
wyprowadzać (vi-pro-va-dzach)
v. lead out; move out; trace
wypróbować (vi-proo-bó-vach)
v. test; try out;put to test
wypróżniać (vi-proozh-ńach) v.
empty; clear out; evacuate
wyprzedawać (vi-pzhe-dá-vach)
v. sell out; clear out(stock)
wyprzedaż (vi-pzhe-dash) v.
(clearance) sale
wyprzedzać (vi-pzhe-dzach) v.
pull ahead;outpace;overtake
wyprzęgać (vi-pzhan-gach) v.
unharness; unhitch (a horse)
wypukły (vi-pook-wi) adj. m.
convex; bulging; cambered
wypuscić (vi-poosh-cheech) v.
let out; set free; let go;
omit;release;launch;lease out
wypychac (vi-pi-khach) v. oust;
push out; stuff;pack; fill;cram
wypytywać (vi-pi-ti-vach) v.
question;ask questions;inquire
wyrabiac (vi-ra-byach) v.
1. make; form; 2. play pranks
wyrachowany (vi-ra-kho-vá-ni)
adj. m. scheming; thrifty
wyratować (vi-ra-tó-vach) v.
rescue; save (a life etc.)
wyraz (vi-ras) m. word; expression; look; term (in vocabulary)
wyraźny (vi-rázh-ni) adj. m.
explicit; clear; distinct
wyrażać (vi-rá-zhach) v. express
wyrażenie (vi-ra-zhé-ńe) n.
expression; utterance; phrase ;
statement
wyrąb (vi-rownp) m. clearing;
felling; cutting ; slash;fell
wyrąbać (vi-równ-bach) v. cut
out (with axe); clear; hack out
wyręczać (vi-ran-chach) v. help
out; replace; relieve of tasks
wyrobnik (vi-rób-ńeek) m. laborer; day-laborer ; navvy

wyrocznia (vi-roch-ña) f. oracle

wyrodny (vi-ród-ni) adj. m. degenerate;unnatural(son);base

wyrodzic się (vi-ro-dżheech śhäñ) v. degenerate;deteriorate

wyrok (vi-rok) m. sentence; verdict; judgment; pronouncement

wyrostek (vi-ros-tek) m. outgrowth; stripling; teenager

wyrosnięty (vi-rosh-nän-ti)adj. m. grown up ; overgrown

wyrozumiały (vi-ro-zoo-mya-wi) adj. m. indulgent; lenient

wyrozumienie (vi-ro-zoo-mye-ñe) n. sympathetic understanding

wyrób (vi-roob) m. manufacture

wyrównać (vi-roov-nach) v. equalize; pay up; smooth

wyrównanie (vi-roov-ná-ñe) m. leveling;balancing(accounts)offset

wyróżniać (vi-roozh-ñach) v. distinguish ; favor; single out

wyruszyć (vi-roo-shich) v. start out;set out;march out;sail away

wyrwać (vir-vach) v. extract; tear out; pull out; run away

wyrywki (yi-riv-kee) pl. random

wyryć (vi-rich) v. engrave; root up; dig out;gully;furrow;incise

wyrzec się (vi-zhets śhäñ) v. renounce;give up; forgo;repudiate

wyrzucać (vi-zhoo-tsach) v. expel; throw out; dump; reproach

wyrzut (vi-zhoot) m. reproach

wyrzutnia (vi-zhoot-ña) f. launch (ing)pad; chute; launcher

wyrzutek (vi-zhoo-tek) m. outcast

wyrzynać (vi-zhi-nach) v. cut out; carve; slaughter; bang; slap

wysadzić (vi-sá-dżheech) v. set out;land; blow up ; eject;plant

wyschnąć (vis-khnowñch) v. dry up

wysepka (vi-sép-ka) f. islet

wysiadać (vi-śha-dach) v. get out (from car etc.); go bust;get off

wysiadywać (vi-śha-di-vach) v. sit out; hatch out; sit late

wysiedlac (vi-śhed-lach) v. expel (from home); resettle;eject

wysilać (vi-śhee-lach) v. exert

wysiłek (yi-śhee-wek) m. effort

wyskoczyć (vi-sko-chich) v. jump out; pop up;run out;bale out

wyskok (vis-kok) m. 1. fling; freak; 2. cam;ledge;run out

wyskokowy (vis-ko-ko-vi) adj. m. alcoholic; intoxicating

wyskrobać (vi-skro-bach) v. scratch out; erase ;scratch

wyskubać (vi-skoo-bach) v. pluck out; pull out(hair etc.)

wysłać (vi-swach) v. send off; dispatch ;emit; let fly

wysłaniec (vi-swa-ñets) m. messenger; envoy ; deputy

wysłowić (vi-swo-veech) v. express ;say; utter; speak

wysłuchać (vi-swoo-khach) v. hear out ;give a hearing

wysługiwać się (vi-swoo-gee-vach śhäñ) v. lackey; use s.o.

wysmarować (vi-sma-ro-vach) v. smear ;lubricate; soil;stain

wysmażony (vi-sma-zho-ni) adj. m. well done (meat);cooked

wysmukły (vi-smook-wi) adj.m. slender ; slim and tall

wysoce (vi-so-tse) adv. highly

wysoki (vi-so-kee) m. tall; high ; soaring; lofty;towering

wysokość (vi-so-koshch) f. height; altitude;level;extent

wysokosciomierz (vi-so-kosh-cho-myesh) m. altimeter

wyspa (vis-pa) f. island; isle

wyspać się (vis-pach śhäñ) v. sleep enough; sleep off

wyspowiadac się (vis-po-vya-dach śhäñ) v. confess

wyssać (vis-sach) v. suck out ; suck dry

wystarać się (vi-sta-rach śhäñ) v. procure ;obtain; secure

wystarczyć (vi-står-chich) v. suffice ; do enough;be enough

wystawa (vi-sta-va) f. exhibition; display (window dressing)

wystawać (vi-sta-vach) v. stand out; stand long time ;stick out

wystawca (vi-stav-tsa) m. exhibitor; signer (of check)

wystawiac (vi-stav-yach) v. put out; stick out; sign (check) ; exhibit ;expose

wystawienie (vi-sta-vye-ñe) n. exposition; exposure ;display

wystąpić (vi-stown-peech) v.
step forward;perform;resign
wystąpienie (vi-stown-pye-ne)
n. withdrawal; appearance
występ (vi-stanp) m. protrusion;
(stage) appearance; utteramce
występek (vi-stan-pek) m. felony; crime; vice; offense
występny (vi-stanp-ni) adj. m.
criminal; immoral; illicit
wystraszyć (vi-stra-shich) v.
frighten away; terrify; scare
wystroić (vi-stro-eech) v. dress
up ; trig out; deck out; adorn
wystrzał (yi-stzhaw) m. shot
wystrzegać się (vi-stzhe-gach
shan) v. avoid ; beware; shun
wystrzelić (vi-stzhe-leech) v.
fire a gun ;shoot out; go off
wystrzępić (vi-stzhan-peech) v.
ravel out ; fray; unravel
wystygać (vi-sti-gach) v. cool
off ; grow cold;get cold
wysuszyć (vi-soo-shich) v. dry
up ; wither;parch; shrivel
wysuwać (vi-soo-vach) v. shove
forward; protrude; put out
wyswobodzić (vi-svo-bo-dzheech)
v. liberate; deliver; free
wysychać (vi-si-khach) v. dry out
wysypać (vi-si-pach) v. pour out
wysypka (vi-sip-ka) f. (skin)
rash ; eruption ;exanthema
wysysać (vi-si-sach) v. suck
wyszczególnić (vi-shche-gool-
neech) v. specify;detail out
wyszeptać (vi-sheptach) v. whis-
per(at vibrating the vocal rchords)
wyszkolić (vi-shko-leech) v.
train ;school; educate ;instruct
wyszpiegować (vi-shpye-go-vach)
v. spy out; spy out that...
wyszukać (vi-shoo-kach) v. find
out ; hunt up; search out
wyszukany (vi-shoo-ka-ni) adj.m.
choice; unusual ; elaborate
wyszydzać (vi-shi-dzach) v.
scoff at ; jeer; deride
wyszynk (vi-shink) m. liquor
store; liquor retail on licence
wyszywać (vi-shi-vach) v. embroider;desing with needlework

wyścielać (vi-shche-lach) v.
pad; line; strew;cushion
wyścig (vish-cheek) m. race;
contest ; rivalry ;(horse)race
wyśledzić (vi-shle-dzheech) v.
spy out; track out ;detect
wyślizgnąć się (vi-shleez-nownch
shan) y. slip out;slide out
wyśmiać (vish-myach) v. laugh
at; deride ;mock;ridicule
wyśmienity (vish-mye-nee-ti)
adj. m. choice; excellent
wyśpiewać (vi-shpye-vach) v.
squeal; sing; say ;sound praises
wyświadczyć (vish-vyad-chich)
v. do (favor); do (good);do (wrong)
wyświechtany (vi-shvyekh-ta-ni)
adj. m. well worn; beat up
wyświetlać (vish-vyet-lach) v.
clear up; project (film)
wytaczać (vi-ta-chach) v. roll
out ; set forth; draw ;turn
wytargować (vi-tar-go-vach) v.
buy by haggling; haggle a lot
wytarty (vi-tar-ti) adj.m.
worn out; thread bare;shabby
wytchnąć (vi-tkhnownch) v. rest
up ; relax ;take a rest;breathe
wytchnienie (vi-tkhne-ne) n.
rest; break; relax; truce
wytępić (vi-tan-peech) v.extermi-
nate; eradicate; wipe out
wytężać (vi-tan-zhach) v. strain
wytknąć (vit-knownch) v. put out;
point out; reproach; trace
wytłuc (vi-twoots) v. kill off;
break up ; ruin; beat up
wytłumaczenie (vi-two-ma-che-
ne) n. explanation; excuse
wytłumaczyć (vi-twoo-ma-chich)
v. explain; excuse; justify
wytrawny (vi-trav-ni) adj. m.
experienced; dry (wine) ;seasoned
wytrącać (vi-trown-tsach) v.
knock of ; deduct; snatch
wytrwały (vi-trva-wi) adj. m.
enduring; persevering; dogged
wytrwanie (vi-trva-ne) n. endurance; persistence ;lasting
wytrwać (vi-trvach) v. persevere
wytrych (vi-trikh) m. pick-a-
-lock; pass-key ; skeleton-key

wytrząść (vi-tzhownshch) v.
shake out ; empty; jolt
wytrzebić (vi-tzhe-beech) v.
devastate; exterminate ; clear
wytrzeźwieć (vi-tzheźh-vyech) v.
sober up;;get sober; sober down
wytrzymać (vi-tzhi-mach) v. endure; stand;hold out; keep
wytrzymałość (vi-tzhi-ma-woshch)
f. endurance ; stamina;strength
wytrzymały (vi-tzhi-ma-wi) adj.
m. enduring ; tough; durable
wytworny (vi-tvor-ni) adj. m.
exquisite ;elegant; stylish
wytwórca (vi-tvoor-tsa) m. producer; manufacturer,; maker
wytwórczość (vi-tvoor-choshch)
v. productivity ;,output ;product
wytwórnia (vi-tvoor-ňa) f. manufacture; factory; plant ;works
wytyczna (vi-tich-na) f. direc-
tive; guideline: guiding rule
wyuzdanie (vi-ooz-da-ňe) n. unbridled license ;adv.dissolutely
wywiad (vi-vyat) m. interview;
reconnaissance ; espionage
wywiązać się (vi-wyown-zach shaň)
v. develop; arise; discharge
(duty); result; set in; evolve
wywierać (vi-vye-rach) v. exert
wywiercać (vi-vyer-tsach) v. bore
out; sink a well;drill a hole
wywlekać(vi-vle-kach) v. drag
out ; tug; bring out :pull out
wywietrzać (vi-vyet-zhach) v.
ventilate ; air; nose out
wywłaszczać (vi-vwash-chach) v.
expropriate ;dispossess
wywłaszczenie (vi-vwash-che-ňe)
n. expropriation ;dispossession
wywnioskować (vi-vňos-ko-vach)
v. infer; draw a conclusion
wywodzić (vi-vo-dźheech) v. lead
out; derive ; deduce ;lead nowhere
wywojować (vi-vo-yo-vach) v.
fight out ; gain by force
wywołać (vi-vo-wach) v. call;
cause; develop (film); recall
wywozić (vi-vo-żheech) v. export
wywód (vi-voot) m. deduction
wywóz (vi-voos) m. export ;removal
wywracać (vi-vra-tsach) v. overturn; overthrow; reverse ;upset

wywyższać (vi-vizh-shach) v.
exalt; elevate;extol;rise
wyzbyć się (viz-bich shaň) v.
get rid;sell out; get over
wyzdrowieć (vi-zdro-vyech) v.
recover; get well;recuperate
wyziębić (vi-zhaň-beech) v.
chill ;let get cold ;cool
wyzionąć (vi-żho-nownch) v.
expire; give up(the ghost)
wyznaczać (vi-zna-chach) v.
mark out; appoint; point out
wyznanie (vi-zna-ňe) n. denomination; declaration;creed
wyznawać (vi-zna-vach) v. profess;
declare ; hold a belief;confess
wyznawca (vi-znav-tsa) m. believer; follower; advocate
wyzuć (vi-zooch) v. deprive;
take off (shoe) ; strip;divest;
bereave
wyzywać (vi-zi-vach) v. challenge ; call names;abuse;revile
wyzwalać (vi-zva-lach) v. liberate; free;let loose; exempt
wyzwolenie (vi-zvo-le-ňe) n .
liberation; release;exemtion
wyzwolić (vi-zvo-leech) v. liberate; free; release; set free
wyzysk (vi-zisk) m. exploita-
tion; sweating(of labor)
wyzyskiwacz (vi-zis-kee-vach) m.
exploiter; slave driver
wyż (vizh) m. hight; highland;
high pressure; peak; atm.high
wyżarty (vi-zhar-ti) adj. m.
over-fed; corroded; bloated
wyżej (vi-zhey) adv. higher;
above; mentioned above;higher up
wyżeł (vi-zhew) m. pointer
wyżerać (vi-zhe-rach) v. eat
away; corrode; erode; eat up
wyżłobić (vi-zhwo-beech) v.
hollow out ;gully; erode;groove
wyżłobienie (vi-zhwo-byé-ňe) n.
groove; gully; erosion;channel
wyższość (vizh-shoshch) f. superiority; excellence;predominance
wyższy (vizh-shi) adj. m. higher
(up),; taller; superior;top(floor)
wyżyć (vi-zhich) v. use up;
hardly live ; make ends meet;
pull through;survive;pull through:
find an outlet for...

wyżyć się (vi-zhich shán) v.
live up; fulfill oneself
wyżymaczka (vi-zhi-mach-ka) f.
wringer (also machine)
wyżymać (vi-zhi-mach) v. wring
wyżyna (vi-zhi-na) f. high
ground; upland;summit(of glory)
wyżywić (vi-zhi-veech) v. feed
wyżywienie (vi-zhi-vye-ne) m.
food; board; subsistance;diet
wzajemny (vza-yem-ni) adj. m.
mutual; reciprocal; inter-
w zamian (vza-myan) adv. in
exchange; instead; in return
wzbić się (vzbeech shán) v.
soar (up); shoot up; rise
wzbogacić (vzbo-ga-cheech) v.
enrich; add to; dress;make rich
wzbraniać (vzbra-nach) v. forbid; prohibit
wzbroniony (vzbro-no-ni) adj.m.
forbidden; prohibited
wzbudzać (vzboo-dzach) v. excite; inspire;arouse; stir
wzburzenie (vzboo-zhe-ne) n.
agitation; unrest; tumult
wzburzyć (vzboo-zhich) v. stir
up; agitate;dishevel;covulse
wzdać (vzdównch) v. puff up;fan
wzdłuż (vzdwoosh) prep. along
wzdrygać się (vzdri-gach shán)
v. flinch; object; shudder
wzdychać (vzdi-khach) v. sigh
wzgarda (vzgár-da) f. contempt
wzgardliwy (vzgard-lee-vi) adj.
m. disdainful; scornful
względność (vzgland-noshch) f.
relativity (of understanding...)
względny (vzgland-ni) adj. m.
relative; indulgent; kind of
względy (vzglán-di) pl. favors
wzgórze (vzgoo-zhe) n. hill
wziąć (vzhównch) v. take;possess
wziernik (vzher-neek) m. peep-
hole; scope;view-finder;spy-hole
wzięty (vzhán-ti) adj. m. popular;in demand; in vogue
wzlot (vzlot) m. ascend; rise
wzmacniać (vzmats-nach) v. reinforce; brace up; fortify
wzmagać (vzma-gach) v. intensify
wzmianka (vzmyán-ka) v. mention

wzniesienie (vzne-she-ne) n.
elevation; height;erection
wznieść (vzneshch) v. raise;
elevate; erect; lift; rear
wzniosły (vznos-wi) adj. m.
lofty; noble; elevated;sublime
wznowić (vzno-veech) v. renew
wznowienie (vzno-vye-ne) n.
resumption; come back;reissue
wzorowy (vzo-ro-vi) adj. m.
exemplary ;model; perfect
wzór (vzoor) m. pattern; model;
formula; fashion; standard
wzrok (vzrok) m. sight; vision
wzrost (vzrost) m. growth;size;
height; increase; rise;stature
wzruszać (vzroo-shach) v. move;
touch; affect; thrill; stir
wzruszający (vzroo-sha-yown-tsi)
adj. m. touching; moving;pathetic
wzuć (vzooch) v. put on (shoe)
wzuwacz (vzoo-vach) m. shoe
horn(for pulling boots,shoes on)
wzwyż (vzvizh) adv. up; upwards
skok wzwyż (skok vzvizh) m.
high jump
wzywać (vzi-vach) v. call; call
in; summon; cite; ask in
z (z) prep. with; off; together
ze (ze) prep. with; off; together;from(the ceiling etc.)
za (za) prep. behind; for; at;
by; beyond; over(a wall)
zabarwić (za-bar-veech) v. stain;
dye ; tint; color;tinge;tincture
zabarwienie (za-bar-vye-ne) n.
color(ing); pigmentation; tinge
zabawa (za-ba-va) f. play; fun;
party; game; recreation;amusement
zabawiać (za-bav-yach) v. entertain ;amuse;dwell;stay; last
zabawka (za-bav-ka) f. toy;trife
zabawny (za-bav-ni) adj. m.
funny; comical; ridiculous
zabezpieczenie (za-bez-pye-che-
ne) n. protection ; safety
zabezpieczyć (za-bez-pye-chich)
v. safeguard; secure ;protect
zabić (za-beech) v. kill; slay;
plug up; nail down;beat(a card)
zabieg (za-byek) m. measure;
procedure; exertions; fuss

zabiegać (za-bye-gach) v. strive;
try hard; court; woo; fuss over
zabierać (za-bye-rach) v. take
away; take along; take on (up)
zabierać się (za-bye-rach shän)
v. clear out; get ready for
zabijać (za-bee-yach) v. kill;
deaden ; wear out; exhaust
zabijaka (za-bee-ya-ka) m. bully;
blusterer; swaggerer; hector
zabity (za-bee-ti) adj. m. killed; dead; out-and-out;thorough
zablizniać (za-bleezh-nach) v.
form cicatrize ; scar up
zabłądzić (za-bwown-dzheech) v.
go astray; get lost; stray
zabłąkany (za-bwown-ka-ni) adj.
m. stray (bullet, man, steer, etc)
zabłocić (za-bwo-cheech) v. get
muddy ; muddy (shoes etc)
zabobon (za-bo-bon) m. superstition;belief in omens, stars etc.
zaboleć (za-bo-lech) v. ache
zaborca (za-bór-tsa) m. invader
zabójca (za-booy-tsa) m. killer
zabójczy (za-booy-chi) adj. m.
murderous ; seductive ;lethal
zabójstwo (za-booy-stvo) n. killing; murder ; homicide
zabór (za-boor) m. annexed territory ; annexation;rape(of Peru..)
zabraniać (za-bra-nach) v. forbid
zabrudzać (za-broo-dzach) v. dirty;
soil; make a mess (of something)
zabudować (za-boo-do-vach) v.
build over; build upon; close
zabudowania (za-boo-do-va-ña) pl.
buildings (on farm, factory etc.)
zaburzenie (za-boo-zhe-ñe) n.
disorder; rout; agitation
zabytek (za-bi-tek) m. relic;
monument(of art, nature etc.)
zachcianka (zakh-chan-ka) f. fad;
fancy; caprice ; whim ;megrim
zachęta (za-khan-ta) f. encouragement; stimulus ;incentive;spur
zachłanność (za-khwan-noshch) f.
greed ; rapacity ;cupidity
zachlysnąć się (za-khwis-nównch
shän) v. choke;swallow a bad way
zachmurzyć (za-khmoo-zhich) v.
cloud; become gloomy;overcloud

zachmurzenie (za-khmoo-zhe-ñe)
n. cloudiness; gloom;gloominess
zachodzić (za-kho-dzheech) v.
call on; occur; arise; become;
set; creep from behind;drop in
zachodni (za-khod-ñee) adj. m.
western; westerly
zachorować (za-kho-ró-vach) v.
get sick; fall ill;be taken ill
zachowanie (za-kho-va-ñe) n.
behavior; maintainance;manners
zachowawczy (za-kho-vav-chi)
adj. m. conservative
zachowywać (za-kho-vi-vach) v.
preserve; maintain;keep(calm)
zachowywać się (za-kho-vi-vach
shän) v. behave; survive;go on
zachód (za-khoot) m. west;sunset;
pains; trouble; endeavor
zachód słońca (za-khoot swoñ-
tsa) m. sunset
zachrypnięty (za-khrip-ñan-ti)
adj. m. hoarse;of a hoarse voice
zachwalać (za-khva-lach) v.
praise; crack up;boost;cry up
zachwiać (zakh-vyach) v. rock;
shake; unsettle (balance etc.)
zachwycać (za-khvi-tsach) v.
fascinate; charm ;delight;enchant
zachwyt (zakh-vit) m. fascination; rapture ;enchantment
zaciąg (za-chowng) m. recruitment; levy; draft ;conscription
zaciągać (za-chown-gach) v.
recruit; drag to; run in debt
zaciekać (za-ché-kach) v. leak;
stain; run down ; fill(up)
zaciekawić (za-che-ka-veech) v.
interest; puzzle; intrigue
zaciekawienie (za-che-ka-vye-ñe)
n. interest; curiosity
zaciekły (za-chek-wi) adj. m.
stubborn; bitter; rabid;stiff
zaciemnić (za-chem-ñeech) v.
obscure; dim; darken ;black out
zacieniać (za-che-ñach) v.
shade; darken ;throw shade
zacierać (za-che-rach) v. efface; erase; hush up ;cover up
zaciesniać (za-chesh-nach) v.
tighten up ; narrow; limit
zacięty (za-chan-ti) adj. m.
obstinate; stubborn ;dogged

zacinac (za-chee-nach) v. notch;
cut; lash; hack; taper;set(teeth)
zaciskac (za-chees-kach) v.
tighten; clench; squeeze;clasp
zacisze (za-chee-she) n. retreat
zacny (zats-ni) adj. m. worthy;
good; upright;respectable
zacofany (za-tso-fa-ni) adj.m.
backward;old fashioned
zaczaic się (za-cha-eech shan)
v. lie in ambush; lurk; hide
zaczarowac (za-cha-ro-vach) v.
enchant; bewitch; cast a spell
zaczac (za-chownch) v. start;
begin; fire away; go ahead
zaczepiac (za-chep-yach) v.
hook on; accost; touch upon
zaczepny (za-chep-ni) adj. m.
aggressive; offensive;provocative
zaczerpac (za-cher-pach) v.
scoop up; dip up; draw; lade
zaczerwienic (za-cher-vye-neech)
v. redden; blush; flush;paint red
zaczynac (za-chi-nach) v. start;
begin; cut (into a new loaf)
zacmienie (zach-mye-ne) n. e-
clipse ; obfuscation
zad (zad) m. posterior; rump
zadac (za-dach) v. give; put;
deal; associate; treat with
zadanie (za-da-ne) n. task; charge; assignment; problem;job;stint
zadatek (za-da-tek) m. earnest
money; down payment;installment
zadławic (za-dwa-veech) v. choke
zadłuzyc się (za-dwoo-zhich shan)v.
get in debt;debit; take mortgage
zadłuzenie (za-dwoo-zhe-ne) n.
debts; indebtedness; liabilities
zadowalajacy (za-do-va-la-yown-
tsi) adj. m. satisfactory; fair
zadowolic (za-do-vo-leech) v.
satisfy; gratify; please;suffice
zadowolony (za-do-vo-lo-ni) adj.
m. satisfied; content;pleased
zadra (za-dra) f. sliver; splinter (in one's finger etc.)
zadrapac (za-dra-pach) v. scratch
open; make a scratch; scratch
zadrasnac (za-dras-nownch) v.
scratch ; wound (pride etc)
zadraznic (za-drazh-neech) v.
irritate; embitter; inflame

zadrgac (zadr-gach) v. twitch;
vibrate ; tremble; flicker
zadrwic (za-drveech) v. sneer
zaduch (za-dookh) m. bad air;
stuffy air; stink;fustiness;fug
zaduma (za-doo-ma) f. meditation; reverie;musing;wistfulness
zadusic(za-doo-sheech) v.throttle;
smother; choke ;strangle;suffocate
Zaduszki (za-doosh-kee) n.
All Souls Day
zadymka (za-dim-ka) f. snow-
storm; blizzard
zadyszany (za-di-sha-ni) adj.
m. breathless; panting
zadzierac (za-dzhe-rach) v.
tear open; turn up; quarrel
zadzierzysty (za-dzher-zhis-
ti) adj. m. defiant; perky
zadziwiac (za-dzheev-yach) v.
astonish; amaze; astound
zadzwonic (za-dzvo-neech) v.
ring; ring up ; ring for
zagadka (za-gad-ka) f. puzzle;
riddle ;crux; problem;quizz
zagadnienie (za-gad-ne-ne) n.
problem ; question; issue
zagajnik (za-gay-neek) m. grove
shubbery ; scrub ;coppice;copse
zagiac (za-gyownch) v. bend
zaginiony (za-gee-no-ni) adj.
m. lost; missing (person)
zagladac (za-glown-dach) v.
peep; look up; look into
zaglada (za-gwa-da) f. extinc-
tion ; extermination;annihilation
zaglebic (za-gwan-beech) v.
plunge; sink; dip;immerse
zaglodzic (za-gwo-dzheech) v.
starve to death; starve out
zagluszac (za-gwoo-shach) v.
silence; jam; drown out; stifle
zagmatwac (za-gmat-vach) v.
entangle; confuse; embroil
zagniewany (za-gne-va-ni) adj.
m. angry; cross; sore;in a huff
zagospodarowywac (za-gos-po-da-
ro-vi-vach) v. make property
productive ; manage (an estate)
zagotowac (za-go-to-vach) v.
boil; start boiling; flare up
zagrabic (za-gra-beech) v. rake
over; grab; seize;carve out

zagradzać (za-gra-dzać) v. bar;
fence; obstruct; intercept
zagranica (za-gra-nee-tsa) f.
foreign countries;ouside world
zagraniczny (za-gra-neech-ni)
adj. m. foreign;external(trde...)
zagrażać (za-gra-zhać) v.
threaten; impend;be imminent
zagroda (za-gro-da) f. farm
house with yard; enclosure
zagrodzić (za-gro-dżeeć) v.
fence in; bar; enclose;obstruct
zagrożony (za-gro-zho-ni) adj.
m. threatened; endangered
zagrzebać (za-gzhe-bać) v.
bury (in the grave,in the past...)
zagrzewać (za-gzhe-vać) v.heat;
warm up; animate;inspire;spur
zahaczać (za-kha-chać) v. hook;
question; accost;find fault
zahamować (za-kha-mo-vać) v.
restrain; put brakes on; stop
zaimek (za-ee-mek) m. pronoun
zainteresowanie (za-een-te-re-
so-va-ne) n. interest;concern
zaiste (za-ees-te) adv. truly;
indeed; very true; verily; yea
zajadać (za-ya-dać) v. enjoy
eating ; gorge;eat heartily
zajadły (za-yad-wi) adj. m.
fierce; rabid;bitter driveway
zajazd (za-yazt) m. motel; inn;
zając (za-yownts) m. hare
zając (za-yownch) v. occupy
zajechać (za-ye-khać) v. drive
up; block; stump; pull in ;stink
zajęcie (za-yan-che) v. occupation; work;trade; interest
zajmować(zay-mo-vać) v. occupy
zajmujący (zay-moo-yown-tsi) adj.
m. interesting; absorbing
zajście (zaysh-che) n. incident
zakalec (za-ka-lets) m. slack
baked bread(or cake)
zakatarzony (za-ka-ta-zho-ni)
adj. m. having a cold
zakatować (za-ka-to-vać) v.
flog to death;torture to death
zakaz (za-kas) m. prohibition
zakazić (za-ka-zheeć) v. infect
zakazywać (za-ka-zi-vać) v.
forbid ; ban; suppress;prohibit;
forbid to do;suppress(activity...)

zakaźny (za-kazh-ni) adj. m.
infectious ; contagious
zakąska (za-kowns-ka) f. snack
zaklęcie (za-klan-che) n. spell;
curse;incantation;charm;entreaty
zakład pogrzebowy (za-kwat po-
gzhe-bo-vi) m. funeral parlor
zakład (za-kwat) m. plant;shop;
institute; bet; wager; fold
zakładać (za-kwa-dać) v.
found; initiate; put on; lay
zakładka (za-kwad-ka) f. fold;
book- mark;tuck;pleat;splice
zakładnik (za-kwad-neek) m.
hostage (for ransom etc.)
zakłamanie (za-kwa-ma-ne) n.
hypocrisy ;mendacity;distortion
zakłopotanie (za-kwo-po-ta-ne)
n. embarrassment;confusion
zakłócać (za-kwoo-tsać) v.
disturb; unsettle;ruffle
zakłuwać (za-kwoo-vać) v. stab
to death ; prick ;stick (a pig)
zakochać się (za-ko-khać shań)
v.fall in love ;become infatuated
zakochany (za-ko-kha-ni) adj.m.
in love ; infatuated;enamorated
zakomunikować (za-ko-moo-nee-ko-
vać) v. communicate; let
know; convey a message; notify
zakon (za-kon) m. monastic
order ;convent; sisterhood
zakonnica (za-kon-nee-tsa) f.
nun ;religious (woman)
zakonnik (za-kon-neek) m. monk
zakończenie (za-koń-che-ne) n.
end; ending; termination;tip
zakopać (za-ko-pać) v. bury
zakorkować (za-kor-ko-vać) v.
plug up;cork up;jam(the traffic)
zakorzenić się (za-ko-zhe-neech
shań) v. get roots in;take roots
zakorzeniony (za-ko-zhe-no-ni)
adj. m. rooted; deep rooted
zakradać się (za-kra-dać shań)
v. creep; steal; sneak(into)
zakrapiać (za-krap-yać) v.
put drops in; sprinkle; have
a drink;instil(in one's eyes)
zakres (za-kres) m. range;field;
scope; domain; sphere;realm
zakreślić (za-kresh-leech) v.
outline; mark off; encircle

zakręcić (za-kran-cheech) v.
turn; twist; turn off; curl
zakręt (za-krant) m. curve;bend
turn ⌠turnbuckle ; cap; nut;
zakrętka (za-krant-ka) f. latch;
zakrwawić (za-krva-veech) v.
stain with blood;draw blood
zakryć (za-krich) v. cover; hide
zakrzatnąc sie (za-kzhownt-
nownch shan) v.get busy;bustle
zakrztusic (za-kzhtoo-sheech)v.
choke (on food,fish bone etc.)
zakrzywic (za-kzhi-veech) v.
bend; bend down; bend back
zaksięgować (za-kzhan-go-vach)
v. post; enter in the books
zakup (za-koop) m. purchase
zakurzony (za-koo-zho-ni) adj.
m. dusty;covered with dust
zakuty (za-koo-ti) adj. m.
shackled; chained; dull (witted)
zakwitnąć (za-kveet-nownch) v.
blossom out; go moldy
zalążek (za-lown-zhek) m. germ;
ovule;seed; origin;embryo
zalecac (za-letsach) v. recommend; advise; enjoin; court; woo
zaledwie (za-led-vye) adv. barely;
scarcely; merely; but; only just
zalegac (za-le-gach) v. be behind (in paying);lie useless;fill
zaległy (za-leg-wi) adj. m. unpaid; overdue;unaccomplished
zalepic (za-le-peech) v. glue (up)
over; gum up; paste over;seal up
zalesienie (za-le-she-ne) n.
forestation; afforestation
zaleta (za-le-ta) f. virtue;
advantage; quality; good point
zalew (za-lev) m. flood; bay;
invasion; deluge;lagoon
zalewać (za-le-vach) v. pour
over; flood;submerge;swarm;spill
zależec (za-le-zhech) v. depend
zależny (za-lezh-ni) adj.m.
dependent; contingent;subordinate
zaliczac (za-lee-chach) v. include; count in; credit;rate;accept
zaliczka (za-leech-ka) f. earnest
money; down payment;installment
zalotnica (za-lot-nee-tsa) f.
flirt; coquette; kitten(slang)

zalotnik (za-lot-neek) m. suit-
or ; wooer; wheedler
zaloty (za-lo-ti) adj. m.
courtship;wooing;love making
zaludniac (za-lood-nach) v.
populate ;bring in population
zaludnienie (za-lood-ne-ne) n.
population;population density
załadowac (za-wa-do-vach) v.
load up; embark;ship(goods)
załagodzic (za-wa-go-dzheech)
v. mitigate; alleviate; soothe
załamac (za-wa-mach) v. break
down; collapse; crash; slump
załamanie (za-wa-ma-ne) n.
break down; (light) refraction
załatwiac (za-wat-vyach) v.
settle; transact; deal;dispose
załączac (za-wown-chach) v.
enclose ; connect;annex;plug in
załącznik (za-wownch-neek) m.
enclosure; attachment; annex
załoga (za-wo-ga) f. crew;
garrison; staff; personnel
założenie (za-wo-zhe-ne) n.
layout; foundation; assumption
założyciel (za-wo-zhi-chel) m.
founder; initiator;promotor
zamach (za-makh) m. attempt;
swing; sweep; coupd'état;spar
zamaczac (za-ma-chach) v. steep;
dip; wet; soak; drench
zamarzły (za-mar-zwi) adj.m.
frozen; frezen over;frozen stiff
zamarznąc (za-mar-znownch) v.
freeze up;freeze over;congeal
zamaskowac (za-mas-ko-vach) v.
mask; conceal; hide; disguise
zamaszysty (za-ma-shis-ti) adj.
m. brisk; vigorous;dashing;heavy
zamawiac (za-ma-vyach) v. reserve; order ;book; engage(workers)
zamazac (za-ma-zach) v. smear
over; soil up; daub;blur(a picture)
zamącic (za-mown-cheech) v.ruffle;
disturb; make turbid; stir a liquid
zamążpójscie (za-mownzh-pooy-
shche) n. marriage
zamek (za-mek) m. lock; castle
zamek błyskawiczny (za-mek
bwis-ka-veech-ni) m. zipper
zamęt (za-mant) m. confusion;welter

zamężna (za-mánzh-na) adj. f.
married(woman in married state)
zamiana (za-mya-na) f. exchange
zamianować (za-mya-no-vach) v.
nominate ; appoint;design
zamiar (za-myar) m. purpose ;
zamiast (za-myast) prep. instead of;in place;in lieu
zamiatać (za-mya-tach) v. sweep
zamieć (za-myech) f. snowstorm;
blizzard;snow in a windstorm
zamiejscowy (za-myeys-tso-vi)
adj. m. out of town;long distance
zamienić (za-mye-neech)v. change;
convert; replace;swap;turn into
zamienny (za-myen-ni) adj. m.
exchangeable;interchangeable
zamierać (za-mye-rach) v. die
out; fade out ; wither;die away
zamierzać (za-mye-zhach) v. intend; mean;propose;plan;think
zamierzenie (za-mye-zhe-ne) n.
aim; purpose ; plan; project
zamieszać (za-mye-shach) v. stir
up; blend; mix up ; involve
zamieszanie (za-mye-sha-ne) n.
confusion ; disarray;turmoil;stir
zamieszkać (za-myesh-kach) v.
take residence ;put up;live
zamieszkiwać (za-myesh-kee-vach)
v. inhabit ; reside ;occupy;live
zamilknąć (za-meel-knownch) v.
became silent ; be hushed
zamiłowanie (za-mee-wo-va-ne) n.
predilection ; fondness ;liking
zamknąć (zam-knownch) v. close;
shut; lock ;wind up; fence in
zamoczyć (za-mo-chich) v. wet;
soak; steep; drench ;submerge
zamorski (za-mor-skee) adj. m.
overseas; from overseas
zamożny (za-mozh-ni) adj. m.rich;
wealthy ; affluent ;well to do
zamówić (za-moo-veech) v. order;
reserve ; commission ;book;engage
zamówienie (za-moo-vye-ne) n.
order ; commission ;custom order
zamrażać (za-mra-zhach) v. freeze
zamroczyć (za-mro-chich) v. dim;
gloom; confuse; darken ;bewilder
zamsz (zamsh) m. chamois; suede
zamulić (za-moo-leech) v. fill
with slime ; silt up (a harbor)

zamurować (za-moo-ro-vach) v.
brick over ; brick up ;wall up
zamydlić (za-mid-leech) v.
soap over ;pull wool over eyes
zamykać (za-mi-kach) v. shut;
conclude ; close (the view etc.)
zamysł (za-misw) m. design
zamyślać się (za-mish-lach shan)
v. contemplate; muse; ponder
zamyślenie (za-mi-shle-ne) n.
reverie; pondering; meditation
zanadto (za-nad-to) adv. too
much ; excess ;beyond measure
zaniechać (za-ne-khach) v.
give up ; wave; desist from
zanieczyścić (za-ne-chish-cheech)
v. soil ; dirty; litter;grime
zaniedbanie (za-ned-ba-ne) n.
neglect; negligence ;sloppiness
zaniemóc (za-ne-moots) v. become ill ; fall ill ;get sick
zaniemówić (za-ne-moo-veech)
v. become speechless (dumb)
zaniepokoić (za-ne-po-ko-eech)
v. alarm; up set; disturb
zaniepokojenie (za-ne-po-ko-ye-
ne) n. anxiety ; alarm; concern
zanieść (za-neshch) v. carry
zanik (za-neek) m. disappearance
zanikać (za-nee-kach) v. disappear ;vanish; decay; wither
zanim (za-neem) conj. before ;
zanocować (za-no-tso-vach) v.
stay over night ; put up at
zanotować (za-no-to-vach) v.
note; write down ;take down
zanurzyć (za-noo-zhich) v. dip
zaocznie (za-och-ne) adv. in
absence;(judgement)by default
zaognić (za-og-neech) v. inflame ; irritate ;excite;kindle
zaokrąglić (za-o-krowng-leech)
v. round off ; make even
zaopatrzenie (za-o-pa-tzhe-ne)
n. supplies;equipment;provision
zaopatrzyć (za-o-pa-tzhich) v.
provide; equip; supply ;fit out;
furnish;stock
zaorać (za-o-rach) v. plough
over(a field etc.);plough up
zaostrzyć(za-os-tzhich) v. sharp-
en; whet; tighten (restrictions);
stimulate(the appetite);intensify

zaoszczędzić (za-osh-chán-
dzheech) v. save ; spare(trouble)
zapach (zá-pakh) m. smell;aroma
zapadać (za-pá-dach) v. fall in;
sink ; set in; drop; settle
zapakować (za-pa-kó-vach) v.
pack up ; stow away; pack off
zapalczywy (za-pal-chí-vi) adj.
m. hotheaded; impetuous
zapalenie (za-pa-lé-ńe) n. ignition ; inflammation(of the skin...)
zapaleniec (za-pa-le-ńets) m.
fanatic ; enthusiastic;hot head
zapalić (za-pa-leech) v. switch
on light; set fire ; animate
zapalniczka (za-pal-ńeech-ka)
f. (cigarette) lighter
zapalnik (za-pál-ńeek) m. fuse
zapalny (za-pál-ni) adj. m.
inflammable ; ardent; impetuous
zapał (zá-paw) m. enthusiasm
zapałka (za-paw-ka) f. match
zapamiętać (za-pa-myán-tach) v.
remember ; memorize;keep in mind
zaparcie (za-pár-che) n. constipation; denial
zaparzać (za-pá-zhach) v. draw
(tea);brew; gall;make(tea);heat
zapas (zá-pas) m. stock; store;
reserve ; supply ;fund;refill
zapasowy (za-pa-só-vi) adj. m.
spare ; emergency(door,part,etc)
zapaść (zá-pashch) v. collapse
zapaśnik (za-pásh-ńeek) m.
wrestler
zapatrywać się (za-pa-tri-vach
śhan) v. have opinion; consider; stare ; take example
zapatrywanie (za-pa-tri-va-ńe)
n. opinion; view ;slant
zapełnić (za-pew-ńeech) v. fill
up ; stop a gap ;fill(a space etc.)
zaperzyć się (za-pe-zhich śhan)
v. flare up ; be testy;get mad
zapewne (za-pev-ne) adv. cer-
ly ; surely; doubtless ;I daresay
zapewnić (za-pév-ńeech) v. assure
zapewnienie (za-pev-ńe-ńe) n. assurance ; protestation;assertion
zapieczętować (za-pye-chán-to-
vach) v. seal up;seal with wax
zapierać się (za-pye-rach śhan)
deny; disavow ;resist;repudiate

zapinać (za-pee-nach) v. button up; fasten;buckle up
zapis (zá-pees) m. registration;
bequest; record; notation
zapisać (za-pee-sach) v. note
down; prescribe; enroll; bequeath; record; write down
zapisek (za-pee-sek) m. note
zaplątać (za-plówn-tach) v.
entangle ;snarl;involve
zaplecze (za-plé-che) n. hinterland; base(of supplies etc.)
zapłacić (za-pwa-cheech) v. pay
zapłakany (za-pwa-ka-ni) adj.
m. in tears; tearful;tear stained
zapłata (za-pwa-ta) f. payment
zapłodnić (za-pwód-ńeech) v.
fertilize ; inseminate;fecundate
zapłon (za-pwon) m. ignition
zapobiegać (za-po-bye-gach) v.
prevent;avert; ward off;stave off
zapobiegliwy (za-po-bye-glee-
vi) adj. m. anticipating;thrifty
industrious;thrifty;provident
zapodziać (za-pó-dźhach) v.
misplace;mislay; get lost
zapominać (za-po-mee-nach) v.
forget;neglect; unlearn
zapomnienie (za-pom-ńe-ńe) n.
oblivion; forgetfulness
za pomocą (za-po-mo-tsówn) adv.
by means; with help(of a tool...)
zapomoga (za-po-mó-ga) f. hand
out; relief; benefit; grant
zapora (za-pó-ra) f. dam; obstacle ; barrier;check;barrage
zapotrzebowanie (za-po-tzhe-bo-
va-ńe)n.(demand) requisition
zapowiadać (za-po-vya-dach) v.
announce ; forecast; pretend
zapoznać (za-póz-nach) v. acquaint ;introduce;instruct
zapożyczać (za-po-zhi-chach) v.
borrow; adopt from ;take from
zapracować (za-pra-tsó-vach) v.
earn; get by hard work
zapracowany (za-pra-tso-vá-ni)
adj. m. earned; overworked
zapraszać (za-pra-shach) v.
invite(to dinner etc.);offer
zaprawa (za-prá-va) f. mortar;v.
seasoning; training;work out

zaprawdę (za-praw-dän) adv. in
deed ; to tell you the truth...
zaprawic (za-pra-veech) v. season ;train; learn;dress;spice
zaproszenie (za-pro-she-ne) n.
invitation (to dinner etc.)
zaprowadzic (za-pro-va-dzheech)
v. lead in; establish ;initiate
zaprząg (za-zhowng) m. team
zaprzeczac (za-pzhe-chach) v.
deny ; contest ; dispute
zaprzeczenie (za-pzhe-che-ne) n.
denial ; negation;contradiction
zaprzepascic (za-pzhe-pash-
cheech) v. loose; waste ; miss
zaprzestac (za-pzhes-tach) v.
discontinue; stop ; cease;quit
zaprzęg (za-pzhäng) m. team; cart;
harness ; yoke; carriage;turn out
zaprzyjaznic się (za-pzhi-yazh-
neech shän) v. make friends
zaprzysiąc (za-pzhi-showñts) v.
swear by oath ;vow; pledge
zaprzysiężony (za-pzhi-shän-zho-
ni) adj. m. sworn in ;pledged
zapusty (za-poos-ti) pl.carni-
val; Shrovetide
zapuszczac (za-poosh-chach) v.
let in (dye); grow (hair);
neglect ; let down;sink into
zapychac (za-pi-khach) v. stuff;
cram ;fill;block ;choke;crowd
zapytanie (za-pi-ta-ne) n. question; inquiry ; query; asking
zapytywac (za-pi-ti-vach) v. ask
zarabiac (za-rab-yach) v. earn
zaradczy (za-rad-chi) adj. m.
preventive ; remedial(measure)
zaradny (za-rad-ni) adj. m. resourceful (man, boy etc.)
zaranie (za-ra-ne) n. downing
zarastac (za-ras-tach) v. overgrow; cicatrize (a wound)
zaraz (za-ras) adv. at once;
directly;right away; soon
zaraza (za-ra-za) f. infection;
plague ; epidemic ;pestilence
zarazek (za-ra-zek) m. virus;
germ ; microbe ;(disease)bacteria
zarazem (za-ra-zem) adv. at the
same time ; as well; also
zarazic (za-ra-zheech) v. infect

zarażenie (za-ra-zhe-ne) n.
infection (with a disease etc.)
zardzewiec (zar-dze-vyech) v.
rust ; get rusty;corrode
zaręczyny (za-rañ-chi-ni) n.
betrothal; engagement ;engagement-
zarobek (za-ro-bek) m. gain;bread;
earnings; wages;livelihood;living
zarobkowac (za-rob-ko-vach) v.
earn working ; earn a living
zarodek (za-ro-dek) m. embryo
zarosły (za-ros-wi) adj. m.
overgrown (with vegetation etc.)
zarost (za-rost) m. beard; hair
zarosla (za-rosh-la) n. thicket
zarozumiały (za-ro-zoo-mya-wi)
adj. m. conceited ; uppish
zarówno (za-roov-no) adv. equally; as well ; alike ; both
zarumienic się (za-roo-mye-neech
shän) v. blush ;flush; brown
zaryglowac (za-rig-lo-vach) v.
bolt a door; bar an entrance
zarys (za-ris) m. sketch; outline ; broad lines;design;draft
zarząd (za-zhownd) m. management ; administration; board
zarządca (za-zhownd-tsa) m.
administrator ; manager
zarządzenie (za-zhown-dze-ne)
n. administrative order
zarzucac (za-zhoo-tsach) v. fill;
give up; reproach ; fling ;cast
zarzut (za-zhoot) m. reproach;
objection ; accusation; blame
zasada (za-sa-da) f. principle;
alkali; base ; law ;rule;tenet
zasadniczy (za-sad-nee-chi) adj.
m. fundamental; essential; basic
zasadzka (za-sadz-ka) f. ambush
zasądzic (za-sown-dzheech) v.
sentence ; adjudge to (somebody)
zasępiony (za-sañ-pyo-ni) adj.
m. gloomy; despondent ;dejected
zasiadac (za-sha-dach) v. take
a seat; sit down; settle down
zasięg (za-shänk) m. reach ;scope
zasięgać rady (za-shän-gach ra-
di) v. consult; seek advice
zasiłek (za-shee-wek) m. hand-
out; grant ;relief;subvention
zaskarżyć (za-skar-zhich) v. sue

zasklepić się (za-skle-peech
śhań) v. scab; shut oneself
up (in); seal up; vault;wall up
zaskoczyć (za-sko-chich) v. surprise; attack unawares;click;lock
zaskórny(za-skoor-ni) adj. m.
subcutaneous;underground(water)
zasłabnąć (za-swab-nownch) v.
faint; get sick;grow faint;swoon
zasłać (za-swach) v. cover (bed)
zasłona (za-swo-na) f. blind;
veil; screen; curtain;shield
zasłonic (za-swo-ñeech) v.
curtain; shade ; shield;cover up
zasługa (za-swoo-ga) f. merit
zasługiwać (za-swoo-gee-vach)
v. deserve ; be worthy;merit
zasłużony (za-swoo-zho-ni) adj.
m. man of merit ;just; fair
zasmucic (za-smoo-cheech) v.
sadden ; pain; distress;grieve
zasmucony(za-smoo-tso-ni) adj.
m. sad; grieved;distressed
zasnąć (za-snownch) v. fall a-
sleep; sleep;drop off to sleep
zasobnik(za-sob-ñeek) m. container; tank;storage tank
zasób (za-soop) m. store; resource ; stock; supply
zaspa (zas-pa) f. snowdrift;
dune; drifted sand;drifted snow
zaspac (zas-pach) v. oversleep
zaspokoic (za-spo-ko-eech) v.
satisfy; quench; appease;provide
zastanowic sie (za-sta-no-veech
śhań) v. reflect; puzzle;ponder
zastaw (za-stav) m. pawn; deposit; security;pledge;forfeit;lien
zastawic (za-sta-veech) v.
1. bar; 2. pledge; 3. set a
table ; cram a room;lay(snares)
zastąpic (za-stown-peech) v. replace; bar passage;do duty for
zastepca (za-stanp-tsa) adj.m.
proxy; substitute; deputy
zastepczo (za-stanp-cho) adv.
replacing; temporary; in lieu
zastepstwo (za-stanp-stvo) n.
replacement ;proxy; agency
zastosowac (za-sto-so-vach) v.
adopt; apply ; employ;make use
zastosować sie (za-sto-so-vach
śhań) v. comply ; toe the line

zastosowanie (za-sto-so-va-ñe)
n. application; use compliance
zastoj (za-stooy) m. stagnation
zastraszyc (za-stra-shich) v.
intimidate ;cow;bully;bulldoze
zastrzał (za-stzhaw) m. (knee)
brace; strut; boom; cramp
zastrzec (za-stzhets) v. reserve ; stipulate;condition
zastrzeżenie (za-stzhe-zhe-ñe)
n. reservation; proviso
zastrzyk (za-stzhik) m. injection ; shot(in the arm)
zastygnąć (za-stig-nownch) v.
congeal ; set; harden;petrify
zasuszyc (za-soo-shich) v. dry
up ; wither ; shrivel(the skin)
zasuwa (za-soo-va) f. bar;
(door) bolt;valve ;shutter
zasuwka (za-soov-ka) f. small
bolt ;damper; valve
zasypac (za-si-pach) v. bury;
cover; add (to soup);fill up
zasypiac (za-sip-yach) v. cat
nap; doze off; fall asleep
zaszczepiac (za-shche-pyach)
v. inoculate; graft;instill
zaszczycac (za-shchi-tsach) v.
honor; dignify; favor; grace
zaszczyt (zash-chit) m. honor;
distinction; privilege;dignity
zaszkodzic (za-shko-dźheech) v.
harm; hurt; damage; injure
zasznurowac (za-shnoo-ro-vach)
v. tie up; lace(shoes);tighten
zaszyc (za-shich) v. sew up
zaszyc sie (za-shich śhań) v.
hide; burrow ; conceal oneself
zas (zaśh) conj. but; whereas;
and ; while; specially
zaslepic (za-śhle-peech) v.
blind; infatuate;blind to facts
zaslepiony (za-śhle-pyo-ni) adj.
m. infatuated; fanatic ;blind
zaslubic (za-śhloo-beech)v.
marry ; get married
zaslubiny (za-śhloo-bee-ni) pl.
wedding ; marriage ;nuptials
zasmiecic (za-śhmye-cheech) v.
litter ; clutter up (a room etc.)
zaśniedziały (za-śhne-dźha-wi)
adj. m. rusty; stagnant

zasrubować (za-shroo-bó-vach) v. screw tight ; screw on (a lid)

zaświadczenie (za-shvyad-che-ne) n. certificate ;affidavit

zaświadczyć (za-shvyád-chich)v. certify; attest; witness

zaświecić (za-zhvye-cheech) v. put light on ; light up ;turn on

zataczać (za-ta-chach) v. roll in; describe(a circle) ; stagger;wheel

zataić (za-tá-eech) v. conceal; suppress; keep secret ;hold back

zatamować (za-ta-mo-vach) v. dam up; stop ; block ;impede

zatańczyć (za-tań-chich) v. dance; perform a dance

zatapiać (sa-tap-yach) v.flood; sink ; penetrate ;inundate;scuttle

zatarasować (za-ta-ra-so-vach) v. obstruct; block up; bolt

zatarg (zá-tark) f. conflict

zatem (zá-tem) adv. then; consequently; therefore ; and so

zatemperować (za-tem-pe-ro-vach) v. sharpen a pencil etc.

zatkać (za-tkach) v. stop up

zatlić się (za-tleech shań) v. catch fire ; smoulder

zatłoczony (za-two-cho-ni) adj. m. crowded ; crammed; cluttered

zatoka (za-tó-ka) f. bay; gulf

zatonąć (za-to-nownch) v. sink

zator (zá-tor) m. (traffic) jam

zatracić (za-trá-cheech) v. lose; waste ; lose all sense of

zatroskać(za-tros-kach) v. grieve

zatrucie (za-troo-che) n. poisoning ; intoxication; toxaemia

zatruć (za-trooch) v. poison

zatrudniać (za-trood-nach) v. employ ; engage ;take on(workers)

zatrzask (zá-tzhask) m. (door) latch; (snap) fastener lock

zatrzymać (za-tzhi-mach) v. stop; retain; detain ;arrest; hold

zatwardzenie (za-tvar-dze-ne) n. constipation; costiveness

zatwierdzać (za-tvyer-dzach) v. approve ;confirm; ratify;affirm

zatwierdzenie (za-tvyer-dze-ne) n. ratification; approval;assent

zatwierdzić (za-tvyer-dzheech) v. ratify; approve ;confirm;validate

zatyczka (za-tich-ka) f. plug

zatykać (za-ti-kach) v. stop up ; plug up; insert a plug

zaufać (za-oo-fach) v. confide

zaufanie (za-oo-fá-ne) n. confidence ; trust ;faith; reliance

zaufany (za-oo-fá-ni) adj. m. reliable; confidential;trusted

zaułek (za-oo-wek) m. alley; back street ; lane ;recess; nook

zauważyć (za-oo-vá-zhich) v. notice ; catch sight;remark

zawada (za-vá-da) f. obstruction; nuisance; hindrance

zawadiaka (za-vad-yá-ka) m. bully; blusterer;swashbuckler

zawadzać (za-vá-dzach) v. hinder; scrape; touch ;be a drag

zawalać (za-vá-lach) v. soil

zawalić (za-vá-leech) v. collapse; obstruct; bury;bungle

zawartość (za-vár-toshch) f. contents ; subject (of a book)

zawczasu (za-vcha-soo) adv. in good time ;in advance

zawczoraj (za-vcho-ray) adv. the day before yesterday

zawdzięczać (za-vdzhán-chach) v. owe (gratitude) ; be indebted

zawezwać (za-vez-vach) v. call; summon; call in (a doctor etc)

zawiadomić (za-vya-do-meech) v. inform; give notice ;let know

zawiadomienie (za-vya-do-mye-ne) n. notification ;information

zawiadowca stacji (za-vya-dóv-tsa státs-yee) m. stationmaster ;superintendent

zawiasa (za-vyá-sa) f. hinge

zawiązać (za-vyown-zach) v. tie up ; bind; set up (a club)

zawieja (za-vyé-ya) f. blizzard

za wiele (za vye-le) adv. too much ; too many (expenses etc.)

za widna (za veed-na) adv. in day light; in light;before dark

zawierać (za-vyé-rach) v. contain; conclude; shut; strike up

zawierucha (za-vye-roo-kha) f. wind storm ; gale; (war)clouds

zawieszenie broni (za-vye-shé-ne bro-ńee) n. armistice ;truce; cessation of hostilities

zawietrzna (za-vyétzh-na) f.
lee side(sheltered from the wind)
zawijac (za-vee-yach) v. wrap
up; tuck in; put in at a port
zawikłac (za-veek-wach) v. complicate; entangle;embroil;tangle
zawiły (za-vee-wi) adj. m. intricate; baffling;knotty(problem)
zawinąc (za-vee-nownch) v. wrap
zawinic (za-vee-neech) v. be
guilty;commit an offense
zawisły (za-vees-wi) adj. m.
dependent(on somebody etc.)
zawistny (za-veest-ni) adj. m.
envious;jealous (of something...)
zawisc (za-veeshch) f. envy
zawitac (za-vee-tach) v. call
on; come and see   ſwrap
zawlec (za-vlets) v. drag;tug;
zawodnik (za-vod-neek) m. competitor (in sport);contestant
zawodowiec (za-vo-do-vyets) m.
professional; specialist
zawody (za-vo-di) pl. (sport)
competition;match;race;game;event
zawodzic (za-vo-dźheech) v.
1. lead; 2. disillusion;lament
zawołac (za-vo-wach) v. call out;
exclaim; shout; cry out; summon
zawołany (za-vo-wa-ni) adj. m.
excellent; perfect;born(poet etc.)
zawozic (za-vo-źheech) v. convey;
take to; cart; deliver;give rides
zawod (za-vood) m. 1. profession;
2. disappointment; deception
zawor (za-voor) m. valve; vent
zawrot głowy (za-vroot gwó-vi) m.
dizziness; vertigo;giddiness
zawstydzic (za-vsti-dźheech) v.
shame; embarrass ;overwhelm
zawsze (záv-she) adv. always;
evermore;(for)ever;at all times
zawszyc (zav-shich) v. louse up
zawziąc się (záv-żhownch śhan) v.
be obstinate; persist ; set on
zawziętosc (zav-żhán-toshch) f.
persistence; obstinacy; keenness
zazdrosny (zaz-drós-ni) adj. m.
jealous; envious;resentful
zazdrosc (záz-droshch) f. envy
zaziębic się (za-żhan-beech śhan)
v. catch a cold

zaznaczyc (za-zna-chich) v.
mark ; make a note; state;
zaznac (záz-nach) v. experience;
taste;   enjoy; undergo
zaznajomic (za-zna-yó-meech)
v. acquaint ; introduce to
zazwyczaj (za-zvi-chay) adv.
usually ; generally; ordinarily
zażalenie (za-zha-lé-ńe) n.
complaint; grievance
zażarty (za-zhár-ti) adj. m.
fierce; bitter;vehement
zażądac (za-zhówn-dach) v.
demand ; require; order
zażenowac (za-zhe-no-vach) v.
shame ;embarrass;confuse;abash
zażyły (za-zhí-wi) adj. m. familiar; intimate ;close;chummy
zażywac pigułki (za-zhí-vach
pee-goów-kee) v. take pills
ząb (zównp) m. tooth; fang;
prong; cog;otch;indentation
ząb mleczny (zównp mléch-ni)
m. milk tooth (of a child etc.)
ząb trzonowy (zównp tzho-nó-vi)
adj. m. molar
ząbkowac (zównb-ko-vach) v.
teethe; jag;cut one's teeth
zbaczac (zba-chach) v. deviate
zbankrutowany (zban-kroo-to-vá-
ni) adj. m. bankrupt; insolvent
zbawca (zbáv-tsa) m. savior
zbawiciel (zba-vee-chel) m.
savior; redeemer; Saviour
zbawicielka (zba-vee-chel-ka)
f. savior; redeemer
zbawic (zbá-veech) v. save;
redeem ; rescue;take(time)
zbawienie (zba-vyé-ńe) n. salvation;deliverance;rescue;redemption
zbesztac (zbésh-tach) v. scold
zbezczescic (zbez-chésh-cheech)
v. desecrate; defile;profane
zbędny (zbánd-ni) m. superfluous ; redundant; needless;useless
zbieg(zbyek) m. fugitive; runaway
zbieg okolicznosci (zbyek o-ko-
leech-nósh-chee) m. coincidence ;occurrence at the same time
zbiegac (zbyé-gach) v. run down
zbiegowisko (zbye-go-vees-ko)
n. concourse; throng; crowd

zbieracz (zbye-rach) m. collector; gatherer ; picker
zbierać (zbye-rać) v. gather;
pick; summon; clear; take in
zbieżny (zbyezh-ni) adj. m.
convergent; tapering;concurrent
zbijać (zbee-yać) v. knock
together; refute;beat down
zbiornik (zbyor-neek) m. tank;
reservoir; container;receptacle
zbiór (zbyoor) m. harvest; collection; set; crop;class;series
zbiórka (zbyoor-ka) f. rally;
assembly ;meeting;gathering
zbir (zbeer) m. thug; ruffian
zbity (zbee-ti) adj. m.close;
1 beaten up; 2. compact;dense
zblednąc (zbléd-nownćh) v.pale;
grow pale; fade;turn pale
z bliska (zbleés-ka) adv. from
near ; close up;from near
zbliżać (zblee-zhać) v. nearby
zbliżyć się (zblee-zhićh śhań)
v. become close; approach;be near
zbliżenie (zblee-zhe-ńe) n. rap-
prochement; close-up
zbliżony (zblee-zho-ni) adj. m.
approximate; nearing;congenial
zbłądzić (zbwown-dźheećh) v.
go astray; make mistake; lose
trail;err; wander off;err;blunder
zbocze (zbo-che) n. (hill) slope
zboczenie (zbo-che-ńe) n. deviation; aberration;drift;sag
zbolały (zbo-lá-wi) adj. m. aching ; sore; woeful; wretched
zboże (zbo-zhe) n. corn; grain
zbój (zbooy) m. bandit; robber
zbór ewangielicki (zboor e-van-
ge-leets-kee)m. Protestant
Church; Evangelical Church
zbratać się (zbra-tać śhań) v.
fraternize; chum up (with)
zbroczony krwią (zbro-cho-ni
krvyówn) adj. m. blood-stained
zbrodnia (zbrod-ńa) f. crime
zbrodniarz (zbrod-ńash) m. criminal; felon; malefactor
zbroić (zbro-eećh) v. arm
zbroja (zbro-ya) f. armor
zbrojony beton (zbro-yó-ni beton) m. reinforced concrete

zbrojownia (zbro-yov-ńa) f.
arsenal; armory ; gunroom
zbryzgać (zbriz-gać) v. spatter ; bespatter; splash
zbrzydnąc (zbzhid-nownćh) v.
grow ugly; lose good looks
zbudować (zboo-do-vać) v. build
zbudzić się (zboo-dźheećh śhań)
v. wake up ; awake; be roused
zbujać (zboo-yać) v. fool;
hoax ; pull one's leg
zburzyć (zboo-zhićh) v. demolish
zbutwieć (zboo-tvyećh) v. mold-
er. ; rot;decompose;decay;spoil
zbydlęcić (zbi-dlań-ćheećh) v.
imbrute;turn into a brute
zbyt (zbit) adv. too, (much)
zbyt wiele (zbit vye-le) adv.
too much ; excessively;over-
zbyt (zbit) m. sale; market
zbyteczny (zbi-tech-ni) adj. m.
superfluous ;needless;redundant
zbytek (zbi-tek) m. frills;
luxury ;pl.:pranks;follies
zbytni (zbit-nee) adj. m. excessive; undue;more than needed
zbytnik (zbit-neek) m. rogue
zbywać (zbi-vać) v. dispose;
dismiss; put off;sell;lack;want
z czasem (z cha-sem) adv.
eventually;later
z dala (z da-la) adv. from far
z daleka (z da-le-ka) adv. from
far; from afar; away from
zdalnie (zdal-ńe) adv. remote;
from afar; by remote control
zdanie (zda-ńe) n. opinion;
judgment; sentence; proposition
zdanie sprawy (zda-ńe spra-vi)
n. report; account;giving account
zdarzać się (zda-zhać śhań) v.
happen; take place;occur
zdarzenie (zda-zhe-ńe) n. happening; event; incident
zdatność (zdat-noshćh) f. fitness; capability;suitability
zdatny (zdat-ni) adj. m. able;
fit; apt;suitable (for the purpose)
zdawać (zda-vać) v. entrust;
submit;turn over;give up;pass(tests)
zdawać się (zda-vać śhań)
1. seem; 2. surrender; 3.rely

z dawien dawna (zda-vyen dáv-na) adv. from way back

z dawna (zdáv-na) adv. since a long time;from way back

zdążyć (zhówn-zhich) v. come on time; keep pace; tend

zdechlak (zdékh-lak) m. weakling

zdechły (zdékh-wi) adj. m. peaky; dead (animal); weakly; sickly

zdecydować się (zde-tsi-dó-vach śhań) v. decide ; determine

zdejmować (zdey-mó-vach) v. take off ; strip(clothes); snap(photo)

zdenerwowany (zde-ner-vo-vá-ni) adj. m. nervous ; excited

zderzak (zdé-zhak) m. bumper

zderzenie (zde-zhé-ńe) n. collision; clash; crash;smash-up

zderzyć się (zdé-zhich śhań) v. collide ; clash; run into

zdjęcie (zdyáń-che) n. snapshot

zdjęcie rentgenowskie (zdyáń-che rent-ge-nóv-skye) n. X-ray picture;X-ray phtograph

zdmuchiwać (zdmoo-khee-vach) v. blow off ; blow out; blow away

zdobić (zdo-beech) v. decorate

zdobycz (zdó-bich) f. booty; spoils;prey; prize;trophy

zdobyć (zdó-bich) v. conquer

zdolność (zdól-nośhch) f. ability; capacity ; talent;aptitude

zdolny (zdól-ni) adj. m. clever; able ; capable; fit ;competent

zdołać (zdó-wach) v. be able

zdrada (zdrá-da) f. treason

zdradliwy (zdrad-lee-vi) adj.m. treacherous; tricky; unsafe

zdradzać (zdrá-dzach) v. betray

zdrajca (zdráy-tsa) adj. m. traitor; informer; turncoat

zdrapać (zdrá-pach) v. scratch off ; scrape off; loosen up

zdrętwieć (zdráht-vyech) v. grow numb ; stiffen ;grow torpid

zdrętwienie (zdrant-vyé-ńe) n. numbness;stiffnes; torpidity

zdrobniały (zdrob-ńá-wi) adj.m. diminutive; grown smaller

zdrojowisko (zdro-yo-vees-ko) n. spa ; health resort ;baths

zdrowie (zdróv-ye) n. health ; good constitution;being well

zdrowotne jedzenie (zdro-vót-ne ye-dzé-ńe) n. health food

zdrowy (zdró-vi) adj. m. healthy; sound; mighty ;in good health

zdrożny (zdrózh-ni) adj. m. vicious ; wicked; wrong ;fatigued

zdrój (zdrooy) m. spring; spa

zdrów i cały (zdroóv ee tsá-wi) m. safe and sound

zdrzemnąć się (zdzhém-nównch śhań) v. doze off; sleep light; catnap; take a nap

zdumienie (zdoo-myé-ńe) n. astonishment ; amazement

zdumiony (zdoo-myó-ni) adj.m. astonished ; flabbergasted

zdun (zdoon) m. stove fitter

zdwajać (zdvá-yach) v. double

zdychać (zdi-khach) v. die

zdyszany (zdi-shá-ni) adj.m. breathless ; panting;out of breath

zdziałać (zdżhá-wach) v. accomplish ; achieve ;manage to do

zdziczeć (zdżhee-chech) v. grow wild; become savage; turn wild

zdziecinnieć (zdżhe-cheen-ńech) v. grow childish(in the old age)

zdzierać (zdżhe-rach) v. strip off; fleece; tear down; peel

zdzierstwo (zdżher-stvo) n. extortion; exorbitance

zdziwaczeć (zdżhee-vá-chech) v. become odd; grow whimsical

zdziwić (zdżhee-veech) v. surprise; astonish;make wonder

zdziwienie (zdżhee-vyé-ńe) n. surprise; wonderment;astonishment

zebra (zé-bra) f. zebra

zebrać(zé-brach) v. gather;clear

zebranie (ze-brá-ńe) n. meeting

zecer (zé-tser) m. type setter

zechcieć (zékh-chech) v. be willing; feel inclined; choose

zegar (zé-gar) m. clock ;meter

zegar słoneczny (zé-gar swo-néch-ni) sundial

zegarek (ze-gá-rek) m. watch

zegarmistrz (ze-gár-mees tsh) m. watchmaker; watchmaker's shop

zejście (zéysh-che) n. descent

zejść (zeyśhch) v. descend

zejść się (zeyśhch śhań) v. meet; rendez vous;have a date

zelówka (ze-loov-ka) f.(shoe)sole
zelżeć (zél-zhech) v. lighten
up ;ease; let up ;diminish;abate
zemdleć (zem-dlech) v. faint;
pan out ; swoon; feel weak
zemsta (zem-sta) f. revenge
zepchnąć (zép-khnownch)v. push
down; drive out ;shove down
zepsuć (zép-sooch) v. damage;
spoil; worsen; pervert;harm;injure
zepsuty (zep-soo-ti) adj. m.
damaged; spoiled ; corrupt ;bad
zerkać (zér-kach) v. squint;peep
zero (zé-ro) n. zero; nought; nil
zerwać (zér-vach) v. pick off;
snap loose; break off; sprain
zerwanie (zer-vá-ñe) n. rupture
zeskakiwać (ze-ska-kée-vach) v.
jump down ; dismount;jump off
zeskrobywać (se-skro-bí-vach) v.
scrape off ; erase;srcape clean
zesłać (ze-swach) v. deport;
send down ; send into exile
zesłanie (ze-swa-ñe) n. deportation ; exile; penal colony
zespolić (ze-spo-leech) v. unite
zespół (ze-spoow) m. team; group;
gang ; crew; set; troupe;complex
zestarzeć się (ze-sta-zhech śhań)
v. grow old ; age; stale;get old
zestawienie (ze-sta-vye-ñe) n.
comparison; balance sheet; list
zestrzelenie (ze-stzhe-le-ñe) n.
shotting down; downing(a plane)
zeszłoroczny (ze-shwo-rocz-ni)
adj. m. last year's (crop etc.)
zeszpecić (ze-shpe-cheech) v.
disfigure ; make look ugly ;deface
zeszyt (ze-shit) m. notebook
ześlizgiwać się (ze-śhleez-gée-
vach śhań) v. glide down; slip
zetknąć się (zét-knownch śhań)
v. meet face-to-face; get in
touch; contact; meet;put in touch
zew (zef) n. call ; appeal;slogan
zewnątrz (zév-nowntsh) adv.& prep.
out; outside; outwards;outdoors
zewnętrzny (zev-nańtzh-ni) adj.
m. exterior;external; outward
zewsząd (ze-vsho“wnt) adv. from
everywhere; from all points
zez (zez) m. squint; crosseye

zeznawać (zez-na-vach) v. declare; testify ;give evidence
zezować (ze-zó-vach) v. squint
zezwalać (ze-zva-lach) v. allow ; give permission;permit
zezwolenie (zez-vo-le-ñe) n.
permission ; leave;license
zębaty (zań-ba-ti) adj. m.
toothed ; cogged; indented
zębate koło (zań-ba-te ko-wo)
n. cog wheel; gear (wheel)
zęby (zań-bi) pl, teeth; cogs
zgadywać (zga-di-vach) v.
guess ; anticipate ;give a guess
zgadzać się (zga-dzach śhań)
v. agree ;fit in;see eye-to-eye
zgaga (zgá-ga) f. heartburn
zganić (zga-ñeech) v. blame
zgarnąć (zgar-nównch) v. rake
together ;gather; brush aside
zgasić (zga-śheech) v. put out;
extinguish; switch off; dim
zgęszczenie (zgań-shche-ñe) n.
condensation ; compression
zgiełk (zgyewk) m. uproar;
clamor ; turmoil; tumult
zgięcie (zgyan-che) n. bend;
fold ; inflection ;inflexion
zginać (zgee-nach) v. bend
(over); fold; stoop ; bow
zgliszcza (zgléesh-cha) pl.
cinders ; ashes ;site of fire
zgłaszać (zgwa-shach) v. notify; call for; tender ;submit
zgłębić (zgwań-beech) v. probe;
sound out ; deepen;go deeply
zgłodniały (zgwod-ná-wi) adj.
m. hungry ; starving ;hungering
zgłosić (zgwó-śheech) v. notify
zgłoska (zgwos-ka) f. syllable
zgłupieć (zgwoo-pyech) v. grow
silly ; grow stupid ;be astounded
zgnębić (zgnań-beech) v. depress ; deject; oppress ;dishearten
zgnić (zgñeech) v. rot ;decay;ret
zgnieść (zgñeśhch) v. crush;stub;
squash ; suppress; quell ;squeeze
zgnilizna (zgñee-leez-na) f.
rot; corruption; foul smell
zgniły (zgñee-wi) adj. rotten;foul
zgoda .zgó-da) f. concord; assent;
consent ;unity; approval;harmony

zgodnie (zgód-ńe) adv. according;
in concert ; peaceably ;in unison
zgodność (zgod-nośhćh) f. accord
agreement ; unanimity ;consistence;
zgodny (zgód-ni) adj. m. compatible ; good-natured ;unanimous
zgoić się (zgó-eećh śháń) v.
heal up; heal over ;heal a wound
zgon (zgon) m. death; decease
zgorszyć (zgór-shićh) v. horrify;
scandalize ; shock; arouse
zgorzkniały (zgozh-kńá-wi) adj.
m. sour; embittered;acrimonious
zgotować (zgo-tó-vach) v. prepare;cook; give (an ovation)
z góry (zgoo-ri) adv. in advance
zgrabny (zgráb-ni) adj. m.skill-
ful; clever; deft; smart;neat;
shapely ; slick; deft;well-built
zgraja (zgrá-ya) f. gang; mob
zgromadzenie (zgro-ma-dzé-ńe) n.
assembly ; congress; meeting
zgromadzać się (zgro-má-dzach
śhań) v. assemble ; gather
zgroza (zgró-za) f. horror
z grubsza (zgroob-sha) adv.
roughly; approximatively
zgryzota (zgri-zó-ta) f. grief
zgryźliwy (zgriżh-lee-vi) adj.
m. sarcastic; peevish; harsh
zgrzać się (zgzhách śhań) v.
get hot; sweat; become hot
zgrzebło (zgzhéb-wo) n. horse-
comb ; harrow ;curry comb;comb
zgrzyt (zgzhit) m. screech;jar
zguba (zgoo-ba) f. loss; doom;
undoing ; ruin; destruction
zgubić (zgoo-beećh) v. lose;
undo;drop;bring to ruin;destroy
zgubić się (zgoo-beećh śhań) v.
get lost; get mixed up ;be mislaid
zgubny (zgoob-ni) adj. m. disastrous; fatal; ruinous ;calamitous
zgwałcić (zgvaw-ćheećh) v. rape
ziarnisty (żhar-ńees-ti) adj.m.
granular ; grainy ;whole grain-
ziarno (żhár-no) n. grain; corn
ziele (żhé-le) n. weed; herb
zieleń (żhe-leń) f. greenery
zielonawy (żhe-lo-ná-vi) adj. m.
greenish;of greenish color
zielony (żhe-ló-ni) adj. m.green;
young and inexperienced (man)

ziemia (żhém-ya) f. earth; land
ground; soil ;native land;district
ziemianin (żhe-myá-ńeen) m.
squire; landowner ; mortal
ziemianka (żhe-myáń-ka) f.
1. dugout; 2. landowner's wife
ziemniak (żhém-ńak) m. potato
ziemski (żhém-skee) adj. m.
earthly ; worldly; landed ;land-
ziewać (żhe-vách) v. yawn; gape
zięba (żhaη-ba) f. finch;chaffinch
ziębić (żhan-beećh) v. cool;
chill;expose to the cold
zięć (żháńćh) m. son-in-law
zima (żhee-ma) f. winter
zimno (żheem-no) n. cold ;chill
zimno (żheem-no) adv. coldly
zimny (żheem-ni) adj. m. cold
zimować (żhee-mo-vách) v.
hibernate; winter;pass the winter
zioło (żhó-wo) n. herb(mint,sage...)
ziszczać (zeesh-chach) v. realize; fulfill ; carry out (a plan)
zjadać (zya-dách) v. eat; eat
up ; have food; ruin ; drain
zjadliwy (zya-dlee-vi) adj.m.
biting; caustic ; spiteful ;vicious
zjawa (zyá-va) f. apparition:
ghost ; vision;specter; phantom
zjawisko (zya-vées-ko) n. fact;
event; phenomenon ;vision ;occurence
zjazd (zyazt) m. meeting; coming; descent ; downhill drive ;slide
zjednoczenie (zyed-no-che-ńe) n.
union ; unification ;association
zjeść (zjéśhćh) v. eat up ;outdo
zjeżdżać (zyéżh-dzhách) v. ride
down; slide down ;make way;slate
zlecać (zle-tsách) v. commission;
order ;entrust; instruct;charge with
zlecenie (zle-tse-ńe) n. commission; order ; errand; message
z ledwoscia (zled-vósh-chown)
adv. hardly; with difficulty
z lekka (zlék-ka) adv. lightly;
softly ; slightly; gently
zlepek (zle-pek) m. agglomerate
zlew (zlef) m. sink;kitchen sink
zlewać (zle-vách) v. pour off;
pour together ; mix ;flunk;whip
zliczyć (zlee-chićh) v. count
up; total; add up ; reckon ;tot up

zlikwidować (zlee-kvee-do-vach) v. liquidate; wind up; destroy

zlodowacenie (zlo-do-va-tse-ne) n. freezing; glaciation

zlot (zlot) m. rally; flocking in

złagodzenie (zwa-go-dze-ne) n. mitigation; softening

złagodzić (zwa-go-dżheech) v. mitigate; soothe; lessen; soften

złamać (zwa-mach) v. break; smash

złamanie (zwa-ma-ne) n. fracture

złazić (zwa-żheech) v. climb down; get off; come off; peel off

złączenie (zwown-che-ne) n. connection; junction; weld; link; fuse

złączyć (zwown-chich) v. join;

złe (zwe) n. evil; wrong; ill

zło (zwo) n. evil; devil; harm

złocenie (zwo-tse-ne) n. gilding

złocić (zwo-cheech) v. gild

złoczyńca (zwo-chiń-tsa) m. evildoer; criminal; malefactor

złodziej (zwo-dżhey) m. thief

złodziejka (zwo-dżhey-ka) f. thief; electrical adapter

złom (zwom) m. scrap; waste

złość (zwoshch) f. anger; malice; spite; soreness; resentment

złośliwy (zwosh-lee-vi) adj.m. malignant; spiteful; malicious

złotnik (zwot-neek) m. goldsmith

złoto (zwo-to) n. gold; gold work

złoty (zwo-ti) adj. m. 1, golden m. 2. Polish money unit

złowić (zwo-veech) v. catch; net; hook (a fish, a husband etc)

złowrogi (zwo-vro-gee) adj.m. ominous; sinister; protentous

złoże (zwo-zhe) n. stratum; bed

złożony (zwo-zho-ni) adj. m. complex; multiple; intricate

złuda (zwoo-da) f. illusion

złudny (zwood-ni) adj. m. illusory; deceptive; illusive

zły (zwi) adj. m. bad; evil; ill; vicious; cross; poor; rotten

zmagać się (zma-gach shań) v. struggle with; grapple with

zmaganie (zma-ga-ne) n. struggle

zmarły (zmar-wi) adj. m. deceased; dead; defunct; the late

zmarszczka (zmarshch-ka) f. wrinkle; crease; fold; pucker

zmartwienie (zmar-tvye-ne) n. worry; sorrow; grief; trouble

zmartwychwstać (zmar-tvikh-vstach) v. rise form the dead

zmartwychwstanie (zmar-tvikh-vsta-ne) n. resurrection

zmarznąć (zmar-znownch) v. freeze; freeze over; be cold

zmawiać się (zma-vyach shań) v. conspire; plot; arrange; collude

zmaza (zma-za) f. stain; blemish; blot; wet dream; slur

zmazywać (zma-zi-vach) v. wipe out; efface; erase; expiate

zmęczenie (zmań-che-ne) n. fatigue; weariness; lassitude

zmiana (zmya-na) f. change; variation; shift; relay; exchange

zmiatać (zmya-tach) v. sweep up

zmiażdżyć (zmyazh-dzhich) v. crush; overwhelm (the enemy etc.)

zmienić (zmye-neech) v. change

zmierzać (zmye-zhach) v. aim; tend; make one's way; drive at

zmierzch (zmyezhkh) m. dusk; twilight; decline; fall; dark; at dark

zmierzyć (zmye-zhich) v. measure; gauge; take aim; make for

zmieszanie (zmye-sha-ne) n. mix up; confusion, embarrassment

zmiłowanie (zmee-wo-va-ne) n. mercy; pity; disposition to forgive

zmniejszenie (zmney-she-ne) n. reduction; decrease; relief

zmniejszyć (zmney-shich) v. diminish; lessen; abate; reduce

zmoczyć (zmo-chich) v. wet; soak

zmora (zmo-ra) f. nightmare; bane

zmorzyć (zmo-zhich) v. overpower

zmordować (zmor-do-vach) v. tire; wear; do in; tire out; exhaust

zmowa (zmo-va) f. conspiracy; collusion; plot; secret deal

zmrok (zmrok) m. dusk; twilight

zmurszały (zmoor-sha-wi) adj.m. mouldy; decaying; rotten; musty

zmuszać (zmoo-shach) v. coerce; compel; force; oblige; constrain

zmykać (zmi-kach) v. cut and run; bolt; scoot off; scurry away

zmylić (zmi-leech) v. fool; mislead; deceive; lose way; outwit

zmysł (zmïsw) m. sense; instinct;knack;aptitude;reason
zmysłowy (zmis-wo-wi) adj. m.
sensual;sensory;sense-; lewd
zmyślać (zmïsh-lać) v. invent;
trump up ; fake up; bluff;cook up
zmyślony (zmïsh-ló-ni) adj.m.
fictitious; invented ; unreal
znaczący (zna-chówn-tsi) adj.
m. significant; emphatic;telling
znaczek (zná-chek) m. sign;stamp
znaczny (znach-ni)adj.m. notable;
znać (znać) v. know;know how
znajdować (znay-do-vać) v.
find ; see; meet; experience
znajomość (zna-yo-moshćh) f.
acquaintance ; knowledge
znajomy (zna-yo-mi) adj. m.well
acquainted;well known;familiar
znak (znak) m. mark; sign; stamp
znakomity (zna-ko-mee-ti) adj.
m. excellent; illustrious
znalazca (zna-láz-tsa) m. finder
znaleźne (zna-leźh-ne) n.find-
er's reward;finder's share
znamienny (zna-myén-ni) adj.m.
significant ; characteristic
znamię (zná-myáń) n. stigma;
mole ; trait; birthmark
znany (zna-ni) adj. m. noted;
known; famed; familiar;well known
znawca (znáv-tsa) m. expert
znęcać się (znáń-tsać shań) v.
torment; harass ; ill-treat
znękany (znáń-ka-ni) adj. m.
dejected; harassed ; wasted
znicz (zneech) m. (holy) fire;
fireside ; pilot-light
zniechęcać (zne-kháń-tsać) v.
discourage ; sicken; indispose
zniecierpliwić się (zne-cher-
pleé-veech shań) v. grow impatient; get vexed;lose patience
znieczulić (zne-choo-leech) v.
anesthetize ; deaden; harden
zniedołężniały (zne-do-wáń-zhna-
wi) adj. m. impotent; decrepit;
infirm; disable; feeble(old man)
zniekształcać (zne-ksztáw-tsać)
v. deform; disfigure ;distort
zniemczać (zném-chach) v.German-
ize; make into a German;force
to accept German identity

znienacka (zne-náts-ka) adv.
all of a sudden;unawares
znienawidzieć (zne-na-vee-
dźheech) v. grow to hate;loathe
znieprawić (zne-pra-veech) v.
deprave; demoralize; debauch
zniesienie (zne-she-ne) n.
abrogation; abolition;repeal
zniesławienie (zne-swa-vye-ne)
n. defamation; slander
zniewaga (zne-vá-ga) f. insult
zniewalać (zne-vá-lać) v.
coerce; captivate; win
znikać (znee-kać) v. vanish
zniewieściały (zne-vyesh-chá-
wi) adj. m. effeminate;sissy
znikąd (znee-kownt) adv. from
nowhere; out of nowhere
znikomy (znee-kó-mi) adj. m.
perishable; negligible;minute
zniszczeć (zneesh-chech) v. decay; go to ruin; be worn out
zniszczenie (zneesh-che-ne) n.
destruction; ravage;ruin;havoc
zniszczyć (znéesh-chich) v. destroy; ruin; ware out;ravage
zniweczyć (znee-ve-chich) v.
annihilate; wreck; lay waste
zniżać (znee-zhać) v. lower
zniżka (znéezh-ka) f. reduction;
decline; slump; drop; fall
znosić (zno-sheech) v. annul;
endure; carry down;ware out
znośny (znósh-ni) adj. m. tolerable; bearable; so-so; fair
znowu (zno-voo) adv. again;anew
znój (znooy) m. toil; sweat
znów (znoof) adv. again; anew
znudzenie (znoo-dzé-ne) n.bore-
dom; till one is sick and tired
znużenie (znoo-zhe-ne) n. weariness; fatigue (people,metals etc.)
zobaczyć (zo-bá-chich) v. see
zobojętnić (zo-bo-yánt-neech)
v. neutralize;make indifferent
zobojętnieć (zo-bo-yánt-nech)
v. grow indifferent;grow listless
zobowiązać (zo-bo-vyown-zać)
v. oblige ;obligate to do
zobowiązanie (zo-bov-yown-za-
ne) n. obligation;commitment
zobrazować (zob-ra-zó-vać) v.
illustrate; describe ;depict

zogniskować (zog-nees-ko-vach) v. focus; concentrate

zohydzać (zo-khi-dzach) v. defame; make loathsome;sicken of

zoolog(zo-ó-log) m. zoologist

zorza północna (zo-zha poow-nóts-na) f. aurora borealis

zostać (zos-tach) v. remain;stay; become; get to be; be left

zostawiać (zos-táv-yach) v. leave;abandon; put aside

z powodu (zpo-vó-doo) prep. because of; owing to;due to

z powrotem (zpov-ró-tem) adv. back; backwards;on the way back

zrabować (zra-bo-vach) v. rob

z rana (zrá-na) adv. in the morning;during the morning

zranić (zra-neech) v. wound; injure; hurt(feelings);mangle

zrastać (zras-tach) v. grow into one; fuse; heal up;blend

zrazu (zrá-zu) adv. at first

zrażać (zra-zhach) v. discourage; set against; alienate

zrąb (zrownp) m. frame (work); clearing; trunk; shell

zrąbać (zrown-bach) v. hew; cut down; hack; chop; pick to pieces

zrealizować (zre-a-lee-zo-vach) v. realize; actualize; execute

zredagować (zre-da-go-vach) v. draw up; compose; edit; draft

zreszta (zresh-town) adv. 1. moreover; besides; 2.after all; though; any way;in the end

zręczność (zranch-noshch) f. cleverness; dexterity; skill

zrobić (zro-beech) v. make; do; turn; execute; perform

zrodzić (zro-dzheech) v. give birth; beget; originate

zrosnąć się (zros-nownch shán) v. grow into one; fuse;blend

zrozpaczony (zros-pa-chó-ni) adj. m. desperate; brokenhearted

zrozumiały (zro-zoo-myá-wi) adj. m. intelligible; understandable

zrozumieć (zro-zoo-myech) v. understand;grasp;see;make out

zrozumienie (zro-zoo-myé-ne) n. understanding;sympathy; sense; grasp; comprehension; spirit

zrównać (zroov-nach) v. level; make even; align; equalize

zrównoważyć (zroov-no-vá-zhich) v. balance; equalize;equilibrate

zróżniczkować (zroozh-neech-ko-vach) v. differentiate

zryć (zrich) v. dig up; furrow

zrywać (zri-vach) v. rip; tear off; tear down; pick; quarrel

z rzadka (zzhad-ka) adv. rarely

zrządzenie losu (zzhown-dzé-ne ló-soo) n. fate ;decree of fate

zrzeczenie się (zzhe-ché-ne shán) n. resignation; renunciation ; renouncement;abdication

zrzeszenie (zzhe-shé-ne) n. association; union

zrzęda (zzhán-da) m. grumbler

zrzucać (zzhoo-tsach) v. throw (down); buck off; drop; shed

zrzut lotniczy (zzhoot lot-nee-chi) m. drop (from plane)

zsiadać (zshá-dach) v. dismount

zstąpić (zstown-peech) v. descend;step down (one time)

zstępować (zstán-po-vach) v. descent; step down

zsyłać (zsi-wach) v. deport;exile

zsyłka (zsiw-ka) f. deportation

zsypywać (zsi-pi-vach) v. heap up; pour off;shoot into

zszyć (zshich) v. sew together

zubożeć (zoo-bó-zhech) v. impoverish; grow poor;pauperize

zuch (zookh) m. brave fellow

zuchwalstwo (zookh-vál-stvo) n. insolence; audacity; impudence

zuchwały (zookh-vá-wi) adj. m. insolent; impudent; bold

zupa (zoo-pa) f. soup

zupełny (zoo-pew-ni) adj. m. entire;whole;total;out and out

zużycie (zoo-zhi-che) n. consumption; wear and tear; waste

zużytkować (zoo-zhit-ko-vach) v. utilize ; use up; exploit

zużyty (zoo-zhi-ti) adj.m. worn out; used up; wasted; trite

zwać (zvach) v. call; name

zwalczyć (zval-chich) v. overpower; overcome; cope; strive

zwalić (zva-leech) v. demolish; fell; collapse; pile up;knock down zwalniac (zval-ñach) v. release; loosen; let go; slow dawn;vacate

zwał (zvaw) m. heap; bank ; pile

zwapnienie (zvap-ñe-ñe) n. calcification ; adv.densely; closely

zwarcie (zvár-che) n. short (cirquit); contraction;infighting

zwariować (zvar-yo-vach) v. go mad ; go crazy; alter (a score...)

zwarzyc (zva-zhich) v. boil; nip; frost damage ; turn sour ;blight

zważać (zva-zhach) v. pay attention ; weigh (words);consider

zważyć (zva-zhich) v. weigh; consider ; give heed ;regard

zwąchac (zvown-khach) v. smell out; get wind; sniff ;scent

zwątpic (zvównt-peech) v. despair of ; lose hope ;give up

zwedzic (zvah-dzheech) v. swipe

zweglic (zvang-leech) v. carbonize ; char; get charred

zwęzic (zvan-zheech)v. narrow down ; contract; restrict ;confine

zwiady (zvya-di) pl. reconnaissance ; scouting ;reconnoitring

zwiastować (zvyas-to-vach) v. announce ; herald ;foreshadow

zwiastowanie (zvyas-to-vá-ñe) n. Annunciation

zwiastun (zvyas-toon) m. harbinger ; herald; omen ;forerunner

związać (zvyown-zach) v. bind; fasten; join; tie up;strap;frame

związek (zvyown-zek) m. alliance; connection; bond· compound ;tie

zwichnąc (zveekh-nownch) v. strain; dislocate; disjoin; luxate ;warp

zwichnięcie (zveekh-nan-che) n. dislocation ; luxation; sprain

zwiedzac (zvye-dzach) v. visit; see the sights ; tour; see ;inspect

zwiedzanie (zvye-dza-ñe) n. sightseeing ;touring

zwierciadło (zvyer-chad-wo) n. mirror ; reflection ;looking glass

zwierz (zvyesh) n. beast of prey

zwierzać się (zvyc-zhach shán) v. disclose a secret; confide in...

zwierzchnik (zvyezh-khñeek) m. boss; superior ; chief; lord ; master; suzerain;feudal lord

zwierzchnictwo (svyezh-khñeetstvo) n. sovereignty; superior authority; supremacy; control

zwierzę (zvye-zhañ) n. animal

zwierzyna (zvye-zhi-na) f. game (animals); game

zwierzyniec (zvye-zhi-ñets) m. zoo; zoological garden ;zodiac

zwieszac (zvye-shach) v. hang low;droop; dangle ; hang down

zwietrzec (zvye-tzhech) v. decompose ; go stale; spoil

zwiewac (zvye-vach) v. cut and run; blow away ; run away

zwiedły (zvyand-wi) adj. m. withered; wilted ;faded

zwiędnąc (zvyand-nownch) v. wither; wilt; fade

zwiększyc (zvyank-zhich) v. increase; magnify ; heighten

zwięzły (zvyanz-wi) adj. m. concise; brief; terse;compact

zwijac (zvee-yach) v. roll up; wind up;coil; twist up ;furl

zwilżac (zveel-zhach) v. moisten; wet; dampen(often)

zwilżyc (zveel-zhich) v. moisten; wet; dampen(one time)

zwinąc (zvee-nownch) v. roll up; wind up; coil up; twist up

zwinny (zveen-ni) adj. m. agile; nimble; deft; dexterous ;lissome

zwisac (zvee-sach) v. hang down; droop; dangle ;sag;beetle

zwlekac (zvle-kach) v. delay

zwłaszcza (zvwash-cha) adv. particularly; chiefly; especially; most of all;specially

zwłoka (zvwo-ka) f. delay;respite

zwłoki (zvwo-kee) n. corpse

zwodzic(zvo-dżheech) v. delude; deceive; let down; lower

zwolenniczka (zvo-len-ñeech-ka) f. adherent; follower;advocate

zwolennik (zvo-len-ñeek) m. adherent; follower; advocate

zwolna (zvol-na) adv. slowly

zwolnic (zvol-ñech) v. slow down; slack off; relax ;slacken

zwolnienie (zvol-ñe-ñe) n. 1. dismissal; release; acquittal; sack;exemption;2.slowing

zwoływać (zvo-wi-vaćh) v. call
together: assemble; convene
zwój (zvooy) m. roll;reel;coil
zwracać (zvra-tsaćh) v. return;
give back; pay(attention)
zwrot (zvrot) m. 1; turn; 2. restitution 3.revulsion;4.phrase
zwrotka (zvrot-ka) f. stanza
zwrotnica (zvrot-nee-tsa) f.
switch (large); steering
zwrotnik (zvrot-neek) m. tropic
zwrotny (zvrot-ni) adj. m. flexible; returnable ;repayable
zwrócić się (zvroo-cheech śhań)
v. turn (to); give back
zwycięski (zvi-chans-kee) adj.
m. victorious;triumphant;winning
zwycięstwo (zvi-chans-tvo) n.
victory; triumph; win
zwyciężać (zvi-chan-zhaćh) v.
conquer; win; prevail;overcome
zwyczaj (zvi-chay) m. custom;
habit; fashion; usage;practice
zwyczajny (zvi-chay-ni) adj. m.
usual; ordinary; common;simple
zwyczajowy (zvi-cha-yo-vi) adj.
m. customary; regular; usual
zwykły (zvik-wi) adj. m. common
zwyrodniały (zvi-rod-na-wi) adj.
m. degenerate; degenerated
zwyrodnienie (zvi-rod-ne-ne) n.
degeneration; degradation
zwyżka (zvizh-ka) f.rise;advance
zwyżka cen (zvizh-ka tsen) f.
price rise ;price increase
zygzak (zig-zak) m. zigzag
zysk (zisk) m. gain; profit
zyskać (zis-kaćh) v. gain ;earn
zyskowność (zis-kov-noshćh) f.
profitability;remunerativeness
zyskowny (zis-kov-ni) adj. m.
profitable; lucrative
zza (z-za) prep. from behind
zziajać się (zzha-yaćh śhań) v.
get out of breath;tire oneself out
zzielenieć (zżhe-le-nećh) v.
turn green; become green
zziębnąć (zzhanb-nownćh) v. feel
cold;be chilled to the bone
zziębnięty (zżhanb-nan-ti) adj.
m. chilled(to the bone)
zżyć się(zzhićh śhań) v. grow
familiar ;grow accustomed

zżymać (zzhi-maćh) v. wring
zżynać (zzhi-naćh) v. cut
down; reap; mow (the grass etc.)
zżywać się (zzhi-vaćh śhań) v.
grow familiar; reconcile
zdźbło (żhdżhbwo) n. stalk;
blade;trifle; a bit; a little
źle (żhle) adj. n,& adv. ill;
wrong; badly; falsely;mistakenly
źrebak (żhre-bak) m. colt
źrebię (żhre-byań) n. foal;colt
źrenica (żhre-nee-tsa) f. pupil
źródlany (żhrood-la-ni) adj.m.
spring (water); of spring
źródło (żhrood-wo) n. spring;
source; well;fountainhead
źródłosłów (żhrood-wo-swoof) m.
root word; etymology; radical
źródłowy (żhrood-wo-vi) adj.m.
original; spring (water)
żaba (zha-ba) f. frog
żaden (zha-den) pron. none;
neither; not any; no one; no-
żagiel (zha-gel) m. sail
żakiet (zha-ket) m. jacket
żal (zhal) m. regret; grief;
sorrow; remorse;grudge; rancor
żalić się (zha-leech śhań) v.
complain; lament;find fault
żaluzja (zha-looz-ya) f. blind
żałoba (zha-wo-ba) f. mourning
żałobny marsz (zha-wob-ni marsh)
m. funeral march
żałosny (zha-wos-ni) adj. m.
lamentable; wretched;plaintive
żałość (zha-woshćh) f. grief;
desolation; sorrow ;deep sorrow
żałować (zha-wo-vaćh) v. regret
żar (zhar) m. heat; glow; ardor
żarcie (zhar-che) n. swill;dub
żargon (zhar-gon) m. jargon
żarliwość (zhar-lee-voshćh) f.
ardor; zeal; earnestness
żarliwy (zhar-lee-vi) adj. m.
ardent; zealous;fervent
żarłoczny (zhar-woch-ni) adj.m.
greedy;voracious; gluttonous
żarłok (zhar-wok) m. glutton
żarówka (zha-roov-ka) f. light
bulb; electric bulb; bulb
żart (zhart) m. joke; jest;quip;
żartować (zhar-to-vaćh) v. joke
make fun; poke fun; trifle ;jest

żarzyć (zha-zhićh) v. glow;anneal
żąć (zhównćh) v. mow; cut; reap
żądać (zhówn-daćh) v. demand;
require; exact; stipulate
żądanie (zhówn-da-ńe) n. demand;
claim;requirement;stipulation
żądło (zhównd-wo) n . sting;fang
żądny (zhównd-ni) adj. m. eager;
anxious; greedy;avid (of fame etc)
żądny przygód (zhównd-ni pzhi-
goot) adventurous (man)
że (zhe) conj. that; then; as
żebrać (zhe-braćh) v. beg
żebraczka (zhe-brach-ka) f. beggar ; pauper (girl, woman)
żebrak (zhe-brak) m. beggar (man)
żebranina (zhe-bra-ńee-na) f.
beggary; begging; alms
żebro (zhe-bro) n. rib;fin
żeby (zhe-bi) conj. so as; in
order that;if;may;if only
żeglarski (zhe-glár-skee) adj.m.
nautical; seaman's (life etc.)
żeglarstwo (zhe-glár-stvo) n.
sailing;navigation;seamanship
żeglarz (zhé-glash) m. seaman;
sailor ; mariner; seafarer
żeglować (zhe-gló-vaćh) v. sail;
navigate (the seas,the ocean)
żeglowny (zhe-glów-ni) adj. m.
navigable (river, canal etc.)
żegluga (zhe-gloo-ga) f. navigation ; shipping; sailing
żegnać (zhég-naćh) v. bid farewell; bless;bid good-bye;see off
żelatyna (zhe-la-ti-na) f.jelly
żelazko (zhe-láz-ko) n. press-
iron ; cutting iron; edger
żelazny (zhe-láz-ni) adj. m. iron
żelazo (zhe-lá-zo) n. iron ;armor
żelazobeton (zhe-la-zo-bé-ton)
m. reinforced concrete
żelaztwo (zhe-láz-tvo) n. scrap
iron; hardware;iron junk
żelbet (zhél-bet) m. reinforced
concrete
żeliwo (zhe-lée-vo) n. cast iron
żenić (zhe-ńeech) v. marry
żenować (zhe-nó-vaćh) v. embarrass
żeński (zhéń-skee) adj. m. female
żer (zher) m. food; prey; feeding
żerdka (zhérd-ka) f. (small)perch

żerdz (zherdźh) f. perch
żłobek (zhwó-bek) m. crib
żłobić (zhwó-beećh) v. channel; erode; furrow; groove
żłób (zhwoop) m. trough; crib
żmija (zhmee-ya) f. viper;
adder; poisonous snake
żmudny (zhmoód-ni) adj. m.
uphill; toilsome; strenuous
żniwiarka (zhńee-vyár-ka) f.
harvester; reaper
żniwo (zhńee-vo) n. harvest
żołądek (zho-wówn-dek) m.
stomach
żołądź (zho-wówndźh) f. acorn
żołd (zhówd) m. (soldier's)
pay
żołdactwo (zhow-dáts-tvo) n.
soldiery ;the soldiery
żołnierz (zhow-ńesh) m. soldier
żona (zho-na) f. wife
żonaty (zho-ná-ti) adj. m.
married; family man
żółć (zhoowćh) f. bile
żółciowy (zhoow-ćhó-vi) adj.m.
gall; peevish; harsh; biting
żółknąć (zhoow-knównćh) v. turn
yellow; become yellow
żółtaczka (zhow-tach-ka) f.
jaundice; the yellows
żółtawy (zhow-tá-vi) adj. m.
yellowish;nankeen; sallow
żółtko (zhoówt-ko) n. yolk
żółty (zhoów-ti) adj. m. yellow
żółto-blady (zhoow-to-bla-di)
adj. yellow-pale; sallow
żółw (zhoowf) m. turtle;tortoise
żółwi krok (zhoow-vee krok) m.
snail's pace; turtle's gait
żrący (zhrówn-tsi) adj. m.
corrosive; caustic; biting
żubr (zhoobr) m. (European-Po-
lish) bison; aurochs
żuchwa (zhoókh-va) f. jawbone
żuć (zhooćh) v. chew;masticate
żucie (zhoó-ćhe) n. chewing;
mastication; chew;munducation
żuk (zhook) m. beetle;dung beetle
żulik (zhoó-leek) m. swindler;
rogue; cheat; street urchin
żuławy (zhoo-wa-vi) pl. marsh-
land ; lowlands;fertile lowlands

żupa (zhoo-pa) f. saltworks
żupan (zhoo-pan) m. old Polish
costume; (hist.) district chief
żur (zhoor) m. soup of fermented meal; sour soup
żuraw (zhoo-rav) m. crane;gantry
żurawina (zhoo-ra-vee-na) f.
cranberry
żurnal (zhoor-nal) m. fashion
magazine
żużel (zhoo-zhel) m. slag; cinder; scoria;clinker;cinder track
żużlobeton (zhoo-zhlo-be-ton) m.
slag concrete
żwawo (zhva-vo) adj. m. briskly;
alertly; apace ; jauntily
żwawy (zhva-vi) adj. m. brisk;
quick; lively; spry;sprightly
żwir (zhveer) m. gravel upkeep
życie (zhi-che) n. life ;pep;
życiodajny (zhi-cho-day-ni) adj.
m. life-giving ; vivifying
życiorys (zhi-cho-ris) m. biography; life history
życzenie (zhi-che-ne) n. wish;
desire ; request ; greeting
życzliwy (zhich-lee-vi) adj.m.
favorable; friendly; kindly
żyć (zhich) v. be alive; live;
exist; subsist; get along
Żyd (zhid) m. Jew
żydowski (zhi-dov-skee) adj.m.
Jewish; Judaic; Yiddish
żydostwo (zhi-dos-tvo) n. Jewry
Żydówka (zhi-doov-ka) f. Jewess
żyjący (zhi-yown-tsi) adj.m.
living ; pl. the living
żyjatko (zhi-yownt-ko) n. ani-
malcule ; tiny animal
żylak (zhi-lak) m. varix
żylakowy (zhi-la-ko-vi) adj.m.
varicose; of varicose vein
żylasty (zhi-las-ti) adj. m.
venous; stringy; sinewy
żyletka (zhi-let-ka) f. (razor)
blade; safety razor blade
żyla (zhi-wa) f. vein; seam;
core; strand; streak; string
żyłka (zhiw-ka) f. veinlet; thread
żyrafa (zhi-ra-fa) f. giraffe
żyrant (zhi-rant) m. endorser
żyrować (zhi-ro-vach) v. endorse

żytni (zhit-nee) adj. m. rye
żytniówka (zhit-noov-ka) f.
corn vodka ; gin; rye vodka
żyto (zhi-to) n. rye
żywcem (zhiv-tsem) adv. alive
żywe srebro (zhi-ve sreb-ro)
n. mercury; restless person
żywica (zhi-vee-tsa) f. resin
żywiec (zhi-vyets) m. cattle
for slaughter; live bait
żywić (zhi-veech) v. feed;
nourish; cherish ; feel
żywioł (zhi-vyow) m. element
żywiołowy (zhi-vyo-wo-vi) adj.
m. elemental; spontaneous;
impulsive; impetuous
żywność (zhiv-noshch) f. food;
provisions; eatables; fodder
żywo (zhi-vo) adv. quickly;
briskly ;exp.: make it snappy!
żywopłot (zhi-vo-pwot) m. hedge
żywość (zhi-voshch) f. animation; liveliness; vivacity;
vitality; vigor; esprit
żywot (zhi-vot) m. life; womb;
belly ; life (of a saint)
żywotnie (zhi-vot-ne) adv. vi-
tally; exuberantly;luxuriantly
żywotność (zhi-vot-noshch) f.
vitality ; liveliness ;vivacity
żywotny (zhi-vot-ni) m. vital
żywy (zhi-vi) adj. m. alive;
lively; vivid; intense; gay;
brisk; live;acute; keen; bright
żyzność (zhiz-noshch) f. fertility ; fruitfulness ;richness
żyzny (zhiz-ni) adj. m. fertile;
generous (soil): fruitful; fat;
fecund; rich

ENGLISH-POLISH

a (ej) art.jeden; pewien;
pierwsza litera angielskiego
alfabetu; pierwszej kategorii
A-O'k (ej okej) zupełnie gotów
aback (e'baek) adv. wstecz;
w tył: do tylu: nazad
abandon (e'baendon) v. opuszczać ; porzucić : zarzucić
abandonment (e'baendonment) s.
opuszczenie:brak pohamowania
abashed (e'baeszt) adj. speszony: zmieszany (czymś)
abate ('ebejt) v. osłabiać;
zmniejszać: mitygować:uciszyć
abbey ('aebi) s. opactwo
abbreviate (e'bry:wjejt) v.
skrócić: skracać
abbreviation (e'bry:wjejszyn)
s. skrót: skrócenie; skracanie
ABC ('ej'bi:'si) alfabet
abdicate ('aebdykejt) v. zrzekać się ; abdykować
abdomen ('aebdemen) s. brzuch
abduct (aeb'dakt) v. uprowa-
dzić: porwać: porywać
abhor (eb'ho:r) v. mieć odrazę
abide, abode, abode (e'bajd,
e'boud, e'boud)
abide (e'bajd) v. znosić; obstawać: dotrzymywać: trwać
ability (e'bylyty) s. zdolność
abject ('aebdżekt) adj. podły;
nędzny: nikczemny: skrajny
abjure (eb'dżuer) v. poprzysiąc
able ('ejbl) adj. zdolny; zdatny: utalentowany: poczytalny
abnormal (aeb'no:rmel) adj.
anormalny: nieprawidłowy
aboard (e'bo:rd) adv. na pokła-
dzie; na statku: w pociągu
abode (e'boud) v. był posłuszny
abode (e'boud) s. mieszkanie;
v. zob. abide
abolish (e'bolysz) v. obalić;
znieść: znosić; obalać
abolition (aebe'lyszyn) n. obalenie; zniesienie(zwyczaju etc)
A-bomb ('ejbom) s. bomba atomowa: bomba jądrowa
abominable (e'bomynebl) adj.
ohydny; wstrętny: obrzydliwy

abortion (e'bo:rszyn) s.przerwa-
nie ciąży; poronienie
abound (e'baund) v. obfitować
about (e'baut) adv. naokoło;
około:dookoła; po: o; wobec:przy
about (e'baut) prep. o; przy;
odnośnie: naokoło: wokoło
about to (e'baut tu) gotów do
above (e'baw) adv. powyżej;
w górze: wyżej: na górze
above (e'baw) prep. nad; ponad
above (e'baw) adj. powyższy
abreast (e'brest) adv. obok;
rzędem: ramię przy ramieniu
abridge (e'brydż) v. skrócić
abroad (e'bro:d) adv. zewnątrz;
za granicą: za granicę; w dal
abrogate ('aebrogejt) v. obalić:
unicestwić; odwoływać; znosić
abrupt (e'brapt) adj. nagły;
szorstki: urwany: ostry; oschły
abscess ('aebses) s. wrzód:ropień
absence ('aebsens) s. brak;
nieobecność: niestawiennictwo
absent ('aebsent) adj. nieobecny;v. być nieobecnym
absent-minded ('aebsent'majndyd)
adj. roztargniony
absolute ('aebselu:t) adj. abso-
lutny; zupełny: nieodwołalny
absolutely ('aebselu:tly) adv.
absolutnie; oczywiście
absolve (eb'zolw) v. rozgrzeszyć;
darować: uwolnić; oczyścić
absorb (eb'zo:rb) v. chłonąć;
tłumić; absorbować: łagodzić
abstain (eb'stejn) v. powstrzymywać się: być abstynentem
abstention (eb'stenszyn) s.
wstrzymanie się(od jedzenia...)
abstinence ('aebstynens) s.
wstrzemięźliwość: abstynencja
abstract ('aebstraekt) adj.
oderwany; abstrakcyjny;
s. abstrakcja; streszczenie;
v. streszczać; abstrahować;
odrywać: ukrasć: sprzątnąć
absurd (eb'se:rd) adj. absurdalny: bezsensowny: niedorzeczny
abundance (e'bandens) s. obfitość: znaczna ilość; dostatek

abundant (e'bandent) adj. obfity;liczny;bogaty; zasobny;płodny

abuse (e'bju:s) s. nadużycie; obelga; (e'bju:z) v. obrażać; nadużywać;łżyć;obrzucać obelgami

abyss (e'bys) n. otchłań; przepaść; głębia;pierwotny chaos

acacia (e'kejsze) s. akacja

academic (,aeke'demyk) adj. akademicki;jałowy; s.uczony

academy (e'kaedemy) s. akademia

accelerate (aek'selerejt) v. przyśpieszać; przyśpieszyć

accelerator (aek'selerejter) s. przyśpieszacz; gaźnik; akcelerator; katalizator

accent ('aeksent) s. wymowa; akcent; (aek'sent) v. akcentować; uwydatniać; znakować

accept (ek'sept) v. akceptować; zgadzać się na;zechcieć wziaść

acceptable (ek'septebl) adj. do przyjęcia; znośny; zadawalający; mile widziany

access ('aekses) s. dostęp

accessible (aek'sesybl) adj. dostępny; przystępny

accession (aek'seszyn) s. wstąpienie; dostęp; dojście; przystąpienie;objęcie(urzędu)

accessory (aek'sesery) s. dodatek; adj. dodatkowy; pomocniczy

access road ('aekses roud) droga dojazdowa

accident ('aeksydent) s. traf; wypadek; katastrofa;awaria

accidental (,aeksy'dentl) adj. przypadkowy; nieważny;uboczny

acclimatize (e'klajmetajz) v. aklimatyzować

accommodate (e'komedejt) v. przystosować; zakwaterować; wyświadczyć; załagodzić(spór)

accommodation (e,kome'dejszyn) s. wygoda; dostosowanie; kwatera; pogodzenie się; ugoda

accompaniment (e'kampenyment) s. towarzyszenie; akompaniament

accompany (e'kampeny) v. towarzyszyć;odprowadzać;akompaniować

accomplice (e'komplys) s. współsprawca; współwinny

accomplish (e'kamplysz) v. dotykonać; spełnić; zrealizować

accomplished (e'kamplyszt) adj. utalentowany; znakomity; wykończony; z ogładą;skończony

accomplishment (e'kamplyszment) s. osiągnięcie; realizacja; dokonanie;wykonanie: ogłada

accord (e'ko:rd) s. zgoda; v. uzgadniać; dać; licować

according (e'ko:rdyng) prep. według; zależnie od

accordingly (e'ko:rdyngly) adv. odpowiednio; więc; zatem

accost (e'kost) v. zaczepić (kogoś);zagadnąć;przystąpić do

account (e'kaunt) s. rachunek; sprawozdanie; v. wyliczać; wytłumaczyć; uważać; oceniać

account for (e'kaunt fo:r) v. dać powód; wytłumaczyć

accountant (e'kauntent) s. księgowy

accounting (e'kauntyng)s. księgowość

accumulate (e'kju:mju,lejt) v. gromadzic;zbierać;piętrzyć

accuracy ('aekjuresy) s. ścisłość; dokładność; celność

accusation (aekju:zejszyn) s. oskarżenie;winienie;posądzenie

accuse (e'kju:z) v. oskarżać

accused (e'kju:zd) adj. oskarżony; oskarżona

accustom (e'kastem) v. przyzwyczajać; przyzwyczaić

accustomed (e'kastemd) adj. przyzwyczajony; zwykły;zwyczajny

ace (ejs) s. as; oczko(in cards)

ache (ejk) s. ból; v.boleć

achieve (e'czi:w) v. dokonać; osiągnąć(cel);zdobywać(sławę)

achievement(e'czi:wment) s. osiągnięcie; wyczyn;zdobycz

aching ('ejkyng) adj. bolący

acid ('aesyd) adj. kwaśny; s. kwas; kwaśna substancja

acid trip ('aesyd tryp) halucynacje po narkotyku

acknowledge (ek'noʔlydż) v. uznać; potwierdzić; przyznać

acknowledgement (ek'nożlydżmen)
s. przyznanie; potwierdzenie;
uznanie; dowód uznania
acoustics (e'ku:styks) pl. akus-
tyka
acquaint (e'kżejnt) v. zaznajo-
mić; zapoznać; zapoznawac(kogoś)
acquaintance (e'kżejntens) s.
znajomość; znajomy
acquiesce (,aekży'es), v. zgadzać się; przyzwalać (bez oporu); przychylić się(do prośby)
acquire (e'kżajer) v. nabywać
acquisition (,aekży'zyszyn) s.
nabytek; nabycie; zdobycz
acquit (e'kżyt) v. zwolnić; wywiązać się;spłacić;uniewinnić
acquittal (e'kżytl) s. zwolnienie;uiszczenie;wywiązanie się
acre (ejker) s. akr; morga;
4047 m²
acrid ('aekryd) adj. żrący;
ostry; cierpki;kwaskowaty
acrimonious (,aekry'mounjes)
adj. szorstki; zjadliwy;
cierpki; zgorzkniały
acrobat ('aekrebaet) s. akrobata
across (e'kros) adv. w poprzek;
na krzyż; prep. przez; na prze-
żaj; po drugiej stronie (czegoś)
act (aekt) v. czynić; działać;
postępować; s. czyn; akt; uczynek;akt sztuki;uchwża;ustawa
action ('aekszyn) s. działanie;
czyn; akcja; ruch;poces
active ('aektyw) adj. czynny;
obrotny; rzutki; ożywiony;żywy
activity (aek'tywyty) s..dzia-
żalność; czynność;ożywienie;ruch
actor ('aekter) s. aktor
actress ('aektrys) s. aktorka
actual ('aekczuel) adj. istotny;
faktyczny; bieżący; obecny
actually ('aekczuely) adv. rzeczywiście; obecnie;istotnie;nawet
acute (e'kju:t) adj. ostry;
przenikliwy; bystry;przenikliwy
ad (aed) s. ogżoszenie (reklama)
(slang)
adapt (e'daept) v. dostosować;
przerobić;przystosować;dostrajać

adaptation (,aedaep'tejszyn)
s. przystosowanie;dostrojenie
add (aed) v. dodać; doliczyć
addict (aedyktĕ) s. nażogowiec;
v. oddawać; poświęcać się
addicted (e'dyktyd) adj. nażo-
gowy; nałogowo poswięcający się
addition (e'dyszyn) s. dodawanie; dodatek; (ponadto)
additional (e'dyszynl) adj.
dodatkowy; dalszy
address (e'dres) s. adres; mowa; odezwa; v. zwracać się;
adresować; skierować(prośbę)
addressee (,aedre'si:) s. ad-
resat; adresatka
adequate ('aedykżyt) s. stosowny; dostateczny;wżaściwy
adhere (ed'hjer) v. lgnąć; należeć; trzymać; przylegać
adhesion (ed'hi:żyn) s. lep-
kość; zrost;przynależność
adhesive (ed'hi:syw) adj. lepki; przylegający; s. plaster
adjacent (e' dżejsent) adj.
przylegży; sąsiedni
adjective ('aeddżyktyw) s.
przymiotnik;adj.dodatkowy
adjoin (e'ddżoyn) v. stykać się;
sąsiadować; dołączać
adjourn (e'ddże:rn) v. odraczać;
przerywać; zakończyć (obrady)
adjust (e'ddżast) v. dostosowywać; uregulować; nastawić
administer (ed'mynyster) v. dawać; sprawować; administrować
administration (ed,myny'strejszyn) s. zarząd; rząd; administracja; ministerstwo; wymiar
administrative (ed'mynystrej-
tyw) adj. administracyjny
administrator (ed'mynystrejtor)
s. zarządca; administrator
admirable ('aedmerebl) adj.
godny podziwu;zachwycający
admiral ('aedmyrel) s. admirał
admiration (aedmy'rejszyn) s.
podziw;zachwyt;przedmiot podziwu
admire (ed'majer) v. podziwiać
admirer (ed'majrer) s. wielbiciel; wielbicielka

admissible (ed'mysybl) adj. dopuszczalny; do przyjęcia
admission (ed'myszyn) s. wstęp: dostęp; przyznanie; uznanie; (dopływ); bilet wstępu
admission ticket (ed'myszyn'tykyt) bilet wstępu
admit (ed'myt) v. wpuszczać; uznać; przyjmować; przyznać
admittance (ed'mytens) s. dostęp; przyjęcie;przyznanie się
admonish (ed'monysz) v. upominać; ostrzegać; pouczać
ado (e'du) s. wrzawa; kłopot; trudności; grymasy; narzekania
adolescence (,aede'lesns) s. młodość(pokwitanie-dojrzałość)
adolescent (,aede'lesnt) adj. młodociany; dorastający
adopt (e'dopt) adoptować; przyjmować; akceptować; wybierać
adoption (e'dopszyn) s. adopcja; adaptacja; przyjęcie; przysposobienie;akceptacja; wybór
adorable (e'do:rebl) adj. godny uwielbienia; bardzo miły
adoration (,aede:rejszyn) s. uwielbienie; wielka miłość
adore (e'do:r) v. czcić; uwielbiać; bardzo lubić; kochać
adorn (e'do:rn) v. zdobić; upiększać; być ozdobą
adrift (e'dryft) adv. na fali; na wodzie bez steru zdany na los
adult ('aedalt) adj. dorosły; dojrzały; s. osoba dorosła
adulterate (e'dalterejt) v. fałszować; podrabiać;zatruwać
adultery (e'daltery) s. cudzołóstwo
advance (ed'waens) v. iść naprzód; pospieszać; awansować; przedkładać; popierać; pożyczać; adj. wysunięty; wcześniejszy; w przodzie
advanced (ed'waenst) adj. postępowy; światły; wysunięty naprzód; stary; przedwczesny
advanced reservation (ed'waenst, rezełwejszyn) rezerwacja z góry zamówiona

advantage (ed'waentydż) s. korzyść; pożytek; przewaga
advantageous (,aedwan'tejdżes) adj. korzystny; zyskowny
adverb ('aedwe:rb) s. przysłówek(oznaczający czas,sposób...)
adversary ('aedwersery) s. przeciwnik; wróg; oponent
adverse ('aedwe:rs) adj. wrogi; przeciwny; szkodliwy;niekorzystny
advertise ('aedwertajz) v. ogłaszać; reklamować
advertisement ('edwertysment) s. ogłoszenie; reklama
advertising ('aedwertajzyng)s. reklama; ogłoszenia handlowe
advice (ed'wajs) s. rada; informacje;porada;pouczenie
advisable (ed'wajzebl) adj. wskazany; rozsądny;ostrożny
advise (ed'wajz) v. radzić; powiadamiać; pouczać
adviser (ed'wajzer) s. doradca; radca(prawny etc.)
advocate ('aedwekejt) v. zalecać; bronić;s.rzecznik;orędownik
aerial ('eerjel) adj. powietrzny; s. antena (radiowa etc.)
aeronautics (eere'no:tyks) s. aeronautyka; lotnictwo
aeroplane ('eereplejn) s. samolot
aesthetic (i:stetyk) adj. estetyczny;wrażliwy na piękno
afar (e'fa:r) adv. daleko;z daleka
affair (e'feer) s. sprawa; interes; romans; przedsięwzięcie
affect (e'fekt) v. wpływać; oddziaływać;wzruszać;dotyczyć;udawać
affected (e'fektyd) adj. dotknięty;przejęty; sztuczny
affection (e'fekszyn) s. uczucie; przywiązanie; choroba; miłość
affectionate (e'fekszynyt) adj. czuły; kochający;tkliwy;przwiązany
affidavit (aef'ydejwyt) s. poręczenie pod przysięgą
affinity (e'fynyty) s. pokrewieństwo;przyciąganie;powinowactwo
affirm (e'fe:rm) v. potwierdzać; zapewniać;zaręczać

affirmation (,aefe:r'mejszyn) s. twierdzenie; oświadczenie; zapewnienie;zatwierdzenie(wyroku)

affirmative (e'fe:rmetyw) adj. pozytywny; twierdzący

afflict (e'flykt) v. gnębić

affliction (e'flykszyn) s. przygnębienie; choroba;ból;cierpienie

affluence ('aefluens) s. dostatek; bogactwo;obfitosc;natłok

affluent ('aefluent) adj. zamożny; s. dopływ (rzeki)

afford (e'fo:rd) v. zdobyć się; dostarczyć; stać na coś

affront (e'frant) v. znieważać

afficionado (éfisienado) s. entuzjasta (walki byków etc.)

aflame (e'flejm) adv. w ogniu; w podnieceniu

afraid (e'frejd) adj. przestraszony;wyrażający rezerwę

African ('aefryken) adj. afrykański

Afro ('aefro) s. (niby) styl afrykański (uczesania,ubioru)

after ('a:fte:r) prep. po; za; odnośnie; według;poniekąd

after all ('a:fte: o:l) prep. jednak; przecież;mimo wszystko

after that ('a:fte: daet) następnie ; potem

afternoon ('a:fte:rnu:n) s. popołudnie; adj. popołudniowy

afterwards ('aftełerdz) adv. poźniej; potem; następnie

again (e'gen) adv. ponownie; znowu;na nowo;więcej;ponadto

again and again (e'gen end e'gen) wciąż; ciągle

against (e'genst) prep. przeciw; wbrew; na; pod;na wypadek

age (ejdż) s. wiek;stulecie;czasy

aged ('ejdżyd) adj. stary; sędziwy;wiekowy;w podeszłym wieku

age ten (ejdż ten) w wieku lat dziesięciu

agency ('ejdżensy) s. ajencja; działanie;pośrednictwo

agenda (e'dżende) s. agenda; lista;porządek dzienny

agent ('ejdżent) s. pośrednik; ajent; czynnik;przedstawiciel

aggravate ('aegrewejt) v. pogarszać; rozjątrzać ;denerwować

aggression (e'greszyn) s. napaść; agresja;napastliwość

aggressive (e'gresyw) adj. napastliwy; zaczepny;napastniczy

aggressor (e'grese:r) s. napastnik; agresor

aghast (e'gaest) adj. przerażony; osłupiały;skonsternowany

agile ('aedżyl) adj. zwinny; obrotny;zręczny;ruchliwy

agitate ('aedżytejt) v. poruszać; miotać; agitować

agitation (,aedżytejszyn) s. poruszenie; agitacja;podniecenie

agitator ('aedżytejter) s. agitator; mieszadło; trzęsarka

agnostic (áegnostyk) s. agnostyk; adj. agnostyczny

ago (e'gou) adv. przed; ...temu

agonize ('aegenajz) v. męczyć się; dręczyć się

agony ('aegeny) s. smiertelna męka; agonia;katusze; spazm

agree (e'gri:) v. godzić się; zgadzać się; uzgadniać

agree about (e'gri: e'baut) v. zgadzać się co do...

agree to (e'gri: tu) v. zgadzać się na...

agreeable (e'gri:ebl) adj. zgodny; miły; chętny;sympatyczny

agreement (e'gri:ment) s. zgoda; umowa;porozumienie;układ

agricultural(,aegry'kalczerel) adj. rolniczy; rolny

agriculture (,aegry'kalczer) s, rolnictwo; uprawa ziemi

agriculturist (,aegry'kalczeryst) s. rolnik

ague ('ejgju:) s. febra; dreszcze;malaria; zimnica

ahead (e'hed) adv. naprzód; dalej; na przedzie;z przodu

aid (ejd) s. pomoc; pomocnik; v. pomagać; subwencjonować

aide (ejd) s. asystent;pomocnik

ailing ('ejlyŋg)s. choroba

aim (ejm) s. zamiar; cel; v. celować; mierzyć; zamierzać;skierować;dążyć

aimless (éjmlys) adj. bezcelowy
air (eer) s. 1. powietrze;
2. mina; postawa;wygląd;nastrój
air ('eer) v. 1. wietrzyć;
2. obnosić się; nadawać
air base ('eerbejs) s. baza lotnicza (wojskowa)
air brake ('eer,brejk) s. hamulec na sprężone powietrze
air-conditioning (,eer-ken'dy-
szynyn) s. klimatyzacja
air compressor (,eer-kem'presor)
s. sprężarka
aircraft ('eer-kra:ft) s. samolot;lotnictwo(wiedza,flota etc.)
aircraft carrier ('eer-kra:ft'
kaerje:) s. lotniskowiec
airfield ('eer-fi:ld) s. lotnisko (do startowania i lądowania)
air force ('eer fo:rs) s. lotnictwo (wojskowe)
airline ('eerlajn) s. linia lotnicza (system transportu)
airmail ('eermejl) s. poczta
lotnicza
airplane ('eerplejn) s. samolot
airport ('eerpo:rt) s. lotnisko
air raid ('eerejd) atak lotniczy
air show ('eerszou) pokaz lotniczy
airsickness ('eersyknys) s.cho-
roba powietrzna
airtight ('eertajt) adj. hermetyczny
air traffic ('eer-traefyk) ruch
lotniczy(samolotów, pasażerów)
airway ('eerłej) linia lotnicza
airy ('eery) adj. przewiewny
aisle (ajl) s. przejście; nawa
boczna(kościoła)
ajar (e'dża:r) adv. uchylony;
pół otwarty;nieco otwarty
akin (e'kyn) adj. pokrewny
alacrity (e'laekryty) s. ochota;
gotowość; żwawość; skwapliwość
alarm (e'la:rm) s. popłoch;
strach; sygnał alarmowy;trwoga;
v. alarmować; trwożyć;płoszyć
alarm clock (e'la:rm,klok) s.
budzik
alas ! (e'laes) excl. niestety
alcohol ('aelkehol) s. alkohol;
spirytus

alcoholic (,aelke'holyk) s.
alkoholik; adj.alkoholowy
alcove ('aelkouw) s. altanka;
alkowa; nisza
alder ('o:lder) s. olcha; ol-
sza
ale (ejl) s, piwo (gorzkie,
angielskie)
alert (e'le:t) adj. czujny;
raźny; żwawy; s.alarm
algae ('aeldżi:) pl. glony;
algi
alias ('ejliaes) adv. inaczej;
alias; vel; s. pseudonim
alibi ('aelybaj) s. alibi; wymówka; v.usprawiedliwiać się
alien ('ejljen) adj. obcy
alienate ('ejljenejt) v. od-
stręczać; odrywać; zrażać
alike (e'lajk) adj. jednakowy;
podobny; adv. tak samo; jedna-
ko; podobnie; zarówno; także
alimony ('aelimeny) s. alimenty
alive (e'lajw) adj. żywy; żyjący; ożywiony;pełen życia
all (o:l) adj.& pron. cały;
wszystek; każdy; adv. całkowicie; w pełni; s. wszystko
all of us (o:l ow as) my
wszyscy; my wszyscy razem
all at once (o:l et łans)wszys-
cy na raz; wszyscy jednocześnie
all the better (o:l dy bete:)
tym lepiej
all told (o:l told) wszystkiego
razem ; razem wziąwszy
alleged(e'ledżd) adj. rzekomy
alleviate (e'li:wjejt) v. łagodzić; zmniejszać
alley ('aely)s. aleja; przejście; zaułek; boczna ulica ;tor
alliance (e'lajens) s. związek;
sojusz; powinowactwo;skoligacenie
allot (e'lot) v. przydzielać;
losować; wyznaczać;wyasygnować
allotment (e'lotment) s. przydział; działka; asygnata
allow (e'lau) v. pozwalać; użyczać; uznawać; uwzględniać
allow for (e'lau fo:r) v.
uwzględniać; dawać (czas)
allowance (e'lauens) s. przydział; pozwolenie; kieszonkowe

alloy ('aeloj) s. stop; próba; domieszka;stop kilku metali

all—round (o:l-raund) adj. wszechstronny; universalny

allude (e'lu:d) v. robić aluzje

allure (e'lju:) v. wabić; kusić; oczarować;nęcić;znęcić;zwabić

allusion (e'lu:żyn) s. aluzja; przymówka;przytyk;napomknienie

ally (e'laj) v. sprzymierzać się; łączyć;połączyc;skoligacić

ally ('aelaj) s. sprzymierzeniec; sojusznik

almighty (o:l'majty) adj. wszechmogący;ogromny;straszliwy

almond (am 'end) s. migdał

almost ('o:lmoust) adv. prawie; niemal;jak gdyby;o mało;ledwo

almost never ('o:lmoust'newer) prawie nigdy; rzadko kiedy

alms (a:mz) s, jałmużna

aloft (e'loft) adv. wysoko;hen; w górze; w górę; do góry

alone (e'loun) adj. sam; samotny;w pojedynkę;sam jeden;jedyny

along (e'lo:ng) adv. naprzód; wzdłuż; z sobą

alongside (e'lo:ngsajd) adv. obok; wzdłuż ;przy(molu,burcie...)

aloof (e'lu:f) adv. z dala; na uboczu; z daleka

aloud (e'laud) adv. głośno

alphabet ('aelfebyt) s. alfabet

already (o:l'redy) adv. już; wcześniej;poprzednio;uprzednio

also (o:lsou) adv. także;również

altar ('o:lter) s, ołtarz

alter (o:lter) v. zmieniać; poprawiać;odmienić;przemienić

alteration (o:lte'rejszyn) s. zmiana; poprawka;przemiana

alternate ('o:lternejt) v. zmieniać się (kolejno);brać kolejno

alternate ('o:lternyt) adj. co drugi; na zmianę;kolejny

alternating current (o:lternejtyŋgkarent) prąd zmienny

alternative (ol-ter'netyw) s. alternatywa; adj.alternatywny

although (o:lżou) conj. chociaż

altitude ('aeltytju:d) s. wysokość(nad poziomem morza)

altogether (o:lte'gedze:r)adv. zupełnie; całkowicie

aluminum (e'lumynem) s. aluminium

alumnus (e'lamnes) s. byłý student uczelni

always ('o:lłejz) adv. stale; zawsze;ciągle;wciąż

am (aem) v. jestem

amass (e'maes) v. gromadzić

amateur ('aemecze:r)s, miłosnik; amator;dyletant

amaze (e'mejz) v. zdumiewać; zadziwiać;wprawić w zdumienie

amazement (e'mejzment) s. zdumienie; osłupienie

amazing (e'mejzyŋg)adj. zdumiewający; zadziwiający

ambassador (aem'baesede:r)s. ambasador; poseł

amber ('aembe:r)s. bursztyn

ambient ('aembient) adj. otaczający

ambiguous (aem'bygjues) adj. dwuznaczny;mętny;zagadkowy

ambition (aem'byszyn) s. ambicja;chęć wybicia się

ambitious (aem'byszes) adj. ambitny; żądny

ambulance ('aembjulens) s. ambulans

ambush ('aembusz) s. zasadzka

amen (ej'men) amen

amend (e'mend) v. poprawiać

amendment (e'mendment) s. poprawa; ulepszenie; uzupełnienie

amends (e'mendz) s. odszkodowanie; zadośćuczynienie

American (e'meryken) s. Amerykanin; adj. amervkański

amiable ('ejmjebel) adj. miły; uprzejmy; sympatyczny

amicable ('aemykebl) adj. polubowny; przyjacielski

amid (e'myd) prep. wśród; pośród; między; pomiędzy

amidst (e'mydst) prep. wśród; pośród; między; pomiędzy

amiss (e'mys) adv. na opak; błędnie; źle;niefortunnie

ammo ('aemou) s. amunicja

ammunition (,aemju'nyszyn) s. amunicja

amnesty (aemnysty) s. ułaskawienie; amnestia
among (e'mang) prep. wśród; pomiędzy; miedzy; pośród
amongst (e'mangst) prep. wśród;
pomiędzy; miedzy; pośrod
amount (e'maunt) v. wynosić;
s. suma; kwota; wynik
amount to (e'maunt tu) v. wy-
nosić(w sumie)
ample ('aempl) adj. rozległy;
dostatni;hojny;suty;obfity
amplifier ('aemplyfajer) v.
wzmacniacz; amplifikator
amplify ('aemplyfy) v. rozszerzać; wzmacniać; przesadzać
amplitude ('aemplytju:d) s.
amplituda; wielkość; obfitość
amply ('aemply) adv. obszernie;
szeroko;zupełnie wystarczajaco
amulet ('aemjulyt) s. amulet
amuse (e'mju:z) v. bawić;ubawić;
śmieszyć; zabawić;rozśmieszać
amusement (e'mju:zment) s. rozrywka; zabawa
amusing (e'mju:zyng)adj. zabawny: śmieszny
an (aen; en) art. jeden ;jakiś
anemia (e'ni:mja) s. anemia
anesthetic (e'nystetyk) s.
środek znieczulający
analogous (e'naeleges) adj.
analogiczny; zbieżny
analogy (e'naeledży) s. podobieństwo; analogia
analysis (e'naelysys) s. analiza
analyze (e'naelajz) v. analizować; rozpatrywać; zanalizować
anathema (e'naetyma) s, klątwa
anatomize (e'naetemajz) v. rozbierać; anatomizować
anatomy (e'naetemy) s. anatomia
ancestor ('aensester) s. przodek
ancestry ('aensestry) s. przod-
kowie; starożytność rodu
anchor ('aenker) s. kotwica
anchovy ('aenchewy) s. sardela
ancient ('ejnszent) adj. starodawny; stary;sędziwy;wiekowy
and (aend; end) conj. i; coraz
anecdote ('aenyk,dout)s. dykte-
ryjka ; anegdota

anew (e'nju:) adv. na nowo
angel ('ejndżl) s. anioł
anger ('eanger) s. gniew;
złość;v.gniewac;irytować
angina (aendżajna) s. angina
angle ('aengl) s. kąt; narożnik; kątówka v. kluczyć
Anglican ('aenglyken) adj.
anglikański
Anglo-Saxon (aenglou'saeksen)
adj. anglo-saski
angry (aengry) adj. zagniewany
anguish (aengłysz) s. udręka;
męka;udręczenie;boleść;ból
angular ('aengjuler) adj. kanciasty; narożny; kątowy; gra-
niasty
animal ('aenyml) s. zwierzę;
stworzenie;adj.zwierzęcy
animate ('aenymejt) v. ożywiać;
adj. ożywiony; żywy
animated cartoon ('aenymejtyd
'ka:rtu:n) film rysunkowy;kres-
kówka
animation (,aeny'mejszyn) s.
ożywianie; ożywienie; żywość
animosity (,aeny'mosyty) s.
uraza; niechęć; animozja
ankle ('aenkl) s. kostka u stopy;staw między stopą i łydką
annex ('aeneks) v. przyłączać;
wcielać;s.przybudówka;załącznik
annihilate (e'najelejt) v. unicestwić; niszczyć;niweczyć
anniversary (,aeny've:rsery) s.
rocznica adj. doroczny(obchód)
annotation (,aene'tejszyn) s.
uwaga; komentarz;przypis
announce (e'nauns) v. zapowiadać; ogłaszać;oznajmiać
announcement (e'naunsment) s.
zapowiedź; zawiadomienie
announcer (e'naunser) s.
1. zapowiadacz; 2. (radio)
speaker; konferansjer
annoy (e'noj) v. dokuczać;
drażnić; nękać;trapić;martwić
annoyance (e'nojens) s. udręka;
przykrość;irytacja ; kłopot
annoyed (e'nojd) adj. rozgnie-
wany; rozdrażniony;strapiony
annual ('aenjuel) adj. coroczt-
ny; s. rocznik;jednorocznik

annuity (e'njuyty) s. renta
roczna; renta dożywotnia
annul (e'nal) v. unieważniac;
anulować; skasować; kasować
anodyne ('aenedajn) s. anodyna;
środek od bólu ,łagodzący
anomalous (e'nomeles) adj. nienormalny; nietypowy
anonym ('aenenym) s. anonim
anonymous (e'nonymes) adj. bez-
imienny; anonimowy
another (e'nadzer) adj.& pron.
drugi;inny; jeszcze jeden
another time (e'nadzer,tajm)
kiedy indziej;innym razem
answer ('aenser) s. odpowiedź;
v. odpowiadać; spełnić(prośbę)
answer for ('aenser fo:r) v.
odpowiadać za(przed kimś)
ant (aent) s. mrówka
antagonist (aen'taegenyst) s.
przeciwnik; przeciwniczka
antagonize (aen'taege'najz) v.
zrażać; narażać; zwalczać
antelope ('aentyloup) s. anty-
lopa
anterior (aen'tierjer) adj. poprzedni;uprzedni;wcześniejszy
anthem ('aentem) s. hymn narodowy
anti ('aenty) pre . przeciw-
anti-aircraft ('aentaj'e:r-
kra:ft) adj. przeciwlotniczy
antibiotic ('aentybajotyk) s.
antybiotyk
antic ('aentyk) adj. dziwaczny;
groteskowy; s. figiel; dzi-
wactwa; błazeństwo
anticipate (aen'tysypejt) v.
przewidywać; uprzedzać
anticipation (aen'tysypejszyn)
s. uprzedzenie; przewidywanie;
przyśpieszenie;oczekiwanie
anticlimax ('aenty'klajmaeks)
s. rozczarowanie; zawód
anticyclone (,aenty'sajkloun)
s. antycyklon; wyż(atmosf.)
antidote ('aentydout) s. odtrutka ; antidotum
antifreeze('aentyfri:z) s. mieszanka niemarznąca
antiknock ('aentynok) s. mieszanka przeciwstukowa

antipathy (aen'typety) s. odraza; niechęć (do kogoś)
antiquated ('aentykłejtyd) adj.
przestarzały; staroświecki
antique (aen'ti:k)adj.stary;
starożytny; staromodny
antiquity (aen'tykłyty) s. starożytność; zabytki
antiseptic (aenty'septyk) adj.
antyseptyk; przeciwgnilny
antlers ('aentlerz) pl. rogi
(np. jelenia)
anvil ('aenvyl) s. kowadło
anxiety (aeng'zajety) s. niepokój; troska; pożądanie
anxious ('aenkszes) adj. zaniepokojony; zabiegający;pragnący
anxious about ('aenkszes e'baut)
troskliwy o...;niepokojący się o...
anxious for ('aenkszes fo:r)
pragnący bardzo czegoś
anxious to ('aenkszes tu) pragnący żeby;mający ochotę na
any ('eny) pron. jakikolwiek;
któryś; jakiś;żaden;lada;byle
any farther ('eny fa:rdzer) trochę dalej;nieco dalej
any more ('eny mo:r) trochę
więcej; teraz; obecnie
anybody ('eny'body) pron. ktoś;
ktokolwiek; każdy; nikt
anyhow ('enyhau) adv. jakkolwiek
anyone ('enyłan) pron. ktokolwiek; każdy; ktoś; nikt
anything ('enytyng)pron. coś;
cokolwiek; wszystko(oprócz);nic
anything else ('enytyngels)
jeszcze coś; coś więcej
anyway ('enyłej) adv. w każdym
razie; jakkolwiek;byle jak
anywhere ('enyhłeer) adv.gdzie-
kolwiek;byle gdzie; nigdzie
apart (e'pa:rt) adv. osobno;
niezależnie;na boku;od siebie
apart from (e'pa:rt, from) niezależnie od...;poza;oprócz;prócz
apartment (e'pa:rtment) s.
mieszkanie; izba; pokój
apartment house (e'pa:rtment,
haus)blok mieszkalny;kamienica
apathetic (aepe'tetyk) adj.
apatyczny;obojętny;bez uczuć

ape (ejp) s. małpa (bezogonowa)
v. małpować;naśladować;błaznować

apex ('ejpeks) s. szczyt; czubek; wierzchołek

apiary ('ejpjery) s. pasieka

apiece (e'pi:s) adv. na osobę;
od sztuki;za sztukę; każdy

aplomb (e'plom) s. pewność siebie; opanowanie; zimna krew

apologize (e'poledżajz) v.
usprawiedliwiać; przepraszać

apology (e'poledży) s. usprawiedliwienie; obrona;przeprosiny

apoplexy ('aepopleksy) s. apo-
pleksja ; udar

apostle (e'posl) s. apostoł

apostolic (,aepe'stolyk) adj.
apostolski

apostrophe (e'postrefy) s.
apostrof; apostrofa

appal (e'po:l) v. przerażać

apparatus (aepe'rejtes) s. aparat; urządzenie;przyrząd;organ

apparent (e'paerent) adj. jawny; pozorny; oczywisty;widoczny

appeal (e'pi:l) v. apelować;
odwoływać się;uciekać się do

appeal to (e'pi:l tu) v. zwracać się do...;zwracać się z apelem

appear (e'pier) v. ukazywać się;
zjawiać się;pokazywać się

appearance (e'pierens) s. wygląd;
pozór; wystąpienie;zjawienie się

appease (e'pi:z) v. łagodzić;
uśmierzać; zaspakajać;ugłaskać

append (e'pend) v. dołączać; do-
czepiać;dodawać;zawieszać

appendicitis (ependy'sajtys) s.
zapalenie wyrostka robaczkowego

appendix (e'pendyks) s. dodatek;
uzupełnienie;ślepa kiszka

appetite ('aepitajt) s. apetyt

appetizing ('aepitajzing) adj.
apetyczny; smakowity

applaud (e'plo:d) v. oklaskiwać;
klaskać;bić brawo;przyklasnąć

applause (e'plo:z) s. aplauz;
oklaski;poklask;pochwała;aprobata

apple ('aepl) s. jabłko

apple-pie('aeplpaj) s. placek
jabłkowy ; szarlotka

applesauce ('aepl so:s) s.
purée z jabłek

apple tree ('aepltri:) s. jabłoń

appliance (e'plajens) s. przyrząd; urządzenie;akcesoria

applicant ('aeplykent) s. petent; zgłaszający się;kandydat

application (,aeply'kejszyn)
s. podanie; użycie; zastosowanie;przykładanie:pilność

apply (e'plaj) v. używać; stosować; odnosić się;naciskać

apply for (e'plaj fo:r) v. starać się o...;wnosić podanie o

apply to (e'plaj tu) v. zwracać
się do..;zgłaszać się do(o coś)

appoint (e'point) v. mianować;
wyznaczać; ustanawiać;ustalić

appointment (e'pointment) s.
nominacja; oznaczenie czasu
i miejsca; umówione spotkanie

apportion (e'po:rszyn) v. wyznaczać; wydzielać;przydzielać

appreciate (e'pri:szjejt) v.
cenić wysoko; zyskiwać na wartości;ocenić; oszacować;docenić

appreciation (e'pri:szjejszyn)
s. ocena; uznanie; wzrost wartości;zrozumienie czegoś

apprehend (,aepry'hend) v. ująć;
pojmać; rozumieć

apprehension (,aepry'henszyn) s.
obawa; pojęcie; aresztowanie;lęk

apprehensive (,aepry'hensyw)
adj.obawiający się; pojętny

apprentice (e'prentys) s. czeladnik; uczeń; terminator

apprenticeship (e'prentysszyp)
s. termin;nauka rzemiosła

approach (e'proucz) v. zbliżać
się; podchodzić;s. dostęp

approach road (e'proucz,roud)
droga dojazdowa

appropriate (e'prouprjejt) adj.
właściwy; odpowiedni;stosowny

appropriation (e'prouprejszyn)
s. asygnowanie; przywłaszczenie;przeznaczenie; kredyty

approval (e'pru:wel) s. aproba-
ta; uznanie; zatwierdzenie

approximate (e'proksymyt) adj.
zbliżony; przybliżony; mniej
więcej;v.zbliżać(się);być około

apricot ('ejprykot) s. morela

April ('ejprel) s. kwiecień

apron ('ejpren) s. fartuch;
płyta przednia;przedpole

apropos (aepre'pou) adv. do tego celu; w związku z tym

apt (aept) v. mieć skłonność

apt to (aept tu) v. być skłon-
nym do...;często coś robić

aquarium (e'kłerjem) s. akwarium

aquatic (e'kłaetyk) adj. wodny

aquatic sports (e'kłaetyk
spo:rts) sport wodny

aqueduct ('aekłydakt) s. wodociąg; akwedukty rzymskie

aquiline ('aekłylajn) adj. orli

Arabic (ae'rebyk) adj. arabski

arable ('aerebl) adj. orny

arbitrary ('a:rbytrery) adj. dowolny; samowolny

arbor ('a:rber) s. altanka; wał
napędowy; oś maszyny; drzewo

arc (a:rk) s. łuk

arc lamp (a:rk lemp) lampa łu-
kowa

arcade (a:r'kejd) s. arkada;
podcienie

arch (a:rcz) s. łuk; sklepienie;
podbicie;v. tworzyć łuk

arch (a:rcz) adj.chytry; wierutny;
arcy...;figlarny

archaeologist (a:rky'oledżyst)
s. archeolog

archeology (a:rky'oledży) s.
archeologia

archaic (a:rkejyk) adj. archai-
czny; przestarzały; staroświecki

archangel ('a:rkejndżel) s.
archanioł

archbishop ('a:rczbyszep) s.
arcybiskup

archer ('a:rczer) s. łucznik

archery ('a:rczery) s. łucznic-
two; łuki i strzały

architect ('a:rkytekt) s. architekt;twórca;budowniczy

architecture ('a:rkytekczer) s.
architektura;styl budowy

archives ('a:rkajwz) pl. archi-
wa ; archiwum

archway ('a:rczłej) s. skle-
pione przejście ; brama

arctic ('a:rktyk) adj. arktycz-
ny ; polarny

ardent ('a:rdent) adj. rozpalo-
ny; prażący ;płonący;gorliwy

ardor ('a:rder) s. żar; żarliwość; gorliwość; zapał

arduous ('a:rdżues) adj. mozolny; wytrwały; stromy;żmudny

are (a:r) v. są ;jesteś;jesteście

area ('e:rje) s. obszar; zakres;
powierzchnia;teren;okolica;strefa

Argentine ('a:rdżentajn) adj.
argentyński

argot ('a:rgou) s. żargon
(złodziejski)

argue ('a:rgju:) v. wykazywać;
rozumować; spierać się; rozpatrywać; dowodzić ;udowadniać

argument ('a:rgjument) s. argument; dowód; sprzeczka ;spór

argumentation (,a:rgjumen'tejszyn) s. roztrząsanie; argu-
mentacja; rozumowanie

arid ('aeryd) adj. suchy; jałowy; oschły;wypalony;spieczony

arise (e'rajz) arose, arisen (e'rajz;
e'rouz; e'ryzn)

arise (e'rajz) v. powstawać;
wstawać; wynikać;nadarzyć się

arithmetic (,aeryt'metyk) s.
rachunki; adj. arytmetyczny;
rachunkowy

ark (a:rk) s. arka; skrzynia

arm (a:rm) s. ramię; odnoga;
konar; rękaw; poręcz

arm (a:rm) s. broń (rodzaj);
uzbrojenie; v. uzbroić; opan-
cerzyć; nastawiać (zapłon)

armament ('a:rmement) s. uzbrojenie; zbrojenia; siły zbrojne

armament race ('a:rmement, rejs)
wyścig zbrojeń

armchair (,a:rm'cze:r) s. fotel

armistice ('a:rmystys) s. zawieszenie broni;rozejm

armor ('a:rmer) s. zbroja;
opancerzenie ;v.zbroić w płyty
pancerne;opancerzać

armored car ('a:rmerd,ca:r)
samochód pancerny
arm-twisting ('a:rm,tɫystyŋ)
napór na (kogoś); (wykręcanie
ręki);nagabywanie kogoś
arms ('a:rmz) pl. broń; uzbrojenie; herby; herb
army ('a:rmy) s. wojsko; armia
aroma (e'roume) s. aromat
arose (e'rouz) v. powstał;
wstał; wynikł; zob. arise
around (e'raund) prep. dokoła;
naokoło; wokoło; adv. wokół;
tu i tam; około; wszędzie
arousal (e'rauzel) s. pobudze-
nie do czynu (działania)
arouse (e'rauz) v. pobudzić;
budzić; wzniecać(uczucia)
arraign(e'rejn) v. pozwać;
oskarżyć;atakować pogląd
arrange (e'rejndż) v. układać;
szykować; porządkować;ustalać
arrangement (e'rejndżment) s.
układ; ułożenie się; urządzenie; zaaranżowanie;porządek;szyk
array (e'rej) v. szykować; przybrać; rozmieszczać; s. szyk;
szereg; uszeregowanie;wystawa
arrears (e'rierz) pl. zaległości;
dɫugi;zaległe prace(płatności)
arrest (e'rest) s. areszt;
aresztowanie; zatrzymanie;
v. aresztować; zatrzymywać;
wstrzymywać;przyciągać(uwagę)
arrival (e'rajwel) s. przyjazd;
przybysz; rzecz nadeszła
arrive (e'rajw) v. przybyć;
dojść; osiągnąć;wspólnie ustalać
arrive at (e'rajw,aet) v. dojść
do...;wspólnie ustalać
arrogance ('aeregens) s. zarozumiałość; buta; arogancja
arrogant ('aeregent) adj. butny; arogancki; wyniosły
arrow ('aerou) s. strzała;
strzałka (kierunkowa)
arrow head ('aerou hed) s. grot
arse (a:rs) s. vulg. rzyć; zadek; dupa ; dupsko
arsenal ('a:rsynl) s. arsenał
arsenic ('a:rsnyk) s. arszenik;
arsen; ('a:rsenyk) adj. arse-
nowy

arson ('a:rsen)s. podpalenie
(zbrodnia); podpalanie
art (a:rt) s. sztuka; chytrość;
zręczność; rzemiosło;fortel
arterial (a:r'tyerjal) adj.
tętniczy; magistralny
arterial road(a:r'tyerjal,roud)
magistrala;główna szosa
artery (a:rtery) s. arteria;
tętnica; arteria ruchu
artful ('a:rtful) adj. chytry;
zręczny; pomysłowy;dowcipny
article ('a:rtykl) s. rodzajnik;
artykuł; warunek;paragraf;temat
articulate (a:rtykjulejt) v.
wyrażać jasno; adj. artykuło-
wany; wyraźny;stawowy
artifact (,a:rty'faekt) s. wytwór ludzkiej ręki
artificial(,a:rty'fyszel) adj.
sztuczny;udany;symulowany
artillery (a:r'tylery) s. artyleria
artisan ('a:rtyzaen) s. rzemieślnik
artist ('a:rtist) s. artysta;
artystka
artiste (a:r'ty:st) s. artysta;
odtwórca; artysta estradowy
artless ('artlys) adj. niewinny; niedołężny;szczery;otwarty
as (aez; ez) adv. pron. conj;
jak; tak; co; jako; jaki; skoro; żeby; choć; z (dniem)
as... as (ez...ez) tak jak
as far as (ez fa:r ez) co do
as many (ez meny) tak wiele
as well (ez łel) również
as well as (ez łel ez) jak także ; tak jak; jak również
as for (ez fo:r) co się tyczy
asbestos (aez'bestes) s. azbest
ascend (e'send) v. piąć się;
iść w górę; wznosić się; wracać w przeszłość; wstępować
ascension (e'senszyn) s. wznoszenie się; Wniebowstąpienie
ascent (e'sent) s. wzlot;
wzrost;stok; postęp;wchodzenie
ascertain (aeser'tejn) v.
stwierdzać; ustalać;konstatować
ascetic (e'setyk) s. asceta;
adj. ascetyczny;odmawiający sobie

ascribe (e'skrajb) v. przypisywać; przypisać(coś komuś)
aseptic ('eseptyk) adj. jałowy;
wyjałowiony; aseptyczny
ash (aesz) s. popiół ;jesion
ashamed (e'szejmd) adj. zawstydzony ;zażenowany
ashamed of (e'szejmd ow)adj.
wstydzący się czegoś
ash can (aesz kaen) wiadro na
śmieci; wiadro na popiół
ashen ('aeszen) adj. popielaty
ashes ('aeszyz) s. popioły
ashore (e'szo:r) adv. na brzeg;
na brzegu ; na ląd; na lądzie
ashtray ('aesztrej) s. popielniczka
Ash Wednesday (,aesz'łenzdy) -
Środa Popielcowa
Asiatic (,ej ży'atyk) adj. azja-
tycki
aside (e'sajd) adv. na stronę;
na stronie; na boku;na uboczu
aside from (e'sajd,from) adv.
oprócz; z wyjątkiem; poza:prócz
asinine ('aesynajn) adj. ośli;
głupi; idiotyczny
ask (aesk) v. pytać ;zapytywać
ask a question ('aesk ej'kłesz-
czyn) stawiać pytanie; pytać
ask to dinner ('aesk tu'dyner)
zapraszać na obiad
ask for ('aesk fo:r) prosić o...
askance (es'kaens) adv. z ukosa;
zezem ; niepewnie; podejrzliwie
askew (es'kju:) adv. krzywo;
skośnie ; z ukosa
aslant (es'sla:nt) adv. ukośnie;
skośnie ; na ukos; w poprzek
asleep (e'sli:p) adv. we śnie;
adj. śpiący;zdrętwiały;ścierpły
asparagus (es'paereges) s. szparag
aspect ('aespekt) s. aspekt; wygląd; wyraz; faza; postać;
strona;mina;przejaw;wystawa domu
aspen ('aespen) s. osika; osina
asphalt ('aesfo,lt) s. asfalt
aspire (es'pajer) v. dążyć; marzyć; wzdychać do...
aspire after (es'pajer'a:fter)
aspirować; dążyć do (czegoś);
mieć aspiracje żeby...

ass (aes) s. osioł;wulg.: dupa
assail (e'sejl) v. napadać;
przystępować;atakować;uderzać
assailant (e'sejlent) s. napastnik
assassin (e'saesyn) s. morderca (najęty); zamachowiec
assassinate (e'saesynejt) v.
zamordować; dokonać zamachu
assassination (e,saesy'nejszyn)
s. morderstwo;zabójstwo;zamach
assault (e'sa:lt) s. napad;
atak; zgwałcenie;v.atakować;bić
assemblage (e'semblydż) s. zebranie; zbiór; zmontowanie
assemble (e'sembl) v. zbierać;
montować;nagromadzać;złożyć
assembly (e'sembly) s. zebranie; zbiórka; montaż
assembly line (e'sembly,lajn)
taśma montażowa;linia montażowa
assent (e'sent) s. zgoda; pogodzenie się;v.zgadzać się;uznawać
assent to (e'sent tu) v. zgadzać się na coś;zatwierdzać coś
assert (e'se:rt) v. twierdzić;
upominać się;dowieść;stawiać się
assess (e'ses) v. szacować;
oceniać; wymierzać; opodatkować;nałożyć podatek
assets ('aesets) pl. własność;
aktywa; wartościowi pracownicy
assign (e'sajn) v. przydzielać;
ustalać; odnosić; przekazywać
assignment (e'sajnment) s. przy-
dzielenie; przypisanie; przekazanie;przydział;podział
assimilate (e'symylejt) v. upodabniać; wcielać; wchłaniać;
asymilować;przyswajać sobie
assist (e'syst) v. pomagać;
brać udział; być przy
assistance (e'systens) s. pomoc;
asysta; wsparcie
assistant (e'systent) s. asystent; pomocnik;adj.pomocniczy
assizes (e'sajzyz) pl. okresowe
sesje sądu (wyjazdowe)w Anglii
associate (e'souszjejt) s. towarzysz; wspólnik-sprzymierze-
niec; rzecz związana z czymś
v. łączyć;obcować ; kojarzyć;
brać do spółki;adj.towarzyszący

association (e,souszy'ejszyn) s.
łączenie; współpraca; kojarzenie; przyłączanie sie ;związek
assort (e'so:rt) v. sortować;
dobierać; obcować; klasyfikować
assorted (e'so:rtyd) adj. dobrany; posortowany; mieszany
assortment (e'so:rtment) s.
asortyment; wybór; sortowanie
assume (e'sju:m) v. zakładać;
obejmować; przybierać; przypuszczać ;wdziewać;udawać
assurance (e'szu:rens) s. zapewnienie; pewność; ubezpieczenie
assure (e'szu:r) v. zapewniać;
ubezpieczać; zabezpieczać
assured (e'szu:rd) adj. pewny
(siebie); s. ubezpieczony
asthma (aesma) s. dusznica;
astma ; dychawica
astigmatic (,aestyg'maetyk) adj.
astygmatyczny
astir (e'ste:r) adv. poruszony;
w ruchu; na nogach ;ożywiony
astonish (es'tonysz) v. zadziwiać; zdumiewać ;zdziwić
astonished (es'tonyszt) adj.
zdumiony ; bardzo zdziwiony
astonishment (es'tonyszment) s.
zdumienie ; zdziwienie
astray (es'trej) adv. na błędną
drogę; na bezdrożu ;na manowce
astride (es'trajd) adv. okrakiem;
rozstawionymi nogami
astringent (es'tr ndżent) adj.
ścigający; surowy ;wstrzymujący
astrodome('aestre,doum)s. astro-
kopuła (nad stadionem sportowym)
astrologer (es'troledżer) s.
astrolog
astronaut ('aestreno:t) s. astro-
nauta
astute (es'tu:t) adj. bystry;
przebiegły ;wnikliwy
asunder (e'sander) adv. oddziel-
nie; na boki; na strony
asylum (e'sajlem) s. azyl; schronisko ; przytułek; schronienie
at (aet; et) prep. w; na; u;
przy; pod; z ;za; do; o; po
ate (ejt) v. jadłem; jadłeś; jadł
etc; zob. eat

athlete ('aetli:t) s. atleta;
siłacz; sportowiec
athletic ('aet'letyk) adj.
atletyczny; sportowy
athletics (aet'letyks) pl.atle-
tyka; sport;wychowanie fizyczne
Atlantic (et'laentyk) adj.
atlantycki
atlas ('aetles) s. atlas
atmosphere('aetmesfier) s.
atmosfera ;otoczenie;nastrój
atoll ('aetol) s, atol
atom ('aetem) s. atom
atom bomb ('aetem bom) s. bomba atomowa
atomic (e'tomyk) adj. atomowy
atomic age (e'tomyk ejdż)
epoka atomowa
atomic pile (e'tomyk pajl)
stos atomowy
atomic weight (e'tomyk łejt)
ciężar atomowy
atomize ('aetemajz) v. rozbijać
na atomy ; rozpylać
atomizer ('aetemajzer) s. rozpylacz (cieczy)
atone (e'toun) v. odpokutować;
okupić; załagodzić
atrocious (e'trouszes) adj.
potworny; okropny ;skandaliczny
atrocity (e'trosyty) s. okrucieństwo ;okrutny czyn;ohyda
attach (e'taecz) v. przywiązywać; przyczepiać; przydzielać;
łączyć ;przymocowywać;nalepiać
attachment (e'taeczment) s. załącznik; przymocowanie ;więź
attack (e'taek) v. napadać;
atakować; s. atak; uderzenie
attempt (e'tempt) v. usiłować;
czynić zamach; próbować
s. próba; usiłowanie; zamach
attend (e'tend) v. uczęszczać;
leczyć; obsługiwać;towarzyszyć
attendance (e'tendens) s. obsługa; opieka; uczęszczanie
attendant (e'tendent) s. obecny; służący ;adj.towarzyszący
attention (e'tenszyn) s. uwaga;
uprzejmość ;troska;opieka
attentive (e'tentyw) adj. uważny; gorliwy; uprzejmy ;pilny

attest (e'test) v. poświadczyć;
stwierdzać;zalegalizować
attic ('aetyk) s. poddasze;
attyka; strych
attitude ('aetitu:d) s. postawa; ustosunkowanie się;poza
attorney (e'te:rny) s. pełnomocnik; adwokat;prawnik
attract (e'traekt) v. przyciągać;zwabić; być pociągającym
attraction (e'traekszyn) s.
przyciąganie;powab;urok;atrakcja
attractive (e'traektyw) adj. pociągający;przyciągajacy; miły
attribute ('aetrybju:t) s, przymiot; cecha;właściwość
attribute (e'trybju:t) v. przypisywać komuś; odnosić do czegoś
attrition (e'tryszyn) s. wy-
niszczenie; ścieranie; skrucha
auburn ('o:bern) adj. (barwa)
kasztanowa; złotobrązowa
auction ('o:kszyn) s. licytacja;
aukcja
auction off ('o:kszyn of) v.
licytować; sprzedawać na licytacji;wystawiać na licytację
audacious (o:'dejszes) adj. odważny; śmiały; zuchwały
audacity (o:'daesyty) s. śmiałość; odwaga; zuchwałość
audible ('o:dybel) adj. słyszal-
ny:odbierany słuchem
audience ('o:djens) s. publiczność; audiencja
audit ('o:dyt) s. sprawdzenie
rachunków; rozliczenie;
v. kontrolować rachunki
aught (a:t) s. coś; nic; zero
August ('o:gest) s, sierpień
august ('o:gast) adj. wyniosły;
dostojny;majestatyczny
aunt (aent) s. ciotka; wujenka;
stryjenka
aurora (o:'ro:re) s. brzask;
jutrznia; jutrzenka; zorza po-
larna
austere (o:s'tier) adj. surowy;
poważny; prosty;czysto użytkowy
austerity (o:s'teryty) s. surowość; powaga; prostota;srogość;
charakter czysto użytkowy

Australian (o:s'trejljen) adj.
australijski
Austrian ('o:strjen) adj.
austriacki;s. Austryjak
authentic (o:'tentyk) adj.
autentyczny; prawdziwy
author ('o:ter) s. autor; pisarz; sprawca
authoritative (o:'torytejtyw)
adj. stanowczy; miarodajny
authority (o:'toryty) s. władza; autorytet; znaczenie;
powaga;moc rozkazywania
authorize ('o:terajz),v. upoważniać; zatwierdzać;aprobować
authorship ('o:terszyp) s.
autorstwo;zawod pisarza
autobiography ('o:tebaj'ogrefy)
s. autobiografia
autograph ('o:tegraef) s. podpis; autograf
automat ('o:temaet) n . restauracja z automatem na monety
automatic (,o:te'maetyk) adj.
automatyczny; machinalny
automation (,o:te'mejszyn) s.
automatyzacja
automobile ('o:temeby:1) s. samochód; auto
autumn ('o:tem) s. jesień
auxiliary (o:g'zyljery) adj.
pomocniczy
avail (e'wejl) v. pomagać;
znaczyć; być przydatny
available (e'wejlebl) adj.
dostępny; osiągalny
avalanche ('aewelaencz) s. lawina; v. spadać lawiną
avarice ('aewerys) s. chciwość;
skąpstwo
avaricious (,aewe'ryszes) adj.
chciwy; skąpy
avenue ('aewynju:)s. bulwar;
aleja;ulica;dojazd;dojście
average ('aewerydż) adj. przeciętny; średni; s. średnia;
przeciętna; v. osiągać średnio; obliczać średnią; wy-
posrodkowywać;pracować średnio..
averse (e'we:rs) adj. niechętny; czujący odrazę;przeciwny
aversion (e'werżyn) s. odraza;
niechęć

avert (e'we:rt) v. odwracać
(np. myśli; oczy); oddalić(cios)
aviation (,ejwy'ejszyn) s. lotnictwo
aviator ('ejwyejter) s.lotnik
avid ('ewyd) adj. chciwy; zachłanny
avoid (e'woyd) v. unikać; uchylać się; stronić
avow (e'wau) v. wyznawać
avowal (e'wauel) s. wyznanie;
przyznanie się; zeznanie
await (e'łejt) v. czekać; oczekiwać;być a oczekiwaniu
awake; awoke; awoke (e'łejk;
e'łouk; e'łouk)
awake (e'łejk) v. budzić się;
otwierać oczy na...; adj. czujny; przebudzony; na jawie
awaken (e'łejkn) v. budzić;
uświadamiać komuś (kogoś)
award (e'ło:rd) v. przysądzać;
wyznaczać; s. nagroda; zapłata; grzywna sądowa
aware (e'łeer) adj. świadomy
away (e'łej) adv. precz; z dala
awe (o:) s. lęk; nabożna część
awful ('o:ful) adj. straszny;
budzący lęk i szacunek
awhile ('ehłajl) adv. na krótko;
przez chwilę;chwilę; króciutko
awkward ('o:kłerd) adj. niezgrabny; niezdarny; kłopotliwy;
nieporęczny;zaklopotany;trudny
awning ('o:nyng)s. dach z płótna; markiza; zasłona; stora
awoke (e'łouk) v. zbudzony;
zob. awake
awry (e'raj) adv. skośnie; krzywo; na opak; adj. krzywy; błędny; opaczny; wypaczony
ax (aeks) s. siekiera; topór;
v. obcinać siekierą;redukować
axe (aeks) = ax
axes (aeksyz) pl. osie;siekiery
axis ('aeksys) s. oś ;oska
axle ('aeksel) s. oś (koła);
oska(łącząca tylnie koła wozu)
azimuth ('aezymet) s. azymut
azure ('aeżer) s. błękit; lazur;
adj. błękitny; lazurowy

b (bi) b; druga litera alfabetu angielskiego
babble ('baebl) v. paplać; gadać; s. paplanina; gadanina
babe (bejb) s. niemowlę
baboon (be'bu:n) s. pawian
baby ('bejby) s. niemowlę
baby carriage ('bejby kaerydż)
s. wózek dziecinny
babyhood ('bejbyhud) s. nie-
mowlęctwo
bachelor ('baecheler) s. niezamężna; nieżonaty; stopień
uniwersytecki (najniższy)
back (baek) s. tył; grzbiet;
v. cofać się; wycofać się
backbone ('baekboun) s. kręgosłup; stos pacierzowy
back.door ('baek'do:r) s. tylne
drzwi;adj.zakulisowy;potajemny
backfire ('baek'fajer) s. wybuch odwrotny; zawisć; v.
spalić na panewce
background ('baekgraund) v. tło;
dalszy plan; przeszłość czyjaś
back number ('baeknamber)s. zaległy numer;stare wydanie pisma
backseat ('baek'si:t) s. tylne
siedzenie;wycofanie się z akcji
backstairs ('baeksteerz) s.
tylne schody;adj.zakulisowy
backstroke ('baek'strouk) s.
pływanie na plecach; rzut
odbity od lewa w tenisie
back tire ('baek'tajer) s. tylna
opona samochodowa (slang)
backward ('baekłerd) adj. tylny; zacofany;zapóźniony
backwards ('baekłerds) adv.
w tyle; odwrotnie; do tyłu
back wheel('baekhłil) s. tylne
koło (samochodu,ciężarówki)
bacon ('bejkn) s. słonina; boczek; bekon
bacon and eggs ('bejkn end egz)
jajka z boczkiem
bacterium (baek'tierjem) s.
bakteria
bacteria (baek'tierje) pl.
bakterie
bad (baed) adj. zły; niedobry;
przykry;sfałszowany;słaby;zdrożny

bade (baed) v. proponował; ofe-
rował cenę; kazał; zob.: bid
badge (baedź) s. odznaka; oznaka (członkostwa, rangi etc.)
badger ('baedźer) s. borsuk;
v. zadręczać (narzekaniem)
badly ('baedly) adv. źle; bardzo
badly wounded ('baedl 'Łu:ndyd)
ciężko ranny ;ciężko zraniony
badminton ('baedmynten) s. rodzaj tenisa (piłka z piórkiem)
bad mouth('baedmaus) v. oczerniać; obgadywać obmawiać
baffle ('baefl) v. udaremniać;
łudzić ;niveczyć;s.przegroda
bag (baeg) s. torba; worek;
babsztyl; v. pakować; zwędzić
baggage ('baegydź) s. bagaż
baggage check ('baegydź,czek)
kwit bagażowy
baggy ('baegy) adj. workowaty
bag-pipe ('baegpajp) s. kobza
bail (bejl) s. kaucja; poręka
bail out (bejl'ałt) v. zwolnic
za kaucją ;wywinąć się z opresji
bailiff ('bejlyf) s. woźny sądowy; komornik ;rządca majątku
bait (bejt) s. przynęta; pokusa
bake (bejk) v. piec; wypalać
baker ('bejker) s. piekarz
bakery (bejkery) s. piekarnia
baking powder ('bejkyŋ,pałder)
proszek do pieczenia
balance ('baelens) s. waga; bilans; równowaga; v. równoważyć; bilansować; wahać się
bald (bo:ld) adj. łysy ;jawny
bale (bejl) s. zwój płótna; bela; v. zob. bail
balk (bo:k) v. opierać się;
przeszkadzać; zniechęcać;
s. belka ;miedza; zawada
ball (bo:l) s. 1. piłka; pocisk;
kłębek; 2. bal;zabawa taneczna
ballad ('baeled) s. ballada;
pieśń (sentymentalna opisowa)
ballast ('baelest) s. balast;
v. obciążać balastem
ball bearing ('bo:l'bearyŋ)
łożyska kulkowe
ballet ('baelej) s. balet ;
zespół baletowy(tancerzy)

ball game('bo:lgejm) s. rozgrywka; gra w piłkę
ballistic (be'lystyk)adj. ba-
listyczny
balloon (be'lu:n) s. balon
ballot ('bealet) s. (tajne)
głosowanie; kartka; v. tajnie
głosować
ballot box ('baeletboks) s.
urna wyborcza
ball-point pen ('bo:l-point-
pen) s. kulkowy pisak;długopis
balm (ba:m) s. balsam
balmy ('ba:my) adj. błogi;
balsamiczny
balustrade (,baeles'trejd) s.
poręcz; balustrada
bamboo (baem'bu:) s. bambus
ban (baen) s. zakaz; klątwa;
v. zabraniać;wyjąć spod prawa
banana (be'na:ne) s. banan
band (baend) s. szajka; kapela;
taśma; v. wiązać się; przepa-
sywać opaską ;zrzeszać
bandage ('baendydź) s. bandaż;
v. bandażować ; obandażować
bandmaster ('baend,ma:ster) s.
kapelmistrz
bandstand ('baendstaend) s.
estrada
bang (baeŋg) s. huk; zryw; uciecha; bęc; v. trzaskać ;walnąć
banish ('baenysz) v. wygnać;
usunąć; wykluczać ;wypędzać
banishment ('baenyszment) s.
wygnanie ; banicja
banisters ('baenystez) pl. ba-
nistry (schodów); poręcze
banjo ('baendźou) s. rodzaj
gitary okrągłej pokrytej skórą
bank ('baeŋk) s.1.brzeg;Łacha;na-
syp; szkarpa; 2. bank; 3. stoł
roboczy; 4. rząd;5.nachylenie toru
v. 1. prowadzić bank; 2. składać w banku; 3. piętrzyć; pochylać; 4. polegać;5.obwałować
bank bill ('baeŋk,byl) s.
banknot
banker ('baeŋker) s. bankier
banking ('baeŋkyŋg)s. bankowość
bank note('baeŋknout) s. banknot ; papierowy pieniądz

bankrate ('baeŋkrejt) s. stopa dyskontowa;stopa procentowa

bankrupt ('baeŋkrept) s. bankrut

banner ('baener) s. chorągiew; transparent; tytuł (czołowy)

banns (baenz) pl. zapowiedzi

banquet ('baenkłyt) s. bankiet

baptism ('baeptyzem) s. chrzest

baptize ('baeptajz) s. chrzcić

bar (ba:r) s. belka; drąg; rogatka; krata; v. zagradzać; hamować; prep.: oprócz

bar (ba:r) s. 1. izba adwokacka, sądowa; 2. bar; bufet z wyszynkiem ;szynkwas

barb (ba:rb) s. haczyk; docinek; kolec; skaza (na odlewie);szew

barbarian (ba:r'bearjen) s. barbarzyńca; adj. barbarzyński

barbed wire ('ba:rbd,łajer) drut kolczasty

barber ('ba:rber) s. fryzjer (męski); golibroda

barbiturate (ba:r'byczeret) s. lek uspakajający ;nasenny lek

bare (beer) adj. nagi; goły; łysy; v. obnażać ;odkrywać

barefoot ('beerfut) adj.& adv. boso; bosy

bareheaded ('beerhedyd) adj. z gołą głową

barely ('beerly) adv. ledwie; otwarcie; ubogo; zaledwie

bargain ('ba:rgyn) s. ubicie targu; dobre kupno; v. targować się; spodziewać się

barge (ba:rdż) s. barka; v. pakować się; trynić się

bark (ba:rk) s. 1. kora; 2. szczeknięcie; v. zdzierać korę; garbować korę; szczekać; pyskować; kaszleć;warkliwie mówić; wyszczekać; zakaszleć

barley ('ba:rly) s. jęczmień

barmaid ('ba:rmejd) f. bufetowa kelnerka; szynkarka

barn (ba:rn) s. stodoła; stajnia; obora; wozownia ;remiza

barometer (be'romyter) s. barometr

barracks ('baereks) pl. koszary; baraki; budyn'i koszarowe etc.; wygwizdywanie (zawodników,graczy)

barrel ('baerel) s. beczka; lufa; rura;cylinder;walec;bęben

barren ('baeren) adj. jałowy; wyczerpany;nieurodzajny

barricade (,baery'kejd) s. barykada; v. barykadować się

barrier ('baerjer) s. zapora; zastawa; rogatka;ogrodzenie

barrister ('baeryster) s. adwokat;adwokatka;obrońca;obrończyni

barrow ('baerou) s. taczki

bartender ('ba:rtender) s. barman; bufetowy;bufetowa;barmanka

barter ('ba:rter) v. wymieniać; handlować; s. handel wymienny

base (bejs) n. podstawa; nasada; adj. podły; nędzny; niski

baseball ('bejsbo:l) s. palant amerykański(grany piłką i maczugą)

baseless ('bejslys) adj. bezpodstawny;nieuzasadniony

basement ('bejsment) s. suterena; piwnica ;podziemie

bashful ('baeszful) a. wstydliwy;nieśmiały;trwożliwy;lękliwy

basic ('bejsyk) a. podstawowy; zasadniczy ;zasadowy

basin ('bejsn) s. miednica; zbiornik; dorzecze; zagłębie

basis ('bejsys) pl. fundamenty; podstawy;podłoże;grunt;zasada

bask (baesk) v. wygrzewać się na słońcu;wylegiwać się;pławić się

basket ('ba:skyt) s. kosz; koszyk;v. wrzucać do kosza

basketball ('ba:skytbo:l) s. koszykówka; piłka do koszykówki

bass (bejs) s. bas (głos,śpiewak)

bass (baes) s. okoń; łyko lipowe ; okoń morski lub rzeczny

bastard ('baesterd) s. bękart; bastard;adj. nieślubny;nędzny

baste (bejst) v. fastrygować; polewać tłuszczem pieczeń

bat (baet) s. nietoperz; maczuga; kij;v. mrugać; hulać(slang)

bath (ba:s) s. kąpiel; łazienka

bathe (bejż) v. kąpać; moczyć; rosić; przemywać; wykąpać

bathing (bejżyŋg)s. kąpanie

bathing cap ('bejżyŋgkaep) czapka kąpielowa

bathing suit ('bejzyŋ sju:t)
strój kąpielowy;kostjum kąpielowy
bathing trunks ('bejzyŋ traŋks) s.
spodenki kąpielowe
bathrobe ('ba:zroub) s. płaszcz
kąpielowy
bathroom ('ba:zru:m) s. łazienka;ubikacja;ustęp;klozet
bath towel ('ba:z tałel) ręcznik kąpielowy
bathtub ('ba:ztab) s. wanna
baton ('baeton) s. buława; pałka;batuta;paleczka dyrygenta
battalion (be'taeljen) s. batalion ;pododdział pułku
batter ('baeter) v. tłuc; walić
battered ('baeterd) adj. pobity
battery ('baetery) s. bateria;
komplet; pobicie;zestaw armat
battle ('baetl) s. bitwa ;walka
battleship ('baetlszyp) s. okręt
wojenny
baulk (bo:k) s. przeszkoda;
rozczarowanie;v.przeszkadzać
bawl (bo:l) v. wrzeszczeć; drzeć
się; krzyczeć; zwymyślać
bay (bej) adj. czerwono-brązowy;
gniady (koń); wawrzyn;laur
bay (bej) s. zatoka; wnęka;
przęsło; v. ujadać ; wyć
bay window ('bej'łyndoł) okno
we wnęce
bazaar(be'za:r) s. bazar
be; was; been (bi:; łoz; bi:n)
be (bi:) v. być; żyć; trwać;
dziać się ;istnieć;stawać się
beatnik (bi:tnyk) s. nonkonfor-
mista; (-tka)
be reading (bi:'ry:dyŋ) czytać
właśnie;być w trakcie czytania
beach (bi:cz) s. brzeg; plaża
beachhead ('bi:czhed) s. przyczółek (nad wodą)
beachwear ('bi:człe:r) s.odzież
plażowa ;kostiumy,plażcze etc.
beacon ('bi:ken) s. sygnał (og-
niowy); latarnia morska
bead (bi:d) s. paciorek; kora-
lik; v. nawlekać korale; per-
lić się ;ozdabiać paciorkami
beak (bi:k) s. dziób ; belfer

beam (bi:m) s. belka; dźwigar;
promień; radosny uśmiech
v.promieniować; nadawać sygnał; rozpromieniać się
bean (bi:n) s. fasola; bób;
ziarnko; łeb; animusz
bear; bore; borne (beer; bo:r;
bo:rn)
bear (beer) s. niedźwiedź;
v. dźwigać; ponosić; znosić;
trzymać się ; rodzić;miec(podpis)
beard (bierd) s. broda (zarost)
bearer ('beerer) s. nosiciel;
okaziciel; zwiastun;karawaniarz
bearing ('beeryŋg)s. zachowanie;
wzgląd; wspornik; rodzenie;łożysko
beast (bi:st) s. bestia; bydle
beastly ('bistly) adj. bydlęcy;
potworny;adv.straszliwie;okrutnie
beast of prey ('bi:st ow prej)
s. drapieżnik
beat; beat; beaten (bi:t; bi:t;
bi:tn)
beat (bi:t) v. bić; bić się;
ubijać;tłuc;trzepotać;zbić;kuć
beat it ! ('bi:t,yt) excl.:
precz !wynoś się; wynoście się !
beaten ('bi:tn) adj. ubity; wy-
deptany; wyczerpany; znany
beautiful ('bju:teful) adj.
piękny;cudny;wspaniały;swietny
beautify ('bju:tyfaj) v.upięk-
szać; upiększyć
beauty ('bju:ty) s. piękność;
piękno ;uroda;piekna kobieta
beauty parlor ('bju;ty'pa:rler)
salon kosmetyczny
beaver ('bi:wer) s. bóbr;
przedsiębiorczy człowiek
because (bi'ko:z) conj. dlatego; że; gdyż; adv. z powodu
beckon('beken) v. skinąć; nęcić; s. skinienie
become; became; become (bi'kam;
bi'kejm; bi'kam)
become (bi'kam) v. stawać się;
nadawać się ;zostawać kimś(czymś)
becoming ('bikamyŋg)adj. stosowny; odpowiedni;twarzowy
bed (bed) s. łoże; łożysko;klomb;
grządka; ławica ;podkład;nocleg

bedclothes ('bedklouz) s. pościel; przescieradła,kołdry etc.

bedding ('bedyng)s. pościel

bed linen ('bed,lynyn) s. pościel ;bielizna pościelowa

bedridden ('bed,rydn) adj. obłożnie chory ;złożony chorobą

bedroom ('bedrum) s. sypialnia

bedside ('bedsajd) przy łożu

bedsore ('bedso:r) s. odleżyna

bedtime ('bedtajm) s. pora do spania ;pora snu

bee (bi:) s. pszczoła

beech (bi:cz) s. buk ;adj.bukowy

beef (bi:f) s. wołowina; siła; narzekanie ;wyrzekanie(slang)

beefsteak ('be:f'stejk) s. befsztyk (do smażenia lub pieczenia)

beefy ('bi:fy) adj. krzepki; flegmatyczny ;muskulary

beehive ('bi:hajw) s. ul

beekeeper ('bi:kiper) s. pszczelarz

beeline ('bi:lajn) s. najkrótsza droga ;linia powietrzna

been (bi:n) v. były, zob. be

beer (bier) s. piwo

beet (bi:t) s. burak

beetle ('bi:tl) s. tłuczek; ubijak;v.ubijać;wystawać;zwisać

beetroot ('bi:tru:t) s. burak

befall (by'fo:l) v. zdarzać się; przydarzać się; przytrafiać się

before (by'fo:r) adv. przedtem; dawniej; z przodu;na przedzie

beforehand (by'fo:rhend) adv. uprzednio; przedtem; z góry

befriend (by'frend) v. zaprzyjaźniac się; wspomagać

beg (beg) v. prosić; żebrać

began (b 'gaen) v. zaczęty; zob. begin

beget; begot; begotten (by'get; by'got; by'gotn)

beget (by'get) v. płodzić; rodzić ; powodować ;wywoływać

beggar ('beger) s. żebrak

begin; began; begun (by'gyn; by'gaen; by'gan)

begin (by'gyn) v. zaczynać

beginner (by'gyner) s. początkujący :nowy(człowiek)

beginning (by'gynyŋg)s. początek :rozpoczęcie

begun (by'gan) v. p.p. zob. begin

behalf (by'hae:f) s. w imieniu kogoś ; poparcie

behave (by'hejw) v. zachowywać się; prowadzić się

behavior (by'hejwjer) v. postępowanie; zachowanie się

behind (by'hajnd) adv. w tyle; z tyłu; do tyłu; prep. za; poza; being ('by:yŋg)s. byt; ⌐s.tyłek istnienie; istota

belated (by'lejtyd) adj. spóźniony ;zapoźniony;późny

belch (belcz) v. zionąć; odbijać się; s. bekanie; buchanie; huk ;odbijanie się

belfry ('belfry) s. dzwonnica

Belgian ('beldżen) adj. belgijski

belief (by'li:f) s. wiara; wierzenie; zaufanie;przekonanie

believe (by'li:w) v. wierzyć; sądzić;mieć przekonanie;zakładać

believer (by'li:wer) s. wyznawca; wierzący ;zwolennik

bell (bel) s. dzwon; dzwonek

belligerent (by'lydżerent) adj. wojujący; wojowniczy;wojenny

bellow ('belou) v. ryczec; s. ryk ;ryczenie;porykiwanie

bellows ('belouz) s. miech; płuca;przedmiot podobny do miecha

belly ('bely) s. brzuch;żołądek

belong (byloŋg) v. należec

belongings (byloŋgyŋz) pl. rzeczy; bagaż; przynależności

beloved (by'lawd) adj. ukochany; drogi;s.kochana osoba

below (by'lou) adv. niżej; w dole; na dół; pod spodem; prep. poniżej; pod ;w piekle

belt (belt) s. pas; pasek; strefa; v. bić pasem ;opasywać

bench (bencz) s. ława; ławka; stół; terasa;miejsce sędziego

bend; bent; bent (bend; bent; bent)

bend (bend) s. zgięcie; krzywa; v. giąć;wyginać;przeginać;zginać

beneath (by'ni:s) prep. pod;
niżej; pod spodem; na dół
benediction (,beny'dykszyn) s.
błogosławieństwo
benefactor (,beny'faekter) s.
dobroczyńca; dobrodziej
beneficient(bi'nefyszent)adj.
dobroczynny
beneficial (,beny'fyszel) adj.
pożywny;korzystny;dobroczynny
benefit ('benyfyt) s. korzyść;
dobrodziejstwo;pożytek;zasiłek
benevolent (by'newelent) adj.
dobroczynny;życzliwy;łaskawy
bent (bent) s. sitowie; skłonność; zgięcie; adj. skłonny;
zgięty; zdecydowany;uparty
benzene ('benzi:n) s. benzen
benzine ('benzi:n) s. (lekka)
benzyna (do czyszczenia)
bequeath (by'kłys) v. zostawiać
w spadku;przekazać potomności
bequest (by'kłest) s. zapis;
spadek;spuścizna; legat
bereave; bereft; bereaved
(by'ri:w, by'reft; by'ri:wd)
bereave (by'ri:w) v. pozbawiać;
odzierać;wyzuwać; osierocić
bereft (by'reft) adj. osierocony; pozbawiony;wyzuty
beret ('berej) s. beret
berry (by'bery) s. jagoda;ikra
berth (be:rs) s. koja; łóżko;
stoisko;miejsce postoju statku
beseech; besought; besought
(by'si:cz; by'so:t; by'so:t)
beseech (by'si:cz) v. błagać;
upraszać; zaklinać
beside (by'sajd) adv. poza tym;
ponadto; inaczej; prep. obok;
przy; w pobliżu; w porównaniu
besides (by'sajdz) adv. prócz
tego; poza tym; prep. oprócz;
poza;ponadto w dodatku
besiege (by'si:dż) v. oblegać
best (best) adj.& adv. najlepszy; najlepiej;v.okpiwać
best wishes (best'łyszys) naj-
lepsze życzenia
best of all (best ow o:l) najlepszy: najlepiej ;a najlepiej...

bestow (by'stou) v. podarować;
składać ;nadawać;użyczać;darzyć
bet (bet) s. zakład; v. zakładać się ;iść o zakład
betray (by'trej) v. zdradzić;
mylić; zawodzić dawać dowód
betrayal (by'trejel) s. zdrada
betrayer (by'trejer) s. zdrajca
better ('beter) adv. lepiej;
lepszy; v. poprawić; przewyż-
szyć ;prześcignąć;prześcigać
better than ('beter dzaen) exp.
więcej (slang); ponad ; lepiej
between (by'tłi:n) prep. między
adv. w pośrodku; tymczasem
beverage ('bewerydż) s. napój
beware (by'łe:r) v. strzec się
beware of the dog (by'łe:r ow
dy dog) strzec się psa; zły
pies
bewilder (by'łylder) v. zmieszać (kogoś);oszołamiać
bewilderment (by'łylderment) s.
zaczarowanie ;oszołomienie;chaos
bewitch (by'łycz) v. zaczarować;oczarować;ujać(kogoś czymś)
beyond (by'jond) adv.& prep.
za; poza; dalej niż; nad; ponad ;dalej(położony etc.)
bias ('bajes) s. uprzedzenie;
fałsz; kierunek; v. skłonić;
nachylić; uprzedzić ;usposabiać
biased ('bajest) adj. stronniczy; uprzedzony;nastawiony
bib (byb) s. śliniak ;v.popijać
Bible ('bajbl) s. Biblia
bicycle ('bajsykl) s. rower
bid (byd) v. oferować cenę; licytować; kazać; s. oferta na
licytacji ;stawka; zaproszenie
bid farewell (byd fa:rłel)
żegnać się ;pożegnać kogoś
bier (bjer) s. mary (pod trumną)
big (byg) adj. & adv. duży;
wielki; ważny ;głośny;godny
big business (byg'byznys) wielkie interesy ;wielkie korporacje
big wig (byg łyg) s. wielka
szyszka ; ważniak;gruba ryba
bike (bajk) s. rower
bilateral (baj'laeterel) adj.
dwustronny; obustronny

bile (bajl) s. żółć;zgorzkniałość
bilious ('byljes) adj. żółciowy;zrzedny;popędliwy;tetryczny
bill (byl) s. dziób;pika;cypel
bill (byl) s. rachunek; kwit;
afisz; plakat; v. ogłaszać;
afiszować;oblepiać afiszami
billboard ('byl,bo:rd) s. tablica ogłoszeniowa
billfold ('byl,fould) s. port-
fel(na dokumenty i pieniądze)
billiards ('byljerdz) s. bilard
billion ('byljen) s. tysiąc
milionów (USA); miliard
bill of exchange ('byl,ow'
eksczendż) weksel
billow ('bylou) s. bałwan; kłąb;
v. piętrzyc; falować;balwanić
bin (byn) s. skrzynia; paka;
v. pakować; chować do skrzyni
bind (bajnd) v. wiązać; zobowiązywać; opatrywać; oprawiać
binding ('bajndyng)adj. wiążący;
s. połączenie; oprawa;wiązanie
binoculars (bajnokjulez) pl.
lornetka(polowa,teatralna etc.)
biography (baj'ogrefy) s. bio-
grafia;opis życia i działalności
biology (baj'oledży) s. biologia
birch (be:rcz) s. brzoza
bird (be:rd) s. ptak ;dziwak
bird of passage ('be:rd ow
paesydż) przelotny ptak
bird of prey ('de:rd ow prej)
drapieżny ptak
bird's eye view ('be:rds aj,wju)
widok z lotu ptaka
birth (be:rt) s. urodzenie
birth control ('be:rt kon,troul)
kontrola urodzin
birthday ('be:rtdej), s. urodziny; początek czegoś
birthday party ('be:rtdej'
pa:rty) przyjęcie urodzinowe
birthplace ('be:rt-plejs)
miejsce urodzenia
biscuit ('byskyt) s. bułka;
sucharek lekko strawny
bishop ('byszep) s. biskup
bison ('bajsn) s. bizon
bit (byt) s. wędzidło; ostrze;
wiertło; ząb; szczypta;odrobina;
12½centów;moment;krótki czas

bitch (bycz) s. suka;wulg.kurwa
bite; bit; bitten (bajt; byt;
bitn)
bite (bajt) v. gryźć; kąsać;
docinać; s. pokarm; przynęta;
ukąszenie;ciętość:lekki posiłek
bitter ('byter) adj. gorzki;
ostry; zły;zgorzkniały;przykry
blab (blaeb) v. paplać; gadać;
s. plotkarz; gaduła;plotkarka
black (blaek) adj. czarny; ponury; s, murzyn;v.czernić
blackberry ('blaekbery) s. jeżyna
blackbird ('blackbe:rd) s. kos
blackboard ('blackbo:d) s. tablica
blacken ('blaekn) v. czernić
black eye ('blaekaj) s. pod-
bite oko
blackhead ('blaekhed) s. wągier
blackmail ('blaemejl) s. szantaż; wymuszenie
black-market ('black ma:rkyt)
s. czarny rynek
blackout ('blaekaut) s. za-
ciemnienie (miasta, okien)
black pudding ('blaek'pudyng)
s. kaszanka; kiszka
blacksmith ('blaeksmys) s. ko-
wal(wiejski)
bladder ('blaeder) s. pęcherz
blade (blejd) s. zdźbło; liść;
ostrze;płetwa;klinga;wesołek
blame (blejm) s. wina; nagana;
v. tajać; ganić ;winić
blame for ('blejm fo:r) v. winić za (coś)
blameless ('blejmlys) adj. bez
winy; niewinny
blank (blaenk) adj. biały;
pusty; s. puste miejsce; nie-
wypełniony formularz;ślepak
blanket ('blaenkyt) s. koc wełniany ;ciepły koc
blasphemy ('blaesfymy) s. bluź-
nierstwo;pogarda dla Boga
blast (bla:st) s. wybuch; podmuch; odgłos eksplozji;
v. wysadzić w powietrze; de-
tonować; niszczyć
blast furnace ('bla:st,fe:rnys)
s. wielki piec hutniczy

blatant ('blejtent) adj. krzykliwy; ryczący; przesądny
blaze (blejz) s. błysk; płomień; wybuch; v. płonąć
bleach (bli:cz) v. wybielać
bleak (bli:k) adj. ponury;
smutny;wystawiony do wiatru
blear (blier) adj. metny; zamglony; niewyraźny
bleat (bli:t) v. beczeć
bleed; bled; bled (bli:d; bled;
bled)
bleed (bli:d) v. krwawić
blemish ('blemysz) s. plama;
wada; v. zniekształcić; splamić;poplamić;pobrudzić
blend; blent; blent (blend;
blent; blent)
blend (blend) v. mieszać się;
łączyć się; s, mieszanina
bless (bles) v. błogosławić
bless my soul ('bles,maj'so:l)
excl.: o Boże !
blessed ('blesyd) adj. błogosła-
wiony;święty; kojący
blessing ('blesyng)s. błogosławieństwo ;aprobata;dobra rzecz
blew (blu:) v. zob.: blow
blight (blajt) s. zniszczenie;
zaraza ;v.niszczyć
blind (blajnd) adj. ślepy;
v. oślepić; s. zasłona
blind alley ('blajnd,alej)
ślepa ulica
blindfold ('blajnd,fould)
adj.& adv. na ślepo; z zawiąza-
nymi oczami; v. zawiązywać
oczy;s. zasłona oczu
blink (blynk) v. mrugać;
s. błysk oka;mignięcie
bliss (blys) s. radość; błogość
blithe ('blajz) adj. wesoły
blizzard ('blyzerd) s. śnieżyca;
zawieja ; zadymka;zamieć
bloat (blout) v. nadymać; nabrzmiewać ;uwędzić;wędzić
bloater ('blouter) s. śledź wędzony ; pikling
block (blok) s. blok; kloc; zeszyt; przeszkoda; v. tamować;
wstrzymywać;tarasować;zatykać;
zablokować;blokować;zatamować

block up ('blokap) v. zablokować ;zablokowywać;zamurować
blockade (blo'kejd) s. blokada;
v. blokować ;robić zator
blonde (blond) s. blondynka
blood (blad) s. krew ;pokrewieństwo
bloodshed ('bladszed) s. krwi
rozlew ; rozlew krwi
bloodshot ('bladszot) adj. nabrzmiały krwią ;zaszły krwią
blood vessel ('bląd,wesl) s.
naczynie krwionośne
bloody ('blady) adj. krwawy
bloom (blu:m) s. kwiecie;
v. kwitnąć ;rozkwitać
blooming (blu:myng) adj. kwitnący; przeklęty (slang)
blossom ('blosem) v. kwitnąć;
s. kwiecie ; kwiat
blot (blot) s. plama; v. plamić
blot out ('blot aut)v.wymazać;
usunąć ;wykreślać;zamazywać
blotter (bloter) s. bibularz;
rejestr aresztowań;suszka
blotting paper ('blotyng,pejper)
bibuła ;suszka
blouse (blauz) s. bluza
blow; blew; blown (blou; blu;
blołn)
blow (blou) s. cios; rzut; rozkwit; v. zakwitać; rozkwitać
blue (blu:) adj. niebieski;
smutny; v. farbować na niebiesko ;pomalować na niebiesko
bluebell ('blu:bell) s. dzwonek
(kwiat)
blues (blu:s) pl. smutek; przygnębienie ;smutne piosenki
bluff (blaf) s. oszustwo; nabieranie; adj. szorstki; stromy; v. wprowadzać w błąd
bluish ('blu:ysh) adj. niebieskawy
blunder ('blander) s. ciężki
błąd ;v.popełniać błąd (gafę)
blunt (blant) adj. tępy; nieczuły; v. stępić ;przytępić
blur (ble:r) s. plama v. zatrzeć; splamić; zamazać
boar (bo:r) s. dzik; odyniec
board (bo:rd) s. deska; władza
naczelna ;tablica;rada;pokład

boarder ('bo:rder) s. pensjo-
nariusz; pasażer;stołownik
boardinghouse ('bo:rdyŋghaus)
s. pensjonat
boarding school ('bo:rdyŋ,sku:l)
s. szkoła z internatem
boardwalk ('bo:rd łok) chodnik z desek
boast (boust) v. chwalić się;
s. samochwalstwo;przechwałki
boat (bout) s. łodź; statek
boat race('bout rejs) s. regaty; wyścigi łodzi
bob (bob) v. kiwać się; krótko
strzyc; szturchnąć; s. wisiorek; kłęb włosów; szturchnięcie
bobby ('boby) s. angielski policjant
bobsled ('bob sled) s. bob-
slej; sanki z kierownicą etc.
bodice ('bodys) s. stanik
bodily ('bodyly) adj.& adv.
osobiście; fizycznie; całkowicie;gremialnie; cieleśnie
body ('body) s. ciało; karoser-
ja; korpus;grupa;gromada;ogół
bodyguard ('bodyga:rd) s. straż
przyboczna;ochrona osobista
bog (bog) s. bagno
boil (bojl) v. wrzeć; kipieć;
gotować; s. wrzenie; czyrak
boil over ('bojl,ouwer) v. wygotować; wygotować się
boiled eggs ('bojld egs) gotowane jajka
boiler ('bojler) s. kocioł
boisterous ('bojsteres) adj.
hałaśliwy;niesforny;burzliwy
bold (bould) adj. śmiały; zuchwały; zauważalny;wyraźny
bolster ('boulster) s. miękka
podkładka; v. miękko podeprzeć
bolt (boult) s. zasuwa; bolec;
piorun; wypad; v. zasuwać;
rzucić się; wypaść;czmychać
bomb (bom) s. bomba; v. bombar-
dować;atakować bombami
bombard (bom'ba:rd) v. bombardo-
wać(artylerią lub bombami)
bond (bond) s. więź; obligacja
bone (boun) s. kość;osc
bonfire ('bonfajer) s. płonący
stos ;ognisko (obozowe etc.)

bonnet ('bonyt) s. czapka
(damska) ; czepek
bonny ('bony) adj. piękny; ładny
bonus ('bounes) s. premia
bony ('bouny) adj. kościsty
book (buk) s. książka; v. księgować; rezerwować; aresztować
booked up ('bukt ap) adj. wyprzedany; pełny
bookcase ('bukkejs) s. półka
na książki
booking clerk ('bukyŋ,klerk)
s. kasjer kolejowy
booking office ('bukyŋ,ofys)
biuro biletowe-rezerwacyjne
bookkeeper ('buk,ki:per) s.
księgowy; księgowa
bookkeeping. ('buk,ki:pyŋg)s.
księgowość
booklet ('buklyt) s. książeczka
bookseller ('buk,seler) s. księgarz
book shop('bukszop) s. księgarnia
bookstore ('buksto:r) s. księgarnia
boom (bu:m) s. huk; nagła zwyżka; v. zwyżkować; podbijać ceny
boomerang ('bu:meraeŋg) s. bumerang;v.działać jak bumerang
boor (bu:r) s. prostak; gbur;
chłop; prostaczka
boost (bu:st) v. forsować; podnosić znaczenie; zachwalać;
wzmacniać;rozreklamować
boot (bu:t) s. but; cholewa
booth (bu:s) s. budka; stragan
booty('bu:ty)s.łup. zdobycz
booze('bu:z)s. alkohol pitny
border ('bo:rder) s. granica;
brzeg; rąbek; v. obrębiać;
graniczyć;oblamować;obszyć
bore (bo:r) v. wiercić; drążyć;
nudzić; s. otwór; nudy; nudziarz;natręt;rzecz nieznośna
bore (bo:r) v. zob. bear
born (bo:rn) adj. urodzony
borough ('be:rou) s. miasteczko
borrow ('borou) v.(za)pożyczać
bosom ('busem) s. (łono) piers
boss (bo:s) s. szef; v. rządzić
botany ('botenv) s. botanika
botch (bocz) s. fuszerka; lata-
nina; v. partaczyć; fuszerować

both (bous) pron.& adj. obaj;
obydwaj ;obie;obydwie;oboje
bother (bodzer) s. kłopot;
v. niepokoić; dokuczać;dręczyć
bother about (,bodzer e'baut)
v. kłopotać się czymś
bottle ('botl) s. butelka
bottom ('botem) s. dno; spód;
dolina; głąb; adj. dolny;
spodni; podstawowy; v. sięgać
dna; wstawiać dno ;osiagać dno
bough (bau) s. konar ;gałąź
bought (bo:t) v. kupiony; zob.:
buy (zakupiony,przekupiony...)
boulder ('boulder) s. głaz
bounce (bauns) v. odbijać się;
podskakiwać; s. gwałtowne odbicie ;odskok;samochwalstwo
bound (baund) s. granica; adj.,
będący w drodze; v. graniczyć
boundary (baundry) s. linia
graniczna ;adj. graniczny
boundless (baundlys) adj. bezgraniczny ; niezmierzony
bouquet (bu:'kej) s. bukiet
kwiatów; zapach (wina)
bout (baut) s. okres; runda;
próba sił ;atak(choroby)
bow (bau) s. łuk; kabłąk; smyczek; ukłon; v. zginać się;
kłaniać się ;wygiąc w kabłąk
bowels ('bauelz) pl. trzewia;
wnętrzności
bower ('bauer) s. altana; chat-
ka; kotwica przednia
bowl (boul) s. miska; czerpak;
stadion; szala; v. grać kulami (w kręgle); toczyć koło
box (boks) s. skrzynka; pudełko;
loża; boks; v. pakować; oddzielać; uderzać pięścią
boxer ('bokser) s. pięściarz;
bokser
boxing ('boksyng)s. pięściarst-
wo; boks
box office('boks,ofys) s. kasa
w teatrze ;kasa biletów wstepu
bov (boj) s. chłopak; służący
boycott ('bojkot) s. bojkot;
v. bojkotować
boyfriend ('boy-frend) przyjaciel (dziewczyny);kochanek

boyhood('bojhud) s. wiek chłopięcy ;dzieciństwo chłopca
boyish ('bojysz) adj. chłopięcy
boy-scout ('boj-skaut) harcerz
bra (bra:) s. biustnik; stanik;
biustonosz
brace (brejs) s. klamra; korba;
podpora; v. wzmacniać; krzepić;
podpierać :spiać klamrą;związać
brace up (brejs ap) v. wytężyć
się; zebrać siły; orzeźwić
bracelet ('brejslyt) s. bransoletka; kajdanek
bracket ('braekyt) s. wspornik;
ramię; nawias; grupa; klamra;
v. brać w nawiasy; grupować
brag (braeg) v. chełpić się
braggart('braegert) s. samochwał; pyszałek ;bufon;fanfaron
braid (brejd) s. warkocz; plecionka; v. pleść; opasywać
brain (brejn) s. mózg; rozum
brain wave(brejnłejw) s. świetny pomysł :swietna myśl
brake (brejk) s. hamulec
bramble ('braembel) s. krzak ja-
gody ;krzak jeżyny; jeżyna
branch (bra:ncz) s. gałąź; odnoga; filja; v. odgałęziać się;
zbaczać ;rozwidlać się
brand-new (,braen'nju) adj. nowiutki;nowiusieńki;jak z igły
brass (braes) s. mosiądz; spiż;
ranga; starszyzna; instrumenty
dęte :forsa;pieniadze;czelność;
śmiałość;przedmioty z mosiądzu
brass band(,braes'baend) s. kapela dęta ;orkiestra dęta
brassiere (bre'zier) s. biustnik;
stanik; biustonosz
brat (braet) s. brzdąc; bachor
brave (brejw) adj. dzielny zuch;
v. stawiać czoło ;odważyć się
Brazilian (Bre'zyljen) a. bra-
zylijski ;s.Brazylijczyk
breach (bry:cz) s.naruszenie;
wyłom; zerwanie; v. przełamać
(się); zrobić wyłom ;przerwać się
bread (bred) s. chleb; forsa
(slang);środki utrzymania
bread and butter (bred-en-bater)
chleb z masłem ;środki utrzymania

breadth (breds) s. szerokość;
rozmach; szerokość poglądów
break; broke; broken (brejk;
brouk; brouken)
break (brejk) v. łamać; rujnować; przerywać; s. załamanie;
wyłom; nagła zmiana; wada
break away ('brejk ełej) v.
oderwać (się);uciekać
break down ('brejk dałn) v. za-
łamać(się); s. zepsucie się;
upadek; rozbiór;awaria
break in ('brejkyn) v. włamać
(się);wtargnąć;wtrącić się
break off ('brejkof) v. urwać;
odłamać;zerwać stosunki
break out ('brejkaut) v. wyrwać
(się);pokryć się pryszczami
break up ('brejkap) v. połamać
(sie) ;rozpadać się;rozejść się
breakable('brejkebel) adj. kruchy; łamliwy;łatwy do zbicia
breakfast ('brekfest) s. śniadanie; v. jeść śniadanie
breast (brest) s. pierś
breaststroke ('brest,strouk)
pływanie żabką
breath (bres) s. oddech; tchnienie ;dech;oddychanie;powiew
breathe (bri:z) v. oddychać;
tchnąć; żyć; dać wytchnać; powiewać;natchnąć;wionąć;szepnąć
breathing ('bri:zyng) s. oddech; wytchnienie ;adj.żywy
breathless (breslys) adj. bez
tchu ;zasapany;zadyszany;zziajany
bred (bred) zob.: breedwychowany
breeches ('bry:czyz) pl. spodnie do konnej jazdy; bryczesy
breed; bred; bred; (bri:d; bred;
bred)
breed (bri:d) v. rodzić; rozmnażać; hodować; s. chów; rasa;
ród ;plemię; ród ludzki
breeder ('bri:der) s. hodowca;
rozsadnik (choroby);rozpłodnik
breeding (bri:dyng) s. hodowla;
obejście; dobre wychowanie
breeze (bri:z) s. wietrzyk;zwada;
v. wiać; śmigać;odejść;oszukać
brevity ('brewyty) s. zwięzłość;
krótkość ; krótkotrwałość

brew (bru:) v. warzyć (piwo);
knuć; s. napój uwarzony; preparat;warzenie;parzenie;odwar
brewery (bru:ery) s. browar
bribe (brajb) v. dawać łapówkę;
przekupywać; s. łapówka
bribery ('brajbery) s. przekupstwo; łapownictwo;korupcja
brick (bryk) s. cegła; kostka;
adj. ceglany; v. obmurować;
zamurować(okno;drzwi,etc.)
bricklayer ('bryk,lejer) s.
murarz
brickwork ('brykłork) s. muro-
wanie;wykonana robota murarska
brickyard ('brykja:rd) s. cegielnia
bridal ('brajdel) adj. ślubny;
weselny;s.ślub;wesele
bride (brajd) s. panna młoda
bridegroom ('brajdgru:m) s, pan
młody; nowożeniec
bridesmaid ('brajdzmejd) s.
druhna ;drużka
bridge (brydż) s. most; mostek;
v. łączyć mostem;zapełnić lukę
bridgehead ('brydżhed) s. przyczółek mostowy ;przyczółek
bridle ('brajdl) s. uździenica;
uzda; cuma; v. kiełzać; powściągać ;opanowywać;okiełzać
bridle path ('brajdl,pas) s.
ścieżka do konnej jazdy
brief (bri:f) s. streszczenie;
odprawa; krótkie majtki;
v. zwięźle streścić; pouczyć;
informować; adj. krótkotrwały;
treściwy; zwięzły ;krótki
briefcase ('bri:f,kejs) s.
teczka
brigade (bry'gejd) s. brygada
bright (brajt) adj. jasny;
świetny; bystry; adv. jasno
brighten ('brajtn) v. rozjas-
nić; błyszczeć; promieniować
brightness (brajtnys) s. jasność;światło;blask;żywość
brilliance ('bryljens) s.blask;
wielkie zdolności ;świetność
brilliancy ('bryljensy) s.
świetność ; blichtr; połysk
jasne światło;blask;jasność

brilliant ('bryljent) adj. błyszczący; świetny; wybitny
brim (brym) s. brzeg (naczynia); rondo (kapelusza);v.napełniać
brimful ('brym'ful) adj. pełen po brzegi;przepełniony
bring; brought; brought (bryng; bro:t; bro:t)
bring (bryng)v. przynosić; przyprowadzać;powodować;zmusić (się)
bring an action ('bryngen'aekszyn) v. wszczynać działanie, akcje
bring about ('bryng e'baut) v. uskutecznić;wywoływać;dokonać
bring forth ('bryng,fo:rs) v. ujawniać; wywoływać;urodzić
bring in (bryngyn)v. wprowadzać; przynosić;wydawać(wyrok etc.)
bring up (bryngap) v. poruszyć; przynieść na górę; przysunąć
brink (brynk) s. skraj; brzeg
brisk (brysk) adj. żywy; raźny; rześki;trzaskający;wesoły
bristle ('brysl) s. szczecina
British ('brytysz) adj. brytyjski; Anglik
brittle ('brytl) a. kruchy
broach (broucz) v. żłobić; zaczynać; poruszać;s.szydło;rożen
broad (bro:d) adj. szeroki; z rozmachem; wyraźny; obszerny s. szeroka płaszczyzna; wulg.: kobieta; adv. szeroko;z akcentem
broadcast ('bro:dka:st) v. transmitować; rozsiewać; szerzyc
broadminded ('bro:d'majndyt) adj. pobłażliwy; z otwartą głową
brochure ('brouszjuer) s. broszura
broke (brouk) adj. złamany; bez grosza; zob. break
broken (brouken) adj. połamany; zepsuty; zob. break
broker (brouker) s. pośrednik; ajent;makler;handlarz narkotyków
bronchia ('bronkje) pl. oskrzela
bronze (bronz) s. brąz; adj.brązowy; v. brązować; brązowieć
brooch (broucz) s. brosza; spinka
brood (bru:d) s. wyląg; potomstwo; v. wysiadywać; tkwić; rozmyślać ponuro;być pogrążonym w myślach

brook (bruk) s. potok;v.ścierpieć
broom (bru:m) s. miotła; v. zamiatać;wymiatać;obmiatać
broth (bros) s. rosół;bulion
brothel ('brodzel) s. burdel
brother ('bradzer)s. brat
brothers and sisters ('bradzers, en'systers) rodzeństwo
brotherly ('bradzerly) adj. braterski
brought (bro:t) adj. przyniesiony; zob. bring
brow (brau) s. brew; czoło; nawias;szczyt;pomost;kładka
brown (braun) adj. brunatny; brązowy; opalony; v. brązowieć; opalać się;przyrumieniać (mięso)
brown paper ('braun,pejpe:r)s. papier pakunkowy
bruise (bru:z) s. siniak; stłuczenie; v. tłuc; otłuc; połamać kości; ranić;zgnieść;wyklepać
brush (brasz) s. szczotka; pędzel; draśnięcie; v. szczotkować; otrzepać; pędzlować
brush up ('brasz ap) v. wygładzić; odświeżyć;zgarnąć szczotką
brutal ('bru:tl) a. brutalny; zmysłowy;zwierzęcy
brutality (bru:'taelyty) s. brutalstwo ; brutalność
brute (bru:t) s. bydlę; zwierzę ludzkie; adj. tępy; brutalny; bezduszny; bydlęcy;nieokrzesany
bubble ('babl) s. bąbel; bańka; kipienie; v. kipieć; burzyć się; wydzielać bańki;musować
buck (bak) s. kozioł; fircyk; dolar adj. rogowy; męski; zwykły (szeregowy); v. skakać narowiście; opierać się;dugować
bucket ('bakyt) s. wiadro; czerpak (koparki);tłok;miska
buckle ('bakl) v. spinać; łączyć; wichrować; s. spinka; sprzączka
buckle on ('bakl on) v. pozapinać się ; zapiąć pas ;przypiąć
buckskin ('bakskyn) s. wyprawiona koźla skóra (też sarnia)
bud (bad) s. pączek; v. pączkować; wyrastać;być w zarodku;rozwijać się;dobrze zapowiadać się

buddy ('bady) s. bliski kolega
budget ('badżyt) s. budżet;
v. budżetować;asygnować
buffalo ('bafelou) s. bawół
buffer ('bafer) s. bufor;
zderzak;odbój
buffet ('bafyt) s. bufet; kułak; cios;raz;uderzenie
buffet ('befej) s. niski kredens;dania barowe
bug (bag) s. owad; pluskwa;
defekt; amator;insekt;robak
bugle ('bju:gl) s. róg (do
trąbienia);v.trąbić;zatrąbić
build; built; built (byld;bylt;
bylt)
build (byld) v. budować; rozbu-
dowywać;stworzyć;wznosić
builder ('bylder) s. budowniczy
building ('byldyng)s. budowla
built (bylt) adj. zbudowany;
zob. build
bulb (balb) s. cebula; żarówka
bulge (baldż) v. wzdymać; wybrzu-
szać; wydymać; wytrzeszczać;
s. wypukłość; wzdęcie; wzdyma-
nie się;wybrzuszenie;przewaga
bulk (balk) s. masa; kolos;
większość;v.gromadzić;komasować
bulky ('balky) adj. wielki;otyły;
ciężki; masywny;nieporęczny
bull (bul) s. byk; duży samiec;
głupstwo;nonsens=bull-shit(bul-
szyt)
bullet ('bulyt) s. kula (nabój)
bulletin ('buletyn) s. komunikat; biuletyn
bulletin board ('buletyn,bo:rd)
s. tablica na ogłoszenia
bullion ('buljen) s. złoto i
srebro w sztabach
bully ('buly) v. dręczyć; tyranizować; s. awanturnik; kłotnik; najęty drab; adj. byczy;
żywy; wesoły;świetny;kapitalny
bum (bam) s. włóczęga; nierób;
popijawa; zadek; v. włóczyć
się; cyganić; pić; adj. marny
bumblebee ('bambl-bi:) s.
trzmiel
bump (bamp) v. zderzyć się; łup-
nąć; odbić się z łomotem; nabić guza; s. zderzenie; grzmotnięcie; guz;wybój;wstrząs; uderzenie; wypukłość; zdolności

bumper ('bamper) s. zderzak;
pełny kielich;rekord
bun (ban) s. ciastko drożdżowe;
kok(włosów)
bunch (bancz) s. pęk; banda;
zgraja; guz; v. składać w pęki; skupiać się; kulić się
bunch of grapes ('bancz,ow
grejps) kiść (gałązka) winogron; pęk winogron
bundle ('bandl) s. tłumok;
wiązka;v.pakować(w tobół)
bundle up ('bandl,ap) v. zawinąć się;zebrać;zbierać
bungalow ('bangelou) s. domek
letni parterowy
bungle ('bangl) s. partactwo;
v. partaczyć; bałaganić
bunion ('banjen) s. zapalenie
stawu w stopie(bolesny guz)
bunk ('bank) s. koja;banialuki
bunk bed ('bank,bed) s. łóżko
piętrowe; łóżko do podnoszenia
bunny ('bani) s. królik; trus
buoy (boj) s. boja; znak pływający;pława;v.znaczyć bojami
burden ('be:rdn) s. brzemię;
ciężar; obowiązek; v. obciążać;
przygniatać; obładowywać
bureau ('bjurou) s. komoda;
biuro;sekretarzyk; urząd
bureaucracy (bju'rokresy) s.
biurokracja
burglar (be:rgler) s. włamywacz
burglary ('be:rlery) s. włama-
nie(zwłaszcza w nocy)
burial ('berjel) s. pogrzeb
burly ('be:rly) adj. krzepki;
tęgi;duży i silny
burn; burnt; burnt (be:rn;
be:rnt; be:rnt)
burn (be:rn) v. palić; płonąć;
zapalić; s, oparzelizna;
dziura wypalona;oparzenie
burner ('be:rner) s. palnik
burning ('be:rnyng) s. palenie
burnt (be:rnt) v. spalony;
zob. burn(przypalony,opalony...)
burst; burst; burst (be:rst;
be:rst; be:rst)
burst (be:rst) v. rozsadzać;
rozrywać; s. wybuch;pęknięcie;
salwa; zryw;szał;grzmot;hulanka

burst of laughter ('be:rst,ow
'lafter) wybuch śmiechu
burst into flames ('be:rst,
yntu'flejms) buchać ogniem
burst into tears ('be:rst,
yntu'tiers) wybuchnąć płaczem ;zalać się łzami
bury ('bery) v. pochowac; zagrzebac; chować ;zakopywać
bus (bas) s. autobus
bush (busz) s. krzak; gąszcz
bushel ('buszel) s. korzec
(8 galonów);v.przerabiać
bushy ('buszy) adj. nastroszony;
krzaczasty ;gęsty
business ('byznys) s. interes;
zajęcie ;sprawa;przedsiębiorstwo
business hours ('byznys,aurs)
godziny urzędowe
business letter ('byznys,leter)
oficjalny list
businesslike ('byznys,lajk)
adj. rzeczowy ;solidny;poważny
businessman ('byznysman) s.
przedsiębiorca; człowiek interesów ;handlowiec
business trip ('byznys,tryp)
podróż służbowa
bus stop ('bas-stop)s.przystanek autobusowy
bust (bast) s. popiersie; biust;
v. rujnować; psuć; rozwalić;
niszczyc ;bankrutować;wybuchnąć
bustle ('basl) v. krzątać się;
zapędzać do pracy; s. rozgardiasz; krzątanina ;bieganina
busy ('byzy) adj. zajęty;
skrzętny; wścibski; ruchliwy
busybody ('byzy,body) wścibski;
złośliwy ;plotkarz;intrygant
but (bat) adv. conj.prep. lecz;
ale; jednak; natomiast; tylko;
inaczej niż; z wyjątkiem
but for ('bat fo:r) exp. oprócz;
bez ; gdyby nie
but now ('bat nau) exp. dopiero
teraz ;dopiero w tej chwili
but once ('bat łans) exp. tylko
raz ;chociaż tylko raz
butcher ('buczer) s. rzeźnik ;kat;
v.zarzynac; mordować; masakrować;brutalnie zabijać;partaczyć

butt (bat) 1. s. drzewce; kolba; nasada; niedopałek papierosa; pośladki; cel; przedmiot
kpin; ofiara; tarcza; v. bość;
trącać; przytykać; 2. s. styk;
zetknięcie: uderzenie głową
butt in ('bat yn) v. wtrącać
się;przerywać rozmowę
butter ('bater) s. masło; v.
smarować masłem ;przychlebiać
buttercup ('baterkap) s. jaskier
butterfly ('baterflaj) s. motyl;
adj. motyli
buttocks ('bateks) pl. pośladki
button ('batn) s. guzik;v.zapinąc
button up ('batn ap) v. zapinać
się ; zapinać na guziki
buttonhole ('batnhoul) s. dziurka od guzika;v.zmuszać do słuchania
buttress ('batrus) s. podpora
buxom ('baksem) adj. dorodny;
okazały;pełny(biust);ładna(babka)
buy; bought; bought (baj; bo:t;
bo:t)
buy (baj) v. kupować ;przekupić
buyer (bajer) s. nabywca
buzz (baz) s. brzęczenie;
v. brzęczeć ;przelotywać nisko
buzzard ('bazed) s. myszołów
by (baj) prep. przy; koło; co(dzień);
przez; z; po;w(nocy);o;według
by myself ('baj majself) ja sam
by and large ('baj end'la:rdż)adv.
ogólnie mówiąc; ogólnie biorąc
by twos ('baj,tuz) dwójkami
by the dozen('baj dy 'dazn) tuzinami
by the end ('baj dy,end) przy
końcu ;ku końcowi;z końcem
by land ('baj,laend) lądem
by bus ('baj,bas) autobusem
by day ('baj,dej) za dnia
by-and-by ('baj-end-baj) s.
przyszłość; adv. wnet ;po chwili
bye-bye ! ('baj'baj) excl.: pa !
by-election (,baj-e'lekszyn) s.
wybory uzupełniające
bygone ('bajgon) adj. miniony;
przestarzały ;s.zdarzeria minione
bygones ('bajgonz) pl. przeszłość; dawne urazy ;dawne zatargi

bylaw ('bajlo:) s. przepis;
zarządzenie (miejscowe etc.)
byname ('bajnejm) s. przydomek
bypass ('baj-pas) s. droga dojazdowa; objazd ;v.objeżdżać
by-product (,baj-'prodakt) s.
produkt uboczny
byroad (,baj-'roud) s. boczna
droga ;droga drugorzędna
bystander (,baj-'stander) s.
przygodny widz
bystreet (,baj-'stri:t) s.
boczna ulica (drugorzędna)
byway ('baj-łej) s. boczna
droga ;boczne przejście
byword ('baj-,łe:rd) s. przysłowie; przydomek (pogardliwy)
by work ('baj,-łe:rk) s. praca
uboczna poza zajęciem głównym
c (si:) litera "c"; trzecia litera alfabetu angielskiego
cab (kaeb) s. taksówka; dorożka-
szoferka ;budka maszynisty
cabaret (,kaebe'rej) s. lokal
taneczny ; kabaret;serwis na tacy
cabbage ('kaebydż) s. kapusta
cabin ('kaebyn) s. kabina; chat-
ka ;prymitywnie zbudowany domek
cabinet ('kaebynyt) s. szafka;
rada ministrów, adj.tajny
cabinetmaker ('kaebynyt,mejke:r)
s. stolarz meblowy
cable ('kejbl) s. przewód; lina;
depesza; v. depeszować; umoco-
wywać liną ;przesyłać kablem
cable-car ('kejbl,ka:r) s. wóz
linowy ; kolejka; linowa
cabman ('kaebmen) s. taksówkarz
cabstand ('kaeb staend) s. postój taksówek
cackle ('kaekl) v. gdakać; gę-
gać; chichotać; s. gdakanie;
gęganie; chichot
cacti ('kaektaj) pl. kaktusy
cactus ('kaektes) s. kaktus
cad (kaed) s. ordynus; cham
café ('kaefej) s. kawiarnia;
kawa ;restauracja; bar
cafeteria (,kaefy'tierja) s.
restauracja samoobsługowa
cage (kejdż) s. klatka; kosz;
v. zamykać w klatce

cake (kejk) s. ciastko; kostka
(mydła);smażony placek(z ryby)
cake tin ('kejk,tyn) s. forma
na ciastko
calamity (ke'laemyty) s. nieszczęście; klęska ;niedola
calculate ('kaelkjulejt) v.
rachować; sądzić; oceniać
calculation (,kaelju'lejszyn)
s. liczenie ;ostrozność
calendar ('kaelynder) s, kalendarz ;terminarz
calf (kaef) s. cielak; łydka
caliber ('kaelyber) s. średnica wewnętrzna; kaliber;
wzorzec; sprawdzian
call (ko:l) v. wołać; wzywać;
telefonować; odwiedzać; zawijać do portu; wyzywać;
s. krzyk; wezwanie; apel; powołanie; wizyta ;nazwanie;rządanie
call for help ('ko:l,fo:r help)
wołanie o pomoc ;wzywanie pomocy
call names ('ko:l,nejmz) przezywać; wyzywać ;ubliżać
call back ('ko:l,baek) odtele-
fonować; odwoływać z powrotem
call at ('ko:l,aet) odwiedzać
call for ('ko:l,fo:r) żądać;
chodzić po coś(żeby otrzymać)
call on ('ko:l,on) odwiedzać
(kogoś);prosić o wypowiedź
call up ('ko:l,ap) telefonować
caller ('ko:ler) s. gość; od-
wiedzający ;adj.rzeźki;świerzy
calling ('ko:lyng) s. zawód;
powołanie ;zatrudnienie;fach
callous ('kaeles) adj. stwardniały; nieczuły;zrogowaciały
calm (ka:m) adj. spokojny; cichy; s. spokój; cisza; opanowanie;
v. uspokajać; uciszać ;uciszyć się
calm down ('ka:m,dałn) v. uciszyć się ;uspokoić się
calorie ('kaelery) s. kaloria
calves (ka:wz) pl. cielaki;
łydki
camber ('kaember) v. wyginać;
s. wygięcie ;wypukłość (jezdni)
came (kejm) v. przyszedł; zob.
come

camel ('kaemel) s. wielbłąd

camera ('kaemere) s. aparat fotograficzny; prywatna izba

camomile ('kaemoumajl) s. rumianek

camouflage ('kaemufla:ż) s. maskowanie; v. maskować (wojsk.)

camp (kaemp) s. obóz; v. obozować: rozlokowywać w namiotach

camp out (kaemp aut) v. obozować w namiocie

campaign (kaem'pejn) s, kampania; akcja; v, odbywać kampanię; agitować

camp bed ('kaemp,bed) s. łóżko polowe;łóżko składane

camper ('kaemper) adj.obozujący;s. wóz lub przyczepa do obozowania; mieszkalny wóz(turystyczny)

camping ('kaempyng) s. obozowanie; życie obozowe

camping ground ('kaempyng,graund) obozowisko; miejsce do obozowania

campus ('kaempes) s. teren uniwersytecki lub szkolny

can (kaen) s., puszka blaszana; ustęp; v. móc; konserwować; wyrzucać;umieć;zdołać;potrafić

Canadian (ke'nejdjen) adj. kanadyjski

canal (ke'nael) s. kanał ;kanalik

canard (kae'na:rd) s. kaczka dziennikarska; plotka

canary (ke'nery) s. kanarek

cancel ('kaensel) v. znosić; kasować;odwoływać;skreślać

cancer ('kaenser) s. rak (choroba); nowotwór

candid ('kaendyd) adj. szczery; bezstronny;otwarty

candidate ('kaendydyt) s. kandydat;kandydatka

candied ('kaendyd) adj. pocukrzony; lukrowany

candle ('kaendl) s. świeca

candlestick ('kaendlstyk) s. świecznik; lichtarz

candy ('kaendy) s. cukierki; lukier;cukier lodowaty

cane (kejn) s. trzcina; laska; pałka; v. chłostać ;wyplatać trzciną; ukarać trzciną

canned (kaend) adj. zakonserwowany w puszce

cannery (kaenery) s. fabryka konserw

cannibal ('kaenybel) s. ludożerca; adj. ludożerczy

cannon ('kaenen) s. działo,

cannot ('kaenot) v. nie móc (od cannot);nie potrafić

canoe (ke'nu:) s. czółno; kajak; v. jeździć kajakiem; wiosłować

canopy ('kaenepy) s. baldachim; okap;firmament; sklepienie

cant ('kaent) s. żargon; frazes

can't (ka:nt) v. nie móc(od can);nie potrafić

canteen (kaen'ti:n) s. manierka; menażka; kantyna

canvas ('kaenves) s. płótno impregnowane

canvass ('kaenves) s. badanie; zabieganie; v.zabiegać; badać; starać się o głosy

cap (kaep) s. czapka; pokrywa; wieko; kapiszon;beret

cap (kaep) v. wkładać czapkę lub nakrywkę; wieńczyć; zakładać spłonkę; zakasować

capability (,kaepe'bylyty) s. zdolność;zdatność; możliwość

capable (,kejpebl) adj. zdolny

capacity (ke'paesyty) s. zdolność; kompetencja; pojemność; właściwość;nośność;objętość

cape (kejp) s. 1. peleryna; 2. przylądek

caper (kejper) v. wywijać kozły; s. hołubiec; sus; skok

capital ('kaepytl) s. stolica; kapitał; adj. główny; zasadniczy; stołeczny; fatalny

capital crime ('kaepytlkrajm) s. morderstwo

capitalism ('kaepytlysem)s. kapitalizm

capital letter ('kaepytl,leter) duża litera

capital punishment ('kaepytl 'panyszment) kara śmierci

capricious (ke'pryszes) adj. kapryśny

capsize (kaep'sajz) v. wywracać
(statek) dnem do góry
capsule ('kaepsju:l) s. kapsuł-
ka;torebka;pochewka;kabinka
captain ('kaeptyn) s. kapitan;
naczelnik;v.dowodzić
caption ('kaepszyn) s. nagłówek;
napis ;poświadczenie;aresztowanie
captivate ('kaeptywejt) v. ująć;
czarować; urzekać:zniewalać
captive ('kaeptyw) adj. jeniec
captivity ('kaeptyvyty) s. niewola
capture ('kaepczer) s. owładnię-
cie; łup; v. pojmać; owładnąć
car (ka:r) s, samochód; wóz
caravan('kaerevaen) s. karawana;
wóz kryty;przyczepka mieszkalna
carbohydrate ('ka:rbe'hajdrejt)
s. węglowodan
carbon ('ka:rben) s. węgiel;
kopia (kalka)
carbon dioxide ('ka:rben
daj'oksajd) s. CO$_2$ dwutlenek
węgla
carbon paper ('ka:rben,pejper)
s. kalka
carburetor ('ka:rbjureter) s.
gaźnik
car carrier (ka:r-'kaerjer) s.
wóz do przewozu aut
carcass ('ka:r-kes) s. ścierwo;
padlina; szkielet
card ('ka:rd) s. karta; bilet;
pocztówka;legitymacja; atut
cardboard ('ka:rdbo:rd) s. tektura;adj.tekturowy
card box('ka:rdboks) s. karton
cardigan ('ka:rdygen) s. wełniana kurta (kamizelka)
cardinal ('ka:rdynl) adj. główny; kardynał
card index ('ka:rd yndeks) s.
kartoteka
car papers (ka:r pejpers) s. dokumenty samochodowe
care (keer) s. opieka; troska;
ostrożność:zgryzota;dozór:uwaga
care of (keer ow) c/o: adres
(u kogos)
care for (keer fo:r) v. dbać
o kogoś:lubić;kochać;mieć ochotę

career (ke'rier) s. kariera;
zawód;tok;pęd;bieg;v. cwałować
carefree (keerfri:) adj. beztroski
careful (keerful) adj. ostrożny;
troskliwy;dbały;pieczołowity
careless (keerles) adj. niedbały; nieuważny;nieostrożny
caress (ke'res) s. pieszczota;
v. pieścić; popieścić
caretaker ('keertejker) s.
dozorca; stróż
careworn ('keerło:rn) s.zgnę-
biony kłopotami
carfare ('ka:rfeer) s. opłata
za jazdę
cargo ('ka:rgou) s. ładunek
caricature (,kaeryke'czjuer)
s. karykatura;v.karykaturować
car mechanic (ka:r-my'kaenyk)
s. mechanik samochodowy
carnation ('ka:r'nejszyn) 1.
s.& adj. ciemno-czerwony;cielis-
ty;2. goździk ogrodowy
carnival ('ka:rnywel) s. karnawał;zapusty
carnivorous (ka:r'nyweres) adj.
mięsożerny
carol ('kaerel) s. kolenda;
v. kolendować
carp (ka:rp) s. karp; v. czepiać się;ganić;przycinać
car parking ('ka:r-pa:rkyŋg)
s. parking samochodowy
carpenter (ka:rpynter) s.
cieśla; stolarz
carpet ('ka:rpyt) s. dywan;
v. wyścielać dywanem
carriage ('kaerydż) s. wagon;
powóz; postawa;kareta;chód
carrier ('kaerjer) s. firma
przewozowa; nośnik; tragarz;
rozsadnik (zakażenia); lotniskowiec;okaziciel
carrion ('kaerjen) s. padlina
carrot ('kaeret) s. marchewka
carry ('kaery) v. nosić; wozić; zanieść; unosić
carry off ('kaery,of) v. upro-
wadzić; zabrać;zdobywać(nagrodę)
carry on ('kaery,on) v. kontynuować;wytrwać;awanturować się

carry out ('kaery,aut) v. wykonać; przeprowadzić;spełnić

cart ('ka:rt) s. woz

cartel ('ka:rtel) s. kartel

carter ('ka:rter) s. woźnica

cart horse ('ka:rthors) s. koń pociągowy

carton ('ka:rten) s. karton

cartoon (ka:r'tun) s. karykatura;v. rysować karykatury

cartoonist (ka:r'tunyst) s. karykaturzysta

cartridge ('ka:rtrydż) s. nabój

cartwheel ('ka:rt-hłi:l) s. kołodziej

carve ('ka:rw) v. rzeźbić; krajać;cyzelować;pociać an części

carver ('ka:rwer) s. snycerz

carving ('ka:rwyng) s. rzeźba

cascade (kaes'kejd) s. wodospad;v.spadać jak wodospad

case (kejs) s. 1. wypadek; sprawa; dowod; 2. skrzynia; pochwa; torba; 3. sprawa sądowa; v. zamykać w pochwie; otaczać czymś ;oszalować; oprawić

casement ('kejsment) s. rama okienna; okno z kwaterami

cash (kaesz) s. gotowka; pieniądze; v. spieniężać; inkasować; płacić (gotówką)

cash on delivery (kaesz on dy'lywery) zapłata przy odbiorze; C.O.D.

cashier (kae'szjer) s. kasjer

cash register(kaesz'redżyster) s. kasa (zmechanizowana)

casing ('kejsyng)s. 1. powłoka; pochwa; 2. obudowa; oprawa; 3. łuska; 4. opancerzenie

cask (kaesk) s. beczułka

casket (kaeskyt) s. trumna; urna; szkatuła

cassock ('kaesek) s. sutanna

cast; cast; cast (ka:st; ka:st; ka:st)

cast (ka:st) s. rzut; odlew; gips; odcień: v, rzucać; łowić; odlewać; powalić; dzielic role teatralne

castaway ('ka:st,e'łej) s. wyrzutek ;rozbitek

cast down (ka:st dałn) adj. przygnębiony,v.deprymować

caste (ka:st) s. kasta

cast iron(ka:stajren) s. żeliwo

castle ('ka:sl) s. zamek

castor oil ('ka:ster,ojl) s. olej rycynowy

cast steel ('ka:st,sti:l) s. lana stal

casual ('kaeżuel) adj. przypadkowy; niedbały;dorywczy

casualty ('kaeżuelty) s. wypadek; ofiara wypadku; lista strat;nieszczęście

cat (kaet) s. kot;jędza

catalog ('kaetelog) s. katalog

catamaran (,kaeteme'raen) s. dwu-czołnowa łódź

cataract ('kaeteraekt) s. katarakta; ulewa;wodospad

catarrh (ke'ta:r) s. katar

catastrophe (ke'taestrefy) s. katastrofa

catch; caught; caught (kaecz; ko:t; ko:t)

catch (kaecz) v. łapać; łowić; ujmować; słyszeć; wybuchać; nabawić się; s. łup; połow

catch cold (kaecz kold) v. zaziębiać się

catch fire (kaecz fajer) v. zapalać się

catch up (kaecz ap) v. dogonić

catching (kaeczyng)adj. zaraźliwy;s.tryby;uchwyt;zazębienie

category ('kaetygery) s. kategoria

cater ('kejter) v. dostarczać żywności; obsługiwać

caterpillar ('kaetepyler) s. gąsie nica (traktora.czołgu etc)

cathedral (ke'ti:drel) s. katedra

Catholic ('kaetelyk) adj. katolicki; s. katolik

cattle (kaetl) s. bydło rogate

caucus ('ko:kes) s. tajne narady partyjne; klika

caught (ko:t) złapany; zob. catch

cauldron ('ko:ldren) s,kocioł

cauliflower ('kalyflauer) s. kalafior

cause (ko:z) s. przyczyna; sprawa;racja;motywacja;proces

causeless(ko:zles) adj. przypadkowy ; bezpodstawny

caution ('ko:szyn) s. ostroż-
nosc; uwaga;v.ostrzegac

cautious ('ko:szes) adj. ostrożny;rozważny;roztropny;uważny

cavalry ('kaevelry) s. kawaleria

cave (kejw) s. pieczara; jaskinia; v. zapadac sie; drążyc

cavern ('kaewen) s. jama; jaskinia; grota; pieczara

cavity ('kaewyty) s. wklęsłosc;
dziura(w zębie);dół;wydrążenie

cease (sy:s) v. ustawac; prze-
stawac; położyc kres

ceaseless (sy:slys) adj. bezustanny;ciągły; nieprzerwany

cede (si:d) v. ustąpic; cedowac

ceiling ('sy:lyng)s. sufit; pułap; gorna granica

celebrate ('selybrejt) v. swię-
cic ;uczcic;sławic;obchodzic

celebrated ('selybrejtyd) adj.
sławny; słynny; głosny

celebration ('selybrejszyn) s.
obchod; odprawianie; swięcenie

celebrity ('sylebryty) s. sławna
osoba;sława;znakomita osobowosc

celery ('selery) s. seler (jarzyna)

celibacy ('selybesy) s. bez-
żenstwo; celibat

cell (sel) s. cela; komórka

cellar ('seler) s. piwnica

Celtic (keltyk) adj. celtycki

cement (sy'ment) s. cement;
v. cementowac; kleic; utwier-
dzac ;spoic; złączyc

cemetery ('semytry) s. cmentarz

censor ('sensor) s. cenzor

censorship ('senserszyp) s. cenzura

censure ('senszer) s. nagana;
krytyka; v. krytykowac

cent (sent) s. cent

centenary (sentynery) adj. stuletni; s. stulecie; setna rocznica

centennial ('sen'tenjel) s.
stulecie; adj. stuletni

center ('senter) s. osrodek;
v. zesrodkowywac

centigrade ('sentygrejd) adj.
stustopniowy(termometr)

centimeter ('sentymi:ter) s.
centymetr

central ('sentral) adj. srod-
kowy; czołowy ; s. centrala

Central Europe ('sentral
juerop) Europa Srodkowa

central heating ('sentrel
hi:tyng)centralne ogrzewanie

centralize ('sentrelajz) v.
centralizowac;zesrodkowywac

center ('senter) s. osrodek
centrum; v. zesrodkowywac;
centrowac ;skupiac się

century ('senczury) s.stulecie

cereals ('syerjelz) pl, zboża

cerebral ('serybrel) adj. moz-
gowy

ceremonial (,sery'mounjel) adj.
ceremonialny; s. rytuał; ceremonial; ceremonialnosc

ceremonious (,sery'mounjes)
adj. drobiazgowy; ceremonialny

ceremony ('serymeny) s. ceremonia;v.sztywno się zachowywac

certain ('se:rtyn) adj. niejaki; pewien;pewny;ustalony;jakis

certainly ('se:rtnly) adv. napewno; oczywiscie;bezwzględnie

certainty ('se:rtynty) s. pewnosc; pewnik; rzecz pewna

certificate (se'rtyfykyt) s.
swiadectwo; poswiadczenie;
v. zaswiadczac ;dyplomowac

certify ('se:rtyfaj) v. zaswiadczac; zapewniac; uznawac za

certitude ('se:rtytju:d) s.
pewnosc; przeswiadczenie

chafe (czejf) v. trzec; otrzec;
irytowac; s. tarcie; otarcie;
irytacja; rozdrażnienie; złosc

chaff(cza:f) s. 1. sieczka;
2. żart; naciąganie; wysmiewac żartobliwie; naciągac

chagrin ('szaegryn) s. smutek; rozczarowanie; v.upo-
karzac;rozczarowywac bolesnie

chain (czejn) s. łańcuch; syndykat; trust; v, wiązać na łań-
cuchu; mierzyć;uwiązać; zakuć
chair (czeer) s. krzesło; stołek; fotel; katedra; v. prze-
wodniczyć; sadzać na krześle
chair lift ('czeerlyft)s. wyciąg linowy
chairman ('czeermen) s. przewodniczący; prezes ___ ſkredą
chalk (czo:k) s. kreda;v.pisać
challenge ('czaelyndż) s. wyzwanie; zadanie; v. wyzywać; zarzucać; wzywać;korcić;prowokować
chamber ('czejmber) s. izba; komora;sala;pokój;v.wydrążyć
chambermaid ('czejmbermejd) s.
pokojowa
chamois ('szaemła:) s. giemza;
ircha; zamsz
champagne ('szaem'pejn) s. szampan
champion ('czaempjen) s. mistrz;
obrońca; v. bronić; walczyć o...
championship ('czaempjenszyp)
s. mistrzostwo
chance (cza:ns) s. okazja; przypadek; szczęście; szansa;ryzyko;
adj. przypadkowy; przygodny;
v. zdarzać się; ryzykować; próbować;przytrafić się;natknąć się
chancellor (cza:seler) s. kanclerz; pierwszy sekretarz (amba-
sady);najwyższy sędzia
chandelier (szaendy'lyer) s.
żyrandol; świecznik
change (czejndż) s, zmiana; wymiana; drobne; v. zmienić;
przebierać (się); wymieniac
change one's mind ('czejndż,
łans'majnd) zmienić czyjeś
zdanie (przekonania etc.)
change trains ('czejndż,trejns)
v. przesiąść się (na kolei)
changeable('czejndżebl) adj.
zmienny;podległjący zmianom
channel ('czaenl) s. kanał; koryto; łożysko; v, żłobić;
przesyłać drogą (urzędową)
chaos ('kejos) s. chaos
chap (czaep) s. chłop; chłopiec;
człek; v.pękać; powodować
pęknięcia (warg);zarysowywać

chapel ('czaepel) s. kaplica
chaplain ('czaeplyn) s. kapelan
chaps (cza:ps)pl. skórzane no-
gawice (kowboja);ochraniacze
chapter ('czaepter) s. rozdział;
oddział; v. dzielić na rozdzia-
ły
character ('kaerykter) s. charakter; typ; cecha; reputacja;
moralność; facet; znak
characteristic ('kaerykterystyk)
adj. charakterystyczny; typowy; s. cecha; własność; właściwość
characterize ('kaerykterajz) v.
charakteryzować (opisywać)
charge (cza:rdż) s. ciężar; ładunek; obowiązek; piecza; podopieczny; zarzut; opłata; należność; szarża; godło; v. ładować; nasycać; obciążać; zadać;
liczyć sobie; oskarżać; atakować; szarżować
charge account (cza:rdż e'kaunt)
s. otwarty kredyt (w banku)
charge card (cza:rdż'ka:rd) s.
karta kredytowa do zakupów
chariot ('czaerjet) s. wóz; rydwan
charitable ('czaerytebl) adj.
litościwy; dobroczynny
charity ('czaeryty) s. miłosierdzie; dobroczynność
charm (cza:rm) s, czar; urok;
amulet; v. czarować; oczarować
charming (cza:rmyŋg)adj. czarujący
chart (cza:rt) s. wykres; mapa
morska; v. robić wykres; wytyczać; pokazywać (jak)
charmless (cza:rmlys) adj. bez
wdzięku
charter (cza:rter)s. statut;
przywilej; dyplom; akt nadania
prawa do... v. nadawać; zakładać na statutach; wynajmować
statek lub samolot
charter plane (cza:rter plejn)
s. wynajęty grupowo samolot
charwoman ('cza:rłumen) s.
sprzątaczka; dochodząca sprzataczka;posługaczka

chase 1. (czejs) s. pościg; pogoń; polowanie; v. gonić; ścigać; polować; wyganiać
chase 2. (czejs) s. łożysko; wgłębienie; wykop; v. złobić
chasm ('kaezem) s. otchłań
chaste (czejst) adj. czysty; niewinny;nieskażony;cnotliwy
chastity ('czaestyty) s. niewinność; prostota;dziewictwo
chat (czaet) s. pogawędka; v. gawędzić; gadać;rozmawiać
chatter (czaeter) v. szczebiotać; klapać; s.szczebiot; klapanie; klekot;paplanie;terkot
chatterbox (czaeterboks) s. trajkotka;gaduła;pleciuga
chauffer ('szoufer) s. zawodowy kierowca; przenośny piecyk
cheap (czi:p) adj. tani; marny
cheapen (czi:pen) v. taniec; obniżać wartość;spadać w cenie
cheat (czi:t) s. oszust; oszustwo; v. oszukiwać; zdradzać (w małżeństwie);okpiwać
check (czek) s. wstrzymanie ; przerwa; sprawdzenie; czek; kwit; szach; a. szachownicowy; kontrolny; pokreślony; v. hamować; sprawdzać; zakreślać; nadawać; zgadzać się; szachować;ganić;krytykować;opanowywać
check in (czek yn) v. wmeldowywać się (w pracy,w wojsku etc.)
check out (czek aut) v. wymeldowywać się;zapłacić za hotel
checked (czekt) adj, w kratkę
checkroom (czekrum) s. przechowalnia (bagażu);szatnia
cheek (czi:k) s. policzek; bezczelne gadanie; v. mówić bezczelnie do kogoś; stawiać się
cheeky ('czi:ky) adj. bezczelny; zuchwały;pełen tupetu;z tupetem
cheer (czier) s. brawo; hurra; radość; jadło; v. krzyczec; rozweselać;dodawać otuchy
cheer on ('czier on) v. zachęcać ;zagrzewać;dodawać otuchy
cheer up ('czier ap) v. pocieszać; nabrać otuchy;rozpogodzić
cheerful ('czierful) adj. pogodny; wesoły; ochoczy;rozweselający

cheerless ('czierlys) adj. ponury; smutny; przybity
cheery ('cziery) adj. wesoły; radosny; pogodny
cheese ('czi:z) s. ser
chef (czef) s. kuchmistrz
chemical ('kemykel) adj. chemiczny;s.substancja chemiczna
chemicals ('kemykels) pl. chemikalia;leki:lekarstwa
chemise (sze'mi:z) s. damska koszula luźna i długa
chemist ('kemyst) s. chemik; aptekarz
chemistry ('kemystry) s. chemia
cheque (czek) s. czek (poza USA)
chequered ('czekerd) adj. kratkowany; urozmaicony; burzliwy
cherish ('czerysz) v. lubić; tulić; żywić (uczucie);miłować
cherry ('czery) s. czeresnia; wiśniowy kolor; vulg.:prawiczka; adj. wiśniowy; vulg.: prawiczy; czerwony
chess (czes) s. szachy
chess-board (czes-bo:rd) s. szachownica
chess man(czesmen) s. figurka szachowa
chest (czest) s. skrzynia; komoda; piers ;płuca;kufer;skrzynka
chestnut ('czesnat) s. kasztan
chest of drawers (czest ow dro:ers) komoda
chew (czu:) v. żuć; przeżuwać; besztać; gderać; s. żucie; tyton do żucia; prymka
chewing gum('czu:yn&gam) s. guma do żucia
chicken ('czykyn) s. kurcze; adj.tchórzliwy; bojący się
chicken out ('czykyn aut) v. stchórzyć;ustąpić ze strachu
chide; chid; chidden (czajd; czyd; czydn)
chide (czajd) v. łajać; droczyć się; skarżyć;besztać; łajać
chicken pox('czykyn poks) s. ospa wietrzna
chief (czy:f) s. wódz; szef; adj. główny; naczelny
chilblain ('czylblejn) s, odmrożenie

child (czajld) s. dziecko
childish ('czajldysz) adj.
dziecinny
childless ('czajldlys) adj. bezdzietny
childlike ('czajldlajk) adj.
dziecięcy; jak dziecko
children('czyldren) pl. dzieci
chill (czyl) s. chłód; dreszcz;
v. studzić; mrozić ;oziębiać
chilly (czyly) adj. chłodny;
adv. chłodno; zimno
chime ('czajm) s. dzwony grające
rytm; kurant; v. bić w dzwony;
wydzwaniać; rymować;zabrzmieć
chimney ('czymny) s. komin; wylot; szkło lampy naftowej
chimney sweeper ('czymny,słi:per)
s. kominiarz;adj. kominiarski
chin (czyn) s. broda; v. podciągać brodę do drążka;s.podbródek
china ('czajna) s. porcelana
chinese ('czaj'ni:z) adj. chiński;Chinese s. chińczyk
chink('czynk) 1. s. brzęk; v.po-
brzękiwać; brzęczeć; 2. szpara;
szczelina; v. zapychać szpary
chip (czyp) s. drzazga; odłamek;
skrawek; v. otłuc; obijać; dokuczać; nabierać; ciosać;
ćwierkać; piszczeć; nogę podstawiać; złuszczać się;odłupać
chirp (czy:rp) s. świergot;
v. ćwierkać; szczebiotać
chisel ('czyzl) s. dłuto; przecinek; v. ciąć; rzeźbić;oszukać
chivalrous ('czywelres) adj.
rycerski
chivalry ('czywelry) s. rycer-
stwo; rycerskość
chive (czajw) s. szczypiorek
chlorine ('klo:ry:n) s. chlor
chloroform ('klo:refo:rm) s.
chloroform; v. maczać w chlo-
roformie;usypiać chloroformem
chock (czok) s. klin; v. osadzać na klinach; adv. szczelnie; ciasno; mocno ; w pełni
chocolate ('czoklyt) s. czekolada;adj. czokoladowy(kolor etc.)
choice (czoys) s. wybor; wybran-
ka; adj.wyborowy;doborowy

choir ('kłajer) s. chór
choke (czouk) v. dusić; zadu-
sić; tłumić; dławić; s. durze-
nie; dławik; gardziel; prze-
wężenie;odgłosy duszenia;zawór
choke down (czouk dałn) v. dławić;zmniejszać gardziel
choke up (czouk ap) v. zatykać
(rurę); zadławić(motor etc.)
choose; chose; chosen (czu:z;
czouz; czouzn)
choose (czu:z) v. wybierać; wolec; postanowić;zadecydować
chop (czop) v. rąbać; obcinać;
s. rąbnięcie; kotlet;krótka fala
chop down (czop dałn) v. powalić (drzewo etc.); ściać;zrąbać
chord (ko:rd) s. struna; cięciwa;struna głosowa
chorus ('ko:res) s. chór;
v. mówić chórem;śpiewać chórem
chose (czouz) v. wybrał; zob.
choose
chow (czau) s. jadło (slang)
Christ (krajst) Chrystus
christen ('krisn) v. ochrzcić
Christian ('krystjen) adj.
chrześcijański; s. chrześci-
janin(slang:cywilizowany)
Christianity (krys'czaenyty) v.
chrześcijaństwo
Christian name ('krystjen,nejm)
s. imię(inne niż nazwisko)
Christmas ('krysmas) s. Boże
Narodzenie
Christmas Day ('krysmas dej)
Dzień Bożego Narodzenia
Christmas Eve ('krysmas i:w)
wilia, wigilia Bożego Narodzenia
chromium ('kroumjem) s. chrom
chronic ('kronyk) adj. chroniczny;strawszliwy (ból)
chronicle ('kronykl) s. kronika
chronological (krone'lodżykel)
adj. chronologiczny
chubby ('czaby) adj. pucołowaty; pyzaty;mały i gruby
chuck (czak) v. rzucać; gdakać;
cmokać; s. kurczątko; dziecina;
kochanie;gdakanie;cmokanie

chuckle (czakl) v. chichotać;
s. chichot; zduszony śmiech
chum (czam) v. przyjaźnić się
blisko; s. serdeczny kolega;
współlokator;v.przyjaźnić sie
church (cze:rcz) s. kościół
churchyard (tze:rczja:rd) s.
cmentarz; dziedziniec kościelny; adj. cmentarny
churn (cze:rn) v. robić masło;
kłócić się; burzyć się; kotłować sie; pienić sie; s. maślni-
ca; maślniczka;bańka na mleko
chute (szu:t) s. koryto zrzuto-
we; spadek; wodospad; spadochron; tor zjażdżalni dla dzieci
chutzpah (hucpa) s. nachalnosc;
śmiałość;tupet(po nowohebrajsku)
cider ('sajder) s. wino z jabłek
cigar (sy'ga:r) s. cygaro
cigaret(te) (sige'ret) s. papieros
cinder ('synder) s. popiół; żużel; v. spalać na żużel
cinderella (,synde'rele) s. kopciuszek; Kopciuszek
cinder track ('synder-traek) s.
bieżnia żużlowa;tor żużlowy
cine camera ('syni-'kaemere) s.
aparat filmowy
cinema ('syneme) s. kino
cinema projector ('syneme-
prodżekter) s. rzutnik filmowy
cipher ('sajfer) s. cyfra; szyfr;
zero; v. szyfrować; rachować
circle ('se:rkl) s. koło; krąg;
obwód; v. otaczać; kręcić się
w koło; opasywać; krążyć;okrążać
circuit ('se:rkyt) s. obwód;
okrężna; okólna (podróż)
circular ('se:rkjuler) s. okólnik; adj. okrągły; kolisty
circulate ('se:rkjulejt) v.
krążyć; cyrkulować; puszczać
w obieg; być w obiegu
circulation ('se:rkjulejszyn)
s. krążenie; obrót; nakład
circumference (se'rkamfyrens)
s. obwód (koła etc.)
circumcision (se:rkem'syżyn)s.
obrzezanie;obcięcie napletka

circumscribe (,se:rkem'skrajb)
v. opisywać; zakreślać
circumstance ('se:rkemstaens)
s. okoliczności; szczegóły
circus ('se:rkes) s. cyrk;
okrągły plac;rondo; desant(sl.)
cistern ('systern) s. zbiornik
na wodę; cysterna
cite (sajt) v. cytować; przy-
taczać; pozywać; wymieniać
w komunikacie;wzywać do sądu
citizen ('sytyzn) s. obywatel
citizenship ('sytyzenszyp) s.
obywatelstwo;cnoty obywatelskie
city ('syty) s. (wielkie) miasto; centrum finansowe;ośrodek
city center ('syty,senter) s.
centrum miasta
city guide ('syty'gajd) s. plan
miasta;przewodnik po mieście
city hall('syty,ho:l) s. zarząd
miasta; magistrat
civics ('sywyks) s. nauka praw
i obowiązków obywatela[uprzejmy;
civil ('sywl) adj. społeczny;
obywatelski;cywilny(kodeks);
civilian (sy'wyljen) adj. cywilny; s. cywil; obywatel
civility (sy'wylyty) s. uprzejmość; grzeczność
civilization (,sywylaj'sejszyn)
s. cywilizacja;całość kultury
civilize ('sywylajz) v. cywili-
zować; ucywilizować
civil marriage ('sywl'maerydż)
s. ślub cywilny
civil rights ('sywl,rajts) s.
prawa obywatelskie
civil service ('sywl'se:rwys)
s. służba państwowa
civil war ('sywl,ło:r) s. wojna domowa
clack (klaek) v. klekotać; gdakać; s. klekot; wieko
clad (klaed) adj. odziany; zob.
clothe
claim (klejm) v. żądać; twierdzić; s. żądanie; twierdzenie;
działka;skarga;zażalenie;dług
claimant (klejment) s. rości-
ciel; pretendent;adj.pilny;rażący

clammy ('klaemy) adj. mokro-
lepki;wilgotny i zimny
clamor ('klaemer) s. zgiełk;
krzyk; v. krzyczeć; robić
wrzawę; wymuszać krzykiem
clamorous ('klaemeres) adj.
zgiełkliwy; krzykliwy
clamp (klaemp) s. klamra; zacisk;v.zaciskać (jak)klamrą
clan (klaen) s. klan; szczep
szkocki;v.tworzyć klikę
clandestine (klaen'destyn) adj.
potajemny; skryty; tajny
clang (klaeng) s.dźwięk: szczęk;
klekot; v. dzwięczeć; szczękać;
klekotać;rozbrzmiewać;dzwonić
clank (klaenk) s. chrzęst;
brzęk; v. brzękać; chrześcić
clap (klaep) s. huk; klaskanie;
v. łopotać; oklaskiwać; klepać
claret ('klaeret) s. czerwone
wino; bordo; slang:krew
clarify ('klaeryfaj) v. wyjaśniać; rozjaśniać; oczyszczać
clarity ('klaeryty) s. czystość;
jasność; przejżystość;klarowność
clash (klaesz) s. brzęk; starcie;
v. brzęczeć; ścierać się; kolidować; uderzać w coś
clasp (klaesp) s. klamra; uchwyt; okucie; v. spinać; ściskać
clasp knife ('klaesp-najf) s.
scyzoryk;kozik; nóż składany
class (klaes) s. klasa; lekcja;
rocznik; grupa; v. klasyfikować ;segregować; sortować
classmate ('kla:s,mejt) s. kolega szkolny
classroom ('kla:s,rum) s. klasa
(w szkole); sala szkolna
class struggle (,kla:s'stragl)
s. walka klas w społeczeństwie
classic ('klaesyk) s. klasyk;
studia klasyczne; adj. klasyczny; uznany autotytet;klasyk
classical ('klaesykel) adj. typowy; klasyczny;humanistyczny
classification (klaesyfy'kejszyn)
s. klasyfikacja;klasyfikowanie
classify ('klaesyfaj) v. klasyfikować; sortować; zaklasyfikować
clatter ('klaeter) v. brzeczeć;
klapać; s. brzęk;łoskot;gwar

clause (klo:z) s. klauzula;
zdanie; punkt umowy
claw (klo:) s. pazur; szpon;
łapa; kleszcze; v. drapać; wydrapać; łapać w szpony
clay (klej) s. glina; sl.trup
clean (kli:n) adj. czysty; wyraźny; zgrabny; adv. całkiem;
zupełnie; poprostu; v, oczyścić; opróżniać; ogołocić; wygrać; uprzatnąć;dużo zyskać(sl,)
clean out ('kli:n aut) v. oczyścić; opróżniać;wyczyścić
clean up ('kli:n ap) v. po-
sprzątać; wygrać; zrobić na
czysto;robić porządek
cleaner ('kli:ner) s. czyści-
ciel; oczyszczalnik; właściciel pralni;pralnia chemiczna
cleaning ('kli:nyng) s. czyszczenie; sprzątanie;porządki
cleanliness ('klenlynys) s.
czystość;zamiłowanie do czystości
cleanly ('klenly) adj. czysty;
adv. czysto; schludnie
cleanness ('kli:nnys) s. czystość;zamiłowanie do czystości
cleanse (klenz) v. czyścić;
zmywać (grzechy);oczyszczać
clear (klier) adj. jasny; czysty; bystry; adv. jasno; wyraźnie; z dala; zupełnie; dokładnie; s. wolna przestrzeń
clear away ('klier,eřej) v. usunąć (przeszkodę etc.)
clear up ('klier,ap) v. wyjaśnić
clear-cut ('klier,kat) adj. wyraźny; czysty ; poprawny
clearing ('klieryng) s. karczo-
wisko; rozrachunek;obrachunek
clearly ('klierly) adv. wyraźnie; jasno; oczywiście
cleave; cleft; cleft (kli:w;
kleft; kleft)
cleave (kli:w) v. 1. łupać; pękać; rozdwajać; 2. trzymać się
wiernie ; nie odstępować
clef (klef) s. klucz (muzyczny)
cleft (kleft) s. szczelina;
pęknięcie; zob. cleave
clemency ('klemensy) s. miłosierdzie;łagodność (klimatu etc.)

clench (klencz) v. ściskać; zaciskać; zewrzeć się; s. uścisk; zacisnięcie; zagięcie;ubić(targu

clergy ('kle:rdży) s. duchowieństwo ;kler

clergyman ('kle:rdżymen) s. duchowny; ksiądz; pastor

clerical ('klerykel) adj. urzędniczy; duchowny; biurowy

clerk (kla:rk) s. subjekt; urzędnik; pisarz; ekspedient

clever ('klewer) adj. zdolny; sprytny; zręczny;pomysłowy;uprzejmy

click (klyk) v. szczękać; cmokać; trzaskać; dopiąć swego; wygrać; s. trzask; zatrzask; klamka;mlaśniecie;klekot;brzęk

client ('klajent) s. klient

cliff (klyf) s. urwisko; stroma ściana; ściana skalna

climate ('klajmyt) s. klimat

climax ('klajmaeks) s. szczyt; zakończenie; v. stopniować; szczytować; kulminować

climb (klajm) s.wspinaczka; miejsce wspinania; v. piąć się; wspinać; wzbijać się;wdrapać się

climb up (klajm ap) v. wspinać się w górę; wdrapywać się

climber (klajmer) s.taternik; karierowicz; pnący (roślina)

clinch (klyncz) v. zaciskać; zaginać; zanitować;zakończyć

cling: clung; clung (klyng;klang; klang)

cling (klyng)v. trzymać się; chwytać się; czepiać się;trwać

clinic ('klynyk) s. klinika; poradnia; adj. kliniczny

clink (klynk) s. dzwonienie; ciupa ; v. dzwonić (kluczami etc.)

clip 1. (klyp) s. sprzączka v. spinać; 2. s. strzyżenie; nożyce; v. strzyc; orżnąć

clippings ('klypyns) pl . wycinki (z gazet);okrawki;obrzynki

cloak (klouk) s. płaszcz;maska; v. okryć płaszczem;wdziewać

clock (klok) s. zegar ścienny

clockwise ('klokłajz) adj. (obrót) w prawo wg.zegarka

clod (klod) s. gruda; ziemia; gamoń.v.obrzucać grudkami ziemi

clog (klog) s. kłoda; chodak; v. zatykać; zapychać;zawadzać

cloister ('klojster) s. krużganek; klasztor

close (klouz) v. zamykać; zatykać; zakończyć; zwierać; zgodzić się; s. zakończenie; koniec; miejsce ogrodzone; adv. szczelnie; blisko; prawie adj. zamknięty; skąpy; gęsty; bliski; ścisły;ekskluzywny;skąpy

close to ('klous tu) przy;tuż obok

close by ('klous baj) obok

close down ('klouz dałn) v. zamykać;kończyć (działalność etc.)

close in (klouz yn) v. nadchodzić; ogarniać; okrążyć;otoczyć

closet ('klozyt) s. pokoik; klozet; kredens

close-up ('klousap) s. zdjęcie zbliżone; zbliżenie

closing time ('klouzyng,tajm) s. koniec pracy; zamknięcie (sklepu);koniec urzędowania

clot (klot) s. skrzep; v. ścinać się; skrzepnąć;zsiadać się

cloth (klos) s. materiał; szmata; szafa; obrus;sukno;żagiel

cloth-bound (klos baumd) s. oprawny w płótno

clothe (klouz) s. materiał; sukno;v.przywdziewać; zamaskować

clothes (klouz) pl. ubranie; pościel; pranie; odzierz;ubiór

clothes brush ('klouz,brasz) s. szczotka do ubrań

clothes hanger ('klouz,hanger) s. wieszak do ubrań

clothesline ('klous,lajn) s. sznur na bieliznę do suszenia

clothespin ('klouz,pyn) s. spinacz do bielizny

clothing (klouzyng) s. odzież; osłona; bielizna;odzienie

cloud (klaud) s. chmura; obłok; zasępienie; v. chmurzyć; sępić; rzucać cień ;ufarbować

cloudy ('klaudy) adj. chmurny; posępny; zamglony; mętny

clove (klouw) s. goździk; ząbek
czosnku: zob. cleave
clover (klouwer) s. koniczyna
clown (klaun) s. błazen; prostak; v. błaznować; wygłupiać się
club (klab) s. klub; pałka;
kij; v, bić pałką; zbijać; łączyć; zrzeszać;stowarzyszać się
_lue (klu:) s. klucz; ślad;
wątek; v. informować(o wątku)
clumsy ('klamzy) adj. niezgrabny; nietaktowny;niekształtny
clung (klang)v:przywarty; zob.
cling
cluster ('klaster) s. grono;
kiść; pęk; kupka; v. tworzyć
pęki; skupiać się; zbierać się
clutch (klacz) s. chwyt; szpon;
sprzęgło;v.trzymać się kurczowo
clutch pedal ('klacz,pedl) s.
pedał sprzęgła
coach (koucz) s. wóz pasażerski;
trener; v. jechać wozem; trenować; uświadamiać;pouczać
coagulate (kou'aegjulejt) v.
stężać; skrzepnąć;koagulować
coal (koul) s. węgiel
coalfield ('koul'fi:ld) s. zagłębie węglowe
coalition (,koue'lyszyn) s.
związek; koalicja;przymierze
coal mine(koul-majn) s. kopalnia
węgla
coal pit ('koul-pyt) s. kopalnia
węgla ;szyb kopalniany
coarse (ko:rs) adj. pospolity;
gruboziarnisty ; szorstki
coast (koust) s. brzeg; v. jechać bez napędu;płynąć `rzegiem
coastguard ('koustga:rd) s.
straż przybrzeżna
coat (kout) s. marynarka; surdut; powłoka; v. okrywać; pokrywać warstwa ;powlekać(farbą)
coat hanger('kouthaenger) s.
wieszak (do ubrania)
coating (koutyng) s. powłoka;
warstwa ;pokrycie
coat of arms('kout ow,a:rms) s.
herb; godło
coax (kouks) v. namówić pochleb-
stwem; udobruchać;przymilać się;
wycyganiać; wyczrowywać(z butelki)

cob (kob) s. głąb; kucyk; łabędź samiec;kaczan;kutwa;bochenek
cobra ('koubre) s. kobra
cobweb ('kobłeb) s. pajęczyna
cock (kok) s. kogut; kurek;
kran; kutas (vulg.) v. postawić; nastroszyć; napiąć; odwodzić; podnieść; zadzierać;wznieść
cock-and-bull ('koken'bul) exp.:
o żelaznym wilku
cockchafer ('kok,chejfer) s.
chrząszcz
cockle ('kokl) s. kąkol;piecyk
cockpit ('kokpyt) s. kokpit;
kabina;arena do walki kogutów
cockroach('kokroucz) s. karaluch
cocksure ('kokszuer) adj. pewny siebie; zarozumiały
cocktail ('koktejl) s. cocktail
coco ('koukou) s. palma kokoso-
wa; kokos
cocoa ('koukou) s. kakao
coconut ('koukenat) s. orzech
kokosowy
cocoon (ke'ku:n) s. kokon;
oprzęd
cod(kod)s.dorsz;sztokfisz;wąt-
łusz;v.wystrychnąć na dudka
coddle ('kodl) v. podgotować;
pieścić; tuczyć; zepsuć
code (koud) s. kodeks; szyfr;
v. szyfrować ;pisać szyfrem
cod-liver oil ('kod,lywer ojl)
s. tran (lekarski)
coexist ('kouyg'zyst) v. współ-
istnieć ;koegzystować
coexistence ('kouyg'zystens)
s. współistnienie,współżycie
coffee('kofy) s. kawa
coffee bean ('kofy-bi:n) s.
ziarno kawy
coffee mill ('kofy-myl) s. młynek do kawy
coffeepot ('kofy-pot) s. maszynka do kawy
coffin ('kofyn) s. trumna
cogwheel ('kog-hłil) s. koło
zębate; tryb
coherence (kou'hierens) s. sens;
spoistość ;związek logiczny
coherency (kou'hierensy) s.
sens; zwartość ;spójność

coherent (kou'hierent) adj. logiczny; zwarty; spoisty

cohesive (kou'hi:syw) adj. spoisty; zwarty ; kleisty

coiffure (kła:'fjuer) s. fryzura; styl uczesania

coil (kojl) s. zwój; cewka; lok; v. zwijać; skręcać; wić się

coin (koyn) s. moneta; v. bić monety; spieniężać; ukuć (nowe pojęcie) ;tłoczyć

coinage (koynydż) s. bicie monety; monety; system monetarny; wymysł;nowe słowo

coincide (kouyn'sajd) v. zbiegać się; pokrywać się; przystawać do siebie; pasować

coincidence (kou'ynsydens) s. zbieg okoliczności; zgodność; przystawanie; zgodność faktów

coke (kouk) s. koks; kokaina; Coca-Cola; v. koksować

cold (kould) s. zimno; przeziębienie; adj.zimny;chłodny;mrożny

cold storage room(kould-storedżru:m) chłodnia

colic ('kolyk) s. kolka (w brzuchu);ostry ból w brzuchu

collaborate (ke'laeberejt) v. współpracować;kolaborować

collaboration (ke'laeberejszyn) s. współpraca; kolaboracja

collapse (ke'laeps) s. załamanie się; v. załamać się; upaść; opaść; zawalić sie;załamywać

collapsible (ke'laepsebl) adj. składany (mebel,,stół,łóżko etc.)

collar ('koler) s. kołnierz; szyjka; pierścień; obroża; chomąto; piana (na piwie) v.wkładać obrożę; pojmać; ująć

collarbone ('koler-boun) s. obojczyk

colleague ('koli:g) s. kolega (po fachu);współpracownik

collect ('ke'lekt) v. zbierać; odbierać; inkasować

collected (ke'lektyd) adj. skupiony; opanowany ;spokojny

collection (ke'lekszyn) s. zbiór; kolekcja; inkaso ;zainkasowane pieniądze

collective ('ke'lektyw) adj. zbiorowy; wspólny;s. kolektyw

collector ('ke'lektor) s. inkasent; poborca; zbieracz

college ('kolydż) s. uczelnia; kolegium;zrzeszenie;akademia

collide (ke'lajd) v. zderzyć się; kolidować;wejść w kolizję

colliery ('koljery) s. kopalnia węgla

collision (ke'lyżen) s. zderzenie; kolizja

colloquial (ke'loukłjel) adj. potoczny (język);familiarny

colon ('koulen) s. grube jelito; dwukropek

colonel('ke:nl) s. pułkownik

colonial (ke'lounjel) a. kolonialny;s. mieszkaniec kolonii

colonialism (ke'lounjelyzem)s. kolonializm

colonist ('kolenyst) s. osadnik ;mieszkaniec kolonii

colonize ('kolenajz) v. osiedlać; kolonizować

colony ('koleny) s. kolonia

color ('kaler) s. barwa; farba; koloryt; v. barwić; farbować; koloryzować; rumienić się

color bar ('kaler ba:r) s. oddzielenie ras

colored ('kaleret) s. murzyn; kolorowy;adj.przekręcony

colcred man ('kaleret men) s. murzyn

colored people ('kaleret'pi:pl) s. murzyni

colorful ('kalerful) adj. pstry; barwny ;żywy;kolorowy

coloring ('kaleryng) s. koloryt; kolorowanie; rumieńce

colorless ('kalerlys) adj. bezbarwny; nudny;monotonny

colorline ('kalerlajn) s. przedział rasowy

color print ('kaler,prynt) s. chromodruk

colt (koult) s.źrebak

column ('kolem) s. kolumna; stos; trzon; szpalta;formacja

coma ('koume) s. omdlenie; koma; śpiączka;ogon(komety)

comb (koum) s. grzebień; grzbiet
(fali); v. czesać; kłębić się
combat ('kombet) s. walka;
v. zwalczać; walczyć
combatant ('kombetent) adj.
walczący; s. kombatant;bojownik
combination (komby'nejszyn)s.
kombinacja; zespół;związek
combine-harvester (kembajn-
ha:rwyster) s. kombajn
combustible (kem'bastebl) adj.
palny; s. paliwo; materiały
palne;opał;adj;popędliwy
combustion (kem'bastszyn) s.
spalanie; zapłon
come; came; come (kam; kejm;
kam)
come (kam) v. przybyć; pochodzić; wynosić;dziać się;być
come about ('kam,e'baut) v. zdarzyć się;stać się;odwracać się
come across ('kam,e'cros) v.
natknąć się;dać się przekonać
come along ('kam,e'long) v.
pospieszyć się; nadejść
come around ('kam,e'raund) v.
zmienic zdanie; odwiedzić
come at ('kam,et) v. podejść;
dotrzeć; przyjść o (czwartej...)
come by ('kam,baj) v. dojść do
czegoś; minąć; nabyć
come for ('kam,for) v. przyjść
po coś
come loose ('kam,luz) v. ob-
luźniac się
come off ('kam,of) v. odpaść;
odlecieć;puszczać;mieć miejsce
come on ('kam,on) v. chodz-że;
przestań; daj spokój!
come round ('kam,raund) v. zmienić zdanie; przechytrzyć;obejść
come to see ('kam tu si:) v. odwiedzić;przyjść z wizytą
come up to ('kam ap tu) v. podejść do...;wejść na sam(szczyt)
come-and-go ('kam-en'-go) s.
bieganina;ruch tam i z powrotem
comeback ('kam-'baek) s. powrót ; bystra odpowiedź;poprawa
comedian (ke'mi:djen) s. komik;

comedy('komydy) s.komedia

comer ('kamer) s. przybysz
comet ('komyt) s. kometa
comfort ('kamfert) s. wygoda;
pociecha; v. pocieszać; czynić wygodnym;dodawać otuchy
comfortable ('kamfertebl) adj.
wygodny; zadowolony;spokojny
comforter ('kamferter) s. po-
cieszyciel; kołdra;smoczek
comical ('komykel) adj. zabawny; śmieszny;komiczny
comic strips ('komyk,stryps) s.
seryjne obrazkówki;kreskówki
comma ('kome) s. przecinek
command (ke'maend) v. rozkazy-
wać; kazać; rozporządzać; panować nad; dowodzić; s. rozkaz;
nakaz; komenda;dowództwo
commander (ke'maender) s. dowódca; komendant;kapitan(fregaty)
commander-in-chief (ke'maender
yn'czi:f) głównodowodzący
commandment (ke'maendment) s.
przykazanie (boskie)
commend (ke'mend) v. chwalić;
zalecać; polecać opiece
comment ('koment) s. objaśnie-
nie; v. robić uwagi krytyczne
lub złośliwe;wypowiadać zdanie
comment on('koment on) v. ko-
mentować; oceniać (utwór etc.)
commentary ('komentery) s. komentarz;uwaga; notatka
commentator('komentejter) s.
komentator; sprawozdawca
commerce ('kome:rs) s. handel
commercial (ke'ke:rszel) adj.
handlowy;s.ogołoszenie(w radiu...)
commissar (,komy'sa:r) s. komisarz w ZSRR
commission (ke'myszyn) s. zlecenie; misja; urząd; v. delegować; powierzać; objąć; zlecać;zamianować;upoważniać
commissioner (ke'myszener) s.
delegat; pełnomocnik; komisarz
rządowy;członek komisji rządowej
commit (ke'myt) v. powierzać;
przekazywać; odsyłać; popełniać; wciągać; zobowiazywać
się;oddawać w opiekę;zamykć w
(domu wariatów);obiecywać

commitment (ke'mytment) s. zobowiązanie; dopuszczenie się;
przekazanie;zaangażowanie się
committee (ke'mytiż) s. komitet;
komisja;opiekuń(umysłowo chrego)
commodity (ke'modyty) s. towar;
rzecz przydatna;artykuł handlu
common ('komen) adj. wspólny;
publiczny; ogólny; pospolity;
zwyczajny;prosty;publiczny
commoner ('komener) s. człowiek
z gminu; nie szlachcic
common law marriage ('komen,lo:
'maerydż) pożycie na wiarę
common market ('komen'ma:rkyt)
wspólny rynek (Zach.Eur.)
commonplace ('komen-plejs) s.
banał; adj. banalny;oklepany
common sense ('komen,sens)
zdrowy rozsądek
commonwealth ('komen,łels) s.
wspólnota; rzeczpospolita
commotion (ke'mouszyn) s. zamieszki; tumult; poruszenie
commune ('komju:n) s. gmina;
komuna; v. obcować; rozmawiać
communicate (ke'mju:ny,kejt) v.
dzielić się; komunikować; łączyć się;przenosić (ciepło etc.)
communication (ke,mju:ny'kejszyn)
s. łączność; komunikacja; po-
rozumiewanie się;zakomunikowanie
communicative (ke'mju:nykejtyw)
adj. otwarty; rozmowny; towarzyski; przystepny
communion (ke'mju:njen) s. obcowanie; uczestnictwo; wspólnota; komunia;wyznanie wiary
communism ('komju,nyzem) s. komunizm;ruch komunistyczny
communist ('komjunyst) s. komunista;adj. komunistyczny
community (ke'mju:nyty) s. środowisko; społeczność; gmina;
kolektyw; wspólnota ;koło;zakon
commute (ke'mju:t) v. zamieniać;
zastępować; łagodzić; dojeżdżać
do pracy;brać bilet okresowy
comose ('koumous) adj. włochaty;
puszysty ;włóknisty
compact (kem'paekt) adj. gęsty;
zbity; zwarty; v. ubijać; zbijać; zagęszczać ;s.puderniczka

compact ('kempaekt) s. 1. ugoda;
porozumienie; 2. puderniczka
samochód średniej wielkości(USA)
companion (kem'paenjen) s. towarzysz; (coś) do pary
companionship (kem'paenjenszyp)
s. koleżeństwo; towarzystwo
company ('kampeny) s. towarzystwo; załoga; goście; partnerzy;
spółka; kompania ;trupa teatralna
comparable ('komperebl) adj.
porównywalny ;wytrzymujący porów-nanie
comparative (kem'paeretyw) adj.
porównawczy; względny; stosunkowy ;s. stopień wyższy(przymiot-nika
compare (kem'peer) v. porówny-
wać; dawać się porównać; stopniować (gram)
comparison (kem'paeryson) s. porównanie ;zestawienie
compartment (kem'pa:rtment) s.
przedział; przegroda; komora
wodoszczelna
compass ('kampes) s. kompas;
busola; obwód; obręb;cyrkiel
zasięg v. obchodzić; otaczać;
ogarniać;osiągać ;dopiąć
compassion (kem'paeszyn) s;
litość ; współczucie
compassionate (kem'paeszynyt)
adj. litościwy ;v.litować się
compatible (kem'paetebl) adj.
zgodny ;licujący; do pogodzenia
compatriot (kem'paetryet) s.
rodak; ziomek ;rodaczka
compel (kem'pel) v. zmuszać;
wymuszać (coś) ;wzbudzać
compensate ('kompen,sejt) v.
wyrównywać; nagradzać; wypłacić
odszkodowanie; kompensować
compensation (,kompen'sejszyn)
s. rekompensata; wynagrodzenie;
odszkodowanie ;wyrównanie
compete (kem'pi:t) v. konkuro-
wać; rywalizować; ubiegać się
compete for (kem'pi:t,fo:r) v.
(o coś) współzawodniczyć;
współubiegać się ;prześcigać się
competence (kem'kompytens) s. fa-
chowość; kwalifikacja; uzdolnienie; zasobność; dobrobyt
competent (kem'kompytent) adj. właściwy;kwalifikowany;odpowiedni;
kompetentny

competition (,kompy'tyszyn) s.
konkurencja; konkurs; zawody;
współzawodnictwo;tuniej
competitor (kem'petyter) s.
rywal; konkurent; współzawodnik;współzawodniczka;rywalka
compile (kem'pajl) v. zbierać;
zestawiać; kompilować
complacent (kem'plejsnt) adj.
zadowolony (z siebie; ze świata);błogi
complain (kem'plejn) v. żalić
się; narzekać; skarżyć; wnosić
zażalenie;wnosić skargę
complaint (kem'plejnt) s. skarga; zażalenie; dolegliwość
complete (kem'pli:t) adj. całkowity; zupełny; kompletny;
v. uzupełniać; udoskonalić;
ukończyć;wypełniać (formularz)
completion (kem'pli:szyn) s.
ukończenie; uzupełnienie;
udoskonalenie;spełnienie(woli)
complexion (kem'plekszyn) s.ce-
ra; płeć; postać; aspekt (charakter);wygląd
complicate ('komply,kejt) v.
wikłać; splatać; komplikować
compliment ('komplyment) s.
komplement; gratulacje; ukło-
ny; uszanowanie; v. mówić
komplementy; gratulować
comply (kem'plaj) v. zastosować
się; spełnić; podporządkować
się;uczynić zadość;przestrzegać
comply with (kem'plaj,łyß) v.
spełniać;przestrzegać czegoś
component (kem'pounent) s.
składnik; część składowa; siła
składowa;adj.składowy
compose (kem'pouz) v. składać;
układać; tworzyć; komponować;
skupiać (myśli); uspokoić; załagodzić;uspokajać się
composed (kem'pouzd) adj. opanowany; spokojny;stateczny
composer (kem'pouzer) s. kompozytor;kompozytorka
composition (,kempe'zyszyn) s.
skład; układ; ugoda; wypracowanie; budowa;usposobienie
composure (kem'pouźer) s. spokój; opanowanie;zimna krew

compote ('kompout) s. kompot
(z puszki);kompotiera
compound (kom'paund) adj. złożony; sprężony; s. związek(chem.)
mieszanka; złożenie; v. mieszać; składać; powiększać;
łączyć;zawrzeć;załatwić
comprehend (,kompry'hend) v.
pojmować; rozumieć; zawierać
comprehensible (,kompry'hensebl)
adj. zrozumiały;pojętny
comprehensive (,kompry'hensyw)
adj. obszerny; szeroki;rozumo-
wy; wyczerpujący;ogólny;wszech-
stronny
compress (kem'pres) v. ściskać;
s. kompres; okład;v.streszczać
comprise (kem'prajz) v. włączać; obejmować;składać się
compromise ('kompre,majz) s.
kompromis; ugoda; kompromitacja; narażenie; v. załatwiać
ugodowo; kompromitować
compulsion (kem'palszyn) s.
przymus; siła przymusu
compulsory (kem'palsery) adj.
przymusowy;przymuszający
compunction (kem'pankszyn) s.
skrucha;żal za grzechy
computation (,kompju'tejszyn) s,
obliczenie; kalkulcja
computer (kem'pju:ter) s. kalku-
lator; komputer; przelicznik
comrade ('komread) s. kolega;
druh; współpracownik
comradeship ('komraedszyp) s.
koleżeństwo; braterstwo
conceal (ken'si:l) v. taić;
ukrywać;przemilczać;zataić
concede (ken'si:d) v. przyznawać; ustępować; poddawać się
conceit (ken'si:t) s. próżność;
zarozumiałość;mniemanie;koncept
conceited (ken'si:tyd) adj.
próżny; zarozumiały
conceivable (ken'si:webl) adj.
wyobrażalny; zrozumiały
conceive (ken'si:w) v. wymyślić;
wyobrażać; rozumieć; ujmować;
zajść w ciążę;pojać;redagować
concentrate ('konsentrejt) v.
skupiać się; stężać;s.roztwór
conception (ken'sepszyn) s. pomysł; poczęcie (dziecka);początek

concern (ken'se:rn) s. interes;
troska; związek; v. tyczyc się;
dotyczyc; obchodzic; niepokoic
się o...;wchodzić w grę
concerned (ken'se:rnd) adj. zainteresowany; zaaferowany;
strapiony; niespokojny
concert ('konsert) s. koncert;
porozumienie; v. ułożyc; ukar-
towac;porozumieć się
concession (ken'se, szyn) s.
koncesja; ustępstwo;przyzwolenie
conciliate (ken'syly,ejt) v.
zjednywac; jednac; godzic; łagodzić; pogodzić;udobruchać
conciliatory (ken'syljeto:ry)
adj. pojednawczy
concise (ken'sajs) adj. zwięzły;
treściwy ;krotki i węzłowaty,
conclude (ken'klu:d) v. zakoń-
czyc; zawierac; wnioskować;
postanawiać ;kończyć się
conclusion (ken'klu:żyn) s. zakończenie; wynik; postanowienie; wniosek; konkluzja; zawar-
cie układu ;wynik ostateczny
conclusive (ken'klu:syw) adj.
rozstrzygający; dowodny
concord ('konko:rd) s. zgoda;
jedność; harmonia;v. zgadzać się
concrete ('konkri:t) s. beton;
konkret; adj. rzeczywisty;
realny; zwarty; stały; konkretny; specyficzny; betonowy
concur (ken'ke:r) v. zgadzać
sie; schodzic się;wspołdziałać
concurrence (ken'ke:rens) s.
zgodność; zbieżność ; zgoda
concussion (ken'kaszyn) s.
wstrząs (mozgu); uderzenie
condemn (ken'dem) v. potępiac;
skazywac ;krytykować ;wybrakować
condemnation (,kendem'nejszyn)
s. potępienie; skazanie
condense (ken'dens) v. kondenso-
wac; zgęszczać;streszczać
condenser (ken'denser) s. kondensator; skraplacz
condescend (,kondy'send) v.
zniżac się; raczyc; zezwalac;
zachowywać się z wyższością

condition (ken'dyszyn) s. stan;
warunek; zastrzeżenie; poprawka; v.uwarunkowywac; zastrzegac; naprawiac; przygotowy-
wac; przyzwyczajac;klimatyzować
conditional (ken'dyszynl) adj.
warunkowy;uzależniony;zależny
condole (ken'doul) v. składac
kondolencje;wspołczuć;ubolewać
condolence (ken'doulens) s.
wyrazy wspołczucia;kondolencje
conduct (kon'dakt) s. prowadzenie; sprawowanie; prowadzenie
się; sprawowanie się; kierownictwo; v. prowadzic; wiesc;
przewodzic;dyrygować;dowodzić
conduction (kon'dakszyn) s.
przewodzenie (fiz.)
conductor (kon'dakter) s. kierownik; przewodnik; dyrygent;
przewód;odgromnik;piorunochron
cone (koun) s. stożek; szyszka;
v. nadawać kształt stożka
confection (ken'fekszyn) s.
sporządzanie; konfitura; słodycze; konfekcja (damska)
confectioner (ken'fekszyner) s.
cukiernik;właściciel cukierni
confectionery (ken'feksznery)
s. cukiernia; wyroby cukier-
nicze
confederacy (ken'federesy) s.
konfederacja; sojusz; związek; spisek; sprzysiężenie
confederate (ken'federyt) adj.
sprzysiężony; v. jednoczyc;
spiskować; knuć;sprzymierzac
confederation (ken,fede'rejszyn)
s. sprzymierzenie; skonfedero-
wanie; konfederacja
confer (ken'fe:r) v. naradzac
się; nadawac ;przyznawać
conferee (,konfe'ri:) s. uczestnik konferencji; nagrodzony
conference ('konferens) s. narada; liga;zebranie;zjazd
confess (ken'fes) v. wyznac;
przyznać się; spowiadać się
confession (ken'feszen) s. wyznanie; spowiedź; przyznanie
się ; religia

confessor (ken'feser) s. spowiednik; ksiądz spowiednik
confide (ken'fajd) s. ufać (komuś); zwierzać sie; powierzać
confidence ('konfydens) s. zaufanie; bezczelność; pewność;
ufność; zwierzenie;śmiałość
confident ('konfydent) adj.
dufny; bezczelny ;przekonany
confidential (,konfy'denczel)
adj. tajny; poufny; zaufany;
poufały;intymny
confine ('konfajn) v. ograniczać; odosabniać;s.kres;granica
confinement (kon'fajnment) s.
uwięzienie; ograniczenie; odosobnienie; połóg; poród
confirm (ken'fe:rm) v. potwierdzać; zatwierdzać; umacniać;
bierzmować;utwierdzać;pokrzepić
confirmation (,konfer'mejszyn)
s. potwierdzenie; zatwierdzenie; bierzmowanie;pokrzepienie
confiscate ('konfyskejt) v. kon-
fiskować; skonfiskować
conflagration (,konfle'grejszyn)
s. pożar; pożoga
conflict ('konflykt) s. zatarg;
starcie; konflikt; kolizja
conform (kon'fo:rm) v. dostosować; upodabniać;dostrajać
conformity (kon'fo:rmyty) s.
zgodność; dostosowanie się
confound (kon'faund) v. mieszać;
zawieść; pokrzyżować;poplątać
confound it ! (kon'faund,yt) exp.
do licha ! niech to diabli wezmą!
confront (ken'frant) v. stawiać
czoło; konfrontować;unaocznić
confuse (ken'fju:z) v. zmieszać
(kogoś; siebie);wikłać;gmatwać
confusion (ken'fju:żyn) s. nieład; zamieszanie;bałagan;chaos
congeal (ken'dźi:l) v. mrozić;
ścinać; marznąć;zakrzepnąć
congestion (ken'dżestczyn)s.
przeludnienie; przeciążenie
(ruchu); przekrwienie
conglomerate (ken'glomerejt) v.
skupiać; zlewać w jedną masę
congratulate (ken'graetju,lejt)
v. gratulować ;składać(komuś)
gratulacje;pogratulować

congratulation (ken,graetju'-
lejszyn) s. gratulacje; gra-
tulowanie; gratulacja
congregate ('kongry,gejt) adj.
zbiorowy; v. skupiać; zbierać
(się); gromadzić (się)
congregation (,kongry'gejszyn)
s. zbieranie; zgromadzenie
congress ('kongres) s. zjazd;
zebranie; parlament USA
conjecture (ken'dżekczer) s.
domysł; przypuszczenie;
v. przypuszczać; mniemać
conjugal ('kondżugel) adj.
małżeński
conjugate ('kondżu,gejt) v.
odmieniać się; kopulować;
parzyc się;adj.połączony
conjugation (,kondżu'gejszyn)
s. koniugacja; zespalanie się;
kopulacja;odmiana czasownika
conjunction (ken'dżankszyn) s.
zbieg; związek; skojarzenie;
spójnik; połączenie
conjunctive mood (ken'dżanktyw,
mu:d) s. tryb łączący
conjure (kan'dżuer) v. zaklinać; błagać;robić sztuczki
conjure ('kandżer) v. czarować
conjurer ('kandżerer) s. czarownik; magik;kuglarz
connect (ke'nekt) v. łączyć;
wiązać;mieć połączenie
connected (ke'nektyd) a. zwarty (logiczny); ustosunkowany
connection(xion) (ke'nekszyn)
s. połączenie; pokrewieństwo
conquer ('konker) v. zdobyć;
zwyciężyć; pokonać
conqueror ('konkerer) s. zdobywca; zwyciezca
conquest ('konkłest) s. podbój; zdobycie;zawojowanie
conscience ('konszyns) s. sumienie;świadomość zła i dobra
conscientious (,konszy'enszes)
adj. sumienny;skrupulatny
conscious ('konszes) adj. przytomny; świadomy;naumyślny
consciousness ('konszesnys) s.
świadomość;całość mysli i uczuć
conscript ('konskrypt) s.& adj.
poborowy ;s.rekrut;v.rekwirować;
brać do wojska

consecrate ('konsy,krejt) v.
poświęcać;adj.poświęcony
consecutive (ken'sekjutyw)
adj. kolejny;nieprzerwany;skut-
consent (ken'sent) s. zgoda;kowy
v. zgadzać się;przyzwalać
consequence ('konsykļens) s.wy-
nik; znaczenie; konsekwencja
consequently ('konsykļently)
adv. a zatem; przeto; tym samym;w skutek tego; więc
conservative (ken'se:rwatyw)
adj. ostrożny; zachowawczy;
konserwatywny; s. konserwatys-
ta; środek konserwujący
conserve (ken'se:rw) v. konserwować; zachowywać; zabezpieczać; s. konserwa owocowa
consider (ken'syder) v. rozważać; rozpatrywać; uważać; szanować; mieć wzgląd;sądzić
considerable (ken'syderebl)
adj. znaczny;adv.znacznie
considerate (ken'syderyt) adj.
myślacy; uważający; troskliwy
consideration (ken,syde'rejszyn)
s. wzgląd; rozważanie; warunek;
uprzejmość; rekompensata
consign (ken'sajn) v. przekazać;
powierzać;złożyć do(banku,grobu..)
consignment(ken'sajnment) s.
przesyłka ; powierzenie
consist (ken'syst) v. składać
się; polegać;zgadzać się
consistency (ken'systensy) s.
konsystencja; solidność; stałość; zgodność;logiczność
consistent (ken'systent) adj.
zgodny; stały; konsekwentny
consolation (,konse'lejszyn) s.
pocieszenie; pociecha;ukojenie
console (ken'soul) v. pocieszać;
s. konsola; wspornik;podpora
consolidate (ken'solydejt) v.
utwierdzać; scalać; jednoczyć
consonant ('konsenent) s. spółgłoska; adj. spółgłoskowy;
zgodny; harmonijny
conspicuous ('ken'spykjues) adj.
widoczny; zwracający uwagę
conspiracy (ken'spyresy) s. spisek; konspiracja; zmowa; umowa

conspirator (ken'spyreter) s.
spiskowiec; konspirator
conspire (ken'spajer) v. konspirować;spiskować;uknuć
constable ('kanstebl) s. policjant; posterunkowy
constant ('konstent) adj. stały; trwały;s. liczba stała
consternation (,konste:rnejszyn)
s. przerażenie;osłupienie
constipation (,konsty'pejszyn)
s. zatwardzenie; zaparcie
constituency (ken'stytjuensy)
s. okręg wyborczy; wyborcy
constituent (ken'stytjuent)
adj.,składowy; s. wyborca;
część składowa; element
constitute ('konsty,tju:t) v.
stanowić; ustanawiać; wyznaczać
constitution (,konsty'tju:szyn)
s. statut; konstytucja; struktura; założenie;układ psychiczny
constitutional (,konsty'tu:szenl)
adj. zasadniczy; istotny; zdrowotny;s.przechadzka dla zdrowia
constrain (ken'strejn) v. wymuszać; zmuszać; ograniczać;
więzić; zniewalać;przymuszać
constraint (ken'strejnt) s.
przymus; skrępowanie; ograniczenie swobody(ruchów etc.)
construct (ken'strakt) v. budować; tworzyć; rysować(figury geom.)
construction (ken'strakszyn)
s. budowa; konstrukcja;układ;
konstruowanie;ujęcie;interpretacja
constructive (ken'straktyw)
adj. twórczy; konstruktywny
consul ('konsel) s. konsul
consular ('konsjuler) adj.
konsularny
consulate ('konsjulyt) s. konsulat;uprawnienia konsula
consulate general ('konsjulyt'
'dżenerel) s. konsulat generalny
consult (ken'salt) v. radzić
się; informować się
consultation (,konsel'tejszyn)
s. porada; konsultacja
consultative (ken'saltetyw) a.
doradczy; konsultatywny

consume (ken'sju:m) v, spożyw-
wać; zużywać; trawić; niszczeć; marnieć;uschnąć
consumer (ken'sju:mer) s. kon-
sumer; spożywca;odbiorca
consummate(ken'samyt) a. doskonały;wielkiej miary;skończony
consummate('kensemejt) v. spełniać małżeństwo
consumption (ken'sampszyn) s.
zużycie; suchoty; pylica
contact ('kontaekt) s. styczność; stosunki; znajomości
v. kontaktować; porozumiewać
się;stykać się;zetknąć się
contact lenses ('kontaekt,lenzys)
pl. szkła kontaktowe
contagious (ken'tejdżes) a. zaraźliwy ; zakaźny;udzielający się
contain (ken'tejn) v. zawierać;
opanowywać się; wiązać;hamować
się
container (ken'tejner) s. zasób-
nik; zbiornik; naczynie
contaminate (ken'taemynejt) v.
zakazić;skalać;deprawować
contamination (ken'taemynejszyn)
s. kontaminacja; zakażenie; ska-
żenie; ujemny wpływ
contemplate ('kontemplejt) v.
oglądać; rozważać; liczyć się
z (czyms) ; medytować;planować
contemplation ('kontemplejszyn)
s. oglądanie; kontemplacja;
rozważanie;planowanie;medytacja
contemplative ('kontemplejtyw)
adj. kontemplacyjny; zamyślony
contemporary (ken'temperery)
adj.& s. współczesny (rówiesnik)
contempt (ken'temt) s. pogarda;
lekceważenie;obraza (sądu etc.)
contemptible (ken'temtebl) adj.
godny pogardy, lekceważenia
contemptuous (ken'temtjues) adj.
pogardliwy;nadęty;lekceważący
contend (ken'tend) v. spierać
się; walczyć;rywalizować;upierać
się
content 1. (ken'tent) adj. zadowolony; s. zadowolenie; v. zadowalać
content 2. ('kontent) s. zawartość; tresć; objętość; pojemność;powierzchnia;kubatura;istota

contented (ken'tentyd) adj. zadowolony; zaspokojony
contents ('kontents) s. zawar-
tosć(pojemnika,treści
contest ('kontest) s. rywalizacja; spór; v. walczyć; spierać się; ubiegać; kwestionować
context ('kontekst) s. kontekst
continent ('kontynent) s. kontynent; część świata
continental ('kontynentl) adj.
kontynentalny; s. mieszkaniec
kontynentu
continual (ken'tynjuel) adj.
ciągły; powtarzający się;stały
continuance (ken'tynjuens) s.
ciągłosć; trwanie; przebieg;
ciąg dalszy;odroczenie;pobyt
continuation (ken,tynju'ejszyn)
s. kontynuacja; ciąg dalszy
continue (ken'tynju:) v. kontynuować;ciągnac dalej; trwać;
ciągnąć się;odroczyć;upierać
continuous (ken'tynjues) adj.się
nieprzerwany;stały;ciągły
contort (ken'to:rt) v. skręcać;
wykrzywiać;zwichnąć;przekrzywić
contour ('kontuer) s. zarys;
kontur,warstwica;v.konturować
contraceptive (,kontre'septyw)
s. środek zapobiegający za-
płodnieniu ;adj.antykoncepcyjny
contract ('kontraekt) s. umowa;
układ; kontract ;obietnicą
contract (ken'traekt) v. ściągać; kurczyć; zobowiązywać
contractor (ken'traekter) s.
przedsiębiorca (budowlany etc.)
contradict (,kontre'dykt) v.
zaprzeczać ;posprzeczać się
contradiction (,kontre'dykszyn)
s. sprzeczność ;zaprzeczenie
contradictory (,kontre'dyktery)
adj. sprzeczny,przekorny;kłótliwy
contrary ('kontrery) adj. przeciwny; s. przeciwieństwo;
adv. w przeciwieństwie
contrariwise ('kontrery,łajz)
adv. odwrotnie; natomiast
contrast (ken'traest) v.prze-
ciwstawiać; kontrastować;
s.kontrast; przeciwieństwo

contribute (ken'trybjut) v.
przyczynić się; dostarczyć;
współdziałać;zasłużyć się
contribution (,kontry'bju:szyn)
s. przyczynek; wkład; ofiara;
kontrybucja;datek;wsparcie
contributor (ken'trybjuter) s.
ofiarodawca; współpracownik
(pisarz);współpracowniczka
contrite (ken'trajt) adj. skruszony ;pełen skruchy
contrivance (ken'trajwens) s.
pomysł; sztuczka; fortel; wynalazek;wynalazczość;pomysłowość
contrive (ken'trajw) v. wymyslić; wynaleźć; doprowadzić do
czegoś; zaplanować;wykombinować
control (ken'troul) v. sprawdzać; rządzić; kontrolować;
opanować; s. kontrola; sterowanie; regulowanie; ster;władza
controller (ken'trouler) s.
kontroler;regulator;zarządca
controversial (,kentre'we:rżel)
adj. sporny; sprzeczający się
controversy ('kontre,we:rsy)
s. spór;kłótnia;polemika;dysputa
contuse (ken'tju:z) v. stłuc;
kontuzjować
convalesce (,konwe'les) v. wyzdrowieć i odzyskać siły
convalescence (,konwe'lesens)
s. wyzdrowienie
convalescent (,konwe'lesnt) s.
rekonwalescent; ozdrowieniec
convenience (ken'wi:njens) s.
wygoda; korzyść;dogodność
convenient (ken'wi:njent) adj.
wygodny;łatwy do osiągnięcia
convent ('konwent) s. zakon
convention (ken'wenszyn) s.
zjazd; zgromadzenie; układ;
umowa; konwent;zebranie
conventional (ken'wenszynl)
adj. zwyczajowy; konwencjonal-
ny; umowny;powszechnie stosowany
conversation (,konwer'sejszyn)
s. rozmowa; konwersacja
converse (ken'we:rs) v. rozmawiać;obcować;prowadzić rozmowę
converse ('konwe:rs) s. rozmowa;
adj. odwrotny; s.rzecz odwrotna

conversion (ken'we:rżyn) s.od-
wrócenie; przemiana; nawrócenie;przeistoczenie
convert (ken'we:rt) v. zmieniać; nawracać; przekształcać;
odwracać;przemieniać;przystosować
convert ('konwert) s. neofita
convertible (ken'we:rtybl) adj.
wymienialny; s. otwarty samochód z podnoszonym dachem
convey (ken'wej) v. przewozić;
przenosić; przesyłać; przekazywać; komunikować;zapisywać
conveyance (ken'wejens) s. przewóz; przenoszenie; uzmysławia-
nie; pojazd; przekazanie
conveyor belt (ken'wejer,belt)
s. przenośnik taśmowy
convict ('konwykt) s. skazaniec;
więzień; v. udowadniać; przekonywać; uznać winnym
conviction (ken'wykszyn) s.
przeświadczenie; przekonanie;
zasądzenie;skazanie
convince (ken'wyns) v. przekonać;przekonywać
convoy ('konwoj) s. konwój;
eskorta; straż
convoy (kon'woj) v. konwojować
convulsion (ken'walszyn) s.
drgawki; wstrząs; konwulsje
convulsive (ken'walsyw) adj.
konwulsyjny;niepohamowany
cook (kuk) s. kucharz; kucharka; v. gotować; preparować
cooking (kukyng) s. gotowanie
cool (ku:l) adj. chłodny;
oziębły; spokojny; v. chłodzić;
studzić; ochłonąć; s. chłód
cooler ('ku:ler) s. chłodnica;
element chłodzący;więzienie
coolness ('ku:lnys) s. chłód;
zimna krew;opanowanie;spokój
co-op (kou'op) s. spółdzielnia
cooperate (kou'operejt) v.
współpracować; współdziałać
cooperation (kou,ope'rejszyn)
s. współpraca; współdziałanie
kooperacja; spółdzielczość
cooperative (kou,ope'rejtyw)
adj. spółdzielczy; uspołecznio-
ny; uczynny; współpracujący

cooperator (kou'ope,rejter) s. współpracownik; współdzielca

coordinate (kou'o:rdynejt) adj. współrzędny; współrzędna

cop (kop) s. policjant (slang) v. złapać; wygrać; buchnąć; nakryć ;porwać; ukraść(slang)

coPartner (kou'pa:rtner) s. uczestnik; wspólnik; udziałowiec(we wspólnym interesie)

cope ('koup) v. uporać; dawać sobie radę; pokrywać; zwieńczać; s. kapa;peleryna(duża)

copilot ('kou'pajlot) s. kopilot;zastępca pilota

copious ('koupjes) adj. obfity; suty; bogaty;płodny;obfitujący

copper ('koper) s. miedź; v.miedziować; slang: glina; policjant;miedziak;kocioł z miedzi

copy ('kopv) v. kopiować; przepisywać; naśladować; s. kopia; odpis; odbitka; egzemplarz; wzór; model;rękopis do druku

copybook ('kopy,buk) s. zeszyt

copyright ('kopy,rajt) s. prawo autorskie.v.chronić prawem autorskim

coral ('korel) s. koral

cord (ko:rd) s. sznur; lina; v. wiązać; ustawiać w sągi

cordial ('ko:rdżel) adj. serdeczny; nasercowy;s.lek nasercowy

cordiality (,ko:rdy'aelyty) s. serdeczność; kordialność

corduroys ('ko:rde,rojz) pl. sztruksowe spodnie

core (ko:r) s. rdzeń v. usuwać rdzeń; wycinać rdzeń

cork (ko:rk) s, korek;v.korkować

corkscrew ('ko:rk,skru:) s. korkociąg;adj.w kształcie korkociąga

corn (ko:rn) s. 1. ziarno; zboże; kukurydza; 2. nagniotek

corner ('ko:rner) s. róg; narożnik; kąt; zakręt; zapędzać do kąta; zmuszać; monopolizować

cornered ('ko:rnerd) adj. rogaty; schwytany;zapędzony w ślepą ulicę

cornet ('ko:rnyt) s. kornet; trąbka (mosiężna)

cornflakes ('ko:rn,flejks) pl. płatki z kukurydzy

coronary disease('korenery dy 'zi:z)s.choroba wieńcowa[nacja

coronation(,kore'nejszyn)s.koronation(,kore'nejszyn)s.koro-

coroner('korener)s. sędzia śledczy, lekarz sądowy(oględziny zwłok)

corporal ('ko:rperel) adj. cielesny; osobisty; s. kapral

corporation (,ko:rpe'rejszyn) s. korporacja; zrzeszenie; osoba prawna zbiorowa

corpse (ko:rps) s. trup;zwłoki

corpulent ('ko:rpjulent) adj. tęgi; otyły; gruby;tłusty

corral (ke'rael) s. ogrodzenie dla bydła; tabór; v. zamykać w ogrodzeniu; łapać; ustawiać tabor;wpędzać do ogrodzenia

correct (ke'rekt) adj, poprawny; v. korygować; karcić; prostować;leczyć;naprawiać

correction (ke'rekszyn) s. poprawka; korektura ;kara

correspond (,korys'pond) v. odpowiadać; korespondować

correspondence (,korys'pondens) s. zgodność; korespondencja

correspondent (,korys'pondent) s. korespondent; adj. odpowiedni; zgodny z; odpowiadający

corridor ('korydo:r) s. korytarz

corrigible ('korydżybl) adj. dający się poprawić;uległy

corroborate (ke'robe,rejt) v. potwierdzić ;potwierdzać

corrode (ke'roud) v. zżerać; rdzewieć; niszczeć; niszczyć

corrosion (ke'roużyn) s. korozja; zżeranie; niszczenie

corrugate ('korugejt) v. marszczyć; fałdować;karbować

corrugated iron('korugejtyd 'ajron) s. pofałdowana blacha

corrupt (ke'rapt) adj. zepsuty; sprzedajny;v.korumpować;psuć się

corruption (ke'rapszyn) s. zepsucie; korupcja;rozkład;fałszowanie

corset (ko'rsyt) s. gorset; sznurówka;v.wkładać gorset

cosmetic (koz'metyk) s. kosmetyk; adj. kosmetyczny

cosmetician (koz'metyszyn) s. kosmetyczka

cosmonaut ('kozme,no:t) s. kos-
monauta ;astronauta (w USA)
cost; cost; cost (kost; kost;
kost)
cost (kost) v. kosztować;
s. koszt; strata; cena
costly ('kostly) adj. kosztowny; wspaniały;drogi;cenny
costume ('kostju:m) s. kostium;
strój; v. przystroić w kostium
cosy ('kouzy) adj. przytulny;
v. przytulić się
cot (kot) s. łóżko składane;
szałas; schronienie
cottage ('kotydż) s. chata; dworek;domek letniskowy
cottage cheese ('kotydż, czi:z)
s. biały ser krowi z kwaśnego mle-
cotton ('kotn) s. bawełna; v.po-
lubić; kapować;adj.bawełniany
cotton wool ('kotn,łul) s. wata
couch (kaucz) s. tapczan; posłanie; łóżko;v.rozsiadać się;mo-
cougar ('ku:ger) s. puma; kuguar
cough (kof) s. kaszel; v. kaszleć ; wykaszleć;,zakaszleć
could (kud) v. mogłby; zob.:cań;
council ('kaunsyl) s. rada; konsylium; sobór;zarząd (miejski etc.)
councilor ('kaunsyler) s. radny;
radca; członek zarządu
counsel ('kaunsel) s. rada; zamysł; radca prawny; v. radzić;
doradzać; przyjmować radę
count (kaunt) v. liczyć; sądzić;
liczyć się; znaczyć; s. rachuba;
liczenie; suma; zarzut; hrabia
countdown (kaunt-dałn) s. liczenie do startu (rakiety)
count in (kaunt yn) v. brać w rachubę; wliczać; włączyć
count out (kaunt aut) v. wyli-
czyć; nie brać w rachubę
countenance ('kauntynens) s. mina; wyraz twarzy; śmiałość;
pewność siebie; animusz; fantazja; v. zachęcać; popierać;
zatwierdzać;usankcjonować
counter ('kaunter) s. 1. kantor;
lada; licznik; żeton; 2. przeciwieństwo; cios odbijający;
napiętek; adj. przeciwny; prze-

ciwległy; podwójny; v. sprzeciwiać się; reagować; uderzać;
adv. przeciwnie; na przekór;
wbrew (instrukcjom,poleceniom...)
counteract (,kaunter'aekt) v.
przeciwdziałać;neutralizować
counterbalance ('kaunter,-
,baelens) s. przeciwwaga
counterespionage ('kaunter'-
'espje,na:ż) s. kontrwywiad
counterfeit ('kaunterfyt) adj.
fałszywy; podrobiony;v.udawać;
counterintelligence fałszować
('kaunteryn'tylydżens) s.
kontrwywiad
counterpart ('kaunter,pa:rt)
s. odpowiednik; duplikat
countess ('kauntys) s. hrabina; hrabianka
countless ('kauntlys) adj. niezliczony; nie do zliczenia
country ('kantry) s. kraj;
ojczyzna; wieś; prowincja
country house ('kantry-'haus)
s. dom wiejski;dom na wsi
countryman ('kantrymen) s.
rodak; wieśniak;człowiek ze wsi
countryside ('kantry,sajd) s.
okolica; krajobraz;ludzie ze wsi
country town ('kantry,tałn)
s. miasteczko; duża wieś
county ('kaunty) s. powiat;
hrabstwo ;adj.powiatowy
couple ('kapl) s. para; v. łączyć; parzyć się; żenić
coupling ('kaplyng) s. złącze;
skojarzenie; sprzęgło
coupon ('ku:pon) s. odcinek;
kupon wymienny(w sklepie,banku...)
courage ('karydż) s. odwaga
courageous (ke'rejdżes) adj.
odważny; śmiały;dzielny;waleczny
courier ('kurjer) s, posłaniec;
goniec;kurier; agent turystyczny
course (ko:rs) s. bieg; kierunek; ruch naprzód; droga; danie; kolejność; bieżnia;
warstwa; kurs; ciąg; v. gnać;
pędzić; ścigać; uganiać się
court (ko:rt) s. podwórze; hala; dwór; hotel; sąd; v.zale-
cać się; wabić; zabiegać;

courteous ('ke:rczjes) adj.
grzeczny; uprzejmy i miły
courtesy ('ke:rtysy) s. grzeczność; uprzejmość; kurtuazja;
(darmowa) usługa; gest przez
grzeczność; adj.grzecznościowy
courtly ('ko:rtly) adj. układny;wytworny; dworski;dostojny
courtmartial ('ko:rt'ma:rszel) s.
sąd wojenny;v.sądzić sadem wojsko-
court of justice ('ko:rt,ow
'dżastys) s. sad
courtroom ('ko:rt.ru:m) s. sala sądowa (rozpraw)
courtship ('ko:rtszyp) s. zaloty; umizgi do kobiety
courtyard ('ko:rt,ja:rd) s. podwórze; dziedziniec
cousin ('kazyn) s. kuzyn; kuzynka; krewny;cioteczny brat(siostra)
cover ('kawer) s. koc; wieko;
oprawa; osłona; koperta; nakrycie (stołu); pokrycie; v. kryć;
pokryć (klacz); ubezpieczać; dać
opis;nakrywać;rozlać;chować;prze-
coverage ('kawerydż) s. pokrycie ubezpieczeniem; zasięg radiowy; omówienie w prasie
covering ('kaweryng) s. osłona;
pokrycie (dachu);przykrycie
covert ('kawert) s. schronienie;
adj. ukryty; potajemny;przebrany
covet ('kawyt) v. pożadać (cu-
dzego);patrzyć z zawiścią
covetous ('kawytes) adj. chciwy;
pożądliwy; łapczywy;zawistny
cow (kał) s. krowa; v. zastraszyć się; przestraszyć się
coward ('kauerd) s. tchórz;
adj. tchórzliwy; bojaźliwy
cowardice ('kauerdys) s.
tchórzostwo ;tchorzliwość
cowardly ('kauerdly) adj.
tchórzliwy; adv. tchórzliwie
cowboy ('kałboj) s. konny pastuch;pastuch bydła;krowjarz
cower ('kauer) v. skulić się;
kucnąć; przykucać do ziemi
cowherd ('kał,he:rd) s. pasterz
bydła; pastuszka
cowhide ('kał,hajd) s. krowia
skóra; skóra wołowa

cowshed ('kał,szed) s. krowia
szopa; obora
cowslip ('kał,slyp) s. pier-
wiosnek(kwiat bagienny)
coxcomb ('koks,koum) s. błazen;
fircyk; pajac;głupi zarozumialec
coxswain ('kok,słejn) s. sternik na regatach
coy (koj) adj. skromny; nieśmiały; ostrożny; cichy;udający
cozy (kouzy) adj. wygodny;
przytulny;s.okrycie czajnika
crab (kraeb) s. krab; rak;
(wulg.) menda; v. łowić kraby;
krytykować; rujnować;narzekać
crab louse ('kraeb,laus) s.
wesz łonowa
crack (kraek) s. trzask; rysa;
szpara; próba; dowcip;
v. trzaskać; żartować; łupać;
uderzyć; rujnować; adj. wyso-
kiej jakości; doskonały
crack a joke (kraek e dżok) v.
palnąć żart;palnąć kawał
crack a smile('kraek,e'smajl)
v. (slang) uśmiechnąć się
cracker ('kraeker) s. sucharek; petarda; łupacz;kłamstwo
crackpot ('kraekpot) s. wariat;
bez piątej klepki (slang)
crackle ('kraekl) v. trzeszczeć; s. trzeszczenie; pajęczyna; porcelana zdobiona
cradle ('krejdl) s. kołyska;
kolebka; wywrotka; v. kraść
w kołysce; kołysać; kosić
(kosa z ramą);płukać złoto
craft (kraeft) s. rzemiosło;
branża; sztuka; cech; podstęp;
chytrość; biegłość; pojazd
craftsman ('kraftsmen) s. rzemieślnik;mistrz w swoim zawodzie
crafty ('kra-fty) adj. sprytny;
zręczny; podstępny;przebiegły
crag (kraeg) s. skała (stroma);
turnia;nawis skalny
cram (kraem) v. tłoczyć; napychać; opychać; wtłaczać; wkuwać (się); s. tłok; ciżba;
wkuwanie się do egzaminu;ścisk;
kłamstwo; uczenie się do egzaminu
intensywnie i w pośpiechu

cramp (kraemp) s.skurcz; klamra; zwornik; v. sciskac; krepowac; ograniczac; adj. scisnięty; stloczony; nieczytelny; sztuczny ;uchwycony w imadlo
cranberry ('kraenbery) s. żurawina; brusznica blotna
crane (krejn) s. żuraw; dźwig; v. podnosic; wyciągać szyję
crank (kraenk) s. korba; dziwak; bzik; v. puszczac w ruch (korba); kręcic; wydębic
crank up ('kraenk,ap) v. zapuszczac (motor);uruchomic(motor)
crape (kraep) s. gra w kości; brednie; bzdury;nonsens
crape (krejp) s. krepa
crash (kraesz) s. huk; lomot; upadek; katastrofa; ruina; krach; samodzial; v. trzaskac; huczec; roztrzaskiwac; wpasc na...; adv. z hukiem;z trzaskiem ;z lomotem;z halasem
crash helmet ('kraesz,helmyt) s. kask ochronny (motocyklisty)
crash landing ('kraesz;laendyng) s. rozbicie się przy lądowaniu
crate (krejt) s. stare pudlo; skrzynia; paka; v. pakowac w skrzynie;wkladac do pak
crater ('krejter) s. krater
crave (krejw) v. pożadac; pragnąc; prosić usilnie; blagac
crawfish ('kro:fysz) s. rak; v. wycofywac się(rakiem)
crawl (kro:l) v. pelzac; czolgac się; wlec; roic się; s. czolganie; plywanie kraulem; ciarki;basen do hodowli raków
crayfish ('krejfysz) s. rak (rzeczny);rak morski bez kleszczy
crayon ('krejen) s. kredka; rysunek kredką; v. rysowac kredką; szkicowac;narysowac węglem
crazy ('krejzy) adj. zwariowany; pomylony; walący się (np.dom)
crazy about ('krejzy,e'baut) zwariowany na punkcie czegos
creak (kri:k) v. skrzypiec; trzeszczec; s. skrzypienie; pisk; zgrzyt; trzask; trzeszczenie;pisknięcie; zgrzytnięcie

cream (kri:m) s. śmietana; śmietanka; krem; v. ustac się; zbierac śmietankę; zabielac
cream cheese(kri:m,czi:z) s. ser śmietankowy(biały i miękki)
creamy ('kri:my) adj. smietankowy ; jak śmietana
crease ('kri:s) s. falda; kant (spodni); v. faldowac; plisowac; prasowac; zmiąc ;pomiąc
create (kry:'ejt) v. tworzyc; wywoływac ;zapoczątkowac;powodowac
creation (kry'ejszyn) s. stworzenie; kreacja; świat ;wszechświat
creative (kry'ejtyw) adj. twórczy ;wynalazczy;tworzący
creator (kry'ejter) s. tworca
creature ('kry:czer) s. stwór; istota; kreatura (dominowana)
credentials (kry'denszelz) pl. dokumenty; listy uwierzytelniające (tożsamość posla etc.)
credibility gap (,kredy'bylyty gaep) s. niedowierzanie; luka w zaufaniu ;brak zaufania
credible ('kredybl) adj. wiarogodny ; wiarygodny
credit ('kredyt) s. kredyt; wiara; autorytet; powaga; uznanie; chluba; v. dawac wiarę; zapisywac na rachunek; zaliczac ;przypisywac(coś komus)
creditable ('kredidtebl) adj. zaszczytny; chlubny;godny pochwaly
credit card ('kredyt ka:rd) karta kredytowa do zakupów
creditor ('kredyter) s. wierzyciel(handlowy,prywatny etc.)
credulous ('kredjules) adj. latwowierny;zbyt latwowierny
creed (kri:d) s. wiara; wierzenia; glębokie przekonania
creek (kri:k) s. potok; zatoka
creep; crept; crept (kri:p; krept; krept)
creep (kri:p) v. pelzac; wkradac sie; miec ciarki; s. pelzanie; ciarki; obsuwanie; poslizg; nędzny typ;pelzanie się
creeper ('kri:per) s. pnącz
cremate (krymejt) v. spalac zwloki na popiól

crept (krept)v.podpełzał; zob.:
creep
crescent ('kresnt) s. półksiężyc; adj. półksiężycowy; rosnący; przybywający;ɛ.rogalik
cress (kres) s. rzeżucha
crest (krest) s. czub; grzebień; grzywa; pióropusz; kita;
hełm; klejnot; grzbiet; v.for-
mować grzbiet; osiągnąć szczyt
crestfallen (krest-folen) adj.
z opadnietym czubem; speszony;
zawstydzony; przygnębiony
crevasse (kry'waes) s. szczelina; pęknięcie (w lodowcu etc.)
crevice ('krewys) s. szczelina; rysa; pęknięcie; szpara
crew (kru:)s. załoga; drużyna;
zgraja; zob. crow
crib (kryb) s. żłób z pętami;
stajnia; obora; ciupka; pokoik;
domek; kojec; plagiat; v. stła-
czać; wyposażac w żłoby; ocemb-
rować; zwędzić;używać ściągaczki
cricket ('krykyt) s. świerszcz;
krykiet; v. grać w krykieta
crime (krajm) s. zbrodnia
criminal ('krymynl) s. zbrodniarz; kryminalista; adj. :
zbrodniczy; kryminalny
crimson ('krymzn) s. & adj. kar-
mazyn(owy); v. zabarwiac na
karmazynowo; zaczerwieniać się
cringe (kryndż) s. uniżoność;
v. kulić; kurczyć sie; kłaniać
sie; płaszczyć sie (usłużnie)
cripple ('krypl) kulawy; kaleka
v. okulawić; osłabiać; kuleć;
utykać; okaleczyc;przeszkadzać
crisis ('krajsys) s. przesilenie; kryzys;krytyczna sytuacja
crises ('krajsi:z) pl. prze-
silenia; kryzysy; opały
crisp (krysp) adj. rzeski;
chrupki; energiczny; v.robić
kruchym;marszczyc; kędzierza-
wić;fryzować; ufryzować
critic ('krytyk) s. krytyk
critical ('krytykel) adj. kryty-
kujący; krytyczny; trudny do
nabycia; ważny(moment etc.)

criticism ('krytysyzem) s. krytyka; krytycyzm;znajdowanie błędów
criticize ('krytysajz) s. krytykować; ganić; znajdywać błędy
croak (krouk) v. rechotac; krakać;s. rechot;rechotanie;krąkanie
crochet ('krouszej) v. robic
na szydełku : szydełkować
crockery ('krokery) s. naczynia gliniane(dzbany, słoje etc.)
crocodile ('krokedajl) s. krokodyl; adj.krokodylowy
crocus ('kroukes) s. krokus;
szafran(z rodziny irysów)
crook (kruk) s. hak; zagięcie;
krzywizna; kanciarz; krzywic;
wyginać; krasć; kantować
crooked (krukyd) adj. zakrzy-
wiony; krzywy; wypaczony;
zgarbiony; cygański; szachraj-
ski; oszukańczy;zgięty;wygięty
crop (krop) s. plon; biczysko:
bacik; całość; przycinanie;
krótko strzyżone włosy; ucinek;
v. strzyc; skubać; zbierać;
zasiewać; obrodzić; wyłaniac
się; uprawiać ziemię; obradzać
crop up (krop ap) v. nagle
zjawiać się; wyskoczyć nagle
cross (kros) s. krzyż; skrzyżowanie; mieszaniec; kant;
cygaństwo; v. żegnac się;
krzyżować; przecinać coś; isć
w poprzek; przekreślać;
udaremnić; adj. poprzeczny;
skośny; krzyżujący; przeciwny; gniewny; opryskliwy
cross out ('kros,aut) v. wy-
kreślać;skreślać;przekreślać
cross-examination ('kros -
ig'zaemynejszyn) s. przesłuchanie; badanie (w śledztwie)
crossing ('krosyng) s. skrzyżowanie; przejście lub przejazd na druga stronę (rzeki...)
crossroads ('krosroudz) pl.
rozstaje; skrzyżowanie dróg
crossword puzzle ('krosłord-
'pazl) s. krzyżówka
crouch (kraucz) v. kulić się;
kurczyć; przysiąsć;gotować się
do skoku

crow (krou) s. kruk; wrona;
pianie; wesoły pisk; v. piać;
piszczec wesoło;krzyczec z rados-
czec; płakac; urągac; ujadac
crowbar ('krouba:r) s. drąg;
lewar; łom(do podważania etc.)
crowd (kraud) s. tłum; tłok;
banda; mnóstwo; v. tłoczyc;
natłoczyc; napierac; wpychac;
spieszyc; przepełniac
crowded ('kraudyd) adj. zatłoczony; zapchany;przeludniony
crown (kraun) s. korona; wieniec; v. wienczyc; koronowac
crucial ('kru:szel) adj. decydujący; przełomowy; krytyczny
crucifixion (,kru:sy'fykszyn)
s. ukrzyżowanie; krucyfiks
crucify (kru:syfaj) v. ukrzyżo-
wac;torturowac;znęcac się
crude (kru:d) adj. surowy;
szorstki; niepożyty;obskórny
cruel (kruel) adj. okrutny
cruelty ('kuelty) s. okrucien-
stwo; znęcanie się(nad kims)
cruet ('kru:yt) v. flaszeczka;
ampułka;buteleczka(na ocet etc.)
cruise (kru:z) v. krążyc; leciec; podróżowac; s. wycieczka
morska; przejażdżka; rejs
crumb (kram) s. okruch; (slang)
dran; v. kruszyc; drobic; dodawac okruszyn;obtoczyc(w bułce)
crumble ('kramb) v. kruszyc (się)
crumple ('krampl) v. zmiąc;
zmarszczyc;załamywac się
crumple up ('krampl,ap) v. po-
miąc; zawalic się;załamac się
crunch (krancz) v. miażdżyc;
chrupac; s, chrupanie; chrzęst
crusade (kru:'sejd) s. wyprawa
krzyżowa;v.isc z krucjatą
crusader (kru:'sejder) s. krzy-
żowiec;aktywny działacz
crush (krasz) v. kruszyc; miażdżyc; miąc; s, miażdżenie;
tłok; ciżba; zadurzenie się
crusher (kraszer) s. łamacz;
miażdżarka;druzgocący cios
crust (krast) s. skorupa; skóra;
v. zaskorupiac (się)
crutch (kracz) s. kula; podpórka ;laska;v.podpierac się

cry (kraj) s. krzyk; płacz;
wrzask; okrzyk; hasło; v.krzy-
czec; płakac; urągac; ujadac
cry-baby ('kraj,bejby) s. mazgaj; beksa; płaksa(dziecinna)
crying ('krajyŋg) s. wołanie;
płacz adj. płaczący;skandalicz-
cry of rage ('kraj,ow'rejdż) ny
s. krzyk szału (wściekłości)
crypt (krypt) s. krypta
crystal ('krystl) s. kryształ;
szkiełko od zegarka;adj.kryszta-
crystalline ('krystelajn) adj.łowy
krystaliczny;kryształowy
crystallize ('krystelajz) v.
krystalizowac się
cub (kab) s. szczenie (dzikie-
go zwierza); zuch;młodzik
cube (kju:b) s. szescian; kostka; (slang) facet; v. podnosic do szescianu; obliczac
kubaturę;formowac w szesciany
cube root ('kju:b,ru:t) s.
pierwiastek szescienny
cubicle ('kju:bykl) s. pokoik;
mała sypialnia;małe mieszkanie
cuckoo ('kuku) s. kukułka;
głuptas;kukanie;duren
cucumber ('kju:kamber) s. ogórek
cuddle ('kadl) s. tulic;
piescic; kulic się;gnieździc
cudgel ('kadżel) s. pałka; się
v. bic pałką
cue (kju:) s. wskazówka; nastrój; ogonek (do sklepu); kij
bilardowy; warkocz;v.dac wska-
cuff (kaf) s. mankiet; kajdan-zówkę
ki; v. bic pięscią; uderzac;
kułakowac;potarmosic;szturchac
cuff links ('kaf,lyŋks) pl.
spinki do mankietów
culminate ('kalmynejt) y.
szczytowac; kulminowac
culmination (,kalmy'nejszyn) s.
kulminacja; punkt szczytowy
culprit ('kalpryt) s. oskarżony; winowajca;winowajczyni
cultivate ('kaltywejt) v. uprawiac; rozwijac; kultywowac
pielęgnowac; spulchniac

cultivation (,kaltu'wejszyn)
s. uprawa; kultura; kultywo-
wanie;kultura duchowa

cultivator ('kaltyvejter) s.
plantator; kultywator;rolnik

cultural ('kalczerel) adj.
kulturalny;kulturowy

culture ('kalczer) s. kultura;
uprawa; v. uprawiac; hodowac;
kształcic;hodować bakterie

cultured ('kalczerd) adj.
kulturalny;oczytany;wykształcony

cumulative ('kju:mjulejtyw)
adj. łączny; kumulacyjny;
skumulowany; kumulujący się

cunning ('kanyng) s. chytrość;
przebiegłość; adj. chytry;
przebiegły; miły; ładny

cup (kap) s. kubek; kielich;
czasza; filiżanka; v. wgłę-
biac; stawiać bańki

cupboard ('kaberd) s. kredens;
szafka;połka na kubki

cupola ('kju:pele) s. kopuła;
piec kopułowy; żeliwiak

cur (ke:r) s. kundel; szelma

curable ('kjuerebl) adj. uleczalny; wyleczalny

curate ('kjueryt) s. wikary

curb (ke:rb) s. krawężnik;
łancuszek; wędzidło; oszczep;
twarda spuchlizna; v. okiełzać; hamować; ograniczać

curd (ke:rd) s. twaróg; tłuszcz

curdle (ke:rdl) v. ścinać;
zsiadać się;formować w gródki

cure (kjuer) s. kuracja; lek;
lekarstwo; v. uleczyc; wyle-
czyc; zaradzic; wykurować

cure-all ('kjuero:l) s. pana-
ceum;lek na wszystkie dolegliwości

curfew ('ke:rfju:) s. godzina
policyjna: capstrzyk

curio ('kjuerjou) s. okaz;
osobliwość ;unikat; rzadkość

curiosity (,kjurj'osyty) n.
ciekawość; osobliwość

curl (ke:rl) s. kędzior; lok;
pukiel; skręt; spirala; wir
v. kręcić; skręcać; zwijać;
marszczyć; złoscic;skulić się

curl up ('ke:rl ap) v.zwinąć (się)

curly ('ke:rly) adj. kędzierzawy; kręty ;falujący;kręcony

currant ('karent) s. porzeczka;
rodzynek bez pestki

currency ('karensy) s. waluta;
obieg; potocznosc; popularnosc

current ('karent) adj. bieżący; obiegowy; obiegający; powszechnie znany; panujący (pogląd);.s. prąd; bieg; nurt;
tok ;strumień;natężenie prądu

curriculum (ke'rykjulem) s.
plan studiow ;program nauki

curriculum vitae (ke'rykjulem,
wajti:) s. życiorys

curse (ke:rs) s. przekleństwo;
klątwa; v. przeklinac; wykli-
nać; kląć; bluźnic;złorzeczyć

cursed (ke:rsyd) adj. przeklęty; cholerny; adv. paskudnie;
cholernie ;po diable

curt (ke:rt) adj. krótki; zwięzły;lakoniczny;szorstki;suchy

curtail (ke:r'tejl) v. obcinać;
skracac; zmniejszać;uczszuplać

curtain ('ke:rtn) s. zasłona;
firanka; kurtuna; v. zasłaniać

curtsy ('ke:rtsy) s. dyg; v. dy-
gać ;złożyć głęboki ukłon

curve (ke:rw) s. krzywa; krzywizna; krzywka; v. wyginać
(się); wykrzywiać (się);zakręcać

cushion ('kuszyn) s. poduszka

custody ('kastedy) s. opieka;
nadzor; areszt ;przetrzymanie

custom ('kastem) s. zwyczaj;
klientela; zrobiony na zamówienie ;nawyk;stałe zaopatrywanie się

customary ('kastemery) adj. zwyczajny; zwyczajowy,s.zbior praw

customer ('kastemer) s. klient

customhouse ('kastem-haus) s.
komora celna ;urząd celny

custom-made ('kastem-mejd) adj.
zrobiony na zamówienie

customs ('kastemz) pl. cło

customs clearance ('kastemz;
klierens) s. odprawa celna

customs declaration ('kastemz,
decle'rejszyn) s. deklaracja
celna (przy przekraczaniu gra-
nicy etc.)

customs examination ('kastemz
ig,zamy'nejszyn) s. rewizja
celna (bagażu,towarów etc.)
cut; cut; cut; (kat; kat; kat)
cut (kat) s. cięcie; przecięcie; wycięcie; ścięcie; odrzy-
nek; krój; styl (krawiecki);
wykop; drzeworyt; v. ciąc;
zacíać; skaleczyć; ranić; krajać; kroić; przycinać; kosić;
rznać; rzeźbić; szlifować; wycinać; obcinać; uciać; ścinać
cut down ('kat,dałn) v. obnizać;
redukować;wyciąc w pień(wroga)
cut in ('kat,yn) v. wtrącać się
cut off ('kat,of) v. odcinać;
przerwać(dopływ);wydziedziczać
cut out ('kat,aut) v. wykroić;
przestać;zaprzestać (palić etc.)
cut up ('kat,ap) v. posiekać;
skrytykować;wypatroszyć;siec
cute (kju:t) adj. miły; ładny;
chytry; sprytny;ciekawy;bystry
cuticle ('kju:tykl) s. naskórek
cuticle scissors ('kju:tykl'-
syez) s. nożyczki od naskórka
cutlery ('katlery) s. wyroby
nożownicze; sztućce
cutlet ('katlyt) s. kotlet (bity);kotlet mielony(mięsny,rybi)
cut-off ('katof) s. odcięcie;
skrót; wyłącznik; wycinek; za-
wór(wodny,parowy,gazowy etc.)
cutout ('kat aut) = cut-off
cutpurse ('kat pe:rs) s. rzezimieszek; kieszonkowiec;opryszek
cutter ('kater) s. kuter; przecinek; przykrawacz; odcinacz
cutting ('katyŋg) adj. bolesny;
przenikliwy; cięty;s.sadzonka
cycle (sajkl) s. cykl; rower;
v. jechać na rowerze; obiegać
cyklicznie(tam i nazad,w koło...)
cyclist ('sajklyst) s. rowerzysta;
rowerzystka ; cyklista;cykilstka
cyclone ('sajkloun) s. cyklon
cylinder ('sylynder) s. walec;
cylinder;bęben(rewolweru etc.)
cynic ('synyk) s. cynik
cynical ('synykel) adj. cynicz-
ny(pomysł,program człowiek etc.)
cynicism('syny,syzem)s.cynizm

cypress ('sajprys) s. cyprys
cyst (syst) s. cysta; torbiel
czar (za:r) s. car; (od nafty;
sportu;komisarz generalny USA)
Czech (czek) adj. czeski
Czechoslovak ('czekou,slouwaek)
adj. czechosłowacki
d (di) czwarta litera alfabetu
angielskiego; oznaczenie centa
dab (daeb) v. musnąć; klepać;
dotknąć; dziobnać; s. muśnie-
cie; klaps; stuknięcie; dziob-
niecie;plama;bryzg;odrobina
dachshund ('daekshund) s. jamnik ;a.jamniczy;jamnika
dad (daed) s. tato; tatuś
daddy ('daedy) s. tatuś
daffodil ('daefedyl) s. żółty
narcyz ;żonkil;adj.bladożółty
daffy ('daefy) adj. zwariowany
daft ('daeft) adj. pomylony;
głupkowaty; zwariowany
dagger ('daeger) s. sztylet;
v. sztyletować ;s. odsyłacz
daily ('dejly) adj. codzienny;
adv. codziennie; s. dziennik
dainty ('dejnty) adj. wyszukany; wyborowy; delikatny;
gustowny; miły; wybredny
daiquiri ('daikery) s. rum z
sokiem cytrynowym, cukrem
i lodem (po amerykańsku)
dairy ('deery) s, mleczarnia
dairyman ('deerymen) s. mleczarz;właściciel mleczarni
daisy (dejzy) s. stokrotka;
ładny okaz(człowieka)
dale (dejl) s. dolina
dally ('daely) v. marudzić;
igrać; flirtować;tracić czas
dam (daem) s. tama; zapora
damage ('daemydż) s. szkoda;
uszkodzenie; odszkodowanie;
(slang) koszt; v. uszkodzić;
ponieść szkody; uwłaczać
dame (dejm) s. dziewczyna;
kobieta; pani(starsza)
damn (daem) v. potępiać; prze-
klinać; adj. przeklęty
damnation (daem'nejszyn) s. potępienie; excl.: psiakrew; cholera;a niech to piorun trzaśnie!

damp (daemp) v. zwilżyć; skropić; tłumić; ostudzić; amortyzować; butwieć; s. wilgoć; przygnębienie; zwątpienie
dampen ('daempen) v. wilgotnieć; zwilgotnieć;zwilżyć
dance (da:ns) s. taniec; zabawa taneczna; v. tańczyć; skakać; kazać tańczyć; huśtać
dancer ('da:nser) s. tancerz; tancerka; baletnica
dancing ('da:nsyŋg) s. taniec; adj. tańczący;do tańca
dandelion ('daendylajon) s. mniszek lekarski; mlecz
dandruff ('daendref) s. łupież
danger ('dejndżer) s. niebezpieczeństwo; groźba
dangerous ('dejndżeres) adj. niebezpieczny;niepewny(grunt...)
dangle ('daengl) v. dyndać; bujać; kręcić się;nadskakiwać
Danish (dejnysz) adj. duński
dapper ('daeper) adj. wytworny; elegancki;dobrze ubrany;zwinny
dare (deer) v. śmieć; ważyć się; wyzywać; s. wyzwanie
daring ('deeryng) adj. śmiały; s. śmiałość; odwaga
dark (da:rk) adj. ciemny; ponury; s. ciemność; mrok; cień; murzyn;tajemniczość;niewiedza
dark-brown ('da:rk brałn) adj. ciemno-brazowy
darken (da:rkn) v. zaciemniać
darkness ('da:rknys) s. ciemność; ciemnota; śniadość
darling ('da:rlyŋg) s. kochanie; ulubieniec; adj. kochany; ulubiony; ukochany
darn (da:rn) v. cerować; s.cera; adj. (slang) przeklęty
dart (da:rt) s. żądło; szybki ruch; oszczep; zryw; v. pędzić; rzucać; wybuchać;strzelać
dash (daesz) v. roztrzaskać; rzucać się; pędzić; popisywać się; zakropić; opryskać; niwecyzć; mieszać; onieśmielać; odbić; naszkicować; s. uderzenie; zderzenie; plusk; barwna plama; szczypta; przy-

mieszka;myślnik; kreska; pęd; skok; rozmach; rozpęd; popis
dash-board ('daeszbo:rd) tablica rozdzielcza; zestaw zegarów (lotniczych, samochodowych, etc,) ; błotnik
dashing (daeszyŋg) adj. dziarski; z werwą; z rozmachem
data ('dejte) pl. dane; podstawa odniesienia ;dane liczbowe
data processing ('dejte'prousesyŋg) s. przetwarzanie danych
date (dejt) v. datować; nosić datę; chodzić z kims; s. data; spotkanie; randka; umówienie się; palma daktylowa; daktyl
date from ('dejt,from) data z... (dnia, miejsce)
dative case('dejtyw,kejs) trzeci przypadek ;celownik
datum ('dejtem) s, dana (fakt; szczegół);punkt wyjściowy
daub (do:b) v. babrać; mazać; oblepiać; s. tynk; polepa; plama; kicz sknocony ;gips
daughter ('do:ter) s. córka
daughter-in-law ('do:ter,yn lo:) s. synowa
dawdle ('do:dl) v. próżniaczyć; mitrężyć ;wałkonić się
dawdle away ('do:dl,a'łej)v. marnować czas;trcić czas
dawn (do:n) v. świtać; zaświtać; dnieć; jaśnieć; s. świt; brzask; zaranie;zdanie sobie sprawy
day (dej) s. dzień; doba
daybreak('dejbrejk)s.świt;brzask
day by day('dej,baj dej)exp.: dzień w dzień :dzień po dniu
daydream('dejdri:m)s. marzenie;v. marzyć;budować zamki na lodzie
day in day out(dej,yn'dej aut)exp. codziennie; dzień w dzień
daylight('dejlajt)s.swiatło dzienne: bisły dzień [(dzienny)
day nursery('dej,ne:rsery)s.żłobek
day off('dej of)s.dzień wolny
days to come('dejs,tu kam) exp.: przyszłość
day's work('dejz,łe:rk)s. dniówka
daytime ('dejtajm)s. dzień od świtu do zmroku

daze (dejz) v. oszałamiać;
otumaniać; oślepiać; s oszołomienie; otumanienie
dazzle (daezl) v. oślepiać;
olśniewać; zamaskować;
s. oślepiający blask
dead (ded) adj.& s. zmarły;
martwy; wymarły; matowy
dead body (ded'body) s. zwłoki
dead center ('ded'senter) s.
punkt martwy, zwrotny
deaden ('deden) v. zabijać siłę, uczucia etc.: tłumić;
osłabiać; stępiać; zmartwieć;
obumrzeć; pozbawiać blasku,
połysku, zapachu;znieczulać
dead end('dedend)s.ślepa(ulica)
deadline('dedlajn)s.nieprzekra-
czalny termin;ostateczna granica
deadlock ('dedlok) s. impas;
martwy punkt;v. powodować impas
deadly (dedly) adj. śmiertelny;
adv. śmiertelnie;nieludzko
deadweight ('dedłejt) s. ciężar własny (urządzenia); kula
u nogi;kamień u szyi
deaf (def) adj. głuchy
deafen (defn) v. ogłuszać
deafening (defnyng) adj. ogłu-
szający
deal; dealt; dealt (di:l; delt;
delt)
deal (di:l) v. zajmować się;
traktować o: załatwiać; przestawać z; postępować; handlować; rozdzielać (karty)
s. ilość; sprawa;sporo;wiele
deal with ('di:l łyt) v. postępować z …;mieć do czynienia
dealer ('di:ler) s. kupiec;
handlarz;rozdający karty
dealing ('di:lyng)s. postępowanie z; stosunki; transakcje
dealt (delt) zob. deal
dean (di:n) s. dziekan
dear (kier) adj. kochany; drogi
dear Sir ('dier,se:r) exp.: szanowny panie;Drogi Panie
dear me ! (kier mi) exp.: ojej !
mój Boże ! czyżby! ależ nie!
death (des) s. śmierć; zgon
deathly (desly) adj. śmiertelny;
adv. śmiertelnie;grobowo;trupio

debar ('dyba:r) v. wykluczać;
zabraniać (komuś):zakazywać
debase (dy'bejs) v. obniżać;
poniżać; fałszować;upadlać
debate (dy'bejt) v. roztrząsać;
rozważać; debatować;s.debata
debauchery ('dy'bo:czery) s.
rozpusta;wyuzdanie;rozwiązłość
debit ('debyt) s. debet; obciążenie rachunku
debrief (dy'bri:f) s. przesłu-
chania po (akcji); v. przesłuchiwać po (akcji)
debris ('dejbri:) pl. gruzy
debt (det) s. dług
debtor ('deter) s. dłużnik;
dłużniczka
decade ('dekejd) s. dziesięcio-
letni okres
decadence ('dekejdens) s. de-
kadencja; chylenie się ku
upadkowi; schyłek; upadek
decapitate (dy'kaepytejt) v.
ścinać głowę;pozbawić wodza
decay (dy'kej) v. gnić; rozpadać się; psuć się; s. upadek;
ruina; zanik; rozkład; gnicie
decease (dy'si:s) v. umierać;
s. zgon ; śmierć
deceased (dy'si:st) adj. zmarły; s. nieboszczyk
deceit (dy'si:t) s. oszukańst-
wo; podstęp; fałsz
deceitful (dy'si:tfel) adj.
kłamliwy; zwodniczy;podstępny,
deceive (dy'si:w) v. okłamywać
zwodzić; łudzić; zawodzić
deceiver (dy'si:wer) s. oszu-
kaniec; zwodziciel; kłamca
decelerate (dy:'selerejt) v.
zwalniać;zmniejszać szybkość
December (dy'sember) s. grudzień
decency ('di:snsy) s. przyzwoitość; obyczajność;dobre obyczaje
decent ('di:sent) adj. przyzwoity; porządny; znośny
deception (dy'sepszyn) s. łu-
dzenie; okłamywanie; podstęp;
zawód; szachrajstwo;oszukanie
decide (dy'sajd) v. rozstrzygać;
postanawiać; decydować się;
zadecydować; skłaniać się

decided (dy'sajdyd) adj. zdecydowany; stanowczy;definitywny
decimal('desymel) adj. dzie-
siętny;s. ułamek dzisiętny
decipher (dy'sajfer) v. odcyfrować; rozszyfrować;rozwiazać
decision (dy'syżyn) s. rozstrzygnięcie; postanowienie;
decyzja; zdecydowanie; stanowczosc; wygrana na punkty
(sport);ustalenie;rezolutnosc
decisive (dy'sajsyw) adj. decydujący; rozstrzygający;
zdecydowany; stanowczy
deck (dek) s. pokład; pomost;
podłoga; talia; v. pokrywać
pokładem; przystrajać
deck chair (dek,czeer) s. leżak (do opalania się na statku)
declaration (dekle'rejszyn) s.
deklaracja; zapowiedź; oświadczenie (oficjalne)
declare (dy'kle:r) v. deklaro-
wać; oświadczać; zeznawać;
ogłaszać; uznawać za; stwierdzać;wykazać;dawać do oclenia
declension (dy'klenszyn) s. de-
klinacja (gram.); przypadkowa-
nie; odchylenie; upadek
decline (dy'klajn) v. uchylać
(się); pochylać (się);skłaniać
(się); isc ku schyłkowi; opadać; obniżać; podupadać; marnieć; słabnąć; zanikać; przy-
padkować;s.schyłek;utrata;spadek
declivity (dy'klywyty) s. pochyłość; spadzistość;stok;skłon
decode (,dy'koud)v.rozszyfrować
decorate('dekerejt)v.ozdabiać;od-
znaczać; udekorować; upiększać
decompose(,dy:kem'pouz)v.rozkła-
dać się; rozłożyć się;gnić
decoration (,deke'rejszyn) s.
ozdoba; odznaczenie;medal etc.
decorative (,deke'rejtyw) adj.
ozdobny; dekoracyjny
decorator ('dekerejter) s. dekorator; architekt wnętrz
decoy (dy'koj),s. wabik; przy-
nętą; v. wabić; usidlać; zwa-
biać; wciągać w pułapke;zacia-
gać sidła;wabić w pułapkę

decrease ('dy:kri:s) v. zmniejszać; słabnąć; obniżać;
s. zmniejszenie; spadek(cen)
decree (dy'kri:) s. dekret;
rozporządzenie; wyrok rozwodowy; postanowienie o sepera-
cji; v. zarządzać; dekretować;
rozporządzać;nakazywać dekretem
decrepit (dy'krepyt) adj.
zgrzybiały; wyniszczony
decry (dy'kraj) v. potępić;
okrzyczeć;zohydzić;obgadać
dedicate ('dedykejt) v. dedyko-
wać; poświęcać; inaugurować
dedication ('dedykejszyn) s.
dedykacja; poświęcenie;otwarcie
deduce (dy'du:s) v. wnioskować;
dedukować; wywodzić (rodowód)
deduct (dy'dakt) v. potrącać;
odciągać;odejmować;odtrącać
deduction (dy'dakszyn) s. potrącenie; odciągnięcie; wnioskowanie; wniosek;wywód
deed (di:d) s. czyn; wyczyn;
akt; v. przekazywać aktem
(własność);przelewać pieniadze
deep (di:p) adj. głęboki;
s. głębia; adv. głęboko
deepen('di:pn) v. pogłębiać
deep-freeze ('di:p,fri:z) s.
(głębokie) zamrożenie
deeply ('di:ply) adv. głęboko
deep-rooted ('di:p'ru:tyd)
adj. głęboko zakorzeniony
deer (dier) s. jeleń; sarna;
łoś; łania ;daniel;renifer
deface (dy'fejs) v. szpecić -
zniekształcać; zacierać
defame (dy'fejm) v. zniesławić
defeat (dy'fi:t) v. pokonać;
pobić; unicestwić; udaremnić;
uniemożliwić; unieważnić
prawnie;s.klęska;udaremnienie
defect (dy'fekt) s. brak; wada; błąd; defekt; v. odpaść;
skłonić do odstępstwa;odstąpić
defective (dy'fektyw) adj. wadliwy; wybrakowany; niepełny
defence (dy'fens) = defense
defend (dy'fend) v. bronić
defendant (dy'fendent) s. pozwany;oskarżony; obrońca

defender (dy'fender) s. obrońca (prawo i sport)

defensive (dy'fensyw) adj. obronny; defensywny; s. defensywa; być w defensywie

defense (dy'fens) s. obrona

defenseless (dy'fenslys) adj. bezbronny

defer (dy'fe:r) v. odraczać; ustępować; ulegać;mieć wzgląd

defiant (dy'fajent) adj. zbuntowany; nieufny;buntowniczy

deficiency (dy'fyszynsy) s. brak; niedobór; należność niezapłacona; niedostatek;słabość

deficit ('defysyt) s. deficyt; niedobór ; nadwyżka rozchodu

defile ('dy:fail) v. kalać; plugawić; brukać; bezcześcić; iść szeregami;defilować

define (dy'fajn) v. określać; definiować; zakreślać (granice); zarysowąć;określać

definite ('defynyt) adj. określony; wyraźny; pewny; prostolinijny;określający(rodzajnik)

definition (,drfy'nyszyn) s. określenie; definicja; ostrość; czystość;oznaczenie

definitive (dy'fynytyw) adj. ostateczny; definitywny; stanowczy;konkluzywny;definiujący

deflate (dy'flejt) v. wypuszczać powietrze (z dętki); zmniejszać obieg ,znaczenie etc.

deform (dy'fo,rm) v. szpecić; zniekształcać;oszpecać

deformed (dy'fo:rmd) adj. ułomny; szpetny;zniekształcony

defrost ('dy:frost) v. odmrozić

defunct ('dy'fankt) adj. zmarły; zlikwidowany;już nie istniejący

defy (dy'faj) v. stawiać czoło; rzucać wyzwania (by zrobić,wykazać)

degenerate (dy'dżeneryt) adj. zwyrodniały; s. degenerat

degrade (dy'grejd) v. poniżać; obniżać; wyrodnieć ;znieważać

degree (dy'gri:) s. stopień (np. naukowy, ciepła etc.)

dejected (dy'dżektyd) adj. przygnębiony ;zgaszony(człowiek) zdeprymowany;strapiony

dejectedly (dy'dżektydly) adv. z przygnębieniem;z niechęcią

delay (dy'lej) v. odraczać; opóźniać; zwlekać; s. odroczenie; zwłoka; opóźnienie

delegate ('delegejt) s. zastępca; wysłannik; v. delegować; udzielać delegacji; zlecać (władzę);udzielać(władzy)

delegation (,dely'gejszyn) s. delegacja;grupa delegatów

deliberate (dy'lyberejt) adj. rozmyślny; spokojny; v. rozmyślać; rozważać; obradować; naradzać się (dy,ly'berejt)v.

delicacy ('delykesy) s. delikatność; smakołyk;takt

delicate ('delykyt) adj. delikatny; wyśmienity;taktowny

delicatessen (,delyka'tesn) s. sklep z delikatesami

delicious (dy'lyszes) adj. rozkoszny;bardzo smaczny etc.

delight (dy'lajt) s. rozkosz; v. zachwycać się; rozkoszować się; lubować się

delightful (dy'lajtful) adj. zachwycający; czarujący

delinquency (dy'lynkłensy) s. zaniedbanie; wina; przestępstwo;nie płacenie należności

delinquent (dy'lynkłent) a. winny; zaniedbany; zalegający z zapłatą (podatkiem); s. winnowajca; przestępca (nieletni)osoba zalegająca etc.

deliver (dy'lywer) v. doręczać; zdawać;wydawać; wygłaszać; zadawać; uwalniać;podawać

deliverance (dy'lywerens) s. uwolnienie ;wygłoszenie(opinii)

deliverer (dy'lywerer) s. zbawca ;oswobodziciel;wybawca

delivery (dy'lywery) s. dostawa; wydawanie; wygłaszanie; podanie; poród; przekazanie

deluge ('delju:dż) s. potop

delusion (dy'lu:żyn) s. urojenie; zwodzenie ;ułuda:iluzja

delusive (dy'lu:syw) adj. złudny;oszukańczy;bałamutny;zwodniczy

demand (dy'ma:nd)s. żadanie;popyt; v.żadać; dopytywać się

demeanor (dy'mi:ner) s. zachowanie się;postepowanie: postawa

demented (dy'mentyd) adj. obłąkany;oszalały;umysłowo chory

demi-('demy) pref. pół-

demilitarized ('dy:mylyterajzd)
adj. zdemilitaryzowany

demise (dy'majz) s. zgon; przekazanie spadku; v. przekazywać
testamentem lub zgonem

demobilize (dy:,moubylajz) v.
demobilizować;zdemobilizować

democracy (dy'mokresy) s. demokracja

democrat ('demokreat) s. demo-
krata; demokratka

democratic (,deme'kraetyk) adj.
demokratyczny

demolish (dy'molysz) v. burzyć;
niszczyć; obalać; demolowac

demon ('di:men) s. diabeł; demon;doskonały zawodnik sportowy

demonstrate ('demenstrejt) v.
wykazywać; udowadniac; demon-
strować;urządzać manifestację

demonstration (,demen'strejszyn)
s. wykazywanie; okazywanie;
demonstracja;adj.wzorcowy;pogla-
demonstrative (dy'menstrejtyw)
adj. wylewny; dowodowy; wskazujący;dowodzacy;ekspansywny

demurrage (dy'me:rydż) s. prze-
stój; opłata za postojowe

den (den) s. nora; jaskinia;
ustronie; cicha pracownia

denial (dy'najel) s. zaprzeczenie; odmowa;wyparcie się

denomination (dynomy'nejszyn)
s. nazwa; miano; określenie;
wyznanie (rel.);kategoria

denounce (dy'nauns) v. oskarżać;
donosić; wypowiadać;denuncjować

dense (dens) adj. gęsty; zwarty;
tępy (człowiek);niepojętny

density ('densyty) s. gęstość;
zwartość; głupota;spoistość

dent (dent) s. wgłębienie; wrąb;
znaczenie;v.szczerbić;wyginać

dental ('dentl) adj. zębowy;
dentystyczny;stomatologiczny

dentist ('dentyst) s. dentysta;
dentystka; stomatolog

denture (denczer) s. (sztuczne) uzębienie; szczęka

deny (dy'naj) v. zaprzeczyć;
odrzucić; odmawiać; wypierać
się;zdementować; przeczyć

depart (dy'pa:rt) v. odjeżdżać;
odbiegać ;robić dygresje;odejść

department (dy'pa:rtment) s.
wydział; ministerstwo; dział

department store (dy'pa:rtment,
sto:r) s. dom towarowy

departure (dy'pa:rczer) s. odjazd; rozstanie; odchylenie

depend on (dy'pend on) v. polegać na...;zależeć od

depend upon (dy'pend,apon) v.
być zależnym od..;być na utrzymaniu;

depends (dy'pends)v. zależy

deplorable (dy'plo:rebl) adj.
godny pożałowania;opłakany

deplore (dy'plo:r) v. ubolewać;
boleć nad...;wyrażać ubolewanie

depolarize (dy'poulerajz) v.
depolaryzować;rozwiać złudzenia

depopulate (dy'popjulejt) v.
wyludniać;pustoszyć;opustoszyć

deport (dy'po:rt) v. zsyłać;
deportować; zachowywać się

depose (dy'pouz) s. składać;
zeznawać;usunąć(z tronu etc.)

deposit (dy'pozyt) s. osad;
warstwa; kaucja; depozyt;
v. składać; osadzać; deponować; nawarstwiać:złożyć (jaja...)

depositor (dy'pozyter) s. de-
ponent; osadnik

depot (depou) s. stacja kole-
jowa; skład;remiza; kadra

depraved (dy'prejwd) adj. zde-
prawowany;zepsuty moralnie

depress (dy'pres) v. przygnębiać; deprymować; spychać
w dół(ceny);deprymować;martwić

depression (dy'preszyn) s.
przygnębienie; depresja

deprive (dy'prajw) v. odzierac;
wykluczać; umartwiać się; pozbawiać;odwołać (z urzędu etc.)

depth (deps) s. głębokość;
głębia; głębina;dno(nędzy etc.)

deputy ('depjuty) s. zastępca;
deputowany; poseł; wice-

derail (dy'rejl) v. **wykoleić**
(się)(czyjś plan,zamiar etc.)

derange (dy'rejndż) v. **pomie-**
szać; rozstrajać; psuć; zakło-
cać; powodować obłęd

deride (dy'rajd) v. **wyśmiewać**

derision (dy'ryżyn) s. **szyder-**
stwo; pośmiewisko; drwina

derisive (dy'rajsyw) adj.**kpią-**
cy; ironiczny;wart śmiechu

derive (dy'rajw) v. **uzyskiwać;**
czerpać; wywodzić; pochodzić

derogatory (dy'rogeto:ry) v.
pomniejszający; uszczuplający;
uwłaczający ; szkodliwy

descend (dy'send) v. **zejść;spaść**
zniżać się;pochodzić; opadać

descendant (dy'sendent) s. **po-**
tomek(przedka;rodziny;grupy etc.)

descent (dy'sent) s. **zejście;**
spadek; pochodzenie;nagły atak

describe (dys'krajb) v. **opisy-**
wać; określać;przerysowywać

description (dy'skrypszyn)
s. **opis;sposób opisywania**

desegregate (dy'segrygejt) v.
(Am.) **znieść podział rasowy**

desert ('desert) adj. **pustynny;**
pusty; s. pustynia;pustkowie

desert (dy'ze:rt) v. **porzucać;**
opuszczać; dezerterować; s.za-
służenie; zasługa;nagroda;kara

deserted (dy'ze:rted) adj.
opuszczony;bezludny

deserter (dy'ze:rter) s. **dezer-**
ter;dezerterka;zbieg;zbiegła

desertion (dy'ze:rszyn) s.
opuszczenie; dezercja;porzucenie

deserve (dy'ze:rw) v. **zasługi-**
wać na...;mieć zasługi wobec...

design (dy'zajn) s. **zamiar;**
plan; szkic; v. pomyśleć; za-
mierzać; przeznaczać; projekto-
wać;zamyślać;uplanować;kreślić

designate ('dezygnejt) v. **wyzna-**
czać; określać; desygnować

designer (dy'zajner) s. **projek-**
tant; konstruktor; rysownik;
intrygant;projektodawca;autor

desirable (dy'zajerebl) adj. **po-**
żądany;pociągający;atrakcyjny
celowy;mile widziany;wskazany

desire (dy'zajer) v. **pożądać;**
pragnąć; życzyć sobie

desirous (dy'zajeres) adj. **żąd-**
ny;pragnący;spragniony

desk (desk) s. **biuro; referat;**
pulpit; ambona ;ławka szkolna

desk set ('desk set) s. **zestaw**
przyborów do pisania

desolate ('deselyt) adj.
opuszczony; posępny;wyludniony

desolate (deselejt) v. **pusto-**
szyć; wyludniać; opuszczać

desolation (,dese'lejszyn) s.
wyludnienie; spustoszenie;
pustka; żałość; strapienie

despair (dys'peer) s. **rozpacz**
despairingly (dys'peeryngly)
adv. **rozpaczliwie;beznadziejnie**

desperate ('desperyt) adj.
rozpaczliwy;beznadziejny;zacie-
kły

desperation (,despe'rejszyn)
s. **rozpacz; desperacja**

despise (dys'pajz) v. **pogar-**
dzać;gardzić;lekceważyć

despite (dys'pajt) s. **przeko-**
ra; złość; prep. pomimo;
wbrew;na przekór(komuś,czemuś)

despond (dys'pond) v. **przygnę-**
biać się;s.przygnębienie

despondent (dys'pondent) adj.
przygnębiony; zniechęcony

dessert (dy'ze:rt) s. **deser;**
legumina; ciastka

destination (desty'nejszyn) s.
miejsce przeznaczenia

destine ('destyn) v. **przezna-**
czać(z góry);przeznaczyć

destiny ('destyny) s. **przezna-**
czenie(wypadków,ludzi...);los

destitute ('destytju:t) adj.
bez środków;pozbawiony;w nędzy

destroy (dy'stroj) v. **burzyć;**
niweczyć;zabijać;zagładzać

destroyer (dy'strojer) s.**kontr-**
torpedowiec; niszczyciel

destruction (dys'trakszyn) s.
zniszczenie;ruina;zguba;zagłada

destructive (dy'straktyw) adj.
niszczycielski;s.niszczyciel

detach (dy'taecz) v. **odczepić;**
odłączyć; odpiąć; odwiązać;
odkomenderować;odlepiać;urwać

detached (dy'taeczt) adj. odosobniony; obojętny;niezależny
detail ('di:tejl) s. szczegół;
wyszczególnienie; v. wyłusz-
czać; przydzielać do zadań
detain (dy'tejn) v. wstrzymywać; więzić; przeszkadzać
detect (dy'tekt) v. wykrywać;
wysledzić;wypatrzyć;przychwycić
detection (dy'tekszyn) s. wy-
krywanie; wysledzenie
detective (dy'tektyw) s. detek-
tyw; adj. detektywistyczny
detention (dy'tenszyn) s. więzienie; zatrzymanie;przetrzymanie
deter (dy'te:r) v. odstraszać
od...;pohamować;onieśmielać
detergent (dy'te:rdżent) s.&
adj. czyszczący (środek)
deteriorate (dy'tierjerejt) s.
psuc; marnieć;tracić na wartoś-
determination (dyte:rmy'nejszyn)
s. okreslenie; postanowienie;
ustalenie; orzeczenie;wygaśnięcie
determine (dy'te:rmyn) v. rozstrzygać; okreslać; postanawiać; ustalać;zdefiniować
deterrent (dy'terent) adj. od-
straszający; s.(czynnik) od-
straszający;środek zaradczy
detest (dy'test) v. nienawidzić;
czuć wstręt;nie cierpieć
detestable (dy'testebl) adj.
wstrętny; nienawistny;obmierzły
detonate ('detounejt) v. wybuchać; powodować wybuch
detour ('dy:tuer) s. objazd
devaluation (,dy:vaelju'ejszyn)
s. dewaluacja;zdewaluowanie
devaluate('dy:waelju:ejt)v.dewalu-
ować;obniżać wartość;zdewaluować
devastate ('devestejt) v. pustoszyć;niweczyć;dewastować
develop (dy'velop) v. rozwijać
(się); wywoływać (zdjęcia)
development (dy'velepment) s.
rozwój; rozbudowa; osiedle;
wywołanie(filmu);ewolucja
deviate ('di:wyejt) v. zbaczać;
odchylać;schodzić z drogi
device (dy'wajs) s. plan; pomysł;
urządzenie; dewiza; hasło;środek

devil ('dewl) s. chart; diabeł
devilish ('dewlysh) adj. szatański; diabelski;adv.diabelsko
devise (dy'wajz) v. zapisać
(komuś); wymyslać; obmyslać
devoid (dy'woyd) adj. pozbawiony;próżny;czczy;wolny od.;
devote (dy'wout) v. poświęcac;
ofiarować;oddawać się
devoted (dy'vouted) adj. oddany;przywiązany (do kogoś,,)
dew (dju:) s. rosa; świeżość;
powiew; v. rosić; zraszać
dew point ('dju:point)
temperatura powstawania rosy
dexter ('dekster) a. prawy
dexterity (deks'teryty) s.
zręczność; bystrość;sprawność
diabetes (,daje'by:ty:z) s.
cukrzyca;choroba cukrowa
diagram ('dajegraem) s. wykres;
schemat; diagram
dial ('dajel) s. tarcza nume-
rowa (zwł. zegarowa);
v. mierzyć; nakręcać (numer)
dial tone ('dajel,toun) s.
sygnał połączenia (tel.)
dialect ('dajelekt) s. gwara;
narzecze; dialekt
dialog(ue) ('dajelog) s. rozmowa; dialog(na scenie etc,)
diameter (dai'aemyter) s. średnica; długość średnicy
diamond('dajemend) s. diament;
romb; a. diamentowy; romboidalny;s.boisko do gry w palanta
diaper ('dajeper) s. pielusz-
ka; wzór romboidalny;
v. przewijać; ozdabiać w romby
diaphragm ('dajefraem) s. przepona; membrana;przesłona
diarrhea (daje'rye) s. biegunka
diary ('daiery) s. dziennik
dice (dajs) v. grać w kości;
kratkować; pl. od die=kostka do
dictate (dyk'tejt) s. nakaz;
v. dyktować;narzucać(wolę etc.)
dictation (dyk'tejszyn) s.
dyktat; dyktowanie :nakaz
dictator (dyk'tejter) s. dyktator;dyktujący dyktando;dyk-
tujący na głos (tekst;list etc.)

dictatorship (dyk'tejterszyp)
s. dyktatura;władza nieograniczona;
dictionary ('dykszeneeryjs.słow-
nik;mała encyklopedia
did (dyd) v. zrobić; zob.: do
die (daj) v. umierać; zdech-
nąć; zginąć; s. matryca;
sztanca; pl. zob,: dice
die-hard ('daj-ha:rd) adj.
twardy; nieustępliwy; s. zagorzały bojownik(szermierz etc.)
diet ('dajet) s. dieta; zjazd;
sejm; v. trzymać na diecie
differ ('dyfer) v. różnic się;
nie zgadzać się(z opinią etc.)
difference ('dyferens) s. róz-
nica; sprzeczka; nieporozumienie
different ('dyferent) adj. różny; odmienny; niezwykły
difficult ('dyfykelt) adj.
trudny;ciężki; niełatwy
difficulty ('dyfykelty) s.
trudność; przeszkoda
diffident ('dyfydent) adj. nieśmiały; bez wiary we własne
siły;bez zaufania do siebie
diffuse (dy'fju:z) adj. rozwlekły; rozproszony; v. rozlewać; szerzyć; rozpraszać
dig; dug; dug (dyg; dag; dag)
dig (dyg) v. kopać; ryć; rozumieć; ocenić; bawić się; kuć
się; s. szarpnięcie; przytyk;
kujon;szturchnięcie;docinek
digest (dy'dżest) v. trawić;
przetrawiać; s. streszczenie;
skrót; przegląd;zbiór praw
digestible (dy'dżestebl) adj.
strawny;łatwy do przyswojenia
digestion (dy'dżestszyn) s.
trawienie; wygotowanie
diggings ('dygynz) s. kopalnia
(złota); mieszkanie
dignified ('dygnyfajd) adj. dostojny;godny;pełen godności
dignity ('dygnyty) s. godność;
dostojeństwo;powaga;zaszczyt
digress ('daj'gres) v. zbaczać;
odbiegać od rzeczy (tematu etc.)
digs (dygz) s, mieszkanie; pokój; buda; melina
dihedral (daj'hi:drel)adj.(kąt)
między dwoma ścianami

dike (dajk) s. tama; grobla;
rów; v. osuszać rowem; otamować
dilapidated (dy'laepydejtyd)
adj. zniszczony;walący się
dilate (daj'lejt) v. rozszerzać; rozwodzić się;rozciągać
diligence ('dylydżens) n. pilność;przykładanie się do pracy
diligent ('dylydżent) adj. pilny;przykładający się do pracy
dill (dyl) s. koper ogrodowy
dill-pickle ('dyl,pykl) s. kiszony ogorek
dilute (daj'lju:t) v. rozpuszczać; rozcieńczać; rozrzedzać;
adj. rozpuszczony; rozcieńczo-
ny; rozrzedzony; rozwodniony;
wypłukany; wyblady;spłowiały
dim (dym) v. przyćmić; zaciemnić; zamglić; adj. przyćmiony;
blady zamazany; niewyraźny
dime (dajm) s. dziesięcio-
centowa moneta U.SA.
dimension (dy'menszyn) s. wymiar; rozmiar; wielkość
diminish (dy'mynysz) v. zmniejszać; zwężać;uszczuplać;niknąć
diminutive (dy'mynjutyw) adj.&
s. drobniutki; zdrobniały;
zdrobnienie:malutka kobieta
dimple ('dympl) s. dołek (w
twarzy) ; v. robić dołki; mieć
dołki (w twarzy etc.)
dine (dajn) v. jeść obiad;
jeść; mieć na obiedzie
diner (dajner) s. stołówka
wagon restauracyjny; osoba
jedząca;restauracja
dining car ('dajnyng,ka:r) s.
wagon restauracyjny
dining room ('dajnyng,ru:m)
s. jadalnia;pokój jadalny
dinner ('dyner) s. obiad
dinner-jacket ('dyner,dżaekyt)
s. smoking
dinner-party ('dyner,pa:rty)
s. przyjęcie; obiad proszony
dip (dyp) v. zanurzać; czerpać;
farbować; pogrążać; płukać;
nachylać się; opadać; s. zanurzenie; zamoczenie; rozczyn;
nachylenie; obniżenie; łojówka;
sos do maczania;skok do wody

diphtheria (dyfteria) s. dyfteryt; błonica
diploma (dy'plouma) s. dyplom
diplomacy (dy'ploumesy) s. dyplomacja;takt
diplomat ('dyplemaet) s. dyplomata;człowiek taktowny
diplomatic(,dyple'maetyk) adj. dyplomatyczny; taktowny
direct, (dy'rekt) v. kierowac; kazac; zarządzic; dowodzic; zaadresowac;nakierowywac; wymierzac polecic; dyrygowac;adj. prosty; bezpośredni; otwarty; szczery; wyrazny; adv. wprost; prosto; bezpośrednio
direct current (dy'rekt'karent) s. prąd stały
direction (dy'rekszyn) s. kierunek; kierowanie; kierownictwo; zarząd; wskazówka; adres
directions (dy'rekszyns) pl. instrukcje; przepisy; przepis
directly (dy'rektly) adv. bezpośrednio; wprost; od razu; zaraz;natychmiast;dokładnie
director (dy'rektor) s. dyrektor; reżyser; celownik; kierownik;zarządzajacy
directory (dy'rektery) s. książka adresowa; telefoniczna(lub przepisow);skorowidz
dirigible ('dyrydżebl) adj.& s. sterowy; sterowiec
dirt (de:rt) s. brud; błoto; świnstwo; ziemia; język plugawy; mówienie oszczrstw;plotki
dirt-cheap (de:rt'czi:p) adv. za bezcen; adj, bardzo tani; tani jak barszcz;śmiesznie tani
dirty (de:rty) adj. brudny; sprosny; podły; wstrętny
disability (,dyse'dylyty) s. inwalidztwo; niemoc;niemożność
disabled (dysejbld) s. kaleka; inwalida wojenny
disadvantage (dysed'wa:ntydż) s. niekorzysc; wada; strata; szkoda; niekorzystne położenie;v.szkodzic;zaszkodzic(komu)
disadvantageous (dysaedwa:ntejdżes) adj. niekorzystny; szkodliwy;ujemny

disagree (dyse'gri:) v. nie zgadzac się; rożnic się; nie służyc (jedzenie; klimat)
disagreeable (,dyse'gri:ebl) adj. nieprzyjemny; niemiły
disagreement (,dyse'gri:ment) s. niezgoda; różnica
disallow (,dyse'lau) v. niepozwalac; nie dopuszczac
disappear (,dyse'pier) v. znikac;zapodziewac się; przepasc
disappearance (,dyse'pierens) s. zniknięcie;zanik;zginięcie
disappoint (dyse'point) v. zawiesc;rozczarowac;nie spetnic
disappointment (dyse'pointment) s. zawod; rozczarowanie
disapproval (dyse'pru:wel) s. potępienie; niechęc;desaprobata
disapprove (dyse'pru:w) v. potępiac; ganic;żle widziec(kogoś)
disarm (dys'a:rm) v. rozbroic; unieszkodliwic;odebrać broń
disarmament (dys'a:rmement) s. rozbrojenie;a.rozbrojeniowy
disarrange ('dyse'rejndż) v. rozstrajac; dezorganizowac
disarray (,dyse'rej) v. wprowadzac nieład; rozstrajac; s. nieład; zamieszanie; bałagan;niekompletny strój
disaster (dy'za:ster) s. nieszczęście; klęska(żywiołowa etc.)
disastrous (dy'za:stres) adj. katastrofalny; zgubny;fatalny
disbelief ('dysby'li:f) s. niewiara; niedowierzanie:nieufność
disbelieve ('dysby'li:w) v. niewierzyc; niedowierzac
disc (dysk) s. krążek; tarcza; płyta; dysk;płyta gramofonowa
discard (dys'ka:rd) v. wyrzucac; odrzucac;zarzucac;zaniechać
discard ('dyska:rd) s. odrzucenie; odrzucona (rzecz lub osoba);odpadek;rzecz wybrakowana
discern (dy'se:rn) v. rozrożniac;odrożniac;rozpoznawać
discharge (dys'cza:rdż) v. rozładowac; odciążac; zwalniac; wypuscic; wystrzelic; s. rozładowani(ewystrzał; zwolnienie; wydzielina;odpływ;odchody;ropa

disciple (dy'sajpl) s. uczeń;
wyznawca;jeden z apostołów
discipline ('dyscyplyn) s.
dyscyplina; karność; v. karać; ćwiczyć; musztrować
disc-jockey (dysk'dżoki) s.
nadający muzykę z płyt ;
(disk jockey)
disclaim (dys'klejm) v. wypierać się;rezygnować;zrzekać się
disclose (dys'k-ouz) v. odsłaniać; ujawniać;wyjawiać;odkryć
discolor (dys'kaler) v. odbarwiać
discomfort (dys'kamfert) s. niewygoda; niepokój; v. sprawiać
niewygody lub złe samopoczucie;krępować;żenować;dolegać
discompose (,dyskem'pouz) v.
niepokoić; mieszać;zmieszać
disconcert (,dysken'ser:t) v.
żenować; krzyżować plany
disconnect ('dyske'nekt) v. odłączyć; oderwać; odhaczyć
disconnected ('dyske'nektyd)
adj. bez związku; bezładny;
rozłączony; chaotyczny
disconsolate (dys'konselyt) adj.
niepocieszony; posępny
dicontent. ('dysken'tent) s. niezadowolenie; adj. niezadowolony; v. wywoływać niezadowolenie ;wywoływać rozgoryczenie
discontented ('dysken'tentyd)
adj. niezadowolony; rozgory-
czony; zniecierpliwiony
discontinue (,dysken'tynju:) v.
zaprzestawać; przerywać; ustawać;zakończyć; zaniechać
discord ('dysko:rd) s. niezgoda; różnica; dysonans;niesnaski
discordance ('dysko:rdens) s.
niezgodność ;dysonans
discotheque ('dyskoutek) s.
dyskoteka; nocny lokal z muzy-
ką z płyt do tańca
discount ('dyskaunt) s. dyskont;
rabat; odjęcie; v. potrącać;
odliczać; nie dawać wiary
discourage (dys'karydż) v. zniechęcać; odstraszać;być przeciwnym
discover (dys'kawer) v. wynaleźć; odkryć; odsłaniać;zobaczyć

discoverer (dys'kawerer) s.
odkrywca; wynalazca
discredit (dys'kredyt) v. dys-
kredytować; przynosić ujmę;
pozbawiać zaufania; s. utrata zaufania i dobrego imienia;
niewiara;zła opinia(kogo ,czego)
discreet (dys'kri:t) a. rozsądny; dyskretny; z rezerwą
discrepancy (dys'krepensy) s.
sprzeczność ;rozbieżność
discretion (dys'kreszyn) s.
swoboda decyzji; rozwaga;
powściągliwość; dyskrecja
discriminate (dys'krymynejt),
v. odróżniać; dyskryminować;
robić różnicę;wyróżniać
discriminate against (dys'krymynejt e'genst) wprowadzać
dyskryminację w stosunku do..
discuss (dys'kas) v. dyskutować; roztrząsać ;debatować
discussion (dys'kaszyn) s.
dyskusja; debata ;debaty
disdain (dy'dejn) s. pogarda;
wzgarda;v.gardzić;lekceważyć
disease (dy'zi:z) s. choroba
diseased (dy'zi:zd) adj. chory; schorzały;cierpiący na...
disembark ('dysym'ba:rk) v.wy-
ładować; wysiadać; lądować
disengage ('dysen'gejdż) v.
odczepiać; wyłączać;odwikłać
disengaged ('dysyn'gejdżd) adj.
wolny; nie zajęty;zwolniony
disentangle ('dysyntaengl) v.
wyplątać; rozplątać;wywikłać
disfavor ('dys'fejwer) s. niełaska; dezaprobata; v. odnosić się nieprzychylnie; z niechęcią traktować;dezaprobować
disfigure (dys'fyger) v. zniekształcić ;zeszpecić
disgrace (dys'grejs) s. hańba;
niełaska; v. hańbić; zniesławić; pozbawiać łaski;narobić wstydu
disgraceful (dys'grejsfel) adj.
haniebny; hańbiący;sromotny;niecny
disguise (dys'gajz) v. przebierać; ukrywać; maskować; z taić;
s. charakteryzacja; udawanie;
pozory ;zamaskowanie; maska

disgust (dys'gast) s. odraza;
wstręt; obrzydzenie; v. budzić odrazę, wstręt, obrzydzenie, rozgoryczenie,oburzenie
disgusting (dvs'gastyŋg)adj.
wstrętny; obrzydliwy;oburzający
dish (dysz) s. półmisek; naczynie;potrawa; danie; v. nakładać; podawać; drążyć;okpiwać
dishes ('dyszyz) pl. statki;
naczynia;smaczne potrawy
dish-cloth ('dysz,kloš) s.
ścierka do wycierania talerzy
disheveled (dy'szeweld) adj.
rozczochrany; zaniedbany
dishonest (dys'onyst) adj. nieuczciwy; nie godny zaufania
dishonesty (dys'onysty) s. nie-
uczciwość;nieuczciwy postępek
dishonor (dys'oner) s. hańba;
dyshonor; niehonorowanie;v.lżyć
dishonorable (dys'onerebl) adj.
haniebny; podły;bez czci i wiary
dishwasher ('dysh,łoszer) s.
pomywacz(ka)
dish-water (dysz,ło:ter) s. pomyje
disillusion (,dysy'lu:żyn) s.
rozczarowanie;otrzeźwienie
disincline (,dysyn'klajn) v.
zniechęcać; mieć niechęć
disinclined (,dysyn'klajnd) adj.
zniechęcony;źle usposobiony
disinfect (,dysyn'fekt) v. odkażać ;zdyzenfekować
disinfectant (,dysyn'fektent)
s. środek odkażający
disinherit ('dysyn'heryt) v.
wydziedziczyć; wydziedziczać
disintegrate (dys'yntegrejt) v.
rozpadać (się); rozkładać (się)
disinterested (dys'yntrystyd)
adj. bezinteresowny; nie zainteresowany;obiektywny
disjoint(dys'dżoint)v. rozłączać;
rozdzielać;zwichnąć;rozerwać
disk (dysk) s. krążek; tarcza;
płyta gramofonowa; dysk
dislike (dys'lajk) v. nie lubić;
mieć odrazę; s. odraza; niechęć;awersja; wstręt

dislocate,('dyslekejt) v.
zwichnąć; przesunąć;zatrącić
disloyal (,dys'lojel) adj. niewierny; nielojalny; zdradziecki
dismal ('dyzmel) adj. nieszczęsny; ponury; posępny
dismantle (dys'maentl) v. rozmontowywać; ogołacać; odzierać;rozbroić;pozbawiać
dismay (dys'mej) s. trwoga;
przestrach; v. przerażać;
konsternować;skonsternować
dismember (dys'member) v. roz-
członować; rozebrać na części
dismiss (dys'mys) v. odprawiać;
zwalniać; odsuwać od siebie
dismissal (dys'mysel) s. zwolnienie; dymisja;rozejście się
dismount ('dys'maunt) v. zsiadać z konia; wyjmować z opra-
wy; wysadzać z siodła
disobedience (dyse'bi:djens)
s. nieposłuszeństwo; opór
disobedient (dyse'bi:djent)
adj. nieposłuszny; oporny
disobey (,dyse'bej) v. nie-
słuchać; być nieposłusznym
disoblige (,dyse'blajdż) v.
lekceważyć; bagatelizować
disorder (dys'o:rder) s. nieporządek; zamieszki; zaburzenie
disorderly (dys'o:rderly)adj.
nieporządny; niesforny; gorszący; burzliwy;bezładny
disown (dys'oun) v. wypierać
się; zaprzeczać; nie uznawać
disparage (dys'paerydż) v.
poniżać; ubliżać; dyskredyto-
wać;uwłaszczać;lekceważyć
dispassion (dys'paeszyn) s.
beznamiętność; odiektywizm
dispassionate (dys'paeszynyt)
adj. beznamiętny;obiektywny
dispatch (dys'paecz) s. wysył-
ka; wysłanie; sprawność; szybkość; szybkie załatwienie;
v. wysyłać; załatwiać
dispel (dys'pel) v. rozwiewać
(obawy);rozpędzać(chmury)
dispensable (dys'pensebl) adj.
zbędny; niekonieczny;do uchyle-
nia

dispense (dys'pens) v. wydzielać; wymierzać; wydawać; udzielać;sporządzać(lekarstwo)

dispense with (dys'pens łyś) v. pomijać; obyć się

disperse (dys'pe:rs) v. rozpraszać; rozpędzać; rozjeżdżać się; rozsiewać;płoszyć

displace (dys'plejs) v. przemieszczać; wypierać; usuwać

display (dys'plej) v. wystawiać; popisywać się; s. wystawa; popis; pokaz;parada

displease (dys'pli:z) v. urażać; drażnić; gniewać; dotykać; oburzać; irytować

displeased (dys'pli:zd) adj. urażony; zirytowany; niezadowolony;obrażony;poirytowany

displeasure (dys'pleżer) s. niezadowolenie; gniew;irytacja

disposal (dys'pouzel) s. rozkład; zbyt; sprzedaż; przekazanie; rozporządzenie;niszczenie

dispose (dys'pouz) v. rozmieszczać; rozporządzić; pozbyć się; sprzedać;usunąć;niszczyć

disposed (dys'pouzd) adj. skłonny; usposobiony(dobrze,źle etc.)

disposition (dys'pouzyszyn) s. skłonność; pociąg; zarządzenie; dyspozycje;rozporządzanie

disproportionate (,dyspre'po:rsznyt) adj. nieproporcjonalny

dispute (dys'pju:t) s. spór; kłótnia; v. sprzeczać się; kłócić się; kwestionować

disqualify (dys'kłolyfaj) v. dyskwalifikować

disquiet (dys'kłajet) v. niepokoić; s. niepokój; adj. niespokojny;zaniepokojony

disregard (,dysry'ga:rd) v. pomijać; lekceważyć;s.lekceważenie

disrepute (,dysry'pju:t) s. niesława;hańba; zła reputacja

disrespectful (,dysry'spektfel) adj. niegrzeczny; niedelikatny

disrupt (dys'rapt) v. rozrywać; rozdzierać;przerwać; obalić

dissatisfaction ('dysseatys'-faekszyn) s. niezadowolenie

dissatisfied (dys,satys'fajd) adj. niezadowolony

dissension (dy'senszyn) s. waśń; niezgoda; swary

dissent (dy'sent) s. różnica; rozbieżność zdań; v. różnić się w zapatrywaniach;odstępstwo

dissimilar ('dy'symyler) adj. niepodobny; różny

dissipate (dy'sypejt) v. rozpraszać; marnować; trwonić; marnotrawić;rozgonić;hulać

dissociate (dy'sousjejt) v. rozłączać; zrywać(z kimś,czymś)

dissolute ('dyselu:t) adj. rozwiązły; rozpustny

dissolution (,dys'elu:szyn) s. rozkład; zanik; rozpuszczenie; rozwiązanie;smierć;zgon;rozpad

dissolve (dy'zolw) v. rozpuszczać; rozkładać; niszczyć; rozwiązywać; zanikać;skasować

dissuade (dy'słejd) v. odradzać; odwodzić (kogos);wyperswadować

distance ('dystens) s. odległość; odstęp; oddalenie;v.zdystansować

distant ('dystent) adj. daleki; odległy; powściągliwy; z rezerwą

distaste (,dys'tejst) s. niesmak; niechęć; odraza; awersja

distasteful (,dys'tejstful) adj. odstręczający;wstrętny;przykry

distend (dys'tend) v. rozdymać; rozszerzać;nabrzmiewać;nadąć

distill (dy'styl) v. przekraplać; destylować;przesączać;kapać

distinct (dys'tynkt) adj. odmienny; odrębny; wyraźny; dobitny

distinction (dys'tynkszyn) s. rozróżnienie; wyróżnienie; wytworność; podział;wyrazistość

distinctive (dys'tynktyw) adj. odróżniający się;charakterystyczny

distinguish (dys'tyngłysz) v. rozróżniać; klasyfikować;odznaczyć

distinguished (dystyngłyszt) adj. wybitny; znakomity; dystyngowany;odznaczający się

distort (dys'to:rt) v. wykrzywiać; wykręcać; przekręcać

distract (dys'traekt) v. odrywać; rozproszyć; oszołomić

distracted (dys'traektyd) adj.
oszalały; w rozterce; skłopo-
tany;roztargniony;rozproszony
distraction (dys'traekszyn) s.
dystrakcja; roztargnienie;
rozrywka; rozterka; szaleństwo;zamieszanie;odwrócenie uwagi
distress (dys'tres) s. męka;
strapienie; niedostatek; potrzeba; niebezpieczeństwo
distressed (dys'trest) adj.
umęczony; udręczony;w niedoli
distribute (dys'trybju:t) v.
udzielać; rozmieszczać;rozdać
distribution (dys'tryju;szyn)
s. rozdział; podział; dystry-
bucja;roznoszenie;a.rozdzielczy
district ('dystrykt) s. okręg;
powiat; dystrykt;dzielnica;rejon
distrust (dys'trast) s. nieufność; niedowierzanie; v.nie-
ufać; niedowierzać;podejrzewać
disturb (dys'te:rb) v. przeszkadzać; niepokoić; zakłócać;
mącić; zaburzyć;denerwować
disturbance (dys'te:rbens) s.
zakłócenie; zaburzenie; naruszenie;burda;awantura;rozruchy
disuse (dys'ju:z) v. zarzucenie; nieużywanie;s.nieużywanie
ditch (dycz),s. rów; v. kopać;
drenować; utknąć w rowie; rzucać do rowu(samolot w morze)
dive (dajw) v. nurkować; zanurzać się; skakać z trampoliny;
s. nurkowanie; zanurzenie; melina;lot nurkowy;pikowanie;knajpa
diver ('dajwer) s. nurek; skoczek
z trampoliny;ptak nurkujący
diverge (daj'we:rdż) v. rozchodzić się; odchylać się; zbaczać;
odbiegać;rozbiegać się
diverse (daj'we:rs) adj. odmienny; rozmaity;inny;zmienny
diversion (daj'we:rżyn) s.odchy-
lenie;objazd;rozrywka;dywersja
diversion (dy'we:rżyn) s. zboczenie; dywersja; rozrywka;odwróce-
nie uwagi;oderwanie uwagi
diversity (daj'we:rsyty) s. roz-
maitość;różnorodność;urozmaicenie

diversity (dy'we:rsyty) s. od-
mienność;roznorodność;rozmaitość
divert (daj'we:rt) v. odwracać (uwagę); odrywać; rozerwać; rozbawić;bawić(kogoś)
divide (dy'wajd) v. dzielić;
rozdzielać; oddzielać; różnić
divide by (dy'wajd,baj) v.
dzielić przez...(liczbę)
divine (dy'wajn) adj. boski;
boży; v. wróżyć; przepowiadać
diving ('dajwyng) s. skakanie
z trampoliny;pikować samolotem
divinity (dy'wynyty) s. bóstwo;
boskość; teologia
divisible (dy'wyzebl) adj. podzielny (przez,na etc.)
division (dy'wyżyn) s. podział;
rozdział; dzielenie; dział;
wydział; oddział; dywizja
divorce (dy'wo:rs) s. rozwód;
rozdzielenie; y. rozwodzić
się; oddzielać;a.rozwodowy
dizzy ('dyzy) adj. wirujący;
oszołomiony;v.oszałamiać
do (du:) v. czynić; robić; wykonać; zwiedzać;przyrządzać
do away ('du,ełej) v. znieść;
pozbyć się; zabić;skasować
do not ('du not) = don't (dont)
nie(rób);nie(idź);nie(stój,etc.)
do in ('du,yn) v.uwięzić; zlikwidować; zabić;wsadzić do paki
do up ('du,ap) v. przerobić;
odnowić; zmęczyć;upudrować etc.
do well (,du'łel) v. mieć się
dobrze; powodzić się
do without (,du'łysout) v.oby-
wać się bez (kogoś,czegoś)
do you know? (du: ju nou) expr.
czy pan wie (zna) ? czy pan sły-
szał?
docile ('dousajl) adj. uległy;
posłuszny;pojętny;giętki;łagodny
dock (dok) s. dok; basen; molo;
miejsce oskarżonego; v. umieścić w doku; cumować przy molu
dockyard (dokja:rd) s. stocznia
doctor ('dakter) s. lekarz;
doktor (medycyny;filozofii etc.)
doctrine ('daktryn) s. doktryna

document ('dokjument) s. dokument;v. udokumentowac
documentary (,dokju'mentery)s.
adj. dokumentarny (film etc.)
dodge (dodż) v. uchylic; unik-
nąc; zwodzic; s, unik; kruczek; sztuczka;odskok;kiwanie
doe (dou) s. łania ;pl.:does (douz)
does (daz) v. on czyni; robi;
zob.: do
dog (dog) s. pies;uchwyt;klamra
dog-catcher (dog'kaeczer) s.
rakarz; oprawca; hycel
dogged ('dogyd) adj. uparty;
zawzięty;wytrwały
doggie ('dogi) s. psina
dogma ('dogme) s. dogmat
dog-tired ('dog'tajerd) adj.
skonany; ledwo żywy;zmęczony
doings ('du:yngs) pl. sprawki;
uczynki; wyprawiania;psoty
dole (doul) s. zasiłek; zapomoga; smutek;v.mało dawac
doll (dol) s. lalka; (slang)
dziewczyna;v.wystroic się
dollar ('doler) s. dolar
dollish ('dolysz) adj. lalko-
waty(a);lalusiowaty
dolorous ('douleres) adj.
smętny; żałosny; zbolały
dolphin ('dolfyn) s. delfin
dome (doum) s. kopuła; sklepienie;v.nakrywac kopuła.
domestic (de'mestyk) adj. domowy; krajowy; domatorski;
s. służący; służąca
domesticate (de'mestykejt) v.
oswajac; zadomowic
domicile ('domysajl) s, miejsce zamieszkania; v. osiedlac;
zamieszkac na stałe
dominate ('domynejt) v. domi-
nowac; gorowac; przeważac;
panowac;miec zwierzchnictwo
domination ('domynejszyn) s.
władza; panowanie; przewaga
domineer (,domy'nier) v. domi-
nowac; rządzic się; rozkazy-
wac;tyranizowac;panoszyc się
domineering (,domy'nieryng)
adj. tyranizujący; apodyktyczny; despotyczny; władczy

donate (dou'nejt) v. podarowac
donation (dou'nejszyn) s. daro-
wizna, donacja; dar
done (dan) adj. zrobiony; uczy-
niony; zob.: do
donkey ('donky) s. osioł
donor ('douner) s. donator;
dawca (krwi etc.);darujący
doom (du:m) s. zguba; zły los;
śmierc; potępienie; v. potępiac; skazac na zgubę;przesądzac
Doomsday ('du:mzdej) s. dzien
sądu ostatecznego
door (do:r) s. drzwi;brama
door handle ('do:r,haendl) s.
klamka
doorkeeper ('do:r,ki:per) s.
dozorca;portier; oddźwierny
doorknob ('do:r,nob) s. klamka
doormat ('do:r,maet) s, wycieraczka (przy drzwiach)
doorway ('do:r,łej) s. wejscie
dope (doup) s. maź; lakier; narkotyk; informacja (poufna);
głupiec (slang). v. narkotyzowac; zaprawiac;fałszowac
dormitory ('do:rmytry) s. dom
studencki; sypialnia
dose (dous) s. dawka; dodatek;
dawkowanie; v. dawkowac (lekarstwo); mieszac; fałszowac
(wino);leczyc;dozowac
dot (dot) s. kropka; punkt;
v. kropkowac; rozsiewac
dote (dout) v. wariowac; kochac
przesadnie; dziecinniec
double ('dabl) adj. podwojny;
dwukrotny; fałszywy; v. podwajac; adv. podwojnie;w dwojnasob
double up ('dabl,ap) v. składac
się we dwoje; zsuwac się (razem);przybiegac;dzielic pokoj
double bed ('dabl,bed) podwojne
łóżko
double-breasted ('dabl,brestyd)
adj. dwurzędowy(płaszcz,marynarka)
double-decker ('dabl-'deker) s.
dwupokładowiec; dwupiętrowiec
double-park ('dabl²pa:rk) v.
parkowac podwojnie (na jezdni)
double-room ('dabl,ru:m) s.
pokoj dwuosobowy(w hotelu etc.)

doubt (daut) s. wątpliwość; niedowierzanie; v. wątpić; powąt-
piewać; niedowierzać
doubtful ('dautful) adj. wątpliwy; niepewny;niezdecydowany
doubtless ('dautlys) adv. nie-
wątpliwie; bez wątpienia
douche (du'sz) s. natrysk
dough (dou) s. ciasto; (slang)
forsa; pieniądze
doughnut ('dounat) s. pączek
(z dziurą)
dove (daw) s. gołąb(ica)
down (dałn) s. wydma; puch;
meszek ;puszek;piórka
down (dałn) adv. na dół; niżej;
nisko; v. obniżać; poniżać;
przewrócić; strącić; przełknąć
downcast ('dałnka:st) adj.
przybity; przygnębiony; ze
spuszczonymi oczyma
downfall ('dałnfo:l) s. upadek;
klęska; ruina; zguba
downhill ('dałn'hyl) adj. opa-
dający; s. spadek ;adv.na dół
downpour ('dałnpo:r) s. ulewa
downright ('dałnrajt) adv. zupełnie; wprost; adj. zupełny;
szczery; otwarty; uczciwy
downstairs ('dałn'steerz) adv.
na dół; w dole ;na dole;pod nami
downtown ('dałntałn) s. centrum
miasta; adv. w śródmieściu;
adj. śródmiejski
downwards ('dałnłódz) adv.
w dół; ku dołowi ;na dół;z góry
downy ('dałhy) adj. puszysty;
(slang):chytry ;falisty;puchaty
dowry ('dałry) s. posag; wiano;
dar wrodzony ; talent
doze (douz) s. drzemka; v. drzemać; zdrzemnąć się; zasnąć
dozen ('dazn) s. tuzin
drab (draeb) s.& adj. brudno-
brunatny; nudny; szary; brudas;
prostytutka; v. puszczać się
draft (dra:ft) s. szkic; brulion
zarys; przekaz; pobór; rysunek;
v. szkicować; projektować; rysować; odkomenderować ;wyżłobić
draftsman ('dra:ftsmen) s. kreślarz; rysownik; projektodawca

drag (draeg) v. wlec; ciągnąć;
s. pogłębiarka; pojazd; wleczenie; opór czołowy
dragon ('draegen) s. smok
dragonfly ('draegenflaj) s.
ważka
drain (drejn) v. odwadniać;
wysączać; ociekać; s. dren;
spust; ściek rów odwadniający
drainage ('drejnydż) s. odwad-
nianie; wody ściekowe; obszar odpływowy (rzeki)
drainpipe ('drejnpajp) s.dren
drake (drejk) s. kaczor
drama ('dra:ma) s. dramat
dramatic (dre'maetyk) adj.
dramatyczny,jak w sztuce;żywy
drank (draenk) s. pijak; pijany; zob.: drink
drape (drejp) v. upinać; spadać fałdami; drapować;s.kotara
drastic ('draestyk) adj. drastyczny ;gwałtowny; surowy
draught (draeft) s. przeciąg;
ciąg; łyk; dawka; zanurzenie
statku ;wyporność;a.pociągowy
draw; drew; drawn (dro:; dru:;
dro:n)
draw (dro:) v. ciągnąć; wyciągać; przyciągać; czerpać; wdychać; ściągać (wodze); spuszczać (wodę); napinać (łuk);
wlec ;rysować; kreślić
draw near(dro:nier) v. zbliżać
się;przybliżać się
drawback (dro:baek) s. strona
ujemna; v. cofać się(draw back)
draw up (dro:,sp) v. podciągać
(się); redagować; zbliżać się;
zrównać się; ustawiać(wojsko)
drawer ('dro:er) s. szuflada;
kreślarz; rysownik;bufetowy
drawers ('dro:ers) pl. kalesony; majtki(damskie,dziecięce ...)
drawing ('dro:yng) s. rysunek
drawing pen ('dro:yng,pen) s.
grafion ;piórko kreślarskie
drawing room ('dro:yng,ru:m)
s. salon ;wagon salonowy
drawn (dro:n) adj. nierozstrzygnięty; ciągniony; wychudzony;
zob.: draw(wyciągnięta:szabla)

drawn-out (dro:n aut) adj.
przewlekły ;wyciągniety(z pochwy)
dread (dred) s. strach; postrach; lęk; v. bać się bardzo; lękać się; adj. straszny
dreadful (dredful) adj. przeraźliwy; okropny ;straszny
dream; dreamt; dreamt (dri:m;
dremt; dremt)
dream (dri:m) v. śnić; marzyć;
s. sen; marzenie;mrzonka;uro-
je-nie
dreamt (dremt) v. mieć sen,
marzenie; zob.: dream
dreamy ('dri:my) adj. marzycielski; mglisty;niewyraźny
dreary ('dryery) adj. posępny;
ponury;smętny;melancholijny
dregs (dregz) pl. osady; męty
drench (drencz) v. zmoczyć;
przemoczyć ;s. ulewa
dress (dres) s. ubiór; strój;
szata; suknia; v. ubierać;
stroić; opatrywać; czyścić;
czesać; przyrządzać; wykan-
czać; wyprawiać ;wygarbować
dress down ('dres dałn) v.
besztać ; czyścić (konia)
dress up ('dres,ap) v. stroić
dressing ('dresyng) s. przyprawa; opatrunek; nawóz ;ubiór
dressing-case ('dresyng,kejs)
s. neseser
dressing-gown('dresyn,gołn) s.
podomka; szlafrok
dressing-room ('dresyng,ru:m) s.
garderoba ;ubieralnia;umywalnia
dressing-table ('dresyng,tejbl)
s. toaleta (mebel)
dressmaker ('dresmejker) s.
krawiec damski; krawcowa
drew (dru:) zob.: draw
drift (dryft) s. dryf; znoszenie; bierność; prąd; dążność;
treść; zamieć; zaspa; nanos
v. dryfować; znosić; plątać
się; nanosić;płynąć z prądem
drill 1. (dryl) s. świder; wiertarka; dryl; musztra; v. wiercić; świdrować; ćwiczyć; musztrować;drążyć;sortować(wagony)
drill 2. (dryl) s. rowek do sia-
nia; siewnik rzędowy; v. siać;
obsadzać w rowkach

drink; drank; drunk ('drynk;
draenk; drank)
drink ('drynk) v. pić; przepi-
jać; s, napój; woda (morze)
drip (dryp) v. kapać; ociekać;
ciec; s. kapanie; okap; piła(sl);
nudziara ;kapka;kropla(wody etc.)
drip-dry ('dryp,draj) s. bielizna niewymagająca prasowa-
nia (schnąca na wieszaku etc.)
dripping ('drypyng) s. tłuszcz
spod pieczeni; adj. kapiący;
ociekający ; przemoczony
drive; drove; driven (drajw;
drouw; drywn)
drive (drajw) v. pędzić; gnać;
wieźć; powozić; prowadzić; napędzać; jechać; wbijać ;drążyć
s. przejażdżka; obława; napęd;
droga; dojazd ;energia;pościg
drive at (drajw et) v. kierować (rozmowę ku...)
drive out (drajw,aut) v. wyjeżdżać (z garażu);wypędzać
drive-in (drajw,yn) s. obsługa
w samochodzie :bank; jadłodajnia; kino; sklep;poczta
drive-in movies (drajw,yn
mu:wiz) kino do oglądania
z samochodu
driven (drywn) v. napędzany;
zob.: drive
driver (drajwer) s. kierowca
driving license ('drajwyng-
,lajsens) s. prawo jazdy
drizzle ('dryzl) s. mżący
deszcz; v. mżyć; adj. mżący;
drobny (deszcz)
drone (droun) s. truten; bucze-
nie; dudniący mówca; v. zbijać
bąki; buczeć; dudnić(monotonnie)
droop (dru:p) v. opadać; zwisać;
zwieszać (głowę); s. zwis;
spadek (tonu); utrata (otuchy)
drop (drop) v. kapać; ciec;
upuszczać; spadać; opadać;
s. kropla; cukierek; spadek
(temperatury);łyk;kieliszek;zniż-
ka;kotara;upadek;obniżenie
drop in ('drop,yn) v. wpaść (do
kogoś);wejść na chwilę
dropout (dropaut) s. osoba prze-
rywająca (studia lub szkołę)

drove (drouw) zob.: drive

drown (draun) v. tonąc; topic;
tłumic; głuszyc; zagłuszac

drowsy ('drauzy) adj. senny;
spiący; ospały;na pół spiący

drudge (dradż) s. niewolnik;
popychadło; v. harowac

drug (drag) s. lek; lekarstwo;
v. narkotyzowac; przesycac

drug-addict ('drag,aedykt) s.
narkoman

drugstore ('drag,stor) s. apteka; drogeria

drum (dram) s. bęben; v. bębnic;zwoływac bębnieniem;zjedny-
drummer ('dramer) s. dobosz wac

drunk (drank) adj. pijany;
zob.: drink

drunken driving (áranken
drajwyŋg) s. kierowanie po
pijanemu (samochodem etc.)

dry (draj) adj. suchy;wytrawny
(wino) v. osuszac; suszyc;(łzy)
zeschnąc;wyjaławiac;wycierac

dry up (draj,ap) v. wycierac;
wysychac;zapomniec;zaniemówic

dry-clean ('draj kli:n) v.
oczyscic chemicznie (sucho)

dry goods('drajgudz) pl. materiały do szycia;konfekcja

dual ('dju:el) adj. podwójny;
dwoisty;dwudzielny;wspólny

duchess ('daczys) s. księżna

duck (dak) s. kaczka; unik; v.
zanurzyc; zrobic unik; nurkowac

duct (dakt) s. przewód; kanał

dud (dad) s. poroniony pomysł;
safanduła; nieuk; niewypał;
strach na wróble;adj.niezdolny

dude (d(j)u:d) s. elegancik;
laluś; turysta;goguś;wyciecz-ko-
dude ranch ('du:d,ra:nch) ran-cz
czo wakacyjne(dla mieszczuchów)

due (dju:) adj. należny; płatny;
należyty; adv. w kierunku na
(wschód); s. to co się należy;
należności; opłata;składka

due to ('dju:,tu) exp. z powodu

duel ('dju(;)el) s. pojedynek

dug (dag) s. cycek; wymię; zob.:
dig

dug2.(dag)s. dójka

dugout ('dagaut) s. ziemianka;
łódź drążona; okop; schron

duke (dju:k) s. książę

dull (dal) adj. tępy; głuchy;
ospały; niemrawy; nudny; ponury; ciemny;v.tępic;tłumic

duly ('dju:ly) adv. własciwie;
należycie; punktualnie;słusznie

dumb (dam) adj. niemy; milczący; głupi;v.odbierac mowę

dumbfounded (dam'faundyd) adj.
osłupiony;osłupiały;oniemiały

dummy ('damy) s, imitacja; bałwan; manekin; (wulg.) niemowa;
adj. udany; podstawiony; imito-
wany ; na niby; niby to

dump (damp) s. smietnisko; hałda;
magazyn; v. zwalac; rzucac; zarzucac (towarem obcym)

dun (dan) s. wierzyciel; inkasent długów; v. napastowac
o zapłatę długu ;a.ciemnobrązowy

dune (dju:n) s. wydma ;diuna

dung (daŋg)s. nawóz; gnój; bagno moralne; v. nawozic; użyzniac
ziemię; gnoic

dungeon ('dandżen) s. loch;baszta
v. więzic w lochu lub baszcie

dupe (du:p) s. ofiara; wystrych-
nięty na dudka ;v. okpic;nabrac

duplicate ('dju:plykyt) adj.
podwójny; s. duplikat; w dwu
egzemplarzach; v. podwajac;
duplikowac (niepotrzebnie)

duplicity (dju:'plysyty) s. dwu-
licowosc; podstęp;fałsz;obłuda

durable ('djuerebl) adj. trwały

duration (dju'rejszyn) s. trwanie; czas trwania

duress (dju'res) s. przymus

during ('djueryŋg) prep. podczas; w czasie ;w ciągu;przez;za

dusk (dask) s. zmierzch; mrok;
cień; adj. ciemny; mroczny;
v. zacmic; zamroczyc

dust (dast) s. pył; kurz; pro-
chy; pyłek; v. odkurzac; trze-
pac; kurzyc się; posypywac

dust bowl (dast,boul) s. kraj
suszy i burz(zamiec)piaskowych

dustcover ('dast, kawer) s.
obwoluta; pokrowiec od kurzu

duster ('daster) s. odkurzacz;
wiatr z kurzem;zmoitka
dust-pan ('dast,paen) s. śmiet-
niczka;łopatka na śmieci
dust-storm ('dast,sto:rm) s.
wicher z tumanami kurzu
dusty ('dasty) adj. zakurzony;
pokryty kurzem; suchy; nudny
Dutch (dacz) adj. holenderski;
w niełasce; lichy
duty ('dju:ty) s. powinność;
obowiązek; szacunek; służba;
uległość; cło; podatek od
sprzedaży;funkcja;obowiązki
dwarf (dżo:rf) s. karzeł;
krasnoludek; adj. karłowaty;
v. pomniejszać; karleć; skar-
leć;skarłowacieć;zmniejszać
dwell; dwelt; dwelt (dżel; wzrosł
dżelt; dżelt)
dwell (dżel) v. mieszkać; zatrzymywać się; rozwodzić się
(o czyms); zwlekać;przystanąć
dwelling (dżelyng) s. mieszkanie;pomieszczenie mieszkalne
dwelt (dżelt) v. mieszkał...
zob,: dwell
dwindle (dżyndl) v. maleć; top-
nieć; marnieć; kurczyć się;
tracić znaczenie;zwyrodnieć
dye (daj) v. barwić; farbować;
s. barwa; barwik;farba
dying (dajyng) v. umierający;
zanikający; zob.: die
dyke (dajk) s. grobla; rów;
tama;v.ogroblić;ochronić tamą
dynamic (daj'naemyk) adj. dyna-
miczny;energiczny;z wigorem
dynamics (daj'naemyks) s. dyna-
mika (sił działających razem)
dynamite ('dajne,majt) s. dynamit;v.wysadzać dynamitem
dynamo ('dajne,mou) s. dynamo
dynasty ('dajnesty) s. dynastia
dysentery ('dysnetry) s. czer-
wonka; dyzenteria(krwawa)
e (i:) piąta litera angielskiego
alfabetu
each (i:cz) pron. każdy;za(sztukę
each other ('i:cz, odzer)siebie;
nawzajem (dwie osoby);sobie

eager ('i:ger) adj. gorliwy;ostry;
żądny;ożywiony pragnieniem;żywy
eagerness('i:gernyss) s. gorliwość;skwapliwość;pochopność
eagle ('i:gl) s. orzeł;a.orli
ear (ier) s. ucho; słuch; kłos
(zboża);a.uszny;dotyczący uszu
eardrum ('ierdram) s. bębenek
ucha; błona bębenkowa(ucha)
early ('e:rly) adj. wczesny;
adv. wcześnie;przedwcześnie
earn (e:rn) v. zarabiać; zasługiwać;zapracować;zdobywać(sławę)
earnest ('e:rnyst) adj. poważny;
gorliwy; s. powaga;zadatek;dowód
earnings ('e:rnynz) pl. zarobki
earphone ('ierfoun) s. słuchawka;loki ułożone na uszach
earring ('ieryng) s. kolczyk
earshot ('ier,szot) w zasięgu głosu ;w zasięgu słuchu
earth (e:rs) s. ziemia;świat;gle-
ba
earthen ('e:rsen) adj. ziemisty; gliniany;wypiekany z gliny
earthenware ('e:rsen,łe:r) s.
wyroby garncarskie(wypiekane)
earthly ('e:rsly) adj. ziemski
earthquake('e:rs,kłejk) s.
trzęsienie ziemi
earthworm ('e:rs,łe:rm) s.
(glista) ;dżdżownica
ease (i:z) v. łagodzić; uspokoić;
odciążyć; s. spokój; wygoda;
beztroska;ulga;łatwość;bezczynność
easel ('i:zl) s. sztaluga
easily ('i:zyly) adv. łatwo;
lekko; swobodnie;bez trudności
east (i:st) s. wschód; adj.
wschodni; adv. na wschód
Easter ('i:ster) s. Wielkanoc
eastern ('i:stern) adj. wschodni;człowiek wschodu;prawosławny
eastwards ('i:stłerdz) adv. ku
wschodowi;na wschód;adj.wschodni
easy (i:zy) adj. łatwy; beztroski; wygodny; adv. łatwo;
swobodnie; lekko;s.odpoczynek
easy chair ('i:zy,czeer) s.
fotel (klubowy) miękki
eat; ate; eaten (i:t; ejt; i:tn)
eat (i:t) v. jeść (posiłek)

eat up ('i:t,ap) v. wyjeść
eaten (i:tn) adj. zjedzony;
zob. eat
eaves (i:wz) pl. okap(dachu)
eavesdropping ('i:wzdropyŋg)
s. podsłuchiwanie(rozmowy)
ebbtide ('ebtajd) s. odpływ
w morze;v.odpływać(jak morze)
ebony ('ebeny) s. heban
eccentric (ik:sentryk) adj.
dziwaczny; s., ekscentryk;
dziwak; mimosród;dziwaczka
ecclesiastic (ik,ly:zi'eastyk)
adj. kościelny; s. duchowny
echo, ('ekou) s. echo; v. odbijać się echem; powtarzać za
kims; odbijać głos
eclipse (i'klyps) s. zaćmienie;
v. zaciemniac;zaćmiewać
ecology (i'koledży) s. ekologia;
związek między środowiskiem
a organizmem(część biologii)
economic (,i:ke'nomyk) adj;
ekonomiczny;gospodarczy
economical (,i:ke:nomykel) adj.
oszczędny; ekonomiczny
economics (,i:ke'nomyks) pl.
nauka o ekonomii (gospodarce)
economist (i'konemyst) s. ekono-
mista;specjalista od gospodarki
economize (i:kone,majz) v.
oszczędzać;zmniejszać wydatki
economy (i,konemy) s. ękonomia;
gospodarka;oszczędność
economy class (i'konemy,kla:s)
s. druga klasa (w pociągu;
samolocie);klasa turystyczna
ecstasy ('ekstesy) s. zachwyt;
ekstaza; uniesienie;siódme niebo
eddy ('edy) s. wir; v. wirować
edelweiss ('ejdl,wajs) s. szarotka (kwiat górski)
edge (edż) s. ostrze; krawędź;
kraj; v. ostrzyc; obszywać;
wyślizgać się;przysuwać po trochu
edging ('edżyŋg) s. brzeg; ob-
szywka; lamówka;skraj
edgy ('edży) adj. nerwowy;
podniecony;o ostrych kantach
edible('edybl) adj. jadalny
edict ('i:dykt) s. edykt; dekret

edifice ('dyfys) s. budowla;
gmach (duży i imponujący)
edifying ('edyfajyŋg) adj. po-
uczający(zwłaszcza moralnie)
edit ('edyt) v. redagować; wydawać;zarządzać gazetą etc.
edition (i'dyszyn) s. wydanie;
nakład (ksiażki,gazety etc.)
editor (e'dyter) s. redaktor;
wydawca;pisarz"od redakcji"
editorial (,edy'to:rjel) s.
artykuł od redakcji; adj.
redakcyjny; redaktorski
educate ('edju:kejt) v. kształcić; wychowywać;płacić za szko-
education (,edju'kejszyn) s. 'lę
wykształcenie; nauka; oświata;
wychowanie; tresura;wiedza
educational (,edju'kejszenl)
adj. kształcący; wychowawczy
educator ('edju,kejter) s.
wychowawca; wychowawczyni
eel (i:l) s. węgorz
effect (i'fekt) s. skutek; wrażenie; v. wykonywać; dokonywać
effects (i'fekts) pl. ruchomości; dobytek;manatki
effective (i'fektyw) adj. skuteczny; wydajny; rzeczywisty;
efektowny;wchodzący w życie
effeminate (i'femynyt) adj.
zniewieściały;nie męski;słaby
effervescent (,efer'wesnt) adj.
musujący; kipiący;tryskający ży-
efficacy ('efykesy) s. skutecz-'ciem
ność;dawanie porządanych wyników
efficiency (i'fyszensy) s. wydajność; skuteczność; spraw-
ność(przy minimum nakładów)
efficient(i'fyszent) adj. skuteczny; wydajny; sprawny
effigy ('efydży) s, wizerunek;
podobizna; czyjaś kukła
effort ('efert) s. wysiłek;
effusive (i'fju:syw) adj. wylewny;wylany;ekspansywny;wulka-
egg (eg) s. jajko; v. zaćhęcać;'niczny;
namawiać;podbechtać;podniecać
eggcup ('eg,kap) s. kieliszek
na jajko;kieliszek do jaj

egghead ('eg,hed) s. intelektualista (nieżyciowy)

egoism ('egou,zyem) s. egoizm

egress ('i:gres) s. wyjście;
wyjazd; uchodzenie;wypływ

Egyptian (i'dżypszen) adj.
egipski

eiderdown ('ajder,dałn) s. kaczy puch; kołdra;pierzyna

eight (ejt) num.osiem; s. ósemka; ośmioro;ośmiu wioślarzy

eighteen('ejt'i:n) num. osiemnaście; osiemnaścioro;osiemnaście

eightfold ('ejt,fould) num.
ośmiokrotny; adv. ośmiokrot-
nie ;osiem razy

eighty ('ejty) num. osiemdziesiąt; s. osiemdziesiątka

either ('ajdzer) pron. każdy
(z dwu); obaj; obie; oboje;
jeden lub drugi;adv.także;też

either... or ('ajdzer..o:r)
albo... albo

ejaculate (i'dżaekju,lejt) v.
zawołać; krzyknąć;wytrysnąć

eject (i'dżekt) v. wyrzucać
(się); eksmitować;usuwać

elaborate (i'laebe,rejt) v.
opracować; adj. wypracowany;
staranny;skomplikowany

elapse (i'laeps) v. minąć;
przeminąć ;przemijać

elastic (i'laestyk) adj. sprę-
żysty; rozciągliwy; elastyczny; s. guma; gumka(do majtek...)

elated (i'lejtyd) adj. podniecony; uniesiony; dumny

elbow ('elboł) s. łokieć; zakręt; kolanko; v. szturchać;
przepychać się; zakręcać

elbow grease ('elboł,gri:s) s.
ciężka praca; wysiłek

elder ('elder) s. człowiek
starszy; adj. starszy
(z dwóch);należący do starszyz-
ny.

elderly ('elderly) adj. pod-
starzały; starszy;starszawy

eldest ('eldyst) adj. najstar-
szy (syn)(w rodzinie)

elect (i'lekt) v. wybrać; postanawiać; decydować; adj.wy-
brany; wyborny; wyborowy

election (i'lekszyn) s. wybór;
wybory (głosowaniem)

elector (i'lekter) s. wyborca;
elektor;członek kolegium wyborcze-
go

electric (i'lektryk) adj. elektryczny;bursztynowy;electryzujący

electrical engineer (e'lektry-
kel,endży'nier) s. inżynier
elektryk

electric chair (i'lektryk,cze:r)
s. krzesło elektryczne (do
egzekucji) (w USA)

electrician (ilek'tryszen) s.
elektryk (monter) (instalator)

electricity (ilek'trysyty) s.
elektryczność;prąd elektryczny

electrify (i'lektryfaj) v.
elektryfikować; elektryzować

electrocute (i'lektrekju:t) v.
uśmiercić prądem elektrycznym

electron (i'lektron) s. elektron

elegance ('elygens) s. elegancja

elegant ('elygent) adj. elegancki;dostojny;doskonały

element('elyment) s. żywioł;
pierwiastek; część składowa
ogniwo; część podstawowa

elemental (,ely'mentl) adj. żywiołowy; zasadniczy; elementarny; podstawowy;konieczny

elementary (,ely'mentery) adj.
elementarny; zasadniczy; niepodzielny; pierwiastkowy

elementary school (,ely'mentery
sku:l) s. szkoła powszechna

elephant ('elyfent) s. słoń

elevate ('ely,wejt) v. podnosić; unosić; wynosić (wzwyż)

elevation (ely'wejszyn) s. wysokość; godność; fasada; podwyższenie

elevator ('ely,wejter) s. winda; dźwig; wyciąg; spichlerz

eleven (i'lewn) num. jedenaście;
s. jedenastka; jedenaścioro

eleventh (i'lewnt) num. jede-
nasty; jedenastka

eligible ('elydżebl) adj. nadający się; odpowiedni na wybór

eliminate (i'lymy,nejt) v. usuwać; wydzielać;pozbywać się;nie
brać pod uwagę;opuszczać

elimination (i,lymy'nejszyn)
s. eliminacja ;pozbycie się
elk (elk) s. łoś
ell (ell) s. łokieć (miara)
ellipse (i'lyps) s. elipsa
elm (elm) s. wiąz
elongate (i'longejt) v. wydłużać się;adj.wydłużony
elope (i'loup) v. uciekać
z ukochanym (potajemnie)
eloquence ('eloukžens) s. elo-
kwencja; krasomówstwo
eloquent ('elokžent) adj. elo-
kwentny; wymowny(też w piśmie)
else (els) adv.inaczej; bo
inaczej; w przeciwnym razie;
poza tym; jeszcze;adj.różny in-
elsewhere (els'hžer) adv. gdzie
indziej;w innym miejscu
elude (i'lu:d) v. ujść; wymknąć
się;obejść prawo;uchylić się
elusive (ilu:syw) adj. nieuchwytny; wymykający się
emanate ('eme,nejt) v. wydobywać; pochodzić;wydzielać się
emancipate (i'maens,ypejt) v.
wyzwolić; wyemancypować
embalm (im'ba:lm) v. zabalsamo-
wać; napełnić aromatem
embankment (im'baeŋkment) s.
nasyp; grobla; nabrzeże
embargo (em'ba:rgou) s. zakaz
handlowania, wjazdu, wyjazdu
embark (im'ba:rk) v. ładować
(się); wsiadać (na statek);
rozpoczynać (przedsięwzięcie)
embark upon (im'ba:rk e'pon) v.
rozpoczynać ;przedsięwziąć
embarrass (im'baeres) v. zakłopotanie; wikłać; przeszkadzać;powodować zadłużenie
embarrassing (im'baeresyŋg)
adj. żenujący; kłopotliwy;
krępujący;zawstydzający
embarrassment (im'baeresment)s.
zakłopotanie; powikłanie;
skrępowanie;zaaferowanie
embassy ('embesy) s. ambasada
embed (im'bed) v. osadzić; sadzić;wmurować;wryć;wkopać
embedded (im'bedyd) adj. osadzo-
ny; wsadzony;wryty;wmurowany
embellish (im'belysz) v. upiększać;ozdabiać;podkolorowywać

embers ('emberz) pl. niewygas-
łe węgle; żarpalące się polana
embezzle (ym'bezl) v. sprzeniewierzać (pieniądze,własność etc.)
embitter (im'byter) v. rozgoryczać; zatruwać; pogarszać
emblem ('emblem) s. godło; wzór
embody (im'body) v. wcielać;
uosabiać; zawierać;włączać
embolden (im'boulden) v. ośmielać; rozzuchwalać ;dodać śmiałości
embolism (embelyzem) s. zator
embrace (im'brejs) v. uścisnąć
się; obejmować; przystępować!
imać się; korzystać; s. uściak;
objęcie ;włączenie(do kategorii)
embroider (im'brojder) v. hafto-
wać;wyszywać;upiększać opowiadanie
embroidery (im'brojdery) s. haft;
hafciarstwo;upiększanie opowiadania
emerald ('emereld) s. szmaragd
emerge (y'me:rdż) v. wynurzać
się; wyłaniać;wynikać;nasunąć się
emergency (y'me:rdżensy) s.
nagła potrzeba; stan wyjątkowy
emergency brake (y'me:rdżensy,
,brejk) s. ręczny hamulec
w samochodzie;hamulec zapasowy
emergency call (y'me:rdżensy,kol)
s. wzywanie pogotowia (nagłe)
emergency exit (y'me:rdżensy,
,eksyt) s. wyjście zapasowe
emergency landing (y'merdżensy,
, laendyŋg)s. przymusowe lądowanie (samolotu)
emigrant ('emygrent) s. wychodźca; emigrant;adj.wychodźczy
emigrate (em'ygrejt) v. emigro-
wać; wywędrować;przeprowadzać się
emigration (,emy'grejszyn) s.
emigracja; wychodźstwo
emigré ('emygrej) s. emigrant
(polityczny);a.emigracyjny(rząd)
eminent ('emynent) adj. dostojny; wybitny; wyniosły; wysoki
eminently ('emynently) adv.
szczególnie; wybitnie;wysoce
emit (y'myt) v. wydawać; wysyłać (światło; fale radiowe;
ciepło; opinie; wypuszczać
(banknoty);nadawać(audycje)
emotion (y'mouszyn) s. wzruszenie; emocja; uczucie(miłości,stra-
chu,gniewu,oburzenia,współczucia)

emotional (y'mouszynel) adj.
emocjonalny;poruszający uczucia
emperor ('emperer) s. cesarz
emphasis ('emfesys) s. nacisk;
emfaza;uwypuklenie;uwydatnienie
emphasize ('emfesajz) v. podkreślać; kłaść nacisk;uwypuklać
emphatic (ym'faetyk) adj. dobitny; wyrazny; stanowczy;
emfatyczny;mówiący z naciskiem
empire ('empajer) s. cesarstwo;
imperium ;adj.empirowy
emplacement (yn'plejsment) s.
umiejscowienie; stanowisko
employ (ym'ploj) v. zatrudniać;
używać; zajmować się; poświęcać (czas);posługiwać się
employee (,emploj'i:) s. pracownik;siła (robocza,biurowa...)
employer (em'plojer) s. pracodawca;pracodawczyni;szef
employment (ym'plojment) s. za-
trudnienie; używanie; zajęcie
employment agency (ym'plojment
'ejdżensy) agencja pośrednict-
wa pracy;biuro zatrudnienia
empower (ym'pałer) v. upełnomocnić; upoważniać;umożliwiać
empress ('emprys) s. cesarzowa
emptiness ('emptynys) s. pustka
empty ('empty) adj. pusty; próżny; v. wypróżniać; wysypywać;
wylewać;wpływać(do morza)
emulate ('emjulejt) v. rywalizować; współzawodniczyć
enable (y'nejbl) v. umożliwiać;
upoważniać;dawać możność
enact (y'naekt) v. postanawiać;
uchwalać; grać (rolę); odgrywać (sztukę); uprawomocnić
enamel (y'naemel) s. emalia;
szkliwo(na zebach etc.)
encase (yn'kejs) v. wsadzać do
pochwy; oprawiać;wpakowywać
enchant (yn'czaent) v. zaczarować; oczarować; zachwycać
encircle (yn'se:rkl) v. otaczać;
okalać;okrążać;okrążyć;otoczyć
enclose (yn'klouz) v. ogradzać;
zamykać; dołączać; załączać;
zawierać;okrążyć(wroga)

enclosure (yn'kloużer) s. ogrodzenie; załącznik;ogradzanie
encounter (yn'kaunter) s. spotkanie; potyczka; pojedynek;
v. natknąć się; spotykać się;
potykać się; mieć utarczkę
encourage (yn'ka:rydż) v. zachęcać; osmielać; popierać;
dodawać odwagi;pomagać
encouragement (yn'ka:rydżment)
s. zachęta; osmielenie; po-
pieranie;dodanie odwagi
encroach (yn'kroucz) v. wdzierać się; naruszać; wkraczać
na cudze;targnąć się na cudze
encumber (yn'kamber) v. krępować; tarasować; obarczać; zawadzać;obciążać(długami etc.)
end (end) s. koniec; cel;
skrzydłowy w nożnej piłce;
v. kończyć (się); skończyć;
dokończyć;położyć kres
endanger (yn'dejndżer) v. narażać na niebezpieczeństwo
endear (yn'dier) v. czynić
drogim; lubianym;przymilać się
endeavor. (yn'dewer) v. starać
się; usiłować; s. usiłowanie;
wysiłek; dążenie;zabiegi;próba
ending ('endyng) s. zakończenie; końcówka (wyrazu etc.)
endless ('endlys) adj. niekończący się; nieskończony;
ustawiczny;wieczny;ciągły
endorse (yn'do:rs) v. potwierdzać; popierać; podżyrować;
notować na odwrocie
endow (yn'dał) v. uposażyć;
wyposażyć;ufundować;zapisywać
endurance (yn'djuerens) s. wytrzymałość; cierpliwość
endure (yn'djuer) v. znosić
(ból); cierpieć; wytrzymać;
przetrwać; ostać się
enema ('enyme) s. lewatywa
enemy ('enymy) s. wróg; przeciwnik; adj. wrogi; nieprzyjacielski;przeciwny
energetic (,ene:r'dżetyk) adj.
energiczny; z wigorem
energy ('enerdży) s. energia

enervate ('ene:rwejt) v. osłabiać (nerwowo,na zdrowiu)wyczerpywać
enervate (y'ne:rwyt) adj. słaby; bez energii;wyczerpany
enfold (yn'fould) v. zawijać; obejmować;zapakowywać
enfranchise (un'fraenczajz) v. wyzwalać; nadawać prawo wyborcze; uwalniać;uwłaszczać
engage (yn'gejdż) v. zajmować; angażować; skłaniać; scierać się;zaręczyć;zobowiązywać się
engaged (yn'gejdżd) adj. zajęty; zaręczony; włączony
engagement (yn'gejdżmęt) s. zobowiazanie; zaręczyny
engine ('endżyn) s. silnik; parowóz; maszyna; motor
engine-driver ('endżyn,drajwer) s. maszynista (kolejowy)
engineer (,endży'nier) s. inżynier;v.planować;zręcznie prowadzić
engineering (,endży'nieryng)s. technika; mechanika; inżynieria;zarząd dróg,maszyn etc.
engine trouble ('endżyn'trabl) s. zepsucie silnika (samochodowego);kłopot z silnikiem
English ('ynglysz) adj. angielski (język)
english ('ynglysz) v. uderzyć piłkę fałszem; s. fałsz; podkręcona piłka; v. zangielszczyć
engorge (yn'go:rdż) v. pożerać
engrave (yn'grejw) v. rytować; ryć; grawerować;wyryć;wyrytować
engraving (yn'grejwyng) s. sztych;rytownictwo;grawiura
engross (yn'grous) v. pochłaniać; monopolizować (rozmowę)
enigma (y'nygme) s. zagadka
enjoin (yn'dżoyn) v. nakazywać; zarządzać; zakazywać;zalecać
enjoy (yn'dżoj) v. cieszyć się; rozkoszować;mieć;posiadać
enjoyment (yn'dżojment) s. uciecha; korzystanie z uprawnienia; rozkosz; przyjemność
enlarge (yn'la:rdż) v. powiększać; poszerzać;zwalniać z ciupy
enlargement (yn'la: rdżment) s. powiększenie; poszerzenie

enlighten (yn'lajtn) v. oświebiać; oswietlać;objasniać
enlist (yn'lyst) v. zaciągać (się); werbować;wstępować
enliven (yn'lajwn) v. ożywiać
enmesh (yn'mesz) v. wplatać (w sieć); usidlać;usidlić
enmity ('enmyty) s. wrogość; nieprzyjazń;nienawiść
enormous (y'no:rmes) adj. olbrzymi; ogromny; kolosalny
enough (y'naf) adj.,s.& adv. dosyć; dość;na tyle;nie więcej
enounce (y'nauns) v. ogłaszać; wymawiać;wypowiadać;wymówić
enquire (yn'kłajer) v. pytać; dowiadywać się;rozpytywać się
enquiry (yn'kłajry) s, pytanie; śledztwo;badania;pytanie
enrage (yn'rejdż) v. rozwścieczać;doprowadzać do wściekłości
enraged (yn'rejdżd) adj. rozwścieczony; rozwścieczona
enrapt (yn'raept) adj. zachwycony;pogrążony w zachwycie
enrapture (yn'reapczer) v. zachwycać;oczarowywać;porywać
enrich (yn'rycz) v. wzbogacać; użyźniać;ozdobić;ozdabiać
enrol(l) (yn'roul) v. zaciągać (się); zapisywać (się)
ensue (yn'su:) v. wynikać; następować;wypływać (z czegoś)
ensure (yn'szuer) v. zabezpieczać; zapewniać ;asekurować
entangle (yn'taengel) v. gmatwać; wplątać;zmieszać;komplikować
enter ('enter) v. wchodzić; wpisywać; penetrować;wkładać;wpisywać
enter into ('enter,yntu) v. wdawać się; brać udział;zawierać
enter upon ('enter,apon) v. wchodzić w posiadanie; przystępować do tematu; zaczynać
enterprise ('enterprajz) s. przedsięwzięcie; przedsiębiorstwo; przedsiębiorczość
enterprising ('enterprajzyng) adj. przedsiębiorczy;ryzykujący
entertain (,enter'tejn) v. zabawiać; przyjmować; żywić; nosić się;brać pod uwagę

entertainer (,enter'tejner) s.
artysta (kabaretowy)
entertainment (,enter'tejnment)
s. rozrywka; zabawa; uciecha
enthusiasm (yn'tju:zjaezem)
s. zapał; entuzjazm
enthusiast (yn'tju:zaest) s.
entuzjasta;zapaleniec
enthusiastic (yn'tu:zy'aestyk)
adj. entuzjastyczny;zapalony
entice (yn'tajs) v. znęcić;
zwabić(nagrodą,przyjemnością)
entire (yn'tajer) adj. cały;
całkowity;nietknięty
entirely (yn'tajerly) adv.
całkowicie; jedynie; wyłącznie;kompletnie;niepodzielnie
entitle (yn'tajtl) v. uprawniać;
tytułować; zatytułować;nadawać
entity ('entyty) s. byt; istnienie; jednostka;istota
entrails ('entrejlz) pl. jelita
wnętrzności;wnętrze ziemi
entrance ('entrens) s. wejście;
wstęp(za opłatą);dostęp;wjazd
entrance (,entraens) v. przejmować; wprawiać w trans
entrance fee ('entrens,fi:)
opłata za wstęp;bilet wstępu
entreat (yn'tri:t) v. błagać
entreaty (yn'tri:ty) s. błaganie; usilna prośba
entrust(yn'trast) v. powierzać
entry ('entry) s. wejście; wpis;
hasło (słownika);uczestnik wys-
entry permit ('entry,per'myt)
pozwolenie wejścia; wjazdu
enumerate (y'nju:merejt) v.
wliczać; sporządzać wykaz
envelop (yn'welep) v. owijać;
otaczać; ogarniać;okryć(ca-
envelope ('enweloup) s. koperta; otoczka;teczka(papierowa)
envenom (yn'wenem) v. zatruwać
enviable ('enwjebl) adj. godzien zazdrości;godny pażądania
envious (enwjes) adj. zazdrosny; zawistny;pełen zazdrości
environment (yn'wajerenment)
s. otoczenie; środowisko
environmental pollution (yn'wa-
jerenmentel pel'ju:szyn) za-
nieczyszczanie środowiska

environs (yn'wajerenz) s. okolice podmiejskie;przedmieścia
envoy ('enwoj) s. wysłannik
envy ('enwy) s. zawiść; zazdrość; przedmiot zazdrości
epic ('epyk) adj. epicki;
s. epos (o bohaterstwie)
epidemic (,epy'demyk) s. epi-
demia; adj. epidemiczny
epidermis (,epy'de:rmys) s. naskórek; skóra(powierzchnia)
epilepsy ('epylepsy) s. epileps-
ja; padaczka
epilog(ue) ('epylog) s. epilog
episode ('epysoud) s. epizod
epitaph ('epytaef) s. napis
na grobie(ku pamięci zmarłego)
epoch (i:'pok) s. epoka
equal ('i:kłel) adj. równy;
jednaki; jednakowy; jednostajny; zrównoważony; s. równy
(stanem); v. równać się; dorównywać; wyrównywać;wyrównywać
equality (i'kłolyty) s. równość
equalize (i'kłelajz) v. wyrównywać; równać;zrównywać(się)
equanimity (,i:kłe'nymyty) s.
opanowanie; spokój; równowaga
equate (i'kłejt) v. równać;
przyrównywać;stawiać na równi
equation (i'kłejżyn) s. równanie; równoważenie;bilansowanie
equator (i'kłejter) s. równik
equilibrium (,i:kłży'lybrjem) s.
równowaga
equip (i'kłyp) v. wyposażać;
zaopatrywać;uzbrajać;ekwipować
equipment (i'kłypment) s. wyposażenie; ekwipunek;sprzęt
equitable ('ekłytebl) adj.
słuszny; sprawiedliwy
equivalent (i'kływelent) adj.
równowartościowy; równoznaczny; równej wielkości;s.równo-
era ('yere) s. era [ważnik
erase (y'rejz) v. wycierać;
wymazywać;zatrzeć;zacierać
erect (y'rekt) adj. prosty; wy-
prężony; najeżony;v.budować;sta-
erection (y'rekszyn) s. podniesienie; wyprostowanie; najeże-
nie; erekcja; budowla; montaż

erosion (y'roużyn) s. wyżera-
nie; żłobienie; erozja
ermine ('e:rmyn) s. gronostaj
erotic (y'rotyk) adj. erotyczny; miłosny; s. erotyk; ero-
toman; wiersz erotyczny
err (e:r) v. błądzic; być
w błędzie;grzeszyć; zgrzeszyć
errand ('erand) s. posyłka;
zlecenie; cel;sprawunek
erratic (y'raetyk) adj. błędny;
nieobliczalny;dziwny;s.dziwak
erroneous (y'rounjes) adj.
błędny;mylny;fałszywy
error ('erer) s. błąd
erudite ('erudajt) adj. uczony; s. erudyta (b.oczytany etc.)
erupt (y'rapt) v. wybuchac;
wyrzucać; przerzynać (się);
wysypywac się;wybuchać lawa
eruption (y'rapszyn) s. wybuch;
przerzynanie się; wysypka
escalation (,eske'lejszyn) s.
wzmożenie;rozszerzenie się
escalator ('eskelejter) s. ru-
chome schody; ruchoma skala
płac(wg. kosztów utrzymania etc)
escape (ys'kejp) s. ucieczka;
wyciekanie; wchodzenie;ocalenie;
v. wymknąc się; zbiec; wyjść
cało; uchodzic;ratować się ucieczką
escort ('esko:rt) s. eskorta;
konwój; mężczyzna towarzyszą-
cy kobiecie; kawaler;v.eskorto-
escort (i'sko:rt) v. eskortować
especial (ys'peszel) adj.
szczególny; wyjątkowy; specjalny; szczegolny; główny
especially (ys'peszely) adv.
szczególnie; zwłaszcza
espionage (,espje'na:dż) s. wywiad; szpiegostwo;szpiegowanie
esprit (es'pri:) s. żywosc; życie; dowcip;silne poczucie humo-
espy (ys'paj) v. spostrzegac;
wysledzić;wykombinować
essay ('esej) s. esej; szkic
literacki; próba; v. probować;
wyprobować;poddać próbie
essence ('esens) s. esencja;
istota czegos; wyciąg; tresc
istotna tresc;sedno sprawy;olej

essential (y'senszel) adj. niezbędny; istotny; zasadniczy;
zupełny; eteryczny; s. cecha
istotna, nieodzowna, zasadni-
cza;rzecz podstawowa,konieczna
establish (ys'taeblysz) v. zakładac; osadzac; ustalać;
wprowadzac;udowodnić;ufundować
establishment (yz'taeblyszment)
s. założenie; osadzenie; ustalenie; ustanowienie; zakład;
gospodarstwo;koła rządzące;
organizacja państwowa lub wojskowa;firma;przedsiębiorstwo
estate (ys'tejt) s. majątek;
stan majątkowy;położenie w ży-
estate tax (ys'tejt,taeks) s.
podatek spadkowy (majątkowy)
esteem (ys'ti:m) v. cenic;
szanowac; poważać; s. poważanie; szacunek;dobra opinia
estimate ('estymejt) v. oceniać;
szacować; s. szacunek; kosztorys; ocena;opinia;oszacowanie
estimation (,esty'mejszyn) s.
szacowanie; poważanie; szacunek;zdanie;mniemanie;sąd
estrange (ys'trejndż) v. od-
stręczać; zrażać;zniechęcać
estray (ys'trej) s. stworzenie
bezpańskie, zgubione
estuary ('estjuery) s. ujście
(rzeki) do morza (oceanu)
eternal (y'ternl) adj. wieczny;
odwieczny;bez początku i końca
eternity (y'ternyty) s. wiecznosc;trwnie bez końca i odpoczyn-
ether ('i:ter) s. eter
ethics ('etyks) pl. etyka
ethnic ('etnyk) adj. etniczny;
pogański;odrębny zwyczajami i je-
etymology (,ety'moledży) s. ety-
mologia;pochodzenie i rozwój słów
eulogy ('ju:ledży) s, mowa
pochwała (pogrzebowa)
eunuch ('ju:nek) n. eunuch;
rzezaniec;człowiek wykastrowany
European (,ju:re'pi:en) adj.
europejski; s. Europejczyk
evacuate (y'waekjuejt) v. ewa-
kuować; oprożniac; wyprożniac;
wydalac;usuwać; wycofywać się

evacuation (y,waekju'ejszyn) s. ewakuacja; wypróżnienie (się)

evade (y'wejd) v. ujść; uniknąć; obchodzić; wymykać się; wykręcać się; pomijać

evaluate (y'waejluejt) v. obliczać; oceniać; analizować

evaporate (y'waeperejt) v. parować; ulatniać się; poddawać parowaniu;wyparowywać;umrzeć

evasion (y'wejżyn) v. uniknięcie; wymknięcie się; obejście; wykręt;oszustwo(podatkowe);wykręt

evasive (y'wejsyw) adj. wykrętny; wymijający; nieuchwytny

eve (i:w) s. wilia; wigilia

even (i:wen) adj. równy; jednolity; parzysty; adv. nawet; v. równać; wyrównać; zemścić się;wygładzać;ujednostajniać

even-handed ('i:wen,haendyd) adj. sprawiedliwy; bezstronny

evening ('i:wnyng) s. wieczór

evening dress ('i:wnyn, dres)s. strój wieczorowy

evening paper ('i:wnyn'pejper) gazeta wieczorna

evensong ('i:wensong) s. nieszpory; pieśń wieczorna

event (y'went) s. wydarzenie; możliwość; wynik; rezultat; zawody (sportowe);konkurencja

eventful(y'wentful) adj. burzliwy; pamiętny; pełen wydarzeń

eventual (y'wenczuel) adj. w końcu pewny

eventually (y'wenczuely) adv. w końcu napewno

ever ('ewer) adv. w ogóle; niegdyś;kiedyś; jak tylko; ile tylko; kiedykolwiek;jeszcze wciąż

ever after (,ewer'after) do tego czasu;już od tego czasu

ever since (,ewer'syns) od tego czasu ; od kiedy (był etc.)

everlasting (,ewer'lastyng)adj. wieczny; ciągły; nieustanny

evermore ('ewer'mi:re) adv. zawsze; na zawsze; na wieki

every ('ewry) adj. każdy; wszelki; co(dzień, noc, rano etc.)

every other day (,ewry,odzer'dej) co drugi dzień

everybody ('ewrybody) pron. każdy; wszyscy(ludzie)

everyday ('ewrydej) adj. codzienny; powszedni; zwykły

everyone ('ewryłan) pron. każdy; wszyscy;każda rzecz

everything ('ewrytyng) pron. wszystko (co jest, etc.)

everywhere ('ewryhłer) adv. wszędzie; gdziekolwiek

evidence ('ewydens) s. znak; dowód; świadectwo; oczywistość; jasność; v. świadczyć; dowodzić (czegoś);manifestować

evident ('ewydent) adj. oczywisty; widoczny;jawny;jasny

evil ('i:wl) adj. zły;fatalny

evildoer ('i:wl-duer) s. złoczyńca

evince (y'wyns) v, wykazywać; okazywać (życzenie);przejawiać

evoke (y'wouk) v. wywoływać; wydobywać; zdobywać (odpowiedź)

evolution (,ewe'lu:szyn) s. rozwój; ewolucja; rozwinięcie (się); pierwiastkowanie

evolve (y'wolw) v. rozwijać; wypracowywać; wytwarzać (ciepło etc.);rozwijać się stopniowo

ewe (ju:) s. owca

ex-(eks) pref. były; była; prep. bez; ze; s. (litera)"x"

exacerbate (eks'aeserbejt) v. drażnić; pogorszyć; irytować

exact (yg'zaekt) adj. dokładny; ścisły; v. wymagać; ściągać; egzekwować ;wymuszać

exactitude (yg'zaektytju:d)s. ścisłość; dokładność;punktualność

exactly (yg'zaektly) adv. dokładnie; ściśle; własnie; zgadza się ;punktualnie; ostro

exactness (yg'zaektnys) s. dokładność; precyzja

exaggerate (yg'zaedżerejt) v. przesadzać; wyolbrzymiać

exaggeration (yg'zaedże'rejszyn) s. przesada; wyolbrzymienie

exalt (yg'zo:lt) v. wywyższać; podnosić;wychwalać;chwalić

exam (yg'zaem) s. egzamin (slang); klasówka; egzamin w szkole lub na uniwersytecie

examination (yg zaemy'nejszyn)
s. egzamin; badanie;rewizja
examine (yg'zaemyn) v. badać;
sprawdzać; egzaminować; rozpatrywać; rewidować; przesłuchiwać;przeprowadzać śledztwo
example (yg'za:mpl) s. przykład; wzór; precedens
exasperate (yg'za:sperejt) v.
rozjątrzać; rozgoryczać; pogarszać; powodować rozpacz
excavate ('ekskewejt) v. kopać; odkopać; wykopać; drążyć;pogłębiać;wybierać(ziemię)
exceed (yk'si:d) v. przewyższać; celować; przekraczać
exceedingly (ek'si:dynly) adv.
niezmiernie; nadzwyczajnie
excel (yk'sel) v. przewyższać;
wybijać się; celować(w czyms)
excellence (yk'selens) s. wyższość; doskonałość; zaleta
excellent (yk'selent) adj. doskonały; wyborny;świetny;celuja-
except (yk'sept) conj. chyba
że...; żeby;oprucz;poza;wyjąwszy
except (yk'sept) v. wykluczać;
wyłączać; prep. z wyjątkiem;
pominąwszy; wyjąwszy;chyba że
exception (yk'sepszyn) s. wyjątek; wyłączenie; zarzut;obiekcja.
exceptional(yk'sepszenl) adj.
nadzwyczajny; wyjątkowy
excess (yk'ses) s. nadmiar;
nadwyżka;a.nadmierny;nad-
excess fare(yk'ses,fe:r) s. dopłata do biletu
excessive (yk'sesyw) adj. nadmierny;zbytni;nieumiarkowany
excess luggage (yk'ses,lągydż)
nadwyżka bagażu
exchange (yks'czendż) s. wymiana; zamiana; giełda; centrala
telefoniczna; v. wymienić; towy
zamienić (się);a.wymienny;walu-
excitable (yk'sajtebl) adj. pobudliwy;pobudzajacy;podniecaja-
excite (yk'sajt) v. pobudzać;
podniecać;prowokować
excited (yk'sajtyd) adj. podniecony; zdenerwowany

excitement (yk'sajtment)
podniecenie; zdenerwowanie
exciting (yk'sajtyng) adj.
emocjonujący; pasjonujący
exclaim (yks'klejm) v. zawołać;
wykrzyknąć; zaprotestować
exclamation (,ekskla'mejszyn)
s. okrzyk; krzyk; wykrzyknik
exclamation mark (,ekskla'mejszyn,ma:rk) wykrzyknik
exclude (yks'klu:d) v. wykluczać; wydalać; usuwać
exclusion (yks'klu:żyn) n.
wykluczenie; wydalenie; usunięcie; wyłączenie
exclusive (yks'klu:syw) adj.
modny; wykluczający; wyłączny;
jedyny; ekskluzywny
excursion (yks'ker:żyn) s. wycieczka;dygresje;a.wycieczkowy
excuse (yks'kju:z) v. usprawiedliwiać; przepraszać; darować; zwalniać; s. usprawiedliwienie; wymówka ;pretekst
excuse me (yks'kju:z,mi)
przepraszam; przepraszam pana
excusable (iks'kju:zebl) adj.
usprawiedliwiony;wybaczalny
execute ('eksykju:t) v. wykonać (wyrok, plan); stracić
(skazańca);nadawac ważność
execution (,eksy'kju;szyn) s.
wykonanie; egzekucja;stracenie
executive (yg'zekjutyw) adj.
wykonawczy; s. władza wykonaw-
cza; stanowisko kierownicze
exemplary (yg'zemplery) adj.
wzorowy; przykładny; przykła-
dowy;wymierzony dla odstraszenia
exempt (yg'zempt) v. zwalniać;
adj. wolny; zwolniony; s. osoba zwolniona;człowiek zwolniony
exercise ('eksersajz) s. ćwiczenie; wykonywanie (zawodu);
korzystanie; v. ćwiczyć; używać;
wykonywać;spełniać;pełnić
exercise book ('eksersajs,buk)
s. zeszyt (szkolny)
exert (yg'ze:rt) v. wytężać
(się); wysilać (się); wywierać
(nacisk, wpływ, etc);zabiegać

exertion (yg'ze:rszyn) s. wy-
tężenie; wysiłek; wywieranie
exhale (eks'hejl) v. wyziewać;
wydychać; zionąć; parować
exhaust (yg'zo:st) v. wydychać;
wyczerpywać; wyciągać; wypróżniać; odgazować; s. wydech; wydmuch; rura wydechowa; opróżnianie (z powietrza);
aspirator;rura wydechowa(auta)
exhaust fumes (yg'zo:st,fjums)
gazy wydechowe(z motoru)
exhaustion (yg'zo:stszyn) s.
wyczerpanie; opróżnienie; zużycie; pochłonięcie;zmęczenie
exhaust-pipe (yg'zo:st,pajp)
s. rura wydechowa (w aucie)
exhibit(yg'zybyt) s. wystawa;
pokaz; eksponaty; v. wystawiać; okazywać; pokazywać;
wykazywać; popisywać się
czyms;przedkładać;mieć wystawę
exhibition(,eksy'byszyn) s.
wystawa; wystawianie; pokazy-
wanie;pokaz; widowisko;popis
exhibitor(yg'zybyter) s. wystawca; wystawczyni
exile ('eksajl) s. wygnanie;
tułaczka; emigracja; wygnaniec; v. wygnać na banicję
exist (yg'zyst) v. istnieć;być;
żyć; egzystować ;zdarzać się
existence (yg'zystens) s. istnienie; byt; egzystencja
existent (yg'zystent) a. istniejący;bedacy;znajdujący się
exit ('eksyt) s. wyjscie; odejs-
cie; ujscie; wylot; swobodne
wyjście; v, wychodzić; kończyć
(slang);schodzić ze sceny
exit visa ('eksyt,wyza) s. wiza wyjazdowa
expand (yks'paend) v. rozszerzać; powiększać; wzrastać;
rozprężać; rozwijać; rozruszać;rozpościerać;powiększać
expanse (yks'paens) s. bezmiar;
rozległa przestrzeń; ekspansja
expansion (yks'paenszyn) s.
rozszerzanie; rozprężanie się;
ekspansja; rozposcieranie;
rozwijanie (się);ilość ekspansji

expansive (yks'paensyw) adj.
rozszerzalny; rozległy; roz-
prężalny; obszerny; wylewny
expect (yks'pekt) v. spodziewać się; przypuszczać;zgadywać
expectation (,ekspek'tejszyn)
s. oczekiwanie; nadzieja;
widoki;prospekt;przewidywanie
expedient (yks'pi:djent) adj.
celowy; wygodny; oportunistycz-
ny; korzystny; s. środek; zabieg; sposób;wybieg;fortel
expedition (,ekspy'dyszyn) s.
wyprawa; ekspedycja; sprawność;
szybkosć;pośpiech;marsz do,akcji
expel (yks'pel) v. wypędzać;
wydalać; usuwać; wyrzucać
expend (yks'pend) v. wydawać;
zużywać;poświęcać czas etc.
expense (yks'pens) s. koszt;
wydatek;rachunek;strata;ofiara
expensive (yks'pensyw) adj.
drogi; kosztowny;wysoko wycenio-
experience (yks'pierjens) s. ^{ny}
doswiadczenie; przeżycie;
v. doświadczać; doznawać;
poznać (coś);przeżywać;przecho-^{dzić}
experienced (yks'pierjenst)
adj. doswiadczony;doznany
experiment (yks'peryment) s.
próba; eksperyment; doswiadczenie; v, eksperymentować;
robić doświadczenia
expert ('ekspe:rt) s. biegły;
ekspert; znawca; adj. biegły;
światły;mistrzowski;wykonany
           przez eksperta
expiration (,ekspi'rejszyn) s.
wygaśnięcie; upłynięcie; wydech; wyzionięcie ducha:smierć
expire (yks'pajer) v. wygasać;
upływać; wydychać; wyzionąć
ducha;umierać;kończyć się
explain (yks'plejn) v. wyjaśnić; objasnić; wytłumaczyc
explanation (,eks'plaenejszyn)
s. wyjaśnienie; wytłumaczenie
explicable ('eksplykebl) adj.
dający się wyjaśnić
explicit (yks'plysyt) adj. jasny; wyrazny; szczery; otwarty;definitywny;wygadany

explode (yks'ploud) v. wybuchac; explodowac; demaskowac
(fałsz) ;obalić(teorię etc.)
exploit (yks'ploit) v. użytko-
wać; exploatować; wyzyskiwać
exploit ('eksploit) s. wyczyn
exploration (,eksplo:'rejszyn)
s. poszukiwanie; badanie
explore (yks'plo:r) v. badać;
sondować;wybadać;przebadać
explorer (yks'plo:rer) s. badacz; sonda ;odkywca;odkrywczyni
explosion (yks'ploużyn) s.
explozja; wybuch (kłotni etc.)
explosive (yks'plousyw) s, materiał wybuchowy; adj. wybuchowy;mogący wybuchnąć
exponent (yks'pounent) adj.
interpretujący; s. eksponent;
wyraziciel; interpretator;
wykładnik (potęgi);przedstawiciel
export (yks'po:rt) v. wywozic;
eksportować; s. wywóz; eksport;
towar wywozowy;wywożenie
expose (yks'pouz) v. wystawiać
(na wpływ); poddawać (czemuś);
odsłaniać; demaskować; ekspo-
nować; naswietlać; porzucac
(dziecko);zrobić zdjęcie
exposé (,ekspou'zej) s..zdemas-
kowanie; odsłonięcie skandalu
exposition (,ekspe'zyszyn) s.
wystawa; wykład; przedstawienie; wyjaśnienie; opis; na-
świetlenie; ekspozycja; po-
rzucenie (dziecka)
exposure (yks'poużer) s. wystawienie (na zimę. etc); ujawnienie; zdemaskowanie; naświet-
lenie;jedno zdjęcie na filmie
exposuremeter (yks'poużer'mi:ter)
s. swiatłomierz
expound (yks'paund) v. wykładać;
wyjaśnić szczegółowo;przedstawic
express (yks'pres) s. ekspres ;
przesyłka pospieszna; adj. wyraźny; umyslny; dokładny;
adv. pospiesznie;expresem
expression (yks'preszyn) s. wyrażenie; wyraz; ekspresja; ton;
wydawanie; wytłoczenie;zwrot
wyciśnięcie;wyżymanie

expressive (yks'presyw) adj.
wyrażający; wyrazisty:
ekspresyjny;pełen wyrazu
expressly (yks'presly) adv.wy-
raźnie; kategorycznie; naumyslnie;specjalnie;formalnie
express way (yks'pres,łej) s.
droga przelotowa (bez skrzy-
żowan jednopoziomowych)
expulsion (yks'palszyn) s. wydalenie; wyrzucenie; wypędze-
nie;wygnanie;wyparcie
exquisite ('ekskłyzyt) adj.
wyborowy; wyborny; wysmienity;
nadzwyczajny; ostry; przeszywający;s.laluś;goguś;pięknis
extent ('ekstent) adj. pozostały; jeszcze istniejący
extemporaneous (eks,tempe'rejn-
jes) adj. zaimprowizowany
extend (yks'tend) v wyciągac
(się); rozciągac (się);prze-
ciągac (się); rozszerzac (się);
dawac i udzielac; przedłużac;
powiększac;rozposcierac się
extendible (yks'tendybl) adj.
rozszerzalny; rozciągalny
extension (yks'tenszyn) s. rozciąganie; wyciąganie; rozwinięcie; przedłużenie; zasięg;
rozmiar; zakres ;skrzydło(domu)
extensive (yks'tensyw) adj.
obszerny; rozległy ;ekstensywny
extent (yks'tent) s. obszar;
rozmiar; zasięg; miara; stopień; wysokość ;oszacowanie
extenuate (yks'tenjnejt) v.
zmniejszac; łagodzic
exterior (eks'tierjer) s. powierzchowność; wygląd zewnętrzny; strona zewnętrzna ;fasada
exterminate (yks'te:rmynejt) v.
tępic (np; pogląd);wyniszczyc
external (eks'te:rnal) adj.
zewnętrzny, zagraniczny
extinct (yks'tynkt) adj. wy-
gasły; zgasły ;zanikły;wymarły
extinguish (yks'tyngłysz) v.
zgasic; zagasić; niszczyc;
unicestwic; umierac ;tępic
extirpate ('ekster,pejt)v. wy-
korzeniac;plewić; tępic

extol (yks'tol) v. wysławiać;
wynosić pod niebiosa
extort (yks'tort) v. wymuszać;
zdzierać(pieniadze);wydrzeć
extra ('ekstre) adj. specjalny; dodatkowy; luksusowy;
nadzwyczajny; ponad normę;
adv. nadzwyczajnie; dodatkowo;
s. dodatek; dopłata; rzecz
szczególnie dobra;statysta
extra charge ('ekstre,cha:rdż)
s. dopłata;nadpłata
extract ('ekstraekt) s. wyciąg;
ekstrat;wyjątek;wypis
extract (yks'traekt) v. wyciągać; wydobywać; wypisywać
extraction (eks'traekszyn) s.
wyciągnięcie; wydobycie; wyr-
wanie (zęba); pochodzenie;ród
extradite ('ekstredajt) v.
wydawać (przestępcę przez granicę)do miejsca zbrodni
extraordinary (yks'tro:rdnery)
adj. niezwykły; nadzwyczajny
extravagance (yks'traewygens)
s. przesada; rozrzutność;
nieumiarkowanie; głupstwo;
niedorzeczność; ekstrawagancja
extravagant (yks'traewegent)
adj. rozrzutny; przesądny;
zwariowany;wygórowany;szalony
extravaganza (yks,traewe'gaenze)
s. ekstrawagancja;fantazja
extreme (yks'tri:m) adj. skrajny; krańcowy; najdalszy; ostatni; s. kraniec; ostateczna
granica; ostateczność;skrajność
extremity (yks'tremyty) s. koniec; kraniec; skrajność; kran-
cowość; kończyna; krytyczne
położenie;potrzeba;ostateczność
extrude (yks'tru:d) v. wypierać; wyrzucać; przeciągać lub
ciągnąć odlew;wytłoczyć
exuberant (yg'zju:berent) adj.
wybujały; pełen życia; kwitnący; wylewny; płodny; obfity
exult (yg'zalt) v. triumfować;
unosić się radością
eye (aj) s. oko;wzrok;v.patrzeć
eyeball ('ajbo:l) s. gałka oczna
w oczodołach za powiekami

eyeball to eyeball ('ajbo:l,tu
'ajbo:l) oko w oko
eyebrow ('ajbrau) s. brew
eyeglasses ('ajgla:sys) pl.
okulary;lupy;monokle
eyelash ('ajlaesz) s. rzęsa
eyelid ('ajlyd) s. powieka
eyesight ('aj-sajt) s. wzrok
eyewash ('ajłosz) s. woda do
oczu; mydlenie oczu (slang)
eyewitness ('aj'łytnes) s.
świadek naoczny
f (ef) szósta litera angielskiego alfabetu; stopień "f"
failure = niedostatecznie
fable (fejbl) s. bajka
fabric ('faebryk) s. tkanina;
materiał; osnowa; szkielet;
budowa; wytwór;a.sukienny
fabricate ('faebrykejt) v. tworzyć;wymyślać; zmyślać; montować;wyssać z palca;sfałszować
fabulous ('faebjules) adj. ba-
jeczny;legendarny;fantastyczny
facade (fe'sa:d) s. fasada
face (fejs) s. twarz; oblicze;
mina; grymas; czelność; śmiałość; powierzchnia lica; prawa strona; obuch; v. stawiać
czoła; stanąć wobec; napotykać; stać frontem do..; wykładać powierzchnię;oblicować
face-lifting ('fejs-lyftyng) v.
operacyjnie usuwać zmarszczki
facetious (fe'si:szes) adj.
żartobliwy;krotochwilny
facilitate (fe'sylytejt) v.
ułatwiać ; udogadniać;uprzy-
stępniać
facility (fe'sylyty) s. łatwość;
zręczność; udogodnienia; układ-
ność; swada;zgodność
fact (faekt) s. fakt; stan
rzeczywisty;podstawa twierdzenia
factor ('faekter) s. czynnik;
współczynnik; część;okoliczność
faculty ('faekelty) s. zdolność;
władza; wydział; fakultet; gro-
no profesorskie;dar; zmysł
fad (faed) s. moda; kaprys;konik;
bzik;chwilowa moda;dziwactwo
fade (fejd) v. więdnąć; blednąć; zanikać;płowieć;pełznąć

fail (feil) v. chybić; zawodzić; nie udać się; brakować; bankrutować; omieszkać; słabnąć; załamać się; zamierać;zepsuć się

failure ('fejljer) s. niepowodzenie; brak; upadek; zawał (serca); niezdara; stopień niedostateczny; pechowiec

faint (fejnt) adj. słaby; omdlały; bojaźliwy; s. omdlenie; v. mdleć; słabnąć;zasłabnąć

fair (feer) adj. piękny; jasny; uczciwy; honorowy; czysty; pomyślny; niezły; adv. prosto; honorowo; pomyślnie; pięknie; v. wypogadzać się; wygładzać; przepisywać na czysto; s. targ; targi; jarmark;targowisko

fairly ('feerly) adv. słusznie; uczciwie; całkowicie; zupełnie; dość;rzetelnie;wręcz;poprostu

fairplay ('feer'plej) szlachetne postępowanie;czysta gra

fairness ('feernys) s. piękność; jasność; sprawiedliwość; bezstronność; uczciwość;uroda

fairy ('feery) s. czarodziejka; adj. zaczarowany;czarodziejski

fairy-tale ('ferrytejl) s. bajka

faith (fejs) s. wiara; zaufanie; wierność; wyznanie;słowność

faithful ('fejsful) adj. wierny; uczciwy;sumienny;skrupulatny

faithless ('fejslys) adj. niewierny; wiarołomny;zdradziecki

fake (fejk) v. fałszować; oszukiwać; podrabiać; s. fałszerstwo; oszustwo;kant;lipa;szwindel

falcon ('fo:lken) s. sokół

fall; fell; fallen (fo:l; fel: fo:len)

fall (fo:l) v. padać; opadać; wpadać; marnieć; zdarzać się; przypadać; s. upadek; spadek; jesień;opad;schyłek;obniżka

fall back ('fo:l, baek) v. cofać się

fall ill ('fo:l,yl) v. zachorować ;rozchorować się

fall in love ('fo:l,yn'law) v. zakochać się

fallout ('fo:lart) s. skutek uboczny; pył radioaktywny; wrażenie na publiczności i prasie(z wypowiedzi,planów),

fall out ('fo:l,art) v. poróżnić się; rozejść się! (komenda)

fall short ('fo:l,szo:rt) v. nieosiągnąć; niewywiązać się

fallen ('fo:len) upadły; zob. fall

false (fo:ls) adj. fałszywy; kłamliwy;adv.zdradliwie;fałszy-

falsehood ('fo:lshud) s. fałsz; kłamstwo;nieprawda;kłamliwość

falsify ('fo:lsyfaj) v. fałszować; przekręcać; kłamać; zawodzić ;podrabiać;oszukać

falter ('fo:lter) v. chwiać się; wahać się; potykać się; jąkać się; s. chwiejność; jąkanie

fame (fejm) s. sława; wieść;fama

famed (fejmd) adj. sławny; znany; głośny; słynący z

familiar (fe'myljer) adj. zażyły; poufały; znany; obeznany

familiarity (fe,myly'aeryty) s. zażyłość; poufałość; obeznanie;znajomość;zażyłość

familiarize (fe'myljerajz) v. obeznać; obznajomić; oswoić; spoufalić;spopularyzować

family ('faemyly) s. rodzina; adj. rodzinny

family name ('faemyly,nejm) s. nazwisko

family tree ('faemyly,tri:) s. drzewo genealogiczne

famine ('faemyn) s. głód; klęska głodu; ogólne braki wszystkiego

famish ('faemysz) v. głodzić; wygłodnieć; głodować;morzyć głodem

famous ('fejmes) adj. znany; jaki sławny;znakomity;swietny;nie byle

fan (faen) v. wachlować; rozdmuchiwać; wiać; rozpościerać; wywiewać; s. wachlarz; wentylator; wialnia; żagiel i śmigło (wiatraka); entuzjasta; miłośnik;kibic;a.wachlarzowaty

fanatic (fe'naetyk) adj. zagorzały; fanatyczny; s, fanatyk

fanciful ('faensyful) adj. dziwaczny; kaprysny; fantastyczny;zmyslony;wyszukany;fantazyjny
fancy ('faensy) s. urojenie; zludzenie; fantazja; kaprys; humor; pomysł; chetka;a.pstry..
fancy dress ball('faensy'fres, ,bo:l) s. bal kostiumowy
fancy-free ('faensy,fri:) adj. wolny od trosk; niezakochany
fancywork ('faensy,łe:rk) s. robótki reczne
fang (faeng) s. ząb jadowity; kieł;sztyft;korzen;v.dławic pompe
fantastic (faen'taestyk) adj. fantastyczny;s.fantastyk
far (fa:r) adv. daleko
far away ('fa:r,ełej) adv. hen; daleko;adj.daleki;odległy
far from ('fa:r,from) adv. bynajmniej; daleko od
fare (feer) s. pasażer; bilet pasażerski; pożywienie; potrawa; v, byc w położeniu. miec sie; wiesc sie; czuc sie; odżywiac sie; jadac; podróżowac
farewell (,feer'lel) s. pożegnanie; adj. pożegnalny; v. żegnaj; do widzenia
farfetched (,fa:r'feczt) adj. przesadny; naciągany; wyszukany;nierozsadny
far-flung (,fa:r'flang) adj. szeroko rozrzucony; rozgałęziony;zakrojony na szeroka skale
farm (fa:rm) s. ferma; gospodarstwo rolne; kolonia hodowlana; v. uprawiac; dzierżawic; wydzierżawiac; wynajmowac; podstwo dzierżawiac;prowadzic gospodar-
farmer ('fa:rmer) s. rolnik; farmer; dzierżawca;hodowca
farmhand ('fa:rm,haend) s. parobek;robotnik rolny
farmhouse ('fa:rm,haus) s. dworek; gospodarski dom mieszkalny
farming ('fa:rmyng)s. rolnictwo; gospodarka rolna; dzierżawa
farm worker (,fa:rm'łe:rker) s. robotnik rolny; parobek
farmyard ('fa:rm,ja:rd) s. podworze fermy;podworze gospodarskie na fermie

farsighted ('fa:r'sajtyd) adj. przewidujacy; dalekowidz; dalekowzroczny:dalekowidz
farther('fa:rdzer) adj. dalszy; adv. dalej;ponadto;poza tym; procz-tego
farthest ('fa:rdzest) adj. najdalszy; adv. najdalej;najpóźniej
fascinate ('faesynejt) v. urzekac; czarowac; fascynowac; hipnotyzowac;zachwycic
fascination (,faesy'nejszyn) s. urok; czar;oczarowanie;olśnienie
fascist ('faesyst) s. faszysta; adj. faszystowski;faszystowska
fashion ('faeszyn) s. moda; fason; kształt; wzór; sposób; v. kształtowac; fasonowac; modelowac; urabiac
fashionable ('faesznebl) adj. modny; s. człowiek wytworny
fast (faest) adj. szybki; przytwierdzony; mocny; twardy; zwodniczy; adv. mocno; pewnie; trwale; v. poscic; s. post
fasten ('faesn) v. umocowac; zamykac;przymocowac
fastener ('faesner) s. przymocowanie (np. gwóżdz); spinacz zatrzask; zasuwka
fastidious (fes'tydjes) adj. wybredny; grymasny; wymagajacy
fat (faet) s. tłuszcz ; tusza; adj. tłusty; tuczny; głupi; tepy;urodzajny;zyskowny
fatal ('fejtl) adj. fatalny; śmiertelny; nieuchronny
fate ('fejt) s. los; przeznaczenie; zguba;fatum;v.los rzadzi...
father ('fa:dzer) s. ojciec
fatherhood ('fa:dzerhud) s. ojcostwo;starszenstwo(w służbie)
father-in-law ('fa:dzerynlo:) s. tesc;ojciec meza lub żony
fatherland ('fa:dzerlaend) s. ojczyzna; ojczysty kraj
fatherly ('fa:dzerly) adj. ojcowski;jak ojciec;dobrotliwy
fathom ('faedzem) s. sążen
fathomless ('faedzemlys) s. bezdenny; niezgłebiony
fatigue (fe'ti:g) s. zmeczenie (człowieka lub materiału);służba porzadkowa;v.trudzic;meczyć

fatten ('faetn) v. tuczyc; tyc;
urzyzniac ziemie: utyc;utuczyc
faucet ('fo:syt) s. kurek (od
wody); czop; tuleja
fault ('fo:lt) s. błąd; wada;
wina; uskok; usterka;brak;defekt
faultless ('fo:ltlys) adj. bezbłędny; nienaganny;doskonały
faulty ('fo:lty) adj. wadliwy;
nieprawidłowy;nieścisły;błędny
favor ('fejwer) s. łuska;uprzej-
mość; upominek; v. sprzyjać;
zaszczycać; faworyzować
favorable ('fejwerebl) adj. życzliwy; łaskawy; sprzyjający;
korzystny(dla kagoś,czegoś)
favorite ('fejweryt) s. ulubieniec; faworyt; adj. ulubiony
fawn (fo:n) v. ocielić; łasić
się; przymilać (się); s. je-
lonek; sarenka; adj. brunatny;
płowy;płaszczyć się(przed kimś)
fear (fier) s. strach; obawa;
v. bać się; obawiać się
fearful ('fierful) adj. okropny;
straszny; wystraszony; bojaźliwy; bojący się;pełen strachu
fearless ('fierlys) adj. nieustraszony;bardzo odważny
feast (fi:st) s. święto; odpust;
biesiada; v. ucztować; sycić
się; ugaszczać pragnienie
feat (fi:t) s. wyczyn; czyn
(bohaterski);(dokazana)sztuka
feather ('fedzer) s. pioro;
v. zdobić piórami
featherbed ('fedzerbed) s. pier-
nat:pierzyna;lekka praca
feathered ('fedzerd) adj. upie-
rzony; pokryty piórami
feathery ('fedzery) adj. pucho-
waty; miękki jak puch:leciutki
feature ('fi:czer) s. cecha;
rys; atrakcja; film długo-
metrażowy;v.cechować;odgrywać
February ('februery) s. luty
fed (fed) adj. karmiony; zob.
feed
federal ('federel) adj. związkowy; federalny
federation (,fede'rejszyn) s.
federacja; konferencja

fee (fi:) s. opłata; wpisowe;
należność; honorarium; v. płacić honorarium;płacić wpisowe
feeble ('fi:bl) adj. słaby
feed: fed; fed (fi:d; fed; fed)
feed (fi:d) v. karmić; paść;
zasilać; s. pasza; obrok; za-
silacz; posuw
feeder (fi:der) s. boczna (droga); dopływ; przewód zasila-
jący
feel; felt; felt (fi:l; felt;
felt)
feel (fi:l) v. czuć (się); odczuwać; macać; dotykać
feel well ('fi:l,łel) v. czuć
się dobrze: być zdrowym
feel bed('fi:l,baed) v. czuć
się źle
feeler ('fi:ler) s. macka; sonda; próbny balon; szperacz
feeling ('fi:lyng) s. dotyk;
uczucie; odczucie; poczucie;
takt; wrażliwość; adj. wrażliwy; czuły; współczujący; szczery; wzruszony; szczery
feet (fi:t) pl. stopy; nogi
fell (fel) v. ścinać (drzewo);
zob. fall
felloe ('felou) s. dzwono(koła)
fellow ('felou) s. towarzysz;
człowiek; chłop; gość; facet;
odpowiednik;wykładowca;adjunkt
fellow being ('felou bi:yng) s.
bliźni
fellow citizen ('felou'sytyzen)
s. współobywatel
fellowship ('felouszyp) s.
udział; wspólnota; związek;
towarzystwo; przyjaźń; cech
felon ('felen) s. przestępca;
adj. okrutny; zły;zbrodniczy
felony ('feleny) s. przestępstwo;
zbrodnia
felt (felt) czuły; zob.; feel
felt (felt) s. wojłok; filc
female ('fi:mejl) s. kobieta;
niewiasta; samica; adj. żeński;
kobiecy; wewnętrzny (gwint)
feminine ('femynyn) adj. żeński;
kobiecy; zniewieściały; s. rodzaj żeński;a.rodzaju żeńskiego

fen (fen) s. bagno; trzęsawisko;nizina bagienna

fence (fens) s. płot; ogrodzenie; szermierka; v. ogrodzić; fechtować się;odpowiadać wykręt-

fencing ('fencyŋg) s. szermierka;płot;ogrodzenie;paserstwo

fend for ('fend,fo:r) v. zaspokajać potrzeby;utrzymywać

fend off ('fend,of) v. odbijać; odparowywać;chronić;ochraniać

fender ('fender) s. błotnik; (zderzak);zasłona;zderzak

fennel ('fenel) s. koper

ferment ('fe:rment) s. ferment; fermentacja; v. wywoływać ferment; podniecać; fermentować

fermentation (,fe:rmen'tejszyn) s. fermentacja; ferment

fern (fe:rn) s. paproć

ferocity (fe'rosyty) s. dzikość; okrucieństwo; srogość

ferry ('fery) v. przeprawiać promem; kursować; s. prom

ferryboat ('ferybout) s. prom

fertile ('fe:rtajl) adj. żyzny; płodny;zapłodniony;obfitujący

fertility (fer'tylyty) z. żyzność; płodność;urodzjność

fertilize ('fe:rtylajz) v. użyźniać;nawozić;zapładniać;zapylać

fertilizer ('fe:rtylajzer) s. nawóz sztuczny

fervent ('fe:rwent) adj. żarliwy; gorący;płomienny;gorliwy

fester ('fester) v. jątrzyć (się) ropieć; gnić; s. ropiejąca rana; mały wrzód;ropniak;zajad

festival ('festewel) adj. świąteczny;odswiętny;s.święto

festive ('festyw) adj. uroczysty; wesoły; radosny;biesiadny

festivity (fes'tywyty) s. wesołość; zabawa; uroczystość

fetch (fecz) v. iść po coś; przynieść; przywieźć;s.odległość

fetter ('feter) v. skuć; spętać

feud (fju:d) s. lenno; waśn rodowa;wojna między klanami

feudal ('fju:dl) adj. feudalny

fever ('fy:wer) s. gorączka

feverish ('fy:werysz) adj. gorączkowy;rozgorączkowany

few (fju:) adj.& pron. mało;kilka; niewielu ; nieliczni;kilku;kilkoro

fiance (fi'a:nsej) s. narzeczony(a)

fib (fyb) s. kłamstwo; v. cyganić:okładać;s. cioś;uderzenie

fiber ('fajber) s. włokno; siła ducha;charakter;łyko;budowa

fibrous ('fajberes) adj. włóknisty; łykowaty

fickle ('fykl) adj. zmienny; niestały;płochy; wietrzny

fiction ('fykszyn) s. fikcja; urojenie; beltrystyka;wymysł

fictitious (fyk'tyszes) a. fikcyjny; urojony; fałszywy

fiddle ('fydl) v. grać na skrzypcach; baraszkować; s. skrzypce

fiddler ('fydler) s. skrzypek; skrzypaczka

fidelity (fy'delyty) s. wierność; dokładność; ścisłosc

fidget ('fydżyt) v. wiercić się; niepokoić się; s. niepokój; człowiek niespokojny

fidgety ('fydżyty) adj. wiercący sie; niespokojny;niecirpliwy

field (fi:ld) s. pole; boisko; drużyna; dziedzina; v. ustawiać na boisku; zatrzymać (piłkę);poprowadzić do akcji

field-events ('fi:ld,y wents) pl. lekkoatletyka

field-glasses('fi:ld,glasys) pl. lornetka polowa

field-gun('fi:ld,gan) s. działo polowe

fiend ('fy:nd) s. zły duch; szatan; demon; nałogowiec; zagorzalec

fierce (fiers) adj. dziki; srogi; zażarty; wściekły; zawziety;nieopanowany;gwałtowny

fiery ('fajery) adj. ognisty; płomienny; palący; zapalny; burzliwy;popędliwy;choleryczny

fife (fajf) s. piszczałka; v. grać na piszczałce (na fujarce)

fifteen ('fyf'ti:n) num. piętnaście;piętnascioro;piętnastka

fifteenth ('fyf'ti:nt) num. piętnasty;jedna piętnasta czesc

fiftieth ('fyftjet) num. pięćdziesiąty;jedna pięćdziesiata

fifty ('fyfty) num. pięćdziesiat

fig (fyg) s. figa; strój

fight; fought; fought (fajt; fo:t; fo:t)

fight (fajt) s. walka; bitwa; zapasy; bój; duch do walki; mecz bokserski; v. walczyć (przeciw lub o coś);bić się

fighter ('fajter) s. bojownik; zapaśnik; samolot myśliwski

figurative ('fygjurejtyw) adj. obrazowy; przenośny;symboliczny

figure ('fyg'er) s. kształt; postać; wizerunek; cyfra; wzór; v. figurować; liczyć; rachować; oznaczać cenami; wyobrażać; przedstawiać

figure out ('fyger,aut) v.obliczać; wynosić;składać się na

figure skating ('fyger, skejtyŋg) s. jazda figurowa na łyżwach

file (fajl) s. rejestr; archiwum; seria; pilnik; v. archiwować; defilować; piłować pilnikiem; wnosić (podanie; skargę);isć rzędem(rzedami);maszerować

fill (fyl) v. napełniać; plombować ząb; obsadzać; s. wypełnienie; napicie i najedzenie do syta; nasyp ;ładunek;porcja

fill in ('ful,yn) v. zapełniać; wypełniać (formularze,blankiety)

fill up ('fyl,ap) v. wypełniać; zapełniać ;nabierać benzyny

fillet ('fylyt) s. wstążki; zraz zawijany; dzwonko; v.przepasywać;wycinać filety

fillet ('fylej) v. dzielić na dzwonka ;wycinać dzwonka

filling ('fylyŋg) s. nadziewka; plomba; wątek ;zapas benzyny

filling station ('fylyŋg,st'ejszyn) s. stacja benzynowa

filly ('fyly) s. źrebica; koza; młoda dziewczyna ;dzierlatka

film (fylm) s. powłoka; błona; warstwa; film; mgiełka; bielmo; v. pokrywać błoną; filmować

filter ('fylter) s. filter; sączek; v. filtrować; przeciekać

filth (fyls) s. brud; plugastwo

filthy (fylsy) adj. brudny; plugawy;niegodziwy;sprośny

fin (fyn) s. płetwa; v. obcinać płetwy; ruszać płetwami

finagle ('fy'nejgl) v. oszukiwać; wyłudzać;nabierać

final ('fajnl) adj. końcowy; ostateczny; s. finał (sport; egzamin etc)coś ostatecznego

finally ('fajnly) adv. w końcu; wreszcie; na końcu;ostatecznie

finance (faj'naens) s. finanse; skarbowość; v. finansować; udzielać pożyczki

financial (faj'naenszel) adj. pieniężny; finansowy

financier (,fynaen'sjer) s. finansista; v. spekulować; sprzeniewierzać pieniądze

finch (fyncz) s. łuszczak;ptak z krótkim dziobem

find; found; found (fajnd; faund; faund)

find (fajnd) v. znajdować; konstatować;dowiedzieć sie

find out ('fajnd, aut) v. wykryć; wynaleźć; dowiedzieć się

finder ('fajnder) s. znalazca; odkrywca;wizier;dalekomierz

finding ('fajndyŋg) s. odkrycie; stwierdzenie ;dane;wniosek

fine (fajn) adj. piękny; misterny; czysty; przedni; wyszukany; świetny; dokładny; adv. świetnie; wspaniale; s. grzywna; kara; v. ukarać grzywną

finery ('fajnry) s. szyk; elegancja; strojny ubiór

finger ('fyŋger) s. palec; kciuk; v. przebierać w palcach; wskazywać palcem;brać palcami

finger nail ('fyŋger,nejl) s. paznokieć

finger print ('fyŋger,prynt) odcisk palca

finish ('fynysz) s. koniec; wykończenie; v. kończyć; skończyć; wykończyć ;dokończyć

finite ('fajnajt) adj. skończony; ograniczony;końcowy

Finnish ('fynusz) adj. fiński

fir (fe:r) s. jodła ;jedlina

fire ('fajer) s. ogien; pożar

fire alarm ('fajer,e'la:rm) s.
sygnał pożarowy ;alarm pożarowy

firearm ('fajera:rm) s. broń
palna (armaty.strzelby etc.)

firebug ('fajer,bag) s. świetlik ;robaczek swietojanski

fire brigade ('fajerbry,gejd)
s. straż pożarna

fire department ('fajer,dy'-
pa:rtment) s. miejska straż
pożarna;straż ogniowa

fire engine ('fajer'endżyn) s.
wóz straży ogniowej(pompa)

fire escape ('fajerys,kejp) s.
wyjście zapasowe;schody zapasowe

fire extinguisher ('fajeryks,-
,tyngłyszer) s. gaśnica

fireman ('fajermen) s. strażak

fireplace ('fajer-plejs) s.
kominek; palenisko

fireproof ('fajerpru:f) adj.
ogniotrwały; ognioodporny

fireside ('fajersajd) s. przy
kominku;kominek;ognisko domowe

firewood ('fajerłud) s. drzewo
opałowe; drewno opalowe

fireworks ('fajerłe:rks) pl.
ognie sztucznie;hałasliwe sceny

firm (fe:rm) s. firma; adv. mocno; adj. pewny; stanowczy;
trwały; v. ubijac; osadzać
(mocno);umacniac sie

firmness ('fe:rmnys) s. stałość; trwałość; stanowczosc;
jędrność;moc;energia

first ('fe:rst) adj. pierwszy;
adv. najpierw; po raz pierwszy;
początkowo; na początku

first of all ('fe:rst,ow'o:l)
przede wszystkim;najpierw

first aid ('fe:rst,ejd) pierwsza pomoc;doraźna pomoc;opatru-
nek

first aid kit ('fe:rst,ejd kyt)
podreczna apteczka; zestaw
pierwszej pomocy(opatrunkow etc.)

firstborn ('fe:rstbo:rn) adj.
pierworodny(syn, dziecko etc.)

first class ('fe:rst'klas) s.
pierwsza klasa;a.najlepszej ja-
gosci

first-class ('fe:rst'klas) adj.
pierwszorzędny; wspaniały

first floor ('fe:rst flo:r) s.
parter(w Anglii pierwsze piętro)

first hand ('fe:rst,haend) adj.
bezpośredni; z pierwszej ręki

firstly ('fe:rstly) adv. po
pierwsze; najpierw

first name ('fe:rst,nejm) s.
imię (chrzestne)

first-rate ('fe:rst,rejt) adj.
pierwszorzędny; adv. pierwszo-
rzędnie ;bardzo dobrze

firth (fe:rs) n. odnoga morska;
zatoka (zwłaszcza w Szkocji)

fish (fysz) s. ryba;v.łowić ryby

fishbone ('fyszboun) s. ość

fisherman ('fyszemen) s. rybak

fishery ('fyszery) s. rybołostwo; teren połowu lub hodowli

fishing ('fyszyng) s. wędkarst-
wo; rybołostwo; połów

fishing line ('fyszyng,lajn) s.
linka; żyłka (od wedki)

fishing rod ('fyszyng,rod)s.
wędka

fishing tackle ('fyszyng,taekl)
s. sprzęt rybacki

fishmonger ('fyszmanger) s.
handlarz ryb;sklep z rybami

fission ('fyszyn) s. dzielenie;
rozbicie (atomu);rozszczepienie;
rozerwanie

fissure ('fyszer) s. szczelina;
pęknięcie; v. rozszczepiać;
pękać; lupać (sie)

fist (fyst) s. pieśc ;v.uderzac

fit (fyt) s. atak (choroby;
gniewu etc.); kroj; dopasowa-
nie; adj. dostosowany; odpowiedni; nadajacy się; gotów;
zdatny; dobrze leżący; v. spros-
tać; dobrze leżeć;przygotowac sie

fit on (fyt on) v. przymierzac

fit out (fyt aut) v. zaopatrywać; s. wyposażenie; umeblowanie

fitness ('fytnys) s. stosownosc;
kondycja;trafnosc(uwagi);przyzwo-
itosc

fitter ('fyter) s,. monter; krawiec dokonywujacy przymiarek;slu-
sarz

fitting ('fytyng) s. okucie;
oprawa; przymiarka; adj. odpowiedni; wlasciwy;trafny;stosowny

five (fajw) num. pięć ;pięcioro;
piąta(godzina);piątka (numer oou-
wła)

fix (fyks) v. umocować; przyczepiać; ustalać; utkwić; ustalać; zgęszczać; tężeć; krzepnąć; urządzic kogoś(źle); usytuować; zaaranżować wynik (zapasów); s. kłopot; dylemat; położenie nawigacyjne (statku,samolotu etc.)

fix up (fyks ap) v. naprawić; uporządkować;ulokować(kogoś)

fixed (fykst) adj. trwały; stały;nieruchomy;niezmienny

fixedly ('fyksydly) adv. stale; trwale; uporczywie

fixture ('fyksczer) s. urządzenie przymocowane

fizz (fyz) s. syk; napój musujący; v. syczeć; musować

flabbergast ('flaebergaest) v. zdumieć; odebrać mowę (ze zdumienia);oszołamiać

flabby ('flaeby) adj. zwiotczały; obwisły; miękki; słaby; niedbały;bez charakteru

flag (flaeg) s. flaga; chorągiew: lotka; v. wywieszać flagę; sygnalizować

flagstone ('flaeg,stoun) s. płyta brukowa; płyta chodnikowa

flak (flaek) s. artyleria przeciwlotnicza (niemiecka)

flake (flejk) s. płatek; łuska; iskra; v. proszyć; odpryskiwać; łuszczyć;padać płatkami

flake oft ('flejk;of) v. złuszczać (się);odpadac płatkami

flame (flejm) s. płomień;miłość; v. zionąć; błyszczeć; płonąć; opalać; migotać;być podnieconym

flank (flaenk) s. bok; flanka; v. flankować; strzec flanki

flannel ('flaenl) s. flanela; v. wycierać flanelą; ubierać we flanelę (lekka wełnę)

flap (flaep) s. trzepot; klapnięcie; klapa; poła; płat; pokrywa; v. trzepotać; zwisać; klapnąć;uderzyc czyms płaskim

flare (fleer) v. błyszczeć; sygnalizować; popisywać się; rozszerzac się;s.jasny płomień

flare up (fleer ap) s. wybuch; błysk; v.wybuchnąć (gniewem, płomieniem);reagować gwałtownie

flash (flaesz) s. błysk; blask; adj. błyskotliwy; fałszywy; gwarowy; v. zabłysnąć; sygnalizować; pędzić; mknąć; wysyłać (natychmiastowo wiadomości etc.)

flashbulb ('flaeszbalb) s. żarówka (do zdjęć);flesz

flashlight ('flaeszlajt) s. latarka (elektryczna)

flashy ('flaeszy) adj. błyskotliwy(chwilowo);jaskrawy;krzykliwy

flask (flaesk) s. flaszka; flakon; kolba;opleciona flaszka wina

flat (flaet) adj. płaski; płytki; nudny; równy; stanowczy; oczywisty; matowy; bezbarwny; adv. płasko; stanowczo; dokładnie; s. płaszczyzna; równina; mieszkanie; przedziurawiona dętka ;v.rozpłaszczyc;matować

flatten ('flaetn) v. spłaszczyć (się);matowieć;wietrzeć;równać

flatter ('flaeter) v. pochlebiać

flattery ('flaetery) s. pochlebstwo; schlebianie komuś

flavor ('flejwer) s. smak; zapach; v. dawać smak;mieć posmak

flaw (flo:) s. skaza; rysa; pęknięcie; v. psuć; pękać

flawless ('flo:les) adj. bez skazy;(przedstawienie)bez usterek

flax (flaeks) s. len

flaxen(fkak'sn)adj.płowy;lniany

flea (fli:) s. pchła

fled (fled) zob. flee

fledgling ('fledźlyŋg) s. świeżo opierzony ptak;żółtodziób

flee (fli:) fled; fled (fli:; fled)

flee (fli:) v. uciekać;pierzchać

fleece (fli:s) s. runo; wełna; czupryna; puch; v. strzyc; skubać; pokrywać puchem

fleet (fli:t) s. flota; park pojazdów; v, mknąc; przemknąć; mijać; adv. płytko;. adj. płytki

flesh (flesz) s. ciało; miąższ

fleshy ('fleszy) adj. mięsisty; tłusty;cielesny;zmysłowy

flew (flu:) zob. fly

flexible (fl'eksybl) adj. giętki; gibki; układny; obrotny; elastyczny;łatwo przystosowujący się; ustępliwy;poddający się

flick (flyk) s. przytyk; śmignięcie; smuga; v. śmignąć;
trzepnąć; rzucać się; trzepotać się;zapalać zapalniczkę
flicker ('flyker) s. mig; mi-
ganie; drganie; trzepot;
v. migać; drgać; trzepotać;
machać;lekko się poruszać
flier ('flajer) s. lotnik;
ulotka;pośpieszny pociąg etc.
flight (flajt) s. lot; przelot; ucieczka;kondygnacja scho-
flight engineer ('flajt,endży'-
nier) s. mechanik pokładowy
flimsy ('flymzy) adj. cienki;
wątły; słaby(papier,wymówka..)
flinch (flyncz) v. uchylać się;
cofać się; drgać;s.unik
fling; flung; flung (flyng;
flang; flang)
fling (flyng) v. rzucać (się);
powalić; wypaść; wierzgać
fling open('flyn,oupen) v.
rozewrzeć (gwałtownie)
flint (flynt) s. krzemień;
krzesiwo;kamyk do zapalniczki
flip (flyp) v. przytykać ; rzucać;wyprztykiwać;s.prztyk
flippant ('flypent) adj. nie-
poważny; impertynencki
flipper ('flyper) s. płetwa
nożna; graba;łapa;błona pławna
flirt (fle:rt) v. flirtować;
machać; s. flirciarz; flir-
ciarka; machnięcie (raptowne)
flirtation (,fle:r'tejszyn) s.
flirt;powierzchowny romans
flit (flyt) v. biegać; fruwać;
wyjechać;poruszać się zwinnie
float (flout) v. unosić się;
pływać na powierzchni; spławiać; puszczać w obieg; lansować; s. pływak; tratwa;
platforma na kołach; gładzik
do tynku;niezdecydowany ruch
flock (flok) s. trzoda; stado;
tłum; v. tłoczyć się; iść
tłumem; gromadzić się
floe (flou) s. kra (lodowa)
flog (flog) v. chłostać; smagać; bić;biczować się
flood (flad) s. powód; wylew;
potok; v. zalewać; nawadniać

floodlights ('flad,lajts) pl.
reflektory (szeroko-stożkowe)
flood tide ('fladtajd) s. przypływ (morza) ;fala powodziowa
floor (flo:r) s. podłoga;dno
floor cloth ('flo:rklo:s) s.
szmata do podłogi;linoleum
floor lamp ('flo:r,laemp) s.
lampa stojąca na podłodze
floor show ('flo:r,szou) s.
przedstawienie kabaretowe
flop (flop) s. klapanie; klapa;
fiasco; v. klapnąć; załamać
się; zrobić klapę;a.dziadowski
florist ('floryst) s. kwiaciarz;
kwiaciarka;hodowca kwiatów
flounder ('flaunder) s. flądra;
brnięcie; v. brnąć; brodzić;
błądzić; wystękać (mowę)
flour (flauer) s. mąka; v. mleć
na mąkę;dodawać mąki(posypywać)
flourish ('flarysz) s. fanfara;
wymachiwanie; v. kwitnąć; zdobić kwiatami; wymachiwać
flow (flou) s. strumień; prąd;
przepływ; dopływ; v. płynąć;
lać się; zalewać;ruszać się płyn-
nie
flower (flauer) s. kwiat;
v. kwitnąć;być w rozkwicie
flown (floun) zob. fly
fluctuate ('flaktjuejt) v.
falować; wahać się;być niezdecydowanym
flu (flu:) s. grypa;influenca
fluent ('fluent) adj. płynny;
biegły i wymowny(mówca;pisarz..)
fluff (flaf) s. puch;v.trzepać;knoc-
fluffy (flafy) adj. puszysty;lekki
fluid ('flu:yd) s. płyn; adj.
płynny;płynnie poruszający się
flung (flang) zob. fling
flunk (flank) v. oblać (egzamin)
spalić (ucznia); nie zdać;zawalić
flurry ('fle:ry) s. wichura;
ulewa; śnieżyca; podniecenie;
rozgardiasz; v. oszałamiać;
denerwować;wprowadzać zamieszanie
flush (flasz) v. rumienić się;
napełniać; spłukiwać; s. rumieniec; rozkwit; blask; adj.
wylewający się; krzepki; rumiany; równy; etc.; adv. równo;
prosto;gładko;pełno;poziomo;sowi-
cie(wyposażać w pieniądze)

fluster ('flaster) s. podniecenie; niepokój; v. podniecać; oszałamiać; kręcić się
flute (flu:t) s. flet;rowkowa-
nie
flutter ('flater) s. trzepotanie; dygotanie; niepokój;
v. trzepotać; drzeć; dygotać;
płoszyć;powodować trzepotanie
flux (flaks) s. prąd; przepływ;
potok; płynność; krwotok;
przypływ;pasta do lutowania
fly (flaj) s, mucha;klapka
fly; flew; flown(flaj; flu;
floun) v. latać; lecieć; powiewać; uciekać; przewozić
samolotem; puszczać (latawca)
fly across (,flaj e'kros) v.
przelatywać (przez)
flyblown ('flaj-bloun) adj.
popstrzony przez muchy
fly into a rage ('flaj,yntu
ej'rejdż) v. wpaść w pasję
flyer ('flajer) s. lotnik
flying ('flajyng)adj. lataja-
cy; lotny; lotniczy; krótkotrwały;samolotowy;pośpieszny
flying boat ('flajynbout) s.
hydroplan (do wodowania)
flying buttress ('flajyn,ba-
trys) s. łuk przyporowy
flying machine ('flajyng
,meszi:n) s. samolot
flying time ('flajyng,tajm) s.
czas przelotu;czas lotu
fly weight ('flaj,łejt) s. waga musza (112 funtów lub mniej)
flywheel ('flajhłi:l) s. koło
zamachowe (do regulowania szybkości
foal (foul) s. źrebię
foam (foum) s, piana; v. pienić się ;a.pianowy;piankowy
foamy ('foumy) adj. pieniący
się;pienisty;spieniony
focus ('foukes) s. ognisko;
ogniskowa; v. skupiać; ognis-
kować; koncentrować;zesrodkowy-
wać
fodder ('foder) s. pasza
foe (fou) s. wróg;przeciwnik
fog (fog) s. mgła;v.otumaniać
foggy ('fogy) adj. mglisty
foible ('fojbl) s. słabostka;lek-
ka słabość charakteru;
słabość; wątłość

foil (fojl) s. folia; tło; floret; trop; ślad; v. udaremnić;
zacierać (ślad);niweczyć
fold (fould) s. fałda; zagięcie;
zagroda (owiec) v. składać;
zaginać (się); splatać; zamykać owce (w owczarni);faidować
folder ('foulder) s. składana
teczka; broszura;falcownik
folding ('fouldyng) adj. składany; rozsuwany;s.fałd;fałda
folding boat ('fouldyng bout)
składana łódź;turystyczna etc.)
folding chair ('fouldyng, czeer)
składane krzesło;kampingowe etc.)
foliage ('fouljydż) s. listowie;
liście (rosnące);ulistnienie
folk (fouk) s. ludzie; krewni;
lud; rasa; adj. ludowy;folklorys-
tyczny
folklore ('fouklo:r) s. folklor
folksy ('fouksy) adj. towarzyski; prosty;ludzki
folk song ('fouksong) s. pieśn
ludowa (regionalna etc.)
follow ('folou) v. iść za; następować za; śledzić; rozumieć
(kogoś) wnikać;gonić;wynikać
follower ('folouer) s. stronnik;
zwolennik; uczeń; pomocnik
following ('folouyng) s. zwolen-
nicy; adj. następujący; następny;s.orszak;świta;posłuch;autory-
tet
folly ('foly) s. szaleństwo
foment (fou'ment) s. podżegać;
podsycać;nagrzewać;pobudzać
fond (fond) adj. kochający; czuły; łatwowierny;głupio czuły
fondle ('fondl) v. pieścić
fondness ('fondnys) s. czułość;
miłość; zamiłowanie;pociąg
food (fu:d) s. żywność; strawa;
pokarm; jedzenie;a.żywnościowy;
odżywczy
fool (fu:l) s. głupiec; głuptas;
błazen; v. błaznować; wyśmiewać;
oszukiwać;okpiwać;partaczyć
foolhardy ('fu:l,ha:rdy) adj.
szaleńczy; wariacki; lekkomyślny;nieroztropny;gwałtowny
foolish ('fu:lysz) adj. głupi
foolishness ('fu-lysznys) s.
głupota; głupstwo;bzdura;nonsens
foolproof ('fu:l,pru:f) adj.
niezawodny;nie do zepsucia

foot (fut) s. stopa; dół; spód; miara (30,5 cm);piechota;v.piechota;v.płafoot the bill ('fut,ty'byl) v. zapłacić rachunek

football ('fut,bo:l) s. piłka nożna; futbol;piłka do nożnej

foot brake ('fut,brejk) s. hamulec nożny(w samochodzie)

foothills ('futhylz) pl. podgórze(przy łancuchu górskim)

foothold ('futhould) s. oparcie (dla nóg); miejsce gdzie można stanąć;pewna pozycja

footing ('futyng) s. fundament; ostoja; podstawa; położenie

footpath ('futpas) s. ścieżka dla pieszych; chodnik

footprint ('futprynt) s. ślad stopy

footstep ('fut,step) s. odgłos kroku; ślad;długość kroku

for (fo:r) prep. dla; zamiast; z; do; na; żeby; że; za; po; co do; co się tyczy; jak na; mimo; wbrew; po coś; z powodu; conj. ponieważ; bowiem; gdyż; albowiem; dlatego że

for two vears ('fo:-tu-je:rs) przez dwa lata

forbade (fe:r'bejd) zob. forbid

forbear ; forbore; forborne (fo:'beer; fe'bo:r; fe'bo:rn)

forbear ('fo:r'beer) v. znosić cierpliwie; powstrzymywać(się) s. wyrozumiałość; przodek

forbid; forbade; forbidden (fer'byd; fe:r'bejd; fer'bydn) forbid (fe'rbyd) s. zakazywać; zabraniać; niedopuszczać; uniemożliwiać;nie pozwalać

forbidding (fe'rbydyng) adj. odpychający; posępny; ponury

forbore (fer'bo:r) zob. forbear

forborne (fer'bo:rn) zob. forbear

force (fo:rs) s. siła; moc; potęga; sens; v, zmuszać; pędzić; wpychać; forsować

forced landing ('fo:rst,laendyng) przymusowe lądowanie

forceps ('fo:rsyps) pl. kleszcze; szczypce;szczypczyki

forcible ('fo:rsybl) adj. gwałtowny; przymusowy; przekonywujący ;mocny;dosadny;bezprawny

ford (fo:rd) v.przeprawiać się brodem; s. bród(płytkie miejsce)

fore (fo:r) adj. przedni; adv. na przedzie; s, przednia część

foreboding (fo:r'boudyng) s. przeczucie (złego) ;złe przeczucie

forecast ('fo:r-ka:st) v. przewidywać; s. przewidywanie

forefather ('fo:r,fa:dzer) s. przodek ; antenat

forefinger ('fo:rfynger) s. palec wskazujący

forefoot ('fo:r-fut) s. przednia noga (zwierzęcia)

foregone (fo:r'gon) adj. przesądzony ;miniony

foreground ('fo:rgraund) s. pierwszy plan (obrazu)

forehead ('fo:ryd) s. czoło

foreign('foryn) adj. obcy; obcokrajowy ;cudzozieski

foreign currency (,foryn'karensy) s. obca waluta

foreigner ('foryner) s. cudzoziemiec; cudzoziemką obcokrajowiec

foreign policy ('foryn,polysy) polityka zagraniczna

foreign trade ('foryn,trejd) handel zagraniczny

foreleg ('fo:rleg) s. przednia noga (zwierzęcia)

foreman ('fo:rmen) s. majster; sztygar; starszy przysięgły

foremost ('fo:r,maust) adj. główny; przedni; adv. przede wszystkim ;w pierwszym rzędzie

forenoon ('fo:rnu:n) s. przedpołudnie ;s.przedpołudniowy

foresee ('fo:rsi:) v. przewidywać ;przewidzieć;wiedzieć z góry

foresight ('fo:rsajt) s. przezorność; przewidywanie; muszka celownika (przy strzelbie etc.)

forest ('foryst) s. las; v. zalesiać ;a. leśny; w lesie

forester ('foryster) s. leśniczy; leśnik;ptak leśny;ćma leśna

forestry ('forystry) s. leśnictwo; lasy ;wiedza o lesie

foretaste ('fo:rtejst) s. przedsmak;zapowiedź tego co ma nasta-
pić;foretell; foretold; foretold
(fo:rtel; fo:'rtould; fo:'r-
tould)
foretell (fo:r'tel) v. przepowiadać; zapowiadać ;wróżyć
forever (fe'rewer) adv. wiecz-
nie; na zawsze; ustawicznie
foreword ('fo:rłe-rd) v. przedmowa; przedsłowie;słowo wstępne
forfeit ('fo:rfyt) s. grzywna;
fant; zastaw; utrata; v. stra-
cić(w skutek konfiskaty);utracić
forge ('fo:rdż) s. kuźnia; huta:
v. kuć; fałszować; posuwać się
z trudem;wykuwać sobie przyszłość
forgery ('fo:rdżery) s. fałszerstwo;podrobiony dokument
forget; forgot; forgotten
(fer'get; fer'got; fer'gotn)
forget (fer'get) v. zapominać;
pomijać; przeoczyć;zaniedbać
forgetful (fer'getful) adj. za-
pominający;zapominalski;niepomny
forget-me-not (fer'getmyna:t) s.
niezapominajka
forgive; forgave; forgiven
(fer'gyw; fer'gejw; fer'gywn)
forgive (fer'gyw) v. przebaczać; darować ;odpuszczać
forgiveness (fer'gywnys) s. przebaczenie; darowanie; wybaczenie
forgiving (fer'gywyŋg)adj. wyrozumiały; pobłażliwy
forgo (fo:r'gou) v. powstrzymywać się; obchodzić się bez
czegoś ;zrzekać się czegoś
forgot (fer'got) zob. forget
fork (fo:rk) s. widły; widelec;
widełki; v. rozwidlać (się);
brać na widły;spulchniać(ziemię)
forlorn (fer'lo:rn) adj. zapuszczony; opuszczony; beznadziejny; rozpaczliwy;niepocieszony
form (fo:rm) v. formować (się);
kształtować (się); utworzyć
(się); organizować (się); wy-
tworzyć; s, forma; kształt;
postać; formuła; formułka; formularz;.blankiet;styl;układ
formal ('fo:rmel) adj. formalny;
urzędowy; oficjalny;s.strój wieczorowy

formation ('fo:rmejszyn) s. for-
macja; szyk; układ; tworzenie
(się); kształtowanie; formowa-
nie (się); powstawanie;budowa
formative ('fo:rmetyw) adj. for-
mujący; kształtujący; tworzą-
cy (się);słowotwórczy
former ('fo:rmer) adj. & pron.
poprzedni; były; miniony; dawny;s. formierz;giser;wzornik
formerly ('fo:rmerly) adv. dawniej; przedtem; poprzednio
formidable ('fo:rmydebl) adj.
straszny;strszny;potężny;ogrom-
ny
formulate ('fo:rmjulejt) v.
formułować;wyrażać;redagować
fornicate ('fo:rnykejt) v.
cudzołożyć ;spółkować bez ślubu
forsake; forsook; forsaken
(fer'sejk; fer'suk; fer'sejken)
forsake (fer'sejk) v. opuszczać;
porzucać;poniechać;zaprzeć się
fort (fo:rt) s. fort
forth (fo:rŗ) adv. naprzód; dalej;wobec;na zewnątrz etc.
forthcoming (fo:rŗ'kamyŋg) adj.
zbliżający się;nadchodzący
forthwith ('fo:rŗ'łys) adv.
bezzwłocznie;natychmiast
fortieth ('fo:rtyjes) num.
czterdziesty;czterdziesta(część)
fortify ('fo:rtyfaj) s. wzmacniać; fortyfikować;umacniać
fortnight ('fo:rtnajt) s. dwa
tygodnie (czternaście nocy)
fortran ('fo:rtraen) = formula
translation, język dla progra-
mów na komputery
fortress ('fo:rtrys) s. twierdza; forteca ;warownia
fortunate ('fo:rcznyt) adj.
szczęśliwy;pomyślny;udany
fortunately ('fo:rcznytly) adv.
na szczęście; szczęśliwie
fortune ('fo:rczen) s. szczęście; los; majątek;traf;ślepy los
forty ('fo:rty) num. czterdziesci;czterdziestka;czterdzieścioro
forward ('fo:rłerd) adj. przedni; naprzód; postępowy; wczesny; chętny; gotowy; v. przyśpieszać; ekspediować; s. napastnik (w sporcie);gracz w ataku

forwards ('fo:rłerds) adv. naprzod; dalej;adj.frontowy;śmiały
foster-child ('foster.czajld) s. wychowanek; wychowanka
fought (fo:t) zob, fight
foul (faul) adj. zgniły;plugawy; wstrętny; adv. nieuczciwie; wbrew regułom; s, nieuczciwosc; v. zawalac (się); zabrudzic (się);plugawic się;kalac
found (faund) v. 1. uzasadniac; zakładac; odlewac; 2. zob. find
foundation (faun'dejszyn) s. podstawa; załoźenie; fundament; fundacja:podwalina
founder ('faunder) s. odlewnik; załoźyciel; v. zatonąc; przepasc;okulawic;zatopic
foundling ('faundlyng) s. podrzutek ; znajda
fountain ('fauntyn) s. fontanna; zrodło;wodotrysk;poijalnia
fountainpen ('fauntyn,pen) s. wieczne pioro
four (fo:r) num; cztery;czworka;czworo;
fourscore ('fo:rskor) num. osiemdziesiąt
four-stroke engine ('fo:r,strok-'endźyn) motor cztero-taktowy
fourteen ('fo:rti:n) num. czternascie;czternascioro;czternastka
fourth ('fo:rs) num. czwarty
fourthly (fo:rsly) adv. po czwarte;na czwartym miejscu
fowl (faul) s. drob; ptaki
fox (foks) s. lis; v.przechytrzyc
fraction ('fraekszyn) s. ułamek;częśc;odłam;frakcja
fracture ('fraekczer) s. złamanie; v. złamac;łamac się
fragile ('fraedźajl) adj. kruchy; łamliwy;słabowity;watły
fragment ('fraegment) s. fragment;urywek;odłamek;okruch
fragrance ('frejgrens) s. zapach; woń; aromat
fragrant ('frejgrent) adj. pachnący;aromatyczny;wonny
frail (frejl) adj. kruchy; wątły;lekkomyslny;s.kosz;plecionka
frailty ('frejlty) s. słabosc; wątłosc ;chwila słabosci

frame ('frejm) s. oprawa; rama; struktura; szkielet; v. oprawiac; kształtowac; wrabiac
frame of mind ('frejm,ow'majnd) s. nastroj; nastawienie psychiczne;usposobienie do czegos
frame-house ('frejm,haus) s. drewniany dom (typowy w USA)
framework ('frejm,łe:rk) s. struktura; zrąb;szkielet;wiąza-nie
franchise ('fraenczajz) s. przywilej; prawo do prowadze-nia filii lub firmy,do głosowa-nia
frank (fraenk) adj. szczery; otwarty;v.wysyłac bez opłaty
frankness ('fraenknys) s. szczerosc; otwartosc
frantic ('fraentyk) adj. wariacki; szalony;zapamiętały
fraternal (fre'te:rnl) adj. braterski;bratni;bracki
fraternity (fre'te:rnyty) s. braterstwo;korporacja studencka
fraud (fro:d) s. oszustwo;oszust
fray (frej) v. strzępic; wycierac; s. bojka; burda
freak (fri:k) s. kaprys; wybryk; potwor;a.fantazyjny
freckle ('frekl) s. pieg; v.pokrywac piegami;powodowac piegi
free (fri:) adj. wolny; bezpłatny; nie zajęty; v. uwolnic; wyzwolic; oswobodzic; adv.wolno; swobodnie; bezpłatnie
free and easy ('fri:,end'i:zy) adj. beztroski;bez ceremonii
freedom ('fri:dem) s. wolnosc; swoboda;nieskrępowanie;prawo do
freemason ('fri:,mejsn) s. mason; wolnomularz
free port ('fri:, port) s. wolnocłowy port
freethinker ('fri:tynker) s. wolnomysliciel;wolnomyslicielka
freeway ('fri:łej) s. szosa przelotowa wieloliniowa
freewheel ('fri:hłi:l) s. wolne koło (np, od roweru)
freeze (fri:z; frouz; frouzn) v. marznąc; zamarzac;krzepnac;przymarznac; mrozic;wyrugowac(konkurenta)

freezing point ('fri:zyŋ,point) s. punkt zamarzania

freight (frejt) s. przewóz; fracht; v. przewozic; frachtowac statek;a.towarowy(pociag etc)

freighter ('frejter) s. frachtowiec; statek towarowy

French (frencz) adj. francuski

frenzy ('frenzy) s. szał; szalenstwo;v.doprowadzac do szału

frequency ('fri:kłensy) s. częstość; częstotliwość

frequent ('fri:kłent) adj. częsty; rozpowszechniony; v. uczęszczac; odwiedzac; bywac

fresh (fresz) adj. świeży; nowy; zuchwały; niedoswiadczony; adv. świeżo; niedawno;dopiero co

freshman ('freszmen) s. student pierwszego roku

freshness ('fresznys) s. świeżość; zuchwałość;zuchwalstwo

freshwater ('fresz;łoːter) adj. słodkowodny; s. woda słodka

fret (fret) v. gryźć się: niepokoic się; s. rozdrażnienie; niepokój;zdenerwowanie;irytacja

fretful ('fretful) adj. rozdrażniony; draźliwy;nerwowy;wzburzony

friar ('frajer) s. mnich; zakonnik ; biała plamka

friction ('frykszyn) s. tarcie; scieranie się; ucieranie

Friday ('frajdy) s. piątek

fridge (frydż) s. lodówka (slang)

fried (frajd) adj. smażony

friend (frend) s. znajomy; znajoma; przyjaciel;kolega;klient

friendly ('frendly) adj. przyjazny; przychylny ;życzliwy

friendship ('frendszyp) s. przyjaźń osobista; dobra znajomość; znajomość powierzchowna; stosunki koleżenskie lub handlowe

fright (frajt) s. strach;przerażenie;strach na wróble

frighten ('frajtn) v. straszyć

frightened ('frajtnd) adj.przestraszony ;zastraszony;wylękniony

frightful ('frajtful) adj. straszny; przerażający;strszliwy; alarmujacy;nieprzyjemny;wstrętny

frigid ('frydżyd) adj. zimny; lodowaty; oziębły;zimna(kobieta)

frill (fryl) v. plisować; s. falbanka; pl. fochy; fanaberie;niepotrzebne ozdóbki

fringe (fryndż) s. frędzla; obrębek; v. obrębiać; obramowywac; ograniczac;wystrzepić

frisk (frysk) v. brykac; s.sus; podskok; skok;v.rewidowac

frisky ('frysky) adj. rozbrykany; ożywiony; swawolny

fro (frou) exp.: to and fro; tu i tam; tam i z powrotem

frock (frok) s. sukienka; habit;mundur;surdut;anglez

frog (frog) s. żaba; strzałka (w kopycie konia);vulg.Francuz

frolic ('frolyk) s. wybryk;figiel swawola; v. dokazywac; swawolic; figlowac; adj. rozbawiony; swawolny; figlarny

frolicsome ('frolyksem) adj. figlarny; swawolny;rozbawiony

from (from) prep. od; z; przed (zimnem); ze;(ponieważ; żeby)

from under (from ander) prep: spod (czegos)

from... to (from... tu) exp. stąd... dotąd ;od ..,do

front (frant) s. przód; front; czoło; adj. przedni; frontowy; czołowy; v. stawiać czoło; stać frontem; konfrontować

front-door ('frant,doːr) s. główne drzwi wejsciowe

frontier ('frantjer) s. granica ; a. pograniczny

front-page ('frant,pejdż) s. strona tytułowa;a.sensacyjny

front tire ('frant,tajer) s. przednia opona (samochodu)

front-wheel ('frant,hłiːl) s. przednie kóło (wozu)

front wheel drive ('frant, hłiːl'drajw) s. napęd na przednie koła (auta,etc.)

frost (frost) s. mróz; przymrozek; oziębłość;v.zmrozic;oszronic

frostbite ('frost,bajt) s. odmrożenie(nosa,reki,stopy etc.)

frosted ('frostyd) adj. matowy; oszroniony; matowy odcien

frosty ('frosty) adj. mroźny;
oszroniony; lodowaty
froth (froθ) s. piana; szumowiny; v. pienić się;ubijać białko
frothy (froθy) adj. spieniony
frown (fraun) v. marszczyć brwi;
s. zachmurzone czoło; wyraz
dezaprobaty;niezadowolona mina
froze (frouz) zob. freeze
frozen food ('frouzn, fu:d) s.
mrożonki;mrożona żywność
frugal ('fru:gel) adj. oszczędny;tani; skromny(posiłek etc.)
fruit (fru:t) s. owoc; v. owo-
cować;a. owocowy
fruitcake ('fru:t,kejk) s.
świąteczne ciasto z kandyzowa-
nymi owocami i orzechami
fruitful ('fru:tful) adj.
owocny;owocujący;zyskowny;wydaj-
fruitless ('fru:tlys) adj. bezowocny; bezpłodny;nieudany
frustrate (fra'strejt) v. udaremnić; zniechęcić; zawieść
fry (fraj) v. smażyć;s.narybek
frying pan (frajyn,paen) s.
patelnia
fuel (fjuel) s. paliwo; opał
fugitive ('fju:dżytyw) s. zbieg;
adj. zbiegły; przelotny
fulfill ('ful'fyl) v. spełnić;
wykonać; dokonać; skończyć
fulfilment (ful'fylment) s.
spełnienie; wykonanie; dokonanie;wypełnienie;wysłuchanie
full(ful) adj. pełny; pełen; za-
pełniony; całkowity; kompletny;
cały; adv. w pełni; całkowicie
full board ('ful'bo:rd) s. pełne
utrzymanie;wikt i opierunek
full moon ('ful'mu:n) s. pełnia
księżyca
fullness (ful'nys) s. pełność;
dokładność;drobiazgowość
full-time ('ful'tajm) adj. pełno-
etatowy; całkowicie zajęty
fumble ('fambl) v. szperać; partaczyć; s. gmeranie; partactwo;
niezdarność;niezdarne zagranie
fume (fju:m) v. dymić; kopcić;
s. dym (ostry); wyziew(przykry)
gazy spalinowe;zapach;woń;na-
pad gniewu;wybuch gniewu

fun (fan) s. uciecha; zabawa;
wesołość; śmiech;powód do wesołoś-
ci
in fun (yn,fan) adv. żartem;
make fun (mejk fan) v. dokuczać; kpić;wyśmiewać się
function ('fankszyn) v. działać; funkcjonować; s. działanie; funkcja; praca; obowiązek;
impreza; uroczystość;czynność
functionary ('fanksznery) s.
urzędnik; funkcjonariusz
fund (fand) s. fundusz
fundamental (,fande'mentel) adj.
podstawowy; s. zasada; podstawa zasada;nakaz;podstawa
funeral ('fju:nerel) s. pogrzeb;
adj. pogrzebowy;żałosny
funereal (fju'njerjel) adj. żałobny;pogrzebowy
funicular railway (fju'nykju-
ler'rejlłej) kolejka linowa
funnel ('fanl) s. lej; lejek;
komin (maszyny parowej etc.)
funny ('fany) adj. zabawny;
śmieszny; dziwny ;humorystyczny
fur (fe:r) s. futro ;v.okładać
furious ('fjuerjes) adj. wściekły; rozjuszony ;gwałtowny;zaciek-
ły
furl (fe:r) v. składać (się);
złożyć (się) ;s.zwitek;zawinięcie
furnace ('fe:rnys) s. piec
(centralny) ;palenisko;piekło
furnish ('fe:rnysz) v. zaopatrzyć; dostarczyć; umeblować;
wyposażyć ;uzbrajać;meblować
furniture ('fe:rnyczer) s.
umeblowanie; urządzenie
furrier ('farjer) s. kuśnierz
furrow ('farou) s. bruzda;
zmarszczka; koleina; v. orać;
przeorać; zryć ;ryć;pruć;żłobić
further ('fe:rdzer) adv. dalej;
dodatkowo; adj. dalszy; dodatkowy; v. pomagać; ułatwiać;
posuwać naprzód;sprzyjać;popierać
further more ('fe:rdzermo:r) adv.
ponadto; oprócz tego; w dodatku
furtive ('fe:rtyw) adj. skryty;
potajemny ;ukradkowy;skradający
furuncle ('fjuerankl) s. czyrak
fury ('fjuery) s. szał; furja;
pasja; gwałtowna siła; jędza;
megiera;siła burzy;siła wiatru

fuse (fju:z) v. stopić; s. zapalnik; bezpiecznik; korek

fuselage ('fju:zyla:ż) s. kadłub (samolotu)bez skrzydeł i ogona

fusion ('fju:żen) s. stopienie; spawanie; zlewanie się

fuss (fas) v. niepokoić; denerwować; krzątac się; s. wrzawa; zamieszanie; krzątanina

fussy ('fasy) adj. grymaśny; hałaśliwy; nieznośny;zrzędny

futile ('fju:tajl) adj. daremny; bezskuteczny; próżny

future ('fju:tczer) s. przyszłość; adj. przyszły(czas...)

fuzzy ('fazy) adj. kędzierzawy; kręty; puszysty; niewyraźny; zamazany(obraz,pojęcie etc.)

g (dżi:) siodma litera angielskiego alfabetu

gab (gaeb) s. gadanie (slang)

gable ('gejbl) s. szczyt (dachu)trójkąt płaszczyzn dachu

gad-fly ('gaedflaj) s. giez; bąk;osoba zaczepna jak giez

gag (gaeg) s. knebel; v. kneblować; nałożyć kaganiec; zamknąć debate;oszukiwać

gage (gejdż) s. wskaźnik; miara; rękojmia; v, mierzyć; oceniac; zastawiać;sadzić

gaiety ('gejety) s. wesołość

gaily ('gejly) adv. wesoło

gain (gejn) s. zysk; zarobek; korzyść; v. zyskiwać; zdobywać; pozyskiwać; wygrywać; osiągać;mieć korzyść;wyprzedzać

gait (gejt) s. chód;bieg(konia)

gaiter ('gejter) s. kamasz; getr

gale (gejl) s. poryw wiatru; sztorm;wybuch śmiechu;zefir

gall (go:l) s. żółć; złość; gorycz;tupet;otarcie;v.urazić...

gallant ('gaelent) s. bawidamek; galant; adj. piękny; dzielny; waleczny; szarmancki

gallery ('gaelery) s. arkady; galeria; kruźganek;balkon;chór

galley ('gaely) s. galera; kuchnia na statku;szufelka

galley proof ('gaely,pru:f) s. odbitka na korektę(szczotkowa)

gallon ('gaelen) s. miara płynu (ok. 4,5 litra)(am.gal.=3,78,1.)

gallop ('gaelep) v. galopować; s. galop; cwał;galopada

gallows ('gaelouz) s. szubienica;kobylica;szelki;a.szybieniczny

galore (gr'lo:r) s. mnóstwo; adv. w bród;bardzo wiele

gamble ('gaembl) s. hazard; ryzyko; v, uprawiać hazard; ryzykować;igrac;spekulować

gambler ('gaembler) s. gracz hazardzista; ryzykant

gambol (gaembel) v. podskakiwać; s. podskok; skok

game (gejm) s. gra; zabawa; zawody; sztuczki; machinacje; adj. dzielny; odważny; kulawy; v. uprawiać hazard

gamekeeper ('gejm,ki:per) s. gajowy; leśnik

gander ('gaender) s. gąsior

gang (gaeng) s. banda; szajka; grupa;v.łaczyc się w bandę

gangster ('gaengster) s. gangster; bandyta

gangway ('gangłej) s. przejście; kładka;chodnik w kopalni

gaol= jail (dżejl) s. więzienie;ciupa;v.uwiezić;wsadzać do więzienia

gaoler= jailer ('dżejler) s. dozorca więzienny;strażnik więzienny

gap (gaep) s. szpara; luka;otwór; przerwa;odstęp;wyrwa;przełęcz;wyłom

gape (gejp) v. gapić się; ziewać; s. ziewanie; gapienie się

garage (gaera:dż) s. garaż; v. garażować; zagarażować

garbage ('ga:rbydż) s. odpadki; śmieci;bezwartościowe publikacje

garden ('ga:rdn) s. ogród;uprawiać ogród

gardener ('ga:rdner) s. ogrodnik

gardening ('ga:rdenyng) s. ogrodnictwo(warzywne,kwiatowe etc.)

gargle ('ga:rgl) v. płukać gardło;v.płyn do płukania gardła

garland ('ga:rlend) s. girlanda

garlic ('ga:rlik) s. czosnek

garment ('ga:rment) s. część ubrania;szaty;v.odziewać

garnish ('ga:rnusz) v. ozdabiać; s. ozdoba; przybranie (potraw) upiększenia literackie

garret ('gaeret) s. poddasze;
strych; mansarda ¦sl.:łeb
garrison ('gaerysn) s. załoga;
garnizon; v. garnizonować
garter ('ga:rter) s. podwiązka
gas (gaes) s. gaz; benzyna
gaseous ('gejzjes) adj. gazowy
gash (gaesz) s. skaleczyć się;
s. szrama; skaleczenie;blizna
gasket ('gaeskyt) s. uszczelka
gas-meter ('gaes,mi:ter) s.
gazomierz;zegar gazowy
gasoline ('gaesely:n) s. gazolina; benzyna
gasp (ga:sp) v. ciężko dyszeć;
sapać; s. ciężki oddech
gas station ('gaes,stejszyn)
s. stacja benzynowa
gas-stove ('gaes'stouw) s. kuchenka gazowa;kuchnia gazowa
gate (gejt) s. brama; furtka;
wrota; szlaban; ilość publiczności;wpływy kasowe ze wstępu
gateway ('gejtłej) s. przejscie; wjazd; brama wjazdowa
gather ('gaedzer) v. zbierać;
wnioskować;wzbierać;narastać
gather speed ('gaedzer spi:d)
nabierać szybkości;rozpędzać się
gathering ('gaedzeryng) s. zebranie;nagromadzenie; ropień
gaudy (go:dy) adj. jaskrawy;
krzykliwy; s. obchód(uroczysty)
gauge (gejdż) s. wskaźnik; miara; skala; v. kalibrować; oceniać;szacować; oszacować
gaunt (go:nt) adj. chudy; nędzny;wycienczony;ponury;posępny
gauze ('go:z) s. gaza; siatecz-
ka;mgiełka;gaza metalowa
gave (gejw) zob. give
gay (gej) adj. wesoły; jaskrawy; pstry; rozpustny; s. pederasta;pedzio;pedał
gaze (gejz) s. spojrzenie;
v. przyglądać się;przypatrywać się
gaze at (gejz aet) v. wpatrywać
(się)w kogoś, w coś
gear (gier) v. włączyć (napęd)
s. przybory; bieg; układ
gear change ('gier,czeindż)
zmiana biegów

gearbox ('gier,boks) s. skrzynka biegów;skrzynia biegów
gearing ('gieryng) s. przekładnia;mechanizm napędowy
gear wheel ('gier-hłi:l) s.
tryb; koło zębate
geese (gi:s) pl. gęsi
gem (dżem) s. klejnot;perła
gender ('dżender) s. rodzaj;
płec; wytwór; potomstwo
general ('dżenerel) adj. ogólny;
powszechny; generalny; naczelny; główny; nieścisły; ogólni-
kowy; s. generał; wódz
generalize ('dżenerelajz) v.
uogólniać; mówić ogólnikami
generally ('dżenerely) adv.
ogólnie; zazwyczaj; powszechnie; najczęściej; w ogóle
generate ('dżenerejt) v. rodzić;
wytwarzać;płodzić; wywoływać
generation ('dżenerejszyn) s.
powstawanie; pokolenie
generator ('dżenerejter) s.
prądnica; sprawca;generator
generosity ('dżene'rosyty) s.
szczodrość; wspaniałomyślność
generous ('dżeneres) adj. hojny;
wielkoduszny; suty; obfity; bogaty; żyzny;mocny; krzepiący
genial ('dżi:njel) adj. wesoły;
łagodny; miły;jowialny;ożywczy
genitive (dżenytyw) s. (gram.)
dopełniacz;adj.wesoły;łagodny
genius (dżi:njes) s. geniusz;
duch; talent;duch epoki etc.
genocide ('dżenousajd) s. ludo-
bójstwo(stematyczne mordowanie)
gentle ('dżentl) adj. łagodny;
delikatny; subtelny.stopniowy
gentleman ('dżentlmen) s. pan;
człowiek honorowy; dżentelmen
gentlemanly ('dżentlmenly) adj.
dżentelmeński; honorowy
gentleness ('dżentlnys) s. łagodność; delikatność
gentlewomen ('dżentl,łumen) s.
szlachcianka; dama;dama dworu
gentry ('dżentry) s. ziemiańst-
wo; szlachta; światek
genuine ('dżenjuyn) adj. prawdziwy; autentyczny; szczery

geography (dży'ogrefy) s. geografia; fizyczne cechy rejonu
geologist (dży'oledżyst) s. geolog
geology (dży'oledży) s. geologia
geometry (dży'omytry) s. geometria
germ (dże:rm) s. zarodek; zarazek; nasienie; pączek
German ('dże:rmen) adj. niemiecki(jezyk,czlowiek)s.Niemiec
germinate ('dże:rmynejt) v. kiełkowac; rozwijac' się
gerund (dżerend) s. rzeczownik odsłowny(z końcówka:"ing")
gestation ('dżes'tejszyn) s. ciąża
gesticulate ('dżes'tykjulejt) v. gestykylowac; mowic'na migi
gesture ('dżeszczer) s. gest
get; got; got (get; got; got)/
get (get) v. dostac; otrzymac; nabyc; zawołac; łupac; przyniesc; zmusic; music; miec; dostac się; wpływac;wsiadac
get about (,get e'baut) v. poruszac' się;rozchodzic się
get along (,get e'long) v. dawac sobie radę; wspołpracowac
get away (,get e'łej) v. uciec; odejsc;wyjeżdżac;oderwac się
get in (,get'yn) v. wejsc; wsiąsc
get off (,get'of) v. wysiasc
get on (,get'on) v. wdziewac; posuwac sie; robic'dalej
get out (,get'aut) v. wysiasc; wyjmowac; wyciągac;wynosic'się
get to (,get'tu) v. dotrzec; przyjsc; musiec;byc zamuszonym
get together (,get te'gedżer) v. zebrac się; s. zebranie
get up (,get'ap) v. wstac;zbudzic się
get-up ('getap) s.wygląd;ubiór
get ready (,get'redy) v. przygotowac(się);przygotowywac się
get to know ('get,tu'nou) v. zapoznac się (bliżej)
geyser ('gajzer) s. gejzer
ghastly ('ga:stly) adj. ohydny; upiorny; blady;adv.okropnie
gherkin ('ge:rkyn) s, korniszon
ghost (goust) s. duch; cien;widmo

ghostly ('goustly) adj. upiorny
giant ('dżajent) s. olbrzym
gibbet ('dżybyt) s. szubienica
gibe ('dżajb) s. kpina; drwina; v. kpic; szydzic; wysmiewac'
giblets ('dżyblyts) pl. podróbki (np. kurze);podroby
giddy ('gydy) adj. zawrotny; mający zawrót głowy; roztrzepany; v. przyprawiac'o zawrót głowy
gift (gyft) s. dar; upominek; talent; uzdolnienie;a.darowany
gifted ('gyftyd) adj. utalentowany;mający naturalne zdolności
gigantic (dżaj'gantyk) adj. olbrzymi; gigantyczny;kolosalny
giggle ('gygl) s. chichot; v. chichotac;głupio śmiac się
gild (gyld) v. złocic; pozłocic;nadac lepszego wygladu
gill (gyl) s. skrzela; wąwóz; potok;jedna czwarta galona
gilt (gylt) adj. pozłacany; s. złocenie; pozłocenie
gin (dżyn) s. jałowcówka
ginger ('dżyndżer) s. imbir
ginger bread ('dżyndżer,bred) s. piernik;przesadne dekoracje
gingerly ('dżyndżerly) adj. ostrożny; delikatny; adv. ostrożnie; delikatnie; nieśmiało
gipsy ('dżypsy). cygan
giraffe (dży'ra:f) s. żyrafa
gird; girt; girt (ge:rd; ge:rt; ge:rt) na
gird (ge:rd) v. opasac;kpic.s.kpigirder ('ge:rder) s. dzwigar; belka; wzdłużnik
girdle ('ge:rdl) s. pas; v. opasac; okrążyc;opasywac'gorsetem
girl (ge:rl) s. dziewczyna;ukochana
girlhood ('ge:rlhud) s. wiek dziewczęcy; dziewczeta (kraju etc.)
girl scout ('ge:rl skaut) s. harcerka
girl's name ('ge:rls,nejm) s. panieńskie nazwisko
girt (ge:rt) zob. gird
girth (ge:rt) s. popręg; obwód
gist (dżyst) s. tresc; istota; sedno; esencja; osnowa;sens; głowna tresc

give; gave; given (gyw; gejw; gywn)

give (gyw) v. dać; dawać; być elastycznym; zawalić się; ustąpić; s. elastyczność; ustępstwo pod naciskiem

give away (,gyw e'łej) v. wydawać; zdradzać;wydawać córkę

give in (,gyw'yn) v. ustępować; podawać(nazwisko);uznawać w końcu

give up (,gyw'ap) v. poddać się; ustąpić; zaniechać;dać za wygraną

give way (,gyw'łej) v. zrobić miejsce; ustąpić;obsunąć się

glacier ('glaesjer) s. lodowiec

glad (glaed) adj. rad; wesoły; radosny;dający radość;ochoczy

gladly ('glaedly) adv. z przyjemnością; chętnie;właściwie

gladness ('glaednys) s. wesołość; pogoda ducha; przyjemność

glamorous ('glaemeres) adj. czarujący; wspaniały; fascynujący

glance (gla:ns) v. spojrzeć; ześliznąć się; błyszczeć; połyskiwać, s. rzut oka; błysk; rekoszet;odbicie się

glance at (gla:ns et) v. spojrzeć na (coś);rzucić spojrzenie

gland (glaend) s. gruczoł

glare (gleer) v. błyskać; razić; wlepiać wzrok; s.błysk; blask

glass (gla:s) s. szkło; szklanka;lampka;kieliszek;szyba etc.

glasses ('gla:sys) pl. okulary; szkła

glassy ('gla:sy) adj. szklisty; szklany;przezroczysty;bez wyrazu

glaze (glejz) v. szklić; oszklić

glazier ('glejzjer) s. szklarz

gleam (gli:m) s. połysk; v. połyskiwać;zjawić się nagle

glee (gli:) s. wesele; radość

glen (glen) s. dolina(zaciszna)

glib (glyb) adj. gładki; żwawy; płynny; wygadany(zanadto)

glide ('glajd) s. poślizg; szybowanie; v. ślizgać się; szybować; powodować poślizg

glider ('glajder) s. szybowiec

glimmer ('glymer) v. migotać; słabo świecić; s. słabe światło; migotanie;słabe postrzeganie

glimpse (glymps) s. mignięcie; przelotne spojrzenie; v. ujrzeć w przelocie;zerknąć

glint (glynt) s. błysk; odblask; v. błysnąć; zamigotać

glisten ('glysn) s. połysk; v. połyskiwać;lśnić;iskrzyć się

glitter ('glyter) v. świecić się; błyszczeć; s. połysk; blask; pretensjonalność

gloat ('glout) v. napawać się; źle patrzeć;pożerać oczami

gloat over ('glout,ower) v. napawać się (cudzym nieszczęściem);unosić się

globe (gloub) s. globus; kula ziemska;jabłko królewskie;gałka

gloom (glu:m) s. smutek; mrok; przygnębienie; v. zasmucać (się); zaciemniać (się);posępnieć

gloomy ('glu:my) adj. ponury; mroczny;posępny;przygnębiony

glorify ('glo:ryfaj) v. chwalić; wychwalać; gloryfikować

glorious ('glo:rjes) adj. sławny, wspaniały;przepiękny;chlubny

glory ('glo:ry) s. chwała; sława; v. szczycić się; chlubić się;chwalić się;chełpić się

gloss (glos) s. połysk; v. polerować;interpretować(błędnie)

glossary ('glosery) s. słownik (przy tekscie);glosarjusz

glossy ('glosy) adj. lśniący

glove (glaw) s. rękawiczka

glow (glou) v. żarzyć się; pałać; s. jarzenie; zapał; żarliwość;łuna; rumieniec;jasność

glowworm ('glou,łe:rm) s. robaczek świętojański

glue (glu:) s. klej; v. kleić; zalepiać;wlepiać(oczy);zlepić

glutton ('glatn) s. żarłok

gluttonous ('glatnes) adj. żarłoczny;jedzący zbyt dużo

gluttony ('glatny) s. żarłoczność;zwyczaj jedzenia za dużo

glycerine (,glyse'ry:n) s. gliceryna

gnarled ('na:rld) adj. sękaty; wykrzywiony; węzłowaty

gnash (naesz) v. zgrzytać zębami jak w złości

gnat (naet) s. komar;owad

gnaw (no:) v. gryźć; wgryzać; ogryzać; nękać(stałym bólem)

go; went; gone (gou; lent; gon)

go (gou) v. iść; chodzić; jechać; stać się;być na chodzie

go about (,gou e'baut) v. zająć się (czyms)afiszować się

go along (,gou e'long) v. towarzyszyć; zgadzać się ;iść sobie

go away (,go e'łej) v. iść precz; odchodzić;wyjeżdżać

go back (,gou'bek) v. wracać; cofać się ;sięgać wstecz

go by (,gou'baj) v. mijać

go on (,gou'on) v. iść naprzód; ciagnąć dalej; kontynuować

go out (,gou'aut) v. wychodzić (z kims); gasnąć ;bywać(u ludzi)

go through (,gou'tru) v. przechodzić; brnąć przez ;przebrnąć

go under (,gou'ander) v. tonąć; ulegać; zniknąć;umrzeć

goad (goud) s. kolec; bodziec; v. popędzać; drażnić; prowokować;doprowadzać do zrobienia

goal (goul) s. cel; meta; bramka

goalie (gouli) s. bramkarz

go-between (,gouby'tły:n) s. pośrednik; stręczyciel

goblet ('goblyt) s. kieliszek; czara;puchar;kielich na nóżce

goblin ('goblyn) s. chochlik

god (god) s. Bóg; bożek;bóstwo

godchild ('godczajld) s. chrześniak; chrześniaczka

goddess ('godys) s. bogini

godfather ('god,fa:dzer) s. ojciec chrzestny;v.trzymać do chrztu

godless ('godlys) adj. bezbożny;grzeszny;niegodziwy;nikczemny

godmother ('god,madzer) s. matka chrzestna

goggles ('goglz) pl. okulary ochronne; gogle;okrągłe okulary

going ('gouyng)s. chodzenie; jazda;tempo;adj.ruchliwy;istniejący

going rate ('gouyn,rejt) bieżący kurs (dolara,oprocentowania)

gold (gould) s. złoto;adj.złoty

gold digger ('gould,dyger) poszukiwacz złota ; naciągaczka

golden ('gouldn) adj. złoty

gold-plated ('gould,plejtyd) s. plater złoty ;platerowany

goldsmith ('gould,smyg) s. złotnik   golfa

golf (golf) s. golf ;v.grać w

golf course ('golf,ko:rs) s. pole golfowe

gondola ('gondele) s. gondola (np. balonu);otwarty,niski wagon

gone (gon) v. zob. go   towarowy

good (gud) adj. dobry; s. dobro; pożytek; zaleta;wartość

better ('beter) lepszy;

best (best) najlepszy

good at it ('gud,et'yt) dobry w tym; dobrze to robi

good-bye (,gud'baj) s. do widzenia; pożegnanie

good-for-nothing ('gudfe:r,nasyng) s. nicpoń ;hultaj;łobuziak

good-looking ('gud'lukyng)adj. przystojny; ładny

good-natured ('gud'nejczerd) adj. dobroduszny;poczciwy

goodness ('gudnys) s. dobroć

good will ('gud'łyl) s. dobra wola;wartość reputacji firmy

goose(gu:s) s. gęs; pl. geese (gi:s) gęsi;gęsie mięso;dureń

gooseberry ('gusbery) s. agrest

gooseflesh ('gu:sflesz) s. gęsia skórka (z zimna,strachu etc.)

gopher ('goufer) s. suseł; v. grzebać;ryć;plądrować gospodarke

gore (go:r) v. bóść; klinować; s, klin w krawiectwie;posoka

gorge ('go:rdż) s. wąwóz; żarłoczność; treść żołądka; przejedzenie; gardziel; v, obżerać się; pożerać; połykać;opychać się

gorgeous ('go:rdżes) adj. wspaniały; okazały; suty; ozdobny; wystawny;wspaniały;cudowny

gospel ('gospel) s. ewangelia

gossip ('gosyp) s. plotka; plotkarz; plotkarka; v. plotkować;pisać popularne artykuły

got (got) zob. get

Gothic ('gotyk) adj. gotycki

gotten ('gotn) = got; zob. get

gourd (go:rd) s. bania; tykwa

gourmet ('guermej) n. smakosz
gout (gaut) s. gościec;podagra
govern ('gawern) v. rządzić;
kierować; dowodzić;trzymać w ry-
governess ('gawernys) s. guwer-
nantka;nauczycielka;instruktor-
government ('gawernment) s.
rząd; ustrój;okręg;a.rządowy
governor ('gawerner) s. gubernator; zarządca;naczelnik;szef
gown (gaun) s. suknia; toga;
v. układać togę;ubierać suknię
grab (graeb) v. łapać; zagar-
niać; grabić; s. łapanie;
chwyt; zagarnięcie;porwanie
grace (grejs) s. łaska; wdzięk;
przyzwoitość; v. czcić; ozdabiać; dodawać wdzięku;zaszczy-
graceful ('grejsful) adj. pełen
wdzięku; wdzięczny;łaskawy
gracious ('grejszes) adj. łaskawy; miłosierny;exp. goodness gracious!(gudnys'grejszes) Boze miłosierny!
grade (grejd) s. stopień; klasa; nachylenie; v. stopniować;
dzielić na stopnie; cieniować;
równać teren;niwelować;profilo-
grade crossing ('grejd'krosyng)
s. skrzyżowanie dróg; przejazd
przez tory(jedno poziomowe)
grade school('grejd'sku:l) s.
szkoła podstawowa
gradient ('grejdjent) s. nachylenie; stopień nachylenia
gradual ('graedżuel) adj. stopniowy;po trochu
graduate ('graedżuejt) s. absol-
went; v. stopniować; ukończyć
studia;adj. podyplomowy(kurs)
graduation (,graedżu'ejszyn) s.
ukończenie wyższych studiów;
stopniowanie;cechowanie;podział
graft (gra:ft) v. szczepić; dawać łapówkę; przeszczepiać;
s. szczepienie; łapówka; przeszczep;szufla(pełna ziemi)
grain (grejn) s. ziarno; zboże;
odrobina; gran; włókno; słój;
v. granulować; ziarnować
gram (graem) s. gram:1/28uncji
grammar ('graemer) s. gramatyka

grammar school ('graemer,sku:l)
s. szkoła podstawowa
grammatical (gre'maetykel) adj.
gramatyczny(poprawny)
gramme (graem) s. gram (ang.)
gramophone ('graemefoun) s.
patefon; gramofon
grand (graend) adj. wielki; główny; wspaniały; świetny; okazały;
(slang):1000 dolarów;całkowity
grandchild ('graen,chajld) s.
wnuk
granddaughter ('graen,do:ter) s.
wnuczka
grandeur ('graendżer) s. wielkość; dostojność; okazałość;
wspaniałość;majestat;blask;pompa
grandfather ('graend,fa:dzer)s.
dziadek
grandma ('graenma:) s. babcia
grandmother ('graen,madzer) s.
babka
grandpa ('graenpa:) s. dziadzio
grandparents ('graen,pearents)
pl. dziadkowie
grandson ('graensan) s. wnuk
grandstand ('graenstaend) s.
główna trybuna;popisywać się
granny ('graeny) s. babunia
grant (gra:nt) v. nadawać; udzielać; uznawać; zgadzać się na;
przekazywać; s,pomoc; przekazanie tytułu własności;darowizna
granulated ('graenjulejtyd) adj.
ziarnisty;rozdrobniony;granulowa-
grape (grejp) s. winogrona
grapefruit ('grejp-fru:t) s.
greipfrut(owoc lub drzewo)
grape-sugar ('grejp,szuger) s.
cukier gronowy
grapevine ('grejp-wajn) s. winorośl; poczta pantoflowa; szep-
tanka;żródło kaczek prasowych
graph (fraef) s. wykres; krzywa
graphic ('graefyk) adj. graficz-
ny; plastyczny; obrazowy(dosadny)
grasp (gra:sp) v. łapać; chwytać; pojmać; pojmować; dzierżyć; s. chwyt; uchwyt; pojęcie;
panowanie;zrozumienie;kontrola
grass (gra:s) s. trawa; (slang):
marijuana; "pot";haszysz

grasshopper ('gra:s,hoper) s.
konik polny (z czterema skrzydłami; żydouer)
grass widower ('gra:s,łydouer)
s. słomiany wdowiec

grate (grejt) s. krata; ruszt;
v. trzeć; ucierać; zgrzytać;
skrzypieć;irytować;być irytującym

grateful ('grejtful) adj.
wdzięczny;dobrze widziany

grater ('grejter) s. tarko;
tarło;raszpla;tarnik do drzewa

gratification (,graetyfy'kejszyn)
s. zaspokojenie; wynagrodzenie; gratyfikacja;łapówka

gratify ('graetyfaj) v. dogadzać; uprzyjemniać; zadawalać;
przekupywać;wynagradzać

grating ('grejtyŋg) s. krata;
adj. zgrzytliwy; ochrypły

gratis ('grejtys) adv. gratis;
bezpłatnie; adj. bezpłatny;
gratisowy ;darmowy

gratitude ('graetytju:d) s.
wdzięczność(za pomoc etc.)

gratuitous (gre'tjuites) adj.
bezpłatny; niepotrzebny

gratuity (gre'tjuity) s. napiwek; zasiłek przy zwolnieniu

grave ('grejw) s. grób; adj.
poważny; v. wyryć; wryć;wykopać

gravel ('grawel) s. żwir; piasek;v.psypywać żwirem; kłopotać

graveyard ('grejwja:rd) s. cmentarz; nocna zmiana w pracy

gravitation (,graewy'tejszyn)
s. ciążenie(ciał);grawitacja

gravity ('graewyty) s. siła
ciężkości; ciężkość; powaga
(np. sytuacji);ciężar(gatunkowy)

gravy ('grejwy) s. sos mięsny;
sok;dodatkowy zysk;osobista korzyść

gray (grej) adj. szary; zob.
grey ;v.szarzeć;s.szary kolor

graze (grejz) v. paść; drasnąć;
s. draśnięcie; muśnięcie;odarcie

grazing land ('grejzyŋg,laend)
s. pastwisko; pastwiska

grease (gri:s) s. tłuszcz; smar;
v. brudzić; smarować; nasmarować smarem(samochod etc.)

grease gun ('gri:s,gan) s. sma-
rownica wyciskowa ;towotnica

greasy('gri:sy)adj.tłusty;śliski

great (grjet) adj. wielki; duży; świetny; znakomity; wspaniały;zamiłowany;doniosły;pra-

greatcoat ('grejt'kout) s.
palto; płaszcz ;opończa

great grandchild ('grejt'graend-
czajld) s. prawnuk

great grandfather ('grejt'-
graendfa:dzer) s. pradziadek

great grandmother ('grejt'-
grand,madzer) s. prababka

greatness ('grejtnys) s. wielkość; ogrom;wielkoduszność;powaga

greed (gri:d) s. chciwość; zachłanność;żądza(władzy etc)

greedy (gri:dy) adj. chciwy;
zachłanny; łakomy; łapczywy;
żądny;zarłoczny;spragniony

Greek adj. grecki; (niezrozumiały);s.język grecki;Grek

green (gri:n) adj. zielony;
naiwny; młody; niedoświadczo-
ny; świeży; s. zieleń; zieleni-
na; trawnik;v.zielenić;naciągać

greenback ('gri:nbaek) s.
(slang) dolar(banknot)

greenhorn ('gri:nhorn) s. nowicjusz ;żółtodziub

greenhouse ('gri:nhaus) s.
cieplarnia

greenish ('gri:nysh) adj. zie-
lonkawy

greet ('gri:t) v. kłaniać się;
pozdrawiać; ukazać się; dojść
do (uszu);zaprezentować się

greeting ('gri:tyŋg)s. pozdrowienie; powitanie;pozdrowienia

grew (gru:) zob. grow

grey (grej) adj. szary; siwy;
s. szarość; v. szarzeć; siwieć (ortografia brytyjska)

greyhound ('grejhaund) s.
chart(wysoki,chudy,szybki,pies)

grid (gryd) s. krata; sieć;
siatka ;sieć wysokiego napięcia

grief (gri:f) s. zmartwienie;
zgryzota ;smutek;żal

grievance ('gri:wens) s. uraza;
krzywda; skarga; zażalenie

grieve (gri:w) v. martwić;
krzywdzić; smucić ;zasmucić

grievious ('gri:wes) adj. dre-
czący; przykry ;ciężki;smutny

grill (gryl) s. rożen; krata;
potrawa z rusztu; v. smażyć
na różnie; przesłuchiwać
grim (grym) adj. srogi; ponury;
okrutny;grozny;odrażający
grimace (gri'mejs) s. grymas;
v. grymasić
grime (grajm) s. brud; v. bru-
dzic(sadzą, smarem etc.)
grimy ('grajmy) adj. brudny;
wysmarowany; zatłuszczony
grin (gryn) v. szczerzyc zęby;
uśmiechać się; s. uśmiech
grind; ground; ground (grajnd;
graund; graund)
grind (grajnd) v. ostrzyć; toczyć; mleć; zgrzytać; trzeć;
harowac; s. mlenie; harówka;
kujon;ciężka rutyna;kucie się
grindstone ('grajnd,stoun) s.
kamień szlifierski:harówka
grip (gryp) s, uchwyt; trzonek;
rękojesc; uścisk dłoni;walizka;
v. chwycic; złapać; trzymac
gripes (grajps) pl. kolka
gristle ('grysl) s. chrząstka
grit (gryt) s. żwir; piasek;
odwaga; wytrzymałość;charakter;
v. zgrzytać; skrzypieć;posypy-
groan (groun) s. jęk; v. jęczeć
grocer ('grouser) s. właściciel
sklepu spożywczego
groceries ('grouserys) pl. towary spożywcze
grocery ('grousery) s. sklep
spożywczy;artykuł spożywczy
groin (grain) s. pachwina
groom (grum) s, parobek; pan
młody; v. obrzadzać; przygo-
towywac do objęcia stanowiska
groove (gru:w) s. bruzda; rowek; rutyna; v. żłobić; rowko-
wac;nacinac zwojnik;gwintowac
grope (group) v. szukać po omacku; isc po omacku;iść na ślepo
gross (grous) adj. gruby; ordynarny; prostacki; całkowity;
hurtowy; tłusty; niesmaczny;
spasły; wybujały; s. 12 tuzi-
nów; v. uzyskac brutto...
ground (graund) s. grunt;zie-
mia; podstawa; podłoże; teren;
dno(morza);osad;powod;przyczyna

dno; v. 1. osiąść na mieliźnie;
uziemiac; gruntowac; zagrunto-
wac; v. 2. zob. grind
ground control ('graund,ken'troul)
kontrolna stacja (lotów)
ground crew ('graund.kru:) s.
załoga, ekipa na ziemi
ground floor ('graund,flo:r) s.
parter(bliski poziomu gruntu)
ground glass ('graund,glas) s.
tłuczone szkło
groundhog ('graundhog) s. swistak (amerykański)
groundless ('graundlys) adj.
bezpodstawny;gołosłowny
groundnut ('graundnat) s. orzeszek ziemny
ground staff ('graund,staf) s.
personel naziemny(lotnictwa etc.)
groundwork ('graundłerk) s. podstawa; podłoże; zasada; fundament;tło;osnowa;kanwa(utworu)
group (gru:p) s. grupa; v. gru-
powac;rozsegregowywać na grupy
grove (grouw) s. gaj
grow; grew; grown(grou; gru:
groun)
grow (grou) v. rosnąć; stawać
się; dojrzewać; hodowac; sadzic
growl (graul) s. ryk; pomruk;
warczenie; v. mruknąć; warknąc;
burczec; warczec; odburknąc;
gderac;mrukliwie odpowiadać
grown (groun) v. zob. grow
grown-up ('groun,ap) adj. dorosły; s. dorosły człowiek
growth (grous) s. rozwój; wzrost;
uprawa; narosl;porost;przyrost
grub (grab) .v karczowac; dłubac: harowac; wcinac (jedzenie)
grubby (graby) adj. brudny;
niechlujny;robaczywy
grudge (gradż) v. żałowac; ską-
pic; zazdroscic; miec niechęc;
s. żal; uraza; niechęc
gruel (gruel) s. kaszka; kleik;
v. wymęczyc ;zadawać bobu(komuś)
gruesome ('gru:sem) adj. okropny
gruff (graf) adj. burkliwy;
gburowaty; ochrypły;gruby(głos)
grumble ('grambl) v. narzekac;
utyskiwać;gderac;skarżyć się;
s.narzekanie; pomruk;szemranie

grumbler (grambler) s. zrzęda
grunt (grant) s. kwik; v. kwiczec;chrząkac;wymruczec
guarantee (,gaeren'ti:) v.
gwarantowac; poręczac; s. poręczyciel;poręka;rękojmia
guarantor (,gaeren'to:r) s.
poręczyciel; poręczycielka
guaranty (,gaerenty) s. gwarancja; poręka;rękojmia;poręczenie
guard (ga:rd) v. pilnowac;chro-
nic; s. strażnik; opiekun;
obronca; bezpiecznik
guard against ('ga:rd.e'genst)
v. zabezpieczac się przed...
guardhouse ('ga:rdhaus) s.
wartownia;tymczasowy areszt
guardian ('ga:rdjen) s. opiekun; kustosz;adj.opiekunczy
guardianship ('ga:rdjenshyp)s.
opieka; opiekunstwo; kuratela
guess (ges) v. zgadywac; przy-
puszczac; myslec; s. zgadywa-
nie; przypuszczenie;zgadnięcie
guest (gest) s. gosc
guest house ('gesthaus) s. pensjonat; osobny domek dla gości
guest room ('gestru:m) s. pokój goscinny;goscinna sypialnia
guidance ('gajdens) s. kierownictwo; poradnictwo;kierowanie
guide (gajd) s. przewodnik; dzic
doradca;v.wskazywac drogę;prowa-s.
guidebook ('gajdbuk) s. przewodnik (książka)dla turystów
guild (gyld) s. cech; związek
guildhall('gyld'ho:l) s. dom
cechowy; ratusz;dom związkowy
guile (gajl) s. oszustwo
guileless ('gajllys) adj.
szczery; otwarty(w postępowaniu
guilt (gylt) s. wina;przestęp-stwo
guiltless ('gyltlys) adj. niewinny;wolny od zarzutu
guilty ('gylty) adj. winny
guinea pig ('gynypyg) s. swi-ów,
ka morska;przedmiot experymen-
guitar (gy'ta:r) s. gitara
gulf (galf) s. zatoka; przepasc; wir; v. pochłaniac
gull (gal) s. mewa;v.oszukiwac
gullet (galyt) s. przełyk; gardło: gardziel

gully ('galy) s. wąwoz; sciek;
kanał; v. złobic;wyżłobic;poryc
gulp (galp) s. łyk; duży kęs
gulp down (galpdałn) v. łykac;
dławic się; hamowac łzy
gum (gam) s. dziasło; guma;
v. kleic;wydzielac żywicę
gun (gan) s. strzelba; armata;
pistolet;działo;wystrzał armatni
gunpowder ('gan,pałder) s. proch
strzelniczy;proch armatni
gurgle ('ge:rgle) v. bulgotac;
bełkotac;s.bulgotanie;szemranie
gush (gasz) s. ulewa; wylew;
v. tryskac; lac się;wytrysnac
gust (gast) s. podmuch; wybuch
gut (gat) s. kiszka; v. patroszyc;wypalic wnętrze (domu)
guts (gats) pl. wnętrznosci
gutter ('gater) v. wyżłobic;
okapywac; s. rynna; rynsztok;
rów; wyżłobienie; adj. ryn-
sztokowy; brukowy(dziennik)
guy (gaj) s. facet; człek; cuma; v. cumowac; uwiązac
gym (dżym) s. sala gimnastyczna;
gimnastyka(przedmiot w szkole)
gymnasium (dżym'nejzjem) s. sala gimnastyczna;hala sportowa
gymnastics (dżym'naestyks) s.
gimnastyka;cwiczenia fizyczne
gynecologist (,gajny'koledżyst)
s. ginekolog
gypsy ('dżypsy) s. cygan; cy-
ganka;cyganeria;język cygański
gyrate (,dzaje'rejt) v. wirowac;
kręcic się(wg.koła lub spirali)
h (ejcz) osma litera angielskiego alfabetu (prawie niema)
haberdasher ('haeberdaeszer) s.
kupiec galanteryjny;szmuklerz
habit ('haebyt) s. zwyczaj; nałog; usposobienie; przyzwyczajenie; habit; v. odziewac się
habitation (,haeby'tejszyn) s.mie
miejsce zamieszkania;zamieszkiwa-
habitual (he'bytjual) adj.
zwykły; nałogowy; zwyczajny
hack (haek) v. siekac; rąbac;
kopac; kaszlec; s. szrama; motyka; szkapa; najemnik; taksow-
ka; adj. wynajęty; spowszednia-
ły; banalny;okłepany;szablonowy

hacksaw ('haekso:) s. piła do metalu (z drobnymi zębami)

had (haed) zob. have

haddock ('haedek) s. łupacz

h(a)emorrhage ('hemerydż) s. krwotok;v. mieć krwotok

hag (haeg) s. wiedźma; czarownica;brzydka zła kobieta

haggard ('haegerd) adj. wynędzniały; strapiony; wychudły

hail (hejl) s. grad; powitanie; v. grad pada; witać; pozdrawiać; zawołać;walić jak gradem

hair (heer) s. włos; włosy

hairbrush ('heerbrasz) s. szczotka do włosów

haircut ('heerkat) s. ostrzyżenie;styl strzyżenia włosów

hairdo ('heerdu:) s. uczesanie; fryzura;styl uczesania

hairdresser ('heer,dreser) s. fryzjer damski

hairdryer ('heer,drajer) s. suszarka do włosów(elektryczna)

hairless ('h-erlys) adj. bezwłosy; łysy;wyłysiały

hairpin ('heerpyn) s. szpilka do włosów

hairy (heery) adj. włochaty

half (ha:f) s. połowa; adj.pół; adv. na pół; po połowie

half an hour ('ha:f,en'aur) s. pół godziny

half brother ('ha:f,bradżer) s. przyrodni brat

half-breed ('ha:f,bri:d) s. mieszaniec

halftime ('ha:f'tajm) s. przerwa; pół etatu;a.pół-etatowy

halfway ('ha:f'łej) adv. w pół drogi; w połowie drogi

hall (ho:l) s. sień; sala; hala; dwór; gmach publiczny;westybul

hallo ! (he'lou) excl.czesc !

halo ! czolem! dzień dobry!

halo ('hejlou) s. nimb; aureola

halt (ho:lt) v. zatrzymać; utykać; kulec; wahać się; s.postój; przystanek;utykanie

halter ('ho:lter) s. kantar pastewny; stryczek;v.nakładać kantar

halve (ha:w) v. przepołowic;po dzielić się po połowie

ham (haem) s. szynka

hamburger ('haembe:rger) s. siekany kotlet wołowy; bułka z siekanym kotletem wołowym

hamlet ('haemlyt) s. wioska; sioło; malutka wieś

hammer ('haemer) s. młotek; v. bić młotkiem; walić

hammock ('haemok) s. hamak

hamper ('haemper) v. zawadzać; krępować; s. kosz z wiekiem

hamster ('haemster) s. chomik

hand (haend) s. ręka; dłoń; pismo; v. podać; zwijać; pomagać;a.podręczny;przenośny

hand back ('haend,baek) v. oddać; podać do tyłu

hand down ('haend,dałn) v. przekazać; dać w spadku;podać w dół

hand in ('haend,yn) v. wręczyć

hand over ('haend,ouwer) v., wręczyć; podać; dostarczyć

handbag ('haendbaeg) s. damska torebka

handbill ('haendbyl) s. ulotka

handbook ('haend-buk) s. podręcznik; poradnik

hand brake ('haend,brejk) s. hamulec ręczny

handcuff ('haendka:f) s. kajdany; v. zakuwać w kajdany

handful ('haendful) s. garść; garstka; kłopotliwa osoba

handicap ('haendykaep) s. przeszkoda; upośledzenie; trudność

handicraft ('haendykra:ft) s. rzemiosło; rękodzieło (tkactwo etc.)

handkerchief ('henkerczy:f) s. apaszka; chustka do nosa

handle ('haendl) s. trzonek; rękojeść; uchwyt; sposób; v. dotykać; manipulować; traktować; załatwiać; dać radę;

handlować;zarządzać;kontrolować

handlebar ('haendlba:r) s. kierownica(od roweru)

hand luggage ('haend,lagydż) s. bagaż ręczny

handmade ('haend'mejd) adj. ręcznie zrobiony

handrail ('haend,rejl) s. poręcz; bariera;balustrada

handshake ('haend,shejk) s. uścisk dłoni(w pozdrowieniu,także)

handsome ('haensem) s. przystojny; szczodry;znaczny(datek)

handwork ('haend,łe:rk) s. robota ręczna;praca fizyczna

handwriting ('haend,rajtyng) s. pismo; charakter pisma

handy ('haendy) adj. zręczny; wygodny; bliski;pod ręką

hang; hung; hung (haeng; hang; hang)

hang (haeng) s. wieszać; powiesić; rozwiesić; wywiesić; zwisać; s. nachylenie; pochyłość;powiązanie;orientacja

hang around ('haeng e'raund) v. wałęsać się;obijać się

hang out ('haeng'aut) v. wywieszać; wychylać się

hang up ('haeng,ap) v. zaczepić się; powiesić słuchawkę; opóźniać (pracę);wstrzymywać

hangar ('haenger) s. hangar

hang-glider ('haeng'glajder) s. lotnia; skrzydło Rogali

hangings ('haenynz) s. kotary; portiery;draperie;obicia;firanki

hang loose ('haen,lu:z) v. być rozluźniony w akcji (sportowej); zwisać swobodnie

hangover ('haeng,ouwer) s. (slang) kac; przeżytek

hanky-panky ('haenky⊥paenky) s. hokus-pokus;też rozwiązłość

haphazard ('haep'haezerd) s. los szczęścia; przypadek; adj. przypadkowy; dorywczy; adv. przypadkowo;na chybił trafi

happen ('haepen) v. zdarzać się; trafić się; przypadkowo być (gdzieś);mieć(nie)szczęście

happen on ('haepen,on) v. przypadkiem spotkać;natknąć się na

happening ('haepenyng) s. wydarzenie; wypadek;zdarzenie

happily ('haepyly) adv. szczęśliwie;na szczęście;trafnie

happiness ('haepynys) s. szczęście; zadowolenie; radość

happy ('haepy) adj. szczęśliwy; zadowolony;właściwy (wybór); mądra (rada); radosny

happy-go-lucky ('haepy,gou laky) adj. beztroski

harass ('haeres) v. niepokoić; trapić; dręczyć; nękać

harbor ('ha:rber) s. przystań; port; v. gościć; dawać schronienie; zawijać do portu

hard (ha:rd) adj. twardy; surowy; trudny; ciężki; ostry; adv. usilnie; wytrwale; ciężko; z trudem; siarczyście

hard by ('ha:rd,baj) adv. blisko;tuż obok; w pobliżu

hard up ('ha:rd,ap) być w kłopotach pieniężnych

hard of hearing (ha:rd,ow'-hieryng) adj. głuchawy

harden ('ha:rdn) v. twardnieć; uodpornić; stabilizować

hardheaded ('ha:rd'hedyd) adj. trzeźwy; praktyczny;twardy człowiek

hardhearted ('ha:rd'ha:rtyd) adj. nieczuły; niemiłosierny

hardly ('ha:rdly) adv. ledwie; zaledwie; prawie; z trudem; surowo;chyba nie; rzadko

hardness ('ha:rdnys) s. twardość; wytrzymałość;odporność

hardship ('ha:rdszyp) s. trudność; trudy; męka; znój

hardware ('ha:rdłeer) s. wyroby żelazne;towary żelazne

hare (heer) s. zając;królik

harebell ('heer-bel) s. dzwonek okrągłolistny

hark (ha:rk) v. słuchaj; uważaj; odejdź;słuchaj uważnie

harm (ha:rm) s. szkoda; krzywda; v. szkodzić; krzywdzić

harmful ('ha:rmful) adj. szkodliwy;szkodzący;zadający ból

harmless ('ha:rmlys) adj. nieszkodliwy; niewinny

harmonious (ha:rmounjes) adj. harmonijny;melodyjny;zgodny

harmonize ('ha:rmenajz) s. uzgadniać; harmonizować

harmony ('ha:rmeny) s. harmonia (dzwięków,ludzi);zgoda

harness ('ha:rnys) s. uprząż; v. zaprzęgać;zużytkować(wiatr...)

harp (ha:rp) s. harfa; v. gadać w kółko; grać na harfie

harpoon (ha:'rpu:n) s. harpun;
v. ugodzić harpunem

harrow ('haerou) s. brona; v.
bronować; dręczyć; szarpać;
ranić; pustoszyć; niszczyć

harsh (ha:rsz) adj. szorstki;
żrący; ostry; cierpki; przykry; surowy;nieprzyjemny

hart (ha:rt) s. rogacz (dorosły)(powyżej pięcioletni)

harvest('ha:rwyst) s. żniwa;
zbiory; zbiór; urodaj; plony; v. zbierać (zboże); zbierać (plony);sprzątać z pól

harvester ('ha:rwyter) s. żniwiarz; żniwiarka (mechaniczna)

has (haez) (on,ona.ono) ma;
zob. have

hash (haesz) s. siekane mięso;
v. siekać;knocić;przemieszać

haste (hejst) s. pospiech

hasten (hejstn) v.przyspieszać;
spieszyć;być szybkim

hasty ('hejsty) adj. pospieszny; prędki; porywczy;niecier-
pliwy

hat (haet) s. kapelusz

hatch (haecz) v. wysiadywać;
wylęgać; wykłuwać; knuć; za-
kreskować; s. wyląg; łuk;
drzwiczki; śluza; kreska

hatchet ('haeczyt) s. toporek

hatchet man('haeczyt,men) s.
człowiek przeprowadzający
czystkę(odrabiający brudną robotę

hate (hejt) s. nienawiść;
v. nienawidzieć;nieznosić

hateful ('hejtful) adj. nienawistny;zasługujący na nienawiść

hatred ('hejtryd) s. nienawiść

haughtiness ('ho:tynys) s.pysz-
ność; hardość;zarozumialstwo

haughty ('ho:ty) adj. hardy;
pyszny;zarozumialy;wzgardliwy

haul (ho:l) s. wleczenie; holowanie; ładunek; polów; zysk;
v. wlec; ciągnąć; holować;
wozić; transportować;taszczyć

haunch (ho:ncz) s. biodro z uderz

haunt (ho:nt) v. nawiedzać;
s, miejsce często odwiedzane;
melina; spelunka;legowisko

have; had; had (haew; haed;
haed)

have (haew) v. mieć; otrzymać;
zawierac; nabyć; musieć

have-not ('haev,nat) adj. nieposiadający; biedny

have on ('haew on) v. mieć na
sobie;być ubranym w

have to do ('haew,tu'du) v. musieć (coś) robić

haven ('hejwn) s. przystań; port;
v. dawać schronienie; wprowadzać do portu

havoc ('haewek) s. spustoszenie

hawk (ho:k) s. jastrząb; packa;
chrząknięcie; v. polować
z jastrzębiem; sprzedawać na
ulicy; chrząkać głosno

hawthorn ('ho:torn) s. głóg

hay (hej) s. siano

haycock ('hejkok) s. stóg siana

hayfever ('hej'fi:ver) s. uczu-
lenie; katar sienny

hayloft ('hej-loft) s. strych
na siano (w stodole etc.)

hayrick ('hejryk) s. stóg siana

haystack ('hejsta:k) s. stóg
siana (w polu, na łące etc.)

hazard ('haezerd) s. przypadek;
traf; ryzyko; v. ryzykować

hazardous ('haezerdes) adj. ryzykowny; hazardowny; niebezpieczny

haze (hejz) s. lekka mgła

hazel ('hejzl) s. leszczyna;
kolor orzechowy

hazel-nut ('hejzl-nat) s. orzech
laskowy

hazy ('hejzy) adj. mglisty;
zamglony; nieco podchmielony

H-bomb ('ejcz bom) s. bomba wodorowa

he (hi:) pron. on

head (hed) s. głowa: łeb; szef;
naczelnik; nagłówek; szczyt;
v. prowadzić; kierować (się)

head over heels ('hed,ouwer'-
hi:ls) do góry nogami; na łeb
na szyję; panicznie;w panice

head or tail ('hed,o:r'tejl)
orzeł czy reszka

headache ('hedejk) s. ból głowy

headgear ('hedgi:r) s. nakrycie głowy;ubiór głowy

heading ('hedyŋ) s. nagłówek

headland ('hedlend) s. przylądek (daleko wysunięty w morze)

headlights ('hedlajts) pl. główne światła samochodu

headline ('hedlajn) s. nagłówek (w gazecie);wiadomość w skrócie;siec; wrzosowisko

headlong ('hedloŋg) adv. na łeb na szyję; na złamanie karku; na oślep;głową na przód

headmaster ('hedma:ster) s. dyrektor (szkoły)

headphones ('hedfouns) pl. słuchawki(radiowe,gramofonowe)

headquarters ('hed'kło:terz) pl. kwatera główna;główne biuro

headstrong ('hedstroŋg) adj. zawzięty; uparty;bezwzględny

headway ('hedłej) s. postęp

heal (hi:l) v. leczyć; łagodzic; uspakajać;wyleczać się

heal up ('hi:l,ap) v. zagoić

health (hels) s. zdrowie

health resort (hels ry'zo:rt) s. uzdrowisko

healthy (helsy) adj. zdrowy; potężny;spowodowany zdrowiem

heap (hi:p) s. kupa; gromada; v. gromadzić; ładować na stos; obsypywać dużą ilością

hear; heard; heard (hier; he:rd; he:rd)

hear (hier) v. słyszec; usłyszec; słuchac; dowiedzieć się

heard (he:rd) zob. hear

hearing ('hieryŋg)s. słuch; posłuch; przesłuchanie; rozprawa;zasięg głosu;słyszenie

hearsay ('hiersej) s. pogłoska

hearse (he:rs) s. karawan

heart (ha:rt) s. serce; odwaga; otucha; sedno;symbol serca

heartbreaking ('ha:rtbrejkyŋg) adj. rozdzierający serce

heartburn ('ha:rtbe:rn) s. zgaga; pieczenie w żołądku

hearth (ha:rs) s. palenisko

heartless ('ha:rtlys) adj. nieczuły; bez serca

heart transplant ('ha:rt,traens- pla:nt) przeszczepienie serca

hearty ('ha:rty) adj. serdeczny; szczery; otwarty;pożywny;obfity; solidny;dobry;krzepki;rześki

heat (hi:t) s. gorąco; upał; żar; ciepło; uniesienie; pasja; popęd płciowy (zwierząt)

heater ('hi:ter) s. grzejnik; piec

heath (hi:s) s. wrzos; wrzosowisko

heathen (hi:zen) adj. pogański; s. poganin. ciemniak

heather ('hedzer) s. wrzos

heating ('hi:tyŋg)s. ogrzewanie

heave; hove; hove (hi:w; houw; houw)

heave (hi:w) v. unosić; dźwigać; podważać; nabrzmiewać; wyciągać; sapać; s. dźwignięcie; przesunięcie

heaven ('hewn) s. niebo; raj; niebiosa

heavenly ('hewnly) adj. niebieski; niebiański; boski

heaviness ('hewynys) s. ciężkość; ociężałość

heavy ('hewy) adj. ciężki; duży; ponury; zrozpaczony

heavy-handed ('hewy'haendyd) adj. niezgrabny; nietaktowny; bezwzględny

heavy traffic ('hewy'traefyk) ciężki ruch (np. kołowy)

heavyweight ('hewyłejt) s. waga ciężka

hectic ('hektyk) adj. gorący; dziki; niszczący; rozgorączkowany

hedge (hedż) s. płot; żywopłot; ogrodzenie; zapora; ubezpieczenie; v. ogradzać; wykręcać się; ubezpieczac się w spekulacji

hedgehog ('hedżhog) s. jeż; świnka morska

heed (hi:d) s. troska; dbałość; uwaga; wzgląd; ostrożność; v. uważać; baczyć

heedful ('hi:dful) adj. uważny; ostrożny

heedless ('hi:dlys) adj. niedbały; nieostrożny; nieuważny

heel (hi:l) s. pięta; obcas; przechył; łajdak; v.dotykać piętą; podbijać obcas;zaopatrywać; przechylać się;tupać obca-

he goat ('hi:gout) s. kozioł
heifer ('hefer) s. jałówka
height (hajt) s. wysokość;
wzniesienie; wyniosłość;
szczyt;najwyższa granica
heighten (hajtn) v. podnosic,
podwyższac;powiększac etc.
heinous ('hejnes) adj. potworny; ohydny;nienawistny;haniebny
heir (eer) s. spadkobierca;
dziedzic; następca
heiress ('eerys) s. spadkobier-
czyni; następczyni; dziedzicz-
ka (majatku, tytułu etc.)
held (held) zob. hold
helicopter ('helykopter) s.
śmigłowiec; helikopter
hell (hel) s. piekło; psiakrew ! miejsce nędzy i okrucień-
stwa
hello ('he'lou) excl.: hallo !
helm (helm) s. ster;v.sterowac
helmet ('helmyt) s. hełm; kask
help (help) v. pomagac; usługi-
wac; nakładac (jedzenie)
s. pomoc; pomocnik; robotnik
helper ('helper) s. pomocnik
helpful ('helpful) adj. pomocny; przydatny; użyteczny
helping ('helpyng) s. porcja
(jedzenia);udzielanie pomocy
helpless ('helplys) adj. bezradny; bez pomocy ;słaby
helplessness ('helplysnys) s.
bezradność ;słabość
helter-skelter ('helter'skelter)
adv. na łapu-capu; na łeb na
szyję; s. popłoch; bezładny
pospiech(w bałaganie)
hem (hem) s. brzeg; obrąbek;
chrząkanie; v. obrębiac; oto-
czyc; pochrząkiwac; wahac się
hem in ('hem,yn) v. okrążyc;
zamknąc; obrębic
hemisphere ('hemysfier) s. półkula (zachodnia,wschodnia etc.)
hemline ('hemlajn) s. obrąbek
(spódnicy)
hemlock ('hemlek) s. szalej;
cykuta jadowita; drzewo tsuga
hemp (hemp) s. konopie; adj.
konopny (sznur etc.)
hemstitch ('hemstycz) s. mereż-
ka; v. mereżkowac (ozdobnie)

hen (hen) s. kura; kwoka; baba
hence (hens) adv. stąd; odtąd;
a więc; przeto; dlatego
henceforth (hens'fo:rs) adv.
odtąd; na przyszłość;od teraz
hen coop ('henku:p) s. kurnik
hen house ('henhaus) s, kurnik
hen pecked ('henpekt) s. pantoflarz;adj.będący pod pantoflem
her (he:r) pron. ją; jej; adj.
jej (należący)do niej
herald ('hereld) s. zwiastun;
v. zwiastowac; wprowadzac
heraldry ('hereldry) s. heral-
dyka;pompa; ceremonia
herb (he:rb) s. zioło (jednoroczne)
herd (he:rd) s. trzoda; stado;
pastuch; v. isc stadem;zganiac
w stado; pasc;popędzac stadem
herdsman ('he:rdzmen) s. pasterz; pastuch
here (hier) adv. tu; tutaj; oto
here you are (,hier'ju:,a:r)
exp.:tu pan ma ! proszę bardzo !
hereafter ('hier'a:fter) adv.
odtąd; poniżej; potem; w życiu pozagrobowym; s, przyszłość; przyszłe życie
hereby ('hier'bay) adv. przez
to; w ten sposób; skutkiem
tego; w pobliżu
hereditary (hy'redytery) adj.
dziedziczny; odziedziczony;
tradycyjny;przekazany dziedzicznie
herein ('hie'ryn) adv. tutaj;
tam że; wobec tego; w tych
warunkach;w tym(rozdziale etc.)
hereof ('hier'ow) adv. tego;
o tym ;w odniesieniu do tego
heresy ('herysy) s. herezja
hereupon ('hiere'pon) adv.
potem; skutkiem tego; o tym
herewith ('hier'łys) adv. ni-
niejszym ;w ten sposób
heritage ('herytydż) s. spuścizna; spadek; dziedzictwo
hermit ('he:rmyt) s. pustelnik;
odludek;eremita;pustelnica
hero ('hierou) s. bohater
heroic ('hierouyk) adj. bohaterski ;heroiczny;epiczny; bardzo wymowny; podniosły

heroine ('hierouyn) s.bohaterka
heroism ('hierouyzem) s.
bohaterstwo (w czynach i ce-
heron ('heren) s. czapla
herring ('heryŋg)s. śledź
hers (he:rz) pron. jej
herself (he:r'self) pron. ona
sama; ona sobie; ja sama
hesitate ('hezytejt) v. wahać
się ;być niepewnym;zatrzymać się
hesitation (,hezytejszyn) s.
wahanie;być niezdecydowanym
hew; hewed; hewn (hju:; hju:d;
hju:n)
hew (hju:) v. rąbać; ciosać;
kuć; wyrąbywać(ścieżkę etc.)
hewn (hju:n) zob: hew
hey (hej) excl.:hej ! ej że!
heyday ('hejdej) s. pełnia;
rozkwit; świetny nastrój
hi (haj) excl.:hej ! (pozdrowienie) ; cześć! czołem!
hiccup; hiccough ('hykap) s.
czkawka; v. mieć czkawkę
hid (hyd) zob, hide
hidden (hydn) zob. hide
hide; hid; hidden (hajd; hyd;
hydn)
hide (hajd) v. chować; ukrywać;
s. kryjówka; skóra (zwierzęca)
hide-and-seek ('hajd,en si:k)
exp.:zabawa w chowanego
hideous ('hydjes) adj. ochydny;
wstrętny ;paskudny;odrażający
hiding ('hajdyŋg)s. kryjówka;
skórobicie ; lanie;manto
hiding place ('hajdyŋg'plejs)
s. kryjówka; melina
hi-fi ('haj'faj) = high-fideli-
ty ('haj fy'delyty) wiernie
odtwarzający dźwięk (aparat)
high (haj) adj. wysoki; wyniosły; silny;cienki(głos)
highbrow ('hajbrau) s. intelektualista;a. intelektualny
high diving('hajdajwyŋg) s.
skakanie z wieży do wody
high jump ('hajdżamp) s. skok
wzwyż (w sporcie)
highlands ('hajlend) s. pod-
górze; góry,górzysty kraj
highlights ('hajlajts) pl. główne punkty (np. programu)

highly ('hajly) adv. wysoko; wysoce; wielce; zaszczytnie
highness ('hajnys) s. wysokość
(tytuł); wyniosłość
high-pitched ('haj'pyczt) adj.
wysoki; ostry; cienki (głos)
spadzisty; stromy (dach)
high-powered ('haj'pałerd) adj.
potężny
high-pressure ('haj'preszer)
adj. wysokiego ciśnienia; na-
chalny
highroad ('haj'roud) s. szosa;
główna droga
high-school ('haj'sku:l) s.
gimnazjum; szkoła średnia
high-strung ('haj'straŋg)adj.
nerwowy; napięty; wrażliwy
high-tide ('haj'tajd) s. przypływ
highway ('haj'łej) s. szosa
highwayman ('haj,łejmen) s.
rozbójnik
hijack ('hajdżaek) v. rabować;
grabić
hike (hajk) v. włóczyć się;
wędrować; wyciągać do góry;
s. wycieczka; podwyżka
hilarious (hy'leerjes)adj.wesoły;
hałaśliwie wesoły
hill (hyl) s. górka; pagórek;
kopiec; v. sypać kopiec
hillbilly ('hylbyly) s. pro-
wincjał
hillside ('hyl'sajd) s. stok
hilly ('hyly) adj. pagórkowaty;
górzysty
hilt (hylt) s. rękojeść; garda
him (hym) pron. jego; go; jemu;
mu
himself (hym'self) pron. się;
siebie; sobie; sam; osobiście;
we własnej osobie
hind (hajnd) s. parobek; łania;
adj. tylny; zadni
hinder ('hynder) v. przeszkadzać; powstrzymywać
hind leg ('hajnd,leg) s. tylna
noga
hindrance ('hyndrens) s. przeszkoda ; zawada;zawadzanie
hindsight('hajnd,sajt)s.zrozu-
mienie co trzeba było zrobić

hinge (hyndż) s. zawiasa; v.obracać; zależeć; zawiesić na zawiasach;wisieć na zawiasach

hinny (hyny) s. muł (z oślicy i ogiera)

hint (hynt) s. aluzja; przytyk; wskazówka; v. napomknąć; dać do zrozumienia;zrobić aluzję

hinterland ('hynter,laend) s. zaplecze; daleki teren

hip (hyp) s. biodro; naroże dachu; chandra;adj.biodrowy

hippie (hypi:) s. niekonformista; adj. zbuntowany przeciw tradycji (wyobcowany)

hippopotamus (hype'potemes) s. hipopotam

hire (hajer) s. najem; opłata za najem; v. najmować; wynajmować; dzierżawić;odnajmować

hire out ('hajer aut) v. wynajmować(się do pracy,na służbę...)

hire purchase ('hajer'pe:rczys) wynajem - zakup na raty

his (hyz) pron. jego

hiss (hys) v. syczeć; gwizdać; s. syk; gwizd;głoska sycząca

historian (hys'to:rjen) s. historyk;historyczka

historic (hys'toryk) adj. historyczny;sławny w historii

history ('hystory) s. historia; dzieje; przeszłość (znana)

hit (hyt) s. uderzenie; przytyk; sukces; sensacja; v. uderzyć; utrafić; natrafić; zabić

hit and run ('hyt,en'ran) adj. uciekający od wypadku (drogowego); walczący podjazdowo; dorywczy i niepewny

hitman ('hytmen) s. najemny zabójca;najemny morderca

hit or miss (hyt o:r mys) adv. na chybił trafił;przypadkiem

hit upon ('hyte'pon) v. natrafić (na coś,na kogoś)

hitch (hycz) s. zaciśnięcie; węzeł; przeszkoda; szarpnięcie; uchwyt; służba (wojskowa) v. doczepić; uczepić; pociągnąć; szarpnąć; przywiązać; zaczepić się;ciągnąć szarpiąc

hitchhike ('hycz,hajk) v. jechać autostopem

hitchhiker ('hycz,hajker) s. jadący autostopem

hither ('hydzer) adv. dotąd; tutaj;adj. bliżej

hitherto ('hydzer'tu:) adv. dotychczas; do tej pory

hive (hajw) s. ul; rojowisko; v. umieszczać w ulu; wchodzić do ula;zbierać do ula

hoard (ho:rd),v. gromadzić; zbierać; s. zapas. zbiór; skarb

hoarfrost ('ho: r'frost) s. szron(na trawie,włosach etc.)

hoarse (ho:rs) adj. zachrypnięty; v. zachrypnąć;mieć chrapliwy głos

hoax (houks) v. bujać; nabierać; s. bujda; kaczka;kawał

hobble ('hobl) s. pętą; utykanie; v. utykać; kuleć; pętać

hobby ('hoby) s. hobby; pasja (np. filatelistyka)

hobbyhorse ('hobyho:rs) s. konik na kiju do zabawy(na biegunach)

hobgoblin ('hob,goblyn) s. skrzat; chochlik

hobnob ('hobnob) v. być za pan brat;blisko się zadawać

hobo('haubou) s. włóczęga

hock (hok) s. pęcina; v. zastawić (się) w lombardzie

hockey ('hoky) s. hokej

hoe (hou) s. motyka; graca; v. gracować;okopywać motyką

hog (hog) s. wieprz; człowiek zachłanny; y. łapać dla siebie; jechać środkiem; wyginąć; łukowato w środku;zagarniać sobie

hoist (hojst) s. dźwig; wyciąg; v. wyciągać ładunek w górę; wywieszać(flagę);podciągać do góry

hold; held; held (hould; held; held)

hold (hould) v, trzymać; posiadać; zawierać; powstrzymywać; uważać; obchodzić; wytrzymywać; trwać; s. chwyt; pauza; pomieszczenie; więzienie; twierdza;silny wpływ;uchwyt

hold back ('hould,baek) v. powstrzymać; zataić;wahać się

hold on ('hould,oṇ) v. trzymać
się; wytrzymywać;powstrzymać
holdup ('hould'ap) s. zatrzymanie; zator; napad rabunkowy
holder ('houlder) s. właściciel; posiadacz; uchwyt
holding ('houldyṇg) s. posiadłość; portfel akcji; dzierżawa;uchwyt;ujęcie;trzymanie
hole (houl) s. dziura; nora;
dołek; v. dziurawić; przedziurawić;przekopywać(tunel)
holiday ('holedy) s. święto;
wakacje; urlop;adj.wesoły;ra-
dosny
holidaymaker ('holedy,mejker)
s. wczasowicz; letnik; turysta;wycieczkowicz;letniczka
holler ('holer) v. wrzeszczeć;
krzyczeć(po prostacku)
hollow ('holou) s. dziupla;
dziura; kotlina; dolina;
adj. wklesły; dziurawy; fałszywy; głuchy; pusty; czczy;
głodny;nieszczęsny;adv.pusto
hollow out ('holou,aut) v.
drążyć;wydrążyć;żłobić
holly ('holy) s. ostrokrzew
holy ('holy) adj. święty
homage ('homydż) s. hołd
home (houm) s. dom; ojczyzna;
kraj; schronisko; bramka;
adj. domowy; rodzinny; krajowy; wewnętrzny; ojczysty
homeless ('houmlys) adj. bezdomny;bez dachu nad głowa,
homely ('houmly) adj. swojski;
pospolity; nieładny; prosty;
skromny;niewybredny;niewyszu-
kany
homemade ('houm'mejd) adj.
domowego wyrobu; krajowy
homesick ('houm-syk) adj.
stęskniony za domem rodzinnym;
stęskniony za (czymś swoim)
homesickness ('houm,syknys)
s. nostalgia;tesknota za domem
home team ('houm-ti:m) s. drużyna miejscowa (sportowa)
home trade ('houm-trejd) s.
handel wewnętrzny
homewards ('houm,łedz) adv. ku
domowi (ojczyźnie);do domu

homework ('houmłerk) s. zadanie
domowe;odrabianie lekcji
homicide ('homy,sajd) s. zabójca; zabójstwo
honest ('onyst) adj. uczciwy;
prawy; przyzwoity; szczery;
adv. naprawdę
honesty ('onesty) s. zacnosc;
prawosc; rzetelność; uczciwość
honey ('hany) s. miód;słodycz
honeycomb ('hany,koum) s. (woskowy) plaster pszczeli;
v. dziurawić; przenikac
honeymoon ('hany,mu:n) s. miodowy miesiąc;v.spędzić miodowy miesiąc
honk (hoṇk) s. krzyk gęsi; głos
trąbki, klaksonu; v. trąbić;
(slang; wymyślać)
honorary ('onerery) adj. honorowy (np. urząd);bezpłatny
honor ('oner) s. cześć; uczciwość; cnota; tytuł sędziego;
v. czcić; zaszczycać; honorować
honorable ('onerebl) adj. czcigodny; uczciwy; szanowny; honorowy; zaszczytny;poważany
hood (hud) s. kaptur; kapturek;
maska; buda; v. zaopatrywać
w kaptur; przykrywać
hoodlum ('hu:dlem) s. opryszek;
chuligan;łobuz
hoodwink ('hudłynk) v. oczy mydlić; zmylić;zawiązywać oczy
hoof ('hu:f) s. kopyto; v. kopać; iść; tańczyć;iść pieszo
hook (huk) s. hak; v. zahaczyć;
zakrzywic (sie);złapać (meża)
hoop (hu:p) s. obręcz; v. otaczać obręczą;wykrzyknąć
hooping cough ('hu:pyṇg-kof) s.
koklusz; krztusiec;zob.whooping-
cough
hoot (hu:t) s. hukanie; odgłosy
niezadowolenia; v. hukać; gwizdać; wyć; trąbić;wygwizdać
hooves (hu:wz) pl. kopyta
hop (hop) s. chmiel; skok; po-
tancówka; v. podskakiwać; poderwać (sie); przeskakiwać
hope (houp) s. nadzieja; v.
mieć nadzieję;spodziewać sie;ufać;
żywić nadzieję

hopeful ('houpful) adj. pełen
nadziei; ufny; obiecujący;
rokujący nadzieje

hopeless ('houplys) adj. beznadziejny; rozpaczliwy; zrozpaczony;zdesperowany

horde (ho:rd) s. horda; gromada

horizon (he'rajzen) s. horyzont
widnokrąg; warstwa oznaczona

horizontal (,hory'zontel) adj.
poziomy; horyzontalny; widno-
kręgowy; s. płaszczyzna po-
zioma;poziom równy i płaski

horn (ho:rn) s. róg; trąbka;
syrena; kula (siodła)
v. bóść; przebóść;wmieszać się

hornet ('ho:rnyt) s. szerszeń

horny ('ho:rny) adj. rogowy;
zrogowaciały;rogaty;jak róg

horrible ('horebl) adj. straszny; okropny;szokujący;paskudny

horrid ('horyd) adj. straszny;
ohydny; odrażający;paskudny

horrify ('horyfaj) v. przerażać;
oburzać;ciężko szokować

horror ('horer) s. groza; wstręt;
odraza; przerażenie;dreszcz

horse ('ho:rs) s. koń; konnica;
jazda; kozioł z drzewa

horseback ('ho:rs,baek) s.
grzbiet koński;adv. konno

horsefly ('ho:rs,flaj) s.giez

horsehair ('ho:rs,heer) s.
włosie końskie;sztywna tkanina

horseman ('ho:rsmen) s. jeździec

horse opera ('ho:rs'opere) s.
film kowbojski (nie-realistyczny)

horseplay ('ho:rs,plej) s. ordy-
narna zabawa (brutalna)

horsepower ('ho:rs,pałer) s.
koń mechaniczny= 746 watów

horse race ('ho:rs.rejs) s.
wyścigi konne

horseradish ('ho:rs,raedysh)
s. chrzan; a. chrzanowy

horseshoe ('ho:rs,szu) s. podkowa;a.w kształcie podkowy

horticulture('ho:rty,kaltczer)
s. ogrodnictwo

hose (houz) s. pończochy; wąż do
podlewania(wiedza i praktyka)

hosiery ('haouzery) s. trykotaże;
pończochy

hospitable ('hospytebl) adj.
gościnny; szczodry dla gości

hospital ('hospytl) s. szpital;
lecznica;a. szpitalny

hospitality (, hospy'taelyty)
s. gościnność

host (houst) s. gospodarz; ży-
wiciel; chmara;czereda;tłum

hostage ('hostydż) s. zakładnik; zastaw;zakładniczka

hostel ('hostel) s. dom studencki; bursa ;zajazd

hostess ('houstys) s. gospodyni; stewardesa; fordanserka

hostile ('hostajl) adj. wrogi;
nieprzyjemny; antagonistyczny

hostility (hos'tylyty) s. wrogość; stan wojny;ostra opozycja

hot (hot) adj. gorący; palący;
pieprzny; ostry; nielegalny;
świeży; pobudliwy; adv. gorąco

hotbed ('hot,bed) s. inspecty;
wylęgarnia;siedlisko;rozsadnik

hot dog ('hot,dog) s.kiełbas-
ka w bułce;kiełbaska smażona

hotel (hou'tel) s. hotel

hothead ('hot,hed) s. człowiek
zapalczywy; raptus;a.porywczy

hothouse ('hot,haus) s. cieplarnia; oranżeria

hot-pants (,hot'paents) exp.
obcisłe damskie szorty;
vulg.:panna puszczalska

hot water bottle (hot'ło:ter'
botl) s. gorąca butelka

hound (haund) s. ogar; łajdak;
v. tropic; szczuć; podjudzać

hour ('auer) s. godzina; pora

hourly ('auerly) adj. cogo-
dzinny; adv. co godzinę;
ustawicznie;z godziny na godzinę

house (haus) s. dom; zajazd;
teatr; widzowie; v. gościć;
dawać pomieszczenie; mieszkać

housekeeper ('haus,ki:per) s.
najęta gosposia ;pomoc domowa

housekeeping ('haus,ki:pyng) s.
gospodarka domowa

housemaid ('haus,mejd) s. pokojówka; pomoc domowa

housewife ('haus,łajf) s.
gospodyni (niepracująca poza
domem)

housework ('haus,że:rk) s. pra-
ce domowe;sprzątanie i gotowanie

housing ('hauzyŋg) s. pomieszczenie; kolonia; osłona; pokrywa; czaprak;obudowa

hove (houw) zob. heave

hover ('hower) v. unosic się;
kręcic się; byc w niepewności;
s. stan niepewności; unosze-
nie się;wahanie się;przywieranie

how (hau) adv. jak; jak ?sposób

how do you do ('hau,du'ju:du)
exp.:dzień dobry !; dobry
wieczór ! (jak sie pan(i) ma ?)

how are you ('hau,a:r'ju) exp.:
jak sie pan(i) ma ?

how about ('hau,e'baut) exp.:
może ?; pozwolisz ? etc.

how much ('hau,macz) exp.: ile ?

how many ('hau,meny) exp.: ile?
ilu ? jak wielu?

how much is it ? ('hau,macz'yz,
yt) ile to kosztuje ?

however (hau'ewer) adv. jakkolwiek; jednak; niemniej

howl (haul) s. wycie; ryk;
v. wyc; wyganiac (gonic)wrzas-
kiem

howler ('hauler) s. gruby błąd

hub (hab) s. piasta; osrodek;
slang: mąż;środek(rozgrywki)

hubbub ('habbab) s. zgiełk;gwar
awantura; wrzawa;tumult

hubby ('haby) s. meżulek (slang)

huckleberry ('hakelbery) s.
borówka amerykańska(krzak i jagoda)

huddle together ('hadl,tu'gedzer)
v. przytulac się; tulic sie

huddle up ('hadl,ap) v.skulic się
zwinąc się w kłębek

hue (hju:) s. barwa; odcień

hug (hag) s. uscisk; chwyt za-
paśniczy; v. ściskac; przycis-
kac; tulic (się);uściskac

huge (hju:dż) adj. ogromny

hull (hal) s. łuska; kadłub;
v. łuszczyć; godzic w kadłub

hullabaloo ('halebelu:) s.
harmider;zgiełk;wrzawa;gwar

hullo (he'lou) excl.:hola! halo!

hum (ham) v. nucic; buczec; mruczec; chrząkac; s. pomruk;
chrząkanie; wahanie się; blaga

human ('hju:men) adj. ludzki;
s. istota ludzka

humane ('hju:mejn) adj. ludzki; humanitarny ;litościwy

humanitarian (hju,maeny'teerjen) adj. humanitarystyczny;
s. humanitarysta;filantrop

humanity (hju'maenyty) s.
ludzkość; rasa ludzka; cechy
ludzkie; dobre uczynki

humble ('hambl) adj. pokorny;
uniżony; skromny; v. upoka-
żac; poniżac; poniżyć

humbleness ('hamblnys) s. pokora; bezpretensjonalność

humbug ('hambag) s. oszustwo;
blaga; bujdą; oszust; blagier;
v. blagować; oszukiwać; nabierać;wyłudzać opowiadaniem bred-
ni

humdrum ('hamdram) adj. nudny;
banalny; monotonny; s. szarzyzna; banalność; nudziarz

humidity (hju'mydyty) s. wil-
goc: wilgotnosc(powietrza etc.)

humiliate (hju'myly,ejt) v.
upokarzać; poniżać;martwić

humiliation (hju,:myly'ejszyn)
s. upokorzenie; poniżenie

humility (hju'mylyty) s. skrom-
nosć; pokora ducha etc.

humming-bird ('hamyŋg,byrd) s.
koliber

humor ('hju:mer) s.humor; nastroj; kaprys; wesołość;
v. dogadzac; zaspakajac; zadowalać; ustepować; dostosować się do zachcianek etc.

humorous ('hju:meres) adj.
śmieszny; pocieszny; pełen
humoru; zabawny;komiczny

hump (hamp) s. garb; v. garbic się; wyginac w łuk

humpback ('hampbaek) s. garbus

hunchback ('hancz,baek) s. garbus;garb na plecach

hundred ('handred) num. sto;
s. setka;niezliczona ilość

hundredth ('handredt) num.
setny; jedna setna

hundredweight ('handred,łejt)
s. cetnar angielski

hung (haŋg) zob. hang

Hungarian (han'geerjen) adj.
węgierski ;s. Węgier
hunger ('hanger) s. głód;
v. głodować; łaknąc; głodzic
hunger strike ('hanger-strajk)
s. strajk głodowy
hungry ('hangry) adj. głodny;
zgłodniały; pożądliwy; ubogi;
jałowy; nieurodzajny;łaknący
hunt (hant) s. polowanie;
teren łowiecki; v. polowac;
gonic; przeszukiwac; szukac
hunter ('hanter) s. myśliwy
hunting ('hantyng) s. polowanie; adj. myśliwski
hunting ground ('huntyng,graund)
s. teren myśliwski
huntsman ('hantsmen) s. myśliwy; łowca
hurdle ('he:rdl) s. opłotki;
v. porac się; skakac przez
płotki; grodzic;przebijac się
hurdler ('he:rdler) s. zawodnik
wyścigów(z płotkami)
hurdle race ('he:rdl,rejs) s.
wyścigi(z płotkami,przez płotki
hurl (he:rl) s. rzut; v. rzucac
hurrah (he'ra:) excl.: hura !
hurray (he'rej) excl.: hura !;
v. krzyczec hura (z radości etc.)
hurricane ('haryken) n. huragan; orkan tropikalny
hurried ('haryd) adj. pospieszny
hurry ('hary) s. pospiech
hurry up ! ('hary,ap) v. spiesz
się ! ruszaj się!
hurt; hurt; hurt; (he:rt;
he:rt; he:rt)
hurt (he:rt) v. ranic; kaleczyc;
urazic; uszkodzic; bolec; dokuczac; s. skaleczenie; rana;
szkoda; krzywda; uraz; uszkodzenie;ból;ujma;ranka
husband ('hazbend) s. mąż;
v. gospodarowac oszczednie;
wydawac za mąż
husbandry ('hazbendry) s. rolnictwo; uprawa; hodowla
hush (hasz) s. cisza; spokój;
milczenie; v. cicho ! sza !;
uciszyc się; milczec; tuszowac (cos);ululac; załagodzic

hush up ('hasz,ap) v. siedziec
cicho; zatuszowac (cos)
husk (hask) s. łuska; v. łuszczyc; wyłuszczac;złuszczac
husky ('hasky) adj. krzepki;
suchy; zachrypniety; łuszczas-
ty; s. pies eskimoski; język
eskimoski
hustle ('hasl) s. pospiech;
krzątanina; bieganina; popy-
chanie; v. spieszyc się;krzą-
tac się; popychac; pchac się;
szturchac; popedzac; wypchnąc
hut (hat) s. chata; barak; chałupa; v. mieszkac w chałupie
hutch (hacz) s. skrzynia; klatka; domek; v. wkładac cos do
skrzyni;s.kurnik;chlewik;chatka
hybrid ('hajbryd) s. mieszaniec;
adj. mieszany;mieszanego pochodzenia
hydrant ('hajdrent) s. hydrant
hydraulic ('haj'dro:lyk) adj.
hydrauliczny
hydro ('hajdrou) adj. wodo- ;
wodoro-; wodny
hydrocarbon ('hajdrou'ka:rben)
s. węglowodor
hydrochloric acid (,hajdrou'-
klo:ryk,asyd) s. kwas solny
hydrogen ('hajdrydżen) s. wo-
dor
hydrogen bomb ('hajdydżen,bom)
s. bomba wodorowa
hydroplane ('hajdrou,plejn) s.
wodnopłatowiec; slizgacz
hyena (haj'y:ne) s. hiena
hygiene ('hajdżi:n) s. higiena
hymn (hym) s. hymn; v. spiewac
hymn :chwalic hymnem
hyphen ('hajfen) s. łącznik;
v. używac łacznika
hypnotize ('hypne,tajz) v.
hipnotyzowac
hypocrisy (hy'pokresy) s. hipo-
kryzja ;udawanie cnoty etc.
hypocrite ('hypekryt) s. hipokryta :obłudnik;obłudnica
hypocritical (,hypou'krytykel)
adj. obłudny; hipokryzyjny;
dwulicowy ;udający cnotę etc.
hypodermic (,hajpe'de:rmyk)
adj. podskórny (zastrzyk)

hypothesis (haj'po̱tysys) s.
hipoteza;niesprawdzona teoria
hysterectomy (,histe'rektemy)
s. wycięcie macicy
hysteria (hys'tyerje) s. histeria;wybuch podniecenia
hysterical (hys'terykel) adj.
histeryczny;podlegający histerii
hysterics (hys'teryks) pl.
atak histerii
hysterotomy (,histe'rotemy)
s. operacja macicy
I (aj) pron. ja; dziewiąta litera angielskiego alfabetu
I-beam ('aj,bi:m) s. belka
dwuteowka (stalowa)
ice (ajs) s. lód; lody; v. zamrażać; mrozić; lukrować
Ice Age('ajsejdż) s. epoka lodowa;epoka lodowcowa
iceberg ('ajsbe:rg) s. góra lodowa (na morzu)
ice-cream ('ajskri:m) s. lody
icicle ('ajsykl) s. sopel
ice floe ('ajs-flou) s. kra
icing ('ajsyŋ) s. lukier
icy ('ajsy) adj. lodowaty
idea (aj'die) s. idea; pojęcie;
pomysł;wyobrażenie; myśl;plan
ideal (aj'diel) adj. idealny;
s. ideał; model doskonały
idealize (aj'dielajz) v. ideali-
zować;wyidealizować
identical (aj'dentykel) adj.
taki sam; identyczny; tożsamoś-
ciowy;zupełnie podobny
identification (ajdentyfy'kejszyn) s. utożsamienie; identy-
fikacja ;stwierdzenie tożsamości
identification papers (aj,denty-
fy'kejszyn'pejpers) s. dowód
tożsamości; dowód osobisty
identify (aj'dentyfaj) v. utożsamić; identifikować
identity (aj'dentyty) s. tożsamość; identyczność
identity card (aj'dentyty ka:rd)
s. dowód osobisty
ideological (,ajdye'lodżykel)
adj. ideologiczny
idiom ('ydjem) s. wyrażenie
zwyczajowe; wyrażenie idioma-
tyczne; dialekt ;typowy styl

idiot ('ydjet) s. idiota ;dureń
idiotic (,ydy'otyk) adj. idiotyczny ;bardzo głupi
idle ('ajdl) adj. niezajęty;
bezczynny; leniwy; pusty;
czczy; jałowy; zbyteczny;
v. próżnować; być na wolnym
biegu;być bez pracy;obijać się
idle away ('ajdl̦e'łej) v. marnować (czas) ;roztrwonić czas
idleness ('ajdlnys) s. bezczynność; lenistwo; próżniactwo;
daremność;bezpodstawność
idol ('ajdl) s. bożyszcze; bałwan;posąg bożka
idolize ('ajdelajz) v. ubóstwiać; uwielbiać; bałwochwalić
idyl ('ydyl) s. sielanka; idyl-
la;opis raju na wsi(w poezji)
if (yf) conj. jeżeli; jeśli;
gdyby; o ile; gdy; żeby(tylko)
iffy (yffy) adj. wątpliwy
(slang) gdybowany
igloo ('iglu:) s. eskimoska
chata kopulasta ze śniegu
ignite (yg'najt) v. zapalić
ignition (yg'nyszyn) s. zapłon;
zapalenie; elektryczny zapłon
ignition key (yg'nyszyn,ki:)
s. klucz do zapłonu (w aucie)
ignoble (yg'noubl) adj. nędzny;
podły; haniebny; niecny; marny;
niegodziwy;niskiego pochodzenia
ignorance ('ygnerens) s. nie-
świadomość; ignorancja; nieuctwo; ciemnota;obskurantyzm
ignorant ('ygnerent) adj. nieświadomy; ciemny; bez wykształcenia ;zdradzający ignorancję
ignore (yg'no:r) v. pomijac;
lekceważyć; odrzucać;nie zważać
ill (yl) adj. zły; chory; słaby; lichy; s. zło; adv. źle;
nie bardzo ;kiepsko;niepomyślnie
ill-advised ('yled'wajzd) adj.
nierozsądny; nierozważny
ill-affected ('yle'fektyd) adj.
źle usposobiony ;nieżyczliwy
ill-bred ('yl'bred) adj. źle
wychowany ;grubiański
illegal (y'li:gel) adj. bezprawny; nielegalny ;samowolny;
przeciw prawu i ustawom

illegible (y'ledźybl) adj. nieczytelny; źle napisany(wydrukowany)
illegitimate (,yly'dżytymejt) adj. bezprawny; nieprawny; nieprawowity; nieślubny
ill-fated ('yl-fejdyd) adj. fatalny; nieszczęsliwy;nieszczę
ill-humored ('yl'hju:merd) adj. w złym humorze
illicit (y'lysyt) adj. bezprawny; niedozwolony;niewłaściwy
illiterate (y'lyteryt) s. analfabeta; adj. niepiśmienny
ill-judged ('yl'dżadżd) adj. nierozważny; nierozsądny
ill-mannered ('yl'maenerd) adj. źle wychowany;grubiański
ill-natured ('yl'nejczerd) adj. zły; złośliwy; opryskliwy
illness ('ylnys) s. choroba
illogical (y'lodżykel) adj. nielogiczny;nierozsądny
ill-tempered ('yl'temperd) adj. w złym humorze;zły;kłótliwy
ill-timed ('yl'tajmd) adj. nie na czasie;niefortunny
ill-treat ('yl'tri:t) v. maltretować; znęcać się(nad kims)
illuminate (y'lju:mynejt) v. oswietlać; oswiecać; uswietniać
illumination (y,lju:my'nejszyn) s. oświecenie; oświecanie; uświetnianie;rozjaśnienie
illusion (y'lu:żyn) s. złudzenie; iluzja; złuda
illusive (y'lu:syw) adj. złudny; iluzyjny;iluzoryczny;zwodniczy
illusory (y'lu:sery) adj. złudny; iluzoryczny;zwodniczy
illustrate ('yles,trejt) v. wyjaśniać; ilustrować
illustration (,yles'trejszyn) s. ilustracja; ilustrowanie
illustrative ('yles,trejtyw) adj. objaśniający; ilustrujący(przykład,zdarzenie etc.)
illustrious (y'lastrjes) adj. znakomity; wybitny; sławny
ill will ('yl'łyl) s. niechęc
image ('ymydż) s. wizerunek; obraz; wcielenie; v. wyobrażać; odzwierciadlać; ucielesniać: dawać obraz(wyobrażenie)

imagery ('ymydżery) s. wizerunki; podobizny; gra wyobraźni; porównanie przez przykłady
imaginable (y'maedżynebl) adj. wyobrażalny; możliwy;do pomyślenia
imaginary (y'maedżynery) a. urojony; zmyslony;nierzeczywisty
imagination (y,maedży'nejszyn) s. wyobraznia; fantazja; urojenie;tworzenie nowych pomysłów
imagine (y'maedżyn) v. wyobrażać sobie;przypuszczać;myśleć
imbecile ('ymby,syl) adj. uposledzony; głupi; niedorozwinięty; cherlawy; s. człowiek uposledzony; imbecyl(niedorozwiniety)
imitate ('ymytejt) v. naśladować; małpować;imitować;wzorować się
imitation (,ymy'tejszyn) s. nasladowanie; naśladownictwo; imitacja;falsyfikat;podróbka
immaterial (,yme'tierjel) adj. nieistotny; bezcielesny;błachy
immature (,yme'tjuer) adj. niedojrzały;niewyrobiony;niedorosły
immeasurable (y,meżerebl) adj. niezmierzony; ogromny;bezmierny
immediate (y'mi:djet) adj. bezpośredni; natychmiastowy;pilny;nagły
immediately (y'mi:djetly) adv. natychmiast; bezpośrednio
immense (y'mens) adj. olbrzymi;ogromny;świetny;kpitalny
immerse (y'me:rs) v. zanurzać; pograzać;ochrzcić przez zanużenie
immigrant ('ymygrent) s. imigrant; adj. imigrujący;osadniczy
immigrate ('ymygrejt) v. imigrować;przywędrować;sprowadzać osadników
immigration (,ymy'grejszyn) s. imigracja;urzad imigracyjny
imminent ('ymynent) adj. nadchodzący; groźny;nadciągający;bliski
immobile (y'moubajl) adj. nieruchomy;przytwierdzony na stałe
immoderate (y'moderyt) adj. nieumiarkowany;niepohamowany;nadmierny
immodest (y'modyst) adj. nieskromny; bezczelny; zuchwały
immoral (y'morel) adj. niemoralny;nieetyczny;rozpustny
immorality(ym'e-ral'ety)s.rozpusta; niemoralność

immorality (‚yme'raelyty) s. niemoralność;rozpusta

immortal (y'mo:rtl) adj. niesmiertelny; wiekopomny

immortality (‚ymo:r'taelyty) s. niesmiertelność

immovable (y'mu:webl) adj.nieruchomy; niezmienny; nieczuły; nieugięty;niewzruszony

immune (y'mju:n) adj. odporny; uodporniony;wolny(od przepisów)

imp (ymp) s. skrzat; diablik

impact ('ympaekt) v. wgniatać; s. zderzenie; uderzenie; wpływ;wstrząs;kolizja;działanie

impair (ym'peer) v. uszkadzać; osłabiać; nadwyrężać;umniejszać

impart (ym'pa:rt) v. dawać; udzielać;zakomunikować

impartial (ym'pa:rszel) adj. bezstronny; sprawiedliwy

impartiality ('ym,pa:rszy'aelyty) s. bezstronność;sprawiedliwość

impassable (ym'pa:sebl) adj. nieprzebyty; nie do przebycia

impassive (ym'paesyw) adj. niewzruszony; obojętny;nieczuły

impatience (ym'pejszens) s. zniecierpliwienie; niecierpliwość;irytacja(z powodu czegoś)

impatient (ym'pejszent) adj. niecierpliwy; zniecierpliwiony;palący się do;podrażniony

impediment (ym'pedyment) s. przeszkoda; utrudnienie

impend (ym'pend) v. grozić; zbliżać się;zagrażać(z bliska)

impenetrable (ym'penytrebl) adj. nieprzenikniony; niedostepny;niezglebiony;nie do prze-

imperative (ym'peretyw) adj. stanowczy; rozkazujący; konieczny;naglący;niezbędny

imperceptible (‚ym-pe'rseptebl) adj. niedostrzegalny;nieuchwytny

imperfect (ym'pe:rfykt) adj. niedoskonały; niedokończony; wadliwy; niezupełny;niedokonany

imperial (ym'pierjel) adj. cesarski; imperialny; dostojny;rozkazujący;majestatyczny

imperialism (ym'pierjelyzem)s. imperializm(budowanie imperium)

imperil (ym'peryl) v. zagrażać; narazić na niebezpieczeństwo

imperious (ym'pierjes) adj. władczy; naglący;nakazujący

imperishable (ym'peryszebl) adj. niezniszczalny; nieprzemijający;trwały;wieczysty

impermeable (ym'pe:rmiebl) adj. nieprzemakalny; nieprzenikniony;nieprzepuszczający

impersonal (ym'pe:rsenl) adj. nieosobowy; nieosobisty

impersonate(ym'pe:rsenejt) v. wcielać; uosabiać; odgrywać kogoś;personifikować

impertinence (ym'pe:rtynens) s. niestosowność; impertynencja; niewłaściwość; natręctwo ;nietakt

impertinent (ym'pe:rtynnent) adj. niestosowny; impertynencki; bezczelny; natrętny;bez związku

imperturbable (‚ympe:r'te:rbebl) adj. niewzruszony; spokojny

impervious (ym'pe:rwjes) adj. nieprzepuszczalny; niedostępny

impetuous (ym'petjues) adj. popędliwy; porywczy; gwałtowny

implacable (ym'plekebl) adj. nieubłagalny;nieprzejednany

implement ('ymplyment) s. narzędzie; środek; sprzęt; v. uzupełniać; urzeczywistniać; wykonać;uprawomocniać;spełniać

implicate ('ymplykejt) v. uwikłać; owijać; włączać;wplątać;wmieszać

implication (‚ymply'kejszyn) s. uwikłanie; włączenie; sugestia

implicit (ym'plysyt) adj. rozumiejący się sam przez się; niezaprzeczalny;domniemany;ślepy

implore (ym'plo:r) v. błagać

imply (ym'plaj) v. zawierać w sobie; mieścić; sugerować; zakładać;nasuwać wniosek

impolite (‚ympo'lajt) adj. nieuprzejmy; niegrzeczny

import (ym'po:rt) s. import;treść v. oznaczać; importować; przywozić z zagranicy;a.importowy

import ('ympo:rt) s. treść; znaczenie;ważność;doniosłość

importance (ym'po:rtens) s. znaczenie; ważność;doniosłość

important (ym'po:rtent) adj.
ważny; znaczący; doniosły
importation (,ympo:r'tejszyn)
s. przywóz; importowanie
importune (ym'po:rtju:n) v.
dokuczać; żądać natarczywie;
narzucać się;naprzykrzać się
impose (ym'pouz) v. nadawać;
narzucać; oszukiwać; imponować;narzucać;nakładać obowiązek
impose upon (,ym'pouz e'pon)
v. narzucać się komuś;okpiwać
imposing (ym'pouzyng) adj.
imponujący;wspaniały;okazały
impossibility (ym,posy'bylyty)
s. niemożliwość
impossible (ym'posybl) adj.
niemożliwy(do zrobienia,zniesienia)
impostor (ym'poster) s. oszust
(podszywający się);szarlatan
impotence ('ympotens) s. niemoc; zniedołężnienie (płciowe);nieudolność;niesprawność
impotent ('ympotent) s. bezsilny; impotent; nieudolny
impracticable (ym'praektykebl)
adj. niewykonalny;krnąbrny
impregnate ('ympregnejt) v. za-
pładniać; impregnować; nasycać;wpoić;zaszczepić;nasiąkać
impress (ym'pres) v. odcisnąć;
wycisnąć; robić wrażenie;
s. odcisk; odbicie; piętno
impression (ym'preszyn) s. wrażenie; druk; odbicie; nakład
impressive (ym'presyw) adj. robiący wrażenie; uderzający;
podniosły;wstrząsający;frapujący
imprint (ym'prynt) v. odbijać;
wpajać; wydrukować; wbijać
w pamięć;wyryć w pamięci
imprint ('ymprynt) s. odbicie;
nadruk; odcisk;piętno;znak firy
imprison (ym'pryzn) v. uwięzić
imprisonment (ym'pryznment) s.
uwięzienie(kara więzienia)
improbable (ym'probebl) adj.
nieprawdopodobny
improper (ym'proper) adj. niewłaściwy; nieprzyzwoity;zdrożny
improve (ym'pru:w) v. poprawić;
udoskonalić; ulepszać(jakość)

improvement (ym'pru;wment) s.
poprawa; udoskonalenie; wy-
korzystanie(sposobności);poprawa
improvise ('ymprowajz) v. improwizować;sklecić na poczekaniu
imprudent (ym'pru:dent) adj. nierozsądny; nieopatrzny; nierozważny;nieoględny;niebaczny
impudence ('ympjudens) s. bez-
wstyd; bezczelność; tupet
impudent ('ympjudent) adj. bezwstydny; bezczelny;zuchwały;e tu-
impulse ('ympals) s. impuls;poryw;
popęd;pęd;siła napędowa;bodziec
impulsive ('ympalsyw) adj. im-
pulsywny; porywczy; pobudliwy
impunity (ym'pju:nyty) s. bez-
karność;swoboda od skutków(kary)
impure (ym'pjur) adj. nieczysty; zanieczyszczony
impute (ym'pju:t) v. oskarżać;
przypisywać(zbrodnię;błąd etc.)
in (yn) prep. w; we; na; za; po;
do; u; nie-
in and out ('yn,end'aut) exp.:
na wylot; wchodzić i wychodzić
in a week ('yn,ej'łi:k) exp.: za
tydzień;w ciągu tygodnia
in my opinion ('yn,maj e'pynjen)
exp.: według mnie;moim zdaniem
in order that ('yn.o:rder'daet)
exp.: ażeby;w celu;poto żeby
in pairs ('yn,peers) exp.: parami
in Shakespeare ('yn,Szekspir)
u Szekspira;w sztukach Szekspira
inability (,yne'bylyty) s. niezdolność;niemożność
inaccessible (ynaek'sesybl) adj.
niedostępny; nieprzystępny
inaccurate (yn'aekjuryt) adj.
nieścisły; niedokładny
inactive (yn'aektyw) adj. bezczynny;bierny;obojetny;inertny
inadequate (yn'aedykłyt) adj.
nieodpowiedni; niewystarczalny
inadmissible (,yned'mysebl)
adj. niedopuszczalny;nie do przyjęcia
inadvertent (,yned'we:rtent)
adj. nieuważny; niedbały; nie-
rozmyślny;mimowolny;nieumyślny
inalterable (yn'o:lterebl) adj.
niezmienny

inanimate (yn'aenymyt) adj.
martwy; nieożywiony; bezduszny; nieorganiczny
inappropriate (,yne'prouprjyt)
adj. niewłaściwy;niestosowny
inapt (yn'aept) adj. niezdatny
inarticulate (,yna:r'tykjulyt)
adj. nieartykułowany; niewyraźny; niemy;słabo mówiący
inasmuch (,ynez'macz) adv.
o tyle; ponieważ; wobec tego;
że; skoro;zważywszy;jako że
inasmuch as (,ynez'macz,aez)
adv. gdyż ;o tyle że;o tyle o
inattentive (,yne'tentyw) adj.
nieuważny; nie uważający
inaudible (yn'o:debl) adj. niesłyszalny;nie uchwytny dla ucha
inaugural (y'no:gjurel) adj.
inauguracyjny
inaugurate (y'no:gjurejt) v.
otwierać uroczyście; inaugurowac;uroczyście zapoczątkowy-
inborn ('yn'bo:rn) adj. wrodzony ;przyrodzony;z natury
incalculable (yn'kaelkjulebl)
adj. nieobliczalny;nieprzewi-
incapable (yn'kejpebl) adj.
niezdolny; nie będący w stanie
incapacitate ('ynke'paesytejt)
v. czynić niezdatnym; dyskwalifikować;uznać za niezdatnego
incapacity (,ynke'paesyty) s.
niezdolność; nieudolność
incarnate (yn,ka:rnejt) adj.
wcielony; v. wcielać; ucieleś-
niać (się);być wcieleniem
incautious (yn'ko:szes) adj.
nieroważny; niebaczny
incendiary (yn'sendjery) adj.
zapalający; podżegający;
s. podpalacz; podżegacz
incense ('ynsens) s. kadzidło
incense (yn'sens) v. rozwścieczać; doprowadzać do szału
incertitude (un'se:rtytju:d) s.
niepewność; niepokój
incessant (yn'sesnt) adj. ustawiczny; bezustanny; stały
incest ('ynsest) s.kazirodztwo
a.kazirodczy
inch (yncz) s. cal (2.54 cm)
v. posuwać cal po calu

incident ('ynsydent) s. zajście;
wydarzenie; incydent; adj. padający; związany;prawdopodobny
incidental (,ynsy'dentl) adj.
przypadkowy; uboczny;drugorzędny
incidentally (,ynsy'dently) adv.
przypadkowo; ubocznie; nawiasem mówiąc;mimochodem;przy spobnoś-
incinerate (yn'synerejt) v.
spalic; spopielić;palić na popiół
incise (yn'sajz) v. naciąć; wyryć;wyrzezbic;wygrawerować
incision (yn'syżyn) s. nacięcie;
ciecie; cietość; bystrość;ostrość
incisive (yn'sajsyw) adj. przenikliwy; ostry; tnący; bystry;
sieczny; zjadliwy;wcinający się
incisor (yn'sajzer) s. siekacz
(ząb)kazdy z przednich zębów między zębami
incite (yn'sajt) v. zachęcać;
podburzać;podżegać;namawiać
inclement (yn'klement) adj.
surowy;ostry (klimat etc.)
inclination (ynkly'nejszyn) s.
skłonność; nachylenie;pociąg
incline (yn'klajn) v. mieć
skłonność; pochylać się
inclose (yn'klous) v. ogrodzić;
załączyć; włączyć;zamknąć
include (yn'klu:d) v. zawierać;
włączać; wliczać(w cenę);obejmować
inclusive (yn'klu:syw) adj.
włączony;obejmujący;adv.włącznie
incoherent (,ynkou'hierent) adj.
bez związku; nieskoordynowany
income ('ynkam) s. dochód
income tax ('ynkam,taeks) s.
podatek dochodowy
incoming ('yn,kamyng) adj. nadchodzący;następujący; przyrastający; s. przybycie; dochód
incomparable (yn'komperebl)
adj. niezrównany; nie do porównania; nieporównywalny
incompatible (,ynkem'paetebl)
adj. niezgodny; sprzeczny
incompetent (yn'kompytent) adj.
niekompetentny; nieudolny
incomplete (,ynkem'pli:t) adj.
niezupełny; nieukończony
incomprehensible (yn,kompry'-
hensebl) adj. niepojęty; niezrozumiały

inconceivable (,ynken'si:webl)
adj. niepojęty; nieprawdopodobny; nieprawdopodobny
inconclusive (,ynken'klu;syw)
adj. nieprzekonywujacy; nie-
rozstrzygający;nie decydujący
inconsequent (yn'konsykŕent)
adj. bez związku; niekonsekwentny; nielogiczny
inconsiderable (,ynken'sydŗebl)
adj. nieznaczny; niepokaźny
inconsiderate (,ynken'syderyt)
adj. bezwzględny; nierozważny
inconsistent (,ynken'systent)
adj. niejednolity; niekonsekwentny; niezgodny;bez związku
inconsolable (,ynken'soulebl)
adj. niepocieszony;nieutulony
inconstant (yn'konstent) adj.
zmienny; niestały; nieregularny
inconvenience (,ynken'wi:n jens)
s. niewygoda; kłopot; v. niepokoić; przeszkadzać; sprawiać
kłopot;deranżować
inconvenient (,ynken'wi:njent)
adj. niewygodny; niedogodny;
kłopotliwy; uciążliwy
incorporate (yn'ko:rperejt) v.
jednoczyć; wcielać; zrzeszać
(yn'ko:rperyt) adj. zrzeszony
incorporated (yn'ko:rperejtyd)
adj. zarejestrowany; zalegali-
zowany;wcielony; złączony
incorrect (,ynke'rekt) adj. niepoprawny; niecisły: błędny
incorrigible (yn'korydżybl) adj.
niepoprawny;nie do poprawienia
increase (yn'kri:s) v. wzrastać;
zwiększać się; pomnażać się;
wzmagać się;rozmnażać się ; s.
('ynkri:s) wzrost; przyrost;
podwyżka;rozrost;mnożenie się
increasingly (yn'kri:syŋgly)
adv. coraz więcej; coraz bardziej; coraz to; wciąż
incredible (yn'kredebl) adj.
nie do wiary; niewiarygodny;
nieprawdopodobny;nie do pomyśle-
incredulous (yn'kredjules) adj.
nie
incriminate (yn'krymynejt) v.
obwiniać; oskarżać;pomawiać;
objąć (kogoś) oskarżeniem

incubator ('ynkjubejter) s. wy-
lęgarka; inkubator
incur (yn'ke:r) v. narażać się;
ponieść; zaciągać;natknąć się na
incurable (yn'kjuerebl) adj.
nieuleczalny;s.człowiek nieulecza-
indebted (yn'detyd) adj. dłużny;
zobowiązany: wdzięczny;zawdzięcza-
indecency (yn'di:sensy) s. nie-
skromność; nieprzyzwoitość
indecent (yn'di:sent) adj. nieprzyzwoity;obrażający moralność
indecision (,yndy'syżyn) s.
chwiejność; niezdecydowanie
indecisiveness(,yndy'sajsywnys)s.
chwiejność; niezdecydowanie
indecisive (,yndy'sajsyw) adj.
nie rozstrzygnięty; niezdecydowany;chwiejny;nie rozstrzygający
indeed (yn'di:d) adv, naprawdę;
istotnie; rzeczywiście; faktycznie;wprawdzie; co prawda;właściwie
indefatigable (,yndy'faetygebl)
adj. niestrudzony; niezmordowany
indefinite (yn'defynyt) adj.
nieokreślony;niewyraźny;nie spre-
cyzowany
indelible (yn'delybl) adj. nie-
zatarty; trwały;nie do zmazania
indelicate (yn'delykyt) adj. niedelikatny; nietaktowny;niestosowny
indemnify (yn'demnyfaj) v. dawać odszkodowanie; zabezpieczać
przed(np. szkodą);powetować
indemnity (yn'demnyty) s. odszkodowanie; zabezpieczenie
przed...;wynagrodzenie
indent (yn'dent) v. naciać; wy-
ciąć; wyrżnać; zamówić; zawierać umowę; tłoczyć; s. wgłębienie;nacięcie;karbowanie
indent ('yndent) s. wcięcie; nacięcie; karbowanie; zamówienie
independence (,yndy'pendens) s.
niezależność; niepodległość;
niezależność materialna
independent (,yndy'pendent) adj.
niepodległy; niezależny (ma-
terialnie);osobny;oddzielny
indescribable (,yndys'krajbebl)
adj. nieopisany; nie do opisania (poza możliwościami opisania)
indeterminate (,yndy'te:rmynyt)
adj.nieokreślony;niewyraźny

index ('yndeks) s. wskaźnik;
indeks; v. umieszczać spisie (indeksie);robić indeks
Indian ('yndjen) adj. indiański;
hinduski ⌐babie lato
Indian Summer ('yndjen'samer)
exp.: słoneczne dni w jesieni;
India-rubber ('yndje'raber) s.
guma (naturalna,elastyczna)
indicate ('yndykejt) v. wskazywać; stwierdzać; wymagać
indication (,yndy'kejszyn) s.
wskazówka; wskazanie; znak
indicative (yn'dyketyw) adj.
oznajmiający; dowodzący
indicator ('yndykejter) s.
wskaźnik; indykator; licznik
indict (yn'dajt) v. oskarżyć
indictment (yn'dajtment) s.
oskarżenie; akt oskarżenia
indifference (yn'dyferens) s.
obojętność ;nieistotność;bła-chość,
indifferent (yn'dyfrent) adj.
obojętny;mierny;błachy;neutralny
indigent ('yndydżent) adj.
ubogi; biedny;s.biedak;biedaczka
indigestible (,yndy'dżestebl)
adj. niestrawny ;źle strawny
indigestion (,yndy'dżestczyn) s.
niestrawność
indignant (yn'dygnent) adj.
oburzony (na niesprawiedliwość...)
indignation (,yndyg'nejszyn) s.
oburzenie
indirect (,yndy'rekt) adj; pośredni; okrężny; nieuczciwy
indiscreet (,yndys'kri:t) adj.
nierozważny; niedyskretny
indiscretion (,yndys'kreszyn)
s. nierozwaga; niedyskrecja;
uchybienie(słowem,czynem etc.)
indiscriminate (,yndys'krymynyt)
adj. bezkrytyczny; pomieszany
indispensable (,yndys'pensebl)
adj. nieodzowny; niezbędny;
konieczny;niezastąpiony
indisposed (,yndys'pouzd) adj.
niezdrów; niedysponowany; niechętny;bez zapału;niedomagający
indisposition (,yndyspe'zyszyn)
s. niedyspozycja; niechęć; odraza;dolegliwość;niedomaganie

indisputable (,yndys'pju:tebl)
adj. bezsporny;niezaprzeczalny
indistinct (,yndys'tynkt) adj;
niewyraźny;niejasny;mętny
individual (,yndy'wydjuel) adj.
pojedyńczy; odrębny; s. jednostka; osobnik;okaz;chłowiek
individualist (,yndy'wydjuelyst)
s. indiwidualista;individualistka
indivisible (,yndy'wyzebl) adj.
niepodzielny;nieskończenie mały
indolence ('yndelens) s. lenistwo; opieszałość;próżniactwo
indolent ('yndelent) adj. leniwy;opieszały;obojętny;niebolesny
indomitable (yn'domytebl) adj.
nieposkromiony; nieugięty
indoor ('yndo:r) adj. domowy;
wewnętrzny; pokojowy;zakładowy
indoors ('yndo:rz) adv. w domu;
pod dachem ;do domu;do mieszkania
indorse(yn'do:rs) v. potwierdzić (podpisem)
induce (yn'dju:s) v. skłonić;
namówić; powodować; wnioskować;pobudzić;nakłonić;powodować
induct (yn'dakt) v. wprowadzać;
tworzyć; brać do wojska
indulge (yn'daldż) v. pobłażać;
znosić; ulegać; dogadzać; używać sobie ;dawać upust;zaspokajać
indulgence (yn'daldżens) s. dogadzanie; nałóg; oddawanie się;
pobłażanie; odpust;uleganie
indulgent (yn'daldżent) adj. pobłażliwy ;ulegający;folgujący
industrial (yn'dastrjel) adj.
przemysłowy (towar,robotnik etc.)
industrial area (yn'dastrjel'
eerje) s. teren przemysłowy
industrial city (yn'dastrjel'
syty) s. miasto przemysłowe
industrialist (yn'dastrjelyst)
s. przemysłowiec
industrialize (yn'dastrjelajz)
v. uprzemysławiać
industrious (yn'dastrjes) adj.
skrzętny; pilny; pracownity
industry ('yndastry) s. przemysł; pilność; pracowitość;
skrzętność;gałaź przemysłu;właściciele i zarządcy przemysłu

ineffective (,yny'fektyw) adj.
bezskuteczny; niesprawny
inefficient (,yny'fyszent)
adj. niewydajny; niesprawny
inequality (,yny'kłolyty) s.
nierówność; niewystarczalność;
zmienność(krajobrazu);niestałość
inert (y'ne:rt) adj. bezwładny;
ociężały; obojętny; opieszały
inertia (y'ne:rszja) s. inercja; bezwład; ociężałość
inestimable (yn'estymebl) adj.
nieoceniony;bezcenny
inevitable (yn'ewytebl) adj.
nieunikniony; nieuchronny
inexact (,ynyg'zaekt) adj. nieścisły; niedokładny
inexcusable (,ynyks'kju:zebl)
adj. niewybaczalny; nie-
usprawiedliwiony;nie do darowa-
nia
inexhaustible (,ynyg'zo:stebl)
adj. niewyczerpany; nieprzebrany; niestrudzony:bez dna
inexpensive (,ynyks'pensyw) adj.
niedrogi; niekosztowny; tani
inexperience (,ynyks'pierjens)
s. niedoświadczenie;brak wprawy
inexplicable (yn'eksplykebl)
adj. niewytłumaczalny; nie-
wyjaśniony;zagadkowy
inexpressible (,yneks'presebl)
adj. niewysławiony; niewyra-
żalny;niewymowny
inexpressive (,ynyks'presyw)
adj. bez wyrazu
infallible (yn'faelebl) adj.
nieomylny; niezawodny; niechybny;bezbłędny;zawsze słuszny
infamous ('ynfemes) adj. haniebny; niesławny; hańbiący;podły
infamy ('ynfemy) s. hańba; niesława; podłość;utrata praw obywa-
telskich
infancy ('ynfensy) s. nie-
mowlectwo; dzieciństwo
infant ('ynfent) s. niemowlę;
dziecko;noworodek;a.dziecinny
infantile ('ynfentajl) adj.
dziecięcy;infantylny;niemowlecy
infantry ('ynfentry) s. piechota (wojsko)
infatuated with (yn'faetjuejtyd
łvs) adj. szalejący za...;rozko-
chany w;nierozsądnie zakochany

infect (yn'fekt) v. zakazić;
zarazić; zatruwać
infection (yn'fekszyn) s. zakażenie; zarażenie; zaraza
infectious (yn'fekszes) adj. zakaźny; zaraźliwy;infekcyjny
infer (yn'fe:r) v. wnioskować;
zawierać w sobie pojęcie
inference ('ynferens) s. wniosek; konkluzja;domniemanie
inferior (yn'fierjer) adj.
niższy; podrzędny; pośledni
inferior to (yn'fierjer,tu)
adj. ustępujący; gorszy
inferiority (yn,fiery'oryty) s.
niższość;poczucie niższości
infernal (yn'fe:rnel) adj. piekielny; diabelski; szatański
infest (yn'fest) v. nawiedzać;
trapić;być utrapieniem
infidelity (,ynfy'delyty) s.
niewiara; niewierność
infiltrate ('ynfyltrejt) v.
wsiąkać; przesiąkać; przenikać
infinite ('ynfynyt) adj. nieskończony; bezgraniczny; niezliczony; ogromny;bezkresny
infinitive (yn'fynytyw) s. bezokolicznik;adj.nieokreslony
infinity (yn'fynyty) s. nie-
skończoność
infirm (yn'fe:rm) adj. słaby;
niedołężny;dotknięty niemocą
infirmary (yn'fe:rmery) s.
szpital; lecznica; izba chorych
infirmity (yn'fe:rmyty) s. niemoc; słabość; zniedołężnienie
inflame (yn'flejm) v. zapalić;
rozognic; pobudzać;zagrzewać
inflammable (yn'flaemebl) adj.
zapalny; pobudliwy; palny
inflammation (,ynfle'mejszyn)
s. zapalenie; zaognienie
inflammatory(yn'flaemeto:ry)
adj. podżegający; zapalny
inflate (yn'flejt) v. nadąć;
rozdąć: powodować inflacje
inflation (yn'flejszyn) s.
inflacja; nadymanie; nadmu-
chanie;zwyżka cen
inflect (yn'flekt) v. zginać;
skrzywić; odmieniać ;naginać

inflexible (yn'fleksebl) adj. sztywny; nieugięty;nieelastycz-

inflection(yn'flekszyn) s. fleksja; modulacja; końcówka; wygięcie ;nadgięcie;odchylenie

inflict (yn'flykt) v. zadać; narzucać; zsyłać(na kogoś)

infliction (yn'flykszyn) s. zadanie (ciosu) narzucanie; przykrosc;nieszczęście;strapie-

influence ('ynfluens) s. wpływ v. wywierać wpływ;oddziaływać

influential (,ynflu'enszel) adj. wpływowy(polityk etc.)

influenza (,ynflu'enza) s. grypa; influenca

inform (yn'fo:rm) v. powiadomić; nadawać; donosić;ożywić

inform against(yn'fo:rme'genst) v. donosic na (kogoś)

information (,ynfer'mejszyn) s. wiadomość; wiedza; objasnienie;informacja;doniesienie

information desk (,ynfer'mejszyn,desk) punkt informacyjny (w banku,hotelu,na wystawie)

information officer (,ynfer'mejszyn 'ofyser) oficer informacyjny(w banku etc.)

informative (yn'fo:rmetyw) adj. objasniający; pouczający

informer (yn'fo:rmer) s. donosiciel; konfident;konfidentka

infuriate (,yn'fjuerjejt) v. rozwścieczać; rozjuszać

infuse (yn'fju:z) v. wlewać; zalewać; zaparzać;dodać(odwagi)

ingenious (yn'dżi:njes) adj. pomysłowy; dowcipny(pomysł)

ingenuity (,yndży'njuyty) s. pomysłowosc;oryginalność;dowcip

ingot ('yngot) s. sztaba

ingratiate (yn'grejszjejt) v. wkradać się w łaski czyjeś

ingratitude(yn'graetytju:d) s. niewdzięczność

ingredient (yn'gri:djent) s. składnik (mieszanki etc.)

ingress ('yngres) s. wejście

inhabit (yn'haebyt) v. zamieszkiwać; mieszkać

inhabitable (yn'haebytebl)adj. mieszkalny(godny zamieszkania)

inhabitant (yn'haebytent) s. mieszkaniec; mieszkanka

inhale (yn'hejl) v. wdychać; zaciągać się (dymem);wziewać

inherent (yn'hierent) adj. nieodłączny; własciwy;wrodzony

inherit (yn'heryt) v. dziedziczyć; być spadkobiercą

inheritance (yn'herytens) s. spadek; spuscizna; dziedzictwo

inhibit (yn'hybyt) v. wstrzymywać; wzbraniac; zakazywać

inhibition (,ynhy'byszyn) s. zakaz; zahamowanie; wstrzymanie

inhospitable (yn'hospytebl) adj. niegoscinny

inhuman (yn'hju:men) adj. nieludzki; okrutny;brutalny etc.

initial (y'nyszel) adj. początkowy;v.znaczyć własnymi inicjałami

initiate (y'nyszjejt) v. zapoczątkowac; wprowadzac; zainicjować; wtajemniczać;s.nowicjusz

initiation (y,nyszy'ejszyn) s. wprowadzenie;zapoczątkowanie

initiative (y'nyszjetyw) s. inicjatywa; adj. początkowy

inject (yn'dżekt) v. wstrzyknąć

injection (yn'dżekszyn) s. zastrzyk;wstrzyknięcie;a.wytryskowy

injudicious (,yndżu'dyszes) adj. nierozważny; nieroztropny

injure ('yndżer) v. zranic; uszkodzic; krzywdzic; zepsuc

injurious (yn'dżuerjes) adj. szkodliwy; krzywdzący; obelżywy;przynoszący ujmę;obraźliwy

injury ('yndżery) s. szkoda; krzywda; rana; uszkodzenie

injustice (yn'dżastys) s. niesprawiedliwość; krzywda

ink (yŋk) s. atrament; tusz

inkling ('yŋklyŋg)s. wzmianka; podejrzenie; przypuszczenie

ink-pot ('yŋk,pot) s. kałamarz

inland ('ynlend) s. wnętrze kraju; adj. z głębi kraju; wewnętrzny; adv. w głębi; w głąb kraju;w głębi kraju

inlet ('ynlet) s. wstawka; zatoka; wlot; wejście;a.wlotowy

inmate ('ynmejt) s. mieszkaniec; lokator; współ-(więzień etc.)

inmost ('ynmoust) adj. głęboko
utajony; skryty;najtajniejszy
inn (yn) s. gospoda; oberża
innate ('y'nejt) adj. wrodzony
inner ('yner) adj. wewnętrzny
innermost ('ynermoust) adj.
głęboko ukryty; najskrytszy
inner tube ('yner,tju:b) s.
dętka(samochodowa,rowerowa)
innkeeper ('yn,ki:per) s.
oberżysta;właściciel zajazdu
innocence ('ynesns) s. niewinność; naiwność;prostoduszność
innocent ('ynesynt) adj. niewinny; naiwny; nieszkodliwy;
niemądry; s. prostaczek;
niewiniątko; głuptas
innovation (,ynou'wejszyn) s.
innowacja;wprowadzanie zmian
innumerable (y'nju:merebl) adj.
niezliczony; bez liku
inoculate (y'nokjulejt) s.
szczepić;wpajać;oczkować roślin
inoffensive (,yne'fensyw) adj.
nieszkodliwy; spokojny;obojętny
inpatient   ('ynpejszent) s.
pacjent leżący w szpitalu
inquest ('ynkłest) s. śledztwo
inquire (yn'kłajer) s. pytać
się; dowiadywać się; dociekać
inquiry (yn'kłajry) s. badanie;
zasięganie informacji; śledztwo; poszukiwanie;ankieta;wywiad
inquisitive (yn'kłyzytyw) adj.
badawczy; ciekawy;wścipski
insane (yn'sejn) adj. chory
umysłowo;zwarjowany;bez sensu
insanity (yn'saenyty) s. obłęd
insatiable (yn'sejszjebl) adj.
nienasycony;niezaspokojony;chci-
insatiate (yn'sej'szjyt) adj.
nienasycony;niezaspokojony
inscribe (yn'skrajb) v. wpisać
napisać;umieszczać na liście
inscription (yn'skrypszyn) s.
napis; dedykacja
insect ('ynsekt) s. owad
insecure (,ynsy'kjuer) adj. niepewny; niezabezpieczony
insensible (yn'sensybl) adj.
nieświadomy; bez zmysłów;w stanie omdlenia;niedostrzegalny

insensitive (yn'sensytyw) adj.
nieczuły; niewrażliwy
inseparable (yn'seperebl) adj.
nierozłączny;nieodstępny
insert (yn'se:rt) v. wstawiać;
wkładać; s. wkładka; wstawka
insertion (yn'se:rszyn) s. wkładka; wstawka; włożenie; wsta-
wienie;przyczep;przyczepienie
inshore (yn'szo:r) adv. blisko
brzegu; przy brzegu; adj. przybrzeżny; bliski brzegu
inside 'ynsajd) s. wnętrze;
adj. wewnętrzny;adv.wewnatrz
inside (yn'sajd) adv. wewnątrz
inside out ('ynsajd'aut) exp.:
na lewą stronę (np. marynarki)
insight ('ynsajt) s. wgląd;
intuicja;wnikliwość
insignificant (,ynsyg'nyfykent)
adj. mało znaczący;blachy
insincere (,ynsyn'sier) adj.
nieszczery;zwodny;dwulicowy
insinuate (yn'synjuejt) v. in-
synuować; podsuwać;sugierować
insipid (yn'sypyd) adj. mdły;
tępy; bez sensu;głupi;skliwy
insist (yn'syst) v. nalegać;
nastawać;utrzymywać;obstawać
insist on (yn'syst,on) v. domagać się;upierać się;nastawać
insolent ('ynselent) adj. bezczelny;zuchwały;butny;wyniosły
insoluble (yn'soljubl) adj. nierozpuszczalny;nie do rozwiązania
insolvent (yn'solwent) adj. niewypłacalny; s. bankrut;bankrutka
insomnia (yn'somnja) s. bezsenność (nie normalna)
insomuch (,ynsou'macz) adv.
o tyle; do tego stopnia;tak dale-
inspect (yn'spekt) v. ogladać;
doglądać; mieć nadzór;badać
inspection (yn'spekszyn) s.
przegląd; ogladanie; inspekcja;
doglądanie;sprawdzanie;kontrola
inspector (yn'spekter) s. inspektor;nadzorca;kontroler
inspiration (,ynspe'rejszyn) s.
natchnienie;wdech;wdychanie
inspire (yn'spajer) v. natchnąć;
podsunać; zainspirować;wdychać

install(yn'sto:l) v. instalować;
wprowadzać na stanowisko
installation (,ynsto:'lejszyn)
s. instalacja; wprowadzenie
na stanowisko;zamontowanie
instal(l)ment (yn'sto:lment)
s. część całości; rata
instance ('ynstens) s. wypadek;
przykład ;v.przytaczać przykład
instant ('ynstent) adj. nagły;
natychmiastowy; bieżący;
s. moment; chwila (szczególna)
instantaneous (,ynsten'tejnjes)
adj. natychmiastowy; momentalny ;zdarzający się w momencie
instantly (yn'stently) adv.
natychmiast; momentalnie
instead (yn'sted) adv. zamiast
tego; natomiast; w miejsce
instead of (yn'sted,ow) adv.
zamiast (kogoś, czegoś)
instigate ('ynstygejt) v. podżegać;podjudzać;prowokować
instigator ('ynstygejter) s.
podżegacz;prowokator;poduszczy-
ciel
instil(l) (yn'styl) v. wsączać;
wpajać (uczucia etc.);wkraplać
instinct ('ynstynkt) s. instynkt;adj.tchnący(czymś);pełen
instinctive (yn'styŋktyw) adj.
instynktowny; odruchowy
institute ('ynstytju:t) s. instytut; v. zakładać; ustanawiać; zarządzać(śledztwo etc.)
institution (,ynty'tju:szyn) s.
instytucja; ustanowienie
instruct (yn'strakt) v. uczyć
instruction (yn'strakszyn) s.
pouczenie; nauka; instrukcja
instructive (yn'straktyw) adj.
pouczający; kształcący
instructor (yn'strakter) s.
nauczyciel;wykładowca;instruktor
instructress (yn'straktrys) s.
nauczycielka ;instruktorka
instrument ('ynstrument) s.
instrument; przyrząd;dokument
insubordinate (,ynseb'o:rdnyt)
adj. niesforny; nieposłuszny
insufferable (yn'saferebl) adj.
nieznośny; nie do zniesienia
insufficient (,ynse'fyszent)
adj. niedostateczny;nieodpowiedni

insulate ('ynsjulejt) v. izolować;oddzielać;odosabniać
insult ('ynsalt) s. zniewaga;
insult (yn'salt) v. lżyć; znieważać;uchybiać;zelżyć
insupportable (,ynse'po:rtebl)
adj. nie do zniesienia; nieznośny;nieuzasadniony
insurance (yn'szuerens) s.
ubezpieczenie;a.ubezpieczeniowy
insurance policy (yn'szuerens'-
polysy) s. polisa ubezpieczeniowa;polisa asekuracyjna
insure (yn'szuer) v. ubezpieczać
(się);asekurować;zabezpieczać
insurmountable (,ynse:r'maun-
tebl) adj. niepokonany
insurrection (,ynse'rekszyn) s.
powstanie; insurekcja
intact (yn'taekt) adj. nietknięty ;nie uszkodzony
integrate ('yntygrejt) v. scalić; uzupełnić; całkować
integrity (yn'tegryty) s. uczciwość; rzetelność; czystość;
prawość ;niepodzielność
intellect ('yntylekt) s. rozum;
umysł;rozsądek;wybitne umysły
intellectual (,ynty'lekczuel)
adj. intelektualny; umysłowy
s. intelektualista;inteligent
intelligence (yn'telydżens) s.
inteligencja; informacja; wywiad;wiadomości;nowiny;informa-
cja
intelligent (yn'telydżent) adj.
inteligentny;łatwo uczący się
intelligentsia (yn'tely'dżencja)
s. inteligencja (warstwa kraju)
intelligible (yn'telydżybl) adj.
zrozumiały; jasny;wyraźny
intemperate (yn'temperyt) adj.
nieumiarkowany; bez umiaru
intend (yn'tend) v. zamierzać;
przeznaczać; mieć na myśli
intense (yn'tens) adj. napięty;
usilny; gorliwy;wytężony;uczucio-
wy
intensify (yn'tensyfaj) v.
wzmóc; wzmocnić; napiąć;wzmagać
intensity (yn'tensyty) s. inten-
sywność; wzmożenie;natężenie
intensive (yn'tensyw) adj. intensywny; wzmożony ;silny;wzma-
gniający

intent (yn'tent) s. plan; zamiar; adj. uważny; zamierzający; zajęty;pochłonięty;zdecydowany
intent on (yn'tent on) adj. pochłonięty; zajęty czymś
intention (yn'tenszyn) s. zamiar; cel;zamierzenie(czynu)
intentional (yn'tenszenel) adj. umyślny; celowy;zamierzony
inter (yn'te:r) v. grzebać
intercede (,ynte:r'si:d) v. wstawiać się; orędować
intercept ('ynte:rsept) v. przechwycić; przejąć; przerwać; udaremnić; podsłuchać
intercession (,ynter'seszyn) s. wstawiennictwo;orędownictwo
interchange (,ynte:r'czejndż) s. wzajemna wymiana; v. wymieniać się; zmieniać się
intercourse ('ynterko:rs) s. stosunek; obcowanie;spółkowanie
interdict (,ynter'dykt) s. zakaz; v. zakazywać;zabraniać
interest('yntryst),s. zainteresowanie; ciekawość; odsetki; interes;procent;v.zainteresować
interested ('yntrystyd) adj. zaciekawiony; zainteresowany
interesting ('yntrystyng) adj. ciekawy; interesujący
interfere (,ynter'fier) v. wtrącać się; wdawać się; kolidować; zakłócać;dokuczać
interfere with (,ynter'fier,łys) v. mieszać się do kogoś
interference (,ynter'fierens) s. wtrącanie się; zakłócenie
interior (yn'tierjer) adj. wewnętrzny; środkowy; s. wnętrze głąb kraju;głąb duszy(serca)
interior decorator (yn'tierjer 'dekerejter) s. architekt wnętrz; sprzedawca mebli
interjection (,ynter'dżekszyn) s. okrzyk; wykrzyknik
interlude (ynter'lu:d) s. przerwa; antrakt
intermediary (,ynter'mi:diery) adj. pośredni; pośredniczący; s. pośrednik;pśredniczka;pośrednie stadium;pośrednia forma rozmowa; v. mieć wywiad; widzieć się z kimś (dla wywiadu)pośredni produkt; agent

intermediate (,ynter'mi:djet) adj. pośredni; środkowy; średni;s.pośrednik;v.pośredniczyć
intermingle (,ynter'myngl) v. mieszać (się); pomieszać (się)
intermission (,ynter'myszyn) s. przerwa;pauza; antrakt
intermittent (,ynter'mytent) adj. przerywany; niemiarowy
intern (yn'te:rn) v. internować; odbywać praktykę lekarską;
intern ('ynte:rn) s. praktykant lekarski w szpitalu
internal ('ynte:rnl) adj. wewnętrzny; krajowy; domowy
international (,ynter'naeszenl) adj. międzynarodowy; s. międzynarodówka; zawody międzynarodowe;zawodnik międzynarodowy
interpose (,ynter'pouz) v. wstawać; wtrącać (się); przerywać
interpret (yn'ter:pryt) v. tłumaczyć i objaśniać; interpretować;rozumieć(opatrznie etc.)
interpretation (yn,te:rpry'tejszyn) s. interpretacja; tłumaczenie;sposób zrozumienia
interpreter (yn'te:rpryter) s. tłumacz (ustny)
interrogate (yn'teregejt) v. wypytywać; przesłuchiwać
interrogation (yn,tere'gejszyn) s. przesłuchanie; pytanie
interrogative (,ynte'rogetyw) adj. pytający (np. ton)
interrupt (,ynte'rapt) v. przerywać; zasłaniać (widok)
interruption (,ynte'rapszyn) s. przerwa (w czynności etc.)
intersect (,ynte:r'skt) v. przecinać (się);pokrzyżować)się)
intersection (,ynter'sekszyn) s. przecinanie się; skrzyżowanie
interval ('ynterwel) s. odstęp; przerwa;antrakt;okres(pogody)
intervene (,ynter'wi:n) s. wdawać się; interweniować; zdarzyć sie; zajść;być między(dwoma etc.)
intervention (,ynter'wenszyn) s. interwencja; wdanie się
interview ('ynterwju:) s. wywiad;

interviewer ('ynterwju:er) s.
przeprowadzający wywiad
intestines (yn'testynz) pl.
wnętrzności ; jelita
intimacy ('yntymesy) s. zażyłość; intymność; poufałe stosunki(płciowe);poufałość
intimate ('yntymyt),adj. zażyły; wewnętrzny; intymny;
v. zawiadamiać; dawać do zrozumienia;s.serdeczny przyjaciel
intimation (,ynty'mejszyn) s.
zawiadomienie; danie do zrozumienia;napomknięcie;znak(czegoś)
intimidate (yn'tymydejt) v.
zastraszyć; onieśmielić
into ('yntu:) prep. do; w; na
intolerable· (yn'tolerebl) adj.
nieznośny;nie do zniesienia
intolerant (yn'telerent) adj.
nietolerancyjny; nie znoszący
czegoś (cudzych przekonań etc.)
intoxicate (yn'toksykejt) v.
upić; upajać; odurzać się
intransitive (yn'traensytyw)
adj. & s. nieprzechodni
intrepid (yn'trepyd) adj. nieustraszony ;śmiały;odważny
intricate ('yntrykyt) adj. zawiły ;trudny do zrozumienia
intrigue (yn'tri:g) s. intryga;
potajemna miłość; v. intrygować; potajemnie utrzymywać
stosunek miłosny; zaciekawiać
introduce (,yntre'dju:s) v.
wprowadzać (coś lub kogoś);
przedstawiać; rozpoczynać; wsuwać; wysuwać; wkładać;zapoznawać
introduction (,yntre'dakszyn) s.
wstęp; wprowadzenie; włożenie;
wsunięcie; przedstawienie
(kogoś);przedmowa;innowacja etc.
introductory (,yntre'daktery)
adj. wstępny; wprowadzający
intrude (,yn'tru:d) v. wpychać
(się); wciskać (się); wedrzeć
(się); narzucać (się) (komuś)
intruder (yn'tru:der) s. natret;
intruz; nieproszony gość
intrusion (yn'tr:żyn) s. wciśnięcie (się); wepchnięcie (się);
narzucanie (się); wdarcie (się)
w cudze prawa

intuition (,yntju'yszyn) s.
intuicja;przeczucie;wyczucie
inutile (yn'ju:tyl) adj. niepotrzebny; bezcelowy;bezużyteczny
invade (yn'wejd) v. najeżdżać;
wdzierać się; zalewać; owładać; ogarniać; wtargnąć
invader (yn'wejder) s. najeźdźca ;okupant
invalid (yn'weli:d) s. chory;
inwalida ;kaleka;człowiek słaby
invalid (yn'waelyd) adj. nieważny ;nieprawomocny
invalidate (yn'daelydejt) v.
unieważniać (prawnie etc.)
invaluable (yn'waeljuebl) adj.
bezcenny; nieoceniony
invariable (yn'weeryebl) adj.
niezmienny;stały;równomierny
invariably (yn'v-eryebly) adv.
niezmiennie;stale;równomiernie
invasion (yn'wejżyn) s. inwazja; najazd; wdarcie (się)
invective (yn'wektyw) s. inwektywa; obelga; napaść (słowna);obelżywe słowa
invent (yn'went) v. wynaleźć;
wymyślić;zmyślić(coś na kogoś)
invention (yn'wenszyn) s. wynalazek; wymysł; zmyślenie
inventive (yn'wentyw) adj. pomysłowy; wynalazczy
inventor (yn'wentor) s. wynalazca (w nauce,mechanice etc.)
inverse (yn'we:rs) adj. odwrotny; s. odwrotność (czegoś)
inversion (yn'we:rżyn) s. odwrócenie; inwersja; homoseksualizm ;wynicowanie
invert (yn'we:rt) v. odwrócić;
przestawić; s. homoseksualista
inverted commas (yn'we:rtyd -
'komes) cudzysłów
invest (yn'west) v. inwestować;
wyposażać; oblegać; obdarzać
investigate (yn'westygejt) v.
badać; prowadzić dochodzenie
investigation (yn,westy'gejszyn) s. badanie; dochodzenie; śledztwo;rozpatrzenie;dociekanie
investigator (yn'westygejtor)
s. badacz ;agent(prokuratury)

investment (yn'westment) s.
inwestycja; lokata; oblężenie;osaczenie;obleczenie
invincible (yn'wynsebl) adj.
niepokonany; niezwyciężony
inviolable (yn'wajelebl) adj.
nienaruszalny; nietykalny;
niepogwałcony ;nieniszczalny
invisible (yn'wyzybl) adj.
niewidoczny; niewidzialny
invitation (,ynwy'tejszyn) s.
zaproszenie (pisemne,słowne)
invite (yn'wajt) v. zapraszać;
wywoływać; ściągać; nęcić;
zachęcać; prosić o (radę)
invoice ('ynwojs) s. faktura;
v. fakturować
invoke (yn'wouk) v. wzywać;
odwoływać się; wywoływać
involuntary (yn'wolentery) adj.
mimowolny; nieumyślny; bez-
wiedny (czyn,ruch etc.)
involve (yn'wolw) v. gmatwać;
wikłać; wmieszać; komplikowa-
wać; obejmować; wymagać
invulnerable (yn'walnerebl)
adj. nie do zranienia; nienaruszalny; nie do zdobycia
inward ('ynłerd) adj. wewnętrzny; adv. wewnątrz;w sercu etc.
inwards ('ynłerds) adv. wewnątrz ;w duchu ; w myśli
iodine ('ajoudi:n) s. jod
IOU =I owe you ('ajou'ju:) s.
kwit; skrypt dłużny
irascible (y'raesybl) adj.
gniewliwy; popędliwy; wybuchowy;skory do gniewu
iridescent (,yry'desnt) adj.
mieniący się; tęczowy
iris ('ajerys) s. tęczówka
Irish ('ajerysz) adj. irlandz-
ki;s. Irlandczyk
iron ('ajern) s. żelazo; żelazko;(pistolet; rewolwer;)adj.
żelazny; v. zakuwać; prasować
ironic(al) (aj'ronyk(el)) adj.
ironiczny; drwiący;uczczypliwy.
ironing ('ajernyng) s. prasowa-
nie (bielizna etc.)
ironmonger ('ajern,manger) s.
handlarz wyrobów żelaznych;właś-
ciciel sklepu żelaznego

iron mold ('ajernmould) s.
plama od rdzy
ironworks ('ajernłe:rks) s. huta żelaza ;przetwórnia żelaza
irony ('ajereny) s. ironia
irradiate (y'rejdjejt) v. oswietlać; naświetlać; oświecać;
rozjaśniać; rozpromienić
irrational (y'raesznel) adj.
nieracjonalny; nierozumny;
niewymierny;s.liczba niewymierna
irreconcilable (y'rekesajlebl)
adj. nieprzejednany; nie dający się pogodzić(z wiarą etc.)
irrecoverable (,yry'kawerebl)
adj. niepowetowany; nie do
odzyskania;stracony bezpowrotnie
irredeemable (,yry'di:mebl)
adj. niewymienny; beznadziejny;nieodwracalny;nieodkupny
irregular (y'regjuler) adj. nieregularny; nierówny; nieporzą-
ny; nielegalny;nieprawidłowy
irrelevant (y'relwent) adj.
nieistotny; niestosowny; oderwany; od rzeczy;nie do rzeczy
irremovable (,yry'mu:webl) adj.
nieusuwalny;nie do pokonania
irreparable (y'reperebl) adj.
niepowetowany;nie do naprawie-
irreplaceble (,yry'plejsebl) adj.
niezastąpiony;nie do zastąpienia
irrepressible (,yry'presybl)
adj. niepohamowany;nieodparty
irreproachable (,yry'prouczebl)
adj. nienaganny; bez zarzutu
irresistible (,yry'zystybl) adj.
nieodparty;porywający;gwałtowny
irresolute (y'rezelu:t) adj.
niezdecydowany; chwiejny
irrespective (.yrys'pektyw) adj.
niezależny; adv. niezależnie;
bez względu na...;bez szacunku
irresponsible (,yrys'ponsybl)
adj. nieodpowiedzialny;nieobli-
czalny
irretrievable (,yry'tri:webl)
adj. bezpowrotnie stracony
irreverent (y'rewerent) adj.
lekceważący; uchybiający
irrevocable (y'rewekebl) adj.
nieodwołalny; nie do odwołania
irrigate ('yrygejt) v. nawadniać; przepłukiwać; oświeżać

irritable ('yrytebl) adj.
drażliwy; wrażliwy; nerwowy;
przewrażliwiony;skory do gniewu
irritate ('yrytejt) v. denerwować; irytować; drażnić;
rozdrażniać;unieważnić prawnie
irritation (,yry'tejszyn) s.
irytacja; rozdrażnienie
is (yz) v. jest; zob. be
island ('ajlend) s. wyspa;
wysepka (na bruku)
isle (ajl) s. wyspa; v. żyć
na wyspie ;zrobić (jak)wyspę
isn't ('yznt) = is not; exp.:
nie jest (w domu etc.)
isn't it ? ('yznt yt) nieprawda ? czy nie prawda?
isolate ('ajselejt) v. odosabniać; izolować;osamotnić
isolated ('ajselejtyd) adj.
odosobniony;osamotniony
isolation (,ajse'lejszyn) s.
odosobnienie; izolacja; wyodrębnienie;osamotnienie
issue ('yszu:) s. wydanie;
przydział; zeszyt; spór; problem; argument; wynik; koniec;
ujście; wyjście; wypływ; potomstwo; upuszczenie; dochód;
v. wysyłać; wypuszczać; wydawać; dawać w wyniku; wychodzić; pochodzić;emitować
isthmus ('ysmes) s. przesmyk;
międzymorze ;cieśń; węzina
it (yt) pron. to; ono
Italian (y'taeljen) adj. włoski
itch ('ycz) s. swędzenie;
świerzb;chętka; v. czuć swędzenie; swędzić;mieć ochotę
item ('ajtem) s. pozycja; punkt
programu; artykuł; wiadomość;
adv. podobnie; także;też dotyczy
itemize ('ajte,majz) v. wy-
szczególniać(rachunek,spis)
itinerary (aj'tynerery) s. marszruta; szlak; przewodnik;
adj. podróżny; drogowy
its (yts) pron. jego; jej; swój
itself (yt'self) pron. się; siebie; sobie; sam; sama; samo
ivory ('ajwery) s. kość słoniowa;klawisz fortepianu;biel kre-
mowa;adj.z kości słoniowej;biały

ivy ('ajwy) s. bluszcz
j (dżej) dziewiąta litera
angielskiego alfabetu
jab (dżaeb) s. szturchaniec;
dźgnięcie; v. szturchać; dżgać
jack (dżaek) s. lewarek; dźwignia; przyrząd; walet; flaga;
gniazdko elektr.; złącze
jack up ('dżaek,ap) v. podnieść
lewarkiem;wyśrubowanie(cen)
jackal ('dżaeko:1) s. szakal;
sługus;harować za kogoś
jackass ('dżaekaes) s. osioł;
dureń; bałwan;menda;niedojda
jackdaw ('dżaekdo:) s. kawka
jacket ('dżaekyt) s. marynarka;
żakiet; kurtka; okładzina; obwoluta; osłona; v. okrywać; nakładać okładzinę;wkładać do teki
jack-in-the-box ('dżaek-yn-dy-
boks) s. figurka wyskakująca
z pudełka;typ ognia sztucznego
jackknife ('dżaeknajf) s.
scyzoryk; nóż składany
jack-of-all-trades ('dżaek,ow-
'o:1,trejds) majster do
wszystkiego;majster klepka
jackpot ('dżaek,pot) s. główna
wygrana; pula
jackscrew ('dżaekskru:) s. lewar śrubowy (podnośnik)
jag (dżaeg) s. ostry występ;
zadarcie; nacięcie; podniecenie; popijawa; zabawa; v. poszarpać; postrzepić; ząbkować
jagged ('dżaegyd) adj. po-
strzępiony;wyszczerbiony;szczerba-ty
jaguar ('dżaegjuer) s. jaguar
jail (dżejl) s. ciupa; wiezie-
nie;v. więzić; uwięzić(kogoś)
jam (dżaem) s. tłok; zator; korek; zła sytuacja; v. stłoczyć;
zablokować; zaciąć; zagłuszyć
janitor ('dżaenitor) s. portier;
dozorca;sprzątacz biurowy etc.
January ('dżaenjuery) s. styczeń; a.styczniowy (dzień etc.)
Japanese (,dżaepe'ni:z) adj.
japoński; s.Japończyk
jar (dża:r) s. słój; słoik;
zgrzyt; kłótnia; drganie;
v. zgrzytać; drażnić; wstrząsać; kłócić się ;trząsć;razić

jaundice ('džo:ndys) s. żółtaczka ;v.powodować żółtaczkę)

javelin ('dżaewlyn) s. oszczep

jaw (dżo:) s. szczęka; v. ględzic; gadac;wstawiać mowę

jaw-bone ('dżo:boun) s. kosć szczękowa; v. nakłaniac słowami (pod presją)

jazz (dżaz) s. muzyka jazzowa; v. kłamac;adj.zgrzytliwy;krzykliwy

jazz it up ('dżaz,yt'ap) v. ożywiac; ulepszac (coś)

jay (dżej) s. sójka; dudek; pleciuga; gaduła (arogancki)

jay-walker ('dżej,ło:ker) s. nieprawidłowo przechodzący jezdnię ;roztrzepaniec

jealous ('dżeles) adj. zazdrosny; baczny (nadzor);zawistny

jealousy ('dżelesy) s. zazdrość; zawisć ;wybuch zazdrości

jeep (dżi:p) s. łazik; samochód terenowy (silnie zbudowany)

jeer (dżier) s. kpina; szyderstwo; drwina; v. drwic; kpic; wykpiwac (ordynarnie i złośliwie)

jelly ('dżely) s. galareta; kisiel;v.zgalarecied;robic galarete

jellyfish ('dżelyfysz) s. meduza;człowiek słabej woli

jeopardize ('dżepe,dajz) v. narazic na niebezpieczenstwo

jerk (dże:rk) s. szarpnięcie; skręt; skurcz; pchnięcie; bzik; frajer; v. szarpac; targac; pchnąc; rzucac się;wzdrygac się

jerky ('dże:rky) adj. urwany; trzesący; bzikowaty;spazmatyczny

jersey ('dże:rzy) s. sweter

jest (dżest) s. żart; dowcip; zabawa; pośmiewisko; v. żartowac; dowcipkowac;przekomarzac się

jester ('dżester) s. błazen; trefnis; błazen nadworny

jet (dżet) s. strumien; wytrysk; płomien; dysza; rozpylacz; odrzutowiec; v. tryskac;a.czarny jak smoła

jet engine (,dżet'endżyn) s. motor odrzutowy

jet lag ('dżet,laeg) s.ujemny efekt zmiany sfer czasu na pasażera samolotu ódrzutowego

jet plane ('dżet,plejn) s. samolot odrzutowy;odrzutowiec

jet-propelled ('dżet-pre,peld) adj. odrzutowy

jet set ('dżet,set) s. złota młodzież; prominenci

jetty (dżety) s. grobla; molo; adj. czarny jak smoła

Jew (dżu:) s. Żyd; v. (slang): ocyganic;okpic;oszukac;cyganic

jewel ('dżu:el) s. klejnot; drogi kamien; v. ozdabiac klejnotami; osadzac na kamieniach(zamontowac)

jeweler ('dżu:eler) s. jubiler;wlasciciel sklepu jubilerskiego

jewelry ('dżu:elry) s, klejnoty; biżuteria;kosztowności

Jewish ('dżu:ysz) adj. żydowski

jibe (dżajb) v. zgadzac się; pasowac (do czegoś);harmonizowac

jiffy ('dżyfy) s. mig; chwileczka;momencik;skundka

jiggle ('dżygl) v. kołysac; lekko hustac;wstrząsac zrywnie

jingle ('dżyngl) v. brzękac; szczekac; dzwonic; s. brzęk; szczek; wierszyk(rymy);dzwonek

job (dżob) s. robota; zajęcie; zadanie; posada; v. pracowac; robic; handlowac; wynajmowac

job (dżob) v. ukłuc; dżgnac; dziobnąc; s. dżgnięcie;praca; dziobnięcie;zadanie;robota;fach

jobless ('dżoblys) adj. bezrobotny ;bez pracy

job-work ('dżobłerk) s. praca na akord (zob. piece-work)

jockey ('dżoky) s. dżokej; v. oszukac; nabrac;pchac się na pozycje

jocular ('dżokjuler) adj. wesoły; żartobliwy;krotochwilny

jocularity (,dżokju'laeryty) s. wesołość; żartobliwość; żarty;ktotochwilność;figlarność

jocund ('dżoukend) adj. wesoły

jog (dżog) s. potrącenie; poruszenie; trucht; róg;występ; v. potrącac; poruszac; przebiedowac; biec truchtem;telepac się

jog-trot ('dżog'trot) s. trucht;a.monotonny;jednostajny

join (dżoyn) v. łączyć; przy-
łaczac (się); przytykac do;
spotykac się;brac udział
joiner ('dżojner) s. stolarz
joint (dżoynt) v. spajac;łą-
czyc; cwiartowac; kantowac;
s. spojenie; fuga; złącze;
zestawienie; zawiasa francuska;
część; lokal; melina; a. wspólny; połączony;dzielący się z kims
joint stock ('dżoynt,stok) adj.
akcyjny (bank);udziałowy
joke (dżouk) s. żart; dowcip;
figiel; v. żartowac z kogos;
dowcipkowac;wysmiac;zadrwic
joker ('dżouker) s. żartownis;
dowcipnis; gosc; facet; dżo-
ker; pułapka; trudnosc
jolly ('dżoly) adj. wesoły; miły; podochocony; adv. szalenie;
bardzo; v. przychlebiac; nabierac; zachęcac;mitygowac;ugłas-
jolt (dżoult) v. wstrząsac;
podrzucac; s. wstrząs; podrzu-
cenie; szarpnięcie;podskok
jostle ('dżosl) v. rozpychac
(się); roztrącac; szarpac się;
walczyc (z kims); s. pchniecie;
starcie;szturchnięcie;tłok;scisk
jot down ('dżot,dałn) v. zapi-
sac napredce;zanotowac pospiesz-nie
journal ('dże:rnl) s. dziennik;
czasopismo; czop;os w łożysku
journalism ('dże:rnlyzem) s.
dziennikarstwo
journey ('dże:rny) v. podrożowac;
s. podroż;jazda;wycieczka
journeyman ('dże:rnymen) s. cze-
ladnik(nauczony rzemiosła)
jovial ('dżouwjel) adj. wesoły;
jowialny;pełen dobrego humoru
joy (dżoj) s. radosc; uciecha
joyful ('dżoyful) adj. radosny;
wesoły;zadowolony(bardzo)
joyous ('dżojes) adj.=joyful
jubilant ('dżu:bylent) adj.
triumfujący; rozradowany
jubilee ('dżu:byli:) s. jubileusz; wielka radosc;a.jubileuszowy
judge (dżadż) v. sadzic; osadzac;
rozsadzac; s. sedzia; znawca;
znawczyni;człowiek biegły w oce-nach

judgment   ('dżadżment) s.
sąd; sądzenie; wyrok; rozsądek;opinia; ocena; decyzja
judicial (dżu'dyszel) adj. sądowy; sędziowski; bezstronny;
krytyczny;sądownie zastrzeżony
judicious (dżu'dyszes) a. rozsądny;rozumny;wykazujący rozum
jug (dżag) s. dzbanek; koza;
ciupa; v. gotowac; wsadzac do
kozy, ciupy;dusic (potrawkę)
juggle ('dżagl) v. żonglowac;
cyganic; robic sztuczki;
s. kuglarstwo;żonglerka
juggler ('dżagler) s. kuglarz;
żongler;oszust;kanciarz
jugglery ('dżaglery) s. kuglarstwo;podstęp;oszukaństwo;żon-glerka
Jugoslav ('ju:gou'sla:v) adj.
jugosłowianski;Jugosłowianin
juice (dżu:s) s. sok; tresc;
benzyna; elektrycznosc;
v. wyciskac sok; doic
juicy ('dżu:sy) adj. soczysty;
jędrny;barwny;deszczowy etc.
juke box ('dżuk,boks) s. auto-
mat-gramofon(na monety)
July (dżu:laj) s. lipiec
jumble ('dżambl) s. pomieszac;
kotłowac; mieszanina; galimatias; bigos:trzęsąca jazda
jumble-sale ('dżambl,sejl) s.
wyprzedaż wysortowanych to-
warow(często dobroczynna)
jump (dżamp) s. skok; sus; podskok; wyskok; v. skakac; podskoczyc; wskoczyc; wyskoczyc;
wyprzedzac; podnosic cenę;
wykoleic;poderwac się;rzucac się
jumper ('dżamper) s. skoczek;
typ sukni (bez rękawow)
jumpy ('dżampy) adj. nerwowy;
zmienny;nierowny;kapryśny
junction ('dżankszyn) s. połączenie; złącze; stacja węzło-
wa; węzeł;skrzyżowanie(drog)
juncture('dżankczer) s. połączenie; stan rzeczy; krytycz-
na chwila; chwila:przesilenie
June (dżu:n) s. czerwiec
jungle ('dżangl) s. dżungla;
gaszcz zarosli,lian etc.

junior ('dżu:njer) s. junior;
młodszy; student trzeciego
roku (USA);a.młodszy;z młodszych
junk ('dżąnk) s.złom; szmelc;
narkotyki; v. wyrzucać
junkie ('dżąnki) s. narkoman
jurisdiction (,dżurys'dykszyn)
s. wymiar sprawiedliwości;
sądownictwo;zasięg władzy
jurisprudence (,dżurys'pru:-
dens) s. prawoznawstwo
juror ('dzuerer) s. sędzia
przysięgły; ławnik; zaprzysiężony;juror
jury ('dżuery) s. sąd przysięgłych; sąd konkursowy
just (dżast) s. sprawiedliwy;
słuszny; dokładny; adv. właśnie; poprostu; zaledwie; przecież; dokładnie; moment wczes-
niej;ścisłe;równie;tak samo
just now ('dżast,nał) exp.:
właśnie teraz;przed chwilą
justice ('dżastys) s. sprawiedliwość; słuszność; są-
dzia(pokoju,sądu najwyższego)
justification (,dżastyfy'kejszyn) s. uzasadnienie;
usprawiedliwienie;wykazanie
justify ('dżastyfaj) v. usprawiedliwić; wytłumaczyć; umoty-
wować; uzasadnić;dać dowody
justly ('dżastly) adv. słusznie;
poprawnie;właściwie;sprawiedli-
jut (dżat) s. występ;v.wystawać
jut out ('dżat,aut) v. wystawać;
sterczeć(na zewnątrz);występować
juvenile ('dżu:wynajl) adj.
małoletni; nieletni; s. wyrostek; młodzik;podrostek
juvenile court ('dżu:wynajl,-
,ko:rt) s. sąd dla nieletnich
juvenile delinquent ('dżu:wy-
najl,dy'lynkłent) s. młodociany przestępca
juxtaposition (,dżakstepe'zyszyn) s. zestawienie; bezpoś-
rednie sąsiedztwo(tuż obok)
k (kej)jedenasta litera angielskiego alfabetu
kangaroo (,kaenge'ru:) s. kangur;a.samosądny;nielegalny
kayak ('kajaek)s.kajak;s.kajakowy

keel (ki:l) s. stępka; kil;
v. wywracać do góry stępką
keen (ki:n) adj. ostry; dotkliwy; żywy; cięty; serdeczny;
gorliwy; zapalony; bystry;
przenikliwy; wrażliwy; czuły
keen on ('ki:n.on) adj. palący się do..;czujący miętę
keep; kept; kept (ki:p; kept;
kept)
keep (ki:p) v. dotrzymywać;
przestrzegać; dochować; obchodzić; strzec; pilnować; utrzymywać; prowadzić; trzymać(sie)
powstrzymywać sie; mieszkać;
kontynuować; s. utrzymanie;
jedzenie; wikt;umocnienie
keep away ('ki:p,ełej) v. trzymać sie z daleka;odstraszać
keep back ('ki:p,baek) v. powstrzymać; nie zbliżać się
keep down ('ki:p,dałn) v. trzymać w ryzach; tłumić; kulić
się;utrzymywać na niskim poziomie
keep in('ki:p,yn) v. zatrzymywać; nie wychodzić; pozostawać;nie pokazywć się
keep off ('ki:p,of) v. nie dopuszczać; trzymać się z dala
keep on ('ki:p,on) v. kontynuować; iść dalej;nudzić;męczyć
keep on doing ('ki:p,on'du:yng)
v. robić dalej; nie przestawać;nie dawać spokoju;nudzić
keep out ('ki:p, ałt) v. nie
wchodzić; trzymać się na uboczu;nie pozwolić wejść;odpędzać
keep talking ('ki:p'to:kyng)v.
mówić dalej;kontynuować rozmowę
keep time ('ki:p'tajm) v. być
punktualnym;zapisywać czas pracy
keep to oneself ('ki:p,tu'łan-
self) v. trzymać się na uboczu; żyć w odosobnieniu
keep up ('ki:p,ap) v. dotrzymywać; utrzymywać w porządku;
nie dawać iść spać; trzymać
się w dobrym stanie;czuwać
keep up with ('ki:p,ap'łys) v.
śledzić; dotrzymywać (kroku)
keeper ('ki:per) s. opiekun;
dozorca; strażnik; konserwator;
klamra; kotwica magnesu;skobel

keeping ('ki:pyŋ) s. opieka;
zgoda; harmonia;a.do przechowy-
wania
keepsake ('ki:psejk) s. upominek; pamiątka od kogoś
keg (keg) s. beczułka;100 funtów
kennel ('kenl) s. psiarnia;
psia buda; ściek; v. trzymać
w budzie; mieszkać w norze
kept (kept) v. zob. keep
kerb stone ('ke:rb,stoun) s.
krawężnik (ang.) zob. curb
kerchief ('ke:rczyf) s. chustka (na głowę);chustka do nosa
kernel ('ke:rnl) s. jądro;
ziarno;sedno sprawy;istotna rzecz
ketchup ('keczap) s. sos pomidorowy (gotowy) do mięsa
kettle ('ketl) s. kocioł; czajnik; imbryk na herbatę
kettledrum ('ketl,dram) s.bęben-
-kocioł(półkulisty)miedziany
key (ki:) s. klucz; klawisz;
klin; ton; rafa; wysepka;
v. stroić; zamykac kluczem
lub zwornikiem;adj.ważny;kontro-lujący
keyboard ('ki:bo:rd) s. kla-
wiatura (maszyny do pisania etc.)
keyhole ('ki:houl) s. dziurka
od klucza (w drzwiach etc.)
keynote ('ki:nout) s. nuta
kluczowa ;myśl przewodnia
keystone ('ki:stoun) s. zwornik;zasada;główna część
kick (kik) s. kopniak; kopnię-
cie; wierzgnięcie; wykop;
strzał; odrzut; skarga; narzekanie; przyjemność; uciecha;
krzepa; miłe podniecenie; opór;
v. kopać; wierzgać; skrzywić
się; protestować; opierać się
kickback ('kykbaek) s. łapówka
za kontrakt;dawanie łapówki
kick downstairs ('kykdałn'steerz)
v. degradować; zrzucać ze
schodów (kopniakiem)
kick-off ('kykof) s. rozpoczęcie
meczu; pierwszy strzał
kick out ('kyk aut) v. wyrzucić;
wykopać; pozbyć się
kick the bucket ('kik,dy'bakyt)
v. umrzeć; odwalić kitę; wy-
ciągnąc nogi;wykitować

kid (kyd) s. koźlę; dzieciak;
smyk; młodzik; błaga; bujda;
v. urodzić koźlę; bujać; nabierać; żartować;dowcipkować
kid glove ('kydglaw) s. rękawiczka;adj.galowy;delikatny
kidnap ('kydnaep) v. porywać;
uprowadzać;ukraść dziecko etc
kidnapper ('kydnaeper) s. porywacz (dziecka;zakładnika etc.)
kidney ('kydny) s. nerka; rodzaj;a.w kształcie nerki
kidney bean ('kydny,bi:n) s.
fasola szparagowa; piesza
kill (kyl) v. zabijać; uśmiercać; wybić; zatrzymać (piłkę,
motor) ścinać (piłkę); s.upo-
lowane zwierzę; zabicie; mord
kill time (,kyl'tajm) v. zabijać czas; marnować czas
killer ('kyler) s. zabójca;
morderca; narzędzie śmierci
kiln (kyln) s. piec do wypala-
nia lub wysuszania cegieł etc.
kilogram(me) ('kylougraem) s.
kilogram;a. kilogramowy
kilometer ('kyle,mi:ter) s. kilometr; a. kilometrowy
kilt (kylt) s. spódniczka męska (szkocka); v. podkasać;
plisować pionowo;s.spódnica szkocka
kin (kyn) s. rodzina; krewni;
ród; adj. spokrewniony;pokrewny
kind (kajnd) s. rodzaj; jakość;
gatunek; charakter; natura;
adj. grzeczny; uprzejmy;
życzliwy; łagodny;wyrozumiały
kindergarten ('kynder,ga:rtn)
s. przedszkole (do sześciu lat wieku)
kindhearted ('kajnd'ha:rtyd)
adj. dobrotliwy;współczujący
kindle ('kyndle) v. rozpalić;
rozżarzyć; rozniecać; podniecać;zapalać się
kindly ('kajndly) adj. uprzejmie; życzliwie; adj. dobry;
dobrotliwy; życzliwy;adv.uprzej-mie
kindness ('kajndnys) s. dobroć;
uprzejmość; łaskawość; życz-
liwość ;życzliwy postępek
kindred ('kyndryd) s. krewni;
pokrewieństwo; adj.pokrewny

king (kyŋg) s. król
kingdom ('kyŋdom) s. królestwo;monarchia;świat(roslin etc.)
kingsize ('kyŋsajz) adj. wielki; duży;krolewskich wymiarow
kingly ('kyŋgly) adj. krolewski
kinsman ('kynzmen) s. krewny; powinowaty (męszczyzna)
kipper ('kyper) s. śledź wędzony; ryba suszona; v. suszyć; wędzić i solić; zasuszać(ryby)
kiss (kys) s. całus; v. całować; pocałować;lekko dotknąć
kit (kyt) s. przybory; narzędzia; wyposażenie; zestaw; komplet; torba; bagaż; cebrzyk; kubeł;komplet(narzędzi)
kitchen ('kyczn) s. kuchnia
kitchenette ('kyczynet) s. kuchenka(mała w kawalerce etc.)
kite (kajt) s. latawiec;v.szybować
kitten ('kytn) s. kotek
knack (naek) s. spryt; sztuczka; chwyt; dryg; talent
knapsack ('naepsaek) s. plecak
knave (nejw) s. łajdak; łotr; szelma; walet;naciągacz;kanalia
knavery ('nejwery) s. łajdactwo; szelmostwo;niegodziwość
knead ('ni:d) v. miesic; gniesc; masować;kształcić(charakter)
knee ('ni:) s. kolano;v.klękać
knee breeches ('ni:bryczyz) pl. spodnie do kolan
kneel; knelt; knelt (ni:l; nelt; nelt)
kneel ('ni:l) v. klękać
knelt(nelt) zob. kneel
knew (nju:) zob . know
knickerbockers ('nikerbockers) s. pumpy; krótkie spodnie spięte pod kolanami
knickknack ('niknaek) s. cacko; fataraszek; przysmaczek
knife (najf) s. nóż; v. krajać; kłuc nożem; zakluc;zadzgac nożem
knight (najt) s. rycerz; v. nadawać szlachectwo;nobilitować
knit; knit; knit (nyt; nyt; nyt)
knit (nyt) v. robić na drutach; dziać; marszczyc (brwi); łączyć; ściągać;powodować zrośnięcie(kości);spajać(cementem)

knitting (nytyŋg) s. dzianie; trykotarstwo ;dziewiarstwo
knives (najwz) pl. noże; pl.od knife
knob (nob) s. guzik; guz; gałka; sęk;uchwyt;pokrętło;rączka
knock (nok) s. stuk; uderzenie; pukanie; stukac; pukac; zapukac; uderzyc; zderzyc; szturchac;zderzyc się
knock down ('nok,dałn) v. powalic; obniżać cenę;rozkręcac
knock out ('nok,aut) v. nokautowac; wybijac; wymeczyc
knock over ('nok,ower) v. przewracac; przewrócić
knocker ('noker) s. kołatka na drzwiach;malkontent;opukiwacz
knot (not) s. węzeł; kokarda; sęk; zgrubienie; dystans morski 1853 m; v. wiazac; zawiązywac; komplikowac; motać
knotty ('noty) adj. węzłowaty; sękaty; zawiły; zagadkowy
know; knew; known (nou; nju:; noun)
know (nou) v. wiedzieć; umieć; znac; móc odróżniac; poznac
know-how ('nouhau) s. umiejętnosc; znajomość rzeczy
knowingly ('nouyŋgly) adj. świadomie; naumyslnie; chytrze
knowledge ('noulydż) s. wiedza; nauka; znajomość;zasięg wiedzy
knowledgeable ('nolydżebl) adj. dobrze poinformowany; mądry
knuckle ('nakl) s. staw palca; kastet; uderzac kościmi palców
kotow ('kou,tał) = kowtow
kowtow ('koł,tał) v. bic czołem; płaszczyc się; s. ukłon starochiński czołem do ziemi
Kraut (kraut) adj. szkopski (niemiecki) ; kapusciany
kudos ('kju:dos) s. nagroda lub uznanie za znaczne osiągnięcie; sława (slang)
Ku Klux Klan ('kju:,kluks'klaen) s. rasistowska tajna organizacja w USA przeciw murzynom, żydom i katolikom
kulak (ku:'la:k) s. zamożny chłop; kułak

l (el) dwunasta litera alfabetu
angielskiego; klauzura; kolanko (rury); kątownik
lab (laeb) s. (slang):labora-
torium; a. laboratoryjny
label ('lejbl) s. nalepka; etykieta; naklejka; przezwisko;
v. przylepiać etykiety (na
coś; komuś);przezywać
labor ('lejber) s. praca; robota; trud; mozół; wysiłek;
klasa robotnicza; poród;
v. ciężko pracować; mozolić
się; borykać się; łudzić się;
brnąć; opracować; rozwodzić
się; rodzić;szczegółowo opracowywać
laboratory (lae'boretery) s.
laboratorium; pracownia
laborious (le'bo:rjes) adj.
pracowity; mozolny; wypracowany;ciężko pracujący
labor union('lejber'ju:njen)
s. związek zawodowy
laborer ('lejberer) s. robotnik płatny na godzinę(fizyczny)
laborite ('lejberajt) s. członek partii pracy (w Anglii)
lace (lejs) s. sznurówka; sznurowadło; koronka; v. sznurować; przetykać; koronkować;
urozmaicać; chłostać; zakrapiać (wódkę);młócić;bić;walić
lack (laek) s. brak; niedostatek; v. brakować; nie mieć
czegoś;być bez czegoś
laconic (le'konyk) adj. lakoniczny; zwięzły; treściwy
lacquer ('laeker) s. lakier;
v. lakierować;emaliować
lad (laed) s. chłopak; chłopiec
ladder ('laeder) s. drabina;
v. pruć; rozpruć;puszczać oczka
ladder proof ('laeder,pru:f)
adj. nie prujące się (np. pończochy);nie puszczający oczek
laden ('lejdn) adj. obciążony;
obarczony;pogrążony(w smutku)
lading ('lejdyng)s. fracht; za-
ładowanie; ładunek (statku etc.)
ladle ('lejdl) s. warząchew;
czerpak; chochla; v. czerpać;
nalewać warząchwią (czerpakiem)

lady ('lejdy) s. pani; dama
lady killer ('lejdy,kyler) s.
pożeracz serc niewieścich
ladylike ('lejdylajk) adj. wytworny; zniewieściały
lag (laeg) s. zaleganie; opóź-
nianie; zwłoka;v. zalegać;
wlec się z tyłu; nie nadążać
lag behind ('laeg,by'hajnd) v.
pozostawać w tyle;zalegać
lager ('la:ger) s. wystałe piwo
lagoon (le'gu:n) s. laguna
laid (lejd) zob. lay
lain (lejn) zob. lie
lair (leer) s. barłóg; legowisko; szałas; v.iść na legowisko
lake (lejk) s. jezioro;a.jeziorny
lamb (laem) s. jagnię; baranina
lame (lejm) adj. kulawy; ułomny; v. okulawić; okaleczyć
lament (le'ment) s. lament;
biadanie; v. lamentować; biadać; opłakiwać; narzekać; ubolewać;zawodzić;być w żałobie
lamentable ('laementebl) adj.
opłakany; godny ubolewania;
żałosny;wyrażający ubolewanie
lamentation (,laemen'tejszyn) s.
lament; biadanie;lamentacja
lamp (laemp) s. lampa; latarka;
kaganek; v. świecić; oświetlać;
gapić się;zobaczyć;widzieć
lamppost ('laemppoust) s. słup
latarniany ;latarnia uliczna
lamp shade ('laempszejd) s.
abażur
lance (la:ns) s. lanca; lansjer;
lancet; v.kłuć; przebijać lan-
cą lub lancetem; rozcinać
land (laend) s. ląd; ziemia;
grunt; kraj; v. wyciągać na ląd;
wyładować; zdobyć (np. nagrodę)
landholder ('laend,houlder) s.
właściciel ziemski; dzierżawca
landing ('laendyng) s. lądowanie;
pomost; przystań; półpiętrze
landing field ('laendyng,fi:ld)
s. lotnisko polowe ;lądowisko
landing gear ('leandyng,gier)
s. podwozie (z kołami-samolotu)
landing stage ('laendyng,stejdz)
s. pomost pływający ; wyładunek

landlady ('laend,lejdy) s. właścicielka domu; hotelu etc.;gospodyni (pensjonatu)

landlord ('laend,lo:rd) s. właściciel domu czynszowego; gospodarz odnajmujący pokój

landmark ('laendma:rk) s. punkt orientacyjny; słup graniczny

landowner ('laend,oŕner) s. właściciel ziemski

landscape ('laendskejp) s. krajobraz; v. kształtować teren i ogród (upiększać)

landslide ('laendslajd) s. osuwisko; lawina głosów

landslip ('laendslyp) s. osuwisko; obsunięcie się ziemi

lane (lejn) s. tor; uliczka; szlak; przejście; linia ruchu kołowego ;trasa(samolotu)

language ('laengłydż) s. mowa; język mowiony i pisany

languid ('laengłyd) s. ospały; omdlały; słaby; ociężały; powolny; rozmarzony; tęskny

languish ('laengłysz) v. omdlewać; marnieć; ginąc z tęsknoty ;mieć wyraz zadumy

languor ('laenger) s. omdlenie; osłabienie;ociężałość; ospałość; tęsknota; rozmarzenie; powolność;brak wigoru;słabość

lank (laenk) adj, mizerny; wysoki; chudy; wychudzony; prosty; gładki ;długi i płaski

lanky ('laenky) adj. wychudzony; wysoki i chudy

lanolin ('laenolyn) s. lanolina

lantern ('laentern) s. latarnia

lap (laep) s. łono; podołek; pola; okrążenie; zanadrze; dolinka; chlupotanie; lura; v. spowijać; otulać; zakładać (jak dachówki); wystawać; chłeptać; chlupotać;chlupać

lapel (le'pel) s. klapa (płaszcza) dochodząca kołnierza

lapse (laeps) s. lapsus; upływ; okres; omyłka; v. potknąć się; odstąpić; omylić sie; upłynąć; stracić ważność; minąć; przechodzić;pogrążyc się w stan...

larceny ('la:rseny) s. kradzież

larch (la:rcz) s. modrzew

lard (la:rd) s. smalec; v. szpikować; naszpikowywać;ozdabiać;cytatami

larder ('la:rder) s. spiżarnia

large (la:rdż) adj. wielki; rozległy; obfity; hojny

largely ('la:rdżly)adv. znacznie; hojnie; suto; w dużym stopniu; w dużej ilości;głównie

lark (la:rk) s. skowronek; zabawa; uciecha; v. figlować; żartować; przeskakiwać

larva ('la:rwa) s. larwa

larynx ('laerynks) s. krtań

lascivious (le'syvjes) adj. lubieżny;wzbudzający lubieżność

lash (laesz) s. bicz; uderzenie; nagana; rzęsa; v. chłostać; machać; walić; pędzić; uwiązać

lass (laes) s. dziewczyna; dziewczę; młoda kobieta

lasso (lae'su:) s. lasso; v. chwytać na lasso

last (laest) adj. ostatni; ubiegły; ostateczny; adv. po raz ostatni; ostatnio; wreszcie; w końcu; v. trwać; wytrzymać; wystarczyć; długo służyć; s. koniec; kres; wytrzymałość; kopyto szewskie ;ostatnie dziecko

last but one ('laest,bat'łan) exp.: przedostatni

lasting ('la:styŋg) adj. stały; trwały;długo trwały

lastly (la:stly) adv. w końcu; na końcu ;w konkluzji;ostatecznie

last night ('laest,najt) exp. wczoraj wieczór

last name ('laest,nejm) s. nazwisko

latch (laecz) s. zasuwka; rygiel; zatrzask; v. zamykać na zasuwkę, rygiel lub zatrzask

latch onto ('laecz,ontu) v. uczepić się kogoś

late (lejt) adj. & s. późny; spozniony; były; zmarły; adv. późno; poniewczasie; niegdys

lately ('lejtly) adv. ostatnio

later on ('lejter,on) adv. później; potem; dalej

lath (laeθ) s. łata; deseczka; v. pokrywać łatami(do tynkowania)

lathe (lejʑ) s. tokarnia; koło garncarskie; v. toczyć (na tokarni); obrabiać(na obrabiarce)

lather ('laeᵭzer) s. piana; mydliny; v. mydlić (brodę); zapienić (się); prać; łoić

Latin ('laetyn) adj. łaciński; s. łacina; łacinnik

latitude ('laetytju:d) s. szerokość (geograficzna); szerokość poglądów; zakres; rozmiary; wolność; swoboda (np. działania); tolerancja

latter ('laeter) adj, drugi; końcowy; schyłkowy;ostatni

latterly ('laeterly) adv. ostatnio; niedawno; poźniej

lattice ('laetys) s. kratownica; v. kratować;ułożyć w kratę

laudable ('lo:debl) adj. chwalebny ;godny pochwały

laugh (laef) v. smiac się; zaśmiac się ;roześmiać się

laugh at ('laef,et) v. wyśmiewać ;uśmiac sie(z czegoś)

laugh away ('laef,e'łej) v. zbyć śmiechem

laugh off ('laef,of) v. obrócić w żart ;pokryc zmieszanie śmiechem

laughter ('laefter) s. smiech

launch (lo:ncz) v. puszczać w ruch; spuszczac na wodę; miotać; rzucac; zadawac; wydawać; s. szalupa; spuszczenie na wodę (statku,okrętu,etc.)

launching pad ('lo:nczyŋg,paed) s. wyrzutnia (rakiet)

launderette (lo:n'dret) s. pralnia samoobsługowa

laundry ('lo:ndry) s. pralnia; bielizna do prania

laurel ('lorel) s. wawrzyn; laur; v. wieńczyc wawrzynem

lavatory ('laewetery) s. umywalnia; ustęp; umywalka

lavender ('laewynder) s. lawenda; v. wkładac lawendę w bieliznę ;a. lawendowy

lavish ('laewysz) adj. hojny;suty; rozrzutny; v. nie szczedzic pieniędzy, miłości etc.)

law (lo:) s. prawo; ustawa; reguła; sądy;posłuszeństwo prawu

lawful ('lo:ful) adj, legalny; słuszny; prawowity; z prawego łoża; prawnie uznany

lawless ('lo:lys) adj. bezprawny; łamiący prawo; rozpustny

lawn (lo:n) s. trawnik; murawa

lawsuit ('lo:sju:t) s. proces (sądowy) ;sprawa sądowa

lawyer ('lo:jer) s. prawnik; adwokat ;radca prawny

lax (laeks) adj. luzny; nieszczelny; niedbały; nieścisły; mający rozwolnienie;wolny

laxative ('laeksetyw) adj.& s. przeczyszczający (środek)

laxity ('laeksyty) s. luźność; nieścisłość; niedokładność; niedbalstwo;rozwiązłość

lay; laid; laid(lej; lejd; lejd)

lay (lej) v. kłaść; uspokajac; układac; skręcac (się); zaczaic się; spac z kims; s. położenie; układ; spanie (z kims); adj. świecki; laicki; niefachowy; lay- zob. lie

layout ('lejout) s. rozkład; plan ;założenie; układ

lay out ('lej.aut) v. układać; projektowac; powalic; (slang): zabić; wydatkowac; wyłożyc

lay up ('lejap) v. zbierać; gromadzic; przechowywać

layer ('lejer) s. warstwa; odkład; kura niosąca; zakładająca się;pokład

layman ('lejmen) s. człowiek świecki; laik

lazy ('lejzy) adj. leniwy; prozniaczy;ociężały

lead (led) s. ołow; v. pokrywać ołowiem; obciażać ołowiem

lead; led; led (li:d; led;led)

lead (li:d) v. prowadzic; kierowac; dowodzic; naprowadzac; nasunąc; namówic; dyrygowac; przewodzic; s. kierownictwo; przewodnictwo; przewaga; prym; wskazówka ;przykład;powodzenie

leaden ('ledn) adj. ołowiany; ciężki;ociężały;ponury;szary

leader ('li:der) s. przywódca; lider; przewodnik; prowadzący

leading ('li:dyŋg) adj. kierowniczy; naczelny; główny; s. kierownictwo; prowadzenie; przewodnictwo;przywództwo

leaf (li:f) s. liść; kartka; pl. leaves (li:wz)

leaflet (li:flyt) s. listek; ulotka (często złożona)

league (li:g) s. liga; związek; mila; v. łączyć (się) w ligę

leak (li:k) s. dziura; otwór; przeciekanie; v. cieknąć; przeciekać; wyciekać (sekrety);wysączać; zaciekać

leakage (li:kydż) s. przeciekanie (sekretów); wyciekanie (pieniędzy); rozproszenie

leaky ('li:ky) adj. dziurawy; nieszczelny; cieknący; niedyskretny;nie dochowujący sekretu

lean; leant; leant (li:n; lent; lent)

lean (li:n) v. nachylać (się); pochylać (się); opierać(się) (o coś); adj. chudy; s. chude mięso;nachylenie;skłonność

leant (lent) v. zob. lean

leap; leapt; leapt (li:p; lept; lept)

leap (li:p) v. skakać; przeskoczyć; s. skok; podskok

leapt (lept) zob . leap

leap-year ('li:pye:r) s. rok przestępny

learn; learnt; learnt (le:rn; le:rnt; le:rnt)

learn (le:rn) v. uczyć się; dowiadywać się;zapamiętać

learned ('le:rnyd) adj. uczony

learner ('le:rner) s. uczący się; uczeń; uczennica .

learning ('le:rnyŋg) s. nauka; wiedza; erudycja;umiejętności

learnt (le:rnt) v. zob. learn

lease (li:s) s. dzierżawa; v. dzierżawić;wydzierżawić

leash (li:sh) s. smycz

least (li:st) adj. najmniejszy adv. najmniej; w najmniejszym stopniu; s. najmniejsza rzecz; drobnostka najmniej ważna

leather ('ledżer)s. skóra; adj. skórzany; v. pokrywać skórą; oprawiać w skórę;sprać(rzemieniem)

leave; left; left (li:w; left; left)

leave (li:w) v. zostawiać; opuszczać; odchodzić; odjeżdżać; pozostawiać; s. pożegnanie; urlop; pozwolenie

leaven (lewn) s. drożdże

leaves (li:wz) pl. liście; zob. leaf

lecture ('lekczer) s. wykład; nagana; v. wykładać; udzielać nagany;przemawiać do sumienia

lecturer ('lekczerer) s. wykładowca(w uczelni,klasie etc.)

led (led) zob. lead

ledge (ledż) s. występ; stopień; półka; gzyms; listwa; rafa

lee (li:) s. strona zawietrzna; osłona;adj.zawietrzny;osłonięty

leech (li:cz) s. pijawka

leek (li:k) s. por

leer (lier) s. spojrzenie z ukosa; v. łypać okiem znacząco (chytrze,złośliwie,pożądliwie)

left (left) adj. lewy; adv. na lewo; s. lewa strona; zob. leave

left-hand ('left,haend) s. lewa ręka;adj.lewoskrętny;lewostronny

left-handed ('left'haendyd) s. mańkut; adj. leworęki; niezgrabny;wątpliwy;nieszczery

left side ('left,sajd) s. lewa strona (drogi,samochodu etc.)

leg (leg) s. noga; nóżka; podpórka; odcinek;kończyna;udziec

legacy (legesy) s. spadek; spuścizna;dziedzictwo;zapis

legal ('li:gel) adj. prawny; prawniczy ;ustawowy;legalny

legation (li'gejszyn) s. poselstwo (włącznie z posłem)

legend ('ledżend) s. legenda

legendary ('ledżendery) adj. legendarny ;tradycyjny

legible ('ledżebl) adj. czytelny ;łatwo czytelny

legion ('li:dżen) s. legion; legia ;wojsko;wielka ilość; mnóstwo;tłumy;mnogość

legislation (,ledżys'lejszyn)
s. prawodawstwo; ustawodawstwo
legislative ('ledżysletyw) adj.
prawodawczy; ustawodawczy
legislator ('ledżyslator) s.
prawodawca; poseł do parlamen-
tu (sejmu,senatu etc.)
legitimate (ly'dżytymyt) adj.
ślubny; prawowity; słuszny;
uzasadniony;logiczny;rozsadny
leg-pull ('legpu:l) s. kawał;
żart; sztuczka;naciąganie
leisure ('li:żer) s. wolny czas;
swoboda od zajęc;wolne chwile
leisurely ('li:żerly) adv. swobodnie; bez pospiechu; adj.
mający czas; spokojny; robiony
w wolnym czasie
lemon ('lemen) s. cytryna;
tandeta;adj.cytrynowy;z cytryn
lemonade ('lemenejd) s. lemo-
niada(z soku cytrynowego etc.)
lend; lent; lent (lend; lent;
lent)
lend (lend) v. pożyczać; użyczać; udzielać
length (lenks) s. długość
lengthen ('lenksen) v. przedłużać; wydłużać(się);podłużać
lengthwise ('lensłajz) adv. adj.
wzdłuż; na długość
lenient ('li:njent) adj. wyrozumiały; łagodny
lens (lenz) s. soczewka; objektyw ;lupa
lent (lent) s. post; zob. lend
leopard ('leperd) s. lampart
leper ('leper) s. trędowaty;
trędowata
leprosy ('lepresy) s. trąd
less (les) adj. mniejszy; adv.
mniej; s. cos mniejszego;
prep. bez;nie tak dużo(wiele)
lessen (lesn) v, zmniejszać(się)
maleć; pomniejszać
lesser ('leser) adj. mniejszy
lesson (lesn) s. lekcja; nauczka;urywek z Biblji;wykład
lest (lest) conj. ażeby nie; że
let; let; let (let;let;let)
let (let) v. zostawić; wynajmować; dawać; puszczać ; pozwalać

let alone ('let,e'loun) s. zostawić w spokoju; dać spokój
let down ('let,dałn) v. robić
zawód; spuszczać; opuszczać;
upokorzyć;odmawiac pomocy
let go ('let,gou) v, wypuszczać;
zwalniać; pozwolić odejść
let know ('let,nou) v. zawiadomić; donieść;powiadomić
let up ('let,ap) v. zelżec;
złagodnieć; s. zelżenie
lethal ('li:sel) adj. smiertelny; zgubny;śmiercionosny
letter ('leter) s. litera; list;
czcionka; v. drukować; oznaczać literami:kaligrafować
letter-box ('leter,boks) s.
skrzynka pocztowa
letter-carrier ('leter'kaerjer)
s. listonosz
lettuce ('letys) s. sałata (gło-
wiasta);liście sałaty
leukemia (lju'ki:mje) s. białaczka;leukemia
level ('lewl) s. poziom; płaszczyzna; równina; poziomnica;
adj. poziomy; adv. poziomo;
równo; v. zrównywać; celować
level crossing ('lewl'krosypg)
s. skrzyżowanie drog (koli-
zyjne)w jednej płaszczyźnie
lever ('li:wer) s. dźwignia;
lewar; v. podważać; podnosić
dźwigiem(lewarem)
levity ('lewyty) s. lekkomyślnosc
levy ('lewy) v. pobierać; nakładać (podatek); s. pobór
lewd (lu:d) adj. zmysłowy; lubieżny;pożądliwy;sprosny
liability (,laje'bylyty) s.
odpowiedzialność; obowiązek;
obciążenie; zadłużenie;ryzyko
liable ('lajebl) adj. odpowiedzialny; podlegający; podatny;
skłonny;narażony;mający widoki
liable to ('lajebl,tu) adj.
skłonny do...;adv.łatwo(zgnije),
liaison (ly'ejzo:n) s. łącznosc;
związek; romans (nielegalny)
liar ('lajer) s. kłamca; łgarz
libation(laj-bej'szyn)s.libacja

libel ('lajbel) s. paszkwil;
oszczerstwo; zniesławienie
(publiczne w piśmie; filmie
etc.);v.zniesławiać
liberal ('lyberel) s. liberał;a.
liberalny; hojny;tolerancyjny
liberate ('lyberejt) v. uwalniać; zwalniać;wyzwalać
liberation ('lyberejszyn) s.
uwolnienie; oswobodzenie
liberator ('lyberejter) s.
oswobodziciel;wyzwoliciel
liberty ('lyberty) s. wolność;
swoboda;nadużywanie wolności
librarian (laj'breerjen) s.
bibliotekarz
library ('lajbrery) s. biblioteka; księgozbiór
lice (lajs) pl. wszy; zob.
louse
license(ce) ('lajsens) s. licencja; pozwolenie; upoważnienie; swoboda; rozpusta;
v. upoważniać; udzielać poz-
wolenia; nadużywać wolności
licensee (,lajsen'si:) s. posiadacz zezwolenia; koncesjo-
nariusz;właściciel licencji
lichen ('lajken) s. liszaj
lick (lyk) s. liźnięcie; odrobina; cios; raz; wybuch;
energia; v. lizać; polizać;
wylizać; bić; smarować
licking ('lykyŋg)s. (slang):
bicie; pobicie; młocka
lid (lyd) s. wieko; powieka;
pokrywa ;nakrywka;przykrywka
lie !. lay ; lain (laj; lej;
lejn)
lie (laj) v. leżeć; s. układ;
położenie;konfiguracja;legowisko
lie 2. lied; lied (laj; lajd;
lajd)
lie (laj) v. kłamać; s. kłamstwo;łgarstwo;fałsz
lie down('laj,dałn) v. kłaść
się;położyć się;nie reagować
lie in ('laj,yn) v. być w poło-
gu; leżeć w (łóżku)
lie over ('laj,ouwer) v. być
odroczonym; zostać przez noc
lieutenant (lef'tenant; lu:te-
nant) s. porucznik

life (lajf) s. życie; życiorys;
zob. pl. lives
life assurance ('lajfe'szuerens)
s. ubezpieczenie na życie
life belt ('lajfbelt) s. pas
ratunkowy
lifeboat ('lajfbout) s. łódź
ratunkowa
lifeguard ('lajfga:rd) s. ratownik
life insurance ('lajf,yn'szuerens) s. ubezpieczenie na życie
life jacket ('lajfdżaekyt) s.
kurta ratownicza;kamizelka ratunkowa
lifeless ('lajflys) adj. bez
życia; martwy;zamarły;wymarły
lifelike ('lajflajk) adj. jak
żywy(człowiek,osoba,stworzenie)
life sentence ('lajf,sentens)
s. kara dożywocia(wyrok)
life-style ('lajfstajl) s. styl
życia; modła życia;sposób życia
lifetime ('lajf,tajm) s. życie; całe życie
lift (lyft) s. dźwig; winda;
przewóz; podniesienie; wzniesienie; v. podnieść; dźwignąć;
podnosić się; kraść; spłacić
(np. dom); kopnąć;buchnąć;awanso-
wać
lift-off ('lyft,of) s. start
lotu (np. rakiety)
ligament ('lygement) s. ścięgno
ligature ('lygeczuer) s. przywiązanie; ligatura; podwiąza-
nie;bandaż;nić chirurgiczna
light; lit; lit (lajt; lyt;lyt)
light (lajt) s. światło; oświetlenie; ogień; adj. świetny; jasny; łatwy; lekki; błahy; słaby; beztroski; niefrasobliwy; lekkomyślny; v.świe-
cić; oświecać; zapalać; ujaw-
nić; poświęcić; rozjaśnić;
przyświecić; zsiadać; wsiadać;
wpaść; wyjechać; adv. lekko
light up ('lajtap) v. zaświecić; rozjaśnić; oświecić
lighten ('lajtn) v. ulżyć; zel-
żyć; oświecać; rozjaśnić się;
błysnąć; błyskać się
lighter ('lajter) s. zapalniczka; latarnik ;lampiarz

lighthouse ('lajthaus) s. latarnia morska

lighting ('lajtyŋg) s. oświetlenie; oswietlanie

light-minded ('lajt'majndyd) adj. lekkomyślny;roztargniony

lightness ('lajtnys) s. jasnosc; lekkosc; łagodnosc; łatwosc; lekkomyślnosc

lightning ('lajtnyŋg)s. błyskawica; piorun;a.błyskawiczny

lightning rod ('lajtnyŋg,rod) s. piorunochron;odgromnik

lightweight ('lajt-łejt) s. waga lekka; adj. lekkiej wagi; błachy(127 do 135 funtowy boks)

light-year ('lajt,je:r) s. rok swietlny(ok.6x10¹²mil=10x10¹²km.)

lignite ('lygnajt) s. węgiel brunatny; lignit

like (lajk) v. lubiec; upodobac sobie; (chciec); miec zamiłowanie, ochotę; adj. podobny; analogiczny; typowy; adv. podobnie; w ten sam sposob; s. drugi taki sam; rzecz podobna; conj. jak; tak jak;po; w ten sposob; niby to;niczym

like that ('lajk'dzaet) adv. tak; w ten sposob;własnie tak

likelihood ('lajklyhud) s. prawdopodobieństwo

likely ('lajkly) adj. możliwy; prawdopodobny; odpowiedni; nadający się; obiecujący; adv. pewnie; prawdopodobnie

likeness ('lajknys) s. podobieństwo; podobizna; pozory

likewise ('lajkłajz) adv. także; rowniez; podobno; podobnie;w ten sam sposob;tez

liking ('lajkyŋg) s. sympatia; upodobanie; zamiłowanie

lilac ('lajlek) s. bez; adj. lila; liljowy;blado siny

lily ('lyly) s. lilja;a.jak lilia

lily of the valley ('lyly,ow' 'dy,waely) s. konwalia

limb (lym) s. kończyna; konar; brzeg; krawędz;ramie;noga;skrzydło

lime 1. (lajm) s. wapno; v. wapnic; adj. wapienny

lime 2. (lajm) s. lipa; cytrus (dzika cytryna);a.cytrusowy

limelight ('lajmlajt) s. swiatło wapienne; swiatło reflektorow; widok publiczny

limestone ('lajmstoun) s. wapień; a. z wapienia

limey ('lajmy) s. (slang):Brytyjczyk (wulg.) zwłaszcza marynarz

limit ('lymyt) s. granica; kres; v. ograniczac; ustalac granic

limitation (,lymy'tejszyn) s. ograniczenie; zastrzeżenie; prekluzja;przedawnienie

limited liability ('lymytyd,labje'bylyty)s. ograniczona odpowiedzialnosc

limp (lymp) adj. wiotki; bez sił; osłabiony; v. kulec; chromac

line (lajn) s. linia; kreska; bruzda; lina; sznur; przewod; granica; zajęcie; zainteresowania; szereg; rząd; linka; v. liniowac; wyscielac; podbic podszewką;służyc za podszewke; lineup ('lajnap) s. uszeregowanie; rząd; ustawianie w rząd

line up ('lajnap) v. ustawic w rząd; uszeregowac

lineaments ('lynjements) pl. rysy twarzy;cechy szczególne

linear ('lynjer) adj. liniowy; linijny; wąski i długi

linen ('lynyn) s. płotno; bielizna; adj. lniany; płócienny

linen closet ('lynen'klozyt) s. schowek na bieliznę

liner ('lajner) s. samolot pasażerski; statek pasażerski

linger ('lyŋger) v. ociągac się; zwlekac; pozostawac w tyle; marudzic; tkwic; wlec życie

lingerie ('le:nżeri) s. damska bielizna ;damskie artykuły bielizniane

lining ('lajnyŋg) s. podszewka; okładzina; zawartosc

link (lyŋk) s. ogniwo; więz; spinka; 20,1 cm; v. połączyc; zczepiac; związac; sprzęgac; links (lyŋks) pl. wydmy; boisko golfowe;wydmy piaszczyste

lion (lajon) s. lew ;a.lwi;lwie

lioness (lajonys) s. lwica

lip (lyp) s. warga; brzeg; ostrze; bezczelne gadanie; v. dotykać wargami; mruczeć

lipstick ('lypstyk) s. kredka do warg; pomadka do ust

liquid ('lykłyd) s. płyn; adj. płynny;niestały;nie ustalony

liquor ('lyker) s. napój alkoholowy; sok; odwar;bulion

liquorice ('lykorys) s. lukrecja

lisp (lysp) v. seplenić; seplenić jak niemowle;s.seplenienie

list (lyst) s. lista; spis; listwa; krawędz; v. wciągać na listę; obramowywać; przechylać (się); pochylać (się); s. pochylenie; przechył

listen ('lysen) v. słuchać; usłuchać;przysłuchiwać się

listen in ('lysen,yn) v. podsłuchiwać;posłuchać(radia etc)

listen to ('lysen,tu) v. usłuchać kogos (czyjejs rady)

listener ('lysener) s. słuchacz

listless ('lystlys) adj. apatyczny; obojętny; zobojętniały;bierny(z powodu choroby)

lit (lyt) zob. light

liter ('li:ter) s. litr

literal ('lyterel) adj. literalny; dosłowny; prozaiczny; literowy;rzeczowy(umysł etc.)

literary ('lyterery) adj. literacki;obeznany w literaturze

literature ('lytereczer) s. literatura; piśmiennictwo

lithe (lajs) adj. giętki; gibki; łatwo gnący się

litter ('lyter) s. śmieci; podściółka ; barłog; v. śmiecić; podścielać; urodzić szczeniaki;porozrzucać niechlujnie

litter bin ('lyter,byn) s. śmietnik ;kosz na śmiecie

little ('lytl) adj. mały; niski; nieduży; adv. mało; niewiele

little bit ('lytl,byt) adv. trochę ;bardzo mało;troszeczkę

little one ('lytl,łan) s. dziecko ;dziecina;dzieciatko

little by little ('lytl,bay' 'lytl) exp. po trochu; stopniowo;po mału;po małutku

live (lyw) v. życ; mieszkać; przeżywać; przetrwać; ocalić

live (lajw) adj. żywy; żyjący; ruchliwy;energiczny;nieeksplodowany

live on ('lyw,on) v. życ z czegos; życ czyms

live wire ('lajw'łajer) s. przewód pod napięciem

livelihood ('lajwly,hud) s. utrzymanie;środki do życia

lively ('lajwly) adj. żywy; wesoły; ożywiony; żwawy; gorący;rzeski;pełen życia;jaskrawy

liver ('lywer) s. wątroba; wątróbka ;a.wątroby

livery ('lywery) adj. wątrobiany; chory na wątrobę; opryskliwy; s. liberia; utrzymanie konia; wynajem (wozów)

lives (lajws) pl. żywotny; zob. life

livestock ('lajwstok) s. żywy inwentarz ;zwierzęta domowe

livid ('lywyd) adj. siny; wściekły ;posiniaczony

living ('lywyng) s. życie; utrzymanie; tryb życia

living room ('lywyn,ru:m) s. salon; bawialnia; pokój

lizard ('lyzerd) s. jaszczurka

load (loud) s. ładunek; waga; ciężar; obciążenie; v. ładować; załadować; naładować; obciążać; nasycać; fałszować

load up ('loud,ap) v. brać ładunek; opychać się

loader ('louder) s. ładowniczy; maszyna do ładowania

loading ('loudyng) s. ładunek; ładowanie ;a.ładunkowy(pomost)

loaded words ('loudyd,łe:rds) s. słowa tendencyjne (niesprawiedliwe)(uwłaszczające)

loaf (louf) s. bochenek; głowa (cukru); pl. loaves (louvz) v. wałęsać się;marnować czas

loafer ('loufer) s. włóczega; łazik; próżniak ;nierób;wałkoń; wygodny bucik sportowy

loam (loum) s. gleba ilasta;
ił ;zaprawa gliniana(murarska)
loan (loun) s. pożyczka;
v. pożyczać ; pożyczać
loath (louþ) adj. niechętny
loathe (louþ) v. nienawidzieć;
czuć wstręt
loathsome ('louþsem) adj.
wstrętny; obrzydliwy; ohydny
loaves (louwz) zob. loaf
lobby ('loby) s. przedpokój;
kuluar; v. urabiac senatora
lub posła na czyjąś korzyść
(przekupywać)
lobbyist('lobyst) s. inter-
wencjonalista kuluarowy (często oficjalnie rejestrowany
w USA); lobbyista
lobe (loub) s. płat (np. płucny)
lobster ('lobster) s. homar
local ('loukel) adj. lokalny;
miejscowy;s.oddział związku zawo-
locality (lou'kaelyty) s.okolica;
miejscowość; strefa;rejon
localize ('loukelajz) v. umiejscowić; lokalizować
locate ('loukejt) v. umieścić;
znaleźć; osiedlić się
located ('loukejtyd) adj. zamieszkały; umieszczony;znaleziony
location ('loukejszyn) s. położenie; ulokowanie; miejsce
zamieszkania;miejsce zaznaczone
loch (lok) s. jezioro; wąska
zatoka (zwłaszcza w Szkocji)
lock (lok) s. zamek; zamknięcie;
śluza; lok; v. zamykać (na
klucz);przechodzić śluzę
lock in ('lokyn) v. zamykać
(wewnątrz); otaczać (górami etc.)
locker ('loker) s. szafka; kabina; skrzynia; schowek
lock out ('lokaut) v. wykluczać;
s. lokaut (lockout)
locksmith ('loksmyþ) s. ślusarz
locomotive ('louke,moutyw) s.
lokomotywa; adj. ruchomy
locust ('loukest) s. szarańcza;
akacja
lodge ('lodż) s. chata; loża;
kryjówka; domek myśliwski; nora
v. przenocować; zdeponować;
umieszczać; wnosić (skargę)etc.

lodger ('lodżer) s. lokator
lodging ('lodżyng) s. mieszkanie (tymczasowe,wynajęte etc.)
loft (loft) s. strych; poddasze;chór;v.podbić piłkę golfową
lofty ('lofty) adj. wzniosły;
wyniosły; wysoki;dumny;hardy
log (log) s. kłoda; kloc; log;
dziennik operacyjny (statku;
szybu) v. wycinać drzewa;
ciąć na kłody; wciągać do
dziennika okrętowego etc.
logbook ('logbuk) s. dziennik
pokładowy;książka raportowa
log cabin ('log,kaebyn) s. chata (z belek) (z okrąglaków)
logic ('lodżyk) s. logika
logical ('lodżykel) adj. logiczny;rozumujący poprawnie
loin (loin) s. lędźwie; polędwica; comber;krzyże;biodra
loiter (lojter) v. marudzić;
wałęsać się; guzdrać; mitrężyć;kręcić się podejrzanie
lol (lol) v. rozwalać się;
opierać się niedbale; wywieszać
(język psa); zwisać
loneliness ('lounlynys) s. samotność;osamotnienie;odludność
lonely ('lounly) adj. samotny
lonesome ('lounsom) adj.
osamotniony; odludny
long (long) adj. długi; długo-
trwały; v. tęsknić; pragnąć
(czegoś); adv. długo; dawno
long ago (,long'egou) adv.
dawno temu;adj.dawno miniony
long before ('long,befor) adv,
dużo wcześniej;znacznie wcześniej
long since ('long,syns) adv.
dawno temu ; od dawna
long distance call ('long'dystans,kol) s. telefon między-
miastowy;rozmowa międzymiastowa
longing ('longyng) s. pragnienie;
tęsknota;ochota;adj.tęskny
long jump ('long,dżamp) s.
skok w dal
longshoreman . ('long,szo:rmen)
s. doker; robotnik portowy
long-sighted ('lon'sajtyd) adj.
dalekowzroczny; przewidujący
long spun ('lon'span)a.rozwlekły

long-term ('loŋ'term) adj.
długoterminowy;długofalowy
long-winded ('lon'łyndyd)
adj. gadatliwy; długo mówiący;(koń) ze zdrowymi płucami
look (luk) s. spojrzenie; wygląd; v. patrzec; wyglądać
look after ('luk,a:fter) v. doglądać; opiekować się(kimś)
look at ('luk,et) v. patrzec
na (kogoś, na coś)
look for ('luk,fo:r)v. szukać
look forwards ('luk fo:rłerds)
v. oczekiwać; cieszyć się
look into ('luk,yntu) v. badać; wglądać
look on ('luk,on) v. przypatrywać się;przyglądać się;kibicować
look out ('luk,aut) v. być
na baczności;wyjrzeć;wyszukać
look over ('luk,ouwer) v.
przeglądać;przejrzeć
look around ('luk,e'raund) v.
rozglądać się;poszukiwać wzro- kiem
look up ('luk,ap) v. szukać;
odwiedzać; patrzec w górę
looker-on('luker'on) s. widz;
przygladający się ;kibic
looking-glass ('lukyŋglass) s.
lustro; zwierciadło
lookout ('luk,aut) s. widok;
uwaga; czaty;czujność
look out ('luk,aut) v. wyjrzeć;
uważać; wyszukać;być w pogotowiu
loom (lu:m) s. krosna; warsztat
tkacki; v. wynurzać się; zagrażać;grozić;zamajaczyć
loop (lu:p) s. pętla; wezeł;
supeł; v. robic pętlę, kokardę;
podwiązywać;splatać (się)
loophole ('lu:p,houl)s. strzelnica; droga ucieczki (od podatków);wykręt; luka;furtka
loose (lu:s) adj. luzny; roz-
luzniony; obluzniony; wolny;
na wolności; rzadki; sypki;
rozwiązły; s. upust; v. luzować; obluzniać; zwalniać
loosen ('lu:sn) v. rozluzniać
(się); obluzniać (się); roz-
walniac;leczyć zatwardzenie
loot (lu:t) s. łupy; (nadużycia
urzędnika);v.plądrować;szabrować

lop (lop) v. obcinac; ciąć; zwisać; plątać się; wałęsac się;
s. ścięcie; obcięte (gałęzie)
lop off ('lop,of) v. obciąć
lope (loup) v. biec susami;
pędzic krotkim galopem; s.
krotki galop; sus
lord (lo:rd) s. pan; władca;
magnat; Bog; v. grac pana;
nadawać tytuł lorda
lorry ('lory) s. ciężarówka;
platforma; lora;przyczepa
lose; lost; lost (lu:z; lost;
lost)
lose (lu:z) v. stracić; schud-
nąć; zgubic; zabładzic; nie-
dosłyszec; spoznic się; prze-
grac; byc pokonanym,pozbawionym
loss (los) s. strata; utrata;
zguba; ubytek;szkoda;kłopot
lost (lost) adj. stracony; zgu-
biony; zob. lose
lot (lot) s. doba; las; losowanie; udział; działka; par-
cela; grupa; zespoł; partia;
sporo; wiele; v. parcelować;
dzielic; losowac;adv.bardzo du- żo
loth (louθ) adj. niechętny;
wstrętny;z ciężkim sercem
lotion ('louszyn) s. płyn
(leczniczy)
lottery ('lotery) s. loteria
lotto ('lotou) s. loteryjka
loud (laud) adj. głosny; smrodliwy; krzykliwy; adv. na cały
głos; głosno;w głosny sposob
loudspeaker ('laud'spi:ker) s.
głośnik; megafon
lounge (laundż) v. próżnować;
wylegiwac; łazić; s. lokal;
salonik; hall; włóczega;
wolny krok;wygodna kanapa
louse (laus) s. wesz; pl. lice
lousy ('lauzy) adj. zawszony;
wstrętny;dobrze zaopatrzony (sl.)
lout ('laut) s. gbur; prostak
love (law) s. kochanie; miłość;
lubienie; ukochana; ukochanie;
gra na zero; v. kochac; lubić;
byc przywiązanym ;pieścić;umizgac się
love-affair ('lawfeer) s. romans; przygoda miłosna;osobiste
troski w sprawach miłosnych

loveless ('lawlys) adj. nieko-
chany; nie kochający; bez
miłości;nie kochany przez nikogo
lovely ('lawly) adj. śliczny;
uroczy; rozkoszny;przyjemny(bar-
lovemaking ('law,mẹjkyṇg) s.
zaloty; umizgi; społkowanie
lover ('lawer) s. kochanek;
miłośnik; amator czegoś
loving ('lavyṇg) adj. kochający;
s. kochanie; miłość
low (lou) s. ryk (bydła); ryczec; adj. niski; niewysoki;
słaby; przygnebiony; cichy;
podły; mały; adv. nisko; nie-
wysoko; słabo; skromnie; cicho; szeptem; marnie; podle
lower ('louer) adj. niższy;
dolny; młodszy; adv. niżej;
v. obniżać; zniżać; spuszczać; poniżyć; sciszyć;
zmniejszyć; osłabiać; opadać;
spadać;ryczeć(jak bydło)
low-grade ('lougrejd) adj.
niskoprocentowy; niskiej
jakości;kiepski;tandetny
lowland ('loulend) pl. nizina;
adj. nizinny
lowly ('louly) adj. skromny;
adv. skromnie;bez pretensji
low-necked('lou'nekyd) adj.
dekoltowany (głęboko)
low-pressure ('lou'preszer) s.
niskie cisnienie; adj. nisko-
prężny;pod niskim cisnieniem
low tide ('lou'tajd) s. odpływ
(morza)
loyal(lojel) adj. lojalny;
wierny(krajowi,ideałom etc.)
loyalty ('lojelty) s. lojalność;
wierność
lozenge ('lozyndż) s. romb;
tabletka; pastylka
lubber ('laber) s. niezdara;
niedołęga;niezdarny marynarz
lubricant ('lu:brykent) s. smar;
adj. smarujący; smarowniczy
lubricate ('lu:brykejt) v. sma-
rowac; oliwic;robić śliskim
lubrication ('lu:brykejszyn) s.
smarowanie; oliwienie
ubricity(lu:'brysyty)s.smarowność;

lucid ('lu:syd) adj. świecacy;
jasny; błyszczacy; klarowny;
przezroczysty; czysty;oczywisty
luck (lak) s. los; traf; szczęs-
cie; szczęśliwy traf;powodzenie
luckily ('lakyly) adv. na
szczęście; szczęśliwie
luckless ('laklyś) adj. niefortunny; nieszczęśliwy
lucky ('laky) adj. szczęśliwy
lucky fellow ('laky'felou) s.
szczęściarz
ludicrous ('lu:dykres) adj.
śmieszny; nonsensowny; absurdalny;komicznie głupi
lug (lag) v. wlec; pociągać;
przytłaczać; s. wleczenie;
szarpanie; ucho; uchwyt
luggage ('lagydż) s. bagaż; walizki
luggage carrier ('lagydż'kaerjer)
s. bagażowy
luggage rack ('lagydż'raek) s.
półka na walizki
luggage slip ('lagydż'slyp) s.
kwit bagażowy
luggage van ('lagydż'waen) s.
wóz bagażowy
lukewarm ('lu:kło:rm) adj. ciepławy; letni; obojętny; oziębł-
ły; niezainteresowany
lull(lal) v. ukołysać; uciszyć;
usmierzyć; s. cisza; zastój
lullaby ('lalebaj) s. kołysanka
lumbago (lam'bejgou) s. lumbago;
ischias
lumbar ('lamber) adj. lędźwiowy
lumber ('lamber) s. budulec
(drewniany); rupiecie; graty;
v. zwalać; wycinać; ciężko
stąpać; poruszać się ociężale
lumberjack ('lamber'dżaek) s.
drwal(przygotowujący do tartaku)
lumber mill ('lambermyl) s.
tartak
luminous ('lu:mynes) adj.
świetlny; jasny; adj. świecą-
cy; wyjaśniający;zrozumiały
lump (lamp) s. bryła; gruda; masa; hurt; guz; niezdara; niedołęga; v. zwalać; gromadzic;
lubieżność;dojść do ładu;zcierpieć;znosić

lump of('lamp,ow) s. kawałek
lump sugar ('lamp,szu:ger) s.
gruda cukru
lump sum ('lamp,sam) s. suma
całościowa
lunar ('lu:nar) adj. księżyco-
wy;mierzony ruchem księżyca
lunar module ('lu:nar,modjul)
s. kapsula do lądowania na
Księżycu
lunatic ('lu:netyk) s. wariat
(chory umysłowo); adj. obłąkany; zwariowany; lunatyk
lunch (lancz) s. obiad (popołudniowy); v. jeść obiad;
gościć obiadem
lunch-hour ('lancz'auer) s.
przerwa obiadowa (w południe)
lung (lang) s. płuco
lunge (landż) s. wypad;
pchnięcie; v. pchnąć; zrobić
wypad;spowodować wypad
lurch (le:rcz) v. opuszczać
w potrzebie; słaniać się na
nogach; przechylać się; s.
nagłe przechylenie się (na
bok);trudna sytuacja
lure (ljuer) s. przynęta; wabik; urok; powab; v. kusić;
nęcić; wabić;przywabiać
lurk (le:rk) v. czaić się;
s. czaty ; ukrycie
luscious ('laszes) adj. sło-
dziutki; ckliwy ;soczysty
lush (lasz) adj. bujny; soczysty;miękki i pełen soku
lust (last) s. żądza; lubieżność; namiętność; pożądli-
wość; v. pożądać(namiętnie)
luster ('laster) s. blask; połysk; świecznik; świetność;
v. glansować; wyswiecać
lusty ('lasty) adj. krzepki;
pełen wigoru (młodzieńczego)
lute (lu:t) s. lutnia; glina;
v. lepić gliną;kitować
luxate ('laksejt) v. zwichnąć
(np. nogę)(staw)
luxation (lak'sejszyn) s.
zwichnięcie (nogi w kostce;
stawu biodrowego etc.)

luxurious (lag'żjuerjes) adj.
zbytkowny; luksusowy;zmysłowy
luxury ('lakszery) s. zbytek;
luksus;rozkosz;a.od zbytku
lying ('lajyng) adj. kłamliwy;
zob. lie; s. kłamstwo; adj.le-
żący; zob. lie; s. leżenie;
posłanie;pozycja leżąca
lying-in (,lajyng'yn) adj. położniczy; połogowy; s. połóg
lymph (lymf) s, limfa; szczepionka; wysięk; serum, (czy-
sta woda)
lynch (lyncz) v. zlinczować;s.
linczowanie;zabijanie bez wyro-ku
lynx (lynks) s. ryś
lyre ('lajer) s. lira
lyric ('lirik) adj. liryczny;
s. słowa piesni; poemat liryczny;tekst piosenki
lysol ('lajsol) s. lizol
m (em) trzynasta litera alfabetu
angielskiego;cyfra rzymska:1000
ma'am (maem) s. pani (madam)
mac (maek) s.nieprzemakalny materiał (płaszcz) mackintosh
machine (me'szi:n) s. maszyna;
machina (polityczna) v. obrabiać maszynowo;adj.maszynowy
machine-made (me'szi:nmejd) adj.
maszynowy; maszynowo robiony
machine-gun (me'szi:ngan) s.
karabin maszynowy
machinery (me'szi:nery) s, maszyneria;maszyneria;aparat
machinist (me'szi:nyst) s, maszynista (np. tokarz)(szwaczka)
macho (ma:czou) s. bardzo męski
mężczyzna (slang)
mack (maek) s. zob. mac
mackintosh ('maekyntosz) s.
zob. mac
mad (maed) adj. obłąkany; szalony; zły; wściekły; v. doprowadzać do obłędu; być obłąkanym
madam ('maedem) s. pani; (panienka)(w zwrocie:proszę pani)
madcap ('maedkaep) s. narwaniec
madden ('maedn) v. rozwścieczać;
szaleć; wściekać sie;wariować
made (mejd) v. zrobiony; zob.
make (wykombinowany;fabryczny..)

madman ('maedmen) s. wariat;
szaleniec;furiat;obłąkaniec
madness ('maednys) s. obłęd;
obłąkanie; furia; wściekłość;
wścieklizna;szał;szaleństwo
magazine (maege'zi:n) s. czasopismo; magazynek (na kule);
skład broni dla wojska
maggot ('maeget) s. dziwactwo;
chimera; larwa
magic ('maedżyk) s. magia; adj.
magiczny; działający jak magia
magician (me'dżyszyn) s. czarodziej; magik
magistrate ('maedżystrejt) s.
sądownik; stróż prawa
magnanimous (maeg'neanymes)
adj. wielkoduszny
magnet ('maegnyt) s. magnes
magnetic (maeg'netyk) adj.
magnetyczny; przyciągający
magnificence (maeg'nyfysns) s.
wspaniałość; świetność;
okazałość
magnificent (maeg'nyfysnt)adj.
wspaniały; okazały
magnify ('maegnyfaj) v. powiększać; potęgować; wyolbrzymiać
magpie ('maegpaj) s. sroka;
gaduła
maid (mejd) s. dziewczyna;
dziewka; panna ;służąca
maiden ('mejden) s. dziewczyna;
panna; adj. panieński; dzie-
wiczy; świeży; nowy
maidenly ('mejdenly) adj.
dziewczęcy; panieński
maiden name ('mejden,nejm) s.
nazwisko panieńskie
mail (mejl) s. poczta; kolczu-
ga; v. wysyłać pocztą
mailbag ('mejl,baeg) s. worek
pocztowy
mailbox ('mejl,boks) s, skrzynka pocztowa
mailman (mejlmen) s. listonosz
mail-order house ('mejlorder,
,haus) s. firma sprzedająca
przez poczte (z katalogu)
maim (mejm) v. okaleczyć
main (mejn) s. główny (przewód)
adj. głowny; najważniejszy

mainland ('mejnlaend) s. konty-
nent(w odróżnieniu od bliskich
wysp)
mainly('mejnly) adv. głównie;
przeważnie;po większej części
main. road('mejnroud) s. główna
droga;główna szosa
main.street ('mejn.stri:t) s.
głowna ulica
maintain (men'tejn) v. utrzymywać (w dobrym stanie); trzymać (pozycję); podtrzymywać;
zachowywać; twierdzić; mieć
na utrzymaniu;bronić;pomgać
maintenance ('mejntenens) s.
utrzymanie; utrzymywanie; poparcie; wyżywienie
maize (mejz) s. kukurydza
majestic (medżestyk) adj. majestatyczny
majesty ('maedżysty) s. majestat;godność;wielkość
major ('mejdżer) s. major; pełnoletni; przedmiot kierunkowy
specjalizacji; adj. większy;
głowny; ważniejszy; pełnoletni;
starszy;v.specjalizować się w stu-
diach
majorette ('mejdżeret) s. tancerka na defiladach i w przer-
wach meczów w USA
majority (me'dżoryty) s.
większość;a. wiekszościowy
major road ('mejdżer,roud) s.
droga główna;ważniejsza droga
make; made; made (mejk; mejd;
mejd)
make (mejk) v. robić; tworzyć;
sporządzać;powodować; wynosić;
doprowadzać; ustanawiać; stać
się; postanowić etc.
make-believe ('mejk,by'li:w) s.
udawanie; pozory
make off ('mejkof) v. uciec;
uciekać .gwiznąc coś komus
make up ('mejkap) v. uzupełnić;
wynagrodzić; sporządzić; zmonto-
wać; ucharakteryzować
makeup ('mejkap) s. makijaż;
charakteryzacja; układ (gra-
ficzny); stan (kogoś,czegoś)
make up your mind ('mejk,ap'-
'jo:r,majnd) exp.: zdecyduj się
(czego chcesz,co wolisz, na co
masz ochotę,gdzie jedziesz etc.)

maker ('mejker) s. wytwórca;
sprawca; producent; fabrykant;
konstruktor(Maker= Bóg)
makeshift ('mejkszyft) s. namiastka; urządzenie prowizo-
ryczne;adj.prowizoryczny
malady ('maeledy) s. choroba
male (mejl) s. mężczyzna; samiec; adj. męski; samczy;
wewnętrzny; obejmowany
malediction (,maely'dikszyn) s.
przekleństwo; złorzeczenie
malefactor ('maelyfaekter) s.
złoczyńca; zbrodniarz
malevolent (me'lewelent) adj.
niechętny; wrogi
malice ('maelys) s. złośliwość;
zła wola; zły zamiar
malicious (me'lyszys) adj.
złośliwy; zły;powodowany złością
malignant (me'lygnent) adj.
złośliwy; zjadliwy
malnutrition ('maelnju'tryszyn)
s. niedożywienie
malt (mo:lt) s. słód; v. słodo-
wać ;adj. słodowy;zcukrzony
maltreat (mael'tri:t) v. poniewierać; maltretować
mamma (me'ma:) s. mama;gruczoł mlekowy
mammal (me'ma:l) s. ssak;a.ssakowy
man (maen) s. człowiek; mężczyzna; mąż; v. obsadzać (np. zało-
gą); pl. men (men)
manacle ('maenekl) s. kajdany;
v. zakuwać w kajdany
manage ('maenydż) v. kierować;
zarządzać; posługiwać się; obchodzić się; opanowywać; poskramiać; radzić sobie
manageable ('maenydżebl) adj.do
pokierowania (możliwy,łatwy)
management ('maenydżment) s.
zarząd; kierownictwo; dyrekcja;
posługiwanie się; obchodzenie
się ;sprawne zarządzanie
manager('maenydżer) s. kierownik
zarządzający; gospodarz
manageress ('maenydżeres) s.
kierowniczka
mane (mejn) s. grzywa
maneuver (me'nu:wer) s. manewr;
v. manewrować;manipulować

manger ('mejndżer) s. żłób; koryto
mangle ('maengl) s. magiel;
v. maglować; poszarpać; pokale-
czyc; poprzekręcać
manhood ('maenhud) s. męskość;
ludność męska ;wiek męski
mania ('mejnje) s. bzik; obłęd;
mania;zbytni entuzjazm;szał
maniac ('mejnjaek) s. maniak;
szaleniec;adj.umysłowo chory
manifest ('maenyfest) adj. jawny; oczywisty; v. manifestować;
ujawniać; s. manifest okrętowy (szczegółowa lista ładunku)
manifold ('maenyfould) adj.
różnorodny; wieloraki; wielokrotny; v. powielać (tekst)
manipulate (me'nypjulejt) v.
manipulować; umiejętnie; zręcz-
nie pokierować (niesprawiedliwie)
mankind (,maen'kajnd) s. ludzkość; rodzaj ludzki
mankind ('maenkajnd) pl. mężczyź-
ni ;cały rodzaj męski
manly('maenly) adj. dzielny;
mężny; męski;adv.po męsku
manner ('maener) s. sposób; zwyczaj; zachowanie (się); wychowanie; maniera;procedura;rodzaj
manoeuvre (me'nu:wer) s. manewr;
v. namewrować (pisownia brytyjska)
man-of-war ('maenew'ło:r) s.
okręt wojenny;uzbrojony statek
manor ('maener) s. dwor; rezydencja (w Anglii:duży majatek)
man power('maen,pałer) s. siła
robocza; rezerwy ludzkie
mansion ('maenszyn) s. rezydencja; pałac;duży dwór
manslaughter ('maen,slo:ter) s.
zabójstwo (bez premedytacji)
mantelpiece ('maentlpi:s) s.
gzyms kominka (obramowanie)
manual ('maenjuel) s. podręcznik;
manuał; adj. ręczny;ręcznie zrobio-
manufacture (,maenju'faekczer)
v. wyrabiać; s. wyrób; produkcja; produkt (zwłaszcza masowy)
manufacturer (,maenju'faekcze-
rer) s. wytwórca; producent;
fabrykant;przedsiębiorstwo wytwór-cze-

manure (me'njuer) s. nawóz;
v. nawozic (gnój)

manuscript ('maenjuskrypt) s.
rękopis; adj. ręcznie pisany

many ('meny) adj. dużo; wiele

many-sided ('meny'sajdyd) adj.
wielostronny; wieloboczny;
wszechstronny

map (maep) s. mapa; plan;
v. planowac; robic mapę

maple ('mejpl) s. klon

marble ('ma:rbl) s. marmur; kul-
ka do zabawy; adj, marmurowy;
v. marmurkowac (np. papier)

March (ma:rcz) s. marzec

march (ma:rcz) s. marsz; v.ma-
szerowac

mare (meer) s. klacz; kobyła

margarine ('ma:rdże,ri:n) s.
margaryna

margin ('ma:rdżyn) s. margines;
brzeg; krawędz; nadwyżka;
rezerwa

marine (me'ri:n) adj. morski;
s. marynarka; żołnierz piecho-
ty desantowej (USA)

mariner ('maeryner) s. marynarz;
żeglarz

maritime ('maerytajm) adj. morski

mark (ma:rk) s. marka (pieniądz)
slad; znak; oznaczenie; nota;
cenzura; cel; uwaga; v. oznaczac; okreslac; notowac; zwracac uwagę

marked (ma:rkt) adj. wybitny;
wyrazny; znaczny

mark out (ma:rk,aut) v. wyznaczac; wytyczac (np. granicę)

market ('ma:rkyt) s. rynek;
zbyt; targ; v. robic zakupy;
sprzedawac na targu

marketing ('ma:rkytyŋg) s. orga-
nizowanie rynku;handlowanie

market-place ('ma:rkytplejs) s.
rynek; plac targowy

marksman ('ma:rksmen) s. strzelec (doborowy)

marmalade ('ma:rmelejd) s.
marmolada (pomaranczowa)

marmot ('ma:rmet) s. swistak ,
marriage ('maerydż) s. małżen-
stwo (skojarzenie);a.slubny

marriageable ('maerydżebl) adj.
na wydaniu;odpowiedni do małżenstwa

marriage certificate ('maerydż,
,ser'tyfykyt) s. swiadectwo
slubu

married ('maeryd) adj, żonaty;
zamężna; małżenski; slubny

married couple ('maeryd,kapl)s.&
adj. para małżenska

marrow ('mearou) s. szpik
(kostny); dynia

marry ('maery) v. poslubic;
udzielac slubu; ożenic (się)
brac slub; pobierac się;
wychodzic za maż

marsh (ma:rsz) s. moczary; bagno;błota;a.bagienny

marshal ('ma:rszel) s. marszałek; mistrz ceremonii; komisarz policji; v. uszykowac
(uroczyscie); przetaczac wagony;uporządkowac;uszykowac

marshy ('ma:rszy) adj. bagnisty; bagienny;błotnisty

marten ('ma:rtyn) s.kuna

martial ('ma:rszel) adj. wojenny; wojowniczy; wojskowy

martyr ('ma:rter) ,s. męczennik; v. zamęczac;zadręczac

marvel ('ma:rwel) s. cudo; cud;
v. podziwiac; dziwic się

marvelous ('ma:rwyles) adj.
cudowny; zdumiewający

mascot ('maesket) s. maskotka

masculine ('maeskjulyn) adj.
męski;płci męskiej

mash (maesz) s. zacier; papka;
mieszanka; v. warzyc; tłuc na
papkę; umizgac się

mashed potatoes ('maeszt,pe'tej-
tous) s. gniecione ziemniaki

mask (ma:sk) s. maska; v. zamaskowac; maskowac

mason ('mejsn) s. murarz; ka-
mieniarz;v.wymurowac;murowac

masonry ('mejsnry) s. murarstwo;
obmurowanie;kamieniarstwo

masque (ma:sk) s. maskarada;
pantomima (amatorska)

mass (maes) s. msza; masa; rzesza; v. gromadzic; zrzeszac

massacre ('maeseker) s. masakra; v. masakrowac;urządzic rzez

massage ('maesa:ż) s. masaż;
v. masować ;zrobić masaż

massif ('maesyw) s, masyw
górski

massive ('maesyw) adj. masywny;
ciężki;zwarty;bryłowaty;ciężki

mast (ma:st) s. maszt

master ('ma:ster) s. mistrz;
nauczyciel; pan; gospodarz;
szef; kapitan statku; panicz;
v. panować; kierować; nabywać (np.wprawy);owładnąć

master key ('ma:sterki:) s.
wytrych

masterly ('ma:sterly) adj.
mistrzowski

master of ceremony ('ma:ster,ow-
sere'mouny) s. mistrz ceremonii

masterpiece ('ma:sterpi:s) s.
arcydzieło

mastership ('ma:sterszyp) s.
mistrzostwo; władza; panowanie; zwierzchnictwo

mastery ('ma:stery) s. władza;
panowanie; mistrzostwo

mat (maet) s. mata; v. plątać;
adj. matowy(bez połysku)

match (maecz) s. zapałka; lont;
mecz; dobór; małżeństwo;
v. swatać; współzawodniczyć;
dobierać;dorównywać

matchless ('maeczlys) adj. niezrównany;nie mający równego

matchmaker ('maecz,mejker) s.
swat; swatka;aranżujący mecze

mate (mejt) s. kolega; małżonek;
samiec; pomocnik; łączyć ślu-
bem; parzyć (się); pobierać
się;zadawać mata(w szachach)

material (me'tierjal) s. materiał; tworzywo; tkanka; adj.
materialny; cielesny

maternal (me'te:rnl) adj. macierzyński; matczyny

maternity (me'te:rnyty) s. macierzyństwo;adj.położniczy

maternity hospital (me'te:rnyty
'hospytl) s. szpital położniczy

mathematician (,maetyme'tyszyn)
s. matematyk

mathematics (,maety'maetyks) s.
matematyka

math (maeg) s. matematyka
(slang)

matriculate (me'trykjulejt) v.
immatrykulować; zdawać wstępny
egzamin (uniw.);zapisać się na.,.

matrimony ('maetrymeny) s. małżeństwo;akt ślubu

matron ('mejtren) s. matrona;
kobieta zamężna; (gospodyni)

matter ('maeter) s. rzecz;
treść; materiał; substancja;
sprawa; kwestia; v. znaczyć;
mieć znaczenie;odgrywać rolę

matter-of-fact ('maeter,ow'faekt)
adj. rzeczowy; praktyczny

mattress ('maetrys) s. materac

mature (me'tjuer) adj. dojrzały;
płatny; v. dojrzewać; stawać
się płatnym (np.pożyczka)

maturity (me'tjueryty) s. dojrzałość; termin płatności

mauve (mouw) s. kolor różowo-
liliowy ;adj.różowo-liliowy

maw (mo:) s. żołądek; wole

maxim ('maeksym) s. maksyma

maximum ('maeksymem) s. maksi-
mum

May (mej) s. maj

may (mej) v. być może; might
(majt) mógłby

maybe ('mejbi:) adv. być może;
może być;możliwe że

may I ? ('mej aj) czy mogę ?

may-bug ('mejbag) s. chrabąszcz

mayor (meer) s. burmistrz

maypole ('mejpoul) s. słup do
tańca "gaik", l-go maja

maze (mejz) s. labirynt; gmatwa-
nina; v. w błąd wprowadzić;
oszołomić;dezorientować;mieszać

mazurka (me'ze:rke) s. mazur;
mazurek

me (mi:) pron. mi; mnie; mną;
(slang):ja

meadow ('medou) s. łąka

meager ('mi:ger) adj. chudy;
cienki; skromny;nie obradzający

meal (mi:l) s. posiłek; grubo
mielona maka;czas posiłku

mealtime ('mi:l-tajm) s. pora
posiłku(ustalona zwyczajem)

mealy ('mi:ly)adj.mączysty;nie-
szczery;słodziutki; obleśny

mean; meant; meant (mi:n;
ment; ment)

mean (mi:n) v. myśleć; przypuszczać; znaczyć; s. przeciętna; średnia; środek;
adj. ubogi; nędzny; podły;
marny; skąpy;tandetny;skąpy

meaning ('mi:nyŋg) s. znaczenie; sens; treść; adj. znaczący;mający zamiar

meaningless ('mi:nyŋglys) adj.
bez sensu; bez znaczenia

meant (ment) przeznaczony;
zob. mean

meantime ('mi:n'tajm) adv.
tymczasem;w tym samym czasie

meanwhile ('mi:n,hłajl) adv.
tymczasem

measles ('mi:zlz) s. odra

measure ('meżer) s. miara;
miarka; środek; zabieg; sposób; v. mierzyć; mieć rozmiar; oszacować;być…wzrostu

measureless ('meżerlys) adj.
bezmierny; nieskończony

measurement ('meżerment) s.
wymiar; miara; mierzenie

meat (mi:t) s. mięso; danie
mięsne;treść (książki etc.)

mechanic (my'kaemyk) s. mechanik;rzemieślnik;technik

mechanical (my'kaenykel) adj.
mechaniczny

mechanics (my'kaenyks) s. mechanika

mechanism ('mekenyzem) s. mechanizm;maszyneria

mechanize ('mekenajz) v. zme-
chanizować

medal ('medl) s. medal

meddle ('medl) v. wmieszać się;
wtrącać się w cudze sprawy

mediaeval (,medy'i:wel) adj.
średniowieczny

mediate ('my:djejt) adj. pośredni; v. pośredniczyć

mediator ('my:djejt) s. rozjemca; mediator

medical ('medykel) adj. lekarski; medyczny

medical certificate ('medykel,
,sertyfykyt) s. świadectwo lekarskie

medicated ('medykejtyd) adj.
leczony; zaprawiony substancją
leczniczą

medicinal (me'dysynl) adj. leczniczy; lekarski; medyczny

medicine ('medysyn) s. medycyna;
lek; lekarstwo; v. leczyć lekarstwami

medieval (,medy'i:wel) adj.
średniowieczny

mediocre ('my:djouker) adj. mierny: średni; przeciętny

meditate ('medytejt) v. obmyślać;
rozmyślać; medytować

meditation (,medy'tejszyn) s.
rozmyślanie ;planowanie

meditative ('medytejtyw) adj.
zadumany; zamyślony; medyta-
cyjny ;kontemplacyjny

Mediterranean (,medyter'rejnjen)
adj. śródziemnomorski

medium ('mi:djem) s. środek;
średnia; przewodnik; środek
obiegowy; środowisko; rozpuszczalnik; sposób; środkowa droga; adj. średni;adv.średnio

medley ('medly) s. mieszanina;
pstrokacizna; rozmaitości

meek (mi:k) s. potulny; łagodny; skromny ;bez wigoru

meet; met; met (mi:t; met;met)

meet (mi:t) v. spotykać; zbierać
się; gromadzić; iść na kompromis; zgadzać się; zaspokajać;
s. spotkanie; zbiórka; miejsce
spotkania; spotkanie sportowe;
zawody(na bieżni etc.)

meet with ('mi:t,łys) v. spotkać się z (kimś);doświadczyć

meeting ('mi:tyŋg) s. spotkanie;
połączenie się; posiedzenie;
zgromadzenie; wiec; zawody;
konferencja; pojedynek

melancholy ('melenkely) s. melancholia; adj. smutny; melan-
cholijny;zasmucający;ponury

mellow ('melou) adj. słodki;
miękki; soczysty; uleżały; zła-
godzony (wiekiem); łagodny; wesoły; pogodny; podchmielony;
dojrzały; miły; świetny; przyjemny; v. dojrzewać; zmiękczać;
uleżeć się;łagodnieć; łagodzić

melodious (my'loudjes) adj.
melodyjny ;harmonijny

melody ('meledy) s. melodia;
piosenka

melon ('melen) s. melon

melt (melt) s. stop; stopienie;
topnienie; wytop; v. topic;
topniec; roztapiac (się);
rozpuszczac; przetapiac; odlewac; wzruszyc;roztkliwiac

melting point ('meltyng'point)
s. temperatura topnienia

member ('member) s. członek;
człon(odrozniający się)

membership ('memberszyp) s.
członkowstwo; przynaleznosc;
skład członkowski

membrane ('membrejn) s. błona;
przepona; membrana

memoir ('memła:r) s. pamiętnik;
życiorys;autobiogrfia

memorable ('memerebl) adj. pa-
mietny;znaczny

memorial (my'no:riel) s. pomnik; memorial; petycja; posag (na pamiatke)

memorize ('memerajz) v. zapamiętywac; uczyc się na pamięc

memory ('memery) s. pamięc;
wspomnienie

men (men) pl. mężczyzni; robot-
nicy; zob.: man

menace ('menes) s. grozba; za-
grożenie; v. grozic; zagrażac

mend (mend) s. naprawa; na-
prawka; reperowac; zaszyc

menial ('mi:njel) s. sługa;
służalec; adj. czarno-robo-
czy; służalczy; służebny

mental ('mentl) adj. umysłowy;
pamieciowy; psychiatryczny;
s. (slang) umysłowo chory

mental hospital ('mentl'hospytl)
s. szpital psychiatryczny

mentality (men'taelyty) s.
umysłowosc; mentalnosc

mention ('menszyn) v. wspominac; wymieniac; nadmieniac;
wzmiankowac; s. wzmianka

menu ('menju:) s. jadłospis

meow (mi:'au) v. miauczec jak kot

mercantile ('me:rkentajl) adj.
handlowy; kupiecki

mercenary ('me:rsynery) adj.
najemny; wyrachowany; s. najemnik; zołnierz najemny

merchandise('me:rczendajz) s.
towar(y); v. handlowac

merchant('me:rczent) s. kupiec;
handlowiec; adj. handlowy;
kupiecki

merciful ('me:rsyfùl) adj. miłosierny; litosciwy

merciless ('me:rsylys) adj. bezlitosny; niemiłosierny

mercurial (me:r'kjuerjel) adj.
rtęciowy; żywy; bystry; rozgarnięty; zmienny

mercy ('me:rsy) s. miłosierdzie;
litosc; łaska;rzecz pomyslna

mercy killing ('me:rsy'kylyng)
s. eutanazja; zabójstwo z li-
tosci

mere (mjer) adj. zwykły; zwyczajny;nie więcj niż

merely ('mjerly) adv. tylko; jedynie; zaledwie; po prostu

merge (me:rdż) v. roztapiac
(się); zlewac; łączyc (się)

merger ('me:rdżer) s. połączenie; zlanie się; fuzja

meridian (me'rydjen) s. południk; zenit; szczyt; adj. południowy; szczytowy

merit ('meryt) s. zasługa; zaleta; odznaczenie; v. zasługiwac

meritorious (,mery'to:rjes) adj.
chwalebny; zasłuzony

mermaid ('me:rmejd) s. rusałka;
syrena

merriment ('meryment) s. uciecha; radosc; wesołosc

merry ('mery) adj. wesoły; radosny; podochocony;odswiętny;
podchmielony

merryandrew ('mery'aendru:) s.
błazen; trefnis ;wesołek

merry-go-round ('merygou,raund)
s, karuzela

merry-making ('mery,mejkyn) s.
zabawa;uciecha;weselenie się

mesh (mesz) s. siatka; sięc;
układ siatkowy; v. łapac w
sięc; zazębiac;wplątac

mess (mes) s. nieporządek; bałagan; bród; świństwo; paskudztwo; paćka; papka; zupa; bigos; posiłek ('mes'ap); stołówka; wspólny stół; v. zababrać; zapaskudzić; zabrudzić; zabałaganić; pokpić; sfuszerować; obijać się; bawić; dawać jeść (posiłek); stołować się (wspólnie)

mess up (,mes'ap) v. zepsuć; zaprzepaścić; sknocić; zagmatwać; pobrudzić; zabałaganić

message ('mesydż) s. wiadomość; orędzie; morał; wypowiedź; v. komunikować; podawać; posłać

messenger ('mesyndżer) s. posłaniec; zwiastun

messy ('mesy) adj. kłopotliwy; zapaskudzony; sfuszerowany; brudny etc. upaćkany; niechlujny

met (met) v. zob. meet

metal ('metl) s. metal; v. pokrywać metalem; a.metalowy

metallic (my'taelyk) adj. metaliczny; metalowy; metalurgiczny

meteor ('mi:tjer) s. meteor

meteorology (,mi:tjero'ledży) s. meteorologia

meter ('mi:ter) s. metr; licznik; v. mierzyć; a.metrowy

method ('meted) s. metoda; metodyka; metodyczność; sposób

methodical (me'todykel) adj. metodyczny; systematyczny

meticulous (my'tykjules) adj. drobiazgowy; szczegółowy; drobnostkowy; pedantyczny

metric system ('metryk'system) s. system metryczny

metropolitan (,metre'polyten) adj. wielkomiejski; metropolitalny; s. mieszkaniec metropolii; metropolita (duchowny)

mew (mju:) v. miauczeć; pierzyć się

Mexican ('meksyken) adj. meksykański; Meksykanin; Meksykanka

miaow (mi:'au) v. miauczeć

mica ('maike) s. mika; łuszczyk

mice (majs) pl. myszy; zob.: mouse

micron ('majkron)s. mikron

microphone ('majkrefoun) s. mikrofon

microscope ('majkreskoup) s. mikroskop podczas; pośród; między mid (myd) adj. środkowy; prep. w;

midday ('myddej) adj. południowy; s. południe

mid summer (,myd'samer) exp. w środku lata

middle ('mydl) s. środek; kibić; stan; adj. środkowy; v. składać w środku; kopać na środek

middle aged ('mydl'ejdżd) adj. w średnim wieku

Middle Ages ('mydle'ejdżys) s. średniowiecze

middle class ('mydl,kla:s) s. klasa średnia; klasa średniozamożna; a.ze średniozamożnej klasy

middle name ('mydl,nejm) s. drugie imię

middle sized ('mydl,sajzd) adj. średniej wielkości; średni

middleweight ('mydl,łejt) s. waga średnia; adj. średniej wagi (148 do 160 funtów)

middling ('mydlyng) adj. średni; przeciętny; adv. średnio

midge ('mydż) s. muszka

midget ('mydżyt) s. karzełek; maleństwo; adj. miniaturowy

midland ('mydlend) s. środek kraju; adj. leżący w środku kraju; w głębi kraju

midmost ('mydmoust) adj. leżący w samym środku; prep. pośród

midnight ('mydnajt) s. północ; adj. północny; o północy

midway ('myd'łej) s. połowa drogi; adv. w połowie drogi

midwife ('mydłajf) s. położna; okuszerka

might (majt) s. moc; potęga; v. mógłby; zob.: may

mighty ('majty) adj. potężny; adv. bardzo; wielce

migrate ('maj,grejt)v. wędrować; przesiedlać się

migratory ('maj,gretery) adj. wędrowny(ptak etc.)

mild (majld) adj. łagodny; powolny; potulny; słaby; delikatny

mildew ('myldju:) s. pleśń;
v. plesnieć;rdzewieć (o zbożu)
mildly ('majldly) adv. łagod-
nie; umiarkowanie;oględnie
mildness ('majldnys) s. łagodnosc; nieostrosc
mile (majl) s. mila; 1,609 km
mil(e)age ('majlydż) s. milaż;
odległosc w milach
milestone ('majlstoun) s. kamien milowy
military ('mylytery) adj. wojskowy; pl. wojskowy; wojsko
milk (mylk) s. mleko; v. doic
(krowy); wykorzystac; exploatowac;podsłuchiwac (telefon)
milking machine ('mylkyng,ma'-
'szi:n) s. maszyna do dojenia
milkman ('mylkmen) s. mleczarz
milk shake ('mylkszejk) s. mieszany napoj mleczny
milksop ('mylksop) s. mamin-
synek;fajtlapa;oferma;niedołega
milky ('mylky) adj. mleczny;
zniewiesciały; koloru mleka
mill (myl) s. młyn; huta; fabryka; (1/1000); walcownia;
krawędz ząbkowana; v. mleć;
frezowac; pilsnic; kręcic się
miller ('myler) s. młynarz
millet ('mylyt) s. proso
milliner ('mylyner) s, modniarka; modystka
million ('myljen) num. milion
millionaire('myljeneer) s. milioner
millionth ('myljent) num.
milionowy; jedna milionowa
(częśc)
milt (mylt) s. mlecz rybi ;
v. zapładniac ikrą
mimic ('mymyk) s, nasladowca;
imitator; v. nasladowac; małpowac; adj. nasladowniczy;udany;
mimiczny;zmyslony;fikcyjny
mince (myns) v. siekac; mowic
bez ogrodek; cedzic (słowa);
drobic nogami; s. siekane
mięso; nadzienie mięsne
mincing (mynsyng) adj. mizdrzą-
cy sie; afektowany;sztucznie
zachowujący się(wykwintny)

mind (majnd) s. umysł; pamięc;
zdanie; opinia; postanowienie;
zamierzenie; v. pamietac; zważac; przejmowac się; baczyc;
miec cos przeciwko;byc posłusznym
mind your own business ('majnd;-
jo:'ołn'byznys) pilnuj swego
nosa; nie wtrącaj się
minded ('majndyd) adj. nastawiony na; skłonny do; gotow; gotowy
mindful ('majndful) adj. pomny;
dbały; uważający; troskliwy
mindless ('majndlys) adj. nierozumny; niedbały; nieuważający
mine (majn) pron. moj; moje; mo-
ja; s. kopalnia; podkop; mina;
bomba; v. kopac; podkopywac;
exploatowac; minowac
miner ('majner) s. gornik
mineral ('mynerel) s. minerał;
adj. mineralny;zawierający mine-
rały
mingle ('myngl) v. mieszac się;
przyłączac się (do innych)
miniature ('mynjeczer) s. miniatura; adj. miniaturowy
minimum ('mynymem) s. minimum;
adj. minimalny;najmniejszy
mining ('majnyng) s. gornictwo;
adj. gorniczy; kopalniany
miniskirt ('myny,ske:rt) s. spod-
nica (mini) (b. krotka)
minister ('mynyster) s. duchowny;
minister; v. stosowac; przyczy-
niac się; udzielac; pomagac
ministry ('mynystry) s. dusz-
pasterstwo; kler; duchowienstwo;
ministerstwo; gabinet ministrow;
służba; pomoc;posługa
mink (mynk) s. norka; adj. z norek; z futer norek
minor ('majner) adj. mniejszy;
mało ważny; młodszy; nieletni;
s. człowiek niepełnoletni
minority (maj'noryty) s. mniej-
szosc; niepełnoletnosc
minster ('mynster) s. katedra;
kosciół klasztorny
minstrel ('mynstrel) s. bard;
spiewak przebrany za murzyna
mint (mynt) s. mieta; mennica;
majatek; zrodło; v. bic pieniądze; wymyslac; tworzyc; kuc

minute ('mynyt) s. minuta;
chwilką; notątka; v. szkicowac;
protokołowac; (maj'nju:t) adj.
szczegółowy;bardzo mały;znikomy

miracle ('myrekl) s. cud;a.cudowny
miraculous (my'raekjules) adj.
cudowny ;nadprzyrodzony

mirage ('myra:dż) s. miraż;
fata morgana ;złudzenie wzroko-we

mire ('majer) s. muł; błoto;
bagno; v. grzęznąc (w trudnosciach); zabłocic się

mirror ('myrer) s. zwierciadło;
v. odzwierciedlac

mirth (me:rs) s. wesołośc; ra-
dośc ;uciecha(pełna smiechu)

miry ('majry) adj. błotnisty;
mulisty ; bagnisty

mis-(mys) przedrostek: nie; źle;
(błędnie) nie-;źle-

misadventure ('mesed'wenczer)
s. niepowodzenie;zła przygoda

misanthrope ('myzentroup) s.
mizantrop ;wróg ludzkości

misapply ('myse'plaj) v. nadu-
życ; źle zastosowac

misapprehend ('mys,aepry'hend)
v. nie pojąc; źle zrozumiec

misbehave ('mysby'hejw) v. nie-
odpowiednio zachowywac się

miscalculate ('mys'kaelkjulejt)
v. przeliczyc się;przerachowac

miscarriage (mys'kaerydż) s. się
poronienie; omyłka;niepowodzenie

mischief ('myscyf) s. szkoda;
krzywda; psota; utrapienie;
złosliwośc; figiel; figlarnośc;
licho; szkodnik;bieda;niezgoda

mischievous ('myscywes) adj.
szkodliwy; niegodziwy; niesforny; niegrzeczny;psotny

misdeed ('mys'di:d) s. przestępstwo; zły czyn(karygodny)

misdemeano(u)r ('mysdy'mi:ner)
s. wykroczenie;złe sprawowanie

miser ('majzer) s. sknera; chciwiec; skąpiec; kutwa

miserable ('myzerebl) adj. nędzny; chory; marny; żałosny

miserably ('myzerebly) adv.
nędznie; marnie; żałośnie

misfortune ('mys'fo:rczen) s.
nieszczęście; pech; zły los

misgiving (mysgywyŋg) s. złe
przeczucie; obawa;powątpiewanie

misguide (,mys'gajd) v. wprowadzac w błąd;sprowadzac na manowce

mishap ('myshaep) s. (mały; nie-
poważny) wypadek(niepowodzenie)

misinform ('mysyn'form) v. źle
informowac;zwieśc z drogi

mislay (mys'lej) v. zatracic;
zob. lay; zagubic;zapodziac

mislead (mys'li:d) v. wprowadzic
w błąd; zob. lead;zbałamucic

mismanage (,mys'maenydż) v. źle
prowadzic;źle pokierowac

misplace (,mys'plejs) v. zatracic; połozyc; nie na miejscu

misprint (,mys'prynt) v. błędnie wydrukowac; s. omyłka druku; błąd drukarski

mispronounce ('myspre'nauns) v.
błędnie wymawiac;źle wymawiac

misrepresent ('mysrepry'zent)
v. przekręcic; błędnie przedstawic ;falszywie przedstawic

Miss (mys) s. panna; panienka

miss (mys) v. chybic; nie trafic; nie znalezc; nie dostac;
brakowac; tęsknic; zacinac się;
s. pudło; niepowodzenie;
opuszczenie; chybienie

miss out ('mys,aut) v. wypuscic
(słowo); chybic ;nie dostac

missile ('mysajl) s. pocisk; rakieta; adj. nadający się do
rzucania (oszczep;rakieta etc.)

missing ('mysyŋg) adj. nieobecny; brakujący; zaginiony

mission ('myszyn) s. misja; delegacja; v. wysyłac z misją;
zakładac misje ;a.misyjny

missionary ('myszynery) s.
misjonarz ;adj.misjonarski

misspelling ('mys'spelyŋg) s.
błąd ortograficzny

mist (myst) s. lekka mgła;
v. zachodzic parą(mgiełką)

mistake (mys'tejk) s. omyłka;
nieporozumienie; v. pomylic
(się) (co do faktu lub człowieka); źle zrozumiec; mylic się

mistaken (mys'tejken) adj. mylny; błędny ;pomylony;nie mający
zrozumienia sytuacji etc.

mistakenly (mys'tejknly) adv.
błędnie;pomyłkowo;nierozsądnie
Mister ('myster) s. pan (używane z nazwiskiem); skrót Mr.
(bez nazwiska niegrzecznie !)
mistletoe (mysltou) s. jemioł-
ka, jemioła;liście jemioły
mistress ('mystrys) s. kochan-
ka; nauczycielka; (myzys) s.
pani; (skrót Mrs); zob.Mister
mistrust (mys'trast) v. podejrzewać; nie ufać; s. niedowierzanie; nieufność
misty ('mysty) adj. mglisty;
zamglony;niejasny;nieokreślony
misunderstanding ('mysande r-
staendyng) s. nieporozumienie
misuse ('mys'ju:z) v. nadużywać; źle używać; ('mys'ju:s)
s. nadużycie; złe użycie
mite (majt) s. molik; kruszyna;
drobiazg; grosz (wdowi); berbeć;mała sumka pieniędzy
mitigate ('mytygejt) v. koić;
usmierzać; łagodzić; łagodnieć; ukoić;złagodzić
mitten ('mytn) s. rękawiczka
bez palców; (slang):rękawica
bokserska(zimowa etc.)
mix (myks) v. mieszać; obcować;
współżyć; s. mieszanka; mieszanina; zamieszanie
mix-up ('myks'ap) s. gmatwani-
na; platanina;zamieszanie;bójka
mixed up with ('mykst'ap,łyg)
adj. zamieszany (w coś)
mixture ('mykscer) s. mieszanka; mieszanina;mikstura
moan (moun) s. jęk; v. jęczeć;
lamentować;mówić jęcząc
moat (mout) s. fosa; row;
v. opasywać fosą
mob (mob) s. tłum; motłoch;
banda; v. napastować; atakować tłumnie;stłoczyc się
mobile ('moubajl) adj. ruchomy;
ruchliwy; zmienne; s. rzeźba-
kompozycja wisząca(abstrakcyj-
na)
mock (mok) v. wykpić; przedrzeźniać; zmylić; stawiać czoło;
żartować z kogoś; s. kpiny;
przedrzeźnianie;naśladownictwo;
adj.fałszywy; udany; pozorny

mockery ('mokery) s. kpiny;
śmiech; posmiewisko;pokrzywianie się
mode (moud) s. sposób; tryb; moda;rzecz modna(lub zwyczajowa)
model ('modl) s. model; wzór; mo-
delka; manekin; v. modelować
moderate ('moderyt) adj. umiarkowany; średni; s. człowiek umiarkowany (w poglądach etc.)
moderate ('moderejt) v.powsciągać;
uspokoić (się);prowadzić(zebranie)
moderation (,mode'rejszyn) s.
umiarkowanie; umiar;spokój
modern ('modern) adj. współczesny;
nowoczesny; nowożytny
modernize ('modernajz) v. unowocześnić (się);modernizować
modest ('modyst) adj. skromny
modesty ('modysty) s. skromność
modification (,modyfy'kejszyn) s.
modyfikacja; łagodzenie z lekka
modify ('modyfaj) v. modyfikować;
zmieniać częściowo; łagodzić
modulate ('modjulejt) v. modulować; regulować; dostosowywać
module ('modju:l) s. moduł; kabina (astronauty)
moist (mojst) adj. wilgotny
moisten(mojsen) v. wilgnąć; zwilżać (sobie usta etc.);wilgotnieć
moisture ('mojscer) s. wilgoć;
wilgotność;lekkie zamoczenie
molar (mouler) s. trzonowy (ząb);
adj. trzonowy
mole (moul) s. kret; grobla; molo; znamię;brodawka etc.
molecule ('molykju:l) s. molekuła; cząsteczka
molest (mou'lest) v. napastować;
dokuczać; molestować;naprzykrzać się
mollify ('molyfaj) v. łagodzić;
miękczyć; mięknąc;usmierzać
moment ('moument) s. chwila; moment; waga; znaczenie; motyw;
powód;doniosłość;ważność
momentary ('moumentery) adj.
chwilowy; mijający;lada chwila
monarch ('monerk) s. monarcha;
król;duży motyl tropikalny
monarchy ('monerky) s. monarchia
monastery ('monestery) s. klasztor (głównie męski);miejsce za
mieszkania mnichów (zakonnic)

Monday ('mandy) s. poniedziałek; a. poniedziałkowy

monetary ('manytry) adj. monetarny;pieniężny;walutowy

money ('many) s. pieniądze

money-order ('many,o:rder) s.
przekaz pieniężny

monger ('manger) s. handlarz;
przekupień;kupiec

monk (mank) s. mnich

monkey (manky) s, małpa; v. dokazywac; małpowac;wygłupiac sie

monkey business ('manky'byznys)
s. małpie figle (dokuczliwe)

monkey wrench ('manky'rencz) s.
francuski klucz (dostosowywalny)

monolog(ue) ('monelog) s. monolog ;a.monologowy

monopolize (me'nopelajz) v.
monopolizowac; skupiac na sobie uwagę wszystkich etc.

monopoly (me'nopely) s. monopol

monotonous (me'notnes) adj.
monotonny; jednolity

monotony (me'notny) s. monotonia

monster ('monster) s. potwor;
adj. olbrzymi;potworny;okrutny

monstrous ('monstres) adj. potworny; ogromny;okrutnie zły

month (mant) s. miesiąc

monthly ('mantly) adj. miesięcz-
ny; adv. miesięcznie; s. mie-
siecznik;adv.co miesiac;na miesiąc

monument ('monjument) s. pomnik

moo (mu:) v. ryczec; s. ryk
(krowy)

mood (mu:d) s. humor; nastrój;
(gram.) tryb;usposobienie

moody (mu:dy) adj. ponury; mający humory;markotny

moon (mu:n) s. księżyc;a.księżyco-
wy

moonlight ('mu:nlajt) s. światło
księżyca; v. miec kilka posad
równoczesnie

moonlit ('mu:nlyt) adj. oświe-
cony księżycem

moonshine ('mu:nszajn) s. światło księżyca; alkohol pędzony
nielegalnie lub przemycony

Moor (muer) adj. mauretański;
s. Maur

moor (muer) s. otwarty teren łowiecki; wrzosowisko; bagno;
trzęsawisko; v. cumowac; umocowac;przybijac do brzegu

moorings ('mueryns) pl. kotwica
martwa; miejsca przycumowania

moose (mu:s) s. łoś amerykański

mop (mop) s. szmata do podłog;
grymas; v. wycierac; zgarniac;
robic miny;spuscic manto

moral ('morel) s. morał; pl.
moralnosc;adj.moralny;obyczajny

morale (me'rael) s. nastrój;
duch (w wojsku,w narodzie)

morality (me'raelyty) s. moralnosc; moralizowanie; etyka

moralize ('morelajz) v. umoral-
niac; moralizowac

morass (me'raes) s. moczar; bagno;mokradła;grzęzawiska

morbid ('mo:rbyd) adj. chorobliwy; chorobowy;niezdrowy;schorzały

more (mo:r) adv. bardziej; więcej; adj. liczniejszy;dalszy

morel (mo'rel) s. (grzyb)
smardz;psianka;a.psiankowaty

more or less ('mo:r,or'les) adv.
mniej więcej;w przybliżeniu

moreover (mo:'rouwer) adv. co
więcej; prócz tego;nadto;poza tym

morgue (mo:rg) s. morga (na
zwłoki) ; kostnica;a.kostnicy

morning ('mo:rnyng) s. rano;
poranek; przedpołudnie

morose (mo'rous) adj. ponury;
zasępiony;przygnębiony;markotny

morphine ('mo:rfi:n) s. morfina ;a.morfinowy

morsel ('mo:rsel) s. kęs; kąsek;
kawałek; smakołyk; v. dzielic
na kawałki;rozdrabniac;rozparce-
lowywac

mortal ('mo:rtl) s. smiertelnik;
adj. smiertelny; straszny

mortality (mo;'rtaelyty) s.
smiertelnosc;liczba ofiar

mortar ('mo:ter) s. mozdzierz;
zaprawa murarska; v. tynkowac;
kłasc zaprawę; strzelac z
mozdzierza;zwiazac zaprawa

mortgage ('mo:rgydż) s. hipoteka; v. hipotekowac

mortician (mo:r'tyszen) s.
przedsiębiorca pogrzebowy
mortification (mo:rtyfy'kejszyn) s. upokorzenie; umartwia-
nie się;wstyd;gangrena
mortify ('mo:rtyfaj) v. zamierać; ranić (uczucia); upokarzać; umartwiać (się);
powściągać;zgangrenować
mortuary ('mo:rtjuery) s. trupiarnia; kostnica;a.pogrzebowy
mosaic (mou'zejyk) s. mozaika;
adj. mozaikowy;mojżeszowy
mosque (mosk) n. meczet
mosquito (mes'ki:tou) s. komar;
moskit;a.moskitowy
moss (mos) s, mech; v. pokrywać
mchem (torfowiskiem)
most (moust) adj. największy;
najliczniejszy; adv. najbardziej; najwięcej; s. najwięk-
sza ilość;maksimum
mostly ('moustly) adv. przeważnie; głównie;po największej części
moth (mos) s. ćma; mól
moth-eaten ('mos,i:tn)adj.zje-
dzony przez mole;przestarzały
mother ('madzer) s. matka;v.mat-
kować
mother country ('madzer'kantry)
s. ojczyzna;kraj rodzinny
motherhood ('madzer,hud) s. macierzyństwo
mother-in-law ('madzer,yn'lo:)
s. teściowa
motherly ('madzerly) adj. macierzyński
mother tongue ('madzer,tang) s.
język ojczysty
motif (mou'ti:f) s. motyw
(artystyczny);główny temat
motion ('mouszyn) s. ruch; wniosek; stolec; v. kierować skinieniem, znakiem; skinąć na
kogoś znaczącym gestem
motionless ('mouszenlys) adj.
bez ruchu; unieruchomiony
motion picture ('mouszyn'pykczer) s. film ruchomy
motivate ('moutywejt) v. uzasadniać; pobudzać kogoś;zachęcać
motive ('moutyw) s. motyw; podnieta; adj. napędowy;poruszający

motor ('mouter) s. motor; adj.
ruchowy; mechaniczny; samochodowy; v. jeździć; przewozić
samochodem;prowadzić wóz
motorbike ('mouter,bajk) s.
motocykl;rower z motorkiem
motorboat ('mouter,bout) s.
motorówka;łódź motorowa
motorcycle ('mouter,sajkl) s.
motocykl
motorcyclist ('mouter,sajklyst)
s. motocyklista
motoring ('mouteryng) s. jazda
samochodem;automobilizm
motorist ('mouteryst) s. auto-
mobilista; kierowca
motorize ('mouterajz) s. motoryzować;zmotoryzować
mottle ('motl) s. cętka; plamka;
v. cętkować;nakrapiać;upstrzyć
motto (motou) s. motto;dewiza
mo(u)ld (mould) s. pleśń; ziemia;
modła; forma; v. pleśnieć; odlewać; kształtować;urabiać
moulder ('moulder) v. gnić;
pruchnieć; niszczyć się; kruszyć się;zgłupieć;s.odlewacz
mouldy ('mouldy) adj. spleśniały;
zgniły;stęchły;przeżyty;nudny
moult (moult) v. linieć;s.linienie
mound (maund) s. hałda; kopiec
mount (maunt) s. oprawa; podstawa; wierzchowiec; v. stanąć (na);
wsiąść (na konia); podnieść;
wchodzić; oprawić; osadzić; wyposażyć;zmontować;wyreżyserować
mountain ('mauntyn) s. góra; sterta; adj. górski; gorzysty
mountaineer (,maunty'nier) s.
góral; alpinista
mountainous ('mauntynes) adj.
gorzysty;olbrzymi;zawrotny
mourn (mo:rn) v. być w żałobie;
opłakiwać;pogrążać się w smutku
mournful ('mo:rnful) adj. żałobny;ponury;przygnębiony
mourning ('mo:rnyng) s. żałoba
mouse (maus) s. mysz; pl. mice
(majs);podbite oko;v.myszkować
moustache (mos'ta:sz) s. wąsy
mouth (maus) s. usta; ujście; wylot;v.mówić przesadnie (patosem)

mouth (mouθ) v. deklamować; brać w usta; robić złą minę

mouthful ('mausful) s. pełne usta; kęs; dźwięk trudny do wymówienia; powiedzieć do rzeczy; ważne słowa; dużo czegoś

mouthpiece ('mauspi:s) s. ustnik; rzecznik; kiełzno

mouthwash ('mausłosz) s. woda do ust; płukanka do ust

move (mu:w) s. ruch; pociągnięcie; krok; zmiana mieszkania; przeprowadzka; v. ruszać się; posuwać; przesuwać; postępować; przeprowadzać się; wzruszać; nakłonić; zwracać się; wnosić; zrobić ruch; działać

move in ('mu:wyn) v. wprowadzać się; wtargnąć; wejść

move on ('mu:w,on) v. jechać dalej; iść dalej; ruszyć (w drogę)

move out ('mu:w,aut) v. wyprowadzać się; wynieść się

movement (mu:wment) s. ruch; poruszenie; przemieszczenie; mechanizm; wypróżnienie

movies ('mu:wyz) s. (slang) kino; film niemy; film

moving ('mu:wyŋg) adj. ruchomy; wzruszający; s. przeprowadzka

moving violation ('mu:wyŋ,waje'lejszyn) przestępstwo drogowe w czasie jazdy (autem)

mow; mowed; mown (moł; mołd; mołn)

mow (moł) v. kosić (trawę)

mower ('mołer) s. kosiarz

mown (mołn) v. zob. mow

Mr. (myster) s. pan (używane z nazwiskiem)

Mrs. (mysyz) s. zamężna pani (używane z nazwiskiem)

much (macz) adj.& adv. wiele; bardzo; dużą sporo; niemało

much too much (,macz'tu,macz) exp. dużo za dużo; zbyt dużo

mucus ('mju:kes) s. śluz

mud (mad) s. błoto; brud

muddle ('madl) v. nurzać się; mącić; bełtać; mieszać; brnąć; wikłać się; s. powikłanie; trudne położenie; nieład; zamęt

muddle through ('madl,tru:) v. przebrnąć; wybrnąć z kłopotów

muddy ('mady) adj. zabłocony; błotnisty; mętny; v. błocić; mącić

muff (maf) s. zarękawek; fuszerka; fuszer; v. fuszerować

muffle (mafl) v. tłumić; owinąć; otulić; s. pysk (przeżuwaczy, gryzoni)

muffler ('mafler) s. tłumik; szal; rękawica bokserska; szalik

mug (mag) s. dzban; kubek; gęba

mulberry ('malbery) s. morwa

mule (mju:l) s. muł (zwierzę)

mull (mal) v. rozmyślać; pokpić; sfuszerować; zagrzać i zaprawić (np. piwo); s. bałagan; muślin; przylądek; tabakiera

mullion ('malion) s. pret; drążek okienny; słupek okienny

multiple ('maltypl) s. wielokrotna; adj. wielokrotny; złożony

multiplication (,maltyply'kejszyn) s. mnożenie; rozmnażanie się

multiplication table (,maltyply'kejszyn tejbl) s. tabliczka mnożenia

multiply ('małtyplaj) v. mnożyć (się); rozmnażać się; pomnożyć

multitude ('maltytju:d) s. mnóstwo; tłum; pospólstwo; mnogość

mumble ('mambl) v. mruknięcie; bąknięcie; v. mruknąć; bąknąć; żuć bezzębnymi dziąsłami; mamrotać

mummy ('mamy) s. mumia; miazga; brunatny barwik; mamusia

mumps ('mamps) s. (choroba); świnka; zapalenie ślinianki

munch (mancz) v. chrupać; schrupać

municipal (mju:'nysypel) adj. miejski; samorządowy; komunalny

municipality (mju:,nysy'paelyty) s. zarząd miasta; miasteczko

mural ('mjuerel) s. malowidło ścienne; fresk; adj. ścienny

murder ('me:rder) s. mord; mordestwo; v. mordować; paskudzić (rolę)

murderer ('me:rderer) s. mordderca

murderess ('me:rderys) s. morderczyni

murderous ('me:rderes) adj. morderczy; śmiercionośny

murmur ('me:rmer) s. mrucze-
nie; pomruk; pomrukiwanie;
szmer; szmeranie; sarkanie;
v. mruczec; szmerać
muscle ('masl) s. mięsień;
muskuł ;v. pchać się na siłę
muscle bound ('masl,baund) adj.
z zerwanymi mięsniami
muscular ('maskjuler) adj.
mięsniowy; krzepki; muskularny;wykonany muskułami etc.
muse (mju:z) v. dumac ;s.zaduma
museum (mju:'ziem) s. muzeum
mush (masz) s. papka; kulesza
(z kukurydzy);v.iść po śniegu
mushroom ('maszrum) s. grzyb;
pieczarka polna; dorobkiewicz;
v. zbierać grzyby; rozszerzać
się (jak grzyby po deszczu)
music ('mju:zyk) s. muzyka;
nuty ;konsekwencje postępku (sl)
musical ('mju:zykel) adj. muzyczny; muzykalny; s. komedia
lub film muzyczny
music hall ('mju: zykho:l) s.
teatr rewiowy
musician ('mju:zyszen) s. muzyk (zawodowy)
music stand('mju:zyk,staend) s.
pulpit (na nuty)
musk (mask) s. piżmo
musket ('maskyt) s.muszkiet
muskrat ('mask,raet) s.
piżmoszczur; futro piżmoszczura
Muslim ('muslym) adj. muzułmań-
ski; s. muzułmanin
muslin ('mazlyn) s. muslin
musquash ('maskłosz) s. piżmo-
wiec;piżmoszczyr
mussel('masl) s. małż
must (mast) s. moszcz winny;
stęchlizna; szał; v. musiec;
adj. konieczny;nieodzowny
mustache ('mastasz) s. wąsy
mustard ('masterd) s. musztarda
muster ('master) v. musztrować;
zbierać (się); s. przegląd;
zebranie; zbiór; apel;zebrani
muster in ('master,yn) v. zaciągać do wojska (powołać)
muster out ('master,aut) v. zwalniać z wojska

musty ('masty) adj. stęchły; za-
plesniaźy;zbutwiały;przestarzały
mute (mju:t) adj. niemy;v.tłumić
mutilate ('mju:tylejt) v. okaleczyc; psuc;okroic(tekst książki)
mutineer (,mju:ty'nier) s.
buntownik; winny buntu
mutinous ('mju:tynes) s. buntowniczy ; zbuntowany
mutiny ('mju:tyny) s. bunt;v.bun-
towac
mutter ('mater) v. mamrotac; mruczec; szemrac (przeciw); szeptac; pomrukiwac; s. mamrot; pomruk; szemranie; narzekanie
mutton ('matn) s. baranina;a.bara-
ni
mutton chop ('matn,czop) s.
kotlet barani
mutual ('mju:tjuel) adj. wzajemny; wspólny; obustronny;wspólny
muzzle ('mazl) s. wylot lufy;
pysk; kaganiec; v. nakładać
kaganiec (psu;dziennikarzowi etc.)
my (maj) pron. mój;moja;moje;moi
myelitis (,maje'lajtys) s. zapalenie rdzenia pacierzowego
myriad ('myryed) s. krocie; ro-
je; 10.000; miriada; adj. niezliczony; wielostronny
myrrh (me:r) s. mirra
myrtle ('me:rtl) s. mirt
myself (maj'self) pron. ja sam;
sam osobiscie; siebie; sobie
mysterious (mys'tierjes) adj.
tajemniczy;niezgłębiony
mystery ('mystery) s. tajemnica;
tajemniczosc ;misterium
mystify ('mystyfaj) v. wprowadzac w błąd; okrywać tajemnica
myth (mys) s. mit; postać mi-
tyczna; bajka;mistyfikacja
mystic ('mystyk) s. mistyk;
adj. mistyczny; tajemniczy
n (en) czternasta litera
angielskiego alfabetu
nab (naeb) v. capnąć; złapać;
przydybac;aresztowac;przyłapać
nag (naeg).v. gderac; dokuczac;
dreczyc; s. szkapa;kucyk;konik
nail (nejl) s. gwoźdz; pazno-
kiec; pazur; v. przybijać;
utkwić(wzrok); ujawnić(kłam-
przygwozdzic; chwytac   stwo)

naive (na:'i:w) adj. naiwny
naked ('nejkyd) adj. nagi; goły; goła(prawda etc.);obnażony
name (nejm) s. imię; nazwa;
nazwisko; v. nazywać; mianować; wymieniać;naznaczyć(datę)
nameless ('nejmlys) adj. bez-
imienny; nieznany; niesłychany; nieopisany;anonimowy
namely ('nejmly) adv. mianowicie; właśnie;żeby(wyjaśnić)
nanny ('naeny) s. niańka; koza
nanny -goat ('naeny,gout) s.
koza (żywicielka,mlekodajna)
nap (naep) v. drzemać; zdrzemnąć się;s.drzemka; meszek;puch;
włos;stroszenie meszku
nape(nejp) s. kark
nappy ('naepy) adj. mocny;
podchmielony; puszysty; v. napój; piwo; półmisek; serwetka
narcosis (na:r'kousys) s. narkoza;uśpienie narkotykami
narcotic(na:r'kotyk) adj.narko-
tyczny; s. narkotyk; narkoman
narrate (nae'rejt) v. opowiadać (coś);opowiedzieć
narration (nae'rejszyn) s. opowiadanie ;opowieść
narrative ('naeretyw) adj. nar-
racyjny; s. opowiadanie
narrator (nae'rejter) n, narrator;opowiadający;opowiadacz
narrow ('naerou) adj. wąski;
ciasny; ograniczony; s. przesmyk; cieśnina; v. zwężać;
ścieśniać; kurczyć się; zmniejszać się; redukować do...
narrow -minded ('naerou'majndyd)
s. ciasny; ograniczony
nasty ('na:sty) adj. obrzydliwy; wstrętny; nieznośny; groź-
nv: brudny; nieprzyzwoity
nation ('nejszyn) s. naród;
kraj; państwo
national ('naeszenl) adj. narodowy; państwowy; s. członek
narodu; obywatel; ziomek
nationality (,naesze'naelyty)
s. narodowość; obywatelstwo
nationalize ('naesznelajz) v.
upaństwowić; nadawać obywatelstwo (imigrantom etc.)

native ('nejtyw) adj. rodzinny;
krajowy; miejscowy; wrodzony;
naturalny; prosty; s. tubylec;
autochton; człowiek miejscowy
native language ('nejtyw'laengłydż) s. ojczysty język
nativity (ne'tywyty) s. narodzenie
natural ('naeczrel) adj. naturalny; przyrodniczy; przyrodzony; doczesny; fizyczny; przyrodni; pierwotny; nieślubny;
dziki; s. biały klawisz (pia-
nina); kasownik (muzyczny)
naturalize ('naeczerelajz) v.
naturalizować (się); aklimatyzować (się); robić naturalnym;
przyswajać sobie; pozbawiać
cech nadprzyrodzonych
naturally ('naeczrely) adv. na-
turalnie ;z przrodzenia;oczywiś-
cie
natural-science ('naeczerel'sajens) s. przyroda; nauka przy-
rody; przyrodoznawstwo
nature ('nejczer) s. natura;
przyroda; usposobienie; rodzaj
naught (no:t) s. nic; zero
naughty ('no:ty) adj. niegrzeczny; nieposłuszny; nieprzyzwoity
nausea ('no:sje) s. nudność;
mdłość; choroba morska; obrzydzenie; wstręt;chęć wymiotowania
nauseating ('no:sjejtyng)adj.
obrzydliwy; przyprawiający
o mdłości ,wymioty etc.
nautical ('no:tykel) adj. ma-
rynarski; morski
nautical mile ('no:tykel,majl)
s. mila morska; 1853 m.
naval (nejwel) adj. morski
naval base ('nejwel,bejz) s.
baza morska (wojskowa)
nave (nejw) s. 1. nawa; 2. piasta (u koła)
navel ('nejwel) s. pępek (ośrodek)
navigable ('naewygebl) adj.
spławny; żeglowny; sterowny;
podatny do żeglugi
navigate ('naewygejt) v. żeglować; kierować; (np.balonem)
navigation (,naewy'gejszyn) s.
żegluga;podróż morska;nawigacja

navigator ('naewygejter) s.
żeglarz; nawigator

navy (nejwy) s. marynarka
wojenna;granatowy kolor

nay (nej) adv. nie; nawet; co
więcej; s. sprzeciw

near (nier) adj. bliski; dokładny; v. zbliżać się; adv. blisko; prawie; oszczędnie

nearby ('nier'baj) adj. pobliski; sąsiedni; adv. w pobliżu

nearly ('nierly) adv. prawie;
blisko; oszczędnie;nie całkiem

nearness ('niernys) s. bliskość

nearsighted ('nier-sajtyd) s.
krótkowzroczny

neat (ni:t) adj. schludny;
zgrabny;proporcjonalny

neatness ('ni:tnys) s. schlud-
ność;prostota; porządek; gus-
towność;dobre proporcje

necessary ('nesysery) adj. konieczny; potrzebny;wynikający

necessitate (ny'sesytejt) v.
wymagać; czynić koniecznym

necessity (ny'sesyty) s. potrzeba; konieczność; artykuł
pierwszej potrzeby; niedostatek;los;zrządzenie los

neck (nek) s. szyja; kark;
szyjka; przesmyk;v.pieścić się

necklace ('neklys) s. naszyjnik

neck-tie ('nektaj) s. krawat

nee (nej) z domu (nazwisko
panieńskie)

need (ni:d) s. potrzeba; trudności; bieda; v. potrzebować;
musieć; cierpieć biedę

needful (ni:dful) adj. potrze-
bujący; potrzebny;konieczny

needle ('ni:dl) s. igła;v.kłuć

needless ('ni:dlys) adj. niepotrzebny; zbyteczny;zbędny

needy ('ni:dy) adj. będący
w potrzebie, w biedzie etc.

negate (ny'gejt) s. zaprzeczać;
negować ; anulować

negation (ny'gejszyn) s. zaprzeczenie; odmowa; niebyt

negative ('negetyw) adj. przeczący; negatywny; odmowny;
ujemny; s. zaprzeczenie;odmowa;
forma przecząca;wartość ujemna;

negatyw; v. sprzeciwić się;
odrzucać(np. plan)

neglect (ny'glekt) v. zaniedbywać; nie zrobić; s. zaniedbanie; pominięcie; lekceważenie

negligent ('neglydżent) adj.
niedbały; opieszały;nieuważny

negotiate (ny'gousjejt) v. pertraktować; omawiać; załatwiać;
przezwyciężać;przebić się przez

negotiation (ny,gouszy'ejszyn)
s. pertraktacje; omawianie

Negress ('ni:grys) s. murzynka

Negro ('ni:grou) s. murzyn; adj.
murzyński

neigh (nej) s. rżenie; v. rżeć

neighborhood ('nejberhud) s.
sąsiedztwo; sąsiedzi; okolica

neighboring ('nejberyng) adj.
sąsiedni; sąsiadujący

neither ('ni:dżer) pron. & adj.
żaden (z dwóch); ani jeden
ani drugi; ani ten ani tamten;
conj. też nie;jeszcze nie

neither... nor ('ni:dżer...no:r)
exp. ani,.. ani

neon ('ni:en) s. neon;a.neonowy

neon sign('ni:en,sajn) s. reklama neonowa

nephew ('nefju:) s. siostrzeniec; bratanek

nerve (ne:rw) s. nerw; siła;
energia; odwaga; opanowanie;
zuchwalstwo; tupet; czelność;
v. dodawać sił, odwagi

nervous ('ne:rwes) adj. nerwowy

nervousness ('ne:rwesnys) s.
nerwowość; zdenerwowanie

nest (nest) s. gniazdo; wyląg
v. budować; gnieździć się

nestle ('nesl) v. skulić; stulić się; przytulić się;urządzić

nestle down ('nesl,dałn) v. się
usadawiać się (wygodnie)

nestle up to ('nesl,ap'tu) v.
przytulić się (do kogoś)

net (net) adj. czysty; netto;
s. siatka; sieć; v. łowić sie-
cią; trafić w siatkę; zarobić
na czysto (na sprzedarzy etc.)

nettle ('netl) s. pokrzywa;
v. parzyć pokrzywą; drażnić;
irytować;docinać(komuś)dopiekać

network ('net‚łe:rk) s. sieć
(np. elektryczna)
neurosis (njue:rousys) s. nerwica;zaburzenia psychiczne
neuter ('nju:ter) adj. nijaki;
neutralny; bezstronny; bezpłciowy; s. człowiek bezstronny; rodzaj nijaki
neutral ('nju:trel) adj. bezstronny; neutralny; obojętny;
pośredni; nieokreślony; bezpłciowy; s. państwo neutralne
neutrality (nu'traelyty) s.
neutralność;obojętność
neutralize ('ny:trelajz)v.neutra-
lizować;unieszkodliwiać;zobo-
jętniać
neutron ('nu:tron).s. neutron
never ('never) adv. nigdy;
chyba nie; wcale; ani nawet
nevermore ('newer'mo:r) adv.
nigdy więcej(przenigdy)
nevertheless (,newerty'les) adj.
niemniej; jednak; pomimo tego
new (nju:) adj. nowy; świeży;
nowoczesny;adv.znowu;na nowo
newborn ('nju:,bo:rn) adj. nowo urodzony; s. noworodek
newcomer (nju:'kemer) adj. no-
woprzybyły; s. przybysz
news (nju:z) s. nowiny; wiadomości; aktualności;zadrzenia
newscast ('nju:z,ka:st) s. na-
dawanie wiadomości
newspaper ('nju:s,pejper) s.
dziennik (gazeta);tygodnik etc.
newsreel ('nju:sri:l) s. kronika filmowa
newsstand ('nju:staend) s.kiosk
z gazetami
new year ('nju:je:r) s. nowy
rok; pierwszego stycznia
New Year's Eve ('nju:,je:rs'i:w)
s. Sylwester(31go grudnia)
next (nekst) adj. następny;
najbliższy; sąsiedni; adv. następnie; potem; z kolei; tuż
obok;prep.obok;najbliżej
next but one ('nekst,bat'łan)
adj. przedostatni
next day ('nekst,dej) exp. na-
stępnego dnia
next door ('nekst,do:r) adj.
(dom) obok; sąsiedni(budynek)

next to ('nekst,tu) prep. obok
nibble at ('nybl,et) v. obgry-
zać; nadgryzać; brać (przynętę); s. ogryzanie; dziobanie
nice (najs) adj. miły; sympatyczny; przyjemny; uprzejmy;
ładny; wybredny; dokładny
nicely ('najsly) adv. przyjem-
nie; miło; grzecznie; ściśle;
dokładnie; skrupulatnie
nicety ('najsyty) s. delikatność; subtelność; zawiłość;
drobiazgowość; dokładność;
drobny szczegół; małe rozróżnienie;precyzja;akuratność
niche (nycz) s. nisza; v. chować (się)w niszy
nick (nyk) s. karb; otłuczenie;
moment; v. karbować; podcinać;
przecinać; trafić; natrafić;
odgadnąć; oszukać; złapać
nickel ('nykl) s. nikiel; 5 centów USA: v. niklować
nick-nack ('nyk,naek) = knickknack; ozdóbka;świecidełko
nickname ('nyknejm) s. zdrobnia-
łe imię; przezwisko; v. nazywać
zdrobniale; przezywać
niece (ni:s) s. siostrzenica;
bratanica
niggard ('nyged) s. sknera; adj.
żałujący (czegoś); skąpiący
night (najt) s. noc; wieczór
night cap ('najtkaep) s. kieliszek przed snem; czepek do spania;szklanka wina przed snem
nightclub ('najtklab) s. nocny
lokal (rozrywkowy)
nightgown ('najtgałn) s. damska
koszula nocna;nocny ubiór
nightingale ('najtyŋgejl) s.
słowik; a. słowikowy; słowika
nightly ('najtly) adv. co noc;
w nocy;adj. nocny; jak noc
nightmare ('najtmeer) s. koszmar; przerażające doświadczenie
night school ('najtsku:l) s.
szkoła wieczorowa
nightshirt ('najtsze:rt) s.
koszula nocna
nighty ('najty) s. koszulka
nocna (dziecinna,kobieca)

nil (nyl) s. nic; zero

nimble ('nymbl) adj. zwinny; zgrabny;bystry;żywy;żwawy

nine (najn) num. dziewięc; s. dziewiątka;dziewiecioro

ninepins ('najnpynz) pl. kręgle

nineteen ('najn'ti:n) num. dziewiętnaście;dziewiętnastka

nineteenth ('najn't:ng) num. dziewiętnasty;dziewiętnasta część

ninetieth ('najntyyš) num. dziewiędziesiąty

ninety ('najty) num. dziewięcdziesiąt;dziewiędziesiątka

ninth ('najng) num. dziewiąty

ninthly ('najnsly) adv. po dziewiąty (raz)

nip (nyp) v. uszczypnac; przychwycic; odszczepic; stłumic; zmrozic; buchnąc; ukrasć; popędzić; polecieć; ucinac; niszczyc;s.ukąszenie;uszczypnięcie

nipoff ('nypof) v. zemknąc

nipple ('nypl) s. brodawka sutkowa; smoczek; złącze gwintowane rury; wzniesienie; pagorek;bańka;złączka;nasówka

niter ('najter) s. saletra

nitrogen ('najtrydżen) s. azot

no (nou) adj. nie; żaden; odmowa; adv. nie; bynajmniej; nic;wcale nie;s.odmowa;sprzeciw

no one ('nou,łan) adj. żaden; ani jeden; nikt (w ogóle)

nobility (nou'bylyty) s. szlachetnosc; szlachta

noble (noubl) adj. szlachetny; szlachecki; wspaniały; wielkoduszny; s. szlachcic

nobleman (noublmen) s. szlachcic

nobody ('noubedy) s. nikt; człowiek bez znaczenia

nod (nod) v. skinąc głową; ukłonic sie; drzemac; przyzwalac skinieniem;byc nachylonym

noise (nojz) s. hałas; zgiełk; wrzawa; szum; odgłos; szmer; v. rozgłaszac coś;rozgłosić

noiseless ('nojzlys) adj. cichy; bezszelestny;nie hałasliwy

noisy ('nojzy) adj. hałasliwy; krzykliwy; wrzaskliwy

nomadic ('noumaedyk) adj. wędrowny; koczowniczy ;wędrujący

nominal ('nomynl) adj. nominalny; imienny; symboliczny ;tylko z nazwy

nominate ('nomynejt) v. mianowac; wyznaczac; obierac

nomination (,nomy'nejszyn) s. nominacja

nominative ('nomynetyw) s. mianownik (gram.); ta sprawa(sądowa)

non- (non) prefix nie-; bez-;

nonalcoholic ('non,aelke'holic) adj. bezalkoholowy

noncommissioned ('nonke'myszend) adj. bez rangi oficerskiej (podoficer)

noncommital ('nonke'mytl) adj. wymijający;nie zobowiazujący(sie)

nonconducting ('nonken'daktyng) adj. nieprzewodzacy

nonconformist ('nonken'fo:rmyst) dyskontent; niekonformista

nondescript ('nondyskrypt) adj. nieokreslony; s. człowiek nieokreslony(trudny do opisania)

none (non) pron. nikt; żaden; nic; adv. wcale nie; bynajmniej nie

nonexistence (,nony'ksystens) s. niebyt;nie istnienie

nonfiction (,non-',fykszyn) s. reportaże; opowiesce prawdziwa; opisy faktow (w dziennikach etc.)

nonsense ('nonsens) s. niedorzecznosc; nonsens; głupstwo

nonskid ('nonskyd) adj. przeciwslizgowy; nie slizgający się (samochód, opona etc.)

nonsmoker ('non'smouker) s. osoba niepaląca; przedział dla niepalących(w pociągu etc.)

nonstop ('non'stop) adj. bezpośredni;bez lądowania; bez postoju; nieprzerwany (lot etc.)

nonunion ('non'ju:njen) adj. nie należący do związku zawodowego;nie uznający związku zawodowego swego

nonviolence ('non'wajelens) s. (polityka) bez gwałtów

noodle ('nu:dl) s. makaron; kluska; cymbał; pała; głupek;łeb

nook (nuk) s. kącik; zakątek

noon (nu:n) s. południe

noose (nu:s) s. pętla; stryczek; sidła; lasso; v. usidlić; zrobić pętlę

nor (no:r) conj. też nie

norm (no:rm) s. norma;wzorzec; standard

normal ('no:rmel) adj. normalny; prostopadły; prawidłowy; s. stan normalny; prostopadła

normalize ('no:rmelajz) v. normalizować; unormować

Norman ('no:rmen) adj. normański;Normandczyk;Normandka

north (no:rs) adv. na północ; s. północ; adj. północny

northeast (no:rs'i:st) adj. północno-wschodni

northerly ('no:rdzerly) adj. północny; adv. na północ

northerner ('no:rdzerner) s. człowiek z północnych stanów

northward ('no:rsłerd) adj. północny; adv. na północ

northwest ('no:rs'łest) adj. północno-zachodni; adv. na północny-zachód; s. północnyzachód

Norwegian (no:rłi:dżen) adj. norweski ;s.Norweg

nose (nouz) s. nos; węch; wylot; dziób; v. węszyć; pocierać nosem; wtykać nos

nosegay ('nouzgej).s. wiązanka; bukiet

nostril ('noustryl) s. nozdrze; chrapy; dziura w nosie

nosy ('nouzy) adj. wścibski; śmierdzący; aromatyczny; nosacz wielki;stęchły;cuchnący

not (not) adv. nie ;ani(jeden)

not a (not ej) adv. żaden

notable ('noutebl) adj. znakomity; sławny; wybitny; s. dostojnik;wybitny człowiek

notary public ('noutery'pablyk) s. notariusz

notation (nou'tejszyn) s. znakowanie; notacja; symbol

notch (nocz) s. nacięcie; karb; przełęcz; v. nacinać; karbować; rowkować ;s.krok(dalej)

note (nout) s. nuta; znak; znamię; uwaga; notatka; banknot; v. zapisywać; zauważać

note down ('nout'dałn) v. zanotować;zapisywać

notebook ('noutbuk) s. zeszyt; notatnik;notes; notesik

noted ('noutyd) adj. znany; znakomity; wybitny

notepaper ('nout,pejper) s. papier listowy ;blok

noteworthy ('nout,łe:rsy) adj. godny uwagi; wybitny;osobliwy

nothing ('nasyng) s. nic; drobiazg; adv. nic; nie; w żaden sposób;bynajmniej nie;wcale nie

nothing but ('nasyng'bat) s. nic tylko..(coś najlepszego)

notice ('noutys) v. zauważyć; spostrzec; traktować grzecznie; powiadamiać; s. zawiadomienie; uwaga; recenzja ;spostrzeżenie

noticeable ('noutysebl) adj. godny uwagi; widoczny

notification (,noutyfy'kejszyn) s. zawiadomienie ;zgłoszenie

notify (noutyfaj) v. zawiadomić

notion ('nouszyn) s. pojęcie; wyobrażenie; zamiar ;wrażenie

notorious ('nou'to:rjes) adj. notoryczny; osławiony;jawny

notwithstanding (,noutłys'staendyng) adv. jednakże; niemniej; mimo; prep. pomimo(tego);mimo

nought (no:t) s. nic; zero

noun (naun) s. rzeczownik

nourish ('narysz) v. żywić; karmić ;utrzymywać

nourishing ('naryszyng) adj. pożywny ;pokrzepiający

nourishment ('naryszment) s. pokarm; pożywienie; żywienie; karmienie ;żywność; jedzenie

novel ('nowel) s. powieść; opowieść; nowela; adj. nowy; nowatorski; osobliwy ;oryginalny

novelist ('nowelyst) s. powieściopisarz

novelty ('nowelty) s. nowość; innowacja ;oryginalność

November (nou'wember) s. listopad; adj. listopadowy

novice ('nowys) s. nowicjusz;
neofita; początkujący

now (nał) adv. teraz; obecnie;
dopiero co; otóż; a więc;
s. teraźniejszość; chwila
obecna; chwila dzisiejsza

now and again ('nał,ende,gejn)
exp. od czasu do czasu

now and then ('nał,end'dzen)
exp.: nieraz; od czasu do czasu; czasem;co jakiś czas

nowadays ('nałe,dejz) adv.
obecnie; dzisiaj; s. obecne
czasy;dzisiejsze czasy

nowhere ('nouhłer) adv. nigdzie; s. niepowodzenie etc.

noways ('noułejz) adv. bynajmniej ; wcale nie

noxious ('nokszes) adj. szkodliwy; niezdrowy (moralnie etc.)

nozzle ('nozl) s. dysza; rozpylacz; dziób; wylot (rury etc.)

nuclear ('nu:kli:er) adj. jądrowy; o napędzie nuklearnym

nuclear fission('nu:kli:er'fyszyn) v. rozszczepienie jądra

nuclear power plant ('nu:kli:-
er'pałer'pla:nt) s. elektrownia atomowa

nuclear reactor ('nu:kli:er,ri:-
'aekter) s. reaktor nuklearny

nucleus ('nu:kljes) s. jądro

nude (nju:d) adj. nagi; goły;
nie ważny (prawnie); s. człowiek nagi; nagość; akt

nudge (nadż) v. trącać lekko;
s. trącenie łokciem

nugget ('nagyt) s. bryłka; złoty samorodek

nuisance ('nju:sns) s. zawada;
naruszenie porządku publiczne-
go; osoba sprawiająca zawadę

null and void ('nal,end'woid)
exp. nieważny; bez znaczenia;
unieważniony;nic, nie zanczący

numb (nam) adj. ścierpły; zdrętwiały; odrętwiały; v. drętwieć;
odurzać;paraliżować;zdrętwieć

number ('namber) s. liczba; numer; ilość; v. liczyć; numerować; wyliczać; zaliczać

numberless ('namberlys) adj.
niezliczony; bez numeru

number plate ('namber'plejt) s.
płyta z numerem rejestracji
samochodu;motoru etc.

numeral ('nju:merel) adj. liczbowy; cyfrowy; s. liczebnik;
cyfra(pisana,mówiona etc.)

numerous ('nju:meres) adj. liczny; obfity;liczebny;rytmiczny

nun (nan) s. zakonnica:mniszka

nunnery('nanery) s. zakon żeński

nuptials ('napszels) pl. zaślu-
biny;gody;wesele;ślub

nurse (ne:rs) s. pielęgniarka;
pielęgniarz; mamka; osłona;
v. pielęgnować; leczyć; opiekować się; żywić; podsycać;
szanować; obejmować; karmić;
pić powoli(piersią) niańczyć

nursery ('ne:rsery) s. pokój
dziecinny; żłobek; przedszkole; ochronka; wylęgarnia;
szkółka (roślin)(drzewek)

nursery school ('ne:rsery'sku:l)
s. przedszkole

nursing bottle ('ne:rsyng'botl)
s. flaszka do karmienia

nursing home ('ne:rsyn'houm)
s. przytułek - lecznica dla
starych i kalekich;dom zdrowia

nut (nat) s. orzech; bzik; dziwak; nakrętka; zakrętka;
v. szukać i zbierać orzechy

nutcracker ('natkraeker) s.
dziadek do orzechów

nutmeg ('natmeg) s. gałka
muszkatołowa

nutria ('nju:trje) s. nutria
(futro);nutrie

nutrient ('nju:trjent) adj.
pożywny; odżywczy ;s.odżywka

nutriment ('nju:tryment) s.
środek odżywczy

nutrition (nju'tryszyn) s. odżywienie; pokarm

nutritious (nju'tryszes) adj.
pożywny; odżywczy

nutshell ('natszel) s. łupka
od orzecha; istota rzeczy;
sama treść(w paru słowach)

nutty ('naty) adj. orzechowy;
pomylony; zbzikowany;dziwaczny;
zwariowany;pikantny;zakochany

nuzzle ('nazl) v. wsadzać nos,
(w coś); ryć; węszyć; wtulać
się (twarzą w czyjeś ramię)
nylon ('najlon) s. nylon; pończochy nylonowe
nymph (nymf) s. nimfa
nymphomania (,nymfe'mejnia) s.
nimfomania(kobieca żądza miłoś)
o (ou) piętnasta litera
angielskiego alfabetu:zero
oak (ouk) s. dąb;a.dębowy
oar (o;r) s. wiosło; v. wiosłować
oarsman ('o:rzmen) s. wioślarz
oasis (ou'ejsys) s. oaza ;
zielonei żyzne miejsce wśród
pustynnej okolicy
oat (out) s. owies
oatmeal ('outmi:l) s. owsianka [stwo;świętokradztwo etc.
oath (ouš) s. przysięga;przekleń-
obedience (e'bi:djens) s. po-
słuszeństwo
obedient (e'bi:djent) adj. posłuszny
obey (e'bej) v. słuchać; być
posłusznym (rozsądkowi etc.)
obituary ('bytjuery) s. nekrolog; adj. posmiertny; żałobny
object ('obdżykt) s. przedmiot;
rzecz; cel; śmieszny człowiek;
dopełnienie; v. zarzucać coś;
być przeciwnym ;sprzeciwiać się
objection (eb'dżekszyn) s. zarzut; sprzeciw; przeszkoda;
trudność; wada; niechęć
objective (eb'dżektyw) s. cel;
objektyw; adj. przedmiotowy;
obiektywny; rzeczywisty
obligation (obly'gejszyn) s.
zobowiązanie; obowiązek; obligacja;dług(wdzięczności etc.)
oblige (e'blajdż) v. zobowiazywać; spełniać prośbę
obliging (e'blajdżyng) adj.
uprzejmy; uczynny ;usłużny
oblique (e'bli:k) adj.pośredni;
ukosny; skosny; kręty; nieszczery; potajemny;v.iść na ukos,
obliterate (e'blyterejt) s. zacierać; zamazywać; wykreślić;
zniszczyć;skasować (zanczek etc.)

oblivion (e'blywjen) s.
zapomnienie; niepamięć
oblivious (o'blywjes) adj. za-
pominający; niepomny; nieświadomy; dający zapomnienie
oblong('oblong)adj. podłużny;
s. podłużny przedmiot
obscene (ob'si:n) adj. sprośny;
nieprzyzwoity; niemoralny
obscure (eb'skjuer) adj. ciemny;
skromny; niejasny; ukryty; nieznany; v., zaciemniać; przyciemniać; zaćmiewać
obsequies ('obsykłyz) pl. pogrzeb
observance (eb'ze:rwens) s. obrzęd; zwyczaj; przestrzeganie;
szacunek;poszanowanie;rytuał
observant (eb'ze:rwent) adj.
uważny; przestrzegający; spostrzegawczy;bystry; czujny
observation (,obzer'wejszyn) s.
obserwacja; spostrzeżenie;
uwaga;spostrzegawczość
observatory (eb'ze:rweto:ry) s.
obserwatorium;punkt obserwacyjny
observe (eb'ze:rw) v. obserwować;
przestrzegać; obchodzić; zauważać;wypowiedzieć uwagę;zbadać
observer (eb'ze:rwer) s. obserwator;człowiek przestrzegający praw
obsess (eb'ses) v. opętać; prześladować;nie dawać spokoju;nawie-
obsession (eb'seszyn) s. obsesja; dzać
opętanie ;natręctwo (myślowe)
obsolete ('obseli:t) adj. przestarzały; szczątkowy;zarzucony
obstacle ('obstekl) s. przeszkoda; zawada
obstetrics (ob'stetryks) s. po-
łóżnictwo
obstinacy ('obstynesy) s. upior
obstinate ('obstynat) adj. uparty; uporczywy;zawzięty;wytrwały
obstruct (eb'strakt) v. tamować;
zagradzać; zasłaniać; wstrzymywać;wywoływać zator;zawadzać
obtain (eb'tejn) v. uzyskać;
trwać; panować;obowiązywać
obtainable (eb'tejnebl) adj.
osiągalny (do nabycia etc.);
możliwy do nabycia

obtrusive (eb'tru:syw) adj.
natarczywy; natrętny
obvious ('obwjes) adj. oczywisty; rzucający się w oczy
occasion (e'kejžyn) s. sposobność; okazja; powod
occasional (e'kejženl) adj.
przypadkowy; okazyjny;
okolicznościowy; rzadki
Occident ('oksydent) s. Zachod (jako kultura, ekonomia
etc.)-całość geogaficzna
occult (o'kalt) adj. tajemny
occupant ('okjupent) s. mieszkaniec; posiadacz (faktyczny)
occupation (,okju'pejszyn) s.
okupacja; zawod; zajęcie;
zajmowanie;zamieszkiwanie
occupy ('okjupaj) v. okupować;
zajmować (się czyms);zatrudniać
occur (e'ke:r) v. zdarzać się;
przychodzić na mysl; poja-
wiać się;dziać sie;trafić sie
occurrence(e'karens) s. wydarzenie; przypadek;występowanie
ocean ('ouszen) s. ocean;a.ocea-
o'clock (e'klok) adv. na zegarze;według zegara
October (ok'touber) s. październik ;a,październikowy
ocular ('okjuler) adj. oczny;na-
oczny;na oko;okiem;s.okular
oculist ('okjulyst) s. okulista
odd (od) adj. nieparzysty;
dziwny; dziwaczny; zbywający;
pozostały; dodatkowy;od pary
odds (ods) pl. szanse; fory;
nadwyżka; różnica; drobne
szczegoły; spor; nierówność
(w grze);sprzeczność;różnica
odds-and-ends ('ods,end'ends)
exp.; resztki; rupiecie
oddity ('odyty) s. osobliwość;
dziwak;dziwactwo;dziwna rzecz
odor ('ouder) s. odor; won;
slad; reputacja;sława;posmak
of (ow) prep. od; z; o; w
of Cracow (ow'Krakau) exp.;
z Krakowa(pochodzeniem etc.)
of charity (ow'chaeryry) exp.
z miłosierdzia
off (of) adv. od; z; na boku;
precz; zdala; przy;prep.z dala

offshore (of'szo:r) adv. przy
wybrzeżu ;adj.od lądu(na morze)
offense (e'fens) s. obraza; za-
czepka; przekroczenie,ofeęywa
offend (e'fend) v. obrazać; razic; występować przeciw (np.
prawu);zawinić;wykroczyć
offender (e'fender) s. winowajca ;przestępca;strona winna
offensive (e'fensyw) adj. obraźliwy; drażniący; przykry; cuchnący; zaczepny; s. ofensywa;
postawa zaczepna
offer ('ofer) s. oferta; propozycja (np. ślubu); v. ofiarować (się); oświadczyć (się);
oferować; nastręczyć się; nada-
rzyć się;występować z propozycją
offering ('oferyng) s. ofiara
office ('ofys) s. biuro; urząd;
obowiązek; służba urzędowania;
posada;funkcja;stanowisko;gabi-
officer ('ofyser) s. urzędnik;
oficer; policjant; v. obsadzać
kadra; dowodzić; kierować
official (e'fyszel) s. urzędnik;
adj. urzędowy; oficjalny
officious (e'fyszes) adj. narzucający się; natrętny; gorliwy;
nieurzędowy;nieoficjalny
offish ('ofysz) adj. chłodny;
sztywny; z rezerwą;nieprzystępny
offset (o':fset) s. offsetowy
druk; gałąż; odgałęzienie;
odrosl; potomek; wyrownanie;
kompensata;v.wynagradzać;rozras-
offspring ('o:fspryng)s. potomek;
wynik; potomstwo
often ('o:fn) adv. często
oh ! (ou) excl.:och !; ach !
oil (ojl) s. oliwa; olej; ropa;
nafta; farba olejna; v. oliwić;
smarować; przetapiać;pochlebiać
oilcloth ('ojlkloš) s. cerata
oily ('ojly) adj. oleisty;
olejny; tłusty; oblesny;służalczy
ointment ('oyntment) s. masć
O.K., okay ('ou'kej) adv. w porządku; tak; adj. b. dobry;
s. zgoda; v. zaaprobować (coś)
old (ould) adj. stary; staroświecki; doświadczony; były
s.dawne czasy;dawno temu

old age ('ould,ejdź) s. starość
old-age ('ould ejdź) adj. dawny; stary; starczy
old-fashioned ('ould'faeszend)
adj. staromodny; staroświecki
old-time ('ould,tajm) adj.
dawny
old town ('ould,tałn) s. starów-
ka; stare miasto
olive ('olyw) s. oliwka; drzewo oliwne; (kolor) oliwkowy;
oliwa stołowa
olive-branch ('olywbra:ncz) s.
gałązka oliwna
Olympic Games (ou'lympyk,gejms)
pl. igrzyska olimpijskie
ombudsman (om'bu:dz,men) s.
rzecznik ludu - załatwia skar-
gi na biurokratów
omelet(te) ('omlyt) s. omlet
omen ('oumen) s. omen; wróżba;
znak ;v. być wrożbą;być znakiem
ominous ('omynes) adj. złowieszczy ; źle wróżący
omission (e'myszyn) s. opuszczenie; zaniedbanie
omit (ou'myt) v. opuszczac;
pomijać; zaniedbywać
omnipotent (om'nypetent) adj.
wszechmocny;wszechmogący
omniscient (om'nysjent) adj.
wszechwiedzący
on (on) prep. na; ku; przy; nad;
u; po; adv. dalej; przed siebie; naprzod ;przy sobie
on and on ('on,end'on) exp.: coraz dalej;bez końca;wciąż
on demand (,on dy'ma:nd) exp.:
na żądanie
on the street ('on,dy'stri:t)
exp.: na ulicy
on to ('ontu) exp. na; do
once (łans) adv. raz; nagle;
naraz; zaraz; kiedyś; niegdyś;
dawniej; s. raz; conj. raz;
gdy; skoro ;od razy;zarazem etc.
one (łan) num. jeden; adj. pierwszy; pojedyńczy; jedyny; pewien;
s. dowcip; kieliszek; pron. ten;
który;ktoś; niejaki;s.jedynka
one Adams ('łan,aedems) exp.: pewien Adams ;niejaki Adams

one day ('łan,dej) exp.pewnego
dnia; kiedyś;niegdyś
one by one ('łan,baj'łan) adv.
pojedyńczo;jeden za drugim
one antoher (,łan e'nadzer) adv.
jeden drugiego; wzajemnie
oneself (łan'self) pron. się;
siebie; sobie; sam; osobiście;
samodzielnie; samotnie
one-sided ('łan'sajdyd) adj.
jednostronny
one-up-manship ('łan,ap'-men-
szyp) s. "wyścig" nerwów
(w zatargu etc)
one-way ('łan,łej) adj. jedno-
kierunkowy(ruch)
onion ('anjen) s. cebula
onlooker ('onluker) s. widz
only ('ounly) adj. jedyny; jedynak; adv. tylko; jedynie;
ledwo; dopiero; conj. tylko
że;coż z tego ,kiedy...
onward ('onłerd) adj. naprzod;
ku przodowi; adv. naprzod;
dalej;dalej naprzod
ooze (u:z) v. sączyć się; wydzielać się; ciec; s. szlam;
muł; wyciek; rzadkie błoto
opaque (ou'pejk) adj. nieprzezroczysty; matowy; mętny;
niejasny; s. rzecz matowa;
nieprzezroczysta
open ('oupen) adj. otwarty; rozwarty; dostępny; wystawiony;
jawny; odsłonięty; wakujący;
otwarty; wolny; v. otworzyc;
zwierzyć się; umożliwic; rozpoczynać; rozchylić;udostępnić
open air ('oupen,eer) s. świeże
powietrze; wolna przestrzeń
opener ('oupener) s. otwieracz
(np. puszek);przyrząd do otwie-
rania
open-handed ('oupn'haendyd) adj.
szczodry; hojny
open-hearted ('oupn,ha:rtyd) adj.
szczery; serdeczny
opening ('oupnyng) s. otwor; wylot; otwarcie; początek; zbyt;
adj. początkowy; wstępny
openly ('oupnly) adv. otwarcie;
szczerze; publicznie; bez ogrodek;po prostu; wprost(powiedzieć)

open-minded ('oupn'majndyd)
adj. z otwartą głową; bez
przesądów; bez stronny
opera ('opere) s. opera
opera glasses ('operegla:sys) s.
lornetka (teatralna)
operate ('operejt) v. działać;
zadziałać; oddziałać; pracować; operować (kimś; kogoś);
wywoływać; prowadzić; kierować; obsługiwać;spekulować
operation (,ope'rejszyn) s.
działanie; czynności; operacja;
obsługiwanie; akcja
operative ('oprejtyw) adj. skuteczny; działający; praktyczny; operacyjny;s.pracownik;agent
mechanik; robotnik; detek-
tyw; agent wywiadu
operator ('operejter) s. operator; pracownik; obsługujący
maszynę; telefonista; kierownik; przemysłowiec; finansista; spekulant
opinion (e'pynjen) s. pogląd;
opinia; zdanie;zapatrywnie;sąd
opponent (e'pounent) s. przeciwnik; oponent; adj. przeciwny; przeciwległy
opportunity (,oper'tju:nyty)
s. sposobność; okazja
oppose (e'pouz) v. przeciwstawiać; sprzeciwiać się,
opposed (e'pouzd) adj. przeciwny;przeciwdziałający
opposite ('epezyt) adj. przeciwny; przeciwległy; odmienny; adv. na przeciwko;na przeciw
s. przeciwieństwo;odwrotność
opposition (,ope'zyszyn) s.
sprzeciw; opor; opozycja;
przeciwstawienie (się); przeciwieństwo;a.opozycyjny
oppress (e'pres) v. przygniatać; uciskać; ciemiężyć;
gnębić; nużyć; męczyć
oppression (e'preszyn) s. ucisk
oppressive (e'presyw) adj.
uciążliwy; dręczący; gnębiciel-
ski; ciężki; duszny;deprymujący
opt (opt) v. wybierać z dwu
alternatyw;optować na rzecz cze-

optical ('optykel) adj. optyczny; wzrokowy,pomocny w widzeniu
optician (op'tyszen) s. optyk
optimism ('optymysem) s. opty-
mizm;pogodny pogląd na życie
optimize ('optymajz) v. używać
najwydajniej,najsprawniej
option ('opszyn) s. możność wyboru; opcja; wybor; v. wybrać
alternatywę
or (o:r) conj. lub; albo; czy;
ani; inaczej; czyli; s. złoto;
adj. złoty
or else ('o:rels) exp. bo jak
nie..; w przeciwnym razie
oral ('o:rel) adj. ustny; do-
ustny; s. egzamin ustny
orange ('oryndż) s. pomarańcza;
adj. pomarańczowy
orangeade ('oryn'dżejd) s.
oranżada(z pomarańcz ,cukru)
orator ('oreter) s. mówca
orbit ('o:rbyt) s. orbita;
oczodoł; v. latać w orbicie
(ziemi)(słońca etc.)
orchard ('o:rczerd) s. sad
orchestra ('o:rkystra) s.
orkiestra
ordain (o:r'dejn) v. wyświęcać;
mianować; nakazywać; przeznaczać;zarządzać;nakazać
ordeal (o:r'di:l) s. ciężka
próba; ciężkie doświadczenie
order ('o:rder) s. rozkaz; zlecenie; zarządzenie; przekaz;
porządek; szyk; układ; stan;
zakon; order; obrzęd; zamówienie; zadanie; v. rozkazać; zamawiać; komenderować; zarządzać;
wyświecać; porządkować
orderly ('o:rderly) s. posługacz; ordynans; adj. adv.
porządny; czysty; dokładny;
skromny; spokojny; dyżurny
ordinal ('o:rdynl) s. liczebnik
porządkowy; adj. porządkowy
ordinary ('o:rdnry) adj. zwyczajny; zwykły; przeciętny;
pospolity; typowy; s. rzecz
zwykła,codzienna,przeciętna
ore (o:r).s. ruda; kruszec;
a. kruszcowy;rudowy

organ ('o:rgen) s. narząd;
organ; organy;czasopismo
organic ('o:rgaenyk) adj. organiczny;usystematyzowany
organization (,o:rgenaj'zejszyn) s. organizacja; organi-
zowanie;struktura;zrzeszenie
organize ('o:genajz) v. organi-
zowac;zrzeszyć;nadawać ustrój
organizer('o:genajzer) s. organizator
orgy ('o:rdży) s. orgia
Orient ('o:rjent) adj. orien-
talny; wschodni;s.Wschód(bliski)
orient ('o:rjent) v. oriento-
wac;ukierunkowywać;ustawiać
origin('orydżyn) s. pochodzenie;
poczatek;źródło;geneza
original (e'rydżynel) adj.
oryginalny; początkowy;
s. oryginał; dziwak
originality (e,rydży'naelyty)
s. oryginalność
originate (e'rydżynejt) v. zapoczątkować; powstawać
ornament ('o:rnament) s. ozdoba; v. ozdabiac;upiększać
ornamental (,o:rne'mentl) adj.
ozdobny; dekoracyjny; zdobni-
czy;upiększający
orphan ('o:rfen) s. sierota;
adj. sierocy; osierocony
orphanage ('o:rfenydż) s. sie-
rociniec; sieroctwo
orthodox ('o:tedoks) adj. pra-
wowierny; prawosławny
oscillate ('osylejt) v. drgać;
wahac się, oscylować
ostrich ('ostrycz) s. struś
other ('adzer) pron. inny; drugi; adv. inaczej;odmiennie
otherwise ('adzerłajz) adv.
inaczej; poza tym; skądinąd
ought (o:t) v, powinien; trzeba;
żeby; należy; zobowiazany etc.
ounce (auns) s. uncja; odrobina; lampart;l/16 funta
our ('aur) adj. nasz
ours ('auerz) pron. nasz
ourselves (auer'selwz) pl.pron.
my; my sami;(dla)nas etc.
oust (aust) v. usuwac; wypie-
rac; wyrzucac;wywłaszczać

out (aut) adv. na zewnątrz;
precz; poza; na dworze; poza
domem;nieobecnym(być) etc.
out-and-out (auten'aut) adj.
całkowity; adv. całkowicie
out of ('autow) adv. z; bez;
poza ;nie (modne,rozsądne)
outbalance (aut'baelens) v.
przeważyc;przewyższać
outbid (aut'byd) v. przelicy-
towac;dac więcej (niż inny)
outbreak ('autbrejk) s. wybuch
(np. wojny)(epidemii etc.)
outburst ('autbe:rst) s. wybuch (np. gniewu)(vulkanu)
outcast ('autka:st) s. wyrzutek; wygnaniec; adj. wygnany
outcome ('autkam) s. wynik;
rezultat;konsekwencje
outcry ('autkraj) s. okrzyk;
wrzawa;silny protest
outdoors ('aut'do:rz) adj. na
wolnym powietrzu; s. wolna
przestrzeń;adv.zewnatrz(domu)
outer ('auter) adj. zewnętrzny
outermost ('auter'moust) adj.
najbardziej zewnętrzny
outfit ('autfyt) s. wyposażenie; drużyna; zespół; towarzystwo; zestaw narzędzi; v. wyposażyć; zaopatrywać;wyekwipować
outgoing ('aut,gouyng)adj. od-
chodzacy; odjeżdżający; przyjazny;komunikatywny;towarzyski
outgrow (aut'grou) v. przera-
stac; wyrastac z..; wyrość(z ro-
outing ('autyng) s. wycieczka(na
otwarte morze,do lasu etc.);wy-
outlast (aut'la:st) v. prze-
trwac (coś,kogoś);wytrwać dłużej
outlaw ('aut-lo:) v. zakazywac;
wyjmowac spod prawa; s. przestępca; banita;notoryczny krymi-
outlet ('autlet) s. wylot; rynek zbytu; wyjscie; ujscie
outline ('autlajn) s. zarys;
szkic; v. konturowac; szkicowac; przedstawiać(plany etc,)
outlive (aut'lyw) v. przeżyc;
przetrwać;wytrwać dłużej
outlook ('autluk) s. widok; pogląd; obserwacja; widoki
(na przyszłość);czaty

outnumber (aut'namber) v. przewyższać liczebnie;być liczniej-
szym
out-of-date (autew'dejt) adj.
przestarzały; niemodny
outpatient ('aut,pejszent) s.
pacjent dochodzący (z domu)
output ('autput) s. wydajność;
wydobycie; moc; produkcja
outrage ('autrejdż) s, gwałt;
zniewaga; v. gwałcić; znieważać;uragać(zdrowemu rozsądkowi)
outrageous (aut'rejdżes) adj.
wołający o pomstę; bezecny;
gwałtowny;skandaliczny;obrażają-
cy
outright (aut'rajt) adj. całkowity; zupełny; stanowczy; bezpośredni; adv. odrazu; całkowicie; zupełnie; otwarcie
outrun (aut'ran) v. przegonić;
wyścignąć
outside ('aut'sajd) s. okładka;
fasada; strona zewnętrzna; adj.
zewnętrzny; adv. zewnątrz;
oprócz; z wyjątkiem
outside right (aut'sajd'rajt)
exp. na zewnątrz po prawej
outsider ('aut'sajder) s. człowiek obcy; niewtajemniczony;
laik; obcy zawodnik
outsize ('autsajz) s. wielkość
nietypowa, za duża
outskirts ('aut,ske:rts) s.
krańce; kraj; peryferie
outspoken (aut'spouken) adj.
szczery; otwarcie wypowiedzia-
ny, bez ogródek,prosto w oczy
outspread (aut'spred) adj. rozpostarty; rozpowszechniony
outstanding ('autstaendyng)
adj. wybitny; wyróżniający się;
otwarty; niezałatwiony; zaległy; wystający; sterczący
outstretched (aut'streczt) adj.
rozpostarty; wyciągnięty
outward ('autłerd) adj. zewnętrzny; powierzchowny; pozorny;
cielesny; s. strona zewnętrzna;
wygląd zewnętrzny;adv.na zewnątrz
outweigh (aut'łej) v. przeważyć
outwit (aut'łyt) v. przechytrzyć
oval ('ouwel) s. owal; adj.
owalny;owalnego kształtu

oven ('own) s. piekarnik; piec
over ('ouwer) prep. na; po;
w; przez; ponad; nad; powyżej;
adv. na drugą stronę; po powierzchni; całkowicie; od początku; zbytnio; znowu; raz
jeszcze(odrabiać zadanie etc.)
over again ('ouwer,e'gejn) adv.
na nowo; jeszcze raz
over-and-over ('ouwer,end'ouwer) adv. w kółko
overall ('ouwero:l) adj. ogólny; wszystko obejmujący;
pl. s. kombinezon roboczy
overboard ('ouwerbo:rd) adv.
(zaniechać) za burtę (wyrzucić)
overburden (,ouwe'rbe:rden) v.
przeładowywać; s. ciężar po-
kładów (np. nad kopalnią);
nadmiar ciężaru;ciężar warstw
overcast ('ouwerka:st) adj. za-
chmurzony; mroczny; ponury;
obrębiony; v. mroczyć; chmurzyć (się); obrębiać
overcharge (,ouwer'cza:rdż) v.
przeciążać; zdzierać (pieniądze); stawiać za wysokie ceny
overcoat ('ouwerkout) s. płaszcz
overcome (,ouwer'kam) v. pokonać
overcrowd (,ouwer'kraud) s. za-
tłoczyć;przepełniać
overdo (,ouwerdu:) v. przeciążać; przesadzać; przegotowywać;
niszczyć przesadą;robić za dużo
overdraw (,ouwer'dro:) v. wyczerpać (konto); przesadzać;
pisać czeki bez pokrycia
overdue (,ouwer'dju:) adj. zaległy;zapóźniony(pociąg etc.)
overestimate (,ouwer'esty,mejt)
v. przecenić; s. za wysoka
ocena;zbyt duże oczekiwania
overflow (,ouwer'flou) v. przepełniać; przelewać; s. wylew;
przelew;kanał przelewowy etc.
overgrow (,ouwer'grou) v. ob-
rastać; przerastać; rosnąć
nadmiernie;róść zbyt szybko
overhang ('ouwer'haeng) v. zwisać; sterczeć; zagrażać;
s. występ; zwis; nawis (dachu);
występ(skały);zwis(skalny etc.)

overhaul (.ouwer'ho:l) v.gruntownie naprawić; gruntownie zbadać; s. gruntowny remont

overhead ('ouwer'hed) s. wydatki administracyjne; adv. powyżej; na górze; adj. górny

overhear (,ouwer'hier) v. usłyszeć przypadkiem; podsłuchać

overheat ('ouwerhi:t) v. przegrzać; s. nadmiernc gorąco; przegrzanie

overjoyed (,ouwer'dżojd) adj. nieposiadający się z radości

overlap (,ouwer'laep) v. zachodzić na siebie; s. zachodzenie (na siebie)

overload (,ouwer'loud) v.przeładowaćs.nadmierny ciężar; przeciążenie(dachu etc.)

overlook (,ouwer'luk) v. przeoczyć; puszczać płazem; mieć widok z góry; nadzorować; wybaczyć; widok z góry; nadzór

overlord ('ouwerlo:rd) s. suzeren; samodzierżca

over-night ('ouwer'najt) adv. przez noc; poprzedniego wieczoru; adj. nocny; na noc

overpass (,ouwer'oa:s) s.skrzyżowanie wiaduktem; przejazd wiaduktem; v. przecinać; przekraczać; przewyższać; przewyciężać; pomijać(w kolejce etc.)

overrate ('ouwer'rejt) v. przeceniać;spodziewać się zbyt dużo

overrule (,ouwer'ru:l) v. opanowaćuchylać; odrzucać; unieważniać;zmieniać czyjeś postanowienie

overrun (,ouwer'ran) v. najechać; zalewać; przelewać; s. przekraczanie ceny umówionej

overseas ('ouwer'si:z) adv. za morzem; do krajów zamorskich; adj. zamorski

oversee ('ouwer'si:) v. dozorować; doglądać

overseer ('ouwer'si:er) s. nadzorca

overshadow ('ouwer'szaedou) v. przyćmiewać; zaćmiewać

oversight ('ouwersajt) s. przeoczenie

oversleep ('ouwer'sli:p) v. zaspać; przespać

overstrain ('ouwer'strain) v. przemęczać; s. przeciążenie; przemęczenie

overtake ('ouwer'tejk) v. doganiać; przeganiać; zaskoczyć

overthrow ('ouwer'srou) v. przewrócić; obalić; pobić; s. obalenie

overtime ('ouwertajm) s. godziny nadliczbowe; adv. nadprogramowa; adj. nądprogramowy; v. prześwietlić; przeeksponować

overtone ('ouwertoun) s. niedomówienie; sugestia; akcent; główna nuta

overture ('ouwer,tjuer) s. rozpoczęcie rokowań; propozycja; uwertura; v. proponować

overturn (,ouwer'te:rn) v. wywracać; obalać; s. przewracanie; przewrót;podbój

overweight (,ouwer'łejt) s. nadwaga; dodatkowa waga; otyłość; adj. ponad normalną wagę

overwhelm (,ouwer'hłelm) v. przygniatać; przywalać; zalewać; rujnować; ogarniać

overwork ('ouwer'łe:rk) v. przepracowywać się; przeciążać pracą; zmuszać do za ciężkiej pracy; przemęczać się; s. nadmierna praca

ovulate ('ouwjulejt) v. jajeczkować; wytwarzać jaja

ow (oł) v.byc winnym; zawdzięczać

owing ('ołyng) adj. dłużny; należny; prep. z powodu; skutkiem

owing to ('ołyng,tu) prep. ponieważ

owl (aul) s. sowa

own (ołn) v. mieć; posiadać; przyznawać (się); adj. własny; rodzony

owner ('ołner) s. właściciel

ownership ('ołnerszyp) s. własność; posiadanie

ox (oks) s. wół; pl. oxen

oxen ('oksen) pl. wały; zob.ox
oxide ('oksajd) s. tlenek
oxidation (oksy'dejszyn) s.
 utlenienie; oksydacja
oxidize (oksydajz) v. utleniać
oxygen (oksygżen) s. tlen
oyster ('ojster) s. ostryga
ozone ('ouzoun) s. ozon
p (pi:) szesnasta litera
 angielskiego alfabetu
pa (pa:) s. tato
pace (pejs) s. krok; chod;
 v. kroczyć; mierzyć krokami;
 ustalać rytm kroku; ćwiczyć
 krok (np. konia); przebywać
 (drogę);chodzić(tam i na zad)
pacer ('pejser) s. regulator
 rytmu (serca; kroku etc)
pacific (pe'syfyk) adj. spokojny; pokojowy
pacify ('paesyfaj) v. uspakajać; zaspokajać
pack (paek) s. pakunek; tłumok;
 toboł; stek; sfora; okład;
 kupa; v. pakować; opakować;
 owijać; stłoczyć; napychać;
 objuczyć; zbierać w stado
pack up ('paek,ap) v. spakować
package ('paekydż) s. pakunek;
 paczka
package deal ('paekydż'di:l)
 s. przyjęcie złożonej propo-
 zycji bez zmian
packer ('paeker) s. pakier;
 przedsiębiorca od pakowania
 artykułów żywnościowych; maszyna do pakowania
packet ('kaekyt) s. pakiet;
 v. zawijać
packing ('paekyŋg) s. pakowa-
 nie; opakowanie; uszczelka;
 okładzina; tampon
packthread ('paektred) s. szpagat
pact (paekt) s. pakt; układ
pad (paed) s. wyściółka; notes;
 blok (papieru); bibularz; łapa;
 podkładka; v. wyściełać;
 wywoływać; rozdymać
padding ('paedyŋg) s. obicie;
 wyściółka; podbicie; podszy-
 cie; rozwadnianie tekstu

paddle ('paedl) s. wiosełko
 kajakowe; v. wiosłować
paddock ('paedek) s. wybieg
 (koński)
padlock ('paedlok) s. kłódka
 v. zamykać na kłódkę
pagan ('pejgen) s. poganin;
 adj. pogański
page (pejdż) s. stronnica;
 karta; paż; goniec
pagent ('paedżent) s. widowisko
 (np. historyczne)
paid (pejd) adj. zapłacony; płat-
 ɪny; zob. pay
pail (pejl) s. wiadro
pain (pejn) s. ból; cierpienie;
 trud; staranie; v. zadawać ból;
 boleć; dolegać
painful ('pejnful) adj. bolesny;
 przykry
painless (pajnlys) adj. bezbolesny
paint (pejnt) s. farba; szminka;
 v. malować
paintbrush ('pejntbrasz) s. pędzel
painter ('pejnter) s. malarz
painting ('pejntyŋg) s. malarstwo; obraz
pair (peer) s. para; parka; stadło; v. dobierać do pary; stanowić parę
pajamas (pe'dża;mez) pl. piżama
pal (pael) s. kumpel; druh; przyjaciel
palace ('paelys) s. pałac
palate ('paelyt) s. podniebienie
pale (pejl) s. pal; granica; adj.
 blady; v. otaczać palami; blednąć; spowodować blednięcie
pallor ('paeler) s. bladość
palm (pa:m) s. palma; dłoń;
 piedz; v. ukrywać w dłoni; dotykać dłonią
palpitation (,paelpy'tejszyn)
 s. palpitacja; mocne bicie serca;kołatanie serca;drżenie;dygota-
 nie
pamper ('paemper) v. rozpieszczać;przekarmiać;zbyt pobłażać
pamphlet ('paemflyt) s. broszura natury polemicznej na tematy
 bieżące, kontrowersyjne etc.

pan (paen) s. patelnia; rondel; rynka; szalka; panewka; gęba; kra; v. gotować na patelni; udawać sie; krytykować

pancake ('paen,kejk) s. naleśnik; adj. płaski

pane (paen) s. szyba; krata; ścianka; płaszczyzna

panel ('paenl) s. tafla; otoczyna; płyta; wstawka; tablica (rozdzielcza); komitet; lista (przysięgłych; lekarzy etc); czaprak

pang (paeng)s. ostry ból; męka; wyrzuty (sumienia etc.)

panhandler (,paen'haendler) s. kwestarz; ksiadz z tacą

panic ('paenyk) s. panika; popłoch; v.wpaść w panikę; wywoływać panikę ;poddać się panice

pan-Slavism ('paen'sla:wyzem) s. panslawizm

pansy ('paensy) s. bratek

pant (paent) s. zadyszka; v. sapać; dyszeć

panther ('paenter) s. pantera

panties ('paentyz) pl. majtki (damskie)

pantry ('paentry) s. spiżarnia

pants (paents) pl. spodnie; kalesony

panty hose ('paenty'houz) s. rajstopy; pończochy z majtkami

pap (paep) s. papka; bzdury; sutka; brodawka piersiowa

papa ('pa:pe) s. papa; tata

paper ('pejper) s. papier; gazeta; tapeta; rozprawa naukowa; papierowe pieniądze; adj. papierowy; rzekomy; v. zawinąć w papier; tapetować

paper-backed ('pejper.baekt) adj. w papierowej okładce; kieszonkowe wydanie książki

paper-bag ('pejper,baeg) s. torba papierowa

paper-hanger ('pejper,haenger) s. tapeciarz

paper-hangings ('pejperhaengyngs) pl. tapety

paper-money ('pejper'many) s. pieniądze papierowe

paper-weight ('pejper,łejt) s. przycisk

par (pa:r) s. stan równości; norma

parable ('paerebl) s. przypowieść

parachute ('paere,szu:t) s. spadochron

parachutist ('paere,szu:tyst) s. spadochroniarz

parade (pe'rejd) s. parada; pochód; rewia; defilada; popisywać się; obnosić się (z czyms)

paradise ('paere,dajs) s. raj; adj. rajski

paragraph ('paere,gra:f) s. ustęp; odnośnik; notatka; v. dzielić na ustępy; pisać notatkę

parallel ('paere,lel) adj. równoległy; odpowiedni (czemuś) s. równoległa; równoleznik; porównanie; v. być równoległym; kłaść równolegle; zestawiać; znaleźć odpowiednik

paralyze ('paere,lajz) v. paraliżować; porażać

paralysis (pe'raelysys) s. paraliż

paramount ('paere,maunt) adj. główny; najważniejszy; kapitalny; najwyższy

parasite ('paere.sajt) s. pasożyt

parcel ('pa:rsl) s. paczka; działka; v. dzielić; pakować w paczki

parch ('pa:rcz) v. wysuszać (się); prażyć; cierpieć z pragnienia

parchment ('pa:rczment) s. pergamin

pardon('pa:rdn) s. ułaskawienie; przebaczenie; v. przebaczać; darować ;ułaskawiać

pardon me ('pa:rdn,mi:) exp.: przepraszam

pardonable ('pa:rdnebl) adj. wybaczalny

pare (peer) v. obcinać; obierać; obskrobać

parent ('peerent) s. ojciec;
matka; rodziciel;rodzicielka
parental (pe'rentl) adj. ro-
dzicielski
parenthesis (pe'rentysys) s.
nawias
parentheses (pe'renty,si:z) pl.
nawiasy
parings ('peerynz) pl. łupiny;
obrzynki
parish ('paerysz) s. parafia
parishioner (pe'ryszener) s.
parafianin
park (pa:rk) s. park; postój
samochodów; v. parkować
parking ('pa:rkyng) s. postój
samochodów; parkowanie
parking garage ('pa:rkyng'gae-
ra:ż) s. garaż parkingowy
parking lot ('pa:rkyn,lot) s.
plac parkingowy
parking meter ('pa:rkyn'mi:ter)
s. licznik do płacenia za
parking(na ograniczony czas)
parking ticket ('pa:rkyn'tykyt)
s. mandat karny za złe parkowanie lub za niezapłacenie
parkway ('pa:rkłej) s. cztero-
liniowa szosa, przedzielona
roślinnością
parliament ('pa:rlyment) s.
parlament
parliamentary (,pa:rly'mentery)
adj. parlamentarny
parlo(u)r ('pa:rler) s. salon;
sala; pokój (przyjęć)
parquet ('pa:rkej) s. parkiet;
v. wyłożyć parkietem
parrot ('paeret) s. papuga;
v. powtarzać jak papuga
parsley ('pa:rsly) s. pietruszka; a.pietruszkowy
parry ('paery) v. parować; odpierać; s. odparcie
parson ('pa:rsn) s. proboszcz
parsonage ('pa:rsnydż) s. plebania
part (pa:rt) s. część; ustęp;
udział; rola; strona; przedział (włosów); v; rozchodzić
(się); rozdzielać; dzielić;
pękać; robić (przedział); wyjeżdżać;adj.mniejszy niż całość

partake (pa:r'tejk) v. brak
udział; dzielić coś z kims;
zob. take
partaken (pa:r'tejkn) v. zob.
partake
partial ('pa:rszel) adj. stronniczy; częściowy; mający słabość do...;nie pełny
partiality (,pa:rszy'aelyty) s.
stronniczość; upodobanie
participant (pa:r'tysypent) s.
uczestnik;adj.uczestniczący
participate (pa:r'tysypejt) v.
brać udział
particle ('pa:rtykl) s. cząstka;
odrobina; partykuła
particular ('per'tykjuler) adj.
szczególny; szczegółowy; specjalny; prywatny; grymaśny
dokładny; uważny; dziwny; nie-
zwyczajny; ostrożny; s. szczegół; fakt
particularity (per,tykju'laeryty)
s. osobliwość; szczegółowość;
drobiazgowość; wybredność
particularly (per,tykju'laerly)
adv. osobliwie; szczególnie
particulars (per'tykjulers) s.
dane osobiste
parting ('pa:rtyng) s. przedzia-
łek (włosów); rozstanie; rozdział; pożegnanie; rozdroże;
zgon
partition (pa:r'tyszyn) s. podział; rozbiór; rozdział; v.
dzielić; przegradzać
partition off (pa:rtyszyn,of)
v. oddzielać
partly ('pa:rtly) adv. częściowo;po części; poniekąd
partner ('pa:rtner) s. wspólnik
partnership ('pa:rtnerszyp) s.
spółka
partook (pa:r'tuk) v. zob. partake
partridge('pa:łrydż) s. kuropatwa
part-time ('pa:rt,tajm) adv.
na niepełnym etacie; na niepełnym czasie;adj.niepełneta-
towy
party ('pa:rty) s. partia; przyjęcie towarzyskie; towarzystwo;
grupa;strona; uczestnik;osobnik

pass (pa:s) s. przełęcz; odnoga
rzeki; przepustka; wypad; bilet; umizg; sztuczka; v, przechodzić; mijać; pomijać; zdać;
przekazać; wymijać; wyprzedzać;
przeprowadzić; przewyższać;
spędzać; puszczać w obieg; podawać; odchodzić; umierać;
dziać się; krążyć
pass away ('pa:se,łej) v. odchodzić;umierać
pass by ('pa:s,baj) v. mijać;
pomijać
pass for ('pa:s,fo:r) v. udawać (kogoś)
pass out ('pa:s,aut) v. zemdleć;
umrzeć; wyjść
pass round ('pa:s,raund) v.
podawać wkoło (np. gościom)
pass through ('pa:s,tru) v.
przechodzić (przez, na wskroś)
passable ('paesebl) adj. nadający się do przebycia;
(stopień) dostateczny; znośny
passage ('paesydż) s. przejście;
przejazd; przeprawa; przelot;
upływ; korytarz; urywek tekstu
passenger ('paesyndżer) s. pasażer; pasażerka
passer-by ('pa:ser'baj) s. przechodzień
passion ('paeszyn) s. namiętność;
pasja; Męka Pańska; stan bierny
passionate ('paeszenyt) adj. namiętny; porywczy; zapalczywy;
żarliwy ;ognisty
passive ('paesyw) adj. bierny;
s. strona bierna
passport ('pa:s,po:rt) s. paszport
password('pa:s,żo:rd) s. hasło
past (pa:st) adj. przeszły;
miniony; ubiegły; prep. za;
obok; po; przed; adv. obok;
s. przeszłość; czas przeszły
paste ,pejst) ?. pasta; ciasto;
klej mączny; klajster; masa;
makaron: ›derzenie (siang);
v. przylepiać; oblepiać;
obić (kogoś)
pasteboard ('pejst,bo:rd) s.
karton; tektura; adj.tekturo-
wy; kartonowy; lichy

pastime ('pa:s,tajm) s. roz-
rywka(po pracy etc.)
pastry('pejstry) s. wyroby cu-
kiernicze; ciastka
past tense ('pa:st tens) s.
czas przeszły (gram.)
pasture ('pa:sczer) s. pastwisko
pat (paet) s. głaskanie; klepanie; krążek (np. masła);
v. pogłaskać; poklepać; pochwalić (kogoś) adv. trafnie;
w sam raz; adj. trafny; biegły;na czasie;zupełnie właściwy
patch (paecz) s. łata; plama;
skrawek; półko; zagon; grządka; klapka (na oko); przepąs-
ka; v. łatać; załatać; szyć
z łat; sztukować; naprawić;
skleić; załagodzić
patch pocket ('paecz,pokyt) s.
naszywana kieszeń
patchwork ('paecz,łe:rk) s.
łatanina; szachownica
pate (pejt) s. slang: głowa;
łeb; pała ;szczyt głowy
patent ('paetnt) s. patent;
v. opatentować; a. patentowa-
ny; opatentowany ;oczywisty
patent ('pejtnt) adj. jasny;
otwarty; oczywisty ;chroniony
patentem
patent-leather ('paetnt'ledzer)
s. skóra lakierowana
paternal (pe'te:rnl) adj. ojcowski; po ojcu
paternity (pe'te:rnyty) s.
ojcostwo; pochodzenie po ojcu;
autorstwo (książki,planu etc.)
path (pa:s) s. ścieżka; tor;
droga ruchu; zob. paths
pathetic (pe'tetyk) adj. żałosny: smutny; uczuciowy;
wzruszający; rozrzewniający
paths (pa:sz) pl. ścieżki; tory;
drogi ruchu
patience ('pejszens) s. cierpliwość; pasjans
patient ('pejszent) adj. cierpliwy; wytrwały; s. pacjent;
pacjentka; chory; chora
patio ('pa:ti:o) s. ogródek
wewnętrzny ; taras

patriot ('pejtryet) s. patryjota

patriotic(,paetry'otyk) adj. patriotyczny

patriotism ('paetrye,tyzem) s. patriotyzm

patrol (pe'troul) v. patrolować; s. patrolowanie; patrol

patrolman (pe'troulmen) s. policjant (drogowy USA)

patron ('pejtren) s. klient; opiekun; patron

patronage ('paetrenydż) s. opieka; poparcie; klientela; US rozdawanie posad etc.; protekcjonalność; przywileje; posady

patronize ('paetre,najz) v. popierać; protegować; traktować protekcjonalnie

patsy ('paecy) s. oferma przez wszystkich zawsze nadużywana

patter ('paeta) s. stukot; trajkot; trajkotanie; gwara; klepanie; szybka recytacja; żargon; v. stukać; bębnić; trajkotać; klepać (np. pacierze); odklepywać; łapać; gadać

pattern ('paetern) s. próbka; wzór; układ; materiał na suknię lub ubranie (USA); zespół; cechy charakterystyczne; ślady kul (na tarczy) v. wzorować; modelować; ozdabiać wzorami

paunch ('pa:ncz) s. (duży) brzuch; żołądek krowy

paunchy ('pa:nczy) adj. brzuchaty ;z wydatnym brzuchem

pause (po:z) s. przerwa; pauza; v. robić przerwę; wahać się

pave, (pejw) v. brukować; torować drogę

pavement ('pejwment) s. bruk; posadzka; materiał do brukowania

pavement-café ('pejwment'kaefej) s. kawiarnia ze stolikami na chodniku

paw (po:) s. łapa; (slang): tatuś; v. uderzać łapą lub kopytem; mietosić w łapach; macać (poufale)

pawn (po:n) s. zastaw; fant; pionek; v. zastawiać; dawać w zastaw

pawnbroker ('po:n,brouker) s. lichwiarz pożyczający pod zastaw; właściciel lombardu

pawnshop ('po:n-szop) s. lombard; sklep zastawniczy

pay; paid; paid (pej; peid; peid)

pay (pej) v. płacić; zapłacić; wynagradzać; udzielać (uwagi); dawać (dochód); opłacać (się) s. płaca; zapłata; pobory; wynagrodzenie; adj. płatny (np. automat telefoniczny); opłacalny

pay back ('pej baek) v. zwrócić dług; odpłacać

payday ('pej dej) s. dzień wypłaty

pay down ('pej dałn) v. dawać zadatek; płacić pierwszą ratę gotówka

pay for ('pej,fo:r) v. płacić (za coś)

pay in ('pej,yn) v. wpłacać

pay off ('pej,of) v. spłacać

pay out ('pej,aut) v. wydatkować; wypuszczać linę (na statku); wypłacać; płacić

pay up ('pej,ap) v. wyrównywać (dług); zapłacić

payable ('pejebl) adj. płatny; dochodowy; opłacający się

payee ('pej'i:) s. odbiorca płatności

payer ('pejer) s. płatnik

payment ('pejment) s. płatność; wypłata; zapłata

pea (pi:) s. groch; ziarnko grochu

peace (pi:s) s. pokój; pojednanie; spokój

peaceful ('pi:sful) adj. spokojny; pokojowy

peach (pi:cz) s. brzoskwinia; wspaniała rzecz, dziewczyna, człowiek; v. (slang):sypać; donosić (na kogoś)

peacock ('pi:,kok) s. paw; v. pysznić się jak paw; chodzić jak paw; parádować

peak (pi:k) s. (ostry) szczyt;
wierzchołek; daszek (u czapki);
szpic; garb (krzywej)
peak hour ('pi:k'auer) s. godzina szczytu ruchu
peal (pi:l) s. huk; łoskot; bicie w dzwony; huczny śmiech;
zespoł dzwonów; v. huczeć;
bic w dzwony; grac (cos) hucz-
nie
peanut ('pi:nat) s. orzeszek
ziemny; drobnostka; a; drobny;
prowincjonalny
pear (peer).s. gruszka
pearl (pe:rl) s. perła
peasant ('pezent) s. chłop;
wieśniak; adj. chłopski
peat (pi:t) s. torf
peat bog ('pi:t'bog) s. torfowisko
pebble ('pebl) s. kamyk; oto-
czak; v. granulowac; obrzucać
kamykami
peck (pek) v. dziobać; wcinac
(jedzenie); dziobnąc; cmoknąc
(męza); stukac; wydziobac;
dłubac; odziobac; v. dziobnięcie; cmok; slad dziobania
peculiar (py'kju:ljer) adj.
szczególny; dziwny; osobliwy;
charakterystyczny;dziwaczny
peculiarity (py'kju:li'aeryty)
s. właściwosc; cecha; osobli-
wosc; dziwacznosc
pedal ('pedl) s. pedal; nuta
pedałowa; v. pedałowac; nacis-
kac pedal; ('pi:dl) adj. pe-
dałowy; nozny
peddle ('pedl) v. sprzedawac po
domach; byc domokrążcą; wydzie-
lac po trochu
peddler ('pedler) s. domokrążca
pedestal ('pedystl) s. piedestał;
podstawa;Vstawiac na piedestał
pedestrian (py'destrjen) adj.
pieszy; przyziemny; prozaiczny;
s. piechur;pieszy człowiek
pedestrian crossing (pu'destrjen'krosyng) v. przejscie dla
pieszych; zebra; pasy
pedigree ('pedygri:) s. rodowód;
drzewo genealogiczne
pedlar('peler)s.przekupień;hand-

peek ('pi:k) v. podglądać
peel (pi:l) s. skóra; skórka;
łupa; v. obierac; zdzierac;
łuszczyc się; (slang):rozbierac
(się)
peep (pi:p) v. zerkac; podglądac;
wynurzac (się); wychodzic nie-
postrzeżenie
peeping Tom ('pi:pyng,tom) s.
podglądający natręt
peer (pier) s. rowny (komuś)
stanem, pochodzeniem etc.
peerless ('pierlys) adj. nie-
zrownany
peevish ('pi:wysh) adj. draźliwy; zły; gniewny;zirytowany
peg (peg) s. czop; kołek; zatyczka; szpunt; v. zakołkowac;
przymocowac kołkami
pelican ('pelyken) s. pelikan
pelt (pelt) s. futro; kanonada;
grzmocenie; pospiech; v. ostrze-
liwac; obrzucac; obsypywac gradem; rzucac zniewagi; obsypywac
zniewagami; walic
pelvis ('pelwys) s. miednica;
a. miedniczny
pen (pen) s. pioro; kojec; ogrodzenie; schron; (slang):więzie-
nie; v. pisac; układac list;
zamykac w ogrodzeniu
penal ('pi:nl) adj. karny; karalny
penalty ('penlty) s. kara
penalty kick ('penlty,kik) s.
karny strzał (do bramki)
penance ('penens) s. pokuta
pence (pens) pl. grosze; zob.
penny
pencil ('pensl) s. ołowek; rysowac; pisac
pencil sharpner ('pensl'sza:rp-
ner) s. strugaczka do ołowka
pendant ('pendent) s. wisiorek;
proporzec; adj. wiszący; zwi-
sający; nierozstrzygnięty; to-
czący się; do rozstrzygnięcia
pending ('pendyng) adj. niezałatwiony; będący w toku; wiszący; prep.: aż do; podczas
penetrate ('peny,trejt) v. przenikac; przepajac; przedostawac
się przez ;wtargnąc;zanurzyc

penetration (,peny'trejszyn)
s. penetracja; przenikanie;
przenikliwość

pen friend ('penfrend) s. znajomy z listów

penguin ('pengłyn) s. pingwin

penholder ('pen,houlder) s.
piórnik; obsadka; stojak na
pióro

penicillin (,peny'sylyn) s.
penicylina

peninsula(py'nynsjule) s. półwysep

penitent ('penytent) s. żałujący grzesznik; pokutnik; adj.
żałujący; skruszony

penitentiary (,peny'tenszery)
s. więzienie; adj. karany
więzieniem; poprawczy

penknife ('pen.najf) s. scyzoryk

penniless ('penylys) adj. w nędzy; bez grosza

penny ('peny) s. cent; grosz;
pl. pennies ('penyz); Br.pl.
pence (pens)

pennyworth ('penyłe:rs) s. wartość centa; exp. za centa

pension ('penszyn) s. renta;
emerytura; pensjonat; v. wyznaczać pensje; pensjonować

pension off ('penszyn,of) v.
przenosić na emeryturę

pensive ('pensyw) adj. zamyslony

penthouse ('penthaus) s. mieszkanie z ogrodem na szczycie
budynku; przybudówka na dachu

people ('pi:pl) s. ludzie;
ludność; lud; v. zaludniać

pep (pep) s. animusz; werwa;
wigor; adj. ożywiony; wesoły;
dowcipny; dodający animuszu

pep pills ('pep,pyls) pl. pigułki podniecające

pep up ('pep,ap) v. ożywić; dodać animuszu

pepper ('peper) s. pieprz; papryka; v. pieprzyć; kropić;
zasypywać kulami; dać lanie

per (pe:r) prep. przez; za; na;
według; co do;za pośrednictwem

perceive (per'si:w) v. uświadamiać sobie; odczuć; dostrzegać;
spostrzegać

percent (per'sent) s. odsetek;
od sta

percentage (per'sentydż) s. odsetek; procent; od sta

perceptible (per'septebl) adj.
dostrzegalny

perception (per'sepszyn) s.
spostrzeganie;percepcja

perch (pe:rcz) s. okoń; grzęda;
żerdz; pręt; v. siedzieć na
grzędzie; sadzać na grzędzie

percussion (per'kaszyn) s. uderzenie; zderzenie;bicie(bębna)

peremptory (per'emptery) adj.
stanowczy; apodyktyczny; ostateczny; nieodwołalny

perfect ('pe:rfykt) adj. doskonały; zupełny; v. udoskonalić;
wykończyć

perfect tense ('perfykt'tens)
s. gram. czas przeszły dokona-
ny

perfection (per'fekszyn) s.
doskonałość; szczyt; wykończenie; udoskonalenie

perforate ('pe:rferejt) v.
przedziurawiać; dziurkować;
przenikać; przebijać się

perform (per'fo:rm) v. wykonywać; odgrywać; spełniać; występować

performance (per'fo:rmens) s.
przedstawienie; wyczyn; wykonanie; spełnienie

performer (per'former) s. wy-
konawca

perfume ('pe:rfju:m) s. perfuma;
zapach ; (pe'rfju:m) v. perfu-
mować

perhaps (per'haeps, praeps) adv.
może; przypadkiem

peril ('peryl) s. niebezpieczeństwo; ryzyko; v. narazić
na niebezpieczeństwo

perilous ('peryles) adj. niebezpieczny; ryzykowny

period ('pieried) s. okres;
period; menstruacja; kropka;
kres; pauza;miesiączka;a.stylo-
wy

periodic (,piery'odyk) adj.
okresowy; periodyczny
periodical (,piery'odykel) s.
czasopismo; periodyk; adj.
okresowy; periodyczny
perish ('perysz) v. zgiąć;
niszczyć; nękać; trapić; gne-
bić';ginąć (przedwczesną śmier-cią)
perishable ('peryszebl) adj.
zniszczalny; s; łatwo psujący się towar
perjury ('pe:rdżery) s. krzy-
woprzysięstwo; złamanie
obietnicy
perm (pe:rm) s. trwała ondulacja
permanent ('pe:rmenent) adj.
trwały; permanentny
permanent wave ('pe:rmenent,
,łejw) s. trwała ondulacja
permeable ('pe:rmjebl) adj.
przepuszczalny; przenikalny
permission (per'myszyn) s. pozwolenie; zezwolenie
permit (per'myt) s. pisemne
zezwolenie; pozwolenie; v.po-
zwalać; zezwalać; dopuszczać
perpendicular (,pe:rpen'dykju-
ler) adj. prostopadły; s, prostopadła; pion
perpetual (per'petjuel) adj.
wieczny; wieczysty; trwały;
dożywotni
persecute ('pe:rsy,kju:t) v.
prześladować
persecution (,pe:rsy'kju:szyn)
s. prześladowanie
persecutor ('pe:rsy,kju:ter) s.
prześladowca
persevere (,pe:rsy'wier) v.
wytrwać
persist (pe'rsyst) v. obstawać;
wytrwać; upierać się
persistence (per'systens); per-
sistency (per'systensy) s. wy-
trwałość; uporczywość; trwałość
persistent (per'systent) adj. wytrwały; uporczywy; trwały
person ('pe:rson) s. osoba;
człowiek
personage ('pe:rsonydż) s.
osobistość;ważny człowiek

personal ('pe:rsenel) adj. osobisty; robiący osobiste uwagi;
s. wiadomość osobista
personality (,pe:se'naelyty) s.
osobowość; powierzchowność;
postawa; indywidualność; pl.
wycieczki (uwagi) osobiste
personify (pe:r'sony,faj), v.
uosabiać; personifikować
personnel (,pe:rse'n el) s.
personel
personnel manager (,pe:rse'-
'nel'maendżer) s. kierownik
oddziału personalnego; personalny
perspiration (,pe:rspy'rejszyn)
s. pocenie się; pot
perspire (,pe:r'spajer) v. pocić się; wypacać się
persuade (pe:r'słejd) v. przekonywać; namawiać
persuasion (pe:r'słejżyn) s.
perswazja; przekonywywanie;
namawianie; przekonanie; wyznanie; wierzenie
persuasive (pe:r'słejsyw) adj.
przekonywujący; s. motyw; pobudka (do czegoś)
pert (pe:rt) adj. śmiały; arogancki; (slang) żwawy
pertain (per'tejn) v. należeć
do czegoś; być właściwym czemuś; odnosić się; wchodzić
w zakres
perusal (pe'ru:zal) s. przestu-
diowanie; dokładne przeczyta-
nie
peruse (pe'ru:z) v. czytać
uważnie; studiować (np. twarz)
pervade (per'wejd) v. przenikać;
owładnąć; ogarniać; szerzyć się
perverse (per'we:rs) adj. przewrotny; przekorny; wyuzdany
pesky ('pesky) adj. (slang): dokuczliwy; natrętny;cholerny
pessimism ('pesy,myzem) s. pe-
symizm ;spodziewanie się najgor-szego
pest (pest) s. plaga; zaraza
pet (pet) s. faworyt; ulubieniec (np. pies); adj; ulubiony; v. (slang):pieścić; być
w złym nastroju; gniewać się ;
migdalić się; wypieścić

petal ('petl) s. płatek

petition (py'tyszyn) s. petycja; prośba; podanie; v, prosić; wnosić podanie

petrify ('petry,faj) v. zamieniać (się) w kamień; powodować kostnienie

petroleum (py'trouljem) s. ropa naftowa; olej skalny

pet shop ('petszop) s. sklep zwierzątek pokojowych

petticoat ('petykout) s. halka; spódniczka; kobieta; adj. kobiecy

petty ('pety) adj. drobny

petty cash (,pety'kaesz) s. gotówka podręczna

pew (pju:) s. ławka (kościelna)

pharmacy ('fa:rmesy) s. apteka; farmacja

phase (fejz) s. faza (np. rozwojowa); aspekt

pheasant ('feznt) s. bażant

philanthropist (fy'laentrepyst) s. filantrop

philologist (fy'loledżyst) s. filolog ;lingwista;językoznawca

philology (fy'loledży) s. filologia; językoznawstwo;ligwistyka

philosopher (fy'losefer) s. filozof

philosophize (fy'lose,fajz) v. filozofować

philosophy (fy'losefy) s. filozofia

phone (foun) s. telefon (slang)

phonetic (fou'netyk) adj. fonetyczny

phon(e)y (founy) adj. fałszywy; udawany; s. rzecz fałszywa; podrabiana;ktoś udający

photo ('foutou) s. fotka; fotografia; v. fotografować

photograph ('foute,gra:f) s. fotografia; zdjęcie; v. fotografować

photographer (fe'togrefer) s. fotograf; fotografik

photography (fe'tegrefy) s. fotografia; fotografika

phrase (frejz) s. wyrażenie; zwrot; v. wyrażać; wypowiadać wyrażeniami lub słowami

physical ('fyzykel) adj. fizyczny; cielesny

physician (fy'zyszyn) s. lekarz

physicist('fyzysyt) s. fizyk

physics ('fyzyks) s. fizyka

physique (fy'zi:k) s. budowa ciała; rozwój; wygląd fizyczny;kondycja;siła muskularna

piano (py'aenou) s. fortepian; pianino

pick (pyk) v. wybierać; dorabiać; kopać; krytykować; dłubać; obierać; zbierać; usuwać; oskubać; wydziobać; kraść; okraść; s, kilof; dłuto; wybór; czółenko; nitka wątka

pick-off ('pyk,of) v. zedrzeć; wystrzelać pojedyńczo(wrogóy)

pick out ('pyk,aut) v. wybrać; dobrać; doszukiwać się

pick over ('pyk,ouwer) v. przebierać;wybierać co lepsze

pick up ('pyk,ap) v. podnosić; brać; nauczyć się; zarabiać; odnaleźć; odzyskać; przyjść do siebie; poznać się; s. adapter; lekka ciężarówka

picket ('pykyt) s. palik; kół; pikieta; posterunek; v. rozstawiać pikiety strajkowe; służyć jako pikieta; zabezpieczać pikietami

pickle ('pykel) s. kiszony ogórek; marynata; kłopot; łobuz; v. marynować; kisić; wytrawiać

pickpocket ('pyk,pokyt) s. złodziej kieszonkowy; kieszonkowiec

picnic ('pyknyk) s. piknik; majówka; v. brać udział w pikniku, majówce,posiłku na dworze

pictorial (pyk'to:rjel) adj. obrazowy; ilustrowany; malowniczy; malarski; s.(czaso)pismo ilustrowane; ilustracja (trzywymiarowa)techniczna

picture ('pykczer) s. obraz; film; rysunek; rycina; portret; widok; v. odmalowywać; przedstawiać; opisywać; wyobrażać sobie; dawać obraz czegoś

picturesque (,pykcze'resk) adj. malowniczy;żywy i przyjemny

pie (paj) s. placek; szarlotka; pasztet; pasztecik;(ptak) sroka

piece(pi:s) s. kawałek; część; sztuka; moneta; utwor; v. łączyc; zeszyc; łatac; naprawiac

piecework ('pi:s,łe:rk) s. robota na akord

pier (pier) s. pomost ładunkowy; molo; falochron; filar (np. mostu)

pierce (piers) v. przewiercac; wnikać; przedziurawiac; przebijac; przedostawac się

piercing (piersyng) adj. przeszywający; ostry; rozdzierający ;prżenikający

piety ('pajety) s. pobożnośc

pig (pyg) s. wieprz; swinia; prosię; v. prosic się

pigeon ('pydżyn) s. gołąb; v. oszukiwac

pigeon-hole ('pydżyn,houl) s. przegrodka; v. umieszczac w przegrodkach

pigheaded ('pyg'hedyd) adj. uparty ; głupi

pigskin ('pyg,skyn) s. świnska skóra; (slang):piłka; siodło

pigtail ('pyg,tejl) s. warkocz

pike(pajk) s. rogatka; dzida; piłka; szpic; ostrze; szczupak

pile (pail) s. stos; sterta; kupa; pal; słup; puszek; meszek; włos; v. układac w stos; gromadzic na kupę;stawiac w kozły

pile up ('pail,ap) v. walic na kupę; s. zwalenie na kupę

piles (pailz) pl. hemoroidy

pilfer ('pylfer) v. ukrasc; zwędzic; buchnąc

pilgrim ('pylgrym) s. pielgrzym

pilgrimage ('pylgrymydż) s. pielgrzymka

pill (pyl) s. pigułka; tabletka

pillar ('pyler) s. filar; słup; podpora

pillbox('pylboks)s. bunkier; pudełeczko na pigułki;kapelusz

pillion ('pyljen) s. tylne siodełko (np. na motocyklu)

pillory ('pylery) s. pręgierz; v. stawiac pod pręgierzem

pillow ('pylou) s. zagłówek; jasiek; poduszka; podkładka v. spoczywac; opierac (np. głowę)

pillowcase ('pylou,kejs) s. poszewka

pillow slip ('pylou,slyp) s. poszewka

pilot ('pajlet) s. pilot; sternik; v. pilotowac; sterowac; przeprowadzic

pimp (pymp) s. stręczycielka; alfons; v. stręczyc

pimple ('pympl) s. pryszcz; wągier

pin (pyn) s. szpilka; sztyft; sworzen; kołek; kręgiel v. przyszpilic; przymocowac

pincers ('pynserz) pl. kleszcze; obcęgi

pinch (pyncz) v. szczypac; gniesc; cisnąc; przycisnąc; przyskrzynic; krępowac; dokuczac;doskwierac; podważac łomem; s. uszczypnięcie; szczypta; łom; (slang) aresztowanie; obława; kradzież

pinch bar ('pyncz ba:r) s. łom (ze stopką)

pine (pajn) s. sosna; ananas; v. usychac

pineapple ('pajnaepl) s. ananas

pinion ('pynjen) s. kółko zębaste; wrzeciono zębate; wał przekładni; koniec piora; lotka v. podcinac (skrzydła); pętac; przywiazywac

pink (pynk) s. różowy kolor; radykał (komunizujacy); goździk; v. urazic do żywego; przekłuwac

pinnacle ('pynekl) s. szczyt; wieżyczka; v. zwienczac; postawic na szczycie; stanowic szczyt

pint (pajnt) s. półkwarcie; 0.47 litra ; 1/8 galona

pioneer (,paje'nier) s. pionier; saper; v. torowac drogę

pious (pajes) adj. pobożny
pip (pyp) s. pestka; oczko;
gwiazdka; ziarnko; punkcik;
pypec; dzwięk gwizdka; v. piszczec; wykluwac się; pobic;
trafic; postrzelic
pipe (pajp) s. rura; rurka;
przewód; piszczałka; (slang)
łatwizna; drobiazg; v. do-
prowadzac rurami; włączyc;
połączyc; prowadzic dzwiękiem
fujarki; grac na fujarce;
grac na kobzie; gwizdac; piszczec
pipeline ('pajp,lajn) s. rurociąg;(slang) informator;
v. przesyłac rurociągiem
piper (pajper) s. kobziarz
pipes (pajps) s. kobza
pirate (pajeryt) s. korsarz;
pirat; statek piracki; maruder; v. grabic; uprawiac kor-
sarstwo; wydawac bezprawnie
(książki)
pistol (pystl) s. pistolet
piston ('pysten) s. tłok
pit(pyt) s. dół; jama; kopalnia; pestka; v. puszczac do
walki; robic dołki; wkładac
do dołu; wyjmowac pestki
piston-stroke ('pysten,strouk)
s. suw tłoka
pitch (pycz) v. rozbijac (oboz);
umieszczac; rzucac; ustawiac;
chwiac się; upasc ciężko; kołysac (na fali); przechylac;
wybierac; ostro pracowac;
rzucac się na...; smołowac;
s. stopien; najwyższy punkt;
wzniesienie; wzdłuzne kołysanie statku; spadek dachu; odstęp między (falami; zębami
kół etc.);skok (uzwojenia,
sruby); smoła
pitcher ('pyczer) s. dzban;
rzucający piłką
piteous ('pytjes) adj. żałosny;
nędzny
pitfall ('pytfo:l) s. pułapka;
wilczy dół
pith (pyg) s. miękisz; rdzen;
tężyzna; moc; v. wyjmowac
rdzen; przecinac rdzen w celu
zabijania bydła (w rzezni etc.)

pitiable ('pytjebl) s. żałosny;
godny pożałowania
pitiful ('pytyful) adj. litosciwy;
żałosny; nędzny
pitiless ('pytylys) adj. bezlitosny
pity ('pyty) s. litosc; wspołczu-
cie; szkoda; v. litowac się;
wspołczuc; żałowac kogos
pivot ('pywet) s. czop; os;
osrodek ;v.obracac jak na osi
pivotal ('pywetel) s. adj. centralny ;kardynalny;kluczowy;decydu-
jacy
placard ('plaeka:rd) s. afisz;
plakat; (ple'ka:rd) v. rozle-
piac plakaty
place (plejs).s. miejsce; miejsco-
wosc; plac; ulica; dom; mieszkanie; zakład; krzesło; posada;
v. umieszczac; połozyc; uloko-
wac; dac stanowisko; pokładac;
powierzyc; okreslac
placid ('plaesyd) adj. łagodny;
spokojny
plague (plejg) s. plaga; dżuma;
zaraza; v. dręczyc
plaice (plejs) s. płastuga pospo-
lita
plaid (plaed) s. sukno; pled
w kratę;rysunek w kratę
plain (plejn) adj. wyrazny; prosty; gładki; szczery; płaski;
równy; adv. jasno; szczerze;
s. równina
plain clothesman ('plejn,klozmen)
s. tajny policjant
plaintiff ('plejntyf) s. powod
(zaskarżający); powodka
plaintive ('plejntyw) adj. żałosny; płaczliwy
plait (plejt) s. plecionka; warkocz; fałda; zakładka; v. plesc;
splatac; fałdowac
plan (plaen) s. plan; v. planowac; zamierzac
plane (plejn) s. płaszczyzna;
równina; poziom; samolot; płat
(skrzydła); strug; wiornik; gładzik; platan (owoc); v. slizgac;
zeslizgiwac się; heblowac
planet ('plaenyt) s. planeta
plank (plaenk) s. deska; tarcica; punkt programu (polityczne-
go w USA); v.pokrywac deskami

plank down ('plaenk,dałn) v. wybulić gotówkę

plant ('pla:nt) s. roslina; fabryka; zakład; wtyczka; (slang) oszustwo; włamanie; kant; v. zasadzać; zakładać; umieszczać; pozorować; ukrywać; wtykać; sadzić(rośliny)

plantation (plaen'tejszyn) s. plantacja

planter ('pla:nter) s. plantator; maszyna do sadzenia; skrzynka na kwiaty

plaque (plaek) s. tablica (pamiątkowa); odznaka

plaster ('pla:ster) s. tynk; wyprawa wapienna; przylepiec v. tynkować; wyprawiać; powlekać; zalepiać; oblepiać

plaster cast ('pla:ster,ka:st) s. odlew gipsowy; opatrunek gipsowy

plaster of Paris ('pla:ster of 'paerys) s. gips

plastic ('plaestyk) s. plastyk; sztuczne tworzywo; adj. plastyczny; giętki

plastics ('plaestyks) s. tworzywa sztuczne

plate (plejt) s. talerz; danie; płyta; taca; tafla; v. platerować; opancerzać

platform ('plaet,fo:rm) s. platforma; podium; trybuna; rampa; program polityczny

platinum ('plaetynem) s. platyna

platter ('plaeter) s. półmisek

plausible ('plo:zebl) adj. pozornie słuszny, prawdziwy, uczciwy; obłudnie przymilny

play (plej) s. gra; zabawa; sztuka; v. grać; bawić się; zagrać; udawać

play back('plej,baek) v. reprodukować; przegrywać

playboy ('plej,boj) s. lekkoduch

player('plejer) s. gracz; muzyk; aktor; zawodnik

playful ('plejful) adj. wesoły; żartobliwy ;figlarny; filuterny; swawolny;rozbawiony;zabawny; rozbrykany;ożywiony

playground ('plej,graund) s. boisko; park

playhouse ('plej,haus) s. teatr

playmate ('plej,mejt) s. towarzysz zabaw(dziecinnych,intymnych)

play-off ('plejof) s. rozgrywka poremisowa

play off ('plej.of) v. rozgrywać partię poremisową

plaything ('plejtyng) s. zabawka

playwright ('plej,rajt) s. dramaturg

plea (pli:) s. usprawiedliwienie; wywod; apel; prosba

plead (pli:d) v. bronić; błagać; powoływać się

plead guilty ('pli:d'gylty) v. przyznawać się do winy

pleasant ('plesnt) s. przyjemny; miły; wesoły

please (pli:z) v. podobać się; zadowalać

please ! (pli:z) v. proszę

pleased (plizd) adj. zadowolony

pleasing ('pli:zyng) adj. przyjemny; miły

pleasure ('plerer) s. przyjemność; adj. rozrywkowy

pleat (pli:t) s. fałda; v. plisować

pledge (pledż) v. zobowiązywać (się); zastawiać; s. zastaw; gwarancja; przyrzeczenie

plenipotentiary (,plenype'tenszery) s. pełnomocnik; adj. pełnomocny

plentiful ('plentyful) adj. obfity; liczny

plenty ('plenty) s. obfitość; mnóstwo; adv. zupełnie; aż nadto;adj.obfity;liczny;obszerny

pliable ('plajebl) adj. giętki

pliers ('plajerz) pl. szczypce

plight (plajt) s. trudności; stan; położenie; przyrzeczenie; v. ręczyć; dawać słowo

plod (plod) v. mozolić się; śleczeć; s. harowanie; kucie

plod along ('plod,e'long) v. wlec się;mozolić się;trudzić się

plot (plot)s. osnowa; fabuła; spisek;działka; wykres; mapa; v.knuć; spiskować;nanosić na mapę; planować; dzielić

plough (plau) s. pług; v. orać
plow (plau) s. pług; v. orac
plowshare ('plau-szeer) s.lemiesz
pluck (plak) v. wyrwać; zerwać;
szarpnąć
pluck up courage ('plak,ap'karydż) exp.: zdobyc się na odwagę
plucky ('plaky) adj. smiały;
odważny
plug (plag) s. czop; zatyczka;
kurek; reklama; świeca (silnika); v. zatykac
plug up ('plag,ap) v. zatkać
plum (plam) s. sliwka; rodzynka; gratka; adv. pionowo
plumage ('plu:mydż) s. upierzenie
plumb (plam) adj. pionowy; zupełny; adv. pionowo; prosto;
dokładnie; zupełnie; s. pion
murarski; sonda; v. pionować;
sondować
plumber ('plamer) s. hydraulik
plumbing ('plambyng) s.instalacja wodociągowo-ściekowa budynku
plume (plu:m) s. pióro; pióropusz; v. ozdabiać piórami;
czyscic pióra
plummet ('plamyt) s. pion murarski; v. spadać pionowo
plump (plamp) adj. pulchny;
tęgi; stanowczy; otwarty;
v. tuczyć tyć; wypełniac
(się); ciężko upasc; upuscic;
rzucic; popierać w wyborach
masowym głosowaniem; adv. prosto; nagle; ciężko; s. upadek
plum pudding('plam'pudyng)s.
budyn swiąteczny
plunder ('plander) s. grabierz;
rabunek; łup; v. pladrować;
łupić; grabic
plunge (plandż) v. pogrążać
(się) ; zanurzać (się); wpadac;
spadać; s. skok do wody; pływalnia
plunk (plank) v. brząkać; wybulic; s. brzęk; adv. z brzekiem; prosciutko;v.ciskac;rzucać
upaśc ciężko;szarpac(struny);
strzelic do kogos;s.sl.:dolar

pluperfect ('plu:'pe:rfykt)
adj. zaprzeszły; s. czas zaprzeszły; plusquamperfectum
plural ('pluerel) s. liczba
mnoga; adj. pluralny; mnogi
plus (plas) prep. plus; więcej;
adj. dodatni; dodatkowy;
s. znak plus; dodatek
plush (plasz) s. plusz; adj.
pluszowy; okazały
ply (plaj) v. uprawiac gorliwie;
używać czegos; zasypywać (np.
pytaniami) ; kursować po...;
s. warstwa; grubosc; skłonnosc;
pasmo
plywood ('plaj,łud) s. sklejka;
dykta
pneumatic (nju'maetyk) adj.
pneumatyczny
pneumonia (nju'mounje) s. zapalenie płuc
poach (poucz) v. uprawiac kłusownictwo; grzęznąc; rozrabiać;
udeptywac; rozmiękac; gotowac
jajko na miękko bez skorupki
poached egg ('pauczt,eg) s.
jajko gotowane na miękko bez
skorupki
poacher ('poucer) s. kłusownik
pocket ('pokyt) s. kieszen;
dziura (powietrzna) v. wkładac do kieszeni
pocketbook ('pokyt,buk) s.
portfel
pocketknife ('pokyt,najf) s.
scyzoryk
pocket money ('pokyt,many) s.
kieszonkowe
pod (pod) s. strączek; kokon;
stadko; obsada; v. rodzic
strączki; łuszczyc; spędzać
razem
poem (pouim) s. wiersz ; poemat
poet (pouyt) s. poeta
poetess ('pouytys) s. poetka
poetic (pou'etyk) adj. poetyczny ; poetycki;poetycznie piękny
poetry ('pouytry) s. poezja
pogrom ('pougrem, pe'grom) s.
pogrom
poignant ('pojnent) adj.przejmujący; uszczypliwy; cięty;
ostry; dotkliwy;wzruszający

point (point) s. punkt; ostry
koniec; szpiczaste narzędzie;
przylądek; kropka; pointa; cecha; sedno; sens; v. zaostrzac;
celowac; wskazywac; punktowac;
kropkowac;dowodzic;dążyć;pokazy-
wać
point at ('point,aet) v. wyce-
lowac; wskazac
point of view ('point,ow'wju:)
s. punkt widzenia
point out ('point,aut) v. wskazywac; uwydatnic
point to ('point,tu) v. wskazac
kierunek (kogos, cos)
pointed ('pointyd) adj. spiczasty; ostry; cięty; zjadliwy
point-blank ('point'blaenk) adj.
(strzelać) na wprost, bezpośredni; bezceremonialny; bez
ogrodek; adv. bezpośrednio;
z bliska; wprost; bez ogrodek;
w prostej linii; bez zastano-
wienia się
pointer ('pointer) s. wskaznik;
wskazowka
poise (pojz) s. rownowaga; postawa; swoboda; stan zawiesze-
nia; stan niepewności; v. row-
noważyc; ważyc w rękach; za-
wisnąc w powietrzu; byc przy-
gotowanym do ataku
poison ('pojzn) s. trucizna;
v. truc; zatruc; zakazic
poisonous ('pojznes) adj. trujący; jadowity; szkodliwy
poke (pouk) v. wtykac; wpychac;
szturchac; dłubac; sterczec;
wtracac się; plątac
poker ('pouker) s. pogrzebacz;
poker
polar ('pouler) adj. polarny
polar bear ('pouler beer) s.
biały niedzwiedz
Pole (poul) s. Polka; Polak
pole (poul) s. biegun; słup;
żerdz; dyszel; maszt
pole jump ('poul dżamp) s. skok
o tyczce
police (pe'li:s) s. policja;
v. rządzic; pilnowac; utrzy-
mywac porządek
policeman (pe'li:smen) s. policjant

police officer (pe'li:s,ofyser)
s. policjant
police station (pe'li:s,stejszyn)
s. komisariat
policewoman (pe'li:s,łumen) s.
policjantka
policy ('polysy) s. polityka
rządzenia; polityka postępowa-
nia; mądrosc polityczna; polisa ubezpieczeniowa
polio ('pouljou) s. poliomyeli-
tis (,poliou,maje'lajtis) s.
paraliż dziecięcy; choroba
Haine-Medina
Polish ('poulysz) adj. polski
(język) (obywatel etc.)
polish ('polysz) v. polerowac;
gładzic; pochlebiac; nabierac
połysku; s. pasta (do butow);
połysk; politura; polor
polite (pe'lajt) adj. grzeczny;
uprzejmy; kulturalny
politeness (pe'lajtnys) s.
grzecznosc; ogłada; kultura;
uprzejmośc
political (pe'lytykel) adj.
polityczny
politician (,poly'tyszyn) s.
polityk; politykier
politics ('polytyks) s. polityka
poll (poul) s. głosowanie; reje-
strowanie głosow; wyniki głosowania; lista; wykaz; lokal
wyborczy; urny wyborcze; ankieta; głowa; tył głowy; obuch
v. oddawac głosy; obliczac
głosy; rejestrowac; dostawac
głosy; strzyc włosy; obcinac
rogi
pollen ('polyn) s. pył kwiato-
wy
pollute (pe'lju:t) v. zanie-
czyszczac; skazic
pollution (pe'lju:szyn) s. ska-
żenie; zanieczyszczenie
pomp (pomp) s. pompa
pompous ('pompes) adj. napuszony; nadęty; pompatyczny
pond (pond) s. staw
ponder ('ponder) v. rozważac;
rozmyslac;przemysliwac;dumac;
zastanawiac się;zadumac się

ponderous ('ponderes) adj.
ciężki; niezgrabny

pontoon (pon'tu:n) s. ponton

pony ('pouny) s. kuc; bryk;
v. odpisywać; ściągać;zrzynać

poodle ('pu:dl) s. pudel(pies)

pool (pu:l) s. kałuża; sadzawka; pływalnia; v. składać się
razem; zbierać się w grupę

poor (puer) adj. biedny; ubogi; lichy; marny; słaby;
kiepski; nędzny; skromny

poorhouse ('puer,haus) s.
przytułek

poorly ('puerly) adv. licho;
kiepsko; skąpo; skromnie;
biednie; ubogo; adj. nie-
zdrów

pop (pop) s. trzask; puknię-
cie; strzał; napój musujący;
lombard; tatuś (slang);
v. strzelać; pukać; nagle wyrzucać; nagle wsadzać; skakać;
wściekać się

popcorn ('pop,ke:rn) s. su-
cha prażona kukurydza

pop in ('pop,yn) v. wskoczyć

pop out ('pop,aut) v. wyskoczyć

pope (poup) s. papież

poplar ('popler) s. topola

poppy ('popy) s. mak

popular ('popjuler) adj. ludowy; rozpowszechniony; popularny (tani)

popularity (,popju'laeryty) s.
popularnosc

populate ('popjulejt) s. zaludniać

population ('popjulejszyn) s.
ludnosc

populous ('popjules) adj. ludny; gęsto zaludniony

porch (po:rch) s. weranda; ga-
nek; portyk

porcupine ('po:rkjupajn) s.
jeż; jeżozwierz; kolczatka

pore (po:r) v. rozmyslać; slę-
czeć; wpatrywać się; s. por
(skóry)

pore over ('po:r,ouwer) v. rozmyslać nad czymś;slęczeć (nad
książką);zagłębiać się

pork (po:rk) s. wieprzowina

porous ('po:res) adj. porowaty

porpoise ('po:rpes) s. morświn;
ssak morski

porridge ('porydż) s. owsianka

port (po:rt) s. port; przystań;
otwor; otwor ładunkowy; postawa; trzymanie się; prezentowa-
nie (broni); wino porto; lewa
burta; sterowanie w lewo

portable ('po:rtebl) adj. prze-
nosny; polowy

porter ('po:rter) s. tragarz;
kolejarz od sypialnego wagonu

portion ('po:rszyn) s. częsć;
porcja; udział; posag; los;
v. dzielić; przydzielać

portion out ('po:rszyn,aut) v.
wydzielać; wyposażać

portly ('po:rtly) adj. dostojny; godny; tęgi; postawny;
okazały

portrait ('po:rtryt) s. portret

pose (pouz) v. pozować; upozo-
wać; stawiać (np. problem);
kłopotać (za pytaniem); s. poza

posh (posz) adj. elegancki; szykowny; v. wyelegantować się

position (pe'zyszyn) s. położenie; stanowisko; postawa;
twierdzenie; umieszczenie;
v. umieszczać; ulokować

positive ('pozetyw) adj. pozytywny; stanowczy; ustanowiony;
zupełny; dodatni; pozytywistycz-
ny; s. znak dodatni; wartość
dodatnia; pozytyw

possess (pe'zes) v. posiadać;
opanować; opętać; przepajać

possessed (pe'zest) adj. opęta-
ny

possession (pe'zeszyn) s. posiadanie; posiadłość; własność;
dobytek;opanowanie

possessor (pe'zeser) s. posiadacz; właściciel

possibility (pose'bylyty) s.
możliwość; możnosc;ewentualność

possible ('posebl) adj. możliwy; ewentualny

possibly ('posebly) adv. może;
wogóle możliwe; możliwie

post (poust) s. słup; posada;
posterunek; poczta; v. ogłaszać; wywieszać; zalepiać
plakatami
postage ('poustydż) s. opłata
pocztowa
postage stamp ('poustydż,staemp)
s. znaczek pocztowy
postal ('poustel) adj. pocztowy
postal order ('poustel'o:rder)
s. przekaz pocztowy
postcard ('poust,ka:rd) s.
pocztówka
post code ('poust,koud) = zip-
code ('zyp,koud) pocztowy
numer kierunkowy
poster ('pouster) s. plakat
poste restante ('poust'resta:-
nt) s. list lub przesyłka do
odebrania na poczcie
posterity (po'teryty) s. po-
tomność
post-free ('poust'fri:) adj.
wolny od opłaty pocztowej
posthumous ('postjumes) adj.
pośmiertny
postman ('poustmen) s. listonosz
postmark ('poust,ma:rk) s.
stempel pocztowy
postmaster ('poust,ma:ster) s.
naczelnik poczty
post office ('poust,ofys) s.
poczta
post office box ('poust,ofys'-
'boks) s. skrytka pocztowa
postpaid ('poust,pejd) s.
opłata pocztowa z góry uisz-
czona
postpone (poust'poun) v. odłożyć; odroczyć; odwlekać
postscript ('pous,skrypt) s.
dopisek; postscriptum
posture('poszcer) s. postawa;
stan; położenie; v. przybrać
postawę; pozować
postwar ('poust'ło:r) adj.
powojenny
posy ('pouzy) s. bukiet
pot (pot) s. garnek; imbryk;
czajnik; nocnik; doniczka;
wazonik;rondel;dzban;kocioł;
kufel;słój;puchar;więcierz;łuza

szklanka; haszysz; v. wsadzać
do garnka; polować; strzelać
potato (po'tejtou) s. ziemniak
potent ('potent) adj. potężny;
skuteczny; jurny
potion ('pouszyn) s. dawka; napój
potter ('poter) s. garncarz;
v. grzebać się; włóczyc się;
łazić
potter about ('poter,e'baut)
v. włóczyć się
potty ('poty) adj. marny; lichy;
błachy; łatwy; stuknięty; pomylony; zbzikowany
pouch (paucz) s. worek; torba;
brzuszysko; ładownica; sakiewka; v. nadawać formę worka;
łykać
poulterer ('poulterer) s.
handlarz drobiu
poultice ('poultys) s. okład;
v. kłaść okład
poultry ('poultry) s. drób
pounce (pauns) s. szpon; nagły
atak z góry; v. rzucać się na
coś; trybować; pumeksować; posypywać (rysunek) proszkiem
(kolorowym)
pound (paund) s. funt (pieniądz;
waga); stuk; tupot; uderzenie;
tłuczenie; walnięcie; ogrodzenie; magazyn; areszt; v.tłuc;
walić; tupać;biegać; więzić;
zamykać
pour (po:r) v. wysypać; posypać; lać; polać; wylać; rozlać;
nalać
pour out ('po:r,aut) v. wysypać;
wylać
pout (paut) v. dąsać się; wydymać; s. wydęcie warg; kwasna
mina
poverty('powerty) s. bieda;
ubóstwo
powder ('pałder) s. proch; pył;
puder; proszek; v. posypywać;
pudrować; proszkować
powder room ('pałder,ru:m) s.
toaleta damska
power ('pałer) s. potęga; moc;
energia; siła; własność; władza; mocarstwo; v. napędzać;
wspomagać;dostarczać energii

power brake ('pařer,brejk) s. serwohamulec; wspomagany hamulec

powerful ('pařerful) adj, potężny; mocny

powerless ('pařerlys) adj. bezsilny

power plant ('pařer,plaent) s. siłownia

power station ('pařer,stejszyn) s. elektrownia

powwow ('pař,řař) v. naradzać się co do taktyki; leczyć; s. sejmik Indian; odprawa oficerska; czarownik indiański

practicable ('praektykebl) adj. wykonalny; możliwy do przeprowadzenia

practical ('praektykel) adj. praktyczny

practice ('praektys) s. praktyka; ćwiczenie; v. praktykować; uprawiać; ćwiczyć

practise ('praektys) v. = practice

practitioner (praek'tyszener) s. zawodowiec; praktykujący lekarz

prairie('preery) s. preria

praise (prejz) s. pochwała; v. chwalić; sławić

praiseworthy ('prejz,ře:rsy) adj. chwalebny; godny pochwały

pram (praem) s. ręczny wózek

prance (praens) v. stawać dęba; tańczyć; paradować; hasać; kazać koniowi stawać dęba

prank (praenk) b. psota; figiel; v. wystroić; popisywać się

prattle ('praetl) v. paplać; s. paplanina

prawn ('pro:n) s. krewetka; v. łowić krewetki

pray,(prej) y. modlić się; prosić; błagać

prayer ('prejer) s. modlitwa; prośba

prayer book ('prejer,buk) s. modlitewnik; książka do nabożeństwa

pre-(pri:-)prefix,przed-;z góry

preach (pri:cz) v. głosić; kazać; wygłaszać

preacher (pri:czer) s. kaznodzieja; pastor

precarious (pry'keeries) s. niepewny; niebezpieczny; dowolny

precaution (pry'ko:szyn) s, przezorność; środek ostrożności

precede (pry:'si:d) v. poprzedzać; mieć pierwszeństwo

precedence (pry'si:dens) s. pierwszeństwo;nadrzędność

precedent (pry'si:dent) adj. uprzedni; poprzedzający

precedent ('presydent) s. precedens

precept('pry:sept) s. nakaz; przykazanie; nauka moralna; reguła

precinct ('pry:synkt) s. okręg (wyborczy); obręb; granice

precious ('preszes) adj. drogi; cenny; afektowany; wyszukany; wspaniały; adv. bardzo; niezwykle

precipice ('presypys) s. przepaść

precipitate (pry'sypytejt) s. opad; osad; przyspieszać (zdarzenia);skraplać (się); rzucać; spadać

precipitation (pry,sypy'tejszyn) s. opady; przyspieszanie; pochopność; upadek; strącanie

precipitous (pry'sypytes) adj. przepaścisty; spadzisty

precis, ('prejsi:) s. skrót; v. robić skrót

precise (pry'sajs) adj. dokładny; wyraźny; v. precyzować; wyszczególniać

precision (pry'syżyn) s. precyzja; dokładność

precocious (pry'kouszes) adj. przedwczesny; przedwcześnie rozwinięty; kwitnący

preconceived ('pry:ken'si:wd) adj. uprzedzony do; powzięty z góry

predatory ('predetery) adj. łupieżczy; grabieżczy; drapieżny

predecessor ('pry:dyseser) s. poprzednik; przodek

predetermine ('pry:dy'te:rmyn)
v. z góry ustanowić; z góry
określić; z góry zadecydować
predicament (pry'dykement) s,
kłopot; kłopotliwe położenie
predicate ('predy,kejt) v.
opierać się na czymś; łączyć
się z czymś; przypisywać czemuś; orzekać o czymś; mieścić
pojęcie czegoś; ('predykyt) s.
cecha; orzecznik; adj. orzecze-
niowy; dopełnienie orzeczenia
predict (pry'dykt) v. przepowiadać
prediction (pry'dykszyn) s.
przepowiednia
predisposition ('pri:dyspe'zyszyn) s. skłonność; predyspo-
zycja
predominant(pry'domynent) adj.
przeważający; panujący; góru-
jący
predominate (pry'domynejt) v.
górować; przeważać
preface ('prefys) s. przedmowa;
wstęp
prefect ('pry:fekt) s. prefekt
prefer (pry'fe:r) v. woleć;
przekładać; dawać awans
preferable ('preferebl) adj.
lepszy
preferably ('preferebly) adv.
raczej
preference ('preferens) s.
pierwszeństwo; uprzywilejowa-
nie; możność wyboru; rzecz bardziej ulubiona, upodobana
preferment (pry'fe:rment) s.
wybór; awans
prefix ('pry:fyks) s. przedrostek; prefiks; tytuł przed
nazwiskiem; v. umieszczać
przedrostek; umieszczać na
wstępie
pregnancy ('pregnensy) s. ciąża
pregnant ('pregnent) adj. brze-
mienny; doniosły; sugestywny;
płodny ;ciężarna (kobieta)
prejudice ('predżudys) s. uprzedzenie; szkoda; v. uprzedzać się
do kogoś; szkodzić (komuś);
rozpowszechniać uprzedzenie

prejudiced ('predżudyst) adj.
uprzedzony ;mający uprzedzenie
preliminary (pry'lymynery) adj.
wstępny; przygotowawczy;
s. wstęp
prelude ('prelju:d) s. wstęp;
preludium; v. grać preludium;
dawać wstęp do czegoś
premature (,preme'tjuer) adj.
przedwczesny; przedwcześnie
dojrzały
premeditate (pry'medy,tejt) v.
obmyślać; rozważać
premier ('premjer) adj. pierwszy; najważniejszy; premier;
prezes rady ministrów
premises ('premysys) pl. lokal;
obejście
premium ('pri:mjem) s. nagroda;
premia
preoccupied (pry:'okju,pajd)
adj. pochłonięty; zaabsorbowany
preparation (,prepe'rejszyn) s.
przygotowywanie; przyrządzanie
prepare (pry'peer) v. przygotowywać (sie); szykować (się);
przyrządzać
prepay ('pry'pej) v. opłacać
z góry
preposition (,prepe'zyszyn) s.
przyimek
prepossess (,pry:po'zes) v.
wpoić; usposobić; natchnąć
prepossessing (,prype'zesyng)
adj. miły; sympatyczny
preposterous (pry'posteres) adj.
niedorzeczny; absurdalny
prerequisite (pry'rekłyzyt) adj.
& s. (warunek) wstępny; podstawowy
prescribe (prys'krajb) v. przepisać; nakazać; zaordynować
prescribtion (prys'krypszyn) s.
nakaz; przepis; recepta
presence ('presens) v. obecność
presence of mind ('prezens,ow'
majnd) v. przytomność umysłu
present ('preznt) s. upominek;
prezent; teraźniejszość; adj.
obecny; niniejszy; teraźniejszy;v.stawiać się;nadarzyć się

present tense ('presnt,tens) s.
czas teraźniejszy

presentation (,prezen'tejszyn)
s. przedstawienie; ofiarowa-
nie; podarek; darowanie; prze-
dłożenie

presentiment (pry'zentyment) s.
przeczucie

presently ('prezently) adv.
wkrótce; niebawem; zaraz

preservation (,preze:r'wejszyn)
s. zachowanie; ochrona; zabezpieczenie

preserve (pry'ze:rw) v. zachowywać; chronić; przechowywać;
konserwować; ochraniać;
s. konserwa; rezerwat

preside (pry'zajd) v. przewod-
niczyć

president ('prezydent) s. prezydent

press (pres) s. prasa; dzienni-
ki; tłocznia; druk; drukania;
nacisk; tłok; ścisk; pospiech;
v. cisnąć; ściskać; przyciskać;
ciążyć; pracować; naglić; narzucać; wciskać; tłoczyć

press in ('pres-yn) v. wciskać

pressing ('presyng) adj. naglący; natarczywy

pressure ('preszer) s. ciśnienie; napór; parcie

prestige (pres'ty:dż) s. prestiż (szacunek i uznanie)

presumable(pry'zju:mebl) adj.
przypuszczalny

presume (pry'zju:m) v. przypuszczać; wykorzystywać (kogoś);
ośmielać się

presumedly (pry'zju:mdly) adv.
przypuszczalnie

presuming (pry'zju:myng) adj.
zarozumiały

presumption (pry'zampszen) s.
przypuszczenie; założenie;
zarozumiałość

presumptuous (pry'zamptjues)
adj. zarozumiały

presuppose (pry:se'pouz) v.
przypuszczać; zakładać z góry;
stawiać warunek

pretend (pry'tend) v. udawać;
pretendować

pretender (pry'tender) s. pretendent

pretense (pry'tens) s. udawanie;
pozór; pretensja; pretensjonal-
nosc

pretension (pry'tenszyn) s.
aspiracje; roszczenie; pretensjonalność; pretensja

preterite ('preteryt) adj.
przeszły; s. czas przeszły

pretext ('pry:tekst) s. pretekst;
pozór;

pretext (pry'tekst) v. wymawiać
się; powoływać się

pretty ('pryty) adj. ładny;
adv. dość; dosyć

prevail (pry'wejl) v. przeważać;
brać górę; przekonać; panować
(np. zwyczaj)

prevalent ('prewelent) adj. panujący; przeważający

prevent (pry'went) v. zapobiec;
powstrzymywać

prevention (pry'wenszyn) s. za-
pobieganie; środek zapobiegający

preventive (pry'wentyw) adj.
zapobiegawczy; prewencyjny

previous ('pry:wjes) adj. poprzedni; wcześniejszy od...;
przedwczesny; nagły; pochopny

previous to ('pry:wjes,tu) adv.
przed czyms

previously ('pry:wjesly) adv.
wcześniej

prewar ('pri:'ło:r) adj.
przedwojenny

prey (prej) s. zdobycz; łup;
ofiara; v. grabić; trawić

price (prajs) s. cena; koszt;
v. wyceniać

priceless ('prajslys) adv.
bezcenny; nieoceniony

prick (pryk) s. ukłucie;
(wulg.) penis; v. kłuć; przekłuwać

prick up one's ears ('pryk,ap-
'łans,eerz) s. nadstawiać
uszu; postawić uszy

prickle ('prykl) s. kolec;
cierń; v. ukłuć; jeżyć się

prickly ('prykly) adj. kolczasty

pride (prajd) s. duma; pycha;
ambicja; chluba; v. byc dum-
nym z czegos;chełpic się;pysznic;
priest (pri:st) s. kapłan; duchowny
primarily ('prajmeryly) adv.
głownie; przede wszystkim
primary ('prajmery) adj. głowny; zasadniczy; pierwotny;
s. wybor kandydatow (U.S.A.)
primary school ('prajmery,sku:l)
s. szkoła podstawowa
prime ('prajm) adj.,pierwszy;
najważniejszy; głowny;v.przygoto-
prime minister ('prajm-'mynyster)
s. premier
primer ('prajmer) s. elementarz;
podręcznik (elementarny)
primitive ('prymytyw) adj. prymitywny; pierwotny
primrose ('prymrous) s. pier-
wiosnek
prince ('pryns) s. książę
princess (pryn'ses) s. księżna;
księżniczka
principal ('prynsepel) adj.
głowny; s. kierownik; zlecenio-
dawca; kapitał; sprawca
principality (prynsy'paelyty)
s. księstwo
principle ('prynsepl) s. zasada;
reguła;podstawa;żrodło;składnik
prink (prynk) v. stroic się;
muskac się
print (prynt) s. slad; odcisk;
druk; pismo; fotka; v. wy-
cisnąc; wytłoczyc; wydrukowac;
byc w druku;drukowac się;odbic
printed matter ('prynted'maeter)
v. druki;materiały drukowane
printer ('prynter) s. drukarz
printing ('pryntyng) s. druk;
drukowanie; nakład;a.drukarski
printing ink ('pryntyng,ynk) s.
farba drukarska
printing office ('pryntyn,ofys)
s. drukarnia
prior ('prajer) adj. wczesniej-
szy; ważniejszy; s. przeor
prior to ('prajer,tu) adv.
przed czyms;wczesniej od czegos
priority ('praj'oryty) s.
pierwszeństwo;starszeństwo

prison ('pryzn) s. więzienie
prisoner ('pryzner) s. więzień
privacy ('prajwesy) s. odosobnienie; samotnosc; utrzymanie
w dyskrecji (tajemnicy); życie
prywatne, intymne, osobiste
private ('prajwyt) adj. prywatny; tajny; ukryty; s. szerego-
wiec;(private parts=genitalia)
private hotel ('prajwyt,hou'tel)
s. pensjonat
privation (praj'wejszyn) s.
prywacja; niedostatek
privilege ('prywylydż) s. przywilej;prawdziwa satysfakcja
privileged ('prywylydżd) adj.
uprzywilejowany;zaszczycony
prize (prajz) v. podważyc; zajmowac; cenic; nagroda; premia;
wygrana; łup;a.kapitalny.v.cenic
prizefighter ('prajz,fajter)
s. zawodowy bokser
prizewinner ('prajz,łyner) s.
laureat; zdobywca nagrody
pro (prou) s. zawodowiec (slang)
adv. za; dla;prep. pro(forma etc.)
probability (proba'bylyty) s.
prawdopodobieństwo;widoki;szanse
probable ('probebl) adj. prawdopodobny;wiarogodny;mający szanse
probation (pro'bejszyn) s. okres probny; proba;zawieszenie kary
probe (proub) s. sonda; v. son-
dowac; zagłębiac się;badac w sledz-
twie
problem ('problem) s. problem;
zadanie; zagadnienie;a.problemowy
procedure (pre'si:dżer) s. postępowanie; procedura(sądowa)
proceed (pre'si:d) v. isc dalej;
postępowac;kontynuowac;zaskarżać
proceed from (pre'si:d,from) v.
wychodzic z...;isc dalej z...
proceedings (pre'si:dyngs) pl.
sprawozdanie (z sesji etc.)
proceeds ('prousi:dz) pl. zysk;
dochody;przychod (ze sprzedaży)
process ('prouses) s. przebieg;
proces; postęp; v. obrabiac;
przerabiac; załatwiac; proce-
sowac;poddawac procesowi;mlec
procession (pre'seszyn) s. po-
chod; procesja;kontynuowanie;
prowadzenie dalej;dalszy rozwoj

proclaim (pre'klejm) v. proklamować; ogłaszać; zakazywać; wskazywać;wprowadzać ograniczenia
proclamation (,prokle'mejszyn) s. proklamacja; obwieszczenie
procrastinate (pre'kraesty,nejt) v. zwlekać; odkładać na później
procure (pre'kjuer) v. postarać się; stręczyć do nierządu
prodigal ('prodygel) adj. marnotrawny; s. marnotrawca;utracjusz
prodigious (pre'dydżes) adj. niezwykły; cudowny; olbrzymi
prod (prod) v. szturchać; kłuć; drażnić; popędzać; s. dżgnięcie; bodziec; szpikulec
prodigy ('prodydży) s. dziwo; cud;genialne dziecko etc.
produce (produ:s) s. produkty; plony; wynik; produkcja; wydajność; wydobycie;produkty rolne
produce (pre'dju:s) v. wytwarzać; produkować; dostarczać; wydobywać; wystawiać; okazywać
producer ('produ:ser) s. wytwórca (filmowy); producent
product ('predakt) s. produkt; wynik; iloczyn;wytwór(natury etc.)
production (pre'dakszyn) s. wytwórczość; wydobycie; produkcja; utwór;produkty;a.produkcyjny
productive (pre'daktyw) adj. wydajny; produktywny; produkcyjny; urodzajny; żyzny
profess (pre'fes) v. twierdzić; zapewniać; udawać; wyznawać; uprawiać (zawód);być profesorem
professed (pre'fest) adj. jawny; rzekomy; zawodowy
profession (pre'feszyn) s. zawód; wyznanie; zapewnienie; oświadczenie;śluby zakonne
professional (pre'feszenl) s. zawodowiec; adj. zawodowy; fachowy;należący do wolnego zawodu
professor (pre'feser) s. profesor; wyznawca;nauczyciel(tańca)
proficiency (pre'fyszensy) s. biegłość; sprawność
proficient (pre'fyszent) adj. biegły; sprawny; s. mistrz;biegły;znający(obcy język);fachowiec

profile ('proufajl) s. profil; szkic biograficzny; v. przedstawiać z profilu; profilować
profit ('profyt) s. zysk; dochód; korzyść; pożytek; v. korzystać; być korzystnym; przydawać się;mieć zyski
profitable ('profytebl) adj. korzystny;intratny;zyskowny
profiteer (,profy'tier) v.paskować; spekulować; s. paskarz; spekulant(na czarnym rynku etc)
profound (pro'faund) adj. głęboki;gruntowny;s.otchłań
profusion (pro'fju:żyn) s. obfitość; rozrzutność;nadmiar
prognoses (prog'nousi:z) pl. prognozy; rokowania
prognosis (prog'nousys) s. prognoza; rokowanie
program ('prougraem) s. program; plan; audycja; przedstawienie; v. planować
progress ('prougres) s. postęp; bieg; rozwój;kolejne etapy etc.
progress (pro'gres) v. robić postępy; iść naprzód;być w toku
progressive (pro'gresyw) adj. postępowy;stopniowy;s.postępowiec
prohibit (pro'hybyt) v. zakazywać; zabraniać
prohibition (,prouy'byszyn) s. zakaz; prohibicja
project ('prodżekt) s. projekt; plan;przedsięwzięcie;schemat
project (pro'dżekt) v. projektować; miotać; rzutować; sterczeć; wystawać;wyświetlać(na ekranie)
projection (pro'dżeksżyn) s. rzut; planowanie; projektowanie; rzutowanie; wystawanie; projekcja; wyświetlanie
projector (pro'dżekter) s. rzutnik;aparat projekcyjny
proletariat (,proule'teerjet) s. proletariat;robotnicy przemysłowi
prolog ('proulog) s.prolog
prolong (prou'long) v. przedłużać; wydłużać;prolongować(spłaty)
promenade (,promy'nejd) s. przechadzka;przejażdżka; deptak; promenada; v.przechadzać się

prominent ('promynent) adj. wydatny; wybitny; sterczący; wystający; wyróżniający się;sławny

promise ('promys) s. obietnica;
przyrzeczenie; v. obiecywać;
przyrzekać; zaręczać; zapewniać;robić obietnice;zapowiadać się

promising('promysyng) adj. obiecujący; rokujący nadzieje

promontory ('promonto:ry) s.
przylądek; wyrostek

promote (pre'mout) v. popierać;
promować; awansować; (slang)
oszukiwać; kombinować

promoter (pre'mouter) s. organizator;krzewiciel; inspirator

promotion (pre'mouszyn) s. po-
pieranie; ułatwienie; awans;
promowanie; lansowanie

prompt (prompt) adj. szybki;
natychmiastowy; v. nakłaniać;
pobudzać; podpowiadać; sufle-
rować;adv.punktualnie;co do mi-
nuty

prompter ('prompter) s. sufler
(w teatrze);podżegacz

promptly ('promptly) adv. natychmiast; z miejsca; bezzwłocznie; punktualnie

prone (proun) adj. leżący twarzą na dół; stromy; skłonny

prong (prong) s. ząb (wideł);
róg; v. kłuć; przebijać;
zaopatrywać w zęby

pronoun ('prounaun) s. zaimek

pronounce (pre'nauns) v. oświadczać; wymawiać; mieć wymowę;
wypowiadać się

pronto ('prontou) adv. (slang):
prędko; już;natychmiast;zaraz

pronunciation (pra,nansy'ejszyn)
s. wymowa;zapis fonetyczny

proof (pru:f) s. dowód; próba
(np. złota); sprawdzian; wy-
próbowanie; korekta; próbna
odbitka; adj. odporny; wypró-
bowany;sprawdzony;nieprzemakalny

prop(up) ('prop,ap) v. podpierać; s. podpórka;ostoja;oparcie

propagate ('prope,gejt) v. rozmnażać (się); rozszerzać; propagować; przekazywać

propagation (,prope'gejszyn) s.
rozmnażanie się; propagowanie

propel (pre'pel) v. napędzać;
poruszać; pędzić

propeller (pre'peler) s. śmigło;
śruba (okrętowa)

proper ('proper) adj. właściwy;
własny; przyzwoity

properly ('properly) adv. własciwie; słusznie; przyzwoicie

property ('property) s. własność;właściwość;cecha;nierucho-
mość

prophecy ('profysy) s. proroctwo

prophet ('profyt) s. prorok;
apostoł

proportion (pre'po:rszyn) s.
proporcja; stosunek; rozmiar;
część; v. dostosowywać; rozdzielać;dawkować;dozować

proportional (pre'po:rsznl) adj.
proporcjonalny (do czegoś)

proposal (pre'pouzel) s. propozycja; projekt; oświadczyny

propose (pre'pouz) v. proponować; przedkładać; zamierzać

proposition (,prope'zyszyn) s.
propozycja; sąd; zagadnienie;
twierdzenie; v. robić nie-
przyzwoite propozycje

proprietary (pre'prajetery) adj.
należący; będący prywatną
własnością; s. właściciel;
własność

proprietor (pre'prajeter) s.
właściciel;posiadacz;gospodarz

propulsion (pre'palszyn) s. napęd; bodziec; popędzanie

prose (prouz) s. proza;v.nudzić

prosecute ('prosy,kju:t) s. ścigać prawnie; prowadzić (np.
studia);nie zaniedbywać;pilno-
wać

prosecution (,prosy'kju:szyn)
s. oskarżenie

prosecutor ('prosy,kju:ter) s.
prokurator; oskarżyciel

prospect ('prospekt) s. widok;
perspektywa; ewentualny klient;
potencjalne złoża; v. przeszu-
kiwać (okolice); próbnie
exploatować kopalnie; szukać
złota etc.;badać(teren etc.)

prospective (pres'pektyw) adj.
przyszły; ewentualny

prospectus (pres'pektes) s.
prospekt (nowego przedsiębiors-twa)

prosper ('prosper) v. prosperować; sprzyjać powodzeniu

prosperity (pros'peryty) s.
dobrobyt; powodzenie; kon-
junktura; pomyślność

prosperous ('prosperes) adj. mający powodzenie; kwitnący; pomyślny; zamożny

prostate (pros'tejt) s. prostata; gruczoł krokowy

prostitute ('prosty,tu:t) s.
prostytutka; v. prostytuować
(się);adj.wszeteczny;rozpustny

prostrate ('prostrejt) v. powalić (np. ze zmęczenia); adj.
leżący twarzą w dół; powalony;
wyczerpany; bezsilny; kłania-
jący się ;leżący plackiem

protect (pre'tekt) v. chronić;
bronić; ochraniać;zabezpieczać

protection (pre'tekszyn) s. ochrona; opieka; protekcja; list
żelazny; wymuszanie pieniędzy
przez grożenie gwałtem

protective (pre'tektyw) adj.
ochronny;zapobiegawczy

protector (pre'tekter) s. opiekun; protektor; ochraniacz

protest (pro'test) v. protestować; zapewniać;oponować

protest ('proutest) s. protest

protestant ('protystent) s.
ewangielik; protestant

protestation (proutes'tejszyn)
s. uroczyste zapewnienie; protest;zaprotestowanie

protract(pre'traekt) v. przeciągać; przedłużać; wystawiać;
przedstawiać w skali

protrude (pre'tru:d) v. wystawać; wysuwać ;sterczeć

proud (praud) adj. dumny; napa-
wający dumą;piękny;szczęśliwy

prove (pru:w) v. udowadniać;
wykazać (się); uprawomocnić;
poddawać próbie; okazywać się

proverb ('prowe:rb) s. przysłowie ;przypowieść

proverbial (pre'we:rbjel) adj.
przysłowiowy

provide (pre'wajd) v. zaopatrywać; przygotowywać; postarać
się; sprzyjać; postanawiać; zaplanować

provide for (pre'wajd,fo:r) v.
zaopatrywać (dla kogoś)

provided that (pre'wajdyd,daet)
exp.: pod warunkiem że…; o ile

providence ('prowydens) s.
opatrzność; oszczędność; przezorność; skrzętność

province ('prowyns) s. prowincja;
zakres; dziedzina

provincial (pre'wynszel) adj.
zaściankowy; prowincjonalny;
s. człowiek z prowincji

provision (pro'wyżyn) s. klauzula; dostawa; przygotowanie
się; (pl.) prowianty; v. pro-
wiantować; zaopatrywać w żywność;zaprowiantować

provisional (pro'wyżenl) adj.
prowizoryczny; tymczasowy

provocation (,prowe'kejszyn) s.
prowokacja; rozdrażnienie;
podniecenie;spowodowanie

provocative (pro'woketyw) adj.
prowokujący; zaciekawiający;
drażniący;wyzywający

provoke (pre'wouk) v. prowokować; podniecać; pobudzać; wywoływać; podżegać;jątrzyć

prowl (praul) v. grasować;
s. grasowanie (po łup)

proxy ('proksy) s. zastępstwo;
pełnomocnik

prude (pru:d) s. świętoszka

prudence ('pru:dens) s. rozwaga; roztropność ;ostrożność

prudent ('pru:dent) s. rozważny;
roztropny;ostrożny

prudish ('pru:dysz) adj. pruderyjny;przesadnie skromny

prune (pru:n) s. śliwka (suszona) v. obcinać (np. gałązki);
oczyszczać (z czegoś)

psalm (sa:m) s. psalm

pseudonym ('sju:de,nym) s.
pseudonim;fikcyjne nazwisko

psyche ('sajki:) s. dusza; duch;
umysł (zwierciadło odchylone)

psychiatrist (saj'kajetryst) s.
psychiatra

psychiatry (saj'kajetry) s.
psychiatria

psychological (,sajke'lodżykel)
adj. psychologiczny

psychologist (saj'koledżyst) s. psycholog

psychology (saj'koledży) s. psychologia

pub (pab) s. Br., knajpa

puberty ('pju:berty) s. dojrzałość płciowa

public ('pablyk) s. publiczność; adj. publiczny; obywatelski

publication (,pably'kejszyn) s. opublikowanie; ogłoszenie; publikacja;wydanie książki

public house ('pablyk,haus) s. szynk; oberża

publicity (pab'lysyty) s. rozgłos; reklama;a.reklamowy

publish ('pablysz) v. publikować; wydawać; ogłaszać; rozgłaszać;wydać drukiem

publisher ('pablyszer) s. wydawca; nakładca

publishing house ('pablyszyng,-haus) s. firma wydawnicza

pudding ('pudyng) s. budyń

puddle ('padl) s. kałuża

puff (paf) v. pykać; sapać; dmuchać; reklamować; pudrować; s. puszek; pyknięcie; dmuchnięcie; blaga reklamowa; pierzyna;kłab dymu;zwój włosów

puff paste ('paf,pejst) s. francuskie ciasto

puffy ('pafy) adj. dychawiczny; nadęty; pękaty; napuszony; otyły; porywisty;dychawiczny

pull (pul) v. pociągnąć; szarpnąć; wyrwać; wyciągać; przeciągać; wiosłować;zciągnać

pull down ('pul,dałn) v. spuścić; rozbierać (np. budynek); osłabiac;sciagac(store etc.)

pull for ('pul,fo:r) v. popierać

pull in ('pul,yn) v. wciągać

pull off ('pul,of) v. ściągać; zdobywać;potrafic;zdołać;stanąc

pull out ('pul,aut) v. wyrwac; wycofać; s. wycofanie się

pulley ('puli) s. bloczek; blok krążkowy; v. podnosić bloczkiem

pullover ('pul,ouwer) s. pulower

pulp (palp) s, miazga; miąższ; papka; v.rozcierać na miazge

pulpit ('pulpyt) s. ambona; kazalnica;kaznodzieje; kazanie

pulpy ('palpy) adj. papkowaty; miąższowy

pulsate (pal'sejt) v. tętnic; pulsowac;drgać;trząść się

pulse (pals) s. tętno; puls; v. tętnic; pulsować

pulverize ('palwerajz) v. proszkować (się); rozpylać; ścierać w proch;zemleć na proch

pump (pamp) s. pompa; lakierek; v. pompować;pytać uporczywie

pump gun ('pamp,gan) s. strzelba (do repetowania)

pumpkin ('pampkyn) s. dynia

pun (pan) s. gra słów (dwuznacznych); v. robic kalambury

punch (pancz) s. uderzenie (pięscią); poncz; przebijak; krzepa; siła; sztanca; kułak; rozmach; v. dziurkować; tłoczyć; walić; szturchać

punctual ('panktjuel) adj. punktualny; punktowy

punctuate ('panktju,ejt) v. przestankowac; przerywać

punctuation (,panktju'ejszyn) s. interpunkcja

punctuation mark (,panktju'ejszyn ma:rk) s. kropka; znak przestankowy

puncture ('pankczer) s. przebicie; punkcja; v. przekłuwac; przedziurawiać;przebić

pungent ('pandżent) adj. kłujący; ostry; cierpki; zjadliwy; gryzący;sarkastyczny;pikantny

punish ('panysz) v. karać;dac bobu

punishment ('panyszment) s. kara; sromotna klęska (na boisku)

pupil ('pju:pl) s. zrenica; uczeń; wychowanek;małoletni;niepełnoletni

puppet ('papyt) s. kukiełka; marionetka;a.kukiełkowy;marionetkowy

puppet show ('papyt,szou) s. występy marionetek

puppet state ('papyt,stejt) s. państwo marionetkowe

puppy ('papy) s. szczenię; szczeniak; piesek;zarozumialec

purchase ('pe:rczes) s. zakup;
kupno; dźwignią; v. kupić;
okupić;nabywac; podnosic (np.
kotwicę);sprawiac sobie

purchaser (pe:rczeser) s. nabywca; kupujący

pure (pjuer) adj. czysty; zupełny; szczery; niewinny; nie
zepsuty,zwykły;czystej krwi

purgative ('pe:rgetyw) adj. przeczyszczający; s. środek na
przeczyszczenie

purgatory ('pe:rgetery) s. czyściec; adj. oczyszczający

purge (pe:rdż) v. przeczyszczac;
oczyścic; usuwac; dawac na
przeczyszczenie; s. oczyszczenie; czystka; środek przeczyszczający;rafinowanie;klarowanie

purify ('pjuery,faj) v. oczyszczac (się);klarowac;rafinowac

purity ('pjueryty) s. czystość

purloin (pe:rloyn) v. ukrasc;
sciągac;porwac

purple ('pe:rpl) s. purpura;
adj. purpurowy; v. robic purpu-
rowym;robic szkarłatnym

purpose ('pe:rpes) s. cel. zamiar; skutek; decyzja; wola;
v. zamierzac ;miec na celu;planowac

purposeful ('pe:rpesful) adj.
celowy; znaczący; rozmyślny;
zdecydowany; stanowczy

purposeless ('pe:rpeslys) adj.
bezcelowy; bezsensowny; daremny; prożny(wysiłek etc.)

purposely ('pe:rpesly) adv. naumyślnie; celowo; rozmyślnie

purr (pe:r) v. mruczec; mrucze-
nie; pomrukiwac;s.pomruk

purse (pe:rs) s. sakiewka; torebka damska; kiesa; nagroda;
v. ściągac (się);marszczyc(czoło)

pursue (per'sju:) v. scigac; tropic; isc dalej; uprawiac (np.
zawod); działac wg.planu; prze-
śladowac; kontynuowac; towarzy-
szyc;spełniac(obowiązek)

pursuer(per'sju:er) s. ścigający;
prześladowca ;dążący do czegoś

pursuit (per'sju:t) s. poscig; po-
goń; zawod; zajęcie; rozrywka

pursy (pe:rsy) adj. dychawiczny; wydęty; otyły;sciągnięty

purvey (pe:r'wej) v. dostarczyc;
zaopatrywac; byc dostawcą

purveyor (pe:rwejer) s. dostawca

pus (pas) s. ropa

push (pusz) s. pchnięcie; suw;
nacisk; wypad; wysiłek; energia; dryg; bieda; kryzys; zdecydowanie; v. pchac; posunąc;
szturchnąc; nakłonic; dopingo-
wac; odpychac; spychac; pomiatac; robic karierę ;ponaglac

push along ('pusz,e'long) v. isc
dalej; ciagnąc się dalej; jechac dalej; spieszyc się

push around ('pusz,a'round) v.
pomiatac kims

pusher ('puszer) s. popychacz;
(uliczny): sprzedawca narkoty-
kow

puss (pus) s. kociak; dziewczyna; (slang):gębal;kot(tygrys)

pussycat ('pusy,kaet) s. kociak;
pliszka; (wulg) narząd płciowy
żeński; ('pasy) adj. ropny

put; put; put (put; put; put)
put (put) v. kłasc; stawiac;
umieszczac; wsadzac; pouczac;
przedkładac; ujmowac; wystawiac; dodawac; wlewac; szaco-
wac; nakładac; opierac; skłądac;
narażac; wypychac (np. kule);
zanosic (np. prosby);s. rzut;
adj. nieruchomy(pozostający na
miejscu)

put back ('put,baek) v. przesta-
wic do tyłu;odłożyc z powrotem

put down ('put,dałn) v. położyc;
stłumic;spuscic w dół ;zapisywac

put forth ('put,fo:rs) v. wydo-
byc; wytężyc(siły);wydawac(pismo)

put off ('put,of) v. odłożyc;
odroczyc ;zbywac;odwiesc ;pozbyc
się

put on ('put,on) v. wdziewac;
przybierac; tyc;udawac;dodawac

put out ('put,aut) v. zwichnąc;
zgasic; wytężyc (się); produ-
kowac; wydawac;wysunąc(rękę etc.)

put together (,put'tugedzer) v.
łączyc; montowac; powiązac;
zbierac(myśli);kojarzyc;zliczyc

put up('pụt,ap) v. ustawiac;
wywieszac; cierpiec; wetknąc;
schowac;dzwigac do góry;ustawic
putrefy ('pju:try,faj) v.gnic;
ropiec;ulegac zepsuciu
putrid ('pju:tryd) adj. zgniły;
zepsuty; cuchnący; smierdzący;
wstrętny; obrzydliwy
putty ('paty) s. kit; szpachlów-
ka; v. szpachlowac; zakitowac
putty knife ('paty,najf) s.
szpachla
puzzle ('pazl) s. zagadka; łamigłówka; zakłopotanie;
v. intrygowac; wprawiac w zakłopotanie; odgadnąc; wymyślic
puzzler ('pazler) s. łamigłówka
pyjamas (pe'dża:mez) pl. piżama
pyramid ('pyremyd) s. piramida;
ostrosłup; v. zarabiac na
spekulacji; wznosic (się)
piramidalnie;budowac jak piramide
python ('pajsen) s. pyton
q (kju:) siedemnasta litera
angielskiego alfabetu (q.=kwarta)
quack (kłaek) s. znachor; szarlatan; kwakanie; v. uprawiac
znachorstwo; gadac jak szarlatan; kwakac
quad (kłod) (skrót): s. kwadrat;
czworokąt
quadrangle (kło'draengl) s.
czworokąt
quadruped ('kładru,ped) adj.
czworonożny
quadruple (kło'drupl) adj.
czterokrotny; cztery razy
większy;czterokrotnie większy
quadruplets (kło'dru:plets) s.
czworaczki
quail (kłejl) s. przepiórka;
v. drżec przed czyms
quaint (kłejnt) adj, malowniczy; trochę dziwaczny
quake (kłejk) s. trzęsienie
(ziemi); v. trząsc się (np.
z zimna)(ze strachu etc.)
quaky (kłejky) adj. trzesący
się; grząski
qualification (,kłolyfy'kejszyn)
s. warunek; określenie; kwalifikacja; uzdolnienie(do pracy)

qualified ('kłolyfajd) adj. wykwalifikowany; uwarunkowany;
kwalifikujący się
quality ('kłolyty) s. jakość;
gatunek; własciwosc; zaleta
qualm (kło:m) s. mdłosci; nudności; obawa; wyrzuty; skrupuły
quandary ('kłondery) s. zakłopotanie; kłopot;dylemat
quantity ('kłontyty) s. ilość;
wielkosc; hurt; obfitosc
quarantine ('kłorenti:n) s.
kwarantanna; v. izolowac
quarrel ('kło:rel) s. kłótnia;
zerwanie; spor; sprzeczka;
v. kłocic się; sprzeczac się;
zerwac z sobą;robic wyrzuty
quarrelsome ('kłorelsem) adj.
kłotliwy; swarliwy
quarry ('kłory) s. kamieniołom;
kopalnia odkrywkowa; łup; zdobycz; płytka; szybka; v. łamac;
wygrzebywac; wydobywac; exploatowac;szperac(za wiadomościami)
quarter ('kło:ter) v. cwiartowac; kwaterowac; rozpłatac;
stacjonowac; s. cwierc; cwiart-
ka; kwadrans; kwatera; 25 cen-
tow (moneta); kwadra; dzielnica;
strona świata; czynniki wpływo-
we (pl.) sfery(rządzące);kwartal
quarterly ('kło:terly) adj. kwartalny; adv. kwartalnie; s. kwar-
talnik;pismo kwartalne
quartet(te) (kło:r'tet) s. kwar-
tet; czworka
quarto ('kło:rtou) s. format
cwiartkowy
quaver ('kłejwer) s. drżenie
głosu; tryl; v. drżec; drgac;
wibrowac; trelowac
quay (ki:) s. molo;nadbrzeże
queasy ('kłi:zy) adj, przeczulony; mdlejący; grymasny;wrażliwy
queen (kłi:n) s. królowa;królówka
queen bee ('kłi:n.bi:) s. królowa pszczoła
queer (kłir) adj. dziwny; dziwaczny; nieswój; podejrzany; fałszywy; pederasta; v. zepsuc;
wpakowac w złą sytuację; mdlic

quench ('kłencz) v. gasić;
tłumić; nagle oziębiać (metal)
querulous ('kłerules) adj. na-
rzekający; zrzędny;płaczliwy
query ('kłiery) s. zapytanie;
pytajnik; znak zapytania;
v. pytać; kwestionować
quest (kłest) s. poszukiwanie;
śledztwo; v. szukać
question ('kłesczyn) s. pytanie;
zagadnienie; kwestia; wątpli-
wości; v. wypytywać; przesłuchiwać; badać; kwestionować;
pytać się;przeegzaminować
questionable ('kłesczenebl) adj.
wątpliwy (moralnie); sporny;
niepewny; niejasny
question mark ('kłesczyn,ma:rk)
s. znak zapytania
questionnaire (,kłejstje'neer)
s. kwestionariusz
queue (kju:) s. warkocz; ogonek; kolejka; v. czekać
w kolejce;czekać w ogonku
queue up ('kju:,ap) v. ustawiać się w kolejce
quibble ('kłybl) s. kruczek;
v. szukać wykrętów
quick (kłyk) adj. prędki; szybki; bystry; pomysłowy; żywy;
lotny; rudonośny; adv. szybko;
chyżo; v. przyspieszać; ożywiać się;zwiększać szybkość
quicken ('kłyken) v. przyspieszać; pobudzać; ożywiać się;
wrócić do życia
quickly ('kłykly) adv. szybko;
prędko; z pospiechem
quickness ('kłyknys) s. prędkość; ostrość
quicksand ('kłyk,saend) s.
grząski piasek
quicksilver ('kłyk,sylwer) s.
rtęć; żywe srebro
quick-tempered ('kłyk'temperd)
adj. porywczy
quick-witted ('kłyk'łytyd)
adj. bystry; rozgarnięty
quid (kłyd) s. funt szterling;
prymka;kawałek do żucia
quiet ('kłajet) adj. spokojny;
cichy; s. spokój; cisza;

v. uspokoić (się); uciszyć
(się);uspokajać;zciszyć;ucichnąć
quiet down ('kłajet dałn) v.
uspakajać;przyciszyć;ucichnąć
quietness ('kłajetnys) s. spokój; cisza;łagodność;skromność
quietude ('kłajetju:d) s. spokój (ducha)
quill (kłyl) s. lotka; dutka;
kolec; szpulka; pióro
quilt (kłylt) s. pikowana
kołdra; pikowana narzuta;
v. pikować; watować; robić
kołdry; zszywać;sprawić lanie
quince (kłyns) s. pigwa
quinine ('kłajnajn) s. chinina
quintal ('kłyntl) s. cetnar;
kwintal
quintuple ('kłyntjupl) adj.
pięciokrotny
quintuplets ('kłyntjuplyts) pl.
pięcioraczki
quit (kłyt) v. przestać; odejść;
odjechać; zabrać się; wyprowadzić się; opuszczać; porzucać;
rezygnować; adj. wolny;uwolniony
quite (kłajt) adv. całkowicie;
zupełnie; raczej; wcale
quiver ('kływer) s. kołczan;
drżenie; drganie; v. drzeć;
drgać; trzepotać skrzydłami
quixotic ('kłyks,otyk) s. marzyciel w stylu Don Kichota
quiz (kłyz) s. klasówka; egzamin; badanie; przesłuchanie;
kawał; v. egzaminować; badać;
przesłuchiwać przeglądać;kpić
quota ('kłouta) s. udział;
kontyngent;norma
quotation (kłou'tejszyn) s. cytata: cytowanie; notowanie;
przytaczanie(bieżącej ceny)
quotation marks (kłou'tejszyn,
,ma:rks) pl. cudzysłów
quote (kłout) v. cytować; przy-
taczać; umieszczać w cudzysło-
wie; notować; podawać kurs;
powoływać się na kogoś
quotient ('kłouszent) s. iloraz
r (a:r) osiemnasta litera
angielskiego alfabetu
rabbi ('raebaj) s. rabin

rabbit ('raebyt) s. królik

rabble ('raebl) s. motłoch

rabid ('raebyd) adj. wściekły; szalony ;rozjuszony;rozzłoszczony

rabies ('raebi:z) s. wścieklizna; wodowstręt

raccoon (ra'ku:n) s. pracz pospolity

race (rejs) s. rasa; plemię; szczep; ród; rodzaj; bieg; gonitwa; wyścigi; prąd; kanał; v. ścigać (się); gonić (się); pędzić; iść w zawody

racer ('rejser) s. wyścigowiec

racial ('rejszel) adj. rasowy

racing ('rejsyng) adj. wyścigowy; s. wyścigi; biegi

racist ('rejsyst) s. rasista

rack (raek) s. ruina; zagłada; zniszczenie; koło tortur; wieszak; drabina stajenna; półka; stojak; zębatka; szybki kłus; v. niszczeć; łamać kołem; torturować; cedzić; szarpać; męczyć; dręczyć

racket ('raekyt) s. rakieta; rak; zabawa; hulanka; awantura hałas; afera; granda; nieuczciwe interesy; kant; v. hałasować; hulać; bumblować; zabawiać się; awanturować się

racketeer (,raeky'tier) s. szantażysta; opryszek; v. szantażować; robić grandę

racoon (re'ku:n) s. szop

racy ('rejsy) adj. typowy; cięty; żywy; dosadny; aromatyczny; pikantny; nieprzyzwoity

radar ('rejder) s. radar

radiance ('rejdjens) s. promieniowanie; blask; promienność

radiant ('rejdjent) adj. promieniujący; promienny; rozpromieniony ;rzucający promienie

radiate ('rejdyejt) v. promieniować(ciepłem, swiatłem etc.)

radiation (,redy'ejszyn) s. promieniowanie;zrodło promieniowania

radiator ('rejdy'ejter) s. grzejnik; kaloryfer; chłodnica (samochodowa);radiowa antena nadawcza;radioaktywna substancja wydzielająca promienie

radical ('raedykel) s. pierwiastek; radykał; adj. zasadniczy; radykalny; podstawowy; pierwiastkowy; korzeniowy

radio ('rejdjou) s. radio; adj. radiowy; v. nadawać przez radio ;wysyłać drogą radiową

radioactive ('rejdjou'aektyw) adj. radioaktywny; promieniotwórczy

radio set ('rejdjou,set) s. aparat radiowy; odbiornik radiowy

radiotherapy ('rejdjou-'terepy) s. radioterapia

radish ('raedysz) s. rzodkiewka

radius ('rejdjes) s. promień

raffle ('raefl) s. loteria fantowa; rupiecie; v. sprzedawać na loterii; kupować los

raft (raeft) s. tratwa; (slang): mnóstwo; v, spławiać na tratwie; robić tratwę

rafter (raefter) s. krokiew

rag (raeg) s. szmata; łachman; łupek; dachówka; v. (slang): besztać; dokuczać

rage (rejdż) s. szaleć; wściekać się; s. szał; wściekłosć; namiętność

ragged (raegyd) adj. szmatławy; obdarty; podarty; poszarpany; kosmaty; zapuszczony; zaniedbany; wadliwy; chropowaty

raid (rejd) s. obława; nalot; najazd; v, urządzać obławę; najeżdzać ;dokonywać napadu

rail (rejl) s. poręcz; szyna; kolej; listwa; erekcja (slang); v. ogradzać poręczami; kłaść szyny; przewozić koleją; drwić; gorzko narzekać ;pomstować

rail in ('rejl,yn) v. przywozić koleją (materiały,towar)

rail off ('rejl,of) v. wywozić koleją (ludzi;towary etc.)

railing ('rejlyng)s. sztachety; ogrodzenie; poręcz;balustrada

railroad ('rejlroud) s. kolej; v. przewozić koleją; przepychać pospiesznie (np.ustawę); (slang) wpakowywać niesłusznie do więzienia

railway ('rejlłej) s. kolej;
tor kolejowy;tor na szynach
railway man('rejlłej,men) s.
kolejarz
rain (rejn) s. deszcz; v. pada
deszcz; spadać deszczem
rainbow ('rejn,boł) s. tęcza
raincoat ('rejnkout) s. płaszcz
nieprzemakalny
rainfall ('rejn,fo:l) s. opad;
ilość opadów
rainproof ('rejn,pru:f) adj.
nieprzemakalny
rainy ('rejny) adj. deszczowy;
dżdżysty; mokry od deszczu
rainy day ('rejny,dej) exp.
czarna godzina
raise (rejz) v. podnosić;
wskrzeszać; wznosić; wynosić;
hodować; wychowywać; wysuwać;
wytaczać; wzniecać; zrywać;
wywoływać; budzić; zbierać
(np. fundusze); wydobywać;
przerywać (np. oblężenie);
znosić (zakaz); s. podwyżka
(płac); podwyższenie
raisin ('rejzyn) s. rodzynek
rake (rejk) v. grabić; przegrze-
bać; grzebać; ostrzeliwać
(wzdłuż); obrzucać wzrokiem;
nachylać do tyłu; uganiać się
za zwierzyną; s. grabie; grab-
ki; rozpustnik
rake-off ('rejk,of) s. niele-
galna prowizja;łapówka
rake out ('rejk,aut) v. wygrzebywać; wygarniać (popioł etc.)
rakish ('rejkisz) adj. zgrabny;
rozpustny; hulaszczy;(pozornie)
szybki (okręt)(z wyglądu)
rally ('raely) s. zbierać (się);
skupiać (sie); przyjść do siebie; ochłonąć; okrzepnąć; ulegać poprawie (giełda); żartować
z kogoś; s. zbiórka; wiec;
okrzepnięcie; ożywienie walki
bokserskiej; wymiana ciosów;
poprawa (konjunktury)
ram (raem) s. tryk; baran; ta-
ran; tłok; dźwig hydrauliczny;
bijak; v. uderzyć; zderzyć się;
ubijać; wtłaczać; bić taranem;
upychac;ugniatać;najechać;zanu-

ramble ('raemb) v. włóczyć się;
przechadzać się; pnąc się (np.
o bluszczu); mówić bez związku;
odbiegać od tematu;s.wędrówka
ramify ('raemyfaj) v. rozgałę-
ziać (się); odgałęzienie (się)
ramp (raemp) s. rampa; v. rzucać się; stawać na tylnych
łapach;opadać pochyło;szaleć
rampart (raempa:rt) s. wał;
szaniec; v. umacniać (szańcem)
ran (raen) v. zob. run
ranch (raencz) s. rancho (gospodarstwo hodowlane) v. prowadzić rancho(farmę etc.)
rancher ('raenczer) s. właściciel rancha
rancid ('raensyd) adj. zjełczały (tłuszcz, oliwa etc.)
rancor('raenker) s. uraza; za-
jadłość; zawziętość; złość
random ('raendem) s. na chybił
trafił; adj. przypadkowy;
pierwszy lepszy;nie planowany
rang (raeng)v. zob. ring
range (rejndż) s. skala; zasięg;
rozpiętość; nosność; strzelnica; pasmo; obszar; wędrówka;
pastwisko; piec kuchenny;
s. ustawiać; układać; klasyfikować; wędrować; nastawiać teleskop; mieć zasięg; wstrzeliwać się; ciągnąć się; zaliczać
się;rozciągać się;sięgać;nieść
range finder ('rejndż,fajnder) s.
dalekomierz ; odległościomierz
ranger (rejndżer) s. strażnik
leśny; policjant; komandos;
wędrowiec;desantowiec etc.
rank (raenk) s. ranga; stan;
stanowisko; v. ustawiać rzędem;
układać; klasyfikować; zaszere-
gować; przewyższać rangą; mieć
rangę; adj. wybujały; zjełczały;
śmierdzący; zupełny; jaskrawy;
obrzydliwy; sprosny;wierutny
ransack ('raensaek) v. przetrząsać; plądrować;grzebać
ransom ('raensem) s. okup; zwolnienie za okupem; v. wykupić;
zwalniać za okupem
rant (raent)v.deklamować z patosem;s.tyrada;bombastyczna mowa

rap (raep) v. dać klapsa; stukać; krytykować; s. klaps; kołatanie; nagana; zarzut; skazanie na więzienie; odrobina
rapacious (re'pejszes) adj. drapieżny;chciwy
rape (rejp) s. zgwałcenie (kobiety); zniewolenie; splądrowanie; uprowadzenie; v. gwałcić (kobietę); uprowadzać; plądrować;pogwałcić neutralność
rapid ('raepyd) adj. prędki; szybki; bystry; stromy
rapidity('raepydyty) s. szybkość; bystrość;rwący nurt(rzeki)
rapids ('raepyds) pl. progi (na rzece); wodospad
rapt (raept) adj. zaabsorbowany; zachwycony;urzeczony;oczarowany
rapture ('raepczer) s. zachwyt; uniesienie;wzięcie żywcem do nieba
rare (reer) adj. rzadki; niedopieczony (np. kotlet); na pół surowy;nie dosmażony;adv.rzadko
rarity ('reeryty) s. rzadkość
rascal ('raeskel) s. hultaj; łobuz; adj. hultajski
rascally ('raeskely) adj. hultajski; łobuzerski
rash (raesz) s. wysypka skórna; ulewa; powódź; adj. pochopny; popędliwy; nieprzemyślany
rasher ('raeszer) s. płatek (np. szynki)
rasp (raesp) s. raszpla; pilnik; zgrzytanie; v. drapać; skrobać; drażnić; chrapliwie mówić
raspberry (ra:zbery) s. malina
rat (raet) s. szczur; łamistrajk; donosiciel; v. polować na szczury; zdradzać; donosić;zaprzedać
rats (raets) pl. szczury; bzdura
rate (rejt) s. stopa; stosunek; proporcja; wysokość; poziom; szybkość; cena; stawka; opłata; podatek; stopień; klasa; v. szacować; oceniać; ustalać; zaliczać; opodatkować; zasługiwać; besztać; wymyślać
rate of exchange ('rejt of yks'czejndż) s. kurs wymiany
rate of interest (,rejt of 'yntryst) s. stopa procentowa

rather ('raedzer) adv. raczej; chętniej; dość; nieco; do pewnego stopnia ;poniekąd;zamiast
ratify ('raetyfaj) v. zatwierdzać; ratyfikować
ration ('raeszyn) s. przydział; porcja; racja; v. racjonować; sprzedawać na kartki
rational ('raeszynl) adj. rozumny; rozsądny; racjonalny; wymierny ;sensowny
rationalize ('raeszyne,lajz) v. racjonalizować; usprawiedliwiać
rattle ('raetl) v. grzechotać; szczekać; brzęczeć; stukać; trzaskać; terkotać; paplać wiersze; s. grzechotanie; terkot; stuk; paplanina; gaduła
rattler ('raetler) s. grzechotnik
rattlesnake ('raetl,snejk) s. grzechotnik
ravage ('raewydż) s. spustoszenie; zniszczenie; v. pustoszyć; niszczyć ;plądrować
rave (rejw) v. bredzić; majaczyć; szaleć; wściekać się; wyć; zachwycać się; v. wrzask; wycie; zaślepienie; przesadna pochwała (entzjastyczna)
raven (rejwn) s. kruk; adj. kruczy; ('raewen) s. grabież; łup; v. pożerać; szukać łupu; mieć szalony apetyt
ravenous ('raewynes) adj. wygłodniały; zgłodniały; żarłoczny; drapieżny
ravine (re'wi:n) s. parów;jar; wąwóz
raving (rejwyng) adj. bredzący; szalony; porywający (np. pięknością); s. atak furii; bredzenie; majaczenie
ravish ('raewysh) v. porywać (kobietę); gwałcić (kobietę)
raw (ro:) adj. surowy; otwarty (np. rana); wrażliwy; nieokrzesany; brutalny; nieprzyzwoity; s. gołe ciało; surówka; v. ocierać (skórę)
ray (rej) s. promień; promyk; (ryba) płaszczka; v. promieniować; naświetlać; prześwietlać wysyłać promienie(światła etc.)

rayon ('rejon) s. sztuczny jedwab

razor ('rejzer) z. brzytwa

razor blade ('rejzer'blejd) s.
żyletka; ostrze brzytwy

re (ri:) prep. w sprawie; tyczy; dotyczy; przedrostek :
znowu; od nowa

reach (ri:cz) v. osiągać; wyciągnąć (np. rękę) dosięgnąć;
dotrzec; docierać; sięgnąć;
s. sięgnięcie; zasięg; połać;
przestrzeń ;pobliże;granice

reach out ('ri:cz,aut) v. wyciągnąć (rękę etc.)

react (ri:'aekt) v. reagować;
oddziaływać; przeciwdziałać

reactor (ri:'aekter) s. reaktor (np. jądrowy)

read; read; read (ri:d; red;
red)

read (ri:d) v. czytać; tłumaczyć; interpretować

read out ('ri:d,aut) v. wydalać kogoś ;wyczytywać

readout, ('ri:daut) s. odczyt
wyników komputera

read to ('ri:d tu) v. czytać
komuś

reader ('ri:der) s. czytelnik;
korektor; lektor; czytanka;
wypisy;recenzent(wydawnictwa)

readily ('redyly) adv. łatwo;
chętnie;ochoczo;bez tudu

readiness ('redynys) s. gotowość; pogotowie; obrotność;
ciętość; przytomność umysłu

reading ('ri:dyŋg)s. czytanie;
oczytanie; interpretacja;
lektura; czytelnictwo; adj.
czytający

readjust ('ri:e'dżast) v. dopasować na nowo

ready ('redy) adj. gotów; gotowy; przygotowany; adv.
w przygotowaniu; gotowy;
v. przygotowywać

ready-made ('redy'mejd) s.
konfekcja; adj. gotowy

ready-to-wear ('redy,tu'łeer)
s. odzież fabrycznej pro-
dukcji

real (ryel) adj. prawdziwy;
rzeczywisty; realny; istotny;
prawdziwy;autentyczny;faktyczny

real estate ('ryel,ys'tejt) s.
nieruchomość; realność

realism ('ryelyzem) s. realizm

realistic ('ryelyst) s. adj.
realistyczny

reality (ty'aelyty) s. rzeczywistość; realizm; prawdziwość

realization (,ryelaj'zejszyn)
s. realizacja; spełnienie;
wykonanie; spieniężenie; uświadomienie sobie

realize ('ry:e,lajz) v. urzeczywistnić; realizować; uprzytam-
niać; zdawać sobie sprawę;
uzyskiwać; zdobywać (majątek)

really ('ryely) adv. rzeczywi-
cie; naprawdę; doprawdy; faktycznie; istotnie

realm (relm) s. królestwo; dziedzina; sfera; zakres

realpolitik (rej'a:lpouly'tyk)
s. polityka egoistyczna

realtor ('ryelter) s. pośrednik
sprzedaży nieruchomości

realty ('ryelty) s. nieruchomość

reap (ry:p) v. żąc; zbierać
plony, owoce pracy etc.

reaper ('ry:per) s. żniwiarz :
żniwiarka

reappear ('ry:e'pier) v. zjawić
się ponownie;znowu ukazać się

rear (rier) s. tył; tyły; ustęp;
v. stawać dęba; hodować; wychowywać; wznosić (się); wybudować;
wystawiać

rear guard('rier,ga:rd) s. tylna
straż

rear-light ('rier,lajt) s. tylne
światło samochodu

rearm ('ry:'a:rm) v. ponownie
uzbrajać

rearmament ('ry:'a:rmement) s.
remilitaryzacja

rearmost (rie:r,moust) adj.
końcowy ;ostatni

rearview mirror ('rier,wju:'-
'myrer) s. (tylne) lusterko
w samochodzie (do sprawdzania
ruchu za samochodem)

rearrange (**'ry:erejndż**) v.
przestawiać; zmieniać (porządek);poprawić(fryzurę etc.)

rearwards (**'rierłedz**) adv.
wstecz;ku tyłowi; na tył

reason (**'ri:zn**) s. rozum; powód; uzasadnienie; motyw; przesłanka; rozsądek; v. rozumować;
rozważać; wnioskować; rozprawiać; przekonywać; dowodzić

reason out (**'ri:zn,aut**) v.
przemyślać;wrozumować;dociekać

reason with (**'ri:zn,łyg**) v.
przekonywać kogoś

reasonable (**'ri:znebl**) adj.
rozumny; rozsądny; umiarkowany; słuszny; racjonalny

reassure (**,ry:a'szuer**) v. zapewniać; upewniać; ubezpieczać
na nowo; uspakajać; przywracać
zaufanie;upewniać na nowo

reassuring (**,ry:a'szueryng**)
adj. uspokajający

rebate (**ry'bejt**) s. rabat;
zwrot (części kwoty); v. udzielać rabatu; potrącać (z rachunku);zamortyzować;przytępiać

rebel (**'rebel**) s. buntownik;
v. buntować się; adj. zbuntowany; buntowniczy

rebellion (**ry'beljen**) s. bunt;
powstanie

rebellious (**ry'beljes**) adj.
zbuntowany; buntowniczy; niesforny;oporny;zbuntowany

rebirth (**ry'be:rg**) s. odrodzenie;odżywanie

re-book (**'ry:buk**) v. zamawiać
na nowo (program teatralny;
bilety lotnicze etc.)

rebound (**ry'baund**) s. odbicie;
odskok; rykoszet; v. odskakiwać; odbijać (się) (sobie na
kimś)

rebuff (**ry'baf**) s. ofuknięcie;
odrzucenie; v. ofuknąć; dać
odprawę;odesłać z kwitkiem

rebuild (**'ry:byld**) v. odbudowywać; przebudowywać

rebuke (**ry'bju:k**) s. nagana;
v. upominać; łajać

recall (**ry'ko:l**) v. odwoływać;
przypominać (sobie);wycofywać;
cofać (obietnicę);s.nakaz powrotu

recap (**'ry:kaep**) s. opona ponownie gumowana; v. ponownie
wulkanizować opony; powtarzać
dla podsumowania

recapture (**ri:'kaepczer**) v.
odzyskać; s. odzyskanie

recede (**ry'si:d**) v. cofać się;
oddalać się; maleć; słabnąć

receipt (**ry'si:t**) s. pokwitowanie; odbiór; recepta

receive (**ry'si:w**) v. otrzymy-
wać; dostawać; odbierać; przyjmować (np. gości)

receiver (**ry'si:wer**) s. odbiornik (radiowy); słuchawka (telefoniczna); odbiorca; syndyk;
zarządca upadłości

recent (**'ri:snt**) adj. niedawny;
świeży; nowy

recently (**'ri:sntly**) adv. niedawno; świeżo; ostatnio;wspól-
nie;często

reception (**ry'sepszyn**) s. przyjęcie; odbiór; recepcja

reception desk (**ry'sepszyn,desk**)
s. biuro do przyjmowania inte-
resantów;portiernia;biuro przyjęć

receptionist (**ry'sepszynyst**) s.
recepcjonistka; sekretarka
przyjmująca klientów;portier

recess (**ry'ses**) s. przerwa
(między lekcjami); ferie;
wgłębienie; nisza; wnęka;
v. odraczać; wkładać do wnęki;
robić wnękę;rozjeżdżać się na ferie

recession (**ry'seszyn**) s. cof-
nięcie; recesja (gospodarcza);
wgłębienie; wnęka:kryzys;zastój

recipe (**'rysypy**) s. przepis;
recepta

recipient (**ry'sypjent**) adj. od-
biorczy; s. odbiorca; zdobywca
nagrody; osoba obdarowana

reciprocal (**ry'syprekel**) adj.
wzajemny; odwrotny; s. odwrotność (w matematyce)

recital (**ry'sajtl**) s. przedstawienie; opowiadanie; recytacja;
koncert;deklamowanie utworu

recite (**ry'sajt**) s. recytować
(wiersz); wyliczać

reckless (**'reklys**) adj. (nie-
bezpiecznie) lekkomyślny;
nieuważający;na oślep;wariacki
brawurowy;szaleńczy;zuchowaty

reckon ('reken) v. liczyć; sądzić, myśleć że;polegać na
reckon up ('reken,ap) v. zli-
czać ;zsumować; podsumowywać
reckon with ('reken,łys) v.
liczyć się (z kimś)
reckoning ('rekenyng) s. oblicza-
nie (położenia); rachuba; obrachunek;kalkulacja;rozliczenie
reclaim (ry'klejm) v. odzyskiwać (pod uprawę); użyzniac;
przerabiać odpadki; wyprowadzać z (zaniedbania; błędu
etc.);zażądać zwrotu;dochodzić
recline (ry'klajn) v. kłasc się;
wyciągać się; złożyć (np. głowę);spoczywać poł leżąc
recognition (,rekeg'nyszyn) v.
rozpoznanie; uznanie; pozdrowienie; dowód uznania
recognize ('rekeg,najz) v. rozpoznawać; pozdrowić; uznawać;
przyznawać; udzielac (głosu)
recoil (ry'kojl) v. wzdrygać się;
cofać się; kopać (np. kolbą);
odskoczyć; odbijać; s. odskok;
odrzut; odbicie; wzdrygnięcie
się
recollect (reke'lekt) v. wspomi-
nać; przypominać sobie; zbierać
na nowo;przypominać sobie z tru-
recollection (,reke'lekszyn) s.
wspomnienie; pamięć
recommend (reke'mend) v. polecać;
zalecać;dobrze świadczyć
recommendation(,rekemen'dejszyn)
s. polecenie; zlecenie
recompense ('rekem,pens) v. odpłacać; dawać odszkodowanie;
s. wynagrodzenie; zadośćuczynienie;odszkodowanie;rekompensata
reconcile ('rekensajl) v. godzić
(sprzeczności); zażegnać (spór);
pojednać;pogodzić się
reconciliation (,reken,syly'ejszyn) s. pojednanie; pogodzenie
reconsider (,ri:ken'syder) v.
ponownie rozważyć; reasumować
reconstruct (,ri:ken'strakt) v.
odbudowywać; odtwarzać
reconstruction ('ri:ken'strakszyn) s. rekonstrukcja; odbudowa

record ('reko:rd) v. zapisywać;
notować; rejestrować; zaznaczać; nagrywać; s. zapiska;
archiwum; rejestracja; dokument; przeszłość (czyjaś); pamięć o kimś; nagranie; rekord
recorder (ry'ko:rder) s. re-
gistrator; aparat zapisujący;
pisak;pisarz archiwista
record holder ('reko:rd,houlder)
s. rekordzista; mistrz
recording ('reko:rdyng) s. nagranie (płyta)
record player ('reko:rd,plejer)
s. adapter
recourse (ry'ko:rs) s. ucieka-
nie się (ratunek)
recover (ry'kawer) v. odzyskać;
nadrabiać; powetować sobie;
uzyskać; przywracać; wyzdrowieć;
ochłonąć; przyjsć do siebie
recovery (ry'kawery) s. odzyskanie (pozycji); wyzdrowienie;
poprawa (gospodarcza)
recreation (,rekry'ejszyn) s.
rozrywka; zabawa; odtworzenie
recruit (ry'kru:t) s. rekrut;
poborowy; v. werbować; uzupełniać (stan zatrudnienia)
rectangle ('rektaengl) s.
prostokąt; a.prostokątny
rectify ('rektyfy) v. prostować
(np. błąd); poprawiać (np.
plan); usuwać (np. nadużycia)
rector ('rekter) s. proboszcz;
rektor
rectory ('rektery) s. probostwo
recur (ry'ke:r) v. powtarzać
się; przypominać się; nawiązywać do czegoś (wielokrotnie)
recurrent (ry'karent) adj. po-
wracający; nawracający
red (red). adj. czerwony;
s. czerwień; lewicowiec; komunista;radykał(skrajny);forsa(sl.)
red-bait('redbejt) v. oskarżać
o komunizm (USA)
red-blooded('red,bladyd) adj.
męski; krzepki ;jurny
redden ('reden) v. zaczerwie-
nić się ;zarumienić się
reddish ('redysz) adj. czerwo-
nawy

redeem (ry'di:m) v. wykupywać;
okupywać; wybawiać; zbawiać;
odkupić; zamienić;kompensować
redemption (ry'dempszyn) s.
wykup; okupienie; odkupienie;
wybawienie;umorzenie;zbawienie
red-handed ('red'haendyd) adj.
splamiony krwią; exp. na gorącym uczynku
red letter day ('red'leter, dej)
s. dzień specjalny; dzień
świąteczny
redouble (ry'dabl) v. podwoić
(się); zwijać się
reduce (ry'dju:s) v. zmniejszać (się); chudnąć; redukować; ograniczać; obniżać; dostosować; sprowadzać; doprowadzać; rozcieńczać; osłabiać;
odtleniać; wytapiać
reduction (ry'dakszyn) s.
zmniejszenie; redukcja; obniż-
ka; sprowadzenie; dostosowanie; odtlenianie; wytapianie
reed (ri:d) s. trzcina; słoma;
fujarka; strzała; płocha
tkacka; stroik (muzyczny)
reeducation (,ry:edju'kejszyn)
s. przeszkolenie ponowne
reef (ri:f) s. rafa; skała podwodna; ref; v. refować
reek (ri:k) s. odor; para; dym;
v. śmierdzieć; parować; dymić;
wędzić; ociekać (krwią)
reel (ri:l) s. szpula; cewka;
rolka; chwianie się; kręcenie
się; v. nawijać; odwijać; rozwijać; recytować; chwiać się;
zataczać się; kręcić się; dostawać zawrotu głowy; dawać zawrót
głowy;zachwiać się na nogach
reel off ('ri:l,of) v. odwijać
reel up ('ri:l,ap) v. nawijać
reelect ('ri:y'lekt) v. ponownie wybierać
reenter ('ri:'enter) v. ponownie wchodzić (w posiadanie etc.)
reentry ('ri:'entry) s. ponowne wejście;rewindykacja
re-establish (,ry:ys'taeblysz)
v. ponownie: zakładać; ustanawiać; ustalać; wprowadzać

refer (ry'fe:r) v. odsyłać; po-
wiązywać; skierować; odwoływać;
cytować; odnosić się; dotyczyć;
powoływać się
referee (refe'ri:) s. sędzia
sportowy; rozjemca; v. sędziować
reference ('referns) s. odsyłacz; odnośnik; odwoływanie
się; aluzja; informacja; referencja; stosunek; związek;
wzgląd ;przelotna wzmianka
reference book ('referens,bu:k)
s. tekst podręczny;podręcznik
reference library ('referens
laj'brery) s. biblioteka podręczna naukowo-informacyjna
refill (ry:'fyl) s. ponowne;
napełnienie; wypełnienie; nowy
zapas; v. ponownie napełniać,
wkładać,zapełniać etc.
refine (ry'fajn) v. oczyszczać;
rafinować; wysubtelniać; rozprawiać subtelnie
refinement (ry'fajnment) s.
rafinowanie; wyrafinowanie;
subtelność; wytworność
refinery (ry'fajnery) s. rafineria
reflect (ry'flekt) v. odbijać;
odzwierciadlać; rozmyślać; zastanawiać się; krytykować;
przynosić (zaszczyt; ujmę)
reflection (ry'flekszyn) s. odbicie; odzwierciedlenie; odbicie światła; zarzut; rozwaga;
namysł;wzmianka;pomysł;wstyd
reflex ('ry:fleks) s. odruch;
refleks; odbicie; odzwierciedlenie; adj. refleksyjny; odbity; wygięty; v. poddawać
refleksom; wyginać wstecz
reflexive (ry'fleksyw) adj.
odbijający; pełen zadumy;
refleksyjny
reform (ry'fo:rm) v. reformować;
poprawić; usuwać; ulegać refor-
mie; s. reforma; poprawa
reformation (,refor'mejszyn) s.
reformacja; poprawa
reformer (ry'fo:rmer) s. refor-
mator(moralności,warunków etc.)

refract (ry'fraekt) v. załamywać światło;wyginać promień światła

refractory (ry'fraektery) adj. oporny; uporczywy; krnąbrny; odporny; ogniotrwały

refrain (ry'frejn) v. powstrzymywać się; s. refren

refresh (ry'fresh) v. odświeżyć; wzmacniać; pokrzepiać

refreshment (ry'freszment) s. odpoczynek; wytchnienie; odświeżenie; zakąska

refrigerator (ry'frydże,rejter) s. lodówka; chłodnia

refuel ('ry:'fjuel) v. zaopatrzyć w paliwo; dodać paliwa

refuge ('refju:dż) s. schronienie; azyl;przytułek;v.schronić się

refugee (,refju'dżi:) s. zbieg; uchodźca; uciekinier

refund (ry'fand) s. zwrot; spłata; v. zwracać pieniądze

refusal (ry'fju:zel) s. odmowa; prawo opcji; wbijanie do oporu

refuse (ry'fju:z) v. odmawiać; odrzucać; adj. odpadowy; s. odpadki; rupiecie

refute (ry'fju:t) v. zbijać (np. twierdzenie)

regain (ry'gejn) v. odzyskać; wrócić (do zdrowia)

regard (ry'ga:rd) v. spoglądać; zważać; uważać; dotyczyć; s. wzgląd; spojrzenie; szacunek; uwaga;pozdrowienia;ukłony

regarding (ry'ga:rdyng) prep. odnośnie;co się tyczy;w sprawie

regardless (ry'ga:rdlys) adv. w każdym razie; adj. nie zważający; bez względu (na kłopoty etc.);nie licząc się(z wydatkami)

regard of (ry'ga:rd,ow) exp. co się tyczy ; w sprawie etc.

regent ('ri:dżent) s. regent; opiekun; członek zarządu

regime (ry'żi:m) s. ustrój; reżym; tryb życia; system; rządy

regiment ('redżyment) s. pułk; zastęp; v. organizować; koszarować; wcielać do pułku

region ('ri:dżen) s. okolica; sfera; rejon; obszar; dzielnica

register ('redżyster) v. rejestrować; zapamiętywać; wysyłać polecony list; prowadzić rejestr; wstrzeliwać się; wyrażać minami

registered letter ('redżysterd, ,leter) s. list polecony

registration (,redzys'trejszyn) s. rejestracja; meldunek; ilość zarejestrowana

regret (ry'gret),s. ubolewanie; żal; v. żałować czegoś

regrettable(ry'gretebl) adj. godny ubolewania

regular ('regjuler) adj. regularny; stały; zawodowy; poprawny; przepisowy; s. regularny (żołnierz; ksiądz etc.); stały gość; wierny partyjnik

regularity (,regju'laeryty) s. regularność; systematyczność

regulate ('regjulejt) v. regulować;przystosowywać do wymogów

regulation (,regju'lejszyn) s. przepis; regulowanie; adj. przepisowy; zwykły

rehearsal (ry'he:rsel) s. próba; powtarzanie

rehearse (ry'he:rs) v. odbywać próbę; powtarzać

reign (rejn) v. panować; władać; s. władza; panowanie

rein (rejn) v. kierować wodzami; trzymać na wodzach

reins (rejns) pl. wodze

reindeer ('rejn.dier) s. renifer

reinforce (,ri:yn'force) v. wzmocnić;popierać;dodać sił

reject (ry'dżekt) v. odrzucić; odpalić; zwracać; ('rydżekt) s. wybrakowany towar; niezdatny do wojska ;coś odrzuconego

rejection (ry'dżekszyn) s. odrzucenie; odmowa; wybrakowany towar;oblanie studenta;odkosz

rejoice (ry'dżojs) v. radować; cieszyć się; weselić się

rejoicing (ry'dżojsyng) s. radość;uradowanie;adj.uradowany

rejoin ('ri:dżoyn) v. ponownie łączyć (się); zestawiać połamane części; odpowiadać na zarzut

relapse (ry'laeps) s. nawrót;
pogorszenie; v. ponownie popadać; zapadać z powrotem
relate (ry'lejt) v. opowiadać;
referować; łączyć się
related (ry'lejtyd) adj. bliski;
spokrewniony; spowinowacony;
związany;pokrewny;powinowaty
relation (ry'lejszyn) s. sprawozdanie; opowiadanie; stosunek; związek; pokrewieństwo;
powinowactwo; krewny
relationship (ry'lejszynszyp)
s. stosunek; pokrewieństwo;
powinowactwo;zależność
relative ('reletyw) adj.
względny; stosunkowy; podrzędny; zależny; dotyczący;
adv. odnosnie; w sprawie;
s. krewny; zaimek względny
relax (ry'laeks) v. odprężać
(się); osłabnąć; rozluźniać
się; łagodnieć; odpoczywać
relaxation (,ry:laek'sejszyn)
n. odprężenie; odpoczynek;
rozrywka; złagodzenie
relay(ry'lej) s. bieg rozstawny; wzmacniacz;vprzekazywać;
zmieniać (tor);kłaść na nowo
relay race (re'lej,rejs) s.
bieg rozstawny; bieg sztafetowy
release (ry'li:z) v. wypuszczać; uwalniać; zwalniać;
s. zwolnienie; uwolnienie;
puszczenie (do druku); spust;
wyzwalacz;wypuszczenie(filmu)
relent (ry'lent) v. łagodnieć;
mięknąć;dać sie wzruszyć
relentless (ry'lentlys) adj.
nieugięty; bezlitosny; nieprzejednany;nieustępliwy;srogi
relevant ('relewent) adj.
istotny; trafny; na miejscu;
należący do rzeczy
reliability (ry,laje'bylyty) s.
rzetelność; solidność; pewność
reliable (ry'lajebl) adj. pewny; solidny; rzetelny
reliance (ry'lajens) s. zaufanie; otucha
reliant (ry'lajent) adj. ufny
w siebie;liczący na kogoś;zależny od czegoś

relic ('relyk) n. zabytek; relikwia;pozostałość;resztka
relief (ry'li:f) n. odprężenie;
ulga; urozmaicenie; zapomoga;
pomoc; zmiana (np. warty);
płaskorzeźba;uwypuklenie
relieve (ry'li:w) v. nieść pomoc, ulgę; ulżyć (sobie);
oddać mocz; ożywić; zmieniać
wartę; zluzować; uwypuklić
(na tle czegoś);uwydatnić
religion (ry'lydżyn) s. religia;
obrządek; wyznanie; zakon
religious (ry'lydżes) adj. pobożny; religijny; zakonny;
s. zakonnik; zakonnica
relinquish (ry'lynkłysz) v. porzucać; wyrzekać się czegoś;
zaniechać; zrzekać się; rezygnować;wypuścić coś z rąk
relish ('relysz) s. smak; posmak;
przyprawa; przysmak; urok; zamiłowanie; v. smakować w czyms;
czynić smaczniejszym; przyprawiać; mieć dobry smak; być
przyjemnym;dodawać smaku
reluctance (ry'laktens) s. niechęć; opór(magnetyczny);wstręt
reluctant (ry'laktent) adj. niechętny; oporny
rely on (ry'laj,on) v. polegać
na czyms lub kims ;liczyć na
remain (ry'mejn) v. pozostawać
remains (ry'mejns) pl. pozostałości; resztki; przeżytki;
zwłoki; szczątki
remainder (ry'mejnder) s. reszta; pozostałość; remanent
remand (ry'maend) v. odsyłać
(do niższej instancji lub więzienia); s. odesłanie do
więzienia; człowiek odesłany
z powrotem
remark (ry'ma:rk) v. zauważyć;
zrobić uwagę; s. uwaga
remarkable (ry'ma:rkebl) adj.
wybitny; godny uwagi
remedy ('remydy) s. lekarstwo;
środek; rada; v. leczyć; zaradzać ;naprawiać
remember (ry'member) v. pamiętać;
przypominać; pozdrawiać; modlić
się za kogoś;mieć w pamięci

remembrance (ry'membrens) s.
wspomnienie; pamiątka; pamięc; pozdrowienie;ukłony
remind (ry'majnd) v. przypomi-
nac coś komuś;przypomnieć
reminder (ry'majnder) s. przypomnienie; upomnienie; ponaglenie;ktoś przypominający
reminiscent (,remy'nysnt) adj.
przypominający; wspominający;
pełen wspomnień
remiss (ry'mys) adj. niedbały;
ospały; niechlujny
remit (ry'myt) s. przekazywać
(pieniądze); darować (dług);
odpuszczać (grzechy); odsyłać; przywracać; łagodzić;
łagodnieć; słabnąć
remitance (ry'mytens) s. przesyłka pieniężna; wypłata
remnant ('remnent) s. resztka;
pozostałość; ślad czegoś
remodel (ry'modl) v. przerabiać; odnowic; przemodelować
remonstrate ('remenstrejt) v.
protestować
remorse (ri'mo:rs) s. wyrzuty
sumienia; skrupuły
remorseless (ri'mo:rslys) adj.
bezlitosny ;nie skruszony
removal (ry'mu:wl) v. usunięcie; przeprowadzka
remove (ry'mu:w) v. usuwać;
przewozic; zdejmować;przepro-
wadzac się; opuszczać;
s. przeprowadzka; odległość;
stopień;oddalenie
remover (ry'mu:wer) s. usuwacz
(plam); środek do usuwania
renaissance (ry'nesens) s. odrodzenie;renesans;a.renesansowy
rend; rent; rent (rend; rent;
rent)
rend (rend) v. drzeć; targać;
wydzierac; urągać; rozdzierać
render ('render) v. uczynić;
zrobic; oddawać; okazywać;
składać; wydawać; płacić; odpłacać; oczyszczać; wytapiac;
tynkować; s. odpłata (np.
w naturze); pierwsza warstwa
tynku

rendezvous ('ra:ndy,wu:) s.
randka; umówione spotkanie;
miejsce spotkań
renew (ry'nu:) v. odnawiać; po-
nawiac; wznawiać; odświeżać;
prolongować
renewal (ry'nu:el) s. odnowienie (np. kontraktu)
renounce (ry'nauns) v. zrzekać
się; zrezygnować; wyrzekać się;
wypowiadać; odstępować; nie-
uznawać
renovate (ry'nowejt) v. odnowić;
naprawic
renown (ry'naun) s. sława; rozgłos; pogłoska
renowned (ry'naund) adj. sławny
rent l. (rent) v. zob. rend
rent 2. (rent) s. komorne;
czynsz; renta; najem; rozdarcie; szczelina; rozłam; parów;
v. wynajmować; dzierżawić; pobierać czynsz; być wynajmowanym
rental ('rentl) s. czynsz; komorne; wypożyczanie; adj. czynszowy
rental agency ('rentl'ejdżensy)
s. biuro wynajmu (narzędzi;
mieszkań etc)
rent free ('rent'fri:) adj.
wolny od opłaty czynszowej
repair (ry'peer) v. pójść;
uczęszczać; naprawiać; reperować; remontować; powetować;
wynagrodzić; s. naprawa; remont; stan
repair shop (ry'peer,shop) s.
warsztat naprawy
reparation (repa'rejszyn) s.
naprawa; remont; odszkodowanie
repartee (repa:r'ti:) s. ripos-
ta; cięta odpowiedz; odcina-
nie się
repay (ry:'pej) v. spłacić;
zwrócic; wynagrodzić; odwza-
jemnić się; oddać
repeat (ry:'pi:t) v. powtarzać
(się); repetować; odbijać się;
robić powtórkę; robić ponownie;
odtwarzać; s. powtórka; po-
wtórzenie; powtórne zamówienie
a.powtórny;wielokrotny

repel (ry'pel) v. odpierać;
odrzucać; odtrącać; budzić
odrazę ,niechęć, wstręt etc.

repent (ry'pent) v. żałować

repentance (ry'pentens) s.
skrucha; żal

repentant (ry'pentent) adj.
żałujący; pełen skruchy

repetition (,repy'tyszyn) s.
powtorzenie; powtórka

replace (ry'plejs) v. zastępować; zwracać; oddawać; umieszczać z powrotem; przywrócić;
wymienić

replacement (ry'plejsment) s.
zastępstwo; zastępca; zastąpienie; wymiana (części)

replenish (ry'plenysz) v. ponownie napełniać; wypełniać;
uzupełniać

replay (ry'plej) v. ponownie
rozgrywać; ('ry:plej) s. ponowna rozgrywka

reply (ry'plaj) v. odpowiadać;
s. odpowiedź

report (ry'po:rt) v. opowiadać;
meldować; dawać sprawozdanie;
zdawać sprawę; pisać sprawozdanie; referować; s. raport;
sprawozdanie; komunikat;
opinia; huk; wybuch; pogłoska

reporter (ry'po:rter) s. dziennikarz; sprawozdawca; reporter

repose (ry'pouz) s. odpoczynek;
spokój; v. odpoczywać; spoczywać; polegać; opierać; pokładać

represent (,repry'zent) v.
przedstawiać; reprezentować;
wyobrażać; grać (kogoś)

representation (,repryzen'tejszyn) s. przedstawicielstwo;
reprezentacja; przedstawienie;
wyobrażenie

representative (,repry'zentetyw) adj. przedstawiający;
reprezentujący; wyobrażający;
s. przedstawiciel; reprezentant (poseł na sejm)

repress (ry'pres) v. tłumić;
hamować; powstrzymywać; poskromić

reprieve (ry'pri:w) v. zawieszać; odraczać; dawać odroczenie; s. odroczenie; darowanie,
zmiana kary (śmierci)

reprimand ('reprymaend) v. karcić; udzielać nagany; s. nagana

reproach (ry'proucz) v. robić
wyrzuty; wymawiać; s. wyrzut;
zarzut; wymówka

reproachful (ry'prouczful) adj.
pełen wyrzutu

reproduce (,rypre'du:s) v. odtwarzać;reprodukować; rozmnażać; wznawiać

reproduction (,ri:pre'dakszyn)
s. reprodukcja; rozmnażanie
się; płodzenie

reproof (ry'pru:f) s. nagana

reprove (ry'pru:w) v. ganić

reptant ('reptent) adj. pełzający

reptile ('reptajl) s. gad; płaz;
gadzina; adj. pełzający; gadzinowy

republic (ry'pablyk) s. republika; rzeczpospolita

republican (ry'pablyken) adj.
republikański; s. republikanin

repugnance (ry'pagnens) s. odraza; niechęć; niezgodność;
sprzeczność

repugnant (ry'pagnent) adj.
odrażający; oporny; sprzeczny;
niezgodny

repulse (ry'pals) v. odpierać;
odrzucać; odtrącać; s. odparcie; odrzucenie; odmowa

repulsive (ry'palsyw) adj. odrażający; wstrętny; odpychający;budzący odrazę

reputable ('repjutebl) adj.
szanowany; zaszczytny

reputation (,repju'tejszyn) s.
reputacja; sława; dobre imię

repute (ry'pju:t) s. reputacja;
sława; v. uważać za coś

request (ry'kłest) s. prośba;
życzenie; żądanie; zapotrzebowanie; v. prosić o pozwolenie;
upraszać ;poprosić o przysługę

require (ry'kłajer) v. żądać;
nakazywać;wymagać;być wymaganym

required (ry'kłajerd) adj.
obowiązkowy;wymagany;żądany
requirement (ry'kłajerment) s.
wymaganie; zadanie; potrzeba
requisite ('rekłyzyt) adj. wy-
magany; s. rzecz konieczna,
potrzebna; rekwizyt
requisition (,rekły'zyszyn) s.
zadanie; nakaz; zapotrzebowanie; v. wydawać zapotrzebowanie; zapotrzebowywać; rekwiro-
wać;zarzadać dostaw
requite (ry'kłajt) v. odwzajemniać się;wynagradzać;zemścić się
rescue ('reskju:) v. ratować;
wybawiać; odbijać z więzienia;
s. ratunek; odbicie z więzienia; odebranie przemocą
research (ry'se:rcz) s. poszukiwanie; badanie
researcher (ry'se:rczer) s. badacz (naukowy etc.)badaczka
resemblance (ry'zemblens) s.
podobieństwo
resemble (ry'zembl) v. być po-
dobnym (z wygladu)
resent (ry'zent) v. czuć urazę
resentful (ry'zentful) adj.
urażony;obrażony;zawziety
resentment (ry'zentment) s.
uraza;złość;oburzenie;obraza
reservation (,rezer'wejszyn) s.
zastrzeżenie; zarezerwowanie;
miejsce zarezerwowane; rezerwat (np. indiański); rezerwa;
zapas;ograniczenie
reserve (ry'ze:rw) v. odkładać;
zastrzegac; zarezerwować;
s. rezerwa; zapas; rezerwat;
zastrzeżenie; warunek
reserved (ry'ze:rwd) adj.zare-
zerwowany; powściągliwy; pełen rezerwy;z rezerwa;zastrzeżo-
ny
reservoir ('reserwla:r) s.
zbiornik; zbiór; pokład kopalniany; v. składać w zbiorniku
reside (ry'zajd) v. mieszkać;
tkwić;spoczywać w;osadzać sie
residence ('rezydens) s. miejsce zamieszkania; pobyt (stały)
residence permit ('rezydens,-
per'myt) s. prawo pobytu

resident ('rezydent) s. stały
mieszkaniec; adj. zamieszkały;
umiejscowiony;zamieszkujący
residue ('rezydju:) s. reszta;
pozostałość;reszta spadkowa
resign (ry'zajn) v. zrzekać się;
wyrzekać się; godzić się z losem
resignation (,rezyg'nejszyn) s.
dymisja; zrzeczenie się; wyrzeczenie się;pogodzenie sie(z losem)
resigned (ry'zajnd) adj. zrezyg-
nowany;w stanie spoczynku
resin ('rezyn) s. żywica; v. zaprawiać żywicą
resist (ry'zyst) v. opierać się;
stawiać opór; być odpornym;
powstrzymywać się
resistance (ry'zystens) s. opór;
sprzeciw; wytrzymałość; odporność; opornica;a.oporowy
resistant (ry'zystent) adj. odporny; opierający się; s. coś
lub ktoś odporny,opierajacy się
resolute ('rezelu:t)adj. rezolutny; śmiały; zdecydowany
resolution (,rese'lu:szyn) s.
uchwała; postanowienie; rezo-
lucja; śmiałość; rozłożenie;
rozwiązanie;rozkład(sił)
resolve (ry'zolw) s. postanowienie; decyzja; stanowczość;
v. rozkładać; rozwiązywać;
uchwalać; decydować; postanawiać; usuwać;przemieniać;skłaniać
resolved (ry'solwd) adj. zdecydowany; śmiały
resonance ('resnens) s. oddźwięk;
odgłos ; rezonans
resonant ('reznent) adj. rezonu-
jący; rozbrzmiewający
resort (ry'zo:rt) v. uciekać się;
uczęszczać; s. uzdrowisko;
uczęszczanie; ucieczka; ucieka-
nie się; ratunek; wyjście
resort to (ry'zo:rt,tu) v. uciekać się do...
resound (ry'zaund) v. rozbrzmiewać; odbijać; opiewać; obiegać;
wypowiadać się;odbijać się echem
resource (ry'so:rs) s. zasoby;
środki; bogactwa; zaradność;
pomysłowość;zasoby naturalne

resourceful (ry'so:rsful) adj.
zaradny; pomysłowy
respect (rys'pękt) v. szanowac; dotyczyc; zważac;
s. wzgląd; szacunek; poważanie;związek;łacznosć;pozdrowie
respectable (rys'pektebl) adj.
chwalebny; godny szacunku;
poważny; pokaźny
respectful (rys'pektful) adj.
pełen szacunku
respectfully (rys'pektfuly)
adv. z poważaniem; z uszanowa-
niem
respecting (rys'pektyng) prep.
odnośnie do...
respective (rys'pektyw) adj.
odpowiedni;poszczególny
respectively (rys'pektywly)
adv. odpowiednio; każdemu
z osobna;kolejno
respiration (,respy'rejszyn)
s. oddech; oddychanie
respite ('respajt) s. wytchnienie (krótkie); odroczenie;
v. odraczac (stracenie); przynosic (krótką) ulgę
resplendent (rys'plendent) adj.
błyszczący silnie;jasny
respond (rys'pond) v. odpowiadac; reagowac; byc czułym
respondent (rys'pondent) adj.
odpowiadający; wrażliwy;
s. pozwany; obronca
response (rys'pons) s. odpowiedz; odzew; reakcja; od-
dzwięk ;odezwanie się
responsibility (rys,ponse'bylyty) s. odpowiedzialnośc
responsible (rys'ponsebl) adj.
odpowiedzialny (wobec; przed)
rest (rest) s. odpoczynek;
spokój; przerwa; przestanek;
podpórka; pomieszczenie;
schronienie; reszta; v. spoczywac; odpoczywac; dawac odpoczynek; uspokoić; byc spo-
kojnym; podpierac się; polegac
restaurant ('resterent) s. restauracja ;jadłodajnia
restful ('restful) adj. spokojny; uspokajający;wypoczęty

restless ('restlys) adj. niespokojny; bezsenny ;niesforny
restlessness ('restlysnys) s.
niepokój ;zniecierpliwienie
restoration (,reste'rejszyn) s.
odnowienie; rekonstrukcja; restytucja; odtworzenie
restore (rys'to:r) v. przywracac; uleczyc; odnawiac; restau-
rowac; restytuowac; zwracac;
rekonstruowac; odtwarzac
restrain (rys'trejn) v. powstrzymywac; powsciągac; krępowac;
ograniczac;trzymac w ryzach
restraint (rys'trejnt) s. skre-
powanie; uwięzienie; zamknięcie w szpitalu psychiatrycznym;
wstrzemięźliwosc; umiar
restrict (rys'trykt) v. ograniczac do; zamykac w (granicach)
restriction (rys'trykszyn) s.
ograniczenie
rest room('rest,rum) s. ustęp;
toaleta
result (ry'zalt) s. rezultat;
wynik; v. wynikac; dawac w wyniku ;wypływac;pochodzic
result in (ry'zalt,yn) v. kon-
czyc się na
resultant (ry'zaltent) adj. wy-
nikający;(np. siła) wypadkowa
resume (ry'zju:m) v. wznawiac;
ponownie podejmowac; obejmowac;
zajmowac; odzyskiwac; ciagnąc
dalej; streszczac ;odzyskac
resumption (ry'zampszyn) s.
wznowienie; odzyskanie; podjęcie
na nowo ;powrót do czegos
resurrection (,reze'rekszyn) s.
odżycie; zmartwychwstanie;
wskrzeszenie ;wznowienie(zwyczaju)
retail ('ri:tejl) s. detal; adj.
detaliczny; v. sprzedawac de-
talicznie; szczegółowo opowiadac ;adv.detalicznie;a.detaliczny
retailer (ri:'tejler) s. sklepikarz; detalista; plotkarz
retain (ry'tejn) v. zatrzymywac;
zapamiętywac; zgodzic (do pracy);zachowywac(tradycje)
retaliate (ry'taeliejt) v. od-
wzajemniac się; brac odwet

retaliation (ry,taely'ejszyn)
s. odwet;zemsta;odpłata

retell ('ri:'tel) y. ponownie
opowiedziec;powtórzyć

retention (ry'tenszyn) s. zatrzymanie (np. moczu); zdol-
nosc zatrzymywania; pamięć

retinue ('retynu:) s. orszak;
swita;czeladz;poczet(dostojnika)

retire (ry'tajer) v. wycofywać
(się); isć na spoczynek;
pensjonować;s.sygnał odwrotu

retired (ry'tajerd) adj. emery-
towany; ustronny;odosobniony

retirement (ry'tajerment) s.
przejscie w stan spoczynku;
ustronie; odosobnienie; wy-
cofanie(weksla);odwrót

retort (ry'to:rt) v. odpłacać
się; odcinać się; odparować;
ripostować; s. retorta; ri-
posta; odwet; odwrócenie
(oskarżenia); cięta odpowiedź

retrace (ry'trejs) v. odtwo-
rzyć; przypomnieć sobie; badac początek (1)

retrace (ry:'trejs) v. ponownie liniować; kopiować (2)

retract (ry'traekt) v. cofnąc
się; odwołać; chować się;
wciągac(się)(pazury)

retreat (ry'tri:t) v. cofać
się; s. odwrót; wycofanie się
w zacisze; kryjówka; odosobnienie; przytułek;ustronie

retribution (,retry'bju:szyn)
s. odpłata; kara; nagroda

retrieve (ry'tri:w) v. odzys-
kac; powetować; odszukać; ura-
tować; uprzytomnic sobie;
aportować; s. odzyskanie; od-
szukanie; powetowanie; urato-
wanie;ruch wsteczny(powrotny)

retrospect ('retrespekt) s.
spojrzenie wstecz; rozważanie
przeszłości; v. rzucać okiem
wstecz; nawiązywać do (przeszłości);patrzyć w przeszłość

retrospective('retrespektyw)
adj. retrospektywny; działający wstecz;z mocą retroaktywną

return (ry'te:rn) v. wracać;
przynosic dochód;złożyć(zeznanie)

obracać w..; oddawać; odwzajem-
nic; odpowiedziec; wybrać;
s. powrot; nawrot; dochód;
zysk; zwrot; rewanż; sprawozdanie (np podatkowe)

return flight (ry'te:rn,flajt)
s. lot powrotny

return ticket (ry'te:rn,tykyt)
s. powrotny bilet

reunification ('ri:ju:nyfy'kejszyn) s. ponowne zjednoczenie

reunion ('ri:'ju:njen) s. zjazd;
ponowne połączenie; zebranie

revaluation (ri:'waelju'ejszyn)
s. ponowna ocena; przewartoscio-
wanie(po ponownej ocenie)

revaluate (ri:'waelju':ejt)v,
ponownie ocenic; przewartoscio-
wać(dom w celach podatkowych)

revamp (ry:'waemp) v, przerabiac; reorganizować; rewidować;
okapować (buty);odnowic

reveal (ry'wi:l) v. ujawniac;
objawiac; odsłaniac; s. rama
okna w karoserii

revel ('rewl) s. zabawa; hulanka; v. hulac; używać sobie

revelation (,rewy'lejszyn) s.
ujawnienie; objawienie; odsłonięcie; rewelacja;odkrycie

revenge (ry'wendż) s. zemsta;
mściwosć; v. pomscic; zemscic
się(za zniewage,krzywde etc.)

revengeful (ry'wendżful) adj.
mściwy

revenue ('rewy,nu:) s. dochód
(z podatków)

revenue office ('rewy,nu:'ofys)
s. urząd podatkowy (finansowy)

revere (ry'wier) v. czcic;
odnosic się z czcią

reverence ('rewerens) s. cześć;
szacunek; wielebnosć

reverend ('rewerend) adj. czcigodny; wielebny; s. duchowny

reverse (ry'we:rs) s. odwrot-
nosc; rewers; tył; niepowodzenie; wsteczny bieg; adj. odwrotny; przeciwny; wsteczny;
v. odwracac; zmieniac kierunek; obalać (np. przepis)

reverse gear (ry'we:rs,gier) s.
wsteczny bieg(w samochodzie)

reverse side (ry'we:rs,sajd)
s. odwrotna strona
review (ry'wju:) v. przeglądać; pisać recenzje; przeglądać w myśli; dokonywać przeglądu; s. recenzja; przegląd; rewia;ponowny przegląd
reviewer (ry'wju:er) s. recenzent; krytyk
revile (ry'wajl) v. wyzywać; wymyślać; przezywać
revise (ry'wajz) v. przejrzeć; zrewidować; przerabiać
revision (ry'wyżyn) s. rewizja; przejrzane wydanie; przeróbka
revival (ry'wajwel) s. ożywienie; odżywanie; powrót do życia;powrót do stanu użyteczności
revive (ry'wajw) v. wskrzeszać; przywracać do życia; wznawiać; ożywiać; odżywać; wracać do przytomności
revolt (ry'woult) s. bunt; powstanie; v. buntować się; wzdrygać się; mieć odrazę; budzić odrazę
revolution (,rewe'lu:szyn) s. obrót; rewolucja
revolutionary (,rewe'lu:sznry) adj. rewolucyjny; s. rewolucjonista
revolutionist (,rewe'lu:szynyst) s. rewolucjonista
revolutionize (,rewe'lu:szn,ajz) v. zrewolucjonizować; wywoływać rewolucje
revolve (ry'wolw) v. obracać; krążyć; obracać się; obmyślać
revolving (ry'wolwyng) adj. obrotowy
reward (ry'ło:rd) s. nagroda; wynagrodzenie; v. wynagradzać
rheumatism ('ru:metyzem) s. reumatyzm; gościec stawowy
rhubarb ('ru:ba:rb) s. rabarbar; (slang): kłótnia
rhyme (rajm) s. rym; rymować się
rhythm ('rytm) s. rytm
rhythmic ('rytmyk) adj. rytmiczny; miarowy
rib (ryb) s. żebro; żeberko; wręga; v. żeberkować; nabierać; wyśmiewać;droczyć się;płytko orać
ribbed(rybd)adj.żebrowany

ribbon ('ryben) s. tasma; pasek; strzęp; wstążka; v. drzeć na strzępy, paski; ozdabiać wstążką;wić się wstęgą
rice (rajs) s. ryż
rich (rycz) adj. bogaty; kosztowny; suty; obfity; tuczący; pożywny; soczysty; mocny (zapach); pełny; tłusty (np. pokarm); pocieszny (zdarzenie)
riches ('ryczyz) pl. bogactwo; bogactwa
richness ('rycznys) s. bogactwo; pełnia
rick (ryk) s. stóg; v. ustawiać w stogi; stawiać stóg
rickets ('rykyts) s. choroba angielska; krzywica; rachityzm
rickety ('rykyty) adj. chwiejny; koślawy; rachityczny
rid; rid; ridded (ryd; ryd; 'rydyd)
rid (ryd) v. uwalniać się od...; oczyszczać się; pozbywać się
ridden ('rydn) zob. v. ride
riddle ('rydl) s. zagadka; v. zadawać zagadki; mówić zagadkami; rozwiązywać zagadki
ride; rode; ridden (rajd; roud; 'rydn)
ride (rajd) v. pojechać; jechać (też statkiem); jeździć; tyranizować; wozić; nosić; dokuczać; s. przejażdżka; jazda; nabieranie (kogoś); droga
rider ('rajder) s. jeździec; dżokej; dodatek; poprawka; klauzula; ciężarek przesuwany; nasadka;poprawka na dokumencie
ridge (rydż) s. grzbiet (też góry); krawędź; kalenica; pasmo górskie; wał; skiba; grobla; v. pokrywać skibami; robić krawędzie; marszczyć
ridicule ('rydy,kju:l) v. wyśmiewać się; s. kpiny
ridiculous (ry'dykju:les) adj. śmieszny; bezsensowny
riding ('rajdyng) s. konna jazda; adj. jadący;do konnej jazdy
rifle (rajfl) s. karabin; gwintówka; gwint;strzelec; v.gwintować (lufę); strzelać;ograbić; okraść; pokrzyżować

rift (ryft) s. szczelina; różnica zdań; v. rozszczepiać
się ;pęknąć;popękać

rig (ryg) v. zaopatrywać; klecić; montować; stroić; robić
kanty; manipulować ceny;
s. sprzęt (wiertniczy); wóz
z koniem; kostium; machlojka

right (rajt) adj. prawa; prawy; poprawny; prawoskrętny;
prosty (też kąt); właściwy;
słuszny; dobry; odpowiedni;
prawidłowy; w porządku; zdrowy; adv. w prawo; na prawo;
prosto; bezpośrednio; bezzwłocznie: dokładnie; słusznie; dobrze; s. prawa strona;
prawo; dobro; słuszność;
sprawiedliwość; pierwszeństwo;
v. naprostować; naprawić;
sprostować; odpłacać; mścić;
usprawiedliwiać

right ahead ('rajt,e'hed) exp.
wprost ;na wprost;przed siebie

right away ('rajt,e'łej) exp.
zaraz ;natychmiast;już teraz

righteous ('rajtszes) adj.
sprawiedliwy; prawy ;słuszny

rightful ('rajtful) adj. słuszny; sprawiedliwy; prawowity;
należny z prawa;prawy

right-hand ('rajt,haend) adj.
praworęki; położony na prawo

right-handed ('rajt-'haendyd)
adj. praworęczny; dostosowany
do prawej ręki; idący wg.ru-
chu zegara; obracający się
w prawo (gwint etc.)

right of way ('rajt,ow'łej)
exp.; prawo pierwszeństwa na
drodze; prawo przejazdu; grunt
pod drogą (kolej)(pod szosą etc.)

rightist ('rajtyst) s. prawico-
wiec; adj. prawicowy

rightly ('rajtly) adv. spra-
wiedliwie; słusznie; poprawnie; właściwie;na miejscu

rigid ('rydżyd) adj. sztywny;
nieugięty; surowy;nieustępliwy

rigor ('ryger) s. rygor; surowość; zesztywnienie

rigorous ('rygeres) adj. surowy; rygorystyczny

rim (rym) s. brzeg; krawędź;
obręcz; powierzchnia wody
(przy żeglowaniu); v. robić
krawędź; posuwać wzdłuż kra-
wędzi;dawać oprawę(do okularów)

rimple ('rympl) v. marszczyć

rind (rajnd) s. kora; łupina;
skórka; v. zdzierać korę

ring (ryng) s. pierścień; obrączka; kółko; koło; zmowa;
szajka; słój; arena; ring
(bokserski); v. otaczać; kołować; krajać w kółko

ring; rang; rung (ryng; raeng;
rang)

ring (ryng) v. dzwonić; dźwięczeć; brzmieć; rozbrzmiewać;
wydzwaniać; telefonować; wybijać czas na zegarze kontrolnym;
sprawdzać monetę dźwiękiem;
s. dzwonek; dzwony; dźwięk;
brzęk; telefonowanie

ring off ('ryng,of) v. skończyć
rozmowę telefoniczną

ring the bell ('ryng,dy'bel) v.
dzwonić (do drzwi etc.)

ring up ('ryng,ap) v. wybijać
kwotę (na kasie rejestracyj-
nej);zatelefonować(do kogoś)

ringleader ('ryng,li:der) s.
prowodyr; herszt

rink (rynk) s. ślizgawka; tor
jazdy na wrotkach; boisko do
gry w kule

rinse (ryns) v. płukać; s. wy-
płukanie

rinse out ('ryns,aut) v. wypłukać ;przepłukiwać

riot ('rajot) s. zgiełk; zamęt; rozruchy; bunty; rozpusta; hulanka; rozprężenie;
orgia; v. buntować się; robić
rozruchy, zamieszki; hulać;
używać sobie;uprawiać rozpustę

riotous ('rajetes) adj. buntowniczy; rozpustny; hulaszczy;
hałaśliwy; bujny;oporny;niesfor-
ny

rip (ryp) v. odrywać; zrywać;
łupać; rozpruwać; piłować
wzdłuż; pękać; pędzić; s. roz-
prucie; rozpustnik; hulaka;
szkapa; rzecz nie warta nic;
wir;wzburzona powierzchnia wody

ripe (rajp) adj. dojrzały
ripen ('rajpn) v. dojrzewac;
przyspieszac dojrzewanie
ripeness ('rajpnys) s. dojrza-
łosc
ripple ('rypl) s. zmarszczki
(na wodzie); fale (na włosach);
falowanie; grzebien do lnu;
v. marszczyc; falowac; roz-
czesywac; rozwodzic sie
rise; rose; risen (rajz; rouz;
'ryzn)
rise (rajz) v. podniesc sie;
stanac; ystawac; powstawac;
buntowac sie; wzbierac; wzbijac sie; wzmagac sie; spros-
tac; s. wschod; wznoszenie
sie; podwyzka; wzrost; powodzenie; poczatek; stopien
risen ('ryzn) v. zob. rise
riser (rajzer) s. osoba wstaja-
ca; pionowy przewod (tez rura);
podstawka stopnia (na schodach)
rising ('rajzyng) s. wzniesienie; powstanie; zmartwychwstanie; babel; pryszcz; zaczyna-
nie ciasta; adj. podnoszacy
sie; wzrastajacy; wschodzacy
risk (rysk) s. ryzyko; niebezpieczenstwo; v. narazac sie;
ryzykowac; ponosic ryzyko
risky ('rysky) adj. niebezpieczny; ryzykowny; pikantny; drastyczny
rite (rajt) s. obrzadek; obrzed
(slubny); rytuał
rival ('rajwel) s. rywal; wspoł-
zawodnik; v. rywalizowac
rivalry ('rajwelry) s. rywalizacja; wspołzawodnictwo
river ('rywer) s. rzeka
riverboat ('rywer,bout) s. statek rzeczny; łodz rzeczna
riverside ('rywer,sajd) s.
brzeg rzeki
rivet ('rywyt) s. nit; v. nito-
wac; utkwic; przykuc
rivulet ('rywjulyt) s. rzeczuł-
ka; mały strumien; mały potok
road (roud) s. droga; kolej;
reda; v. topic
road hog ('roud,hog) s. pirat
drogowy (lekceważacy przepisy)

road map ('roud,maep) s. mapa
drogowa; mapa samochodowa
roadside ('roud,sajd) s. bok
drogi; adj. przydrozny
roadsign ('roud,sajn) s. znak
drogowy
roam (roum) v. włoczyc sie;
s. włoczega; wedrowka
roar (ro:r) v. ryczec; huczec;
s. ryk; huk (armat); ryk(smiechu)
roars of laughter ('ro:rs,ow-
'lafter) exp. wybuchy smiechu
roast (roust) v. piec; opiekac;
przypiekac; wypalac; osmieszac;
krytykowac ostro; s. pieczen;
pieczenie; kpiny; krytyka
ostra; adj. pieczony
roast beef ('roust,bi:f) s.
pieczen wołowa
roast meat ('roust,mi:t) s.
pieczone mieso
rob (rob) v. grabic; rabowac;
ograbic; pozbawiac (czegos)
robber ('rober) s. rabus
robbery ('robery) s. rabunek
robe (roub) s. podomka; suknia;
szata; płaszcz kapielowy; toga; v. przyodziewac; przyoblekac
robin ('robyn) s. drozd; rudzik
robot ('roubot) s. robot
robust ('roubast) adj. krzepki;
trzezwy; szorstki; hałasliwy;
ciezki; silny; mocny
rock (rok) s. kamien; skała;
forsa; kołysanie; taniec
(rock and roll); pl. kostki
lodu w napoju; v. kołysac sie;
bujac sie; hustac sie; wstrza-
sac; wypłukiwac piasek; płu-
kac (sie); a. kamienny; skalisty
rocker ('roker) s. biegun; łyz-
wa holenderka
rocket ('rokyt) s. rakieta;
v. wznosic sie
rocket power ('rokyt'pałer) s.
naped rakietowy
rocketry ('rokytry) s. bron
rakietowa; technika rakietowa
rocking chair ('rokyng,czeer)
s. krzesło na biegunach
rocky ('roky) adj. skalisty;
chwiejny; kamienisty; skalny

rod (rod) s. pręt; drąg; rózga;
wędka; (pręt = 5.029 m)
rode (roud) v. zob. ride
rodent ('roudent) s. gryzoń
roe (rou) s. sarna; łania;
ikra we wnętrzu ryby;sperma ry-
rogue (roug) s. łobuz; łajdak;
psotnik; słoń samotnik
roguish ('rougysz) adj. psotny;
figlarny; łobuzerski
role (roul) s. rola
roll (roul) s. rolka; zwój;
zwitek; rulon; bułka; rożek;
spis; wykaz; rejestr; lista;
wokanda; wałek; walec; wałek;
kołysanie (się); werbel; huk;v.
toczyć; wałkować; tarzać;
grzmieć; dudnić; rozlegać się;
zataczać beczkę; toczyć koło;
kręcić; obracać; wymawiać "r";
rozwałkowywać ;wałkować
roll up ('roul,ap) v. zawinąć
(rękawy); kłębić się; pod-
jeżdżać; skumulować (się)
roller ('rouler) s. wałek; rolka; kółko; długa tocząca się
fala ;narzędzie do wałkowania
roller coaster ('rouler'kou-
ster) s. kolejka wysokogórska;
wesołe miasteczko
roller-skate ('rouler'skejt) s.
wrotka
rolling mill ('roulyŋ,myl) s.
walcownia
Roman ('roumen) adj. rzymski
romance (rou'maens) s. romans
średniowieczny; powieść miłosna; sprawa miłosna; adj. romański; v. romansować; koloryzować; przesadzać;pisać romanse
romantic (rou'maentyk) adj. romantyczny; s. romantyk
romp (romp) s. urwis; zbytki;
swawole; figle; igraszki;
v. figlować; dokazywać; uganiać; łatwo wygrać (wyścigi)
rompers ('rompers) pl. kombinezon do zabawy dla dziecka
roof (ru:f) s. dach; v. pokrywać dachem
roof over ('ru:f,ouwer) v. pokrywać dachem

rook (ruk) s. gawron; szuler;
wieża (w szachach); v. ograć;
oszukać; zdzierać skórę
room (rum) s. pokój. miejsce;
mieszkanie; izba; wolna przestrzeń; sposobność; powod;
v. dzielić pokój lub mieszkanie;mieszkać lub odnajmować pokój
room-mate ('rum,mejt) s. współ-
mieszkaniec; współlokator
roomy ('rumy) adj. przestronny;
obszerny
roost (ru:st) s. grzęda; v. siedzieć na grzędzie
rooster (ru:ster) s. kogut
root (ru:t) s. korzeń; nasada;
podstawa; istota; źródło; sedno;
pierwiastek; y. posadzić; zakorzenić; ryć; szperać; wygrzebywać; popierać; dopingować
root out ('ru:t,aut) v. wykorze-
niać; wyrywać z korzeniami
rope (roup) s. sznur; powróz;
lina; stryczek; v. związać;
przywiązać; łapać na lasso;
ogradzać sznurami; ciągnąć na
linie; przyciągać; zdobywać;
obśliznąć
rope off ('roup,of) v. ogradzać
linami
rose (rous) s. róża; kolor różowy; rozetka; v. zarożowić;
zob. rise
rosy ('rouzy) adj. różowy
rot (rot) s. zgnilizna; rozkład;
zepsucie; głupstwa; brednie;
motylica; v. gnić; butwieć;
rozkładać się
rotary ('routery) adj. rotacyjny;
obrotowy
rotate ('routejt) v. obracać
(się); kolejno zmieniać (się);
wirować ;adj.kółkowy
rotation (rou'tejszyn) s. ro-
tacja; ruch obrotowy; obracanie
(się); płodozmian; ciągła wymiana; kolejne następstwo
rotor ('router) s. wirnik
rotten ('rotn) adj. zgniły; zepsuty; zdemoralizowany; lichy;
kiepski; marny;chory na moty-
licę ;do niczego;do chrzanu

rotund (rou'tand) adj. okrągły; zaokrąglony; szumny;
przysadkowaty

rough (raf) adj. szorstki; chropowaty; ostry; nierówny; wyboisty; nieokrzesany; brutalny;
drastyczny; cierpki; nieprzyjemny; nieociosany; surowy;
gruby; burzliwy; gwałtowny;
hałaśliwy; ciężki; pobieżny;
przybliżony; prymitywny;
wstępny; szkicowy; adv. ostro;
szostko; grubiańsko; z grubsza; s. nierówny teren; stan
naturalny - nieobrobiony;
hacel;huligan; v. być szorst-
kim; szorstko postępować;
hartować (się); jeżyć (się);
burzyć (się); szlifować z grubsza; pasować z grubsza; obrabiać z grubsza; szkicować;
przebiedować; ujeżdżać (konia);
robic coś z grubsza; podkuwac
hacelami

roughness ('rafnys) s. szorstkość; grubiaństwo; chamstwo

rough-neck ('rafnek) s. członek
obsługi szybu; łobuz; brutal;
chuligan

round (raund) adj. okrągły; zaokrąglony; kolisty; okrężny;
tam i nazad; kulisty; sferyczny; adv. wkoło; kołem; dookoła; prep. dookoła; s. koło;
obwód; kula; obrót; krąg; bieg
cykl; ciąg; zasięg; seria;
objazd; obchod; runda; za-
okrąglenie; pasmo (np. trudności); przechadzka; v. zaokra-
glać; wygładzać; okrążyć; obchodzić; opływać

round off ('raund,of) v. za-
okrąglac

round out ('raund,out) v. za-
okrąglac się; tyć

round up ('round,ap) v. spędzać
(bydło)

round-up ('round'ap) s. spędza-
nie bydła

roundabout ('raundebaut) adj.
okrężny; s. rondo; karuzela

round trip('raund,tryp) s. podroż tam i nazad

rouse (rauz) v. pobudzić;
wzniecać; ruszyc; ożywiac;
podsycać; wyrywac; wypłoszyc;
obudzić się; otrzasnąć się

roustabout ('rauste,baut) s.
robotnik portowy; robotnik
przemysłu naftowego

route (ru:t) s. droga; trasa;
marsz; szlak

routine (ru:'ti:n) s. rutyna;
tok zajęc

rove (rouw) v. wałęsać się;
błądzić wzrokiem; łowic; skręcać włokno; s. niedoprzęd

rover ('rouwer) s. wędrowiec;
włoczęga; korsarz; pirat

row (roł) s. szereg; rząd;
jazda łodzią; v. wiosłować

row (rał) s. zgiełk; hałas;
kłótnia; bójka; burda; nagana;
bura; v. besztac; pokłocić się

row-boat ('roł,bout) s. łodz
wiosłowa

rower ('rołer) s. wioslarz

rowing boat ('rołyngbout) s.
łodz wiosłowa

royal ('rojel) adj. krolewski

royalty ('rojelty) s. krolew-
skość; honorarium autorskie

rub (rab) v. trzec; potrzec;
wytrzec; wycierac; głaskac;
nacierac; s. tarcie; nacie-
ranie

rub down('rab,dałn) v. nacierac;wcierac

rub in ('rab,yn) v. wcierac;
wytykac

rub off ('rab,of) v. zetrzec

rub out ('rab,aut) v. wymazac

rubber('raber) s. guma; masażysta; pl. kalosze; v. pokrywac gumą; odwracac (głowę)

rubberneck ('raber,nek) s.
ciekawski; turysta; gapa

rubber plant ('raber,plaent)
s. kauczukowa roślina

rubbish ('rabysz) s. smiec;
gruz; tandeta; nonsens; brednie; głupstwa; bzdury

rubble ('rabl) s. gruz; rumowisko skalne; kamień łamany

ruby ('ru:by) s. rubin

rucksack ('ruksaek)s. plecak

rudder ('rader) s. ster
ruddy ('rady) adj. rumiany;
czerstwy; czerwony; v. ru-
mienic się
rude (ru:d) adj. szorstki;
niegrzeczny; ostry; surowy;
prosty; pierwotny; nagły;
gwałtowny; krzepki
ruff (raf) s. kołnierz; kreza; batalion; bojownik; bicie atutem; v. przebić atutem
ruffian ('rafjen) s. zbój;
łotr
ruffle ('rafl) s. kreza; ża-
bot; mankiet koronkowy;
kłopot; zamieszanie; marsz-
czenie; v. marszczyć (po-
wierzchnię); rozwiewać; roz-
czochrać; nastroszyć; wzburzyć (się)
rug (rag) s. pled; kilim; dywan
rugby ('ragby) s. (sport) rugby
ruin (,ruyn) s. ruina; v. ruj-
nowac (się); zniszczyć (się)
rule (ru:l) s. przepis; prawo;
reguła; zasada; rządy; panowanie; postanowienie; miarka;
linijka; v. rządzić; panować;
kierować; orzekać; postanawiać; liniować
rule out ('ru:l,aut) v. wykluczać
ruler ('ru:ler) s. władca;
liniał; linijka
rum (ram) s. rum; adj. dziwny
rumble ('rambl) v. dudnić;
grzmieć; turkotać; s. huk;
grzmot; dudnienie; tylne
miejsce w pojeździe na bagaż
lub służącego
ruminant ('ru:mynent) adj.
przeżuwający; s. przeżuwacz
rummage ('ramydż) s. szperanie; przetrząsanie; wyprzedaż
resztek; v. grzebać; przetrząsać
rumor ('ru:mer) s. pogłoska;
słuchy; v. puszczać pogłoski
rump (ramp) s. zad; kuper;
comber; kadłub

rumple ('rampl) v. zmiąć; zmięto-
sić; mierzwic; czochrać
run; ran; ran (ran; raen; raen)
run (ran) v. biec; biegać; pędzić; spieszyć się; jechać; płyn-
nąć; kursować; obracać się;
działać; funkcjonować; pracować;
uciekać; zbiec; prowadzić; toczyć się; wynosić (sumę); rozpływać się; łzawic; głosic;
spotykać; narzucać się; molestować; zderzyć się; sprzeciwiać
się; wpaść etc.; s. bieg; przebieg; bieganie; rozbieg; rozpęd;
przebieg; passa; sekwens; okres;
seria; ciąg; dostęp; wybieg;
pastwisko; zjazd; tor
run about ('ran,e'baut) v. biegać tu i tam; s. wędrowiec;
adj. wędrowny
run across ('ran,e'kros) v. spotkać przypadkowo
run after ('ran,aefter) v. gonić
run away ('ran,e'łej) v. uciekać;
ponieść
run down ('ran,dałn) v. przejechać; wyczerpać; wytropić
run in ('ran,yn) v. wpaść na...;
dotrzec
run off ('ran,of) v. uciekać;
recytować; drukować
run out ('ran,aut) v. skończyć
się; wygasnąć; wydrukować
run over ('ran,ouwer) v. przejechać; przepełniać
run up ('ran,ap) v. dobiec; dojść
do..; dodać; wyśrubować; s. dochodzenie do celu
rung (rang) s. poprzeczka; szczebel; szprycha; v. zob. ring
runner ('raner) s. goniec; biegacz; posłaniec; woźny; akwizytor; łopatka; obsługujący ma-
szynę; chodnik; przemytnik; płoza; łożysko ślizgowe; wałek
running ('ranyng) adj. bieżący;
biegający; będący w biegu; cieknący; ropiejący; w ruchu; ruchomy; ciągły; nieustanny; pochyły;
nieprzerwany; s. bieg; wyścig;
kandydowanie; funkcjonowanie;
ropienie; kierownictwo

running board ('ranyng,bo:rd)
s. stopień; pomost

runway ('ran,lej) s. bieżnia
(do ładowania); tor (jezdny)

rupture ('rapczer) s. złamanie;
zerwanie; przepuklina; v.
przerywać; zrywać; poderwać
się (mieć przepuklinę)

rural ('ruerel) adj. wiejski

ruse (ru:z) s. podstęp

rush (rasz) v. pędzić; poganiać; ponaglać; rzucać się na
coś; przeskakiwać; wysyłać
pospiesznie; zdobywać szturmem; zdzierać (pieniądze);
słać sitowiem; s. pęd; ruch;
pospiech; napływ; atak; intensywny popyt; sitowie

rush hour ('rasz,auer) s. godzina szczytu; chwila uderze-
nia

Russian ('raszyn) adj. rosyjski ;s.Rosjanin

rust (rast) s. rdza (zbożowa)
v. rdzewieć ;niszczyć się

rust-eaten ('rast.i:tn) adj.
zardzewiały

rustic ('rastik) adj. wiejski;
prostacki; s. wieśniak; prostak

rustle ('rasl) v. szeleścić;
kraść bydło; krzątać się;
s. szelest

rusty ('rasty) adj. zardzewiały; zaniedbany; wyszły z wprawy ;podniszczony

rut (rat) s. koleina; bruzda;
utarty szlak; rutyna; nawyk;
rowek; wyżłobienie; ruja;
·rokowisko; rykowisko

ruthless ('ru:tlys) adj. bezlitosny; bezwzględny; niemiłosierny

rutted ('ratyd) adj. rozjeżdżo-
ny; wyjeżdżony

rutty ('raty) adj. wyjeżdżony

rye (raj) s. żyto; żytniówka

rye whisky (raj,hłysky)
szkocka żytnia wódka

s (es) dziewiętnasta litera
alfabetu angielskiego

's skrót: is, has, us

saber ('seiber) s. szabla; pałasz; v. ciąć; ranić; ścinać

sable ('sejbl) s. soból; czerń;
adj. czarny ;sobolowy(z futer)

sabotage ('saebeta:ż) s. sabotaż; v. sabotować

sabre ('sejber) s. szabla; zob.
saber

saccharin ('saekeryn) s. sacharyna

sack (saek) s. worek; torebka;
sak; luźny płaszcz; plądrowa-
nie; v. pakować do worków;
zwalniać z pracy; plądrować

sacrament ('saekrement) s. sakrament

sacred ('sejkryd) adj. poświęco-
ny; nienaruszalny

sacrifice ('saekryfajs) s. ofiara; wyrzeczenie (się); v. ofia-
rowywać; poświęcać; wyrzekać
się w zamian za coś innego

sacrilegious (,saekry'lydżes)
adj. świętokradzki

sad (saed) adj. smutny; bolesny;
posępny; ponury; okropny

sadden ('saedn) v. zasmucać (się);
posmutnieć

saddle ('saedl) s. siodło;
v. siodłać; obarczać; wkładać
ciężar (komuś)(na kogoś)

sadness ('saednys) s. smutek

safe (sejf) adj. pewny; bezpieczny; s. schowek bankowy;
kasa pancerna; spiżarnia
wietrzona; (slang):kondon

safeguard ('seifga:rd) v. ochraniać; zabezpieczać; gwarantować;
s. zabezpieczenie; gwarancja

safety ('sejfty) s. bezpieczeństwo; zabezpieczenie; bezpiecznik ; adj.dający bezpieczeństwo

safety belt ('sejfty,belt) s.
pas bezpieczeństwa (np. w samochodzie)

safety lock ('sejfty,lok) s. zamek bezpieczeństwa

safety pin ('sejfty,pyn) s.
agrafka

safety razor ('sejfty,rejzer) s.
maszynka do golenia się żyletka-
mi (które się wymienia po zużyciu)

safety-valve ('sejfty,waelw)
s. klapa bezpieczeństwa; zawór bezpieczeństwa
sag (saeg) v. obwisać; zwisać; wyginać (się); przechylać się; spadać w cenie; s. zwis; wygięcie; spadek ceny
sagacity (se'gaesyty) s. rozwaga; mądrość; roztropność; bystrość
said (sed) v. zob. say
sail (sejl) s. żagiel; podróż morska; żaglować; kroczyć okazale; sterować okrętem; bawić się modelem statku
sail-boat ('sejl,bout) s. żaglówka
sailing-ship('sejlyng,szyp) s. statek żaglowy
sailor ('sejlor) s. żeglarz; marynarz
saint (sejnt) s. & adj. święty
sake (sejk) s. czyjeś dobro; wzgląd
salad ('saeled) s. sałata
salary ('saelery) s. pensja; pobory; wynagrodzenie
sale (sejl) s. sprzedaż; wyprzedaż
saleslady ('sejls'lejdy) s. sprzedawczyni
salesman ('sejlsmen) s. sprzedawca
salesmanager (,sejls'maenydżer) s. kierownik działu sprzedaży
saliva (se'lajwa) s. ślina
sallow ('saelou) adj. ziemisty; blady; żółtawy; v. dawać żółtawy odcień; s. iwa (wierzba)
sally ('saely) s. wypad; wycieczka z oblężenia; docinek (cięty)
sally out ('saely,aut) v. wyruszać w podróż
salmon ('saemen) s. łosoś; adj. łososiowy; łososiowego koloru
saloon (se'lu:n) s. bar; szynk; sala (zabaw); salon (na okręcie)
salt (so:lt) s. sól; adj; słony; v. solić
saltcellar ('so:lt,seler) s. solniczka

salt-free ('so:lt,fri:) adj. bezsolny;pozbawiony soli
salty ('so:lty) adj. słony
salutation (,saelju:'tejszyn) s. pozdrowienie; przywitanie
salute (se'lu:t) s. pozdrowienie; salutowanie; honory wojskowe; salwa (powitalna); v. pozdrowić; powitać; salutować; odbierać defiladę; przejść przed kompania honorową
salvation (sael'wejszyn) s. zbawienie; ratunek; wybawienie
salve (sa:w) v. natrzeć; złagodzić; uspokoić; s. maść; balsam
same (sejm) adj. ten sam; taki sam; jednostajny; monotonny; adv. tak samo; identycznie; bez zmiany; pron. to samo
sample ('sa:mpl) s. próbka; wzór; v. próbować; dawać próbki
sanatorium (,saene'to:rjem) s. sanatorium
sanctify ('saenkty,faj) v. uświęcać; poświęcać
sanction ('saenkszyn) v. usankcjonować; s. sankcja
sanctuary ('saenkczuery) s. przybytek; azyl
sand (saend) s. piasek; v. posypywać piaskiem; obrabiać papierem sciernym
sandal ('saendl) s. sandał; rzemyk; v. wkładać sandały; przywiązywać rzemykiem
sandwich ('saendłycz) s. kanapka; sandwicz; v. wkładać (między)
sandy ('saendy) adj. piaskowy; piaskowego koloru
sandy beach ('saendy,bi:ch) s. plaża
sane (sejn) adj. zdrowy na umyśle; rozsądny; normalny
sang (saeng) v. zob. sing
sanitarium (,saeny'teerjem) s. sanatorium
sanitary ('saenytery) adj. higieniczny; zdrowy
sanitary napkin ('saenytery 'naepkyn) s. podpaska higieniczna

sanitation (,saeny'tejszyn) s. higiena; kanalizacja; urządzenia sanitarne

sank (saeŋk) v. zob. sink

Santa Claus (,saenta'klo:z) s. Dziadek Mróz; Święty Mikołaj

sap (saep) s. żywica; sok; głupiec; kujon; nudziarstwo; sapa; podkopywanie; v. wyciągać soki; usuwać biel z drzewa; podkopywać; podmywać; kopać sapę

sappy('saepy) s. soczysty; pełen wigoru; energiczny

sarcasm ('sa:rkaezem) s. sarkazm

sardine (sa:r'di:n) s. sardynka

sash (saesz) s. szarfa; rama okienna do pionowego suwania okien; v. instalować ramy okienne

sash window('saesh'żyndou) s. suwane okno

sat (saet) v. zob. sit

Satan ('sejtn) s. szatan

satchel ('saeczel) s. torba z rzemieniami na plecy

satellite ('saete,lajt) s. satelita

satin ('saetyn) s. atlas; adj. atlasowy; v. satynować (papier)

satire ('saetajer) s. satyra

satirize ('saety,rajz) v. wykpiwać; wyśmiewać; satyryzować

satisfaction (,saetys'faekszyn) s. zadowolenie; satysfakcja; spłacenie długu ;zaspokojenie

satisfactory (,saetys'faektery) adj. zadawalający; odpowiedni

satisfy ('saetys,faj) v. zaspokoić; uiścić; spełnić; zadowalać; odpowiadać; przekonywać

Saturday ('saeterdy) s. sobota

sauce (so:s) s. sos; kompot; v. przyprawiać jedzenie; nagadać komuś ;stawiać się

saucebox ('so:s,boks) s. impertynent ;zuchwalec

saucepan ('so:spen) s. patelnia; rondel

saucer ('so:ser) s. spodek

saunter ('so: nter) s. przechadzka; przechadzać się; chodzić powolnym krokiem

sausage ('sosydż) s. kiełbasa

save (sejw) v. ratować; oszczędzać; zachowywać pozory; zbawiać; uniknąć; zyskiwać (czas); prep. oprócz; wyjąwszy; poza; pominąwszy; conj. że; poza tym; chyba że; z wyjątkiem

save for a car ('sejw,fo:r'ej- ,ca:r) exp.: oszczędzać na samochód

saver ('sejwer) s. osoba oszczędzająca; przedmiot oszczędzający (np, czas)

saving ('sejwyŋg) adj. zbawienny; oszczędny; prep. wyjąwszy

savings-bank ('sejwynz'baeŋk) s. kasa oszczędności

savior ('sejwjer) s. zbawca; zbawiciel

savor ('sejwer) s. smak; aromat; powab; v. mieć smak; pachnieć; smakować; nadawać smak

savory ('sejwery) adj. smaczny; apetyczny; smakowity; pikantny; aromatyczny

saw; sawed; sawn (so:; so:d; so:n)

saw (so:) v. zob. see; piłować; s. piła

sawdust ('so:,dast) s. trociny

sawmill ('so:,myl) s. tartak

Saxon ('saeksn) adj. saksoński; saski ; s. Sas

say; said; said (sej; sed; sed) v. mówić; powiedzieć; odprawiać; twierdzić

sayso ('sejso) s. rozkaz; powiedzenie; ostatnie słowo

saying ('sejyŋg) s. powiedzonko; powiedzenie

scab (skaeb) s. strup; parch; świerzb; łamistrajk

scaffold ('skaefeld) s. rusztowanie; platforma; estrada; szafot; v. stawiać rusztowanie

scaffolding ('skaefeldyŋg) s. rusztowanie

scald (sko:ld) v. oparzyć; wyparzyć; pasteryzować; s. oparzenie

scale (skejl) s. skala; podziałka; układ; drabina;
szalka; łuska; kamień nazębny;
v. wyłazic; wdzierac się;
mierzyc (podziałką); ważyc;
łuszczyc; łuskac; złuszczac
się

scale down ('skejl,dałn) v.
zmniejszac (proporcjonalnie)

scale up ('skejl,ap) v. po-
wiekszac (proporcjonalnie)

scales ('skejls) pl. waga

scalp ('skaelp) s. skalp; skora na głowie; v. oskalpowac;
złosliwie krytykowac

scan (skaen) v. badawczo prze-
glądac; skandowac; miec rytm

scandal ('skaendl) s. skandal;
zgorszenie; oszczerstwo;
plotki

scandalous ('skaendeles) adj.
skandaliczny; gorszący;
oszczerczy

Scandinavian (,skaendy'nejw-
jan) adj. skandynawski

scant (skaent) adj. skąpy;
ograniczony; ledwo wystarcza-
jacy; niedostateczny

scapegoat ('skejp,gout) s. kozioł ofiarny

scar (ska:r) s. blizna; szrama;
wyrwa; urwisko; v, pokieresze-
wac (się); zabliźniac się

scar over ('ska:r,ouwer) v.
zabliźnic

scarce (skeers) adj. rzadki;
niewystarczający

scarcely ('skeersly) adv. zaledwie; ledwo; z trudem;
z trudnością

scarcity ('skeersyty) s. niedostatek; niedobor; brak

scare (skeer) s. popłoch; panika; strach; v. nastraszyc;
przestraszyc; siac popłoch

scare away ('skeere,łej) v.
odstraszac

scarecrow ('skeer,krou)s.
straszydło; strach na wroble

scarf (ska:rf) s. szalik;
chustka na szyję; szarfa

scarfs (ska:rfs) pl. styk;
złącza

scarlet ('ska:rlyt) s. szkarłat;
adj. szkarłatny

scarlet fever ('ska:rlyt,fi:wer)
s. szkarlatyna ; płonica

scarp (ska:rp) s. skarpa; urwisko

scarred (ska:rd) adj. poznaczo-
ny bliznami; poszarpany

scarves (ska:rwz) pl. zob.scarf;
chusty na szyję; szarfy etc.

scathing ('skejzyng) adj. kostyczny; zjadliwy; niszczący

scatter ('skaeter) v. rozpra-
szac (się); rozsypywac; roz-
rzucac; rozwiewac; posypywac;
rozpierzchnąc (się)

scavenge ('skaewyndż) v. czyscic; oczyszczac; wyrzucac spa-
liny; byc zamiataczem ulic

scene (si:n) s. scena; miejsce
zdarzen; widowisko; widok; obraz; awantura publiczna

scenery (si:nery) s. widok;
krajobraz; dekoracje sceniczne

scent (sent) v. węszyc; wiet-
rzyc; wydawac zapach; s. zapach; nos (węch); perfumy

sceptic ('skeptyk) s. sceptyk;
adj. sceptyczny ;powątpiewający

sceptical ('skeptykel) adj.
sceptyczny;powątpiewający we
wszystko

schedule ('skedżul) s. rozkład
jazdy; wykaz; zestawienie; tabela; taryfa; harmonogram; lista; plan; v. planowac; wciagac
na listę ;naznaczac wg planu

scheme (ski:m) s. intryga; podstęp; plan

scholar ('skoler) s. uczony;
stypendysta; uczen ;student

scholarship ('skolerszyp) s.
poziom naukowy; stypendium;
erudycja ;systematyczna wiedza

school (sku:l) s. szkoła; katedra;
ra; nauka; ławica; adj. szkolny; v, szkolic; kształcic; nauczac; wycwiczyc; tworzyc ła-
wicę ;karcic; sprawdzac naukę

schoolboy ('sku:l,boj) s.
uczen

schoolgirl ('sku:l,ge:rl) s.
uczennica

schooling ('sku:lyŋg) s. nauka;
szkolenie; wykształcenie
schoolmaster ('sku:l,ma:ster)
s. kierownik szkoły
schoolmate ('sku:l,mejt) s. kolega szkolny
school of driving ('sku:l,ow-
'drajwyŋg) s. nauka jazdy
(samochodem)
schooner ('sku:ner) s. skuner;
szklanka na piwo
science ('sajens) s. wiedza;
nauka; umiejętność
scientific ('sajentyfyk) adj.
naukowy; umiejętny
scientist ('sajentyst) s. uczony; przyrodnik; naukowiec
scissors ('syzez) s. nożyce;
nożyczki
scoff (skof) v. szydzić; kpić;
drwić; s. pośmiewisko; szyderstwo; kpiny; drwiny
scold (skould) v. besztać;
skrzyczeć; obrugać; łajać;
złorzeczyć; s. jędza; sekutnica; megiera
scone (skon) s. placek trójkątny z jęczmiennej mąki
scoop (sku:p) v. zaczerpnąć;
wygarnąć; wybrać; s. czerpak;
szufelka; chochla; kubeł; sensacyjna wiadomość
scooter ('sku:ter) s. skuter;
hulajnoga
scope (skoup) s. zasięg; zakres;
dziedzina; meta; sposobność;
możliwość
scorch (sko:rcz) v. spalić;
przypiekać; przypalać; dopie-
kać; wypłowieć; pędzić samochodem jak szalony; s. poparzenie
score (sko:r) v. zdobyć (punkt);
podkreślić; zanotować; zapisać;
wygrać; osiągnąć; strzelić
bramkę; s. ilość (zdobytych
punktów lub bramek); zacięcie;
rysa; znak; dwadzieścia
scorn (sko:rn) s. lekceważenie;
wzgarda; v. lekceważyć; gardzić;odrzucać z pogardą
scornful('sko:rnful) adj. pogardliwy (i zagniewany);odrzuca-
jący z gniewem i pogardą

Scot (skot) adj. szkocki
Scotch (skocz) adj. szkocki
scot-free ('skot'fri:) adj.
cały; nietknięty; niezraniony;
gratis; bezpłatny
scoundrel ('skaundrel) s. kanalia; łotr
scour ('skauer) v. podmyć; szorować; przepłukiwać; poszukiwać; grasować; przetrząsać;
s. podmycie; przemywanie;
przepłukiwanie
scout (skaut) s. harcerz; zwia-
dowca; v. iść na zwiady; robić
rekonesans
scoutmaster ('skaut,ma:ster)
s. harcmistrz
scowl (skaul) v. chmurzyć się;
patrzeć spode łba; groźnie;
patrzeć; s. zła mina; groźne
spojrzenie; krzywa mina
scramble ('skraembl) s. ubija-
nie się; gramolenie się; do-
bijanie się; robienie jajeczni-
cy; v. ubijać się; gramolić się;
dobijać się; robić jajecznicę
scrambled eggs ('skraembld,egs)
s. jajecznica
scrap (skraep) s. szmelc; odpadki; skrawki; wycinki; bójka; v. wyrzucać na szmelc; odrzucać; wycofać; bić się
scrape (skrejp) s. skrobanie;
tarapaty; szurnięcie; ciułanie;
draśnięcie; v. skrobać; drasnąć;
ciułać; szurnąć
scrape off ('skrejp,of) v. ze-
skrobać
scrape out ('skrejp,aut) v. wyskrobać
scrape together (skrejp,tu'gedzer) v. uciułać
scrap iron('skraep,ajern) s.
złom żelazny
scrappy ('skraepy) adj. niejednolity; bez związku; frag-
mentaryczny
scratch (skraecz) s. draśnięcie;
zadrapanie; rozdarcie; skrobanie; linia startu; adj. do pisania (np, brulion; brulionowy);
v. drapać (się); zadrasnąć;
gryzmolić; wydrapać; wykreślić

scream (skri:m) s. krzyk; pisk;
gwizd; kawał; v. krzyczeć
przenikliwie; śmiać się hałaśliwie i histerycznie

screech(skri:cz) s. zgrzyt;
pisk; skrzypienie; v. zgrzytać; piszczeć; skrzypieć

screen (skri:n) s. zasłona; osłona; siatka na komary; ekran;
sito; siewnik; filtr (światła)
v. zasłaniać; osłaniać; zabezpieczać; wyświetlać; przesiewać; sortować; badać; przesłuchiwać; filmować; izolować

screw (skru:) s. śruba; propeler; śmigło; zwitek; wyzyskiwacz; dusigrosz; (slang): stosunek płciowy; v. przyśrubować; wyduszać; naciskać; wykrzywiać; zabałaganić; obracać się; (slang):spółkować;
wkopać (kogoś);oszukać

screwdriver ('skru:,drajwer) s.
śrubokręt; wódka z sokiem pomarańczowym

scribble ('skrybl) s. gryzmoły;
bazgranina; v. gryzmolić;
bazgrać; pisać naprędce

script (skrypt) s. rękopis;
scenariusz

scripture ('skrypczer) s. Pismo Święte

scroll (skroul) s. zwitek;
krzywa; spirala

scrub (skrab) s. zarośla; zagajnik; karłowate drzewo; pętak; niepozorny człowiek; szorowanie; v. szorować; oczyszczać;adj.lichy;marny;małeawy

scruple ('skrupl) s. skrupuł;
v. wahać się; mieć skrupuły

scrupulous ('skru:pjules) adj.
sumienny; dokładny; skrupulatny; pedantyczny

scrutinize ('skru:tynajz) v.
badać szczegółowo

scrutiny ('skru:tyny) s. dokładne badanie

scuff (skaf) s. włóczenie nogami; wytarte miejsca; v. powłóczyć nogami; wycierać; rozrzucać; porysować ;musnąć;zedrzeć;zdzierać;szurać

scuffle (skafl) s. włóczenie nogami; szamotanie się; utarczka;
bójka; v. szamotać się; bić się;
powłóczyć nogami;szurać;zaszurać

sculptor ('skalpter) s. rzeźbiarz

sculpture ('skalpczer) s. rzeźba;
v. rzeźbić

scum (skam) s. szumowiny; v.
zbierać szumowiny, wytarzać

scurf (ske:rf) s. łupież;strup;parchy

scurvy ('ske:rwy) s. szkorbut;
adj. podły; nędzny

scuttle ('skatl) s. wiaderko;
szybka ucieczka; właz; v. pędzić; uciekać; robić dziury
w dnie; zatapiać

scuttlebutt ('skatelbat) s. kadź;
pogłoska

scythe (sajz) s. kosa; v. kosić

sea (si:) s. morze; fala

sea breeze ('si:'bri:z) s. wiatr
od morza

seafarer ('si:,feerer) s. żeglarz;
podróżnik morski

seafood ('si:fu:d) s. potrawy
morskie (ryby; skorupiaki)

sea gull ('si:gal) s. mewa

seal (si:l) s. foka; futro foki;
uszczelka; zagadka; plomba;
pieczątka; piętno; znak; v.polować na foki; uszczelniać; plombować; pieczętować; zalakować

seal up ('si:l,ap) v. zaplombować; uszczelnić; zamknąć; zalakować; zapieczętować

sea level('si:,lewl) s. poziom
morza

sealskin ('si:lski:n) s. futro
z fok

seam (si:m) s.szew; rąbek; pokład; blizna; szpara; szczelina; v. łączyć szwami; pękać;
pokiereszować

seaman ('si:men) s. marynarz;
żeglarz

seamstress ('semstrys) s.
szwaczka

seaplane ('si:,plejn) s. hydroplan

seaport ('si:,po:rt) s. port
morski

sea-power ('si:,paľer) s. potęga morska

search (se:rcz) s. poszukiwanie; badanie; szperanie; rewizja; v. badać; dociekać; szukać; przetrząsać; rewidować

searching ('se:rczyng) adj. badawczy; przenikliwy

seashore ('si:,szo:r) s. wybrzeże; brzeg morski

seasick ('si:,syk) adj. chory na morską chorobę

seaside ('si:'sajd) s. wybrzeże morskie

season ('si:zn) s. pora roku; pora; sezon; v. zaprawiać; przyprawiac; okrasić

seasonable (si:znebl) adj. stosowny; odpowiedni; właściwy na porę roku; w porę

seasonal ('si:zenl) adj. sezonowy

seasoned ('si:znd) adj. zaprawiony; wdrożony; przyprawiony; pikantny; wystały

seasoning ('si:znyng) s. przyprawa

season ticket ('si:sn'tykyt) s. abonament; karta wstępu; bilet (np. na serię przedstawień)

seat (si:t) s. siedzenie; ławka; krzesło; miejsce siedzące; siedlisko; siedziba; gniazdo; v. posadzić; usadowić; wybierać (do sejmu); siąsć; osadzić

seat belt ('si:t,belt) s. pas ochronny w samolocie lub samochodzie; pas bezpieczeństwa

seaward ('si:ľerd) adv. ku (otwartemu) morzu; adj. skierowany ku morzu

seaweed ('si:ľi:d) s. wodorost

seaworthy ('si:,ľe:rgy) adj. zdatny do podróży morskiej (m.in. wodoszczelny)

secession (sy'seszyn) s. secesja; oddzielenie się

seclude (sy'klu:d) v. odosabniać (się)

secluded (sy'klu:dyd) adj. odosobniony

seclusion (sy'klu:żyn) s. odosobnienie; ustronie; zacisze

second ('sekend) adj. drugi; wtórny; powtórny; ponowny; zastępczy; zapasowy; drugorzędny; v. poprzeć; sekundować; s. sekunda; moment; chwila; drugi; sekundant; delegat; zastępca

secondary ('sekendery) adj. drugorzędny; wtórny; pochodny

secondary school ('sekendery-,sku:l) s. szkoła średnia

second floor ('sekend,flo:r) s. pierwsze piętro

secondhand ('sekend,haend) adj. z drugiej ręki; używany

secondly ('sekendly) adv. po drugie

second-rate ('sekend'-rejt) adj. drugorzędny; lichy; kiepski

secrecy ('si;krysy) s. tajemnica; skrytość; dyskrecja

secret ('si:kryt) adj. tajny; tajemny; sekretny; skryty; ustronny; dyskretny; s. tajemnica; sekret; pl. wstydliwe części ciała

secretary ('sekretry) s. sekretarz; sekretarka; sekretarzyk

secretary of state ('sekretry-,ow'stejt) minister spraw zagranicznych USA

secrete (sy'kri:t) v. wydzielać; ukrywać

secretion (sy'kri:szyn) s. wydzielina; wydzielanie; ukrycie

section ('sekszyn) s. część; wycinek; etap; oddział; grupa; dział; ustęp; paragraf; sekcja; przekrój; żelazo profilowe; przedział; drużyna robocza; v. dzielić na części; robić przekrój

sector ('sekrer) s. wycinek; odcinek

secular ('sekjuler) adj. świecki; wiekowy; stuletni; s. ksiądz świecki

secularize (,sekjulerajz) s. sekularyzować

secure (sy'kjuer) v. zabezpieczać (się); umacniać; uzyskiwać; zapewniać sobie; adj;
spokojny; bezpieczny; pewny
security (sy'kjueryty) s. bezpieczeństwo; zabezpieczenie;
pewność; zastaw; papier wartościowy; zbytnia ufność
sedan (sy'daen) s. samochód
4-osobowy
sedate (sy'dejt) v. uspokajać
(lekarstwami); adj. spokojny;
opanowany; zrównoważony
sedative ('sedetyw) adj. & s.
(środek) uspakajający, nasen-
ny
sediment ('sydyment) s. osad;
nanos; (skała osadowa)
seduce (sy'du:s) v. uwodzić
seduction (sy'dakszyn) s. uwo-
dzenie; pokusa; poneta; powab
seductive (sy'daktyw) adj. kuszący; necący
sedulous ('sedjules) adj. pilny; skrzętny; staranny; skwapliwy
see; saw; seen (si:, so:,si:n)
see (si:) v. zobaczyć; widzieć;
ujrzeć; zauważyć; spostrzegać; doprowadzić; odprowadzić;
zwiedzać; zrozumieć; odwiedzać; przeżywać; dożyć; uważać; zastanawiać się; dopilnować
see off ('si:,of) v. odprowadzać
see out ('si:,aut) v. odprowadzić do drzwi
see through ('si:,tru:) v.prze-
prowadzić do końca; doczekać
się końca
see to ('si:,tu) v. troszczyć
się o...
seed (si:d) v. obsiewać; obsypywać się; zasiewać; wybierać;
s. nasienie; zarodek; plemię
seek; sought; sought (si:k;
so:t; so:t)
seek (si:k) v. szukać; starać
się; chcieć; zadać; nastawać;
usiłować; próbować; przetrząsać; dażyć

seek out ('si:k,aut) v. odszuki-
wać; wykrywać
seem (si:m) v. zdawać się; robić
wrażenie; okazywać się; mieć
wrażenie
seeming (si:myng) adj. pozorny;
widoczny
seemingly ('si:myngly) adv. na
pozór; widocznie
seemly ('si:mly) adj. właściwy;
przyzwoity
seen (si:n) v. zob. see
seep (si:p) v. sączyć się; wyciekać
seesaw ('si:so:) s. huśtawka
(na desce); adj. wahadłowy;
huśtawkowy; s. huśtać się; wahać się; adv. (poruszać czyms)
do góry i na dół
segment ('segment) s. odcinek;
segment; v. podzielić na częs-
ci
segregate('segry'gejt) v. oddzielać; segregować
segregation ('segry'gejszyn) s.
oddzielenie; segregacja
seize (si:z) v. uchwycić; złapać; zrozumieć; owładnąć; sko-
rzystać; zaciąć się; zatrzeć
się; zablokować się
seizure ('si:zer) s. zagarnięcie;
zawładnięcie; zajęcie; napad;
atak apopleksji; zatarcie; za-
blokowanie ;atak drgawek
seldom ('seldem) adv. rzadko;
z rzadka
select (sy'lekt) v. wybierać;
wyselekcjonować; adj. wybrany;
doborowy; ekskluzywny
selection (sy'lekszyn) s. wybór;
dobór; selekcja
self (self) prefix. samo; auto-
matycznie; s. jaźń; osobowość;
własne dobro; pl.selves (selwz)
self-acting ('self'aektyng) adj.
samoczynny
self-command ('self,ke'ma:nd) s.
spokój; panowanie nad sobą;
opanowanie
self-confidence ('self,konfydens)
s. pewność siebie; tupet
self-conscious ('self'konszes)
adj.nieśmiały; zażenowany

self-control ('self,ken'troul)
s. zimna krew; opanowanie
self-defense ('self,dy'fens) s.
samoobrona
self-employment ('self,ym'plojment) samozatrudnienie
self-government ('self'gawen-
ment) s. samorząd; autonomia
self-interest ('self'yntryst)
s. interesowność; własne dobro
selfish ('selfysz) adj. samolubny; egoistyczny
self-made ('self'mejd) adj.
przez samego siebie osiągnięty
self-possessed ('self,pe'zest)
adj. opanowany; spokojny
self-reliant ('self,ry'lajent)
adj. na sobie polegający
self-respect ('self,rys'pekt) s.
poczucie własnej godności
self-righteous ('self'rajczes)
adj. nadmiernie pewny siebie
self-service ('self'se:rwys) s.
samo-obsługa
sell; sold; sold (sel; sould;
sould)
sell (sel) v. sprzedawać; za-
przedawać; sprzeniewierzyć;
wykiwać; mieć zbyt; być na
sprzedaż; wyprzedawać
sell out ('selaut) v. wyprzedawać
seller ('seler) s. sprzedawca
selves (selwz) pl. zob. self
semblance ('semblens) s. pozór;
podobieństwo
semen ('si:men) s. nasienie
semicolon ('semy'koulen) s.
średnik
semifinal ('semy'fajnl) s. pół-
finał
senate ('senyt) s. senat
senator ('seneter) s. senator
send; sent; sent (send; sent;
sent)
send (send) v. posyłać; wysyłać;
nadawać; transmitować; wystrze-
liwać; sprawiać; wywoływać
send away ('send,e'łej) v. odprawiać; wypędzać
send for ('send,fo:r) v. zawołać; zamawiać; kazać przynieść

send in ('send,yn) v. posłać;
nadesłać
send off ('send'o:f) v. wysyłać;
odprowadzać (np. na lotnisko);
pożegnać kogoś (na stacji)
sender ('sender) s. nadawca;
nadajnik (np. radiowy)
send-off ('send'o:f) s. pożegnanie
senior ('si:njer) adj. starszy
(np. rangą); s. starszy człowiek; senior; student ostat-
niego roku
sensation (sen'sejszyn) s. wrażenie; doznanie; uczucie; sensacja
sensational (sen'sejszenl) adj.
sensacyjny; wrażeniowy
sense (sens) s. zmysł; poczucie; uczucie (np. zimna); świadomość (czegoś); rozsądek;
znaczenie; sens; v. wyczuwać;
czuć; rozumieć
senseless ('senslys) adj. bez
sensu; nierozumny; nieprzytomny
sensibility (,sensy'bylyty) s.
wrażliwość
sensible ('sensybl) adj. rozsądny; świadomy; przytomny;
wrażliwy; odczuwalny; pozna-
walny; sensowny
sensitive ('sensytyw) adj.
wrażliwy; delikatny
sensual ('senszuel) adj. zmysłowy (też seksualnie)
sensuous ('senszues) adj. zmysłowy (nie seksualnie)
sent (sent) v. zob. send
sentence ('sentens) s. zdanie;
powiedzenie; wyrok; sentencja;
v. wydawać wyrok; skazywać
sentiment ('sentyment) s. sentyment; uczucie; opinia; zdanie;
życzenie; sentymentalność
sentimental (,senty'mentl) adj.
uczuciowy; sentymentalny
sentimentality (,senty'ment'aelyty) s. uczuciowość; czułost-
kowość; sentymentalność
sentry ('sentry) s. posterunek;
wartownik

separable ('seperebl) adj. roz-
łączny

separate ('seperejt) v. rozłą-
czyc; rozdzielic; oddzielic;
oderwac; odseparowac (się);
odgrodzic; rozszczepic;

separate ('sepryt) adj. odrębny;
oddzielny; osobny; indywidualny; poszczególny

separation (,sepe'rejszyn) s.
separacja; rozdzielenie; oddzielenie; rozłączenie

September (sep'tember) s.
wrzesien

septic ('septyk) adj. septyczny;
zakazny

sepulcher ('sepelker) s. grób;
v. składac do grobu

sequel ('si:kłel) s. ciąg dalszy; wynik; następstwo

sequence ('si:kłens) s. następstwo; kolejnosc; porządek;
progresja

serene (sy'ri:n) adj. pogodny;
spokojny; s. spokojne morze;
pogodne niebo etc. v. rozpogo-
dzic

sergeant ('sa:rdżent) s. sierżant

serial('sierjel) a. seryjny;
periodyczny; kolejny; odcin-
kowy

series ('sieri:z) pl. seria;
szereg; rząd

serious ('sierjes) adj. poważny

sermon ('se:rmen) s. kazanie;
nagana

serpent ('se:rpent) s. wąż

serum ('sierem) s. surowica

servant ('se:rwent) s. służący;
sługa; służąca; urzędnik
(panstwowy)

serve (se:rw) s. służyc; odby-
wac służbę (też kadencję;
praktykę etc.); nadawac się;
obsłużyc; podawac; sprzedawac;
dostarczyc; wręczyc; potrakto-
wac; postepowac; spełniac
fukcje; sprawowac urząd; odby-
wac karę (więzienia); zaserwo-
wac

service ('se:rwys) s. służba;
obsługa; praca; urząd; zaopatrzenie; instalacja;
uprzejmosc; grzecznosc; przysługa; pomoc; użytecznosc;
nabożenstwo; serw; serwis
(stołowy); wręczenie; v. do-
glądac; naprawic; kryc (sami-
ce)

serviceable ('se:rwysebl) adj.
pożyteczny; użyteczny; praktyczny; wygodny; mocny; trwały

service-station('se:rwys-'stejszyn) s. stacja obsługi
i sprzedaży benzyny

session ('seszyn) s. posiedzenie; siedzenie; półrocze

set; set; set (set; set; set)

set (set) v. stawiac; ustawiac;
wstawic; urządzic; umieszczac;
przykładac; nastawiac; osadzac;
wbijac; wyznaczac; ustalac;
sądzic; nakrywac; składac;
wysadzac (czyms); scinac się;
okrzepnąc; adj. zastygły; nieruchomy; zdecydowany; stały;
ustalony; s. seria; garnitur;
skład; komplet; zespół; grupa;
szczepek; zachod: ustawienie;
układ; twardnienie; gęstosc;
rozstęp; oszalowanie

set at ease ('set,et'i:z) v.
uspokoic

set-back ('setbaek) s. pogorszenie; nawrot; zahamowanie

set free ('set,fri:) v. uwolnic

set off ('set,of) v. uwydatnic;
wyodrębnic; wystrzelic; wysa-
dzic; wywołac; wyruszyc; wy-
jeżdżac

set out ('set,aut) v. wystawiac;
ozdabiac; wykładac; wyruszac;
zaczac się

set to ('set,tu) v. zabierac
się (do czegos)

set up ('set,ap) v. ustawiac;
zakładac; zaczynac; zaopatrywac; roscic; wysuwac; przywracac; podnosic; założyc; podawac
się (za kogos)

settee (se'ti:) s. kanapa; sofa
setting ('setyŋg) s. otoczenie;
oprawa; ułożenie; układ; inscenizacja
settle (setl) v. osiedlić (się);
umieścić (się); uregulować;
osadzić (się); ustalić; roz-
strzygnąć; zapłacić (dług);
zamieszkać; usadowić (się);
uspokoić (się); zawierać (umowę); układać (się)
settle down ('setl,dałn) v.
ustatkować się; osiedlić się;
zabrać się do czegoś
settlement ('setlment) s. osiedle; osada; kolonia; osiadanie;
sedymentacja; załatwienie; rozstrzygnięcie; ustalenie
settler ('setler) s. osadnik;
kolonista
set-up ('set,ap) s. postawa;
układ; drużyna; dodatki do
alkoholu; (slang):ukartowane
zawody; łatwa sprawa
seven ('sewn) num. siedem;
s. siódemka
seventeen ('sewn'ti:n) num.
siedemnaście; s. siedemnastka
seventh ('sewent) adj. siódmy
seventy ('sewnty) num. siedemdziesiąt; s. siedemdziesiątka
sever ('sever) v. odrywać; odłączyć; zrywać; urywać; rozchodzić się
several ('sewrel) adj. kilku;
kilka; kilkoro
severe (sy'wier) adj. surowy;
srogi; ostry; dotkliwy; bolesny; zacięty
severity (sy'weryty) s. surowość; srogość; ostrość; za-
ciętość; ciężki stan
sew; sewed; sewn (sou; soud;
soun)
sew (sou) v. szyć; uszyć
sewage ('sju:ydż) s. ścieki
sewer ('suer) s. kanał ścieko-
wy; v. kanalizować;
sewer ('souer) s. osoba szyjąca
sewerage ('su:erydż) s. kanalizacja; system kanalizacyjny
sewing ('souyŋg) s. szycie

sewing-machine ('souyŋgme,szi:n)
s. maszyna do szycia
sewn (soun) v. zob. sew
sex (seks) s. płeć
sex appeal ('sekse'pi:l) s.
atrakcyjność płciowa; seksapil
sexton ('seksten) s. grabarz
sexual ('seksjuel) adj. seksualny; płciowy
Sejm (sejm) s. sejm
shabby ('szaeby) adj. brudny;
skąpy; odrapany; wytarty;
nędzny; podły
shack (szaek) s. buda; szałas;
dom
shack up ('szaek,ap) v. spędzać
noc z kimś (slang)
shackle ('szaekl) s. kajdany;
klamra; pęta; v. zakuwać;
szczepiać
shade (szejd) s. cień; odcień;
abażur; stora; pl. ustronie;
piwnica na wino; v. zasłaniać;
zamroczyć; cieniować
shadow ('szaedou) s. cień
(czyjś); v. pokrywać cieniem;
śledzić kogoś
shady ('szejdy) adj. cienisty;
nieczysty; mętny
shaft (szaeft) s. drzewce; trzon;
strzała; promień; wał; trzonek;
dyszel; szyb
shaggy ('szaegy) a. włochaty;
krzaczasty
shake; shook; shaken (szejk;
szuk; szejken)
shake (szejk) v. potrząsać;
uścisnąć dłoń; grozić (palcem);
wstrząsać; drżeć; dygotać;
s. dygotanie; dreszcze; drżenie; potrząsanie
shake-up ('szejkap) s. otrząśnię-
cie (się); czystka (slang)
shaky ('szejky) adj. drżący;
rozklekotany; słaby; zachwiany;
chwiejący się
shale (szejl) s. łupek
shall (szael) v. będę; będziemy;
musisz; musi; muszą (zrobić)
shallow ('szaelou) s. mielizna;
adj. płytki; powierzchniowy;
v. spłycać; płycieć; obniżać
poziom (wody)

sham (szaem) adj. fałszywy;
oszukańczy; sztuczny; udawany; symulowany; upozorowany;
s. poza; symulowanie; symu-
lant; pozór; udawanie; v.uda-
wać, symulować

shambles ('szaemblz) pl. jatki; rzeź

shame (szejm) s. wstyd; v.wsty-
dzić się

shame on you ! ('szejm,on'ju:)
exp.: wstydź się !

shameful ('szejmful) adj. sromotny; haniebny

shameless ('szejmlys) adj. bezwstydny; bezczelny

shampoo (szaem'pu:) s. szampon;
mycie głowy szamponem; v. myć
szamponem

shank (szaenk) s. goleń; trzonek; uchwyt

shape (szejp) v. kształtować;
rzeźbić; modelować; formułować; wyobrazić; s. kształt;
kondycja; postać; zjawa; widmo; model

shaped ('szejpt)adj. ukształto-
wany

shapeless('szejplys) adj. bezkształtny; nieforemny; niezgrabny

shapely ('szejply) adj. kształtny; foremny; zgrabny

share (szeer) s. udział; należ-
na część; lemiesz; v. rozdzie-
lić; dzielić (się); podzielać;
brać udział

share-holder ('szeer,houlder)
s. akcjonarjusz

shark (sza:rk) s. rekin

sharp (sza:rp) adj. ostry; bystry; pilny; wyraźny; chytry; do-
minujacy; inteligentny; adv.
punktualnie; szybko; biegiem

sharpen ('sza:rpen) v. ostrzyć;
temperować; obostrzyć; za-
ostrzyć

sharpener ('sza:rpner) s. temperówka; narzędzie do ostrze-
nia

sharpness ('sza:rpnys) s. ostrość; bystrość; chytrość; pilność

sharp-witted ('sza:rp'łytyd)
adj. bystry; dowcipny; rozgarnięty

shatter ('szaeter) v. gruchotać; roztrzaskac; niweczyć;
szarpać

shave; shaved; shaven (szejw;
szejwd; szejwn)

shave (szejw) v. golić (się);
oskrobać; strugać; s. golenie;
muśnięcie

shaven (szejwn) v. zob. shave

shaving ('szejwyng) v. golenie;
skrobanie; wiórkowanie; s.
wiór

shawl(szo:l) s. szal

she (szi:) pron. ona

sheaf (szi:f) s. snop; wiązka;
wiązanka; plik; pl. sheaves
(szi:wz)

shear; sheared; shorn (szier;
szierd; szo:rn)

shear (szier) v. ścinać; uci-
nać; ostrzyc; s. ścinanie; pl.
nożyce (shears)

sheath (szi:s) s. pochwa; futerał; powłoka; prezerwatywa

sheaves (szi:wz) pl. od sheath

shed (shed) s. szopa; buda;
v. zrzucać; strącać; pozbywać
(się); pogubić; ronić; przelewać (krew); wydzielać; promieniować

sheep (szi:p) pl. owce

sheep dog ('szi:p,dog) s. owczarek

sheepish ('szi:pysz) adj. bojaźliwy; nieśmiały; zakłopota-
ny; zbaraniały; ogłupiały

sheer (szier) v. schodzić z kur-
su; skręcać nagle; adj. zwykły;
jawny; czysty; zwyczajny; stromy; prostopadły; pionowy;
przejrzysty; przewiewny; lekki;
adv. zupełnie; pionowo; stromo

sheet (szi:t) s. arkusz; prześcieradło; gazeta; tafla; obszar; warstwa; v. pokrywać
prześcieradłem; okrywać brezen-
tem

sheet iron ('szi:t,ajren) s.
blacha stalowa

shelf (szelf) s. półka; rafa;
mielizna; pl. shelves (szelwz)
shell (szel) s. łupina; skorupa; powłoka; osłona; łupina;
pancerz; muszla; szkielet;
łuska; pocisk; granat; gilza;
v. ostrzeliwać z armat; wyłus-
kiwać
shellfish ('szel,fysz) s. sko-
rupiak; mięczak
shelter ('szelter) s. schronienie; ochrona; osłona; v, chronić; osłaniać; udzielać schro-
nienia; zabezpieczać
shelve (szelv) v. odkładać (na
półkę); wkładać do szuflady;
opadać (wzdłuż stoku)
shelves (szelwz) pl. zob.shelf
shepherd ('szeperd) s. pastuch;
pasterz; v. paść; (pilotować)
prowadzić
shield (szi:ld) s. tarcza;
osłona; v. osłaniać; ochraniać
shift (szyft) v. zmieniać (np.
biegi); przesuwać; przełączyć;
zwalić; s. przesunięcie; zmiana; szychta; wykręt; wybieg
shiftless ('szyftlys) adj. niezaradny
shifty ('szyfty) adj. zmienny;
fałszywy; chytry
shilling ('szylyng) s. szyling
shin (szyn) s. goleń; v. kopać
w goleń
shine; shone; shone (szajn;
szon; szon)
shine (szajn) v. zabłyszczeć;
zajaśnieć; oczyścić na połysk;
s. jasność; blask; (slang):
granda; awantura; sympatia
shingle ('szyngl) s. gont; szyld;
wywieszka; kamyk; v. pokryć
gontami; krótko ostrzyc
shingles ('szynglz) pl. półpa-
siec
shiny('szajny) adj. błyszczący;
wypolerowany
ship (szyp) s. okręt; statek;
samolot; v. załadować; zaokre-
tować; posyłać
shipment ('szypment) s. załadunek; przesyłka; fracht

shipowner ('szyp,ołner) s. armator
shipping ('szypyng) s. flota
handlowa; żegluga; załadunek;
usługi żeglugowe; przesyłka;
adj. spedycyjny; okrętowy
shipping company ('szypyng'kampeny) s. firma okrętowa; armator
shipwreck ('szyp,rek) s. rozbicie statku; v. ulec rozbiciu;
spowodować rozbicie statku;
rozbić się
ship-wrecked('szyp,rekt) s. rozbitek
shipyard('szyp,ja:rd) s. stocznia
shire ('szajer) s. hrabstwo
(powiat)
shirk (sze:rk) v. uchylać się;
wymigiwać się; s. nierób; wy-
migiwacz
shirt (sze:rt) s. koszula
shirt sleeves ('sze:rt,sli:wz)
pl. rękawy od koszuli; bez
marynarki; adj. prosty; domowy
shit (szyt) v. wulg.: srać;s.gów-
no
shitty ('szyty) adj. wulg.: za-
srany
shiv (szyw) s. majcher (slang)
shiver ('szywer) v. drżeć;
trząsć się; rozbijać się w kawałki; s. dreszcz; kawałek
shock (szok) s. wstrząs; cios;
uderzenie; starcie; porażenie;
czupryna; kopka; v. wstrząsać;
gorszyć; oburzać; porazić
shock absorber ('szok-eb,so:r-
ber) s. tłumik drgań; amorty-
zator
shocking('szokyng) adj. okropny; wstrętny; skandaliczny;
oburzający; niestosowny
shoddy ('szody) adj. tandetny
shoe; shod; shod (szu:, szod,
szod)
shoe (szu:) s. but; półbucik;
trzewik; okucie; podkowa;
nakładka (hamulca); obręcz;
nasada; v. obuwać; podkuwać

shoehorn ('szu:,ho:rn) s. łyżka do butów; wzuwacz

shoelace ('szu:,lejs) s. sznurowadło

shoemaker ('szu:,mejker) s. szewc

shoestring ('szu:,stryŋg) s. sznurowadło; bardzo mały kapitał

shoeshine ('szu:,szajn) s. czyszczenie butów (na połysk)

shone (szon) v. zob. shine

shook (szuk) v. zob. shake

shoot (szu:t; szot; shot (szu:t; szot; szot)

shoot (szu:t) v. strzelić; wystrzelić; zastrzelić; rozstrzelać; zrobić zdjęcie; nakręcić film; mknąć; przemknąć; spłynąć; rwać; kiełkować; s. pęd; kiełek; polowanie; progi; plac zwozu śmieci

shooter ('shu:ter) s. strzelec; rewolwer

shooting ('shu:tyŋg) adj. mknący; pędzący; strzelający

shooting gallery ('shu:tyŋg,gaelery) s. strzelnica

shooting-star ('shu:tyŋg,sta:r) s. spadająca gwiazda

shooting-party ('shu:tyŋg,pa:rty) s. wyprawa łowiecka; polowanie

shop (szop) s. sklep; pracownia; warsztat; zakład; v. robić zakupy

shopkeeper ('szop,ki:per) s. kupiec; sklepikarz

shoplifter ('szop,lyfter) s. złodziej sklepowy

shopping center ('szopyŋg,senter) s. skupisko sklepów; osrodek zakupów

shopping mall ('szopyŋg,mol) s. skupisko sklepów wzdłuż krytej hali ;pasaż handlowy

shop·window('szop'łyndoł) s. wystawa

shore (szo:r) s. brzeg; wybrzeże; podpora; v. podpierać; podstęplowac

shorn (szo:rn) v. zob. shear

short (szo:rt) adj. krótki; niski; zwięzły; oschły; niecały; niewystarczający; adv. krótko; nagle; za krótko; s. skrót; zwarcie; pl. szorty

shortage ('szo:rtydż) s. brak; niedobór; deficyt

short circuit ('sho:rt'se:rkyt) s. krótkie spięcie; zwarcie

shortcoming ('sho:rt'kamyŋg) s. wada; niedociągnięcie; brak; niedobór

shorten ('szo:rtn) v. skracać

shorthand ('szo:rthaend) s. stenografia

shortly ('szo:rtly) adv. wkrótce; niebawem

shortness ('szo:rtnys) s. krótkosć; niedobór

shorts ('szo:rts) pl. szorty; kalesony (krótkie)

shortstory ('szo:rt,sto:ry) s. nowela

short-sighted ('szo:rt'sajtyd) adj. krótkowzroczny; nieprzewidujący

short-term ('szo:rt'term) adj.. krótkoterminowy; krótkotrwały

short-winded ('szo:rt'łyndyd) adj. zasapany; krótko mówiący

shot (szot) v. zob. shoot; ładowac broń; s. strzał; pocisk; śrut; zastrzyk; docinek; adj. mieniący się

shotgun ('szotgan) s. dubeltówka; śrutówka; strzelba

should (szud) v. tryb warunkowy od shall

shoulder ('szoulder) s. ramię; plecy; łopatka; pobocze; v. brac na ramię; rozpychac się

shout (szałt) s. krzyk; okrzyk; wrzask; v. krzyczec; wykrzykiwać

shove (szaw) v. popychac; posuwac (coś); s. pchnięcie

shovel ('szawl) s. łopata; szufla; v. przerzucac łopatą lub szuflą

show; showed; shown (szou; szoud; szoun)

show (szou) v. pokazywać; wskazywać; s. wystawa; przedstawienie; pokaz

show around ('szou,e'raund) v. oprowadzać

show off ('szou,o:f) v. popisywać się; paradować; starać się imponować

show up ('szou,ap) v. demaskować; zjawiać się; ukazywać się

show business ('szou'byznyz) s. przemysł widowiskowy

shower (szaier) s. tusz; prysznic; przelotny deszcz; grad; stek; przelotnie kropić; obsypywać; oblewać

shower bath ('szaier,ba:t) s. tusz; prysznic

shown (szołn) v. zob. show

showy ('szołi) adj. ostentacyjny; okazały

shrank (szraenk) s. zob. shrink

shred (szred) s. strzęp; v. ciąć na strzępy

shrew (szru:) s. złośnica; sekutnica; sorek

shrewd (szru:d) a. przenikliwy (np. obserwator)

shriek (szri:k) v. wrzeszczeć; piszczeć; rechotać; s. wrzask; pisk; gwizd (ostry)

shrill (szryl) adj. ostry; przenikliwy; przeraźliwy; v. rozlegać się przenikliwie; adv. przenikliwie

shrimp (szrymp) s. krewetka; karzełek; v. łowić krewetki

shrine (szrajn) s. przybytek; relikwiarz; v. umieszczać w przybytku

shrink (szrynk; szrank; shrunk (szrynk; szraenk; szrank)

shrink (szrynk) v. kurczyć (się) wzbraniać (się) wzdrygać się; s. kurczenie się; (slang):psychiatra

shrinkage ('szrynkydż) s. kurczenie się; ubytek na wadze

shrivel ('szrywl) v. kurczyć (się)

Shrovetide ('szrouwtajd) s. ostatki; zapusty

Shrovetide Tuesday ('szrouwtajd'tju:zdy) s. tłusty wtorek

shrub (szrab) s. krzew; krzak

shrubbery ('szrabery) s. krzaki

shrubby ('szraby) adj. krzaczasty

shrug (szrag) s. wzruszenie ramion; v. wzruszyć ramionami

shrunken ('szrankn) v. zob. shrink

shudder ('szader) s. dreszcz; (slang):nudziarz; v. zadrzeć; wzdrygać się

shuffle ('szafl) v. wlec się; powłóczyć; kręcić; tasować; mieszać; s. krok suwany; krętactwo; tasowanie (kart); wleczenie się; szuranie

shun (szan) v. unikać; wystrzegać się; s. baczność; uwaga

shut; shut; shut (szat; szat; szat)

shut (szat) v. zamykać (się); przytrzasnąć; adj. zamknięty

shut down ('szat,dałn) s. zamknięcie; wstrzymanie pracy; v. zamykać; kłaść koniec; zasłaniać; (o zakładzie) stanąć

shut up ('szat,ap) v. pozamykać; zamknąć gębę; zamilknąć; bądź cicho; wulg.:stul pysk!

shutter ('szater) s. okiennica; zasłona; migawka; regulator organów; v. zamykać okiennice

shy (szaj) adj. płochliwy; wstydliwy; niesmiały; nieufny; ostrożny; skąpy; szczupły; v. płoszyć się; stronić; rzucać; s. rzut (w coś)

shyness ('szajnys) s. skromność; niesmiałość

shyster ('szajster) s. chytry (polityk) bez zasad; adwokat-krętacz

sick (syk) adj. chory; znudzony; chorowity; skażony zarazkami; chorobowy

sickbed ('sykbed) s. łóżko chorego; łoże boleści

sick benefit ('syk'benefyt) s. zasiłek chorobowy

sicken ('sykn) v. zaczynać chorować; wywoływać obrzydzenie; brzydzić (się)

sickle ('sykl) s. sierp

sick leave ('sykli:w) s. zwolnienie lekarskie; urlop chorobowy

sickly ('sykly) adj. chorowity; słabowity; niezdrowy; chorobliwy; ckliwy

sickness ('syknys) s. choroba; wymioty; nudności

sick room ('syk-ru:m) s. izba chorych; pokój chorego

side (sajd) s. strona; adj. uboczny; v. stać po czyjejś stronie

side by side ('sajd,baj'sajd) exp.: obok siebie; jeden przy drugim

side arms ('sajda:rmz) pl. broń boczna (np. szable)

sideboard ('sajdbo:rd) s. kredens

sidecar ('sajd,ka:r) s. przyczepa do motocykla

sided ('sajdyd) adj. stronny; mający strony

side dish ('sajd,dysz) s. przystawka

side-kick ('sajdkyk) s. (slang): kompan; pomagier

sideroad ('sajd,roud) s. boczna droga

side line ('sajd,lajn) v. odsuwać na bok; zapobiegać

sidewalk ('sajd-ło:k) s. chodnik; trotuar

sidewalk café ('sajdło:kaefej) s. kawiarnia na chodniku

sidewards ('sajdłedz) adv. bokiem; w bok

sideways ('sajdłejz) adv. bokiem; na poprzek; adj. boczny

side with ('sajd,łys) v. brać czyjąś stronę

siege (si:dż) s. oblężenie

sieve (syw) s. sito; rzeszoto; przetak; v. przesiewać

sift (syft) v. przesiewać; przebierać; oddzielać; proszyć; posypywać

sigh (saj) s. westchnienie; v. wzdychać

sight (sajt) s. wzrok; widok; celownik; przeziernik

sighted ('sajtyd) adj. spostrzeżony

sightly ('sajtly) adj. dający dobry widok; miły; przyjemny

sight seeing ('sajtsi:yng) s. zwiedzanie; adj. turystyczny

sight seeing tour ('sajtsi:yng,tu:r) s. zwiedzanie z wycieczką; wycieczka krajoznawcza

sightseer ('sajtsi:er) s. turysta; zwiedzający

sign (sajn) s. znak; omen; godło; napis; wywieszka; szyld; skinienie; oznaka; objaw; ślad; znak drogowy; hasło; odzew; v. znaczyć; naznaczyć; podpisać; skinąć

sign up ('sajn,ap) v. zapisywać się

sign out ('sajn,aut) v. wypisywać się

signal ('sygnl) s. sygnał; znak; v. sygnalizować; zapowiadać; dawać znak

signature ('sygnyczer) s. podpis; sygnatura; klucz

signature-tune('sygnyczer,tju:n) s. oznaczenie tonacji

signboard ('sajnbo:rd) s. wywieszka; szyld; godło

signet ('sygnyt) s. sygnet; pieczątka; v. pieczętować

significance (syg'nyfykens) s. wyraz; ważność; znaczenie

significant (syg'nyfykent) adj. istotny; znaczący; doniosły; znamienny; ważny

signification (syg'nyfykejszyn) s. znaczenie

signify ('sygnyfaj) v. znaczyć; mieć znaczenie; oznaczać; zaznaczać

signpost ('sajn,poust) s. drogowskaz

silence ('sajlens) s. milczenie; cisza; v. nakazywać milczenie; cicho !

silencer ('sajlenser) s. tłumik
silent ('sajlent) adj. milczący;
cichy; małomówny
silk (sylk) s. jedwab; adj.
jedwabny
silken ('sylkn) adj. jedwabny;
jedwabniczy
silky ('sylky) adj. jedwabisty
sill (syl) s. próg; podkład;
parapet
silly ('syly) s. głupiec; adj.
głupi; ogłupiały
silver ('sylwer) s. srebro;
v. posrebrzać; adj. srebrny;
srebrzysty
silvery ('sylwry) adj. srebrzysty
similar ('symyler) adj. podobny; rzecz podobna
similarity (,symy'laeryty) s.
podobieństwo
simmer ('symer) v. wolno gotować (się); burzyć się wewnątrz;
s. gotowanie na wolnym ogniu
simple ('sympl) adj. prosty;
zwykły; naturalny; szczery; naiwny; głupkowaty; zwyczajny
simplicity(sym'plysyty) s.
prostota
simplification (,symplyfy'kejszyn) s. uproszczenie
simplistic ('symplystyk) adj.
zbyt upraszczający
simplify ('symplyfaj) v.upros-
cić; ułatwić
simply ('symply) adv. po prostu
simulate ('symjulejt) v. udawać; naśladować
simultaneous (symel'tejnjes)
adj. równoczesny; jednoczesny
sin (syn) s. grzech; v. grze-
szyć
since (syns) adv. odtąd; potem;
conj; skoro; ponieważ; od czasu jak
sincere (syn'sier) adj. szczery
sincerely (syn'sierly) adv.
szczerze
sincerity (syn'seryty) s. szczerość
sinew ('synu:) s. ścięgno
sinews ('synu:s) pl. muskulatu-
ra; siła; moc

sinewy ('synuy) adj. muskularny; mocny
sing; sang; sung (syng; saeng;
sang)
sing (syng) v. śpiewać; wyć;
zawodzić; bzykać; świstać;
opiewać; s. śpiew; świst
singe (syndż) v. opalać; osma-
lać
singer (synger) s. śpiewak
single ('syngl) adj. pojedynczy; jeden; samotny; szczery;
uczciwy; s. bilet w jedną
stronę; gra pojedyncza; v. wybierać; wyróżniać
single out ('syngl,aut) v. wybierać
single-handed ('syngl'haendyd)
adj. adv. w pojedynkę; na
własną rękę; samodzielny; samodzielnie
single room ('syngl'ru:m) s.
pojedynczy pokój
single ticket ('syngl'tykyt) s.
bilet w jedną stronę
singles bar ('syngls,ba:r) s.
bar dla samotnych
singular ('syngjuler) adj.
osobliwy; niezwykły; pojedynczy; liczba pojedyncza
singularity (,syngju'laeryty)
s. osobliwość; niezwykłość;
niezwykły człowiek
sinister ('synyster) adj.
zbrodniczy; złowieszczy; lewy
sink; sank; sunk (synk; saenk;
sank)
sink (synk) v. zatonąć; zato-
pić; zagłębić (się); opuścić;
obniżyć; pogrążyć; zanikać;
zmaleć; wykopywać; ukrywać;
wyryć; zainwestować; amortyzować; s. zlew; ściek; bagno
zepsucia
sinking ('synkyng)s. uczucie
mdłości (np. z przerażenia)
sinner ('syner) s. grzesznik
sip (syp) s; łyk; popijanie;
v. popijać
sir (se:r) s. pan; v. nazywać
panem; exp.: proszę pana !
sirloin (se:rloyn) s. polędwica
sister (syster) s. siostra

sister in law ('syster yn,lo:) s. szwagierka

sit; sat; sat (syt; saet; saet)

sit (syt) v. siedzieć; przesiadywać; usiąść; zasiadać; obradować; leżeć; pozować

sit down ('syt,dałn) v. usiąść

sit up ('syt,ap) v. wyprostować się siedząc; czuwać; usiąść prosto

site (sajt) s. miejsce; plac (np. budowy); położenie; v. umieszczać

sitting ('sytyŋg) s. posiedzenie; sesja

sitting-room ('sytyŋg,ru:m) s. bawialnia; salon

situated ('sytjuejtyd) adj. umieszczony; stojący; usytuowany

situation (,sytu'ejszyn) s. położenie; posada; sytuacja

six (syks) num. sześć; s. szóstka

sixteen ('syks'ti:n) num. szesnaście; s. szesnastka

sixth (sykst) num. adj. szósty; s. jedna szósta

sixthly ('sykstly) adv. po szóste

size (sajz) s. wielkość; numer; format; klajster; krochmal; rzadki klej; v. sortować wg wielkości; oceniać wielkość; nadawać się; krochmalić; usztywnić klejem

sized-up ('sajzd,ap) adj. oceniony (co do wielkości, siły lub ważności)

sizzle ('syzl) v. skwierczeć; s. skwierczenie

skate (skejt) s. łyżwa; wrotka; płaszczka; szkapa; pętak; patałach; v. ślizgać się; jeździć na wrotkach

skater ('skejter) s. łyżwiarz; wrotkarz

skeleton ('skelytn) s.szkielet

skeptic ('skeptyk) adj. sceptyczny; s. sceptyk

sketch ('skecz) s. szkic; skecz; zarys; v. szkicować ;przedstawić w ogólnych zarysach(w krótkich słowach);robić wstępny rysunek

sketch block ('skecz,blok) s. szkicownik

sketchbook ('skecz,bu:k) s. szkicownik

ski (ski:) s. narta; wyrzutnik bomb; v. jeździć na nartach

skid (skid) s. deska; płoza; podpórka; klin hamowniczy; poślizg; zarzucenie; v. ślizgać się; zarzucać; umieszczać na płozach; hamować

skier ('ski:er) s. narciarz

skiing ('skiyŋg) s. narciarstwo; jazda na nartach

ski lift ('ski lyft) s. wyciąg narciarski

skill ('skyl) s. zręczność; wprawa

skilled ('skyld) adj. wykwalifikowany; wykonany fachowo

skillful ('skylful) adj. zręczny; wprawny

skillet (skylyt) s. patelnia; (slang): draka

skim (skym) v. zbierać (śmietankę); szumować; przebiegać wzrokiem; puszczać po powierzchni; szybować; s. zbieranie; mleko zbierane; adj. zbierany

skimmer ('skymer) s. warzęchwa; cedzidło

skimp (skymp) v. skąpić

skimpy (skympy) adj. skąpy; za mały; niewystarczający

skin (skyn) s. skóra; skórka; cera; szawłok; (slang):oszust; v. zdzierać skórę; pokrywać naskórkiem; ściągać z siebie

skin-deep('skyn'di:p) adj. powierzchowny

skindiver ('skyn'dajwer) s. płetwonurek

skindiving ('skyn'dajwyŋg) s. sportowe nurkowanie (z płetwami) [skóra i kości

skinny ('skyny) adj. chudy ;

skip (skyp) v. skakać; przeskakiwać; odskakiwać; pomijać; (slang):uciekać; s. skok; przeskok; kapitan sportowy

skipper ('skyper) s. szyper; kapitan statku; skoczek; kapitan drużyny

skirt ('ske:rt) s. spódnica;
poła; wulg.:kobietka; przepona; brzeg; v. jechać brzegiem;
obchodzić; leżec na skraju
skit ('skyt) s. skecz; satyra;
mnóstwo
skoal (skoul) excl.:na zdrowie!
skull (skal) s. czaszka
sky (skaj) s. niebo; klimat
skyjack ('skaj,dżaek) s. porwanie samolotu w locie; v. porwać samolot w locie(uprowadzać)
skyjacker ('skaj,dżaeker) s.
pirat powietrzny
skylark ('skajla:rk) s. skowronek; v. dokazywać; swawolić
skylight ('skajlajt) s. okno
dające górne światło; okno
w suficie
skyscraper ('skaj.skrejper) s.
drapacz chmur
skywards ('skajłerdz) adv.
ku niebu
slab ('slaeb) s. płytka; v. kra-
jac na płytki (kromki)
slack (slaek) adj. luźny; wolny; rozlazły; opieszały; ospały; leniwy; niedbały;
v. zluźniać; zwalniać; popuszczać; zaniedbywać; gasić (np.
ogień); s. luźna część; lenistwo; zastój; bezczelność;
miał węglowy ;zwis;impertynencja
slacken (slaeken) v. rozluźniac
(się); zwalniać; poluźniać
(się); popuszczać; zaniedbywać; gasić (np. wapno)
slacks (slaeks) pl. (luźne)
spodnie
slain (slejn) zabity; zob.slay
slake (slejk) v. gasić (np.
wapno); wywierać (np.zemstę)
slam (slaem) v. zatrzasnąć (się)
(slang) krytykować ostro; pobić; s. trzaśnięcie; ostra
krytyka; ciupa
slang (slaeng) s. gwara; żargon;
slang; adj. gwarowy; żargonowy;
v. nawymyślać komuś
slangy (slaengy) adj. gwarowy
slant (sla:nt).s. pochyłość;
skos; tendencja; punkt widze-

nia; spojrzenie; adj. ukosny;
v. isć skośnie; pochylać (się);
odchylać (się); być nachylonym
slap (slaep) s. klaps; plaśnię-
cie; v. plasnąć; dać klapsa;
uderzyć; narzucić; adv. nagle;
prościutko; regularnie
slapstick ('slaep,styk) s. laska
arlekina; błazeńska komedia
slash ('slaesz) v. pokiereszować; przeciąć; hłostać; smagać;
walić; ciąć; s. cięcie; szrama;
przecięcie; wyrąb; odpadki
drzewne; porosłe (krzakami) moczary
slate(slejt) s. łupek; dachówka
łupkowa; tabliczka do pisania;
lista (kandydatów w USA); v.po-
krywac dachówkami; umieszczać
na liście kandydatów; łajać;
wymyślac; krytykować
slate pencil ('slejt'pensl) s.
rysik
slattern ('slaete:rn) s. brudas;
flejtuch; kocmołuch
slaughter ('slo:ter) v. rznąć;
zabijać; wymordować; s. ubój;
rzeź; masakra
Slav (sla:w) adj. słowiański
slave (slejw) adj. niewolniczy;
s. niewolnik; v. harować
slavery ('slejwery) s. niewol-
nictwo
slay; slew; slain (slej; slu:,
slejn) v. zabić; uśmiercać
sled (sled) s. sanie; v. wozić
saniami
sledge hammer ('sledż-haemer)
s. oburęczny młot
sleek (sli:k) adj. gładki; uli-
zany; v. gładzić; wygładzać
sleep; slept; slept (sli:p;
slept; slept)
sleep (sli:p) v. spać; spoczywać; dawać nocleg; s. sen;
spanie; drzemka
sleep off ('sli:p,of) s. ode-
spać ∫wtyczka (szpiegowska etc)
sleeper ('sli:per) s. człowiek
śpiący; dźwigar; potencjalny
przedmiot rozgłosu;truteń;leń
sleeping-bag ('sli:pyng,baeg)
s. śpiwór

sleeping car ('sli:pyng,ca:r)
s. wagon sypialny

sleeping partner ('sli:pyng-
'pa:rtner) s. cichy wspólnik

sleeping pill ('sli:pyng,pyl)
s. pigułka nasenna

sleepless ('sli:plys) adj. bezsenny

sleepwalker ('sli:p,ło:ker) s.
lunatyk

sleepy ('sli:py) adj. śpiący

sleet (sli:t) s. słota; deszcz
ze śniegiem; gołoledź

sleeve (sli:w) s. rękaw; tuleja; łuska; nasadka; tuba;
zanadrze

sleeved ('sli:wd) adj. z ręka-
wami

sleigh (slej) v. saneczkować
(się); jechać saniami

slender ('slender) adj. wysmukły;szczupły; wiotki; nikły;
skromny; niewielki; słaby

slept (slept) v. zob. sleep

slew (slu:) v. zob. slay

slice (slajs) s. kromka; płatek;
plasterek; kawałek; łopatka
kuchenna; v. krajać na kromki;
kawałki etc. przecinać; wiosłować; wyjmować łopatką

slick (slyk) adj. gładki; tłusty; oślizgły; miły; pociągający; pierwszorzędny; adv. gładko; prościutko; s. tłusta plama (na morzu); szerokie dłuto

slicker ('slyker) s. gładki
płaszcz od deszczu; oszust

slid (slyd) v. zob. slide

slide; slid; slid (slajd; slyd;
slyd)

slide (slajd).v. suwać (się);
sunąć (się); ślizgać (się);
s. ślizganie się; suwak; pro-
wadnica ślizgowa; poślizg;
przeźrocze; zrzutnia

slide rule('slajd,ru:l) s. suwak logarytmiczny

slight (slajt) adj. wątły; niewielki; drobny; skromny; nieznaczny; v. lekceważyć;
s. lekceważenie

slim (slym) adj.szczupły; wysmukły; słaby; (slang):chytry;
v. wyszczuplać; odchudzać (się)

slime (slajm) s. szlam; muł;
śluz; płynna smoła ziemna;
v. zamulać; odmulać; zwilżać
(np. śliną)

slimy (slajmy) adj. mulisty;
zamulony; oblesny; oślizgły

sling; slung; slung (slyng;
sląg; sląg)

sling (slyng) s. proca; rzut;
pętla (np. do ładowania dźwigiem); temblak; rzemień do
strzelby itp. v. rzucać;
strzelać z procy; podnosić na
pętli; zawieszać na (np. rze-
mieniu)

slinger ('slynger) s. procarz

slinky ('slynky) adj. ukradko-
wy; (slang):mający ruchy węża

slip; slipped; slipped (slyp;
slypd; slypd)

slip (slyp) v. pośliznąć (się);
wyśliznąć (się); ześliznąć
(się); popełnić nietakt; zrobić błąd; przepuścić (np.okaz-
je); wymknąć się; zerwać się;
zapomnieć; spuszczać (np. ze
smyczy); s. poślizg; potknięcie; pomyłka; błąd; przemówienie się; zsuw; halka; świstek
(papieru); pochylnia

slip off ('slyp,of) v. zdejmować; rozbierać się; ześlizgiwać się; spadać

slip on ('slyp,on) v. wdziewać

slip out ('slyp,aut) v. wymknąć się

slip up ('slyp,ap) s. błąd; za-
chwianie się; przemówienie się;
zsuw; ślizg; v. zrobić błąd;
pomylić się; potknąć się

slipper ('slyper) s. pantofel

slippery ('slypery) adj. śliski; niebezpieczny; ryzykowny;
nieuczciwy; nieczysty; drażliwy; delikatny; wykrętny;
chytry

slit; slit; slit (slyt; slyt;
slyt)

slit (slyt) v. rozszczepić;
rozedrzeć wzdłuż; s. szpara;
szczelina; rozcięcie
slobber ('slober) s. ślina; roz-
czulenie; v. oslinic się; roz-
czulic się
slogan ('slougen) s. slogan;
hasło; powiedzonko (np. rekla-
mowe)
sloop (slu:p) s. slup (łódź)
slop (slop) v. rozlewać; przepełniać płynem; rozpryskiwać;
s. kałuża; brudna woda; pomyje; lura
slop over ('slop,ouwer) v.
przelewać się przez wierzch
slope (sloup) s. pochyłosc;
spadek; nachylenie; spadzis-
tosc; stok; skarpa; zbocze;
pochylnia; v. byc pochylonym;
miec nachylenie; nachylać;
pochylac; wałęsac się; łazi-
kować
sloping (sloupyng) adj. pochyły; skosny
sloppy ('slopy) adj. błotnisty;
pochlapany; zaniedbany; rozlazły; ckliwy
slot (slot) s. szczelina; rozcięcie; trop; ślad; v. roz-
ciąc; naciąć; wyżłobic
sloth (slous) s. lenistwo; le-
niwiec
slot-machine ('slotme,szi:n)
s. (grający lub sprzedający)
automat na monety
slouch (slaucz) s. przygarbie-
nie; niedbała postawa; wałkoń;
v. garbić się; isc ociężale;
opuszczac rondo kapelusza
slough (slau) s. bagno; trzęsawisko
slaugh (slaw) v. leniec; zrzucać skorę
sloven ('slawn) s. niechlujny;
brudas; flejtuch; fuszer;
partacz
slovenly ('slawnly) adj. niechlujny; partacki
slow (slou) adj. powolny; nie-
gorliwy; nieskory; opieszały;
leniwy; tępy; nudny; adv. wolno; powoli

slow down ('slou,dałn) v. zwalniac; przyhamować
slow-motion ('slou'mouszyn) s.
zwolnione tempo; w zwolnionym
tempie
slowworm ('slou,łe:rm) s. padalec
sluggish ('slagysz) adj. ospały; leniwy; powolny
sluice ('slu:s) s. śluza; sciek;
rynna; v. puszczać wodę (ze
stawu etc). spłukiwać; zalewać; chlusnąć; spływać ze
śluzy
slums (slamz) s. dzielnica nędzy
slumber ('slamber) v. spac lekko; drzemac; s. sen; drzemka;
spokój; bezczynnosc
slung (slang) v. zob . sling
slush (slasz) s. chlapa; odpadki tłuszczowe; smar; fundusz
z odpadków; smar; fundusz na
przekupstwo; v. opryskac; wysmarować; pokrywac zaprawą
slut (slat) s. flejtuch; kocmołuch; plucha; pinda; szmata;
flądra; suka
sly (slaj) ad. szczwany; chytry;
filuterny
slyboots ('slajbu:ts) s. urwis;
spryciarz; chytrus (udający
głupiego)
smack (smaek) s. posmak; odrobina; trzask; mlasnięcie;
cmoknięcie; klaps; jednomasz-
towiec; v. cmokac; strzelac
z bata; dac w pysk; oblizywac
(wargi)
smacking ('smaekyng) adj.
zgrabny; raźny; mocny (wiatr)
small (smo:l) adj. mały; drobny; niewielki; skromny; ciasny;
nieliczny; nieznaczny; małostkowy; adv. drobno; na małą ska-
lę; cicho; s. drobna rzecz;
mała częsc
small change ('smo:l,czejndż)
s. drobne (pieniądze)
small hours ('smo:l,auers) pl.
bardzo wczesne ranne godziny
smallish ('smo:lysz) adj. ma-
ławy

small of the back ('smo:l,ow-
'dy,baek) s. krzyże
smallpox ('smo:l,poks) s. ospa
smart (sma:rt) adj. dotkliwy;
cięty; zreczny; żwawy; dowcipny; szykowny; zgrabny; elegancki; v. piec; palic (np.
w oczy); cierpieć; szczypać;
parzyć; odczuwać boleśnie;
pokutować
smart aleck ('sma:rt,alek) s.
Jedrek-medrek
smash (smaesz) v. rozbić; rozwalić; roztrząskać; zmiażdżyc;
potłuc; palnąć; rozgromić;
upadać: zbankrutować; ścinać
piłkę
smashing ('smaeszyng) adj. nadzwyczajny; niezwykły
smattering ('smaeteryn) s. zna-
jomosci po łebkach; wiedza
powierzchowna
smear (smier) v. osmarować;
zasmarować; wlepić komuś sma-
ry; s. plama; smar
smell; smelt; smelled (smel;
smelt; smeld)
smell (smel) s. węch; won; zapach; odor; smród; v. pachnieć; tracić; miec zapach;
śmierdzieć; miec powonienie;
obwachiwać; czuc zapach;
zwietrzyć; zwąchać; poczuc
smelt (smelt) v. sob. smell;
stapiac; wytapiac (metal);
s. stynka (ryba)
smile (smajl) v. usmiechać się;
s. usmiech
smite; smote; smitten (smajt;
smout; 'smytn)
smite (smajt) v. uderzać; po-
razic; powalic; zabic; nękac;
karac; oczarować; s. cios;
uderzenie;sprobo
smith (smys) s. kowal
smithy (smysy) s. kuźnia
smitten ('smytn) v. zob.smite
smock (smok) s. chałat; kitel;
v. ubierac chałat; ozdabiać
rysunkiem szachownicy
smog (smog) s. mgła zanieczysz-
czona dymem (Londyn,Los Angeles)

smoke (smouk) s. dym; palenie;
papieros; v. dymic; kopcic; wy-
kurzac; wyjawiac; wykadzac; oka-
dzać; okopcic; uwędzic; przypa-
lac; palic (tytoń)
smoke-dried ('smouk,drajd) adj.
wędzony
smoker ('smouker) s. palący; pa-
lacz
smoking ('smoukyng) s. palenie
(tytoniu)
smoking car ('smoukyng,ka:r) s.
wagon dla palących
smoking compartment ('smoukyng-
kaem,pa:rtment) s. przedział
dla palących
smoky ('smouky) adj. dymiący;
przydymiony; zadymiony; okopcony
smolder ('smoulder) v. tlic się;
s. tlenie się; dym
smooch (smu:cz) v. brudzic; walac; całować się; sciskac się;
migdalic się
smooth (smu:s) adj. gładki; spokojny; łagodny; v. gładzic; łagodzic; adv. gładko; s. wygła-
dzenie
smooth down ('smu:s,dałn) v.
wygładzic; uspakajac (się)
smother ('smadzer) v. stłumic;
stłamsic; obcałowywać; zatuszowac; okrywać
smudge (smadż) v. poplamic; zabrudzic; s. plama; kleks; brud
smuggle ('smagl) v. przemycac
smuggler ('smagler) s. przemytnik
smut (smat) v. poplamic; s. brud
z sadzy; sprosności; tłuste
kawały; śniec
smutty ('smaty) adj. sprosny;
brudny od sadzy
snack (snaek) s. zakąska
snack bar ('snaek,ba:r) s. bufet; bar
snafu (snae'fu:) v. zabałaganic;
s. bałagan (slang)
snail (snejl) s. ślimak
snake (snejk) s. wąż; v. wic
sie; wlec (za sobą);pełzać jak
wąz;przybierać kształt węża

snap (snaep) v. łapać zębami;
warczeć; błysnąć; urwać; złamać; chwytać; zapalić się do;
przerwać szorstko; poprawić
się; mieć się na baczności;
zatrzasnąć (się); strzelać
z bicza; pstryknąć; sfotogra-
fować; spiesznie załatwiać;
machnąć ręką lekceważąco;
s. ugryzienie; warknięcie;
trzask; zatrzask; dociskacz;
zdjęcie; rzecz łatwa; adj.
prosty; łatwy; doraźny; nagły
snap bolt ('snaep,boult) s.
zatrzask u drzwi
snap fastener('snaep,fa:sner)
s. zatrzask
snappish ('snaepysz) adj.
zgryźliwy; kostyczny
snappy ('snaepy) adj. zgryźliwy; kostyczny; żwawy; prędki
snapshot ('snaepszot) s. zdjęcie migawkowe; strzał na chybił trafił
snare (sneer) v. usidłać; łapać w sidła; s. sidła; pułapka
snarl (sna:rl) s. warknięcie;
plątanina; v. warczeć; plątać (się); zaplątać; robić
zator
snatch (snaecz) v. złapać;
wyrwać; s. złapanie; urywek;
strzęp; mig
sneak (sni:k) v. chyłkiem zakradać się; przemykać się;
zerkać; zwiać; s. podły
tchórz
sneakers ('sni:kers) pl. trze-
wiki; trampki
sneer (snier) v. uśmiechać się
szyderczo; kpić; drwić; s.
szyderstwo; szydercze spojrzenie
sneeze (sni:z) v. kichać;
s. kichnięcie
sniff (snyf) v. prychać; po-
ciągąc nosem; krzywić się na
coś; powąchać; obwąchać; zwąchać; wyczuć; s. prychnięcie;
pociągnięcie nosem

sniffle ('snyfl) s. katar; po-
ciąganie nosem; v. pociągać
nosem
snipe (snajp) s. bekas; strzał
z ukrycia; v. z ukrycia: strzelać; trafić, zabić
sniper ('snajper) s. strzelec
wyborowy; strzelec z ukrycia
snivel ('snywel) s. śluz z nosa;
biadolenie; udawanie; v. smarkać się; skamleć; biadolić;
płakać; rozczulać się
snob (snob) s. człowiek wywyższa-
jący się
snoop (snu:p) v. myszkować;
wścibiać nos; s. szpicel
snoop around ('snu:p,e'raund)
v. przemyszkowywać; szpiegować
snooze (snu:z) s. drzemka;
v. drzemać; zdrzemnąć się
snore (sno:r) v. chrapać; s.
chrapanie
snort (sno:rt) v. parskać;
s. parsknięcie
snout (snaut) s. ryj; pysk; morda; wylot
snow (snou) s. snieg; (slang):
kokaina; heroina; v. ośnieżyć;
śnieg pada; zasypać śniegiem;
pobić na głowę; omamiać
snowball ('snoubo:l) s. kula
śnieżną; v. bić się śniegiem;
rosnąć jak lawina
snow blindness ('snou'blajndnys)
s. śnieżna ślepota
snowdrift ('snou'dryft) s. zas-
pa śnieżna
snowdrop ('snoudrop) s. śnie-
życzka
snow job ('snou,dżob) s. naciąganie pochlebstwami
snow-white ('snou'hłajt) adj.
śnieżnobiały
snowy ('snoły) adj. śnieżny;
śniegowy
snub (snab) v. ofuknąć; dać po
nosie; traktować lekceważąco;
nagle zatrzymać; adj. perkaty;
zadarty nos; s. bura; ofuknięcie;ostra odprawa;afront;ucie-
ranie nosa komuś;przywodzenie
kogoś do porządku

snuff (snaf) s. tabaka; proszek do zażywania przez nos; zapach; opalony koniec knota; v. zażywać tabakę; pociągać nosem; czyścić koniec knota

snug (snag) adj. przytulny; wygodny; ukryty; v. tulić się; zrobić przytulnym

snuggle ('snagl) v. przytulić się

so (sou) adv. tak; a więc; w takim razie; a zatem; też; tak samo; bardzo to; także; excl.: to tak ! no, no !

so far ('sou fa:r) adv. jak dotąd ; jak do tej pory

soak (souk) v. moczyć (się); nasycać (się); przenikać; namoknąć; (slang):wyciągać (od kogoś) pieniądze; mocno uderzyć; s. moczenie (się); woda do moczenia; popijawa; zastaw

soap (soup) s. mydło; pochlebstwo; wazelinowanie się (komuś); v. mydlić (się); pochlebiać; adj. mydlany; mydlarski

soap box ('soup,boks) s. skrzynia od mydła; mównica (np. uliczna). v. przemawiać na ulicy, w parku etc.

soap opera ('soup'opere) s. (popołudniowe) przedstawienie radiowe lub telewizyjne pełne małżeńskich kryzysów, tragedii, cierpień, płaskiej czułostkowości i melodramatycznych zakończeń

soar (so:r) v. wznosić się; osiągać wyżyny; iść w górę (np. ceny)

sob (sob) v. łkać; szlochać; s. łkanie; szloch

sober ('souber) adj. trzeźwy; wstrzemięźliwy; stateczny; zrównoważony; rzeczowy; poważny; spokojny; v. trzeźwieć; wytrzeźwieć; wytrzeźwiać ; otrzeźwieć; opanować się

sober up ('souber,ap) v. wytrzeźwieć

sober-minded ('souber,majndyd) adj.stateczny; zrównoważony

so-called ('sou-ko:ld) adj. tak zwany

soccer ('soker) s. piłka nożna

sociable ('souszebl) adj. towarzyski; przyjacielski; gromadny; stadny

social ('souszel) adj. społeczny; socjalny; s. zebranie towarzyskie

social democrat ('souszel'demekraet) s. socjaldemokrata

socializm ('souszelyzem) s. socjalizm

social security ('souszelsy'kjueryty) s. ubezpieczenia społeczne

socialist ('souszelyst) s. socjalista; adj. socjalistyczny

social worker ('souszel'łerker) s. pracownik społeczny; pracownik urzędu opieki społecznej

socialize ('souszelajz) v. upaństwowić; uspołecznić

social welfare ('souszel,łelfeer) s. opieka społeczna

society (so'sajety) s. towarzystwo; społeczeństwo; społeczność; spółka (np. akcyjna)

sock (sok) s. skarpetka; cios; szturchaniec; v. cisnąć w kogoś; uderzyć; walnąć; adv. prosto (np. w nos)

socket ('sokyt) s. oprawka; oczodół; zębodół; gniazdko; wydrążenie

sod (sod) s. darń; darnina; wulg.; skurwysyn; sodomita

sofa ('soufe) s. kanapa; sofa

soft (soft) adj. miękki: delikatny; przyciszony; łagodny; słaby; głupi; wygodny; zmięknąć

soft drink ('soft,drynk) s. napój bezalkoholowy

soft goods ('soft,gu:ds) pl. tekstylia

soften ('softn) v. zmiękczyć; osłabić; złagodzić; złagodnieć; zmięknąć

soil (sojl) s.gleba; rola; ziemia; brud;plama; v.zabrudzić; powalać; poplamić;wysmarować

sojourn ('sedże:rn) s. pobyt;
v. przebywać; zatrzymywać (się)

sold (sould) v. sprzedany; zob.
sell

soldier ('souldżer) s. żołnierz
najemnik; adj. żołnierski;
v. służyć w wojsku

sole (soul) s. podeszwa; podwa-
lina; zelówka; stopa; spodek;
sola; adj. jedyny; wyłączny

solemn ('solem) adj. solenny;
uroczysty; poważny

solicit (se'lysyt) v. prosić;
zwracać się (o coś); nagabywać; ubiegać się; zwracać (np.
uwagę)

solicitor (se'lysyter) s. radca prawny; akwizytor; agent
firmowy

solicitous (se'lysytes) adj.
pragnący; troszczący się o...;
niepokojący się

solicitude (se'lysytju:d) s.
troska; pieczołowitość;
troskliwość

solid ('solyd) adj. stały; masywny; lity; trwały; mocny;
rzetelny; solidny; ciało stałe; bryła

solidarity ('soly'daeryty) s.
solidarność

solidity (so'lydyty) s. masyw-
ność; trwałość; rzetelność

soliloquy (se'lylekły) s. monolog; mówienie do siebie

solitary ('solytery) adj. samotny; odosobniony; odludny;
pojedynczy; wyjątkowy; adj.
pustelnik; odludek; samotnik

solitude ('solytju:d) s. samotność; osamotnienie; odludne
miejsce

solo ('soulou) adj. adv. w pojedynkę; adj. jednoosobowy;
s. solo

soloist ('soulyst) s. solista

soluble ('soljubl) adj. rozpuszczalny; możliwy do rozwiązania

solution (so'ljuszyn) s. rozczyn; roztwór; rozwiązanie
(problemu)

solve (solw) v. rozwiązywać
(np. problemy)

solvent ('solwent) adj. wypłacalny; rozpuszczający; s.
rozpuszczalnik

somber ('somber) adj. mroczny;
ciemny; posępny; ponury

some (sam) adj. jakiś; pewien;
niejaki; nieco; trochę; kilku;
kilka; kilkoro; niektórzy;
niektóre; sporo; niemało; nie
byle jaki; adv. niemało; mniej
więcej; jakieś; pron.: niektórzy; niektóre; kilku; kilka

some more ('sam,mor) exp.: nieco
więcej

somebody ('sambedy) pron. ktoś;
s. ktoś ważny

someday ('samdej) adv. kiedyś

somehow ('samhał) adv. jakoś;
w jakiś sposób

someone ('samłan) pron. ktoś;
s. ktoś

somersault ('samerso:lt) s.
salto; koziołek

something ('samsyng) s. coś;
coś niecoś; ważna osoba; adv.
trochę; nieco; (slang):co się
zowie

sometime ('samtajm) adj. były;
adv. kiedyś; swego czasu

sometimes ('samtajmz) adv. niekiedy; czasem; czasami

someway ('sam,łej) adv. jakoś

somewhat ('samhłot) adv. nieco;
do pewnego stopnia; niejaki

somewhere ('samhłe:r) adv.
gdzieś

son (san) s. syn

song (song)s. pieśń; śpiew

song-bird ('songbe:rd) s. ptak
śpiewający

song-book ('songbuk) s. śpiewnik

sonic ('sonyk) adj. dźwiękowy

sonic boom ('sonyk,bu:m) s.
grzmot samolotu przekraczają-
cego szybkość dźwięku

son-in-law ('san,ynlo:) s. zięć

sonnet ('sonyt) s. sonet

soon (su:n) adv.wnet; niebawem;
wkrótce; zaraz; niedługo

sooner ('su:ner) adv. wczes-
niej; adj. chętnie
soot (sut) s. sadza; kopeć;
v. brudzić sadzą; użyźniać
sadzą
soothe (su:z) v. uspakajać;
uciszać
sooty ('suty) adj. okopcony;
zakopcony; czarny jak sadza
sophisticated (se'fystykejtyd)
adj. wyszukany; wyrafinowany;
wymyślny; doświadczony
sophomore ('sofemo:r) s. student drugiego roku
sorcerer ('so:rserer) s. czarownik; czarodziej
sorceress ('so:rserys) s. czarodziejka
sorcery ('so:rsery) s. czary
sordid ('so:rdyd) adj. brudny
(np. zysk); nikczemny; podły;
skąpy
sore (so:r) adj. bolesny; drażliwy; wrażliwy; dotkliwy; dotknięty; złoszczący się; zmartwiony; adv. srodze; bardzo;
akrutnie
sore throat ('so:r,trout) s.
zapalenie gardła; ançina
sorrow ('sorou) s. zmartwienie;
żal; smutek ; narzekanie;
v. martwić się; boleć za...
sorrowful ('sorouful) adj.
smutny; zmartwiony; przykry
sorry ('so:ry) adj. żałujący;
zmartwiony; przygnębiony;
nędzny; marny
sorority (se'ro:ryty) s. korporacja studentek (w USA)
sort (so:rt) s. rodzaj; gatunek; sorta; v. sortować
sortie ('so:rty) s. wypad wojskowy; lot bojowy
so-so ('sou-sou) adj. taki sobie; adv. tak sobie
sought (so:t) v. zob. seek
soul (soul) s. dusza
soulless (soulys) adj. bezduszny
sound (saund) s. dźwięk; ton;
szmer; cieśnina wodna; pęcherz
pławny; sonda; v. dźwięczeć;

brzmieć; grać (na trąbce); bić
na alarm; głosić; opukiwać;
wymawiać; zabierać głos; chwalić się; sondować; zanurzać
się do dna
soundless ('saundlys) adj. bezdźwięczny
soundproof ('saundpru:f) adj.
dźwiękoszczelny
soundwave ('saundłejw) s. fala
dźwiękowa
soup (su:p) s. zupa
sour ('sauer) adj. kwaśny;
skwaszony; cierpki; v. kisnąć;
kwasić się; zniechęcać się
source (so:rs) z. źródło
south (saus) adj. południowy;
z. południe; adv. na południe
southeast ('saus'i:st) s. południowy wschód; adj. południowo-
wschodni; adv. na południowy
wschód
southern ('sadzern) adj. południowy; s. południowiec
southernmost (,sadzern'moust)
adj. najbardziej na południe
southwards ('sausłerdz) adv.
ku południowi; na południe
southwest ('saus'łest) s. południowy zachód; adj. południowo-zachodni; adv. na południowy zachód
southwesterly ('saus'łesterly)
adj. południowo zachodni
souvenir ('su:venier) s. pamiątka
sovereign ('sawryn) s. suweren;
władca; adj. suwerenny; wyniosły; najwyższy
sovereignty('sawrenty) s. su-
werenność; zwierzchnictwo;
najwyższa władza
Soviet ('souwjet) adj. sowiecki;
radziecki
sow; sowed; sown(sou; soud;
soun)
sow (sou) v. siać; zasiewać; posiać
sow (sau) s. maciora; koryto
odlewnicze
sown (soun) v. zob. sow
spa (spa:) s. zdrojowisko; zdrój
mineralny; (USA) sport zdrowotny za opłatą

space (spejs) s. przestrzeń;
miejsce; obszar; odstęp; okres;
przeciąg (czasu); chwila;
v. robić odstępy; rozstawiać
spacecraft ('spejs,kra:ft) s.
pojazd międzyplanetarny
spaceship ('spejs,szyp) s. statek międzyplanetarny(kosmiczny)
space suit ('spejs;sju:t) s.
kombinezon międzyplanetarny
spacious ('spejszes) adj. przestronny; obszerny
spade (spejd) s. łopata; v. kopać łopatą
spades (spejdz) pl. piki (w kar-
tach)
spadework ('spejd-łe:rk) s.
praca przygotowawcza
span; spanned; spanned (spaen;
spaend; spaend)
span (spaen) v. zob. spin; sięgać (np. przez rzekę); rozciągać się (np. nad rzeką); obejmować (pamięcią); mierzyć pię-
dzią; posuwać się stopniowo;
łączyć brzegi; s. piędz; rozpiętość; przeswit; przęsło;
przeciąg (czasu) zasięg; roz-
ciągłość; para; zaprzęg
spangle ('spaengl) s. świecidełko; błyskotka; v. pokrywać
świecidełkami; błyszczeć świecidełkami
spangled ('spaengld) adj. pokryty (świecidełkami)
Spanish ('spaenysz) adj. hiszpański
spank ('spaenk) s. klaps; v. dawać klapsa; popędzać klapsami;
iść kłusem
spanking (spaenkyng) s. skoro-
bicie; lanie; adj. chyży; zamaszysty; silny; solidny; świetny; adv. bardzo (slang)
spanner ('spaener) s. ścięgno
(mostu); klucz do nakrętek
gąsienica miernikowa
spare (speer) v. oszczędzać; zaoszczędzić; odstępować; obywać
się; zachować; przeznaczać;
szanować (uczucia); szczędzić;
a. zapasowy; oszczędny; skromny;

drobny; szczupły; wolny (np.
czas) s. część zapasowa; koło
zapasowe
spare time ('speer,tajm) s.
wolny czas
spare tire ('speer,tajer) s.
koło zapasowe
sparing ('speeryng) adj. oszczędny; wstrzemięźliwy
spark (spa:rk) s. iskra; zapłon;
wesołek; zalotnik; v. iskrzyć
się; sypać iskrami; zapalać się;
dawać początek; zalecać się
grać galanta
spark plug ('spa:rk,plag) s.
świeca samochodowa (zapłonowa)
sparrow ('spaerou) s. wróbel
sparse (spa:rs) adj. rzadki;
z rzadka; rozsiany; szczupły
spasm ('spaezem) s. skurcz;
spazm; napad (kaszlu)
spastic ('spaestyk) adj. skur-
czowy; spazmatyczny; chory na
paraliż kurczowy
spat (spaet) v. zob . spit;
kłócić się; dawać klapsy; składać jaja (przez ostrygi); s.
jaja mięczaków; kłótnia;
klaps; lekki cios
spatial ('spejszel) adj. przestrzenny
spawn (spo:n) s. ikra; skrzek;
nasienie; v. składać (ikrę;
skrzek); wylęgać się; płodzić;
zasiewać grzybnię
spayed (spejd) adj.(samica)
z usuniętymi jajnikami; bez-
płodna: wytrzebiona
speak; spoke; spoken (spi:k;
spo:k;'spoken)
speak (spi:k) v. mówić; przemawiać; szczekać na rozkaz; grać;
sygnalizować do statku
speak out ('spi:k,aut) v. wypowiadać (się); mówić otwarcie;
mówić głośno
speak up ('spi:k,ap) v. wypowie-
dzieć się bez osłonek
speaker ('spi:ker) s. mówca;
głośnik; marszałek sejmu; przewodniczący

spear (spier) s. dzida; włócznia; oszczep; kopia; oścień; zdźbło; v. przebijać dzidą; kłuć; wystrzelić w górę

spearhead ('spierhed) s. ostrze dzidy; czołówka; v. prowadzić; być na czele

special ('speszel) adj. specjalny; wyjątkowy; osobliwy; dodatkowy; nadzwyczajny; s. dodatkowy autobus; nadzwyczajne wydanie; reklamowa dzienna zniżka ceny w sklepie

specialist ('speszelyst) s. specjalista

speciality (,speszy'aelyty) s. specjalność; specjalna cecha

specialize ('speszelajz) v. wyspecjalizować (się); wyszczególniać; precyzować; różniczkować(się); ograniczać (się)

specially ('speszely) adv. specjalnie; szczególnie

specialty ('speszelty) s.specjalność; specjalizacja

species ('spi:szi:z) s. gatunek; rodzaj; postać czegoś

specific (spy'syfyk) adj. określony; wyraźny; gatunkowy; charakterystyczny; specyficzny

specify ('spesyfaj) v. wyszczególniać; precyzować; konkretyzować; sporządzić specyfikację

specimen ('spesymyn) s. okaz; przykład; wzór; typ; próba; numer okazowy

spectacle ('spektekl) s. widowisko

spectacles ('spektekls) pl. okulary

spectacular (spek'taekjuler) adj. widowiskowy; efektowny; sensacyjny; okazały; s. film widowiskowy "wielki"

spectator ('spektejter) s. widz

speculate ('spekjulejt) v. spekulować; rozmyślać nad..; rozważać

speculation (,spekju'lejszyn) s. spekulacja; domysł; rozmyślanie

sped (sped) v. zob. speed

speech (spi:cz) s. mowa; przemówienie; język; wymowa; przemowa

speechless ('spi:czlys) adj. (chwilowo) niemy; oniemiały; (slang): pijany (kompletnie)

speed; sped; sped (spi:d; sped; sped)

speed (spi:d) v. pospieszyć; popędzić; pędzić; odprawić; kierować spiesznie; popierać (np. sprawę); s. szybkość; prędkość; bieg

speedboat ('spi:dbout) s. ślizgacz

speed limit ('spi:d,lymyt) s. ograniczenie szybkości

speedometer (spi'domyter) s. szybkościomierz

speed up ('spi:d,ap) v. przyspieszyć; s. przyspieszenie

speedy ('spi:dy) adj. szybki

spell; spelled; spelt (spel; speld; spelt)

spell (spel) v. przeliterować (poprawnie); napisać ortograficznie; znaczyć; mozolnie odczytywać; sylabizować; zaczarować; urzec; dać (wytchnienie); odpoczywać; zaczarować; pracować na zmiany; s. chwila pracy; chwila; okres; pewien czas; zaklęcie; czar

spellbound ('spel baund) adj. zaczarowany; urzeczony; oczarowany

spelling ('spelyng) s. pisownia

spelt (spelt) v. zob. spell

spend; spent; spent (spend; spent; spent)

spend (spend) v. wydawać (np. pieniądze); spędzać (czas); zużywać (się); wyczerpywać; tracić (np. siły); składać ikrę

spent (spent) v. wyczerpany; wydany; zob. spend

sperm (spe:rm) s. sperma; nasienie męskie

spew (spju:) v. wypluwać; wymiotować; wyrzucać z siebie

sphere (sfier) s. kula; globus;
ciało niebieskie; sfera (np.
działalności)

spice (spajs) s. wonne korzenie;
pikanteria; v. przyprawiać
korzeniami; dodawać pikanterii

spicy ('spajsy) adj. korzenny;
zaprawiony korzeniami; aromatyczny; pikantny; nieco nieprzyzwoity; elegancki; żywy;
ostry

spider (spajder) s. pająk

spike (spajk) s. ćwiek; bretn-
al; kolec; gwoźdz do szyn;
szpic; ostrze; fanatyk religijny; kłos; v. przymocowywać
gwoździami; zaostrzać końce;
ranic kolcami; zagważdzać
armatę; zaprzeczać pogłoskom;
odpierać; zakrapiać alkoholem;
wspinac się na słup ostrymi
okuciami (na butach)

spiky ('spajky) adj. kolczasty;
wydłużony; ostro zakończony;
fanatyczny religijnie

spill; spilled; spilt (spyl;
spyld; spylt)

spill (spyl) v. rozlewać (się):
rozsypywać (się); uchylać żagiel z wiatru; wyśpiewać; wygadać (się); powiedzieć
wszystko; popsuc sprawę; s.roz-
lanie; rozsypanie; ilosc roz-
lana; ilosc rozsypana; odłamek;
zatyczka; upadek; fidybus do
zapalania świec

spilt (spylt) v. zob. spill

spin; spun; span (spyn; span;
spaen)

spin (spyn) v. snuć; prząść;
kręcić (się); puszczać bąka;
toczyć na tokarni; łowić ryby
na błyszczkę; zawirować;
s. kręcenie (się); zawirowanie;
ruch wirowy; przejażdżka; korkociąg (w locie)

spinach ('spynycz) s. szpinak

spinal column ('spajnel'kolem)
s. stos pacierzowy ;kręgosłup

spinal cord ('spajnel'ko:rd)
s. rdzeń kręgowy

spindle ('spyndl) s. wrzeciono;
oś; wał; 14400 jardów lnu;
15120 jardów bawełny; v. miec
kształt wrzecionowaty

spine ('spajn) s. kręgosłup;
grzbiet; cierń

spinning mill ('spynyŋg,myl)
s. przędzarnia

spinster ('spynster) s. stara
panna

spiny ('spajny) adj. ciernisty;
kolczasty; trudny

spiral ('spajerel) s. spirala;
adj. spiralny; v. poruszać się
spiralnie; szybko iść w górę
(np. ceny); nadawać kształt
spirali

spire ('spajer) s. iglica; hełm
wieży; zwoj; spirala; ostry
szczyt; szpic; pęd; v. strzelac w górę; nakładać hełm na
wieżę

spirit ('spyryt) s. duch; intelekt; umysł; zjawa; odwaga;
nastawienie; nastrój; v. zachęcać; ożywiać; rozweselac; zabierać (potajemnie)

spirits ('spyryts) s. spirytus;
alkohol

spirited ('spyrytyd) adj. ożywiony; z werwą; napisany
z zacięciem

spiritual ('spyryczuel) adj.
duchowy; duchowny; natchniony;
s. murzyńska pieśń religijna

spit; spat; spat (spyt; spaet;
spaet)

spit (spyt) v. pluć; zionać;
splunąć; wypluc; lekceważyc;
fuknąc; parsknac; mżyć; kropić; pryskać; nadziewać na rożen; s. plucie; ślina; parska-
nie; mżenie; jaja owadow; rożen; językowaty półwysep;
głebokość łopaty

spite (spajt) s. złość; uraz;
złośliwość; v. zrobic na złość;
in spite of= wbrew; pomimo

spiteful ('spajtful) adj. złośliwy; mściwy

spittle ('spytl) s. plwocina;
ślina

splash (splaesz) v. chlapać;
pryskać; plusnąć; rozpryskać;
upstrzyc; s. rozprysk; plusk;
zakropienie; plamka; sensacja

splash down ('splaesz,dałn) v.
wodować; s. wodowanie

spleen (spli:n) s. śledziona;
przygnębienie; splin; złość

splendid ('splendyd) adj.
wspaniały; świetny; doskonały

splendor ('splender) s. wspaniałość; przepych, blask

splint (splynt) s. łupek; szyna; patyk; kość piszczelowa;
v. wstawiać w szyny złamaną
kość

splinter ('splynter) s. drzazga;
odłamek

split; split; split (splyt;
splyt; splyt)

split (splyt) v. łupać; pękać;
rozszczepiać (się); dzielić;
oddzielać (się) odchodzić;
s. pęknięcie; rozszczepienie;
rozdwojenie; odejście

splitting ('splytyŋg) adj. roz-
sadzający; ostry; gwałtowny

splutter ('splater) v. pryskać;
opryskać; mówić bezładnie;
s. pryskanie; szybka gadanina;
zgiełk

spoil; spoilt; spoiled (spojl;
spojlt; spojld)

spoil (spojl) v. psuć (się);
zepsuć (się); (slang): kraść;
sprzątnąć; przetrącić

spoils (spojls) pl. łupy (też
w polityce)

spoilsport ('spojl'spo:rt) s.
psujący zabawę

spoilt ('spojlt) v. zob.spoil

spoke (spouk) v. zob. speak;
s. szczebel; szprycha

spoken ('spoukn) v. zob. speak

spokesman (spouksmen) s. rzecznik

sponge (spandż) s. gąbka; wycior; tampon; pieczeniarz; pasożyt; v. myć gąbką; chłonąć;
łowić gąbki; wyłudzać; wsysać;
pasożytować

sponger ('spandżer) s. pasożyt;
pieczeniarz (slang)

sponge cake ('spandż'kejk) s.
biszkopt

spongy ('spandży) adj. gąbczas-
ty

sponsor ('sponser) s. patron;
organizator; gwarant; ojciec
chrzestny; v. wprowadzać; być
gwarantem; popierać; opłacać
(np. program telewizyjny)

spontaneous (spon'tejnjes)
adj. spontaniczny; samorzutny;
naturalny; odruchowy

spook (spuk) s. zjawa; duch;
upiór

spool (spu:l) s. cewka; rolka;
szpulka; nawijać na (rolkę
etc).

spoon (spu:n) s. łyżka; v. czerpać (łyżką); durzyć się w kims

spoon out ('spu:n,aut) v. drążyć; nabierać

spoon-fed ('spu:n,fed) adj. roz-
pieszczony; łyżką karmiony

spoonful ('spu:nful) s. łyżka
czegoś

spore (spo:r) s. zarodnik;
v. wytwarzać zarodniki

sport (spo:rt) s. sport; zawody;
zabawa; rozrywka; sportowiec;
(slang): człowiek dobry, elegancki, lubiący zakładać się;
v. bawić się; uprawiać sport;
obnosić się z czymś; popisywać się; wyśmiewać się

sportive ('spo:rtyw) adj. żartobliwy

sportsman (spo:rtsmen) s.
sportowiec; myśliwy

sporty ('spo:rty) adj. (slang):
sportowy; krzykliwy (ubiór);
modny

spot (spot) s. plama; skaza;
kropka; cętka; plamka; miejsce;
lokal; odrobina; punkt; dolar;
krótkie ogłoszenie; v. plamić
(się); umiejscowić (np. zepsucie); poznawać; wyróżniać;
rozmieszczać; adj. gotowy;
gotówkowy; dorywczy

spotless ('spotlys) adj. bez
skazy

spotlight ('spotlajt) s. reflektor szczelinowy; v. rzucać światło (na coś)
spout (spaut) s. wylot; rynna;
wylew; dziobek; strumień;
pochyłe koryto; v. wyrzucać
z siebie płyn; tryskać;
chlusnąć; recytować
sprain (sprejn) s. bolesne
wykręcenie (nie zwichnięcie);
v. wykręcić
sprang (spraeŋg) v. zob.
spring
sprat (spraet) s. szprotka
(śledź); v. łowić szproty
sprawl (spro:l) v. rozwalać
się; gramolić się; rozłazić
się; rozrzucać; być rozrzu-
conym; s. rozwalenie się;
rozłażenie się; rozkrzewia-
nie się
spray (sprej) s. rozpylony
płyn; krople z rozpylacza;
płyn do rozpryskiwania;
spryskiwacz; grad (kul); gałązka; v. opryskiwać; rozpryskiwać (się)
spread (spred; spread (spred;
spred; spred)
spread (spred) v. rozpościerać (się); rozszerzać (się);
posiać; rozsmarowywać; rozkładać; pokrywać; nakrywać;
rozklejpywać; s. rozpostar-
cie; rozpiętość; zasięg;
szerokość; pasta; narzuta;
(slang): smarowidło na chleb
sprig (spryg) s. gałązka;
latorośl; młokos; szyft;
v. ozdabiać gałązkami
sprightly ('sprajtly) adj. żywy; dziarski; wesoły
spring; sprang; sprung (spryŋg;
spraeŋg; spraŋg)
spring (spryŋg) v. skakać;
sprężynować; wypłynąć; puścić
pędy (pąki); zaskoczyć; spowodować wybuch; paczyć się;
puszczać oczko; pękać; s.wios-
na; skok; sprężyna; źródło;
zdrój; prężność; adj. wiosenny; sprężynowy; źródlany

springboard ('spryŋg,bo:rd)
s. trampolina; odskocznia
springtime ('spryŋgtajm) s.
wiosna
sprinkle ('spryŋkl) v. posypać;
pokropić; s. deszczyk
sprint (sprynt) s. krótki bieg;
krótki zrywny wysiłek; v.bieg
na krótki dystans
sprinter (sprynter) s. sprinter;
biegacz krótkodystansowy
sprout (spraut) s. pęd; odrośl;
v. puszczać pędy; wyrastać
spruce (spru:s) s. świerk;
smrek; adj. elegancki; schludny; v. stroić się
sprung (spraŋg) v. zob. spring
spun (span) v. zob. spin
spur (spe:r) v. pogardliwie odtrącać; pospieszyć; popędzać;
s. odtrącenie z pogardą
sputter ('spater) v. pryskać
(śliną); bełkotać; s. pryskanie; plwociny; bełkot
spy (spaj) s. szpieg; tajniak;
szpiegowanie; v. szpiegować;
wybadać; czatować; wypatrzeć
squabble ('skłobl) s. sprzeczka; sprzeczać się
squad (skłod) s. oddział; grup-
ka; (lotny) patrol; wóz patro-
lowy; v. formować grupki
squall (skło:l) s. szkwał; kłopot; wrzask; v. wiać gwałtownie; wrzeszczec
squander ('skłonder) s. marnotrawstwo; v. trwonić; marnotrawić
square ('skłeer) s. kwadrat;
czworobok (budynków); plac;
katownik; węgielnica; adj.
kwadratowy; prostokątny; prostopadły; uporządkowany; zupełny;
uczciwy; v. robić kwadratowym
prostym; podnosić do kwadratu;
płacić (dług); adv. w sedno;
rzetelnie; wprost
squash (skłosz) v. ubijać (się);
gnieść (się); miażdżyć;
s. miazga; tłok; rodzaj tenisa;
napój owocowy; mała dynia
squat; squat; squat (skłot;
skłot; skłot)

squat (skłot) v. kucac; przy-
cupnąc; nielegalnie koczowac
na gruncie; adj. przysadzisty;
niski; szeroki; s. osoba przy-
sadzista; kucki

squeak (skłi:k) v. piszczec;
skrzypiec; mowic piskliwie;
(slang): zdradzac (sekrety);
sypac; przepychac się z trudnością; s. pisk; trudne osiągnięcie czegos

squeal (skłi:l) v. piszczec;
kwiczec; (slang): awanturowac
się; sypac; wydawac (kogos);
s. pisk; kwik; sypanie (kogos, czegos)

squeamish ('skłi:mysz) adj.
wybredny; pruderyjny; przesadny; wrażliwy

squeegee ('skłi:dżi:) s. przyrząd w kształcie litery T do
usuwania wody z mytych szyb

squeeze (skłi:z) v. sciskac;
wyciskac; wygniątac; wciskac;
odciskac; sciesnic; s. ucisk;
nacisk; odcisk; tłok; scis-
nięcie

squeezer ('skłi:zer) s. wy-
ciskacz (soku)

squid (skłyd) s. przynęta
z mątwy; kałamarnica (ryba),

squint (skłynt) s. zez; ukosne
spojrzenie; zerknięcie; skłonnosc; v. mrużyc oczy; wysiłac
wzrok; zezowac; skłaniac się;
adj. zezowaty; zerkający

squirm (skłe:rm) v. wic się
(z bolu); płonac (ze wstydu);
kręcic się niespokojnie;
s. skrecanie się

squirrel ('skłó:rel) s. wiewiórka

squirt (skłe:rt) v. strzykac;
tryskac; s. strzykawka; struga; pętak

stab (staeb) v. dzgnąc; pchnąc;
ugodzic; ranic; s. pchnięcie;
dzgnięcie; rana kłuta

stability (ste'bylyty) s.sta-
łosc; statecznosc; stabil-
nosc; równowaga

stabilize ('stejbylajz) v.
ustalac; stabilizowac

stable ('stejbl) s. stajnia;
stadnina; v. trzymac konie
w stajni; adj. stały; stanowczy; trwały

stack (staek) s. stóg; stos;
sterta; komin; kupa; v. układac w stogi; ustawiac w kozły;
układac podstępnie przeciwko
komus

stadium('stejdjem) s. stadion;
faza; stadium (czegos)

staff (staef) s. laska; drzewce; sztab; personel; adj.
sztabowy; v. obsadzac persone-
lem

stag (staeg) s. rogacz; jeleń;
samotny mężczyzna

stage (stejdż) s. scena; stadium; etap; rusztowanie; pomost; postój; v. wystawiac;
odegrac (sztukę); urządzac;
inscenizowac; adj. teatralny;
sceniczny

stagecoach ('stejdż-koucz) s.
dyliżans

stage-manager ('stejdż'maenydżer) s. reżyser

stagflation ('staegflejszyn)
s. stagnacja, rosnące bezrobocie i inflacja jednocześnie

stagger ('staeger) v. zataczac
się; wahac się; chwiac się;
układac w zygzak lub w odstę-
pach; porażac; s. układ skosny; zachodzący na siebie w od-
stępach lub zygzakowaty; zataczanie się; pl. zawroty głowy

staggering ('staegeryng) adj.
przerażający; oszałamiający;
rozbrajający

stagnant ('staegnent) adj. za-
stały; stojący; będący w za-
stoju

stain (stejn) v. plamic (się);
brudzic; szargac; barwic; ko-
lorowac; farbowac; drukowac
tapety; s. plama;barwik; bej-
ca do drzewa

stained ('stejnd) adj. zabar-
wiony (np. szkło)

stainless ('stejnlys) adj. nierdzewny (stal); nieskalany

stair (steer) s. stopień; pl.
schody

stair case ('steer,kejs) s.
klatka schodowa

stair way ('steerłej) s. schody

stake (stejk) s. słup; słupek;
kołek; palik; stawka; kowa-
dełko blacharskie; v. przy-
twierdzać kołkami; wytaczać;
przywiązywać do słupa; stawiać na coś

stake out ('stejk,aut) v.
wziąć pod obserwację; wyznaczać granicę

stake-out ('stejkaut) s. zasadzka (slang)

stale ('stejl) adj. stęchły;
nieświeży; zwietrzały;
czerstwy; przestarzały;
v. czuć nieświeżym

stalk (sto:k) v. kroczyć; podkradać się; podchodzić; s.(majestatyczny) chód; podkrada-
nie się; podchodzenie; wysoki komin; łodyga; nóżka (kie-
liszka)

stall (sto:l) v. działać opóź-
niająco; zwlekać; przewlekać;
kręcić; zwodzić; przetrzymy-
wać; dławić motor; utykać;
grzęznąć; trzymać bydło w obo-
rze; zaopatrywać w przegrody
s. stajnia; obora; stragan;
kiosk; przegroda; komora
(w kopalni); (slang): trik;
kruczek

stallion ('staeljen) s. ogier

stalwart ('sto:lłert) s. bojownik partyjny; adj. dzielny;
krzepki; stanowczy

stammer ('staemer) v. jąkać się;
s. jąkanie się

stamp (staemp) v. stemplować;
wytłaczać; tupać; kruszyć;
wbijać (w pamięć); przylepiać
znaczki pocztowe; s. stempel;
pieczątka; znaczek; piętno;
cecha; pokrój; tupnięcie; ubijak do kruszenia (rudy)

stanch (staencz) v. tamować
krwotok; adj. wierny; stały;
krzepki; szczelny

stand; stood; stood (staend;
stud; stud)

stand (staend) v. stać; stanąć;
wytrzymać; znosić; przetrzymać;
zostać; utrzymywać się; stawiać
opór; znajdować się; być; postawić; (slang): płacić; s. stanie;
stanowisko; stojak; trybuna;
postój; łan; ława dla świadków;
unieruchomienie; umywalka

stand back ('staend,baek) v.
stać w tyle; zachowywać rezerwę

stand by ('staendbaj) v. popierać; być w stanie pogotowia

stand off ('staend,of) v. cofać
się

stand-off ('staend,of) s. nie-
rozegrana (równowaga sił)

stand out ('staend,aut) v. wyróżniać się; kontrastować;
wytrwać

stand up ('staend,ap) v. wstawać; powstawać; stawać w obro-
nie; nie ustępować; stawiać
czoło

standard ('staenderd) s. sztandar; norma; miernik; wzorzec;
wskaźnik; stopa (życiowa);
próba; słup; podpórka; adj.
znormalizowany; normalny; typowy; przeciętny; wzorcowy;
klasyczny; literacki (język)

standardize ('staenderdajz) v.
normalizować; dostosowywać do
normy; mierzyć wzorcem; porów-
nywać z wzorcem

standing ('staendyng) adj. stojący; na pniu; pionowy; stały;
s. stanie; stanowisko; znaczenie; poważanie; reputacja;
czas trwania

standing room ('staendyng,ru:m)
s. miejsce stojące

standoffish ('staend'ofysz) adj.
nieprzystępny; trzymający się
z dala

standpoint ('staend,poynt) s.
punkt widzenia; punkt obserwacyjny

standstill ('staendstyl) s. zastój; przerwa; martwy punkt;
unieruchomienie

stank (staeŋk) v. zob. stink
star (sta:r) s. gwiazda;
gwiazdor; gwiazdka; v. ozdabiać gwiazdkami; być gwiazdo-
rem; adj. gwiezdny; występu-
jący w głównej roli
starboard ('sta:rberd) s. prawa burta; v. sterować na prawo
starch (sta:rcz) s. skrobia;
sztywność; krochmal; v. na-
krochmalić;(slang):siła
starchy ('sta:rczy) adj. na-
krochmalony; skrobiowaty;
sztywny
stare (steer) v. patrzec; gapić się; wpatrywać się; zwracać uwagę; s. nieruchomy
wzrok; wytrzeszczone oczy;
zagapione spojrzenie
stare at ('steer,aet) v. gapić
się na...
stark (sta:rk) adj. sztywny;
zupełny; czysty; wierutny;
ponury; posępny; adv. zupełnie; całkowicie
starling ('starlyŋg) s. szpak
starlit ('sta:rlyt) adj.
gwiaździsty; oświetlony
gwiazdami; wygwieżdżony
starry ('sta:ry) adj. gwiaździsty; usiany gwiazdami; promienny; marzycielski; rozmarzony
stars-spangled ('sta:r-spaeŋgld)
adj. usiany gwiazdami (flaga
USA)
start (sta:rt) v. zacząć; ruszyc; startować; zerwać się;
podskoczyc; wyruszyć; zabierać się; uruchamiac; obsuwać;
rozpoczynać; wszczynać; s.po-
czątek; start; wymarsz; poderwanie się; obsunięcie się;
zdobywanie przewagi
starter ('sta:rter) s. starter;
rozrusznik; startujący zawodnik; pierwsze danie; kierownik ruchu
startle ('sta:rtl) v. zasko-
czyc; zaniepokoić; podrywać;
wzdrygać się; przestraszać;

s. zaniepokojenie; poderwanie
się
startling ('sta:rtlyŋg) adj.
sensacyjny; zdumiewający; niepokojący
staryation (sta:r'wejszyn) s.
głód; głodowanie; głodzenie;
przymieranie głodem
starve (sta:rw) v. głodowac;
zagłodzić; przymierać z głodu,
zimna; łaknąc; zmuszać (głodem, brakiem)
stash (staesz) v. (slang): chowac na potem; s.schowanie;
schowek
state (stejt) s. państwo; stan;
zajęcie; parada; pompa; cere-
moniał; stan prac; adj. państwowy; stanowy; uroczysty;
paradny; formalny; v. stwier-
dzac; wyrażać; okreslać; wyrażać (też symbolami)
state department ('stejt,dy'-
'pa:rtment) w USA ministerstwo spraw zagranicznych
stately ('stejtly) adj. uroczysty; okazały; adv. uroczyscie; okazale
statement ('stejtment) s. wyrażenie; twierdzenie; sprawozdanie; wyciąg; oświadczenie;
deklaracja; zeznanie
state room ('stejt,rum) s. prywatny pokój; kabina; przedział
state side ('stejt,sajd) adj.
amerykański; w stanach
statesman('stejtsmen) s. mąż
stanu
statesmanship('stejtsmenszyp)
s. rozum polityczny
static ('staetyk) adj. statycz-
ny; nieruchomy
station ('stejszyn) s. stacja;
stanowisko; stan; pozycja życiowa; godność; punkt; stacja
telewizyjna; radiowa, etc.
stationary ('stejsznery) adj.
niezmienny; stały; nieruchomy;
pozycyjny
stationmaster ('stejszyn,ma:-
ster) s. naczelnik stacji

station wagon ('stejszyn,łaegn)
s. samochod typu kombi

statistics (ste'tystyks) s.
statystyka

statue ('staeczu:) s. posąg

statute ('staetju) s. ustawa;
prawo; statut; nakaz

staunch (sto:ncz) v. tamować
krwotok; tamponować; adj. oddany; wierny; zagorzały

stay; stayed; staid (stej;
stejed; stejd)

stay (stej) s. pobyt; zwłoka;
odroczenie; opóźnienie; zawieszenie; podpora; wanta;
zatrzymanie; przerwa; wytrzymałość; v. zostać; przebywać;
wytrzymać; odraczać; kłasc
kres; zaspakajać (głod)

stay away ('stej,ełej) v.
trzymać się z dala

stay up ('stej,ap) v. nie siadać

stay with ('stej,łys) v. mieszkać u kogos

stead (sted) s. miejsce; na
miejsce; pożyteczność

steadfast ('sted,fa:st) adj.
stały; nieruchomy; niezachwiany; niewzruszony; mocny;
pewny

steady ('stedy) adj. mocny;
silny; pewny; stały; rzetelny;
rowny; stateczny; excl.:powo-
li ! prosto ! naprzod ! stoj !
v. dawać równowagę; odzyskiwać
rownowagę; s. podpora; (slang):
ukochany

steak (stejk) s. stek; befsztyk; płat (np. mięsa)

steal; stole; stolen (sti:l:
stoul; stoulen)

steal (sti:l) v. krasć; wykrasć;
wejsć ukradkiem; zakradać się;
skradać się; s. kradzież;
rzecz ukradziona; rzecz ku-
piona prawie że za darmo; dar-
mocha (slang)

stealth (stels) s. tajemni-
czość; ukradkowość

stealthy ('stelsy) adj. ukrad-
kowy; tajemny

steam (sti:m) s. para; v. parować; dymić; płynąć pod parą;
gotować w parze; umieszczać
pod parą

steam up ('sti:m,ap) v. zamglić
(się); zajsć mgłą lub parą

steamer ('sti:mer) s. parowiec

steamship ('sti:m,szyp) s. parowiec

steel (sti:l) s. stal; pręt
stalowy; adj. stalowy; ze
stali; v. pokrywać stalą; kar-
tować

steelworks ('sti:l,łe:rks) s.
stalowania

steep (sti:p) v. moczyć się;
rozmiękczać; impregnować; po-
grażyć się; rozpijać się;
adj. stromy; nieprawdopodobny;
wygorowany; przesadny

steepen ('sti:pn) v. nagle
podnosić ceny; robić stromym

steeple ('sti:pl) s. strzelista
wieża; ostra wieżyczka

steer (stier) v. sterować; kierować; prowadzić; s. wskazówka; młody wół na mięso

steering wheel ('stieryng,hłi:l)
s. kierownica; koło sterowe

stem (stem) s. pień; łodyga;
szpulka; trzon; trzonek; noż-
ka; v. pochodzić; tamować; powstrzymywać; isć pod prąd;
zwalczać

stench (stencz) s. smrod; odor;
fetor

stenographer ('stenegraefer) s.
stenograf; stenografistka

step (step) s. krok; stopień;
takt; szczebel; schodek;
v. stąpać; kroczyć; isc; tan-
czyć; podnosić; wzmagać; przyciskać nogą; mierzyć (krokami)

stepchild ('step,czajld) s.
pasierb

stepfather ('step,fa:dzer) s.
ojczym

stepmother ('step,madzer) s.
macocha

stereo ('steriou) s. stereoskop;
dwugłosnikowe radio-adapter;
adj. stereofoniczny

sterile ('sterajl) adj. wyjałowiony; jałowy; sterylny; bezpłodny

sterilize ('stery,lajz) v. wyjałowić; wysterylizować

sterling (,ste:rlyŋg) s. pieniądz pełnowartościowy; adj. solidny; niezawodny

stern (ste:rn) adj. surowy; srogi; s. rufa; zad; zadek; tył; pośladki

sternness('ste:rnys) s. surowość; srogość

stew (stu:) v. gotować;dusić (się); martwić się; wkuwać się; s. potrawa duszona; kłopot; staw na ryby

steward ('stu:erd) s. zarządca; ekonom; kelner; v. zarządzać; być stewardem

stewardess ('stu:erdys) s. stewardesa

stewpan ('stu:,paen) s. rondel; garnek

stick (styk) stuck;stuck (styk; stak; stak)

stick (styk) v. wtykać; przekłuwać; kłuć; wbijać; zarzynać; przyklejać; naklejać; utkwić; utknąć; ugrzęznąć; przyczepiać (się); trzymać się (tematu); oszukiwać; s. pałka; patyk; laska; kij; tyczka; żerdź

stick out ('styk,aut) v. wystawiać; sterczeć; zadać

stick to ('styk,tu) v. trzymać się (tematu); przylepiać

stick up ('styk,ap) v. terroryzować (bronią); brać w obronę; podnosić; przeciwstawiać się

sticky ('styky) adj. lepki; kleisty; grząski; parny; (slang): marny; nieprzyjemny

stiff (styf) adj. sztywny; twardy; kategoryczny; zdrętwiały; "słony"; wygórowany; trudny; ciężki; silny; s. (slang): trup; umrzyk; niedojda; włóczęga; facet; pedant

stiffen ('styfn) v. usztywniać; podnieść (wymagania); zgęszczać; zesztywnieć

stifle (stajfl) v. dusić (się); tłumić; przygaszać; tuszować

stile (stajl) s. przełaz; kołowrót; pionowa rama drzwi

still (styl) adj. spokojny; cichy; nieruchomy; martwy (przedmiot); milczący; adv. jeszcze; jednak; wciąż; dotąd; niemniej; mimo to; v. uspokoić (się); uciszyć; destylować; s. destylarnia (też wódki)

stillness ('stylnys) s. cisza; spokój; bezruch

stilt (stylt) s. szczudło

stilted ('styltyd) adj. na szczudłach; nienaturalny; sztuczny; na wspornikach

stimulant ('stymjulent) s. bodziec; podnieta; alkohol; środek podniecający; zachęta; adj. pobudzający

stimulate ('stymjulejt) v. pobudzać; zachęcać

stimulating ('stymjulejtyŋg) adj. podniecający; pobudzający

stimulation ('stymjulejszyn) s. podnieta; zachęta; podniecenie

stimulus ('stymjules) s. bodziec; zachęta; podnieta

sting; stung; stung (styŋg; staŋg; staŋg)

sting (styŋg) v. kłuć; parzyć; kąsać; szczypać; palić; rwać; gryźć; s. żądło; ukłucie; poparzenie; piekący ból; uszczypliwość; zjadliwość

stingy ('styndży) adj. skąpy

stink; stank; stunk (styŋk; staeŋk; staŋk)

stink (styŋk) v. cuchnąć; śmierdzieć; zasmradzać; wyganiać smrodem; (slang): poczuć smród s. smród

stipulate ('stypjulejt) v. zażądać; uwarunkować; zastrzegać w umowie

stir (ste:r) v. ruszać; poruszać; grzebać; mieszać; wzniecać; podniecać; s. poruszenie; podniecenie; ruch; (slang): więzienie

stirrup ('styrep) s. strzemię;
pocięgiel; okucie do wspinania się
stitch (stycz) s. szew; ścieg;
oczko; kłucie; v. szyc; zaszyc; zeszywac
stoat (stout) s. gronostaj; v.
zaszywac niewidocznym ście-
giem
stock (stok) s. zapas; zasób;
bydło; pien; strzon; kłoda;
łożysko; ród; rasa; surowiec;
kapitał udziałowy; akcje giełdowe; obligacje; wywar; v. zaopatrywac; zagospodarowac; za-
rybiac; miec na składzie;
adj. typowy; seryjny; w stałym zapasie; repertuarowy
stockade (sto'kejd) s. palisada;
częstokół; oboz
stockbroker ('stok,brouker) s.
makler giełdowy
stock exchange ('stok,eks'-
'czejndz) s. giełda
stockholder ('stok,houlder) s.
akcjonariusz; udziałowiec
stocking ('stokyng) s. pończocha
stocky ('stoky) adj. krępy
stock market ('stok-'ma:rkyt)
s. giełda
stole (stoul) v. zob. steal;
s. stula; etola
stolen ('stouln) v. zob. steal
stolid ('stolyd) adj. obojętny;
flegmatyczny
stomach ('stamek) s. żołądek;
brzuch; apetyt; ochota;
v. jesc; przełykac (obelgę);
znosic
stone (stoun) s. kamien; głaz;
skala; pestka; adj. kamienny;
v. ukamieniowac; obkładac
(mur) kamieniem; wyjmowac
pestki; upijac (się) na umór
stonewall ('stoun-łc:l) v. od-
mówic zaciekle jakiejkolwiek
kooperacji
stoneware ('stoun-łeer) s. naczynia kamionkowe
stony ('stouny) adj. kamienny;
kamienisty; skamieniały;
pestkowy

stood (stud) v. zob. stand
stool (stu:l) s. stołek; sedes;
taboret; stolec; klęcznik; podnóżek; pniak puszczający pędy;
wabik; v. puszczac pędy
stoop (stu:p) v. schylac się;
ugiąc się; poniżyc się; raczyc;
garbic się; s. pochylenie;
przygarbione plecy; weranda;
taras (przy domu)
stooping ('stu:pyng) adj. przy-
garbiony
stop (stop) v. zatrzymywac;
powstrzymywac; wstrzymywac;
zatykac; zaplombowac; zagrodzic;
zablokowac; zamknąc; zaprzesta-
wac; niedopuscic; stanąc; prze-
stac; exp.:przstan ! stój !
dosyc tego !; s. zatrzymanie
(się); stop; postój; przystanek; zatkanie; zator; zatyczka;
zderzak; ogranicznik
stop by ('stop,baj) v. wstąpic
do kogos na chwilę
stopover ('stop'ouwer) s. zatrzymanie się w podróży
stoppage ('stopydz) s. wstrzymanie; zatrzymanie (się); zatwardzenie
stopper ('stoper) s. korek; zatyczka; v. zatykac; umocowac
liną
stopping ('stopyng) s. plomba
(w zębie); zatrzymanie; zatkanie
storage ('sto:rydz) s. skład;
przechowywanie; magazynowanie
store ('sto:r) s. zapas; sklep;
skład; mnostwo; składnica;
v. magazynowac; miescic w sobie; zaopatrywac; wyposażac
store up ('sto:r,ap) v. zama-
gazynowac; zachowac
storehouse ('sto:rhaus) s.
skład; magazyn; skarbnica; kopalnia
storekeeper ('sto:r,ki:per) s.
sklepikarz; kupiec
storey ('sto:ry) s. piętro
storeyed ('sto:rjed) adj. pięt-
rowy (angielska pisownia)
storied ('sto:rjed) adj. pięt-
rowy

stork (sto:rk) s. bocian

storm (sto:rm) s. burza; wichura; sztorm; zawierucha; szturm; v. szalec (burza etc.) wpasc do pokoju; wypasc z pokoju (jak burza); rzucac gromy; szturmowac; brac szturmem

stormy ('sto:rmy) adj. burzliwy; zwiastujący burzę

story ('sto:ry) s. opowiadanie; opowiesc; powiastka; historia; bajka; anegdota; gawęda; zmyslanie; nowela; piętro

story teller ('sto:ry,teler) s. gawędziarz; kłamczuch

stout (staut) adj. dzielny; krzepki; gruby; s, mocny np. porto (wino); mocne piwo; tęga osoba

stove (stouw) s. piec (też kuchenny); cieplarnia; v. zob. stave; hodowac w cieplarni

stow (stou) v. wypełniac; układac szczelnie; miescic; wsuwac; chowac; przesłac (slang)

stow away ('stou,e'łej) v. jechac na gapę

stowaway ('stouełej) s. pasażer na gapę

straggling ('straeglyng) adj. sporadyczny; rozposcierający się; rzadki

straight (strejt) adj. prosty; bezposredni; celny; szczery; otwarty; rzetelny; zwykły; s. prosta linia; prosty odcinek (toru); adv. prosto; wprost; na przełaj; po prostu; pod rząd; należycie; nieprzerwanie; ciągiem

straightaway ('strejt,ełej) adv. natychmiast ;bez zwłoki

straight ahead ('strejt,ehed) adv. na wprost

straighten ('strejtn) v. wyprostowac (się); poprawic (się)

straightforward (strejt'fo:rłerd) adj. łatwy; jasny; prosty; prostolinijny; szczery; uczciwy

strain (strejn) v. prężyc; naprężac; naciągac; wytężac; odkształcac; nadużywac; nadwerężac; przeciążac; robic gwałtowne wysiłki; cedzic; przecedzac; s. naprężenie; napięcie; obciążenie; przemęczenie; zwichnięcie; nadwerężenie; wysiłek; odkształcenie; rasa; odmiana; rys

strainer ('strejner) s. sito; sączek; cedzidło; rozciągacz; napinacz

strait (strejt) v. sciesniac; byc w trudnosciach

straited circumstances ('strejtyd,ser'kamstenses) s. kłopoty pieniężne

straiten ('strejtn) v. zbiedniec; zubożec

strait jacket ('strejt'dżaekyt) s. kaftan bezpieczenstwa

straits (strejts) pl. ciesnina morska; kłopoty finansowe; braki czegos

strand (straend) s.skręt; zwitek; pasmo; nitka; warkocz; sznur; rys; kosmyk; brzeg; plaża; v. splatac; osadzac na mieliznie; osiąsc na mieliznie

strange (strejndż) adj. obcy; dziwny; niezwykły; nieznany; niewprawny

stranger ('strejndżer) s. obcy; nieznajomy; człowiek nieobeznany; exp.:panie tego !

strangle ('straengl) v. dusic; trzymac za gardło; zadusic

strap (straep) s. rzemien; pasek; rzemyk; tasma; uchwyt; rączka; chłosta; bicie; v. na pasku umocowywac; ostrzyc; bic paskiem; zalepiac plastrem

strategic (stre'ti:dżyk) adj. strategiczny

strategy ('straetydży) s. strategia; taktyka

straw (stro:) s. słoma

strawberry ('stro:bery) s. truskawka

stray (strej)v. zabłądzic; zabłąkac się; schodzic na manowce; s. zbłąkane zwierzę; dziecko bez opieki; adj.zabłąkany

strays (strejs) pl. zaburzenia
atmosferyczne (np. w radiu)
streak (stri:k) s. smuga; pasek; pasmo; prążek; rys;
pierwiastek;passa; v. rysować paski, prążki; błyskawicznie poruszać się; wpadać
nagle dokądś
streaky ('stri:ky) adj. prążko-
wany; w paski; zmienny; nierówny (slang)
stream (stri:m) s. strumień;
potok; rzeka; struga; prąd;
v. płynąć (strumieniami);
ociekać; tryskać; powiewać
street (stri:t) s. ulica
streetcar ('stri:tka:r) s.
tramwaj
strength (strenkθ) s. moc; siła; stężenie; natężenie;
ilość; skład (ludzi)
strengthen ('strenkθn) v.
wzmocnić (się); wzmagać; dać
przewagę
strenuous (strenjues) adj.
męczący; żmudny; mozolny; wy-
tężony; zawzięty; pracowity;
energiczny; silny
stress (atręs) s. nacisk; akcent; napór; wysiłek;
v. kłaść nacisk; podkreslać;
naciskać
stretch (strecz) s. naciągać
(się); naprężać; napinać; nad-
użyać; przeciągać; rozciągać (się); ciągnąć się; sięgać; powiesić (kogoś); s. napięcie; rozciąganie; przeciąganie się; nadużycie; połać;
okres służby; przeciąg czasu;
prosty odcinek toru; (slang):
pobyt w więzieniu
stretcher ('streczer) s. nosze
strew; strewed; strewn (stru:,
stru:d; stru:n)
strew (stru:) s. posypać; roz-
rzucić; porozrzucać
strewn (stru:n) v. zob. strew
stricken (stri:ken) v. zob.
strike; adj. dotknięty; nawie-
dzony; rażony; udręczony
stride; strode; stridden
(strajd; stroud; stridn)

stride (strajd) v. kroczyć;
przekroczyć; stać okrakiem
(nad czymś); s. krok; rozkrok
strife (stajf) s. spór; walka;
współzawodnictwo
strike; struck; stricken (strajk;
strak; strykn)
strike (strajk) v. uderzać; bić
(monetę); walić; kuć; wykrze-
sać; zapalić (zapałkę); natrafić; zastrajkować; porzucać
robotę; chwytać (przynętę);
s. strajk; strychulec; wybicie
monety; natrafienie (żyły, np.
złotodajnej); chwycenie przy-
nęty; nieudane uderzenie palan-
tem; zwalenie wszystkich kręgli
naraz
strike off ('strajk off) v. od-
rapywać; ścinać; wykreslać;
drukować kilka egzemplarzy
strike out ('strajk‚aut) v.
uderzać na odlew; zacząć; ukuć;
wymyslić
striker ('strajker) s. strajku-
jący; młotek (w dzwonku)
striking ('strajkyŋg) adj.
uderzający
string; strung; strung (stryŋg;
straŋg; straŋg)
string (stryŋg) v. zawiązać;
przywiązać; zaopatrzyć w struny; stroić; napinać; podniecać;
powiesić kogoś; ciągnąć sie
(klej); obwieszać; s. sznurek;
szpagat; powróz; sznurowadło;
tasiemka; cięciwa; struna;
żyła; włókno; rząd; stek
(głupstw)
strip (stryp) v. obdzierać;
ogałacać; obnażać; zdzierać;
rozbierać (się); wydobyć do
końca; ścierać (gwint); ciąć
na paski; s. pasek; skrawek;
seria komiksów
strip-tease ('strypti:z) s.
rozbieranie się na scenie
stripes (strajps) pl. paski;
prążki; naszywki; chłosta;
cięgi
striped ('strajpt) adj. pa-
siasty; w pasy

strive; strove; striven
('strajw; strouw; strywn)
strive (strajw) v. starac się;
usiłowac; dążyc; borykac się;
zwalczac
striven ('strywn) v. zob.strive
strode (stroud) v. zob. stride
stroke (strouk) s. uderzenie;
cios; cięcie; raz; porażenie;
ciąg; pociagnięcie (pióra);
rys; kreska; ruch (wiosła);
wysiłek; suw; skok (tłoka);
takt; głaskanie; v. znaczyc;
przekreślac; nadawac tempo;
głaskac; ugłaskac
stroke of luck ('strouk,ow'lak)
exp.: los szczęścia
stroll (stroul) v. przechadzac
się; spacerowac; wędrowac;
s. przechadzka
stroller ('strouler) s. space-
rowicz; włóczęga; aktor
wędrowny; wózek (dziecięcy)
strong (strong) adj. mocny;
silny; będacy w liczbie...;
mocarstwowy; potężny; trwały;
solidny; wyskokowy; przekonywujący; ordynarny
strongbox ('strong,boks) s.
sejf; kasa ogniotrwała
strongroom ('strong,rum) s.
skarbiec
strove (strouw) v. zob.strive
struck (strak) v.zob. strike
structure ('strakczer) s. budowa; struktura; budowla; wiązanie; splot; v. nadawac
kształt
struggle ('stragl) v. szarpac
się; szamotac się; walczyc;
usiłowac; s. walka;borykanie
strum (stram) v. rzępolic;
brzdąkac; s. brzdęk; brzdąkanie
strung (strang) v. zob. string;
adj. napięty
strut (strat) v. kroczyc ma-
jestatycznie; rozpierac;
s. krok majestatyczny; zastrzał; rozpora
stub (stab) s. pniak; korzen;
resztka; niedopałek; grzbiet

(biletu); v. karczowac; gasic (papierosa)
stubble ('stabl) s. rżysko;
ściernisko; twardy zarost
stubborn ('stabern) adj. uparty
stuck (stak) v. zob. stick
stud (stad) s. sworzen; gwóźdź;
guz; trzon; słup; rozporka;
ogier; stadnina; v. nabijac
(np. gwoździami; guzami);
usiewac czyms; byc rozsianym;
podpierac (słupami)
student ('stju:dent) s. student;
badający cos; znawca czegos
studio ('stju:djou) s. studio;
pracownia
studio couch ('stju:djou,kaucz)
s. tapczan
studious ('stu:djes) adj. pilny; staranny; dbały; wyszukany
study ('stady) s. pracownia;
gabinet; nauka; przedmiot nauki, staran, troski, zadumy,
marzenia; v. badac; studiowac;
dociekac; uczyc się
stuff (staf) v. napychac; opy-
chac (się); tuczyc (się); fa-
szerowac; wpychac; wkuwac;
s. materia; materiał; glina;
rzecz; rupiecie (brednie)
stuffing ('stafyng) s. nadzienie; farsz; nadziewka; wyściółka
stuffy ('stafy) adj. zatęchły;
duszny; ciężki; nudny; zatka-
ny (nos); (slang): ważny;
tępy; skwaszony; zły; purytan-
ski
stumble ('stambl) v. potykac
(się); utykac; natknąc się;
zawahac (kogos); miec skrupuły; czuc się dotkniętym;
s. potknięcie się
stumblebum ('stambl,bam) s.
(slang): zawalidroga; próżniak
stump (stamp) s. pniak; głąb;
kikut; ogarek; resztka; niedopałek; kulas; krzykactwo; agitacja (polityczna); kuc; klocek;
przysadkowaty człowiek; v. karczowac; obcinac; zdumiec (się);
agitowac; wyzwac kogos; chodzic na protezie

stun (stan) v. ogłuszyć; oszołomić; s. oszołomienie (uderzenie hukiem)

stung (stąng) v. zob. sting

stunk (stąnk) v. zob . stink

stunning ('stanyng) adj. nadzwyczajny; szlagierowy; kapitalny

stupefy ('stu:pyfaj) v. ogłu-
piać; odurzać; wprawiać
w osłupienie

stupid ('stu:pyd) adj. głupi;
odurzony; nudny; s. głupiec

stupidity ('stu:pydyty) s.
głupota; głupstwo

stupor ('stu:per) s. osłupienie; odurzenie; apatia

sturdy ('ste:rdy) adj. krzepki; dzielny; solidny; s. motylica

stutter ('stater) v. jąkać (się)
s. jąkanie się

sty (staj) s. chlew; burdel;
jęczmień (w oku); v. żyć w
chlewie; trzymać w chlewie

style (stajl) s. styl; maniera;
sposób; fason; wzór; kształt;
rylec; szyjka; tytuł; nazwa;
format; wskazówka; v. formować stylowo; określać mianem

stylish (stajlysh) adj. szykowny; stylowy; wytworny

suave (sła:w) adj. gładki; łagodny; uprzejmy

subdivision (,sabdy'wyżyn) s.
dzielnica (miasta; osiedla);
podział

subdue (seb'du:) s. ujarzmiać;
poskramiać; przyciszać; tłumić; łagodzić; podbijać

subject ('sabdżykt) s. podmiot;
przedmiot; temat; tresć; tworzywo; (sab'dżekt) motyw;
poddany; osobnik; v. podporządkować; ujarzmić; podbić;
narazić; poddać czemuś; adj.
poddany; uległy; podległy;
narażony; podatny; podlegający; ujarzmiony; adv. pod warunkiem; z zastrzeżeniem;
z uwzględnieniem czegos

subjective('sabdżektyw) adj.
subiektywny; podmiotowy

subjunctive mood (seb'dżanktyw,
,mu:d) s. tryb warunkowy

sublime (se'blajm) adj. wzniosły; wyniosły; podniosły

submachine-gun ('sabme'szi:ngan)
s. (automatyczny) pistolet maszynowy

submarine (sabme'ri:n) s. łódź
podwodna

submariners (sabme'ri:ners) pl.
załoga łodzi podwodnej

submerge (seb'me:rdż) v. zalewać; zatapiać; zanurzać (się);
zakrywać

submission (seb'myszyn) s.
uległość; poddanie się; przed-
łożenie (opinii)

submissive (seb'mysyw) adj.
uległy

submit (seb'myt) v. poddawać
(się); przedkładać

subnormal (sab'no:rmel) adj.
niżej normy; cofnięty w roz-
woju

subordinate(se'bo:rdnyt) adj.
zależny; podporządkowany;
s. podwładny; (se'bo:rdnejt)
v. podporządkowywać

subordinate clause (se'bo:rd-
nyt,klo:z) s. zdanie podrzędne

subscribe (seb'skrajb) v. za-
prenumerować; podpisywać (np.
obraz); pisać sie na coś; dawać na cel

subscribe for (seb'skrajb,fo:r)
v. zapisywać się na (nową)
książkę

subscribe to (seb'skrajb,tu) v.
abonować gazete

subscriber (seb'skrajber) s.
abonent; człowiek popierający

subscription (seb'skrypszyn) s.
prenumerata; przedpłata; pod-
pisanie; zgoda pisemna; podpis dołączony

subsequent ('sabsykłent) adj.
następny

subsequently ('sabsykłently)
adv. następnie

subside (seb'sajd) v. klęsnąc;
opadać; osadzać się; osiadac;
uspokajać się

subsidiary (seb'sydjery) adj.
pomocniczy; subsydiowany (zależny); s. pomocnik

subsidiary company (seb'sydjery'kampeny) s. firma zależna
od innej firmy

subsidize ('sabsydajz) v. za-
siłkować; zasilać; opłacać;
przekupywać

subsidy ('sabsydy) s. zasiłek
(państwowy); subwencja; danina

subsist (seb'syst) s. istnieć;
egzystować; utrzymywać się
przy życiu; żyć czyms

subsistence (seb'systens) s.
utrzymanie; istnienie

substance ('sabstens) s. istota; treść; sens; sedno; substancja; znaczenie; rzeczywistość; majątek

substandard (sab'staenderd)
adj. poniżej poziomu; ordynarny (język)

substantial (sab'staenszel)
adj. materialny; rzeczywisty;
solidny; zasadniczy; ważny;
bogaty; wpływowy; konkretny;
treściwy

substantive ('sabstentyw) adj.
rzeczywisty; niezależnie
istniejący; zasadniczy; poważny; rzeczownikowy; wyrażający
istnienie; s. rzeczownik

substitute ('sabstytut) s. namiastka; zastępca

substitution (,sabsty'tuszyn)
s. zastępstwo; zastąpienie

subtitle ('sabtajtl) s. pod-
tytuł; napis na filmie

subtle ('sabtl) s. subtelny;
delikatny; cienki; rzadki;
chytry; bystry

subtract (sab'traekt) v. odejmować

suburb ('sabe:rb) s. przedmieście

suburban ('sabe:rben) adj.
podmiejski

subway ('sabłej) s. kolejka
podziemna

succeed (sek'si:d) v. mieć po-

wodzenie; udawać się; następować po kims

success (sek'ses) s. powodzenie;
sukces; rzecz udana; człowiek
mający sukces

successful (sek'sesful) adj.
udały; mający powodzenie

succession (sek'seszyn) s. następstwo; kolej; kolejność;
sukcesja; spadkobiercy; szereg

successive (sek'sesyw) adj.
kolejny

successor (sek'seser) s. następca; dziedzic; spadkobierca

succumb (se'kam) v. ulegać (po-
kusie); poddawać się; umierać

such (sacz) adj. taki; tego
rodzaju; pron. taki; tym podobny

suck (sak) v. ssać; korzystać;
wyzyskiwać; wchłaniać; wciągać;
(slang): nabierać; dać się nabrać; podlizywać się komuś;
s. ssanie; wciąganie; (slang):
łyk

suckle ('sakel) v. karmić piersią; dawać piers; ssać piers

suckling ('saklyng) s. osesek;
młode w okresie ssania

sudden ('sadn) adj. nagły

sudden death ('sadn,det) s.
nagła śmierć; rozstrzygnięcie
w następnej rozgrywce

suddenly ('sadnly) adv. nagle;
raptowanie; nieoczekiwanie

suds (sadz) pl. mydliny; (slang):
piwo

sue (su:) v. skarżyć; zaskarżać;
pozywać; upraszać; ubiegać się

suede (slejd) s. zamsz

suet ('su:yt) s. łój; adj. ło-
jowy

suffer ('safer) v. cierpieć;
ucierpieć; ścierpieć; doznać
(czegoś); zostać straconym

suffer from ('safer,from) v.
być chorym(na coś)

sufferable ('saferebl) adj.
znośny

sufferer ('saferer) s. cierpiący

suffice (se'fajs) v. wystarczyc

sufficiency (se'fyszensy) s. wystarczająca ilość; zapasy

sufficient (se'fyszent) adj. dostateczny; wystarczający

suffix ('safyks) s. przyrostek

suffocate ('safokejt) v. udusic; zadusic

sugar ('szuger) s. cukier; słodkie dziecko; (slang): forsa; v. słodzic

sugar-cane ('szugerkejn) s. trzcina cukrowa

suggest (se'dżest) v. sugerowac; proponowac; nasuwac; podsuwac; poddawac (mysl)

suggestion (se'dżestszyn) s. sugestia; wskazówka; mysl; poddawanie; podsuwanie; slad (czegos)

suggestive (se'dżestyw) adj. przypominający; nasuwający (mysl). dwuznaczny

suicide (,su:y'sajd) s. samobójstwo; samobójca; v. popełnic samobójstwo

suit (su:t) v. dostosowac; odpowiadac; słuzyc; wybrac; byc odpowiednim; zadowalac; pasowac; s. garnitur; ubranie; komplet; skarga; proces; prosba; zaloty; staranie się; zestaw

suit yourself ('su:tjor,self) exp.:rób co chcesz

suitable ('su:tebl) adj. własciwy; stosowny; odpowiedni

suitcase ('su:tkejs) s. walizka

suite (sli:t) s. swita; orszak; szereg; zestaw (mebli); apartament; garnitur; komplet; suita

suitor ('su:ter) s. zalotnik; petent; pretendent; strona; konkurent

sulfate ('salfejt)s. siarczan; v. zakwaszac; zamieniac na siarczan

sulfur ('salfer) s. siarka; v. siarkowac

sulk (salk) v. byc w złym humorze; s. zły humor; człowiek w złym humorze

sulky ('salky) adj. w złym humorze; ponury; s. jednokonny dwukołowy wózek

sullen ('salen) adj. ponury; posępny; flegmatyczny; powolny

sulphur ('salfer) s. siarka; v. siarkowac

sultry ('saltry) adj. parny; duszny; gwałtowny; gorący; namiętny

sum (sam) s. suma; w sumie; rachunek; v. dodawac; zbierac; podsumowywac

sum up ('sam,ap) v. dodawac; zbierac; podsumowywac

summarize ('samerajz) v. streszczac; zbierac; podsumowywac

summary ('samery) s. streszczenie; skrót; adj. pobiezny; dorazny; krotki

Summer ('samer) s. lato; v. spędzac lato

Summer resort ('samer ry'so:rt) s. letnisko

Summer school ('samer,sku:l) s. szkoła w lecie, w czasie wakacji

summit ('samyt) s. szczyt

summon ('samen) v. wzywac (oficjalnie); zdobywac się(na odwagę)

summons ('samens) pl. wezwanie urzędowe; v. doręczac wezwanie urzędowe

sun (san) s. słonce; v. nasłoneczniac (się)

sunbath ('sanba:s) s. kąpiel słoneczna

sunbathe ('sanbejg) v. opalac się

sunbeam ('sanbi:m) s. promien słonca

sunburn ('sanbe:rn) s. opalenizna

Sunday ('sandy) s. niedziela

sundial ('sandajel) s. zegar słoneczny

sundries ('sandryz) s. różności;
rozmaitości

sundry ('sandry) adj. różny;
rozmaity

sung (sang) v. zob. sing

sunglasses (san,gla:sys) pl.
okulary od słońca

sunk (sank) v. zob. sink

sunken ('sanken) v. zob. sink;
adj. zapadnięty; zatopiony;
podwodny

sunny ('sany) adj. słoneczny

sunny side up ('sany,sajd ap)
exp.: jaja sadzone

sunrise ('san-rajz) s. wschód
słońca

sunshade ('sanshejd) s. parasol
od słońca

sunset ('sanset) s. zachód
słońca

sunshine ('sanszajn) s. blask
słońca; pogoda. wesołość

sunstroke ('sanstrouk) s. porażenie słoneczne

sup (sap) s. łyk; v. częstować
kolacją; zjeść kolacje; pić
małymi łykami

super ('su:per) adj. pierwszorzędny; wspaniały; kwadratowy;
prefix: nad-; prze-; s. statysta; nadzorca; szlagier;
przeboj (filmowy); najlepszy
gatunek

superabundant ('su:per,e'bandent) adj. nadmierny; przebo-
gaty

superb (se:'pe:rb) adj. wspaniały

super-duper (,su:per-'du:per)
adj. (slang): b. dobry; luksusowy; bardzo elegancki

superficial (,su:per'fyszel)
adj. powierzchowny; powierzchniowy

superfluous (su'pe:rflues)
adj. zbędny; zbyteczny

super-highway (su'per-hajłej)
s. (m.in. 4-pasmowa) autostrada

superhuman(,su:per'hju:man)
adj. nadludzki

superintend (,su:peryn'tend)
v. nadzorować; doglądać; kierować

superintendent (,su:peryn'tendent) s. nadzorca; dozorca;
nadinspektor

superior (su:'pierjer) adj.
wyższy; nieprzeciętny;
pierwszorzędny; przewyższa-
jący; lepszy; nadęty; wyniosły;
s. zwierzchnik; przełożony;
starszy rangą

superiority (su:,pie:ry'oryty)
s. wyższość

superlative (su:'pe:rlatyw)
adj. najwyższy; s. szczyt;
superlatyw; stopień najwyższy

superman ('su:permen) s. nadczłowiek

supermarket ('su:per'ma:rkyt)
s. supersam; duży sklep samo-
obsługowy (żywnościowy)

supernatural (,su:per'naeczerel) adj. nadprzyrodzony

supernumerary (,su:per'nju:me-
ryry) adj. nadliczbowy; nie-
etatowy; statysta

superscription (,su:per'skrypszyn) s.napis u góry; nadpis;
adres; napis

supersede (sju:per'si:d) v.
zastąpić; wypierać; zajmować
miejsce

supersonic (,su:per'sonyk)
adj. ultradźwiękowy; ponad-
dźwiękowy

superstition (su:per'styszyn)
s. zabobon; przesądy

supervise ('su:perwajz) v.
nadzorować; doglądać

supervisor ('su:perwajzer)
s. inspektor; nadzorca

supper ('saper) s. wieczerza;
kolacja

supple ('sapl) adj. giętki;
gibki; v. stawać się gibkim

supplement ('saplyment) s.
dodatek; uzupełnienie;
v. uzupełniać

supplementary ('saplymentery)
adj. dodatkowy; uzupełniają-
cy

supplication (,saply'kejszyn)
s. błaganie; prośba

supplier (se'plajer) s. dostawca

supply (se'plaj) s. zapas;
aprowizacja; zaopatrzenie;
dostarczenie; dostawy; kredyty; podaż; dopływ; zasilanie;
v. dostarczać; zaopatrywać;
zaradzić; zastępować

support (se'po:rt) s. utrzymanie; podtrzymanie; podpora;
poparcie; pomoc; wspornik;
dźwigar; rama; łożysko; podłoże; ostoja; v. podtrzymywać; utrzymywać; podpierać;
popierać; wytrzymywać; znosić; tolerować

suppose (se'pouz) v. przypuszczać; zakładać; sądzić

supposed (se'pouzd) adj. domniemany; przypuszczalny;
rzekomy

supposedly (se'pouzdly) adv.
rzekomo; przypuszczalnie

supposition (sape'zeszyn) s.
przypuszczenie; domniemanie

suppress (se'pres) v. tłumić;
zgniatać; znosić; zatrzymywać (krwawienie); usuwać;
taić

suppression (se'preszyn) s.
stłumienie; zgniecenie;
zniesienie; usunięcie; przemilczenie; zatajenie

suppurate ('sapjurejt) v. ropieć

supremacy (se'premesy) s.
zwierzchnictwo; przewaga; najwyższa władza; supremacja

supreme (se'pri:m) adj. najwyższy; doskonały; ostateczny

surcharge (se:r'cza:rdż) s.
nadpłata; nadmierny ciężar;
dodatkowy ciężar; opłata (karna); przeładowanie; v. ściągać opłatę podatkową; nakładać grzywnę; przeładować;
przedrukować (znaczek)

sure (szuer) adj. pewny; niezawodny; niemylny; bezpieczny;
exp.: napewno !; zgadza się !

adv. z pewnością; pewnie; napewno; niezawodnie; niechybnie

sure enough ('szuer,y'naf) adv.
faktycznie

surely ('szuerly) adv. pewnie;
z pewnością

surety ('szuerty) s. ręczyciel;
gwarancja; zabezpieczenie;
kaucja; pewność

surf (se:rf) s. (łamiące się)
fale przybrzeżne

surface (se:rfys) s. powierzchnia; v. wypływać na powierzchnię; wykańczać powierzchnię

surfboard ('se:rfbo:rd) s. pojedyncza (deska); narta wodna;
v. jeździć na desce na falach
ku brzegowi

surfriding ('se:rf,rajdyng) v.
zjeżdżać z fal ku brzegowi

surge (se:rdż) s. gwałtowny
impuls; fala uskokowa; falowanie; fala; v. nagle wzbierać;
drgać; popuścić; kołysać;
hustać; zeslizgiwać się

surgeon ('se:rdżen) s. chirurg

surgery ('se:rdżery) s. chirurgia; operacja; sala operacyjna

surgical ('se:rdżykel) adj.
chirurgiczny

surly ('se:rly) adj. grubiański;
zgryźliwy

surmise ('se:rmajz) s. domysł;
v. domyślać się czegoś

surmount (ser'maunt) v. pokonywać; wychodzić na (górę);
przechodzić przez; pokrywać;
wznosić się

surmounted by (ser'mauntyd baj)
adj. pokonany przez

surname ('se:rnejm) s. nazwisko;
przydomek; (se:r'nejm) v.
przezywać; nadawać przydomek

surpass (se:r'paes) v. przewyższać; przechodzić (oczekiwania)

surpassing (se:r'paesyng) adj.
nieprześcigniony; niezrównany

surplus (se:r'plas) s. nadwyżka; nadmiar; superata; nadwyżka
produkcyjna; wartość dodatkowa;
adj. stanowiący nadwyżkę; nadwyżkowy; zbywający

surprise (ser'prajz) s. niespodzianka; zaskoczenie; zdziwienie; v. zaskoczyć; zdziwić; zmuszać; złapać na gorącym uczynku; adj. nieoczekiwany; niespodziewany

surprised (ser'prajzd) adj. zaskoczony; złapany na gorącym uczynku

surrender (se'render) s. poddanie się; wyrzeczenie się; v. poddawać się; oddawać się; wyrzekać się czegoś

surround (se'raund) v. otaczać; okrążać

surroundings (se'raundyngs) pl. otoczenie

survey (se:r'wej) s. przegląd; oględziny; inspekcja; pomiary; plan (topograficzny); opis; ankieta; statystyka; v. przeglądać; robić pomiary; wymierzać; oglądać

surveying (se:r'wejyng) s. miernictwo

surveyor (se:r'wejer) s. mierniczy; inspektor celny

survival (ser'wajwel) s. przeżycie; przeżytek

survive (ser,wajw) v. przeżyć; dalej żyć

survivor (ser'wajwer) s. człowiek pozostały przy życiu

susceptible (se'septybl) adj. wrażliwy; drażliwy; podatny; dopuszczający

suspect (ses'pekt) v. podejrzewać kogoś; ('saspekt) adj. podejrzany

suspected (ses'pektyd) adj. podejrzany

suspend (ses'pend) v. zawiesić; powstrzymać (się chwilowo)

suspended (ses'pendyd) adj. zawieszony w czynnościach

suspenders (ses'penders) pl. podwiązki; szelki

suspense (ses'pens) s. niepewność; zawieszenie; nierozstrzygnięcie

suspension (ses'penszyn) s. zawieszenie; zawiesina; wstrzymanie

suspension bridge (ses'penszyn ,brydż) s. wiszący most

suspicion (ses'pyszyn) s. podejrzenie; v. podejrzewać

suspicious (ses'pyszes) adj. podejrzany; nieufny

sustain (ses'tejn) v. podtrzymywać; dźwigać; cierpieć; doznawać; ponosić; potwierdzać; utrzymywać; uznawać (słuszność)

sustenance ('sastynens) s. pożywienie; utrzymanie

swab (słob) s. wycior; wacik chłonący; ścierka na kiju; gamoń; epoleta; v. wycierać; ścierać; wuszorować

swab up ('słob,ap) v. wytrzeć

swagger (słaeger) v. paradować; dumnie chodzić; chełpić się; pysznić się;odstraszyć; nakłaniać strachem

swallow ('słolou) v. połykać (np. zniewagę); przełykać; dać się nabrać; odwołać (słowa); s. przełykanie; łyk; kęs; przełyk; jaskółka

swam (słaem) v. zob. swim

swamp (słomp) s. bagno; v. zalewać; pochłaniać; przysłaniać; grzęznąć

swampy (słompy) adj. bagnisty; błotnisty

swan (słon) s. łabędź

swap (słop) v. zamieniać (się); wymieniać (się); s. zamiana; wymiana

swarm (sło:rm) s. mrowie; mnóstwo; rój; v. roić (się); wyroić; obfitować (w coś); wspinać się; wdrapywać się

swarthy ('sło:rty) adj. śniady; smagły

swathe (słejz) v. spowijać; s. zawinięcie; bandaż

sway (słej) v. kołysać (się); chwiać (się); zachwiać (się); rządzić czyms; władać; s. chwianie się; władza

swear; sware; sworn (słeer; sło:r; sło:rn)

swear (słeer) v. przysięgać; poprzysiąc

sweat (słet) s. poty; pot; harówka; v. pocic sie; pracować ciężko; (slang): hárować; szwejsować; fermentować; wyświechtywać monety; wydzielać (żywice)

sweat out (słet,aut) v. wypacać (się); (slang): ciężko pracować; wyduszać z kogoś coś; wyciagać pieniadze szantażem; wyciagać odpowiedzi torturami; odsiadywać więzienie

sweater ('słeter) s. sweter; wyzyskiwacz robotników

sweatshop ('słet,szop) s. zakład wyzyskujacy robotników

sweatshirt ('slet,sze:rt) s. koszula trykotowa

Swedish ('słi:dysz) adj. szwedzki

sweep; swept; swept (słi:p; słept; słept)

sweep (słi:p) v. zamiatać; wymiatać; zmiatać; oczyszczać; wygrywać (np. wszystkie medale); porywać (słuchaczy); przewalić sie przez coś (burza; wichura; powódź); ogarniać; obejmować; rozciagać sie; sunać uroczyście; ślizgać sie; śmigać; zwalać (kogoś z nóg); ostrzeliwać; etc. s. zamiatanie; zdobycie; zagarniecie; ogołocenie; śmieci; śmignięcie; machnięcie; zasięg; robienie zakrętu; etc.

sweeper ('słi:per) s. zamiatacz; zamiataczka; zmiotka

sweeping ('słi:pyng) adj. szeroki; wspaniały; rozległy; daleko idacy

sweepings ('słi:pyngs) pl. śmieci

sweepstake ('słi:pstejk) s. wyścigi; loteria; nagroda (zbiorowa) w wyścigach

sweet (słi:t) adj. słodki; przyjemny; miły; rozkoszny; dobrze osłodzony; deserowy; melodyjny; świeży; łagodny; zakochany

sweeten ('słi:tn) v. słodzić; osładzać; stawać się słodkim; (slang): zwiększać stawkę; zwiększać zastaw

sweetheart ('słi:t-ha:rt) s. ukochana; ukochany

sweetness ('słi:tnys) s. słodycz

sweetpea ('słi:tpi:) s. groszek pachnący

swell; swollen; swelled (słel; słoulen; słeld)

swell (słel) v. puchnąć; wzdymać (się); nadymać (się); wydymać (się); rozdymać; wzbierać; wzrastać; potęgować się; s. wydęcie; zgrubienie; nabrzmienie; wzbieranie; wzburzona fala (morze); (slang): wytworniak; gruba ryba

swelling ('słelyng) s. spuchlizna; wzdęcie; obrzęk; wezbranie (rzeki)

swept (słept) v. zob. sweep

swerve (słe:rw) s. odchylenie; zboczenie; v. zbaczać; odchylać (się)

swift (słyft) adj. prędki; rączy; chyży; żywy; s. nawijak przędzy; traszka; jaszczurka; jerzyk

swiftness ('słyftnys) s. prędkość; chyżość

swim; swam; swum (słym; słaem; słam)

swim (słym) v. płynąć; przepływnąć; pływać (w wyścigach); pławić; ociekać czyms; unosić się na powierzchni; iść z prądem; kręcić się (w głowie); s. pływanie; nurt (życia); woda (do pływania); głębia; pęcherz pławny

swimmer ('słymer) s. pływak

swimming ('słymyng) s. pływanie

swimming pool ('słymyng,pu:l) s, pływanlnia

swimming suit ('słymyng,sju:t) s. kostium kąpielowy

swindle (słyndl) s. oszustwo; v. oszukiwać

swine (słajn) s. świnia

swing ; swung; swang (słyng;
słang;słaeng)

swing (słyng) v. huśtać (się);
kołysać (się); wahać (się);
bujać (się); machać; wywijać;
przerzucać (się) na coś; porywać (za sobą); pociągać
(za sobą); s. huśtanie (się);
kołysanie (się); ruch wahadłowy; zmiana pracy; objazd (te-
renu); rytm; przerzucanie się;
kołyszący chód; taniec (swing)

swing bridge ('słyng,brydź) s.
most wahadłowy

swing door ('słyng,do:r) s.
drzwi wahadłowe

swing wheel ('słyng,hłi:l) s.
koło rozpędowe (zamachowe)

swirl (słe:rl) s. wir; wirowanie; skręt; lok; v. wirować;
kręcić się; unosić się (wiru-
jąc)

Swiss (słys) adj. szwajcarski

switch (słycz) s. pręt; zwrotnica; przekładnia; wyłącznik;
przełącznik; kontakt; śmignięcie; v. bić prętem; machać;
wyrywać; zmieniać; przełączać;
włączać; rozłączać (się); wyłączać (się); włączać (np.
światło)

switch off ('słycz,of) v. wyłączać

switch on ('słycz,on) v. włączać

switchboard ('słyczbo:rd) s.
tablica rozdzielcza; łącznica
(telefoniczna etc.)

swollen ('słoulen) v. zob.swell
adj. opuchnięty; wzdęty;
wezbrany

swoon (słu:n) v. zemdleć; omd-
leć; zamierać; s. omdlenie

swoop down on ('słu:p,dałn on)
v. zaatakować z góry; runąć
na coś

swoop up ('słu:p,ap) v. porywać; s. spadnięcie; porwanie

swop (słóp) v. zamieniać; wymieniać; s. zamiana; wymiana

sword (so:rd) s. pałasz; szpada;
miecz; szabla; bagnet (slang)

swore (sło:r) v. zob. swear

sworn (sło:rn) v. zob. swear;
adj. zaprzysiężony; przy-
sięgły

swum (słam) v. zob. swim

swung (słang) v. zob. swing

sycamore ('sykemo:r) s. jawor;
klon; figowiec

syllable ('sylebl) s. sylaba;
zgłoska

symbol ('symbel) s. symbol;
v. symbolizować

symbolic (,sym'bolyk) adj.
symboliczny

symbolism ('symbelyzem) s.
symbolizm

symmetric (sy'metryk) adj. symetryczny

symmetry ('symytry) s. symetria

sympathetic (,sympe'tetyk) adj.
współczujący; życzliwy; sympatyczny; współbrzmiący;
s. współczulny; łatwy do za-
hipnotyzowania

sympathize ('sympetajz) v.
współczuć; mieć zrozumienie;
sympatyzować z kimś

sympathy ('sympety) s. współczucie; solidarność; sympatia

symphony ('symfeny) s. symfonia

symptom (sympten) s. symptom

synagogue ('synegog) s. bożni-
ca; synagoga

synchronize ('synkrenajz) s.
działać równocześnie; synchronizować; pokazywać jednakowo
(czas); uzgadniać (zegary)

synonym ('synenym) s. synonim

synonymous (sy'nonymes) adj.
równoznaczny z czyms

syntax ('syntaeks) s. składnia

synthesis ('syntysys) s. synteza

syntheses ('syntysi:s) pl. syn-
tezy

synthetic (syn'tetyk) adj.
sztuczny; syntetyczny

syphilis ('syfylys) s. kiła; sy-
filis

syringe ('syryndż) s. strzykawka; v. strzykać (wodą)

syrup ('syrep) s. syrop
system ('systym) s. system
systematic (,systy'maetyk)
adj. systematyczny
t (ti:) dwudziesta litera
alfabetu angielskiego
tab (taeb) s. patka; wieszak
(przyszyty); język (buta);
naszywka; języczek; ucho;
przywieszka; rachunek; kontrola; pilnowanie; v. prowadzić
ewidencję; tabelować; za-
opatrywać w (języczek lub
ucho etc.)
table ('tejbl) s. stół; stolik; tablica; tabela; tabliczka (np. mnożenia); płyta;
płaskowyż; blat; v. kłaść
na stole; odraczać (na długo);
wciągać na agendę; adj.sto-
łowy
tablecloth ('tejbl,kloθ) s.
obrus
tableland ('tejbl-laend) s.
płaskowyż
tablespoon ('tejbl-spu:n) s.
łyżka stołowa (do zupy)
tablespoonful ('tejblspu:nful)
s. pełna łyżka (pół uncji)
tablet ('taeblyt) s. tabletka;
tabliczka (do pisania)
taboo (te'bu:) s. tabu; v.za-
kazywać; adj. zakazany
tacit ('taesyt) adj. milczący;
cichy; niemy
taciturn ('taesyte:rn) adj.
małomówny
tack (taek) s. gwóźdź tapicer-
ski; papiak; pluskiewka;
fastryga; kurs (polityki);
taktyka; stan lepki; prowiant;
żywność; jedzenie; v. przyczepiać; przybijać (lekko); fastrygować; zmieniać kurs; lawirować; hałasować
tackle ('taekl) s. zestaw przyborów (do łowienia, golenia);
wielokrążek; takielunek; złapanie i trzymanie; v. zewrzeć
się; borykać (się); złapać
i trzymać; zmagać (się); brać
się do czegoś (ostro); umoco-
wywać; porać (się)

tacky ('taeky) adj. lepki; niemodny; marny
tact (taekt) s. takt; wyczucie;
dotyk
tactful ('taektful) adj. taktowny
tactics ('taektyks) pl. taktyka
tactile ('taektajl) adj. doty-
kowy; dotykalny
tactless ('taektlys) adj. nietaktowny
tad (taed) s. berbeć
tadpole ('taedpoul) s. kijanka
tag (taeg) s. skuwka; etykieta;
kartka; strzęp; przywieszka;
znaczek tożsamości; marka;
mandat karny (pisany); ucho;
igliczka; wieszadło (przyszyte);
błyszczka; dodatek; morał; frazes; banał; cytat; refren;
ogon; zabawa w gonionego;
v. przyczepiać: skuwkę; kartkę;
znaczek, markę; ucho; wieszadło, igliczkę, ogon; dawać;
mandat karny, morał, bawić się
w gonionego; tańczyć odbijanego;
wymierzać wyrok; przeznaczać;
włóczyć się za kimś; dołączyć
do czegoś
tail (tejl) s. ogon; tył; koniec;
tren; poła; pośladki; buńczuk;
warkocz; świta; cień (chodzący za kimś); v. dodawać ogon;
obrywać ogonki; śledzić (krok
w krok); zamykać pochód
tailcoat (,tejl'kout) s. frak
taillight ('tejl,lajt) s.
tylne światło (wozu)
tailor ('tejler) s. krawiec;
v. szyć odzież
tailor-made ('tejlermejd) adj.
uszyty na zamówienie
tail wind ('tejlłynd) s. wiatr
w plecy
taint (tejnt) s. skaza; zaraza;
plama; v. plamić; kazić; zepsuć; plugawić
taintless ('teintlys)adj. bez
skazy
take; took; taken (tejk; tuk;
'tejkn)

take (tejk) s. brać; wziąć; łapać; chwytać; zdobywać (twierdzę); zajmować (miejsce); rezerwować; zażywać; pić; jeść; odczuwać; rozumieć; pojechać; notować; zrobić (zdjęcie); zadać sobie (trud); dostawać (napadu); przyjmować (radę; karę; etc.); mierzyć swoją temperaturę; godzić się(na traktowanie); nabierać (połysku); iść (za przykładem) s. połów; zdjęcie; wpływy (do kasy)

take along (,tejke'long) v. zabrać ze sobą

take down ('tejk,dałn) v.zdejmować; rozmontowywać

take-in ('tejk'yn) s. oszukanie; naciąganie

take off ('tejk,of) v. rozbierać; kasować; małpować; wystartować; odjąć; usunąć

takeoff ('tejkof) s. start; skok; skocznia; karykatura; parodia; naśladowanie; odbicie; lista materiałów

take out (tejk aut) v. podejmować (poza domem); wyprowadzać; wynieść;wyrywać; wykupić; odjąć; oddzielić

takeover ('tejkouwer) s. opanowanie firmy przez manipulacje giełdowe lub finansowe

take over ('tejk,ouwer) v. przejmować (firmę); przyjmować (obowiązki);dominować

take up ('tejk,ap) v. ponosić; wchłonąć; wziąć (miejsce); zacząć (uczyć się); zadawać się;brać;zcieśniać; besztać

taken ('tejkn) v. zob. take; adj. zabrany; porwany; zdobyty; nabrany; oszukany

talc(taelk) s. talk; v. posypywać talkiem

tale (tejl) s. opowiadanie; plotka; wymysł

talent ('taelent) s. talent (do czegoś); dar; uzdolnienie

talk (to:k) v. mówić; rozmawiać; plotkować; namawiać;

s. rozmowa: dyskusja; pogadanka; plotka: gadanie; mowa

talkative ('to:ketyw) adj. rozmowny; gadatliwy

talk-to ('to:k,tu) s. bura

tall (to:l) adj. wysoki; (slang): nieprawdopodobny

tall talk ('to:l,to:k) s, przechwałki

tallow ('taelou) s. łój; v. tuczyć; smarować łojem

talon ('taelen) s. szpon; pazur; rygiel; łapa ludzka; palec

tame ('tejm) v. oswajać; poskramiać; ujarzmić; okiełzać; łagodzić; przytłumić; upokorzyć

tamper ('taemper) s. ubijak; v. majstrować; manipulować; zmieniać coś nielegalnie

tan (taen) s. opalenizna; kolor (brązowy) brunatny; kora garbarska; v. garbować; opalać się (na słońcu); brązowieć; wyłoić komuś skórę

tangent ('taendżent) adj. styczny; s. styczna; szczegół oderwany; zmiana tematu (od rzeczy); zmiana kierunku rozmowy

tangerine (taendże'ri:n) s. mandarynka

tangle ('taengl) s. plątanina; v. plątać (się); wikłać (się); (slang): pobić się z kimś

tank (taenk) s. tank; zbiornik; cysterna; czołg; (slang): więzienie; v. nabierać do zbiornika; (slang): popić sobie

tankard ('taenkerd) s. kufel

tanner ('taener) s. garbarz

tantalize ('tae ntalajz)v. dręczyć (zwodną) nadzieją; łudzić

tantrum ('taentrem) s. napad złości

tap (taep) v. stukać; odszpuntować; napoczynać; robić punkcje; naciąć; ciągnąć sok; wykorzystywać; gwintować; podsłuchiwać (telefon); s. czop; szpunt; kurek; zawór; gwintownik; zaczep; odczep

tape (tejp) s. tasma; tasiemka; tasiemiec; (slang): wodka; v. wiązać tasmą (przylepcem); mierzyć; (slang):oceniac kogoś

tape measure ('tejp,mežer) s. miara na tasmie (krawiecka)

taper ('tejper) s. stopniowe zwężanie (się); stożek; ubytek; osłabianie; stoczek; świeczka

taper off ('tejper,of) v. zwężać się stopniowo; cichnąc stopniowo; kończyć się spiczasto

tape recorder ('tejp-ry,ko:rder) s. magnetofon

tape recording ('tejp;ry,ko:rdyŋg) s. nagranie na tasmę

tapestry ('taepystry) s. gobelin; arras; v. zdobić gobelinami

tapeworm ('tejpłor:m) s. soliter; tasiemiec

tar (ta:r) s. smoła; dziegieć; ter; v. smołować; terować

target ('ta:rgyt) s. cel; obiekt; tarcza strzelnicza; v. kierować do celu; celować; ustalać cel

tariff ('taeryf) s. cło; taryfa; cennik; c. clic wg taryfy; układać taryfę celną

tarnish ('ta:rnysz) v. matowieć; przyćmiewać; brudzić (się); brukać (się); tracić połysk; s, matowienie; skaza

tart ('ta:rt) adj. cierpki; zgryzliwy; s. ciastko owocowe; (slang): kurewka

tartan ('ta:rten) s. materiał w kratę szkocką

task ('taesk) s. zadanie (specjalne); lekcja zadana; przedsięwzięcie; v. wyznaczać zadanie; wystawiac na próbę; rugać

taskforce ('taesk,fo:rs) s. oddział (grupa) do specjalnego zadania

taskmaster ('taesk,ma:ster) s. nadzorca (kontrolujący wykonanie zadania)

tassel ('taesel) s. kutas; kitka; v. ozdabiać kutasami; kitkami

taste (tejst) s. smak; gust; posmak; zamiłowanie; v. smakować; kosztować; czuć smak; miec smak; doznawać (czegoś)

tasteful ('tejstful) adj. gustowny; w dobrym smaku

tasteless ('tejstlys) adj. bez gustu; bez smaku

tasty ('tejsty) adj. smakowity; smaczny

ta-ta (tae'-ta:) exp. do widzenia; pa ! pa !

tattoo (te'tu:) v. bębnic palcami; tatuować; s. capstrzyk; tatuaż

taught(to:t) v. zob. teach

taunt (to:nt) v. urągać; wymyslać komus; zwymyślać kogoś; s. urąganie; wymyślanie; adj. wysoki (np, maszt)

taut (to:t) adj. napięty; naprężony; w dobrej formie; w dobrym stanie

tax (taeks) s. podatek; wysiłek; ciężar; obciążenie; v. opodatkować; obarczać; obciążać; nadwerężać; sprawdzać; wymagać wysiłku; zarzucać coś

taxation (taek'sejszyn) s. opodatkowanie

tax collector ('taekske,lekter) s. poborca podatkowy

taxi ('taeksy) s. taksówka; v. jechać taksówką;wieźć taksówką

taxidriver ('taeksydrajwer) s. taksówkarz

taximeter ('taeksy,mi:ter) s. licznik (w taksówce); taksometr

taxpayer ('taeks,pejer) s. podatnik

tax return ('taeks,ry'te:rn)s. podatek (zapłata ze sprawozdaniem)

tea (ti:) s. herbata; herbatka; podwieczorek; v. pić i częstować herbatą

teabag ('ti:baeg) s. woreczek papierowy z herbatą

teach; taught; taught (ti:cz; to:t; to:t)

teach (ti:cz) v. uczyc (się); nauczac; wykładac

teacher (ti:czer) s. nauczyciel

teacup ('ti:kap) s. filiżanka na herbatę

teakettle ('ti:,ketl) s. imbryk; czajnik

team (ti:m) s. zespoł; drużyna; zaprzęg; v. zaprzęgac; jezdzic zaprzęgiem

team up ('ti:map) v. łączyc się razem (do pracy etc.)

teamwork ('ti:młe:rk) s. praca zespołowa

teapot ('ti:pot) s. mały czajnik

tear; tore; torn (teer; to:r; to:rn)

tear (teer) v. drzec; targac; rwac; kaleczyc; wydrzec (rane) pędzic; s. dziura; rozdarcie; wybuch pasji; kropla; łza; (slang) hulanka

tearoom ('ti:ru:m) s. herbaciarnia

tease (ti:z) v. drażnic; nudzic; s. dokuczanie; nudziarstwo

teat (tyt) s. cycek (wulg.kobiecy)

technical ('teknykel) adj. techniczny; formalny; spekulacyjny

technician ('teknyszyn) s. technik

technique (tek'ni:k) s. technika malowania, rzeźby etc.

tedious ('ti:dies) adj. nudny

teem (ti:m) v. roic sie; obfitowac; oprożniac; wylewac

teen (ti:n) s. szkoda; zgryzota

teens (ti:nz) pl. wiek 12 do 18 lat

teeny ('ti:ny) adj. maleńki

teeth (ti:s) pl. zęby; zob. tooth

teethe (ti:s) v. ząbkowac

teetotaler (ti:'toutler) s. abstynent

telegram('telygraem)s. telegram

telegraph ('telygra:f) s. telegraf

telephone ('telyfoun) s. telefon; v. telefonowac

telephone booth('telyfoun,bu:s) s. kabina telefoniczna

telephone call('telyfoun,ko:1) s. rozmowa telefoniczna

telephone directory ('telyfoun, dyrektory) s. książka telefoniczna

telephone exchange ('telyfouneksczendż) s. centrala telefoniczna na zagranice

telephone kiosk ('telyfounkiosk) s. kiosk telefoniczny

teleprinter ('tely,prynter) s. dalekopis

telescope ('telyskoup) s. teleskop

teletypewriter (,tely'tajprajter) s. dalekopis

televise ('telywajz) v. nadawac przez telewizję

television ('telywyżyn) v. telewizja

television set('telywyżyn,set) s. telewizor; odbiornik telewizyjny

televisor ('telywajzer) s. telewizor

tell;told; told (tel; tould; tould)

tell (tel) v. (o kims; o czyms): mowic; opowiadac; powiedziec; wskazywac; pokazywac; kazac; poznac; sprawdzic; policzyc; poznawac; wiedziec; doniesc; oskarżyc; skarżyc; miec znaczenie; odbijac się na kims; odrożniac

teller ('teler) s. narrator; kasjer; liczący głosy

telltale ('teltejl) s. plotkarz; okolicznosc ostrzegawcza; wskaźnik odchylenia (steru); aparat sprawdzający, ostrzegawczy; adj. ostrzegawczy; wymowny

temper ('temper) s. usposobienie; humor; gniew; złosc; domieszka;mieszanka; stan; hartownosc; v.łagodzic; hartowac

temperament ('temprement) s.
temperament; usposobienie;
skala temperowana; temperatura skali

temperance ('temperens) s.
umiarkowanie; powściągliwość;
obstynencja; wstrzemięźliwość

temperate ('temperyt) adj.
umiarkowany; powściągliwy;
wstrzemięźliwy

temperature ('tempereczer) s.
temperatura; ciepłota

tempest ('tempyst) s. burza;
v. zaburzać

tempestuous (tem'pestjues) adj.
burzliwy

temple ('templ) s. świątynia;
skroń; ucho od okularów; rozciągacz tkacki

temporal ('temperel) adj. doczesny; czasowy; skroniowy;
s. kość skroniowa

temporary ('temperery) adj.
chwilowy; tymczasowy

tempt (tempt) v. kusić; nęcić

temptation (temp'tejszyn) s.
pokusa; kuszenie

tempting ('temptyŋg) adj. ponętny; nęcący; kuszący

ten (ten) num. dziesięc; s.
dziesiątka

tenacious (ty'nejszes) adj.
wytrwały; nieustępliwy; trwały; wierny; czepny; ciągliwy;
mocny; spoisty

tenant ('tenent) s. lokator;
dzierżawca; v. zamieszkiwać;
dzierżawić

tend (tend) v. skłaniać się:
zmierzać; służyć; doglądać;
obsługiwać

tendency ('tendensy) s. skłonność; tendencja

tender ('tender) adj. delikatny; miękki; kruchy; wrażliwy;
czuły; niedojrzały; młody;
młodociany; uważający; dbały; łamliwy; drażliwy; wywrotny; v. oferować; przedłożyć; założyć; s. oferta; środek płatniczy; dozorca; tender; statek pomocniczy-zaopatrzeniowy

tenderloin ('tenderloyn) s.
polędwica

tenderness ('tendernyss) s. czułość; dbałość; delikatność

tendon (tenden) s. ścięgno

tendril (tendryl) s. wąs; wic

tenement house (tenymenthaus) s.
dom czynszowy

tennis ('tenys) s. tenis

tennis court ('tenys'ko:rt) s.
kort tenisowy

tense (tens) s. czas (np. przyszły) adj. naprężony; napięty

tension (tenszyn) s. naprężenie;
napięcie; prężność

tent (tent) s. namiot

tentacle (tentekl) s. macka;
czułek

tenth (tenŋ) adj. dziesiąty

tenthly (tenŋly) adv. po dziesiąte

tepee ('ti:pi:) s. namiot indiański (stożkowy)

tepid ('tepyd) adj. letni; ciepławy; bez zapału

term (te:rm) s. okres; czas
trwania; przeciąg; semestr; kadencja; termin; wyrażenie;
określenie; kres; v. określać;
nazywać;

terms (te:rms) pl. warunki
(kontraktu, porozumienia) stosunki wzajemne

terminal ('te:rmynel) adj. końcowy; terminowy; ostateczny;
s. zakończenie; końcówka;
uchwyt; końcowa stacja

terminate ('te:rmynejt) v. skończyć; zakończyć; kończyć (się)
ograniczać; upływać; rozwiązywać (umowę); ustawać; wygasać;
upływać; wymawiać pracę

termination (,te:rmy'n ejszyn)
s. koniec; wypowiedzenie (pracy); wygaśnięcie; zakończenie;
końcówka

terminus (te:rmynes) s. końcowa stacja; kres; koniec; granica

termite ('te:rmajt) s. termit

terrace ('teres) s. taras; terasa; ulica wzdłuż zbocza;
v. robić tarasy

terraced ('terest) adj uformowany w terasy

terrible ('terybl) adj. straszliwy; straszny; okropny

terrific ('te'ryfyk) adj. przerażający; (slang): fantastyczny; pierwszej klasy

terrify ('teryfaj) v. przerażać

territorial (,tery'torjel) adj. terytorialny

territory ('teryto:ry) s. obszar; rejon; (terytorium bez praw stanu np. w USA)

terror ('terer) s. terror; przerażenie; postrach

terrorize ('tereraiz) v. siać strach; przerażać; terroryzować

test (test) s. próba; sprawdzian; test; egzamin; odczynnik; skorupa; v. sprawdzać; poddawać próbie; oczyszczać (metal)

testament ('testement) s. testament

testify ('testyfaj) v. świadczyć; dawać świadectwo; zaświadczać; poświadczać

testimonial (,testy'mounjel) s. świadectwo (moralności); polecenie; nagroda w uznaniu zasług

testimony ('testymouny) s. świadectwo

testy ('testy) adj. drażliwy; popędliwy; pobudliwy

tetanus ('tetenes) s. tężec

text (tekst) s. tekst

textbook ('tekstbuk) s. podręcznik

textile ('tekstail) s. tkanina; adj. tkacki; tekstylny

texture ('teksczer) s. budowa; tkanina; struktura; tkanie

than (dzaen) con, aniżeli; niż; od

thank (taenk) v. dziękować; s. podziękowanie; dzięki

thank you ('taenkju:) exp.: dziękuję

thank you very much ('taenkju:-'wery,macz) exp.:bardzo dziękuję

thankful ('taenkful) adj. wdzięczny; dziękczynny

thankless ('taenklys) adj. niewdzięczny

thanks ('taenks) pl. podziękowanie; dzięki

Thanksgiving Day ('taenksgy-wyng,dej) s. dzień święta dziękczynienia (USA)

that (daet) adj. & pron. pl. thouse (dzous); tamten; tamta; tamto; ten; ta; to; ów; owa; owo; pl. tamci; tamte; ci; te; owi; owe; adv. tylu; tyle; conj. że; żeby; aby; skoro

thatch (taecz) s. strzecha; v. pokrywać strzechą

thaw (tso:) s. odwilż; rozkrochmalenie się; v. tajać; odtajać; taje; jest odwilż

the (przed samogłoską dy; przed spółgłoską de; z naciskiem dy:) przyimek określony rzadko kiedy tłumaczony; ten; ta; to; pl. ci; te; ten właśnie , etc. adv. tym; im...tym

theater ('tieter) s. teatr; kino; widownia; amfiteatr

theatrical (ti:aetrykel) adj. teatralny; sceniczny; aktorski

theatricals (ti:'aetrykels) pl. przedstawienie (amatorskie)

theatrics (ti:'aetryks) s. sztuka teatralna

thee (di:) archaiczna forma; ty używana przez kwakrów

theft (teft) s. kradzież

their (dzeer) zaimek; ich

theirs (dzeers) zaimek dzierzawczy: ich

them (dzem) przypadek zależny od: they , (np.: im; nimi; nich)

theme (ti:m) s. temat; zadanie; wypracowanie

themselves (dzem'selwz) pl.oni sami; one same

then (dzen) adv. wtedy; wówczas; po czym; potem; następnie; później; zatem; zaraz; poza tym; ponadto; conj.a więc; no to;wobec tego; ale przecież; adj.ówczesny;s.przedtem;uprzednio; dotąd; odtąd;

theologian (tie'loudżjen) s.
teolog

theology (tie'oledży) s. teologia

theoretic(al) (tie'retyk-el)
adj. teoretyczny

theory (tiery) s. teoria

therapy (terepy) s. leczenie;
terapia

there (dzeer) adv. tam; w tym;
co do tego; oto; własnie; potem; tędy; dlatego; z tego;
na to; s. ta miejscowość; to
miasto; to miejsce

thereabout ('dzeerebaut) adv.
w tych stronach; gdzies tam
mniej więcej; cos około tego

thereafter ('dzeera:fter) adv.
pózniej; odtąd

there are (dzeer'a:r) exp.: są

thereby ('dzeer'baj) adv. przez
to; w ten sposób; skutkiem
tego

therefore ('dzeer,fo:r) adv.
dlatego; zatem więc

therein (,dzeer'yn) adv. w tym;
w nim; w niej

there is (,dzeer'ys) exp.: jest

thereupon ('dzeer,e'pon) adv.
skutkiem tego

therewith (,dzeer'łys) adv.
tym; z tym; w następstwie tego

there you are (,dzeer'ju:,a:r)
exp.: proszę; tu jest to !
tu pan to ma ! etc.

thermometer (ter'momyter) s.
termometr

thermos ('termos) s. termos

these (di:z) pl. od this

thesis ('ti:sys) s. teza; praca dyplomowa; pl. theses
('ti:syz)

they (dżej) pl. pron. oni; one
(ci; którzy)

they say (dżej sej) exp.:podob-
no (mówią)

thick (tyk) adj. gruby; gęsty;
zbity; rzęsisty; stłumiony;
niewyrazny; mętny; ponury;
tępy; ochrypły; (slang): blat-
ny; spoufalony; s. gruba częsc;
duren; głuptas; adv. gęsto;
grubo; ochryple; tępo

thicken ('tykn) v. pogrubiac
(sie); zagęszczac (się)

thicket ('tykyt) s. gaszcz;
gęstwina

thickness ('tyknys) s. grubosc;
warstwa; gęstosc

thief (ti:f) s. złodziej;
pl. thieves (ti:ws)

thigh (taj) s. udo

thimble ('tymbl) s. naparstek;
koncówka (metalowa liny)

thimbleful ('tymblful) s. odrobina; naparstek

thin (tyn) adj.cienki (sos;
głos etc). rzadki; szczupły;
słaby (kolor.etc.); (slang):
paskudny; v. rozcienczac;
szczuplec;przerzedzac(się)

thine (tajn) sob. thy; stara
forma: twój; twoje

thing (tyng) s. rzecz; przedmiot;
uczynek; cos; krzyk mody; warunek; urojenia; przywidzenia;
pl. zwierzęta; rzeczy; odzież;
ubrania; ruchomosci; sytuacja;
koniunktura:wszystko; nierucho-
mosci; głupstwa

think; thought; thought (tynk;
'to:t;'to:t)

think (tynk) v. myslec; pomyslec;
zastanawiac się; rozważac; rozmyslac (się); wymyslic; wyobra-
żac sobie; uważac za; miec zdanie; miec za; zapomniec (roz-
myslnie); miec na mysli; roz-
wiązywac; etc.

think over ('tynk'ouwer) v. prze-
mysliwac; zastanawiac się

think up ('tynk,ap) v. wymyslac;
wykombinowac; rozwiązac

third (te:rd) adj. trzeci

third degree (,te:rd dy'gri:)
exp.: trzeci stopien (przesłuchi-
wania na policji—głupi, przykry i męczący)

thirdly ('te:rdly) adv. po trzecie

third party (,te:rd'pa:rty) s.
strona trzecia; osoby trzecie

thirdrate ('te:rd'rejt) adj.
trzeciorzędny

Third World ('te:rd'₤e:rld) s. trzeci świat (poza Europą, Chinami, Indią oraz Ameryką)

thirst ('te:rst) s. pragnienie; żądza; v. pragnąc

thirsty ('te:rsty) adj. spragniony; żądny; suchy; wyschnięty; (slang): ciężki

this (tys) adj. & pron. pl. these (ti:z) ten; ta; to; tak; w ten sposob; tyle; obecny; bieżący; adv. tak; tak daleko; tyle; tak dużo

thistle ('tysl) s. oset

thorn ('to:rn) s. kolec; ciern; krzak cierniowy; v. kłuc; drażnić

thorny ('to:rny) adj. kolczasty; ciernisty; drażliwy

thorough (terou) adj. dokładny; zupełny; całkowity; sumienny; adv. na wskros; na wylot

thoroughbred ('te:rou,bred) adj. rasowy; czystej krwi; s. koń rasowy

thoroughfare ('te:rou,feer) s. arteria komunikacyjna; przejazd; ulica

thoroughly (te:rouly) adv. zupełnie; dokładnie; całkowicie; na wskros; sumiennie; gruntownie

those (douz) pl. od that

thou (dau) biblijne: ty

though (tou) conj. chociaż; choćby; gdyby; adv. jednak; pomimo tego; przecież

thought (to:t) v. zob. think; s, mysł; namysł; zastanowienie się; pomysł; oczekiwanie; rozwaga; zamiar; pl. zdanie; pogląd; odrobina; troszkę

thoughtful ('to:tful) adj. zamyslony; zadumany; rozważny; uważający; dbały; uprzejmy; (oryginalnie) myślący

thoughtless ('to:tlys) adj. bezmyślny; nieuważający; nierozważny

thousand ('tauzend) num. tysiąc

thousandth ('tauzendt) adj. tysięczny

thrash (traesz) s. młocic; walic; bic; prac; dyskutować; s. młocenie; walenie

thrashing (traeszyng) s, młocka; lanie

thread (tred) s. nic; nitka; przędza; sznurek; wątek; żyłka; krok (śruby); zwojnik (nici); gwint; v. nawlekać (igłę); przetykać; nacinać gwint (zwojnik); przepychać się

threadbare (tredbeer) adj. wytarty; wyświechtany; wyszarzały

threat (tret) s. grożba; pogrożka

threaten ('tretn) v. grozic; zagrażać; odgrażać się

threatening ('tretnyng) adj. grożący; zagrażający; groźny

three (tri:) num. trzy; s. trójka

threefold ('tri:fold) adj. potrójny

threescore ('tri:sko:r) num. sześćdziesiąt

threestage ('tri:stejdż) adj. trójfazowy; trzystopniowy

thresh (tresz) v. młocic; roztrząsać; obgadać szczegółowo; omówić gruntownie; s. młocka

thresher ('treszer) s. młockarnia

threshing ('treszyng) s. młocenie

threshing machine ('treszyng,me-'szi:n) s. młockarnia

threshold ('treszould) s. prog

threw (tru:) v. zob. throw

thrice (trajs) adj. trzykrotnie

thriftless (tryftlys) adj. rozrzutny

thrifty (tryfty) adj. oszczędny; rozrastający sie; kwitnący

thrill (tryl) v. przejmować (się); drgać; s. dreszcz; dreszczyk; drganie; powieśc sencacyjna; szmer (serca)

thriller (tryler) s. dreszczowiec; powieśc sensacyjna (kryminalna); sztuka sensacyjna; opowieśc sensacyjna

thrilling (trylyŋg) adj. podniecający; przejmujący; sensacyjny

thrive; throve; thriven (trajw; trouw; trywn)

thrive (trajw) v. dobrze: rosnąc, chowac się, rozwijac się, miewac się, kwitnac, prosperowac

thro(tru:) = through

throat (trout) s. gardło; szyja; wlot; gardziel; wąskie przejscie; v. żłobic; żłobkowac; mowic gardłowo

throb (trob) v. pulsowac; drgac; bic; tetnic; rwac; s. pulsowanie; drganie; bicie serca; dreszcz; warkot maszyny

thrombosis (trom'bousys) s. skrzep

throne (troun) s. tron; v. tronowac; wprowadzac na tron

throng (tro:ng)s. tłum; tłok; rzesza; masa; v. tłoczyc się; zatłaczac; napierac na

throstle (trosl) s. drozd; przędzarka

throttle ('trotl) s. gardziel; dławik; przepustnica; zawor dławiący; v. dusic; regulowac dławikiem

through (tru:) prep. przez; poprzez; po; wskros; na wylot; ze; z; skutkiem; na skutek;za; dzięki; z powodu; adv. na wskros; na wylot; adj. przelotowy; bezposredni; skonczony (np. życiowo)

throughout ('tru:,aut) prep. poprzez; przez cały; od początku do konca; wszędzie; całkowicie; adv. na wskros

throw (trou) v. zob. thrive

throw; threw; thrown (trou; tru:, troun)

throw (trou) v. rzucac; ciskac; zarzucac; zrzucac; skrecac; powalic; narzucac; modelowac na kole; odrzucac; marnowac; s. rzut; ryzyko; szal; narzuta; uskok

throw up ('trou,ap) v. wymiotowac; rzucac w gorę; podrzucac

thrown ('troun) v. zob. throw

thru (tru:) = through

thrum (tram) v. rzępolic; bębnic; robic z nitek; odcinac luzne nitki; s. brzdąkanie; odcięta nitka; krajka

thrush (trasz) s. drozd; choroba strzałki kopyta konskiego; plesniawka

thrust; thrust; thrust (trast; trast; trast)

thrust (trast) v. wpychac; wsadzac; wtykac; wrazic; pchac (się); przepychac się; wysuwac (się); szturchac; przebijac; wepchnąc; narzucac (się); wtracac (się); zadawac pchnięcie; pchnąc; s. pchnięcie; dzgnięcie; wypad; wypchnięcie; nacisk; siła : napędu, ciągu, pędu; zrzut; parcie; uwaga; przytyk

thud (tad) s. łomot; łoskot (głuchy); v. łomotac; upadac z łoskotem

thug (tag) s. bandyta; zbir

thumb (tam) s. kciuk; duży palec; władza (domowa); talent ogrodniczy; zasada (praktyczna); v. kartkowac; brudzic palcami; niszczyc; walac; grac niezgrabnie; prosic o podwiezienie; wyprosic (gestem)

thumb a lift (tam a lyft) v. prosic o podwiezienie (autostopem)

thumbtack ('tam-taek) s. pineska; pluskiewka

thump ('tamp) s. grzmotnięcie; v. grzmocic; walic; isc ciężko

thunder ('tander) s. grzmot; burza; grom; piorun; v. grzmiec; rzucac gromy; piorunowac; miotac (grozby)

thunderstorm ('tander-sto:rm) s. burza z piorunami

thunderstruck ('tander-strak) adj. rażony piorunem; oszołomiony

Thursday ('te:r-zdej) s. czwartek

thus (tas) adv. tak; w ten sposób; tak więc; a zatem

thus far ('tas,fa:r) adv. jak dotąd

thus much ('tas,mach) adv. tyle

thwart ('tło:rt) v. udaremnic; pokrzyżowac; psuc szyki; adj. poprzeczny; przeciwny; niepomyslny; s. poprzeczna ławka wioslarska

thy (taj) pron. twoj; twoje; zob. thine

tick (tyk) s. kleszcz; tykanie; moment; wsyp; kredyt; sprawne działanie; v. tykac; kupowac na kredyt; sprzedawac na kredyt (slang); ustalac sprawne działanie

tick away ('tyke'łej) v. znaczyc tykaniem

tick off ('tykof) v. odliczac; besztac; odfajkowac

ticker ('tyker) s. telegraf; zegarek; serce (slang)

ticket ('tykyt) s. bilet; kwit; znaczek; wywieszka; lista kandydatow (USA); v. zaopatrywac w bilet, etykietkę; umieszczac na liscie kandydatow

ticket office ('tykyt'ofys) s. kasa biletowa

tickle ('tykl) v. łaskotac; łechtac; swędzic; rozsmieszac; bawic; cieszyc; s. łaskotanie; łechtanie; swędzenie

tidal wave ('tajdelłejw) s. olbrzymia fala przypływu skutkiem trzęsienia ziemi

tide (tajd) n. przypływ & odpływ morza; fala; okres; v. przypływac falą; płynąc z falą; wybrnąc

tidy ('tajdy) adj. schludny; czysty; niemały; spory; s. zbiornik na odpadki; pokrowiec na mebel; v. oporządzic; sporządzac; oporządzac (się); porządkowac

tie (taj) v. wiązac; zawiązac; przywiązac; łączyc; sznurowac; remisowac; zawrzec slub; unieruchomic; s. węzeł; krawat; podkład kolejowy; prog; remis; sznur; rozgrywka; połbucik

tie up ('taj,ap) v. zawiązywac; unieruchamiac

tier (tier) s. piętro; rząd; węzeł; zwoj; kondygnacja; rzecz wiążąca; fartuszek; v. spiętrzac się (też warstwami)

tiger ('tajger) s. tygrys; jaguar; kugar; zawadiaka; pracujący zapamiętale

tight (tajt) adj. zacisnięty; mocny; zwarty; szczelny; spoisty: obcisły; wąski; nabity; wstawiony; zalany; skąpy; niewystarczający; silny; mocny; uparty; adv. zwarcie; ciasno; szczelnie; obcisle; mocno; silnie

tighten ('tajtn) v. zaciskac (się); uszczelniac; napinac (się)

tightfisted ('tajt-,tystyd) adj. sknera; kutwa

tight fitting ('tajt-fytyng) adj. obcisły; opięty

tightrope ('tajt-roup) s. lina akrobatyczna

tights (tajts) pl. trykot baletnicy, akrobaty etc.; w Anglii rajstopy

tigress ('tajgrys) s. tygrysica

tile (tajl) n. dachowka; kafelek; dren; (slang): cylinder; v. pokrywac dachowkami; wykładac kaflami (płytami)

till (tyl) prep. aż do; dopiero; dotychczas; aż; dopoki nie; dotąd; v. uprawiac (ziemię); s. szufladka na pieniądze; kasa podręczna

tilt (tylt) s. przechylenie; przechył; nachylenie; natarcie kopią; plandeka; daszek; v. przechylac (się); nachylac (się); nacierac kopią; (pełnym) pędem leciec; zaopatrywac w daszek

timber ('tymber) s. drzewo; budulec; drewno; belka; wręga;
las; charakter; v. zaopatrywać w budulec; podpierać belką
timberland ('tymber'laend) s.
obszar lasu budulcowego
timberwork ('tymber:łe:rk) s.
konstrukcja drewniana
timber yard ('tymber,ja:rd) s.
skład (drzewa) budulca
time (tajm) s. czas; pora; raz;
takt; v. obliczać czas zużyty;
ustalać czas; wybierać czas;
robić we właściwym czasie; nastawiać (przyrząd); regulować
(zegar); synchronizować; harmonizować; trzymać takt;
excl.: czas ! (zamykać lokal
etc.)
time and again ('tajm end,e'-
'gen) exp.: ciągle; ustawicznie
time bomb ('tajm,bom) s. bomba
zegarowa
time is up ('tajm'ys,ap) exp.:
koniec (zabawy; rozmowy etc)
timely ('tajmly) adv. na czasie;
w porę; adj. aktualny; odpowiedni; właściwy; punktualny
timetable ('tajm,tejbl) s. rozkład jazdy, zajęć etc.
timeless ('tajmlys) adj. wieczny; ponadczasowy (niekończący
się)
timid ('tymyd) adj. nieśmiały;
bojaźliwy
timidity (ty'mydyty) s. bojaź-
liwość
timorous ('tymeres) adj. bojaźliwy
tin (tyn) s. cyna; blacha; puszka blaszana; blaszanka; folia
cynowa; pieniądze; adj. cynowany; blaszany; dziadowski (kubek); v. cynować
tinfoil ('tynfojl) s. folia
metalowa; cynfolia; staniol
tinge (tyndż) s. odcień; lekkie
zabarwienie; v. zabarwiać lekko
tingle ('tyngl) s. mrowienie;
świerzbienie; kłucie; v. czuć
kłucie; mrowienie; kłuć

tinkle ('tynkl) v. dzwonić;
brzęczeć;(siusiać) s. dzwonienie
tinned (tynd) adj. cynowany
tinopener ('tyn,oupner) s.
otwieracz puszek (narzędzie)
tint (tynt) s. odcień; zabarwienie; v. zabarwiać
tinware ('tynłeer) s. wyroby
blaszane
tiny ('tajny) adj. drobny; ma-
lusieński; malutki
tip (typ) s. koniec (np. palca);
koniuszek; szczyt; zakończenie; skuwka; okucie; napiwek;
poufna informacja; wiadomość;
rada; wskazówka; trącenie;
przechylenie; skład śmieci;
v. wykańczać koniec; okuwać;
przechylać (się); ważyć; przewracać (się); dać napiwek; informować (poufnie); trącać
lekko; dotykać; uderzać uko-
sem (piłkę); przeważać
tip off ('typ,of) v. ostrzegać
tip-off ('typof) s. poufne
ostrzeżenie (informacja)
tipster ('typster) s. człowiek
udzielający poufnych informacji (o wyścigach etc.)
tipsy ('typsy) adj. podchmielony; pijany; chwiejny; niepewny
tiptoe ('typtou) s. koniec palca u nogi; v. chodzić na palcach; adv. na palcach (u nóg)
tire ('tajer) v. męczyć (się);
nudzić (się); nakładać obręcz,
oponą; przystroić; s. obręcz;
opona; strój
tired ('tajerd) adj. zmęczony;
znużony; znudzony
tireless ('tajerlys) adj. niestrudzony
tiresome ('tajersem) adj. męczący; nudny
tissue ('tyszu:) s. tkanka;
tkanina; siatka; bibułka
tissue paper (tyszu:,pejper) s.
bibułka; papier toaletowy;
papier płótnowany

tit (tyt) s. sikora
tit for tat ('tyt,fo:r taet)
exp.: wet za wet
titbit ('tytbyt) s. smakołyk
titilate ('tytylejt) s. łechtac
title ('tajtl) s. tytuł; nagłówek; napis; tytuł rodowy; tytuł prawny; prawo; czystość
złota w karatach
titled ('tajtld) adj. utytuło-
wany
titter ('tyter) v. chichotać;
s. chichot
tittle-tattle ('tytl-'taetl)
v. plotkować; s. plotkowanie
to (tu:; tu) prep. do; aż do;
ku; przy; w stosunku do;
w porównaniu z; w stosunku
jak; stosownie do; dla; wobec;
względem; za (zależnie od
ustaleń zwyczajowych)
toad (toud) s. ropucha
to and fro ('tu:end,rou) exp.:
tam i z powrotem
toast (toust) s. grzanka; toast;
v. robić granki;wznosić toast
tobacco (te'baekou) s. tyton
tobacconist (te'baekounyst) s.
sprzedawca wyrobów tytoniowych
toboggan (te'bogen) s. saneczki;
v. sankować się; spadać (ceny)
today (te'dej) adv. dzisiaj;
dziś; s. dzień dzisiejszy
toddle ('todl) v. dreptać; drobić nóżkami; s. drobienie nóżkami; dreptanie; pędrak
toddler ('todler) s. pędrak;
berbeć
to-do (te'du:) s. zamieszanie;
rwetes
toe (tou) s. palec u nogi; nosek;
szpic; stopa wału (tamy); występ z przodu; przednia część
kopyta; hacel; dno odwiertu;
v. kopnąć; cerować palec u pończochy; podporządkować się;
stawać na starcie; stosować się
do linii (też partyjnej); ukośnie wbijać gwoździe; krzywo
chodzić (palcami zbyt do wewnątrz lub na zewnątrz)

toffee ('tofi) s. karmelek
toffy ('tofy) s. karmelek
(śmietankowy)
together (te'gedzer) adv. razem; wspólnie; naraz; równocześnie
toil (tojl) s. znój; mozół;
trud; mozolić się; trudzić
się; harować
toilet ('tojlyt) s. ustęp;
toaleta; ubranie; adj. toaletowy
toilet paper ('tojlyt,pejper)
s. papier toaletowy
toils (tojlz) s. sidła; matnia
token ('toukn) s. znak; dowód
autentyczności; symbol; pamiątka; żeton; bon; adj. symboliczny; niewiążący
told (tould) v. zob. tell
tolerable ('tolerebl) adj.
znośny; nienajgorszy; dosyć
zdrowy
tolerance ('tolerens) s. tolerancja; luz; wyrozumiałość
tolerant ('tolerent) adj. to-
lerancyjny; wyrozumiały; tole-
rancki
tolerate ('tolerate) v. znosić;
tolerować; cierpieć
toleration (,tole'rejszyn) s.
znoszenie; tolerancja; tolero-
wanie
toll (toul) s. opłata (np. telefoniczna); myto: mostowe;
drogowe; miejski podatek; try-
but; danina; dzwonienie;
v. uiszczać opłatę; wydzwaniać;
dzwonić jednostajnie; wabić
(zwierzynę)
toll bar ('toulba:r) s. szlaban
tollgate ('toulgejt) s. rogatka
wjazdowa na płatny most lub
autostradę
tomato (te'mejtou) s. pomidor
tomatoes (te'mejtouz) pl. pomidory
tomb (tu:m) s. grób; grobowiec;
v. pochowanie
tombstone (tu:m-stoun) s. kamien nagrobny; nagrobek

tomcat ('tom'kaet) s. kocur

tomorrow (te'mo:rou) s.& adv. jutro

ton (tan) s. tona (2000 funtów) (slang); mnóstwo

tone (toun) s. ton; normalny stan (np. ciała; organizmu); brzmienie; v. stonować się; stroić; harmonizować

tone down ('toun,dałn) v. złagodzić; stonować

tongs (tonz) s. szczypce; kleszcze; obcęgi

tongue (tan) s. język; mowa; ozór; v. dotykać językiem; łajać; mleć językiem

tonic ('tonyk) adj. wzmacniający; elastyczny; krzepiący; s. środek tonizujący

tonight (te'najt) s. dziś wieczór; dzisiejsza noc; adv. dziś wieczorem; gwara: ubiegłej nocy; wczoraj wieczór

tonnage ('tanydż) n. tonaż; opłata od tony ładunku

tonsil ('tonsel) s. migdałek

tonsillitis (,tonsy'lajtys) s. zapalenie migdałków

tony (touny) adj.(slang):szykowny

too (tu:) adv. tak; także; ponadto; do tego; zbytnio; zanadto; zbyt; za; na dodatek; też

took (tuk) v. zob. take

tool (tu:l) s. narzędzie; obrabiarka; v. obrabiać; oporządzać

tool up ('tu:l,ap) v. oprzyrządzać

tools (tu:ls) pl. przybory; sprzęt

tooth (tu:s) s. ząb; pl. teeth (ti:s) v. uzębiać; wcinać zęby; ząbkować; szczepiać zębami trybów

tooth ache ('tu:s ejk) s. ból zęba

tooth brush ('tu:s,brasz) s. szczotka do zębów

toothless('tu:slys) adj. bezzębny

toothpaste ('tu:spejst) s. pasta do zębów

toothpick ('tu:spyk) s. wykałaczka

top (top) s. wierzchołek; czubek; szczyt; wierzch; powierzchnia; góra; bocianie gniazdo; przykrywka; bąk; fryga; adj. wierzchni; zewnętrzny; górny; wyższy; najwyższy; szczytowy; maksymalny; v. nakrywać; wieńczyć; uwieńczać; przewyższać; stanowić wierzch; osiągać szczyt; ścinać szczyt; przeskoczyć (przez coś); położyć kres; mierzyć wysokość; wznosić się

topaz ('toupez) s. topaz

topic ('topyk) s. temat (rozmowy)

topple ('topl) v. przechylać; wywracać

topple down ('topldałn) v. przewrócić

top secret (,topsi:kryt) adj. ściśle tajny

topsy-turvy ('topsy'te:rwy) adj. do góry nogami; v. przewracać do góry nogami; s. rozgardiasz; bałagan; galimatias

torch (to:rcz) s. pochodnia; znicz; kaganek; palnik (do lutowania etc.)

tore (to:r) v. zob. tear

torment ('to:rment) s. męka; udręka; (to:r'ment) v. męczyć; dręczyć

torn (to:rn) v. zob. tear

tornado (,to:r'nejdou) s. trąba powietrzna; tornado

torrent ('to:rent) s. potok (rwący); ulewny deszcz; burza

torsion (to:rszyn) s. skręt; skręcanie

tortoise ('to:rtes) s. żółw (słodkowodny)

torture ('to:rczer) s. tortura; męka; v. torturować; męczyć; dręczyć; wykręcać; przekręcać

tosh (tosz) s. bzdury; brednie; banialuki

toss (to:s) v. rzucać się;
podrzucać; zarzucać; podnosic;
niepokoic; kłopotac; przewracac się (w łóżku); podbijać
(piłkę); wypasć z pokoju;
kołysać się na boki; s. rzut;
losowanie; upadek (z konia)
toss about (,to:s e'baut) v.
przewracać się (po czyms)
toss up ('to:s,ap) v. przewracac; grac w orła i reszkę
toss-up ('to:sap) s. 50%
prawdopodobieństwa; orzeł
czy reszka ?;rzecz wątpliwa
total ('total) a. ogólny; zupełny; całkowity; totalny;
kompletny; v. zliczac; wyno-
sic ogółem; (slang): niszczyc
całkowicie (np. samochód
w wypadku)
totalitarian (tou,taely'tear-
jen) adj. totalitarny; tota-
listyczny; s. totalista
totter ('toter) v. chwiac się;
zataczac się; s. chwianie
się; zataczanie się (dziecka)
touch (tacz) v. dotykac; sty-
kac się; wzruszac (sie);
poruszac (cos); brać; wydobywać; zabarwiac;lekko uszka-
dzac; cechowac; mierzyc; re-
tuszowac; rabnac kogos na
pieniądze (slang); s. dotyk;
dotknięcie; pociagnięcie;
odrobina; kontakt; lekka (choroba); rys; nuta (np.złości);
obmacywanie;cecha; probierz;
naciąganie na pieniądze(slang)
touch down ('tacz,dałn) v. lądować;uzyskiwac 6 punktów
touchdown (taczdałn) s. lądowanie;gol w futbolu(6 punktów)
touching ('taczyng) adj. wzruszający; rozrzewniający; adv.
odnośnie (do czegos)
touchy ('taczy) adj. draźliwy;
obraźliwy; przewrażliwiony
tough (taf) adj. twardy;trudny;
ciężki; łobuzerski; adv. trudno; s. człowiek: trudny, twardy; łobuz; chuligan

tour (tuer) s. objazd; wycieczka; tura; przechadzka; służba
(wojskowa); v. objeżdżać; ob-
wozic
tourist ('tueryst) s. turysta;
klasa turystyczna
tourist-agency ('tueryst'ejdżensy) s. biuro podróży
tournament ('tuernement) s.
turniej
tousle ('tauzl) v. szarpac;
mierzwic; czochrać; targać;
s. rozczochrane włosy;rozczo-
chranie
tow (tou) v. holowac; ciągnąc;
s. holowanie; lina holownicza;
przedmiot holowany; włókna
lniane; paździory
towards (to:rdz; 'tołerdz) prep.
ku; w kierunku; dla; w celu;
na (cos)
tow-boat ('taubout) s. holownik
towel ('tauel) s. ręcznik;
v. wycierac ręcznikiem
tower ('tauer) v. wieża; wznosic (się); sterczec; wzbijać
się
town (tałn) s. miasto
town councilor (,tałn'kaunsyler)
s. radny miejski
town hall ('tałn,ho:l) s. ratusz
towrope ('touroup) s. lina
holownicza
toy (toj) s. zabawka; cacko;
v. bawic się; cackać się; robic niedbale; flirtowac (też
np. z pomysłem)
toxic ('toksyk) adj. trujący;
jadowity
trace (trejs) s. ślad;postronek;
drążek przekaznikowy; v. isć
śladami; kopiowac rysunek;
przypisywać czemus; wytyczać;
nakreslac; kreslic
track (traek) s. tor; koleina;
ślad; trop; bieżnia; rozstaw
kół; v. śledzic; tropic; zo-
stawiac ślady; zabłocic; zawalac; zakładac tor; mieć
rozstęp kół; ciągnąc liną
z brzegu

track down ('traek,dałn) v.
wytropić; wyśledzić; schwytać
track and field events ('traek-
,end-fi:ldy'wents) s. lekkoatletyka
track events (traek y'wents)
s. biegi; zawody na bieżni
traction engine (traekszyn-
endżyn) s. lokomotywa; pociągowy motor; traktor
tractor ('traekter) s. ciągnik;
traktor
trade (trejd) s. zawód; zajęcie;
rzemiosło; handel; wymiana;
klientela; branża; kupiectwo;
v. handlować; wymieniać; frymarczyć; przewozić towary;
kupczyć; przehandlować
trademark ('trejd,ma:rk) s.
znak ochronny; v. przybijać
znak ochronny; rejestrować
znak ochronny
trader ('trejder) s. handlowiec;
statek handlowy; spekulator
giełdowy
trade-union ('trejd'ju:njen)
s. związek zawodowy
trade unionist ('trejd'ju:n-
jenyst) s. działacz związku
zawodowego
tradition (tre'dyszyn) s. tradycja
traditional (tre'dyszynel) adj.
tradycyjny
traffic ('traefyk) s. ruch(kołowy, pasażerski,towarowy,
telegraficzny, telefoniczny,
drogowy, etc.); v. handel
czyms; frymarczyć; kupczyć
traffic island ('traefyk-aj-
lend) s. wysepka na jezdni
traffic jam('traefyk-dżaem)
s. zator ruchu
traffic lights ('traefyk-
lajts) pl. semafory uliczne
traffic regulation ('traefyk,re-
gju'lejszyn) s. przepisy ruchu
traffic sign ('traefyk,sajn)
s. znak drogowy
traffic-cop ('traefyk,kop) s.
policjant ruchu (drogowego)

tragedy ('traedżydy) s. tragedia
tragic ('traedżyk) adj. tragiczny
tragical ('traedżykel) = tragic
trail (trejl) v. pociągnąć (się);
powlec (się);holować; wlec (się)
pozostawać w tyle; iść za tro-
pem; ścigać; wydeptywać (ścieżkę); nosić (karabin poziomo
przy boku); s. szlak; ścieżka;
trop; ogon; smuga; struga;
bruzda; koleina
trailer ('trejler) s. przyczepa
(do samochodu); przyczepa to-
warowa, mieszkalna, turystyczna, etc.; maruder; pnąca (się)
roślina
train (trejn) v. szkolić; kształcić; przyuczać; wytresować;
ćwiczyć (się); trenować (się);
kierować na kogoś (np. wzrok);
wlec; s. pociąg; tren; ogon;
sznur; szereg; następstwo;
orszak; świta; porządek; wątek;
łańcuch
trainer ('trejner) s. trener;
instruktor; samolot szkolny
training ('trejnyng) s. zaprawa; trening; ćwiczenie; szkolenie
trait (trejt) s. cecha
traitor ('trejtor) s. zdrajca
tram (traem) s. tramwaj
tramp (traemp) v. stąpać; włóczyć się; wędrować pieszo;
iść pieszo; s. włóczęga;tramp;
wędrowiec; statek (nieregular-
nej żeglugi)
trample ('traempl) v. deptać
trance (tra:ns) s. trans; uniesienie; ekstaza
tranquil ('traenkłyl) adj. spokojny
tranquility ('traen'kłylyty) s.
spokój
tranquilize ('traenkłylajz) v.
uspokajać
tranquilizer ('traenkłylajzer)
s. środek uspakajający
transact (traen'saekt) v. załatwiać; pertraktować; przeprowadzać

transaction (traen'saekszyn)
s. transakcja; przeprowadze-
nie sprawy; pl. sprawozdania
naukowe; rozprawy

transalpine (traens'aelpajn)
adj. transalpejski

transatlantic (traenzet'laentyk) adj. transatlantycki

transcend (traen'send) v.
przewyższać; prześcignąć;
górować

transcribe (traens'krajb) v.
nagrywać na taśmie; przepisywać

transcript ('traenskrypt) s.
kopia; transkrypcja

transfer (traens'fe:r) v.
przemieścić; przenieść (się);
przewozić; przekazać; s.prze-
niesienie; przewóz; przedruk;
przekaz; przelew; odstąpienie

transferable (traens'fe:rebl)
adj. przenośny

transform (traens'fo:rm) v.
przekształcić; zmienić postać

transformation (,traensfer'-
'mejszyn) s. przekształcanie;
przeobrażenie

transfuse (traens'fjuz) v.
przelać; przetoczyć (krew)

transfusion (traens'fjużyn) s.
transfuzja

transgress (traens'gres) v.
naruszyć; zgrzeszyć

transgression (traens'greszyn)
s. naruszenie; grzech; wykroczenie

transgressor (traens'greser)
s. grzesznik

transient ('traenzjent) adj.
przechodni; przejeżdżający;
przelotny

transistor (traen'syster) s.
tranzystor

transit ('traensyt) s.przejazd;
przelot; przewóz; tranzyt;
teodolit

transition (traen'syszyn) s.
przejście; zmiana

transitive ('traensytyw) adj.
przechodni

translate (traens'lejt) v. przetłumaczyć; przełożyć

translation (traens'lejszyn)
s. tłumaczenie; przekład

translator (traens'lejter) s.
tłumacz

translucent (traenz'lu:sent)
adj. przeswiecający; pół-
przeźroczysty

transmission (traenz'myszyn) s.
przekładnia; transmisja

transmit (traenz'myt) v. przekazywać; nadawać; transmitować

transmitter (traenz'myter) s.
nadajnik; przekaźnik

transparent (traens'peerent)
adj. przeźroczysty

transpire (traens'pajer) v. pocić się; wyparować; okazywać
się; zdarzyć się

transplant (traens'pla:nt) v.
przeszczepiać; przesadzać;
s. przesadzanie; przeszczep

transport (traens'po:rt) v.
przewozić; zachwycać; s.prze-
wóz; zachwyt; uniesienie

transportation (,traenpo:r'tejszyn) s. przewóz; transport;
deportacja; zesłanie

trap (traep) s. pułapka; potrzask; sidła; zasadzka; podstęp; syfon; skała wylewna;
(slang): jadaczka; pl.:manatki;
v. złapać w pułapkę; zaopatrywać w pułapkę; zatrzymywać
(w czymś); przykrywać czapra-
kiem; puszczać rzutki

trap-door ('traep'do:r) s.
drzwi zapadowe; zapadnia

trapeze (tre'pi:z) s. trapez

trapper ('traeper) s. traper;
myśliwy; zastawiający pułapki;
nadzorca szybów powietrznych
w kopalni

trappings (traepyŋgz) s.ozdoby;
strój ozdobny; czaprak

trash (traesz) s. śmieci; ru-
pieci; tandeta; odpadki; bzdury; hołota; v. obdzierać (z
liści, gałązek)

travel ('traewl) v. podróżować
(też za interesem); poruszać
się (części maszyny); przesuwać się; biec (w terenie);
przechodzić (oczami po czymś);
poruszać się żwawo; błądzić;
s. (daleka) podróż; ruch (pojazdów); suw (maszynowy);
przesunięcie

travel agency ('traewl'ejdżensy)
s. biuro podróży

traveler ('traewler) s. podróżnik; wodzik nitkowy; komiwojażer

traveler's check ('traewlers,-
,czek) s. z góry wykupiony
czek do użytku w podróży

traveling bag ('traewlyng,baeg)
s. torba podróżna

traverse (trae'we:rs)v. przecinać; przesuwać na bok; przechodzić; omawiać; pokrzyżować;
zaprzeczyć formalnie; nakiero-
wywać (działo); obracać (się)
jak na osi

travesty ('traewysty) s. trawe-
stia; parodia; v. trawestować;
parodiować

trawl (tro:l) s. włok; włók;
trał; niewód; sieć - worek do
holowania;v.ciągnąć niewód; łowić niewodem, włókiem, wędką
ciągnioną za łodzią

trawler ('tro:ler) s. trawler

tray (trej) s, taca; szufladka
(też wkładowa)

treacherous ('treczeres) adj.
zdradziecki; niebezpieczny;
zdradliwy; zawodny; perfidny

treachery ('treczery) s. zdrada; zdradzieckość; zdradliwość;
perfidia

treacle ('tri:kl) s. syrop; melasa; sok (drzewny)

tread (tred) s. trod; tro(den), (tred;
trod; 'trodn)

tread (tred) v. deptać; stąpać
(po czymś); nadepnąć; tłoczyć;
wdeptywać; iść (ścieżką); wydeptać (ścieżkę); gnieść;
s. stąpanie; krok; podnóżek;

guma opony dotykająca jezdni;
szyna; bieżnik; podeszwa (dotykająca ziemi); stopień

treadle ('tredl) s. pedał;
v. pedałować

treadmill ('tredmyl) s. kierat
(cylindryczny ze stopniami)

treason('tri:zn) s. zdrada

treasure ('treżer) s. skarb;
v. zaskarbiać; cenić; strzec
skarbu

treasure up ('treżer,ap) v.
przechowywać jak skarb

treasurer ('treżerer) s. skarbnik

treasury ('treżery) s. urząd
skarbowy; skarbnica

Treasury Department ('treżery,-
,dy'pa:rtment) s. ministerstwo
skarbu (USA)

treat (tri:t) v. traktować; po-
traktować; obchodzić się z
kimś; uważać kogoś za; brać
coś (za żart); leczyć coś; poddawać działaniu; pertraktować;
fundować (komuś); s. przyjęcie;
uczta; majówka; poczęstunek;
zabawa; przyjemność; rozkosz

treatise ('tri:tys) s. traktat;
rozprawa

treatment ('tri:tment) s. traktowanie; leczenie

treaty ('tri:ty) s. traktat;
układ; umowa

treble ('trebl) adj. potrójny;
wysoki; ostry; przenikliwy;
sopranowy; s. sopran; wysoki
dźwięk; v. potrajać (się)

tree (tri:) s. drzewo; forma;
kopyto; rama siodła; belka;
nadproże; krokiew; szubienica;
v. zapędzić (na drzewo); wsa-
dzić (na kopyto)

treeless ('tri:lys) adj. bez-
drzewny

tree-trunk ('tri:,trank) s.
pień roślina trójlistna;

trefoil ('trefojl) s. koniczyna trójlistna;adj.trójlistny

trellis ('trely) s, krata; altana; v. kratować winorośl;
nadawać formę kraty

tremble ('trembl) v. trząść
się; drżeć; dygotać; s.drże-
nie; drżączka
tremendous (try'mendes) adj.
straszny; olbrzymi
tremor ('tremer) s. drżenie;
drganie; trzęsienie (ziemi)
tremulous ('tremjules) adj.
drżący
trench (trencz) s.rów; okop;
bruzda;. cięcie; rów strzelec-
ki; v. kopać rów; okopywać
się; kłaść do rowu; żłobić;
ciąć; przecinać; podkopywać
się; graniczyć
trench up ('trencz,ap) v.
wdzierać się (bezczelnie)
w cudze (prawa etc.)
trend (trend) s. dążność; ogól-
na tendencja; ogólny kierunek;
v. dążyć; mieć tendencję;
kształtować się; ciągnąć się
trespass ('trespas) v. wdzierać się w cudze; nadużywać;
naruszać; wykraczać; grze-
szyć; v. przekroczenie; wykroczenie; grzech; szkoda wy-
rządzona na cudzym terenie
trespasser ('trespaser) s.
człowiek naruszający przepisy,prawo (czyjeś)
tress (tres) s. warkocz; v.za-
platać warkocz
trestle (tresl) s. kozioł;
kobylica; most filarowy
trial ('trajel) s. próba; proces sądowy; zmartwienie; zawody eliminacyjne; adj. próbny; doświadczalny
trial and error ('trajel end'-
'erer) exp.: chaotyczne próby
(w nieznane)
triangle ('trajaengl) s. trójkąt
triangular (traj'aengjular) adj.
trójkątny
triangulate (traj'aengjulejt)
v. mierzyć (trójkatami) przy
pomocy triangulacji
tribe (trajb) s. plemię; szczep
tribunal (traj'bju:nl) s. trybunał ; sąd

tribune ('trybju:n) s. trybuna;
mównica; gazeta; trybun (ludu)
tributary ('trybjutery) adj.
pomocniczy; płacący daninę;
haracz; s. dopływ; kraj płacący daninę
tribute ('trybju:t) s. haracz;
danina
trick (tryk) s. podstęp; chwyt;
sztuczka; sposób; nawyk; maniera; psota; fortel; (slang):
dziecko; dziewczynka; v. oszukać; okpić; wyłudzić; płatać
figla; zawodzić; zaskakiwać
trick up ('tryk,ap) s. wystroić
trickle ('trykl) v. sączyć (się);
przeciekać; przesączyć; puszczać ciurkiem; kroplami;
s. struga (mała)
tricky ('tryky) adj. podstępny;
chytry; sprytny; trudny; zawiły; zręczny
tricycle ('trajsykl) s. rower
na trzech kołach
trifle ('trajfl) s. drobiazg;
drobnostka; błachostka; bagatela; odrobina; głupstewko; byle
co; stop cyny i ołowiu; biszkopt z kremem; v. nie brać po-
ważnie; poflirtować; baraszkować; paplać; bagatelizować
trifling ('trajflyng) adj. płochy; błachy; znikomy
trigger ('tryger) s. spust;
cyngiel; zapadka; v. pociągać
za spust; wywoływać; dawać początek; zaczynać (akcję)
trill (tryl) s. trel; wibrująca
spółgłoska; v. wymawiać z wi-
bracją; trząść głosem; trelować; wymawiać wibrująco
trillion ('tryljen) = USA billion ('byljen) num. trylion
trim (trym) v. oporządzać;
usuwać niepotrzebne (gałezie;
tłuszcz etc.); przybierać (li-
stwą; tasmą etc); rozkładać
poprawnie ładunek; poprawiać
(opinię); być oportunista;
zmyć komus głowe; dać komus lanie; wyprowadzić w pole; besztać; rugać; s. stan; forma;

nastrój; gotowość; porządek;
strój; ozdoby; listwy; tasmy;
wstążki do poprawienia wyglądu; dekoracja wystawy; oporzą-
dzenie; obcięcie; równowaga
lotu; wyposażenie wnętrza
(np. samochodu, domu etc,)
adj. schludny; porządny;
uporządkowany; wysprzątany
trimming ('trymyŋg) s. ozdoby;
uporządkowanie; przystrzyżenie;
garnirowanie
trimmings ('trymyŋgs) s. zrzyn-
ki i obrzynki z przybierania;
dodatki do potraw; obcinki
Trinity ('trynyty) s.Trójca Sw.
trinket ('trynkyt) s. ozdóbka
(na suknie); świecidełko;
błahostka
trip (tryp) s. podróż; wycieczka; jazda; trans narkomana;
potknięcie; podstawienie nogi;
zgrabny krok; wyzwalanie za-
padkowe lub wychytlowe; błąd;
pomyłka; v. potknąć się; iść
lekkim krokiem; drobić nóżkami;
tańczyć (lekko); pomylić się;
podstawiać nogę; złapać na błędzie; wyzwalać; odczepiać kotwicę; przesuwać wychytem kot-
wicowym; obracać reje; spuszczać nagle częsć maszynv
tripe (trajp) s. flaki (też potrawa); byle co; paskudztwo;
lichota
triple (trypl) adj. potrójny;
s. potrójna ilość; trójka;
v. potrajać (się)
triplets ('tryplyts) pl. trojacz-
ki
tripod ('trajpod) s. trójnóg;
statyw
triumph ('trajemf) s. triumf;
v. triumfować
triumphal (traj'amfel) adj.
triumfalny
triumphant (traj'amfent) adj.
zwycięski; triumfalny
trivial ('trywiel) adj. trywialny; błahy; płytki; banalny;
znikomy
trod (trod) v. zob. tread

trodden ('trodn) v. zob. tread
trolley car ('troly car) s.
tramwaj; wywrotka (woz)
trombone (trom'boun) s. puzon
troop (tru:p) s. grupa; gromada; trupa teatralna; rota;
pół szwadronu; s. isć gromadą;
gromadzić się; formować w ro-
ty (pułk)
trophy ('troufy) s. trofeum
tropic ('tropyk) adj. podzwrotnikowy; tropikalny; s. zwrotnik
tropical ('tropykel) adj. tropikalny; gorący; namiętny
trot (trot) s. kłus; trucht;
bryk (szkolny); (slang): biegunka
trouble ('trabl) s. kłopot;
zmartwienie; zaburzenie; niepokój; trud; dolegliwość; fatyga; bieda; awaria; uszkodzenie; defekt; v. martwić (się);
dręczyć (się); dokuczać; niepokoić (się); kłopotać (się)
troublesome ('trablsem) adj.
kłopotliwy
trough (trof) s. koryto; rynna;
rów (też między falami); niec-
ka; łęk; synklina
trouser leg ('trauserleg) s.
nogawka
trousers ('trauzez) pl. spodnie
trouseau ('tru:sou) s. wyprawa
(ślubna)
trout (traut) s. pstrąg; v. łowić pstrągi
truant ('tru:ent) s. wagarowicz;
opuszczający pracę; adj. próż-
niacki; wałęsajacy (się); v.,
chodzić na wagary; opuszczać
pracę
truce (tru:s) s. rozejm; zawieszenie broni
truck (trak) s. ciężarówka;
taczki; wózek; podwozie na kołach; lora; drobne towary; warzywa; wymiana; interes; śmieci; brednie; stosunki z kimś;
v. przewozić wozem; ładować na
wóz; wymieniać się z kims; obnosic towar; utrzymywać stosunki z kims

truck farm ('trak,fa:rm) s.
gospodarstwo warzywne

trudge (tradż) s. trudny marsz;
v. trudzić się marszem; odbywać z trudem drogę

true (tru:) adj. prawdziwy;
wierny; ścisły; dokładny; praw-
domowny; czysty; faktyczny;
szczery; lojalny; dobrze do-
pasowany; s. prawda; właściwe
położenie; v. regulować; wyre-
gulować; adv. prawdziwie; dokładnie; exp.:to jest prawda !

truly ('tru:ly) adv. prawdziwie;
dokładnie

true-blue ('tru:blu:) adj. bez-
kompromisowy; prawdziwie oddany

trump (tramp) s. atut; as; zuch;
złoty człowiek; trąba; v. bić
atutem; roztrąbić

trump up ('tramp,ap) v. wyssać
z palca; zmyślać (zarzuty);
preparować (zarzuty)

trumpet ('trampyt) s. trąbka;
dźwięk; trębacz; v. grać na
trąbie; trąbić; roztrąbić

truncheon ('tranczen) s. pałka
policjanta; buława marszałka

trunk (trank) s. pień; trzon;
tułów; tors; kadłub; główny kanał; główna linia; trąba słoniowa; kufer; bagażnik;
pl. spodnie (krótkie)

trunk line ('trank-lajn) s.
linia międzymiastowa (też telefoniczna w Anglii)

trunk road ('trank-roud) s.
szosa główna

truss (tras) s. wieżba; wspornik;
kratownica; wiązanie dachowe;
wiązka (siana); pas przepukli-
nowy; v. związać (np. dach);
przywiązać; wieszać (zbrodnia-
rza)

trust (trast) s. pewność; zaufanie; wiara; nadzieja; kredyt;
opieka; powiernictwo; trust;
v. zaufać; mieć zaufanie; ufać;
wierzyć; polegać (na pamięci
swojej etc.) powierzać; kredytować

trustful ('trastful) adj. ufny

trusting ('trastyng) adj. ufny;
pełen zaufania

trustworthy ('trast,łe:rty) adj.
godny zaufania; pewny

truth (tru:s) s. prawda; prawdziwość; rzetelność

truthful ('tru:sful) adj. prawdo-
mówny; prawdziwy (np. opis)

truths (tru:sz) pl. prawdy

try (traj) v. próbować; wypróbować; sądzić; sprawdzić; kosztować; doświadczyć; starać się;
męczyć; s. próba. usiłowanie;
wysiłek

trying (trajyng) adj. przykry;
męczący; nieznośny; irytujący;
ciężki

try on ('traj,on) s. przymierzać

try out ('traj,aut) v. wypróbo-
wywać

T-square ('ti:,skłeer) s. węgielnica

tub (tab) s. balia; ceber; kadź;
wanna; kąpiel; łódź terningowa
(wiosłowa); oszalowanie;
v. wsadzać do wanny; prać;
szalować

tube (tju:b) s. rura; wąż; dętka; tubka; tunel (kolei pod-
ziemnej); v. zamykać w rurze;
zaopatrywać w rury; nadawać
kształt rury

tuberculosis (tjube:rkju:lou-
sys) s. gruźlica

tuck (tak) v. wtykać; wsuwać;
podwijać; zawijać (rąbek);
otulać; zbierać w fałdy; obrębiać; schować; (slang): pa-
łaszować; wcinać; wieszać
(skazańca); s. fałd; fałda;
obręb; koncha

tuck in ('takyn) v. otulać
(w łóżku)

tuck up ('tak,ap) v. podkasać

Tuesday ('tju:zdy) s. wtorek

tuft (taft) s. pęk; peczek;
kiść; kępa; kitka; bródka;
pikowanie; v. robić pęki; dawać pęki; rość pękami; pikować

tug (tag) v. ciągnąć (z trudem)
holować; wciągać; s. holownik;
gwałtowne pociągnięcie
tug-of-war ('tag,ow łor) s.
przeciąganie liny (próba sił;
zawody); zażarta walka o przewagę
tuition (tju'yszyn) s. czesne;
nauczanie; lekcje (płatne)
tulip ('tju:lyp) s. tulipan
tumble ('tambl) v. upasć; zwalić (się); potknąć się; zataczać się; kołysać się; hustać
się; wywalić się; gramolić się;
rzucać się; biegać na oślep;
cisnąć; zwichrzyć; (slang):
kapować; iść do łóżka; v.zwa-
lenie; pobicie rekordu; upadek;
sztuka akrobatyczna; bałagan
tummy ('tamy) s. żołądek;
brzuch (dziecka)
tumor ('tu:mer) s. tumor;
obrzęk; guz ; nowotwór
tumult ('tu:malt) s. zgiełk;
wrzawa; tumult; podniecenie;
zaburzenie
tumultuous ('tu:altjues) adj.
burzliwy; podniecony; hałaśliwy
tun (tan) s. beczka; kadź (252
galonów); v.wlewać do beczki;
przechowywać w beczce
tuna ('tu:na) s. tuńczyk
tune (tu:n) s. melodia; nastrój;
harmonia; v. stroić; dostroić;
harmonizować; nucić
tune in ('tu:n,yn) v. nastawiać
(radio etc.)
tune up ('tu:n,ap) v. nastrajać
(np. motor)
tunnel ('tanl) s. tune;; nora;
v. przekopywać tunel, korytarz,
norę; przekopywać się
turbine ('te:rbyn) s. turbina
turbot ('te:rbet) s. skarptur-
bot (ryba)
turbulent ('te:rbjulent) adj.
wzburzony; burzliwy; gwałtowny;
buntowniczy
turf (te:rf) s. torf; darń;
v. pokrywać darniną; (slang):
drażować (piechotą)
Turk (te:rk) adj. turecki

turkey ('te:rky) s. indyk;
v.mówić bez ogródek
Turkish ('te:rkysz) adj. turecki
Turkish bath ('te:kysz,ba:s)
s. parówka; kąpiel parowa;
łaźnia
turmoil (te:rmojl) s. zamieszanie; zgiełk; niepokoj; podniecenie
turn (te:rn) v. odwrócić (się);
odkręcić (się); przekręcać
(się); skręcać (się); zwracać
(się); odwracać (się); odpierać
(atak); napadać; zmieniać się;
nawracać (się); popełniać
(zdradę); stawać się (np. kato-
likiem); wyswiadczać; obracać;
kierować; robić skręt; wyprawiać; odprawiać; toczyć (na
kole); puścić w ruch; okazać
się; zdarzać się; zwolnić; wyganiać; wyrzucać etc.
s. obrót; kolej; z kolei; po
kolei; tura; zakręt; zwrot;
skręt; punkt zwrotny; przełom;
kształt; forma; przechadzka;
transakcja; wstrząs; atak;
przysługa; numer (popisowy);
kolejność; postępowanie wobec
kogoś
turn away ('te:rn,e'łej) v. odwracać się od ; porzucić
turn back ('te:rn,baek) v. za-
wrócić (z drogi)
turn down ('te:rn,dałn) v. odmówić; przyciszać; odrzucać
turn off ('te:rn,of) v. zakręcić (kurek); skręcić; wyłączać
(światło). odprawić
turn on ('te:rn,on) v. puszczać
(wodę); włączać (światło); od-
kręcać (kurek)
turn out ('te:rn,aut) v. wyrzucać (za drzwi); wyrabiać; zwalniać (z pracy)
turn over ('te:rn'ouwer) v. odwracać; rozważać; mieć obrót;
wydawać (policji);przekazywać
turn round ('te:rn raund) v.
przekręcać; odwracać; zmieniać
przekonania ;przekabacić

turn to ('te:rn,tu) v. zabrać
się (do czegoś)

turn up ('te:rn,ap) v. odwracać;
zawinąć (rękawy); podkręcać;
przychodzić; zgłosić się;
przytrafić (się)

turncoat ('te:rn,kout) s. zdrajca

turning point ('te:rnyŋg,poynt)
s. punkt zwrotny

turnip ('te:rnyp) s. rzepa

turnout ('te:rnaut) s. stawie-
nie się; ilość obecnych;ekwipunek

turnover ('te:rn,ouwer) s. zmiana; kapotaż; przewrócenie; placek; przemieszczanie (ludzi,rzeczy)

turnpike ('te:rn,pajk) s. kołowrot; rogatka;autostrada(płatna)

turnstile ('te:rnstajl) s. koło-
wrot(do wchodzenia pojedynczo)

turnup ('te:rnap) s. traf; zamieszanie; część wywrócona;
coś podwiniętego; podwinięcie

turpentine ('te:rpentajn) s.
terpentyna; v. terpentynować;
zbierać terpentynę

turret ('te:ryt) s. wieżyczka;
imak wielonożowy

turtle ('te:rtl) s. żółw (morski)

turtledove ('te:rtl,daw) s.
turkawka

tusk (task) s. kieł; ząb (u bro-
ny); v. bość; kłuć; rozdzierać
kłami

tutor ('tu:ter) s. nauczyciel
prywatny; korepetytor; opiekun
(studentów); v. uczyć kogoś;
mieć opiekę nad kimś; powściągać
(się); być korepetytorem; uczyć
się pod nadzorem nauczyciela

tutorial ('tu:terjel) adj. wychowawczy; opiekuńczy

TV (ti:wi:) s. telewizja

tuxedo (tak'si:dou) s. smoking
(USA)

twang (tdaeŋg) s. brzęk (struny);
mowienie przez nos; v. brzęczeć;
rzępolić; brzdąkać; mówić przez
nos

tweed(tłi:d) s. materiał wełniany lub wełniano-bawełniany z
szorską powierzchnią

tweet (tłi:t) s. ćwierkanie;
v. ćwierkać

tweezers (tli-zez) s. szczypczyki (kosmetyczne itp.)

twelfth (tłelfs) adj. dwunasty

twelve (tłelw) num. dwanaście;
s. dwunastka

twentieth ('tłentyjes) adj.
dwudziesty

twenty (tłenty) num. dwadzies-
cia; s. dwudziestka

twice (tłajs) adv. dwa razy;
podwojnie; dwukrotnie

twiddle ('tłydl) s. obracanie;
v. kręcić; obracać; przebierać palcami; próżnować

twig (tłyg) v. zrozumieć; po-
łapać się; spostrzec; zauważyć; rozpoznawać; s. gałązka;
rozdzka czarodziejska

twilight ('tłajlajt) s. zmrok;
półcień; półmrok; zmierzch

twin (tłyn) s. bliźniak; adj.
bliźniaczy; v. rodzić się jako bliźnięta; łączyć (się)
ściśle ze sobą

twin-engined ('tłyn'endżynd)
adj. dwumotorowy

twinkle (tłynkl) v. migotać;
błyszczeć; mrugać; s. migotanie; błysk; mrugnięcie

twirl (tłe:rl) v. wirować;
kręcić (się); s. wirowanie;
kręcenie się; zakrętas; piruet

twist (tłyst) v. skręcać (się);
zwijać (się); zwichnąć (się);
zawirować; wykrzywiać (twarz);
przekręcać; pokręcić (się);
wić (się); powikłać (się);
tańczyć (twista); wykręcać;
przewijać się (przez tłum)
s. skręt; szpagat; przędza;
lina (skręcona); splot; obrót;
przekręcenie (znaczenia);
zwichnięcie; skłonność;
strucla

twitch(tłytcz)v. szarpać; wyrwać; wydrzeć; wykrzywić (się);
poruszyć się gwałtownie;
s. skurcz; szarpnięcie;pociąg-
nięcie(za rękaw);drgawka; tik;
drganie(powieki);spazm;kurcz

twitter ('tłyter) v. ćwierkać; świergotać; chichotać; drzeć (ze strachu etc.); s. świergot; chichot; podniecenie; zdenerwowanie

two (tu:) num. dwa; s. dwójka

two-bit ('tu:byt) adj. tandetny; marny; (slang): wart 25 centów; rzecz mała; rzecz bez znaczenia

twofold ('tu:fould) adj. podwójny; adv. podwójnie; dwojako

two-piece ('tu:pi:s) adj. dwuczęściowy

two stroke ('tu:,strouk) adj. dwutaktowy; dwusuwowy

two-way ('tu:,łej) adj. dwukierunkowy (np. ruch); dwutorowy; dwuwartościowy

type (tajp) s. typ; wzór; przykład; symbol; klasa; okaz; czcionka; kaszta (drukarska); v. pisać na maszynie; ustalać typ; symbolizować; wyznaczać role

typewriter ('tajp,rajter) s. maszyna do pisania

typhoid ('tajfoyd) adj. tyfusowy; s. tyfus; dur brzuszny

typhoon (taj'fu:n) s. tajfun; burza (morska) w układzie wielkiego wiru

typhus ('tajfes) adj. tyfusowy

typical ('typykel) adj. typowy; charakterystyczny

typify ('typyfaj) v. uosabiać; stanowić typ; zapowiadać

typist ('tajpyst) s. maszynistka

tyrannical (ty'raenykel) adj. tyranski

tyrannize ('tyrenajz) v. tyranizować

tyranny ('tyreny) s. tyrania

tyrant ('tajerent) s. tyran

tyre ('tajer) s. opona; obręcz; v. nakładać oponę (obręcz)

u (ju:) dwudziesta pierwsza litera alfabetu angielskiego

ubiquity (ju'bykłyty) s. wszechobecność

U-boat ('ju:bout) s. łódź podwodna (niemiecka)

udder ('ader) s. wymię

ugly ('agly) adj. brzydki; paskudny

uhlan ('u:la:n) s. ułan

ulan ('u:la:n s. ułan

ulcer ('alser) s. wrzód

ultimate ('altymyt) adj. ostateczny; ostatni; końcowy; podstawowy; s. ostateczny wynik; podstawowy fakt

ultimatum (alty'mejtem) s. ultimatum

umbrella (am'brela) s. parasol

umpire ('ampajer) s. sędzia sportowy; rozjemca; v. sędziować; rozstrzygać jako arbiter

unabashed ('ane'baeszt) adj. niespeszony; niezmieszany; nie zbity z tropu

unabated ('an,e'bejtyd) adj. niesłabnący; niezmniejszony

unable ('an'ejbl) adj. niezdolny; nieudolny

unacceptable ('ane'kseptebl) adj. nie do przyjęcia

unaccountable ('ane'kauntebl) adj. niewytłumaczony; niezrozumiały; dziwny; nie tłumaczący się nikomu

unaccustomed ('ane'kastemd) adj. niezwykły; nie przyzwyczajony

unacquainted ('ane'kłejntyd) adj. nie obznajomiony

unaffected (,ane'fektyd) adj. niekłamany; naturalny

unanimous (ju'naenymes) adj. jednogłosny

unapproachable (,ane'prouczebl) adj. niedostępny; niezrównany

unarmed ('an'a:rmd) adj. bezbronny; nie uzbrojony

unashamed ('an,e'szejmd) adj. bezwstydny

unassisted ('an,e'systyd) adj. nie wspomagany

unassuming ('an,e'sju:myng) adj. skromny; bezpretensjonalny

unauthorized ('an'o:terajzd) adj. nieupoważniony

unavoidable ('an,e'wojdebl) adj. nieunikniony; niechybny

unaware ('ane,e'Ẑeer) adj.nie-
świadomy; niepoinformowany
unawares ('ane'Ẑeerz) adv.nie-
świadomie; znienacka; niespo-
dziewanie ;nic nie wiedząc
unbalanced ('an'baelensd) adj.
niezrównoważony
unbar ('an'ba:r) v. odryglować
unbearable (an'beerebl) adj.
nieznośny; nie do wytrzymania
unbecoming ('an,by'kamyŋg)adj.
niestosowny; niewłaściwy;
nieodpowiedni; nietwarzowy
unbelievable (,anby'li:webl)
adj. niewiarygodny; nieprawdopodobny
unbelieving (.anby'li:wyŋg)
adj. niewierzący; niedowierza-
jacy
unbending ('an'bendyŋg) adj.
nieugięty; niezłomny
unbiased ('an'bajest) adj.
bezstronny
unbidden ('an'bydn) adj. nieproszony
unborn baby ('an'bo:rn'bejby)
adj. przyszłe dziecko; nie-
urodzone (jeszcze) dziecko
unbounded (an'naundyd) adj.
bez granic; bezgraniczny
unbroken (an'brouken) adj.
nieprzerwany; niezbity; nie
ujeżdżony (koń)
unbutton ('an'batn) v. odpiać;
rozpiać (sie)
uncalled-for ('an'ko:ld,fo:r)
adj. niewłaściwy; niezasłużony;
niczym nie usprawiedliwiony
uncanny (an'kaeny) adj. niesamowity
uncared-for ('an'keerd,fo:r)
adj. porzucony; zaniedbany
unceasing (an'si:syŋg) adj.
bezustanny; nieprzerwany
uncertain (an'se:rtn) adj. niepewny; wątpliwy
unchallenged (an'chaelyndżd)
adj. niekwestionowany
unchangeable (an'chejndżebl)
adj. stały; niezmienny
unchanged (an'chejndżd) adj.
niezmieniony

unchecked (an'czekt) adj. niepowstrzymany; niepohamowany;
nieposkromiony
uncivil ('an'sywyl) adj. niegrzeczny; nieuprzejmy; nieokrzesany; grubiański
uncivilized ('an'sywylajzd)
adj. dziki; niecywilizowany;
barbarzyński
uncle ('ankl) s. wujek; stryjek
unclean ('an'kli:n) adj. nieczysty; plugawy; sprosny
uncomparable ('an'komperebl) adj.
nieporównywalny
uncommon ('an'komen) adj. niezwykły; rzadki; adv. niezwykle;
nadzwyczaj
uncommunicative ('an-ke'mju:ny-
ketyw); adj. małomówny; skryty;
niekomunikatywny
uncomplaining ('an-kem'plejnyŋg)
adj. cierpliwy; nienarzekający
unconcern ('anken'se:rn) s,
beztroska; niefrasobliwość;
obojętność
unconcerned ('anken'se:rnd) adj.
obojętny; niefrasobliwy; beztroski
unconditional ('an-ken'dyszynl)
adj. bezwarunkowy
unconfirmed ('an-ken'fe:rmd) adj.
nie potwierdzony
unconscious (an'kouszes) adj.
nieprzytomny; zemdlony; nieświadomy; s. podświadomość
unconsciousness (an'konszesnys)
omdlenie; nieprzytomność
unconstitutional ('an,konsty'-
'tju:szynl) adj. niezgodny
z konstytucja
uncontrollable ('an,kon'troulebl)
adj. nieposkromiony; niepohamowany
unconventional ('an-ken'wenszynl)
adj. niekonwencjonalny; oryginalny
unconvinced ('an-ken'wynst) adj.
nieprzekonany
unconvincing ('an-ken'wynsyŋg)
adj. nieprzekonywujący
uncouth (an'ku:s) adj. nieokrzesany; niezręczny; niezgrabny

uncover (an'kawer) v. odkryć;
demaskować
uncultivated ('an'kaltywejtyd)
adj. nieuprawny; leżący odłogiem; niekulturalny
uncultured ('an'kalczerd) adj.
niewykształcony; niekulturalny
undamaged ('an'daemydżd) adj.
nieuszkodzony
undecided ('an-dy'sajdyd) adj.
niezdecydowany; niepewny;
nieokreślony; nierozstrzygnięty
undefined ('andy'fajnd) adj.
nieokreślony; mglisty
undeniable (,andy'najebl) adj.
niezaprzeczalny
under ('ander) prep. pod; poniżej; w; w trakcie; zgodnie
z; z; adv. poniżej; pod spodem; adj. spodni; niższy;
dolny; podrzędny; podwładny
underbid ('ander'byd) v. zob.
bid; składać niższą ofertę
w przetargu
undercarriage ('ander,kaerydż)
s. podwozie
underclothes ('ander;klousz)
pl. bielizna
underclothing ('ander-klousyng)
s. bielizna
underdeveloped (ander,dy'we-
lept) adj. zacofany; nie wywołany poprawnie; niedorozwinięty
underdone ('ander'dan) adj.
półsurowy; niedogotowany
underestimate ('ander'estymejt)
v. niedoceniać; za nisko
oszacować
underfed ('ander'fed) v. niedo-
żywiony
undergo (,ander'gou) v. zob.go;
doznawać czegoś; przechodzić
coś; doświadczyć; poddawać się
(operacji)
undergraduate (,ander'graedjuit)
s. student bez stopnia bachelor
underground ('ander,graund) adj.
podziemny; zaskórny; tajny;
s. kolej podziemna; ruch oporu;

adv. (,ander'graund)pod ziemią;
skrycie; tajnie
undergrowth ('ander-grous) s.
poszycie (lasu)
underline ('anderlajn) v. podkreślać; s. podkreślenie; podpis pod ilustracją; zawiadomienie (u spodu afisza teatralne-
go) o następnej sztuce
undermine (,ander'majn) v. podkopywać (zdrowie etc.) podmywać (brzegi etc.)
undermost ('andermoust) adj.
najniższy
underneath (,ander'ni:s) adv.
pod spodem; poniżej; na dole;
pod spód
underpass (,ander'pa:s) s.
przejazd poniżej poziomu (w
skrzyżowaniu bezkolizyjnym)
underpay ('ander'pej) v. za mało płacić
underprivileged ('ander'prywylydżd) adj. upośledzony
undershirt ('andersze:rt) s.
podkoszulek
undersigned ('ander'sajnd) adj.
(niżej) podpisany
undersized ('ander'sajzd) adj.
zbyt mały; małego wzrostu
under soil ('ander,sojl) s.
podglebie
understaffed ('ander'sta:ft)
adj. mający zbyt mały personel
understand; understood; understood (,ander'staend; ander'-
stud; ,ander'stud)
understand (,ander'staend) v.
rozumieć; domyślać się; orien-
tować się; znać; wywnioskować;
wiedzieć jak; umieć dobrze
understandable (,ander'staend-
ebl) adj. zrozumiały
understanding (,ander'staendyng)
adj. pełen zrozumienia; s. zrozumienie; warunek; (wyższa)
inteligencja; porozumienie;
rozum
understatement (,ander'stejtment) s. zbyt skromne wyraża-
nie się; niedomówienie

undertake (,ander'tejk) v.zob.
take; przedsiębrać; podejmować się; ręczyć; zobowiązywać się do czegoś; być przed-
siębiorcą pogrzebowym
undertaker (,ander'tejker) s.
przedsiębiorca pogrzebowy
undertaking (,ander'tejkyng) s.
przedsięwzięcie; zobowiązanie;
obietnica; przyrzeczenie;
przedsiębiorstwo pogrzebowe
undervalue (,ander'waelju) v.
niedoceniać; za nisko szacować
underwear ('anderłeer) s. bielizna
underwood ('ander,łu:d) s. poszycie (lasu)
underworld ('ander,łe:rld) s.
podziemie; świat podziemny;
pl. antypody
underwrite ('ander-rajt) v.
zob. write; zakontraktować
(ubezpieczenie); podpisać(się);
wydawać (polisę ubezpieczenio-
wą); zobowiązywać się
underwriter ('ander-rajter) s.
ajent ubezpieczeniowy
undeserved ('andy'ze:rwd) adj.
niezasłużony; niesłuszny
undesirable (andy'zajerebl)
adj. niepożądany; niedogodny;
s. człowiek niepożądany
undeveloped (andy'welopt) adj.
nierozwinięty; niewywołany
undies (andyz) pl. bielizna
(damska i dziecięca)
undignified (an'dygnyfajd) adj.
niegodny; bez godności
undiminished (an'dymynszt) adj.
niezmniejszony
un-disciplined (an'dysyplind)
adj. niezdyscyplinowany; nie-
karny
undisputed (,andys'pju:tyd)
adj. bezsporny; niezaprzeczony
undisturbed ('andys'te:rbd) adj.
niezakłócony
undo; undid; undone ('an'du;
'an'dyd, an'dan)
undo ('an'du:) v. robić nieby-
łym; unieważniać; usuwać;
niszczyć; rujnować; rozpakować;

rozwiązać; otwierać; rozpinać;
przekreślać
undreamt-of ('an'dremt,ow)
adj. nieprawdopodobny; nie do
pomyślenia; niesłychany
undress (an'dres) v. rozbierać
(się); odbandażowywać; s. negliż; zwykłe ubranie
undressed (an'drest) adj. nie
przyrządzony; chropowaty; nie
opatrzona (rana); rozebrany
undue (an'dju:) adj. przesadny;
nadmierny; postronny; niewłas-
ciwy; jeszcze niepłatny (np.
rachunek)
undutiful (an'djutyful) adj.
nieobowiązkowy
uneasy (an'i:zy) adj. niespokojny; niepokojący; nieswój;
zażenowany; nieprzyjemny;
krępujący; budzący niepokój
uneducated (an'edjukejtyd)
adj. niewykształcony; bez
wykształcenia
unemployed (an'emplojd) adj.
bez pracy; bezrobotny; nie-
wykorzystany; nie zużytkowany
unemployment (an'emplojment)
s. bezrobocie
unendurable ('anyn'djuerebl)
adj. nie do zniesienia
unenviable ('an'enwjebl) adj.
nie do pozazdroszczenia
unequal ('an'i:kłol) adj. nierówny; nie na wysokości (zadania)
unequaled ('an'i:kłold) adj.
niezrównany
unequivocal ('any'kływokel) adj.
niedwuznaczny; wyraźny; jasny
unerring ('an'e:ryng) adj.
nieomylny; niezawodny
uneven ('an'i:wen) adj. nieparzysty; niejednolity; nierówny
uneventful ('an,y'wentful) adj.
adj. nieurozmaicony; spokojny;
jednostajny
unexpected ('anyks'pektyd)
adj. niespodziewany; nieoczekiwany
unfailing (an'tejlyng) adj.
niezawodny; niewyczerpany

unfair (an'feer) adj. niesprawiedliwy; krzywdzący; nieuczciwy; nieprzepisowy

unfaithful (an'fejsful) adj.
niewierny; wiarołomny; nieścisły

unfamiliar ('anfe'myljer) adj.
nieznany; nieobznajomiony;
obcy

unfashionable ('an'faeszenebl)
adj. niemodny

unfasten ('an'fa:sn) v. odczepić (się); odpiąć (się); od-
wiązywać (się); odryglować
(się); rozluźnić (się)

unfavorable ('an'fejwerebl)
adj. niepomyślny; nieżyczliwy;
niesprzyjający; nieprzychylny

unfeasible (an'fi:sebl) adj.
niewykonalny

unfeeling (an'fi:lyng) adj.
bez uczucia; bez serca; okrutny

unfinished ('an'fynyszt) adj.
niewykończony; niedokończony

unfit ('an'fyt) adj. nie nadający się; niezdatny; niezdolny; nieodpowiedni; v. czynić
niezdolnym do czegoś

unflappable ('an'flaepebl) adj,
nie do wytrącenia z równowagi

unfold ('an'fould) v. ujawniać
(się); rozwijać (się); otwierać; odsłonić

unforseen ('an'fer,si:n) adj.
nieprzewidziany; niespodziewany

unforgettable ('an-fer'getebl)
adj. pamiętny; niezapomniany

unforgiving ('an-fer'gywyng)
adj. niewybaczający; nieprzejednany

unforgotten ('an-fer'gotn)adj.
niezapomniany

unfortunate (an'fo:rcznyt) adj.
niefortunny; pechowy; niepomyślny; nieszczęśliwy

unfortunately (an'fo:rcznytly)
adv. niestety; nieszczęśliwie

unfounded (an'faundyd) adj.
bezpodstawny

unfriendly (an'frendly) adj.
nieprzyjazny; nieprzychylny

unfurnished (an'fe:rnyszt) adj.
nieumeblowany

ungainly (an'gejnly) adj. niezdarny; niezgrabny

ungenerous (an'dżeneres) adj.
małostkowy; nie szczodry

ungentle (an'dżentl) adj. nie-
łagodny

unget-at-able ('anget'aetbl)
adj. niedostępny (slang)

ungovernable (an'gawernebl)adj.
dziki; niesforny; krnąbrny;
nieopanowany

ungraceful (an'grejsful) adj.
niewdzięczny; nieuprzejmy

ungrateful (an'grejful) adj.
niewdzięczny

unguarded ('an'ga:rdyd) adj.
niebaczny;nieopatrzny; nierozważny; niestrzeżony

unhappy (an'haepy) adj. nieszczęśliwy; pechowy; zmartwiony;nieudany

unharmed ('an'ha:rmd) adj. nietknięty

unharness ('an'ha:rnys) v. wyprzęgać; zdejmować zbroję; etc.

unhealthy (an'helsy) adj. niezdrowy

unheard-of (an'he:rd,ow) adj.
niesłychany; niebywały; nieprawdopodobny

unheeded (an'hi:dyd) adj. niezauważony; niedostrzeżony

unheeding (an'di:dyng) adj. nieuważający; niedostrzegający

unhesitating (an'hezytejtyng)
adj. nie wahający się

unhoped-for (an'hopt,fo:r) adj.
niespodziewany; nieoczekiwany

unhurt (an'he:rt) adj. nieuszkodzony; bez szwanku

unicorn ('ju:nyko:rn) s. jedno-
rożec; jednoróg

unification (,ju:nyfy'kejszyn)
s. zjednoczenie; zcalenie;
ujednolicenie

uniform ('ju:nyfo:rm) adj.
jednolity; równomierny; jednostajny; s, mundur; uniform

uniformity ('ju:ny'fo:rmyty)
s. jednolitość; jednostajność;
ujednolicenie;ujednostajnienie

unilateral ('ju:ny'laeterel) adj. jednostronny

unimaginable (any'maedżynebl) adj. nie do pomyślenia

unimaginative (any'maedżynejtyw) adj. bez wyobraźni; bez polotu

unimportant ('anym'po:rtent) adj. nieważny; błahy; mało ważny

uninhabitable('anyn'haebytebl) adj. nie do mieszkania; nie do życia

uninhabited ('anyn'haebytyd) adj. niezamieszkały

uninjured ('an'yndżerd) adj. bez szwanku; nie uszkodzony; bez obrażeń

uninspired ('anyn'spajerd) adj. banalny

unintelligible ('anyn'telydżebl) adj. niezrozumiały

unintentional ('anyn'tenszynl) adj. mimowolny; nie zamierzony

uninteresting ('anyn'terestyng) adj. nudny; nieciekawy; nie-interesujący

uninterrupted ('anyn'teraptyd) adj. nieprzerwany; ciągły; bezustanny

uninvited ('anyn'wajtyd) adj. nieproszony

uninviting ('anyn'wajtyng) adj. nie zachęcający; odpychający; nieapetyczny

union ('ju:njen) s. połączenie; złącze; łączność; związek; zjednoczenie; małżeństwo; zgoda; łącznik; złączka; godło

unionist ('ju:njenyst) s. związkowiec; zwolennik związku

union Jack ('ju:njen'dżaek) s. flaga angielska

unique (ju:'ni:k) adj. wyjątkowy; jedyny; niezrównany

unisex ('ju:ny'seks) adj. styl (wyrobów) do użytku obu płci; odzież, przybory toaletowe, zakład fryzjerski etc.

unison ('ju:nyzn) adj. zgodnie (razem)

unit ('ju:nyt) s. jednostka; zespół

unite (ju:'najt) v. łączyć; jed-noczyć; zjednoczyć

united (ju:'najtyd) adj. połą-czony; zjednoczony; łączny

unity ('ju:nyty) s. jedność (czasu, miejsca, działania, etc); jednostka; jednolitość; har-monia; zgoda

universal (ju:ny've:rsel) adj. powszechny; ogólny; uniwersalny

universe ('ju:nyvers) s. wszech-świat; świat; ludzkość; kosmos

university (,ju:ny'wersyty) s. uniwersytet; wszechnica; uczel-nia

unjust ('an'dżast) adj. nie-sprawiedliwy

unkempt ('an'kempt) adj. nie-uczesany; rozczochrany; nie-chlujny

unkind (an'kajnd) adj. niedobry; okrutny

unknown ('an'noun) adj. nieznany; niewiadomy

unlace ('an'lejs) v. rozsznurować

unlawful ('an'lo:ful) adj. bez-prawny; nielegalny

unlearn ('an'le:rn) v. oduczać (się); zob. learn

unless (an'les) conj. jeżeli nie; chyba że

unlike ('an'lajk) adj. niepodob-ny; odmienny; prep. odmiennie; inaczej; w przeciwieństwie

unlikely (an'lajkly) adj. nie-prawdopodobny; nieoczekiwany; nie rokujący

unlimited (an'lymytyd) adj. nieograniczony; bezgraniczny; dowolny

unload ('an'loud) v. rozładowy-wać; zrzucać ciężar

unlock ('an'lok) v. otwierać zamek; otworzyć

unlocked ('an'lokt) adj. otwar-ty; niezamknięty

unlooked-for (an'lukt,fo:r) adj. nieoczekiwany; niespodzie-wany; nieprzewidziany

unloosen ('an'lu:sn) adj. roz-luźniony; rozwiązany; rozsznu-rowany unlucky (an'laky) adj. pechowy; niefortunny; niepomyślny; nieszczęśliwy

unmanageable (an'maenydżebl) adj. niesforny; krnąbrny

unmanly (an'maenly)adj. zniechecający; odbierający odwage; adv. zniechecająco

unmarried (an'maeryd) adj. nieżonaty; niezameżna

unmistakabe ('anmys'tejkbl) adj. niewątpliwy; wyraźny; niedwuznaczny

unmoved ('an'm:wd) adj. niewzruszony

unnatural (an'naeczrel) adj. sztuczny; nienaturalny; wbrew naturze; nienormalny

unnecessary (an'nesysery) adj. zbędny; zbyteczny; niepotrzebny

unnoticed ('an'noutyst) adj. niezauważony; (pominięty)

unobtainable ('anęb'tejnebl) adj. nie do nabycia(otrzymania)

unobtrusive ('aneb'tru:syw) adj. skromny; dyskretny; nie narzucający się

unoccupied ('an'okjupajd) adj. wolny; nie zajęty

unoffending ('ane'fendyng) adj. nieszkodliwy; (niewinny)

unofficial ('ane'fyszel) adj. nie urzędowy; nieoficjalny

unpack ('an'paek) v. rozpakowywać (się)

unpaid ('an'pejd) adj. niezapłacony; (bezinteresowny)

unparalleled (an'paereleld)adj. niezrównany; niespotykany; bezprzykładny; niesłychany

unpardonable (an'pa:rdnebl) adj. niewybaczalny

unperceived (an'per'si:wd)adj. niespostrzeżony

unperturbed ('an-per'te:rbd) adj. spokojny; nie zaniepokojony; nie przejmujący się

unpleasant (an'plezent) adj. nieprzyjemny; przykry; niemiły

unplug (an'plag) v. odczopować; wyciągnąć z kontaktu

unpolished ('an'polyszt) adj. niewyczyszczony; niewygładzony

unpopular (an'popjuler) adj. m. niepopularny; niemile widziany

unpopularity ('an,popju'laeryty) s. niepopularność; złe przyjęcie

unpractical ('an'praektykel) adj. niepraktyczny; nierealny

unpracticed (an'praektyst) adj. nie wypraktykowany; niewprawny

unprecedented (an'presydentyd) adj. bezprzykładny; bez precedensu; niesłychany

unprejudiced (an'predżudyst) adj. bezstronny; nie mający przesądów

un-premeditated ('anpry:'medytejtyd) adj. bez premedytacji; nienaumyślny

unprepared ('anpry'peerd) adj. nieprzygotowany; nieprzyrządzony

unprincipled (an'prynsepld) adj. bez skrupułów; niegodziwy

unproductive (an'prodaktyw) adj. niewydajny; nie wytwórczy; niepłodny;

unprofitable (an'profytebl) adj. niepopłatny; niekorzystny; nierentowny

unprovided-for ('an-pre'wajdyd-,fo:r) adj. niezabezpieczony; bez środków do życia

unqualified ('an'kłolyfajd) adj. niewykwalifikowany; bez kwalifikacji; niesprecyzowany; nieograniczony (np. zaufanie)

unquestionable (an'kłesczynebl) adj. bezsporny; niewątpliwy

unquestioned (an'kłesczynd) adj. niezaprzeczony; niepytany

unreasonable (an'ri:znebl) adj. nierozsądny; niedorzeczny; wygórowany (w cenie)

unrefined ('anry'faind) adj. niesubtelny; niewyrafinowany; niewykształcony

unreliable ('anry'lajebl) adj. niepewny; niesolidny

unreserved ('anry'ze:rwd) adj.
otwarty; szczery; bez zastrzeżeń; całkowity; niezarezerwowany

unresisting ('anry'zystyŋg)
adj. nieodporny; nieopierający się

unrest ('an'rest) s. niepokój;
zamieszki; niepokoje

unrestrained ('anrys'trejnd)
adj. niepowstrzymany; niepohamowany; nieopanowany

unrestricted ('anrys'tryktyd)
adj. nieograniczony; (niedostępny)

unrip ('an'ryp) v. porozpruwać

unripe ('an'rajp) adj. niedojrzały

unrivaled (an'rajweld) adj.
niezrównany; bezkonkurencyjny

unroll ('an'roul) v. rozwinąć
(zwój; rolkę)

unruffled (an'rafld) adj. niezmącony; niezakłócony; zachowujący równowagę

unruly (an'ru:ly) adj. niesforny

unsafe ('an'sejf) adj. niepewny;
ryzykowny; niebezpieczny

unsanitary ('an'saenytery) adj.
niehigieniczny; szkodliwy; niezdrowy

unsatisfactory ('an,saetys'faektery) adj. niezadawalający;
niedostateczny

unsatisfied (an'saetysfajd) adj.
niezadowolony; niezaspokojony

unsavory ('an'sejwery) adj.
niesmaczny; przykry

unscrew('an'skru:) v. odsrubować; rozsrubować; odkręcić
(gwint)

unscrupulous ('an'skru:pjules)
adj. bez skrupułów; niegodziwy

unseen (an'si:n) adj. nie widziany; niewidoczny

unselfish (an'selfysz) adj. bezinteresowny

unsettled ('an'setld) adj. zaburzony; zakłócony; nieustalony; niezapłacony; rozstrojony

unshaven (an'szejwn) adj. nieogolony

unshrinkable (an'szrynkebl)
adj. nie kurczący się (w praniu)

unshrinking (an'szrynkiŋg) adj.
nie wahający się; nie wzdrygający się

unskilled (an'skyld) adj. niewprawny; niewykwalifikowany

unskilful (an'skylful) adj.
niewprawny; niezręczny

unsociable (an'souszebl) adj.
nietowarzyski

unsocial (an'souszel) adj. niesocjalny; niespołeczny

unsolvable (an'salwebl) adj.
nierozwiązalny; nierozpuszczalny

unsolved (an'solwd) adj. nierozwiązany; nierozpuszczony

unsophisticated (,anso'fystykejtyd) adj. prosty; naturalny; prawdziwy

unsound (an'saund) adj. niezdrowy; sprochniały; słaby;
niepewny; ryzykowny; błędny;
niesolidny

unspeakable (an'spi:kebl) adj.
niewypowiedziany;nie do opisania

unspoiled (an'spojld) adj.
niezepsuty; nierozpieszczony
(dziecko)

unspoken ('an'spouken) adj.
nie mówiony (np. prawo)

unspoken-for (an'spoukn;fo:r)
adj. niezamówiony

unspoken-of (an'spoukn) adj.
nie omawiany

unstable (an'stejbl) adj. niepewny; chwiejny;niezrównoważony

unsteady ('an'stedy) adj.
chwiejny; chwiejący się; niezdecydowany; nieustabilizowany;
zmienny; niepewny

unstressed ('an'strest) adj.
nieakcentowany; niepodkreślony;
nieobciążony

unsuccessful ('an-sek'sesful)
adj. nieudany; bez powodzenia;
nieudały; nie mający powodzenia; bezowocny

unsuitable ('an'sju:tebl) adj.
niewłaściwy; niestosowny;
nieodpowiedni

unsure (an'szuer) adj. niepewny; zawodny

unsurpassed ('an-ser'pa:st)
adj, nieprześcigniony; niezrównany

unsuspected ('an-ses'pekyd)
adj. (zupełnie) niepodejrzany

unsuspecting('an-ses'pektyng)
adj. nieczego nie podejrzewa-
jący

unsuspicious ('an-ses'pyszes)
adj. ufny; niepodejrzliwy

unthinkable ('an'tynkebl) adj.
nie do pomyślenia; nieprawdopodobny

unthinking ('an'tynkyng) adj.
bezmyślny

untidy (an'tajdy) adj. niechlujny;niestaranny; rozczor-
rany; zaniedbany; nie posprzą-
tany

untie(an'taj) v. rozwiązywać
(się); rozsupłać; uwalniać
(się) z więzów; usuwać (trudności)

until (an'tyl) prep. & conj.
do; dotychczas; dopiero; aż

untimely (an'tajmly) adj. nie
w porę; przedwczesny; nie na
czasie; wczesny; adv. przedwcześnie; w nieodpowiedniej
chwili

untiring (an'tajeryng) adj.
niezmordowany

unto ('antu:) prep.,= to; do;
ku; aż do

untold (an'told) adj. niewypowiedziany; nieprzeliczony

untouchable (an'taczebl) adj.
niedotykalny

untouched (an'taczt) adj. nietknięty; nieskazitelny; nieczuły

untried (an'trajd) adj. niewy-
próbowany

untroubled (an'trabld) adj.
spokojny; beztroski

untrue ('an'tru:) adj. nieprawdziwy; fałszywy; niewierny;
sprzeniewierzający się

untrustworthy ('an'trast,łe:rsy)
adj. niegodny zaufania; niepewny

untruth ('an'tru:s) s. nieprawda;
kłamstwo

unused ('an'ju:zd) adj. nie używany; nie przyzwyczajony; nie
stosowany

unusual (an'ju:żuel) adj. niezwykły; wyjątkowy

unutterable (an'aterebl) adj.
niewysłowiony; niewypowiedziany

unvarying (an'weery-yng) adj.
jednostajny; nieurozmaicony;
nie zmieniający (się)

unvoiced (an'wojst) adj. bez-
głosny; bezdźwięczny

unwanted (an'łontyd) adj. niepożądany; niepotrzebny; zbędny; zbyteczny

unwarranted ('an'łorentyd) adj.
nieusprawiedliwiony; bezpodstawny

unwholesome ('an'houlsem) adj.
niezdrowy; szkodliwy

unwilling ('an'łylyng) adj.
niechętny

unwind ('an'łajnd) v. zob.wind;
rozwijać (się); odprężać (się);
(slang): odpoczywać sobie

unwise ('an'łajz) adj. niemądry;
nieostrożny; nieroztropny

unworthy (an'łe:rsy) adj. niegodny; niegodziwy; niewart;
niezasługujący; ujemny

unwrap ('an'raep) v. rozwijać
(się); rozpakować; odsłonić
(się); odwijać (się)

unyielding ('an'ji:ldyng) adj.
nieustępliwy; twardy; nieugięty

up (ap) adv. do góry; w górę;
w zwyż; w górze; wyżej; na;
tam (gdzie); na górze; wysoko;
wyżej; aż (do); aż (po); na
(piętro); pod (górę); v. podnosić; zrywać się; podbijać
(cenę); zaczynać

up-and-about ('apend,ebaut).
exp.:(znowu) na nogach (po chorobie)

up-and-coming ('ap,end'komyŋg)
exp.:(slang): obiecujący; rzutki; przedsiębiorczy (człowiek)

up-and-doing ('ap,end'duyŋg)
exp.:(slang): czynny; ruchliwy

up-and-up ('ap,end'ap)być uczciwym

up to('ʌp,tu)adv.aż do;pogodny

upbeat('apbi:t)adj.optymistyczny;

upbringing (' ,p,bryŋgyŋg) s.
wychowanie; wychowywanie

uphill ('ap'hyl) adj. wznoszący (się); stromy; trudny; uciążliwy; adv. stromo; pod górę; w górę

upholster (ap'houlster) v.
obijać (meble); wyścielać; pokrywać; urządzać

upholsterer (ap'houlsterer)
s. tapicer; dekorator

upholstery(ap'houlstry),s.
tapicerstwo; meble wyściełane

upkeep ('apki:p) s. utrzymanie; koszty utrzymania szanie się

upmanship('apmen,szyp)s.wywyższanie się

upon (e'pon)prep.=on; na; po
upper ('aper) adj. wyższy; górny; wierzchni; s. przyszwa

uppermost ('aper,moust) adj.
najwyższy; adv. na górze; na górę

uppish ('apysh),adj. zadzierający nos do góry (slang)

upright ('ap'rajt) adj. wyprostowany; prosty; uczciwy; prawy; adv. pionowo; s. pionowy słup; podpora; pianino; pozycja pionowa

uprising (ap'rajzyŋg) s. powstanie; wstawanie

uproar ('ap,ro:) s. zgiełk; wrzawa; harmider; tumult

upset ('apset) v. zob. set; przewracać (się), pokonywać; wzburzać; rozstrajać; rozkuwać; pogrubiać; skręcać; rozklepywać; s. wywrócenie (się); porażka; podniecenie; zaburzenie; rozstrój; niepokój;

bałagan; sztanca do kucia

upside-down ('apsajd'dałn)adv.
do góry nogami; do góry dnem;
adj. odwrócony do góry nogami

upstairs ('ap'steerz) adv. na górę; na górze

upstart ('ap-sta:rt) s. parwenjusz

upstream ('ap'stri:m) adv. pod prąd; w górę rzeki

uptight ('ap'tajt) adj. (slang); napięty; naprężony (nerwowo)

up-to-date ('ap-tu-'dejt) adj.
bieżący; nowoczesny

upwards (apłerdz) adv. w górę; ku górze; na wierzch; wyżej; powyżej (czegoś)

uranium (ju'rejnjem) s. uran

urbane (e:r'bejn) adj. grzeczny; układny; wytworny

urchin ('e:rczyn) s. ulicznik; urwis; łobuz; smyk; jeżowiec; jeżak; czesak

urge (e:rdż) v. poganiać; popędzać; ponaglać; przyspieszać; nalegać; pilić; namawiać; s. pragnienie; impuls; tęsknota; pociąg; bodziec

urge on ('e:rdż,on) v. namawiać na cos

urgent (e:rdżent) adj. pilny; naglący; gwałtowny; natarczywy; nalegający

urine ('jueryn) s. mocz; uryna

urn (e:rn) s. urna

usage ('ju:sydż) s. zwyczaj; praktyka; obchodzenie (się); używanie (zwrotów, języka poprawnego)

use (ju:s) s. użytek; używanie; użycie; posługiwanie; zastosowanie; pożytek; korzyść; zwyczaj; praktyka; obrządek; przyzwyczajenie; v. używać; korzystać; wykorzystać; używać; zużyć; wyczerpać; traktować; obejść się; mieć zwyczaj

used (ju:zd) adj. przyzwyczajony; używany; stosowany

useful ('ju:zful) adj. użyteczny; pożyteczny; dogodny; wygodny; (slang):doskonały; sprawny; biegły; zdolny

useless ('ju:zlys) adj. niepotrzebny; bezużyteczny; zbyteczny; bezcelowy; nieużyteczny; do niczego

use up ('ju:s,ap) v. zużyć
(wszystko); wyczerpać (np.
pracą

usher ('aszer) s, odźwierny;
woźny; bileter; rozprowadza-
jący na miejsca (w kinie;
w kościele etc.) v. wprowadzać; zapoczątkować

usher in ('aszer,yn) v. wprowadzać do

usherette (,asze'ret) s. bi-
leterka (rozprowadzająca)

usual ('ju:zuel) adj. zwykły;
zwyczajny; normalny; zwyczajowy; utarty

usually ('ju:zuely) adv. zwykle; zazwyczaj

usurer ('ju:żerer) s. lichwiarz

usury ('ju:żury) s. lichwa

utensil (ju'tensyl) s. sprzęt;
naczynie; narzędzie

utility (ju'tylyty) s. pożytek;
użyteczność; firma dostarcza-
jąca gaz, elektryczność lub
wodę ludności w USA

utilize ('ju:tylajz) v. zużytkować; spożytkować; wykorzystać

utmost ('atmoust) adj. najwyższy; ostateczny; skrajny; największy; najdalszy; ostatni

utter ('ater) adj. całkowity;
zupełny; kompletny; skończony; skrajny; ostatni; v. wydawać (głos); powiedzieć; wy-
powiedzieć (hasło itp.); wyrażać; wystawiać (czeki); podrabiać (np. dokumenty); puszczać (w obieg)

utterance ('aterens) s. wypowiedź; wymowa; wyrażenie;
zeznanie; oświadczenie

uvula ('ju:wjula) s. języczek
miękkiego podniebienia

v (wi:) dwudziesta druga litera
alfabetu angielskiego

vacancy ('wejkensy) s. wolne
mieszkanie; wolne pokoje mote-
lowe; wakans; próżnia; pustka;
bezczynność

vacant ('wejkent) adj. pusty;
próżny; wolny; wakujący;bez-
czynny; bezmyślny; obojętny

vacate (we,kejt) v. opróżniać;
opuszczać; unieważniać

vacation (we,kejszyn) s. wakacje
ferie; opróżnienie; zwolnienie
(mieszkania); ewakuacja

vaccinate ('waeksynejt) v.
szczepić

vaccination ('waeksynejszyn)
s. szczepienie

vaccine ('waeksi:n) s. szczepionka

vacuum ('waekjuem) s. próżnia

vacuum bottle ('waekjuem'botl)
s. termos

vacuum cleaner ('waekjuem'kli:-
ner)s. odkurzacz

vacuum flask ('waekjuem,fla:sk)
s. termos

vagabond ('waegebond) adj.
włóczęgowski; wędrowny;
s. włóczęga; nierób; próżniak

vagary ('wejgery) s. kaprys;
chimera

vague (wejg) adj. niejasny; niewyraźny; nieokreślony; nieuchwytny; niewyraźny; wymijający; niezdecydowany

vain (wejn) adj. próżny; zarozumiały; czczy; pusty; gołosłowny; daremny; bezcelowy

valance ('waelens) s. krótka
podłużna zasłona (światła);
rodzaj adamaszku

vale ('wejl) s. dolina; pożegnanie; excl.;żegnajcie !

valerian (we'lerjen) s. waleria-
na

valet ('waelyt) s. służący;
v. usługiwać

valiant ('waeljent) adj. dzielny;
s. zuch

valid ('waelyd) adj. słuszny;
ważny; uzasadniony

valley ('waely) s. dolina; koryto fali; wewnętrzny kąt płaszczyzn dachu

valor ('waelɑɾ) s. dzielność

valuable ('waeljuebl) adj.
wartościowy; cenny; kosztowny;
s.(pl)kosztowności;biżuteria

valuables ('waljuebls) pl.
kosztowności

valuation (,walju'ejszyn) s.
oszacowanie; cena

value ('waelju:) s. wartość;
cena; stopień jasności barwy
(w obrazie); v. szacować; cenić; oceniać

valueless ('waelju:lys) adj.
bezwartościowy

valuer ('waelju:er) s. taksa-
tor

valve (waelw) s. zawór; wentyl;
klapa; zastawka

van (waen) s. kryty wóz (cię-
żarowy); czoło armii; v. przewozić krytym wozem; badać rudę pukaniem

vane (wejn) s. chorągiewka (od
wiatru); łopatka śmigła;
brzechwa bomby; skrzydło wiatraka

vanilla (we'nyle) s. wanilia

vanish ('waenysz) v. znikać;
zanikać

vanity ('waenyty) s. próżność;
pycha; marność; czczość; toaleta; źródło próżności; rzecz
bez wartości

vanitycase ('waenyty,kejs) s.
kosmetyczka

vantage ('waentydż) s. korzyst-
na pozycja; przewaga (w tenisie)

vaporize ('wejporajz) v. wyparować; zamieniać sie w pare

vapor (wejpor) s. para; mgła;
v. parować; ględzić

vaporous ('wejperes) adj.
mglisty; zamglony

variable ('weerjebl) adj. zmienny; niestały; s, zmienny wiatr

variance ('weerjens) s. rozbieżność; niezgodność

variant ('weerent) s. odmiana;
wariant; adj. odmienny; różny

variation (,weery'ejszyn) s,
zmiana; odmiana; wariant;
wariacja

varicose vein ('waerykous,wejn)
s. żylak

varied ('waeryd) adj. różnorodny;
różny; urozmaicony

variety (we'rajety) s. rozmai-
tość; urozmaicenie; różnorod-
ność; wielostronność; teatr
rozmaitości; kabaret; szereg;
odmiana

various ('weerjes) adj. różny;
rozmaity; urozmaicony; wiele;
kilka; kilkakrotnie

varnish ('wa:rnysz) s. pokost;
politura; werniks; polewa;
v. pokostować; werniksować

Varsovian (wa:r'souwjen) adj.
warszawski; s.warszawiak

vary ('weery) v. zmieniać (się);
urozmaicać; różnić się; nie podzielać zdania

vase (wejz) s. waza; wazon

vat (waet) s. zbiornik; kadź;
cysterna

vault (wo:lt) s. sklepienie;
podziemie; piwnica; grobowiec;
skok o tyczce; v. przesklepiać;
osklepić; przeskoczyć; skoczyć
o tyczce

vaulting horse ('wo:ltyŋg,ho:rs)
s. kozioł (przyrząd gimnastyczny)

veal(wi:l) s. cielęcina

vegetable ('wedżytebl) s. jarzyna

vegetarian (,wedży'teerjen) adj.
jarski; s. jarosz; wegetarianin

vegetate ('wedżytejt) v. wegetować; rosnąc

vehemence ('wi:ymens) s. gwałt-
towność; porywczość; wybucho-
wość

vehement ('wi:yment) adj. gwałtowny; porywczy; wybuchowy

vehicle ('wi:ykl) s. pojazd;
środek; narzędzie; przymieszka
do farby

veil (wejl) s. welon; woalka;
wstąpienie do klasztoru; zasłona (maska); chrypka; v. zasłaniać; ukrywać

vein (wejn) s. żyła (też złota);
usposobienie; natura; nastrój;
wena; v. żyłkować

velocity (wy'losyty) s. szybkość

velvet ('welwyt) s. aksamit;
delikatna skórka; (slang);
zarobek; forsa; adj. aksamit-
ny
venal ('wi:nl) adj. sprzedajny
vend (wend) v. sprzedawać
vender ('wender) s. (uliczny)
sprzedawca; automat do sprzedaży
vending machine ('wendyŋg,me'-
'szi:n) s. automat do sprzedaży
venerable ('wenerebl) adj.
czcigodny; wielebny
venerate ('wenerejt) v. czcić
venereal (wy'njerjel) adj.
weneryczny; chory wenerycznie;
przeciwwenervczny; płciowy
Venetian blind (wy'ni:szyn,-
,blajnd)s. żaluzja (wenecka)
vengeance ('wendżens) s. zem-
sta; pomsta
venison ('wenzn) s. dziczyzna
venom ('wenem) s. jad
venomous('wenemes) adj. jadowity
vent (Went) s. odwietrznik;
wentyl; otwór wentylacyjny;
rozcięcie w tyle marynarki;
ujście; upust; v. dawać upust
czemus; wyładowywać (złość);
rozgłaszać; wietrzyć; viercić
otwór wentylacyjny
ventilate ('wentylejt) v.
wentylować; wietrzyć; prze-
dyskutować
ventilator ('wentylejtor) s.
wentylator; wietrznik
ventriloquist (wen'trylokłyst)
s. brzuchomówca
venture ('wenczer) s. ryzyko;
stawka; spekulacja; impreza;
interes; próba; v. odważać
się; osmielać się; ryzykować;
smieć; narazić się
veranda (we'raende) s. weranda
verb (we:rb) s. czasownik;
słowo
verbal ('we:rbel) adj. ustny;
słowny; werbalny; czasownikowy
verdict ('we:rdykt) s. wyrok;
werdykt; osąd; orzeczenie

verdure ('we:rdżer) s. zieleń
verge ('we:rdż) s. skraj; brzeg;
krawędź; v. graniczyć; zbliżać
się; chylić się; skłaniać się;
verge on ('we:rdż,on) v. graniczyć
verification (,weryfy'kejszyn)
s. uwierzytelnienie; sprawdzenie
verify ('weryfaj) v. sprawdzać;
potwierdzać; udowadniać
vermicelli (we:rmy'sely) s. cienki makaron
vermiform appendix (we:rmy'fo:rm-
e'pendyks) s. ślepa kiszka;
wyrostek robaczkowy
vermin ('we:rmyn) s. robactwo;
świat przestępczy
vernacular (we:r'naekjuler) adj.
rodzimy; miejscowy; krajowy;
s. gwara; język rodzinny; do-
sadne powiedzenie
versatile ('we:rsetail) adj.
wszechstronny
verse (we:rs) s. wiersz; strofa
versed ('we:rst) adj. doświadczony; wprawiony (w czyms)
version ('we:rżyn) s. wersja;
przekład; przekręcenie macicy
vertebra ('we:rtybre) s. krąg
vertebrae ('we:rtybri:) pl.
kręgi
vertical ('we:rtykel) adj. pionowy; szczytowy; s. pionowa
płaszczyzna; linia
very ('wery) adv. bardzo; absolutnie; zaraz; własnie; adj.
prawdziwy; sam; skończony(drań)
vessel ('wesl) s. naczynie; pojemnik; statek; okręt
vest (west) s. kamizelka; v. nadawać; przekazać; przysługiwać
komuś; przypadać komuś; odzie-
wać w szaty; przykrywać ołtarz
vestry ('westry) s. zakrystia
vet (wet) s. weterynarz
veteran ('weteran) s. weteran
veterinary ('weterynery) s.
weterynarz
veto ('wi:tou) s. weto; v. zakładać weto

vex (weks) v. złościć; dręczyć; dokuczać

vexation (wek'sejszyn) s. dokuczanie; drażnienie; zniecierpliwienie; irytacja; udręka; przykrość; zaniepokojenie

vexatious (wek'sejszes) adj. dokuczliwy; irytujący; przykry; nieznośny

via ('waje) prep. przez; wia

vibrate (waj'brejt) v. zadrgać; zadrzeć; oscylować; wprawiać w drganie lub ruch wahadłowy

vibration (waj'brejszyn) s. drganie; drżenie; wibracja; oscylacja; ruch wahadłowy

vibrator (waj'brejter) s. wibrator; oscylator

vicar ('wyker) s. wikary; wikariusz; zastępca

vice (wajs) imadło; zacisk; rozpusta; występek; nałóg; narów; wada; v. zaciskać w imadle

vice versa ('wajsy'we:rsa) adv. odwrotnie

vicinity (wy'synyty) s. sąsiedztwo; pobliże

vicious ('wy'szes) adj. błędny; występny; złośliwy; wadliwy; zepsuty; dokuczliwy; narowisty; rozpustny

victim ('wyktym) s. ofiara

victor ('wykter) s. zwycięzca

victorian (wyk'to:rjan) adj. wiktoriański

victorious (wyk'to:rjes) adj. zwycięski

victory ('wyktery) s. zwycięstwo

victuals ('wytlz) s. prowianty; wiktuały

video ('wydjou) s. telewizja; adj. telewizyjny

view (wju:) v. oglądać; rozpatrywać; zbadać; zapatrywać się; s. obejrzenie; spojrzenie; wizja; zasięg wzroku; widok; przegląd umysłowy; pogląd; zapatrywanie; intencja; zamiar; cel; ocena

viewer ('wju:er) s. widz (telewizyjny etc.)

viewpoint ('wju:,pojnt) s. punkt widzenia; zapatywanie

vigil ('wydżyl) s. czuwanie; wigilia

vigilance ('wydżylens) s. czujność; bezsenność

vigilant ('wydżylent) adj. czujny

vigor ('wyger) s. krzepkość; tężyzna; rześkość; energia; siła; moc

vigorous ('wygeres) adj.krzepki; mocny; jędrny; energiczny

vile (wajl) adj. podły; nędzny; marny

village ('wylydż) s. wieś

villager ('wylydżer) s. wieśniak (raczej nieokrzesany)

villain ('wylen) s. łajdak; łotr; nikczemnik; łobuziak

villainous ('wylenes) adj. łajdacki; niegodziwy

villainy ('wyleny) s. łajdactwo

vim (wym) s. tężyzna

vincible ('wynsybl) adj. przezwyciężalny

vindicate ('wyndykejt) v. oczyszczać z zarzutu, oskarżenia, podejrzenia; rehabilitować; usprawiedliwiać; bronić; dochodzić; dowodzić

vindication (,wyndy'kejszyn) s. obrona; windykacja; usprawiedliwienie; oczyszczenie się (z zarzutu); rehabilitacja

vindictive (wyn'dyktyw) adj. mściwy; karzący

vine (wajn) s. winna latorośl; winorośl

vinegar ('wynyger) s. ocet; v. kwasić

vineyard ('wynjerd) s. winnica

vintage ('wyntydż) s. rocznik wina; winobranie; robienie wina; model (roczny)

violate ('wajelejt) v. gwałcić; zgwałcić (kobietę)

violation (,waje'lejszyn) s. pogwałcenie; zgwałcenie; gwałt; zbeszczeszczenie; naruszenie (też praw ruchu) violence ('wajelens) s. gwałtownosc; gwałt; przemoc

violent ('wajelent) adj. gwałtowny; niepohamowany; wsciekły

violet ('wajelyt) s. fiołek; adj. fioletowy (np. promien)

violin (,waje'lyn) s. skrzypce

violinist (,waje'lynyst) s. skrzypek

viper ('wajper) s. żmija

virgin ('we:rdżyn) s. dziewica

virginity (we:r'dżynyty) s. dziewictwo

virile ('wyrajl) adj. męski

virility (wy'rylyty) s. męskosc; wiek męski; cechy męskie

virtual ('we:rczuel) adj. zasadniczy; własciwy; faktyczny; prawdziwy; rzeczywisty

virtually ('we:rczuely) adv. rzeczywiscie; faktycznie; praktycznie biorąc

virtue ('we:rczju:) s. cnota; prawosc; czystosc; skutecznosc; siła; moc

virtuoso (,we:rczju'ouzou) s. wirtuoz; miłosnik- znawca sztuki

virtuous (,we:rczjues) adj. cnotliwy; prawy

virulent ('wyrulent) adj. jadowity; złosliwy; zjadliwy

virus ('wajeres) s. wirus; jad (chorobowy)

visa ('wi:za) s. wiza; v. wiza; v. wizowac

viscosity (wys'kosyty)s.lepkosc; ─kleistosc

visibility (,wyzy'bylyty) s. widocznosc

visible (wyzybl) adj. widoczny; wyrazny; widzialny

vision ('wyżyn) s. widzenie; wzrok; wizja; dar przewidywania; v. okazywac wizję; miec wizję

visit ('wyzyt) v. odwiedzac; wizytowac zwiedzac; nawiedzac; karac; udzielac się; gawędzic; s. wizyta; odwiedziny; pobyt

visitor ('wyzyter) s. gosc; przyjezdny; zwiedzający; inspektor

vista ('wysta) s. perspektywa; wizja; widok

visual ('wyżjuel) adj. wzrokowy; optyczny

visualize ('wyżjuelajz) v. wyobrazac sobie; uwidaczniac; uzmysławiac

vital ('wajtl) adj. witalny; życiowy; żywotny; zasadniczy; smiertelny

vitality (waj'taelyty) s. żywotnosc; żywosc

vitamin ('wajtemyn) s. witamina

vivacious (wy'wejszes) adj. żywy

vivacity (wy'waesyty) s. żywosc

vivid ('wywyd) adj. żywy

vivify ('wywyfaj) v. ożywiac

vivisection ('wywysekszyn) s. wiwisekcja

vixen ('wyksen) s. liszka; lisica; jędza

vixenish ('wyksenysz) adj. jędzowaty

vocabulary (wou'kaebjulery) s. słownik (specjalny); słownictwo

vocal ('woukel) s. samogłoska; adj. głosowy; wokalny; głosny; natarczywy

vocalist ('woukelyst) s. spiewak; wokalista

vocation (wou'kejszyn) s. zawód; zamiłowanie; powołanie; skłonnosc

vogue (woug) s. moda; popularnosc

voice (wois) s. głos; dzwięk samogłoskowy; strona (czasownika); v. wymawiac; wyrazac; dawac wyraz czemus; wymawiac dzwięcznie; udzwięczniac; pisac partie głosowe do muzyki; stroic

void (woid) s. próznia; pustka; adj, prózny; pusty; pozbawiony czegos; wolny od czegos; wakujący; niewazny; v. uniewazniac; wydalac; wyprózniac (się); oddawac (mocz)

void of ('woid,ow) exp.:bez

volatile ('woletyl) adj. lotny;
uiatniający się; zmienny
volcano (wol'kejnou) s. wulkan
volley ('woly) s. salwa; potok;
odbicie (piłki); wolej;
v. dać salwę; wypuszczać salwę; podawać wolejem; miotać
potokiem (przekleństw);lecieć
salwą; odbijać w locie
volleyball ('woly,bo:l) s.
siatkówka
volt (woult) s. wolt (elektr.)
wolta; v. robić woltę
voltage ('woultydż) s. napięcie
prądu; woltaż
voluble ('woljubl) adj. gładki;
potoczysty; ze swadą
volume ('wolju:m) s. tom; objętość; masa; ilość; pojemność;
rozmiar; siła
voluntary ('wolentery) adj.
ochotniczy; dobrowolny; wolą
kontrolowany; spontaniczny;
samorzutny; s. specjalny wyczyn z wyboru sportowca; gra
solo na organie
volunteer ('wolentier) s. ochotnik (bezpłatnie pracujący);
v. robić z własnej ochoty;
zgłaszać się na ochotnika;
podejmować coś dobrowolnie;
być ochotnikiem
voluptuous (we'lapczues) adj.
zmysłowy; lubieżny
vomit ('womyt) v. wymiotować;
wyrzucać; pobudzać do wymiotów; s. wymioty; środek wymiotny
voodoo ('wu:du:) s. wiara w
czary; czarownik;v.zaczarować
voracious (we'rejszes) adj.
żarłoczny
voracity ('we'raesyty) s. żarłoczność
vote (wout) s. głos; głosy;
głosowanie; prawo głosowania;
uchwała; wotum (zaufania);
v. głosować; uchwalać; orzekać; uznawać powszechnie za
cos
vote down ('wout,dałn) v. odrzucać w głosowaniu

voting paper ('woutyŋg'pejper)
s. kartka wyborcza
vouch (waucz) v. ręczyć; gwarantować; potwierdzać; zapewnić
voucher ('wauczer) s. dowód
kasowy
vouch for ('waucz,fo:r) v. ręczyć za kogoś
vouch safe (waucz'sejf) v. (łaskawie) raczyć
vow (wau) s. ślub (też zakonny);
przymierze; v. przysięgać;
ślubować; składać śluby
vowel ('wałel) s. samogłoska
voyage ('wojydż) s. podróż
(statkiem)
voyager ('wojedżer) s. podróżnik
vulcanize ('walkenajz) s. wulkanizować
vulgar ('walger) adj. ordynarny;
wulgarny; prostacki; gminny;
pospolity; powszechny
vulgarity ('wal'gaeryty) s.
wulgarność; wyrażenie wulgarne
vulnerable ('walnerebl) adj.
czuły; wrażliwy; mający słabe
miejsce; narażony na cios; podatny na zranienie; niezabezpieczony
vulpine ('walpajn) adj. lisi;
przebiegły; chytry ____[szakal
vulture ('walczer) s. sęp;(slang)
vulturine (walczeryn) adj. sępi
w ('dablju:) dwudziesta trzecia
litera alfabetu angielskiego
wabble ('łobl) v. (slang); rozklekotać; roztrząsąć; rozchwiać;
s. rozchwianie; rozklekotanie
wack (łaek) s. (slang); oryginał;
dziwak
wacky ('łaeky) adj.(slang):
zwariowany;zdziwaczały; nieobliczalny
wad (łod) s. tampon; wałek (zwinięty); wata (w uszach); przybitka naboju w strzelbie;
(slang): forsa; plik (banknotów)
v. zatykać (tamponem); watować;
przybijać (nabój); wypychać;
zwijać w wałek
wadding ('łodyŋg) s. watowanie;
watolina; wata; wełna (do utykania); podkład; przybitka

waddle ('łodl) v. chodzić kołysząc się w biodrze jak
kaczka; v. kaczy krok

wade (łejd) y. brodzić; brnąć;
przechodzić w bród; brodze-
nie

wafer ('łejfer) s. wafel;
opłatek; naklejka urzędowa
(pieczątkowa); v. zapieczę-
towywać naklejką

waffle ('łofl) s. wafel z ciasta naleśnikowego

waft ('łaeft) v. popychać (lekko); posuwać; posyłać (cału-
sa); przepędzać; unosić (w
powietrzu). s. śmignięcie
skrzydła; powiew; podmuch;
tchnienie; przelotne uczucie;
smuga (światła)

wag (łaeg) v. kiwać (ogonem);
poruszać się; wahać się; chodzić tam i spowrotem; merdać

wage (łejdż) s. płaca; zarobek;
zapłata; v. prowadzić (np.
wojnę)

wage earner ('łejdż,e:rner) s.
człowiek zarobkujący

wages ('łejdżyz) s. zapłata

wager ('łejdżer) s. zakład;
v. zakładać się o coś

wagon ('łaegen) s. ciężki wóz
(kryty); lora; wóz policyjny;
furgon

wail (łejl) v. zawodzić; lamentować; opłakiwać; v. zawodze-
nie; lament; płacz

wainscot ('łejnsket) s. boazeria;
ozdobne obicie ścian drzewem

waist (łejst) s. talia; stan;
pas; kibić; stanik; środokrę-
cie; zwężenie

waistcoat ('łeiskout) s. kamizelka

wait (łejt) v. czekać; oczekiwać;
czyhać; czatować; czaić się;
obsłużyć; obsługiwać kogoś;
s. czekanie; oczekiwanie; zasadzka; czaty

wait at table('łejtettejbl) v.
usługiwać przy stole

waiter ('łejter) s. kelner

wait on('łejton) v.obsługiwać

waiting (łejtyng) s. czekanie;
oczekiwanie; wyczekiwanie; zasadzka

waiting list (łejtyng,lyst) s.
lista kolejności (kandydatów,
klientów)

waiting room(łejtynrum) s.po-
czekalnia

waitings (łejtyns) pl. kolędni-
cy

waitress (łejtryss) s. kelnerka

wake; woke; woken (łejk; łouk;
łoukn)

wake (łejk) v. obudzić (się);
nie spać; pobudzić; rozbudzić;
wzbudzić; wskrzesić; czuwać
przy (zwłokach); s. niespanie;
czuwanie przy zwłokach; kilwater; fala w ślad za statkiem
(motorówką); ślad (po kims, po
czyms)

wake up ('łejk,ap) v. obudzić
(się); ocknąć się; oprzytomnieć; zdawać sobie sprawę;
zbudzić

wakeful ('łejkful) adj. czuwa-
jący; bezsenny; czujny

waken (' łejkn) = woken (łouken)
v. zob. wake

waken ('łejkn) v. zbudzić;
obudzić; ożywiać; wzbudzić;
wskrzesić (np. zmarłego)

walk (łо:k) v. iść; przechadzać się; chodzić; kroczyć;
iść stępa; jechać stępa;
wejść; zejść; s. chód; krok;
przechadzka; spacer; marsz;
deptak; aleja; odległość prze-
byta

walk about ('łо:ke,baut) v.
włóczyć się; łazić

walk along ('łо:ke,long) v.
chodzić sobie

walk away ('łо:ke,łej) v. odchodzić; (w zawodach): łatwo
wygrywać

walk back ('łо:k,baek) v. wracać

walk down ('łо:k,dałn) v. schodzić

walk in ('łо:k,yn) v. wchodzić

walk off ('ło:k,of) v. odchodzić; zniknąć; ulotnić się (z czymś)

walk out ('ło:k,aut) v. wyjść; opuścić

walk over ('ło:k,ouwer) v. wygrywać łatwo; traktować pogardliwie

walk up ('ło:k,ap) v. podejść; wejść na górę

walker ('ło:ker) s. piechur

walkie-talkie ('ło:ky-'to:ky) s. przenośny, mały odbiornik-nadajnik radiowy

walking (ło:kyng) s. chodzenie; marsz; wycieczka piesza; adj. chodzący; wędrowny

walking papers ('ło:kyn'pejpers) pl. zwolnienie z pracy na piśmie

walking stick ('ło:kyng,styk) s. laska

walking-tour ('ło:kyng,tu:r) s. wycieczka piesza; zwiedzanie piechotą

walk-out ('ło:kaut) s. strajk

walk-over ('ło:k-over ('ło:k-ouwer) s. walkower (sport)

wall (ło:l) s. ściana; mur; przepierzenie; wał; v. obmurować

wall in ('ło:l,yn) v. otaczać

wall up ('ło:l,ap) v. zamurować

wallboard ('ło:l,bo:rd) s. licówka (ściany)

wallet ('łolyt) s. portfel

wallop ('łolep) v. walić; łoić; prać; pobić na głowę; galopować; łazić ciężko i niezgrabnie; s. wyrżnięcie (cios); galop; ruch ciężki i niezgrabny

wallow ('łolou) v. tarzać się; kłębić się; kołysać się; s. tarzanie się

wallpaper ('łol,pejper) s. tapety; v. tapetować

Wall Street ('łolstri:t) s. ośrodek finansowy (USA)

walnut ('ło:lnat) s. orzech włoski

walrus ('ło:lres) s. mors

waltz ('ło:ls) s. walc; v. tańczyć walca; (slang): ruszać się żwawo

wan (łon) adj. blady; wybladły; blednąć

wand (łond) s. laseczka; pałeczka; pręt; buława

wander ('łonder) v. wędrować; błądzić; błąkać się

wanderer ('łonderer) s. wędrowiec

wane (łejn) v. zanikać; gasnąć; s. zanik

wangle ('łaengl) v. (slang): wycyganić; wyłudzić; sfałszować; s. krętactwo; kant

want (ło:nt) s. brak; potrzeba; niedostatek; niedopatrzenie; bieda; nędza; v. pragnąć; chcieć; brakować; potrzebować; pożądać

wanted ('ło:ntyd) adj. poszukiwany

wanting ('ło:ntyng) adj. brakujący; kiepski; niedokładny; pozbawiony; nie na poziomie; słaby na umyśle; prep. bez; mniej;przy braku

want in ('ło:nt,yn) v. chcieć wejść

wanton ('łonten) adj. złośliwy; krzywdzący; bez powodu; bezmyślny; samowolny; bezczelny; nieokiełzany; wyuzdany; lubieżny; bujny; zbytkowny; s. lubieżnik; lubieżnica; v. oddawać się rozpuście; używać sobie; swawolić; rość bujnie; trwonić; psocić; figlować; bawić się

want out ('ło:nt,aut) v. chcieć wyjść

war (łor) s. wojna; v. wojować; zawojować

warble ('łorbl) v. nucić; jodłować; s. nucący głos; nucona pieśń; guz od siodła na grzbiecie konia; guz wywołany larwą gza bydlęcego

ward (ło:rd) s. dzielnica; cela; sala; oddział; podopieczny; opieka; kuratela; postawa obronna; parada; straż; v.odparowywać (cios); odsuwać (niebezpieczeństwo);umieszczać na oddziale

ward off ('ło:rd,of) v, odparowywać cios; odsuwać (zagro-
żenie)

warden ('ło:rdn) s. dyrektor
więzienia; dozorca; nadzorca;
gatunek twardej gruszki

warder ('ło:rder) s. strażnik
więzienny; posterunek; buława

ward heeler('ło:rd,hi:ler) s.
naganiacz partyjny

wardrobe ('ło:droub) s. garderoba; szafa na ubranie

ware (łeer) s. towar; wyrób;
ceramika; v. uwaga na coś;
trzymać się z dala od czegoś;
excl.: strzeż się !

warehouse ('łeerhaus) s. magazyn; składnica; dom składowy;
v. magazynować; składować

warm (ło:rm) adj. ciepły; świeży (trop); bliski znalezienia;
zadomowiony (na posadzie);
zamożny

warm up ('ło:rm,ap) v. ożywiać
(się); podgrzewać (się); ogrze-
wać (się); rozgrzewać (się)

warmup ('ło:rmap) s. ćwiczenia
rozluźniające (przed zawodami
etc); zagrzanie się

warmth ('ło:rms) s. ciepło;
serdeczność; zapał

warn (ło:rn) v. ostrzegać;
przypominać; wzywać; zapowiadać; uprzedzać

warn against(ło:negejnst) v.
ostrzegać przed czymś

warning ('ło:rnyng) adj. ostrzegawczy; s. ostrzeżenie; przestroga; znak ostrzegawczy;
wypowiedzenie (posady)

warp (ło:rp) v. wypaczyć (się);
zwichrować (się); wykrzywić
(się); spaczyć (się); przyholo-
wywać do miejsca utwierdzenia
liny lub łańcucha; użyźniać
(przez zalewanie osadem);
s. spaczenie; wypaczenie; osnowa; szew skośny; lina holownicza; osad

warrant ('łorent) v. usprawiedliwiać; uzasadniać; gwarantować; s. upoważnienie; gwarancja;

nakaz prawny (aresztu; rewizji,
etc). pełnomocnictwo dla ad-
wokatów; patent starszego pod-
oficera (USA)

warranty ('łorenty) s. gwarancja; poręka; rękojmia; podstawa; usprawiedliwienie; upoważnienie; dokument sądowy

warren ('ło:ryn) s. królikarnia

warrior ('ło:rjor) s. wojownik;
żołnierz; adj. wojowniczy

wart (ło:rt) s. brodawka; ku-
rzawka

wary ('łeery) adj. ostrożny

was (łoz) v. zob. be

wash (ło:sz) v. myć (się); prać;
prać (się); oczyszczać; zraszać; lekko barwić; lawować;
umyć się; sunąć; płynąć z
pluskiem; płukać (rudę);
s. mycie; pranie; płyn (czyszczący); fale; plusk; pomyje;
lura; wypłukane miejsce w ziemi; ględzenie; zaburzenie wody za statkiem; zaburzenie powietrza za samolotem; ziemia
na tacy zawierająca złoto; pod-
mywanie przez fale; mielizna;
kanał wyżłobiony przez wodę;
mielizna naniesiona wodą; la-
wowanie; cienka warstwa metalu;
kilwater; ślad wodny

wash away (ło:sze,łej) v. spłukać; zmyć; unosić

wash down ('ło:sh,dałn) v. zmywać strumieniem wody; popić
jedzenie

wash off (ło:sh,of) v. odeprać;
wymywać

wash out ('ło:sh,aut) v. wypłu-
kiwać (się) (z pieniędzy etc.)

wash up ('ło:sh,ap) v. zmywać
naczynia; wymyć się

wash and wear ('ło:sz,end'łeer)
s. bielizna i odzież gotowa
do noszenia po praniu bez pra-
sowania

washbowl ('ło:sz,boul) s.mied-
nica; umywalka; umywalnia

washcloth ('ło:sz,clos) s. zmy-
wak; szmatka do zmywania

washer ('ło:szer) s. uszczelka; podkładka; maszyna do prania

washing ('łoszyŋg)s. mycie; pranie; przemywanie; woda z prania; popłuczyny; wypłukane złoto; wypłukany żwir; bielizna do prania

washing machine ('ło:szyŋg,meszi:n) s. pralka; maszyna do prania

washing powder ('ło:szyŋ'pałder) s. proszek do prania

washing up ('ło:szyŋg,ap) v. obmycie się

washleather ('ło:sz,ledzer) s. ircha; zamsz

washout ('ło:szaut) s. zapadnięcie się; podmycie; (slang): klapa; niepowodzenie

washtub ('ło:sztab) s. balia

washy ('ło:szy) adj. wodnisty; rzadki; blady; cienki; wypłowiały

wasn't = was not

wasp (łosp) n. osa; (slang): biały-anglosaksonin-protestant

waspish ('łospysh) adj. zjadliwy; cienki w pasie (jak osa)

wastage ('łejstydż) s. strata; zużycie

waste (łejst) adj. pustynny; pusty; nieużyty (ziemia); opustoszały; wyludniony; leżący odłogiem; zużyty; niepotrzebny; zbyteczny; odpadowy; v. pustoszyć; psuć; niszczyć (się); stracić (też zabić); zmarnować; ginąć; zużywać (się); zapuścić; zaniedbać; s. pustynia; marnowanie; trwonienie; zniszczenie; ubytek; zużycie; odpady; bezmiar (np. wody); zaniedbanie; marnotrawstwo

waste away ('łejst,e'łey) v. marnieć

wasteful ('łejstful) adj. rozrzutny; marnotrawny

wastepaper basket ('łejst-pejper-ba:skyt) s. kosz na śmieci

waste pipe ('łejstpajp) s. rura odpływowa; rura ściekowa

waster ('łejster) s. marnotrawca; zepsuty materiał; artykuł wybrakowany; nicpoń

watch (ło:cz) s. czuwanie; pilnowanie; czaty; czujność; wachta; zegarek; mieć się na baczności; oczekiwanie na coś; wyglądanie czegoś; v. czuwać; oczekiwać; czatować; pilnować; opiekować się; uważać; mieć na oku; mieć się na baczności; wyglądać czegoś; obserwować; szpiegować; przyglądać się; patrzyć; oczekiwać sposobności; śledzić

watch out ('ło:czaut) v. uważać; strzec się; uwaga !; uważaj !

watchdog ('ło:czdog) s. pies podwórzowy

watchful ('ło:czful) adj. czujny; baczny

watchmaker ('ło:cz,mejker) s. zegarmistrz

watchman ('ło:czmen) s. stróż; dozorca

watchtower ('ło:cz,tauer) s. strażnica; wieża strażnicza

watchword ('ło:cz'e:rd) s. hasło; slogan

watch your step ('ło:cz,jo:r'-'step) exp.: uważaj !; pilnuj się !

water (ło:ter) s. woda; wysięk; przypływ; odpływ; pl. zdrój; wody lecznicze; ocean; morze; jezioro; rzeka; v. polewać; podlewać; pokropić; poić; iść do wodopoju; nawadniać; rozwadniać; rozcieńczać; skrapiać; łzawić się; ślinić się

water anchor ('ło:ter'aenker) s. kotwica dryfująca

water blister ('ło:ter,blyster) s. pęcherzyk z wodą

waterborne ('ło:ter,born) adj. przenoszony lub przekazywany przez wodę

water bottle ('ło:ter,botl) s. karafka; manierka

water brush ('ło:ter,brasz) s.
zgaga

water but ('ło:ter,bat) s.
zbiornik na deszczówkę

water-cart ('ło:ter,ca:rt) s.
beczkowóz

water closet ('ło:ter'klozet)
s. ustęp

watercolor ('ło:ter'kaler) s.
akwarela

water cool ('ło:ter,ku:l) v.
chłodzić wodą

watercourse ('ło:ter,ko:rs)
s. strumień; rzeka ; kanał

watercress ('ło:ter,kres) s.
rzeżucha wodna

water-cure ('ło:ter,kjuer) s.
kuracja wodna

water-dog ('ło:ter,dog) s. pies
myśliwski aportujący z wody;
(slang): amator pływania, etc)

water down ('ło:ter,dałn) v.
rozwadniać

waterfall ('ło:ter,fo:l) s.
wodospad

waterfowl ('ło:ter,faul) s.
ptactwo wodne

waterfront ('ło:ter,frant) s.
wybrzeże; doki; dzielnica
portowa

watergap ('ło:ter,gaep) s.
przełom rzeki

water gate('ło:ter,gejt) s.
śluza

water gauge('ło:ter,gejdż) s.
wodowskaz; licznik wodny

water-glass ('ło:ter,gla:s) s.
szklanka; naczynie; kubek;
szklany wodowskaz; przeziernik podwodny

water hammer ('ło:ter,haemer)
s. silny wstrząs wywołany na-
głym zatrzymaniem wody w rurze

water hen ('ło:ter,hen) s. kur-
ka wodna

water hole ('ło:terhol) s. stojąca woda (w suchym łożysku
rzeki); wodopój

water ice ('ło:ter,ajs) s. sor-
bet

watering place ('ło:teryng-
plejs) s. wodopój; kąpielisko;
zdrojowisko

waterless ('ło:terlys) adj.
bezwodny; pozbawiony wody

water lily ('ło:ter,lyly) s.
grzybień biały; lilia wodna

water level ('ło:ter'lewl) s.
poziom wody

waterline ('ło:terlajn) s.
linia zanurzenia statku

waterlogged ('ło:ter,logd) adj.
przesycony wodą

watermain ('ło:ter,mejn) s.
główna rura wodociągów

waterman ('ło:termen) s. prze-
woźnik; wioślarz

watermark ('ło:terma:rk) s.
znak wodny; wodowskaz; v. robić znak wodny

watermelon ('ło:ter,melen) s.
arbuz; kawon

water meter('ło:ter'mi:ter) s.
wodomierz; licznik wodny

water mill ('ło:ter,myl) s.
młyn

water mocassin ('ło:ter,mokesyn)
s. żmija wodna w USA

water motor ('ło:ter'mouter) s.
motor wodny

water plane ('ło:ter'plejn) s.
hydroplan

waterpower ('ło:ter'pałer) s.
siła wodna; prawo do używania
wody

water pot ('ło:ter,pot) s.ko- -
newka; polewaczka

waterproof ('ło:ter,pru:f)
adj. nieprzemakalny; v. robić
nieprzemakalnym

water-rat ('ło:ter,raet) s.
szczur wodny

water rate ('ło:ter,rejt) s.
opłata za wodę; cena wody

waterscape ('ło:ter,skejp) s.
krajobraz morski

watershed ('ło:ter,szed) s,
dział wodny; (slang): ważna
granica

water-ski ('ło:ter,ski:) s.
narta wodna

water·spout('řo:ter,spaut) s.
trąba wodna; rynna pionowa

water supply ('řo:terse,plaj)
s. zaopatrzenie w wodę; sieć
wodociągowa

water table ('řo:ter,tejbl) s.
poziom (w ziemi) wody zaskórnej

watertight ('řo:ter,tajt)
adj. wodoszczelny

water·tower ('řoter,tauer) s.
wieża ciśnień

water wave ('řo:ter,řejw) s.
ondulacja wodna

waterway ('řo:ter,řej) s.
droga wodna; kanał; rzeka
spławna

waterwheel ('řo:ter,hři:l) s.
koło (młyńskie) wodne

water witch ('řo:ter,řycz) s.
różdżkarz

waterworks ('řo:ter,ře:rks) s.
wodociągi; fontanna

watery ('řo:tery) adj. wodnisty;
zalzawiony; śliniący się; wróżący deszcz

watt (řot) s. (electr.) wat

waul (řo:l) v. miařczeć ostro
i przeciągle

wave (řejw) s. fala; falistość;
ondulacja; pokiwanie ręką;
gest ręka; v. falować; ondulować; machać do kogoś

wave away ('řejwe'řej) v. odprawiać machnięciem ręki

wave back ('řejw,baek) v. przywoływać (spowrotem) machnięciem ręki

wavelength ('řejw,lenks) s.
długość fali

wave meter('řejwmi:ter) s. falomierz

waver ('řejwer) v. zachwiać(się);
zamigotać; być niezdecydowanym;
załamywać się; drzeć; zawahać
się; kołysać się; trzepotać
się;schwianie (się)

wavy ('řejwy) adj. falisty; sfalowany; drżący; migocący;
karbowany

wawl ('řo:l) v. wrzeszczeć jak
kot

wax (řaeks) s. wosk; adj. woskowy; v. woskować; stawać się

waxen ('řaeksn) adj. woskowy;
miękki jak wosk

wax paper ('řaeks'pejper) s.
papier woskowy

waxwork ('řaeksře:rk) s. figura woskowa; v. modelować
z wosku

waxy ('řaeksy) adj. woskowy;
woskowaty; (slang): wściekły;
zły; okrutny

way (řej) s. droga; szlak;
trakt; przejście; wolna droga;
odległość; kierunek; strona;
sposób; zwyczaj; bieg; tok;
sens; stan; położenie

way back (řej baek) adv. dawno
temu; daleko w tyle; dawno

waybill ('řejbyl) s. list
przewozowy; fracht

wayfarer ('řej,feerer) s. podróżnik (pieszy)

waylay (řejlej) v.zob. lay;
zaskoczyć kogoś; czyhać na
kogoś; czatować

way of life ('řej ow,lajf) s.
styl życia; sposób życia

way-out ('řej,aut) s. wyjście;
rozwiązanie; adj. (slang):
nadzwyczajny; nadzwyczaj;
dobrze zrobiony; nadzwyczaj
zdolny; (zob. far-out)

wayside ('řej,sajd) s. skraj
drogi; adj. przydrożny

way station (,řej'stejszyn) s.
przystanek

-ways (řejz) (przyrostek)
w taki sposób (np:sideways)

wayward ('řejřerd) adj. przewrotny; uparty; kaprysny;
nieobliczalny; chimeryczny

we (ři:) pron. my

weak (ři:k) adj. słaby

weaken ('ři:kn) v. osłabiać;
słabnąć; rozcieńczać

weak-kneed ('ři:kni:d) adj.
słaby

weakling ('ři:klyng) s. słabeusz; cherlak; człowiek słaby; adj. słaby

weakly ('łi:kly) adj. słabowity; adv. słabo
weak-minded ('łi:k,majndyd)
adj. słaby na umyśle; słabe-
go charakteru
weakness (łi:knys) s. słabość;
słabostka
wealth (łels) s. bogactwo; dobrobyt
wealthy ('łelsy) adj. bogaty
wean (łi:n) v. odłączać od
piersi; oduczać; odrywać
weanling ('łi:nlyng) s. dziecko świeżo odsunięte od piersi
weapon ('łepon) s. broń
wear; wore; worn (łeer; ło:r;
ło:rn)
wear (łeer) v. nosić; chodzić
w czyms; ścierać się; wycierać się; żłobić; zacierać się;
przechodzić; mijać; zdzierać;
nużyć; męczyć; wyczerpywać;
długo trwać; długo służyć;
s. noszenie; rzeczy noszone;
moda; zużycie; wytrzymałość
wear away ('łeer,e'łej) v.
zużywać; wlec się
wear off ('łeer,of) v. zetrzeć (się); zacierać (się);
mijać
wear on ('łeer,on) v. wlec się
wear out ('łeer,aut) v. zdzierać (się); wyczerpywać (się)
wearing ('łieryng)adj.przezna-
czony do noszenia na sobie
wearisome ('łierysem) adj.
męczący; nużący; nudny
weary ('łiery) adj. zmęczony;
znużony; znudzony; męczący;
nużący; nudny; v. męczyć;
nudzić; naprzykrzać się;
uprzykrzać sobie
weasel ('łi:zl) s. łasica
weather ('łedzer) s. pogoda;
adj. atmosferyczny; odwietrz-
ny; pogodny; v. zwietrzać;
okrywać się patyną (śniedzią)
weather-beaten ('łedzer,bi:tn)
adj. zaharowany; skołatany
przez burze
weather-bound ('łedzer,baund)
adj. zatrzymany przez pogodę
(statek)

weather bureau ('łedzer,bjuerou)
s. instytut meteorologiczny
weather chart ('łedzer,cza:rt)
s. wykres meteorologiczny
weathercock ('łedzer,kok) s.
chorągiewka na dachu; kurek
na dachu; człowiek niestały
weather forecast ('łedz,fo:r-
ka:st) s. komunikat meteorologiczny
weather vane ('łedzer,wejn) s.
wiatrowskaz; chorągiewka na
dachu
weave (łi:w; łouw;
łouwn)
weave (łi:w) v. tkać (tkaninę);
knuć (spisek); układać (intry-
gę; opowiadanie) spleść; splatać; zajmować się tkactwem
weaver ('łi:wer) s. tkacz
weaving ('łi:wyng) s. tkactwo
web (łeb) s. tkanina; sztuka
(materiału); stek (kłamstw);
pajęczyna; błona (nietoperza);
tkanka łączna; usztywnienie
wed (łed) v. zaślubiać; łączyć
się; pobrać się; adj. zaślubiony
wedded ('łedyd) adj. zaślubiony; ślubny; oddany (sprawie)
wedding ('łedyng) s. ślub; wesele; adj. ślubny; weselny
wedding ring ('łedyng,ryng) s.
obrączka ślubna
we'd (łi:d) = we had; we would;
we should
wedge (łedż) s. klin; trójkątny
kawałek (tortu); golfowy kijek
z klinowym zakończeniem; v.kli-
nować; zaklinować; rozklinować;
łupać
wedge in ('łedż,yn) v. wpychać
(się); wciskać (się)
wedge off ('łedż,of) v. wypychać (się)
wedlock ('łedlok) s. małżeństwo
Wednesday ('łenzdy) s. środa
weed (łi:d) s. chwast; zielsko;
cygaro; (slang): chuchro; cherlak; mizerak; szkapa; v. pie-
lić; odchwaszczać
weeder ('łi:der) s. pielnik;
wypielacz

weed grown ('łi:dgroun)adj.
zachwaszczony

weed out ('łi:d,aut) v. wypie-
lać; usuwać

weeds ('łi:ds) pl. krepa żałobna; strój żałobny

weedy ('łi:dy) adj. zachwaszczony; chudy; wysoki

weed killer ('łi:d,kyler) s.
trucizna na chwasty

week (łi:k) s. tydzień

weekday ('łi:kdej) s. dzień
powszedni

weekend ('łi:kend) s. niedziela oraz części wolne
soboty i poniedziałku;
v. spędzać weekend

week in-week out ('łi:k,yn-
'łi:k,aut) adv. exp.: co tydzień

weekly ('łi:kly) adj. tygodniowy; adv. tygodniowo; s.
tygodnik

weep; wept; wept (łi:p; łept;
łept)

weep (łi:p) v. płakać; opłakiwać; zapłakać; lamentować;
cieknąć; wyciekać; ociekać;
s. płacz; cieknięcie

weeper ('łi:per) s. płaczek;
płaczka; welon żałobny; krepa żałobna

weep away ('łi:pe,łej) v. wy-
płakać się

weeping willow ('łi:pyng,ły-
lou) s. wierzba płacząca

weep for joy ('łi:p-fo:r-dżoj)
v. płakać z radości

weep out ('łi:p,aut) v. powiedzieć z płaczem

weigh (łej) v. ważyć (się);
rozważać; mierzyć; równoważyć;
podnosić (kotwicę); s. waże-
nie

weigh in ('łej,yn) v. ważyć
(boksera; dżokeja przed zawodami)

weigh out ('łej,aut) v. wywa-
żyć człowieka przed zawodami

weigh up ('łej,ap) v. rozważyć

weigh upon ('łej,apon) v. przygniatać; ciążyć na kims

weight (łejt) s. ciężar; waga;
obciążenie; ciężarek; odważnik;
przycisk; grubość (odzieży);
znaczenie; doniosłość; odpowiedzialność; v. obciążać; pogrubiać sztucznie tkaninę

weight lifting ('łejt lyftyng)
s. (sport) podnoszenie ciężarów

weightless ('łejtlys) adj. lekki;
bez ciężaru

weighted-with(łejyd,łys) adj.
obarczony (np. wiekiem)

weighty ('łejty) adj. ciężki;
ważki; doniosły; ważny; poważny ; przekonywujący; rozważony;
przemyślany

weir (łier) s. jaz; grobla

weird (łierd) adj. niesamowity;
tajemniczy; nadprzyrodzony;
dziwny; dziwaczny; s. los

welcome ('łekem) exp.: witaj !
witajcie ! s. powitanie; adj.
mile widziany; mający pozwolenie; mogący korzystać; v. powitać; witać (z radością)

weld (łeld) v. spawać (się);
spajać; zespalać; zgrzewać;
s. spoina; spawanie; spojenie;
miejsce spojenia

welder (łelder) s. spawacz;
spawarka; przyrząd do spawania

welfare ('łelfeer) s. dobro;
dobrobyt; powodzenie; pomyślność; szczęście

welfare-state ('łelfeer'stejt)
s. państwo o bardzo wysokich
świadczeniach społecznych

welfare-work ('łelfeer,łe:rk)
s. praca społeczna; społecz-
nictwo; praca dobroczynna

well; better; best (łel; beter;
best) adv. dobrze; lepiej; najlepiej

well (łel) s. studnia; otwór
wiertniczy; odwiert; źródło;
klatka (schodowa); adv. dobrze;
należycie; porządnie; mocno; so-
lidnie; szczęśliwie; całkiem;
wyraźnie; łatwo; lekko; słusznie; adj. dobry; zdrowy; zadawalający; pomyślny; w porządku;
exp.: dobrze ! a więc ?

well-balanced ('łel'baelenst)
adj. zrównoważony

well-behaved ('łelby'hejwd)
adj. dobrze wychowany

well-being ('łel'bi:yŋg)s.
dobrobyt; powodzenie; po-
myślność

well-born ('łel'bo:rn) adj.
dobrze urodzony

well-bred ('łel'bred) adj.
rasowy; dobrze wychowany

well-connected ('łel'konektyd)
adj. dobrze skoligacony

well-disposed ('łeldys'pouzd)
adj. życzliwie usposobiony

well done ('łeldan) exp.:
brawo ! dobrze zrobione !

well-fed ('łelfed) adj. dobrze
odżywiony

well-founded ('łelfaundyd)
adj. uzasadniony

wellhead ('łel'hed) s. źródło

well-heeled ('łel'hi:ld) adj.
slang): forsiasty (ma forsę)

Wellingtons ('łelyŋtenz) s.
buty z wysokimi holewami
(też z gumy)

well-informed ('łel-ynfo:rmd)
adj. dobrze poinformowany;
wykształcony

well-intended ('łel-'yntendyd)
adj. dobrze pomyślany

well-judged ('łel-'dżadżd) adj.
rozsądny; roztropny; dobrze
pomyślany

well-knit ('łel'nyt) adj.
zwarty; dobrze zbudowany;
jędrny

well-known ('łel'nołn) adj.
dobrze znany

well-meant ('łel'ment) adj.
zrobiony w najlepszej intencji

well-nigh ('łel'naj) adv. nieledwie; o mało co; o mało nie

well-off ('łel'o:f) adj. dobrze sytuowany; zamożny

well point('łel'poynt) s. rura
do usuwania wody podskórnej
(przed kopaniem)

well-read ('łel'red) adj.
oczytany

well-sinker ('łel'syŋker)s.
studniarz

well-spoken ('łel'spouken) adj.
uprzejmy; pięknie mówiący;
dobrze powiedziany

wellspring (łel'spryŋg)s.
źródło

well-timed ('łel'tajmd) adj.
na czasie; odpowiedni

well-to-do ('łel-te'du:) adj.
zamożny; dobrze sytuowany

well-wisher ('łel'łyszer) s.
sympatyk

well-worn ('łel'ło:rn) adj.
wytrwały; wyświechtany; oklepany; dobrze noszony

welsh (łelsz) adj. walijski;
s. wykręcanie się od płacenia;
v. uciekać nie zapłaciwszy,

welter ('łelter) v. falować;
tarzać się; s. falowanie;
powódź; zamęt; kolos; silne
uderzenie

wench (łencz) s. dziewucha;
ulicznica; v. latać za dziew-
kami

Wendish (łendysz) adj. łużycki

went (łent) v. zob. go

wept (łept) v. zob. weep

were (łe:r) v. zob. be

we're (łier) = we are

werewolf('łe:rłuf) s. wilkołak

west (łest) s. zachód; adj.
zachodni; adv. na zachód; ku
zachodowi

westerly ('łesterly) adj. zachodni; adv. na zachód

western ('łestern) adj. zachodni; pochodzący z zachodu

westward ('łestłerd) adj. zachodni; ku zachodowi; na zachód

wet (łet) adj. mokry; wilgotny;
zmoczony; przemoczony; słotny;
deszczowy; dżdżysty; (slang):
w błędzie; s. wilgoć; wilgotność; trunek; v. moczyć (się);
zwilżać; zraszać

wet nurse ('łet,ne:rse) s.
mamka; v. karmić

wether ('łedzer) s.skop (ka-
strowany baran)

wet through ('łet'tru:) v.
przemoczyć (na wylot)

we've (łi:w) = we have

whack (hłaek) v. walić; grzmocić; (slang: dzielić się
czymś; s. walnięcie; trzas-
nięcie; (slang): część; próba;
stan (rzeczy)

whacker ('hłaeker) s. kolor

whacking ('hłaekyŋg) adj. kolosalny

whale (hłejl) s. wieloryb;
rzecz wspaniała; v. polować
na wieloryby; (slang): bić

whale-boat ('hłejl,bout) s.
łódź do połowu wielorybów;
łódź strażnicza; ratunkowa

whalebone ('hłejlboun) s, fisz-
bin

whale-fin ('hłejlfyn) s. fisz-
bin

whale-oil ('hłejl,ojl) s. tran
wielorybi

whaler ('hłejler) s. statek do
połowu wielorybów

whammy ('hłaemy) s. (slang):
urok (rzucony na kogoś)

whang (hłaeŋg) s. grzmotnięcie;
huczenie; v. walić; grzmocić;
huczeć

wharf (hło:rf) s. przystań (wy-
ładunkowa); nabrzeże; v. cumować do wyładunku; wyładowywać
w przystani

wharves (hło:rfs) pl. nabrzeża
wyładunkowe

what (hłot) adj. jaki; jaki
tylko; ten; który; ten...co;
taki... jaki; tyle.., ile;
pron. co; to co; cos;
excl.:co ? czego ? jak to !

what about ('hłote,baut) exp.:
a co z... ?; co powiesz o...?

whatever ('hłot'ewer) adj.
jakikolwiek; pron. cokolwiek;
wszystko co; co tylko; bez
względu; obojętnie co

what for('hłotfo:r) s. (slang):
bura; lanie; exp.:za co ?

what next ('hłot,nekst) exp.:
co dalej ?

whatnot ('hłotnot) s. etażerka;
cacka; (slang): cokolwiek;
obojętnie co; wszystko

whatsit ('hłotsyt) s. jak się
to nazywa; ten (przedmiot)

whatsoever ('hłotsou'ewer) adj.
jakikolwiek by; cokolwiek by;
co tylko by; pron. wszystko
co tylko

wheat (hłi:t) s. pszenica

wheaten ('hłi:tn) adj. prze-
niczny

wheel ('hłi:l) s. koło; kółko;
ster; kierownica; v. obracać
(się); wrócić (się); prowadzić
taczki (rower); wozić taczkami
etc.

wheelbarrow ('hłi:l,baerou) s.
taczki

wheel chair('hłi:l,czeer) s. fotel na kółkach

wheeler-dealer ('hłi:ler,di:ler)
s. cwaniak; politykier

wheelwright ('hłi:lrajt) s.
kołodziej

wheeze ('hłi:z) v. sapać; s. sa-
panie; (slang); dowcip; komunał

wheezy ('hłi:zy) adj. sapiący;
zasapany

when (hłen) adv. kiedy; kiedyż;
wtedy; kiedy to; gdy; przy;
podczas gdy;
s. czas (zdarzenia)

whenas (,hłen'aez) conj. kiedy;
podczas gdy

whence (hłens) adv. & conj. skąd

whenever ('hłenewer) adv. kiedy
tylko; skoro tylko

whensoever ('hłensou'ever) adv.
skoro tylko; skądkolwiek

where (hłeer) adv. & conj. gdzie;
dokąd

whereabout ('hłeere'baut) adv.
gdzie ?

whereabouts ('hłeere'bauts) adv.
zważywszy; gdzie; mniej więcej;
s. miejsce zamieszkania;(pobytu)

whereas('hłeer'aez) conj. podczas
gdy

whereat ('hłeer,et) conj. podczas
gdy

whereby ('hłeer,baj) adv. po
czym ? po kim ? po którym; za
pomocą którego? jak?którym

wherefore('hłeerfo:r) adj.
dlaczego; dlatego; z tego
powodu

wherefrom (hłeer'fro:m) adv.
skąd; z czego

wherein (hłeer'yn) adv. w czym;
w ktorym

whereof (hłeer'ow) adv. z czego; z którego

whereon (hłeer'on) adv. na
czym; na ktorym

wheresoever (,hłeersou'ever)
adv. wszędzie by; dokądkolwiek
by; gdzie tylko by

whereupon (,hłeere'pon) adv.
na czym; po czym

wherever (,hłeer'ever) adv.
dokądkolwiek; wszędzie; gdzie
tylko

wherewith (,hłeer'łyz) adv.
(z) czym ?

wherewithal (,hłeerły'so:l) s.
potrzebne środki (fundusze,
przybory)

whet (,hłet) v. naostrzyc;
zaostrzyc (też apetyt);
s. ostrzenie; zakąska

whether ('hłedzer) conj. czy-
czy; czy tak, czy owak

whetstone (,hłet,stoun)s. oseł-
ka; kamien szlifierski

whey (hłej) s. serwatka

which (hłycz) pron. ktory; co;
którędy; dokąd; w jaki (sposob)

whichever (hłycz,ewer) adj.
ktorykolwiek; jaki; każdy...
jaki; który tylko; pron.
ktorykowiek; każdy

whichsoever (,hłyczsou'ewer)
adj. pron. = whichever (z naciskiem)

whiff (hłyf) s. powiew; podmuch; tchnienie; zapach; dym;
lekki wybuch gniewu; v. dmu-
chac; dymic; palic; lekko
wiac

while (hłajl) s. chwila; pewien czas; po chwili; niebawem; wkrotce; conj. podczas
gdy; jak długo; dopóki; poki;
natychmiast; chociaż co prawda

while ago ('hłajl'egou) adv.
(nie)dawno

while away ('hłajle'łej) v.
spędzac czas; skracac sobie
czas

whim ('hłym) s. kaprys; zachcianka; fantazja; fanaberia;
kołowrot gorniczy

whimper ('hłymper) v. piszczec;
kwilic; skomlec; skowyczec;
s. kwilenie; skowyt; skamlanie

whimsical ('hłymzykel) adj.
kaprysny; dziwaczny; cudaczny

whimsy ('hłymzy) s. kaprys

whim-wham('hłymhłaem)s. cacko

whine ('hłajn) v. skomlec; ję-
czec; powiedziec jękliwie;
s. skomlenie; jęk

whip (hłyp) s. bat; bicz; pomocnik; woznica; naganiacz;
uderzenie biczem; bita śmietana; v. chłostac ; zacinac (batem); ubijac (śmietanę); sma-
gac; przyrządzac na prędce;
zwyciężyc; zakasowac (kogos);
owijac; windowac; smigac;
zbierac; wyjechac (pospiesznie)

whip in ('hłyp,yn) v. zapędzac
batem

whip off ('hłyp'o:f) v. zerwac
cos; czmychnąc z czyms

whip on ('hłyp'on) v. popędzac
batem

whip out ('hłyp,aut) v. wyciąg-
nąc błyskawicznie

whip round ('hłyp,raund) v. od-
wrocic się znienacka

whip together ('hłyp te'gedzer)
v. zganiac batem; zwalac na
kupę; montowac na gwałt

whipped cream ('hłypt'kri:m) s.
bita śmietana

whipper-snapper ('hłyper'snae-
per) s. chłystek; smarkacz

whipping boy ('hłypyng,boj) s.
kozioł ofiarny (chłopak chło-
stany za innego)

whipping top ('hłypyng,top) s.
bąk do podbijania

whippy (,hłypy) adj. giętki;
elastyczny

whipsaw (,hłyp'so) s. wąska
piłeczka; v. ciąc piłką;
wygrac podwojnie; pobic podwójnie

whipstock (,hłyp'stok) s. biczysko

whirl (hłé:rl) v. kręcic (się);
wirowac; zawirowac; porywac
w wir; s. wirowanie; ruch
wirowy; wir; (slang): próba
(czegos)

whirlpool ('hłé:rl'pu:l) s.
wir

whirlwind ('hłé:rl'łynd) s.
trąba powietrzna; wir po-
wietrzny

whirlybird (hłé:rly'be:rd) s.
helikoper (USA)

whirr (hłé:r) v. furgotac;
warkotac; s. furgot; warkot
(maszyny)

whisk (hłysk) s. wiechec;
smignięcie; trzepaczka (do
jajek etc.); miotełka;
v. otrzepac; odpędzac; porywac; szybko odwozic; przywozic; czmychac; wymachiwac;
smigac

whisk away ('hłyske'łej) s.
strzepnąc; przewiezc lotem
strzały; czmychnac

whiskers ('hłyskers) pl. baki;
bokobrody; wąsy

whisky ('hłysky) s. (wodka)
whiskey

whisper ('hłysper) v. szeptac;
mowic cicho; szmerac; szeles-
cic; s. szeptanie; szmer

whistle ('hłysl) v. gwizdac;
swistac; zagwizdac; s. gwizdanie; gwizd; swist; gwizdek;
gardło

whistle away ('hłysle'łej) v.
pogwizdywac sobie

white (hłajt) adj. biały; bezbarwny; blady; czysty; niepokalany; uczciwy; rzetelny;
niewinny; s. biel; biały (człowiek); białko; białe wino

white coffee (hłajt'kofi) v.
kawa z mlekiem

white-collar('lajt,koler) adj.
zajęci biurowo(urzędnicy etc.)

white elephant (hłajt'elyfent)
s. towary wybrakowane; buble

white collar worker ('hłajt,ko-
ler łerker) s. pracownik
umysłowy

white frost ('hłajt'fro:st) s.
szron

white-headed ('hłajt'hedyd) adj.
siwowłosy

white heat (hłajt'hi:t) biały
żar

white lie (hłajt'laj) s. kłamstwo; wykręt towarzyski

white paper ('hłajt,pejper) s.
oficjalna publikacja wykazują-
ca, że rząd ma zawsze rację
(USA)

whiten ('hłajtn) v. wybielac;
pobielac; bielic; zbieleć

whiteness ('hłajtness) s. biel

whitewash (,hłajt'łosz) s.
wapno; wybielanie czegos lub
kogos; v. wybielac; wymywac
na czysto; uniewinnic; uspra-
wiedliwic; pobic na sucho
(na zero)

Whitsuntide ('hłajtsntajd) s.
Zielone Swięta

whittle down ('hłytl,dałn) v.
strugac; zestrugac; wystrugac;
obstrugac

whity ('hłajty) adj. białawy

whizz (hłyz) s. swist; (slang):
mistrz; rzecz wspaniała;
v. swistac; suszyc

who (hu:) pron. kto; który

whodunit (hu:danyt) s. (slang):
"kryminał"; powieść detekty-
wistyczna

whoever (hu:'ewer) pron. ktokolwiek

whole (houl) adj. cały; pełno-
wartosciowy; zdrowy; s. całosc

wholehearted ('houl'ha:rtyd)
adj. serdeczny; szczery

whole hogger ('houl'hoger) s.
człowiek idący na całego

whole length ('houl'lenks) s.
(portret) w całości

wholesale ('houl,sejl) s. hurt;
handel hurtowy; adj. hurtowy;
masowy; adv.hurtem; masowo

wholesaler ('houl,sejler) s.
hurtownik
wholesale trade ('houlsejl-
,trejd) s. handel hurtowy
wholesome ('houlsem) s. zdrowy;
zdrowotny
whole-time ('houltajm) adj.
pełno-etatowy (czasowy)
whole-wheat ('houl'hłi:t) adj.
pełno-ziarnisty (chleb)
who'll (hu:l) = who shall;
who will
wholly ('houly) adv. całkowicie
whoom (hu:m) pron. kogo ?
zob. who
whoop (hu:p) s. okrzyk (wesoły
np.)
whooping ('hu:pyŋg) adj.(slang):
ogromny
whooping cough ('hu:pyŋ,kof)
s. koklusz
whore (ho:r) s. wulg.: kurwa;
dziwka; v. kurwic się; gonic
za dziwkami
whorelet ('ho:rlyt) s. wulg.:
kurewka
whose (hu:z) pron. & adj. czyj;
czyja; czyje; ktorego
why (hłaj) adv. dlaczego; czemu; czemuż; dlatego; własnie;
s. przyczyna; powod; exp.: jak
to ! własnie ! patrzcie;
no wiesz !;no to co !
why so ('hłaj'sou) adv. dlaczego
wick (łyk) s. knot; tampon
wicked ('łykyd) adj. niegodziwy; niedobry; frywolny; paskudny; złosliwy; zły; nikczemny
wickedness ('łykydnys) s.
nikczemnosc; niegodziwosc
wicker basket ('łyker,ba:skyt)
s, pleciony kosz
wicker chair (łyker,czeer) s.
plecione krzesło
wicket (łykyt) s. furka; kołowrot; okienko kasowe; bramka;
cel; drzwi na pół wysokosci
(otworu)
wide (łajd) adj. szeroki; rozległy; szeroko otwarty; ob-

szerny; wielki; pokazny; znaczny; duzy; daleki; szeroko otwarty; adv. szeroko; z dala
(od czegos)
wide-awake ('łajde,e'łejk) adj.
czujny; rozbudzony; bystry;
z szeroko otwartymi oczami
widen ('łajdn) v. poszerzyc;
rozszerzac
wideness ('łajdnys) s. szerokosc;
rozległosc; bezmiar
wide-open (,łajd'oupen) adj.
szeroko otwarty
widespread (,łajd'spred) adj.
rozprzestrzeniony; szeroko
rozpostarty
widow ('łydou) s. wdowa; v. wdowiec
widower ('łydouer) s. wdowiec
width (łyds) s. szerokosc
wife (łajf) s. zona; pl. wives
(łajwz)
wig (łyg) s. peruka; v. zaopatrywac w peruke
wild (łajld) adj. dziki; dziko
rosnący; gwałtowny; wściekły;
szalony; burzliwy; rozwichrzo-
ny; pustynny;zdziczały; rozwydrzony; fantastyczny; nierealny; podniecony; s. pustynia;
dziki teren; adv. na chybił
trafił
wildcat ('łajld,kaet) adj. porywczy; awanturniczy; nadzwyczajny (np. pociąg); s. żbik;
szyb naftowy na nowym terenie;
awanturnicze przedsiębiorstwo;
spekulacja; samotna łokomotywa;
porywcza osoba; v. szukac nafty na niesprawdzonych terenach
wilderness (łajldernys) s.
pustynia; puszcza; odludzie
wildfire (,łajld'fajer) s.
błyskawicznie rozprzestrzenia-
jący się ogien; ogien grecki;
biedny ognik
willful('łylful) adj. rozmyslny;
umyslny; zamierzony; swiadomy;
samowolny; uparty
will (łyl) s. wola; testament;
siła woli; v. postanowic; zarzą-
dzac; zapisywac (w testamencie)
zmuszac; chciec

willing (,ľylyŋg) adj. skłonny (coś zrobić); chętny; pełen dobrej woli

willow ('ľylou) s. wierzba

willowy ('ľyloľy) adj. smukły; gibki; giętki; obfitujący w wierzby

will power ('ľyl,pałer) s. siła woli

willy-nilly ('ľyly'nyly) adv. chcąc nie chcąc

will you ? ('ľyl,ju:) exp.: czy zrobisz; czy zechcesz ?;czy obiecasz ?

wilt (ľylt) v. więdnąc; opadać; oklapnąć; powodować zwiędnięcie; opadać z sił; s. więdnięcie; osłabienie; depresja

wily (ľajly) adj. chytry

win; won; won (ľyn; łon; łon)

win (ľyn) v. wygrywać; zwyciężać; zdobywać; zarabiać; osiągać; pozyskać; przedostać się; przezwyciężać; s. wygrana; zwycięstwo

win over (ľynouwer) v. pozyskać sobie; przekonać

wince (ľyns) v. skrzywić się (z bólu) drgać; s. drgnięcie; skrzywienie

winch (ľyncz) s. korba; wyciąg; kołowrot; v. podnosić; wyciągać kołowrotem lub korbą

wind (ľajnd; wound; wound (ľajnd; łaund; łaund)

wind (ľajnd) v. nawijać; zwijać; zwinąć; owinąć (się); wić (się); zakończyć (ľynd) s. wiatr; podmuch; oddech; dech; zapach; puste słowa; gadanie; v. trąbić; dąć w rog; przewietrzyć; zwietrzyć; poczuć; zmęczyć; dać wytchnąc

windbag ('ľyndbaeg) s. czczy gaduła

windfall ('ľynd fo:l) s. gratka; owoc zrzucony wiatrem

winding (ľajndyŋg) adj. kręcony; kręcący się

winding-stairs (łajdyŋgsteers) s. kręcące się schody

wind-instrument (ľynd,ynstrument) s. intrument dęty

windlass (ľyndles) s. wyciąg; kołowrot

windmill ('ľynmyl) s. wiatrak

wind off(ľajnd,o:f) v. odwinąć (się)

wind up (ľajnd,ap) v. nakręcać (zegar); kończyć (mowę; zamykać zebranie)

window ('ľyndou) s. okno; okienko

window dressing ('ľyndou,dressyŋg) s. dekoracja wystawy sklepowej

windowpane ('ľyndou,pejn) s. szyba okienna

window shade ('ľyndou,szejd) s. żaluzja

window shopping ('ľyndouszopyŋg) v. oglądać wystawy (a nie kupować)

window-sill ('ľyndou,syl) s. parapet

windpipe ('ľynd,pajp) s. tchawica

windshield ('ľyndszyld) s. szyba ochronna (przednia) w samochodzie

windshield wiper ('ľyndszyld-'łajper) s. wycieraczka szyby ochronnej

windy ('ľyndy) adj. wystawiony na wiatr; wietrzny; gadatliwy

wine ('łajn) s. wino

wineglass ('łajngla:s) s. kieliszek do wina

wine-press ('łajnpres) s. wytłaczarka do winogron

wing (łyŋg) s. skrzydło; ramię kulisa; dywizjon; lot; v. uskrzydlać; przewozić na skrzydłach; przelecieć (przez coś); lecieć; szybować

wing commander ('łyŋg-ke,ma:nder) s. dowódca dywizjonu lotnictwa (podpułkownik)

wink ('łyŋk) v. mrugać (na kogoś); przymykać oczy; s.mrugnięcie

winner ('łyner) s. zdobywca nagrody; człowiek wygrywający; laureat winning ('łynyŋg) s. otwór do wydobywania węgla; adj. ujmujący; zwycięski

winning post ('łynyŋg,poust) s. meta

winnings ('łynyŋgs) pl. wygrana

winsome ('łynsem) adj. ujmujący; pociągający

winter ('łynter) s. zima; adj. zimowy; v. zimować

winter crop('łynter,krop) s. ozimina

winterize ('łynterajz) v. dostosowywać, przygotowywać do zimy

wintry ('łyntry) adj. zimowy; chłodny; obojętny

winy ('łajny) adj. podchmielony; winny

wipe (łajp) v. wycierać; ocierać; ścierać; wymazać; zamachnąć się; s. starcie; wytarcie; bicie

wipe away ('łejpe,łej) v. wycierać; wymazać

wipe off ('łajp,o:f) v. zetrzeć (plamę etc.)

wipe out ('łajp,aut) v. wytrzeć; wymazać; wyniszczyć; zgładzać

wipe up ('łajp,ap) v. wytrzeć (podłogę etc,)

wire (łajer) s. drut; przewód; telegram; kabel; struna metalowa; sidła; v. drutować; zadrutować; złapać (w sidła); założyć przewody (w domu); zatelegrafować; ciągnąć za sznurki zakulisowe

wire cutter ('łajer,kater) s. szczypce do cięcia drutu

wire haired ('łajer,heerd) adj. ostrowłosy (pies)

wireless ('łajerlys) adj. radiowy; bez drutu

wireless set ('łajerlys,set) s. radio

wire netting ('łajer,netyŋg) s. siatka druciana

wire-pulling ('łajer,pulyŋg) s. używanie protekcji; wpływów

wire rope ('łajer,roup) s. lina stalowa

wiry ('łajery) adj. twardy; żylasty; muskularny; druciany

wisdom ('łyzdem) s. mądrość

wisdom tooth ('łyzdem.tu:s) s. ząb mądrości

wise (łajz) s. sposób; adj. mądry; roztropny

wiseacre ('łajz,ejker) s. mądrala; mędrek

wise after('łajz,a:fter) adj. mądry po...

wisecrack ('łajzkra:k) s. dowcipna uwaga; v. robić dowcipy

wise guy ('łajzgaj) s. nadęta wielkość

wise saw('łajzso:) s. przysłowie

wish (łysz) v. życzyć (sobie); pragnąć; chcieć; s. pragnienie; życzenie; chęć; powinszowanie; ochota; rzecz upragniona

wishbone ('łyszboun) s. kość widełkowa (ptaków)

wish for ('łysz fo:r) v. życzyć sobie (np. pogody)

wishful ('łyszful) adj. pragnący

wishful thinking ('łyszfultynkyŋg) s. pobożne życzenie

wish well ('łysz,łel) v. dobrze życzyć

wishy-washy ('łyszy,łoszy) adj. bez treści; wodnisty; lurowaty

wisp (łysp) s. wiązka; garść; pęczek; kosmyk; wstęga (dymu)

wistful ('łystful) adj. smutny; zadumany; pełen tęsknoty

wit (łyt) s. umysł; rozum; dowcip; człowiek dowcipny; inteligencja; olej w głowie

witch (łycz) s. czarownica; czarodziejka; v. zaczarować; oczarować

witchcraft ('łycz.kra:ft) s. czary; czarnoksięstwo

witch doctor ('łycz,dakter) s. czarownik; znachor

witchery ('łyczery) = witchcraft

witch hunt('łyczhant) s. tropienie czarownic; polityczne głosne śledztwo (propagandowe) w celu udowadniania działalności wywrotowej

with (łys) prep. z (kims; czyms)
u (kogos); przy (kims); za pomocą); (stosownie) do; (cierpliwosc) dla

withdraw (łys'dro:) v. zob.
draw; cofac (się); wycofywac
(się); odwolac (cos); odebrac (ze szkoły); odsuwac
(zasłonę)

withdrawał (łys'dro:el) s.
wycofanie

wither ('łydzer) v. powodowac
więdnięcie, usychanie; zabijac (spojrzeniem); usychac;
usuwac się (w cien itp)

withers ('łydzers) pl. kłęby
(u konia między łopatkami)

withhold (łys'hould) v.zob.
hold; wstrzymywac; odmawiac;
wycofac

within (łys'yn) adv. wewnątrz;
w domu; u siebie; w (czyms):
w duchu; do wnętrza; w obrębie; w odległosci (np. mili);
w ciągu (np..dnia); w zasięgu (wzroku); s. wnętrze

without (łysaut) prep. bez;
poza; na zewnatrz; adv. na
zewnatrz; pozá domem; s. strona zewnętrzna

withstand (łys'staend) v. zob.
stand; opierac się; przeciwstawiac się; byc wytrzymałym;
wytrzymywac

witling ('łytlyng) s. dowcipnis

witness ('łytnys) s. swiadek;
widz; swiadectwo; v. byc
swiadkiem; swiadczyc (też
podpisem)

witness box ('łytnys,boks) s.
miejsce dla swiadka w sądzie
(USA)

witness stand ('łytnys,staend)
s. miejsce dla zeznawania
w sadzie (USA)

witticism ('łytysyzem) s. złosliwy dowcip; dowcipkowanie

witty (łyty) adj. dowcipny

witty at someone's expense
('łyty et'somłans,yks,pens)
exp.: dowcipny cudzym kosztem

wives (łajwz) pl. żony; zob.
wife

wiz (łyz) s. (slang): znawca;
mistrz; rzecz wspaniała

wizard ('łyzerd) s. czarownik;
czarodziej; adj. czarodziejski;
(slang): wspaniały

wo (ło:u) exp.:prrr (na konia,
żeby stanął)

wobble ('łobl) v. chwiac się;
ruszac się chwiejnie; chodzic
chwiejnie; jechac kołysząc się;
mowic drżąco; grac drżąco (melodię); drgac; wahac się; byc
niezdecydowanym

wobbler ('łobler) s. człowiek
chwiejny

wobbly (łobly) s. chwiejący
się; chwiejny

woe (łou) s. nieszczęscie

woebegone ('łoubi,go:n) adj.
nieszczęsny

woeful ('łouful) adj. bolesny;
żałosny

woke (łouk) v. zob . wake

woken (łoukn) v. zob. wake

wolf (łulf) s. pl. wolves
(łulvz); wilk; (slang): kobieciarz; v. żrec; pożerac; połykac jak wilk; polowac na
wilki

wolf down ('łulf,dałn) v. pożerac jak wilk

wolfcall ('łulf,ko:1) s. (slang):
gwizdanie na kobietę (z podziwem, zaczepką etc.)

wolf-cub ('łulf,kab) s. wilczek;
wilcze; młodszy harcerz

wolf-dog ('łulfdog) s. wilczur

wolfhound ('łulfhaund) s.
wilczur rosyjski lub alzacki

wolfish ('łulfysz) adj.wilczy

wolf skin('łulf'skyn) s. wilcza
skora (na podłoge etc.);
wilczura (okrycie)

wolf whistle('łulfhłysl) =
wolfcall

wolverene (,łulve'ri:n) s.
rosomak; mieszkaniec stanu
Michigan

woman ('Łumen) s. pl. women
('Łymyn); kobieta; baba; żona; v. mówić per "kobieta";
umieszczać między kobietami
woman doctor ('Łumen'dakter)
s. lekarka
womanhood ('Łumenhud) s. kobiety; kobiecość (dojrzała)
womanish ('Łumenysz) adj. bab-
ski; zniewieściały
womanize ('Łumenajz) v. ba-
bieć; niewieścieć; gonić za
kobietami
womankind ('Łumen,kajnd) s.
kobiety; ród niewieści
womanlike ('Łumen,lajk) adj.
kobiecy
womanly ('Łumenly) adj. kobiecy
womb (Łu:m) s. macica; Łono;
żywot
women (Łymyn) pl. zob, woman
womenfolk ('Łymynfouk) =
womankind
won (Łan) v. zob. win
wonder ('Łander) s. zdumienie;
cud; v. dziwić się; być cie-
kaw; zastanawiać sie
wonderful ('Łanderful) adj.
cudowny
wonderland ('Łanderlaend) s.
kraina cudów (czarów)
wonderment ('Łanderment) s.
zdziwienie; zdumienie
wondering ('Łanderyng) adj.
zdumiony; niedowierzający
wonderwork ('ŁanderŁe:rk)
s. cud
wonder-worker ('ŁanderŁe:rker)
s. cudotwórca
wonder-working ('ŁanderŁe:rkyng)
adj. sprawiający cuda
wondrous ('Łandres) adj. cudowny; adv. cudownie
wont; wont; wonted (Łont;
Łont; Łantyd)
wont (Łant) v. przyzwyczajać;
mieć zwyczaj; s. zwyczaj;
przyzwyczajenie
won't (Łcount) = will not
wonted ('Łantyd) adj. zwykły

woo (Łu:) v. zalecać się (do
kobiety): umizgać się; ubiegać
się; namawiać do czegoś
wood (Łud) s. drzewo; drewno;
lasek; pl; lasy; puszcza;
v. obsadzać drzewami; dostarczać drzewo
woodbine ('Łudbajn) s. powój
wonny; wiciokrzew pomorski
woodblock ('Łudblok) s. drzeworyt (do odciskania)
wood carving ('Łudka:rwyng) s.
drzeworytnictwo
woodchuck ('Łudczak) s. świstak
wood coal ('Łudkoul) s. węgiel
drzewny
woodcock ('Łudkok) s. słomka
woodcraft ('Łudkra:ft) s. znajomość lasu
woodcraftsman ('Łudkra:ftsmen)
s. myśliwy; traper
woodcut ('Łudkat) s. drzeworyt
woodcutter ('Łudkater) s.
drwal; drzeworytnik
wooded ('Łudyd) adj. lesisty;
zalesiony
wooden ('Łudn) adj.drewniany;
tępy
wood engraver (,Łudyn'grejwer)
s. drzeworytnik
wood engraving(,Łudyn'grejwyng)
s. drzeworytnictwo
wooden head ('Łudn,hed) s. głupiec
woodland ('Łudlaend) s. las;
lesisty okręg; adj. lesisty
leśny
woodman ('Łudmen) s. drwal;
leśnik
wood notes('Łudnouts) s. dźwię-
ki lasu
woodpecker ('Łud,peker) s. dzięcioł
wood pulp ('Łud,palp) s. miazga
drzewna
woodruff ('Łudraf) s. marzan-
na (wonna)
woodshed ('Łud,szed) s. drwal-
nia; drewutnia
woodsman ('Łudsmen) s. mieszkaniec lasu; drwal

wood sorrel('łudserel) s. szcza-
wik zajęczy

woodsy (łudzy) adj. leśny

wood wind ('łud,łynd) s.(dęty)
instrument drewniany

woodwork (łudłe:rk) s. wyroby
drzewne; części drewniane (np.
ramy okien etc.); drewniana
część budowy; budowa drewniana; stolarka; ciesiołka

woody ('łudy) adj. lesisty;
drewniany

wooer ('łu:er) s. zalotnik

woof (łu:f) s. wątek

wool (łul) s. wełna (czesana,
strzyżona, zgrzebna); czupryna; włosy (wełniste); owcze
runo; wełniane rzeczy

wool-bal ('łulbo:l) s. kłębek
wełny

woolen ('łuln) adj. wełniany;
s. wyrób wełniany

wool fat ('łulfaet) s. lanolina

woolfell, ('łulfel) s. barani-
ca; skóra owcza

woolgathering ('łul,gaedzeryng)
adj. głupio rozmarzony (roztargniony); s. głupie marzy-
cielstwo

woollen ('łulyn) adj. wełniany;
pl, tkanina wełniana

woolly ('łuly) adj. wełnisty;
oschły (głos); mętny umysł;
nie soczysty; mączasty;
włókniasty (owoc); zamazany;
(slang): surowy i niekulturalny; s. wełniana odzież; (slang):
owca

wooly ('łuly) = woolly

woozy ('łu:zy) adj. (slang):
wstawiony; otumaniony; niezdrów

word (łe:rd) s. słowo; wyraz;
słówko; komplement; przechwał-
ka; obelga; mowa; wieść; rozkaz; adv. ustnie; słownie;
adj. słowami wyrażony; v. wyrazić; redagować; sformułować;
ubierać w szatę słowną; przybierać w słowa

wordage ('łe:rdydż) s. ilość
słów

word-blind('łe:rd,blajnd) adj.
niezdolny do rozumienia pisma

wordbook ('łe:rd,buk) s. słownik

wording ('łe:rdyng) s. ujęcie,
wyrażenie słowami

wordplay, ('łe:rd,plej) s.
gra słów

word-splitter('łe:rd,splyter)
s. pedant słowny

word-splitting ('łe:rd,splytyng)
s. sofistyka; dzielenie włosa
na czworo

wordy ('łe:rdy) adj. rozwlekły;
gadatliwy; słowny (wojna słów)

wore (ło:r) v. zob. wear

work ; worked; worked (łe:rk;
łe:rkt; łe:rkt)

work (łe:rk) s. praca; robota;
zajęcie; energia; zadanie;
dzieło; utwór; uczynek;
pl. fabryka; huta; fortyfika-
cje; ozdoby; v. pracować;
działać; funkcjonować; skutkować; oddziaływać; wywoływać;
sprawiać; wykonywać; kazać
robić; prowadzić; obsługiwać;
poruszać (motor); posuwać (się);
przesuwać (się); wprawiać w
(pasję); nadawać kształt;
przeprowadzać przez coś; obrabiać; urabiać (się); wyszywać; robić robótkę; (slang):
wykorzystywać (znajomości);
drgać; burzyć; falować; fermentować; trzeszczeć (statek);
źle działać (maszyna); wyczerpać się; odrabiać; wypracować;
wytwarzać; uzyskiwać z trudem;
podniecać (się) stopniowo; za-
znajamiać się z czyms; mieszać
w całość; dokazywać (cudów);
wywierać (wpływ); urabiać; fa-
sonować; exploatować (kopalnie itp.)

work away ('łe:rke,łej) v.
pracować zawzięcie

work in ('łe:rkyn) v. pasować;
wprowadzać coś

work off ('łe:rko:f) v. pozbywać się czegoś

work on ('łe:rkon) v. pracować dalej

work out ('łe:rkaut) v. przeprowadzać; realizować; obliczać; rozwiązywać; wyczerpywać; wyeksploatować; skończyć; wynosić (w sumie)

work up ('łe:rkap) v. podniecać(się); doprowadzać (się); opracowywać; wyrabiać; rozwijać; wspinać się; podnosić (się)

workable ('łe:rkebl) adj. możliwy (do obróbki, uprawy etc.); opłacalny; wykonalny; realny; możliwy do przeprowadzenia; w stanie używalności

workaday ('łe:rkedej) adj. codzienny; roboczy; powszedni

work-basket ('łe:rk,ba:skyt) s. koszyk z robótką

workbook ('łe:rk,buk) s. podręcznik ze wskazówkami; dziennik pracy

workbox ('łe:rkboks) s. pudełko z przyborami do szycia

workday ('łe:rkdej) adj. dzień roboczy; dzień powszedni

worker ('łe:rker) s. pracownik; robotnik

workhouse ('łe:rk,haus) s. dom poprawczy; przytułek

working ('łe:rkyng) adj. pracujący; pracowniczy; roboczy; praktyczny; działający; czynny; ruchomy; powszedni; s. praca; robota; działanie; ruch; roboczodniówka; obróbka

working capital ('łe:rkyng - kaepytl) s. kapitał obrotowy

working knowledge ('łe:rkyng- 'nolydż) s. wiedza praktyczna

working-class ('łe:rkyng'- kla:s) s. klasa robotnicza

working day ('łe:rkyngdej) s. dzień pracy

working hours ('łe:rkyng,auers) s. godziny pracy

working load ('łe:rkyng,loud) s. ciężar użyteczny; nośność

workingman ('łe:rkyng,men) s. robotnik

working pressure ('łe:rkyng,preszer) s. ciśnienie robocze

workless ('łe:rklys) adj. & s. bezrobotny

worklike ('łe:rklajk) adj. dobrze wykonany; dobrze nastawiony do pracy

workman ('łe:rkmen) s. pl. workmen ('łe:rkmen); robotnik (fizyczny); fachowiec

workmanship ('łe:rkmanszyp) s. wykonanie; jakość wykonania; faktura; twór

work of art ('łe:rk-ow,a:rt) s. dzieło sztuki

workout ('łe:rkaut) s. trening; zaprawa; danie komuś szkoły

workroom ('łe:rk'rum) s. pracownia

works council ('łe:rks'kansl) s. rada zakładowa

workshop ('łe:rkszop) s. pracownia; warsztat; zakład; posiedzenie

workshy ('łe:rkszaj) s. próżniak

worktable ('łe:rktejbl) s. biurko

workup ('łe:rkap) s. podniecenie (się); powalanie podczas druku

workwoman ('łe:rkłumen) s. pl. workwomen ('łe:rkłymyn) ; robotnica; pracownica fizyczna

world (łe:rld) s. świat; ziemia; kula ziemska; sfery; masa; mnóstwo; zatrzęsienie czegoś; bezmiar; wielka ilość adj. światowy

worldling ('łe:rldlyng) s. człowiek oddany sprawom doczesnym

worldly ('łe:rldly) adj. światowy; ziemski; doczesny

worldminded ('łe:rld'majndyd) adj. oddany sprawom doczesnym

world old ('łe:rld,old) adj. stary jak świat

world power ('łe:rld'pałer)
s. potęga światowa; wielkie
mocarstwo

world-series ('łe:rld'sieri:z)
s. mistrzostwa palanta
(baseball) USA

world-war ('łe:rld'łor) s. wojna światowa

world-weary ('łe:rld'łeery)
adj. zmęczony życiem

world-wide ('łe:rld,łajd) adj.
światowy

world wise ('łe:rld,łajz) adj.
obyty; doświadczony

worm (łe:rm) s. robak; robaczek; glisda; dżdżownica;
gwint; zwojnik; śruba (nie
ostra); wężownica; v. wkradać się; wykradać; czołgać
się; wyciągać(tajemnicę z
kogoś); czyścić (zwierzę)
z robaków; czyścić (grządkę)
z robaków

wormcast ('łe:rm,ka:st) s.
gleba wydalana przez dżdżow-
nicę

worm-eaten ('łe:rm,i:tn) adj.
robaczywy; stłoczony przez
robaki; (slang); przestarzały

worm-fishing ('łe:rm,fyszyn)
s. łowienie ryb na robaki

worm gear('łe:rm,gier) s.
przekładnia ślimakowa

wormhole ('łe:rm,houl) s.
dziura wygryziona przez roba-
ka

wormseed ('łe:rm.si:d) s.
rośliny stosowane przeciw
robakom

worm-wheel ('łe:rm,hłi:l) s.
koło przekładni ślimakowej

wormwood ('łe:rm,łud) s. pio-
łun;(też) przykrość

wormy ('łe:rmy) adj. robaczywy

worn (ło:rn) v. zob. wear;
adj. używany; noszony; pomarszczony

worn-out ('ło:rn,aut) adj. zużyty; zniszczony; wynoszony

worried ('łe:ryd) adj. zatros-
kany; zaniepokojony

worriment ('łe:ryment) s. zmartwienie

worrisome ('łe:rysem) adj. tra-
piący; lubiący się martwić

worry ('łe:ry) v. dręczyć (się);
martwić (się); trapić (się);
zadręczać; zamartwiać; naprzykrzać (się); narzucać (się);
napastować; kąsać; szarpać zębami; s. zmartwienie; troska;
kłopot; kąsanie (zdobyczy przez
psa)

worry along ('łe:rye,long) v.
uporać się z trudnościami

worry dawn ('łe:ry,dałn) v. połykać łapczywie

worry out ('łe:ry,aut) v. rozwiązać z wysiłkiem (np. problem)

worse (łe:rs) adj. gorszy (niż:
bad; evil; ill); podniszczony;
słabszy; bardziej chory;
s. coś gorszego; to co najgor-
sze; najgorszy stan; najgorszy
wypadek; v. pogarszać się;
adv. gorzej; bardziej

worsen ('łe:rsn) v. pogorszyć
(się)

worship ('łe:rszyp) s. cześć;
kult; uwielbienie; nabożeństwo;
bałwochwalstwo; v. czcić;
wielbić; uwielbiać; brać udział
w nabożeństwie

woshipful ('łe:rszypful) adj.
pełen czci; czcigodny

worship(p)er ('łe:rszyper) s.
czciciel

worst (łe:rst) adj. najgorszy;
s. coś najgorszego; najgorszy
wypadek; adj. najgorzej; najbardziej; (slang): bardzo
v. pokonać; wziąć nad kims górę; zadać klęskę; pobić

worsted ('łustyd) adj. czesan-
kowy; s. kamgarn; przędza wełniana czesana; czesanka

worth (łe:rs) s. wartość; cena;
adj. wart; opłacający się

worthless ('łe:rslys) adj. bezwartościowy

worth reading ('łe:rs'ri:dyng)
adj. wart czytania

worth·seeing ('łe:rs̩'si:yn͡g)
adj. wart widzenia
worthwhile ('łe:rgh̩ła̦jl) adj.
wart zachodu; opłacający się
worthy ('łe:rg̦y) adj. godny;
wartosciowy; poczciwy;
s. godny człowiek; wybitny
człowiek (też żartem)
would (łud) v. zob. will
(forma warunkowa)
would be ('łud,bi:) adj. rzekomy; niedoszły; adv. rzekomo;
niby to
wound (łu:nd) s. rana; v. ranic; zob.: v. wind
wounded ('łu:ndyd) adj. ranny;
urażony
wove (łouw) v. zob.: weave
woven ('łouwn) v. zob.: weave
wow (łau) (slang): s. szlagier;
swietna rzecz; v. miec powodzenie; wywoływac zachwyt
excl.: au !;cudownie !
wrack (raek) s. = wreck (age);
chwasty morskie wyrzucone na
brzeg; używane na nawoz̦
wraith (rejs) s. sobowtor;
cien (duch)
wrangle ('raengl) s. kłotnia;
burda; v. kłocic się; (slang):
pilnowac koni
wrangler ('raengler) s. kłotnik;
pastuch konski (kowboj)
wrap; wrapt; wrapt (raep;
raept; raept)
wrap (raep) v. zawijac; owijac;
zapakowywac; spowijac; otulac
się; okrywac (się); zachodzic
na siebie; s. szal; chusta;
okrycie
wrap up ('raepap) v. owijac
(się); pakowac
wrapper ('raeper) s. opakowanie; opaska; obwoluta; bande-
rola; papierek; bibułka; osłona; podomka (damska); pako-
wacz
wrapping ('raepyng̦) s. opakowanie
wrapping paper ('raepyng̦ pejper) s. papier do pakowania

wrapt (raept) v. zob. wrap
wrasse (raes) s. (ryba) wargacz
wrath (ra:s̩) s. gniew; oburzenie
wrathful (ra:s̩ful) adj. gniewny
wreak (ri:k) v. wywierac (zem-
stę); dawac upust; wyładowac
(gniew)
wreath(ri:s̩) s. wieniec
wreathe (ri:z̩) v. wienczyc; wic
się; splatac̦; spowijac; plesc
się; kłębic się̦ (dym etc.)
wreck (rek) s. ruina; wrak;
rozbicie się (np.statku); katastrofa; szczątki (np. na wodzie); zniszczenie; rozbitek
życiowy; kaleka; wypadek;
v. rozbic (pojazd); zniweczyc
(nadzieje); burzyc̦; byc roz-
bitym; spowodowac rozbicie;
zrujnowac; miec wypadek
wreckage ('rekydz̦) s. rozbicie;
szczątki; gruzy
wrecked ('rekt) adj. rozbity;
zniszczony; zepsuty
wrecking company ('rekyng̦'kampeny) s̩. przedsiębiorstwo
rozbiorki budynkow
wrecking service ('rekyng̦'se:r-
wys) s. przewoz zepsutych sa-
mochodow
wrecker ('reker) s. sprawca wypadku; ciężarowka (z dźwigiem)
do przewozu zepsutych samocho-
dow; kierowca przewożacy ze-
psute samochody; przedsiębiorca rozbiorki budynkow; przedsiębiorca wydobywania zatopio-
nych statkow; człowiek kradnący
szczątki statku; szkodnik; roz-
bijacz małżenstwa
wren (ren) s. strzyżyk
wrench (rencz) s. gwałtowne
skręcenie; ukręcenie; szarpnięcie; wykręcenie; zwichnięcie; przekręcenie (faktow);
bol (rozstania); klucz maszynowy; klucz nasadowy; klucz
nakrętkowy; v. szarpnąc;
skręcic; wykręcic̦; zwichnąc
(nogę); przekręcac(fakty);
ukręcac

wrench open ('rencz'oupen) v.
odkręcić; otwierać; odśrubowywać

wrench off ('rencz,o:f) v. wyrywać; wykręcić; ukręcić
(głowę)

wrest (rest) v. wykręcać; wyrywać; przekręcać (fakty);
wydobywać zeznania; s. wykręcanie; wyrywanie; klucz
do strojenia (harfy)

wrest from ('restfrom) v. wyrwać komuś

wrestle ('resl) v. mocować
się; zmagać się; borykać się;
walczyć; s. zapasy; walka

wrestler ('resler) s. zapaśnik

wrestling ('reslyng) s. zapaśnictwo

wrestpins ('rest,pynz) pl. kołki na struny fortepianowe

wretch (recz) s. nieszczęśnik;
biedaczysko; biedak; nędzarz;
łajdak; łotr; nikczemnik

wretched ('reczyd) adj. nieszczęśliwy; pechowy; biedny;
nędzny; marny; fatalny;
ochydny; wstrętny; nadzwyczajny (łotr)

wrick (ryk) v. lekko zwichnąć;
nadwyrężyć; s. zwichnięcie;
lekkie naderwanie

wriggle ('rygl) v. wić się;
wkręcać (się); kręcić; wywinąć się; s. ruch wijący
się; wicie

wriggle along ('rygle'long)
v. posuwać się wijąc

wriggle in ('rygl,yn) v. wkręcać się

wriggle out ('ryglaut) v. wykręcać się

wright (rajt) s. robotnik;
twórca

wring; wrung; wrung (ryng;
rang; rang)

wring (ryng) v. wyżymać; wykręcać; ukręcić (łeb); przekręcać (słowa); ściskać (serce); uściskać (rękę); wymóc
(coś na kimś); zniekształcić;
s. wyżymanie; uścisk; ściskanie; wyżęcie; wyciśnięcie;

wringer (rynger) s. wyżymaczka

wrinkle ('rynkl) s. zmarszczka;
fałda; zmarszczenie; (slang):
ciekawy pomysł; rada
v. marszczyć (się); być pomarszczonym; zmiąć (się)

wrinkle up ('rynkl ap) v. pomarszczyć

wrinkly (rynkly) adj. pomarszczony

wrist (ryst) s. przegub; ruch
ręki w przegubie

wristband ('rystbaend) s. mankiet u koszuli

wristwatch ('ryst,łocz) s.
zegarek na rękę

writ (ryt) s. nakaz pisemny;
prawny

writ for ('ryt,fo:r) s. rozpisanie (wyborów)

write; wrote; written (rajt;
rout; rytn)

write (rajt) v. pisać; napisać;
zapisać; wypisać; komponować;
wstawiać (czek); spisywać;
sławić (piórem)

write back ('rajt,baek) v. odpisywać (komuś)

write down ('rajtdałn) v. spisywać; notować; określać (ujemnie)

write home ('rajt,houm) v. pisać do domu

write-in ('rajt,yn) v. wpisywać; dopisywać

write-off ('rajt,of) v. odpisywać (na straty); pisać na
prędce

write out ('rajt,aut) v. wypisywać; sporządzać

write-up ('rajt,ap) v. zapisywać; opisywać; przesadnie szacować; pochwalić

writer ('rajter) s. pisarz;
niżej podpisany; powieściopisarz

writhe (rajs) v. wić się (z bólu); cierpieć (zniewagę);
skręcać się (ze wstydu)

writing ('rajtyng) s. pismo;
utwór; artykuł; pisanie;
piśmiennictwo; sztuka pisania;
praca literacka; napisana rzecz

writing desk ('rajtyng,desk)
s. biurko; pulpit

writing ink ('rajtyng,ynk)
s. atrament

writing paper ('rajtyng,pej-
per) s. papier listowy; papier do pisania

writing table ('rajtyng,tejbl)
s. biurko

written ('rytn) v. zob.: rite;
adj. pisany

wrong (ro:ng) adj. zły; niewłaściwy; błędny; nie w porządku; mylny; niekorzystny;
niesprawiedliwy; s. zło; wykroczenie; krzywda; wina; pomyłka; grzech; strata; nie-
sprawiedliwosc; v. skrzyw-
dzic; niesłusznie posądzac;
byc niesprawiedliwym;
adv. mylnie; niewłasciwie;
błędnie; zle; zdroznie; nie-
korzystnie

wrongdoer ('ro:ng'du:er) s.
krzywdziciel; grzesznik;
winowajca

wrongdoing ('ro:ng'duyng) s.
nadużycia; wykroczenia;
grzechy; przestępstwa

wrongful ('ro:ngful) adj.zły;
krzywdzący; niesprawiedliwy;
bezprawny

wronghead ('ro:ng'hed) v.
przekręcac (słowa etc.)

wrongheaded ('ro:ng'hedyd)
adj. uparty; przewrotny

wrote (rout) v. zob. write

wroth (ro:g) adj. gniewny

wrought (ro:t) v. zob. work

wrought iron ('ro:t'ajern)
s. kute żelazo

wrought-up ('ro:t,ap) adj.
napięty; zdenerwowany

wrung ('rang) v. zob. wring

wry (raj) adj. krzywy; okrzy-
wiony

wryneck ('rajnek) s. zastrzał
szyi; kręcz karku

wynd (łajnd) s. (kręta) uliczka

x (eks) dwudziesta czwarta litera angielskiego alfabetu;
rzymska cyfra 10; niewiadoma

xenon ('zenon) s. ksenon

xenophobia (,zene'foubje) s.
ksenofobia

Xmas ('krysmes) = Christmas

x-ray ('eks'rej) adj. rentge-
nowski; v. prześwietlac; robic
zdjęcie rentgenowskie

x-ray diagnosis ('eks'rej,da-
jeg'nouzys) s. rozpoznanie
rentgenowskie

x-ray examination ('eks'rej-
yg'zaemynejszyn) s. badanie
rentgenowskie

x-ray picture ('eks'rej'pykczer)
s. zdjecie rentgenowskie

x-rays ('eks'rejs) pl. promienie rentgenowskie

xylem ('zajlem) s. drewno

xylophagous (zaj'lofeges) adj.
drzewożerny

xylophone ('zylefoun) s. ksylo-
fon

y (łaj) dwudziesta piąta litera
angielskiego alfabetu

yabber ('jaeber) v. gadac

yacht (jot) s. jacht; y. płynąc
jachtem; urządzac wyscigi jach-
towe

yachting ('jotyng) s. sport
żeglarski

yak (jaek) s. jak; (slang): gadanie; smiech; v. gadac; smiac
się

yap (jaep) v. ujadac; (slang):
paplac; s. ujadanie; paplanina;
krzykacz; jadaczka

yard (ja:rd) s. jard (91.44 cm);
podwórze; dziedziniec; v. umieszczac w ogrodzeniu

yarn (ja:rn) s. włokno; przędza;
historyjka; v. opowiadac histo-
ryjki

yawn (jo:n) v. ziewac; ziąc; zio-
nąc; s. ziewnięcie; ziewanie

ye (ji:) pron. wy (biblijne)

yea (jej) adv. tak; s. głosowanie "tak"

yeah (jej) (slang): tak; excl.:
tak !; nie wierzę !

year (je:r) s. rok

yearly (je:rly) adj. roczny;
coroczny; adv. corocznie;
s. rocznik;adv.raz na rok

yearn (je:rn) v. tęsknić

yeast (ji:st) s. drożdże; ferment; piana; v. fermentować; pienić (się)

yell (jel) v. wrzeszczeć; s.wrzask; dopingowanie

yellow ('jelou) adj. żółty; (slang): tchórzliwy; zawistny; żółty z zazdrości; n. żółty kolor; żółtko; v. żółknąć; powodować zółknięcie

yelp (jelp) s. skowyt; v. skowyczeć

yeomen ('joumen) s. podoficer marynarki; (dawniej) wolny chłop

yep (jep) adv. (slang): tak

yes (jes) adv. tak; v.potakiwać

yesterday ('jesterdy) adv. & s. wczoraj

yet (jet) adv. & conj. dotąd; jeszcze do tej pory; na razie; jak dotąd; jednak; ani też; mimo to

yew (ju:) s. cis

Yiddish (jydysz) s. język żydowski

yield (ji:ld) v. wydawać; dawać; rodzić; przynosić; oddawać (się); porzucać; ustępować; s. plon; zysk; wydajność

yielding(ji:ldyng) s. wydajność; adj. ustępliwy

yogurt ('jouguert) s. jogurt

yoke (jouk) s. jarzmo; v. zaprzęgać; nakładać jarzmo; (slang): zaskakiwać (przechodnia) w celu rabunku

yolk (jouk) s. żółtko; rodzaj łoju

yonder ('jonder) adj. & adv. tam dalej; tamten

you (ju:) pron. ty; wy; pan; pani; panowie; panie

you'd (ju:d) = you would; you had

you'll (ju:l) = you shall; you will

young (jang) adj. młody; młodzieńczy; młodociany

youngster ('jangster) s. dziecko; młodzik

your (ju:r) adj. twój; wasz; pański

you're (jo:r) = you are

yours (juers) pron. twój; wasz; pański (z poważaniem)

yourself (,juer'self) pron. ty sam

yourselves (,juer'selvz) pron. wy sami

youth (ju:s) s. młodość

youths (ju:dz) pl. młodzież; młodzieniec

youthful ('ju:sful) adj. młody; młodzieńczy

youth-hostel ('ju:s'hostl) s, schronisko młodzieżowe

you've ('ju:w) = you have

Yugoslav ('ju:gou'sla:w) adj. jugosłowiański

z (zi:) dwudziesta szósta litera alfabetu angielskiego

zany ('zejny) adj. pocieszny; błazenski; s. błazen; głupek

zeal (zi:l) s. gorliwość

zealous ('zeles) adj. gorliwy

zebra ('zi:bre) s. zebra; (slang): mulat; adj.pręgowany

zebra crossing ('zi:bre'krosyng) s. pasami znaczone przejście jezdni dla pieszych

zenith ('senit) s. zenit; szczyt (sławy)

zero ('zierou) s. zero; v. ustawiać na zero; brać na cel

zest (zest) s. smak; pikanteria; rozkosz; zamiłowanie; v. dodawać pikanterii

zigzag ('zygzaeg) s. zygzak; adj. zygzakowaty; adv. zygzakiem

zinc (zynk) s. cynk; v. cynkować

zip (zyp) s. świst; wigor; v. śmigać; gnać; zapinać zamek błyskawiczny

zip code ('zyp,koud) s. numeracja pocztowa miejscowości

zipper ('zyper) s. zamek błyskawiczny

zippy ('zypy) adj. żywy; zgrabny
zloty ('zlouty) s. złoty (pieniądz polski); adj. golden
zodiac ('zoudjaek) s. zodiak
zombie ('zomby) s. bóg-pyton;
(slang); bałwan; tuman
zone (zoun) s. strefa; zona; v.
opasywać; dzielić na zony

zoo (zu:) s. ogród zoologiczny
zoology (zou'oledży) s. zoolo-
gia
zoom (zu:m) v. buczec; wzlatywać;
wzbijac się szybko; śmigac;
s. poderwanie (samolotu);
soczewka zbliżająca w aparacie
do filmowania oraz w aparacie do
fotografowania

Appendix

ABBREVIATIONS – SKRÓTY

a.	— attribute	– przydawka
adj.	– adjective	– przymiotnik
adj. f.	– adjective feminine	– przymiotnik żeński
adj. m.	– adjective masculine	– przymiotnik męski
adj. n.	– adjective neuter	– przymiotnik nijaki
adv.	– adverb	– przysłówek
am.	– American	– amerykański
chem.	– chemistry	– chemia
conj.	– conjunction	– spójnik
constr.	– construction	– budowa
etc.	– and so on	– i tak dalej
excl.	– exclamation	– wykrzyknik
expr.	– expression	– wyrażenie
f.	– substantive feminine	– rzeczownik żeński
gram.	– grammar	– gramatyka
hist.	– history	– historia
hyp.	– hyphen	– łącznik
indecl.	– indeclinable	– nieodmienny
inf.	– infinitive	– bezokolicznik
m.	– substantive musculine	– rzeczownik męski
m.in.	– among others	– między innymi
n.	– substantive neuter	– rzeczownik nijaki
num.	– numeral	– liczebnik
part.	– particle	– partykuła
pl.	– substantive plural	– rzeczownik liczba mnoga
poet.	– poetry	– poezja
polit.	– politics	– polityka
p.p.	– past participle	– imiesłów czasu przeszłego
prep.	– preposition	– przyimek
pron.	– pronoun	– zaimek
s.	– substantive	– rzeczownik
sb.	– somebody	– ktoś
slang	– slang	– gwara, żargon
v.	– verb	– czasownik
vulg.	– vulgarity	– ordynarność
wg	– according to	– według
W.W. II	– World War II	– druga wojna światowa
zob.	– see	– zobacz

SAY IT IN POLISH!

POLISH CONVERSATIONS FOR TRAVELERS TO POLAND
WITH COMPLETE PRONUNCIATION GUIDE AND WITH A
DETAILED DESCRIPTION OF POLISH FOOD

1

Excuse me, where is the passport control?

Przepraszam, gdzie jest kontrola paszportowa?
pshe-pra-sham, gdźhe yest kon-tró-la pash-por-tó-va

The passport control booth is straight ahead.

Kontrola paszportowa znajduje się tam na wprost.
kon-tró-la pash-por-tó-va znay-dóo-ye śhäñ tam na vprost

Your passport, please.

Proszę o pański paszport.
pró-shäñ o páñ-skee pásh-port

Here is my passport.

Oto mój paszport.
o-to mooy pásh-port

2

Thank you, your visa is in order.

Dziękuję, pańska wiza jest w porządku.
dźhan-kóo-yäñ, páñ-ska veé-za yest v po-zhóẅnd-koo

Could you tell me where to exchange my money vouchers?

Czy mógłby pan mi powiedzieć gdzie mogę zrealizować kwit wymiany?
chi móogw-bi pan mee po-vyé-dźhech gdźhe mó-gäñ zre-a-lee-zó-vach kveet vi-myá-ni

Money exchange is inside on your right.

Wymiana waluty jest wewnątrz po prawej stronie.
vi-myá-na va-loó-ti yest vév-noẅntsh po prá-vey stro-ñe

Thank you.

Dziękuję.
dźhäñ-kóo-yäñ

3

Please, exchange my voucher.

Proszę zrealizować mój kwit wymiany.
pró-shäñ zre-a-lee-zó-vach mooy kveet vi-myá-ni

I would like to exchange a fifty-dollar bill.

Chciałbym wymienić banknot pięćdziesięciodolarowy.
khcháw-bim vi-myé-ñeech bánk-not pyáñch-dźhe-śhäñ-cho-do-la-ró-vi

Here is your exchange receipt.

Oto pański dowód wymiany.
o-to páñ-skee dó-voot vi-myá-ni.

Here is your money.

Oto pańskie pieniądze.
ó-to páñ-ske pye-ñóẅñ-dze

Thank you.

Dziękuję panu.
dźhäñ-kóo-yäñ pá-noo

4

Please, remember that you will need your exchange receipt later during your stay in Poland.

Proszę pamiętać że dowód wymiany będzie panu potrzebny później, w czasie pobytu w Polsce.
pró-shäñ pa-myáñ-tach zhe dó-voot vi-myá-ni bäñ-dźhe pá-noo po-tsheb-ni póóźh-ñey, v chá-śhe po-bí-too v póls-tse

I am glad you told me that.

Dziękuję że pan mi to powiedział.
dźhäñ-kóo-yäñ zhe pan mee to po-vyé-dźhhaw

Have a good time.

Życzę przyjemnego pobytu.
zhí-chäñ pshi-yem-né-go po-bí-too

Thank you, where are the customs?

Dziękuję, gdzie jest odprawa celna?
dźhäñ-kóo-yäñ, gdźhe yest odprá-va tsél-na

5

You will find the customs near
the exit.

Odprawa celną jest przy wyjściu.
od-prá-va tsel-na yest pshi víy-sh-
choo

I'll see you later.

Do widzenia.
do-vee-dzé-ña

Here is my baggage.

Oto mój bagaż.
ó-to mooy bá-gazh

Do you have anything to declare?

Czy ma pan coś do oclenia?
chi ma pan tsosh do o-tslé-ña

No I have only personal items.

Nie, mam tylko rzeczy osobiste.
ñe, mam tíl-ko zhé-chi o-so-beés-te

6

Please, open this suitcase!

Proszę otworzyć tą walizkę!
pró-shañ ot-vó-zhich tówñ va-leéz-kañ

What is in this package?

Co jest w tym zawiniątku?
tso yest v tim za-vee-ñówñt-koo

Small gift- toy for a child.

Mała zabawka, podarunek dla dziecka.
ma-wa za-báv-ka, po-da-roó-nek dla
dźéts-ka

You may close your suitcase.

Może pan zamknąć walizkę.
mó-zhe pan zámk-nówñch va-leéz-kañ

What do you have in this bag?

Co ma pan w tej torbie?
tso ma pan v tey tór-bye

7

Mainly small personal things and
magazines and a book.

Głównie drobne rzeczy osobiste, cza-
sopisma i książkę.
gwoóv-ñe drob-ne zhé-chi o-so-beés-te
cha-so-peés-ma ee kshówñzh-kañ

Thank you, you may proceed.

Dziękuję, może pan iść.
dźáñ-koó-yañ, mó-zhe pan eeshćh

Porter, please, take my luggage
to a taxi.

Bagażowy, proszę zanieść mój bagaż
do taksówki.
ba-ga-zhó-vi, pró-shan zá-ñeshćh
mooy bá-gazh do tak-soóv-kee

Here   you are.

Proszę, to dla Pana.
pró-shañ, to dla pa-na

8

I want to go to the Hotel Forum.

Chcę jechać do hotelu Forum.
khtsáñ yé-khach do kho-té-loo fó-rum

Do you know where it is?

Czy pan wie gdzie to jest?
chi pan vye gdźhe to yest

Of course!

Oczywiście!
o-chi-veésh-che

Do you speak English?

Czy pan mówi po angielsku?
chi pan móvee po an-ǵél-skoo

I speak a little English;
please, speak slowly.

Mówię trochę po angielsku; proszę
mówić powoli.
moóv-yañ tró-khañ po an-ǵél-skoo;
pró-shañ moó-veech po-vó-lee

9
How far is it to the hotel?

Jak daleko jest do hotelu?
yak da-lé-ko yest do kho-té-loo

Almost half an hour's ride, about ten kilometers.

Prawie pół godziny jazdy, około dziesięciu kilometrów.
pra-vye poow go-dzhée-ni yáz-di, o-kó-wo dzhé-shánch kee-lo-mét-roov

How much is the fare?

Ile kosztuje przejazd?
ée-le kosh-too-ye pshé-yazd

The fare is a hundred fifty zl.

Opłata za przejazd wynosi sto pięćdziesiąt złotych.
o-pwa-ta za pshe-yazd vi-nó-shee sto pyánch-dźhé-shownt zwó-tikh

Please get in.

Proszę wsiadać.
pro-shǎñ vshá-dach

10
Here is your money!

Proszę, to dla Pana.
pro-shǎñ, to dla pa-na

Keep the change.

Proszę zatrzymać resztę.
pro-shañ za-tshi-mach resh-tǎñ

I like your service, how can I reach you again?

Jestem zadowolony, jak można pana znaleźć?
yés-tem za-do-vo-ló-ni, yak mózh-na pá-na zná-leźhch?

My telephone number is two zero zero thirty.

Mój numer telefonu jest dwa zero zero trzydzieści.
mooy noó-mer te-le-fó-noo yest dva zé-ro zé-ro tshi-dźéśh-chee

11
Please, write your number here.

Proszę mi ten numer tu zapisać.
pró-shǎñ mee ten noó-mer too za-pée-sach

Thank you very much.

Dziękuję bardzo.
dźhǎñ-koó-yǎñ bár-dzo

Goodbye.

Do widzenia.
do-vee-dzé-ña

I have a reservation here.

Mam tu rezerwację.
mam too re-zer-va-tsyǎñ

What is your name?

Jak Pana nazwisko?
yak pá-na naz-veés-ko

12
My name is Jimmy Karter.

Nazywam się Jimmy Karter.
na-zí-vam shǎñ dzhí-mi Kár-ter

I have a room for you.

Mam dla pana pokój.
mam dla pá-na pó-kooy

Please register.

Proszę się zarejestrować.
pró-shǎñ shǎñ za-re-yes-tró-vach

You can pick up your passport tomorrow.

Może pan odebrać paszport jutro.
mó-zhe pan o-déb-rach pásh-port yoót-ro

Porter, room two zero two for Mister Karter.

Portier, pokój dwa zero dwa dla pana Karter'a.
pór-tyer, pó-kooy dva zé-ro dva dla pá-na Kar-té-ra

13

The room is on the third floor.

Pokój jest na trzecim piętrze.
pó-kooy yest na tshé-cheem pyan-tshe

Let us take the elevator.

Pojedźmy windą.
po-yedźh-mi veén-down

After you, madam.

Pani pierwsza.
pá-ñee pyérv-sha

Press the button, please.

Proszę przycisnąć guzik.
pró-shañ pshi-chees-nównch goó-żheek

Open the door, please.

Proszę otworzyć drzwi.
pró-shañ ot-vó-zhich dzhvee

14

Let us go left then right.

Choćmy na lewo a potem na prawo.
khóch-mi na lé-vo a pó-tem na prá-vo

Here is the bath and here is the closet.

Tu jest łazienka a tu jest szafa.
too yest wa-żhén-ka a too yest shá-fa

The telephone is beside the TV set.

Tu jest telefon obok telewizora.
too yest te-lé-fon ó-bok te-le-vee-zó-ra

Press this button for the maid.

Proszę przycisnąć ten guzik aby wezwać pokojową.
pró-shañ pshi-chees-nównch ten goó-żheek á-bi véz-vach po-ko-yó-vown

Here is your key.

Oto pański klucz.
ó-to páñ-skee klooch

15

Please, show me the soap and the towels.

Proszę mi pokazać mydło i ręcznik.
pró-shañ mee po-ká-zach míd-wo ee ráñch-ñeek

May I have my suit dry cleaned here in the hotel?

Czy mogę oddać moje ubranie do pralni chemicznej tu w hotelu?
chi mó-gañ ód-dach mó-ye oo-brá-ñe do pral-ñee khe-méech-ney too v kho-te-loo

I want my shoes shined.

Chciałbym mieć wyczyszczone buty.
khcháw-bim myech vi-chish-chó-ne boó-ti

May I have my suit pressed.

Chciałbym mieć wyprasowane ubranie.
khcháw-bim myech vi-pra-so-vá-ne oo-bra-ñe

16

I would like to have my shirts washed.

Chciałbym mieć koszule wyprane.
khcháw-bim myech ko-shoo-le vi-prá-ne

When is the restaurant open?

Kiedy jest retauracja otwarta?
ké-di yest res-taw-ráts-ya ot-vár-ta

The restaurant is open from 7 a.m. till 11 p.m.

Restauracja jest otwarta od siódmej rano do jedenastej wieczorem
res-taw-ráts-ya yest ot-vár-ta od shoód-mey rá-no do ye-de-nás-tey vye-chó-rem

Would you like to eat?

Czy chciałby Pan coś zjeść?
chi khcháw-bi pan cosh zyeść

I am hungry.

Jestem głodny./yés-tem gwód-ni/

17

Is there a swimming pool in this hotel?

Czy jest w tym hotelu basen kąpielowy?
chi yest v tim ho-té-loo bá-sen kown-pye-ló-vi

Yes, there is a swimming pool in the basement.

Tak, basen kąpielowy jest w podziemiu.
tak, bá-sen kown-pye-ló-vi yest v pod-źhém-yoo

The swimming pool is open from six a.m. till ten p.m.

Basen kąpielowy jest otwarty od szóstej rano do dziesiątej wieczorem.
bá-sen kown-pye-ló-vi yest ot-vár-ti od shóós-tey rá-no do dźhe-shówn-tey vye-chó-rem

18

Let us go to the restaurant.

Chodźmy do restauracji.
khóch-mi do res-taw-ráts-yee

Let me make reservations.

Pozwól mi zrobić rezerwacje.
póz-vool mee zró-beech re-zer-váts-ye

May I reserve a table for three for dinner at 8 p.m. today.

Chciałbym zarezerwować stół na trzy osoby na obiad dziś o ósmej wieczorem.
khchaw-bim za-re-zer-wó-wach stoow na tshi o-só-bi na ob-yad dźheesh o óós-mey vye-chó-rem

Good evening, sir.

Dobry wieczór panu.
dob-ri vye-choor pá-nu

Follow me, please.

Proszę iść za mną.
pró-shan eeshch za mnown

19

Here is the menu.

Proszę, jadłospis.
pró-shan, yad-wós-pees

Which waiter serves at this table?

Który kelner obsługuje ten stół?
któó-ri kél-ner ob-swoo-góó-ye ten stoow

What do you wish?

Co pan sobie życzy?
tso pan só-bye zhí-chi

What kind of cuisine do you have?

Jaki rodzaj kuchni tu prowadzicie?
yá-kee ró-dzay koókh-ñee too pro-va-dźheé-che

Polish traditional and general European.

Polską tradycyjną i ogólną europejską.
pól-skówn tra-di-tsiy-nówn ee o-góól-nówn e-oo-ro-péy-skówn

20

What are the consommés Polish style?

Jakie są polskie zupy?
yá-ke sówn póls-ke zóó-pi

Polish consommés are traditionally seasoned beef or chicken broth.

Polskie rosoły z wołowiny lub kury są tradycyjnie przyprawiane.
pól-ske ro-só-wi z vo-wo-veé-ni loop koó-ri sówn tra-di-tsiy-ñe pshi-pra-vyá-ne

Consommé with raw egg yolk.

Rosół z żółtkiem.
ró-soow z zhoówt-kem

Consommé with salty biscuit.

Rosół z diablotką.
ró-soow z dyab-lót-kówn

Consommé in a cup.

Rosół w filiżance.
ro-soow w fee-lee-zhán-tse

21

Polish soups cooked of bones and served with sour cream.

Polskie zupy gotowane na kościach i podawane z kwaśną śmietaną.
pól-ske zoó-pi go-to-va-ne na kósh-chakh ee po-da-ya-ne z kvásh-nówñ shmye-tá-nówñ

Polish beet-root soup with stuffed patties with meat or mushrooms.

Barszcz podany razem z pasztecikami z mięsem lub grzybami.
barshch po-dá-ni rá-zem z pash-te-chee-ká-mee z myáñ-sem loop gzhi-bá-mee

Polish barley kasha soup.

Krupnik.
kroóp-ñeek

Yellow cheese soup with browned butter, flour and sour cream

Neapolitańska z żółtego sera.
ne-a-po-lee-táñ-ska z zhoow-té-go sé-ra

22

Polish mushroom and noodle soup.

Zupa z grzybów suszonych z lanym ciastem.
zoó-pa z gzhí-boof soo-shó-nikh z lá-nim chás-tem.

Polish style tomato soup with rice.

Zupa pomidorowa z ryżem.
zoó-pa po-mee-do-ró-va z rí-zhem

Vegetable soup.

Zupa jarzynowa.
zoó-pa ya-zhi-nó-va

Pea and smoked ham soup.

Zupa grochowa na wędzonce.
zoó-pa gr-khó-va na van-dzówñ-tse

Sour cabbage soup.

Kapuśniak.
ka-poósh-ñak

23

Potato soup with browned butter and flour.

Zupa ziemniaczana.
zoó-pa zhem-ña-cha-na

Cauliflower soup.

Zupa kalafiorowa.
zoó-pa ka-la-fyo-ró-va

Fermented meal soup with browned bacon.

Żur z wędzonką.
zhoor z vãñ-dzón-kówñ

Fermented meal soup with browned sausage.

Żur z kiełbasą.
zhoor z ķew-ba-sówñ

Polish-Jewish bean soup with noodles.

Zupa fasolowa po żydowsku.
zoó-pa fa-so-ló-va po zhi-dós-koo

24

Asparagus soup.

Zupa szparagowa.
zoó-pa shpa-ra-gó-va

Chicken soup with mushrooms.

Zupa z kury z grzybami.
zoó-pa z koó-ry z gzhi-bá-mee

Duck soup.

Zupa z kaczki.
zoó-pa z kách-kee

Goose soup.

Zupa z gęsi.
zoó-pa z gãñ-shee

Minced liver soup.

Zupa z wątroby.
zoó-pa z vówñ-tró-bi

Lobster soup.

Zupa z homara.
zoó-pa z kho-má-ra

25
Barley soup with mushrooms.

Zupa jęczmienna z grzybami.
zoó-pa yańch-myén-na z gzhi-bá-mee

Calf's brain soup.

Zupa z móżdżku cielęcego.
zoó-pa z móżhj-koo che-lâń-tsé-go

Fish soup.

Zupa rybna.
zoó-pa ri-bó-va

Turtle soup.

Zupa żółwiowa.
zoó-pa zhoow-vyó-va

Bread soup with egg.

Zupa chlebowa.
zoó-pa khle-bó-va

Onion soup.

Zupa cebulowa.
zoó-pa tse-boo-ló-va

26
Lemon soup with rice.

Zupa cytrynowa z ryżem.
zoó-pa ci-tri-nó-va z rí-zhem

Caraway seed soup.

Zupa kminkowa.
zoó-pa kmeen-kó-va

Tart sorrel soup with eggs.

Zupa szczawiowa z jajkami.
zoó-pa shchav-yó-va z yay-ká-mee

Lentil soup with ham.

Zupa soczewicowa z szynką.
zoó-pa so-che-vee-tsó-va z shín-kowń

Spring vegetable soup.

Zupa z młodych jarzyn.
zoó-pa z mwo-dikh ya-zhin

Mixed vegetable soup.

Zupa jarzynowa.
zoó-pa ya-zhi-nó-va

27
Dill pickle soup.

Ogórkowa zupa z koperkiem.
o-goor-kó-va zoó-pa z ko-pér-ḱem

Chesnut broth with vegetables.

Zupa orzechowa.
zoó-pa o-zhe-khó-va

Ukrainian barshch with Polish
sausage.

Barszcz ukraiński z polską kiełbasą.
Barshch oo-kra-eéń-skee z pól-skowń
kél-ba-sowń

Fermented beetroot for barshch.

Kwas.
kvas

Clear barshch with mushrooms.

Czysty barszcz z grzybami.
Chís-ti barshch z gzhi-bá-mee

Polish barshch with sour cream.

Polski barszcz ze śmietaną.
pól-skee barshch ze śhmye-tá-nowń

28
Lenten barshch with mushrooms.

Barszcz postny z grzybami.
barshch póst-ni z gzhi-bá-mee

Zhoor on sour rye bread.

Żur na zakwaszonym chlebie.
zhoor na za-kva-shó-nim khle-bye

Oatmeal soup with Polish sausage.

Zupa wielkanocna na kiełbasie.
zoó-pa vyel-ka-nóts-na na kél-bá-śhe

Oatmeal soup with salami.

Zupa wielkanocna na salami.
zoó-pa vyel-ka-nóts-na na sa-lá-mee

Beer soup with sour cream.

Zupa piwną ze śmietaną.
zoó-pa peév-na ze śhmye-tá-ńowń

Pumpkin soup with rice.

Zupa z dyni z ryżem.
zoó-pa z di-ńee z rí-zhem

29
Vegetable broth with egg yolk.

Rosół jarzynowy z żółtkiem.
ró-soow ya-zhi-nó-vi z zhoówt-ḱem

Rice soup with onions.

Zupa ryżowa z cebulą.
zoó-pa ri-zhó-va z tse-boó-lówn

Vegetable soup with browned flour.

Zupa jarzynowa zasmażana.
zoó-pa ya-zhi-nó-va za-sma-zhá-na

Vegetable soup with sour cream.

Zupa jarzynowa ze śmietaną.
zoó-pa ya-zhi-nó-va ze shmye-tá-nówn

Kashoobyan vegetable soup.

Zupa kaszubską.
zoó-pa ka-shoob-ska

Milk soup with kasha.

Zupa mleczna z kaszą.
zoó-pa mlech-na z ka-shówn

30
What cold soups do you serve?

Jakie zimne zupy można dostać?
Yá-ḱe zeém-ne zoó-pi mózh-na dós-tach

Buttermilk soup with vegetables.

Chłodnik.
khwoód-ñeek

Barshch and cucumber soup.

Zupa ogórkowa na barszczu.
zoó-pa o-goor-kó-va na barsh-choo

Apple soup with sweet cream.

Zupa jabłkowa.
zoó-pa yabw-kó-va

Blackberry soup with sour cream.

Zupa ożynowa ze śmietanką.
zoó-pa o-zhi-nó-va ze shmye-tán-kówn

Raspberry soup.

Zupa malinowa.
zoó-pa ma-li-nó-va

31
Cold almond soup.

Zimna zupa migdałowa.
żheém-na zoó-pa meeg-da-wó-va

Plum soup with sour cream.

Zupa śliwkowa.
zoó-pa shleev-kó-va

Fruit soup with milk and eggs.

Zupa owocowa.
zoó-pa o-vo-tsó-va

Milk soup with vanilla.

Zupa waniliowa.
zoó-pa va-ñeel-yó-va

Cold tomato soup.

Chłodna zupa pomidorowa.
khwoód-na zoó-pa po-mee-do-ró-va

Raspberry soup with wine

Malinowa zupa z winem.
ma-lee-nó-va zoó-pa z veé-nem

32
What additions to soups are available?

Jakie dodatki do zup można dostać?
Yá-ḱe do-dát-kee do zoop mózh-na dós-tach

Potato dumplings.

Kluski ziemniaczane.
kloós-kee żhem-ña-chá-ne

Potato balls in bread crumbs.

Krokiety osmażane.
kro-ḱé-ti os-ma-zhá-ne

Polish style meat stuffed ravioli.

Uszka nadziewane mięsem.
oósh-ka na-dźhe-vá-ne myáñ-sem

Polish ravioli with mushrooms.

Uszka z grzybami.
oósh-ka z gzhi-bá-mee

33
Polish patties with meat.

Paszteciki z mięsem.
pash-te-chéekee z myáń-sem

Polish patties with mushrooms.

Paszteciki z grzybami.
pash-te-chee-kee z gzhee-bá-mee

Egg balls with grated cheese.

Krokiety z jajka.
kro-ké-ti z yáy-ka

Stuffed cucumbers.

Nadziewane ogórki.
na-dźhe-vá-ne o-góor-kee

Dumplings with meat.

Pierożki z mięsem.
pye-rózh-kee z myáń-sem

Dumplings with chicken.

Pierożki z kurą.
pye-rózh-kee z koó-rówń

34
What are the Polish fish dishes?

Jakie są polskie potrawy rybne?
yá-ke sówń póls-ke po-tra-vi rib-ne

Cod with horseradish sauce.

Dorsz w sosie chrzanowym.
dorsh w só-śhe khzha-nó- vim

Stuffed pike.

Szczupak faszerowany.
shchoó-pak fa-she-ro-vá-ny

Boiled pike with horseradish sauce.

Gotowany szczupak z sosem chrzanowym.
go-to-vá-ny shchoó-pak z só-sem
khsha-nó-vim

Baked pike with horseradish sauce.

Pieczony szczupak z sosem chrzanowym.
pye-chó-ni shchoó-pak z só-sem
khsha-nó-vim

35
Haddock fillet in batter.

Łupacz w cieście.
woó-pach w chéśh-che.

Carp in jelly.

Karp w galarecie..
Karp w ga-la-ré-che

Carp in grey sauce.

Karp a szarym sosie.
Karp w shá-rim só-sie.

Carp with red cabbage.

Karp w czerwonej kapuście.
karp w czer-vó-ney ka-poóśh-che

Carp Jewish style.

Karp po żydowsku.
Karp po zhi-dóv-skoo

Carp in mushroom sauce.

Karp w sosie grzybowym.
karp w só-śhe gzhi-bó-vim

36
Baked pike with anchovies.

Pieczony szczupak z sardelami.
pye-chó-ni shchoó-pak z sar-de-lá-mee

Pike Jewish style.

Szczupak po żydowsku.
shchoó-pak po zhi-dóv-skoo

Perch with white wine.

Okoń na białym winie.
ó-koń na byá-wim veé-ñe

Perch with hard boiled eggs.

Okoń z jajkami na twardo.
ó-koń z yay-ká-mee na tvár-do

Broiled perch with mushrooms.

Okoń z rożna z grzybami.
ó-koń z rózh-na z gzhi-bá-mee

Stewed eel in wine.

Duszony węgorz w winie.
Doo-shó-ni vań-gosh v veé-ñe

37
Sole in white wine.

Sola w białym winie.
só-la v bya-wim veé-ñe

Stewed sole with tomatoes.

Duszona sola z pomidorami.
doo-shó-na só-la z po-mee-do-rá-mee

Minced cod balls in tomato sauce.

Zrazy mielone z dorsza w sosie pomidorowym.
zrá-zi mye-ló-ne z dór-sha v só-she po-mee-do-ró-vim

Fried herring in bread crumbs.

Smażony śledź w bułce tartej.
sma-zhó-ni śhledźh v boów-tse tár-tey

Minced cod cutlet.

Kotlet mielony z dorsza.
kót-let mye-ló-ni z dór-sha

38
Fillet of sole with grated cheese.

Filet z soli z tartym serem.
Feé-let z só-lee z tár-tim sé-rem

Fillet of flounder with grated cheese.

Filet z flądry z tartym serem.
feé-let z flównd-ri z tár-tim sé-rem

Trout with parsley.

Pstrąg z pietruszką.
pstrówng z pyet-roósh-kówn

Fricassee of fish with grated cheese.

Potrawka z ryby z tartym serem.
po-tráv-ka z ri-bi z tár-tim sé-rem

Cod steamed with vegetables.

Dorsz parzony z jarzynami.
dorsh pa-zhó-ni z ya-zhi-ná-mee

39
Salmon in jelly.

Łosoś w galarecie.
wo-sosh v ga-la-ré-ĉhe

Salmon with stuffing.

Łosoś nadziewany.
wo-sosh na-dźhe-vá-ni

Sturgeon with sour cream.

Jesiotr z kwaśną śmietaną.
Ye-śhotr z kvaśh-nówn śhmye-tá-nówn

Lobster with sour cream.

Homar ze śmietaną.
khó-mar ze śhmye-tá-nówn

Oyster cakes with mushrooms and grated cheese.

Krokiety z ostryg z grzybami i z tartym serem.
kro-ké-ti z óst-rig z gzhi-bá-mee ee z tár-tim sé-rem

40
What are your meat specialities?

Jakie są tu dania mięsne?
Yá-ĉe sówn too dá-ña myáns-ne

Here is the menu.

Proszę, jadłospis.
pro-shán, yad-wó-spees

Veal cutlets in mushrooms and white wine.

Kotlety cielęce z grzybami w białym winie.
kot-lé-ti ĉhe-lán-tse z gzhi-bá-mee v byá-wim veé-ñe

Veal with paprika.

Cielęcina z papryką.
ĉhe-lán-ĉhe-na z pap-rí-kówn

Pounded veal chops with Bechamel.

Bite zrazy cielęce z Beszamelem.
Beé-te zra-zi ĉhe-lán-tse z be-sha-mé-lem

41
Pounded veal stewed with onion.

Bite zrazy cielęce duszone z cebulą.
beé-te zra-zi che-lań-tse doo-szó-ne
z tse-boó-lówn

Fried minced veal patties.

Paszteciki z siekanej cielęciny.
pash-te-chee-kee z she-ká-ney che-
lań-chee-ni

Veal patties with sour cream.

Paszteciki cielęce ze śmietaną.
pash-te-chee-kee che-lań-tse ze
shmye-tá-nówn

Veal roast with garlic.

Pieczeń cielęca z czosnkiem.
pye-cheń che-lań-tsa z chósn-kem

Stuffed veal cutlets.

Nadziewane kotlety cielęce.
na-dzhe-vá-ne kot-lé-ti che-lań-tse

42
Veal brain cutlets.

Kotlety z mózgu cielęcego.
kot-lé-ti z moóz-goo che-lań-tsé-go

Veal steak.

Stek cielęcy.
stek che-lań-tsi

Fried veal liver.

Smażona wątroba cielęca.
sma-zhó-na vówn-tro-ba che-lań-tsa

Pounded veal chops.

Bite zrazy cielęce.
beé-te zra-zi che-lań-tse

Veal chops with mushroom sauce.

Zrazy cielęce w sosie grzybowym.
zrá-zi che-ań-tse w só-she gzhi-bó-
vim

43
Pot roast of beef.

Pieczeń wołowa, duszona.
pye-cheń vo-wó-va, doo-shó-na

Cooked beef with horseradish
sauce.

Wołowina gotowana z sosem chrzanowym.
vo-wo-vee-na go-to-vá-na z só-sem
khsha-nó-vim

Pot roast with sour cream.

Pieczeń wołowa ze śmietaną.
pye-cheń vo-wó-va ze shmye-tá-nówn

Pot roast with mushrooms.

Pieczeń wołowa z grzybami.
pye-cheń vo-wó-va z gzhi-bá-mee

Beef steak with horseradish.

Befsztyk z chrzanem.
béf-shtik z khshá-nem

44
Simmered beef Radecki style with
mushrooms.

Duszona wołowina Radeckiego z grzybami.
doo-shó-na vo-wo-vee-na ra-dets-ké-
go z gzhi-bá-mee

Meat loaf with sour cream.

Rolada mięsna ze śmietaną.
ro-lá-da myáns-na ze shmye-tán-kówn

Meat loaf Cracov style.

Rolada mięsna po krakowsku.
ro-lá-da myáns-na po kra-kóv-skoo

Stuffed roast husar style

Pieczeń wołowa po husarsku.
pye-cheń vo-wó-va po hoo-sár-skoo

Boiled beef with horseradish
sauce

Sztuka mięsa z sosem chrzanowym.
shtoó-ka myáń-sa z só-sem khsha-nó-
vim

45
Steak Tartare.

Befsztyk po tatarsku.
béf-shtik po ta-tár-skoo

Meat loaf stuffed with eggs.

Klops nadziewany jajkami.
klops na-dźhe-vá-ni yay-ká-mee

Meat loaf stuffed with sausage.

Klops nadziewany kiełbasą.
klops na-dźhe-vá-ni kél-ba-sówn.

Meat loaf with sour cream sauce.

Klops w sosie śmietanowym.
klops v só-she śhmye-ta-nó-vim

Meat loaf with mushrooms.

Klops z grzybami.
klops z gzhi-bá-mee

Goulash meat stew.

Gulasz.
goó-lash

46
Beef tongue with carrots.

Ozór wołowy z marchewką.
ó-zoor yo-wó-yi z mar-khév-kówn

Fried tongue.

Ozór smażony.
ó-zoor sma-zhó-ni

Beef chops with onion.

Zrazy wołowe z cebulą.
zrá-zi vo-wó-ve z tse-boó-lówn

Cooked tongue, browned in horse-radish sauce.

Ozór zapiekany w sosie chrzanowym.
ó-zoor za-pye-ká-ni w só-she khsha-nó-vim

Cooked beef, browned in horse-radish sauce.

Sztuka mięsa zapiekana w sosie chrzanowym.
shtoó-ka myán-sa za-pye-ká-na w só-she khsha-nó-vim

47
What pork products do you have?

Jakie wyroby masarskie można tu dostać?
vá-ke vi-ró-bi ma-sár-ske mózh-na too dós-tach?

We have a great variety of Polish trditional pork products.

Mamy urozmaicony wybór polskich tradycyjnych wyrobów masarskich.
má-mi oo-roz-ma-ee-tsó-ni vi-boor pól-skeekh trá-di-tsíy-nikh vi-ro-boof ma-sár-skeekh

Lean ham smoked and cooked.

Chuda szynka wędzona gotowana.
khoó-da shín-ka vân-dzó-na go-to-vá-na

Pork ribs cooked with vegetables.

Żeberka wieprzowe gotowane z jarzynami.
zhe-bér-ka vyep-shó-ve go-to-vá-ne z ya-zhi-ná-mee

48
Pork loin cutlets.

Kotlety schabowe.
kot-lé-ti skha-bó-ve

Ground pork cutlets.

Kotlety wieprzowe mielone.
kot-lé-ti vyep-shó-ve mye-ló-ne

Pounded ham cutlets.

Bite kotlety z szynki.
beé-te kot-lé-ty z shín-kee

Cold cooked ham.

Szynka gotowana na zimno.
shín-ka go-to-vá-na na zheém-no

Pork chops.

Zrazy wieprzowe.
zrá-zi vyep-shó-ve

Stewed pork chops.

Zrazy wieprzowe duszone.
zrá-zi vyep-shó-ve doo-shó-ne

49

Minced pork chops with rice.

Siekane zrazy wieprzowe z ryżem.
she-ká-ne zrá-zi vyep-shó-ve z
rí-zhem

Pounded minced lean pork chops-
royal bitki.

Bite zrazy wieprzowe po królewsku.
beé-te zrá-zi vyep-shó-ve po kroo-
lév-skoo

Lean pork meat balls with
anchovies.

Krokiety wieprzowe z sardelami.
kro-Ké-ti vyep-shó-ve z sar-de-lá-mee

Sauer cabbage with pork ribs.

Żeberka wieprzowe z kiszoną kapustą
zhe-bér-ka vyep-shó-ve z kee-shó-nówn
ka-poós-tówn

Roast loin of pork.

Schabowa pieczeń wieprzowa.
skha-bó-va pyé-cheń vyep-shó-va

50

Ham baked in dough.

Szynka pieczona w cieście.
shín-ka pye-chó-na v cheśh-che

Young pork liver.

Wątróbka wieprzowa.
vównt-roób-ka vyep-shó-va

Pork brain cutlets.

Kotlety z mózgu wieprzowego.
kot-lé-ti z moóz-goo vyep-sho-vé-go

Pork brain Polish style.

Mózg wieprzowy po polsku.
moózg vyep-shó-vi po póls-koo

Pork goulash.

Gulasz wieprzowy.
goó-lash vyep-shó-vi

Stuffed piglet.

Prosię nadziewane.
pro-śhań na-dźhe-vá-ne

51

Spare ribs stewed with kohlrabi.

Żeberka wieprzowe duszone z kalarepą.
zhe-bér-ka vyep-shó-ve doo-shó-ne z
ka-la-ré-pówn

Ground pork chops with tomato
sauce

Mielone zrazy wieprzowe w sosie pomidorowym.
mye-ló-ne zrá-zi vyep-shó-ve v só-śhe
po-mee-do-ro-vim

Smoked sausage with onion sauce.

Kiełbasa wędzona w sosie cebulowym.
kéł-bá-sa vań-dzó-na v so-śhe tse-
boo-ló-vim

Sausage served hot.

Kiełbasa na gorąco.
kéł-bá-sa na go-równ-tso

Franks served hot.

Parówki na gorąco.
pa-roóv-kee na go-równ-tso

52

Pig's foot jelly.

Golonka gotowana.
go-lón-ka go-to-vá-na

Pork kidneys with groats.

Nerki wieprzowe z kaszą.
nér-kee vyep-shó-ve z ka-shówn

Baked bacon.

Boczek pieczony.
bó-chek pye-chó-ni

Pork meat loaf.

Klops z wieprzowiny.
klops z vyep-sho-veé-ni

White pork sausage with onion.

Kiełbasa biała z cebulą.
kel-bá-sa byá-wa z tse-boó-lówn

53
How about lamb?

Czy jest baranina?
chi yest ba-ra-ńéé-na

Lamb roast with sour cream.

Pieczeń barania ze śmietaną.
pye-cheń ba-rá-ña ze śhmye-tá-nówn

Lamb roast with garlic.

Pieczeń barania z czosnkiem.
pye-cheń ba-rá-ña z chósn-kem

Roast lamb shoulder.

Łopatka barania pieczona.
wo-pát-ka ba-rá-ña pye-chó-na

Fricassee of lamb.

Potrawka z baraniny.
po-tráv-ka z ba-ra-ńéé-ni

Lamb shish kebab with bacon.

Szaszłyk barani z boczkiem.
shásh-wik ba-rá-ńee z bóch-kem

54
Pounded lamb chops.

Bite zrazy baranie.
bée-te zrá-zi ba-rá-ńe

Lamb chops with grated cheese.

Zrazy baranie z tartym serem.
zrá-zi ba-ra-ńe z tár-tim śé-rem

Marinated lamb with Polish
sausage.

Marynowana baranina z polską kiełbasą
ma-ri-no-vá-na ba-ra-ńéé-na z pols-
kówn kel-ba-sówn

Lamb chops with mushrooms.

Zrazy baranie z grzybami.
zrá-zi ba-rá-ńe z gzhi-bá-mee

Lamb cooked with cabbage.

Baranina gotowana z kapustą.
ba-ra-ńéé-na go-to-vá-na z ka-
poós-tówn

55
Cooked lamb with onion sauce.

Baranina gotowana z sosem cebulowym.
ba-ra-ńéé-na go-to-vá-na z só-sem
tse-boo-ló-vim

Cooked lamb shoulder.

Łopatka barania gotowana.
wo-pát-ka ba-rá-ña go-to-vá-na

Ground lamb cutlets.

Kotlety baranie mielone.
kot-lé-ti ba-rá-ńe mye-ló-ne

Lamb brisket cutlets.

Kotlety z mostka baraniego
kot-lé-ti z móst-ka ba-ra-ńé-go

Lamb stewed with vegetables.

Baranina duszona w jarzynach.
ba-ra-ńéé-na doo-shó-na v ya-zhí-nakh

56
Lamb-veal-beef meat balls in
dough.

Kołduny zawijane w cieście.
kow-doó-ni za-vee-yá-ne w chésh-che

Lamb stewed with tomatoes.

Baranina gotowana z pomidorami.
ba-ra-ńéé-na go-to-vá-na z po-mee-
do-rá-mee

Lamb and beans.

Baranina z fasolą.
ba-ra-ńéé-na z fa-só-lówn

Lamb stewed with potatoes.

Baranina gotowana z ziemniakami.
ba-ra-ńéé-na go-to-vá-na z żhem-
ńa-ká-mee

Calf's liver, veal, and pork
meat loaf with bacon, eggs and
mushrooms.

Pasztet.
pásh-tet

57

Tripe with soup bone and
vegetables.

laki.
lá-kee

Liver pudding.

asztet z wątroby.
ásh-tet z vown-tro-bi

Chopped liver and pork with groats.

iszka.
eésh-ka

Sour cabbage with diced pork,veal,
beef, ham,sausage and mushrooms.
stewed, then fried.

igos.
ée-gos

Black pudding.

rwawa kiszka.
rvá-va keésh-ka

58

What poultry dishes do you
recommend?

akie potrawy z drobiu pan poleca?
á-ke po-trá-vi z drób-yoo pan
o-lé-tsa

Chicken Polish style cooked with
vegetables and chopped mushrooms.

urczę po polsku.
oór-chań po póls-koo

Chicken fricassee.

otrawka z kury,
o-tráv-ka z koó-ri

Fricassee of giblets.

otrawka z podróbek,
o-tráv-ka z po-droó-bek

Chicken in dill sauce.

urczak w sosie koperkowym.
oór-chak v so-she ko-per-kó-vim

59

Chicken stuffed with pea puree.

Kurczę nadziewane z puree z groszku.
koór-chań na-dźhe-vá-ne z pee-re z
grósh-koo

Chicken stewed with pepers.

Paprykarz z kurcząt.
pap-ri-kash z koór-chownt

Roast stuffed chicken.

Pieczone kurczę nadziewane.
pye-chó-ne koór-chań na-dźhe-vá-ne

Baked chicken with sour cream.

Kurczę pieczone ze śmietaną.
Koór-chań pye-chó-ne ze shmye-tá-nown

Caesar's chicken with mushrooms.

Kurczę po cesarsku z grzybami.
koór-chan po tse-sárs-koo z gzhi-
bá-mee

60

Chicken stewed with tomatoes.

Kurczę duszone z pomidorami.
koór-chań doo-shó-ne z po-mee-do-
rá-mee

Chicken breast cutlets.

Smażone kotlety z piersi kury.
sma-zhó-ne kot-lé-ti z pyér-shee
koó-ri

Chicken cutlets with mushrooms.

Kotlety z kury z grzybami.

Chicken livers with rice and
cheese.

Wątróbki z kurczęcia z ryżem i serem.
Vown-troób-kee z koor-chań-cha z
ri-zhem ee se-rem

Fricasse of pigeons with nuts.

Potrawka z gołębi z orzechami.
po-tráv-ka z go-wań-bee z o-zhe-khá-
mee

61

Baked stuffed turkey with cranberries.

Pieczony nadziewany indyk z żurawinami.
pye-cho-ni na-dźhe-va-ni een-dik z zhoo-ra-vee-na-mee

Minced turkey cutlets.

Siekane kotlety z indyka.
she-ka-ne kot-le-ti z een-di-ka

Fried chicken.

Kurczak pieczony.
koor-chak pye-cho-ni

Duck stewed with cabbage and apples.

Kaczka duszona w kapuście z jabłkami.
kach-ka doo-sho-na v ka-poosh-che z jabw-ka-mee

Roast goose.

Pieczona gęś.
pye-cho-na gansh

62

Fried goose liver.

Smażona gęsia wątróbka.
sma-zho-na gan-sha vown-troob-ka

Goose with liver stuffing.

Gęś z nadzieniem wątrobianym.
gansh z na-dźhe-ńem vown-tro-bya-nim

Goose baked with apples.

Gęś pieczona z jabłkami.
gansh pye-cho-na z jabw-ka-mee

Duck baked with apples.

Kaczka pieczona z jabłkami.
kach-ka pye-cho-na z yab-ka-mee

Partridge baked in bacon.

Kuropatwa pieczona w słoninie.
koo-ro-pat-va pye-cho-na v swo-ńee-ńe

Roast venison.

Pieczona dziczyzna.
pye-cho-na dźhee-chiz-na

63

Roast venison with sour cream.

Dziczyzna pieczona w śmietanie.
dźhee-chíz-na pye-cho-na v shmye-ta-ńe

Pounded venison chops with wine.

Bite zrazy z dziczyzny w winie.
bee-te zra-zi z dźhee-chíz-ni v vee-ńe

Pounded venison cutlets.

Bite kotlety z dziczyzny.
bee-te kot-le-ti z dźhee-chíz-ni

Fried minced venison patties.

Paszteciki z siekanej dziczyzny.
pash-te-chee-kee z she-ka-ney dźhee-chíz-ni

Fricassee of hare.

Potrawka z zająca.
po-tráv-ka z za-yown-tsa

64

Hare meat loaf with onions and bacon.

Pasztet z zająca.
pash-tet z za-yown-tsa

Fricassee of rabbit.

Potrawka z królika.
po-tráv-ka z kroo-lee-ka

Rabbit hunting style.

Marynowany królik po myśliwsku.
ma-ri-no-va-ni kroo-leek po mish-leev-skoo

Marinated wild duck stewed.

Dzika kaczka.
dźhee-ka kach-ka

Marinated wild goose with olives.

Dzika gęś z oliwkami.
dźhee-ka gansh z o-leev-ka-mee

65

Baked marinated deer haunch in sour cream Polish style.

Udziec sarni w śmietanie po polsku.
oó-dźhets sár-ñee w śmye-tá-ñe po póls-koo

Boar ham stewed and baked.

Pieczeń duszona z dzika.
pye-cheń doo-shó-na z dźheé-ka

Marinated boar cutlets.

Kotlety z dzika.
kot-lé-ti z dźheé-ka

Venison meat loaf.

Pasztet z dziczyzny.
pásh-tet z dźhee-chíz-ni

Fricassee of venison.

Potrawka z dziczyzny.
po-tráv-ka z dźhee-chíz-ni

66

What sauces do you have?

Jakie ma pan sosy?
yá-ke ma pan só-si

Let us start with the hot sauces.

Zacznijmy od sosów gorących.
zach-neéy-mi od só-soof go-równ-tsikh

White sauce.

Sos mleczny.
sos mléch-ni

Cheese sauce.

Sos serowy.
sos se-ró-vi

Horseradish sauce.

Sos chrzanowy.
sos khsha-nó-vi

67

Mushroom sauce.

Sos grzybowy.
sos gzhi-bó-vi

Dried mushroom sauce.

Sos z grzybów suszonych.
sos z gzhí-boof soo-shó-nikh

Dill sauce with sour cream.

Sos koperkowy ze śmietaną.
sos kop-er-kó-vi ze śhmye-tá-nówn

Tomato sauce with sausage.

Sos pomidorowy z kiełbasą.
sos po-mee-do-ró-vi z kél-ba-sówn

Tomato sauce with sour cream.

Sos pomidorowy ze śmietaną.
sos po-mee-do-ró-vi ze śhmye-tá-nówn

Onion sauce.

Sos cebulowy.
sos tse-boo-ló-vi

68

Polish egg sauce.

Polski sos jajowy.
pól-skee sos ya-yo-vi

Polish gray sauce.

Polski szary sos.
pól-skee shá-ri sos

Raisin sauce with wine.

Sos rodzynkowy z winem.
sos ro-dzin-kó-vi z veé-nem

Mustard sauce.

Sos musztardowy.
sos moosh-tar-dó-vi

Pickle sauce.

Sos ogórkowy.
sos o-goor-kó-vi

Anchovy sauce.

Sos sardelowy.
sos sar-de-ló-vi

69

There are many good Polish cold sauces.

Jest wiele dobrych polskich zimnych sosów.
yest vyé-le dób-rikh póls-keekh źheém-nikh só-soof

Tartare sauce.

Sos tatarski.
sos ta-tár-skee

Beet sauce.

Ćwikła.
ćhveék-wa

Mayonnaise sauce.

Sos majonezowy.
sos ma-yo-ne-zó-vi

Mayonnaise sauce with wine.

Sos majonezowy z winem.
sos ma-yo-ne-zó-vi z veé-nem

70

Vegetables served Polish style:

Jarzyny podane po polsku.
ya-zhí-ni po-dá-ne po póls-koo

Polish potato dishes.

Polskie dania ziemniaczane.
póls-ke dá-ña źhem-ña-chá-ne

Browned mashed young potato pies.

Smażone placki z młodych gniecionych ziemniaków.
sma-zhó-ne pláts-kee z mwó-dikh gñe-ćho-nikh źhem-ña-koof

Cabbage and onion dish.

Kapusta gotowana z cebulą.
ka-poós-ta go-to-vá-na z tse-bóo-lówn

Sour beans dish.

Fasola na kwaśno.
fa-só-la na kváśh-no

71

Green peas.

Zielony groszek.
źhe-ló-ni gró-shek

Asparagus dish.

Szparagi.
shpa-rá-gee

String beans.

Szparagowa fasola.
shpa-ra-gó-va fa-só-la

Beet dish.

Buraczki.
boo-rách-kee

Brussels sprouts.

Brukselka.
brook-sél-ka

Kohlrabi dish.

Kalarepa.
ka-la-ré-pa

72

Peas and carrots.

Marchewka z groszkiem.
mar-khév-ka z grósh-kem

Horseradish sauce.

Sos chrzanowy.
sos khsha-nó-vi

Spinach with eggs.

Szpinak z jajkami.
shpeé-nak z yay-ká-mee

Broccoli with butter.

Brokuły z masłem.
bro-koó-wi z más-wem.

Turnips and potatoes on bacon.

Brukiew po mazursku.
broó-kev po ma-zoór-skoo.

Browned turnips with bacon.

Brukiew zasmażana.
broó-kev za-sma-zhá-na

73

Turnips with carrots on bacon.

Brukiew z marchewką.
broó-kev z mar-khév-kówn

Turnips with tomato sauce.

Brukiew w sosie pomidorowym.
broó-kev w soó-she po-mee-do-roó-vim

Browned beets with vinegar.

Zasmażane buraki z octem.
zas-mazhá-ne boo-rá-kee z óts-tem

Beets with rhubarb.

Buraki z rabarbarem.
boo-rá-kee z ra-bar-bá-rem

Onion stew on bacon.

Cebula duszona.
tse-boó-la doo-shó na

Pumpkin with potatos on bacon.

Dynia po mazursku.
di-ña po ma-zoór-skoo

74

Pumpkin with Polish pickles.

Dynia z kiszonymi ogórkami.
di-ña z kee-sho-ní-mee o-goor-ká-mee

Beans in tomato sauce.

Fasola w sosie pomidorowym.
fa-só-la w soó-she po-mee-do-roó-vim

Cauliflower in sour cream sauce.

Kalafior w sosie śmietanowym.
ka-láf-yor w soó-she shmye-ta-noó-vim

Cauliflower with bread-crumbs.

Kalafior z bułeczką tartą.
ka-láf-yor z boo-wéch-kówn tár-tówn

Cauliflower with cheese in
Béchamel sauce.

Kalafior z serem w sosie beszamelowym.
ka-láf-yor z sé-rem w soó-she be-sha-me-ló-vim

75

Polish style shreded cabbage with
bacon and onion.

Kapusta szatkowana z cebulą na boczku.
ka-poós-ta shat-ko-vá-na z tse-boó-lówn na bóch-koo

Cabbage with apples and sour
cream.

Kapusta z jabłkami ze śmietaną.
ka-poós-ta z yabw-ká-mee ze shmye-tá-nówn

Browned cabbage with apples.

Kapusta zasmażana z jabłkami.
ka-poós-ta za-sma-zhá-na z yabw-ká-mee

Sour shreded cabbage with browned
onion.

Kiszona szatkowana kapusta z zasmażaną
cebulą.
kee-shó-na shat-ko-vá-na ka-poós-ta z zas-ma-zhá-nówn tse-boó-lówn

76

Browned white cabbage with
tomatoes.

Kapusta biała zasmażana z pomidorami.
ka-poós-ta byá-wa zas-ma-zhá-na z po-mee-do-rá-mee

White cabbage chunks with potato.

Biała kapusta "parzybroda".
byá-wa ka-poós-ta pa-zhi-bró-da

Red cabbage browned with apples.

Kapusta czerwona zasmażana z jabłkami.
ka-poós-ta cher-vó-na zas-ma-zhá-na z yabw-ká-mee

Sour cabbage with peas.

Kapusta kiszona z grochem.
ka-poós-ta kee-shó-na z gró-khem

Sour cabbage with mushrooms.

Kapusta kiszona z grzybami.
ka-poós-ta kee-shó-na z gzhi-bá-mee

77

Sour cabbage shredded and boiled.

Kapusta kiszona "parzonka".
ka-poós-ta kee-shó-na pa-zhón-ka

Cabbage rolls with mushrooms.

Gołąbki z grzybami.
go-wównb-kee z gzhi-bá-mee

Cabbage rolls with minced pork.

Gołąbki z mięsem.
go-wównb-kee z myáń-sem.

Carrot and potato chunks
Mazovian style.

Marchew po mazursku.
már-khev po ma-zoór-skoo

Carrots browned with butter and
flour, Polish style.

Marchew zasmażana.
már-khev za-sma-zhá-na

78

Carrots with turnips with
marjoram, Polish style.

Marchew z brukwią.
már-khev z broók-vyówn

Carrots with kohlrabi dish.

Marchew z kalarepą.
már-khev z ka-la-ré-pówn

Browned tomatoes Polish style.

Pomidory osmażane.
po-mee-dó-ri os-ma-zhá-ne

Tomatoes stuffed with pickles.

Pomidory nadziewane mizerią.
po-mee-dó-ri na-dźhe-vá-ne mee-zér-yówn

Tomtoes stuffed with mixed
vegetable salad.

Pomidory nadziewane sałatką.
po-mee-dó-ri na-dźhe-vá-ne
sa-wát-kówn

79

Tomatoes with cheese and chives
filling.

Pomidory z serem i szczypiorkiem.
po-mee-dó-ri z sé-rem ee shchi-pyór-kem

Tomatoes stuffed with rice and
mushrooms.

Pomidory nadziewane ryżem i grzybami.
po-mee-dó-ri na-dźhe-vá-ne rí-zhem ee
gzhi-bá-mee

Tomatoes with meat filling.

Pomidory nadziewane mięsem.
po-mee-dó-ri na-dźhe-vá-ne myáń-sem

Tomatoes in batter.

Pomidory w cieście.
po-mee-dó-ri- v ćhéśh-ćhe

Meat stuffed tomatoes with sour
cream.

Nadziewane pomidory ze śmietaną.
na-dźhe-vá-ne po-mee-dó-ri ze śhmye-tá-nówn

80

Celery fried in batter.

Selery smażone w cieście.
se-lé-ri sma-zhó-ne v ćhéśh-ćhe

Celery stewed in wine.

Selery duszone w winie.
se-lé-ri doo-shó-ne v veé-ńe

Baked cucumbers stuffed with
mushrooms and onions.

Pieczone ogórki nadziewane grzybami
z cebulą.
pye-ćhó-ne o-goór-kee na-dźhe-vá-ne
gzhi-bá-mee z tse-boó-lówn

Asparagus with grated cheese.

Szparagi z tartym serem.
shpa-rá-gee z tár-tim sé-rem

Asparagus with sour cream.

Szparagi ze śmietaną.
shpa-rá-gee ze śhmye-tá-nówn

81
Browned leeks.

Pory zasmażane.
pó-ri za-sma-zhá-ne

Leeks with butter.

Pory z masłem.
pó-ri z más-wem

Artichokes boiled.

Karczochy gotowane.
kar-chó-khi go-to-vá-ne

Artichokes stewed.

Karczochy duszone.
kar-chó-khi doo-shó-ne

Artichokes with wine.

Karczochy z winem.
kar-chó-khi z vée-nem

Baked stuffed artichokes.

Pieczone nadziewane karczochy.
pye-chone na-dźhe-vá-ne kar-chó-khi

82
Stuffed red peppers.

Nadziewana czerwona papryka.
nadźhe-vá-na cher-yo-na pap-ri-ka

Baked stuffed yellow peppers.

Pieczona nadziewana żółta papryka.
pye-chó-na na-dźhe-vá-na zhóów-ta
pap-ri-ka

Stuffed green peppers.

Nadziewana zielona papryka.
na-dźhe-vá-na źhe-ló-na pap-ri-ka

Spinach with sour cream.

Szpinak z kwaśną śmietaną.
shpeé-nak z kvásh-nówn shmye-tá-nówn

Fried spinach patties.

Smażone paszteciki ze szpinaku.
sma-zhó-ne pash-te-chée-kee ze shpee
ná-koo

83
Early spinach with butter.

Szpinak wczesny z masłem.
shpeé-nak vchés-ni z más-wem

Spinach and radishes with sour cream sauce.

Szpinak z rzodkiewką w sosie śmietanowym.
shpeé-nak z zhod-ḱév-kówn v só-śhe
shmye-ta-nó-vim

Spinach with grated Parmesan.

Szpinak z tartym parmezanem.
shpeé-nak z tár-tim par-me-zá-nem

Spinach with mushroom sauce.

Szpinak w sosie grzybowym.
shpeé-nak v só-śhe gzhi-bó-vim

Green peas with mushroom.

Groszek z grzybami.
gro-shek z gzhi-bá-mee

84
Potato pancakes Polish style.

Smażone placki ziemniaczane.
sma-zhó-ne pláts-kee żhem-ňa-chá-ne

Boiled potatoes with parsley.

Gotowane ziemniaki z pietruszką.
go-to-vá-ne żhem-ňá-kee z pyet-roósh-
kówn

Mashed potatoes.

Ziemniaki tłuczone.
żhem-ňá-kee twoo-chó-ne

Fried potatoes.

Ziemniaki smażone.
żhem-ňá-kee sma-zhó-ne

Early potatoes with dill and butter

Młode ziemniaki z masłem i koprem.
mwó-de żhem-ňá-kee z más-wem ee
kóp-rem

85

Baked potatoes.

Ziemniaki pieczone.
Zhem-ńá-kee pye-chó-ne

Potatoes stewed with onions and bacon.

Ziemniaki duszone po "szewsku".
Zhem-ńá-kee doo-shó-ne po shév-skoo

Fried potato balls.

Smażone krokiety ziemniaczane.
sma-zhó-ne kro-ké-ti zhem-ńa-chá-ne

Potato balls with mushrooms.

Krokiety ziemniaczane z grzybami.
kro-ké-ti zhem-ńa-chá-ne z gzhi-bá-mee

Potato pancakes with onions.

Placki ziemniaczane z cebulą.
pláts-kee zhem-ńa-chá-ne z tse-bóo-lóẃn

86

Potato-milk mix pancakes.

Ziemniaczane placki parzone.
Zhem-ńa-chá-ne pláts-kee pa-zhó-ne

Potato and eggs with sour cream casserole.

Zapiekane ziemniaki z jajkami i śmietaną.
za-pye-ká-ne zhem-ńa-kee z yay-ká-mee ee shmye-tá-nóẃn

Potato and eggs with mushroom sauce casserole.

Zapiekane ziemniaki z jajkami i sosem grzybowym.
za-pye-ká-ne zhem-ńa-kee z yay-ká-mee ee so-sem grzi-bó-vim

Potatoes stuffed with meat.

Ziemniaki nadziewane mięsem.
Zhem-ńá-kee na-dźhe-vá-ne myáń-sem

87

Potatoes stuffed with mushrooms.

Ziemniaki nadziewane grzybami.
Zhem-ńá-kee na-dźhe-vá-ne gzhi-bá-mee

Potatoes stuffed with grated cheese.

Ziemniaki nadziewane tartym serem.
Zhem-ńá-kee na-dźhe-vá-ne tár-tim sé-rem.

Stewed potatoes with barley and sour cream.

Ziemniaki duszone z jęczmieniem i kwaśną śmietaną.
Zhem-ńá-kee doo-shó-ne z yáń-myé-ńem ee kvásh-nóẃn shmye-tá-nóẃn

Potato noodles stuffed with meat.

Pyzy.
pí-zi

Potato and cheese noodles.

Kluski ziemniaczane.
klóos-kee zhem-ńa-chá-ne

88

Potato and milk puree.

Ziemniaki przecierane z mlekiem-purée
Zhem-ńá-kee pshe-che-ra-ne z mlé-ḱem

Potato salad with smoked fish.

Sałatka z ziemniaków z rybą wędzoną.
sa-wát-ka z zhem-ńá-koof z ri-bóẃn vań-dzó-nóẃn

Potato salad with onion.

Sałatka z ziemniaków z cebulą.
sa-wát-ka z zhem-ńá-koof z tse-bóo-lóẃn

Potato salad with chives and dill.

Sałatka z ziemniaków ze szczypiorkiem i koprem.
sa-wát-ka z zhem-ńá-koof ze shchip-yór-ḱem ee kóp-rem

Potato salad with celery.

Sałatka z ziemniaków z selerem.
sa-wát-ka z zhem-ńá-koof z se-lé-rem

89
Potato salad in egg sauce with lemon and wine.

Sałatka z ziemniaków w sosie jajowym.
sa-wát-ka z źhem-ńá-koof v so-śhe ya-yó-vim

Potato salad with eggs and mushrooms.

Sałatka z ziemniaków z grzybami.
sa-wát-ka z źhem-ńá-koof z gzhi-bá-mee

Potato salad with apples and capers.

Sałatka z ziemniaków z jabłkami i z kaparami.
sa-wát-ka z źhem-ńá-koof z yabw-ká-mee ee z ka-pa-rá-mee

Potato salad with anchovies.

Sałatka z ziemniaków z sardelami.
sa-wát-ka z źhem-ńá-koof z sar-de-lá-mee

90
Red beet salad with horseradish.

Ćwikła.
Chyeék-wa

Herring salad with mustard.

Sałatka śledziowa z musztardą.
sa-wát-ka śhle-dźhó-va z moosh-tár-down

Herring salad with mayonnaise.

Sałatka śledziowa z majonezem.
sa-wát-ka śhle-dźhó-va z ma-yo-né-zem

Jellied lobster salad

Sałatka w galarecie z homara.
sa-wát-ka v ga-la-ré-che z kho-má-ra

Royal salad with herring.

Królewska sałata ze śledziem.
kroo-lév-ska sa-wá-ta ze śhle-dźhem

91
Cauliflower salad with mayonnaise.

Sałatka z kalafiora z majonezem.
Sa-wát-ka z ka-la-fyó-ra z ma-ya-né-zem

Mixed cooked vegetable salad.

Mieszana sałatka jarzynowa.
mye-shá-na sa-wát-ka ya-zhi-nó-va

Asparagus tips salad.

Sałatka szparagowa.
sa-wát-ka shpa-ra-gó-va

Jellied vegetable salad.

Sałatka jarzynowa w galarecie.
sa-wát-ka ya-zhi-nó-wa w ga-la-ré-che

Tomato and grated onion salad.

Sałatka pomidorowa z cebulą.
sa-wát-ka po-mee-do-ro-va z tse-bóó-lówn

92
String bean salad.

Sałatka z fasoli szparagowej.
sa-wát-ka z fa-só-lee shpa-ra-gó-vey

Sardine salad with mustard.

Sałatka z sardynek w musztardzie.
sa-wát-ka z sar-dí-nek w moosh-tár-dźhe

Vegetable salad with tomatoes.

Sałatka jarzynowa z pomidorami.
sa-wát-ka ya-zhi-nó-va z po-mee-do-rá-mee

Sliced fruit salad with wine.

Sałatka owocowa z winem.
Sa-wát-ka o-vo-tsó-va z veé-nem

Onion salad with tarragon.

Sałatka z cebuli z estragonem.
sa-wát-ka z tse-bóó-lee z es-tra-gó-nem

93

What are the Polish mushroom dishes?

Jakie są polskie potrawy grzybowe?
ya-ke sown pols-ke po-tra-vi gzhi-bo-ve

Minced mushroom cutlets.

Siekane kotlety grzybowe.
she-ka-ne kot-le-ti grzi-bo-ve

Stuffed mushrooms.

Grzyby nadziewane.
gzhi-bi na-dzhe-va-ne

Mushrooms stewed in sour cream.

Grzyby duszone w śmietanie.
gzhi-bi doo-sho-ne w shmye-ta-ne

Marinated mushrooms.

Grzyby marynowane.
gzhi-bi ma-ri-no-va-ne

94

May I see the list of your dairy dishes?

Czy mógłbym zobaczyć listę potraw z nabiału?
chi moogw-bim zo-ba-chich lees-tan po-trav z na-bya-woo

We have a list of dairy dishes right here.

Tutaj właśnie mamy listę potraw z nabiału.
too-tay vwash-ne ma-mi lees-tan po-trav z na-bya-woo

Stuffed eggs.

Jajka nadziewane.
yay-ka na-dzhe-va-ne

Scrambled eggs with ham.

Jajecznica z szynką.
ya-yech-nee-tsa z shin-kown

95

Scrambled eggs with chives.

Jajecznica ze szczypiorkiem.
ya-yech-nee-tsa ze shchi-pyor-kem

Scramble eggs with sausage.

Jajecznica z kiełbasą.
ya-yech-nee-tsa z kew-ba-sown

Scrambled eggs with tomatoes.

Jajecznica z pomidorami.
ya-yech-nee-tsa z po-mee-do-ra-mee

Eggs sunny side up.

Jajka sadzone.
yay-ka sa-dzo-ne

Soft boiled eggs in a glass.

Jajka na miękko w szklance.
yay-ka na myän-ko v shklan-tse

Soft boiled eggs in an egg cup.

Jajka na miękko w kieliszku.
yay-ka na myän-ko v ke-leesh-koo

96

Poached eggs.

Jajka w koszulkach.
yay-ka v ko-shool-kakh

Poached eggs in a sauce.

Jajka w koszulkach w sosie.
yay-ka v ko-shool-kakh v so-she

Poached eggs in sour cream.

Jajka w koszulkach w śmietanie.
yay-ka v ko-shool-kakh v shmye-ta-ne

Egg cutlets.

Kotleciki z jaj.
kot-le-chee-kee z yay

Omelette.

Omlet naturalny.
om-let na-too-ral-ni

Omelette with spinach.

Omlet ze szpinakiem.
om-let ze shpee-na-kem

97

Omelet with peas.

Omlet z groszkiem zielonym.
óm-let z grósh-kem zhe-ló-nim

Omelet with cauliflower.

Omlet z kalafiorem.
óm-let z ka-la-fyó-rem

Omelet with ham.

Omlet z szynką.
óm-let z shín-kówn

Hard boiled eggs.

Jaja na twardo.
yá-ya na tvár-do

Eggs in a horseradish sauce.

Jaja w sosie chrzanowym.
yá-ya v só-she khzha-nó-vim

Egg noodles with ham.

Kluski na jajach z szynką.
Kloós-kee na yá-yakh z shín-kówn.

98

Egg noodles with poppy seed.

Kluski na jajach z makiem.
kloós-kee na yá-yakh z má-kem

Noodles with cheese and milk.

Kluski z mlekiem i serem.
kloós-kee z mlá-kem ee sé-rem

Noodles with cottage cheese.

Kluski z białym serem.
kloós-kee z byá-wim sé-rem

Baked noodles.

Kluski pieczone.
kloós-kee pye-chó-ne

Polish ravioli with cheese.

Pierogi leniwe z serem.
pye-ró-gee le-ñeé-ve z sé-rem

Ravioli with Cracov kasha.

Pierogi z kaszą krakowską.
pye-ró-gee z ka-shówn kra-kóv-skówn

99

Pancakes with sour cream.

Naleśniki ze śmietaną.
na-lesh-ñeé-kee ze shmye-tá-nówn

Pancakes with cottage cheese.

Naleśniki z białym serem.
na-lesh-ñeé-kee z byá-wim sé-rem

Pancakes with yeast and sour cream.

Bliny.
bleé-ni

Pancakes with jam.

Naleśniki z dżemem.
na-lesh-ñeé-kee z je-mem

Polish dumpling with prunes.

Knedle ze śliwkami.
knéd-le ze shleev-ká-mee

100

Polish dumplings with plum.

Knedle z rodzynkami.
knéd-le z ro-dzin-ká-mee

Polish dumplings with apricots.

Knedle z morelami.
knéd-le z mo-re-lá-mee

Polish dumplings with cherries.

Knedle z czereśniami.
knéd-le z che-resh-ñá-mee

Polish dumplings with cream of wheat.

Knedle z grysikiem.
knéd-le z gi-sheé-kem

Boiled browned flour with bacon.

Prażucha.
pra-zhoó-kha

101

I have heard about the Polish gourmet desserts.

Słyszałem o polskich przysmakach deserowych.
swi-shá-wem o póls-keekh pshi-smá-kakh de-se-ró-vikh.

Would you like to look at the list of our desserts?

Czy chciałby pan popatrzeć na spis naszych deserów?
chi khćháw-bi pan po-pá-tshech na spees ná-shikh de-sé-róof

I would really like to.

Z chęcią.
z khán-chówn

Here you can make your selection.

Z tego może pan wybrać.
z té-go mó-zhe pan vi-brach

Thank you.
Dziękuję.
dźhán-kóo-yán

102

Raisin pudding.

Budyń rodzynkowy.
bóo-diń ro-dzin-kó-vi

Vanilla pudding.

Budyń waniliowy.
bóo-diń va-ńeel-yó-vi

Almond pudding.

Budyń migdałowy.
bóo-diń meeg-da-wó-vi

Nut pudding.

Budyń orzechowy.
bóo-diń o-zhe-khó-vi

Milk pudding.

Budyń mleczny.
bóo-diń mlech-ni

Cheese pudding.

Budyń z sera.
bóo-diń z sé-ra

103

Chocolate pudding.

Budyń czekoladowy.
bóo-diń che-ko-la-dó-vi

Wine pudding.

Budyń winny.
bóo-diń veén-ni

Chestnut pudding with fruit.

Kasztanowy budyń z owocami.
kash-ta-nó-vi bóo-diń z o-vo-tsá-mee.

Bread pudding with sour cream.

Budyń chlebowy ze śmietaną.
bóo-diń khle-bó-vi ze śhmye-ta-nówn

Potato pudding.

Budyń ziemniaczany.
bóo-diń źhem-ńa-chá-ni

Rice pudding.

Budyń z ryżu.
bóo-diń z rí-zhoo

104

Cranberry pudding.

Budyń z żurawin.
bóo-diń z zhoo-rá-veen

Rum pudding with raspberries.

Budyń na rumie z malinami.
bóo-diń na róo-mye z ma-lee-ná-mee

Sherry pudding with cherries.

Budyń na winie z czereśniami.
boo-diń na vee-ńe z che-reśh-ńá-mee

Frozen pudding with apricots.

Mrożony budyń z morelami.
mró-zho-ni bóo-diń z mo-re-lá-mee

Apricot compote /stewed/.

Kompot morelowy.
kóm-pot mo-re-ló-vi

Stuffed apple compote.

Kompot z nadziewanych jabłek.
kóm-pot z na-dźhe-vá-nikh yab-wek

105
Orange and apple compote.

Kompot z pomarańcz i jabłek.
kóm-pot z po-má-rańch ee yáb-wek

Strawberry compote with wine.

Kompot truskawkowy z winem.
kóm-pot troos-kav-kó-vi. z veé-nem

Rhubarb compote.

Kompot z rabarbaru.
kóm-pot z roo-bar-bá-roo.

Pear compote.

Kompot z gruszek.
kóm-pot z groó-shek

Blueberry compote.

Kompot z czarnych jagód.
kóm-pot z chár-nikh ya-goot

Marinated cherry compote.

Kompot z marynowanych czereśni.
kóm-pot z ma-ri-no-vá-nikh che-résh-
ńee

106
Melon stuffed with berries.

Melon nadziewany jagodami.
mé-lon na-dźhe-vá-ni ya-go-dá-mee

Pears in wine sauce.

Gruszki w sosie winnym.
groósh-kee w só-śhe veén-nim

Pears in rum.

Gruszki w rumie.
groósh-kee v roó-mye

Stuffed peaches.

Brzoskwinie nadziewane.
bzhos-kveé-ńe na-dźhe-vá-ne

Strawberries with sour cream.

Truskawki ze śmietaną.
troos-káv-kee se śhmye-tá-nówn

Fresh fruit salad.

Surówka owocowa.
soo-roóv-ka o-vo-tsó-va

107
Baked apples.

Pieczone jabłka.
pye-chó-ne yáb-ka.

Sour milk jelly.

Galaretka z kwaśnego mleka.
ga-la-rét-ka z kvash-né-go mlé-ka

Fried fruit juice jelly.

Galaretka ze smażonych soków owoco-
wych.
ga-la-rét-ka ze sma-zhó-nikh só-koof
o-vo-tsó-vikh

Currant jelly.

Galaretka porzeczkowa.
ga-la-rét-ka po-zhech-kó-va

Boiled apple jelly.

Galaretka jabłkowa.
ga-la-rét-ka yab-kó-va.

108
Cooked cherry jelly.

Galaretka z wisien gotowanych.
ga-la-rét-ka z veé-shen go-to-vá-nikh

Raw raspberry jelly.

Galaretka surowa malinowa.
ga-la-rét-ka soo-ró-va ma-lee-nó-va

Sour cream souffle.

Suflet śmietanowy.
soof-let shmye-ta-nó-vi

Coffee souffle.

Suflet kawowy.
soof-let ka-vó-vi.

Tea souffle.

Suflet herbaciany.
soof-let kher-ba-ńha-ni

Lemon souffle.

Suflet cytrynowy.
soof-let tsi-tri-nó-vi

109
Wheat grain and honey dessert.

Kutia.
koot-ya

Apple soufflé.

Suflet jabłkowy.
soof-let yab-kó-vi

Apple slices in batter.

Krajane jabłka smażone w cieście.
kra-yá-ne yáb-ka sma-zhó-ne v che-sh-che

Grated carrots and apples.

Marchewka tarta z jabłkami.
mar-khév-ka tár-ta z yap-ká-mee

Coffee layer cake.

Tort kawowy.
tort ka-vó-vi

110
Chocolate layer cake.

Tort czekoladowy.
tort che-ko-la-dó-vi

Almond and strawberry layer cake

Tort migdałowo truskawkowy.
tort meeg-da-wó-vo troos-kav-kó-vi

Nut layer cake.

Tort orzechowy.
tort o-zhe-khó-vi

Chestnut cake.

Tort kasztanowy.
tort kash-ta-nó-vi

Cheese layer cake.

Tort serowy.
tort se-ró-vi

Round coffee cake.

Babka.
báb-ka

111
Poppy seed roll.

Makownik.
ma-kov-neek

Fried cookies Polish style.

Chrust   =   Faworki.
khroost   =   fa-vór-kee

Yeast batter balls fried.

Pączki.
pównch-kee

Cherry stuffed batter balls.

Pączki z wiśnią.
pównch-kee z veésh-nown

Batter balls with preserved
rose petals.

Pączki nadziewane konfiturą z róży.
pównch-kee na-dźhe-vá-ne kon-fee-
too-równ z roó-zhi

112
Creamed apples.

Mus jabłkowy.
moos yab-kó-vi

Creamed strawberries.

Mus truskawkowy.
moos troos-kav-kó-vi

Lemon cream.

Krem cytrynowy.
krem tsi-tri-nó-vi

Strawberry cream.

Krem truskawkowy.
krem troos-kav-kó-vi

Chocolate sweet sauce.

Słodki sos czekoladowy.
swód-kee sos che-ko-la-dó-vi

Sweet cream sauce.

Krem śmietanowy.
krem shmye-ta-no-vi.

113

Almond sauce.

Sos migdałowy.
sos meeg-da-wo-vi

Apricot sauce.

Sos morelowy.
sos mo-re-lo-vi

Raspberries sauce.

Sos malinowy.
sos ma-lee-no-vi

Vanilla sauce.

Sos waniliowy.
sos va-ñeel-vo-vi

Fruit juice sauce.

Sos na soku owocowym.
sos na so-koo o-vo-tso-vim

Fruit sauce.

Sos owocowy.
sos o-vo-tso-vi

114

What kind of appetizers do you have?

Jakie państwo macie zakąski?
ya-ke páñs-tvo má-che za-kówñ-skee

Stuffed eggs Polish style.

Jaja faszerowane po polsku.
ya-ya fa-she-ro-va-ne po póls-koo

Stuffed eggs with sauce.

Jaja faszerowane z sosem.
ya-ya fa-she-ro-va-ne z so-sem

Eggs stuffed with ham.

Jaja faszerowane szynką.
ya-ya fa-she-ro-va-ne z shín-kówn

Eggs stuffed with herring.

Jaja nadziewane śledziem.
ya-ya na-dzhe-va-ne shle-dzhem

115

Eggs in horseradish sauce.

Jaja w sosie chrzanowym.
ya-ya v so-she khzha-no-vim

Eggs in mustard sauce.

Jaja w sosie musztardowym.
ya-ya v so-she moosh-tar-do-vim

Marinated mushrooms.

Grzyby marynowane.
gzhi-bi ma-ri-no-va-ne

Marinated herring.

Śledzie marynowane.
shle-dzhe ma-ri-no-va-ne

Herring in sour cream.

Śledzie w kwaśnej śmietanie.
shle-dzhe v kvásh-ney shmye-tá-ñe

Canapés Polish style.

Wybór kanapek.
vi-boor ka-ná-pek

116

Browned onion and mushroom ravioli.

Pierożki.
pye-rózh-kee

Chicken pâté.

Pasztet z kury.
pásh-tet z koo-ri

Pork pâté.

Pasztet z wieprzowiny.
pásh-tet z vyep-sho-vee-ni

Venison pâté.

Pasztet z dziczyzny.
pásh-tet z dzhee-chíz-ni

Cod fish pâté.

Pasztet z dorsza.
pásh-tet z dór-sha

Smoked meat (and fish) plate.

Wędliny.
wånd-lee-ni

117
Refreshments.

Napoje orzeźwiające.
na-pó-ye o-zhezh-vya-yówn-tse

Rhubarb beverage.

Napój z rabarbaru.
ná-pooy z ra-bar-bá-roo

Cranberry beverage.

Napój z żurawin.
ná-pooy z zhoo-rá-veen

Honey beverage.

Napój z miodu.
ná-pooy z myó-doo

Mint beverage.

Napój z miety.
ná-pooy z myán-ti

Linden flower beverage.

Napój z kwiatu lipowego.
ná-pooy z kvyá-too lee-po-vé-go

118
Hot drinks.

Napoje gorące.
na-pó-ye go-równ-tse

Black coffee.

Czarna kawa.
chár-na ká-va

Coffee with milk.

Biała kawa.
byá-wa ká-va

Coffee with cream.

Kawa ze śmietanką.
ká-va ze śhmye-tán-kówn

Tea.

Herbata naturalna.
her-bá-ta na-too-rál-na

Cocoa.

Kakao.
ka-ká-o

119
Retail of alcoholic drinks.

Wyszynk.
vî-shink

Bison vodka.

Żubrówka.
zhoo-broóv-ka

Rye vodka.

Żytnia wódka.
zhít-ña voód-ka

Choice vodka, grain vodka.

Wódka wyborowa.
voód-ka vi-bo-ró-va

Caraway seed vodka.

Kminkówka.
kmeen-koóv-ka

Rowanberry vodka.

Jarzębiak.
ya-zháñb-yak

120
Sweet, after dinner vodkas.

Słodkie wódki.
swód-ke voód-kee

Apricot vodka.

Wódka morelowa.
voód-ka mo-re-ló-va

Orange vodka.

Pomarańczówka.
po-ma-rañ-choóv-ka

Lemon vodka.

Cytrynówka.
tsi-tri-noóv-ka

Peppercorns, vanilla, honey vodka.

Krupnik.
kroóp-ñeek

Sweet sedge vodka.

Ajerówka.
a-ye-roóv-ka

121
Wine brandy.

Winiak.
vee-ñak

Cherry cordial.

Wiśniówka.
veesh-ñoóv-ka

Plum brandy.

Śliwowica.
shlee-vo-veé-tsa

Golden vodka.

Złota woda.
zwó-ta vó-da

Eggnog vodka.

Ajerkoniak.
a-yer-kó-ñak

Mead, honey wine.

Miód pitny.
myood peét-ni

122
Beer.

Piwo.
peé-vo

Light beer.

Jasne piwo.
yás-ne peé-vo

Dark beer.

Ciemne piwo.
chém-ne peé-vo

Hot beer with egg yolks.

Gorące piwo z żółtkami
go-rów-tse peé-vo z zhoowt-ká-mee

Malt liquor.

Piwo słodowe.
peé-vo swo-dó-ve

Hot wine with cloves.

Gorące wino z goździkami.
go-rów-tse veé-no z gozh-dźhee-ká-mee

123
Operator, how do I make a telephone call outside the hotel?

Proszę mi powiedzieć jak się mogę połączyć z miastem?
pró-shañ mee po-vyé-dźhech yak shañ mó-gañ po-wówñ-chich z myás-tem

Please, dial nine and then the number you want.

Proszę nakręcić dziewiątkę a potem numer panu potrzebny.
pró-shañ na-kráñ-cheech dźhev-yówñt-kañ a pó-tem nóo-mer pá-noo po-tshéb-ni

University, may I help you?

Uniwersytet, słucham.
oo-ñee-ver-sí-tet, swóo-kham

Extention seven two one, please.

Proszę o wewnętrzny siedem dwa jeden.
pró-shañ o vev-nóñtsh-ni shé-dem dva yé-den

124
Good morning, may I talk to Mr. Barski?

Dzień dobry, czy mogę mówić z panem Barskim?
dźheñ dób-ri, chi mó-gañ móo-veech z pá-nem Bárs-keem

Barski speaking, who is calling?

Mówi Barski, kto przy telefonie?
móo-vee bárs-kee, kto pshi te-le-fó-ñe

This is Jimmy Parker.

Przy telefonie Jimmy Parker.
pshi te-le-fó-ñe Jimmy Parker

Oh, how nice to hear from you. Where are you now?

Jak to miło cię usłyszeć. Gdzie jesteś?
yak to meé-wo chañ oo-swi-shech. gdźhe yés-tesh

I am in the Hotel Forum.

Jestem w hotelu Forum.
yés-tem v kho-té-loo fó-room

125

What is your room number?

Jaki masz numer pokoju?
yá-kee mash noó-mer po-kó-yoo

My room number is two zero two.

Mam pokój numer dwa zero dwa.
mam pó-kooy noó-mer dva zé-ro dva

Are you free this morning?

Czy masz czas dziś rano?
chi mash chas dżheesh rá-no

Yes, I am free.

Tak, jestem wolny.
tak, yés-tem vól-ni

Could we get together for a few minutes?

Czy moglibyśmy spotkać się na parę minut?
chi móg-lee bísh-mi spót-kach shãn na pá-rãn meé-noot

126

Fine.

Bardzo dobrze.
bar-dzo dób-zhe.

I would like to invite you to my appartment or I can come to your hotel.

Chciałbym cię zaprosić do mego mieszkania, albo mogę przyjść do twojego hotelu.
khcháw-bim chãn za-pró-sheech do mé-go myesh-ká-ña, ál-bo mó-gãn pshiy-shch do tvo-yé-go kho-té-loo

Since I do not know my way around, could you come to the hotel?

Ponieważ nie znam miasta, czy mógłbyć przyjść do hotelu?
po-ñe-vazh ñe znam myás-ta, chi moógw-bish pshiy-shch do kho-té-loo

With pleasure.

z przyjemnością.
z pshi-yem-nó'h-chõwn

127

I shall be at your hotel at ten thirty a.m.

Będę u ciebie w hotelu o dziesiątej trzydzieści.
bãn-dãn oo chéb-ye v kho-té-loo o dżhe-shówn-tey tshi-dżhésh-chee

I can not wait to see you, Ed.

Nie mogę się doczekać żeby cię zobaczyć Edziu.
ñe mó-gãn shãn do-ché-kach żhé-bi chãn zo-bá-chich, e-dżhoo

I shall see you soon, Jimmie.

Zobaczymy się wkrótce, Jimmie.
zo-ba-chí-mi shãn vkroót-tse, Jimmie

Hello, room two zero two.

Halo, pokój dwa zero dwa?
khá-lo, pó-kooy dva zé-ro dva

Yes indeed, Parker speaking.

Tak jest, mówi Parker.
tak yest, moó-vee pár-ker

128

Mr. Barski is waiting for you in the hotel coffee shop.

Pan Barski czeka na pana w kawiarni hotelowej.
pan bárs-kee ché-ka na pá-na v kav-yár-ñee kho-te-ló-vey

Thank you, please, tell him that I shall come down shortly.

Dziękuję, proszę mu powiedzieć że zaraz przyjdę.
dżhan-koó-yãn, pró-shãn moo po-vyé-dżhech zhe zá-raz pshíy-dãn

Good morning Ed, I am glad you came.

Dzień dobry Edziu, cieszę się że przyszedłeś.
dżheñ dób-ri é-dżhoo, ché-shãn shãn zhe pshi-shéd-wesh

I am glad to see you again, Jimmie.

Miło mi cię znowu zobaczyć, Jimmie.
meé-wo mee chãn znó-voo zo-bá-chich, Jimmie

129

It must be nearly ten years since
we were in school together.

Prawie dziesięć lat minęło od czasu
kiedy studiowaliśmy razem.
prá-vye dźhé-śhanćh lat mee-nán-wo od
chá-soo ke-dī stoo-dyo-ya-leéśh-mi
rá-zem

Yes, the time is really flying.

Tak, czas rzeczywiście leci szybko.
tak, chas zhe-chi-veéśh-che lé-ćhee
shíb-ko

I am glad you came to Warsaw.

Cieszę się że przyjechałeś do Warszawy.
ćhe-shan śhan zhe pshi-ye-khá-weśh do
var-shá-vi

Let us sit down.

Usiądźmy.
oo-śhówndźh-mi

130

You might find the Polish coffee
rather strong, so you might want
a lot of cream.

Polska kawa może ci się wydawać zbyt
mocna, tak że może będziesz chciał
sporo śmietanki.
póls-ka ká-va mó-zhe ćhee śhan vi-dá-
vaćh zbit móts-na, tak zhe mó-zhe
bań-dźhesh khćhaw spó-ro śhmye-tan-kee

I would love to try the Polish
coffee.

Bardzo chciałbym spróbować polskiej
kawy.
bár-dzo khćhaw-bim sproo-bó-vaćh póls-
key ká-vi.

Strong coffee might help you recover from jet lag.

Mocna kawa może ci pomóc przystosować się do zmiany godzin.
mats-na ka-va mo-zhe ćhee po-moots
pshi-sto-so-vaćh śhan do zmya-ni
go-dźheen

131

Miss, would you give us two small
black coffees?

Proszę dwie małe czarne kawy.
pró-shań dvye má-we chár-ne ká-vi

Would you like anything else?

Czy panowie pozwolą coś jeszcze?
chi pa-nó-vye poz-vó-lówn tsośh
yéśh-che

No, thank you.

Nie dziękuję.
ńe dźhań-koó-yán

Jimmie, my wife and I would like
to have you for dinner tonight.

Jimmie, zapraszamy cię na kolację
do nas dziś wieczór.
Jimmie, za-pra-sha-mi ćhań na kola-
ts-yan do nas dźheeśh vye-choc

That is a splendid idea.

To wspaniały pomysł.
to vspa-ńá-wi pó-misw

132

Janka can not wait to meet my old
school friend.

Janka nie może się doczekać żeby poznać mego starego przyjaciela ze studiów.
yán-ka ńe mó-zhe śhań do-che-kaćh zhe-
bi póz-naćh mé-go sta-re-go pshi-ya-
ćhe-la ze stoód-yoof

Edward, you have to help me overcome the language and custom gap.

Edward   musisz mi pomóc radzić sobie
z różnicami w mowie i zwyczajach.
Ed-vard   moó-śheesh mee pó-moots rá-
dźheećh sób-ye z roozh-ńe-tsá-mee v mó-
vye ee zvi-chá-yakh

You are smart, Jimmie, to notice
this gap.

To dowcipnie z twojej strony że   zauwa-
żyłeś tę różnicę.
to dov-ćheép-ńe z tvó-yey stró-ni zhe
za-oo-va-zhi-weśh tań roozh-ńeé-tsań

133
I remember how you used to ask
me about such things in America.

Pamiętam jak o takie rzeczy pytałeś
mnie w Ameryce.
pa-myán-tam yak o tá-ke zhé-chi pi-
tá-wesh   mñe v a-me-ri-tse

Now we have a chance to talk
about them in Poland.

Teraz mamy okazję porozmawiać o nich
w Polsce.
té-raz ma-mi o-káz-yáñ po-roz-máv-
yach o ñeekh v póls-tse

I notice that people in Poland do
not use the family name with the
word mister as we do in America.

Zauważyłem że w Polsce nie używa się
nazwiska ze słowem pan, tak jak to
robi się w Ameryce.
za-oo-ya-zhí-wem zhe v póls-tse ñe
oo-zhi-va sháñ naz-veés-ka ze swo-
vem pan, tak yak to sháñ ró-bee y
a-me-ri-tse

134
You are right.

Masz rację.
mash ráts-yáñ

In Poland it sounds unpleasantly
official to use the family name
with the word mister.

W Polsce używanie nazwiska ze słowem
pan brzmi zbyt oficjalnie.
w póls-tse oo-zhi-vá-ñe naz-veés-ka
ze swó-vem pan bzhmee zbit ofee-tsyál-
ñe

In America it is impolite to call
anyone mister without using his
family name.

W Ameryce jest niegrzecznie mówić do
kogoś per pan i jednocześnie nie wymieniać jego nazwiska.
v a-me-rí-tse yest ñe-gzhéch-ñe mó-
veech do kó-gosh per pan ee yed-no-
chésh-ñe ñe vi-mye-ñach yé-go naz-
veés-ka

135
In a conversation in Poland the
words Mister, Mrs   are
used without the family name.

W Polsce.w rozmowie.słowa pan, pani
     są używane bez nazwiska.
v póls-tse v roz-mó-vye swó-va pan,
pá-ñee   sówn oo-zhi-vá-ne
bez naz-veés-ka

How do you say politely in Polish
Please, pass me the coffee.

Jak się grzecznie mówi po polsku:
Proszę podać mi kawę.
yak sháñ gzhech-ñe móó-vee po póls-
koo : pro-sháñ pó-dach mee ká-váñ

Your expression is correct.

Twoje wyrażenie jest poprawne.
tvó-ye vi-ra-zhé-ñe yest po-práv-ne

It depends on who is being
addressed.

Zależy z kim rozmawiasz.
za-lé-zhi z keem roz-máv-vyash

136
Miss, could you pass me the
coffee?

Czy mogłaby pani podać mi kawę?
chi mog-wá-bi pa-ñee pó-dach mee
ká-váñ

Waiter,could you pass me the
coffee?

Czy mógłby pan podać mi kawę?
chi moogw-bi pan pó-dach mee
ká-váñ

Little girl, could you pass me
the coffee?

Dziewczynko, czy mogłabyś podać mi
kawę?
dzhev-chín-ko, chi mog-wá-hish pó-
dach mee ká-váñ

Little boy, could you pass me
the coffee?

Chłopczyku, czy mógłbyś podać mi
kawę?
khwop-chí-koo, chi moogw-bish pó-
dach mee ká-váñ

137

The Polish word "pan" is used like English "you","Mister" and "Sir"

Polskie słowo "pan" używa się jak w angielskim "you", "Mister" i "Sir".
póls-ḱe swó-vo pan oo-zhí-va śhañ
yak v an-ḋéls-keem you, mister ee sir.

I hope that these tips will help me make a good impression at the dinner party.

Mam nadzieję że te wskazówki pomogą mi zrobić dobre wrażenie na przyjęciu u ciebie.
mam na-dźhé-yáñ zhe te vska-zoóf-kee po-mó-gówñ mee zró-beech dób-re vra-zhé-ñe na pshi-yáñ-choo oo ćhéh-ye

What are some other typical Polish customs?

Jakie są inne typowe polskie zwyczaje?
yá-ḱe sówñ eén-ne ti-pó-ve póls-ḱe zvi-chá-ye

138

Cut flowers are always an acceptable gift in Poland.

W Polsce bukiet kwiatów jest zawsze dobrze widziany.
v póls-tse boó-ḱet kvyá-toof yest záv-she dób-zhe vee-dźhá-ni

In Poland the guest may compliment the hostess directly about her beauty, her dress or her cooking.

W Polsce gość może wprost mówić komplementy pani domu o jej urodzie, jej sukni czy też jej gotowaniu.
v póls-tse gośhćh mó-zhe vprost moó-veech kom-ple-mén-ti pá-ñee dó-moo o yey oo-ró-dźhe, yey soók-ñee chi tezh yey go-to-vá-ñoo

In America we usually tell the husband about the beauty and the elegance of his wife.

W Ameryce my zwykle mówimy mężowi o piękności i elegancji jego żony.
v a-me-rí-tse mi zvik-le moo-veé-mi man-zhó-vee o pyáñk-nóśh-ćhee ee e-le-gánts-yee yé-go zhó-ni

139

What about table manners in Poland?

Jakie są polskie zwyczaje przy stole?
yá-ḱe sówñ póls-ḱe zvi-chá-ye pshi stó-le

The guest of honor sits at the head of the table.

Gość honorowany zasiada na pierwszym miejscu.
gośhćh kho-no-ro-vá-ni za-śhá-da na pyérv-shim myéys-tsoo

In the family the lady of the house sits at the head of the table.

W rodzinie.pani domu zasiada na pierwszym miejscu.
v ro-dźheé-ñe pá-ñee dó-moo za-śhá-da na pyérv-shim myéys-tsoo

The host pours the drinks.

Pan domu nalewa napoje.
pan dó-moo na-lé-va na-pó-ye

140

The guest of honor is the first to be served.

Gościowi honorowanemu podaje się jedzenie jako pierwszemu.
gośh-ćhó-vee kho-no-ro-va-né-moo po-dá-ye śhañ ye-dzé-ñe yá-ko pyerv-shé-moo

In the family the lady of the house serves herself first.

W rodzinie pani domu pierwsza nabiera sobie jedzenie.
v ro-dźheé-ñe pá-ñee dó-moo pyérv-sha na-byé-ra só-bye ye-dzé-ñe

Everybody takes as much food as he is sure to eat.

Każdy bierze tyle jedzenia ile zje.
kázh-di byé-zhe ti-le ye-dzé-ña eé-le zye

That makes sense.

To jest słuszne.
to yest swoósh-ne

141

In Poland, it is considered impolite to leave a quantity of food on one's plate.

Tak, w Polsce nie należy do dobrych
manier zostawiać jedzenie na talerzu.
tak, v póls-tse ńe na-lé-zhi do dób-
rikh má-ńer zos-táv-yaćh ye-dzé-ńe na
ta-lé-zhoo

In Poland you may use your fork with either your right or your left hand.

W Polsce można używać widelca prawą
lub lewą ręką.
v póls-tse móżh-na oo-zhí-vaćh yee-
dél-tsa prá-vówh loob lé-vówh rán-kówh

Most Americans hold the fork in their left hand while cutting food, then transfer the fork to their right hand for placing food in their mouths.

Amerykanie jedzą widelcem tylko prawą
ręką.
a-me-ri-ká-ńe ye-ć-ówh vee-dél-tsem
til-ko pra-vówh rán-kówh

142

It is funny how these habits differ.

Ciekawe jak się zwyczaje różnią.
ćhe-ká-ve yak śhäñ zvi-chá-ye roózh-
ńówh

I hope I will remember what you have told me.

Mam nadzieję że zapamiętam co mi po-
wiedziałeś.
mam na-dźhe-yan zhe za-pz-myáń-tam
tso mee po-vye-dźhá-weśh

What time should I arrive?

O której godzinie powinienem przyjść?
o ktoó-rey go-dźheé-ńe po-vee-ńé-nem
pshiy-śhćh

You are invited for seven p.m.

Jesteś zaproszony na siódmą wieczorem.
yés-teśh za-pro-shó-ni na śhoód-mówh
vye-chó-rem

143

However, the guests are usually fifteen minutes late.

Zwykle goście spóźniają się piętnaście minut.
zvík-le góśh-ćhe spooźh-ńá-yówh śhäñ
pyant-náśh-ćhe meé-noot

That gives the hostess an extra quarter of an hour.

To daje pani domu dodatkowy kwadrans.
to dá-ye pá-ńee dó-moo do-dat-kó-vi
kvád-rans

It is not polite to be much more than fifteen minutes late.

Nie jest uprzejmie spóźniać się więcej niż kwadrans.
ńe yest oo-pshéy-mye spoóżh-ńach śhäñ
vyáñ-tsey ńeezh kvád-rans

That is good to know.

To dobrze wiedzieć.
to dób-zhe vyé-dźhećh

144

In America at dinner parties we try to avoid discussing politics religion and women.

W Ameryce na przyjęciu unikamy rozmów
o polityce, religii i kobietach.
v a-me-ri-tse na pshi-yáñ-choo oo-ńee-
ká-mi róz-moof o po-lee-tí-tse, re-
leég-yee ee ko-byé-takh

Is there such a custom in Poland?

Czy jest taki zwyczaj w Polsce?
chi yest tá-kee zvi-chay v póls-tse

In Poland conversation starts light and then turns to more serious subjects.

W Polsce rozmowa zaczyna się lekko a
potem zwraca się do poważniejszych
tematów.
v póls-ts roz-mó-va za-chí-na śhäñ
lék-ko a po-tem zvrá-tsa śhäñ do po-
vazh-ńéy-shikh te-má-toof

You have to be tactful.

Musisz być taktowny.
moó-śheesh bićh tak-tóv-ni.

145

Your Polish ladies seem most attractive.

Polskie kobiety wydają się bardzo interesujące.
póls-ke ko-byé-ti vi-dá-yõwn shañ bár-dzo een-te-re-soo-yõwn-tse

Polish woman have a reputation for selecting clothes to enhance their best features.

Polskie kobiety znane są z dobrego doboru twarzowych sukienek.
póls-ke kob-yé-ti zná-ne sõwn z dob-ré-go dob-bó-roo tva-zhó-vikh soo-ké-nek

Yes, I have not seen anybody walking around in hair curlers.

Tak, nie widziałem nikogo na ulicy w papilotach.
tak, ñe vee-dźha-wem ñee-kó-go na oo-leé-tsi v pa-pee-ló-takh

146

You have good sight-seeing weather today.

Masz dziś dobrą pogodę do zwiedzania.
mash dźheeśh dó-brown po-gó-dan do zvye-dzá-ña

I would like to go on a general tour of the capital, first.

Chciałbym naprzód ogólnie zwiedzić stolicę.
khćháw-bim ná-pshoot o-goól-ñe zvyé-dźheeśh sto-leé-tsän

You can join a guided tour here at the hotel.

Możesz przyłączyć się do wycieczki z przewodnikiem tu w hotelu.
mó-zhesh pshi-wówn-chiśh śhań do vi-ćhéch-kee z psze-vod-ñeé-kem too v kho-te-loo

That is convenient.

To wygodnie.
to vi-gód-ñe

147

The "Orbis" travel agency handles the tours here at the hotel.

Agencja "Orbis" tu w hotelu załatwia sprawy wycieczek.
a-génts-ya ór-bees too v kho-té-loo za-wát-vya sprá-vi vi-ćhé-chek

I hope they do have English speaking guides.

Mam nadzieję że mają przewodników mówiących po angielsku.
mam na-dźhé-yań zhe má-yõwn pshe-vod-ñeé-koof moov-yõwn-tsikh po an-géls-koo

Most guides speak English.

Większość przewodników mówi po angielsku.
vyáñk-shoshćh pshe-vod-ñeé-koof moó-vee po an-géls-koo

Let us go to "Orbis".

Chodźmy do "Orbisu".
khodźh-mi do or-beé-soo

148

"Orbis" is located between the coffee shop and the florist.

"Orbis" znajduje się między kawiarnią i kwiaciarnią.
ór-bees znaj-doó-ye śhań myáñ-dzi ka-yyár-ñõwn ee kvya-ćhár-ñõwn

Good morning.

Dzień dobry.
dźheñ dób-ri

May I help you?

Czym mogę służyć?
chem mó-gań swoó-zhiśh

I would like to go on a sight-seeing tour this afternoon.

Chciałbym dziś popołudniu zwiedzać z wycieczką.
khćháw-bim dźheeśh po-po-woód-ñoo zvye-dzaćh z vi-ćhéch-kõwn

149

There are seats on the Wilanów
tour and on the Żelazowa Wola tour.

Są miejsca na wycieczkę do Wilanowa i
do Żelazowej Woli.
sown myéys-tsa na vi-chéch-kan do vee-
la-nó-va ee do zhe-la-zó-vey vó-lee

Which tour is more interesting?

Która wycieczka jest ciekawsza?
ktoó-ra vi-chéch-ka yest che-káv-sha

That depends on you.

To zależy od pana.
to za-lé-zhi od pá-na

The tour to Żelazowa Wola is lon-
ger.

Wycieczka do Żelazowej Woli jest dłuż-
sza.
vi-chéch-ka do zhe-la-zó-vey vó-lee
yest dwoózh-sha

150

Żelazowa Wola is the birthplace
of Chopin.

Żelazowa Wola jest miejscem urodzenia
Szopena.
zhe-la-zó-va vó-la yest myéys-tsem
co-ro-dzé-ña sho-pé-na.

Wilanów palace belonged to King
John III Sobieski, the Supreme
Commander of the Allied Christian
Army at Vienna in 1683.

Pałac wilanowski należał do króla Ja-
na trzeciego Sobieskiego, naczelnego
wodza zjednoczonej armii chrześcijań-
skiej pod Wiedniem w tysiąc sześćset
osiemdziesiątym trzecim roku.
pá-wats yee-la-nóv-skee na-lé-zhaw do
kroó-la yá-na tshe-ché-go so-byes-ké-
go, na-chel-né-go vó-dza zyed-no-cho-
ney ármy-yee khshe'h-chee-vań-skey pod
vyéd-ñem v ti-śhównts shé'shch-set o-
śhem-dźhe-śhówn-tim tshé-cheem ró-koo

151

Wilanów palace is one of the best
examples of the Polish baroque.

Pałac wilanowski jest jednym z najlep-
szych przykładów polskiego baroku.
pá-wats yee-la-nóv-skee yest yéd-nim
z nay-lép-shikh pshi-kwá-doof pols-
ké-go ba-ró-koo

I would like to go on the Wilanów
tour first.

Chciałbym naprzód pojechać na wycieczkę do Wilanowa.
khcháw-bim ná-pshood po-yé-khach na
vi-chéch-kàñ do vee-la-nó-va

Your tour starts at two p.m.; here
is your ticket.

Pańska wycieczka wyrusza o drugiej po
południu; oto pański bilet.
páñ-ska vi-chéch-ka vi-roó-sha o
droó-gey po po-woód-ñoo, ó-to páñ-
-skee beé-let

152

The ticket costs 200 zloties.

Bilet kosztuje dwieście złotych.
beé-let kosh-toó-ye dvyéśh-che zwó-
tikh

I have a thousand zloty bill.

Mam banknot   tysiąc-złotowy.
man bánk-not   ti-śhownts zwo-to-vi

Your change: 800 zloties.

Pańska reszta: osiemset złotych,
páñ-ska resh-ta: o-śhém-set zwó-tikh

Does "Orbis" handle the air
tickets?

Czy "Orbis" załatwia bilety lotnicze?
chi ór-bees za-wátv-ya bee-lé-ti lot-
ñee-che

No, the air tickets are handled
by "Lot".

Nie, bilety lotnicze załatwia "Lot".
ñe, bee-lé-ti lot-ñeé-che za-wát-vya
lot

153

"Orbis" handles bus and railroad tickets and sight seeing tours.

"Orbis" załatwia bilety kolejowe i autobusowe oraz zwiedzanie.
ór-bees za-wát-vya bee-lé-ti ko-le-yó-ve ee aw-to-boo-só-ve ó-raz zvye-dzá-ńe

Where is the "Lot" office?

Gdzie jest biuro "Lotu"?
gdźhe yest byóo-ro ló-too

The "Lot" office is on the second floor.

Biuro "Lotu" jest na drugim piętrze.
byóo-ro ló-too yest na dróo-geem pyáńt-she

Thank you.

Dziękuję.
dźháń-koo-yáń

154

Good morning to you.

Dzień dobry pani.
dźheń dób-ri pa-ńee

May I help you?

Czym mogę służyć?
chim mo-gáń swoó-zhich

I have an open return ticket on the Polish airline "Lot".

Mam bilet z otwartą datą powrotu na polskie linie lotnicze "Lot".
mam beé-let z ot-vár-tówn dá-tówn po-vró-too na póls-ke leéń-ye lot-ńeé-che lot

May I see your ticket?

Czy mogę zobaczyć pański bilet?
chi mo-gáń zo-bá-chich páń-skee beé-let?

155

When would you like to fly back?

Kiedy chciałby pan lecieć z powrotem?
ké-di khćháw-bi pan lé-ćhećh z po-vró-tem

I would like to fly in two weeks.

Chciałbym lecieć za dwa tygodnie.
khćháw-bim lé-ćhećh za dva ti-gód-ńe

I will check the Saturday flight.

Sprawdzę lot w sobotę.
správ-dzáń lot v so-bó-tań

The Saturday flight is sold out.

Sobotni lot jest wyprzedany.
so-bót-ńee lot yest vi-pshe-dá-ni

There are several passengers wait-listed for this flight.

Jest kilku pasażerów na liście oczekujących (zwolnień miejsc) na ten lot.
yets keél-koo pa-sa-zhé-roof na leeśh-ćhe o-che-koo-yówn-tsikh zvól-ńeń na ten lot

156

I would like to have confirmed flight reservations.

Chciałbym mieć potwierdzoną rezerwację lotu.
khćháw-bim myećh po-tvyer-dzó-nówn re-zer-váts-yáń ló-too

Friday and Sunday flights still have a few seats available.

Piątkowy i niedzielny lot mają po kilka wolnych miejsc.
pyównt-kó-vi ee ńe-dźhél-ni lot má-yówn po keél-ka vól-nikh myeysts

I will take the Friday flight.

Polecę w piątek.
po-le-tsan v pyówn-tek

Fine, here is the confirmation of your departure.

Dobrze, oto potwierdzenie pańskiego odlotu.
dób-zhe o-to pot-vyer-dźé-ńe pańs-ké-go od-ló-too

157

Have a pleasant flight.

Życzę przyjemnego lotu.
zhi-cháñ pshi-yem-né-go ló-too

Thank you and good-bye.

Dziękuję i do widzenia.
dźhan-kóo-yáñ ee do vee-dzé-ña

It's going to rain.

Deszcz będzie padał.
deshch ban-dźhe pá-daw

You need an umbrella.

Potrzebny jest Panu parasol.
po-tshéb-ni yest pá-noo pa-rá-sol

I ought to buy an umbrella.

Powinienem kupić parasol.
po-vee-ñe-nem koo-peech pa-rá-sol

Let's go to the store.

Chodźmy do sklepu,
khódźh-mi do sklé-poo

158

Excuse me.

Przepraszam.
pshe-prá-sham

Do you have an umbrella?

Czy ma pani parasol?
chi ma pá-ñee pa-rá-sol

Certainly, sir.

Tak jest, proszę pana.
tak yest, pró-shañ pá-na

I want the black umbrella.

Proszę o ten czarny parasol.
pró-shañ o ten chár-ni pa-rá-sol

Do you need a raincoat?

Czy jest Panu potrzebny płaszcz
przeciwdeszczowy?
chi yest pá-noo po-tshéb-ni
pwashch pshé-cheev desh-chó-vi

159

Yes, I need a raincoat.

Tak, potrzeba mi płaszcza od deszczu.
tak, po-tshé-ba mee pwásh-cha od désh-choo

What size?

Jaki wymiar?
yá-kee vim-var

Please try this on.

Proszę ten spróbować.
pró-shañ ten sproo-bó-vach

It doesn't fit.

Nie pasuje mi.
ñe pa-sóo-ye mee

Let's try a larger size.

Spróbujmy o numer większy.
sproo-bóoy-mi o nóo-mer vyáñk-shi

160

I don't like the color.

Kolor mi się nie podoba.
kó-lor mee shañ ñe po-dó-ba.

What color do you like?

Jaki kolor panu odpowiada?
yá-kee kó-lor pá-noo od-po-vyá-da

I want a gray coat.

Chciałbym szary płaszcz.
khcháw-bim shá-ri pwashch

What about this one?

Jak się panu ten podoba?
yak shañ pá-noo ten po-dó-ba

This suits me fine.

Ten mi odpowiada.
ten mee od-po-vyá-da

Very good.

Bardzo dobrze.
bár-dzo dób-zhe

161
We have suits on sale.

Mamy ubrania na wyprzedaży.
má-mi oo-brá-ña na vi-pshe-dá-zhi

I have heard that the Polish tailors are very good.

Słyszałem że polscy krawcy są bardzo dobrzy.
swi-shá-wem zhe póls-tsi kráv-tsi sówñ bár-dzo dób-zhi

I would like to buy a jacket made in Poland.

Chciałbym kupić marynarkę uszytą w Polsce.
khcháw-bim koó-peech ma-ri-nár-kåñ oo-shi-tówñ v póls-tse

Do you prefer wool or cotton?

Czy woli pan wełnę czy bawełnę?
chi vó-lee pan véw-nåñ chi ba-véw-nåñ

162
I want a brown cotton jacket.

Chciałbym mieć brązową marynarkę z bawełny.
khcháw-bim myeñch brówñ-zó-vówñ ma-ri-nár-kåñ z ba-véw-ni

I am sorry, sir.

Niestety nie mamy.
ñe-sté-ti ñe má-mi

Where is the sales lady?

Gdzie jest sprzedawczyni?
gdźhe yest spshe-dav-chí-ñee

How much is this dress?

Ile kosztuje ta suknia?
ée-le kosh-toó-ye ta soók-ña

4000 zloties.

Cztery tysiące złotych.
chté-ri ti-shówñ-tse zwó-tikh

163
That is very expensive.

To jest bardzo drogo.
to yest bár-dzo dró-go

Where are the blouses and the sweaters?

Gdzie są bluzki i swetry?
gdźhe sówñ hloóz-kee ee svét-ri

Where are the shirts and the skirts?

Gdzie są koszule i spódnice?
gdźhe sówñ ko-shoó-le ee spood-ñée-tse

We have many hats on sale.

Mamy wiele kapeluszy na wyprzdaży.
má-mi vyé-le ka-pe-loó-shi na vi-pshe-dá-zhi

These are very cheap.

Te są bardzo tanie.
te sówñ bár-dzo tá-ñe

164
Do you like these ties?

Czy podobają się panu te krawaty?
chi po-do-bá-yówñ śhåñ pá-noo te kra-vá-ti?

Are they rayon?

Czy są ze sztucznego jedwabiu?
chi sówñ ze shtooch-né-go yed-váb-yoo

They are silk.

Są z jedwabiu.
sówñ z yed-váb-yoo

Do you have a jewelry department.

Czy macie dział jubilerski?
chi má-che dźhaw yoo-bee-lér-skee?

A jeweler is across the street.

Jubiler jest po drugiej stronie ulicy.
yoo-beé-ler yest po droó-gey stró-ñe oo-leé-tsi

165
May I show you some watches?

Czy mogę panu pokazać zegarki?
chi mó-găn pá-noo po-ka-zach ze-gár-kee

I am looking for a diamond ring.

Chciałbym kupić pierścionek z brylantem.
khcháw-bim koó-peech pyersh-chó-nek z bri-lán-tem

Do you handle signet rings?

Czy sprzedajecie sygnety?
chi spshe-da-yé-che sig-né-ti

Yes, we also have an engraving service.

Tak, mamy też rytownictwo.
tak, má-mi tezh ri-tov-níeéts-tvo

That is very good.

To bardzo dobrze.
to bár-dzo dób-zhe

166
Your driver's license, please.

Proszę o pańskie prawo jazdy.
pró-shan o páńs-ke prá-vo yáz-di

You have a flat tire.

Pan ma przebitą dętkę.
pan ma pshe-beé-tówn dént-kăn

I need gasoline.

Potrzebuję benzyny.
po-tshe-boó-yăn ben-zí-ni

Where is a gas station?

Gdzie jest stacja benzynowa?
gdźhe yest státs-ya ben-zi-nó-va

Let's change the oil.

Zmieńmy oliwę.
zmyéń-mi o-leé-văn

There is the garage.

Tam jest garaż.
tam jest gá-razh

167
How far is it to Warsaw?

Jak daleko jest do Warszawy?
yak da-lé-ko yest do var-shá-vi

Which road goes to Cracov?

Która droga prowadzi do Krakowa?
ktoó-ra dró-ga pro-vá-dżhee do Kra-kó-va

Do not drive so fast.

Nie jedź tak szybko.
ńe yedźh tak shíb-ko

The road is good.

Droga jest dobra.
dró-ga yest dób-ra

The road is very steep.

Droga jest bardzo stroma.
dró-ga yest bár-dzo stró-ma

168
I want to rent a car.

Chciałbym wynająć samochód.
khcháw-bim vi-ná-yównch sa-mó-khoot

How much does it cost to rent it?

Ile kosztuje wynajęcie samochodu?
eé-le kosh-toó-ye vi-na-yán-che sa-mo-kho-doo

Twenty dollars per day.

Dwadzieścia dolarów dziennie.
dva-dźhéśh-cha do-lá-roof dźhén-ńe

Which car do you like?

Który samochód panu się podoba?
ktoó-ri sa-mó-khoot pá-noo śhăn po-dó-ba

I like this blue Fiat.

Podoba mi się ten niebieski Fiat
po-dó-ba mee-śhăn ten ńe-byés-kee fyat

169
Let us go to write the rental contract.

Chodźmy spisać kontrakt wynajmu.
khóch-mi spee-sach kón-trakt vi-náy-moo

For how many days?

Na ile dni?
na eé-le dñee

Do you want complete insurance?

Czy chce pan pełne ubezpieczenie?
chi khtse,pan péw-ne oo-bez-pye-ché-ñe

I need a road map.

Potrzebna mi jest mapa samochodowa.
po-tsheb-na mee yest má-pa sa-mo-kho-dó-va.

You start with a full tank.

Zaczyną pan z pełnym bakiem.
za-chi-na pan z péw-nim bá-kem

170
What town are we in?

W jakim mieście jesteśmy?
v yá-keem myéh-che yes-téh-mi

You are in Poznań.

Jesteście państwo w Poznaniu.
yes-téh-che páñs-tvo v poz-ná-ñoo

No parking.

Zakaz postoju,
zá-kaz pos-tó-yoo

Please don't close the window.

Proszę nie zamykać okna.
pró-sháñ ñe za-mi-kach ók-na

Be careful.

Proszę uważać.
pró-sháñ oo-va-zhach

The motel is on the next corner.

Motel jest na następnym rogu.
mó-tel yest na nas-táñp-nim ró-goo

171
I do not understand any Polish.

Wcale nie rozumiem po polsku,
vtsá-le ñe ro-zoóm-yem po póls-koo

I understand a little Polish.

Rozumiem trochę po polsku.
ro-zoóm-yem tró-kháñ po póls-koo

I speak little Polish.

Mało mówię po polsku.
má-wo moóv-yáñ po póls-koo

Please, speak slowly.

Proszę mówić powoli.
pró-sháñ moó-veech po-vó-lee

Are you from America?

Czy jesteście państwo z Ameryki?
chi yes-téh-che páñs-tvo z a-me-ri-kee

Yes, we are from America.

Tak jesteśmy z Ameryki.
tak, yes-téh-mi z a-me-ri-kee

172
Where is the railroad station?

Gdzie jest dworzec kolejowy?
gdźhe yest dvó-zhets ko-le-yó-vi

It isn't near by.

Nie jest blisko.
ñe yest bleéz-ko

Where is the bus stop?

Gdzie jest przystanek autobusowy?
gdźhe yest pshi-stá-nek aw-to-boo-só-vi

Does this bus go to the railroad station?

Czy ten autobus dojeżdża do dworca kolejowego?
chi ten aw-tó-boos do-yézh-dzha do dvór-tsa ko-le-yo-vé-go

How much is the fare?

Ile kosztuje bilet?
eé-le kosh-toó-ye beé-let

173
Do you want a one way or a
round trip ticket.

Czy chce pan bilet w jedną stronę
czy powrotny?
chi khtse pan beé-let v yed-nówn
stró-nän chi po-vrót-ni

Do you have a time table?

Czy ma pani rozkład jazdy?
chi ma pá-ńee róz-kwad yáz-di

What time does the train for
Gdańsk leave?

Kiedy odjeżdża pociąg do Gdańska?
Ké-di od-yézh-dzha pó-chówñg do gádñ-
ska

Please tell me where to get off.

Proszę mi powiedzieć gdzie mam wysiaść
pró-shäñ mee po-vye-dźhech gdźhe mam
vi-śhówñshćh

174
What time does the train from
Lublin arrive?

Kiedy przyjeżdża pociąg z Lublina?
Ké-di pshi-yézh-dzha pó-chówñg z loob-
leé-na

Is this seat occupied?

Czy to miejsce jest zajęte?
chi to myéys-tse yest za-yäñ-te

No, please sit down.

Nie, proszę usiąść.
ñe, pró-shäñ oó-śhówñshćh

Please, open the window.

Proszę otworzyć okno.
pró-shäñ ot-vó-zhićh ók-no

Please, close the window.

Proszę zamknąć okno.
pró-shäñ zámk-nówñćh ók-no

175
No smoking.

Nie palić. = Palenie wzbronione.
ñe pá-leećh= pa-lé-ñe vzbro-ñó-ne

I would like to smoke a cigaret

Chciałbym zapalić papierosa.
khćháw-bim za-pá-leećh pa-pye-ró-sa

Do you have a cigarette?

Czy ma pan papierosa?
chi ma pan pa-pye-ró-sa

Do you have matches ?

Czy ma pan zapałki?
chi ma pan za-páw-k ee

Do you see the sign "no smoking"

Czy widzi pan napis "palenie wzbronione"?
chi veé-dźhee pan ná-pees "pa-lé-ñe
vzbro-ñó-ne"

176
Please write it down.

Proszę zapisać.
pró-shäñ za-peé-saćh

Do you have a pen?

Czy ma pan pióro?
chi ma pan pyoó-ro

I lost my pen.

Zgubiłem moje pióro.
zgoo-beé-wem mo-ye pyoo-ro

Do you have a pencil?

Czy ma pan ołówek?
chi ma pan o-woó-vek

Here is pencil and paper.

Oto ołówek i papier.
ó-to o-woó-vek ee pá-pyer

Thank you.

Dziękuję.
dźháñ-koó-yäñ

177

Are you sick?

Czy źle się pan czuje?
chi źhle źhañ pan choo-ye

I am sick at my stomach.

Jest mi niedobrze.
yest mee ńe dób-zhe

I am nauseated.

Mam nudności.= Nudzi mnie.
mam nood-nósh-chee=noo-dźhee mńe

Please call the doctor.

Proszę wezwać lekarza.
pró-shañ véz-vach le-ká-zha

How do you feel?

Jak się pan czuje?
yak źhañ pan choo-ye?

I have a stomach ache.

Boli mnie żołądek.
bó-lee mńe zho-wówń-dek

178

You must stay in bed.

Musi pan pozostać w łóżku.
moó-shee pan po-zós-tach v woózh-koo

Do you feel better?

Czy czuje się pan lepiej?
chi choo-ye źhañ pan lé-pyey

I feel much better.

Czuję się dużo lepiej.
choo-yáń źhañ doó-zho lé-pyey

I have a headache.

Boli mnie głowa.
bó-lee mńe gwó-va

You can get headache pills at
the "Ruch" news-stand.

Może pan dostać proszki na ból głowy
w kiosku "Ruchu".
mó-zhe pan dós-tach prósh-kee na bool
gwó-vi v kyós-koo roó-khoo

179

Headache pills and aspirin are
available at "Ruch" news-stand.

Pastylki od bólu głowy i aspirynę można dostać w kiosku "Ruchu".
pas-tíl-kee od boó-loo gwó-vi ee as-
pee-ri-náñ mózh-na dós-tach v kyós-
koo roó-khoo

"Ruch" news-stands also sell some
basic cosmetics, shaving supplies
etc.

Kioski "Ruchu" również sprzedają nie-
zbędne artykuły kosmetyczne, przybory
do golenia etc.
kyós-kee roó-khoo róov-ñezh spshe-dá-
yóvń ñez-báńd-ne ar-ti-koó-wi kos-me-
tích-ne, pshi-bó-ri do go-lé-ña
et-tsé-te-ra

Polish drugstores sell medicines
only.

Polskie apteki sprzedają wyłącznie le-
karstwa.
póls-ke ap-té-kee spshe-dá-yóvń vi-
wóvńch-ñe le-kárs-tva

180

What do you call the cosmetics
supply store?

Jak się nazywają sklepy z kosmetykami?
yak źhañ na-zi-vá-yóvń sklé-pi z kos-
me-ti-ká-mee

"Drogeria" is the Polish word
for a cosmetics supply store.

Polskie słowo na sklep z kosmetykami
jest "drogeria".
póls-ke swó-vo na sklep z kos-me-ti-
ká-mee yest dro-gér-ya

I want to buy some toothpaste.

Chciłbym kupić pastę do zębów.
Khcháw-bim koó-peech pás-tán do záń-
boof

I also need a tooth brush.

Potrzebuję również szczoteczkę do zębów.
po-tshe-boó-yáń roóv-ñezh shcho-tếch-
kań do záń-boof.

POLISH — ENGLISH PHONETICS

POLISH VOWELS

Schematic ellipse of the tip of the tongue positions

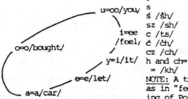

u=oo/you/

i=ee /feel/

o=o/bought/

y=i/it/

e=e/let/

a=a/car/

Polish nasalized vowels:
A, ą /ōñh/ one nasalized sound
E, ę /āñ/ two sounds:
short "a" and nasalized "n"
dąb /dōñp/   kęs /kāñs/
wąs /vōñs/   gęś /gāñsh/

SPEECH ORGAN DIAGRAM
for Polish consonants not used in the English language

vocal chords

"dż","dzi"/dżh/ and "ć","ci"/ćh/ air compressed behind lips and teeth then suddenly released /ex-plosives/;
"ź","zi"/żh/ and "ś","si"/śh/ air flow with continuous friction /fricatives/;
In each case the tip of the tongue is at the tooth ridge.

POLISH CONSONANTS

UNVOICED	VOICED	NASALS
p	b	m
t	d	n
k and ḱ	g and ǵ	ń and ni
f	w /v/	/ñ/
s	z	
ś /śh/	ź /żh/	GLIDES
sz /sh/	ż /zh/	r /flut-
c /ts/	dz	tered/
ć /ćh/	dź /dżh/	j /y/
cz /ch/	dż /j/	ł /w/
h and ch= = /kh/		

NOTE: A trace of the sound "ee" as in "feel" is typical in softening of Polish consonants as in: "kie","gie","pie","bie","mie",and "wie" in the phonetic notation:"ḱ", "ǵ","pye","bye","mye" and "vye". The softened consonant is followed by vowel "e" /as in "let"/, without which it is impossible to pronounce.

POLISH SOUND "R"
is fluttered and may be pronounced alone like Scottish "R"

vocal chords

Mouth is slightly open; tip of the tongue is raised; it vibrates on exhaling impulse and strikes the toothridge; sides of the tongue touch back teeth. Tongue does not glide as far as needed to pronounce the English "R". DWG. OF SPEECH ORGANS BY PROF. JERZY STARCZEWSKI

BY IWO CYPRIAN POGONOWSKI

SAMOGŁOSKI ANGIELSKIE

Schematyczna elipsa pozycji języka dla dwunastu samogłosek angielskich /wymowa amerykańska/.

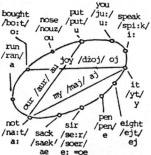

bought /bo:t/ o:

put /put/ u

you /ju:/ u:

nose /nouz/ ou

speak /spi:k/ i:

run /ran/ a

joy /dżoj/ oj

our /aur/ au

my /maj/ aj

it /yt/ y

not /na:t/ a:

sack /saek/ ae

sir /se:r/ /soer/ e:

pen /pen/ e

eight /ejt/ ej

=oe

Trzy podstawowe dwugłoski angielskie: diphtongs /'dyftons/ są zaznaczone wewnątrz elipsy

SPÓŁGŁOSKI ANGIELSKIE

Bezdźwięczne	Dźwięczne	Nosowe
p	b	m
t	d	n
k	g	n jak w
f	v /w/	"ng"i"nk"
th /t̯/ /s̯/	th /d̯/	przejś-
	/dż/ /z̯/	ciowe:
s	z	r
sh /sz/	/ż/ vision	
	/'wyżyn/	y /j/aj/
ch /cz/	j /dż/	w /l/
h hw /hl/	ł	
why /hłaj/		

Uwaga: Często spółgłoski angielskie dźwięczne na końcu słowa są wymawiane dźwięcznie / w przeciwieństwie do polskich, które na końcu słowa wymawia się bezdźwięcznie/.

ANGIELSKI DŹWIĘK "TH"

struny głosowe

angielska spółgłoska "th" "seplemiona", koniec i przód języka szeroko spłaszczony, widzialny między zębami; ciągły przelot powietrza między zębami i wargami.

Bezdźwięczna: thank /taenk/
bath /ba:s/
Dźwięczna: they /dzej/
those /douz/
bathing /bejzyng/

ANGIELSKI DŹWIĘK "R"

struny głosowe

Angielska spółgłoska "r": usta nieco otwarte; koniec języka uniesiony wklęsłym podgięciem ku tyłowi, nie dotyka podniebienia; boki języka dotykają zębów; wymowa możliwa tylko w przejściu od lub do samogłoski. Dźwięk angielski spółgłoski "r" przypomina lekkie rzężenie.